A GUIDE TO THE BIRDS OF PANAMA

Sponsored by the
International Council for Bird Preservation
(United States and Pan American Sections),
The Academy of Natural Sciences of Philadelphia,
and the New York Zoological Society

Second Edition

A GUIDE TO THE

Birds of Panama

with Costa Rica, Nicaragua, and Honduras

BY ROBERT S. RIDGELY

and JOHN A. GWYNNE, JR.

PRINCETON UNIVERSITY PRESS

Library of Congress Cataloging in
Publication Data will be found on the last
printed page of this book

This book has been composed in Baskerville

ISBN 0-691-08529-3
ISBN 0-691-02512-6 (pbk)

10 9 8 7 6 5 4

Production services by Fisher Duncan & Company,
Chiswick, London, United Kingdom
Printed in Singapore

CONTENTS

FOREWORD TO THE FIRST EDITION

The long isthmus of Panama offers a varied and attractive avifauna to the birdwatcher, amateur and professional. In its western and central areas there are representatives of tropical kinds found through Central America, and in the east in San Blas and Darién, those of affiliation with South America. Among the residents at the proper season there appear many migrants from the north, present in this warmer climate as a winter home, or in passage to and from more distant regions farther to the south. The avifauna in total, as compiled by the authors, includes over 880 species that have been recorded by naturalists over a period of more than one hundred years. Valuable additions to the text are the 32 color plates and numerous line drawings in which the artist, John Gwynne, Jr, carefully portrays details of color and form from museum specimens, photographs, and his personal field experience.

The common birds of the lowlands in Panama are widely distributed, and many are easily found. On first encounter some immediately suggest kinds familiar in more northern haunts. (If it is winter, these should be examined carefully to make certain they are not northern migrants.) Others may be both strange and unusual in appearance and mannerism. Highland species are seen most readily in a journey west to Boquete and Cerro Punta in the mountains of Chiriquí; to find species from Darién may require longer time and special arrangements.

Local interests in birds has increased in recent years, and there is now an active chaper of the Florida Audubon Society. Travelers remaining in Panama for a period may find its scheduled meetings and bird walks helpful.

The present volume, based on the broad field experience of the authors throughout the isthmus, is certain to be a valuable guide to the bird student, be he tyro or expert in the field.

Alexander Wetmore
Smithsonian Institution
July 1974

INTRODUCTION TO THE FIRST EDITION

The Republic of Panama comprises an area of 75,648 square kilometres (29,208 square miles) (somewhat smaller than the state of South Carolina), which includes a strip about 16 km (10 miles) wide bordering the Panama Canal leased "in perpetuity" to the United States, and has long been a region of special interest to those interested in birds. Located at the southern end of Middle America, Panama is a land bridge where the faunas of North and South America meet and intermingle. Largely because of this geographical position, Panama's avifauna is exceptionally large: at the time of writing this some 883 species have been reported from the Republic, considerably more species than are recorded from all of North America north of Mexico. People have been studying Panama's birdlife for over a century, and today it is one of the best known (in an ornithological sense) countries in the neotropics. Nonetheless, as will be noted repeatedly on the following pages, there is still much to be learned and some areas remain little explored. The conscientious observer is in a position to add materially to our knowledge.

The first man to make large bird collections in what was formerly the Canal Zone was James McLeannan, who in the mid-nineteenth century was stationmaster at Lion Hill on the Panama Railroad (now submerged under Gatun Lake). He collected many birds around Lion Hill (Harpy Eagles were then not uncommon) and sent them to leading American and British ornithologists; from these specimens a number of new species were described, chiefly by George Lawrence and Osbert Salvin. Other collectors worked in different parts of Panama, most notably Enrique Arcé in "Veragua," which then encompassed much of present-day western Panama (including Bocas del Toro and Chiriquí). Available data were included in the *Aves* volumes of *Biologia Centrali-Americana* by O. Salvin and F. DuC. Godman (1879–1904); but it was the influx and interest of North Americans, partly stimulated by Canal construction, that prompted the intense zoological exploration of Panama and the beginning of popular study.

A number of bird collections were made in little-known regions of the country during the first third of the century, notably by W. W. Brown, T. Barbour, E. A. Goldman, L. Griscom, R. R. Benson, H. Wedel, H. E. Anthony and W. B. Richardson, F. H. Kennard, J. Aldrich, and others. These collections established the distributional outlines of Panama's avifauna and were used in publications by either the collectors of such leading ornithologists as O. Bangs, F. M. Chapman, J. L. Peters, and C. Hellmayr. Robert Ridgway's great, though uncompleted, multi-volume work, *The Birds of North and Middle America* (1901–1919), provided the descriptive and taxonomic foundation for subsequent Middle American studies. In 1918 W. Stone produced the first checklist of Canal Zone birds, based partly on a collection made by L. L. Jewel. In 1935 L. Griscom published the first complete checklist of the birds then known from the Republic. Work on seabirds in the Gulf of Panama was done by

R. C. Murphy, and collections over many years by T. B. Mönniche on the Volcán de Chiriquí massif were later reported upon by E. R. Blake (1958). Detailed ecological and behavioral studies, as well as public interest, were promoted by the establishment in 1923 of a biological research station on Barro Colorado Island, Canal Zone, under the supervision of James Zetek. This former hilltop, isolated by rising waters when the Chagres River was dammed to form Gatun Lake, has been a mecca for naturalists, many of whom have repeatedly returned to Panama, or have sent their students. Its fame was spread by F. M. Chapman's delightful books, *My Tropical Air Castle* (1929) and *Life in an Air Castle* (1938). Some personnel associated with the operation or defense of the Canal developed an interest in the varied avifauna of the area, and this was markedly assisted by the preparation of a popular book, *Field Book of Birds of the Panama Canal Zone* in 1928 (long since out of print) by B. B. Sturgis, wife of a former Canal Zone commanding general.

Succeeding decades have seen an increase in the number of visiting naturalists and residents interested in the local birdlife. Of these, the two who have made by far the most significant contributions are Dr Alexander Wetmore and Dr Eugene Eisenmann. Since the 1940s, Wetmore, one of the world's leading ornithologists, has collected birds virtually throughout Panama, and it is largely through his efforts and those of his collaborators in the Gorgas Memorial Laboratory that something is known about the birds found in certain of the less accessible parts of the country. Dr Wetmore's research has culminated in the publication of a lengthy and very important multi-volume treatise on the birds of the country. Eisenmann has also been conducting personal field work in Panama since the 1940s (in addition to having been born in the country), gathering distributional, ecological, and behavioral data, publishing on Panama birds, and encouraging and assisting students of its ornithology. Barro Colorado Island was placed under the jurisdiction of the Smithsonian Institution, and subsequently (particularly in the last fifteen years under its recent director, Dr Martin Moynihan) the Smithsonian has greatly expanded its local organization until it is now a major center for research into many aspects of tropical biology. During the early 1960s, Florida State University established a branch in the Canal Zone, and under its auspices the Center for Tropical Studies was created in 1963, directed until recently by Dr Horace Loftin. This organization has sponsored many research visits by graduate students and others, and offers a course in ornithology. Popular nonprofessional clubs and societies have existed sporadically through the period, and recently the Panama Audubon Society (chartered in 1968 an an affiliate of the Florida Audubon Society) has done a great deal to foster the study and appreciation of Panama's birdlife. In 1973 a chapter of the Amigos de la Naturaleza was also organized in Panama City.

I arrived in Panama as an Army lieutenant in the fall of 1967, and, as a birder from early boyhood in the United States, was elated at the prospect of several years in the neotropics, but being accustomed to North America's superbly written and illustrated bird guides, I was not fully prepared for the difficulties in field recognition that I would encounter in Panama. Toucans and the other large showy species were no problem, but what of the many more difficult groups such as the hummingbirds, woodcreepers, antbirds, and above all the wealth of confusing flycatchers? The references available at the time — the Sturgis book mentioned above and de Schauensee's *Birds of Columbia* — were both useful up to a point, but neither was easy to use in the field. I now remember those first few months as being greatly exciting but also rather frustrating. A growing friendship with Dr Eisenmann proved invaluable at this point. I soon was given permission to copy his unpublished ''Diagnostic List of Panama Birds'' with its 100 pages of brief field diagnoses of Panama birds, this in return for making available to him any of my personal field observations. I found this manuscript to be immensely valuable over the next few years, and with time I gained in field proficiency. But its use was highly restricted by the author, who at the time was still considering expanding and publishing it. I and many others felt that what was needed was a generally available, more comprehensive and detailed book, and above all one which would include color illustrations.

Soon after my return to Princeton University in the fall of 1969, I made the decision to write the book I would have like to have had myself. Eisenmann agreed to let me use his ''Diagnostic List'' as the basis for the projected work, having by then realized that with his other commitments he would never find the time to do the work himself, on the understanding that all royalties would accrue to some nonprofit ornithological or conservation organization. Since then he has given freely of his vast storehouse of knowledge, providing information on distribution, morphology, behavior, and taxonomy, and has labored untold hours over the pages of manuscript I sent him to examine. By a stroke of good fortune, a fellow undergraduate at Princeton, John Gwynne, Jr, had an interest in birds and a remarkable artistic talent, and he agreed to do the illustrations. Gwynne had never done such work, but his proficiency increased rapidly, and I feel certain the results are a valuable contribution to neotropical ornithology.

It has taken five years to complete the work, far more time, and effort than either Gwynne or myself had anticipated. All along we have been students with many other concerns, and never have we been able to devote any extended, full-time effort to our project. Throughout that period, assistance, direct and indirect, has been rendered by a great many individuals and organizations, in this case far too many for all to be mentioned here, but the following are among the most important.

A trip to Panama during the summer of 1970 for Gwynne and myself was financed in part by a grant from the National Science Foundation undergraduate summer study program at Princeton, and in part from funds made available by Dr Robert MacArthur of the Princeton Biology Department. While in Panama, Captain and Mrs Gaylord Lyon USN furnished us with accommodations, while Mr and Mrs Roy Sharp loaned us one of their cars; both these couples, as well as many other persons, extended many kindnesses to us during that delightful sojourn. On that and my subsequent visits, the staff of STRI have gone out of their way to be helpful, as have Drs Edwin Tyson and Horace Loftin of the Florida State branch, and several of the Panama Audubon Society, especially Dr Jaime Pujals. Dr Pedro Galindo, of the Gorgas Memorial Laboratory, kindly afforded Eisenmann, Gwynne, and myself the hospitality of the Gorgas camp above the Bayano River near Majé in late January 1973, and he also provided invaluable assistance in setting up my trip to Santa Fé, Veraguas, in early January 1974. Dr Jorge Campabadal, director of the Organization for Tropical Studies in Costa Rica, was helpful in providing transportation and lodging during my visit to that country during the winter of 1972–1973. An abundance of information has been gleaned from Eisenmann's copious unpublished data, compiled by him over the years from his personal observations, study of specimens and the literature, and notes given him by numerous observers. A comprehensive listing of these contributions would be too lengthy (they are credited in the text when the observation is unusual), but I owe all of them a great debt of gratitude, in particular (other than those mentioned elsewhere in this introduction): James E. Ambrose, Major F. O. Chapelle, Eugene S. Morton, Richard Ryan, Dennis R. Sheets, and Edwin O. Willis. Dr Wetmore's volumes have of course been invaluable, and he has graciously taken the time to answer many specific queries as well. Peter Alden, David O. Hill, James R. Karr, Neal G. Smith, F. Gary Stiles, and Guy Tudor have all been very patient in replying to my persistent queries. Many people thus contributed information and advice, but responsibility for all the statements made in this book rests, of course, with the author.

Several people (among them Alden, John Dunning, Karr, Michel Kleinbaum, Hill, and Smith) have kindly lent photographs of certain species needed by Gwynne for more accurate portrayals. Guy Tudor, one of the finest living bird artists, has also given Gwynne much technical advice for which Gwynne is grateful. We are indebted to the American Museum of Natural History (in particular to Dr Dean Amadon and Charles O'Brien), the Museum of Comparative Zoology (and Dr Raymond A. Paynter, Jr), and the Smithsonian Institution (and Dr George E. Watson) for access to and loan of specimens in their collections. Both of use are immensely grateful to Eugene Eisenmann, without whose aid and encouragement the book would never have gotten off the ground. Drs S. Dillon Ripley and Thomas Lovejoy have given valuable advice, and Warren King has also been helpful. The Pan American and United States Sections of the International Council for Bird Preservation provided a needed boost by agreeing to sponsor the book, while the generosity of Mrs Carll Tucker and the Marcia Brady Tucker Foundation helped make its actual publication possible; Mrs Tucker's deep interest is greatly appreciated. Finally, both Gwynne's and my parents gave support and encouragement when needed.

Robert S. Ridgely
August 1974

INTRODUCTION TO THE SECOND EDITION

Ever since the publication of *A Guide to the Birds of Panama* in 1976 it has been our goal to see the work come out in a Spanish language translation. Such efforts always seem to require much time and energy, and this one has been no exception. Gradually, however, royalties from the sale of the first edition accumulated in a special account established for this by the United States Section of the International Council for Bird Preservation, and by the early 1980s funds seemed to be sufficient to entertain seriously thoughts about commencing such an effort. It took several years more, but eventually an appropriate (and available) translator surfaced, and now John Guarnaccia, with able assistance from his wife Mercedes Villamil, has virtually completed that difficult task.

We recognized early on that the publication of a Spanish language edition would entail producing a number of new color plates to show various northern migrant species which we had expressly avoided illustrating in the original English edition, out of consideration for costs. It was also our intention to re-paint several of the original plates, especially for those groups whose coverage was relatively incomplete. It seemed reasonable, therefore, to also plan for a more or less simultaneous English language edition incorporating this new artwork. What was not, however, entirely anticipated was the virtual explosion in our new knowledge about Panama's birds, obtained both locally and in neighboring countries. Much of this cried out to be included in a revised and updated text, and the decision was taken to incorporate as much as was practicable. A further complication became the publication in 1983 of the Sixth Edition of the American Ornithologists' Union's *Check-list of North American Birds* which for the first time extended its coverage south to include Panama. With its appearance, the taxonomy and nomenclature of Middle American birds was very substantially updated, and the differences between it and *Panama* were quite marked — the Honeycreeper family was no more, and so on. It seemed advisable to follow their systematic approach, and this we have done in all but a few cases (or where new information has come to light). Finally, there remained the problem of the countries to the north of Panama in Central America. *A Guide to the Birds of Panama* was helpful here, particularly in Costa Rica, but its Appendix covering species not found in Panama was clearly inadequate, and numerous colleagues urged us to expand upon it. Eventually we were convinced, and that section has now been greatly enlarged. The logical next step was also to illustrate some of these birds, and in due course this too was agreed upon, the result being eight new plates depicting mainly Central American species.

The end product has been, as will be obvious to users of the first edition, transformation into an almost entirely new book, one which we hope will better meet the needs of the growing legion of people, both visitors and residents, with an interest in Central American birds. As always, its preparation depended on the good will and assistance of numerous individuals and organizations. Among those who have been most helpful to RSR in Panama are the following: Francisco Delgado, who shared many of his discoveries concerning Azuero Peninsula birds (a large proportion still otherwise unpublished); Dodge and Lorna Engleman, indefatigable birders who revised and greatly expanded the Bird Finding section and passed on to me, through a voluminous correspondence, information about their latest finds and those of numerous others, given to Dodge in his capacity as record-keeper for the Panama Audubon Society; Pedro Galindo, former Director of the Gorgas Memorial Laboratory, who invited RSR to participate on various expeditions into areas of Panama he knew relatively poorly or not at all, and who also substantially aided him in reaching other destinations, notably his first expedition to Darién and his memorable trip to Coiba Island; Jaime Pujals, Panama's most active birder until his departure several years ago (his enthusiasm will always be remembered by those who knew him); and Neal Smith, who continues in his capacity as resident bird expert at the Smithsonian Tropical Research Institute, and advisor, official and otherwise, to legions of students and scientists, among them RSR (who will never forget, though it was 20 years ago, Neal teaching him that that call he was hearing everywhere was produced by the Little Tinamou!). Various other individuals have shared their observations with RSR, with the following having been especially helpful in this regard: John Arvin, Bob Behrstock, John Blake, Victor Emanuel, Doug Graham, John Guarnaccia, Mark Letzer, Mark Robbins, and Bret Whitney.

We should here note that both Alexander Wetmore and Eugene Eisenmann passed away during the 15 years between Editions. Their passing leaves a void; we miss them both, and can only hope that they would approve of our present efforts.

Since 1982, RSR has benefitted from the companionship and stimulating atmosphere of the Bird Department of the Academy of Natural Sciences in Philadelphia, and the Academy's superb collection of bird specimens has been of inestimable value in the production of this work, for us both. Collections in the American Museum of Natural History in New York helped fill in the gaps in the Academy's holdings, and we are very grateful for continued access to it. JAG also benefitted greatly from the artistic advice of Guy Tudor, not to mention access to the latter's unparalleled photographic collection. The final accolade must, for RSR, be reserved for his wife Peg, who gently but insistently prodded him into greater productivity and provided the atmosphere for this massive task to be completed — all in his "spare" time.

Robert S. Ridgely
John A. Gwynne
July 1989

CLIMATE

Panama lies between 7° and 10° north of the Equator, hence its climate is essentially warm tropical; only the highlands of the west and east have cooler conditions. This is not to say that the climate of the country is uniform; it varies significantly between regions, and in most areas also fluctuates seasonally.

In a tropical climate one finds that the variation between the average daily maximum and minimum temperatures is greater than the variation in the average monthly figures. Table I demonstrates this for Balboa and Cristobal, representative localities on the Pacific and Caribbean coasts of central Panama, respectively. Variation in the monthly averages at Balboa is only 3°F, and at Cristobal is even less. Variation between daily highs and lows is greater on the Pacific slope than on the Caribbean, primarily because of its lower humidity and less persistent cloud cover. In general, temperatures in the Panama lowlands are hot during daylight hours and pleasant during the hours of darkness; one should plan one's activities accordingly.

A major factor of most tropical lowland climates is the seasonal variability in precipitation; i.e. there is a definite alternation between dry and rainy seasons. Table II shows that this is clearly the pattern in Panama. For the five localities given (placed in order from Balboa on the Pacific coast to Cristobal and Portobelo on the Caribbean), considerable differences in the average annual totals can be seen (ranging from 68.9 in. in Balboa to 158.6 in. at Portobelo). For each locality, however, there is a distinctly drier period (January–April) and a rainier period (May–December). The same annual pattern holds for most of the Panama lowlands, with heaviest precipitation occurring in Caribbean western and eastern (not central) Panama; in Bocas del Toro and rainfall tends to be more uniformly distributed. As the table indicates, dry season on the Caribbean slope is much less pronounced than on the Pacific, though here, too, notably less precipitation falls than during the rainy season. A pattern somewhat similar to that of the Caribbean slope also prevails on the Pacific slope in most of Darién and in western Chiriquí and on the western side of the Azuero Peninsula. The remainder of the Pacific slope has a more pronounced dry season, most severe in southern Coclé, Herrera, and adjacent Veraguas. Here many trees then lose their leaves (this happens to ralatively few species in Caribbean slope forests), the grass turns brown, and many areas are burned over. Not surprisingly, this seasonal fluctuation in rainfall has a pronounced effect on birdlife. Many species time their breeding cycles so that they will be feeding young about the time when the rains begin, when food is most abundant, this peaking April–June. Furthermore, a growing body of evidence indicates that a number of species engage in local movements correlated with seasonal change; e.g. they migrate to more humid areas during the dry season and then back again (see section on Migration and Local Movements). One other interesting point

TABLE I

TEMPERATURE DATA FOR FORMER CANAL ZONE (DEG. F.)

	Jan.	Feb.	Mar.	Apr.	May	June	July	Aug.	Sept.	Oct.	Nov.	Dec.
BALBOA												
Avg.	80.0	80.5	81.6	82.2	80.9	80.2	80.4	80.3	79.8	79.2	79.2	79.9
Avg. Max.	88.3	89.4	90.7	90.5	87.6	86.2	86.9	86.7	85.9	85.2	85.4	87.0
Avg. Min.	71.7	71.7	72.6	73.9	74.4	74.1	74.0	73.8	73.7	73.3	72.9	72.6
CRISTOBAL												
Avg.	80.3	80.3	80.8	81.4	81.1	80.8	80.5	81.9	80.7	80.3	79.5	80.1
Avg. Max.	83.9	83.8	84.4	85.2	85.6	85.5	84.9	84.9	85.8	85.6	84.0	84.1
Avg. Min.	76.6	76.7	77.3	77.6	76.7	76.0	76.2	75.9	75.5	75.0	75.0	76.1

SOURCE: Panama Canal Company, Meteorological and Hydrographic Branch

can be made about rainfall in Panama and in some other tropical areas. Rainfall in much of the temperate zone characteristically occurs during storms that often last for a day or more. In the Panama lowlands, by contrast rain may come down unbelievably hard, but usually it lasts no more than an hour or two, frequently less. The classic rainy season pattern is for clouds to build during the day, and for a heavy shower to fall in the late afternoon or evening, followed by nighttime clearing. This "schedule" is by no means invariable — especially during October–November, the peak of the rainy season, when it often rains in the morning — but is of regular enough occurrence to take into consideration when planning a day's trip.

The main cause of this annual cycle of dry and rainy seasons is the trade winds. In Panama the northwest trades blow most strongly during the dry season, when they drop their moisture chiefly on the Caribbean slope of the highlands. The winds build up during the day so that on some afternoons there may be a gusty breeze blowing, especially over the open Pacific savannas where they further desiccate an area already made dry by a lack of rain and a hot sun unobstructed by clouds. The constant trades at this season also sometimes cause an upwelling in the Gulf of Panama: warm surface waters are pushed away from the land by the wind, and cooler, more nutrient-rich, underlying water is forced up to take the warm water's place, thereby creating a rich feeding ground for great flocks of birds. During the rainy season, the trades subside and are more variable, though most afternoons a breeze will spring up; strong gusty winds may occur around squalls and showers. It should finally be pointed out that Panama lies well south of the normal hurricane track, though very occasionally a weak tropical depression may skirt the Caribbean coast.

Most of the preceding description is especially applicable to the lowlands, but some of the same patterns also hold in the highlands. Temperatures in the highlands are, as expected, lower, and at high elevations can become rather

TABLE II

PRECIPITATION DATA FOR CENTRAL PANAMA AND VICINITY (INCHES)

	Jan.	Feb.	Mar.	Apr.	May	June	July	Aug.	Sept.	Oct.	Nov.	Dec.	Ann.
BALBOA													
Avg.	1.1	0.6	0.6	3.0	7.8	7.8	7.3	7.7	7.5	10.2	9.9	5.4	68.9
Max.	5.2	4.9	5.0	7.8	15.2	16.3	15.8	15.6	17.3	20.8	20.5	15.0	93.1
Min.	0	0	0	Tr.	2.2	2 .4	3.4	1.3	2.5	3.4	3.2	0.2	48.9
SUMMIT													
Avg.	0.9	0.4	0.4	3.1	10.1	9 .2	10.1	10.0	9.9	12.2	12.6	5.8	84.8
Max.	5.3	2.9	3.0	8.9	22.8	16.4	20.4	18.7	14.8	18.8	31.4	24.4	111.2
Min.	0	0	0	0	3.3	3.6	2.9	5.2	4.5	4.3	6.0	0.5	67.6
BARRO COLORADO ISLAND													
Avg.	2.2	1.3	1.2	3.4	11.0	10.9	11.7	12.5	10.3	14.0	17.9	10.6	107.3
Max.	9.0	7.3	5.5	18.3	19.0	19.4	28.6	21.9	20.0	22.2	41.6	28.2	143.4
Min.	0.2	Tr.	Tr.	Tr.	3.1	3.8	5.4	5.9	5.7	6.1	7.2	1.2	76.6
CRISTOBAL													
Avg.	3.3	1.6	1.5	4.0	12.4	13.2	15.6	15.3	12.5	15.7	22.5	12.2	129.7
Max.	12.2	12.4	9.0	21.4	20.4	21.2	27.7	26.6	23.0	42.2	43.1	34.4	183.4
Min.	0.3	Tr.	Tr.	0.1	1.6	5.9	4.4	5.8	3.1	5.8	6.6	0.9	86.5
PORTOBELO													
Avg.	5.1	3.0	2.6	6.4	17.5	16.9	18.3	19.3	13.2	15.6	24.5	16.1	158.6
Max.	20.9	11.6	9.7	30.2	30.6	25.9	29.0	33.5	23.0	42.2	53.3	58.2	237.3
Min.	0.7	0.4	0.6	0.5	5.0	6.5	7.4	8.7	6.5	4.8	7.7	2.2	118.0

SOURCE: Panama Canal Company, Meteorological and Hydrographic Branch

cold. One notices a significant and pleasant drop in temperature at elevations over 600 m (2000 ft), as on Cerro Campana and Cerro Azul. In Chiriquí at elevations over 12000 m (4000 ft), nights can be cold, and frosts are not unknown, especially at higher elevations, while days are usually in the 60s or low 70s F (lower in inclement weather). Seasonal fluctuations in rainfall are not as marked as in most of the lowlands. The Caribbean slopes tend to be more humid than those on the Pacific, in part a result of frequent low-hanging mist and clouds. Series of several rainy, unpleasant days are not infrequent in the highlands, especially on the Caribbean slope. A typical pattern is for the sky to be crystal clear at daybreak, for clouds to form rapidly during the morning, and for the clouds to lower and precipitation to occur on and off through the afternoon, often in the form of a drenching mist or drizzle (locally called *bajareque*). Some days, though, are delightful and sunny, especially invigorating after the heat of the lowlands. At elevations above 2100 m (7000 ft), temperatures become progressively colder, clouds and precipitation are likely at any time of the year, and frosts occasionally occur, especially during the dry season. Snow has been reported falling briefly on the summit of the Volcán Barú (*fide* Eisenmann).

Out of Panama's total avifauna of 929 species (including species newly recorded since the 1976 edition), and excluding its 33 hypothetical species, 122 species occur only as long-distance migrants, i.e. they are not known and are unlikely to breed in the country. This total (Table III) includes only those species that probably occur regularly, though some may occur only in small numbers. Another 62 species (Table IV) have been recorded on but a few occasions, some of them being purely casual or accidental (e.g. Snowy Plover, Vermilion Flycatcher), while others may have only been overlooked (e.g. Elegant Tern, Black-whiskered Vireo). Note that this total does *not* include hypothetical species. Another 13 species are basically pelagic (Table V) and occur only as nonbreeding visitants; most are rarely seen from shore, and several are known from very few (or even one) records. More collecting and observation in Panama waters will undoubtedly add to this pelagic list.

Practically all of the long-distance migrants are temperate or arctic North American breeders; only one landbird breeding in South America is known to migrate regularly to Panama (Brown-chested Martin), though a few others (e.g. Southern Martin, Ashy-tailed Swift, and the Patagonian race of the Blue-and-white Swallow) may be more regular than the few records would indicate. Migration from South America and from farther north in Middle America may be more extensive but in numerous cases involves populations of species or even subspecies that also breed in Panama, and separating migrants from local breeders is difficult or impossible without having marked birds (examples include Fork-tailed Flycatcher of Middle America, Streaked Flycatcher, Gray-breasted Martin). Only five species that breed in Panama are definitely thought to migrate out of the country during their nonbreeding season. All five are generally absent during the peak of the rainy season and returning in January or later (American Swallow-tailed and Plumbeous Kites, Common Nighthawk, Piratic Flycatcher, Yellow-green Vireo).

At some times of the year, especially during the northern autumn and spring migration periods, migrant passerines constitute a conspicuous element in the Panamanian avifauna. Some northern breeding species (e.g. Yellow Warbler, Orchard Oriole) arrive in Panama so early and leave so late that they spend considerably more of their year in their winter quarters than in their breeding grounds. In general, most northern migrants shun the forest interior in favor of borders, lighter woodland and man-disturbed areas such as clearings and gardens; however, certain species (e.g. Arcadian Flycatcher, Kentucky Warbler, and others) do require forest or mature second-growth woodland during most or all of their period of residence in Panama, and others depend on forest at least at times. In more wooded areas migrant passerines frequently join mixed flocks of resident species, while in more open areas they are apt to occur in groups of their own species or with other migrants. Northern migrants are most numerous during their periods of

TABLE III
REGULAR MIGRANTS
(not known to breed in Panama)

Great Blue Heron	Eastern Wood-Pewee
Glossy Ibis	Yellow-bellied Flycatcher
Blue-winged Teal	Acadian Flycatcher
American Wigeon	Willow Flycatcher
Lesser Scaup	Alder Flycatcher
Osprey	Great Crested Flycatcher
Mississippi Kite	Sulphur-bellied Flycatcher
Northern Harrier	Eastern Kingbird
Sharp-shinned Hawk	Gray Kingbird
Broad-winged Hawk	Scissor-tailed Flycatcher
Swainson's Hawk	Purple Martin
American Kestrel	Brown-chested Martin
Merlin	Northern Rough-winged Swallow
Peregrine Falcon	Sand Martin
Sora	Cliff Swallow
American Coot	Barn Swallow
Black-bellied Plover	Veery
American Golden Plover	Gray-cheeked Thrush
Semipalmated Plover	Swainson's Thrush
Killdeer	Wood Thrush
Greater Yellowlegs	Gray Catbird
Lesser Yellowlegs	Cedar Waxwing
Solitary Sandpiper	Yellow-throated Vireo
Willet	Philadelphia Vireo
Spotted Sandpiper	Red-eyed Vireo
Upland Sandpiper	Blue-winged Warbler
Whimbrel	Golden-winged Warbler
Marbled Godwit	Tennessee Warbler
Ruddy Turnstone	Yellow Warbler
Surfbird	Chestnut-sided Warbler
Red Knot	Magnolia Warbler
Sanderling	Yellow-rumped Warbler
Semipalmated Sandpiper	Black-throated Green Warbler
Western Sandpiper	Blackburnian Warbler
Least Sandpiper	Palm Warbler
White-rumped Sandpiper	Bay-breasted Warbler
Baird's Sandpiper	Cerulean Warbler
Pectoral Sandpiper	Black-and-white Warbler
Stilt Sandpiper	American Redstart
Buff-breasted Sandpiper	Prothonotary Warbler
Short-billed Dowitcher	Worm-eating Warbler
Common Snipe	Ovenbird
Laughing Gull	Northern Waterthrush
Franklin's Gull	Louisiana Waterthrush
Ring-billed Gull	Kentucky Warbler
Herring Gull	Mourning Warbler
Gull-billed Tern	Common Yellowthroat
Royal Tern,	Hooded Warbler
Sandwich Tern	Wilson's Warbler
Common Tern	Canada Warbler
Least Tern	Summer Tanager
Black Tern	Scarlet Tanager
Black Skimmer	Western Tanager
Black-billed Cuckoo	Rose-breasted Grosbeak
Yellow-billed Cuckoo	Blue Grosbeak
Chuck-will's-widow	Indigo Bunting
Chimney Swift	Painted Bunting
Belted Kingfisher	Dickcissel
Yellow-bellied Sapsucker	Bobolink
Olive-sided Flycatcher	Orchard Oriole
Western Wood-Pewee	Northern Oriole

TABLE IV
VERY RARE OR CASUAL VISITANTS
(not breeding in Panama)

Peruvian Booby	Inca Tern
American White Pelican	Dark-billed Cuckoo
Guanay Cormorant	Gray-capped Cuckoo
American Bittern	Burrowing Owl
Buff-necked Ibis	Whip-poor-will
Jabiru	White-chinned Swift
Fulvous Whistling-Duck	Chapman's Swift
White-faced Whistling-Duck	Ashy-tailed Swift
Northern Pintail	Ruby Topaz
Northern Shoveler	Ruby-throated Hummingbird
Ring-necked Duck	Least Flycatcher
Cinnamon Teal	Vermilion Flycatcher
Snail Kite	Southern Martin
Harris' Hawk	Tree Swallow
Snowy Plover	Violet-green Swallow
American Avocet	White-eyed Vireo
Wandering Tattler	Solitary Vireo
Long-billed Curlew	Black-whiskered Vireo
Hudsonian Godwit	Northern Parula
Dunlin	Cape May Warbler
Ruff	Black-throated Blue Warbler
Long-billed Dowitcher	Townsend's Warbler
Wilson's Phalarope	Hermit Warbler
Bonaparte's Gull	Yellow-throated Warbler
Band-tailed Gull	Prairie Warbler
Lesser Black-backed Gull	Blackpoll Warbler
Caspian Tern	Connecticut Warbler
Elegant Tern	MacGillivray's Warbler
Forster's Tern	Lincoln's Sparrow
Yellow-billed Tern	White-crowned Sparrow
Large-billed Tern	Yellow-headed Blackbird

TABLE V
PELAGIC VISITANTS

Wedge-tailed Shearwater	Masked Booby
Sooty Shearwater	Red-footed Booby
Wilson's Storm-Petrel	Red-necked Phalarope
Wedge-rumped Storm-Petrel	Pomarine Jaeger
Black Storm-Petrel	Parasitic Jaegar
Markham's Storm-Petrel	Sabine's Gull
Least Storm-Petrel	

transience in the fall and spring, often occurring im marked waves; they are less numerous during the northern winter months (December–February). However, some migrants remain common, notably in the foothills and highlands, all through the winter, though the reasons for this contrast with the lowlands are uncertain. Several other migrant groups besides the passerines occur in significant numbers in Panama. Migrant ducks, though limited in species, are in the aggregate more numerous than all the resident waterfowl together. Certain species of diurnal raptors (Turkey Vulture, Broad-winged and Swainson's Hawks) provide an almost unbelievable spectacle during their migrations (for photos see N. G. Smith, *Am. Birds 27*: 3–5, 1973). Many of the shorebirds also gather in impressive flocks, and the variety of species is often notable.

Some Panamanian breeding species may engage in local movements, in most cases of an unknown magnitude. Information on this phenomenon is scant, for it requires long-term observations, population studies, and banding of individuals at specific areas. One problem is that the entire population of a species may not take part in the local movement; i.e. the presence of a few individuals may "mask" the absence of others. What we see for some species is a seasonal fluctuation in abundance, probably caused by seasonal variations in the food supply, or by dispersal of immatures, or both. The Ruddy-breasted and Yellow-bellied Seedeaters are good examples, both seemingly "disappearing" from their breeding areas from the end of the rainy season through most of the dry season. Other species also fluctuate markedly on a local basis, e.g. in the Canal area, Blue Ground-Dove and Lesser Elaenia. Various species of hummingbirds almost unquestionably engage in similar local movements (e.g. White-necked Jacobin), probably in order to find sufficient flowering trees and other plants. Again it must be emphasized that these comments are of a preliminary nature, and are included merely to indicate how much has yet to be learned about this interesting and until recently unrecognized phenomenon.

Altitudinal movements are also undertaken by some Panamanian breeding species, in all known cases involving birds that breed in the highlands or foothills and descend to the lowlands in their nonbreeding seasons. Again these movements are little documented in Panama except in the case of two large cotingas, the Three-wattled Bellbird and Bare-necked Umbrellabird, both of which breed in the western highlands and subsequently descend to the lowlands, especially during the peak of the rainy season. Movements of this type are most likely to be noted in lowland areas adjacent to some mountains, which largely eliminates central Panama, where most of the sustained bird observation work to date has taken place. Also, because most of the species involved are forest birds, areas that are still largely covered with forest are required, thus eliminating much of Pacific western Panama. Other species besides the bellbird and umbrellabird that may in part move down-slope after the breeding season include several parrots (Sulphur-winged and Barred Parakeets and Red-fronted Parrotlet), several hummingbirds (Violet-headed Hummingbird, Snowcap), White-ruffed Manakin, Olive-striped Flycatcher, Pale-vented and White-throated Thrushes, Silver-throated Tanager, and probably a number of others (in part as to Costa Rica, *fide* F. G. Stiles, oral comm.). Much further field work will be required before the extent of these movements is known. Bocas del Toro, Caribbean slope Veraguas, and Darién would seem the most promising areas for such studies.

RECENT DEVELOPMENTS IN PANAMA
ORNITHOLOGY AND CONSERVATION

As might have been expected, there have been numerous changes in the Panama ornithological and conservation scene since the text of *A Guide to the Birds of Panama* was completed in 1974. The purpose of these next few pages is to summarize some of the more important of these developments, and to suggest certain directions for the future. It should be noted that from a bird *finding* perspective, the many changes which have occurred in the intervening 15 years have been dealt with in the substantially re-written and expanded chapter on finding birds, and will not be dealt with here.

Perhaps the most fundamental change has involved what was formerly called the Panama Canal Zone. In 1979 the treaty under which the United States had held numerous rights over the Canal Zone was formally modified, with most of those rights reverting to Panama. This resulted in a substantial and gratifying reduction in tensions between the two nations, and while inevitably certain inequities could not be resolved to everyone's complete satisfaction, solutions to most of the outstanding differences were found. Particularly successful was the resolution of many of the environmental concerns which had been raised. Under the treaty, and subsequent to it, not only was Barro Colorado Island and a substantial portion of nearby Gatun Lake shoreline protected as the Barro Colorado Natural Monument, but so too was the entire expanse of forest from the Pipeline Road area south across the Chagres River and extending to incorporate Madden Forest. This area is now called Soberanía National Park, and much of it is now well protected; hunting is virtually a thing of the past, and numbers of certain depleted species appear to be gradually recovering (and perhaps soon the reintroduction of the one locally extirpated species, the Great Green Macaw, can even be attempted). Furthermore, in order better to regulate the flow of water needed for the Canal operation during the dry season, various measures have recently been started to protect forest in the Chagres River's drainage area above Madden Lake.

These moves have all been extremely beneficial, and Panama is to be congratulated for having been so far-sighted; but it must be pointed out that even more can and should be done. For instance, the valuable and exceptionally rich coastal forest along the Caribbean coast in the Fort Sherman/Achiote area needs to be protected when that area's lease to the US Military expires in 1999; the Military provides reasonably good protection for the present. Permanent protection is also needed for some or all of the fine deciduous forest and woodland still found on Fort Kobbe and Howard Air Force Base, now virtually unique on the Pacific mainland.

Much progress has also been made at the national level. Panama now has a functioning National Park system, though much of the land it includes is either remote and difficult of access, or is protected mainly on paper and not on the ground. INRENARE, the governmental agency in charge of park management (as well as other functions), is chronically under-funded and under-staffed, but despite this the situation has much improved since 1974, in part due to the prodding and assistance of vigorous new non-governmental private conservation organizations such as ANCON (Asociación Nacional para la Conservación de la Naturaleza). Panama's premier protected area is the huge Darién National Park in eastern Darién, encompassing a vast sweep of wild country along the Colombian frontier and including all of the Cerro Pirre and Cerro Tacarcuna massifs. It is doubtless the richest and most important protected area for wildlife in Middle America. Visitor access remains difficult (see discussion in the section on bird finding), but will hopefully be made easier in the not-too-distant future—this is an area which people should be able to experience without having to mount a full-fledged expedition. At the other end of the country, the upper level of Panama's highest mountain, Volcán Barú in western Chiriquí, now has its own National Park, but here too it is hard to reach most of the park, and visitors do not seem to be encouraged (certainly not along the telecommunications tower road west of Boquete). One cannot help but make the somewhat invidious comparison with various protected montane areas in Costa Rica—Monteverde springs to mind. These thrive and attract attention the world round precisely because they provide visitor amenities: a large number of visitors, both nationals and foreigners, are thus permitted to experience and savor the area, they learn to cherish it, and soon want to protect it. Panama could do the same.

One area in the Comarca de San Blas deserves mention as the first real attempt to foster this sort of development in Panama. Not only have the Kuna Indians, who have jurisdiction over all of San Blas and can restrict access, established a major reserve in the western portion of the Comarca, but they have also constructed a limited infrastructure for visitor access at Nusagandi, an area rich for birds situated square on the Continental Divide. Hopefully this effort will be successful, and others will emulate it.

Panama's park system encompasses a number of other areas, too many to mention here. However, we might point out that two of Panama's most imperilled faunal areas remain completely unprotected. One is the humid lowland forest once found in western Chiriquí. The only significant remaining tract of this forest, so rich in species not found elsewhere in the country (though all do occur in neighboring Costa Rica, so none is endangered at the global level), is found on the Burica Peninsula. Here what is left continues to be gradually felled, so that even now much of what remains lies on the Costa Rican side of the border. Protection of what remains should receive the highest priority. The second involves the deciduous forest once found on the Pacific slope of western Panama from central Chiriquí to the western side of the Azuero Peninusla. On the mainland virtually all of this has now been destroyed—flying over the area is a discouraging prospect indeed— leaving the only important remnant that found on Coiba Island off the coast. Here forest cover remains extensive, given as it is de facto protection as a result of the island's continuing status as a penal institute. It is much to be urged that a substantial portion of the island, which supports Panama's only viable population of the once much more widespread Scarlet Macaw (as well as numerous other species of interest, including one endemic), be permanently protected as a national park or reserve. Consideration might even be given to introducing to the island certain rare species (such as the Great Curassow) which have apparently been incapable of colonizing the island naturally but which should thrive there.

Happily, interest in Panamanian birds has never been greater than at the present: we like to think that *Birds of Panama* has played a role in this. One important change has been the great increase in the number of natural history and birding tours offered to the country (and of course to neighboring Costa Rica and elsewhere). We view this as a beneficial development, for not only does it bring a substantial and much needed infusion of foreign exchange into the country, it also provides an additional incentive for protecting various natural habitats. One result of the upsurge in nature-related tourism has been the increased number of keen and perceptive birders who have been active in the country. Their prowess has resulted in numerous new records and other interesting observations; the contribution of the portable tape recorder must be especially singled out, as it has so facilitated the learning of numerous vocalizations of previously little-known birds. We are grateful to many of these international birders for sharing many of their observations and tape recordings. Of course local residents have also played an extremely important role in fostering and encouraging increased knowledge of Panama's birds. Most notable perhaps has been the role of the Panama Audubon Society, particularly its "Field Editor" Dodge Engleman (and his wife Lorna). They are the pair who, among many other things, so superbly organize the "Atlantic Side" Christmas bird count, routinely the top count in North America in terms of species observed (upwards of 350 having been found in a single year!). More recently, far more Panamanian citizens have begun to develop an interest in looking at and enjoying birds, a positive and hopeful sign indeed and one which we hope will be further stimulated by the publication of *Birds of Panama* in Spanish. Francisco Delgado, the present head of the Panama section of the International Council for Bird Preservation and a professor from

Chitre in Herrera has been especially effective in this role, though there have of course been numerous others as well. Lastly, the more scientifically oriented influence of the Smithsonian Tropical Research Institute continues to be substantial, serving as it does as the primary center for biological research in the country. In particular, James Karr's ongoing research on forest bird population dynamics has become something of a model for such studies, and has also been the catalyst for bringing numerous individuals, both amateurs and scientists, to Panama in the first place.

A staggering amount of new information concerning the distribution and abundance of Panama's birds has accumulated over the past 15 or so years, so much so that we believe it is safe to say that Panama is now about as well known in this regard as any other tropical American country. Working on the solid systematic framework provided by the late Alexander Wetmore, whose fourth and final volume in his monumental series was at last published in 1982, records have poured in from virtually all parts of Panama. RSR has been fortunate to have been able to participate in, or to organize, numerous productive trips to various poorly known localities. The three which stand out were the two to the exceptionally rich Fortuna area in central Chiriquí (the first in the pre-dam era of 1976), and to the Burica Peninsula in extreme western Chiriquí (whose avifauna as noted above is more threatened in Panama than any other). Other areas which have proven exceptionally interesting in recent years have included: the southern end of the Azuero Peninsula, where Delgado made his stunning discovery of the Painted Parakeet, and still the area most likely to harbor new, conceivably even undescribed, species; the Cana and Cerro Pirre area in Darién, site of a major Louisiana State University expedition in 1980, and of numerous shorter trips since, surely the single finest locality in the province and well worth the effort to get there; the El Copé region of Coclé, with its legion of western foothill species surprisingly far to the east, and the best site in Panama to view the exquisite and rare Snowcap; and the foothills of western San Blas, first investigated only in 1985 by John Blake and since visited by others with notable results. It might be pointed out here that despite the substantial collecting efforts of the past, there still remains a real need for this activity to continue in certain poorly known areas (including, surprisingly, western San Blas where the racial affinity of some forms, still unknown, will be of major biogeographic interest). Furthermore, it will only be through the collection of additional material for biochemical and anatomical study that the relationships of many Panama birds will be firmly established.

Doubtless the most remarkable ornithological event to have occurred in Panama over the past 15 years was the astounding incursion of unusual oceanic and coastal birds which occurred subsequent to the exceptionally strong "El Niño" event in 1982. In fact water temperatures increased only somewhat in Panama, far less than they did off the western coast of South America, but massive numbers of apparently displaced and randomly dispersing birds did come in. For several months, for example, the Peruvian Booby, a bird never before recorded from Panamanian waters, was the most numerous booby in the bay. Within about a year most of the incursive birds had either died or further dispersed, so the event caused no permanent change in bird distribution. It was, however, truly unparalleled in its magnitude while it lasted, and one can only wish that a more systematic effort to document the occurrence could have been mounted, for it is unlikely to be repeated for a very long time indeed.

Looking toward the future, what remains to be done? Of course, the answer is inumerable things! The basic outlines of bird distribution and abundance may now be known, but natural history information on numerous species remains scanty or is even entirely lacking, and there will always remain the need to monitor avifaunal change in the face of continuing habitat alterations; and only now are the ecological relationships of the legion of northern migratory species to those permanently resident in Panama beginning to be seriously investigated. In terms of distribution, pelagic species remain the least known in Panama. We continue to expect that a number of unrecorded or under-recorded species will be found to occur more or less regularly in the deep water south of the Azuero Peninsula. The breeding status of the three pelagic terns (and possibly other species as well?) on islands off Punta Mala needs to be established once and for all, while the recent observation of Cory's Shearwater off Colon leads us to suspect that the Caribbean too would repay some observational effort. The southern end of the Azuero Peninsula may remain ornithologically the least known part of Panama, but genuine surprises also turn up elsewhere. What is the status of the recently recorded Rose-throated Becard in Chiriquí? What will the new Clapper Rail found by Wilberto Matinez in Bocas de Toro turn out to be? Will Blackpoll Warblers continue to be regular, if sparse, visitants during the northern winter? Will increased observer coverage continue to result in records of various casual migrants (Cape May Warbler, Black-throated Blue Warbler, White-eyed Vireo, etc.) so that the assessment of their status will have to be revised, and to what extent might this reflect other possible changes elsewhere? Will Shiny Cowbirds continue to spread and increase westward? What of other mainly South American species (Southern Lapwings and the like) now spreading through Panama, and in some cases on into Costa Rica as well? The questions are endless, limited only by one's capabilities to accurately observe, record, and publish (or somehow make known) observations. We look forward to the next 15 years with keen anticipation, confident that they will see discoveries every bit as notable as we have enjoyed these past few years, and hopeful that the move to protect adequately Panama's avifauna has only just begun.

POSTSCRIPT

Some readers may be interested in the following list of the 46 species added to Panama's avifauna since the publication in 1976 of the first edition of *Birds of Panama*. Note that one, the Rock Dove, was previously not considered to be a feral bird in Panama; that another, the Black Rail, is now admitted on the basis of new information concerning an old record; that another, the Markham's Storm-Petrel, is also admitted on the basis of an old specimen record; and that the Purple-throated Woodstar is added on the basis not only of a 1980 specimen but also as a result of the re-identification of an old specimen previously identified as Gorgeted Woodstar, which has now been deleted from the Panama list.

Cory's Shearwater
Townsend's Shearwater
Markham's Storm-Petrel
Peruvian Booby
American White Pelican
Reddish Egret
Pearl Kite
Black Rail
Clapper Rail
Paint-billed Crake
American Avocet
Hudsonian Godwit
Lesser Black-backed Gull
Forster's Tern
Yellow-billed Tern
Inca Tern
White Tern
Rock Dove
Dusky Pigeon
Common Ground-Dove
Painted Parakeet
Dwarf Cuckoo
Dark-billed Cuckoo

Gray-capped Cuckoo
Ocellated Poorwill
Black Swift
Ruby Topaz
Purple-throated Woodstar
Hammond's Flycatcher
Cattle Tyrant
Western Kingbird
Rose-throated Becard
Lovely Cotinga
White-collared Manakin
Cave Swallow
European Starling
Nashville Warbler
Northern Parula
Prairie Warbler
Yellow-collared Chlorophonia
Ashy-throated Bush-Tanager
Lesson's Seedeater
Peg-billed Finch
Lark Sparrow
White-crowned Sparrow
House Sparrow

In the first edition in 1976, 883 species were credited to Panama. Of these, the 1983 AOU Check-list split four species in which both of the component forms occur in Panama (Common and Mangrove Black-Hawks, Blue-chested and Charming Hummingbirds, Purple-throated and White-throated Mountain-gems, and Northern and Southern Rough-winged Swallows), while three species were lumped (both component forms occurring in Panama), these being Green and Striated Herons, Rufous-tailed and Black-chinned Jacamars, and Yellow and Mangrove Warblers. This results in a net change of one additional species to the list of 1976. Thus the present Panama list totals 929 species. Of this total, 33 species are considered to be of hypothetical status (for my operating definition of "hypothetical," see under Plan of the Book, p.20). These are given in Table VI.

PLAN OF THE BOOK

Those who have had field experience observing birds, especially in the neotropics, will find this book much easier to use than those who are just starting out in this fascinating study. A certain amount of knowledge has had to be assumed. However, we have tried to make the book both understandable to the beginner and useful to the experienced amateur and professional. Thus, some information is included that only the beginner will need (such as how to tell an ibis from a heron), and also data that only those will experience will know how to use (such as how to distinguish the two dowitcher species).

In this section we will discuss the major headings found under each family and species account, and define the more important terms used.

FAMILY ACCOUNTS

The sequence of families followed is that of the 1983 AOU Check-list. The family accounts themselves follow a relatively standardized format in order to facilitate comparison. First, the general distribution of the family is given, and its approximate size is indicated. Generalizations about the family that may be helpful to the field student are made, with emphasis on distinctive family characteristics. Data on food preferences, general behavior, and style of nest are included here for the Panamanian members of the family as a whole, rather than in the individual species accounts. Finally, where appropriate, special identification problems in the family are outlined, and its current status in Panama may be discussed. The number of species recorded for the family in Panama is given in parentheses in the heading.

SPECIES ACCOUNTS

Some discussion of classifcation and nomenclature is essential at this juncture. The species is the basic unit in biology. Most zoologists now accept the view than an animal species consists of a group of populations whose members interbreed freely, or would do so if their ranges met. Different species are usually also morphologically distinct, i.e. they "look different," though this is not a prerequisite, and some geographical populations of the same species look very different and yet interbreed freely where their ranges meet. Many species contain several such subspecies or geographic races, which inhabit different portions of the range of the species. Subspecies generally differ only slightly in appearance. Only those subspecies occurring in Panama that differ markedly from each other are mentioned in the main text. This all seems simple in theory, but in practice it often proves difficult. The problem that most concerns the nonsystematist arises when zoologists differ as to whether or not a particular population or populations, usually isolated and of distinctive appearance, represents a valid species or is merely a subspecies or group of subspecies. Final resolution of many of these problems may depend on various forms of biochemical analysis, but meanwhile *some* decision as to names employed must be made.

This book attempts to steer a middle-of-the-road course in scientific nomenclature. In general, the policy has been to retain most reasonably distinct forms as valid species where such treatment has been customary in the literature. In this book, when a serious taxonomic question at the species (or sometimes higher) level involves Panama populations, it is mentioned in the hope that work in Panama might help to resolve it.

Most nonprofessionals are not usually concerned with the scientific name except insofar as they generally wish to list only what are regarded as full species. Of greater concern to them is the English name that each species has been given. In temperate North America and Europe these names have been generally standardized and accepted, though a few changes must always be made in order to conform with new taxonomic findings. In the neotropics, however, where ornithology is now little more advanced than it was in the United States soon after the turn of the century, a single species may have been given several different English names by various authors. This obviously creates difficulties for those who are not accustomed to using the scientific names —one often cannot be sure what bird is being talked about. A giant step toward the standardization of these names for neotropical birds was taken with the publication of Eisenmann's *The Species of Middle American Birds* (1955) and Meyer de Schauensee's *The Species of Birds of South America* (1966), the latter prepared with considerable assistance from Eisenmann. These names have been followed more or less, by most recent authors, and were used in the 1983 AOU Check-list in the main. The problem of English names is a thorny one: everyone has their personal preferences, and one usually wants to retain names that are familiar to him. But the primary issue is one of utility and standardization. Therefore the names used in this book are those of the 1983 AOU Check-list with but a few exceptions, all of these explained.

After much consideration, we still opted not to include Spanish names, as there seems as yet to be so little agreement on the subject. A few widely used popular names have been mentioned.

The sequence of species within each family is that of the 1983 AOU Check-list, with only minor deviations (notably in the Psittacidae).

Each species account is divided into up to six headings, as follows; one or more may be omitted where there is insufficient information.

DESCRIPTION

First the species' average total length in inches (from tip of bill to end of tail) is given; other lengths are also mentioned when appropriate (hummingbird bills, elongated tail feathers, etc.). The first sentence is designed as a "warning sentence", and is included when the species is not widespread in its Panama range. For example, "found only in western highlands" means that in Panama it ranges only in the highlands of Chiriquí, Veraguas, and sometimes Bocas del Toro. Thus any observation away from this area would be highly unusual and should be carefully checked. Another phrase "Known only from . . . ," is similar, but implies that while the species has been recorded only from the area given, the species is little known and may be more widespread. The next sentence gives distinguishing features of shape and soft-part colors, when these are particularly helpful in species recognition.

Adult males are described first, followed by females, immatures, juveniles, and aberrant plumages where appropriate (often all that it indicated is how they differ from the adult male). For each, a diagnosis of the entire plumage is given. The description is kept simple, with details not considered important to identification omitted. The most distintive characters of the species are italicized. In a few cases where a less well-known species closely resembles another better known bird, reference is made to the latter and only distinguishing points are given. Many North American migrants (but, interestingly, very few resident species: one is the male Red-legged Honeycreeper) have a breeding and a nonbreeding ("winter") plumage. In Panama these migrants are most often seen in nonbreeding plumage, hence that is usually treated first.

SIMILAR SPECIES

Comparison is made here between the species under discussion and others known from Panama with which it might be confused. For a few difficult groups, wing and tail measurements (in millimeters) are included as an aid to mist-netters. When the species is not likely to be confused, this paragraph is omitted.

STATUS AND DISTRIBUTION

In this paragraph, the known range of the species in Panama, its relative abundance, its period of occurrence when not a resident, and its known habitat preferences are given. For some species, specific, accessible localities where they may be more easily found than elsewhere are included. If information on some (or all) of these points is scanty, this is clearly indicated in the hope that further work will fill in some of these gaps in our knowledge. For many of the less common species, specific records are mentioned. In the case of sight reports of such rarities, the name of the observer(s) is given. Collector's names are usually included only when the record was not mentioned by Wetmore or when some special situation is involved. Emphasis has been placed on documenting reports not included in Wetmore's volumes, or which occurred subsequent to preparation of his volumes, especially when such reports have significantly altered the status or range of that species in Panama.

In order to describe the status of transient and migratory species, the vast majority of which breed in North Amnerica, it has been expedient to use seasonal terms such as "winter", etc. We well realize that such terms have little or no bearing on seasonality in Panama, and would have preferred not to use them. However, not doing so inevitably and frequently results in syntax which is awkward and wordy. Thus, with reluctance, we continue to employ them. So, unless otherwise stated (through use of the term ''austral'', which connotes seasonality in the *Southern* Hemisphere), all seasonality terms refer to seasons in the *Northern* Hemisphere.

Accents have been included only on proper names thought not to be well known to English readers. Thus Panama, Galapagos, Peru, Yucatan, Colon have not been accented (though they are in Spanish, e.g. Panamá, Colón, Yucatán), while other, less familiar names have had their accent retained, in part as a pronunciation guide (e.g. Chiriquí, Darién, Coclé, Calovévora, etc.).

Abundance Terms

The abundance terms used here are necessarily subjective and thus require explanation. Many species in Panama, especially those of forest and undergrowth, are difficult to see; one hears them many times for each time seen. In estimating relative abundance of these species, we have relied heavily on thier often very distintive vocalizations, and this fact must be borne in mind. For example, we have listed the Spectacled Antpitta as ''fairly common'' though we have not seen it (other than in mist-nets or in response to a tape recording) more than a half-dozen times. Nonetheless it is known to be fairly common in suitable habitat because its distinctive far-carrying call is so often heard. The numerical abundance of certain furtive, undergrowth species is much better indicated by mist-net captures than by sight observations (leaftossers are prime examples), and consideration has also been given to this factor.

Two further qualifications must be made. First, our field experience is to some extent biased toward the Canal area, where we have spent most of our time in Panama (though RSR has, over the past 15 years, made a concerted effort to pass some time in *all* parts of Panama, however remote). The abundance terms used thus tend to be slanted to an indeterminable extent by experiences in central Panama. In some cases the problem has been overcome by separating ranges into several parts, while in a few others no abundance term has been used at all. One should also remember that, in general, as one approaches the geographical limit of the range of a species, that species becomes less numerous (for example, the Black-tailed Trogen and Sirystes are both rather scarce at the northwestern limit of their range in the Canal area, but become more numerous as one moves into eastern Panama). Second, abundance terms must be approached in a relative sense: hawks should be compared with hawks, and flycatchers with flycatchers, but not hawks with flycatchers. The Double-toothed Kite and Forest Elaenia are both listed as fairly common, but there are not nearly as many kites ''per acre'' as there are elaenias. There is thus a double standard , one for large birds, another for smaller ones. In general, moreover, birds of open situations, being more easily seen, will appear more numerous than those of forest or woodland, though again they may not be any more numerous "per acre". Here, too, there is a double standard, one for more or less open country, one for wooded areas.

The abundance terms used are explained below. A "trip" is considered to be a day's field work. The terms must be viewed in a relative, not absolute, sense. It should be emphasized that the terms refer to the frequency with which the experienced observer, especially one familiar with vocalizations, notes them; clearly the beginner will not be as successful.

Abundant. Recorded on all field trips in proper habitat and season, often in large numbers. These are usually birds of open areas or water habitats. Examples: Tropical Kingbird, Western Sandpiper.

Very common. Almost invariably recorded on trips in proper habitat and season, but not observed in as large numbers as the preceding category. Examples: Slaty Antshrike, Lesser Greenlet.

Common. Recorded on most (at least 75%) trips in proper habitat and season, but usually not in large numbers. Examples: Boat-billed Flycatcher, Slaty-tailed Trogon.

Fairly common. Recorded on about half of trips in proper habitat and season. Examples: Blue-chested Hummingbird, White-winged Tanager. From this category on, numbers recorded on any trip are usually small.

Uncommon. Recorded on less than half (between 25 and 50%) of trips in proper habitat and season. Examples: Ocellated Antbird, Gray-headed Kite.

Rare. Recorded on fewer (usually considerably fewer) than 25% of trips in proper habitat and season. Examples: Plumbeous Hawk, Dull-mantled Antbird.

Very rare. Records extremely few anywhere in Panama, and always in small numbers, but presumed to be a resident within the country, or within the expected range of a migrant or wanderer. Examples: Least Flycatcher, Lanceolated Monklet.

The following terms relate to distributional status or regularity, rather than primarily to numbers.

Casual. Records very few in Panama; a migrant or wandering species that ranges regularly not too far from Panama, but that cannot be expected to occur in the country except at intervals (usually long). Examples: Buff-necked Ibis, Yellow-throated Warbler.

Accidental. Usually only one record for Panama, and hardly to be expected again though possible; a species whose normal range is a considerable distance from Panama. Examples: Burrowing Owl, White-crowned Sparrow.

Hypothetical. A species for which there is no incontrovertible proof of occurrence in Panama. Species have been admitted to full status on the Panama list if: a) a specimen has been collected and preserved, or b) a recognizable photograph has been taken (some of these are now archived in the VIREO collection at the Academy of Natural Sciences; more should be), or c) there are at least three independent sight reports by at least three competent observers of a species that can be identified in the field. Failure to meet one of these criteria relegates a species to the hypothetical list for Panama. A few additional species have been placed on the hypothetical list because there is doubt as to whether it reached Panama unassisted or whether the specimen attributed to Panama was actually collected in the country. By these criteria, 33 species are on Panama's hypothetical list; see Table VI. In the text the English names for each of these species is placed in brackets.

TABLE VI
PANAMA HYPOTHETICAL SPECIES

Wandering Albatross	White Tern
Waved Albatross	Dusky Pigeon
Gray-headed Albatross	Dwarf Cuckoo
Dark-rumped Petrel	Ocellated Poorwill
Black Petrel	Black Swift
Cory's Shearwater	Hammond's Flycatcher
Townsend's Shearwater	Cattle Tyrant
White-vented Storm-Petrel	Western Kingbird
Galapagos Penguin	Lovely Cotinga
Reddish Egret	Cave Swallow
Scarlet Ibis	European Starling
Mallard	Nashville Warbler
Long-tailed Jaegar	Yellow-throated Euphonia
South Polar Skua	Ashy-throated Bush-Tanager
Gray-hooded Gull	Lesson's Seedeater
Gray Gull	Lark Sparrow
Swallow-tailed Gull	

Local. A relatively subjective term indicating that a species seems not to be found in all areas that, on the basis of present knowledge, appear suitable. Numerous forest species seem to be local, though this may at least in part be due to the furtive habits of many and a lack of sufficient field work (some may have very narrow ecological tolerances). Examples: Wing-banded Antbird, Grass Wren.

Irregular. A migrant or wandering species whose numbers fluctuate considerably from year to year, i.e. in some years it may be locally numerous while in others it is rare or even absent. Examples: Cedar Waxwing, Yellow-rumped Warbler.

Scarce. Used occasionally as a general term to refer to an uncommon or rare species, especially in the case of migrants.

Elevation Terms

To indicate elevation, four terms have been used. There is considerable overlap between adjacent zones, and a good deal of variation occurs depending on local climatic conditions. On the more humid Caribbean slope the upper zones tend to extend somewhat lower. For still controversial reasons, many birds of higher elevations tend to occur somewhat lower where the mountain ranges are low than where the mountains are high; thus many basically montane species occur notably lower in Veraguas and Darién than they do in Chiriquí. Measurements used are given first in meters (m), then feet (ft).

Lowlands. Areas ranging from sea level up to about 600 m (2000 ft).

Foothills. (Sometimes hill country). Areas ranging between about 500 m (1500 ft) and 1200 m (4000 ft).

Highlands. Areas above about 900 m (3000 ft); used in a general sense.

Mountains. Areas above about 1800 m (6000 ft) (found chiefly in Chiriquí). Timberline in Chiriquí occurs at about 3000 m (10,000 ft).

Habitat Terms

The habitat terms used also require some discussion. As will be seen, many species occur in more than one, and the habitats themselves often merge almost imperceptibly. The following are the terms most frequently employed.

Forest, humid forest, and deciduous forest. In mature tropical forest the trees are tall (averaging about 30 m: 100 ft in height with occasional taller emergent trees), and in fairly level areas they form a more or less solid canopy that so reduces the amount of sunlight reaching the ground that there is little undergrowth. *Forest* is used in a general sense for tall mature canopied woodland, and has been subdivided into two major types. *Humid forest* is luxuriant and occurs where the climate is sufficiently wet that most trees retain their leaves throughout the year. *Deciduous forest* occurs where the climate is drier; here the dry season is marked, at which time a larger number of trees lose their leaves. *Humid forest* includes Holdridge's "rain forest," "wet forest," and "moist forest"; *deciduous forest* is equivalent to Holdridge's "dry forest." Humid forest is found (where not removed by man) in the Caribbean lowlands, in much of the foothill zone on both slopes, and in parts of eastern Panama province and Darién. Deciduous forest occurred on most of the Pacific slope lowlands, but much of it has been destroyed except on the western side of the Azuero Peninsula, in eastern Panama province, and in western and southern Darién. The term *cloud forest* has not been used in the descriptions; the forest found in the highlands of Panama are simply called *forest* or *montane forest*, though in the sense that many other authors use the term, it is cloud forest. It should be mentioned that unless one is willing to mount a full-fledged "expedition," one is not going to see much "virgin" forest in Panama, for virtually all of the reasonably accessible forest has been cut over at one time or another. But much forest is fully mature, and mature and virgin forest are scarcely distinguishable from each other in their structure (though in tree species composition they may differ), and their bird faunas are essentially identical.

In a structural sense, forest can be divided into five components, each with its own characteristic set of birds: ground (Great Tinamou); undergrowth, within about 3 m (10 ft) of the ground (Spotted Antbird); lower growth, between about 1.5 and 6 m (5 and 20 ft) of the ground (Olivaceous Flatbill); middle tree levels, roughly 4.5–15 m (15–20 ft) above the ground (Rufous Piha); and upper levels, everything higher, including the top of the canopy (Green Shrike-Vireo, Blue Cotinga). These divisions are, of course, generalizations, but are useful in describing where a bird is most apt to be found, and are frequently employed throughout the text. Tropical forests are noted for their remarkable diversity of tree species, and also for their profuse growth of epiphytes, lianas, and many species or orchids. In tropical forests is also found the highest diversity of bird species, and many of the most interesting to the observer.

Second-growth woodland. A relatively mature regrowth stage found over large areas, this will in time develop into true forest. Woodland eventually covers an area that was cleared in the fairly recent past but has subsequently been allowed to grow back to trees. The trees in woodland are not as tall as in forest, averaging not more than 15 or 22 m (50 or 75 ft) in height. In its more mature stages, the canopy is more or less closed, but a greater amount of light gets through than in forest and hence there is more undergrowth, which at borders may especially be very dense.

Dry woodland. Here the trees are even smaller and spaced farther apart than in second-growth woodland, and the undergrowth is often very dense. Many species of trees lose their leaves during the dry season. Dry woodland occurs near the Pacific coast of the Canal and on many of the Pearl Islands; again much of it has been highly disturbed. If left alone for sufficiently long periods of time, even this woodland will develop into a fine tall deciduous forest, as it has on Coiba Island.

Gallery woodland or forest. A special type of woodland or forest (depending on the size of the trees), referring to the growth of trees along streams or other watercourses in otherwise mostly open country. In Panama, gallery forest or woodland is usually man-created, and is a remnant of a more extensive forest that has been largely destroyed. Examples can be seen in the Tocumen/ Chepo area of eastern Panama province, and in the Chiriquí lowlands.

Forest or woodland borders. Describes the edge of either forest or woodland with a more open area such as a road, clearing, stream or river, or even where a tree has fallen, often taking down many of its neighbors. The vegetation is usually dense, in humid areas often with *Heliconia* and other big-leaved monocots, and it more closely resembles the popular conception of a "jungle" than does the interior of forest or woodland. Tangled viny growth is also often frequent. Borders are interesting habitats for the bird observer, for the variety is often great, visibility is usully better than inside forest or woodland, and many upper-level or canopy species often come lower, while many undergrowth species may venture briefly into the open.

Shrubby areas and clearings. The regrowth stage preceding woodland. Here an area that had been recently cleared is being allowed to grow up with shrubs, small trees, and dense thickety growth with interspersed areas of tall grass.

Many stages of this habitat occur, of course, and with time trees gradually become dominant. Shrubby clearings have a surprisingly rich avifauna, though many species are difficult to observe because of the dense growth. Bird activity during the first few hours of the days is high, but afterwards seems to taper off even more markedly than in forest.

Scrubby areas. A distinctive habitat of the Pacific lowlands. It is a relatively permanent growth (probably in whole or in part maintained by fire) of low and often straggly bushes and small trees with grass interspersed, unusually found in areas with a relatively dry climate and poor or much eroded soil. In its relative permanence, it is unlike the shrubby growth found in clearings in more humid areas or areas with better soil, which if undisturbed will revert to woodland and ultimately forest. Characteristic areas occur in southern Coclé and adjacent western Panama province.

Savannas and grassland. Also found most extensively on the Pacific slope, although there are increasingly large grassy cleared areas on the Caribbean as well. The two terms are used here more or less interchangeably to describe the open grassy plains that dominate much of the Pacific lowlands except in eastern Panama. Such habitat in Panama is apparently not natural, though some of it is ancient, being artificially maintained through seasonal burning. Trees are found along fencelines (the "live fences"), along watercourses (gallery woodland), and a few are planted around habitations or are retained to shade cattle.

Residential areas and gardens. The man-maintained areas around habitations, with planted trees, shrubs, and lawns. A suprisingly rich bird habitat, especially if it is near an undisturbed area. The best such areas are found in the Canal area, notably at Ancon Heights and Summit Gardens.

Swamps. Low areas where water stands most of the year with considerable tree growth. Natural fresh water swamps are rare in Panama except in Bocas de Toro and Darién.

Marshes. Low areas where water stands most of the year, supporting emergent vegetation, but where trees do not grow. Likewise not extensive in Panama, found primarily in the Pacific lowlands.

Mangroves. A distinctive association found locally in the intertidal zone on both slopes, consisting of a few species of trees, flooded to varying depths at high tide, characterized by their stilt-like roots. Rather extensive in Panama, but usually difficult of access. In Chiriquí and along some other coasts, the mangroves are tall and form an impressive forest.

Ocean. The Gulf of Panama comprises that section of the Pacific lying north of a line connecting the Azuero Peninsula with Darién; Panama Bay is that portion of the Gulf lying north of the Pearl Islands. The largest numbers of seabirds usually occur around driftlines, often found south of the Pearl Islands and off Darién and the Azuero. Relatively few seabirds have been reported from the Caribbean Sea (but possibly more intensive effort than has occurred to date would prove rewarding).

HABITS

This paragraph summarizes behavioral information about the species, most of which is intended as an aid to identification (such as whether of not it ocurs in groups of mixed foraging flocks). Special attention is given to transcriptions of vocalizations, recognition of which is so important to bird identification in the tropics. Much new behavioral and vocal information has been incorporated into this Edition; if the species remains relatively unfamiliar to RSR, credit has been given to the observer providing the data.

RANGE

A summary of the entire range of the species is included here.

NOTE

When there is a current dispute as to the taxonomic status of the species, this is here briefly noted. These are usually included only in one or the other of the following two situations: the English or scientific names we employ differ from those used in the first edition of *Birds of Panama* ; or the English or scientific names we employ differ from those found in the 1983 AOU Checklist. In the latter case, an explanation for our treatment is given. Also included under this heading are other more or less similar species that have not yet been recorded from Panama, but that seem rather likely to occur, and for which one should be alert. In general, these are species whose known ranges closely approach Panama either in Costa Rica or northwestern Colombia. For each, a brief diagnosis of its appearance and range is given.

A CHECKLIST OF THE BIRDS OF SOUTHERN MIDDLE AMERICA

Use this list to mark off the species you see in each country.

	Panama	Costa Rica	Nicaragua	Honduras
Great Tinamou				
Highland Tinamou				
Little Tinamou				
Thicket Tinamou				
Slaty-breasted Tinamou				
Choco Tinamou				
Least Grebe				
Pied-billed Grebe				
Wandering Albatross				
Waved Albatross				
Gray-headed Albatross				
Dark-rumped Petrel				
Black Petrel				
Cory's Shearwater				
Greater Shearwater				
Wedge-tailed Shearwater				
Sooty Shearwater				
Townsend's Shearwater				
Audubon's Shearwater				
Wilson's Storm-Petrel				
White-vented Storm-Petrel				
Wedge-rumped Storm-Petrel				
Black Storm-Petrel				
Markham's Storm-Petrel				
Least Storm-Petrel				
Galapagos Penguin				
Red-billed Tropicbird				
Masked Booby				
Blue-footed Booby				
Peruvian Booby				
Brown Booby				
Red-footed Booby				
American White Pelican				
Brown Pelican				
Neotropic Cormorant				
Guanay Cormorant				
Anhinga				
Magnificent Frigatebird				

	Panama	Costa Rica	Nicaragua	Honduras
Least Bittern				
Pinnated Bittern				
American Bittern				
Rufescent Tiger-Heron				
Fasciated Tiger-Heron				
Bare-throated Tiger-Heron				
Great Blue Heron				
Cocoi Heron				
Great Egret				
Snowy Egret				
Little Blue Heron				
Reddish Egret				
Tricolored Heron				
Cattle Egret				
Green-backed Heron				
Agami Heron				
Capped Heron				
Black-crowned Night-Heron				
Yellow-crowned Night-Heron				
Boat-billed Heron				
White Ibis				
Scarlet Ibis				
Glossy Ibis				
Green Ibis				
Buff-necked Ibis				
Roseate Spoonbill				
Wood Stork				
Jabiru				
Fulvous Whistling-Duck				
White-faced Whistling-Duck				
Black-bellied Whistling-Duck				
Muscovy Duck				
Comb Duck				
Green-winged Teal				
Mallard				
Northern Pintail				
Blue-winged Teal				
Cinnamon Teal				
Northern Shoveler				
American Wigeon				
Canvasback				
Ring-necked Duck				
Lesser Scaup				
Ruddy Duck				

	Panama	Costa Rica	Nicaragua	Honduras
Masked Duck				
Black Vulture				
Turkey Vulture				
Lesser Yellow-headed Vulture				
King Vulture				
Osprey				
Gray-headed Kite				
Hook-billed Kite				
American Swallow-tailed Kite				
Pearl Kite				
White-tailed Kite				
Snail Kite				
Slender-billed Kite				
Double-toothed Kite				
Mississippi Kite				
Plumbeous Kite				
Northern Harrier				
Tiny Hawk				
Sharp-shinned Hawk				
White-breasted Hawk				
Bicolored Hawk				
Cooper's Hawk				
Crane Hawk				
Plumbeous Hawk				
Semiplumbeous Hawk				
Barred Hawk				
White Hawk				
Common Black-Hawk				
Mangrove Black-Hawk				
Great Black-Hawk				
Savanna Hawk				
Harris' Hawk				
Black-collared Hawk				
Solitary Eagle				
Gray Hawk				
Roadside Hawk				
Broad-winged Hawk				
Short-tailed Hawk				
Swainson's Hawk				
White-tailed Hawk				
Zone-tailed Hawk				
Red-tailed Hawk				
Crested Eagle				
Harpy Eagle				

	Panama	Costa Rica	Nicaragua	Honduras
Black-and-white Hawk-Eagle				
Black Hawk-Eagle				
Ornate Hawk-Eagle				
Red-throated Caracara				
Crested Caracara				
Yellow-headed Caracara				
Laughing Falcon				
Barred Forest-Falcon				
Slaty-backed Forest-Falcon				
Collared Forest-Falcon				
American Kestrel				
Merlin				
Aplomado Falcon				
Bat Falcon				
Orange-breasted Falcon				
Peregrine Falcon				
Gray-headed Chachalaca				
Plain Chachalaca				
White-bellied Chachalaca				
Black Guan				
Highland Guan				
Crested Guan				
Great Curassow				
Buffy-crowned Wood-Partridge				
Marbled Wood-Quail				
Black-eared Wood-Quail				
Black-breasted Wood-Quail				
Tacarcuna Wood-Quail				
Spotted Wood-Quail				
Singing Quail				
Ocellated Quail				
Tawny-faced Quail				
Crested Bobwhite				
Black-throated Bobwhite				
Ocellated Crake				
Ruddy Crake				
White-throated Crake				
Gray-breasted Crake				
Black Rail				
Clapper Rail				
Gray-necked Wood-Rail				
Rufous-necked Wood-Rail				
Uniform Crake				
Sora				

	Panama	Costa Rica	Nicaragua	Honduras
Yellow-breasted Crake				
Colombian Crake				
Paint-billed Crake				
Spotted Rail				
Purple Gallinule				
Common Moorhen				
American Coot				
Sungrebe				
Sunbittern				
Limpkin				
Double-striped Thick-knee				
Southern Lapwing				
Black-bellied Plover				
American Golden Plover				
Collared Plover				
Snowy Plover				
Wilson's Plover				
Semipalmated Plover				
Killdeer				
American Oystercatcher				
Black-necked Stilt				
American Avocet				
Northern Jacana				
Wattled Jacana				
Greater Yellowlegs				
Lesser Yellowlegs				
Solitary Sandpiper				
Willet				
Wandering Tattler				
Spotted Sandpiper				
Upland Sandpiper				
Whimbrel				
Long-billed Curlew				
Hudsonian Godwit				
Marbled Godwit				
Ruddy Turnstone				
Surfbird				
Red Knot				
Sanderling				
Semipalmated Sandpiper				
Western Sandpiper				
Least Sandpiper				
White-rumped Sandpiper				
Baird's Sandpiper				

	Panama	Costa Rica	Nicaragua	Honduras
Pectoral Sandpiper				
Dunlin				
Stilt Sandpiper				
Buff-breasted Sandpiper				
Ruff				
Short-billed Dowitcher				
Long-billed Dowitcher				
Common Snipe				
Wilson's Phalarope				
Red-necked Phalarope				
Pomarine Jaeger				
Parasitic Jaeger				
Long-tailed Jaeger				
South Polar Skua				
Laughing Gull				
Franklin's Gull				
Gray-hooded Gull				
Bonaparte's Gull				
Gray Gull				
Band-tailed Gull				
Ring-billed Gull				
Herring Gull				
Lesser Black-backed Gull				
Sabine's Gull				
Swallow-tailed Gull				
Gull-billed Tern				
Caspian Tern				
Royal Tern				
Elegant Tern				
Sandwich Tern				
Roseate Tern				
Common Tern				
Forster's Tern				
Least Tern				
Yellow-billed Tern				
Bridled Tern				
Sooty Tern				
Large-billed Tern				
Black Tern				
Inca Tern				
Brown Noddy				
White Tern				
Black Skimmer				
Rock Dove				

	Panama	Costa Rica	Nicaragua	Honduras
Pale-vented Pigeon				
Scaled Pigeon				
White-crowned Pigeon				
Red-billed Pigeon				
Band-tailed Pigeon				
Short-billed Pigeon				
Ruddy Pigeon				
Dusky Pigeon				
White-winged Dove				
Eared Dove				
Mourning Dove				
Inca Dove				
Common Ground-Dove				
Plain-breasted Ground-Dove				
Ruddy Ground-Dove				
Blue Ground-Dove				
Maroon-chested Ground-Dove				
White-tipped Dove				
Gray-headed Dove				
Caribbean Dove				
Gray-chested Dove				
Olive-backed Quail-Dove				
White-faced Quail-Dove				
Chiriqui Quail-Dove				
Purplish-backed Quail-Dove				
Buff-fronted Quail-Dove				
Russet-crowned Quail-Dove				
Violaceous Quail-Dove				
Ruddy Quail-Dove				
Blue-and-yellow Macaw				
Great Green Macaw				
Scarlet Macaw				
Red-and-green Macaw				
Chestnut-fronted Macaw				
Green Parakeet				
Pacific Parakeet				
Crimson-fronted Parakeet				
Olive-throated Parakeet				
Orange-fronted Parakeet				
Brown-throated Parakeet				
Sulphur-winged Parakeet				
Painted Parakeet				
Barred Parakeet				
Spectacled Parrotlet				

	Panama	Costa Rica	Nicaragua	Honduras
Orange-chinned Parakeet				
Red-fronted Parrotlet				
Blue-fronted Parrotlet				
Brown-hooded Parrot				
Saffron-headed Parrot				
Blue-headed Parrot				
White-crowned Parrot				
White-fronted Amazon				
Yellow-lored Amazon				
Red-lored Amazon				
Yellow-naped Amazon				
Yellow-crowned Amazon				
Mealy Amazon				
Dwarf Cuckoo				
Black-billed Cuckoo				
Yellow-billed Cuckoo				
Dark-billed Cuckoo				
Gray-capped Cuckoo				
Mangrove Cuckoo				
Squirrel Cuckoo				
Little Cuckoo				
Striped Cuckoo				
Pheasant Cuckoo				
Lesser Ground-Cuckoo				
Lesser Roadrunner				
Rufous-vented Ground-Cuckoo				
Greater Ani				
Smooth-billed Ani				
Groove-billed Ani				
Common Barn-Owl				
Pacific Screech-Owl				
Whiskered Screech-Owl				
Vermiculated Screech-Owl				
Tropical Screech-Owl				
Bare-shanked Screech-Owl				
Crested Owl				
Spectacled Owl				
Great Horned Owl				
Northern Pygmy-Owl				
Andean Pygmy-Owl				
Least Pygmy-Owl				
Ferruginous Pygmy-Owl				
Burrowing Owl				
Mottled Owl				

	Panama	Costa Rica	Nicaragua	Honduras
Black-and-white Owl				
Fulvous Owl				
Stygian Owl				
Striped Owl				
Unspotted Saw-whet Owl				
Short-tailed Nighthawk				
Lesser Nighthawk				
Common Nighthawk				
Common Pauraque				
Ocellated Poorwill				
Chuck-will's-widow				
Rufous Nightjar				
Tawny-collared Nightjar				
Buff-collared Nightjar				
Whip-poor-will				
Dusky Nightjar				
White-tailed Nightjar				
Spot-tailed Nightjar				
Great Potoo				
Common Potoo				
Oilbird				
Black Swift				
White-chinned Swift				
Spot-fronted Swift				
Chestnut-collared Swift				
White-collared Swift				
Chimney Swift				
Vaux's Swift				
Chapman's Swift				
Short-tailed Swift				
Ashy-tailed Swift				
Band-rumped Swift				
Gray-rumped Swift				
White-throated Swift				
Lesser Swallow-tailed Swift				
Great Swallow-tailed Swift				
Bronzy Hermit				
Rufous-breasted Hermit				
Band-tailed Barbthroat				
Green Hermit				
Long-tailed Hermit				
Pale-bellied Hermit				
Little Hermit				
White-tipped Sicklebill				

	Panama	Costa Rica	Nicaragua	Honduras
Tooth-billed Hummingbird				
Green-fronted Lancebill				
Scaly-breasted Hummingbird				
Wedge-tailed Sabrewing				
Violet Sabrewing				
White-necked Jacobin				
Brown Violet-ear				
Green Violet-ear				
Green-breasted Mango				
Black-throated Mango				
Ruby Topaz				
Violet-headed Hummingbird				
Emerald-chinned Hummingbird				
Rufous-crested Coquette				
Black-crested Coquette				
White-crested Coquette				
Green Thorntail				
Fork-tailed Emerald				
Garden Emerald				
Crowned Woodnymph				
Fiery-throated Hummingbird				
Violet-bellied Hummingbird				
Sapphire-throated Hummingbird				
Blue-headed Sapphire				
Blue-throated Goldentail				
White-eared Hummingbird				
Violet-capped Hummingbird				
Rufous-cheeked Hummingbird				
White-bellied Emerald				
Honduran Emerald				
Blue-chested Hummingbird				
Mangrove Hummingbird				
Azure-crowned Hummingbird				
Indigo-capped Hummingbird				
Berrylline Hummingbird				
Blue-tailed Hummingbird				
Steely-vented Hummingbird				
Snowy-bellied Hummingbird				
Rufous-tailed Hummingbird				
Buff-bellied Hummingbird				
Cinnamon Hummingbird				
Stripe-tailed Hummingbird				
Black-bellied Hummingbird				
White-tailed Emerald				

	Panama	Costa Rica	Nicaragua	Honduras
Coppery-headed Emerald				
Snowcap				
White-vented Plumeleteer				
Bronze-tailed Plumeleteer				
Green-throated Mountain-gem				
Green-breasted Mountain-gem				
Amethyst-throated Hummingbird				
White-bellied Mountain-gem				
White-throated Mountain-gem				
Purple-throated Mountain-gem				
Garnet-throated Hummingbird				
Green-crowned Brilliant				
Magnificent Hummingbird				
Greenish Puffleg				
Purple-crowned Fairy				
Long-billed Starthroat				
Plain-capped Starthroat				
Magenta-throated Woodstar				
Slender Sheartail				
Sparkling-tailed Hummingbird				
Purple-throated Woodstar				
Ruby-throated Hummingbird				
Wine-throated Hummingbird				
Volcano Hummingbird				
Glow-throated Hummingbird				
Scintillant Hummingbird				
Black-headed Trogon				
White-tailed Trogon				
Baird's Trogon				
Violaceous Trogon				
Mountain Trogon				
Elegant Trogon				
Collared Trogon				
Orange-bellied Trogon				
Black-throated Trogon				
Black-tailed Trogon				
Slaty-tailed Trogon				
Lattice-tailed Trogon				
Golden-headed Quetzal				
Resplendent Quetzal				
Tody Motmot				
Blue-throated Motmot				
Blue-crowned Motmot				
Rufous Motmot				

	Panama	Costa Rica	Nicaragua	Honduras
Keel-billed Motmot				
Broad-billed Motmot				
Turquoise-browed Motmot				
Ringed Kingfisher				
Belted Kingfisher				
Green Kingfisher				
Amazon Kingfisher				
Green-and-rufous Kingfisher				
American Pygmy Kingfisher				
Barred Puffbird				
White-necked Puffbird				
Black-breasted Puffbird				
Pied Puffbird				
White-whiskered Puffbird				
Lanceolated Monklet				
Gray-cheeked Nunlet				
White-fronted Nunbird				
Dusky-backed Jacamar				
Rufous-tailed Jacamar				
Great Jacamar				
Spot-crowned Barbet				
Red-headed Barbet				
Prong-billed Barbet				
Emerald Toucanet				
Collared Aracari				
Fiery-billed Aracari				
Yellow-eared Toucanet				
Keel-billed Toucan				
Chestnut-mandibled Toucan				
Olivaceous Piculet				
Acorn Woodpecker				
Golden-naped Woodpecker				
Black-cheeked Woodpecker				
Red-vented Woodpecker				
Red-crowned Woodpecker				
Hoffmann's Woodpecker				
Golden-fronted Woodpecker				
Yellow-bellied Sapsucker				
Ladder-backed Woodpecker				
Hairy Woodpecker				
Smoky-brown Woodpecker				
Red-rumped Woodpecker				
Rufous-winged Woodpecker				
Stripe-cheeked Woodpecker				

	Panama	Costa Rica	Nicaragua	Honduras
Golden-green Woodpecker				
Golden-olive Woodpecker				
Spot-breasted Woodpecker				
Northern Flicker				
Cinnamon Woodpecker				
Chestnut-colored Woodpecker				
Lineated Woodpecker				
Crimson-bellied Woodpecker				
Crimson-crested Woodpecker				
Pale-billed Woodpecker				
Pale-breasted Spinetail				
Slaty Spinetail				
Rufous-breasted Spinetail				
Red-faced Spinetail				
Coiba Spinetail				
Double-banded Graytail				
Spotted Barbtail				
Beautiful Treerunner				
Ruddy Treerunner				
Buffy Tuftedcheek				
Striped Woodhaunter				
Lineated Foliage-gleaner				
Spectacled Foliage-gleaner				
Slaty-winged Foliage-gleaner				
Buff-fronted Foliage-gleaner				
Buff-throated Foliage-gleaner				
Ruddy Foliage-gleaner				
Streak-breasted Treehunter				
Plain Xenops				
Streaked Xenops				
Tawny-throated Leaftosser				
Gray-throated Leaftosser				
Scaly-throated Leaftosser				
Sharp-tailed Streamcreeper				
Plain-brown Woodcreeper				
Tawny-winged Woodcreeper				
Ruddy Woodcreeper				
Olivaceous Woodcreeper				
Long-tailed Woodcreeper				
Wedge-billed Woodcreeper				
Strong-billed Woodcreeper				
Barred Woodcreeper				
Black-banded Woodcreeper				
Straight-billed Woodcreeper				

	Panama	Costa Rica	Nicaragua	Honduras
Buff-throated Woodcreeper				
Ivory-billed Woodcreeper				
Black-striped Woodcreeper				
Spotted Woodcreeper				
Streak-headed Woodcreeper				
Spot-crowned Woodcreeper				
Red-billed Scythebill				
Brown-billed Scythebill				
Fasciated Antshrike				
Great Antshrike				
Barred Antshrike				
Black Antshrike				
Black-hooded Antshrike				
Slaty Antshrike				
Speckled Antshrike				
Russet Antshrike				
Plain Antvireo				
Streak-crowned Antvireo				
Spot-crowned Antvireo				
Pygmy Antwren				
Streaked Antwren				
Checker-throated Antwren				
White-flanked Antwren				
Slaty Antwren				
Rufous-winged Antwren				
Dot-winged Antwren				
White-fringed Antwren				
Rufous-rumped Antwren				
Dusky Antbird				
Jet Antbird				
Bare-crowned Antbird				
White-bellied Antbird				
Chestnut-backed Antbird				
Dull-mantled Antbird				
Immaculate Antbird				
Spotted Antbird				
Wing-banded Antbird				
Bicolored Antbird				
Ocellated Antbird				
Black-faced Antthrush				
Black-headed Antthrush				
Rufous-breasted Antthrush				
Black-crowned Antpitta				
Scaled Antpitta				

	Panama	Costa Rica	Nicaragua	Honduras
Spectacled Antpitta				
Fulvous-bellied Antpitta				
Ochre-breasted Antpitta				
Silvery-fronted Tapaculo				
Tacarcuna Tapaculo				
Narino Tapaculo				
White-fronted Tyrannulet				
Sooty-headed Tyrannulet				
Paltry Tyrannulet				
Yellow-bellied Tyrannulet				
Brown-capped Tyrannulet				
Northern Beardless-Tyrannulet				
Southern Beardless-Tyrannulet				
Mouse-colored Tyrannulet				
Northern Scrub-Flycatcher				
Yellow-crowned Tyrannulet				
Forest Elaenia				
Gray Elaenia				
Greenish Elaenia				
Yellow-bellied Elaenia				
Lesser Elaenia				
Mountain Elaenia				
Torrent Tyrannulet				
Olive-striped Flycatcher				
Ochre-bellied Flycatcher				
Sepia-capped Flycatcher				
Slaty-capped Flycatcher				
Yellow Tyrannulet				
Yellow-green Tyrannulet				
Rufous-browed Tyrannulet				
Bronze-olive Pygmy-Tyrant				
Black-capped Pygmy-Tyrant				
Scale-crested Pygmy-Tyrant				
Pale-eyed Pygmy-Tyrant				
Northern Bentbill				
Southern Bentbill				
Slate-headed Tody-Flycatcher				
Common Tody-Flycatcher				
Black-headed Tody-Flycatcher				
Brownish Twistwing				
Eye-ringed Flatbill				
Olivaceous Flatbill				
Yellow-olive Flycatcher				
Yellow-margined Flycatcher				

	Panama	Costa Rica	Nicaragua	Honduras
Stub-tailed Spadebill				
White-throated Spadebill				
Golden-crowned Spadebill				
Royal Flycatcher				
Ruddy-tailed Flycatcher				
Tawny-breasted Flycatcher				
Sulphur-rumped Flycatcher				
Black-tailed Flycatcher				
Bran-colored Flycatcher				
Tawny-chested Flycatcher				
Black-billed Flycatcher				
Common Tufted-Flycatcher				
Olive-sided Flycatcher				
Greater Pewee				
Dark Pewee				
Ochraceous Pewee				
Western Wood-Pewee				
Eastern Wood-Pewee				
Tropical Pewee				
Yellow-bellied Flycatcher				
Acadian Flycatcher				
Willow Flycatcher				
Alder Flycatcher				
White-throated Flycatcher				
Least Flycatcher				
Hammond's Flycatcher				
Yellowish Flycatcher				
Buff-breasted Flycatcher				
Black-capped Flycatcher				
Black Phoebe				
Vermilion Flycatcher				
Pied Water-Tyrant				
Long-tailed Tyrant				
Cattle Tyrant				
Bright-rumped Attila				
Speckled Mourner				
Rufous Mourner				
Sirystes				
Dusky-capped Flycatcher				
Panama Flycatcher				
Ash-throated Flycatcher				
Nutting's Flycatcher				
Great Crested Flycatcher				
Brown-crested Flycatcher				

	Panama	Costa Rica	Nicaragua	Honduras
Lesser Kiskadee				
Great Kiskadee				
Boat-billed Flycatcher				
Rusty-margined Flycatcher				
Social Flycatcher				
Gray-capped Flycatcher				
White-ringed Flycatcher				
Golden-bellied Flycatcher				
Golden-crowned Flycatcher				
Streaked Flycatcher				
Sulphur-bellied Flycatcher				
Piratic Flycatcher				
Tropical Kingbird				
Cassin's Kingbird				
Western Kingbird				
Eastern Kingbird				
Gray Kingbird				
Scissor-tailed Flycatcher				
Fork-tailed Flycatcher				
Barred Becard				
Cinereous Becard				
Cinnamon Becard				
White-winged Becard				
Black-and-white Becard				
Gray-collared Becard				
Rose-throated Becard				
One-colored Becard				
Masked Tityra				
Black-crowned Tityra				
Rufous Piha				
Turquoise Cotinga				
Lovely Cotinga				
Blue Cotinga				
Black-tipped Cotinga				
Yellow-billed Cotinga				
Snowy Cotinga				
Purple-throated Fruitcrow				
Bare-necked Umbrellabird				
Three-wattled Bellbird				
Thrushlike Mourner				
Broad-billed Sapayoa				
Gray-headed Piprites				
Green Manakin				
White-collared Manakin				

	Panama	Costa Rica	Nicaragua	Honduras
Golden-collared Manakin				
Orange-collared Manakin				
White-ruffed Manakin				
Lance-tailed Manakin				
Long-tailed Manakin				
White-crowned Manakin				
Blue-crowned Manakin				
Golden-headed Manakin				
Red-capped Manakin				
Sharpbill				
Purple Martin				
Gray-breasted Martin				
Southern Martin				
Brown-chested Martin				
Tree Swallow				
Mangrove Swallow				
Violet-green Swallow				
Blue-and-white Swallow				
Black-capped Swallow				
White-thighed Swallow				
Northern Rough-winged Swallow				
Southern Rough-winged Swallow				
Sand Martin				
Cliff Swallow				
Cave Swallow				
Barn Swallow				
Steller's Jay				
White-throated Magpie-Jay				
Black-chested Jay				
Green Jay				
Brown Jay				
Bushy-crested Jay				
Azure-hooded Jay				
Black-throated Jay				
Silvery-throated Jay				
Unicolored Jay				
Common Raven				
Brown Creeper				
Black-capped Donacobius				
White-headed Wren				
Band-backed Wren				
Rufous-naped Wren				
Rock Wren				
Sooty-headed Wren				

	Panama	Costa Rica	Nicaragua	Honduras
Black-throated Wren				
Black-bellied Wren				
Bay Wren				
Riverside Wren				
Stripe-throated Wren				
Stripe-breasted Wren				
Rufous-breasted Wren				
Spot-breasted Wren				
Rufous-and-white Wren				
Banded Wren				
Carolina Wren				
Buff-breasted Wren				
Plain Wren				
House Wren				
Rufous-browed Wren				
Ochraceous Wren				
Grass Wren				
White-bellied Wren				
Timberline Wren				
White-breasted Wood-Wren				
Gray-breasted Wood-Wren				
Northern Nightingale-Wren				
Southern Nightingale-Wren				
Song Wren				
American Dipper				
Tawny-faced Gnatwren				
Long-billed Gnatwren				
White-lored Gnatcatcher				
Tropical Gnatcatcher				
Slate-throated Gnatcatcher				
Eastern Bluebird				
Brown-backed Solitaire				
Black-faced Solitaire				
Varied Solitaire				
Slate-colored Solitaire				
Black-billed Nightingale-Thrush				
Orange-billed Nightingale-Thrush				
Ruddy-capped Nightingale-Thrush				
Slaty-backed Nightingale-Thrush				
Black-headed Nightingale-Thrush				
Spotted Nightingale-Thrush				
Veery				
Gray-cheeked Thrush				
Swainson's Thrush				

	Panama	Costa Rica	Nicaragua	Honduras
Wood Thrush				
Sooty Thrush				
Black Thrush				
Mountain Thrush				
Pale-vented Thrush				
Clay-colored Thrush				
White-throated Thrush				
Rufous-collared Thrush				
Gray Catbird				
Black Catbird				
Tropical Mockingbird				
Blue-and-white Mockingbird				
Yellowish Pipit				
Cedar Waxwing				
Black-and-yellow Silky-Flycatcher				
Long-tailed Silky-Flycatcher				
European Starling				
White-eyed Vireo				
Mangrove Vireo				
Bell's Vireo				
Solitary Vireo				
Yellow-throated Vireo				
Yellow-winged Vireo				
Warbling Vireo				
Brown-capped Vireo				
Philadelphia Vireo				
Red-eyed Vireo				
Yellow-green Vireo				
Black-whiskered Vireo				
Yucatan Vireo				
Scrub Greenlet				
Tawny-crowned Greenlet				
Golden-fronted Greenlet				
Lesser Greenlet				
Green Shrike-Vireo				
Yellow-browed Shrike-Vireo				
Rufous-browed Peppershrike				
Blue-winged Warbler				
Golden-winged Warbler				
Tennessee Warbler				
Orange-crowned Warbler				
Nashville Warbler				
Northern Parula				
Tropical Parula				

	Panama	Costa Rica	Nicaragua	Honduras
Crescent-chested Warbler				
Flame-throated Warbler				
Yellow Warbler				
Chestnut-sided Warbler				
Magnolia Warbler				
Cape May Warbler				
Black-throated Blue Warbler				
Yellow-rumped Warbler				
Townsend's Warbler				
Hermit Warbler				
Black-throated Green Warbler				
Golden-cheeked Warbler				
Blackburnian Warbler				
Yellow-throated Warbler				
Grace's Warbler				
Pine Warbler				
Prairie Warbler				
Palm Warbler				
Bay-breasted Warbler				
Blackpoll Warbler				
Cerulean Warbler				
Black-and-white Warbler				
American Redstart				
Prothonotary Warbler				
Worm-eating Warbler				
Swainson's Warbler				
Ovenbird				
Northern Waterthrush				
Louisiana Waterthrush				
Kentucky Warbler				
Connecticut Warbler				
Mourning Warbler				
MacGillivray's Warbler				
Common Yellowthroat				
Olive-crowned Yellowthroat				
Masked Yellowthroat				
Gray-crowned Yellowthroat				
Hooded Warbler				
Wilson's Warbler				
Canada Warbler				
Red-faced Warbler				
Painted Redstart				
Slate-throated Redstart				
Collared Redstart				

	Panama	Costa Rica	Nicaragua	Honduras
Golden-crowned Warbler				
Fan-tailed Warbler				
Rufous-capped Warbler				
Golden-browed Warbler				
Black-cheeked Warbler				
Pirre Warbler				
Three-striped Warbler				
Buff-rumped Warbler				
Wrenthrush				
Yellow-breasted Chat				
Olive Warbler				
Bananaquit				
White-eared Conebill				
Plain-colored Tanager				
Gray-and-gold Tanager				
Emerald Tanager				
Silver-throated Tanager				
Speckled Tanager				
Bay-headed Tanager				
Rufous-winged Tanager				
Golden-hooded Tanager				
Spangle-cheeked Tanager				
Green-naped Tanager				
Scarlet-thighed Dacnis				
Blue Dacnis				
Viridian Dacnis				
Green Honeycreeper				
Shining Honeycreeper				
Purple Honeycreeper				
Red-legged Honeycreeper				
Blue-crowned Chlorophonia				
Golden-browed Chlorophonia				
Yellow-collared Chlorophonia				
Scrub Euphonia				
Yellow-crowned Euphonia				
Thick-billed Euphonia				
Yellow-throated Euphonia				
Blue-hooded Euphonia				
Fulvous-vented Euphonia				
Spot-crowned Euphonia				
Olive-backed Euphonia				
White-vented Euphonia				
Tawny-capped Euphonia				
Orange-bellied Euphonia				

	Panama	Costa Rica	Nicaragua	Honduras
Blue-gray Tanager				
Yellow-winged Tanager				
Palm Tanager				
Blue-and-gold Tanager				
Olive Tanager				
Lemon-spectacled Tanager				
Gray-headed Tanager				
Black-throated Shrike-Tanager				
White-throated Shrike-Tanager				
Sulphur-rumped Tanager				
Scarlet-browed Tanager				
White-shouldered Tanager				
Tawny-crested Tanager				
White-lined Tanager				
Red-crowned Ant-Tanager				
Red-throated Ant-Tanager				
Black-cheeked Ant-Tanager				
Hepatic Tanager				
Summer Tanager				
Scarlet Tanager				
Western Tanager				
Flame-colored Tanager				
White-winged Tanager				
Crimson-collared Tanager				
Crimson-backed Tanager				
Scarlet-rumped Tanager				
Flame-rumped Tanager				
Rosy Thrush-Tanager				
Dusky-faced Tanager				
Common Bush-Tanager				
Tacarcuna Bush-Tanager				
Pirre Bush-Tanager				
Sooty-capped Bush-Tanager				
Yellow-throated Bush-Tanager				
Ashy-throated Bush-Tanager				
Yellow-backed Tanager				
Black-and-yellow Tanager				
Swallow Tanager				
Streaked Saltator				
Grayish Saltator				
Buff-throated Saltator				
Black-headed Saltator				
Slate-colored Grosbeak				
Black-faced Grosbeak				

	Panama	Costa Rica	Nicaragua	Honduras
Yellow-green Grosbeak				
Black-thighed Grosbeak				
Rose-breasted Grosbeak				
Black-headed Grosbeak				
Blue-black Grosbeak				
Blue Bunting				
Blue Grosbeak				
Indigo Bunting				
Painted Bunting				
Dickcissel				
Sooty-faced Finch				
Yellow-thighed Finch				
Yellow-green Finch				
Large-footed Finch				
Yellow-throated Brush-Finch				
Chestnut-capped Brush-Finch				
Black-headed Brush-Finch				
Orange-billed Sparrow				
Olive Sparrow				
Green-backed Sparrow				
Black-striped Sparrow				
Prevost's Ground-Sparrow				
White-eared Ground-Sparrow				
Blue-black Grassquit				
Slate-colored Seedeater				
Variable Seedeater				
White-collared Seedeater				
Lesson's Seedeater				
Yellow-bellied Seedeater				
Ruddy-breasted Seedeater				
Nicaraguan Seed-Finch				
Lesser Seed-Finch				
Blue Seedeater				
Yellow-faced Grassquit				
Slaty Finch				
Cinnamon-bellied Flowerpiercer				
Slaty Flowerpiercer				
Peg-billed Finch				
Saffron Finch				
Grassland Yellow-Finch				
Wedge-tailed Grass-Finch				
Stripe-headed Sparrow				
Botteri's Sparrow				
Rusty Sparrow				

	Panama	Costa Rica	Nicaragua	Honduras
Chipping Sparrow				
Grasshopper Sparrow				
Lark Sparrow				
Savannah Sparrow				
Lincoln's Sparrow				
Rufous-collared Sparrow				
White-crowned Sparrow				
Volcano Junco				
Bobolink				
Red-winged Blackbird				
Red-breasted Blackbird				
Eastern Meadowlark				
Yellow-headed Blackbird				
Melodious Blackbird				
Nicaraguan Grackle				
Great-tailed Grackle				
Shiny Cowbird				
Bronzed Cowbird				
Giant Cowbird				
Black-cowled Oriole				
Black-vented Oriole				
Orchard Oriole				
Yellow-backed Oriole				
Orange-crowned Oriole				
Yellow-tailed Oriole				
Streak-backed Oriole				
Spot-breasted Oriole				
Altamira Oriole				
Northern Oriole				
Yellow-billed Cacique				
Scarlet-rumped Cacique				
Yellow-rumped Cacique				
Crested Oropendola				
Chestnut-headed Oropendola				
Montezuma Oropendola				
Black Oropendola				
Red Crossbill				
Black-headed Siskin				
Yellow-bellied Siskin				
Lesser Goldfinch				
House Sparrow				

TINAMOUS: Tinamidae (4)

The tinamous are an exclusively neotropical group of terrestrial birds much sought after as game; Panama's four species range in size from that of a quail to a grouse. They are compact in build, with thin slightly decurved bills, small heads, slender necks, and very short tails. All are cryptically colored in shades of brown and gray, often barred or spotted darker. Panama's representatives are shy and infrequently seen inhabitants of forest, woodland, or brushy areas (others in South America are found in open country). None flies often or particularly well. Many have beautiful, tremulous, whistled calls; all are heard much more often than seen. Their food is primarily vegetable matter. Tinamous are known for their lovely unicolored eggs with a glazed, almost enamel-like surface. So far as known, incubation is exclusively by the male; females may lay eggs at several sites for different males to incubate, and two or more females may lay at one site for a single male.

GREAT TINAMOU
Tinamus major   Plate 1

Description: 16–18. *Large. Mostly olive brown,* barred with dusky especially on upperparts and flanks. Birds from western Caribbean slope (*fuscipennis*) have crown sooty olive brown; on Pacific slope and in eastern Panama crown chestnut brown; *distinctly crested* from eastern Colon and eastern Panama provinces eastward (*saturatus*).

Similar species: Much larger than Little or (in extreme eastern Darién) Choco Tinamous. Highland Tinamou of Chiriquí highlands is browner above with blackish cap, rufescent below.

Status and distribution: Fairly common in humid forest in lowlands and foothills on both slopes, ranging up in smaller numbers into lower highlands (to about 1500 m: 5000 ft) in Chiriquí and Darién; absent from dry open Pacific lowlands from eastern side of Azuero Peninsula to western Panama province, but does occur in remaining deciduous forest on Pacific slope (e.g. on Azuero Peninsula and in upper Bayano valley in eastern Panama province). Now very local in Chiriquí due to deforestation, with only recent reports from Burica Peninsula (June 1982; Ridgely). A highly esteemed table bird, it becomes less numerous and more wary near settled areas. Still reasonably common in forested areas on Caribbean slope of Canal area, particularly on Pipeline Road.

Habits: Usually shy and not often observed, normally walking away quietly or hiding, but occasionally flushes with a great rush like a grouse. Roosts at night on a branch or liana. Heard far more often than it is seen; the call consists basically of two beautiful, long, tremulous whistles, the first slightly lower pitched and sometimes repeated two or three times, the second note sliding down; it calls chiefly at dawn and dusk, occasionally during the day or at night. The eggs, placed between the buttresses of a large forest tree, are a beautiful glossy turquoise blue or blue-green.

Range: Southern Mexico to northern Bolivia and Amazonian Brazil.

HIGHLAND TINAMOU
Nothocercus bonapartei   Plate 1

Description: 15–16. Known only from Chiriquí highlands. *Crown and sides of head blackish*; otherwise dark brown above, finely vermiculated with black, more rufous on nape; wings and rump spotted with buff; *almost uniform rufous below*, brightest on throat, buffier on belly, narrowly and sparsely barred with black except on throat, more heavily barred black on sides and flanks.

Similar species: Slightly smaller than Great Tinamou and richer brown and rufous generally (not so olive), especially on underparts; Great Tinamou in Chiriquí has chestnut brown (not black) crown.

Status and distribution: Rare in forest in highlands of western Chiriquí, mostly above 1500 m (5000 ft). Recently recorded from forested slopes above the Boquete Trail above Cerro Punta, and from Finca Lerida above Boquete.

Habits: Little known in Panama, with a restricted range (so far only from slopes of Volcán Barú); reclusive and infrequently seen. The call is reported to be a two-noted, loud deep slightly nasal *caw-oh* or *kooyoo* (Eisenmann, in Venezuela, but similar calls presumed to be this have been heard in Chiriquí).

Range: Costa Rica and western Panama; Colombia to northern Venezuela and northern Peru.

LITTLE TINAMOU
Crypturellus soui   Plate 1

Description: 9–9½. *The smallest Panama tinamou. Nearly uniform brown with no barring,* more rufous on rump and tail, whitish on throat and more gray on chest. Some birds are more grayish brown. Females are brighter brown, especially below.

Similar species: Easily identified by its small size, lack of barring, and usually its non-forest habitat. In extreme eastern Darién see Choco Tinamou.

Status and distribution: Common in forest borders, second-growth woodland, overgrown clearings, and scrubby areas in lowlands and foothills on both slopes, ranging up in reduced numbers to lower highlands (to about 1500 m: 5000 ft) in western Chiriquí; found also on Pearl Islands (Rey) where possibly introduced by Amerindians.

Habits: Extremely furtive, and though frequently heard rarely seen. Almost exclusively terrestrial, keeping to dense thickets, and rarely flying. There are two main calls, one a series of clear tremulous whistles, each higher in pitch than the preceding, increasing in volume and rapidity and usually ending abruptly; the other somewhat resembling that of the Great Tinamou, sliding up about a half tone, then down about a full tone; neither call is nearly as resonant as the Great Tinamou's.

Range: Southern Mexico to northern Bolivia and southern Brazil.

CHOCO TINAMOU
Crypturellus kerriae

Description: 12. Known only from eastern Darién. *Legs reddish. Crown blackish, sides of head slaty gray;* otherwise dark warm brown above indistinctly barred with dusky; upper throat white, lower throat gray, remaining underparts dull cinnamon brown. Female has breast and flanks slaty gray and is somewhat darker above.

Similar species: The only Panamanian tinamou with reddish legs. Little Tinamou is smaller and almost uniform brown, with no black or gray on head.

Status and distribution: Apparently uncommon to rare in humid forest in lower foothills (300–750 m: 1000–2500 ft) of eastern Darién; first recorded only in 1970–1971 on slopes of Cerro Quía, with two specimens taken (Wetmore and P. Galindo). More recently, believed heard on slopes of Cerro Pirre above Cana (but not confirmed by specimens or sightings; various observers).

Habits: Not well known. Call believed to be a hollow, mournful *whoh, whoh-ah*, not dissimilar from that of Slaty-breasted Tinamou of Middle America.

Range: Extreme eastern Panama and northwestern Colombia.

GREBES: Podicipedidae (2)

Panama's two members of this widespread family are found exclusively on fresh water lakes, ponds, and marshes. They have lobed toes and are expert divers, feeding on aquatic invertebrates and to a lesser extent fish. Their nests are floating structures attached to aquatic vegetation.

LEAST GREBE

LEAST GREBE
Tachybaptus dominicus   Plate 3, p.52

Description: 9. *Slender black pointed bill.* Cap and throat black, sides of head and neck sooty, with *prominent pale orange to yellow eye*; otherwise brownish gray above; paler below, whitish on center of breast and belly, more cinnamon on chest. In flight shows white wing patch. Juvenile has whitish throat, striped face and neck. Nonbreeding birds have whitish throat.
Similar species: Smaller and slenderer than Pied-billed Grebe with narrower black bill (not stout and whitish) and darker head. The pale eye often stands out at a distance.
Status and distribution: Fairly common on shallow ponds and lakes, especially those with marshy borders, in lowlands on both slopes; ranges up to lower highlands of western Chiriquí on Volcán Lakes; found also on Coiba Island. Widespread in Canal area in suitable habitat.
Habits: Almost invariably seen swimming, usually singly or in pairs, in favorable areas in scattered groups. Obtains most of its food by diving underwater. Often seen on same lakes as Pied-billed Grebe, but will occupy small ponds too shallow for that species. Has a high pitched nasal *yank*.
Range: Southern Texas and Mexico to central Argentina; West Indies.
Note: Formerly placed in the genus *Podiceps*.

PIED-BILLED GREBE
Podilymbus podiceps   Plate 3

Description: 12–14. *Thick short white bill,* with black ring in breeding plumage. *Mostly grayish brown,* somewhat paler below, with black throat patch in breeding plumage and white under tail-coverts. Shows no white on wing in flight. Juvenile has dusky and white stripes on sides of head and neck.
Similar species: Least Grebe is smaller and darker on head and neck, with narrow pointed black bill.
Status and distribution: Fairly common locally on ponds and lakes in lowlands on both slopes in western and central Panama; not recorded from San Blas (though seems likely to occur), and only one report from Darién (a single bird, likely a migrant, on the Tuira River above El Real on March 6, 1981; Ridgely *et al.*). Some migrants from North America have been recorded, but local breeding is recorded from western Bocas del Toro, western Chiriquí (Volcán Lakes in lower highlands), Herrera, both slopes of Canal area, and eastern Panama province.
Habits: Much like Least Grebe but more reluctant to fly and favors somewhat deeper and more open water. Like other grebes often submerges slowly, leaving only the head and neck above water. The usual call, often heard in the breeding season, is a loud *cuk-cuk, cuk-cuk, cuk-cuk, cow-cow-cow.*
Range: Canada to southern South America; West Indies.

ALBATROSSES: Diomedeidae (3)

Albatrosses are very large seabirds found primarily in southern oceans, with three species in the North Pacific and one other nesting on the Galapagos Islands. All are characterized by their exceptionally long and very narrow wings and stout, strongly hooked bills; several species are among the largest flying birds in the world. They feed on squid and other marine animals. Albatrosses are best known for their marvelous powers of flight, gliding without a flap over the water for extended periods of time. They are entirely pelagic except when nesting, usually on small islands. No albatross is regular in Panama waters, and all three recorded species must be regarded as hypothetical for one reason or another.

[WANDERING ALBATROSS]
Diomedea exulans

Description: 40–50. One record. *Very large* with long narrow wings (spread of 9–10 ft, sometimes more). Heavy pinkish bill. Old adult is *all white* with black wing-tips and tipping to secondaries; adult female has brown rear crown and some brown vermiculations on back. Juvenile brown with *white facial area* and *white under wing surface* (as in adults); they become progressively whiter with age, requiring more than 10 years to attain full adult plumage.

Similar species: So much larger than most other albatrosses that confusion is most unlikely; one of the largest flying birds. In all plumages, *entire* under wing surface is white except for dark tip to primaries and line along rear edge.

Status and distribution: One yearling was captured alive in Panama Bay in August 1937 and brought to Balboa, where it was photographed and released. No subsequent records. This bird possibly was captured in southern waters, kept on a ship coming north to transit the Canal, and then released (or escaped) in Panama Bay.

Range: Breeds on subantarctic islands; in America, ranges north as nonbreeder to off Peru and Argentina, with single records from Panama and California.

[WAVED ALBATROSS]
Diomedea irrorata

Description: 35. Two sight reports. *Heavy yellow bill. Head and neck yellowish white; otherwise sooty with narrow wavy white barring above and narrow white freckling below*; under wing-coverts grayish white with dusky markings.

Similar species: Gray-headed Albatross has partly or mainly black bill and adults have white underparts (whitish in immatures). Wandering Albatross is much larger.

Status and distribution: Apparently an occasional wanderer to Pacific offshore waters; no specimens. Two reports: one seen west of Piñas Bay, Darién on February 26, 1941 (R. C. Murphy, who also collected one just south of the Panama–Colombia border near the Octavio Rocks on March 8,

1941); three seen during gale SW of Pearl Islands (Galera) on September 27, 1964 (N. G. Smith).

Range: Breeds on Galapagos Islands, and on La Plata Island off Ecuador; nonbreeders range eastwards to off Ecuador and Peru, casually to Colombia and Panama.

Note: Also known as Galapagos Albatross.

[GRAY-HEADED ALBATROSS]
Diomedea chrysostoma

Description: 32–36. One unsatisfactory record from Pacific coast. *Bill black* with orange-yellow stripe down culmen and another on underside of lower mandible. *Head and neck light bluish gray* (though becoming whiter with age and wear), back and tail gray, wings blackish; rump and *underparts white; under wing-surface mostly white* with broad black leading edge and narrower black trailing edge.

Similar species: See Waved Albatross. Probably not safely identified in the field in Panamanian waters as confusion is likely with other "mollymawk" albatrosses (some of which are actually more likely to occur than this far southern species).

Status and distribution: One old record of a bird supposedly collected on the "Coast of Panama" (variously later attributed to "Bay of Panama" or "off coast of Chiriquí") in 1855 or 1856. Wetmore doubts whether the bird was taken in Panamanian waters at all, and could not find the specimen in the British Museum.

Range: Breeds on subantarctic islands; in America, ranges north as nonbreeder to off Peru and Argentina, with unsatisfactory records from Panama, California, and Oregon.

SHEARWATERS AND PETRELS: Procellariidae (7)

The shearwaters and petrels are pelagic birds found throughout the oceans of the world, coming ashore only to nest on islands, usually in burrows. A number of species are highly migratory. Only one species breeds in Panama, with the others occurring only as migrants off the Pacific ocean. Typical shearwaters have a characteristic stiff gliding flight low over the water on set wings, interspersed with short flaps, similar to but less accomplished than the flight of albatrosses. Some of the smaller shearwaters have a weaker, more fluttery flight, while the gadfly-petrels (*Pterodroma* spp.) have a distinctive dashing flight, often arcing well above the surface. All feed on various marine organisms and also on refuse. Field identification in Panama presents considerable difficulty, in part because of variability in color and pattern, in part because the status of so many species is still inadequately known. Additional pelagic field work, especially off the Azuero Peninsula and also off Darién, is needed and will surely result in the addition of several species not as yet recorded from Panama. Rather than describe the various "possible" species here, it is suggested that the interested reader refer to P. Harrison's *Seabirds: An Identification Guide* (1983).

[DARK-RUMPED PETREL]
Pterodroma phaeopygia

Description: 16–17. Three sightings from off Pacific coast. Bill black; legs bluish flesh. *Cap, nape, and sides of neck blackish*, forming partial hood, *contrasting sharply with white forehead and entire underparts*; upperparts otherwise dark brown, with many birds showing a whitish patch on either side of rump; *underwing mostly white* with blackish tip, trailing edge, and leading edge extending back as diagonal bar across coverts, and blackish patch on axillars.

Similar species: The contrasting white forehead should readily distinguish this rare petrel from other procellariids recorded from Panama. Wings are distinctly long, with outer part usually held angled sharply back, and tail fairly long and somewhat wedge-shaped; the silhouette is often distinctive.

Status and distribution: Three sightings believed to be this species: one seen off Azuero Peninsula on March 31, 1935 (J. Chapin); several seen south of Pearl Islands (Rey) on September 9, 1937 (R. C. Murphy); and 11 seen SW of Pearl Islands (Galera) on September 27, 1964 (N. G. Smith). Specimen confirmation needed in this difficult genus.

Habits: Flight much like that of similarly sized *Puffinus* shearwaters; in strong winds may bank up steeply until it is well above the water, then glide downward for a very long distance, while under calmer conditions gliding is regularly interspersed by several slow flaps.

Range: Breeds on Galapagos Islands and on Hawaii (considered endangered on both), with Galapagos race (nominate *phaeopygia*) dispersing eastward to off Middle America, Ecuador, and Peru.

Note: Also known as Hawaiian Petrel.

[BLACK PETREL]
Procellaria parkinsoni

Description: 17–18. Several sightings off Pacific coast. *Bill whitish*, with dark tip and line on culmen; *legs black*. *Entirely brownish black*; from below, bases to primaries are silvery. Immature similar but with indistinct whitish edging to feathers of mantle.

Similar species: Larger than any all-dark *Puffinus* shearwater recorded in Panama. Sooty has dark bill, and all but a very few birds have whitish under wing-linings. Dark-phase Wedge-tail likewise has dark bill, but it also has flesh-colored legs, wedge-shaped tail.

Status and distribution: Several sight records: one almost surely this species seen 56 km (35 miles) SE of Punta Mala, Azuero Peninsula, on April 7, 1965 (G. Watson); one probably this seen W of Punta Mala on March 31, 1935 (J. Chapin); one seen on Gulf of Panama on November 9–10, 1958 (C. R. Robins), was perhaps this (Eisenmann); and two likely this seen in Panama Bay on June 14, 1983 (N. G. Smith). Perhaps regular off Pacific coast; most likely period of occurrence seems to be March–June.

Habits: Flight is strong, with slow measured wingbeats interspersed with long glides, often swinging high above the waves when the wind is strong. Sometimes attracted to boats, where it feeds on scraps thrown overboard (J. Jehl).

Range: Breeds on islands off New Zealand (where considered endangered), dispersing east across tropical Pacific to off Middle America and Ecuador.

Note: Also known as Parkinson's Petrel.

[CORY'S SHEARWATER]
Calonectris diomedea

Description: 18–21. One recent sighting from Caribbean off Colon. *Bill yellowish* tipped darker. *Above pale grayish brown*, sometimes with some whitish on upper tail-coverts; below white, but showing *relatively little contrast with upperparts*.

Similar species: Only other shearwater known from Caribbean waters in Panama is the much smaller Audubon's, but see also the possible Greater Shearwater (below).

Status and distribution: One report of a single bird seen 19 km off Colon on September 20, 1985 (R. Pitman).

Range: Breeds on islands in Mediterranean Sea and the eastern Atlantic Ocean, in nonbreeding season dispersing westward in the Atlantic, and south to off South America and Africa.

Note: Greater Shearwater (*Puffinus gravis*) is known from one record of washed-up remains on Tortuguero Beach in northeastern Costa Rica, and is as likely to occur in Caribbean waters off Panama as the Cory's. Greater differs in having black bill, blacker crown (resulting in a much more "capped" look), more prominent white on upper tail-coverts, and blackish smudge on belly (latter often hard to discern at sea). Greater nests on islands in South Atlantic Ocean, dispersing north into North Atlantic when not breeding.

WEDGE-TAILED SHEARWATER
Puffinus pacificus

Description: 16–17. Recorded off Pacific coast. Tail rather long, and is wedge-shaped, but this is rarely a useful field character (when swimming, tail extends beyond wing-tips). Bill slaty gray; *legs flesh.* Occurs in two phases. Dark phase is entirely dark brown, *including entire underwing.* Pale phase brown above, contrasting with *mostly white underparts*; sides, flanks, and under tail-coverts mottled brownish gray; underwing also mostly white, with leading and trailing edge brown, and some brown mottling on coverts.

Similar species: Dark phase distinguished from Sooty Shearwater by its dark under wing-linings (pale in Sooty). Only other shearwaters recorded from Panama waters which have white underparts are the much smaller Audubon's and Townsend's Shearwaters; Dark-rumped Petrel has bold white forehead, etc.

Status and distribution: Uncertain. Only one specimen record, that of two birds (one in either phase) taken off southern Darién on March 5, 1941 (R. C. Murphy); Murphy also saw large flocks of 60–80 birds in both phases off Piñas Bay, Darién, on February 26, 1941. Shearwaters believed to be light phase Wedge-tails were seen off the Pearl Islands on April 21, 1930 (J. Chapin), and off Taboga Island on July 13, 1952; and one believed to be a dark phase Wedge-tail was seen off the Pearl Islands on May 2, 1976 (Ridgely).

Habits: Tends to hold wings somewhat "bowed", slightly above level of body and well forward (P. Harrison).

Range: Breeds on various, mostly tropical, islands in Pacific and Indian Oceans (including the Revillagigedo Islands off Mexican coast), ranging eastward as far as off Panama and Ecuador.

SOOTY SHEARWATER
Puffinus griseus Plate 4

Description: 16–18. Apparently the only numerous medium-sized shearwater in Panama waters. *Bill slender, slaty; legs blackish.* Wings long and narrow, back swept; tail short and rounded. *Sooty brown,* somewhat paler and more grayish below, with *whitish* (occasionally pale gray) *under wing-linings* (showing well as the bird banks). A rare light phase has throat whitish and breast mottled gray and grayish white.

Similar species: Dark phase Wedge-tailed Shearwater has dark under wing-linings, somewhat longer tail, and sometimes pale bill. See also Flesh-footed and Short-tailed Shearwaters (below).

Status and distribution: Apparently a fairly common transient along Pacific coast, recorded mostly June–September with a few at other times. Occasionally seen from shore. Though not recorded from Caribbean, perhaps occurs.

Habits: Usually seen well offshore, scaling low over the water on stiff wings, flapping only occasionally, banking to change direction. On calm days frequently seen swimming.

Range: Breeds on islands off extreme southern South America, Falkland Islands, and New Zealand, dispersing northward as far as arctic regions on Pacific and Atlantic Oceans.

[TOWNSEND'S SHEARWATER]
Puffinus auricularis

Description: 13. One sighting in Gulf of Panama. *Closely* resembles Audubon's Shearwater, but *legs blackish* (not flesh), blacker (not so brown) above and on under tail-coverts, and with *white on flanks extending up* ("wrapping around") *on to sides of rump; underwing whiter* (with trailing dark edge narrower, and leading edge mostly reduced to area around carpal joint). Townsend's is also slightly larger.

Status and distribution: One sighting of a bird believed this species in the Gulf of Panama on October 30, 1977 (R. G. B. Brown). Needs specimen or photographic confirmation.

Habits: Similar to Audubon's Shearwater, and also with a low fast flight, but wingbeats between glides perhaps fewer and slower (R. G. B. Brown).

Range: Breeds on Revillagigedo Islands of Pacific coast of Mexico, and in Hawaii, with Mexican race (nominate *auricularis*) apparently dispersing south to waters north of Galapagos Islands and off Panama.

Note: Formerly considered a race of the Manx Shearwater (*P. puffinus*) of Atlantic Ocean, but treated as a full species in the 1983 AOU Check-list.

AUDUBON'S SHEARWATER
Puffinus lherminieri   Plate 4

Description: 11–12. *Panama's smallest shearwater.* Bill black; legs mostly flesh. *Brownish black above*, sharply demarcated on sides of head from *white underparts*; small area on sides of breast and under tail-coverts brown; underwing mostly white, but with broad smudgy brown leading and trailing edges.

Similar species: So much smaller than any other Panama shearwater (aside from the hypothetical Townsend's, which see) that confusion is unlikely.

Status and distribution: Breeds on Tiger Cays off western Bocas del Toro (*loyemilleri*), and recorded occasionally off entire Caribbean coast; the Galapagos breeding race (*subalaris*) is fairly common in Gulf of Panama (not known to breed) from south of Pearl Islands to off Darién, but rare in Panama Bay.

Habits: Has a distinctive sloppy flight, not long sustained, with 5–10 shallow flaps interspersed with a short glide; may approach and circle boats. Frequently feeds over schools of small fish, often with flocks of terns, the terns hovering and plunging headfirst or plucking from the surface, the shearwaters swimming and making short thrusts into the water.

Range: Breeds in Bermuda, West Indies, and on islands off Caribbean coast of Panama and Venezuela and off Tobago; also on Galapagos Islands and many islands in tropical Pacific and Indian Oceans; recorded off both coasts of Panama and Costa Rica.

STORM-PETRELS: Hydrobatidae (6)

Storm-petrels are small seabirds found on oceans throughout the world. Several species are highly migratory, most notably the Wilson's which is also reputed to be one of the most numerous birds in the world (though rare in Panama). Most have an erratic and fluttering flight, somewhat swallow-like, frequently pausing to "dance" on the surface with their feet touching the water; others have longer wings and a more swooping flight. They feed primarily on zooplankton, and some species often follow ships. No member of the family is known to breed in Panama; elsewhere they nest in burrows or crevices on islands. As in the previous family, field identification is critical, often requiring the collection of specimens; various unrecorded species remain possible (for details consult P. Harrison, *Seabirds: An Identification Guide*, 1983).

WILSON'S STORM-PETREL
Oceanites oceanicus

Description: 7–7½. Very rare; one recent specimen from Pacific (but could be overlooked). Bill and long legs black, with *yellow on webs of feet* (sometimes visible while "walking" on surface of water; see below). Sooty black with pale patch on wing-coverts and *bold, rounded white rump-band extending down to lower flanks; tail square.* Some individuals have feathers of under tail-coverts edged white.

Similar species: Resembles the numerous Wedge-rumped Storm-Petrel but slightly larger with white rump band not as extensive and not distinctly triangle-shaped; note also that feet of Wilson's project beyond tail in normal flight (they do not in Wedge-rumped), and its yellow foot webbing (feet all black in Wedge-rumped). Flight and feeding behavior also differ. See also the hypothetical White-vented Storm-Petrel.

Status and distribution: Only one record, a bird collected (specimen in GML collection) in Pearl Islands (near San José) on August 29, 1969 (H. Loftin, Smithsonian Pacific seabird project), identified as the subspecies *chilensis* by Eisenmann. To be looked for during austral winter (especially May-October), and could also occur off Caribbean coast.

Habits: Flight is somewhat swallow-like, steady and direct with rather shallow fluttery wingbeats and relatively little gliding. When feeding hovers while pattering loosely dangled feet on surface, the wings held in a "V" above the back; then it bounds along to a new spot. Frequently follows ships.

Range: Breeds in Antarctica and on subantarctic islands off southern tip of South America; migrates to North Atlantic, Pacific (where rare north of the Equator), and Indian Oceans.

[WHITE-VENTED STORM-PETREL]
Oceanites gracilis

Description: 6–6¼. One report from Pacific. Closely resembles Wilson's Storm-Petrel (likewise with projecting, yellow-webbed feet, and with similarly shaped white rump band), but smaller and with white extending well up onto median belly; underwing with prominent pale area on coverts (underwing basically dark in Wilson's).

Status and distribution: Attributed to Panama on the basis of a report by R. C. Murphy, who told Eisenmann that in early September 1937 he saw this species "in the Gulf of Panama and southward" and definitely observed two at Humboldt Bay, just south of the Darién border, on September 11. This was before the very similar Wilson's Storm-Petrel was known to occur at least casually in the Pacific north of the Equator. Collection will probably prove that both species occur.

Habits: Similar to Wilson's Storm-Petrel. Curiously, no nest of this locally numerous storm-petrel has ever been found.

Range: Galapagos Islands and off western coast of South America from Colombia to central Chile.

Note: Also known as Elliot's Storm-Petrel.

WEDGE-RUMPED STORM-PETREL
Oceanodroma tethys   Plate 4

Description: 6–7. Generally the most numerous storm-petrel off Pacific coast. Bill and legs black. Sooty black with pale patch on wing-coverts; *large triangular white rump patch*, extending down to lower flanks and sides of under tail-coverts; tail very slightly forked.

Similar species: The rump patch on this storm-petrel is so large that at a distance it can look mostly white-tailed with dark only on the corners. Learn this species well as a basis for comparison with the other white-rumped storm-petrels recorded from Panama.

Status and distribution: Often fairly common to common off Pacific coast, sometimes coming well up into Panama Bay, and occasionally visible even from shore. Apparently most numerous May–November, and either rare or absent January–February. Both the nominate race (breeding in Peru) and *kelsalli* (breeding on Galapagos) have been recorded.

Habits: Flight is usually fast and steady, with deep wingbeats and occasional glides. When feeding has more bounding flight, dropping down to the water with legs trailing on surface. On calm days flocks often rest on the water. Less wary than other Panama storm-petrels. Sometimes attracted to boats but not an habitual follower.

Range: Breeds on Galapagos Islands and islands off coast of Peru; disperses north to off Pacific coast of Mexico (casually California), Panama, Colombia, and Ecuador, and south to central Chile.

BLACK STORM-PETREL
Oceanodroma melania   Plate 4

Description: 9. Regular off Pacific coast. Bill and rather long legs black. A *large* storm-petrel, *all brownish black* with somewhat paler brown wing-coverts; tail deeply forked.

Similar species: Large size and lack of white rump sets it apart from other recorded Panama storm-petrels except the very much smaller Least. See also the casual Markham's Storm-Petrel.

Status and distribution: Uncommon but apparently regular in small numbers through the year in Gulf of Panama and off Darién, only rarely coming inshore into Panama Bay.

Habits: Flight is languid and graceful (often recalling a Black Tern), with steady slow deep wingbeats and relatively little gliding; looks rather long-winged. Usually flies well above the surface. In Panama usually seen alone, only occasionally gathering in small loose groups.

Range: Breeds on islands off Baja California, ranging at sea north to central California and south to central Peru.

Note: At least one of the dark-rumped forms of Leach's Storm-Petrel (*O. leucorhoa*) probably occurs off Pacific coast. Four specimens of what was formerly considered the race *chapmani* (see D. Ainley, *Auk 97*: 837–853, 1980), which breeds off southern Baja California and winters south to the Galapagos, were taken on March 30, 1925, by W. Beebe, then en route from Balboa to the Galapagos. Eisenmann plotted his position on that date as some 160–240 km (100–150 miles) from the Azuero Peninsula. This form of Leach's Storm-Petrel resembles Black, but is smaller with shorter wings and less deeply forked tail, and its flight is more bounding and erratic.

MARKHAM'S STORM-PETREL
Oceanodroma markhami

Description: 9. One record from off Pacific coast. *Very* closely resembles Black Storm-Petrel, the two perhaps not being safely distinguished in the field. Differs in its overall more sooty brown coloration (less blackish) with more extensive and longer (reaching to carpal area) pale bar on wing-coverts, its even more deeply forked tail, and apparently in flight characteristics (see below).

Status and distribution: Only record is of a bird collected on June 30, 1937 off Puerto Armuelles, Chiriquí, by R. W. Smith (specimen in ANSP). Smith was the vertebrate collector on the George Vanderbilt South Pacific Expedition; their boat was then en route between Cocos Island and the Panama Canal. We have not been able to locate an actual log or field notebook, but as from other sources it is known they arrived in Balboa on July 3rd, it seems reasonable to believe that the bird was indeed taken in Panama waters, as the tag indicates.

Habits: Similar to Black Storm-Petrel, replacing that species in the cold waters of the Humboldt Current but apparently at least at times dispersing northward. Flight style is, however, reported to differ: it glides much more, and wingbeats are much shallower and faster. Thus typically there are rather long periods of gliding, punctuated by short bouts of three to four fast shallow wingbeats which extend no more than 20–30° above or below horizontal (R. G. B. Brown).

Range: Ranges at sea mostly off coast of Peru and Chile, in small numbers north to off Ecuador and the Galapagos Islands, accidentally to off western Panama and near Cocos and Clipperton Islands.

LEAST STORM-PETREL
Oceanodroma microsoma   Plate 4

Description: 5½–6. Regular off Pacific coast. Bill and legs black. *The smallest storm-petrel.* Sooty black, slightly paler on wing-coverts; tail rather short, *wedge-shaped.*

Similar species: The wedge-shaped effect of the tail can be hard to see (tail sometimes looks rounded, and at sea can seem almost tail-less), but in any case this species is easy to identify on the basis of its small size and all-dark plumage.

Status and distribution: Uncommon to fairly common in the Gulf of Panama and off Darién, occasionally ranging north into Panama Bay, and very rarely seen even from mainland. Apparently less numerous July–October.

Habits: Often found with Wedge-rumped Storm-Petrels. Has a fluttery, somewhat erratic flight, usually very close to the surface of the water.

Range: Breeds on islands off Baja California; ranges at sea to southern California and south to Ecuador.

Note: Formerly placed in the monotypic genus *Halocyptena.*

PENGUINS: Spheniscidae (1)

The penguins are a well-known group of flightless seabirds of colder waters of the Southern Hemisphere. They hardly merit inclusion here as Panama's only recorded species is certainly at most an accidental visitor, and probably would never have occurred but for the aid of man. They are probably most closely related to the Procellariiformes.

[GALAPAGOS PENGUIN]
Spheniscus mendiculus

Description: 19–20. One record from coast of Chiriquí. *Face black bordered above, behind,* and below by white stripe; otherwise slaty above (becoming more brownish as feathers wear); white below with *two slaty bands across chest.* Immature has blackish areas paler, with pattern more obscure but already present.

Status and distribution: Only record is an immature captured alive in the surf at Puerto Armuelles, Chiriqui, by a local fisherman in February 1955. The bird was kept alive for a month, then died, and was ultimately prepared as a specimen, now at the Smithsonian. It seems likely that the bird was captured by some visiting vessel in the Galapagos, then released (or escaped) off Chiriquí.

Range: Galapagos Islands; possibly wanders to Panama.

TROPICBIRDS: Phaethontidae (1)

The tropicbirds are a small group of beautiful seabirds found in warmer waters throughout the world. Adults are characterized by their extremely long central tail feathers, which when fully developed may exceed the length of the body. They nest on small islands, usually in crevices or shady places, at other seasons dispersing at sea where they are generally encountered individually. Their food is fish and squid, obtained by diving from considerable heights.

RED-BILLED TROPICBIRD
Phaethon aethereus

Description: 18–22, excluding *extremely long white central tail feathers (1–2 feet in length)*. *Heavy red bill. Mostly white with black primaries*, black stripe through eye, and *fine black barring on back and rump*. Immature lacks the long tail feathers, and has yellowish bill, coarser barring on back, and black eye-stripe extends back to form partial nuchal collar.

Status and distribution: Breeds in small numbers on Swan Cay off western Bocas del Toro; not reported elsewhere on Caribbean coast though possible; rare visitant to Gulf of Panama (including single individuals collected by H. Loftin on Smithsonian Pacific seabird project on September 20 and October 12, 1968), usually seen singly and well offshore; not known to breed in Pacific Panama waters, but does nest on nearby Malpelo Island off Colombia.

Habits: Strong, dove-like flight. When swimming, the tail is cocked up out of the water.

Range: Breeds on small islands in warmer parts of eastern Pacific Ocean (off Baja California, Malpelo Island, Galapagos Islands), Caribbean Sea, Red Sea, and Indian Ocean; ranges widely in tropical oceans.

Note: White-tailed Tropicbird (*P. lepturus*) might wander to Caribbean coastal waters as it breeds in the Antilles and has been taken off Caribbean coast of Colombia. It resembles Red-billed but is smaller (16 inches without the long tail feathers); adult differs in having unbarred back and black band on scapulars, secondaries, and wing-coverts; immature differs from immature Red-billed in lacking the black nuchal collar.

BOOBIES AND GANNETS: Sulidae (5)

Boobies and gannets are large seabirds with long pointed wings and narrow, wedge-shaped tails. Boobies are found in tropical oceans throughout the world, gannets in temperate oceans except the North Pacific. They have a strong flight, often gliding on set wings like a shearwater or albatross, but are less pelagic, being found primarily near islands rather than far out to sea. All feed on fish captured on a spectacular plunge from considerable heights. They are colonial breeders, most boobies nesting on the ground on small islands, with two species nesting in trees. The common name "booby" is derived from the birds' unsuspicious behavior on their breeding grounds, which enabled early sailors to kill them easily for food.

MASKED BOOBY
Sula dactylatra   Plate 4

Description: 32–36. Bill of male usually bright orange-yellow, duller greenish yellow in female; bare facial skin black; legs usually yellow. Adult *white* with black flight feathers and *black tail*. Immature had grayish legs, is mostly grayish brown above with *white collar across hindneck* and some white on rump; throat grayish brown, with white remaining underparts.

Similar species: See white phase of adult Red-footed Booby (smaller, with white tail and red legs). Immature resembles adult Brown Booby, but latter is smaller and more uniformly dark brown above (lacking the white collar and white on rump), and has yellow (not dark) legs. Immature also much like immature Blue-footed Booby, but latter more cinnamon (not so grayish) brown above and with white patch on upper back (no collared effect).

Status and distribution: Occasionally observed off Caribbean coast, rarely seen from Colon harbor; regular and sometimes quite numerous in Gulf of Panama south of Pearl Islands and off Darién, rarely noted around Pearl Islands, and very rare in Panama Bay. Though regular in occurrence at least off Pacific coast, apparently does not breed in Panama waters.

Habits: Distinctly pelagic. Often in small groups, frequently seen perched on floating debris in drift lines. Feeding dives are more nearly vertical than in other boobies.

Range: Breeds on islands in warmer parts of Atlantic, Pacific, and Indian Oceans; known breeding sites closest to Panama are Malpelo Island off Pacific coast of Colombia and Los Monjes off Caribbean coast of Colombia (breeds also on Galapagos).

BLUE-FOOTED BOOBY
Sula nebouxii   Plate 4

Description: 30–34. Occurs off Pacific coast. Bill dull greenish or bluish gray; *legs bright blue* (somewhat duller in immatures). *Head and neck streaked pale cinnamon brown and white*; above mostly cinnamon brown with *large white patch on upper back*, a smaller white patch on rump, and some white scaling on mid-back and scapulars; underparts white. Immature similar but browner on head and throat.

Similar species: This and the Brown Booby are the two numerous boobies off Pacific coast. Even at a distance the smaller Brown Booby can be distinguished by its *uniform* brown upperparts (whether adult or immature), lacking Blue-footed's white patches on upper back and rump; adult Blue-footed can look quite pale-headed at a distance. See also Peruvian Booby (only a temporary resident in Panama waters), and immature Masked Booby (Masked typically occurs much further offshore than this species, however).

Status and distribution: Locally fairly common on and around several small islands in Panama Bay and on some of the smaller Pearl Islands; disperses to some extent, but generally seems rather sedentary near its favored islands.

Habits: In Panama seems somewhat crepuscular, feeding mostly in early morning and late afternoon, perching inactively most of the day. Feeding dives are sharply angled; often feeds in groups, sometimes close inshore.

Range: Breeds on islands off Baja California, and from Panama to central Peru; recorded off Costa Rica.

PERUVIAN BOOBY
Sula variegata

Description: 28–30. An irregular and temporary visitant to Panama Bay. Bill bluish gray; bare facial skin black; legs bluish gray. Resembles Blue-footed Booby; smaller and legs never ever bright blue. *Entire head and neck pure white* (lacking streaked effect of Blue-footed); above brown with conspicuous white scaling (without Blue-footed's obvious white patch on upper back), with some white at base of tail; below entirely white. Immature similar but with head, neck, and underparts uniformly streaked brownish (imparting a dingy look), upperparts with less white (so looks darker brown).

Status and distribution: Normally a resident of cold Humboldt Current waters along the west coast of South America, this species became numerous in 1983 in Panama Bay (and perhaps elsewhere along Pacific coast), the result of a massive dispersal caused by an unusually severe and prolonged penetration of warm water south along South America's Pacific coast (widely known as the "El Niño" Current). In Panama, Peruvian Boobies apparently first appeared in about March and rapidly built up in numbers; by June they were much the commonest booby, and on 17 June N. G. Smith counted no less than 3490 roosting on Pacheca Island in the Pearl Islands; at that time large numbers could also be seen from shore along the Panama City coastline. Numbers gradually declined (the birds evidently slowly dying off), with a few persisting into early 1984, but apparently none since.

Habits: Much like Blue-footed Booby; likewise basically an inshore booby, usually not occurring too far from land.
Range: Pacific coast from Peru south to central Chile; small numbers occur periodically off southern Ecuador (but does not breed), rarely dispersing north to Panama.

BROWN BOOBY
Sula leucogaster   Plate 4

Description: 26–30. Bill and legs greenish to yellow. Adult *dark brown with sharply contrasting white breast and belly;* under wing-coverts also white. Immature mostly dark grayish brown but already with an indication of adult's pattern below (throat and chest distinctly darker than breast and belly). Adult males of Pacific race (*etesiaca*) have white forehead, darkening on forecrown.
Similar species: Immature Red-footed Booby somewhat resembles immature of this species but lacks the contrast below. See also the larger Blue-footed Booby.
Status and distribution: The most numerous booby on both coasts. Known to breed on islands off Bocas del Toro and eastern Colon province, and on various small islands off Pacific coast and some of the smaller Pearl Islands. Quite frequently seen from shore on both coasts.
Habits: Looks tapered at all ends, with long pointed bill, narrow pointed wings, and long wedge-shaped tail. Sails on rather stiff outstretched wings, usually rather low over the water, much like a large shearwater. Often attempts to fly off with bait being trolled behind fishing boats; occasionally one becomes hooked and must be hauled in to be released.
Range: Breeds on islands in warmer parts of Atlantic, Pacific, and Indian Oceans.

RED-FOOTED BOOBY
Sula sula

Description: 26–30. Bill pale bluish with pinkish at base; facial skin dull blue; legs bright red. White phase adult *mostly white* with black flight feathers and *black carpal patch on underwing; tail usually white* (but blackish in form of white phase found on Galapagos Islands). Brown phase adult mostly grayish brown, usually with *white rump, lower belly, and tail.* Some brown phase birds have these areas brown, while others which have white tail and rearparts also have white head and neck. Adults of all phases often tinged golden buff on head and neck. Immatures have dark legs and are all brown, often darker on belly than elsewhere; they gradually acquire adult plumage of their respective phase, and legs can be yellowish.
Similar species: Red legs are diagnostic (but can be hard to see in flight), as is, if present, the white tail (dark in all other boobies). White phase Red-footeds with dark tail distinguished from Masked Booby by their smaller size, black carpal patch on underwing (lacking in Masked), and absence of Masked's black on scapulars. Immature Brown Booby similar to immature Red-footed, but it already shows at least an indication of adult's pattern on underparts.
Status and distribution: Not well known in Panama waters. Apparently regular at sea off Caribbean coast, but very rarely seen from shore. Only report from the Pacific is of a brown phase adult perched on a cactus on Pachequilla Island in the Pearl Islands on June 17, 1983 (N. G. Smith); its presence there on that date was probably associated with the "El Niño" Current, then at the height of its strength in the eastern Pacific south of Panama.
Habits: A pelagic booby, apparently often recorded feeding at night (its principal food is flying fish). Like the Brown Booby frequently attracted to ships, flying alongside for long periods. The only Western Hemisphere booby which regularly roosts and nests in trees.
Range: Breeds on islands in warmer parts of Atlantic, Pacific, and Indian Oceans; closest known breeding sites to Panama are islands off Belize and Honduras and off Venezuela in Caribbean Sea, and on Revillagigedo Islands off Mexico and Cocos and Galapagos Islands in the Pacific.

PELICANS: Pelecanidae (2)

Pelicans are very large, heavy waterbirds with characteristic long bills and throat pouches. They are widely distributed in tropical and to some extent temperate areas. Most are found on lakes, marshes, and coastal lagoons, but Panama's only regularly occurring species is a coastal bird. Pelicans feed primarily on fish, obtained either by plunging into the water, or by submerging the bill and head while swimming. They nest in colonies, often large, some species on the ground, but the Brown Pelican in bushes or trees. Pesticide contamination caused a decline in Brown Pelican numbers in the United States during the 1950s and 1960s; this decline has to a large extent now been reversed, due to vastly curtailed usage of persistent pesticides, but Panama's still substantial population will doubtless be increasingly imperilled by the ever-greater amounts of pesticides now being applied to Panamanian soils.

AMERICAN WHITE PELICAN
Pelecanus erythrorhynchus

Description: 60–70. One recent record. Unmistakable. Bill and legs orange-yellow. *Mostly white*, with black primaries and outer secondaries. Immature similar but with some brownish mottling on head, neck, and wing-coverts.
Similar species: Brown Pelican can look surprisingly "white" in very strong light.
Status and distribution: One bird was seen and photographed at Playa El Agallito, on the Herrera coast near Chitre, between January 10 and February 3, 1984 (F. Delgado). Up to four or five others were reported by fishermen from nearby Los Santos at the same time.
Habits: Much more of a fresh water bird than Brown Pelican. Obtains its food by dipping bill into water while swimming; regularly feeds in groups, driving fish ahead of them.
Range: Breeds in western North America; winters south to Mexico, casually wandering south to southern Middle America (recent sightings from Costa Rica and Nicaragua, as well as the record from Panama).

BROWN PELICAN
Pelecanus occidentalis   Plate 4

Description: 46–54. Unmistakable. *Very large.* Heavily built with *long bill* and *pouch on lower mandible.* Mostly gray above, the feathers outlined darker; *dark brown below; crown and stripe down sides of neck white.*

Nonbreeding adults have head and neck whitish. Immature is brownish above and on head and neck, whitish below.
Status and distribution: Abundant along Pacific coast, especially in Panama Bay and around Pearl Islands and other islands off Pacific coast; less numerous but still fairly common along entire Caribbean coast. Breeds on many islands off Pacific coast of central Panama and on some of the Pearl Islands, but only known colony from western Panama is on Isla Barca Quebrada off Coiba Island (about 150 pairs with young seen on April 10, 1976; Ridgely); no known colonies along Caribbean coast. The largest colony is on the south side of Taboga Island. Frequently seen crossing the isthmus along the Canal, occasionally elsewhere.
Habits: The head is drawn back so that the bill rests on the neck, both perched and in flight. Flies with a characteristic few flaps and a sail. Lines of pelicans are often seen scaling low over the water; at other times they soar high on thermals. When feeding they fly roughly 9-15 m (30–50 ft) above water, then plunge down headfirst, extending neck just before entering water. Upon resurfacing, Laughing Gulls often attempt to snatch away their quarry. In shallow water pelicans also feed without diving by submerging and opening the bill.
Range: Coasts of southeastern and western United States to the Guianas and extreme northeastern Brazil and northern Peru; West Indies.
Note: Does not include *P. thagus* (Peruvian Pelican) of Peru and Chile.

CORMORANTS: Phalacrocoracidae (2)

The cormorants are a widespread group of aquatic birds, the various species being found both on freshwater rivers, lakes, and marshes, and on seacoasts. They feed primarily on small fish, captured after diving from the surface of the water. Cormorants are colonial breeders, nesting on cliffs, the ground, or in trees (which are slowly killed by their profuse droppings). Several species, notably the Guanay, are extremely important producers of guano.

NEOTROPIC (OLIVACEOUS) CORMORANT
Phalacrocorax olivaceus   Plate 4

Description: 25–27. Long slender blackish bill, hooked at tip; legs black. Adult *entirely black*; in breeding season bare facial skin dull yellow to orange, bordered behind by narrow line of white feathers. Immature more grayish brown above, paler below, almost white on breast. Juvenile almost entirely white below, including sides of head.
Similar species: With its long slender neck, rather long wedge-shaped tail, and blackish plumage easily recognized. See Anhinga and the casual Guanay Cormorant.
Status and distribution: Common (locally and temporarily abundant) along both coasts and on larger bodies of fresh water on both slopes; most abundant along Pacific coast and on the Pearl Islands, where at times in huge flocks numbering in the tens of thousands; immatures occasionally wander up into the lower Chiriquí highlands. Only known breeding colonies are on two of the Pearl Islands (Pacheca and Saboga), and on the lake impounded behind the dam on the Bayano River (where large numbers nested at least in the late 1970s, *fide* P. Galindo). Numbers of this species fluctuate markedly, in part due to local feeding conditions, but die-offs due to disease outbreaks are also believed to have occurred (in the mid 1970s they may have been seriously affected by St Louis encephalitis, *fide* P. Galindo, but numbers since appear to have recovered).
Habits: May occur in staggering numbers in Panama Bay soon after the onset of the dry season when upwelling in inshore waters (caused by constant northeast trade winds) attracts schools of small fish. Swims low in water, sometimes with no more than head and neck visible, bill tilting upwards. Has a strong steady flight (though some difficulty in becoming airborne) with outstretched head and neck slightly angled upward. Perches upright, often with wings outstretched to dry its nonwaterproof plumage.
Range: Very wide-ranging, breeding from extreme southern United States to extreme southern Chile (Cape Horn) and high on Andean lakes; also Bahamas and Cuba.
Note: We continue to favor calling this species the Neotropic Cormorant; the 1983 AOU Check-list calls it the Olivaceous Cormorant, this despite the fact that it is not olivaceous, and that the species has by far the largest range of any of the neotropical cormorants.

[GUANAY CORMORANT]
Phalacrocorax bougainvillii

Description: 27–28. Casual off Pacific coast. *Long narrow yellowish bill*; legs reddish. Adult *glossy bluish black above* with bare red facial skin; *elliptical patch on upper throat and lower foreneck to belly immaculate white*. Immature similar but more brownish above, bare parts duller, and entire foreneck brown (no white throat patch) and somewhat mottled brown on belly.
Similar species: See Neotropic Cormorant, immatures of which are somewhat similar being at least partially white below (but never showing contrast between dark foreneck and white lower parts). Guanay's bill is narrower and longer, its neck even more slender, and its tail shorter; these differences combine to produce a distinctly different flight profile, apparent even from considerable distances.
Status and distribution: An irregular wanderer to Pacific waters. About 100 were seen flying north along coast of southern Darién off Enseñada de Guayabo Chiquito on May 21, 1941 (R. C. Murphy), with others being collected by the same observer off Colombia in March and April of the same year (still the only Colombian records). The presence of these birds was probably correlated with a Niño event in 1940, and the small invasion which occurred in 1983 definitely was. In that year small numbers were present in Panama Bay and around the Pearl Islands from at least March (various observers), but all were evidently gone by the end of 1984.
Habits: In its normal range occurs in vast throngs, at least when numbers have not been recently decimated by El Niño incursions. Swims very low in the water, such that the white on underparts is completely hidden.
Range: Pacific coast from Peru south to central Chile; small numbers occur periodically off southern Ecuador (but does not breed), occasionally dispersing north to Panama and south to southern Chile; another very small population on coast of southern Argentina.

DARTERS: Anhingidae (1)

The darters are a small group of freshwater aquatic birds found in subtropical and tropical areas of the world. They resemble cormorants, differing in their long pointed (unhooked) bill, small head, very long and slender neck, and long tail. Like cormorants they feed mostly on fish, but rather than grasp their prey, darters spear it underwater and then, upon resurfacing, flip it up into the air and catch it as it falls. They nest in small colonies in swamps and along wooded rivers, sometimes with various herons and ibis.

ANHINGA

Anhinga anhinga   Plate 4

Description: 32–36. Long pointed bill, small head, very long slender (*"snaky"*) neck, and *long fan-shaped tail*. Male *glossy black with large silvery area on wing;* tail tipped with brown. Female similar but with *head, neck, and chest pale brown*.

Similar species: Somewhat cormorant-like, but longer and more slender, with pointed (not hooked) bill, silvery wing-patch, and fan-shaped (not wedge-shaped) tail.

Status and distribution: Uncommon to fairly common around fresh water marshes, ponds, lakes, and wooded rivers in lowlands on both slopes (not yet reported from Chiriquí or San Blas, but presumably occurs). Nesting has recently been recorded from eastern Panama province (at least one nest in January 1976 at Tocumen, Ridgely *et al.*, and small numbers nesting with Neotropic Cormorants on the lake impounded behind the dam on the Bayano River in the late 1970s, *fide* P. Galindo), and in Herrera (several pairs in a mixed heronry near Paris, in June–August 1977 and subsequently; F. Delgado).

Habits: Usually seen perched on branches of bushes and trees bordering water, often with wings outstretched to dry its non-water repellant plumage. Normal flight consists of long glides alternating with flapping, but also soars on flat wings a great deal (be aware that cormorants also occasionally soar). Swims low in the water, frequently with only its snake-like head and neck visible, diving for food while swimming.

Range: Southeastern United States to Bolivia, northern Argentina, and Uruguay; Cuba and Grenada.

FRIGATEBIRDS: Fregatidae (1)

The frigatebirds are a small group of spectacular seabirds found in tropical oceans, but generally not far from land. They are typically seen soaring high overhead with no apparent movement of their very long pointed wings; their wingspread is the largest of any bird in proportion to their weight, and accounts for their exceptionally buoyant, effortless appearing flight. Some of their food is obtained by harrying other seabirds (boobies, gulls, terns, etc.), but a good proportion is found independently, the birds swooping over the surface and capturing flying fish and squid; frigatebirds are unique among the seabirds in that they never intentionally settle on the water. In Panama, especially on the Pacific coast, frigatebirds are also often seen feeding on dead fish or other offal floating on the surface. They breed in colonies on islands, the nest usually being placed in bushes and trees.

MAGNIFICENT FRIGATEBIRD

Fregata magnificens   Plate 4

Description: 38–42. Very large with *very long narrow pointed wings* (spread up to 7½ ft), bent back at the "shoulder", and *long deeply forked tail* (often folded so as to appear pointed). Adult male *entirely black* with red throat pouch, which is inflated like a ballon in breeding season (often not apparent at other times). Adult female also mostly black (including throat), but lacks throat pouch and has *sides of neck and entire breast white*, and brown band on upper wing-coverts. Immature resembles female but in addition has *entire head white*.

Status and distribution: Very common along Pacific coast, offshore islands, and on

Pearl Islands; less numerous but still common along Caribbean coast. Breeds on many small islands off Pacific coast, including Pearl Islands and off Veraguas; not recorded as a breeder on Caribbean though possible in Bocas del Toro (ballooning males have been seen). Regularly seen crossing the isthmus along the Canal, less often elsewhere.

Habits: Generally seen soaring high overhead on motionless wings, sometimes in very large congregations, particularly over its nesting and roosting islands.

Range: Breeds on small islands in tropical Atlantic and eastern Pacific Oceans.

Note: The very similar Great Frigatebird (*F. minor*) could wander to Pacific waters, though so far not recorded; it breeds as close

as Cocos and the Galapagos Islands (as well as elsewhere in the tropical Pacific, Indian, and eastern Atlantic Oceans). It would easily be overlooked among Magnificents, and is about the same size (disregard its contradictory English and Latin names). Adult male differs in its brown band on upper wing-coverts (sometimes shown faintly by male Magnificents) and its reddish or brown (not black) legs; adult female differs in its whitish or pale gray (not black) throat and its narrow red (not blue) eye-ring; immatures have head and often breast washed with rusty. All stages have entirely black axillars (whereas in all stages of Magnificent axillars have some whitish tipping). *All* these points are subtle, and extreme care is necessary.

HERONS: Ardeidae (19)

Herons are long necked and long legged wading birds with pointed straight bills found throughout the world. They vary considerably in size, among Panamanian species from the large Great Blue and Cocoi Herons and the heavy tiger-herons to the diminutive Least Bittern. Virtually all the Panamanian species favor the vicinity of water, fresh or salt, though the Cattle Egret regularly forages in dry pastures. They fly with neck retracted and legs extended. Most feed primarily on fish and small vertebrates, obtained on shores and in shallow water. Many species are gregarious and highly colonial during the breeding season, nesting in trees in inaccessible swamps; a few, including the tiger-herons, bitterns, and the Green-backed Heron, nest solitarily or in small groups, the bitterns on or near the ground in dense vegetation. Recent field work by Francisco Delgado has confirmed the existence of several mixed colonies on the eastern side of the Azuero Peninsula, and others continue to be found on islands in Panama Bay and on the Pearl Islands; still others may exist elsewhere (e.g. along the coast of eastern Panama province east from the mouth of the Bayano River). The sequence employed here is that of the 1983 AOU Check-list; note that the Boat-billed Heron, formerly treated as a separate family, is now considered a subfamily within the Ardeidae.

LEAST BITTERN
Ixobrychus exilis Plate 2

Description: 11–13. *Easily the smallest Panama heron. Crown, most of back, and tail black,* with *nape and upper back chestnut; wings pale buff and* (outer half) *dark rufous,* the contrast very prominent in flight; sides of head and neck buff to rufous, becoming buffy white on foreneck and underparts. *Erythromelas* (resident locally) has darker rufous sides of head and neck than the rather pale buff of nominate race (a migrant from the north), and former also lacks nominate's pale stripe down either side of back. Female similar but with dark brown crown and back. Immature like female but somewhat streaked below.

Similar species: Might be confused with several of the rails, especially in brief flight after having been flushed, though no rail shows the conspicuous buffy patch on the wing-coverts. Green-backed Heron is notably larger and has all-dark wings.

Status and distribution: Uncommon and very local in freshwater marshes; has probably been overlooked due to its reclusive habits, and likely is more widespread. So far recorded mainly from Canal area, especially along shores of Gatun Lake and the Chagres River above Gamboa; reported east on Pacific slope to Tocumen, eastern Panama province.

Habits: Very secretive, usually remaining in dense marshy vegetation, climbing among reeds and often attempting to escape detection by "freezing" with long neck and bill pointed upward. When flushed may fly quite strongly for some distance before pitching back into the marsh. Generally quiet, but breeding birds give a soft cooing call, often trebled.

Range: North America south locally to Bolivia, Paraguay, and southeastern Brazil.

AMERICAN BITTERN
Botaurus lentiginosus

Description: 25–30. Only one old record. Brown above mottled with buff and with *broad black stripe down sides of neck; flight feathers slaty*, contrasting with brown wing-coverts; whitish buff below streaked with brown.

Similar species: Immatures of both night-herons are superficially similar but lack the black neck stripe and the slaty flight feathers. See also Pinnated Bittern (below).

Status and distribution: Known only from a specimen taken by McLeannan in 1862, presumably on what is now Caribbean side of Canal area. To be watched for in marshes during northern winter months.

Range: Breeds in North America; winters rarely south through Middle America, casually to Panama, also in West Indies.

Note: Pinnated Bittern (*B. pinnatus*), recorded locally in marshes from southeastern Mexico to Costa Rica and in South America, is unreported from Panama but may yet be found. It resembles American Bittern but differs in its distinctly blackish barred crown and hindneck (this area plain buffy brown in American), in lacking a distinct black stripe down sides of neck, and in being more barred and vermiculated with blackish on back and wings (this area much more uniform in American). Young tiger-herons somewhat resemble Pinnated, but they are much more boldly *banded* with black and buff on upperparts, especially across the wings. Pinnated's call (in Costa Rica) reported to be similar to the deep pumping (*oong-ka-choonk*) of American Bittern, but higher pitched and less hollow (D. E. Birkenholz and D. E. Jenni, *Auk 81*(4): 558–559, 1964).

RUFESCENT TIGER-HERON
Tigrisoma lineatum   Plate 1

Description: 26–28. Stout yellowish to dusky bill; legs dull green. *Head, neck, and chest deep chestnut*, with median white stripe on foreneck; upperparts otherwise brownish finely vermiculated black; lower underparts buffy brown, with flanks barred black and white. Juvenile *mostly cinnamon-buff coarsely barred with black*, with *particularly bold buff and black banding on wings*; throat, median underparts, and belly whitish. Requires about 5 years to attain full adult plumage.

Similar species: Adults of other two tiger-herons look gray (not rufous) on sides of head and neck. Juveniles present more of a problem. Bare-throated, while similar, in all plumages shows an obvious featherless yellow throat, and its wings are more mottled and vermiculated (without the bold banded effect). Juvenile Fasciated is, however, so similar that it is only doubtfully distinguishable in the field; in the hand note its somewhat shorter and heavier bill, shorter legs, and presence of powder downs on back.

Status and distribution: Apparently rare in swampy forest and along forested streams and rivers in lowlands on entire Caribbean slope; on Pacific slope known only from eastern Panama province (mainly from Bayano River valley, with one 1952 report from near Chepo) and Darién. Few reports from Canal area, all from Caribbean slope, but perhaps now slowly increasing.

Habits: Rather inconspicuous and generally solitary in Panama, where it feeds mainly in or near forest (in some parts of South America also regularly in the open). Generally found feeding at edge of water, freezing with hunched neck and not elevating the bill when disturbed. Flushed birds sometimes perch well up in trees. Has a low hooting call, usually a pair of notes, which is often given at night.

Range: Honduras to northern Argentina and Uruguay; one old record (a vagrant?) from southern Mexico.

FASCIATED TIGER-HERON
Tigrisoma fasciatum   Plate 1

Description: 23–25. Dusky bill shorter and heavier than in other tiger-herons, and with slightly arched culmen. Crown black with slaty gray sides of head; *neck and upperparts otherwise slaty black finely vermiculated with pale buff*; median stripe on foreneck white; lower underparts rufous with slaty on flanks. Juvenile very similar to juvenile Rufescent Tiger-Heron; immature and subadult resemble adult but are less strongly patterned.

Similar species: Adult resembles adult Bare-throated Tiger-Heron but is smaller, shows a feathered white throat in all plumages (never the bare yellow of Bare-throated; but note that there *is* some bare yellow at base of bill in Fasciated), and has darker sides of neck and upperparts (buff bars being narrower); note that the two would rarely or never occur together. Juvenile Fasciated difficult to distinguish in the field from other juvenile tiger-herons, but note its smaller size and shorter, heavier bill; normally the three separate out by range and habitat.

Status and distribution: Apparently rare along rapidly flowing streams and rivers in lowlands and foothills on entire Caribbean slope, and on Pacific slope in eastern Panama province (upper Bayano River valley) and Darién. There are relatively few actual reports, but the species is inconspicuous and always occurs at low densities, and is probably widespread in appropriate habitat. Only a few reports from immediate Canal area, all from streams crossing Pipeline Road, the first an adult seen along upper Río Pelón on January 31, 1976 (Ridgely and R. Forster).

Habits: In South America usually seen as it rests stolidly on a gravel bar or boulder in a turbulent stream or river, usually fully in the open but nonetheless not very conspicuous and apt to be overlooked unless you are watching for them. The foothill replacement for the lowland-inhabiting Rufescent Tiger-Heron.

Range: Costa Rica south locally to northwestern Argentina and southeastern Brazil.

BARE-THROATED TIGER-HERON
Tigrisoma mexicanum   Plate 1

Description: 28–32. *Bare throat greenish yellow to orange-yellow in all plumages.* Adult has black crown and *light gray sides of head*; sides of neck and upperparts otherwise blackish *narrowly* barred buff; median stripe down foreneck white bordered black; remaining underparts dull cinnamon brown. Juvenile buff coarsely barred with black, more mottled and vermiculated on wings; throat, median underparts, and belly whitish.

Similar species: Neither of the other tiger-herons has the bare yellow throat which this species shows in all plumages. Otherwise all plumages somewhat resemble Fasciated Tiger-Heron (which see), but note habitat differences.

Status and distribution: Rare to uncommon in Pacific coastal lowlands from Chiriquí to eastern Panama province, both along coast

and in nearby freshwater swamps and marshes; found also on Coiba Island and on the Pearl Islands (fairly common on the latter); only one record from Caribbean slope, that a bird taken in eastern San Blas at Permé on July 25, 1929. Appears to be declining over much or all of its Panama range, due both to persecution (abetted by its remarkably unsuspicious nature) and drainage and development of its habitat; only a few now remain in the Tocumen area, and they are probably gone from La Jagua (now entirely devoted to sugarcane cultivation).

Habits: Usually solitary, feeding on ground near edge of water, but often resting (and also nesting) in trees. Mainly crepuscular, and at times active even at night (as are other tiger-herons). When flushed, often flies off giving a deep harsh croaking, *wok-wok-wok*, vaguely night-heron-like; also has a low throaty guttural *rowhr* or *wowhr*.

Range: Mexico to northwestern Colombia.

GREAT BLUE HERON
Ardea herodias   Plate 2

Description: 40–50. A *very large*, long-necked, *mostly gray* heron. Bill dull yellow to dusky; legs dark. Adult has black crown with *white central stripe*, in breeding dress also with two long black occipital plumes; neck grayish streaked in front with black and white; back and wings bluish gray; lower underparts streaked black and white with *rufous thighs*. Immature is similar but dingier, crown dusky without white.

Similar species: Large size and mostly gray appearance sets it apart from all Panama herons except the Cocoi, which is much whiter generally and has a solid black crown.

Status and distribution: Uncommon winter visitant (mostly September–April) on larger bodies of fresh water in lowlands on both slopes, ranging occasionally to Volcán Lakes in lower highlands of western Chiriquí; a few birds, apparently immatures, are present throughout the year with nesting unproved though possible (not known to breed on continental Middle America south of Mexico); recorded also from Coiba Island, Taboga Island, and the Pearl Islands.

Habits: Usually solitary and rather wary.

Range: Breeds from North America to southern Mexico and in West Indies and islands off Venezuela and on Galapagos Islands; northern birds winter south to northern Colombia and Venezuela (where also may breed).

COCOI (WHITE-NECKED) HERON
Ardea cocoi   Plate 1

Description: 40–50. Superficially like more widespread Great Blue Heron but *much whiter generally*. *Entire crown black* (no white central stripe), when breeding with long occipital plumes black tipped white; *neck and chest white* with a few black streaks on foreneck; *lower underparts black, with thighs white*. In flight *upper wing mostly white* with blackish flight feathers (not gray with slaty flight feathers, as in Great Blue). Immature dingier but already essentially white below with white thighs.
Similar species: See Great Blue Heron.
Status and distribution: Rare in freshwater marshes and along rivers on Pacific slope in eastern Panama province and Darién; wanderers occasionally occur well to the west of their normal range, with single birds having been seen on Bohio Peninsula along shore of Gatun Lake in June 1977 and on April 14, 1978 (N. Brokaw *et al*.), and at the Cienega Las Macanas in Herrera on June 17, 1981 and August 10, 1982 (F. Delgado *et al*.). These latter probably represent post-breeding dispersal, for even in the Tocumen area it has always occurred only in the rainy season (April–October). Actual nesting remains unrecorded, though seems virtually certain in Darién and likely in the upper Bayano valley.
Habits: Similar to Great Blue Heron, which it replaces in South America.
Range: Central Panama to southern Chile and southern Argentina.
Note: We favor employing the English name "Cocoi Heron" for this species, as did Hancock and Elliot (1978), rather than the "White-necked Heron" used by the 1983 AOU Check-list.

GREAT EGRET
Casmerodius albus   Plate 2

Description: 36–40. A large, slender, long-necked heron with *yellow bill* and *black legs*. *Entirely white;* long aigrettes spring from back during breeding season.
Similar species: Snowy Egret and immature Little Blue Heron are also all white, but both are much smaller and have black or partly dark bills.
Status and distribution: Common and widespread both coastally and in freshwater

marshes and along rivers in lowlands on both slopes, ranging rarely to Volcán Lakes in lower highlands of western Chiriquí; found also on all offshore islands; local population is augmented by northern migrants during northern winter, but species is numerous the entire year, occasionally occurring in flocks of several hundred or more. Nesting has been reported from various islands in Panama Bay and the Gulf of Panama (including Changamé, Taborcilla, Taboga, and the Pearl Islands), and has recently also been confirmed on the mainland, with colonies being found on the eastern side of the Azuero Peninsula (near Paris and near Chitre in Herrera, and at Peñon de los Santos in Los Santos) in the late 1970s and early 1980s (F. Delgado).
Habits: Remains motionless for long periods of time when feeding, often with straight neck so that it stands well above other herons and egrets.
Range: Virtually cosmopolitan in warmer areas; in America from United States (wandering north to Canada) to extreme southern Chile and in West Indies.

SNOWY EGRET
Egretta thula   Plate 2

Description: 23–27. *Slender black bill* with yellow lores; legs black with *bright yellow feet* ("golden slippers"). *Entirely white*, with graceful filmy recurved aigrettes springing from crown, back, and chest during nesting season. Immature has greenish yellow back of leg, and gray at base of bill.
Similar species: Great Egret is larger and has longer neck and all yellow bill. Immature Little Blue Heron has bicolored bill and greenish legs.
Status and distribution: Fairly common along both coasts; less numerous in freshwater marshes and along shores of lakes and rivers, ranging occasionally to Volcán Lakes in lower highlands of western Chiriquí; recorded also on Coiba Island and the Pearl Islands; more numerous during northern winter when some northern migrants are present. To date found breeding only on two small islands in Panama Bay (Changamé and Taborcilla); colonies may exist on the mainland as well, particularly near Pacific coast.
Habits: An active feeder, walking, sometimes running in shallow water, stirring up prey with its feet and stabbing repeatedly to catch it. The most elegant and graceful of Panama's herons.

Range: United States (wandering north to Canada) to central Chile and northern Argentina; West Indies.

LITTLE BLUE HERON
Egretta caerulea   Plate 2

Description: 22–26. *Bill basally bluish with blackish tip; legs greenish* (blacker when breeding). Adult *mostly slaty blue* with reddish maroon head and neck; in breeding plumage head and neck somewhat paler, and with plumes on crown, foreneck, and back. Juvenile white except for inconspicuous dusky tipping to primaries; color at base of bill variable, *usually pale greenish to grayish*, varying to pinkish or pale yellowish. Immature white *splotched irregularly with slaty*, giving a pied appearance.
Similar species: Snowy Egret rather resembles juvenile but has all black bill (not bicolored) and black legs with yellow feet (though immature Snowy's legs show greenish stripe down back, which can cause confusion). See also Great Egret and Tricolored Heron.
Status and distribution: Common and widespread both coastally and in freshwater marshes and along rivers in lowlands on both slopes, ranging in small numbers to Volcán Lakes in lower highlands of western Chiriquí; found also on Coiba Island and all larger islands in Panama Bay and Gulf of Panama; considerably more numerous during northern winter months, when local population (presumably resident?) is augmented by northern migrants. No breeding has been recorded in Panama.
Habits: Immatures and juveniles predominate. A fairly active feeder but less graceful in its movements than Snowy Egret.
Range: Eastern United States and Mexico to central Peru, southeastern Brazil, and Uruguay; West Indies.
Note: Formerly placed in the monotypic genus *Florida*.

[REDDISH EGRET]
Egretta rufescens

Description: 29–31. One recent report from Coiba Island. *Bill pinkish flesh*, outer third black; legs bluish slate (bill and leg colors duller in nonbreeding plumage). *Shaggy plumes conspicuous on head, neck, and breast* (longest in breeding plumage but present throughout year). Dark phase has *rufous head, neck, and breast*; otherwise ashy gray. Light phase adult (unlikely in Panama) all white. Immatures like respective adults but with shorter plumes, duller soft part colors; foreparts of dark phase immature often dull cinnamon.
Similar species: The shaggy plumes and bicolored bill are normally diagnostic; note also its unusual feeding behavior (see below). Most likely confused with Little Blue Heron, but notably larger and more plumed in all plumages (never looks slender or sleek).
Status and distribution: A dark phase adult was observed for several hours on the flats off Playa Blanca on Coiba Island on April 12, 1976 (Ridgely); efforts to collect it failed. There has been a recent spate of records from Costa Rica (all of dark phase birds between September and April), mostly from Pacific coast, and also several from Pacific coast of Nicaragua and Honduras, so the species should be watched for in Panama. Almost all of these pertain to birds found at salt evaporation ponds; whether they reflect an increase in the Reddish Egret population, in the number of saltworks, or merely of observers remains uncertain.
Habits: Has a characteristic lurching, acrobatic feeding behavior (but note: does not *always* feed in this manner, and other herons, especially Little Blues, often forage in a somewhat similar way), dashing and staggering about actively in shallow water, sometimes flicking wings out or holding them open.
Range: Southern United States to Colombia and Venezuela.
Note: Formerly placed in the monotypic genus *Dichromanassa*.

TRICOLORED HERON
Egretta tricolor   Plate 2

Description: 24–26. A slender heron with long thin neck and *long slender bill*. Bill usually yellowish (sometimes bluish) with dark tip; legs slaty to greenish olive (in immatures). *Mostly bluish slate above* with white occipital plumes and long light brown scapular feathers which often cover lower back; throat and foreneck white, latter usually strongly tinged chestnut; rump and *belly contrastingly white*. Immature similar in pattern but head, hindneck, and wing-coverts brownish chestnut; lacks occipital and scapular plumes.
Similar species: Adult Little Blue Heron is stockier, entirely dark (bluish slate and maroon) without white belly.

Status and distribution: Fairly common both coastally and in freshwater marshes and along rivers in lowlands on both slopes (most numerous on or near Pacific coast), ranging rarely to Volcán Lakes in lower highlands of western Chiriquí; found also on larger Pearl Islands; more numerous during northern winter when northern migrants are present. Nesting has only recently been documented in Panama, with colonies having been found on Taborcilla Island near Chame, western Panama province (e.g. about 130 pairs on April 25, 1976; Ridgely), and a few nesting pairs have also been located in mixed heronries near Paris and Chitre in coastal Herrera in the late 1970s and early 1980s (F. Delgado).

Habits: An active, graceful feeder which sometimes prances and dashes about much like a Reddish Egret, briefly even shading the water with its wings.

Range: Eastern United States and Mexico to Peru and central Brazil; Greater Antilles.

Note: Formerly placed in the monotypic genus *Hydranassa*, and called Louisiana Heron.

CATTLE EGRET
Bubulcus ibis   Plate 2

Description: 18–20. A small *white* heron with characteristic *heavy jowl*, giving a heavy-headed appearance. Breeding adult has varying amounts of buff on crown, back, and breast, lost at other seasons. *Bill yellow*, becoming red (except at tip) for short period at onset of breeding season; legs dull yellow to greenish, also becoming red at beginning of breeding season. Immatures lack the buff.

Similar species: Snowy Egret and immature Little Blue Heron are larger and slenderer, never have yellow or red bills.

Status and distribution: Common to very common in open country (especially near water and where cattle and other livestock are present) in lowlands on both slopes, ranging into lower highlands around Volcán in western Chiriquí; reported from Taboga Island in 1964 (G. Harrington). Much more numerous and widespread on Pacific slope. First reported in 1954, the Cattle Egret has increased and spread rapidly in Panama, and may still be doing so. Very large numbers are now known to be nesting at various localities on the eastern side of the Azuero Peninsula, with up to 1500 nests having been estimated at one colony (near Paris, Herrera); F. Delgado attributes this increase, which he continues to monitor, to the spread of rice cultivation in the region. Probably nests elsewhere in substantial numbers, but other sizable heronries not reported as yet.

Habits: Notably gregarious, flocks usually feeding among cattle or other grazing animals, sometimes even perching on their backs.

Range: Eastern and southern North America to Chile, northern Argentina, and southern Brazil and in West Indies, still spreading; also warmer parts of Old World (its original range).

GREEN-BACKED (GREEN, STRIATED) HERON
Butorides striatus   Plate 1

Description: 16–18. *A small, dark, chunky heron*. Legs bright orange in breeding adult, yellow otherwise. Crown (with shaggy crest, sometimes raised) black; *sides of head, neck, and chest rich maroon-chestnut*, with narrow white black-bordered median stripe down foreneck; above otherwise greenish black, brownish gray below. The above applies to birds breeding east to the Canal area (*maculatus*, with *margaritophilus* on the Pearl Islands) and to northern migrants (*virescens*). Eastward is found nominate *striatus*, in which the *sides of head, neck, and chest are gray* (not chestnut); some individuals have this area grayish buff (these are believed to be intergrades, the *"patens"* form; Wetmore points out that birds with this coloration also crop up throughout the range of *striatus* in South America). A melanistic phase of *maculatus* occurs on the Caribbean slope (especially in Bocas del Toro), with blackish neck and lacking the white median stripe on foreneck. Immatures of all forms are duller (and essentially indistinguishable) with browner upperparts and *white underparts heavily streaked brown*.

Similar species: Now that the former Green and Striated Herons are considered conspecific, there should be no problem in identification: there is no other small, dark heron in Panama. Attempting to distinguish the forms will, however, continue to be a worthwhile endeavor, and might shed further light on their still rather uncertain relationships.

Habits: Fairly common and widespread both coastally and around fresh water (particularly numerous along shores of lakes and rivers) in lowlands on both slopes; ranges up to Volcán Lakes in lower highlands of western Chiriquí; found also on Pearl Islands (where mostly in mangroves);

resident population augmented by northern migrants during northern winter.

Habits: Usually solitary. Normally hunts by standing on a perch just out of the water (not often wading). When nervous often flicks its tail and raises its crest. Flushed birds often give vent to a loud complaining *kyow* as they fly off.

Range: North America to northern Argentina and Uruguay (casual central Chile); also warmer parts of Africa, Asia, Australia, and islands in western Pacific Ocean.

Note: The 1983 AOU Check-list considered *B. virescens* (Green Heron) conspecific with *B. striatus* (Striated Heron), opting to call the enlarged species the Green-backed Heron. Whether this will ultimately prove the best course remains controversial.

AGAMI (CHESTNUT-BELLIED) HERON
Agamia agami   Plate 1

Description: 28–32. Slender with very long neck and *very long slender bill;* legs short. *Mostly dark glossy green above* with black face and long bluish gray crest; *neck and most of underparts rich chestnut*, with throat and stripe down front of neck white, and patch of bluish gray on chest; bluish gray plumes also spring from back in breeding plumage. Immature dark brown above with blackish crown; throat white, remaining underparts buff.

Status and distribution: Rare and local (but probably mostly just overlooked) along forested streams and in swampy areas in lowlands on entire Caribbean slope (not reported from San Blas, but surely occurs); on Pacific slope known from Canal area east very locally through Darién; one record from Pearl Islands (Rey). In Canal area recently reported most often from streams crossing Pipeline Road (but even here *very* infrequently encountered).

Habits: A solitary, shy, and beautiful heron of shady forest streams and wet depressions; rarely in the open. When disturbed an Agami will sometimes fly up to a perch fairly high in the trees, but more often they retreat into dense lower growth.

Range: Southeastern Mexico to northern Bolivia and central Brazil.

Note: We favor calling this wonderful, exotic-looking heron the ''Agami Heron'', as did Hancock and Elliot (1978), rather than burden it with the prosaic ''Chestnut-bellied''. The 1983 AOU Check-list, alas, employed the latter.

CAPPED HERON
Pilherodius pileatus   Plate 1

Description: 22–24. *Bill and facial skin blue*, becoming more intense in breeding plumage; legs gray. White with *black crown* (not forecrown) and long white occipital plumes. In breeding plumage underparts become strongly tinged with buff. Immature has crown streaked with gray.

Similar species: A striking heron, not to be confused. Rather chunky, in flight often suggesting a white Black-crowned Night-Heron.

Status and distribution: Rare to locally uncommon along rivers and in freshwater marshes and swamps on Pacific slope in eastern Panama province (Tocumen-Chepo area) and Darién; on Caribbean slope known only from upper Chagres River valley above Gamboa; a few recent reports from Pacific side of Canal area (e.g. at Chiva Chiva marsh) presumably represent wanderers. Persists in small numbers in the Tocumen marsh area, but more numerous around El Real, Darién.

Habits: Rather a solitary and wary heron. Usually seen feeding or resting along shore of a river or lake, often not moving for long periods. Usually flies with rather shallow wing-strokes.

Range: Central Panama to northern Bolivia, northern Paraguay, and southeastern Brazil.

BLACK-CROWNED NIGHT-HERON
Nycticorax nycticorax   Plate 2

Description: 24–26. Rather stocky with short neck and rather short black bill and greenish or yellowish legs. *Crown, nape, and back glossy black* with long white occipital plumes (even longer when breeding); *wings and tail gray*; sides of neck and chest pale gray, *white on remaining underparts*. Immature with *lower mandible mostly dull greenish yellow*; brown above *conspicuously* streaked and spotted with white (with especially large spots on wing-coverts; whitish below streaked with brown. Subadults gradually assume adult plumage over 3 years; second-year birds show pattern of full adult but are browner.

Similar species: Boat-billed Heron somewhat resembles adult in pattern but has paler back and rufous and black belly (not white); the bills of course are very different. Immature resembles immature Yellow-crowned Night-Heron, but younger birds always show some pale color on lower mandible (bill always all dark in Yellow-crowned), and are browner (not so slaty) with more obvious streaking above (especially on wing-coverts).

Status and distribution: Uncommon to fairly common along coasts and in freshwater marshes and swamps, more numerous on Pacific side; found also on Taboga Island and the Pearl Islands; numbers are somewhat greater during northern winter months when a few northern migrants are present. Small numbers have been found nesting on various islands in Panama Bay, and also in mixed heronries on the eastern side of the Azuero Peninsula (F. Delgado).

Habits: Nocturnal, only rarely seen abroad by day, usually roosting in leafy trees. Often heard is an abrupt *quok*, given most frequently in the evening as it flies to its feeding areas, also when disturbed.

Range: Virtually cosmopolitan except in holarctic regions and in Australia; in New World from southern Canada to Tierra del Fuego and in West Indies.

YELLOW-CROWNED NIGHT-HERON
Nyctanassa violacea   Plate 2

Description: 24–26. Similar in shape to Black-crowned Night-Heron, but with *stouter bill* and *longer legs*. Adult *mostly gray; head black with white crown and white patch behind eye* and long white occipital plumes (even longer in breeding season). The yellow is restricted to a very small spot on the forecrown. The resident race *caliginus* is a darker sootier gray than the nominate race (which migrates from the north at least to Bocas del Toro), and it has a heavier bill. Immature resembles immature Black-crowned Night-Heron, but is slatier (not so brown) with finer streaking above, *especially on the wing-coverts* (where spotting is small and triangle-shaped in Yellow-crowned, as opposed to the large tear-dropped spots on coverts of Black-crowned). In flight part of legs as well as feet project beyond the tail (only the feet in Black-crowned); *bill always blackish* (mostly or partly dull greenish yellow in Black-crowned immature).

Status and distribution: Common along Pacific coast, less numerous along Caribbean coast and inland in freshwater marshes and along rivers in lowlands on both slopes; common also on Coiba Island, Taboga Island, the Pearl Islands, and other smaller islands off Pacific coast; one subadult seen at the Volcán Lakes in late July 1984 (J. Guarnaccia) is only report

from Chiriquí highlands. Breeding colonies have been recorded on Changamé Island off Pacific entrance to the Canal, and on Taborcilla Island near Chame, western Panama province (e.g. about 100 nests on April 25, 1976; Ridgely), but there doubtless are others as well (likely including some along Caribbean coast). Sizable numbers can generally be seen, even at midday, on mudflats and rocks exposed at low tide around Pacific entrance to Canal and in Panama City.

Habits: Not as nocturnal as Black-crowned Night-Heron. The call is similar but somewhat higher pitched, *quak*.

Range: Eastern United States and Mexico to northern Peru and eastern Brazil (primarily in coastal areas) and in West Indies and Galapagos Islands.

Note: Transferred to the genus *Nycticorax* in the 1983 AOU Check-list, but reversion to *Nyctanassa* is imminent.

BOAT-BILLED HERON
Cochlearius cochlearius   Plate 2, p.74

Description: 18–20. *Very broad and flat bill. Panamensis* (most of the species' Panama range) has *crown* (except white forehead), *long and wide crest, and upper back black;* otherwise dark gray on back, rump, wings, and tail; foreneck and breast pale grayish buff, becoming rusty on mid-belly with *large area on sides and flanks black.* Birds from extreme southern Darién at Jaqué (the mainly South American nominate race) are generally similar but markedly paler gray above and have white foreneck and breast. Immatures strongly washed with cinnamon above and buff below, and they lack crest.

Similar species: In pattern somewhat like adult Black-crowned Night-Heron.

Status and distribution: Uncommon and seemingly rather local in mangroves, freshwater swamps, and along rivers in lowlands on entire Caribbean slope; on Pacific slope known only from Chiriquí, eastern side of Azuero Peninsula, and from Canal area east through Darién; reclusive and strictly nocturnal so doubtless somewhat overlooked. A few can usually be spotlighted in the mangroves along the road in to Galeta Island.

Habits: By day roosts in groups in trees with thick foliage, usually apart from other herons though sometimes at the edge of mixed heronries. At night they disperse to feed solitarily. Foraging techniques apparently vary (perhaps seasonally or geographically?), but at least some scooping and sifting for mud-dwelling fish and crustaceans has been observed (and would be expected, from its shovel-like bill). However, visual techniques are also employed, at least to some extent; in western Mexico their prey was found not to differ from that of the two night-herons. Though usually quite tame at their day roosts, Boat-billed Herons tend to flush quickly at night, and often utter a low duck-like quacking call as they fly off.

Range: Mexico to Bolivia, northern Argentina, and southeastern Brazil.

Note: Formerly in its own family (Cochleariidae), the 1983 AOU Check-list gave the Boat-billed Heron only subfamily rank in the Ardeidae.

BOAT-BILLED HERON

IBISES AND SPOONBILLS: Threskiornithidae (6)

Ibises and spoonbills are large, long legged wading birds, widespread in distribution but particularly numerous in tropical areas. Ibises are known by their long decurved bills, spoonbills by their broad flat bills widened at the tip. They fly with neck outstretched, and a number of species alternate a series of flaps with short glides on somewhat downcurved wings. Their food consists mostly of fish and crustaceans, usually obtained by probing in mud, or (in the case of spoonbills) by sideways movements in mud and shallow water. Many species are gregarious, forming large roosts and nesting colonies in accessible swamps; others (among them the Green and Buff-necked Ibises) are more solitary and are found in at most small groups.

WHITE IBIS
Eudocimus albus   Plate 2

Description: 23–25. *Decurved bill and bare facial skin red;* legs pink. Adult *white with black wing-tips*. Immature has pinkish bill with dark tip, pinkish legs; is grayish brown somewhat streaked with white, with *contrasting white rump and belly.*
Similar species: Egrets and white herons lack black in wings; Wood Stork is larger and has all of flight feathers black. Glossy and Green Ibises are *all* dark, lacking white rump and belly of immature. See also Limpkin.
Status and distribution: Fairly common in mangroves and on coastal mudflats on entire Pacific slope (though less numerous in Chiriquí and Darién), and on Coiba Island and the Pearl Islands; on Caribbean slope known only from a few recent reports from the Galeta Island area (D. Engleman, J. Cubit, *et al.*); occasionally forages slightly inland in freshwater marshes, but basically a coastal bird in Panama. Nesting has been reported from two islands in Panama Bay (Changamé and Taborcilla), and on eastern side of Azuero Peninsula in Herrera and Los Santos (F. Delgado). Can almost always be seen on mudflats exposed at low tide at Pacific entrance to the Canal.
Habits: Rather gregarious. Often become quite soiled by the mud in which they habitually forage. A flock of adults in flight presents an especially attractive sight.
Range: Southeastern United States and Mexico to northwestern Peru and Venezuela; Greater Antilles.

[SCARLET IBIS]
Eudocimus ruber

Description: 22–24. One report. Unmistakable. Decurved bill, bare facial skin, and legs red (sometimes blackish in breeding plumage). *Entirely scarlet* with black wing-tips. Immature closely resembles immature White Ibis.

Status and distribution: Only report is an adult seen on the Farfan mudflats at the Pacific entrance to the Canal "off and on" from January 25, 1967 to February 17, 1967, and again on March 14, 1967 (N. G. Smith). The origin of the bird must remain suspect; the species is often kept in captivity.

Range: Colombia, Venezuela, the Guianas, and eastern Brazil; casual or accidental in southeastern United States (perhaps all escapes) and West Indies.

GLOSSY IBIS
Plegadis falcinellus   Plate 2

Description: 22–24. Rare. *Long decurved bill.* Bare facial skin and lores slaty. *Mostly bronzy chestnut*, with purplish reflections in good light, greener on wings and lower back. Breeding birds have border of facial skin bluish white. Winter adults have whitish streaks on head and neck. Immature like winter adult but duller and grayer.

Similar species: Appears blackish in poor light. Green Ibis is stockier with shorter legs, slight bushy crest, and is greener on neck and chest. Immature White Ibis has white rump and belly. See also White-faced Ibis (below).

Status and distribution: A rare but possibly regular migrant in small numbers to freshwater marshes and ponds and wet grassy areas in lowlands locally on Pacific slope (Herrera, eastern Panama province); on Caribbean slope only in Canal area. Though only one specimen has been taken (near La Jagua on March 18, 1949), there have been a number of recent sight reports, perhaps reflecting the species' recent increase in the United States and West Indies. Though apparently most frequent during fall and winter months, there are also sightings from northern breeding season (May 23 and July 16, 1968; Ridgely). Many of the birds sighted could be identified only as *Plegadis*, chiefly immatures, but all that could be identified to species seemed to be Glossies.

Range: Coastal eastern and southern United States and Greater Antilles; migrating or wandering birds have been recorded with increasing frequency in Middle America and northern South America, though status in these areas uncertain due to confusion with White-faced Ibis, which had erroneously been thought to be resident in

Colombia and Venezuela. Recently found breeding in Venezuela (*fide* P. Schwartz); breeding in Middle America possible but unrecorded. Also found locally in warmer parts of southern Europe, Africa, Asia, and Australia.

Note: White-faced Ibis (*P. chihi*) of western North America and southern South America might possibly occur as a wanderer. It very closely resembles the Glossy, but adults in breeding plumage have bare red facial skin and lores (though this is grayish when not breeding), and this area is narrowly edged with white *feathers*. In all plumages (including immatures and non-breeding adults) iris is *red* (brown in Glossy), but this is usually hard to discern. Bare-faced Ibis (*Phimosus infuscatus*) of South America is also possible; it ranges regularly as close as nearby Caribbean slope Colombia. Compared to Glossy (with which it is most likely to be confused, in part because both occur in open marshy habitat) it is smaller (18–20 in) and distinctly shorter-legged (this is particularly evident in flight when legs do not trail appreciably behind tail, unlike Glossy); its entire bill and face are pinkish to dark reddish; and its plumage is more blackish, without Glossy's bronzy or chestnut overtones.

GREEN IBIS
Mesembrinibis cayennensis   Plate 2, p.76

Description: 20–22. Decurved greenish bill; *short greenish legs. Dark bronzy green, brightest on neck and chest*, with bushy crest (usually not prominent); belly dull black.

Similar species: At a distance or in poor light Glossy Ibis is superficially similar, but it has a more slender build, lacks crest, and adults are purplish chestnut when seen in good light (not as black as this species). See also Bare-faced Ibis.

Status and distribution: Rare to locally fairly common in swampy forest and along forested rivers in lowlands on both slopes; recorded only from western Bocas del Toro (Almirante Bay area), eastern Colon province (up to seven seen regularly in the Río Cascajal/Río Claro area east of Portobelo in January–June 1987; D. Graham), San Blas (only two records, from Mandinga and Puerto Obaldía, but likely more widespread), eastern Panama province (recorded mostly along middle and upper Bayano River, with one 1958 record from near Pacora), and Darién. In Canal area known only from several nineteenth-century specimens, not recorded since.

Habits: Usually found singly or in pairs. Often rather secretive and hard to see, but sometimes feeds in the open on gravel bars on banks of rivers, probing deeply in mud and water between rocks. In some areas best known from their mellow rolling calls, heard at sunrise and dusk, *kro, kro*, or *koro, koro*.
Range: Costa Rica to Paraguay, northeastern Argentina, and southeastern Brazil.

GREEN IBIS

BUFF-NECKED IBIS
Theristicus caudatus

Description: 28–32. Casual. *Large*. Bill decurved. *Head, neck, and chest buffy white*, more orange-rufous on crown and chest, whiter on throat; upperparts otherwise dark gray, wings black with *conspicuous white wing-coverts*; lower underparts black.
Status and distribution: Only one definite record, a bird killed near Pacora, eastern Panama province, on September 18, 1950; another was reported seen in the same general area in September 1958 (Baldomiro Meno, *fide* Wetmore). Decreasing in western Colombia, where now so scarce that it seems likely it will never again wander to Panama.
Habits: Usually seen in pairs or small groups, walking about in open areas, most often near water but regularly on dry ground. The call is a loud unmistakable *tu-túrt, tu-túrt*, given most often in flight.
Range: Colombia (casual in Panama) to Tierra del Fuego.
Note: More than one species is likely to be involved.

ROSEATE SPOONBILL
Ajaia ajaja   Plate 2

Description: 28–32. Long flat bill, broadening at tip into the *unmistakable "spoonbill"*.

Adult has featherless head and white neck; *otherwise mostly pink, wing-coverts red*; tail buffy-orange. Immature has head largely feathered, is more whitish, becoming pinker with age.
Similar species: Even the whitish immatures can be instantly recognized by the spatulate bill.
Status and distribution: Uncommon and local in mangroves, on coastal mudflats, and in freshwater marshes near coast in lowlands on entire Pacific slope; on Caribbean slope apparently occurs only as a wanderer, with a few reports from western Bocas del Toro and from Canal area. Seems to be declining generally in Panama; recent reports are rather few, and none involve more than a few birds. Nesting has not been recorded in recent years, and in fact the only reported colony is one which was said to have existed in mangroves near Cocoli, on Pacific side of Canal area, until about 1930 (*fide* Wetmore).
Habits: Usually seen in small flocks. Forages by swinging bill from side to side in shallow water and mud.
Range: Southeastern United States and Mexico south locally to northern Argentina and Uruguay (casual in central Chile); Greater Antilles.

STORKS: Ciconiidae (2)

The storks are a widespread group of large, long legged wading birds. Resembling herons in many respects, they differ obviously in flying with neck extended. Only three species are found in the New World, of which but two are known in Panama. All storks feed on fish, small animals, and to some extent insects, generally in shallow water or wet grassy areas. The Wood Stork often feeds in a cooperative manner, a group more or less lining up and muddying the water in front of them with their feet, grabbing the fleeing prey with their bill. Some storks (notably the Wood Stork) are highly colonial, often nesting in association with herons and ibises; other species (among them the Jabiru) are solitary nesters.

WOOD STORK
Mycteria americana   Plate 2

Description: 35–42. Very large, with heavy somewhat decurved bill. Mostly white with *bare blackish head and upper neck* and *black flight feathers* and tail. Immature similar but with head and neck more or less feathered, brownish.
Similar species: Egrets and white herons lack black on wings and dark bare skin on head and neck. White Ibis is much smaller, has red bill and facial area, black restricted to wing-tips. Soaring birds somewhat resemble King Vulture in pattern.
Status and distribution: Uncommon to occasionally common, but local and often erratic, in marshes and swamps on entire Pacific slope; less numerous on Caribbean slope, where recorded mostly from Bocas del Toro. In Panama seems generally to avoid salt water. Nesting remains little documented in Panama, with only two colonies having been reported: one of originally 40 or more nests which gradually diminished to only six or eight in a small patch of forest adjacent to mangroves south of Las Lajas, Chiriquí, in February–March 1976 (Ridgely); and another of about 12 nests at the mouth of the Río Pavo, Veraguas, near the southwestern tip of the Azuero Peninsula (F. Delgado). Likely breeds elsewhere as well. Rather infrequent in the Canal area, and then often seen only flying overhead.
Habits: Gregarious. Though rather awkward on the ground or perched in a tree, they are exceptionally graceful in the air, particularly when circling high overhead on outstretched wings.
Range: Southern United States (where decreasing) to northern Argentina and Uruguay.

JABIRU
Jabiru mycteria   Plate 2

Description: 48–55. *Huge size* makes this very rare species unmistakable. Bill very heavy, slightly upturned. *Entirely white* with bare head and neck black becoming red on lower neck. Immature is more brownish gray.
Similar species: Wood Stork is much smaller with black flight feathers and tail.
Status and distribution: Only one definite record, a bird taken at Cricamola, Bocas del Toro, on August 11, 1927. Wetmore mentions that Baldomiro Meno, a local hunter, said that he had seen this species once at La Jagua, eastern Panama province (date not given). Favors extensive marshy areas, nesting solitarily in trees. Given its recent decline in Costa Rica (where at most a few dozen pairs are believed to persist, mainly in Guanacaste), the Jabiru seems unlikely to ever occur again in Panama.
Habits: Usually solitary or in pairs, unlike Wood Stork. Like that species, the Jabiru often soars to great heights.
Range: Occurs from southern Mexico (accidental in southern Texas, with one recent record) south locally to northern Argentina and Uruguay; recorded breeding in Middle America only in Belize and Costa Rica.

DUCKS, GEESE, AND SWANS: Anatidae (14)

Well known and worldwide in distribution, the waterfowl need no introduction. Most of the ducks found in Panama feed primarily on vegetable matter, a few on crustaceans and other small aquatic animals. Nests of the Panamanian breeding species are generally located in hollows in trees, the exception being the Masked Duck, which conceals its nest in dense vegetation on the ground near water. Due to a scarcity of good habitat and the intense hunting pressure on much of what exists, ducks do not form a conspicuous part of Panama's avifauna.

FULVOUS WHISTLING-DUCK
Dendrocygna bicolor

Descriptions: 18–21. Only one record. Bill slaty gray. *Mostly cinnamon brown*, paler and buffier below, with patch of whitish streaks on sides of neck and *prominent creamy white stripes down sides and flanks*. In flight, wings appear very dark and it shows *conspicuous white ring on upper tail-coverts*.
Similar species: See other whistling-ducks. Female *Anas* ducks are differently shaped (shorter neck, shorter legs), show some pattern on wings, and are generally mottled

with dusky; female Pintail is most similar but shows white on wing in flight and lacks creamy white flank stripe.

Status and distribution: Only record is a bird shot at La Jagua, eastern Panama province on June 14, 1936. To be watched for among groups of Black-bellied Whistling-Ducks.

Range: Southern United States south locally to Costa Rica (where now apparently resident in small numbers in the northwest); accidental in Panama; locally in South America south to Argentina; also in eastern Africa and southern Asia.

WHITE-FACED WHISTLING-DUCK
Dendrocygna viduata

Description: 16–18. Now very rare. Bill black. *Forepart of head white* (sometimes stained by mud), remainder of head and neck black (sometimes with patch of white on foreneck); back brown; rump, tail, and most of wings black; chest rufous-chestnut, center of lower underparts black, sides and flanks brown barred with black. In flight shows *no white on wings.* Juvenile has no black or white on head; head mainly gray with rusty face, below light gray barred with darker.

Similar species: Other whistling-ducks lack white on head.

Status and distribution: Apparently extirpated. Recorded only from Canal area on Gatun Lake (where one was shot in June 1924, and a group was reportedly seen in April 1976), and in eastern Panama province in the La Jagua/Pacora area (where single birds were taken in 1928 and 1931, with more reportedly having invaded in the 1930s, some remaining to nest, but all having disappeared by the 1940s with many having been shot). Given the amount of drainage and associated agricultural development that has taken place in the Tocumen/Chepo area over the past several decades, it seems unlikely that this species will ever again reside permanently in Panama; one presumes that the 1976 Gatun Lake birds were only accidental wanderers.

Range: Northwestern Costa Rica; irregular (but now probably only accidental) in central Panama; South America south to Argentina, and in warmer parts of Africa.

BLACK-BELLIED WHISTLING-DUCK
Dendrocygna autumnalis   Plate 3

Description: 20–22. *Bill and legs reddish.* Mostly reddish brown with sides of head and upper neck gray and wash of gray on lower chest; *breast and belly black; wings show broad white band across coverts* (visible at rest and very prominent in flight). Immature is duller and more grayish brown but already shows adult's pattern; bill and legs dusky.

Similar species: See other whistling-ducks. On the ground, whistling-ducks give a gangly impression, with long neck and legs; in the air the wings beat relatively slowly, the neck is drooped, and the long legs extend well beyond the tail.

Status and distribution: Uncommon and local in freshwater marshes and ponds, and in mangroves in lowlands on entire Pacific slope; on Caribbean slope rare, and perhaps occurring only as an irregular wanderer, with a few records from Canal area (but only one recent report, a single bird seen at Galeta Island in 1977) and eastern San Blas. Scarce in the Canal area, though small flocks of up to 10–20 birds have lingered, sometimes for protracted periods, in the Chiva Chiva and Farfan areas. Most numerous in western Panama, but even here numbers have been much reduced by hunting pressure. They once occurred in flocks numbering in the hundreds (C. A. Rogers, oral comm.), but now seeing more than a few dozen at once is unusual.

Habits: Unlike the other two Panama whistling-ducks, this species perches readily in trees, especially on dead branches. Usually in small groups. Has loud high semi-whistled calls, varying in speed and quality, given mostly in flight; these result in its local name of "wichity" or "güichiti". Often kept in captivity around farmyards and pools.

Range: Southern Texas and Mexico to northern Argentina and southeastern Brazil.

MUSCOVY DUCK
Cairina moschata   Plate 3

Description: ♂ 32–35; ♀ 24–26. *Large.* Adult male has fleshy red caruncles over eye and at base of bill. *Glossy black* with slight bushy crest; *upper wing-coverts and entire undersurface of wing white* (very conspicuous in flight). Female similar but much smaller, with no red on bill or face and no noticeable crest. Immature has much less white on wing.

Similar species: Comb Duck has mostly white head, neck, and underparts, and has wholly black wings. Immature in flight showing little white on wings might be confused with Neotropic Cormorant.

Status and distribution: Rare to locally uncommon in freshwater swamps and marshes, and to a lesser extent in mangroves (perhaps only to roost?), in lowlands on Pacific slope, where recorded mainly from eastern Panama province (Tocumen eastward) and Darién, with wanderers occasionally straggling west to the Canal area (e.g. a group of three to four seen on Miraflores Lake on March 12, 1983; R. Behrstock *et al.*), and recently reported also from coastal Veraguas (with pairs being seen regularly near the mouths of the Río Tabasará and Bubí in 1981; F. Delgado); on Caribbean slope recorded only from Canal area, where apparently formerly resident in Chagres River valley but long since extirpated except for wandering birds (though there is some evidence of a recent increase, with a number of sightings from the Gamboa area in 1986–1987); one sighting from Coiba Island (Wetmore). Apparently never widespread in Panama, Muscovy numbers have declined due to hunting pressure and drainage; nonetheless, fair numbers do persist in at least a few areas (e.g. 28 were seen at Tocumen on January 15, 1988; Ridgely *et al.*). Protection from hunting during the nesting season would be extremely worthwhile, as would emulating the successful Mexican program of putting out nesting boxes for this species and the Black-bellied Whistling-Duck.

Habits: Muscovies are frequently domesticated and kept at liberty by country people, so it is sometimes questionable whether or not a bird is truly feral. Wild birds are usually very wary, often a good distinction from captive ones. The species favors wooded swamps and rivers, and perches readily in trees.

Range: Mexico south locally to northern Argentina and Uruguay.

COMB DUCK
Sarkidiornis melanotos　　　　　Plate 3

Description: ♂ 28–30; ♀ 22–24. Large. Adult male has *black fleshy comb* on upper mandible. Crown and hindneck mostly black, feathers recurved forming slight crest; *rest of head and neck and most of underparts white*, the head flecked with black; remaining upperparts (including entire wing) black glossed with green and purple. Female much smaller.

Similar species: Muscovy is all dark with prominent white wing-coverts. Some domesticated Muscovies have white on under-parts (and elsewhere) but always show white on wings.

Status and distribution: Uncommon and local in lowlands of Darién (recorded only from along the Río Chucunaque, but perhaps more widespread); casually wanders west to eastern Panama province (where one of a band of five was shot on March 30, 1949, with others lingering into May; no other reports).

Habits: In South America tends to consort with whistling-ducks, and is most numerous in open to semiopen marshy areas (generally avoiding forested regions). Behavior much like the Muscovy. Seems much prone to long-distance wandering.

Range: Eastern (rarely central) Panama south locally to northern Argentina and Uruguay; also in Africa and southern Asia.

[MALLARD]
Anas platyrhynchos

Description: 22–26. Old reports. Bill yellow in male, *orange and dusky in female*. Male has *glossy green head, narrow white collar around neck, rufous chest*, and mostly pale gray body with black rump and under tail-coverts and white tail. Female mottled brownish with *whitish tail*. In flight, both sexes show violet-blue speculum *bordered in front and behind by a white stripe*.

Similar species: Female can be told from female Northern Pintail by orange on bill, whitish tail, and stripe in front of wing speculum (pintail has stripe only to rear).

Status and distribution: Two rather vague, old reports. One was reported seen, with no corroborating details, at Miraflores, on the Pacific side of the Canal area, on November 26, 1911 (L. Jewel), and the species was also listed as occurring at Lion Hill, on the Caribbean slope of the Canal area, by McLeannan in the nineteenth century (but no specimens were taken). The species requires confirmation from anywhere in southern Middle America.

Range: Breeds in North America, Europe, and Asia; in America winters south to Mexico, rarely to Honduras, reported seen in Nicaragua, Costa Rica, and Panama.

NORTHERN PINTAIL
Anas acuta

Description: 26–30. *Long slender neck* and *pointed tail* (much longer in male). Bill gray. Male has *brown head and white stripe extending up foreneck ending in point*; upperparts and sides mostly pale gray; underparts mostly white with black under tail-coverts. Female is mottled light brownish all over. In flight, both sexes show *white stripe on rear edge only* of green speculum.

Similar species: Females can be known by their streamlined appearance and pointed tail (longer than in other similar female ducks). See Fulvous Whistling-Duck.

Status and distribution: Generally a rare winter visitant (recorded mostly December–February), though on infrequent occasions can be more numerous; reported mostly from Bocas del Toro and eastern Panama province (especially at the since-drained marshes of La Jagua), but also from Los Santos and Coclé (band recoveries). Almost unreported from Canal area, though it was listed by McLeannan for Lion Hill in the nineteenth century, and a female was seen on the Chagres River above Juan Mina on December 18, 1962 (Eisenmann). Seems no longer to occur with any regularity in Panama; there are few, if any, recent reports.

Range: Breeds in North America, Europe, and Asia; American birds winter south to northern South America and in West Indies.

BLUE-WINGED TEAL
Anas discors   Plate 3

Description: 15–16. Bill gray. Male has head and upper neck dark gray (blacker on crown) with *prominent white crescent on forepart of face*; otherwise mostly blackish above, brownish below spotted with blackish; black rump, tail, and under tail-coverts. Female mottled light brownish. In flight, both sexes show *prominent pale blue wing-coverts* (may look white at a distance) and green speculum.

Similar species: Noticeably smaller than most of the ducks with which it consorts; see Cinnamon Teal. Northern Shoveler has similar pale blue wing-coverts but is larger with spoon-shaped bill.

Status and distribution: Despite being a migrant, easily the most numerous and widespread duck in Panama. Locally common on freshwater ponds, marshes, and lakes in lowlands on both slopes, ranging up to the Volcán Lakes in the lower highlands of western Chiriquí; reported also from Coiba Island. Recorded mostly September–April, with a few occasionally lingering through the northern summer months (e.g. 16 seen near El Rincón, Herrera, on July 27, 1975; Ridgely *et al.*), with some of these perhaps

being crippled birds. Numbers on Gatun Lake have increased dramatically since 1966 due to the spread of *Hydrilla* mats along its shoreline.

Habits: Found wherever there is suitable marshy or shallow water habitat and an absence of excessive disturbance. Like most other *Anas* ducks feed by tipping up, submerging the front half of the body. Also like other *Anas* ducks, springs directly into flight, without preliminary pattering along the surface of most of the others. Usually silent, like most other migrant ducks in Panama.

Range: Breeds in North America; winters from southern United States to central Argentina and Uruguay.

Note: Green-winged Teal, *Anas crecca*, of North America and Eurasia could occur as a vagrant to Panama, as it has occurred accidentally south to Costa Rica and Colombia. Male is mostly gray with chestnut head and green band on face; breast buffy, spotted black, with vertical white stripe on sides in front of wing; wing with green speculum. Female much like female Blue-winged Teal, but lacking latter's pale blue wing-coverts.

CINNAMON TEAL
Anas cyanoptera

Description: 15–17. Rare. Bill blackish; *iris red*. Male *mostly bright reddish chestnut*, with black mottling on back and blackish rump and tail. Female virtually identical to female Blue-winged Teal, and cannot be distinguished in the field. In flight both sexes show prominent pale blue wing-coverts and a green speculum (as in Blue-winged Teal).

Similar species: Males in breeding plumage (which is generally assumed by January) are easy to pick out, but when in eclipse plumage they very closely resemble females of both Blue-winged and Cinnamon Teals; they then can be known only by their red eyes (but these can be noted only at close range).

Status and distribution: A rare winter visitor, perhaps overlooked. Known only from one old "Canal Zone" record without details, a sighting of a male from Gamboa on January 5, 1967 (N. G. Smith), and from three band recoveries of shot birds, two taken at the La Jagua marshes in eastern Panama province (January 20, 1955; January 7, 1956), and one from near Chame, western Panama province (November 8, 1957).

Habits: Similar to Blue-winged Teal, and most likely to be spotted consorting with a flock of that species.

Range: Breeds in western North American south to Mexico, these birds wintering south rarely to northern South America; resident populations in the Andes and southern South America.

NORTHERN SHOVELER
Anas clypeata

Description: 17–20. *Oversize spoon-shaped bill* distinguishes both sexes. Male has *head and neck dark green*, back black, chest white, *most of lower underparts dark chestnut* with white area on flanks. Female is mottled brownish. In flight, both sexes show pale blue wing-coverts and green speculum.

Similar species: Told from all other Panama ducks by its large spatulate bill. Female resembles female Blue-winged Teal but is larger with the oversize bill.

Status and distribution: Rare winter visitant (October–March) to freshwater marshes and ponds in lowlands on both slopes; rather local, with reports only from Chiriquí (David), Bocas del Toro (Changuinola), Canal area, and eastern Panama province. Only two reports from Canal area, the more recent being a female at Pedro Miguel on December 17, 1967 (Ridgely). Rather few recent reports from anywhere in Panama.

Habits: Usually holds bill angled downward, almost touching the water. Feeds by sifting through mud and shallow water as it slowly paddles forward.

Range: Breeds in North America, Europe, and Asia; in America winters south to northern South America.

AMERICAN WIGEON
Anas americana   Plate 3

Description: 18–22. Bluish gray bill. Male has *white crown and green patch behind eye*; throat and neck buff with small black dots; otherwise brown above; chest and sides pinkish brown, center of underparts white; white patch in front of black rump and under tail-coverts. Female *mostly ruddy brown with contrasting grayish head and neck*. In flight, both sexes show *prominent white wing-coverts* and a green speculum.

Similar species: Pale bluish wing-coverts of Shoveler and Blue-winged Teal can look white in some lights. Male's white crown is usually very conspicuous.

Status and distribution: Locally fairly common but somewhat irregular winter visitant (October–April) to ponds, lakes, and freshwater marshes in lowlands of western and central Panama; recorded from Bocas del Toro, Chiriquí (sight report of two east of David on November 9, 1968; Ridgely and J. Karr), Canal area (most numerous and regular in the Miraflores Lake/Pedro Miguel area), and eastern Panama province (La Jagua); one band recovery from southern Los Santos in December 1957.

Habits: Swims with more upright carriage than other *Anas* ducks. Males frequently give an easily recognized whistled *whee whee whew* (R. T. Peterson).

Range: Breeds in western North America; winters south to northern Colombia and Venezuela, and in West Indies.

RING-NECKED DUCK
Aythya collaris

Description: 16–18. *Bill bluish gray with white ring* and black tip. Male has head and neck black (glossed purple) with inconspicuous narrow chestnut collar around neck; chest and *back black*; sides light gray with *prominent vertical white mark in front of wing*; center of lower underparts white. Female mostly brown, darkest on crown and back, with *whitish face* and *white eye-ring*; belly white. In flight, both sexes show broad gray stripe on flight feathers.

Similar species: Both sexes resemble Lesser Scaup but have ring on bill (absent in scaup). Male known by its black (not gray) back and white vertical mark in front of wing (lacking in scaup); female by its lack of female scaup's distinct white patch at base of bill (though face is vaguely whitish).

Status and distribution: First reported in February 1951, now known to be an occasional winter visitant (December–February) in very small numbers to ponds, lakes, and freshwater marshes. No Panama specimens; reported from Chiriquí (sighting of a female on Volcán Lakes on February 23, 1971; R. V. Clem, J. H. Dick, and G. Stout), Canal area (a number of sight reports, principally from Miraflores Lakes and Pedro Miguel), and eastern Panama province (reportedly shot occasionally at La Jagua).

Habits: A diving duck, preferring fairly open but not necessarily very deep water. Favors company of the commoner Lesser Scaup.

Range: Breeds in North America (increasing in recent decades, especially to east); winters from United States to Panama (once Venezuela) and in West Indies.

LESSER SCAUP
Aythya affinis   Plate 3

Description: 16–18. Bill bluish. Male has black head (glossed with purple in some lights), neck, and chest; *otherwise mostly grayish* (paler below). Female is brown, darker above, with *well-defined white patch at base of bill*. In flight, both sexes show prominent white strip on flight feathers.
Similar species: See much less numerous Ring-necked Duck.
Status and distribution: Locally fairly common winter visitant (November–March) to less disturbed portions of larger bodies of water in lowlands on both slopes, ranging up to Volcán Lakes in lower highlands of western Chiriquí; recorded also on Coiba Island; apparently not recorded from Darién or San Blas. Most numerous in Canal area on Madden and Gatun Lakes, and on Chagres River above Gamboa.
Habits: Usually seen in flocks on open water, diving frequently.
Range: Breeds in western and northern North America, wintering south in very small numbers to northern South America.

MASKED DUCK
Oxyura dominica   Plate 3

Description: 13–14. *Bill bright blue* (duller in female and nonbreeding male); long stiff tail usually held submerged or flat on surface of water, but sometimes cocked into the air. Breeding male has *black face*; *otherwise mostly rufous-chestnut*, paler and buffier below, with back and sides speckled black. Female and nonbreeding male mostly dark brown above with sides of head more grayish buff and *crossed by two dusky stripes*; buffy brownish below mottled with dark brown. In flight both sexes show *prominent white patch on secondaries*.
Similar species: Small size and chunky squat shape should preclude confusion with any other Panama duck.
Status and distribution: Fairly common but local and erratic in freshwater marshes and shallow ponds on entire Pacific slope; on Caribbean slope recorded only from Gatun Lake in Canal area, and from eastern San Blas; recorded irregularly as high as the Volcán Lakes in the lower highlands of western Chiriquí. Most numerous on various ponds in the Canal area (especially on Gatun Lake around and above Gamboa, and in the Chiva Chiva/Miraflores area), and on the eastern side of the Azuero Peninsula, but everywhere numbers seem to fluctuate, and at times none seem to be present even in the most favored locales.
Habits: Often rather shy and difficult to see, usually remaining in areas of water with thick emergent vegetation. Swim low in the water, diving or merely submerging (grebe-like) to procure food underwater. Males in full plumage are usually much out-numbered by female-plumaged birds.
Range: Southern United States south locally to Argentina and Uruguay.
Note: Perhaps better placed in the monotypic genus *Nomonyx* (B. C. Liverzy, *Auk 103* (4): 737–754, 1986).

AMERICAN VULTURES : Cathartidae (4)

The American Vultures are a well known group of carrion eaters found only in the New World, in greatest numbers in warmer regions. Two species, the Turkey and the Black, are familiar birds in Panama, as elsewhere in the warmer parts of America. Black Vultures in particular are especially numerous around towns and cities; they and the Turkey Vulture roost in large numbers in places such as Ancon Hill. The Panamanian vultures apparently nest in shaded crevices, such as hollow trees or logs on or very near the ground and cavities in rocks. Vultures locate their food primarily through keen eyesight, though recent evidence indicates that, at least in the Turkey Vulture, the sense of smell also plays a role. It has been suggested that the Cathartid vultures are more closely related to the Ciconiiformes than they are to the other Falconiformes.

BLACK VULTURE
Coragyps atratus   p.84

Description: 24–27. *Black*, including featherless head and neck, with *white patch at base of primaries* (prominent in flight).

Similar species: Compared to Turkey Vulture has relatively broad and short wings and tail; Turkey Vulture has red (not solid black) head in adults and lacks the white wing patch.

Status and distribution: Very common to abundant in more or less inhabited and open country and in smaller numbers at forested borders (rare in areas of unbroken forest, occasionally flying over) virtually throughout; particularly numerous around towns and cities; found also on Coiba Island, Taboga Island, the Pearl Islands, and other smaller islands in Panama Bay.

Habits: A familiar carrion feeder in settled areas and around sea bird colonies. In some places (e.g. Panama City) it becomes very unsuspicious and serves a useful function as a supplementary garbage collector. Very large numbers are also to be seen on updrafts around Ancon Hill or going to roosts about Panama City. Ordinary flight consists of several flaps and a sail, unlike the Turkey Vulture, which mainly soars; the Black soars on flat wings (not in a dihedral). Whether the Black Vulture engages in migratory movements is uncertain.

Range: Central United States to central Chile and southern Argentina.

TURKEY VULTURE
Cathartes aura   p.84

Description: 28–32. Black, with *featherless head and neck reddish* (blackish in young birds). The breeding race (*ruficollis*) has several narrow dull yellow bands across back of neck (may look like a pale patch at a distance). *Soars with wings held slightly above the horizontal*; from below contrast between black under wing-coverts and *silvery gray flight feathers* is apparent.

Similar species: Black Vulture has shorter and broader wings and tail, white patch on primaries, and alternates flapping with sailing (soaring much less). Lesser Yellow-headed Vulture is similarly shaped but has mostly yellow head (not just on rear part of neck), usually has whitish patch at base of primaries, and is smaller. Immature King Vulture shows some white below except when very young. Zone-tailed Hawk is smaller with larger feathered head, has white tail bands.

Status and distribution: Common resident throughout, abundant on migration, in greater numbers during northern winter months; probably somewhat more numerous in open country than in forested areas; found also on the Coiba, Taboga, and Pearl Islands. In October and November and again from late February to early April large (sometimes tremendous) flocks of migrants breeding in north pass overhead,

providing the observer who is in the right place at the right time with a breathtaking spectacle; these flocks often number in the many thousands. The greatest flights have been observed in coastal Bocas del Toro and on Pacific slope of Canal area and eastern Panama province, in early March and in October.

Habits: More widespread than Black Vulture, but less numerous around towns and cities. Less gregarious (except on migration) than Black Vulture. A masterful flier, soaring for long periods without a flap, tilting from side to side to take advantage of every favorable air current.

Range: Breeds from southern Canada to Tierra del Fuego; Greater Antilles. Many northern birds winter in Middle America and northwestern South America.

LESSER YELLOW-HEADED VULTURE
Cathartes burrovianus

Description: 23–25. Resembles more familiar Turkey Vulture but slighter and *smaller*; at close range bare head can be seen to be *mostly yellow or orange-yellow* with red forecrown and nape and blue-gray mid-crown (skin colors somewhat variable). In flight shows whitish patch on upper surface of wing at base of primaries, as well as two-toned underwing pattern as in Turkey Vulture. Immature has dusky head with whitish nape.

Similar species: See Turkey Vulture.

Status and distribution: Fairly common locally over savanna grasslands and open marshes in lowlands on Pacific slope from Chiriquí and eastern side of Azuero Peninsula to eastern Panama province. Scarce in Canal area and vicinity, though occasional single birds or small groups have been seen in Panama city and in grassy open areas of Canal area. Fairly numerous in Tocumen/La Jagua area though most common in Coclé and eastern Azuero Peninsula. Seems seasonally more numerous, so perhaps in part migratory; evidently breeds in Panama, however, as juveniles have been observed. Most reports from Panama came from the rainy season (April–December).

Habits: Usually seen sailing low over a grassy area or marsh, or perched on a low branch or fence post; only rarely soars high (when sometimes hard to distinguish from Turkey Vulture).

Left, BLACK VULTURE; right, TURKEY VULTURE

Range: Eastern Mexico; spottily in Central America; Colombia to northern Argentina and Uruguay.

KING VULTURE
Sarcoramphus papa   p.84

Description: 30–34. Very large. Adult *mostly creamy white* with black rump, tail, and flight feathers; at short range *multicolored featherless head and neck* can be seen. Immature blackish brown, becoming progressively whiter on underparts with age. Flight profile of long broad flat wings, *short tail*, and almost headless look is characteristic at great distances.
Similar species: Adults are unmistakable. Immature might be confused with Turkey Vulture but generally shows at least some white and soars with flat (not uptilted) wings.
Status and distribution: Uncommon to locally fairly common in lowlands and foothills on both slopes, mostly in relatively unsettled forested or wooded regions; fairly common also on Coiba Island. Numbers seen are never very large (never even coming close to equalling those of Turkey or Black Vultures), but the species is conspicuous and can be seen almost daily in appropriate habitat, if flying conditions are good. In Canal area much more numerous on Caribbean side, with no evidence of any

KING VULTURE (adult)

decline in numbers. Perhaps commonest in the Darién lowlands and on Coiba Island, where up to four to eight per day can be seen with fair regularity.
Habits: Almost invariably seen soaring effortlessly high overhead, only occasionally perched. Usually seen singly, occasionally in pairs, very rarely more; generally keeps apart from other soaring vultures.
Range: Southern Mexico to Bolivia, northern Argentina, and Uruguay.

HAWKS, EAGLES, AND KITES: Accipitridae (40)

This is a varied group of diurnal birds of prey, worldwide in distribution and well represented in Panama. All are characterized by a strongly hooked bill and gripping feet; most species have rather rounded wings (the exceptions being chiefly several species of kites). The female is larger, sometimes considerably larger, than the male, and a few species show sexual dimorphism in coloration as well. Their food is live prey, ranging in the various species from sizable mammals and birds to insects. Though many Panama species, especially the medium-sized members of the group, are generalists (i.e. they feed relatively opportunistically), a number of others have more specialized feeding habits; several feed mainly on insects captured on the wing, a few feed on snails, several mainly on birds, a number chiefly on snakes and other reptiles, and two on fish. Though they are more conspicuous and easily observed on the open savannas and in gallery woodland, there is a greater diversity of species in humid forest and woodland. Many neotropical birds of prey are difficult to identify in the field, for one often does not get a close or long look at them, and in numerous species there are several plumage phases or age stages to contend with. Most resident species are still poorly known and would amply repay detailed and sustained study. The larger species, in particular the huge Harpy Eagle, have been greatly reduced in numbers around settled areas, and though the Harpy is now officially protected, it as well as other species are still usually shot when the opportunity arises. The taxonomy and sequence employed is essentially that of the 1983 AOU Check-list, with a few minor deviations. Note that the Osprey, formerly treated as a separate family, is now considered a subfamily within the Accipitridae.

OSPREY
Pandion haliaetus p.85

Description: 21–24. Mostly *dark brown above, white below; crown and nape white*, broad stripe through eye black. Immature is similar but more streaked and edged with white and buffy above, washed with buffy below. In flight, wings appear long and rather narrow, with terminal half bent back ("kinked"); underside of wings mostly whitish with *black "wrist" mark* (carpal joint).
Similar species: Contrasting dark upperparts and white underparts and attachment to larger bodies of water are characteristic.
Status and distribution: Fairly common during northern winter months around larger bodies of water in lowlands on both slopes; smaller numbers present throughout the year, especially on or near coast ("summering" birds being immatures); on migration, occurs elsewhere, sometimes accompanying other migrating hawks; noted regularly on Volcán Lakes in western Chiriquí highlands; occurs also on Coiba Island, Taboga Island, and the Pearl Islands. Does not breed in Panama.
Habits: Regularly rests on a high exposed perch near water, from which it flies out to fish. Generally hunts while flying, often hovering heavily, plunging feet first into the water, often from a considerable height and with a great splash. Its feet have been

modified with a rough spiny surface to assist in grasping its slippery prey, and Ospreys do seem successful a good proportion of the time (more so than most other raptors). In normal flight glides on set wings, with deep deliberate wingstrokes interspersed. Calls fairly often in Panama, a loud, yelping, upward-inflected, *cleeyp! cleeyp!* (sometimes singly or in series) being most frequent.

OSPREY

Range: Virtually cosmopolitan, breeding on every continent except South America; during northern winter, North American birds occur south to southern South America (with some individuals "summering" even there); in New World not known to breed south of Guatemala and Belize.

GRAY-HEADED KITE
Leptodon cayanensis   Plate 7, p.88

Description: 18–22. Cere, bare facial area, and legs gray. Adult has *pale gray head contrasting with slaty black upperparts and white underparts*; tail black with two narrow white bands (a third rarely visible) and narrow white tipping. In flight from below, wings rather broad and rounded, *black with bold white barring on flight feathers*, the black wings *contrasting strongly with white body*. Immatures variable and confusing; all have cere, facial skin, and legs yellow to orange-yellow. In pale phase *most of head, neck, and underparts white* with brown on mid-crown and small black streak over eye; back and wings dark brown; tail black with grayish bands; under wing-coverts white (not black as in adult), with flight feathers barred dusky. In dark phase upperparts (including sides of head and neck) dusky brown; underparts buffy whitish variably streaked dusky, usually heavily so, sometimes so coarsely that chest is almost blackish. In an intermediate phase shows only a few fine dusky streaks on throat and breast, these sometimes coalescing into a central throat stripe.
Similar species: Adults are distinctive and should not be confused; looks rather small-headed, this often imparting a "weak" look. Immatures of both phases are, however, tricky. Pattern of pale phase resembles that of the rare Black-and-white Hawk-Eagle; kite is somewhat smaller and with slenderer build, browner above, has yellow lores and cere (not black lores and orange cere), and shorter and weaker legs. See also immature Hook-billed Kite and Ornate Hawk-Eagle. Dark phase can be very troublesome as there are so many other more or less streaked immature raptors. Compare especially to immature Gray Hawk, and Common and Mangrove Black-Hawks, and remember small-headed profile when perched, and round-winged profile when flying.
Status and distribution: Uncommon in forest, second-growth woodland, and borders in more humid lowlands and foothills on both slopes; not reported from

dry Pacific lowlands from eastern side of Azuero Peninsula to extreme western Panama province. Thinly spread throughout Canal area in more wooded areas, more numerous on Caribbean side.
Habits: Usually rather unobtrusive, often remaining perched hidden from view for long periods. Usually perches rather high, sometimes fully in the open in the early morning. Feeds on a large variety of mostly small prey items. Gray-headed Kites soar regularly, and are perhaps most apt to be seen at such times. When breeding they frequently give voice to their loud, apparently territorial call, a repeated *kek kek kek kek* . . . (Wetmore), given both in flight and from a perch in the canopy. Also gives a loud cat-like *miaow* (E. O. Willis).
Range: Eastern Mexico to Bolivia, northern Argentina, and southern Brazil.

HOOK-BILLED KITE
Chondrohierax uncinatus   Plates 7,9, p.88

Description: 16–18. *Heavy and conspicuously hooked bill*, with *greenish cere and facial skin and small yellow-orange spot in front of whitish eye*; legs yellow or orange. Adult male *slaty gray, usually lightly barred with white or buffy below*; upper tail-coverts whitish; tail dark gray with two whitish bands and narrow tip. Some birds are plain gray below and have only one tail band. Adult female dark brown to slaty gray above with *tawny collar on hindneck*; *coarsely barred with brown and white or buffy below*; tail as in male. In flight note distinctive "oval" wing shape, quite rounded but obviously narrowing at base; in both sexes wing linings grayish with flight feathers barred black and white (occasionally more or less uniform below in male). Relatively rare melanistic phase (occurs in both sexes) *entirely brownish black including underwing* (unbarred), tail with one broad white band. Immature dark brown above with *narrow whitish collar on hindneck*; creamy white below becoming progressively more barred with age; tail with three to four grayish or brownish bands; underwing as in adult. Immature of melanistic phase all sooty black with white tail bands.
Similar species: Very variable, but can often be recognized (even immatures) by the odd visage imparted by the big bill and the pale spot in front of eye. Normal adults (with barred underparts) perhaps most likely to be confused with several *Buteo* hawks but more coarsely barred below and on flight feathers than any of them; head shape and flight

profile also differ markedly. Melanistic phase superficially like several other kites (e.g. Snail and Slender-billed) and Plumbeous Hawk. Compare immature to immature Gray-headed Kite of pale phase, Bicolored Hawk immature, and Collared Forest-Falcon.

Status and distribution: Uncommon in humid forest and second-growth woodland in lowlands on both slopes, but rather local and not recorded from the Caribbean slope outside of the Canal area aside from one Bocas del Toro sighting (N. G. Smith), and not recorded from the Azuero Peninsula to Coclé, or from Darién (though seems likely, at least in the latter). In Panama especially fond of swampy areas; elsewhere recorded regularly from foothills and even well up into the highlands, though this does not seem to be the case in Panama. In Canal area most numerous in Achiote Road area.

Habits: Often sluggish and unsuspicious, allowing a close approach once it is spotted though doubtless often overlooked due to its habit of perching for long periods inside foliage. Soars occasionally, but usually not for very long or very high. Its distinctive call is a rapid chuckling *wi-i-i-i-i-i-i-i-uh* (E. O. Willis). Feeds primarily on tree snails.

Range: Southern Texas to Bolivia, northern Argentina, and southern Brazil; Cuba and Grenada.

AMERICAN SWALLOW-TAILED KITE
Elanoides forficatus   p.88

Description: 21–24. Unmistakable. *Head, neck, and underparts white*; back, wings, and tail black, glossed with green on upper back and shoulders (gloss becoming duller blue in worn plumage); *tail very long and deeply forked.*

Status and distribution: Fairly common in forest and forest borders in lowlands and foothills on both slopes, more numerous on Caribbean; ranges up in Chiriquí highlands to over 1800 m (6000 ft). Breeds in Panama, and also occurs as a transient in fairly large numbers (flocks of up to several hundred birds, regularly in associated with Plumbeous Kite) late January–February and late July–early September; appears to be absent mid-September–early January. Breeding birds of southern United States (nominate *fortificatus*) unrecorded but possibly occur as transients en route to their wintering grounds in South America east of the Andes (though perhaps only moving via the West Indies or Caribbean); they cannot be separated in the field from Middle American breeders (*yetapa*).

Habits: A beautiful bird, the most graceful of all birds of prey. Pre-eminently a bird of the sky, only infrequently seen perched, then mostly in cloudy dull weather. Quite gregarious, even when breeding gathering in groups of a dozen or so individuals.

Range: Breeds from southern United States to Bolivia, northern Argentina, and southeastern Brazil; North and Middle American birds withdraw to South America during northern winter; transients recorded in Cuba and Jamaica.

PEARL KITE
Gampsonyx swainsonii   Plate 9

Description: 8. A *small, falcon-shaped* kite of open country which appears to be colonizing Panama. *Mostly slaty blackish above*, with *forehead and cheeks creamy buff* and narrow white nuchal collar; *mainly white below* with patch of blackish on sides of chest and rufous sides. Juvenile similar but with feathers of mantle edged rufous. In flight shows *prominent white border to trailing edge of inner flight feathers*; from below wing essentially all white.

Similar species: Given a reasonable view, not likely to be confused. American Kestrel has similar shape, behavior, and habitat, though kestrel has different facial pattern, is barred above and more or less streaked below, etc.

Status and distribution: First recorded only in 1977 (see J. Pujals *et al., Am. Birds* 31(6): 1099–1111, 1977), the Pearl Kite has since been recorded from a number of semi-open areas in Panama, though nowhere is it yet numerous. Reports are most frequent from eastern Panama province (Panama City area east to around Chepo), but it has also been seen on both slopes of Canal area, and in Coclé, Herrera (including one collected on July 15, 1982; F. Delgado), Bocas del Toro (one seen near Changuinola on April 24, 1980; N. G. Smith), and Darién (one seen at Cana on July 16 and August 3, 1982; M. Robbins *et al.*). Appears to be in the process of colonizing Panama, and though no nesting has yet been recorded, apparent pairs have been seen, and a juvenile was picked up dying (after having been mobbed by Great-tailed Grackles) at La Boca on May 19, 1987 (N. Gale). Colonization has doubtless been from northern Colombia, where forest clearance has permitted an increase in numbers and spread in range (S. Hilty). The parallel with the White-tailed

All adults. Top row, left to right, DOUBLE-TOOTHED KITE, HOOK-BILLED KITE (female), GRAY-HEADED KITE, PLUMBEOUS KITE; second row, BROAD-WINGED HAWK, GRAY HAWK, AMERICAN SWALLOW-TAILED KITE; third row, SHORT-TAILED HAWK (light phase), WHITE-TAILED HAWK, WHITE HAWK; bottom row, SAVANNA HAWK, BLACK- COLLARED HAWK, SWAINSON'S HAWK (typical phase), RED-TAILED HAWK

Kite's spread into Panama during the 1960s is worth noting.

Habits: A conspicuous small raptor, usually seen perched in the open, kestrel-like, on a wire, or on top of a tree or bush. Its flight is swift and usually rather low; may hover momentarily before pouncing down on its prey (mostly insects and small lizards).

Range: Western Nicaragua; Panama; South America south to northern Argentina and southern Brazil.

WHITE-TAILED KITE
Elanus leucurus   Plate 9, p.89

Description: 15–16. Wings fairly long, pointed; tail long, square-tipped. *Mostly white* with pearly gray back and wings and a *black shoulder patch.* Juvenile similar but tinged with brown above, on breast, and on tail.

Similar species: Should be easily recognized. Plumbeous Kite has similar shape but is uniform leaden gray with black tail crossed by white bands; see also Mississippi Kite. Male Northern Harrier is also mostly pale gray and white, but is considerably larger with prominent white rump, lacks black shoulders, and has different proportions.

Status and distribution: First seen only in 1967, but already breeding by 1970; now fairly common to common in open grassy areas and savannas, agricultural terrain, and semi-open clearings on Pacific slope from Chiriquí to eastern Panama province, with a few reports from Darién (first seen on January 14, 1978; N. Brokaw); on Caribbean slope known mainly from Canal area and Colon province (east to around Portobelo), with a few sightings from Bocas del Toro and one from western San Blas (one seen north of Nusagandi on May 13, 1985; J. Blake); in western Chiriquí ranges regularly up into lower highlands (e.g. around Volcán and Boquete), and in central Panama regularly into foothills (e.g. on Cerro Azul/Jefe). This species' dramatic range expansion and population increase through Middle America was described by Eisenmann (*Am. Birds* 25(3): 529–536, 1971).

Habits: Generally very conspicuous. Has a graceful flight with deep wingbeats; often hovers, the body then angled at about 45° (not horizontal as in kestrel). At least partially crepuscular, hunting mostly in the early morning and late afternoon, perching most of the day, often in an exposed situation.

WHITE-TAILED KITE

Range: Southwestern United States to central Panama; northern Colombia to the Guianas; eastern Brazil through Paraguay, northern Argentina, and Chile.

Note: The American *E. leucurus* was considered conspecific with *E. caeruleus* (Black-shouldered Kite) of the Old World by the 1983 AOU Check-list, calling the enlarged species Black-shouldered Kite. Our preference, however, is to maintain *E. leucurus* as a full species. See also D. Amadon et al. (*Proc. W. Found. Vert. Zool.* 3(4): 307, 1988).

SNAIL KITE
Rostrhamus sociabilis   Plate 9

Description: 16–17½. Apparently rare. *Bill black, slender, very sharply hooked. Facial area and legs red* (orange in immature). Adult male slaty black with *upper and under tail-coverts, basal half of tail, and tip of tail white.* Adult female brownish black above; buffy below streaked and mottled with brown; *tail as in male.* Immature like female but brown above and more prominently streaked below.

Similar species: Brightly colored facial skin and legs, strongly hooked bill, and white basal half of tail distinguish any plumage of this species. Slender-billed Kite of Darién lacks white in tail. Hook-billed Kite also has sharply hooked bill but in any plumage lacks reddish facial area. See also female and immature Northern Harrier.

Status and distribution: Uncertain; apparently rare, and perhaps erratic. Only one specimen has been taken, an immature at Permé, San Blas on March 22, 1929. The five sight reports do not reveal any particular pattern: an adult male and an immature at Guataca, eastern Chiriquí on September 27, 1965 (Eisenmann and N. G. Smith); an immature at Tocumen, eastern Panama province in March 1971 (P. Alden and R. Forster *et al.*) and another female there on February 5, 1973 (G. Tudor *et al.*); several pairs evidently breeding (one nest seen) in a marsh near Remedios. Chiriquí on June 19, 1973 (D. Hill); and an immature at the Chiva Chiva marsh, on Pacific side of Canal area on March 16, 1979 (Ridgely *et al.*). Elsewhere known to be somewhat nomadic in response to fluctuations in water levels, and possibly not regular anywhere in Panama (where there is relatively little suitable habitat for it).

Habits: A rather sociable bird of open freshwater marshes where it feeds mostly on *Pomacea* snails, hunting by beating somewhat clumsily over the marsh. Regularly circles at considerable heights above its marsh, and even soars fairly often.

Range: Southern Florida; eastern Mexico south locally to Bolivia, northern Argentina, and Uruguay; Cuba.

SLENDER-BILLED KITE
Rostrhamus hamatus

Description: 15–16½. Known only from eastern Darién. *Bill black, slender, very sharply hooked; facial area and legs orange-red; iris white to yellowish white.* Uniform slaty gray with blackish wing-tips and tail (*no white*). Immature similar but with some whitish barring on underparts, and two to three narrow white bands and tip on tail. In flight note *very chunky profile with short tail barely extending beyond the broad wings.*

Similar species: Snail Kite is lankier, with longer wings and tail and conspicuous white at base of tail; male's iris is red (not pale). Furthermore, the two occupy very different habitats. Adult Slender-billed Kite is *only* dark hawk with an all-black tail. Somewhat similar melanistic phase Hook-billed Kite has different facial and iris colors, and its longer tail is crossed by a broad white band.

Status and distribution: Known only from two specimens taken at Rio Paya in the Tuira River valley of eastern Darién.

Habits: In South America favors swampy forest and woodland, where it perches at varying heights. Rather sluggish, and thus not very conspicuous as it tends to remain within cover. Occasionally circles low over the forest, but only rarely does it soar at any great height. Apparently feeds exclusively on *Pomacea* snails.

Range: Eastern Panama locally to Surinam, Amazonian Brazil, and eastern Peru.

Note: Formerly placed in the monotypic genus *Helicolestes.*

DOUBLE-TOOTHED KITE
Harpagus bidentatus   Plates 7,9, p.88

Description: 13–15. *Accipiter*-like in shape, but without that genus' fierce, capped expression. Cere greenish yellow; iris orange red; legs yellowish. Grayish brown above, head more bluish gray; throat white with *dusky central stripe; chest rufous,* remaining underparts mostly rufous barred with grayish or whitish (females are more uniform rufous below with less barring); tail blackish with three whitish bands and narrow white tip. In flight from below, under wing-coverts whitish, contrasting with dark body, and flight feathers boldly barred blackish and white; *white feathers of crissum fluffy and conspicuous,* often protruding to sides. Immature browner above; creamy whitish below, variably (but usually heavily) streaked with brown, but *already showing adult's throat stripe.*

Similar species: Especially in flight resembles an *Accipiter* in shape; none of those, however, has a throat stripe, and all are much more wary and dashing than this relatively sluggish, tame kite. The throat stripe is diagnostic and usually easy to see, though the "double-tooth", two notches on the upper mandible, is not. See Sharp-shinned Hawk (especially immature), and Broad-winged and Roadside Hawks.

Habits: Usually seen perched quietly at medium heights, often at edge of forest or woodland. Soars regularly; most often low but at times ascending on thermals to great heights. Hunts for lizards and large insects in the canopy and middle levels, and frequently seen accompanying monkey troupes (in Panama most often White-faced Monkeys, though sometimes with others), taking prey the monkeys disturb as they move through the forest. Often gives a high thin *weeoo-weést* or *weeoo-wheép* (N. Brokaw), but this is relatively weak and apt to be overlooked.

Status and distribution: Fairly common in forest, second-growth woodland, and borders in more humid lowlands on both slopes; absent from dry Pacific lowlands from eastern side of Azuero Peninsula to southern Coclé; ranges in reduced numbers up into the foothills and, in western Chiriquí, into the lower highlands (e.g. around Santa Clara); fairly common also on Coiba Island. Widespread in Canal area, though more numerous on Caribbean side, especially on Pipeline Road.

Range: Southern Mexico to Bolivia and southern Brazil.

MISSISSIPPI KITE
Ictinia mississippiensis

Description: 14. Resembles the much more numerous Plumbeous Kite. *Legs dusky* in all plumages. Leaden gray above, *paler gray on head* and below; tail black with *no white bands*; wings with *no rufous in primaries*, but with *pale gray patch on secondaries*. Juvenile more brownish than juvenile Plumbeous Kite, heavily streaked rusty brown below, with three whitish tail bands. Immature resembles adult but retains tail bands.

Similar species: Caution is urged in distinguishing this species from the Plumbeous Kite. *Ictinia* kites are usually seen in flight overhead, when the two major field marks of adult Mississippis (lack of white tail bands, lack of rufous in wing) can often not be unquestionably determined. Perched adults can be known by their paler head (contrasting with back), pale wing patch, solid black tail, and dusky (not orange) legs. Immature is usually not distinguishable in the field, and juvenile is difficult, though it is browner than juvenile Plumbeous Kite.

Status and distribution: Uncommon to briefly common transient in Panama, with records from Bocas del Toro, both slopes of Canal area, eastern Panama province, San Blas, and Darién; so far as known periods of passage are mid-March–late April and October, in both periods migrating later than the Plumbeous Kite (though there may be some overlap). Still no Panama specimen.

Habits: In Panama most likely to be seen flying overhead, often with other passing raptors. As views under such circumstances are often equivocal, it is best to look for these birds in the *early* morning (when they often fly at much lower levels), or during late afternoon as they drop down prior to roosting. Regularly recorded in groups of up to several hundred individuals, but even larger flocks would seem possible as at least the bulk of the population winters in South America.

Range: Breeds in central and southern United States (recently increasing in numbers and regaining its former range);

recorded during northern winter in south-central South America (Paraguay and northern Argentina), but migration routes and exact winter range, particularly in South America, not well known; apparently the entire population moves through Middle America (no records from West Indies).

PLUMBEOUS KITE
Ictinia plumbea　　　　　　Plate 9, p.88

Description: 14. Bill black, cere dark gray; *legs orange. Mostly leaden gray*; wings and tail black, *tail with two white bands, wings with rufous patch in primaries* (conspicuous in flight). Juvenile slaty above edged with buffy whitish; whitish below, heavily streaked with grayish; tail with three white bands; wings usually with some rufous in primaries. Wings long and narrow, usually pointed, but when soaring primaries often spread; rather long tail.

Similar species: See Mississippi Kite. When seen perched can resemble other mostly gray hawks, but note long wings, which extend beyond tip of tail.

Status and distribution: Uncommon to locally (or briefly) fairly common in forest, forest borders, and second-growth woodland in lowlands on both slopes, ranging up in smaller numbers into foothills (particularly as a migrant); during migration may pass over more open, sometimes even quite arid areas; recorded also from Pearl Islands, probably only as a migrant. Middle American nesters withdraw to South America when not breeding, and these are seen in flocks of up to several hundred birds passing over in early February–mid-March (rarely January), and in early August–late September (rarely early October); Plumbeous Kites appear to be absent from Panama between mid-October and mid-January. Except on migration, not a particularly numerous bird in Panama (*much* less so than in South America); no actual nest has yet been reported, though breeding seems virtually certain.

Habits: Often associates with the American Swallow-tailed Kite. Usually seen in flight overhead, often high, where it soars gracefully and captures its primary prey, aerial insects (some insects are also picked off from leaves). Frequently perches on high exposed snags.

Range: Breeds from eastern Mexico to Bolivia, northern Argentina, and southern Brazil; Middle American birds withdraw to

South America during northern winter, but exact distribution unknown.

NORTHERN HARRIER
Circus cyaneus

Description: 18–22. Wings long and narrow, *in flight usually held slightly above horizontal in dihedral*; tail long. Characteristic *white rump patch* in both sexes. Adult male *mostly pale gray*, white on breast and belly. In flight from below, wings whitish with primaries tipped black. Female mostly dark brown above and on face and chest, paler brown below streaked with darker; tail grayish brown barred with blackish; underside of wings strongly barred with grayish brown. Immature like female but more uniform rufous below with less streaking.
Similar species: Note the conspicuous white rump. Female and immature Snail Kite are somewhat similar but have broader wings and heavier body, sharply hooked bill, brightly colored facial area and legs, and white on base of tail. At a distance male might be confused with White-tailed Kite.
Status and distribution: Rare transient and winter resident in open grassy areas and marshes in lowlands, though more numerous on Pacific slope (mid-October–late April, with most spring transients recorded in March); migrants may pass high over any sort of terrain.
Habits: Migrant birds are most likely to be picked out as they pass over among the huge flocks of Broad-winged and Swainson's Hawks. Winterers are usually noted as they quarter back and forth low over the ground. Rarely seen perched, as they usually rest on the ground in tall grass.
Range: Breeds in northern and central Eurasia and in North America; American birds winter south to Panama, rarely to Colombia and Venezuela.

TINY HAWK
Accipiter superciliosus   Plates 7,9

Description: ♂ 8–9; ♀ 10–11. Iris red; cere and legs yellow. Slaty gray above, blacker on crown; white below *narrowly barred throughout with dark gray except on throat*. Tail blackish with three or four grayish bands. Immature has two phases. In brown phase, dusky brown above, buff below narrowly barred with rufous brown except on throat; tail dusky brown with six or seven grayish bands. In rufous phase, bright rufous brown above with dusky crown and some black

barring on mantle, below buff narrowly barred with rufous brown except on throat; tail even brighter rufous, with six or seven grayish bands.
Similar species: Should be known in any plumage by its small size; the smallest Panamanian hawk. Double-toothed Kite is larger and lacks the even, narrow barring below. See also Sharp-shinned Hawk and Barred Forest-Falcon.
Status and distribution: Rare to locally uncommon in humid forest and second-growth woodland on both slopes. Recorded mostly from Caribbean slope, and on Pacific slope known only from a few old Chiriquí and Veraguas specimens, and from eastern Panama province and Darién. There are many recent reports from a variety of areas on the Caribbean slope of the Canal area, where the species is either increasing or observers now know better how to look for and identify it.
Habits: In general a rather secretive hawk of the forest canopy and dense tangled borders, and doubtless often overlooked. Most likely to be seen in the early morning when birds (occasionally pairs) take prominent perches and warm up in the sun; sometimes they again perch conspicuously in late afternoon. In Costa Rica reported at one locality (La Selva) to specialize to some extent in feeding on hummingbirds, literally "traplining", i.e. visiting a series of known territorial singing perches of male hummers, or waiting in ambush near a known perch (F. G. Stiles).
Range: Nicaragua to eastern Peru, Paraguay, northeastern Argentina, and southern Brazil.

SHARP-SHINNED HAWK
Accipiter striatus   Plate 9

Description: ♂ 10; ♀ 14. Short rounded wings and rather long tail as in other Accipiters. *Dark bluish gray above*, darkest on crown; *white below barred with rufous brown*; tail black with three gray bands and white tip. Immature is dusky brown above, whitish below heavily streaked with dusky and brown.
Similar species: Adults most resemble dark phase immature Tiny Hawk, but latter is dusky (not bluish gray) above. Double-toothed Kite is rather similar but has distinctive black throat stripe in both adult and immature. See also Cooper's Hawk (below).
Status and distribution: Uncommon winter visitor to western Chiriquí foothills and

(especially) highlands (late October–late March); occasional birds wander eastward and to lowlands, with sightings from low-lands of Herrera and Los Santos (Wet-more), lowlands of Bocas del Toro and foot-hills of Veraguas (N. G. Smith), and from Caribbean slope of Canal area (one seen at Colon on February 21, 1981; R. Behrstock *et al.*); easternmost report is of an adult near Cerro Jefe, eastern Panama province, on January 25, 1976 (Ridgely).

Habits: Favors woodland borders and clearings; usually inconspicuous, perching in concealment of foliage, but also circles and flies in the open, especially on migration. A bird eater.

Range: Breeds in North America and Mexico, also in Greater Antilles; northern birds winter to western Panama.

Note: Does not inlude South American forms, nor *A. chionogaster* (White-breasted Hawk) of northern Middle America. Cooper's Hawk (*A. cooperii*) of North America has been recorded casually as far south as Costa Rica during northern winter, and is possible in Panama. It rather closely resembles Sharp-shinned Hawk but is larger ($\circ$ 15 in, $\circ$ 18 in) with larger and more projecting head and neck, more blackish crown in adult, and has tip of tail somewhat rounded (not squared off; this visible mainly in flight). Great care would be needed in order to firmly establish its identity.

BICOLORED HAWK
Accipiter bicolor   Plates 7,9

Description: $\circ$ 14, $\circ$ 17. Iris orange; cere and legs yellow. Tail fairly long, somewhat rounded at tip. *Slaty gray above*, blacker on crown; *uniform paler gray below* except for *rufous thighs* (often hidden by belly feathers) and white crissum; tail blackish with three grayish bands and narrow tip. Immature dusky brown above, blacker on crown, *usually showing a partial buff or whitish collar* on hindneck; *below usually buffy white*, but varying from whitish to occasionally rufous, with thighs usually darker or mottled rufous; tail as in adult.

Similar species: The two-toned gray adult with its contrasting rufous thighs is distinctive, but the variable immatures are often confusing. Compare especially to Collared Forest-Falcon (with longer and more graduated tail and black crescentic cheek stripe) and Slaty-backed Forest-Falcon (never showing a collar).

Status and distribution: Rare in forest and forest borders in lowlands and foothills on both slopes; occurs in both humid and deciduous forest. May be most numerous in western Panama (on both slopes), and not recorded at all from eastern side of Azuero Peninsula to southern Coclé (where probably absent), or from eastern Colon province east through San Blas (where doubtless present). Possibly more numerous on Coiba Island than on the mainland, at least seen there regularly. Very few reports from Canal area, but has been seen recently along Pipeline and Escobal Roads (various observers).

Habits: Still a little known, secretive bird, usually remaining within cover and less likely to perch in the open than Tiny Hawk. Hunts at all levels, from canopy to near the ground; very bold and rapacious in pursuit of its prey, primarily birds.

Range: Eastern Mexico south locally to Tierra del Fuego.

Note: More than one species is likely to be involved in South America.

CRANE HAWK
Geranospiza caerulescens   Plate 8, p.100

Description: 17–20. *Lanky and slender* with *very long reddish orange legs*; bill weak, with cere and lores red; iris slaty. Wings rather long and rounded; tail long. *Slaty blackish in west, becoming paler and grayer eastward*; more or less barred with white on lower belly, thighs, and under tail-coverts; tail black with two broad white bands and narrow tip. In flight from below, wings essentially blackish with *prominent white band across primaries* (obscure from above). Immature browner, with whitish streaking on head, and more pronounced buff mottling or barring below.

Similar species: Perched birds are best recognized through their slender shape, with small head and very long legs; in color they resemble a black-hawk or a Zone-tailed Hawk. In flight can be instantly known by the unique white band on primaries.

Status and distribution: Rare to uncommon in humid forest, second-growth woodland, borders, and swamps and marshes in lowlands on both slopes; seems more numerous in eastern Panama province and (especially) Darién. Decidedly scarce in Canal area, with most recent reports coming from the Achiote Road area.

Habits: When feeding in forest hops about rather awkwardly from branch to branch, sometimes even hanging upside down, searching for frogs, lizards, snakes, and large insects in epiphytes and crevices. Also goes to the ground, then seeming very long-legged. At times quarters over open marshy areas much like a harrier; occasionally soars, then appearing rather Buteo-like.

Range: Mexico to Bolivia, northern Argentina, and Uruguay.

PLUMBEOUS HAWK
Leucopternis plumbea   Plate 7

Description: 16–17. In shape like more numerous Semiplumbeous Hawk. *Cere, lores and legs orange. Mostly dark slaty gray*; tail black with *one prominent white band* (in some, especially immatures, another shows). In flight shows *white under wing-coverts*. Immature has under wing-coverts and thighs somewhat barred, belly somewhat flecked with white.

Similar species: Superficially resembles several other dark forest hawks but note orange soft parts and the white tail band. Black phase Hook-billed Kite has strongly hooked bill, greenish cere and lores, and black underside of wing (no white). Plumbeous Kite has dark gray cere, long wings projecting beyond tail at rest, no white on underside of wing. In Darién see also Slender-billed Kite.

Status and distribution: Rare in humid forest in lowlands and lower foothills on both slopes; on Caribbean slope recorded from Veraguas east through San Blas, on Pacific from a single sighting on Cerro Azul, eastern Panama province (Eisenmann), and from Darién. Only recently (1968) found in Canal area, but now known to be a rare but regular resident in Pipeline and Achiote Road areas.

Habits: Similar to Semiplumbeous Hawk. An unsuspicious bird of the forest interior, usually seen at low and middle levels, but in the early morning occasionally perching high on an open branch. Apparently never soars.

Range: Western Panama to extreme northwestern Peru.

SEMIPLUMBEOUS HAWK
Leucopternis semiplumbea   Plate 7

Description: 15–16. Wings short, broad, and rounded. *Cere, base of bill, and legs bright orange to reddish orange. Slaty gray above; white below*, sometimes with a few fine dusky streaks on chest (immatures especially); tail blackish with *one broad white band* (a second narrower one sometimes visible near base). Underside of wings mostly white.

Similar species: Light phase Short-tailed Hawk is superficially similar but lacks orange cere and legs, has indistinctly banded tail, very different habits. Slaty-backed Forest-Falcon is quite similar and is a forest bird like Semiplumbeous, but has three narrow tail bands (not a single broad one) and does not have orange soft-parts.

Status and distribution: Uncommon in humid forest and advanced second-growth woodland in lowlands on entire Caribbean slope; on Pacific slope recorded mostly from eastern Panama province (Bayano River valley) and Darién, though there are several sightings from the Canal area (e.g. Fort Clayton and Rodman areas, where probably a rare resident) and one old specimen from Veraguas. Widespread in forested areas on Caribbean side of Canal area.

Habits: A bird of the interior of forest and shady woodland, rarely leaving their borders. Usually very unsuspicious, generally seen perched on an open branch beneath the canopy (sometimes quite low), in the early morning sometimes on a high exposed perch. Seems never to soar, or even to circle above the canopy. The call is a long, high-pitched *kiteeeeeeeeeeeah* (E. O. Willis), somewhat reminiscent of the whistled call of a Broad-winged Hawk.

Range: Honduras to northwestern Ecuador.

BARRED HAWK
Leucopternis princeps   Plate 8, p.100

Description: 23–25. Known only from highlands of west and east. Broad wings and short tail (in shape, rather like a White Hawk). Base of bill, cere, and legs yellow. *Blackish slate above and on throat and chest; breast and belly white narrowly barred with black*; tail black with one white band. In flight from below, wings whitish barred with gray and dusky.

Similar species: Large size and sharp contrast between black chest and pale lower underparts distinguish this handsome species. The barring below is not prominent at a distance. See the smaller, paler Gray Hawk of lowlands.

Status and distribution: Rare to locally uncommon in humid foothill and montane forest in Chiriquí, Bocas del Toro, Veraguas, southern Los Santos (Cerro Hoya), western San Blas (pair seen at Nusagandi on March 7, 1986; Ridgely and J. Guarnaccia), and eastern Darién (Cerro Pirre). In western Panama occurs mostly on the Caribbean slope; rare, perhaps occurring only as a wanderer, in western Chiriquí around Volcán Barú itself, but more numerous in the much more humid region east of Boquete, e.g. around Fortuna. Recorded in Panama 450–1800 m (1500–6000 ft).

Habits: A magnificent, imposing raptor much given to soaring, particularly on sunny mornings when it may rise to great heights, then fold its wings and sail down the valley. Often noisy while it soars, especially if a pair is flying together (and even more so if that pair is interacting with others, as often occurs); the calls include a loud, screaming hawk-eagle-like *kee-yaaaarr*, sometimes repeated or followed by a series of *weep* notes. Much less often seen perched; apparently hunts mainly from branches inside forest, like other *Leucopternis*.

Range: Costa Rica to Ecuador.

Note: Formerly sometimes called Black-chested Hawk.

WHITE HAWK
Leucopternis albicollis   pp.88, 95

Description: 22–24. Buteo-like in shape, with broad rather rounded wings and fairly short tail. *Entirely white* with black markings on primaries and secondaries and a broad black subterminal band on tail.

Status and distribution: Fairly common in forest and forest borders in more humid lowlands and foothills on both slopes, ranging up to about 1200 m (4000 ft), rarely higher; absent from eastern side of Azuero Peninsula to southern Coclé lowlands, and now very local in Chiriquí and Pacific slope Veraguas due to very extensive deforestation; recently (1976) found also on Coiba Island (Ridgely). More conspicuous than most other forest raptors; thus it may seem proportionately more numerous than it actually is.

Habits: Soars freely, sometimes quite high, presenting a beautiful contrast against blue of sky or dark green of forest canopy. When soaring, often utters a semi-whistled hissing or buzzy *sheeeer*, somewhat like call of Red-tailed Hawk. Often perches on fairly low branches at forest borders and usually rather unsuspicious.

Range: Southern Mexico to Bolivia, central Brazil, and the Guianas.

COMMON BLACK-HAWK
Buteogallus anthracinus   Plate 8, p.100

Description: 20–21. *Only along and near Caribbean coast* (Mangrove Black-Hawk of

WHITE HAWK

Pacific coast now regarded as a distinct species; see following). Very broad wings and short tail. *Cere, lores, and legs yellow.* Mostly black; *tail with one broad white band and narrow white tip.* In flight from below usually shows a small whitish patch at base of primaries. Immature blackish brown above with some buff markings on head and indistinct buff superciliary; *tawny-buff below, streaked and splotched* (sometimes heavily) *with dusky*; tail mostly buff with *five to eight narrow black bars* and wider subterminal band; sometimes shows buff patch on underside of primaries.

Similar species: See the very similar Mangrove Black-Hawk; the two are not known to occur together (but might). This species is also often hard to distinguish from the Great Black-Hawk (particularly its western race *ridgwayi*). Note Common's slightly smaller size and shorter legs, its yellow lores (lores slaty in *ridgwayi*, though also yellow in nominate race of Great Black), and lack of white upper tail-coverts (though feathers may be narrowly tipped with white). Immatures are even harder, but note Great Black's more numerous (10–14) tail bands, and its size. Unless seen well the two can often not be definitely distinguished; habitat and voice are also often helpful clues (see below). Adult when perched can also be confused with Zone-tailed Hawk, and see Crane Hawk and dark phase Short-tailed Hawk; at a distance in flight Common Black's profile is reminiscent of Black Vulture. Immature Common Black also somewhat resembles immature of smaller Gray Hawk, though latter does not show the numerous dark tail bars.

Status and distribution: Fairly common along Caribbean coast, and ranging inland to some extent along larger rivers (but not found far from water normally), and in mangroves. In Canal area particularly numerous in Fort Sherman/San Lorenzo area; only occasionally does it wander inland as far as Gatun Lake.

Habits: Soars freely, then often uttering its characteristic call, a series of loud high-pitched (*spinking*) whistled notes, somewhat Osprey-like, quite different from Great Black's harsh scream. Usually rather unsuspicious. Perches at all heights, but usually rather high except when hunting for its primary food, crabs; then may even walk on ground.

Range: Southwestern United States to northern Colombia, Venezuela, and Guyana; Cuba (perhaps a distinct species, *gundlachii*) and St Vincent.

MANGROVE BLACK-HAWK
Buteogallus subtilis

Description: 18–19. Now considered a species distinct from Common Black-Hawk, *found only along and near Pacific coast. Very* similar to Common Black-Hawk, and could probably not be distinguished were they to occur together (which they are not known to do). *Slightly smaller*, and more likely to show rufous (rather than white) in primaries. An occasional pale plumage, apparently subadult, is known, in which they are mostly buff or clay-colored ("chamois"), sometimes with some fine dusky streaking on crown and underparts; in Panama these are known mainly from Darién (though there is one specimen of it from western Panama province in GML). It is not known to occur in Common Black-Hawk.

Similar species: See Common Black-Hawk.

Status and distribution: Fairly common to locally common along Pacific coast and in mangroves, also occurring inland along rivers and streams and in freshwater swamps and marshes, but not normally found far from water; common also on Coiba Island and on the Pearl Islands. Still quite numerous in mangroves and marshes of eastern Panama province from Juan Diaz eastward.

Habits: Very similar to Common Black-Hawk; even the voice seems to be the same. Though elsewhere reported to be restricted to mangroves, this is definitely not the case in Panama.

Range: Along Pacific coast from El Salvador south to northwestern Peru.

Note: *B. subtilis* was recognized as a distinct species in the 1983 AOU Check-list, the

justification being that *B. anthracinus* and one of the races of *B. subtilis* (*rhizophorae*) are nearly in contact in Honduras, with no evidence of intergradation. The situation in Panama, where the two also come into virtual contact, also needs to be examined in this regard; as the two are so similar morphologically and behaviorally, we remain less than convinced that two species are indeed involved.

GREAT BLACK-HAWK
Buteogallus urubitinga   Plate 8, p.100

Description: 22–25. Very like Common and Mangrove Black-Hawks, but *larger* (especially than Mangrove Black), with *longer legs*. Cere and legs yellow; *lores slaty* in northern race, *ridgwayi*, of most of Panama, but yellow in southern race, the mainly South American nominate *urubitinga*, of eastern Panama. Adult mostly black, with upper tail-coverts white (usually hard to see clearly, and feathers sometimes only white-tipped); *tail with two white bands* (though upper one narrow and often concealed) and narrow white tip; *usually shows some white barring on thighs*. Southern race similar but note soft part differences (above), and has *basal half of tail white* and never seems to show thigh barring. Immature closely resembles immature Common and Mangrove Black-Hawks except for its larger size and more numerous (10–14) narrow black tail bands.

Similar species: Often hard to distinguish from the two other black-hawks. White thigh barring is diagnostic if present. Note also Great Black's larger size and longer legs, less yellow on facial area in northern birds (but remember that *all* black-hawks have a yellow cere), and its white upper tail-coverts and second tail band (when these are visible). Southern birds, with their broad basal half of tail, are relatively easy. See also the very rare Solitary Eagle.

Status and distribution: Uncommon to locally fairly common in canopy and borders of second-growth woodland in lowlands on both slopes, ranging locally up into foothills and in western Chiriquí also up into the highlands to about 1860 m (6200 ft). The mainly South American race (nominate *urubitinga*) is recorded from eastern Darién (in the Tuira drainage) and eastern San Blas, and individuals intermediate toward *ridgwayi* have been taken on Pacific side of Canal area (specimen collected at Rodman on February 14, 1974, by G. Barrett, Jr;

specimen in GML) and seen in the Tocumen area of eastern Panama province.

Habits: Similar to Common and Mangrove Black-Hawks, but less restricted to immediate vicinity of water. Soars freely, often giving its harsh whistled scream (very different from Common and Mangrove Black's calls), *wheeeeeeeuur*.

Range: Northern Mexico to Bolivia, northern Argentina, and Uruguay.

SAVANNA HAWK
Buteogallus meridionalis   Plate 8, p.88

Description: 21–24. Very long broad wings and short tail; looks small-headed and long-necked. Long yellow legs. *Mostly dull cinnamon-rufous*, more gray on back, paler and more cinnamon below and narrowly barred with dusky; tail black with single white band and narrow tip. In flight, *wings mostly rufous* (from above and below), with flight feathers tipped black. Immature blackish brown above with buff forehead and superciliary, and buff or rufous mottling on back and wings; below deep buff heavily mottled and spotted with blackish. Older immatures gradually acquire the rufous of adult.

Similar species: A large hawk with distinctive, mostly rufous coloration. Black-collared Hawk has somewhat similar proportions and rufous color but has whitish head, black collar, and lacks white in tail.

Status and distribution: Uncommon to locally common in open savannas and pastures with scattered trees in lowlands on Pacific slope from Chiriquí to eastern Panama province; still not recorded from Darién (though may appear with clearing of forest). Only a few reports from Caribbean slope: a sighting of an immature from Changuinola, Bocas del Toro (Eisenmann), a few sightings from Canal area since 1973 (but not yet fully established), and one specimen from Permé, San Blas. Most numerous in southern Coclé and Herrera; distinctly scarce in western Chiriquí.

Habits: A conspicuous open country hawk, though rather stolid and sluggish, most often seen perched on a low branch or fencepost. Frequently also rests on the ground, where it often walks about with ease. Numbers often gather at grass fires, or to follow tractors which are plowing. Savanna Hawks soar regularly and powerfully, sometimes rising to considerable heights.

Range: Western Panama (one Costa Rica sighting) to central Argentina and Uruguay.

Note: Formerly placed in the monotypic genus *Heterospizias*.

HARRIS' HAWK
Parabuteo unicinctus

Description: 19–22. Apparently rare. Rather long and narrow wings and tail. Mostly blackish brown with *bright chestnut shoulders* and thighs; tail black with *white rump and basal area* and tip. In flight from below shows chestnut under wing-coverts and black flight feathers. Immature is similar but with upperparts somewhat edged with rufous; underparts variable, ranging from chocolate brown streaked with buff to buffy streaked with dusky; *shows chestnut shoulders* (though not as prominent as in adult) and *whitish base of tail from above* (from below tail more grayish barred with dusky).

Status and distribution: Uncertain. Known only from three old specimens (taken at Santa Fé, Veraguas; Pacora, eastern Panama province; and Almirante, Bocas del Toro), and from small numbers seen on migration from Ancon Hill, on Pacific side of Canal area, in October 1970 and 1971 (N. G. Smith), but none seen since or anywhere else. All dated records are from northern winter or migration months; seems likely to be only a very rare straggler from further north.

Habits: Favors savanna country and open areas with scattered trees, often near water and marshes. Forages chiefly by sailing low over the ground, somewhat suggesting a dark harrier; sometimes soars. Frequently perches low, even on the ground. Sometimes eats carrion.

Range: Southwestern United States south locally (only in drier regions) to central Chile and central Argentina; northern birds are not recorded as being migratory, but the species is a fairly common resident as close as northwestern Costa Rica.

BLACK-COLLARED HAWK
Busarellus nigricollis   Plate 8, p.88

Description: 18–22. Wings broad and long; tail very short and broad. *Mostly bright cinnamon-rufous*, with *head and hindneck buffy whitish* and *a black patch on upper chest*; tail barred black and chestnut with broad black subterminal band. In flight from below, under wing-coverts chestnut, flight feathers mostly black. Immature similar but duller, buffier below, streaked throughout with dusky.

Similar species: A handsome, distinctive hawk; likely to be confused only with Savanna Hawk, which has white tail bands, mostly rufous undersurface of wing, and lacks whitish head and black collar. When perched, Black-collared Hawk seems to have a small head.

Status and distribution: Rare and local in freshwater marshes and around rivers and lakes in lowlands on Pacific slope from Veraguas to Darién; only two records from Caribbean slope, both from Canal area, one a bird collected in 1900 at Lion Hill, the second a soaring bird well seen over the first part of Pipeline Road on May 25, 1986 (M. Letzer and R. Hannigan). Declining in Panamá and only infrequently recorded in recent years; can still occasionally be found in the Tocumen/Chepo area of eastern Panama province, but numbers now unquestionably reduced due to drainage and development. Perhaps now most numerous in Darién, though few recent reports even from there.

Habits: Usually seen perched on trees or bushes near water, but also soars majestically on broad flat wings. Feeds mostly on fish, which it captures near the surface of the water. Spends much time drying its nonwaterproof plumage.

Range: Western and southern Mexico to Bolivia, northern Argentina, and southern Brazil.

SOLITARY EAGLE
Harpyhaliaetus solitarius

Description: 28–30. Very rare. Very long broad wings and *extremely short tail*. Cere, lores, and legs yellow. *Dark slaty gray* with slight bushy crest on nape; *tail with one white band* and narrow white tip. In flight from below, underside of wing uniformly dark. Immature blackish brown above edged and mottled with buff and rufous; buffy whitish below, *heavily streaked and mottled with blackish* (almost solid on chest); tail buffy gray mottled with dusky (but *without distinct barring*). In flight from below, under wing-coverts mottled buff and dusky, flight feathers blackish.

Similar species: Easily confused with Great Black-Hawk. Eagle is larger and more massive with heavier legs; in flight its profile is slightly different, with *short tail barely protruding beyond trailing edge of the wing*, and somewhat longer wings. Adult is also more bluish slate (not so black), and this is easily

evident against a dark background. Immature Great Black-Hawk is not as coarsely marked below as the eagle, and its tail has many very narrow black bands (instead of the irregular mottling of the eagle).

Status and distribution: Apparently very rare and local; few records. Known only from two nineteenth-century specimens taken in Veraguas foothills (Calobre), two sightings from foothills of eastern Panama province (one seen north of Chepo on April 14, 1949, by Wetmore, and two seen north of El Llano on September 9, 1972, by N. G. Smith), and one sighting from eastern Darién (a single adult seen near Cerro Quía on July 15, 1975, by Ridgely).

Habits: In South America usually seen soaring over mountain ridges and valleys, sometimes high. Its loud call, often given in flight, is a long series of piping whistles with quality of Black Hawk-Eagle (thus very different from Great Black-Hawk), the series lasting 1 to 20 seconds, *wheet-wheet-wheet-wheet.* . . .

Range: Northern Mexico south locally to northern Venezuela and northwestern Argentina.

GRAY HAWK
Buteo nitidus   Plates, 8, 9, p.88

Description: 15–18. *Pale gray above*, indistinctly barred with darker gray; white below *narrowly barred with silvery gray*; tail black with two broad white bands (a third near base sometimes shows) and narrow white tip. In flight from below, wings whitish with indistinct gray barring on wing-coverts. Immature dark brown above with buff or whitish edging; *head and underparts buffy whitish*, with crown and nape streaked dusky and *breast with numerous tear-shaped spots of dark brown* (sometimes quite large and bold), and often a prominent dusky moustache; tail blackish with three to four grayish white bands. In flight from above shows *prominent pale buff patch at base of primaries*.

Similar species: Attractive pearly gray adults are likely to be confused only with Roadside Hawk; Roadside has solid grayish head, throat, and chest (no barring there), and prominent rufous in wings in flight. Immatures are more difficult, and can be confused with several other immature hawks and kites, but are generally the palest on head and most spotted (as opposed to streaked) below. Most resembles immature Broad-winged Hawk, but note that Gray's barring on thighs often appears early (in Broad-wing thighs streaked or spotted, sometimes plain but *never* barred), and Gray usually shows whitish on upper tail-coverts (lacking or obscure in Broad-wing).

Status and distribution: Uncommon to locally fairly common in forest borders, lighter usually deciduous woodland, and clearings with scattered trees in lowlands on both slopes, though more numerous and widespread on the Pacific; in western Chiriquí reported up to about 1200 m (4000 ft) in lower highlands around Volcán; not recorded from Bocas del Toro, and seems only recently to have spread into Darién (now regular in small numbers in lower Tuira and Chucunaque River valleys).

Habits: Favors vicinity of water. Soars fairly often, usually not at great heights. Sometimes allows a close approach when perched, but unlike Roadside Hawk does not seem sluggish, remaining alert and watchful. The call is a loud clear descending *schweeeeer*.

Range: Extreme southwestern United States to northern Argentina and southern Brazil.

Note: Perhaps better placed in the monotypic genus *Asturina*.

ROADSIDE HAWK
Buteo magnirostris   Plate 7

Description: 14–16. *Slaty grayish above* (browner on back) *and on throat and chest*; breast and belly barred gray and dull rufous; tail banded inconspicuously with rufous and dusky, *often appearing essentially reddish*; in flight shows *prominent rufous patch in primaries*, visible from above and below. Birds from Bocas del Toro (*argutus*) and extreme eastern Panama (*insidiatrix*) have pale tail bands mainly gray (not reddish). Immature resembles adult but is browner on breast with some dusky streaking, tail with more blackish bands. Juvenile has more brown streaking below, less barring.

Similar species: Grayish general appearance and conspicuous rufous wing patch identify this small open country Buteo. See Gray Hawk.

Status and distribution: Uncommon to locally common in open or semiopen areas with scattered trees, in lighter woodland and scrubby areas, and in clearings in lowlands on entire Pacific slope; on Caribbean slope less numerous (though doubtless increasing at least locally due to deforestation), and recorded from western Bocas del Toro and from northern Coclé east through San Blas; in Chiriquí highlands found regularly up to

around 1500 m (5000 ft); found also on Coiba Island and the Pearl Islands. Inexplicably scarce in Canal area, which in many places has seemingly suitable clearing and edge habitat (possibly the Roadside Hawk is too tame for its own good in this region of many people and many guns), but numerous in savanna and agricultural country on eastern side of Azuero Peninsula and in southern Coclé.

Habits: Usually seen perched fairly low, often on telephone poles or even wires. A sluggish hawk, often very unsuspicious, and a weak flier with very shallow rapid wingbeats interspersed with short periods of gliding. Soars mainly when displaying, rarely very high. Its distinctive call is a squealing buzzy *kzweeeeooo* or *zhweeeeyoo*. Eats mainly reptiles and insects, also birds.

Range: Central Mexico to central Argentina and Uruguay.

BROAD-WINGED HAWK
Buteo platypterus   Plate 9, p.88

Description: 15–18. A chunky small Buteo. Dark grayish brown above; whitish below *broadly barred or mottled with dull grayish rufous*; tail blackish with *two broad white bands* (a third may show near base of tail) and narrow white tip. In flight from below, underside of wings mostly whitish. Immature brown above, whitish below sparsely streaked with dark brown; tail more narrowly banded with dusky and whitish.

Similar species: Double-toothed Kite is smaller and more slender, with dusky throat stripe. Immature resembles immature Gray Hawk but is less heavily streaked below. Roadside Hawk is much grayer generally with prominent rufous in wings.

Status and distribution: Abundant transient in huge migrant flocks, passage occurring mostly in October (some late September and early November) and March–early April, following same routes as Swainson's Hawk; also a common winter resident in forest borders, second-growth woodland, and clearings in lowlands and foothills on both slopes, ranging up to about 1950 m (6500 ft). During winter months perhaps the most numerous hawk in Panama woodlands (certainly the most often seen), although essentially solitary at this season.

Habits: Regularly occurs in aggregations of many thousands of individuals while on migration; the passage of this species, together with the Swainson's Hawks and Turkey Vultures which often accompany them, is Panama's most spectacular avian

All adults. Top row, left to right, ORANGE-BREASTED FALCON, SHORT-TAILED HAWK (dark phase), CRANE HAWK, BARRED HAWK; second row, ZONE-TAILED HAWK, COMMON BLACK-HAWK, GREAT BLACK-HAWK, GREAT BLACK-HAWK (eastern race); third row, BLACK HAWK-EAGLE; bottom row, HARPY EAGLE, CRESTED EAGLE (light phase), ORNATE HAWK-EAGLE sight. On occasion the sky does seem literally "blackened". Over-wintering Broad-wings are usually seen singly, however. Perched birds often seem rather sluggish, allowing a close approach. They soar frequently, and both adults and immatures give their loud shrill whistled *p-teeeeeee* call, identical to that heard on the breeding grounds.

Range: Breeds in North America and West Indies; winters in southern Florida and from southern Mexico to Peru and northern Brazil.

SHORT-TAILED HAWK
Buteo brachyurus   pp.88, 100

Description: 17–18. Two phases, lighter one considerably the more numerous. Light phase adult slaty black above *and on sides of head and neck* (with hooded effect); small patch on forehead and *entire underparts white*; tail dark grayish to brownish with dusky barring. In flight from below, *underwing mainly white* except for some grayish barring on flight feathers, and primaries tipped black; tail whitish with narrow blackish bands and broader subterminal band. Dark phase adult *entirely sooty black except for whitish forehead*; tail as in light phase. In flight from below *mostly whitish flight feathers contrast with black under wing-coverts*; tail as in light phase. Immatures resemble adults of respective phase, but have more bars on tail; light phase has whitish streaking on head, while dark phase has white spotting or mottling below.

Similar species: Often confused. In both phases note absence of prominent tail banding. Light phase best known by its dark cheeks and essentially pale underwing. Dark phase can be trickier. It most resembles Zone-tailed Hawk in pattern, but shape quite different, Short-tail with more typical Buteo proportions (Zone-tail with longer narrower wings and tail, former typically held in dihedral); Zone-tail adult has prominent white tail banding. See also dark phase White-tailed and Swainson's Hawks.

Status and distribution: Uncommon to fairly common (generally conspicuous) in mostly open or partially wooded or forested country in lowlands and foothills on both slopes, apparently more numerous on Pacific side; generally absent from extensively forested regions. No evidence of any migratory movements.

Habits: Almost invariably seen in flight, when it may soar to considerable heights. Hardly ever takes a prominent perch, and

vocalizes very infrequently. Preys mostly on small and mid-sized birds, obtained mostly by rapidly stooping down on them. Has also been seen to capture a lizard (Ridgely).

Range: Florida; Mexico to northern Argentina and southern Brazil.

SWAINSON'S HAWK
Buteo swainsoni   p.88

Description: 19–22. A rather large Buteo with fairly broad wings. Pale phase adult dark brown above; whitish below usually with *broad brown band across chest*; contrasting with white throat; tail brownish gray with numerous blackish bands. In flight from below, under wing-coverts buffy whitish contrasting with dark flight feathers. In dark phase, more or less sooty brown all over, including wings from below. Intermediates between these two phases often occur. Immature is brown above, buffy below streaked to varying degrees with dusky.

Similar species: Typical pale phase adults are relatively easily recognized and usually predominate. Other phases can be very confusing: note lack of prominent tail banding, and that rump and basal half of tail (as seen from above) can look whitish. Dark individuals closely resemble immature White-tailed Hawk, but that species usually shows some white below. Dark phase Short-tailed Hawk is smaller with white on forehead and pale flight feathers contrasting with dark under wing-coverts. See also dark phase Red-tailed Hawk. Swainson's *often carries wings angled in slight dihedral*, suggesting the narrower-winged Zone-tailed Hawk (which somewhat resembles dark phase of this species but has white tail bands and two-toned underwing).

Status and distribution: Common to abundant transient through Panama, sometimes occurring in enormous flocks, with passage mostly March–early April (sometimes as early as late February, or as late as late April), and October–early November (sometimes as early as late September). Most birds winter in southern South America, but a few, usually mostly immatures, linger in open country on Pacific slope (largest numbers in southern Coclé and Herrera). The usual migration route is along the Pacific slope, near the coast in central Panama, along central mountain range in west and east; flights have also been observed on Caribbean slope, in San Blas (Eisenmann) and Bocas del Toro; in Chiriquí highlands, large flights have been noted only during northward passage.

Habits: The Swainson's Hawks generally remain separate from the migrant flocks of Broad-wings, though there are often a few Swainson's among the Broad-wings and vice versa. Migrating birds have been seen roosting at night on the ground in very large fields, re-commencing their passage in early morning. Over-wintering birds are also often seen on the ground in groups, frequently on plowed fields or following tractors.

Range: Breeds in western North America; winters mostly in southern South America, migrating through Middle America; small numbers over-winter locally in southern United States and Middle America.

WHITE-TAILED HAWK
Buteo albicaudatus p.88

Description: 21–25. Slaty above with blackish coming down on sides of head and *prominent rufous area on shoulders*; white below (except black on sides of head sometimes extends over entire throat); *rump and tail strikingly white, tail with broad black subterminal band*. In flight from below, under wing-coverts white, flight feathers grayish. A rare dark phase is all slaty gray, without the rufous shoulders, but *with white tail as in normal phase*. Immature brownish black with variable amounts of white below, especially on mid belly; rump whitish barred with brown, *tail looks pale* brownish or grayish, gradually becoming whiter with age.

Similar species: In flight from below normal phase recalls pattern of light phase Short-tailed Hawk (both show the dark hood on sides of head), but it is smaller and has numerous dusky tail bands. White Hawk is also similar from below, but is very different above and is a forest bird. Immature White-taileds can be difficult, though in most birds rump and tail are sufficiently pale, at least toward base, to make recognition possible. When present their hint of rusty on the wing is also helpful. Compare especially to dark phase Swainson's and Red-tailed Hawks.

Status and distribution: Uncommon and local on grassy savannas and open hillsides on Pacific slope from western Chiriquí (where there are a few sightings from Llanos del Volcán above the town of Volcán, up to about 1800 m: 6000 ft) to eastern Panama province (where a few have been noted in recent years in the Tocumen/Cerro Azul area); only two records from Caribbean slope (old specimens taken at Cricamola, Bocas del Toro, and Calovevora, Veraguas); one sighting also from Taboga Island (Wetmore). Most readily seen in southern Coclé and on the open eroded hillsides near Cerro Campana.

Habits: A handsome hawk of open, usually rather dry or scantily vegetated country. Often perches on or near the ground, or on fenceposts or telephone poles. Soars regularly, often at great heights, and while hunting also often hovers (the only *Buteo* in Panama which regularly does so).

Range: Southern Texas and Mexico south locally to central Argentina and southern Brazil.

ZONE-TAILED HAWK
Buteo albonotatus p.100

Description: 18–23. Wings and tail fairly long. Entirely black, with *three or four white tail bands* (grayer from above; sometimes only two show). In flight from below, *wings noticeably two-toned*, with black under wing-coverts and grayish flight feathers. Immature similar but browner and lightly spotted below with white; tail grayish brown above with narrow black bars, inner webs whitish or pale gray so that from below tail looks whitish.

Similar species: In flight suggests a Turkey Vulture, and like that species flies tilting from side to side and with wings held slightly above horizontal; both also show a similar two-toned effect on wings below. Zone-tail, however, is smaller, and has white tail bands and a larger feathered head. Dark phase Short-tailed Hawk has more typical *Buteo* proportions, and lacks conspicuous tail bands. The various black-hawks are chunkier with shorter tails, and have only one or two tail bands. See also dark phase Swainson's and immature White-tailed Hawks.

Status and distribution: Uncommon, with reports scattered but mostly from lowlands and foothills on Pacific slope, where recorded from Chiriquí (seen once at David airport; E. O. Willis) to Darién (seen near El Real on July 22, 1975; Ridgely), with majority of records from Panama province and Pacific side of Canal area; on Caribbean slope recorded from Bocas del Toro (N. G. Smith), Canal area, and San Blas (three specimens); found also on the Pearl Islands. Though apparently migrating birds have been seen from Ancon Hill in October (N. G. Smith) and in eastern Panama province (one with other migrating raptors over Tocumen on March 12, 1979; Ridgely and J. Baird *et al.*), there are now so many reports from during the northern summer that the existence of a resident breeding population in Panama seems clear (probably augmented by northern migrants). To date, however, there is no actual evidence of nesting in Panama.

Habits: Usually seen flying fairly low over open or broken country. Appears to mimic the Turkey Vulture, thus presumably luring its prey into a very false sense of security. Zone-tails are often almost passed by as Turkey Vultures.

Range: Southwestern United States south locally to northern Argentina, Paraguay, and southern Brazil.

RED-TAILED HAWK
Buteo jamaicensis p.88

Description: 19–24. Large and chunky, with broad wings and rounded tail. In adults the *rufous tail*, brighter from above, is distinctive. Plumage of northern populations (small numbers of which winter south to Panama) highly variable. Dark brown above; whitish below with varying amounts of black streaking, *especially on belly* (in some birds almost forming a band). Some individuals of northern races are entirely blackish aside from the rufous tail, while others are solid rufous brown or whitish below. Adult of western Panama breeding race (*costaricensis*) generally similar but less variable, always showing *rufous thighs* and usually with *rufous-buff extending up on flanks and over most of belly*; they show *little or no black streaking*. Immatures of northern races similar to adults but tail brownish gray with numerous narrow dusky bands; immature *costaricensis* more streaked below than adult, and tail dull cinnamon with numerous narrow dusky bars.

Similar species: The rufous-tailed adults are easily identified; much smaller and slighter Roadside Hawk also has reddish tail in most of Panama but shows reddish on wings in flight. Immatures very difficult, resembling several other large immature Buteos, usually not safely identified away from western mountains. Swainson's Hawk (the most similar) has somewhat more slender proportions, longer and narrower wings, and longer less fan-shaped tail.

Status and distribution: Uncommon resident in montane forest and adjacent cleared areas in highlands of Chiriquí (mostly above 1500 m: 5000 ft) and Veraguas (no evidence of local movements. What are apparently northern migrants have been recorded rarely

in lowlands of Bocas del Toro, Pacific slope Veraguas, Pacific slope of Canal area, and in lowlands and foothills of eastern Panama province (east to Chepo/El Llano area). Racial identity of these birds (recorded mainly November–February) uncertain, and several subspecies could be involved; the one specimen has been identified as of the western North American race *calurus*.

Habits: In the Chiriquí highlands, an individual or pair can often be seen soaring over forested ridges or clearings, sometimes high. Elsewhere seen only rarely, in open or semiopen areas, usually soaring high overhead (often with other Buteos) or resting on a high exposed perch.

Range: Breeds from North America to western Panama and in West Indies; northern birds winter, at least occasionally, to Panama.

CRESTED EAGLE
Morphnus guianensis pp.100, 104

Description: 31–35. A rare large eagle with broad rounded wings and *very long tail*. In all plumages has *pointed blackish occipital crest*, flared up when bird is agitated. Adult has two phases. In normal light phase mostly brownish black above with *head, neck, and chest pale gray tinged brown*, contrasting with white lower underparts, sometimes with a little light tawny barring on thighs; tail black with three broad gray bands. In flight from below, *under wing-coverts white*, flight feathers broadly banded black and gray. Dark or banded phase is similar but with head, neck, and chest dark gray (almost blackish on chest) and *lower underparts boldly barred with black*; *entire underwing* (including wing-coverts) *broadly banded and barred black and gray*. Intermediates and a rare almost wholly black phase are known. Immature has head, neck, and entire underparts white (head and neck becoming grayer with age); mantle with conspicuous whitish mottling; wings and tail as in adult. Several years are required to attain adult plumage.

Similar species: Closely resembles Harpy Eagle, especially when in various immature or subadult plumages. Crested differs in its slightly smaller size, slimmer build, proportionately longer tail, weaker bill, longer and less thick legs, and its single pointed crest; all of these points can be subtle and difficult in the field, and many birds cannot be identified with certainty (especially as they are often seen only briefly). Light phase adult Crested can be

Left, CRESTED EAGLE (light phase adult); right, HARPY EAGLE (adult)

known by its immaculate under wing-coverts (boldly barred in Harpy); dark phase Crested relatively easy. See also the much smaller hawk-eagles, all of which have *feathered legs* (bare in Crested and Harpy).

Status and distribution: Rare in extensively forested areas in lowlands and foothills on entire Caribbean slope; on Pacific slope recorded from southwestern Azuero Peninsula (Cerro Hoya region; F. Delgado), and in eastern Panama province and Darién; sightings from Coiba Island and Chiriquí are considered unsubstantiated. Declining throughout Panama in the face of encroaching civilization; probably now most numerous in Darién, though even here thinly spread and seen only very rarely. Few recent reports from Canal area, though still seen occasionally on Barro Colorado Island; one subadult was photographed at close range near Achiote Road on January 8, 1975 (W. Cornwell).

Habits: Remains imperfectly known, but believed not to differ much from Harpy Eagle, though tending to favor hilly or foothill regions. Does not seem to soar at great heights, though occasionally a bird will glide out over canopy or across a valley. Thus like the Harpy not a very conspicuous

bird, and despite its size probably often overlooked. Perched birds can sometimes be approached surprisingly closely, seeming almost to ignore the observer.

Range: Guatemala south very locally to northern Argentina and southern Brazil.

HARPY EAGLE
Harpia harpyja pp.100, 104

Description: 35–40. A rare, *very large* eagle; massively built, with tarsi 2 in thick, and considered the most powerful bird of prey in the world. Broad rounded wings and long tail. In all plumages has *conspicuous two-pointed blackish crest*. Adult has *head and neck gray, contrasting with black chest*; upperparts otherwise black, feathers indistinctly edged gray; lower underparts white, with thighs barred black; tail black with three broad gray bands and narrow gray tip (whiter from below). In flight from below, *wings white boldly barred and banded with black*, axillars also black. Immature has head, neck, and underparts white; upperparts brownish to pale gray marbled with blackish; tail gray with several dusky bands; underwing as in adult but with white axillars. Several years are required to attain adult plumage; the dark chest band apparently appears rather early.

Similar species: Full adults are unmistakable, but earlier age stages are easily confused with Crested Eagle; for distinctions, see under that species.

Status and distribution: Rare in extensively forested areas in lowlands and foothills on entire Caribbean slope; on Pacific slope recorded from western Panama province (a 1951 sighting by Wetmore from near La Campana; doubtless long since gone from this now well settled area) east through Darién. Formerly apparently more numerous, this spectacular eagle has decreased greatly in recent decades, with few recent verified reports except from Bocas del Toro and Darién (probably also still occurs more or less widely in San Blas, and perhaps also in northern Veraguas). Surprisingly, however, a few do continue to persist on the Caribbean slope of the Canal area (or possibly they wander in from elsewhere?), with several recent sightings from Pipeline Road area. Never very numerous even in entirely wild, unsettled areas, the Harpy declines rapidly in the face of civilization, due both to deforestation and to incidental shooting: sadly, Harpies are often not particularly shy in the presence of man, and hunters almost instinctively shoot them at any opportunity (despite its legally protected status in Panama).

Habits: Harpy Eagles are inconspicuous despite their enormous size, generally staying in or below the canopy, where they hunt from a perch or in surprisingly rapid, agile flight. Only occasionally do they soar, then normally only low and briefly. They prey on a variety of small to mid-sized mammals, sloths and monkeys being especially preferred.

Range: Southern Mexico to northern Argentina and southern Brazil.

BLACK-AND-WHITE HAWK-EAGLE
Spizastur melanoleucus p.106

Description: 22–24. Small eagle with rather *Buteo* -like proportions. *Cere bright orange*; legs feathered to toes. *Head, neck, and entire underparts white; small mask, short bushy crest* (forms a patch), *and entire upperparts black*; tail black with three broad gray bands and narrow gray tip. In flight from below, *underwing essentially white*, with a little black barring on tips of flight feathers. Immature similar but mantle more brownish gray with some white feather edging.

Similar species: Immature of more numerous Ornate Hawk-Eagle is brownish (not black) above, lacks the sharply contrasting black lores (which are surprisingly conspicuous in this species), and has black barring on flanks and thighs (never shown in Black-and-white) and often to some extent on under wing-coverts. Pale phase immature Gray-headed Kite similar in pattern, but slighter in build with notably smaller head; it has yellow lores (thus lacking masked effect of this species), shorter and bare legs, and is more boldly banded on flight feathers.

Status and distribution: Rare and local in forest canopy and borders and in adjacent clearings in lowlands and foothills on both slopes; recorded only from Bocas del Toro, lower highlands or Chiriquí (above Boquete), Veraguas (a nineteenth-century specimen without specific locality), Caribbean side of Canal area, eastern Panama province, and Darién (below Boca de Cupe; Cana). Not regularly seen anywhere in Panama (nor apparently anywhere else in its vast range).

Habits: Generally conspicuous where it does occur, soaring frequently and sometimes perching on high exposed limbs. Does not seem to be as vocal as the *Spizaetus* hawk-eagles, but a shrill *kree-ówow* has been recorded (S. Hilty).

Range: Southern Mexico south very locally to northern Argentina and southern Brazil.

BLACK HAWK-EAGLE
Spizaetus tyrannus p.100

Description: 25–28. Wings broad and rounded, *narrower* at base; tail rather long. Legs feathered to toes. *Mostly black* with short bushy crest, some white about head and white barring on thighs; tail black with three whitish bands. In flight from below, *flight feathers prominently barred black and white*. Immature is mostly dark chocolate brown with white to buff mottling, especially on head, and white barring on back; throat white, most of lower underparts barred with white.

Similar species: A large but rather slender eagle with a very distinctive flight appearance: wings and long tail prominently banded, wing-tips often held forward of head, with rear of wing often seemingly "cut-out" near body. No other mostly dark hawk or eagle has such conspicuous banding on underside of wings

BLACK-AND-WHITE HAWK-EAGLE

(though this is sometimes difficult to see against the light).

Status and distribution: Fairly common in forest, second-growth woodland, and borders in lowlands and foothills on entire Caribbean slope, and in more humid forested areas on Pacific slope (especially from Canal area east through Darién); apparently absent from Azuero Peninsula east through southern Coclé lowlands; in western Chiriquí ranges at least occasionally up into lower highlands (above Boquete). Still frequently noted in Canal area where, for a bird its size, it is numerous and widespread in or near forested or wooded areas on both slopes.

Habits: Very conspicuous, frequently seen soaring high overhead, even in the heat of the day; rarely seen perched. Calls regularly when soaring, an unmistakable loud, mellow *wheet, wheet, wheeteeeeeea*, with long slurred note last; sometimes the last note is given alone.

Range: Eastern Mexico to northern Bolivia, northeastern Argentina, and southern Brazil.

ORNATE HAWK-EAGLE Plate 8, p.100
Spizaetus ornatus

Description: 23–25. Wings broad, rather short and rounded; tail rather long. Legs feathered to toes. *Crown and long pointed crest black; sides of head, hindneck, and sides of chest tawny*; back and wings black; throat and center of chest white, bordered with black malar stripe; *lower underparts white heavily barred with black*; tail black with three grayish bands; underside of wings barred black and white. Immature has head, neck, and underparts white with *long crest* usually white with black tip, *flanks and thighs barred with black*; dark brown above; wings and tail as in adult.

Similar species: Immature can be confused with Black-and-white Hawk-Eagle, which has black area around eye, lacks long crest and black barring on flanks. Immature Black Hawk-Eagle is much darker below. Crested Eagle is much larger.

Status and distribution: Uncommon in forest and forest borders in lowlands and foothills on entire Caribbean slope, and in more humid forested areas on Pacific slope; in western Chiriquí and eastern Darién also ranges up into lower highlands; found also on Coiba Island (where a number were seen in April 1976; Ridgely). Local on Pacific slope, where now found mainly in eastern Panama province and Darién; in Canal area on this side apparently known only from a specimen (in GML) taken at Curundu on August 29, 1973 (G. Barrett, Jr), and only recently (1982) found in southernmost Azuero Peninsula (drainages of Río Pavo and Río Portobelo; F. Delgado). In Panama seems generally to be outnumbered by the Black Hawk-Eagle; in Canal area perhaps most regularly seen on Pipeline Road.

Habits: Does not soar as much nor usually as high as the Black Hawk-Eagle, typically circling fairly low over the canopy, its steady flight occasionally broken by brief bouts of "butterfly-like" shallow wing flutters. Its call is distinctive and often given in flight, *whee-er, whip, whip, whip, whip*, with slurred note first; in pattern the reverse of the Black Hawk-Eagle's call, which has slurred note last. Not often seen perched, though occasionally may survey the canopy from an exposed limb during the early morning. Apparently hunts mainly by ambushing prey from a semi-concealed perch in the canopy or lower.

Range: Eastern Mexico to Bolivia, northern Argentina, and southern Brazil.

FALCONS AND CARACARAS: Falconidae (13)

This family includes a large and widespread group of diurnal birds of prey, separated in most species from the Accipitridae by their notched upper mandible and various anatomical characters. The true falcons (genus *Falco*), a world-wide group, are known by their pointed and rather narrow wings; some of the smaller falcons often hover, while many of the larger ones kill their avian prey by a spectacular stoop from above. Most of the caracaras (entirely American in distribution) eat largely carrion, but one Panamanian species (the Red-throated) specializes in wasp and bee larvae. The forest-falcons (also exclusively American) are inconspicuous accipiter-like birds of dense forest lower growth; they have short rounded wings, long tails (in some strikingly graduated), and an owl-like facial ruff (sometimes not very apparent), and feed mostly on birds. Nesting sites selected by the members of the family are varied, ranging from cliff ledges to old nests of other birds, holes in trees, and stick nests in trees.

RED-THROATED CARACARA
Daptrius americanus   Plate 8

Description: 2–21. Very distinctive in appearance, almost suggesting a small cracid. Bill yellow with gray base; *bare red facial skin, throat, and legs. Mostly glossy black* (though often looking rather scruffy and unkempt) with sharply contrasting *white belly and crissum.*

Status and distribution: This species seems to be undergoing a general, and still unexplained, decline in most of Panama (and apparently almost throughout its former range in Middle America). Formerly recorded widely from the entire Caribbean slope, there are *no* recent records, even from areas where extensive lowland forest habitat remains (such as Bocas del Toro); perhaps it persists in San Blas, where there has been relatively little recent ornithological exploration. It gradually disappeared from the Canal area during the 1950s and 1960s, persisting latest in the Achiote Road area, where last recorded in the early 1970s. Seems to remain in "normal" numbers only in eastern Panama province (upper Bayano River valley) and Darién, where it ranges occasionally up to about 1350 m (4500 ft) though most numerous below 600 m (2000 ft). Formerly also known from Chiriquí to the western side of the Azuero Peninsula, it is surely extirpated from virtually all of this region because of widespread deforestation; however, it persists on the Burica Peninsula south of Puerto Armuelles (where one was seen on June 24, 1982; Ridgely), in Chiriquí, and a few may still be found in remote extreme southwestern Azuero Peninsula (from whence no recent reports, but at least some forest remains). In Costa Rica reported now to be largely confined to the southwest (e.g. at Corcovado Nat. Park); there seem to be no recent reports from *anywhere* north of Costa Rica in Middle America (though it once ranged north to the Pacific slope of Chiapas, Mexico). A study attempting to address the reasons for its spectacular, and unexpected, decline is badly needed; there seems to be no evidence of an equivalent decline in South America.

Habits: Travels in small groups, usually rather high in trees (though rarely flying much above the canopy), but at times coming much lower inside forest, occasionally even to the ground. Its flight is rather weak and labored, and even when perched the birds manage to look awkward and often off balance. At times they are very unsuspicious, sometimes even seeming curious and approaching the observer closely. They feed mostly on wasp and bee larvae, obtained by tearing open the nests of even the most aggressive species; they also eat some fruit. Often very noisy, with unbelievably loud raucous calls, e.g. *ca-ca-ca-cáo*, frequently several birds at once in an incredible cacophony; at a distance they sound like macaws. Known locally as "cacao", for obvious reasons.

Range: Costa Rica (formerly to southern Mexico, but seemingly no recent records from Nicaragua northward) to Peru and southern Brazil.

CRESTED CARACARA
Polyborus plancus   Plate 8

Description: 20–24. Rather long legs. Somewhat crested. *Bare skin of face and base of bill red. Crown black; sides of head, neck, and throat whitish;* otherwise blackish above; breast whitish barred with dusky, becoming solid dusky on belly; *rump and most of tail white* narrowly barred with dusky and with broad black subterminal band; in flight shows *conspicuous white patches on primaries.* Immature recognizably similar though buffier and browner overall and more streaked below.

Similar species: Yellow-headed Caracara is much smaller and less robust, lacks white rump and wing patch (buffy instead) and has head and underparts mostly buffy.

Status and distribution: Fairly common to common in open grassy or scrubby areas and in agricultural regions in lowlands on Pacific slope from Chiriquí to eastern Panama province; single records (doubtless stragglers) from Taboga Island and the Pearl Islands (Pacheca). Uncommon in immediate Canal area, where there is little suitable habitat (most regular at Albrook AFB); since the 1970s a few odd individuals have been turning up in open areas on the Caribbean slope of the Canal area, but there is as yet no evidence of its actually becoming established here.

Habits: Like Yellow-headed Caracara, most common in cattle country. A rather powerful bird of prey whose food is not limited to carrion. Usually forages in pairs or small groups, often seen walking on the ground. Flies strongly but does not seem to soar.

Range: Southwestern United States to Tierra del Fuego; southern Florida and Cuba.

YELLOW-HEADED CARACARA
Milvago chimachima   Plate 8

Description: 16–17. Wings rather long, somewhat pointed; tail fairly long, rounded at tip. *Head, neck, and underparts pale buffy* with *narrow dark brown streak behind eye*; back and wings blackish brown; tail with numerous blackish and buff bands; in flight wings dark with *prominent pale buffy patch on base of primaries.* Immature streaked with brown and buff on head and neck and with brown back; mostly brown below streaked with buff or whitish; tail brownish barred with white; wings as in adult, with primaries barred with cinnamon.

Similar species: Immatures, though less distinctive, can still be recognized by caracara shape, wing patch, and habits. See Crested Caracara and Laughing Falcon.

Status and distribution: Fairly common to common in open grassy or scrubby areas and in agricultural regions in lowlands on Pacific slope from Chiriquí to eastern Panama province (east to Chepo/El Llano area, but likely will spread eastward with clearing), in western Chiriquí highlands ranging up to about 1350 m (4500 ft) in

suitable habitat; has recently begun to colonize the Caribbean slope in Canal area (a number of recent reports of small numbers since the early and mid 1980s) and eastern Colon province (where small numbers were seen regularly in January–June 1987 east to Nombre de Dios by D. Graham), and probably will continue to spread and increase. One of the most numerous raptors of open country on Pacific slope, particularly from western Panama province westward.

Habits: Rather unsuspicious; often in small groups. Much of its food is carrion of all sorts: a good proportion is obtained by patrolling the highways for road-killed animals. Sometimes also seen picking ticks from backs of cattle. The usual call is a harsh *krrr-krrr-krrr*; also heard is a peculiar (part whistle, part hissing) *ksyeh, ksyeh.*

Range: Southwestern Costa Rica to Bolivia, northern Argentina, and Uruguay.

LAUGHING FALCON
Herpetotheres cachinnans   p.109

Description: 18–22. Appears large-headed. Wings rather short and rounded; tail long and rounded. *Head, neck, and underparts buffy white to buff* with *prominent broad black mask through eyes and around hindneck*; crown with a few black shaft streaks; upperparts dark brown; tail black with numerous buffy white bands. In flight shows caracara-like buffy patches on primaries.

Similar species: Yellow-headed Caracara is smaller and lacks the broad mask (only a thin black line through eye).

Status and distribution: Uncommon and perhaps local in forest and woodland borders, galley woodland, and adjacent clearings with scattered trees in lowlands on Pacific slope, though absent from eastern side of Azuero Peninsula to western Panama province; on Caribbean slope recorded only from Bocas del Toro (where rare) and Canal area (e.g. two on Achiote Road on January 25, 1984; Ridgely); in western Chiriquí has occasionally been found up into lower highlands to around 1200 m (4000 ft). Not a particularly numerous bird in Panama, and quite scarce in immediate Canal area, from whence there are recent reports from Madden Forest and Rodman.

Habits: Rather sluggish, often perching for long periods on an exposed branch, erect and motionless. At times notably unsuspicious. Feeds mostly on snakes. Flies with rapid and stiff wing-beats alternating with short glides; does not soar. Best known from

LAUGHING FALCON

its far-carrying calls, most often given in early morning and late afternoon (but also sometimes heard at night), typically a loud *guá-co, guá-co, guá-co. . .* , or *gua-ców, gua-ców, gua-ców. . .* , often continuing for several minutes, initially often as a single note and rather slowly, then gradually increasing in tempo and becoming more rhythmic. Other less frequently heard vocalizations do somewhat suggest muffled maniacal laughter, e.g. *hah, hah, hah-hah-hah-hahhahhah-hah*. The typical vocalization can resemble call of Collared Forest-Falcon, especially at first when the single halting note is being given.
Range: Mexico to Bolivia, northern Argentina, and southern Brazil.

BARRED FOREST-FALCON
Micrastur ruficollis   Plates 7,9

Description: 13–15. Short rounded wings; tail very long and graduated. Cere, *orbital area*, lores, and legs orange-yellow. Blackish slate above (browner in female); throat pale gray, *remaining underparts white finely and evenly barred with black*; tail black with three narrow white bands and narrow white tip. Immature variable, dark brown above with narrow buff collar (sometimes broken or hidden); varying shades of buff below, usually with irregular dusky barring (much coarser than in adult); in a few individuals, underparts uniform deep buff with no barring; tail as in adult.

Similar species: Adult's even barring below is characteristic, but see Tiny Hawk (smaller, with different shape, habits). Collared Forest-Falcon is much larger. Immature Bicolored Hawk lacks barring below, has shorter legs and shorter less graduated tail. See also Slaty-backed Forest-Falcon.
Status and distribution: Apparently uncommon (probably overlooked because of furtive habits) in humid forest in lowlands and foothills on entire Caribbean slope; on Pacific slope found in humid forested areas (mostly in foothills) from Chiriquí to Darién, ranging up in western Chiriquí in lower highlands to 1620 m (5400 ft). More numerous on Caribbean side of Canal area.
Habits: A bird of dense forest undergrowth and borders, shy and not often seen. Follows swarms of army ants persistently, then often terrifying the other small birds in attendance, though it captures mostly large insects, only occasionally going after a bird (E. O. Willis). More often recorded from its vocalizations. The usual call is a sharp stacatto *our!* repeated at intervals, much like the bark of a small dog (Slud). This often reveals the bird's presence, but it is extremely difficult to track down, being ventriloquial and the calling bird being very wary and usually slipping away at one's approach (sometimes will come in to a tape playback, however). When excited, the note is repeated more rapidly, becoming *kĕo, kĕo, kĕo. . . .* Most vocal in the early morning and late afternoon.
Range: Southern Mexico to Bolivia, northern Argentina, and southern Brazil.

SLATY-BACKED FOREST-FALCON
Micrastur mirandollei   Plate 7

Description: 16–18. Shape similar to Collared Forest-Falcon, but tail not as proportionately long and graduated. Base of bill, cere, and legs yellow. *Dark slaty gray above and on sides of neck (with no collar on hindneck)*; below varying from whitish to pale buff with very fine dark shaft streaks; tail blackish with three narrow whitish bands. Immature has mainly yellow bill, is browner above, whitish below with broad dusky scalloping.
Similar species: Caution is urged in identifying this scarce and confusing species. Immature Barred Forest-Falcons that lack black barring below somewhat resemble adults of this species with light buff underparts, but are much smaller, with more graduated tail, are browner or dusky

above, and have pale face and yellow orbital area. This species also resembles immature Bicolored Hawk but has facial ruff, shorter legs, slaty (not rusty) upperparts, and never has a collar (present in most Bicoloreds). Semiplumbeous Hawk has similar color pattern but is chunkier with one prominent white tail band (not three narrow inconspicuous ones).

Status and distribution: Rare to uncommon in humid forest and second-growth woodland in lowlands on Caribbean slope (though unrecorded from Bocas del Toro or Veraguas, it probably occurs); on Pacific slope found only in eastern Panama province and Darién. In Canal area most regularly reported from Achiote Road and vicinity.

Habits: Inconspicuous and infrequently seen, most often recorded only by voice. Usually remains in lower growth inside forest or in heavily overgrown borders. Reported to do some of its hunting on the ground (Wetmore). Has several calls, all apparently with an accelerating effect and slightly rising in pitch; one is a series of up to 10–14 nasal *aah* syllables, the other a more two-parted affair, rising at first then steady in pitch, *ah, ow, ow, ow, ow, ow, ow, úah, úah, úah, úah, úah. . .* (B. Whitney). Like the other forest-falcons it will, with patience, respond to tape playback.

Range: Costa Rica to eastern Peru, Amazonian Brazil, and the Guianas.

COLLARED FOREST-FALCON
Micrastur semitorquatus   Plate 7, p.110

Description: 20–24. Slender with short broad wings; *long graduated tail*. Bill blackish; bare facial skin and cere dull greenish; legs yellow. Three phases in adults. In light phase, blackish above, *black of crown extending down over face in crescent*; white below, extending up over sides of head and neck and forming *collar on hindneck*; tail black with narrow white bands and white tip. Buffy phase similar but with *white replaced by buff to tawny*. Rare dark phase is all sooty black except for white tail banding and small amount of white barring on flanks. Immature variable, with greenish bill; upperparts dark brown edged with tawny, and *whitish to tawny collar*; upperparts varying from whitish to deep buff, brightest on chest, and coarsely barred with blackish or dark brown; tail as in adult. Dark phase immature brownish black with white barring on lower underparts.

IMMATURE COLLARED FOREST-FALCON

Similar species: All phases except dark show contrasting collar. Immature Bicolored Hawk resembles this species' white and buffy phases but is smaller and has shorter ungraduated tail, shorter legs, and lacks white or buff face and dark facial crescent. Barred Forest-Falcon is much smaller and lacks prominent collar, is evenly barred below in adults.

Status and distribution: Uncommon in forest, second-growth woodland, and borders in more humid lowlands on both slopes; apparently absent from southern Coclé and dry lowlands of western Panama province; in western Chiriquí recorded well up into the highlands (e.g. one seen at 1950 m (6500 ft) above Finca Lerida on February 7, 1976; Ridgely and R. Forster). In Canal area more numerous on Caribbean side.

Habits: Usually remains in dense undergrowth and lower trees, and thus often difficult to observe. A bold rapacious hunter, flying from perch to perch, waiting in ambush for its prey (principally birds) then rapidly chasing after it, sometimes crashing through dense cover in wild pursuit. Occasionally even runs on the ground (H.-J. Peters). The call is a slowly repeated, hollow and resonant *ow. . .ow. . .ow. . .*, somewhat suggestive of the Laughing Falcon but slower and without the acceleration. It is usually given in early morning and again in late afternoon (sometimes until well after dusk), generally from a high hidden perch.

Range: Mexico to Bolivia, northern Argentina, and southern Brazil.

AMERICAN KESTREL
Falco sparverius   Plate 9

Description: 9–12. Male *mostly rufous above* with most of crown and *wings bluish gray*;

sides of head white with narrow black moustache stripe and a vertical stripe through eye; buff below, spotted with black on breast and sides; *tail rufous* with broad black subterminal band and white tip. Female has head pattern as in male, *entirely rufous above* (including wings), barred with black; buffy below, lightly streaked with brown; *tail rufous* with many narrow black bands.

Similar species: Striking facial pattern and mostly rufous tail and upperparts will identify both sexes.

Status and distribution: Rare to fairly common transient and winter resident (early October–early April) in open areas in lowlands on Pacific slope from Chiriquí to eastern Panama province (Cerro Azul/Jefe and Chepo area), becoming less numerous eastward; in smaller numbers in suitable habitat on Caribbean slope east to the Canal area; ranges in clearings well up into the highlands of western Chiriquí (to 1950 m: 6500 ft or more); also recorded on Pearl Islands (San José) and on Coiba Island.

Habits: Usually seen perched conspicuously on telephone poles or wires or on an exposed branch, favors open or semi-open country. Often jerks tail up and down upon alighting. Regularly seen hovering while hunting, especially just before it plunges down after its predominately insect prey.

Range: Breeds from northern North America south locally to Nicaragua and through much of South America; northern birds winter south at least to northern South America.

MERLIN
Falco columbarius

Description: 10–13. Male *dark bluish gray above*, tinged with rusty on sides of head and nape; buff to whitish below, *streaked with blackish brown*; tail black with three gray bands and white tip. Female and immature are similar but browner above.

Similar species: Note falcon shape and habits, fairly small size, and streaked underparts. American Kestrel has bright rufous back and tail; Peregrine is much larger with prominent dark moustache.

Status and distribution: Rare to uncommon transient and winter resident in open or semiopen and (especially) coastal areas throughout, mainly in lowlands but also at least occasionally up into western Chiriquí highlands; recorded also from Pearl Islands; recorded in Panama late September–mid-April.

Habits: Usually seen in swift flight low over the ground, or on an exposed perch (but unlike kestrel rarely perches on phone wires).

Range: Breeds in northern Eurasia and northern North America; American birds winter from southern United States to Venezuela and northern Peru and in West Indies.

APLOMADO FALCON
Falco femoralis   Plate 9

Description: 14–17. Very local in savannas of Pacific western Panama. A rather slender falcon with relatively long tail. Mostly bluish gray above with *conspicuous white or pale buff superciliary extending back to encircle crown; narrow but conspicuous black moustache below eye*; sides of neck, throat, and chest whitish to pale buff, *contrasting with black sides and mid-breast* (latter imparting a somewhat vested look, and narrowly barred with white); belly tawny-rufous; tail blackish with several narrow white bars. In flight shows a *narrow but conspicuous whitish trailing edge on inner flight feathers*.

Similar species: Most likely confused with Peregrine, small males of which overlap in size with large females of this species. Peregrines bulk larger and are broader-winged and proportionately shorter-tailed; differently patterned, they are most likely to be confused at a distance in flight, when Aplomado's pale trailing margin on wing is often the best mark.

Status and distribution: Rare to uncommon in grassy savannas and other very open areas with at most a few scattered trees in lowlands on Pacific slope in Herrera and southern Coclé (east to around Penonomé); one sighting from extreme southern Los Santos (near Pedasí) by Wetmore, who also saw another, very anomalous vagrant circling over Barro Colorado Island on February 19, 1954. With the general increase in human population over much of its limited Panama range, and in particular the conversion of so much of it to sugar cane cultivation, the Aplomado Falcon seems to be becoming rare; its population status needs to be monitored.

Habits: Usually perches low and in the open, typically on a fence post, but also in smaller trees and on telephone poles. Can fly very rapidly, often skimming along close to the ground; occasionally hovers. Eats birds and large insects; sometimes seen following grass fires.

Range: Extreme southwestern United States (where apparently extirpated) south very locally to Tierra del Fuego; only one report from Costa Rica (Guanacaste).

BAT FALCON
Falco rufigularis   Plate 7

Description: 9–12. Very long, narrow, pointed wings. Dark bluish slate above and on sides of head; *throat, upper chest, and sides of neck white*, sometimes tinged with tawny; *lower chest, breast, and upper belly black*, narrowly barred with white; lower belly rufous.
Similar species: A small falcon which appears dark in the field except for the white on throat, etc. See the larger (but very similarly plumaged) Orange-breasted Falcon. Bat Falcon's flight silhouette is astonishingly like that of the White-collared Swift, and occasionally a falcon will join a flock of swifts for a while (possibly to ambush unsuspecting prey?).
Status and distribution: Uncommon to locally fairly common in forest and woodland borders and nearby clearings in lowlands on both slopes, occasionally ranging up into the lower highlands; found also on Coiba Island, Taboga Island, and the Pearl Islands (San José). Rather scarce (unaccountably so) in Canal area.
Habits: Usually seen perched on an exposed branch, often in pairs, rather unsuspicious. Seems to feed mostly in early morning and late afternoon; catches its food (larger insects, bats, small birds) in very swift and graceful flight, often even eating its prey while on the wing. Nests in tree holes.
Range: Mexico to Bolivia, northern Argentina, and southern Brazil.

ORANGE-BREASTED FALCON
Falco deiroleucus   p.100

Description: 13–16. Very rare. *Very* closely resembles the *much* more numerous Bat Falcon. Differs in its *proportionately much larger feet* and by its *coarser more rufescent barring on the black band across breast and upper belly*. Note that Bat Falcon regularly shows some orange-rufous on its breast, especially just above the black; *many* Bat Falcons with "orange breasts" are called Orange-breasted Falcons!
Similar species: Differentiation from Bat Falcon is often problematic, and many sightings are unconvincing. In flight Orange-breasted has proportions of a small Peregrine

Falcon; the two are quite similarly colored from above.
Status and distribution: Known only from two nineteenth-century specimens from Chiriquí, and three sightings which were believed to pertain to this species: one near Penonomé, Coclé on March 29, 1957 (Wetmore); one near Cerro Jefe, eastern Panama province on June 25, 1970 (Ridgely); and one at Cana, Darién on March 2, 1981 (Ridgely *et al.*). All of these birds were seen only in flight. Griscom's account of nesting in church towers and belfries in western Panama (*Bull AMNH 64*: 164, 1932) is compromised by the fact that Bat Falcons are known to inhabit such situations, and because elsewhere Orange-breasted Falcons have been found to range only in extensively forested areas.
Habits: Evidently rare and very local throughout its large range. Recent studies in South America have shown that Orange-breasted Falcons are most "numerous" in foothill areas where there are cliffs for their eyries, though they are also known to nest in hollows in tall emergent trees. They prey primarily on birds, overtaking even very fast ones (doves, parrots, swifts, and swallows) in flight. Like the Bat Falcon they are to some extent crepuscular.
Range: Southern Mexico south very locally to northern Argentina and southern Brazil.

PEREGRINE FALCON
Falco peregrinus

Description: 15–20. *Long pointed wings*; rather pointed tail. *Slaty gray above*, blacker on head, with *broad black moustache stripe running down sides of throat*; whitish below, washed with buff and irregularly barred with dusky on breast and belly; tail barred gray and blackish. Immature similar but is dark brown above, buffy whitish below streaked with brown.
Similar species: Large size and long pointed wings mark this species as the largest of Panama's falcons. See the very rare Orange-breasted Falcon.
Status and distribution: Uncommon transient and winter resident (October–early May), with records scattered throughout but chiefly coastally or around larger bodies of fresh water (e.g. especially Gatun Lake); recorded also from Pearl Islands and Coiba Island. Several usually pass the winter at either entrance to the Canal, feeding on the abundant shore and water birds.

Habits: Nearly always seen singly in Panama, either in the air or resting on a high exposed perch. Effortless-looking flight is graceful and can be astonishingly fast (though it often also circles or soars lazily). In Panama their most commonly taken prey are birds, usually obtained by stooping down on them at tremendous speeds, less often by overtaking in direct pursuit; wintering Peregrines have also been seen to feed on emerging bats. North American breeders declined very alarmingly between the 1940s and 1960s, and for a while were totally eliminated as a breeder across much of temperate North America; they are now gradually recovering, thanks to the release of captive-bred birds. Arctic breeders, which may comprise the majority (all?) of the birds in Panama, never declined as much. The decline was entirely attributable to breeding abnormalities caused by the residues of various persistent pesticides and industrial products. Their banning in North America has permitted the Peregrine's gradual recovery, but their continued and often excessive use across much of Latin American may mean that the Peregrine is not out of trouble yet.

Range: Virtually cosmopolitan, though not breeding any closer to Panama than northern Mexico and Ecuador.

CURASSOWS, GUANS, AND CHACHALACAS: Cracidae (4)

This group of superficially pheasant or turkey-like birds is found only in the warmer parts of the New World. Most species are primarily arboreal; curassows, however, do much of their foraging on the ground. Although most species range in forest, chachalacas favor overgrown clearings and woodland borders. They feed chiefly on vegetable matter, particularly fruit. The nest is a simple structure of twigs or sticks and leaves, usually situated rather low in trees. All are much desired gamebirds, and populations of the larger species are quickly reduced by even light hunting pressure.

GRAY-HEADED CHACHALACA
Ortalis cinereiceps Plate 41, p.114

Description: 19–21. Slender with small head (somewhat crested), long neck, long tail. *Mostly grayish brown* with small patch of red skin on throat; *head and neck distinctly gray*; somewhat paler below, becoming whitish on lower belly; *bright chestnut primaries conspicuous in flight*; tail tipped buff.
Similar species: Crested Guan is much larger, has white streaking below, lacks chestnut on wings.
Status and distribution: Fairly common in second-growth woodland and borders and in shrubby clearings in more humid lowlands on both slopes; found also on larger Pearl Islands. Quite numerous and widespread in wooded areas on both slopes of Canal area.
Habits: Usually seen in groups of up to about a dozen individuals; primarily arboreal. Not particularly shy where they are not under intense hunting pressure. Has a variety of vocalizations: groups often greet the dawn with a harsh repeated *chack* or *chacalaca*; also has a soft *hoit, hoit,* or *hweet, hweet* and a *kt-kt-kt*, both given especially when the birds are disturbed.
Range: Honduras to extreme northwestern Colombia.

BLACK GUAN
Chamaepetes unicolor Plate 41, p.114

Description: 21–23. Found only in western highlands. Iris red; *bare blue skin in front of eye and on sides of face*; legs light reddish. *Wholly black.* Immature has breast and belly somewhat more brownish. Unmistakable in its range.
Status and distribution: Rare to locally fairly common in montane forest and forest borders in highlands of Chiriquí, Bocas del Toro, Veraguas (Calovévora and Santa Fé), and

Left, two CRESTED GUANS; center top, BLACK GUAN; center bottom, two GREAT CURASSOWS (female left, male right); right top, two GRAY-HEADED CHACHALACAS

western Coclé (seen above El Copé in mid-February 1987; J. Arvin *et al.*); recorded mostly 900–2250 m (3000–7500 ft), though has been taken as low as 450 m (1500 ft) in Bocas del Toro. In Panama best known from Chiriquí, though numbers there have diminished due to forest destruction and (especially) hunting pressure; scarce now on Volcán Barú, but still moderately numerous in the Fortuna area.

Habits: Usually in pairs, which can be tame in remote areas with little or no hunting (and in areas where hunting has been effectively halted, as at the Monteverde Cloud Forest Reserve in Costa Rica). For the most part Black Guans are arboreal, though at times they do go to the ground, perhaps mostly to feed on fallen fruit.

Range: Costa Rica and western Panama.

CRESTED GUAN
Penelope purpurascens   Plate 41, p.114

Description: 34–36. Very large but rather slender with long neck and tail. Mostly dark olive brown with short, bushy crest and *prominent bare red throat; chest and breast lightly streaked with white*; lower back and tail more chestnut.

Similar species: As long as a curassow, but much more slender with proportionately longer neck and tail. See Baudo Guan (below).

Status and distribution: Locally still fairly common in more remote forests in lowlands and foothills throughout, but overall range and numbers now much reduced by deforestation and heavy hunting pressure. Recorded from entire Caribbean slope; on Pacific slope recorded from Chiriquí (where now virtually extirpated, though a few still survive in remaining forests on the Burica Peninsula, with two being seen on June 26, 1982; Ridgely), southern Veraguas to western side of Azuero Peninsula (where also virtually extirpated, though still numerous in the remaining forested areas in the extreme south, e.g. around Cerro Hoya; F. Delgado), and Canal area (formerly) and eastern Panama province (now largely restricted to upper Bayano valley) east through Darién. Still ranges in reduced numbers in more extensive forested areas on Caribbean side of Canal area; perhaps most numerous on Barro Colorado Island.

Habits: Mainly arboreal, usually being found in pairs (less often small groups) which travel through the canopy walking along branches, these guans (known locally as "pavas") have an elegant carriage and usually move gracefully — only when they are suddenly disturbed do they flop off heavily and clumsily, often accompanied by loud honking calls, e.g. *quonk, quonk, quonk.* A wing-whirring display in which they glide from the top of one tree to another producing a fast vibrating (mechanical) noise is heard mostly in the pre-dawn darkness during the dry season. Highly esteemed gamebirds, guans are quickly reduced in numbers by even light hunting pressure, but they seem better able to persist, albeit in reduced numbers, than do curassows, becoming wary and secretive. In wild areas, such as the more remote parts of Darién, they can be almost stolidly tame.

Range: Mexico to northern Venezuela and western Ecuador.

Note: Baudo Guan (*Penelope ortoni*) of western Colombia and Ecuador may occur in eastern Darién as it has been recorded close to the Panama border (Río Jurado). It is much smaller (26 in) than the Crested Guan, and feathers of underparts are less conspicuously edged with whitish.

GREAT CURASSOW
Crax rubra   Plate 41

Description: 34–38. Restricted to more remote forest. *Very large.* Male *black* with rounded crest of recurved feathers and *globular yellow knob on base of upper mandible*; belly and tail-coverts white. Female lacks yellow knob on bill, is variable in color, mostly rufous brown or blackish washed with rufous, *head, neck, and rounded crest black barred with white*; tail barred buff and brown; belly barred buff and black. Subadult male lacks yellow knob on bill.

Similar species: This magnificent bird should not be confused. Crested Guan is more lightly built, with bare red throat, white streaking below.

Status and distribution: Formerly widespread and presumably numerous in lowland forest on both slopes, the curassow (known locally as the pavón) is one of the first birds to disappear as a region becomes accessible and settled. It is now *very* local in Panama, and nowhere does it seem to be numerous, even in the most remote parts occurring in small, diminishing numbers. Recorded from entire Caribbean slope, and on Pacific slope from Chiriquí (where it once ranged up to about 1500 m: 5000 ft in the western Chiriquí highlands) to western side of Azuero Peninsula, and from Canal area east through Darién. There are no recent reports at all from Pacific western Panama, and few from anywhere on the Caribbean slope (these coming from Bocas del Toro and the Canal area, though it presumably still also occurs in northern Veraguas and San Blas). Its main stronghold in Panama now appears to be eastern Panama province (especially the upper Bayano River valley) and Darién; can be found regularly in small numbers around Cana and on the lower slopes of Cerro Pirre. In Canal area a few manage to hang on, amazingly enough, in the Pipeline Road area, though you have to be *very* lucky to encounter any; one's chances are maximized by wading one of the many small streams which the road crosses. So imperilled is the curassow in Panama that a strong case can be made for attempting to introduce a population into the still largely inviolate forests of Coiba Island; these forests would appear to be suitable habitat, but evidently the curassow has been prevented from reaching them by its inability to cross the ocean barrier (unlike the Scarlet Macaw).

Habits: Curassows are mainly terrestrial, walking about in pairs or (less often) small groups, feeding on fallen fruit. When disturbed they usually flush into trees and there perch motionless, hoping to remain undetected; if pressed too closely, they burst from cover and may fly for a long distance (too far to follow). Males give a long low booming or humming call which constitutes its territorial "song"; of very low frequency, it is extremely ventriloquial and difficult to track to its source (though hunters are good at it!). When alarmed, either sex will give a high pitched whistled *wheep, wheep, wheeeew*, or simply a *whee-eep ?*; this call will occasionally reveal the presence of an otherwise unseen bird. No bird is more desired for the table than the "pavón" in Panama; as a result, though it may be quite tame in areas where hunting is limited or nonexistent, it quickly becomes secretive and wary, and doubtless it is this characteristic which has permitted its survival for so long in, for instance, the Canal area.

Range: Eastern Mexico to western Ecuador.

PHEASANTS, GROUSE, TURKEYS, AND QUAIL:
Phasianidae (7)

This family is most highly developed in the Old World, especially in southern Asia, with only a few groups native to America (these including the two species of turkeys, endemic to North America). It is not very well represented in Panama: one species of quail found in Pacific western savannas is obviously related to the familiar Northern Bobwhite group, and there are six species of infrequently seen wood-quail in humid forests. All Panama species are terrestrial, ranging in small groups (called coveys) and best known from their far-carrying calls. It should be noted that the vocalizations of the various wood-quail species, while distinctive as a group, are confusingly similar to each other — so much so that where more than one species occurs they often cannot be distinguished (at least on the basis of present knowledge). Quail and wood-quail eat a variety of food, mainly seeds and berries but supplemented with insects and other invertebrates. The simple nest is placed on the ground.

MARBLED WOOD-QUAIL
Odontophorus gujanensis   Plate 1

Description: 9–11. *Bare skin around eye orange to red.* Short, bushy crest varying from brown to blackish; *otherwise mostly dark brown*, finely barred and vermiculated with black and buff; neck often gray and scapulars streaked with whitish.

Similar species: More uniformly colored than any other wood-quail, and the only one with reddish orbital area. Black-eared Wood-Quail has dark orbital area, black foreneck, and rufous crown and underparts. Tinamous, while also uniformly colored, are very differently shaped, with smaller heads, longer and more slender necks, and tail-less appearance.

Status and distribution: Rare to locally fairly common in humid forest in lowlands and foothills (to about 1500 m: 5000 ft) on Caribbean slope from Coclé east through San Blas; on Pacific slope known from eastern Panama province (Bayano River valley; formerly west to the Tocumen/Cerro Azul area) and Darién; now very local in lowlands of western Chiriquí (*castigatus*), with only recent record being a pair heard on the Burica Peninsula on June 26, 1982 (Ridgely). Deforestation and hunting have reduced its numbers and overall range substantially; this is especially the case in Chiriquí. Now scarce in the Canal area, even where forest remains; small numbers are still found in the Pipeline Road area (especially).

Habits: Usually found in small groups on the forest floor. Rather shy in most areas, keeping to dense cover and usually preferring to escape by crouching and hiding or by running (not flying). Best known from its very fast rollicking ringing musical call, *córcorovado, córcorovado, córcorovado* . . . (also interpreted as "perro-mulato"), repeated many times for up to several minutes, given most often at dawn or dusk. The call is antiphonal, the male giving the *córcoro*, the female the *vado*.

Range: Costa Rica to Bolivia and Amazonian Brazil.

BLACK-EARED WOOD-QUAIL
Odontophorus melanotis   Plate 1

Description: 9–10. *Bare orbital area purplish blue in male, black in female.* Crown and short crest rufous, feathers of crest tipped with blackish brown; otherwise dark olive brown above mottled with black and buffy; *sides of head, throat, and foreneck blackish; remaining underparts chestnut.* Female similar but brown on sides of neck, throat, and foreneck (no black).

Similar species: Marbled Wood-Quail is more uniform dark brown (not chestnut below), lacks rufous crest, and has red or orange (not dark) orbital area.

Status and distribution: Rare to uncommon and local in humid forest in lowlands and (especially) foothills on Caribbean slope, where recorded from Bocas del Toro (locally down to near sea level), Veraguas, eastern Colon province, and San Blas (locally down to near sea level in Cangandi area; J. Blake); on Pacific slope recorded from Veraguas foothills (Santa Fé), Panama province (Cerro Campana and Cerro Azul/Jefe), and eastern Darién (Cerro Quía and Cerro Pirre); recorded mostly 450–1050 m (1500–3500 ft), locally lower and on Cerro Pirre up to over 1500 m (5000 ft). No known records since the mid 1970s from foothills of Panama province, but regularly encountered (at least heard) on slopes of Cerro Pirre.

Habits: Little known in Panama. A covey on Cerro Jefe was rather unsuspicious, and uttered soft peeping notes before scurrying up the rather open slope of a forested ravine. In Costa Rica reported to forage on the forest floor in small bands; the call, heard mostly in the early morning but also in the late afternoon, is a repeated *kláwcoo kláwcoo* . . . sometimes reversed to *kookláwk* (Slud).

Range: Honduras to eastern Panama.

Note: Middle American birds (*O. melanotis*) are here considered specifically distinct from those found in western Colombia and western Ecuador (true *O. erythrops*, Rufous-fronted Wood-Quail), though the 1983 AOU Check-list considered them conspecific, as do most other recent authors. The ranges of these two distinctly different wood-quail approach each other closely near the Panama–Colombia boundary with no evidence of any intergradation.

BLACK-BREASTED WOOD-QUAIL
Odontophorus leucolaemus   Plate 1

Description: 9–9½. Known only from western highlands. Dark brown above (more blackish on crown and short crest) finely vermiculated with black; *throat usually white, sides of head and neck and most of underparts black* with dull white barring on belly. Considerable individual variation: some birds blacker above with throat speckled with black or even wholly black, others brighter brown above and below (especially on breast).

Similar species: The only Panama wood-quail with largely black head and underparts.

Status and distribution: Uncommon to rare and local in humid forest in foothills and lower highlands (990–1560 m: 3300–5200 ft) of Bocas del Toro, Chiriquí, Veraguas, and Coclé (one old specimen of uncertain locality); most records are from Caribbean slope. Regularly heard in the Fortuna area of central Chiriquí.

Habits: Not well known, and like other wood-quail, very infrequently seen. Ranges forest floor in pairs or small groups; upon an observer's approach, they usually crouch, hoping to avoid detection, but if pressed too closely they flush with a sudden whir, generally not to be seen again. Sometimes a flushed bird will land on a low limb more or less in the open. The call in Costa Rica is reported to be a rushing gabble which breaks

out suddenly from several individuals, two sets of paired syllables, the first accented, repeated over and over (Slud); there is variation, however, and at times this call is difficult to distinguish from that of the Black-eared Wood-Quail.

Range: Costa Rica and western Panama.

TACARCUNA WOOD-QUAIL
Odontophorus dialeucos   Plate 1

Description: 9–10. Found only in highlands of eastern Darién. *Crown and crest black spotted very lightly with white, superciliary white*, neck brown becoming buff on hind-neck; otherwise dull brown above, vermiculated with black; *throat and upper chest white, lower throat crossed by a blackish band*; remaining underparts dull buffy brown mottled with black.

Similar species: The only wood-quail recorded in its restricted range.

Status and distribution: Reported fairly common in forest in highlands of eastern Darién (Cerro Tacarcuna, Cerro Malí), above 1050 m (3500 ft). Discovered only in 1963.

Habits: Little known. A terrestrial forest species, found in pairs or small groups. One was seen perched 7.5 m (25 ft) up in a small tree (Wetmore).

Range: Eastern Panama and adjacent extreme northwestern Colombia.

SPOTTED WOOD-QUAIL
Odontophorus guttatus   Plate 1

Description: 9½–10½. Found only in western Chiriquí highlands. Mostly dark olive brown with blackish crown and rufous crest, wings speckled with white spots; *throat and foreneck blackish streaked with white*; remaining underparts grayish brown *with small elongated black-bordered white spots*. Some birds are brighter brown above and below.

Similar species: The only Panama wood-quail that is spotted below (though the spots are sometimes hard to see in the dim light of the forest). Black-breasted Wood-Quail has white throat (usually) and mostly black sides of head and underparts (no rufous on head).

Status and distribution: Fairly common in montane forest and mature secondary woodland in the highlands of western Chiriquí; recorded mainly 1050–2400 m (3500–8000 ft). This species of wood-quail seems capable of remaining reasonably numerous despite substantial habitat disturbance and fragmentation, more so than any of its Panama congeners; it is still quite common, for instance, in forests on Finca Lerida above Boquete, but there as elsewhere heard far more often than it is seen.

Habits: Like other wood-quail shy and not often seen, ranging the forest floor in small coveys. The call somewhat resembles the Marbled Wood-Quail's, a loud rapidly repeated series of whistled phrases, often antiphonal, *whípa, wipeé-o* . . ., . heard mostly in the early morning.

Range: Southern Mexico to Pacific western Panama.

TAWNY-FACED QUAIL
Rhynchortyx cinctus   Plate 1

Description: 7–8. Male has *sides of head bright tawny* with narrow dark brown stripe through eye; otherwise brown above, mottled with gray and buff on back, wings barred and spotted with black and buff; *throat and breast gray,* lower underparts cinnamon-buff to whitish, flanks lightly barred with black. Female mostly brown with *narrow, pale buffyish superciliary;* throat whitish, chest brown, *lower underparts whitish barred with black.*

Similar species: *Odontophorus* wood-quail are considerably larger. Male easily recognized by its bright tawny face, female by its overall brown appearance and barred lower underparts.

Status and distribution: Rare and local in humid forest in lowlands and foothills on Caribbean slope from Canal area eastward; on Pacific slope known from one 1951 sighting from Cerro Campana, western Panama province, and from eastern Panama province (Cerro Azul/Jefe area, at least formerly, eastward) and Darién (where recorded up to at least 1410 m: 4700 ft). Not recorded from any definite locality in western Panama, though the original nineteenth-century specimens came from "Veragua", a term that then encompassed most of the western area. Only recently found in Canal area (1968; J. Karr *et al.*), where still reported only from Pipeline Road; here, as elsewhere, it is doubtless much overlooked, especially as it seems not to have a loud advertising call which reveals its presence (unlike the *Odontophorus* wood-quails).

Habits: A terrestrial quail, shy and very infrequently encountered. Apparently usually ranges in pairs (though coveys of up to eight birds have been reported); generally they freeze or scurry off upon being accidentally discovered. Disturbed birds have been heard to give a fast nervous cheeping note, reminiscent of the Northern Bobwhite (*Colinus virginianus*) under similar circumstances (J. Karr).

Range: Honduras to northwestern Ecuador.

CRESTED BOBWHITE
Colinus cristatus   Plate 41

Description: 8–9. *Crown, prominent pointed crest, and face buff to white*, hindneck and sides of neck black spotted with white; otherwise brown above spotted and vermiculated with black; buff to chestnut below, with *prominent white spots on breast and flanks*, barred with black on belly. Female similar but duller, crown black and crest brown, throat streaked with black.

Status and distribution: Fairly common in savannas and open scrubby areas in lowlands on Pacific slope from western Chiriquí to western Panama province (Playa Coronado to base of Cerro Campana), ranging to above 1200 m (4000 ft) around Boquete in western Chiriquí; commonest in Herrera, less numerous east of Coclé. Two nineteenth-century specimens labeled "Panama Railroad" may be attributable to the then more open conditions of that area; the only subsequent report from Canal area is a sighting of a small covey near Contractor's Hill in southwestern sector on August 10, 1969 (H. A. Hespenheide). Apparently absent from savannas of eastern Panama province though they would seem to be suitable.

Habits: Similar in most respects to the Northern Bobwhite (*C. virginianus*). Usually found in small coveys on ground; rather shy, generally keeping in or close to cover. Males have an unmistakable, whistled call similar to the northern bird's, though it is faster and huskier, usually triple-noted *quoit bob-white?,* sometimes double-noted, *oh, wheet.* Seems to call mainly during the rainy season.

Range: Guatemala to the Guianas and northeastern Brazil.

Note: Includes the *leucopogon* group of Guatemala to central Costa Rica; this was formerly treated as a distinct species (Spot-bellied Bobwhite), but was considered conspecific with *C. cristatus* in the 1983 AOU Check-list. "True" *cristatus* has recently spread into southwestern Costa Rica, in the Golfo Dulce lowlands.

RAILS, GALLINULES, AND COOTS: Rallidae (15)

This is a cosmopolitan group of small to medium-sized, mostly marsh and swamp inhabiting birds. Many species are secretive (some are crepuscular and even nocturnal) and difficult to study, and a number of the species recorded from Panama are still very poorly known. Wood-rails are relatively large, brightly patterned, almost chicken-like birds of wet forests, swamps, and mangroves. Typical rails have fairly long bills; the crakes have short bills and are smaller; both groups favor marshes and wet meadows. Gallinules and coots are more birds of open water, swimming regularly and the coot (with lobed toes) diving expertly. All members of the family eat a variety of plant and animal matter. The nest is generally on or near the ground in dense vegetation, though in the wood-rails it is placed in a bush or low branch of a tree.

WHITE-THROATED CRAKE
Laterallus albigularis   Plate 1

Description: 6. Short bill dull pale greenish; legs dull yellowish brown. Mostly warm brown above, brighter chestnut on hindneck; throat white, with *sides of head and neck, and breast bright rufous*; belly white, with *flanks and crissum boldly barred black*. Birds from Bocas del Toro and western Caribbean Veraguas (*cinereiceps*) have crown and sides of head gray.
Similar species: Uniform Crake is larger, with red legs, lacks black and white barring on belly. Gray-breasted Crake has head and breast gray (no rufous below).
Status and distribution: Common in marshes, damp pastures, and grassy or tangled areas near streams or ditches on entire Caribbean slope, and on Pacific slope in Chiriquí and southern Veraguas, and from Coclé and western Panama province eastward; mostly in lowlands, but in western Chiriquí ranges regularly up in lower highlands to around 1200 m (4000 ft); found also on Coiba Island. Widespread in suitable areas throughout the Canal area.
Habits: The most numerous small rail in Panama, though it is usually secretive and hard to more than glimpse. Very difficult to actually flush (unless almost literally cornered, the bird preferring to slip away within dense cover), but can sometimes be seen feeding more or less in the open in the early morning and toward dusk. Its call is very distinctive, and will be heard much more often than the bird is seen, a long rattling descending churring, *chirrrrrrrrrr*. Birds regularly call almost at one's feet and yet manage to remain invisible.
Range: Honduras to western Ecuador.

GRAY-BREASTED CRAKE
Laterallus exilis   Plate 1

Description: 6. Seemingly rare and local (perhaps in part just overlooked). Short bill dusky above, greenish below and at base of maxilla; legs yellowish brown. *Head, neck, and breast gray, contrasting with bright chestnut nape and upper back*; above otherwise olive brown, wing-coverts sometimes with some narrow white barring; throat and belly whitish, flanks and crissum barred with blackish.
Similar species: White-throated Crake has head and breast rufous (not gray), but contrast between gray head and brown back of *cinereiceps* race of that species is reminiscent of Gray-breasted Crake (especially in a flushed bird). See also Colombian and Paint-billed Crakes, and the Black Rail.
Status and distribution: Known only from four records from four widely scattered localities: one taken on Coiba Island on January 28, 1956 (Wetmore); one taken at Puerto Obaldía, San Blas, on March 14, 1963 (Wetmore); one seen at Fort Sherman, on Caribbean side of Canal area, on June 9, 1977 (J. Wall and D. Wilcove); and one seen at Tocumen, eastern Panama province, on February 27, 1983 (D. Wolf *et al.*). Another, purchased alive at the Panama city market in 1961 by Mrs Ricardo Marciaq, lived at the Summit Gardens Zoo until at least 1964. In South America recorded from tall grass bordering lakes, grassy marshes, and wet meadows and pastures. In Panama probably more widespread in suitable habitat than the paucity of records would seem to indicate.
Habits: Furtive and generally almost impossible to see casually in its dense habitat; in early morning occasionally one may forage just out from cover. Very hard to flush. More likely to be recorded once its vocalizations are known; these are several, but include a descending churring similar to White-throated Crake's but shorter and not as steady, and irregularly paced single

tinkling notes. They respond to tape playback of both of these calls.

Range: Belize south very locally to northern Bolivia, Paraguay, and Amazonian Brazil.

Note: See F. G. Stiles and D. J. Levey (*Condor* 90(3): 607–612, 1988) for information on this species' occurrence and behavior in Costa Rica.

BLACK RAIL
Laterallus jamaicensis

Description: 5¾. One record. *Bill blackish;* legs greenish. *Head, neck and most of underparts dark gray;* nape dark chestnut, with remaining upperparts dark brownish gray *lightly spotted with white;* flanks and crissum blackish narrowly barred with white.

Similar species: Resembles slightly larger Gray-breasted Crake but darker below and with blackish (not partially greenish) bill and diagnostic white spotting above.

Status and distribution: One was reported flushed, and a domed nest with three eggs was collected, near a marshy depression in a field with tall grass northeast of Tocumen, eastern Panama province, on July 6, 1963 (S. T. Harty and G. B. Reynard *et al.*). There long existed some doubt as to whether this record pertained to this species or to the Gray-breasted Crake (the distinctions between the two were not well understood at the time). The eggs are slightly larger than those reported for Black Rail elsewhere (*fide* J. Bond), but the bird's vocalization, which was recorded by Reynard, is unlike anything known for Gray-breasted Crake: it resembles the usual call of North American Black Rails except for the addition of an extra initial syllable, *dídidee-dunk* (but J. Weske indicates that Maryland Black Rails *do* give such an extra initial syllable up to about 25% of the time; cf. Ripley, 1977, p. 204). There have been no subsequent records despite several searches, both at the precise spot and nearby.

Range: Very locally from United States to Guatemala, in Panama, Peru, and northern Chile, and in Greater Antilles; uncertain records from Honduras and Costa Rica.

CLAPPER RAIL
Rallus longirostris

Description: 14. One recent Bocas del Toro record. Rather long, slightly decurved bill blackish above and yellow-orange below; legs buffy brownish. Crown blackish, with *facial area gray;* otherwise *quite boldly streaked*

blackish and grayish olive above, with dull rufescent wing-coverts; throat white, *breast cinnamon-rufous,* and belly whitish, with *flanks and under tail-coverts boldly banded blackish.*

Similar species: Nothing really similar in Panama. Wood-rails lack the conspicuous banding below and the streaking above, etc. See also Spotted Rail.

Status and distribution: One was mist-netted by W. Martinez at Miramar, Bocas del Toro (23 miles west of Chiriquí Grande) on March 19, 1985, after having been seen by him there since January 25; it was placed in captivity, but died several weeks later. The prepared skin, unfortunately unsexed, was ultimately sent to ANSP. Its racial identity remains uncertain; careful comparison at ANSP, MCZ, and (courtesy of R. Banks) USNM indicates that it cannot be assigned to any of the numerous described races in either the *longirostris* (Clapper Rail) or *elegans* (King Rail) complexes, here regarded as conspecific. Presumably it represents a new undescribed subspecies, but more material is needed before this can be safely done. The description above is taken directly from the skin, and from photographs of the bird before it died; its measurements are: wing 144.5 mm, exposed culmen 49.2 mm, culmen 54 mm, and tarsus 49.1 mm.

Habits: The Bocas bird frequented a freshwater pond with grassy margins just back from the shoreline of the Chiriquí Lagoon. It was shy, but on several occasions was observed capturing insects and crustaceans, often washing the latter before swallowing them (W. Martinez).

Range: United States south locally into Mexico and Belize; West Indies; very locally in coastal South America south to northwestern Peru and eastern Brazil.

Note: Ripley (1977, pp. 125–136) is here followed in considering *R. elegans* (King Rail) as conspecific with *R. longirostris*. The 1983 AOU Check-list considered them distinct species.

GRAY-NECKED WOOD-RAIL
Aramides cajanea   Plate 1

Description: 14–16. Iris and eye-ring red; *rather long bill, yellowish at base, more greenish at tip;* legs red. Head and rather long neck mostly *gray,* browner on crown and more whitish on throat; above otherwise olive brown; breast and sides cinnamon-rufous; *belly, rump, and tail black* (tail often cocked up); primaries rufous-chestnut (usually concealed except in flight). Immature duller with dusky bill and legs.

Similar species: The largest rail in Panama, relatively brightly colored and patterned. Very local Rufous-necked Wood-Rail is smaller and has rufous head and neck.

Status and distribution: Fairly common and widespread along forested streams and rivers, in swampy wooded areas, and in mangrove swamps in lowlands on both slopes; ranges locally up into forested foothills (to about 1200 m: 4000 ft) in Chiriquí, Los Santos, and Darién; found also on Coiba and Cébaco Islands and the Pearl Islands. In Canal area more numerous on Caribbean slope.

Habits: Usually keeps to thick cover and not regularly seen; sometimes, however, feeds partially in the open though never far from concealment. Often feeds at night, but also roosts well above ground. Coastally feeds largely on crabs. Best known from its loud cackling calls, often given in a duet, a rather deliberate repeated *cok, cok*, and a hoarse cackling *co haak* or *co wéy hee* over and over. Calls most often in early morning, late afternoon, and at night. Known in Panama as "cocaleca" or "coclé" because of its calls.

Range: Central Mexico to Bolivia, northern Argentina, and Uruguay.

RUFOUS-NECKED WOOD-RAIL
Aramides axillaris   Plate 1

Description: 12. *Very local in mangroves.* Bill yellowish green; legs red. *Head, neck, breast, and sides rufous-chestnut*, with throat more whitish; *area on nape and upper back bluish gray*, with upperparts otherwise olive brown; *belly, rump, and tail black*; primaries rufous-chestnut (usually concealed except in flight).

Similar species: Overall aspect similar to much commoner Gray-necked Wood-Rail (which *also* can be found in mangroves); Rufous-neck is smaller and has entirely rufous head and foreneck. Uniform Crake is smaller with shorter bill and legs, and is more or less uniform rufous brown (lacking black on rearparts and gray on upper back).

Status and distribution: Apparently rare (but doubtless in part only overlooked) in mangrove swamps on both coasts; seemingly very local, and recorded from only three localities: around Almirante, Bocas del Toro; on the Río Pocrí at Puerto Aguadulce, Coclé; and on Caribbean side of Canal area (one seen at Fort Sherman on

December 28, 1974; D. Gardner). Perhaps more widespread.

Habits: Generally very secretive, and most apt to be seen at low tide when they may emerge from the mangroves in order to forage for crabs on tidal flats and banks (though rarely far from cover). In South America also recorded from floor of humid forest, even at some distance inland from mangroves. The call in Mexico is reported to be a duet, consisting of loud, irregularly paced *kip* and *kow* notes, e.g. *kip-kow-kip, kow-kip-kow, kip-kowkip-kow, kow, kow, kow-kip* . . . (B. Whitney).

Range: Mexico south locally to western Ecuador and the Guianas.

UNIFORM CRAKE
Amaurolimnas concolor   Plate 1

Description: 8–8½. Rare. *Bill short*, thick, yellowish green; legs red. *Mostly dull rufous brown*, more olive brown on rear crown hindneck, and back; *brighter rufous brown below*, paler on throat.

Similar species: Should be recognized by uniform brown color and the short bill. See Rufous-necked Wood-Rail.

Status and distribution: Apparently rare or local, at least infrequently reported. Known from western Chiriquí (Boquerón), western Bocas del Toro (Almirante area), Veraguas (Chitra), Caribbean slope of Canal area (one seen at Achiote Road on January 4, 1975; Ridgely), San Blas (Mandinga), Darién (single sightings from El Real and Matuganti; Wetmore, Ridgely), and the Pearl Islands (San José).

Habits: Favors damp thickets and second-growth woodland near water or swampy areas; usually not in marshes. Extremely furtive though occasionally one will be seen foraging in the semiopen on the shady forest floor, when they have the aspect of a small, short-billed wood-rail. Its song is a series of six to nine upslurred whistles which rise and then fall, *Tooee, Tooeee, TOOEEE, Tooeee, tooee, tooee-twee-tui*; also gives a whistled *toooo* call (F. G. Stiles).

Range: Southern Mexico south locally to Bolivia, Amazonian and southeastern Brazil, and Guyana; Jamaica (perhaps extinct).

SORA
Porzana carolina   Plate 3

Descriptions: 8–9. A plump little rail with *stout, short, yellow bill* and greenish legs. *Black*

face patch and throat (smaller in female); brownish above streaked with black and white; *sides of head and most of underparts gray*, barred with black and white on sides and flanks, lower belly white. Immature lacks black facial area and is buffier below.

Similar species: Larger than the breeding crakes of Panama. Can be known in any plumage by the yellow bill, barred sides, and lack of rufous brown in plumage.

Status and distribution: Locally fairly common winter resident (late September–early April) in freshwater marshes and damp grassy areas in lowlands on both slopes; perhaps somewhat erratic or irregular in numbers, though given proper conditions can be numerous. On Caribbean slope recorded from Bocas del Toro, Veraguas, Canal area, and San Blas; on Pacific slope from Chiriquí (so far only in lower highlands around Volcán, where probably regular in small numbers, but likely also in lowlands), Canal area, and eastern Panama province; recorded also from Coiba Island. In some winters numerous and easily seen in the Tocumen area, eastern Panama province.

Habits: Generally keeps to cover and not easily seen, though sometimes skulks partially in the open. More easily flushed than most rails. Utters a sharp *keek* when disturbed; also gives a distinctive descending whinny.

Range: Breeds in North America; winters from southern United States to central Peru and Guyana.

YELLOW-BREASTED CRAKE
Porzana flaviventer   Plate 1

Description: 5½. Local in marshes. *Very small*. Short, dusky bill; *legs yellow*. Crown and stripe through eye black, superciliary white; otherwise buffy brown above streaked with whitish and black; throat and belly white, *sides of neck and breast buffy*; sides, flanks, and belly barred boldly with black.

Similar species: A tiny mostly buffy crake, the smallest rail in Panama, and easily recognized.

Status and distribution: Local in freshwater marshes and grassy areas near water (often floating vegetation around margin of lakes); Wetmore found it fairly common along the Chagres River between Gamboa and Juan Mina (and there are a few recent reports), and there are also scattered records from western Bocas del Toro (a 1956 sighting at Changuinola; Eisenmann), eastern Chiriquí (one collected and another seen at Playa Jobo south of Las Lajas on January 8, 1955;

Wetmore), Caribbean coast of Canal area (three seen at Galeta Island on January 2, 1984; D. Scott), and eastern Panama province (several sightings from Tocumen); recorded also from Coiba Island (one seen on April 4, 1976; Ridgely).

Habits: Walks and climbs through grass and floating vegetation, often perching and foraging partially in the open during the first hour of daylight. Flushes quite easily, dangling its yellow legs, but quickly pitches back into cover. In Colombia heard to give a hoarse, slightly downscale *zeee-eee-eee-eee* (W. McKay), and in the West Indies a loud ringing almost scraping *clureéco* (G. B. Reynard).

Range: Southern Mexico south locally to northern Argentina and central Brazil; Greater Antilles.

Note: Ocellated Crake (*Micropygia schomburgkii*), found locally in savannas of tropical South America, has been collected once in southwestern Costa Rica and is to be watched for in Panama. It is slightly larger than Yellow-breasted Crake (5½–6 in), mostly ochraceous with prominent black-edged white spots on upperparts, and lacking barring below; its legs are red.

COLOMBIAN CRAKE
Neocrex columbianus   Plate 1

Description: 7½–8. Very local. *Bill yellowish green with red at base* and black tip; *legs red*. Head and most of underparts slaty gray, with hindneck and upperparts brownish olive; throat whitish, lower belly and under tail-coverts pale buff (*with no barring*).

Similar species: Resembles Paint-billed Crake (and the two have been found together at one site), but that species is barred on lower underparts. See also Gray-breasted Crake.

Status and distribution: Known from only two localities, but likely overlooked. The type specimen of the race *ripleyi* was taken by G. Van Horn on November 8, 1965, in a small marshy area on Achiote Road, just beyond the former Canal area border in western Colon province. In February 1982, Colombian Crakes were discovered at Tocumen marsh, eastern Panama province (D. Wolf *et al.*), and they have been seen there on several occasions since, mostly as they congregate near drying ditches. A juvenile, believed still incapable of flight, was seen on February 28, 1982, indicating almost certain breeding here (R. Behrstock, *Am. Birds 37*(6): 956–957, 1983).

Habits: The Tocumen birds have invariably

been seen in the early morning as they skulked along the edges of channels and pools with some standing water, and they rarely stayed in the open for very long. It remains uncertain whether Colombian Crakes are permanently resident in this area, and also whether they only recently appeared in the area, or had been there all along but were overlooked. A specimen would be helpful in order to determine the subspecies involved (conceivably nominate *columbianus* and not *ripleyi*?).

Range: Central Panama to southwestern Ecuador.

PAINT-BILLED CRAKE
Neocrex erythrops   Plate 3

Description: 7½–8. Very local. *Bill yellowish green with red at base* and black tip; *legs red. Head and most of underparts gray*, with hindneck and upperparts brownish olive; throat whitish, *lower belly and crissum boldly barred black and white*.

Similar species: The similar Colombian Crake lacks barring on lower underparts. Gray-breasted Crake is smaller, lacks red on bill and has brownish (not red) legs, and has contrasting bright chestnut on upper back.

Status and distribution: Known from only two localities. Two were collected by W. Martinez and D. C. Booth on November 10, 1981, about 6 km west of the Changuinola airport in western Bocas del Toro; numerous others were seen in the area at that time, mostly as they foraged at dawn and dusk along roadside ditches adjacent to rice fields. Some have been seen in the same area as recently as October 1988 (D. and L. Engleman). Several were also seen at Tocumen marsh in eastern Panama province in late February 1982 (records at least 21–28 February; D. Wolf *et al.*), at the same time and in the same situation as somewhat larger numbers of Colombian Crakes were being seen; unlike the latter, however, no Paint-billeds have been recorded since. One of the Bocas del Toro birds was eventually received by the USNM, where it was examined by S. D. Ripley and found to represent *olivascens*, the wide-ranging race found east of the Andes in South America (nominate *erythrops* being restricted to western Peru and the Galapagos).

Habits: Similar to Colombian Crake. Voice is described as a guttural, buzzy, frog-like *qur-r-r-rk* or *auuk*, sometimes given in series, *qurrrk, auuk, qurrrk, auuk* . . . (S.

Hilty, from P. Schwartz recording). It seems likely that both populations represent recent incursions, but it remains to be seen whether they will stay and breed, and if so whether sympatry with the closely related Colombian Crake can be maintained. It should further be noted that the two recent United States records (specimens from Virginia and Texas), and its apparently recent establishment on the Galapagos Islands, lend some credence to the hypothesis that the species may be undergoing a genuine increase and range expansion.

Range: Colombia and the Guianas south locally to northern Argentina and eastern Brazil (west of the Andes only in Peru), and on Galapagos Islands; outlying (permanent?) populations in Panama, and two recent records from United States.

SPOTTED RAIL
Pardirallus maculatus   Plate 1

Description: 10. Very local. Virtually unmistakable, as *boldly spotted and barred black and white*. Rather long slightly decurved bill greenish yellow with small red spot at base; legs reddish. *Above mostly black spotted and streaked with white*, wings browner with white streaking; *throat and foreneck black spotted with white, breast and belly barred black and white*, with crissum whitish. Immature has black basically replaced by brown, with underparts varying from almost uniform sooty to grayish olive, with amount of barring variable but strongest on belly and flanks.

Status and distribution: Only recently confirmed as a breeding resident in Panama, an adult with a small chick was seen and photographed at the Tocumen marsh, eastern Panama province on January 14–21, 1978 (V. Emanuel *et al.*; see *Am. Birds* 34(2): 214–215, 1980); they have been seen at this location occasionally since (various observers). Known from only two other localities, both on Caribbean coast; an immature at Fort Sherman, in Canal area, on October 20, 1984 (D. Engleman *et al.*; this bird was in mangroves, and seems almost certainly to have been dispersing); and one seen at Mandinga, San Blas on January 22, 1957 (Wetmore).

Habits: Generally reclusive and difficult to see, usually remaining within dense marsh vegetation. However, Spotted Rails seem to regularly emerge to feed in the semiopen during the early morning, and thus if known

to be present in an area, a little patience will often be rewarded. Reported to give a four-noted whistled call, the first high and long, the other three shorter and in rapid succession (D. E. Birkenholz and D. A. Jenni, *Auk 81* (4): *558*–559, 1964).
Range: Mexico south very locally in Middle America, and in South America south to Bolivia, northern Argentina, and Uruguay; Greater Antilles.

PURPLE GALLINULE
Porphyrula martinica Plate 3

Description: 13–14. *Brilliantly colored.* Bill rather stout, red, tipped yellow; *frontal shield pale blue*; legs yellow. *Head, neck, and entire underparts deep purple to violet-blue*; back and wings bronzy green; under tail-coverts white. Immature *brown above*, bluer on wings; mostly whitish below; bill dusky.
Similar species: Beautiful adults are unmistakable; immature might be confused with immature Common Moorhen but is not as grayish and shows more white under tail. Immature jacanas, though also basically brown above and whitish below, are very differently shaped, have extremely long toes, and show much yellow on wings in flight.
Status and distribution: Fairly common to common in freshwater marshes and along edges of ponds, lakes and slow-flowing rivers (the requirement being abundant marshy vegetation) in lowlands on both slopes, ranging up to lower highlands of western Chiriquí on the Volcán Lakes; recently found also on Coiba island (common in April 1976; Ridgely), to which it has only recently spread, probably in response to the great expansion of rice cultivation there. More widespread than the Common Moorhen in the Canal area, though usually does not concentrate in as large numbers.
Habits: Less apt to be seen swimming than Common Moorhen; more often seen walking on floating vegetation, along shores, even perching and climbing about in bushes and emergent vegetation.
Range: Southeastern United States and Mexico to northern Argentina (recorded once in Uruguay and northern Chile); West Indies.

COMMON MOORHEN
Gallinula chloropus Plate 3

Description: 13–14. A chunky somewhat duck-like (swimming) or chicken-like

(perched) bird with *stout red bill* (with yellow tip) *and frontal shield*; legs greenish. Mostly slaty gray, browner on back and wings, with *white stripe on sides and flanks* and white on under tail-coverts. Immature is paler, more olive or brownish gray, with whitish sides of head and throat, gray underparts with white streaks on flanks and belly; bill brown.
Similar species: Purple Gallinule is deep violet-blue (not slaty gray) on head and underparts and lacks white flank stripe; immature Purple is brown above (not olive or grayish) and whitish on breast and belly (not grayish). American Coot has white bill and lacks the flank stripe.
Status and distribution: Locally common on freshwater lakes, ponds, and marshes in lowlands on both slopes; numbers may increase as a result of migration from the north, but known to breed in western Bocas del Toro and on both slopes of Canal area, and breeding likely in Herrera and elsewhere; ranges rarely up into lower highlands of western Chiriquí (but here almost certainly only as a migrant). Widespread in appropriate habitat throughout the Canal area, in largest (and perhaps increasing) numbers on Gatun lake and in the Pedro Miguel area, apparently in response to the spread of the hydrilla mats.
Habits: Usually seen swimming (unlike Purple Gallinule), with head nodding back and forth. Flies relatively little. Has a variety of clucks and cackles.
Range: Nearly cosmopolitan except for Australia; in America from extreme southern Canada to northern Chile and northern Argentina.
Note: Formerly called the Common Gallinule.

AMERICAN COOT
Fulica americana Plate 3

Description: 13–14. *Stout, white bill* with dark ring near tip; inconspicuous reddish brown frontal shield. *Entirely slaty gray* (blacker on head and neck) except for white under tail-coverts and white tips to secondaries (visible in flight). Immature is paler, more olive gray, with whitish on throat; bill whitish.
Similar species: Rather duck-like but note bill shape, small head and short neck pumped back and forth when swimming. Adult gallinules have red bills; immature Common Moorhen is browner than immature Coot and has dark bill and at least a suggestion of a white flank stripe.

Status and distribution: Uncommon to locally common winter resident (October–late April) on lakes and ponds in lowlands on both slopes, though not recorded from eastern Panama (easternmost reports being from eastern Panama province), and recorded occasionally up into lower highlands of western Chiriquí on the Volcán Lakes. Most numerous in Bocas del Toro; numbers seem to have declined somewhat in recent years in the Canal area, though some still winter regularly on Gatun Lake. Not known to breed in Panama, though this remains a possibility.

Habits: Usually seen swimming in open water, frequently in flocks. Dives for its food. Has various cackling notes.

Range: Breeds from North America to Nicaragua and from Colombia to Ecuador; northern birds winter at least to Panama and in West Indies.

Note: *F. ardesiaca* (Slate-colored Coot) of the Andes is maintained as a polymorphic species, following J. Fjeldsa (Bull. BOC *103* (1): 18–22, 1983).

FINFOOTS: Heliornithidae (1)

The finfoots are a small family of tropical aquatic birds, one species being found in the Americas, one in Africa, and one in southern Asia. They are shy and usually not easily observed, and are not very well known. They feed on a variety of aquatic animal life. The nest is a platform of twigs placed in a bush or low tree overhanging the water.

SUNGREBE
Heliornis fulica   Plate 1

Description: 11–12. Slender reddish bill; black-and-yellow banded webbed feet. Small head and slender neck. *Crown and hindneck black with white superciliary, a black stripe on cheeks and down sides of neck, and another white stripe down neck*; otherwise olive brown above; white below; rather wide tail black narrowly tipped white. Female has buffy cheeks.

Similar species: More slender than a grebe or duck; black and white striped head and neck is characteristic. Sunbittern is mostly brown with white striping only on face, does not swim or dive.

Status and distribution: Uncommon and local in lowlands on freshwater ponds, lakes, and quiet streams and rivers with abundant bordering vegetation; recorded only from western Bocas del Toro, Chagres River valley, eastern Panama province (La Jagua), and Darién (Tuira River). Best known from Gatun Lake and the Chagres; can be found regularly in esteros on Gigante Bay on southwestern shore of Barro Colorado Island and on middle Chagres above Gamboa.

Habits: Essentially aquatic; usually seen swimming, but not far from protective shoreline vegetation. Perches on branches hanging low over the water. Dives freely. Sometimes swims, like a grebe, with body submerged and only head and neck above water. When disturbed, flies and patters rapidly along the surface of the water. Reported to give a peculiar "bark" of one, two or three notes (L. Jewel); in Mexico the call has been described as a *eeoó, eeoó, eeoó-eeyéh, eeyéh* (M. Alvarez del Toro).

Range: Southern Mexico to northern Bolivia, northeastern Argentina and southern Brazil.

SUNBITTERNS: Eurypygidae (1)

The Sunbittern is an interesting and beautifully marked bird found along forested streams in the New World tropics. Superficially resembling a heron (but with different proportions and shorter legs), it also looks something like a large sandpiper. It is terrestrial, sedately walking and wading along streams and rivers, feeding on aquatic animal life. The nest, however, is placed on a branch of a tree some ten to twenty feet above the ground, near water's edge.

SUNBITTERN
Eurypyga helias   Plate 1

Description: 17–18. *Bill long and straight*, upper mandible black tipped orange-yellow, lower mandible orange; *short orange legs*. Head notably small, neck long and slender; *long fan-shaped tail*. Head black with narrow white stripe over eye and another across cheeks; *neck and upperparts dull chestnut vermiculated and barred with black*, wing-coverts spotted with white; tail broadly banded chestnut and black and with black vermiculations; throat white, most of remaining underparts buff narrowly barred with black, becoming whitish on belly; *wings with bright orange-rufous patches*, conspicuous in flight and in display.

Similar species: Not likely to be confused. Sungrebe (a swimming, diving bird) has black and white striped neck and white underparts.

Status and distribution: Rare to locally uncommon along forested streams in lowlands and foothills (to about 900 m: 3000 ft) on both slopes (recent records mostly from Caribbean slope and Darién); unreported from dry Pacific lowlands from eastern side of Azuero Peninsula (but recorded from Cerro Hoya in Los Santos) to western Panama province. Rare in Canal area, where in recent years recorded primarily from Pipeline Road and vicinity.

Habits: Usually seen walking deliberately on the ground along or near a stream; sometimes alights on low tree branches, especially when disturbed. Very unsuspicious and tames easily. Has a beautiful display with lowered neck, spread wings, and raised and fanned tail, thus exposing the subtle plumage details and the "sunbursts" on the wings. Utters a low hissing sound like a tire going flat when disturbed (Ridgely, J. Karr); also has an alarm call *ka, ka, ka . . .*, repeated six or eight times; and a sweet and high but very penetrating and far carrying clear note (with quality of a tinamou).

Range: Southern Mexico to northern Bolivia and central Brazil.

LIMPKINS: Aramidae (1)

The Limpkin is a large, brown, superficially ibis-like wading bird of riverbanks and tree-bordered marshes. It is rather scarce and not well known in Panama, though it enjoys a wide range in the warmer parts of the New World. It feeds largely on *Pomacea* snails. The nest is placed on the ground or low in a bush or tree, always near water.

LIMPKIN
Aramus guarauna   Plate 2

Description: 26–28. Long dark legs, long slender neck, and *long slightly drooping bill* impart a somewhat ibis-like appearance. Nominate race (found locally in most of Panama range) is dark brown with relatively narrow *white streaks on head and neck*. Birds from Bocas del Toro (*dolosus*) similar but with wider white streaks, and these extend to wings and body.

Similar species: Ibises have more slender and much more decurved bills with bare facial areas. Immature and winter adult Glossy Ibis also have white streaks on head and neck but are smaller with bare facial area, and are darker and glossier on back and underparts.

Status and distribution: Rare to uncommon and local in freshwater swamps and tree-bordered marshes, and along rivers in lowlands on both slopes; recorded only from western Bocas del Toro (east to Cricamola), Herrera (one seen south of Santa María on May 23, 1968; Ridgely), Canal area (locally on both slopes), and Darién. A small population has long been known to be present along the Chagres River above Gamboa, and this is presumably the source of the birds seen recently (first on December 22, 1984) on Barro Colorado Island, where they are now believed to be breeding (C. Handley), and elsewhere along shores of Gatun Lake, and for the occasional wandering birds seen elsewhere (even on the Pacific side, e.g. in the Pedro Miguel/Chiva Chiva area and at Howard AFB).

Habits: Infrequently seen in Panama, and very local, apparently due to lack of much suitable habitat. Often perches in bushes and low trees. Rather noisy, with a variety of loud wailing calls, *carr-rr-rao, car-rr-rao* (Wetmore). Their flight is jerky and awkward and usually not long sustained, with outstretched neck and dangling legs.

Range: Florida; southern Mexico locally to Bolivia, northern Argentina, and Uruguay; Greater Antilles.

PLOVERS AND LAPWINGS: Charadriidae (8)

The plovers are a generally distributed group of shorebirds, many favoring coastlines and freshwater borders but with other species inhabiting fields, open plains, and marshes. Most species differ from typical sandpipers in their shorter and heavier bills and chunkier proportions. Many species are highly migratory and most are gregarious. They eat a wide variety of animal matter. Most of the species recorded from Panama breed only in North America (mostly in arctic regions), occurring in Panama as transients and winter residents; some individuals of these northern breeding species also pass the summer months in Panama, without breeding (most are apparently first year birds). Two species do breed locally (Collared and Wilson's), the nest being a slight depression in the ground or beach, usually with no lining.

SOUTHERN LAPWING
Vanellus chilensis   Plate 5, p.127

Description: 13–14. Local. Unmistakable. Bill pinkish with black tip; legs pink. *Long pointed black crest.* Mostly brownish gray above with shoulders bronzy greenish; *forehead, throat patch, and breast black*; belly white. In flight has *broad rounded wings* with *prominent large white band on wing-coverts*, white rump, and black tail with narrow white tip.

Status and distribution: Uncommon to rare and local on savannas and other grassy areas near water, and along rivers; though still not numerous in Panama, it does seem to be increasing and spreading westward. Originally known mainly from eastern Panama province (Chepo/La Jagua area), with isolated records from San Blas (Puerto Obaldía) and Darién (El Real), there are a number of recent reports from Darién (lower Tuira River area), Canal area (mostly on Pacific side, but also in Chagres River valley around Gamboa and Madden Lake), eastern Colon province (where up to four were seen regularly along the Río Cascajal east of Portobelo in January–June 1987; D. Graham), and even as far west as Herrera (small numbers seemingly resident since 1981 at the Cienega Las Macanas; F. Delgado), with one also present (possibly the same individual?) at the Volcán Lakes in lower highlands of western Chiriquí from at least January 1980 to January 1988. Actual breeding seems not to have been recorded in Panama, but it is virtually certain that it is now a resident here.

Habits: This attractive, boldy patterned plover is conspicuous, favoring open areas with short grass near water. It flies with distinctive slow floppy wing beats, and is very noisy, giving its loud calls at the slightest provocation, e.g. *kehoo, kehoo . . .* or *kleek! kleek! . . .*

Range: Panama to Tierra del Fuego.

BLACK-BELLIED PLOVER
Pluvialis squatarola   Plate 5

Description: 11–13. Fairly large and chunky; short stout black bill. Nonbreeding plumage: *light grayish to brownish gray above* with whitish mottling and indistinct whitish superciliary; white below, somewhat mottled with dusky on breast. Juveniles are more streaked or mottled with brownish below. Breeding plumage: *upperparts mottled black and silvery white* (looking gray at a distance); white forecrown extending back as broad stripe around sides of head to sides of breast; *face and underparts mainly black*, with white under tail-coverts. In flight shows *white rump and mostly white tail* (latter with some coarse black barring), conspicuous white wing-stripe, and *black axillars* contrasting with white under wing-linings.

Similar species: See the much less common American Golden Plover, and also nonbreeding Red Knot.

Status and distribution: Common transient and winter resident on both slopes; uncommon in summer.

SOUTHERN LAPWING

Habits: Occurs on beaches, mudflats, and grassy areas, though most numerous on extensive tidal flats such as those at Panama Viejo and Juan Diaz. They generally occur in compact flocks only when roosting at high tide, scattering out to forage; feeding is deliberate, with the birds standing erect and motionless, then running ahead a few feet, resuming erect stance or picking at food off the surface. Usually wary. Their distinctive and lovely call, a plaintive slurred whistled *whee-er-eee*, is frequently heard.

Range: Breeds in high arctic; winters in southern United States, Middle and South America, southern Europe and Africa, southern Asia, Australia, and islands in South Pacific.

AMERICAN (LESSER) GOLDEN PLOVER
Pluvialis dominica

Description: 9–11. Overall aspect similar to Black-bellied Plover, but bill slightly slimmer. Nonbreeding plumage: grayish brown above mottled with whitish, and with *fairly prominent whitish superciliary and dusky crown*; buffy whitish below, more or less spotted or mottled with brown. Juvenile *quite heavily mottled with golden yellow on upperparts*. Breeding plumage: blackish brown above *heavily spangled with golden yellow*; white forehead extending back as broad stripe around sides of head to sides of breast; *face and underparts entirely black*. In flight shows *dark rump and wings* with only vague white wing-stripe, and grayish axillars (not black) and wing-linings.

Similar species: Black-bellied Plover is slightly larger and always shows bold white rump and wing- stripe, as well as the black axillars. At rest nonbreeding adults and juveniles can look quite alike (though Golden tends to be darker above, especially on crown, and has more obvious superciliary), so the best policy is to flush the bird whenever possible.

Status and distribution: Rare to locally uncommon transient on or near both coasts (recorded mainly late August–early November, and March–April), with a few individuals straggling through northern winter and southern months. Most reports are from Canal area, with one each from Coiba Island (one seen April 9–11, 1976; Ridgely), Herrera (one collected at Cenegón del Mangle in October 1977; F. Delgado), and Darién (one seen on March 10, 1981 at El Real; Ridgely *et al.*).

Habits: Favors grassy fields over mudflats, but sometimes also on the latter. Usually less wary than the Black-bellied Plover, with which it often occurs. The call is a clear high *queedleet*, without plaintive quality of Black-belly's call.

Range: Breeds in arctic North America; winters mostly in southern South America.

Note: Does not include *P. fulva* (Pacific Golden Plover), shown by P. G. Connors (*Auk 100*(3): 607–620, 1983) to be a distinct species, breeding sympatrically with *P. dominica* in western Alaska. We use the English names suggested by Connors; the 1983 AOU check-list called *P. dominica* the Lesser Golden Plover. The AOU Committee on Nomenclature and Classification has not yet passed on the *P. dominica/P. fulva* situation, but we suspect it will ultimately recognize both as full species, hence *fulva* is mentioned here. Pacific Golden Plover breeds in northern Siberia and western Alaska, and winters mainly on Pacific islands and coasts of Australia and southern Asia; small numbers are recorded regularly south along Pacific coast to California, and there are records from Chile and Galapagos Islands. It should thus be watched for in Panama. Distinguishing Pacific Golden Plover from American Golden requires great care, but *fulva* is slightly smaller and slimmer; nonbreeding adult and juvenile basically yellowish buff (not brownish gray) with considerable golden spotting above and golden mottling on breast (*much* more yellow than in respective plumages of American Golden, but beware molting birds), and yellowish (not whitish) superciliary.

COLLARED PLOVER
Charadrius collaris   Plate 5, p.129

Description: 5½–6. A small plover, reminiscent of the Semipalmated. *Bill slender and all black*; legs yellowish to pinkish. Grayish brown above with fairly large patch of white on forehead; *crown and nape tinged cinnamon, sometimes forming a cinnamon-rufous band around hindneck*; white below, breast crossed by black band. Immature duller with less cinnamon on head.

Similar species: Resembles the more numerous migrant Semipalmated Plover. Collared is a smaller, more dapper bird; it has a narrower, longer, all black bill, lacks the white collar of the Semipalmated, and has a larger white patch on forehead and rufous on head. Wilson's Plover is larger

COLLARED PLOVER

with white superciliary and heavy bill. See also very rare Snowy Plover.

Status and distribution: Fairly common locally after breeding season on sandy and gravelly beaches and on short grass areas in central Panama from July (rarely June) to early March. At other seasons, disperses, apparently to breeding areas on sand and gravel banks in streams and rivers, but actual breeding evidence lacking from Panama. During nonbreeding season readily found on the grass at Coco Solo and Gatun Dam, and at Fort Amador.

Habits: Always less numerous than the migrant plovers. Curiously little is known about their breeding in Panama, though birds collected and others seen on rivers in Bocas del Toro were thought to be nesting.

Range: Western and southern Mexico to Chile and central Argentina.

SNOWY PLOVER
Charadrius alexandrinus

Description: 6. Casual. *Slender black bill* and *slaty gray legs. Very pale sandy gray above*, with black forecrown and ear-coverts; forehead, sides of head, and underparts white; sides of breast black (forming an incomplete collar). Female and immature duller, showing no black on head or on partial collar (which is brownish).

Similar species: Much paler above than any of the other small plovers; most like Collared Plover but with dark gray (not pale) legs. See also the equally pale nonbreeding Sanderling.

Status and distribution: Apparently a casual winter visitant, but perhaps somewhat overlooked. Only two records: one collected at Cocoplum, Bocas del Toro, on October 30, 1927 (R. Benson, specimen in AMNH); and one taken at Punta Chame, western Panama

province, on December 30, 1986 (from a flock of up to 20 birds seen between November 28, 1926, and January 4, 1987; G. Castro and J. P. Myers, specimen in ANSP). Both are of the North American race *nivosus*.

Habits: In its normal range found primarily on sand flats, beaches, alkaline ponds, etc.

Range: Breeds locally in southern and western United States, Mexico, the West Indies, and from coastal Ecuador to northern Chile; also in Europe, North Africa, and Asia; North American birds winter south to Mexico, casually to Costa Rica and Panama.

Note: For details on the Punta Chame record, see G. Castro and J. P. Myers (*Am. Birds 42(3): 374, 1988*).

WILSON'S PLOVER
Charadrius wilsonia   Plate 5

Description: 7–8. *Rather long heavy black bill; legs dull pinkish.* Brown above, sometimes tinged with cinnamon on back of head and ear-coverts; forehead, broad eye-stripe, narrow collar on hindneck, and underparts white; *breast crossed by single broad black band.* Female has brownish breast band.

Similar species: Immature Semipalmated Plover also has an all-black bill, but it is shorter and slimmer than in Wilson's, and its legs are yellowish (not dull pinkish). Wilson's is also frequently confused with Collared Plover; bear in mind that Wilson's seems *never* to occur away from immediate coast, and check bill shape and Collared's more delicate overall appearance.

Status and distribution: Fairly common locally as transient and winter resident along both coasts, but much more numerous and widespread on Pacific; also known to breed locally along Pacific coast. Particularly numerous at Pacific entrance to Canal, where flocks of well over 100 birds have been seen during northern winter months, and where it is known to breed; nesting is also known from western Panama province (Playa Coronado) and Coclé (Aguadulce), and is likely elsewhere. Not yet known to breed along Caribbean coast, but may do so.

Habits: Prefers sandy or pebbly beaches, less often on mudflats. The call is an emphatic whistled *fwit* or *fwheep*.

Range: Coastal southeastern United States, Middle America, northern South America to Guyana, western South America to Peru, and in West Indies; winters to Brazil.

Note: Often called Thick-billed Plover.

SEMIPALMATED PLOVER
Charadrius semipalmatus   Plate 5

Description: 6½–7½. Small and chunky. *Short orange to yellow bill* with black tip; orange to yellow legs. Brown above with white forehead and black band behind it and another on cheeks; below white, with *white collar around hindneck* and *black band across chest.* Nonbreeding plumage birds have duller legs, mostly blackish bills, a brown chest-band, and less distinct facial pattern; juveniles are similar but with wholly black bill.
Similar species: See Collared Plover. Wilson's Plover has stouter all black bill and pinkish (not yellowish) legs.
Status and distribution: Very common transient and common winter resident; fairly common in summer.
Habits: Largely coastal (especially Pacific), on beaches and mudflats, gathering in huge flocks at Panama Viejo in September and April. The distinctive call is a musical two-noted *toor-lee.*
Range: Breeds in northern North America; winters from southern United States south coastally through most of South America.

KILLDEER

KILLDEER
Charadrius vociferus   p.130

Description: 9–11. Fairly long black tail. Bill black; legs flesh. Brown above with *buffy-orange rump*; forehead, eye-stripe, collar on hindneck, and underparts white; *breast crossed by two black bands.*
Similar species: Larger than the other "ringed" plovers, and easily recognized by its *two* breast bands.
Status and distribution: Uncommon and somewhat local transient and winter resident throughout, recorded mostly late October–late March, occasionally lingering to mid-April.
Habits: Favors savannas, short grass areas, golf courses and the like, often far from water. Generally found as scattered individuals or small groups, not in large flocks. The call is a loud insistent *kil-deé* or *kil-deéah*, often repeated.
Range: Breeds in North America and West Indies, also in coastal Peru; northern birds winter south to Ecuador and Venezuela.

OYSTERCATCHERS: Haematopodidae (1)

Various species of oystercatchers (the exact number is still disputed) inhabit coastlines virtually throughout the world. They are characterized by their stout, laterally compressed bills, used to pry open oysters and other shellfish. The nest is a slight hollow in the ground or beach, sometimes lined with grasses or bits of seaweed.

AMERICAN OYSTERCATCHER
Haematopus palliatus   p.131

Description: 17–19. A *large* shorebird, with *stout, bright red bill*, fairly short pink legs, and rather prominent yellow iris and red eye-ring. *Head, neck, and chest black*; remaining upperparts dark brown; *lower underparts white.* In flight shows *very prominent white wing-stripe* and white upper tail-coverts.
Status and distribution: Fairly common but local resident on Pacific coast (possibly formerly more numerous), favoring rocky areas and remote beaches; no records from Darién. Known to breed in Los Santos, in

Punta Chame area of western Panama province, and on Coiba Island and the Pearl Islands, but probably elsewhere as well. Scarce in Canal area, where apparently only an irregular wanderer in very small numbers. Only report from Caribbean coast is of a bird seen repeatedly and photographed at Coco Solo, Canal area, September 27 to October 5, 1973 (J. Pujals *et al.*); this individual could have been a northern migrant.

Habits: Usually in pairs; wary. Extremely noisy, the birds often calling in the middle of the night, a shrill piercing *kleeep!*, repeated over and over. Favors areas where oyster beds are exposed at low tide.

Range: Locally on coasts of United States, Middle America, and South America; also in West Indies and Galapagos Islands.

AMERICAN OYSTERCATCHER

STILTS and AVOCETS: Recurvirostridae (2)

The stilts and avocets are a small group of large, elegant shorebirds, found locally throughout the world. They are characterized by very long slender bills (upturned in the avocets), long legs (exceptionally so in the stilts), and bold, basically black and white plumage patterns. They are gregarious and nest in colonies; as yet the stilt has not actually been found breeding in Panama, but it may well do so locally on the Pacific coast.

BLACK-NECKED STILT
Himantopus mexicanus   Plate 5

Description: 14–15½. A striking black and white shorebird with a *long* (2¼–2¾ in), *needle-like black bill*, and *extremely long red to pink legs*. *Black above*, including wings; white below and on forehead, spot above eye, and rump. Females are browner above, juveniles with some buff edging on upperparts.

Status and distribution: Uncommon to locally and seasonally common on coastal mudflats and salt lagoons, and around freshwater ponds and marshes along or near both coasts, though much more numerous on Pacific. Actual status still uncertain, with numbers fluctuating seasonally (many birds are probably northern migrants, as numbers are greatest September to March) and with water levels; there is still no evidence of nesting in Panama, though this remains possible or even likely along the Pacific coast (e.g. in the Aguadulce area of Coclé or the Punta Chame area of western Panama province). Several to many hundred birds now seem to be over-wintering regularly in the Panama Viejo/Juan Diaz area.

Habits: Feeds actively in shallow water; rather noisy, with several short sharp notes, often given in a series, especially when bird is alarmed. The long legs trail far beyond the tail in flight.

Range: Breeds locally from southern United States south through Middle America and most of South America, also in West Indies; northern birds withdraw southward during northern winter.

Note: Birds of southern South America may represent a separate species, *H. melanurus* (White-backed Stilt).

AMERICAN AVOCET
Recurvirostra americana

Description: 18. One recent record. An elegant shorebird, unmistakable with its *long, distinctly upturned bill* (slightly longer and straighter in males); very long gray legs. *Bold black and white pattern* obvious at all seasons. In nonbreeding plumage, *head and neck pale gray*, becoming white on lower underparts; mid-back and rump white, broad stripe on sides of back black; scapulars white, but wings mainly black above, with white on tertials and near base of wing-coverts. Breeding plumage birds similar but with *head and neck rich cinnamon*.

Status and distribution: One bird in nonbreeding plumage (believed a female) was found at the Aguadulce saltworks in Coclé on September 24, 1986, by R. G. Brown and R. Greenberg, seen again by them there on October 1, and was seen and photographed by D. and L. Engleman on October 18 (photos to VIREO). It was associated with a flock of Black-necked Stilts.

Habits: When not breeding favors pools with shallow water, mudflats, etc. Feeds by wading deeply into water, and sweeping its bill from side to side.

Range: Breeds in western North America; winters mainly from southern United States to southern Mexico; casually south (increasingly rare southward) to Costa Rica and Panama, and in West Indies.

Note: For details on this first Panama record see R. G. Brown and L. Engleman (*Am. Birds 42*(1): 28, 1988).

JACANAS: Jacanidae (2)

Jacanas are found in marshes in tropical and subtropical regions throughout the world. They are conspicuous noisy birds, best known for their extremely elongated toes, which enable them to walk with ease upon lily pads and other floating vegetation. Most species have a sharp spur on the carpal joint of the wing, the exact function of which is uncertain. They feed on a variety of animal and vegetative life. The nest is usually located on floating vegetation. The American species, at least, appear to be polyandrous, the female having two or more mates, each of which incubates a separate clutch of eggs.

NORTHERN JACANA
Jacana spinosa   Plate 1

Description: 9. Found only in western Panama. Bill yellow, with *base of maxilla contrastingly white* and with *three-lobed yellow frontal shield*; long grayish legs and extremely long toes. Head, neck, and chest black; *otherwise rich chestnut; pale greenish yellow flight feathers* (very conspicuous in flight though usually hidden at rest). Immature very different with *buffy white stripe above eye and dusky stripe behind eye*; otherwise grayish brown above and whitish below, with *greenish yellow flight feathers as in adult*; bill brownish with *rudimentary frontal shield yellowish green*.

Similar species: Adult Wattled Jacana (in Panama) is usually mostly black, with two-lobed frontal shield and short wattles on sides of bill dull purplish red. Immatures of the two are very similar but Wattled is blacker on crown and has rudimentary pinkish or blue frontal shield and wattles.

Status and distribution: Common in freshwater marshes and on slow flowing rivers and streams with abundant floating vegetation in lowlands of western Bocas del Toro and lowlands of Chiriquí and extreme western Pacific Veraguas, ranging up to Volcán Lakes in lower highlands of western Chiriquí. Readily seen in marshes and ponds along Pan-American Highway in Chiriquí, especially during rainy season.

Eastern limit of range on Caribbean slope unknown.

Habits: Similar to Wattled Jacana.

Range: Southern Texas (erratic) and Mexico to western Panama; West Indies.

WATTLED JACANA
Jacana jacana   Plates 1, 3

Description: 9. Resembles the preceding species. Bill yellow with *two-lobed frontal shield and short wattles on sides of bill dull red to purplish red* (sometimes lavender); long grayish legs and *extremely long toes*. Mostly *black* (a few birds with maroon-chestnut on wing-coverts, sometimes also on back and even rump, then resembling Northern Jacana); *pale greenish yellow flight feathers very conspicuous in flight*. Immature very different, sooty brown above, *more blackish on crown* with buffy whitish stripe over eye and black stripe behind eye; sides of head and entire underparts whitish; yellow flight feathers as in adult; bill brownish with *rudimentary pinkish or lilac frontal shield and wattles*.

Similar species: Easily recognized as a jacana; in western Panama see Northern Jacana.

Status and distribution: Common in freshwater marshes and along shores of lakes, ponds, and rivers with abundant emergent vegetation in lowlands on Caribbean slope from at least northern Coclé east through San Blas; on Pacific slope from western Veraguas (possibly eastern Chiriquí) east through Darién; once recorded from Coiba Island. Recorded with Northern Jacana on ponds near Remedios, eastern Chiriquí by Griscom in 1920s, but only Northern Jacanas seen there recently. Common and conspicuous in suitable habitat throughout Canal area, particularly on Chagres River and Gatun Lake.

Habits: Usually seen walking on floating vegetation, using their extremely long toes to advantage. Sometimes also feeds in adjacent grassy areas. Rather noisy, with various chatters and clacking calls.

Range: Western Panama to Bolivia, northern Argentina, and Uruguay (casually central Chile).

SANDPIPERS, PHALAROPES, AND ALLIES: Scolopacidae (30)

Most members of this family (now expanded to include the phalaropes, formerly considered to be a separate family, the Phararopodidae, on account of their lobed toes, an aid in their frequent swimming) breed in the Northern Hemisphere, especially in the arctic; none nests in Panama. However, most are highly migratory, and thus a large selection of species occur in Panama as transients and winter residents, with first-year immatures of many also often over-summering. Most "shorebirds" (often used as a general term for the family) are associated with shallow water and muddy or grassy margins, either salt or fresh; many are quite specific in their habitat requirements, and thus occur only locally. Several sites on the Pacific coast are of particular importance for shorebirds, notably the vast tidal flats which stretch along Panama Bay from Panama City eastward to at least the mouth of the Río Bayano (most accessible at Panama Viejo and Juan Diaz), and along the shore of the Gulf of Parita on the eastern side of the Azuero Peninsula and in southern Coclé. The vast throngs of shorebirds which feed here, especially on migration, must be seen to be believed, and these sites are clearly of vital international significance for a number of species. Shorebird numbers elsewhere in Panama are invariably smaller, though locally the variety can often be large; the wet short-grass fields on the Caribbean side of the Canal area are particularly good, though migrating shorebirds are opportunistic, and they may appear wherever there is suitable habitat (even temporary). Identification is often difficult. Many species closely resemble each other, doubly so in their nonbreeding plumages (and it is these plumages, rather than their relatively colorful breeding garb, which are mostly seen in Panama). Furthermore, only recently have some of the subtleties of plumage sequence (especially the often distinct juvenile plumage, worn for varying periods prior to molting into adult nonbreeding plumage) and other variations become known. An attempt has been made here to incorporate some of this new information, where it is relevant to the situation in Panama, into the following species accounts. However, it should be borne in mind that some of it is only tentative, and that certain points remain to be fully worked out. For further details, refer to Hayman, Marchant, and Prater (*Shorebirds, An Identification Guide*, 1986). Perhaps for no other group could the careful observer in Panama contribute so much with such relative ease: all that needs to be done is to carefully monitor a site through one or several seasons, recording which species are present, and in what numbers and plumages.

GREATER YELLOWLEGS
Tringa melanoleuca   Plate 5

Description: 12–14. Long straight bill, *often perceptibly upturned*; *legs yellow to orange-yellow*. Nonbreeding plumage: above brownish gray, spotted and edged with white; throat and chest finely streaked dusky and white, becoming pure white on remaining underparts. In flight shows *dark wings, white rump, and whitish tail*; long legs extend well beyond the tail. Juvenile similar but darker above; breeding plumage birds also similar but more blackish above and more coarsely streaked on foreneck and somewhat barred with blackish on flanks.

Similar species: The very similar Lesser Yellowlegs has a slender straight bill, is somewhat smaller (though largest Lessers are virtually the size of the smallest Greaters), and has a different call (often the best point): Greater's is a loud ringing three- or four-noted whistle *tew-tew-tew*; Lesser's is a softer whistle, characteristically one or two-noted *yew* or *wheep-wheep* (R. T. Peterson).

Status and distribution: Fairly common transient (especially in fall), and uncommon winter resident; a few presumed juveniles over-summer, but recorded mostly August–April.

Habits: Widespread, but in largest numbers on coastal mudflats along Pacific shore such as at Panama Viejo and Juan Diaz; has been found as a transient even at the Volcán Lakes in lower highlands of western Chiriquí. Greater Yellowlegs are wary shorebirds, always seeming to be alert and quick to give an alarm at one's approach. They feed actively by snatching at food from surface of mud or in shallow water (but usually not by probing); occasionally a group will pursue, and often seem to "herd", schools of minnows in shallow water, attacking them by sideways swipes of the bill.

Range: Breeds in Alaska and Canada; winters from southern United States to Tierra del Fuego.

LESSER YELLOWLEGS
Tringa flavipes

Description: 10–11. Closely resembles respective plumages of Greater Yellowlegs, so much so that they rarely can be distinguished on that basis. Lesser Yellowlegs is best known by its *relatively thin and straight bill* (proportionately shorter than in Greater, and lacking that species' slight upturn), and by its *smaller size* (though this is often not apparent unless the two are together). Their voices also differ characteristically, and the two often seem to segregate by habitat, Lesser favoring shallow freshwater pools and wet grassy areas, Greater coastal mudflats (though they also regularly occur together).

Similar species: See Greater Yellowlegs. Solitary Sandpiper is darker above with more prominent white eye-ring (bear in mind that both yellowlegs do often show a narrow eye-ring, however) and dark rump, and has darker, greenish legs. Stilt Sandpiper in nonbreeding plumage has flight pattern similar to a yellowlegs' (and frequently associates with Lessers); it shows a slightly drooped bill, narrow white eye-stripe, and duller greenish yellow legs. See also nonbreeding plumage Wilson's Phalarope (rare).

Status and distribution: Fairly common to locally common fall transient, but much less numerous during return spring passage (which is barely noticeable); uncommon winter resident; a few may over-summer very locally. Highest numbers in Panama occur late August to November; gatherings of several hundred or more occur on Caribbean side of Canal area.

Habits: In Panama most often found in freshwater situations, especially near either coast. Feeds mostly by snatching at food in shallow water, sometimes wading in almost to its belly; frequently in small groups. Not as shy as Greater Yellowlegs, and not nearly as vocal.

Range: Breeds in Alaska and Canada; winters from southern United States to Straits of Magellan.

SOLITARY SANDPIPER
Tringa solitaria   Plate 5

Description: 8–8½. Long slender black bill; *legs olive green.* Dark olive brown above spotted with white and with *prominent white eye-ring;* white below, throat and chest washed and obscurely streaked with brownish. Breeding plumage birds are more strongly spotted and streaked with blackish. In flight shows dark wings and *dark center of rump and tail, with outer tail feathers white barred with brown.*

Similar species: Spotted Sandpiper teeters more (nods less), flies with stiff wingbeats showing white stripe lacking in Solitary. Lesser Yellowlegs has yellow (not dark) legs, white rump in flight.

Status and distribution: Fairly common transient and less numerous winter resident throughout, recorded mostly late August–early April, rarely as early as late July or lingering to late April. This and the Spotted Sandpiper are by far the two most widespread shorebirds in Panama; the Solitary can be found almost anywhere there is shallow water in a semiopen situation.

Habits: As the name implies, often solitary, at most in small loose groups of up to six or eight birds. Found mostly on fresh water, especially around the margins of shallow ponds and marshes, and along sluggish streams. Frequently nods its head and bobs its tail, especially when nervous; then when it flushes almost invariably gives its shrill *peet-weet* or *peet* call, similar to but sharper than Spotted Sandpiper's. Flies with deep, almost swallow-like wing-strokes.

Range: Breeds in Alaska and Canada; winters from southern Mexico to Peru and central Argentina.

WILLET
Catoptrophorus semipalmatus   Plate 5

Description: 14–16. Fairly heavy long blackish bill (sometimes paler at base); *legs bluish gray.* Nonbreeding plumage: *rather drab, pale brownish gray above and on breast,* fading to whitish on throat and belly. Breeding plumage birds are more grayish brown above, barred with blackish; whitish below, barred and streaked with blackish except on mid-belly. In any plumage shows unmistakable flight pattern: *very bold white wing-stripe* and black outer wing, white rump and pale gray tail.

Similar species: Rather nondescript at rest, but cannot be confused in flight. Greater Yellowlegs always has yellow legs (not gray), and its bill is a little longer and not as heavy; at rest the two can look somewhat alike (especially when Willet is in breeding plumage), but once flying they are utterly different.

Status and distribution: Very common transient and winter resident on both coasts though more numerous on Pacific; common also in summer.

Habits: This species and the Whimbrel are easily the two commonest large shorebirds in Panama. Both often roost in mangroves at high tide, up to 15 or 20 ft above the ground or water. Usually occurs in compact flocks but scatters out to feed. The calls are loud and shrill, a repeated *kip-kip-kip*, also *klee-wee-wee*.

Range: Breeds in North America and in West Indies; winters from southern United States south coastally to northeastern Brazil and Peru, occasionally to northern Chile and southeastern Brazil.

WANDERING TATTLER
Heteroscelus incanus

Description: 11. Casual. Bill black; rather short *greenish yellow legs.* Nonbreeding plumage: *uniform dark gray above* with vague whitish superciliary; white below, washed with dark gray across breast. Breeding plumage: similar, but with white *underparts evenly and narrowly barred with dark gray.* In flight shows uniformly dark gray wings, rump, and tail.

Similar species: Sometimes bobs like a Spotted Sandpiper, but latter is much smaller, browner above (not so gray), and shows white wing-stripe in flight.

Status and distribution: Apparently a casual transient or winter resident to rocky places along Pacific shoreline or on Pacific islands. Only five records (has perhaps been somewhat overlooked): one collected on Valladolid Rock in Panama Bay between Chame and Otoque Islands on March 3, 1969 (H. Loftin and R. Crossin; Smithsonian Pacific seabird project); one seen on Isla Barca Quebrada off southern coast of Coiba Island on April 10, 1976 (Ridgely); one almost certainly this at Fort Kobbe, Pacific side of Canal area, on April 22, 1973 (S. West); one seen on the Gatun Dam spillway, Caribbean side of Canal area, on March 18, 1979 (J. Baird, Ridgely *et al.*); and six seen with Surfbirds at Panama Viejo on February 22, 1987 (R. Behrstock *et al.*). All were in nonbreeding plumage.

Habits: Rather strictly associated with rocky coastlines. Teeters and bobs its hindquarters almost continuously as it forages; usually tame. Often associates with other rock-inhabiting shorebirds such as turnstones and Surfbirds, but usually feeds independently.

Range: Breeds locally in mountains of Alaska and northwestern Canada; winters on islands in South Pacific, and also locally on rocky Pacific coasts and islands from California to Peru, and on the Galapagos Islands.

SPOTTED SANDPIPER
Actitis macularia   Plate 5

Description: 7–8. Bill flesh, tipped black; legs flesh. Nonbreeding plumage: olive brown above with white eye-stripe; white below, with *brownish smudge on sides of chest.* Breeding plumage: similar, but somewhat barred with blackish above, *distinctly spotted with black below* (female usually with more spots). In any plumage easily recognized by *almost constant teetering.* In flight shows whitish wing-stripe, *stiff wing-beats.*

Similar species: Soitary Sandpiper is darker above, bobs its head more than it teeters its rear end, and has dark wing and dark rump with white on sides of tail.

Status and distribution: Very common transient and winter resident (mostly early August–mid-May, rarely in late July and to late May) throughout, occurring wherever there is water. Apparently does not over-summer.

Habits: Found scattered individually, not in flocks. Usually stands with body tilted forward, head low, bobbing tail up and down. When flushed, flies low over the water with short stiff wing-strokes below the horizontal, often calling a shrill *peet-weet*.

Range: Breeds in North America; winters from southern United States to southern South America.

UPLAND SANDPIPER
Bartramia longicauda   p.136

Description: 11–12. Rather short yellowish bill; legs also yellow. Distinctive proportions: *small head with large dark prominent eyes, long slender neck, and rather long wedge-shaped tail.* Brown above mottled with blackish and with buff feather-edging imparting a scaly appearance; buffy whitish below, streaked and chevroned with brown on breast and barred on flanks. In flight blackish primaries contrast with mottled brown upperparts.

Similar species: Though it has no single diagnostic mark, this species can be recognized by its characteristic shape and overall brown appearance.

Status and distribution: Uncommon to fairly common fall and rather rare spring transient (mid-August–late December; mid-March–late May) on grassy fields and pastures in lowlands on both slopes.

Habits: Found singly or in small scattered groups, usually apart from other shorebirds. Plover-like in some of its mannerisms, running in spurts and then stopping abruptly. Often flies with stiff wing-beats reminiscent of a Spotted Sandpiper, and frequently holds its wings up for a few seconds after alighting.

Range: Breeds in North America; winters in southern South America, mainly in eastern Argentina.

WHIMBREL
Numenius phaeopus   Plate 5

Description: 16½–18. *Long (3–4 in) decurved blackish bill;* legs grayish. Grayish brown above, feathers edged paler, with *bold blackish and white striping on crown* and black stripe through eye; whitish below, faintly streaked and barred dusky.

Similar species: See much rarer Long-billed Curlew, and Marbled Godwit.

Status and distribution: Common transient and winter resident; fairly common in summer; most numerous on beaches and

UPLAND SANDPIPER

mudflats on both coasts (especially on Pacific), but also on damp grassy fields in lowlands not far from shore.

Habits: Scatters out over flats and beaches to feed, but gathers in large flocks of up to several hundred birds to roost at high tide, at times perching well up in mangroves. Usually wary. When flushed often gives a rapidly repeated series of musical whistles; also has a sharp *kee-kee-kee-kee-kee-kee.*

Range: Breeds in arctic North America and Eurasia; winters from southern United States south coastally through most of South America, and in Europe, Africa, and Australia.

LONG-BILLED CURLEW
Numenius americanus

Description: 22–26. Casual. *Exceptionally long decurved blackish bill* (5–8 in), though shorter (about the same as a Whimbrel's) in juveniles. *Much larger and buffier overall than Whimbrel,* with cinnamon brown tone above and almost uniform buff underparts; *lacks Whimbrel's head-striping.* In flight Long-billed's *bright cinnamon-buff wing-linings* are conspicuous and diagnostic (brownish in Whimbrel).

Status and distribution: Three records, all from Caribbean side of Canal area but to be watched for elsewhere. One was collected (out of two seen) at Fort Sherman on September 24–30, 1966 (H. Loftin *et al.*); another was seen at the same place on December 4, 1967 (Ridgely); and one was seen and photographed at Coco Solo from

November 23 to December 19, 1975 (J. Pujals *et al.*).

Habits: In Panama has been found on airstrips and fields with short grass; elsewhere also found on coastal beaches and mudflats.

Range: Breeds in western North America; winters from southern United States south rarely to Honduras and Costa Rica (where perhaps regular very locally on Pacific coast), casually to Panama.

HUDSONIAN GODWIT
Limosa haemastica

Description: 14–16. One recent record. *Long (3–4 in) slightly upturned bill* pinkish to orange on basal half, blackish on terminal half; legs grayish to black. Nonbreeding plumage: *uniform brownish gray above and on breast*, with whitish superciliary and throat and white lower underparts. In flight note *white upper tail-coverts contrasting with black tail, bold white wing-stripe*, and black under wing-coverts and axillars. Breeding plumage birds have face whitish streaked gray, with mottled brownish black upperparts and *rich chestnut underparts*.

Similar species: Marbled Godwit is larger and buffier generally (never looking gray), and it lacks the wing-stripe and the black and white tail pattern.

Status and distribution: A bird in nonbreeding plumage was seen and photographed at Coco Solo, on the Caribbean side of Canal area, on October 9–25, 1983 (D. Englemen, R. G. Brown *et al.*). The species could begin to occur more regularly, for its overall population now seems to be recovering after having been decimated by market gunners in the late nineteenth and early twentieth centuries.

Habits: The Coco Solo bird was associating with a flock of Black-bellied Plovers on a damp, closely mowed field. Elsewhere Hudsonian Godwits are also regularly seen on coastal mudflats, etc.

Range: Breeds in northern North America; winters in southern South America; migration routes still not well documented, and may be largely non-stop (southward passage is normally far out over the Atlantic, while on northward passage almost never recorded south of central United States).

Note: For details on this first Panama record see R. G. Brown and D. Engleman (*Am. Birds* 40(3): 429, 1986).

MARBLED GODWIT
Limosa fedoa   Plate 5

Description: 17–19. *Long (4–5 in) somewhat upturned bill*, pinkish on basal half, blackish on terminal half; legs grayish. *Brown above* mottled with buff and whistle; *buffy below*, more whitish on throat, indistinctly barred with brown. In flight from below shows cinnamon under wing-linings.

Similar species: A large, buffy brown shorebird with a distinctly upcurved bill. Likely to be confused only with the Whimbrel, which has a decurved bill and is not as buffy (this apparent even at a distance when bill shape cannot be made out). See also Hudsonian Godwit.

Status and distribution: Uncommon and local on coastal mudflats and damp grassy fields; recorded mostly from the vast tidal flats in the Panama Viejo/Juan Diaz area of eastern Panama province (and probably also occurs eastward, where the flats are more or less inaccessible), with a few recent records from Caribbean side of Canal area (mostly at Coco Solo in October; J. Pujals *et al.*); only known record away from Canal area is of four birds at Punta Chame, western Panama province, on April 25, 1976 (Ridgely). Numbers in Panama typically are small, with no more than up to 10–40 birds being present in the Panama Viejo/Juan Diaz area; here they seem to be present more or less year-round. In the 1950s numbers may have been larger, with up to 150 having been seen in March (F. O. Chappelle).

Range: Breeds in western North America; winters from southern United States to Panama, rarely on west coast of South America.

RUDDY TURNSTONE
Arenaria interpres   Plate 5

Description: 8–9. Bill black, very slightly upturned; *short orange legs*. Nonbreeding plumage: head, upperparts, and chest brownish; remaining underparts white. Breeding plumage: much brighter, with *rusty red back and wings*, white head, *chest and stripes on sides of head black*, lower underparts white. In flight in any plumage shows *striking wing and tail pattern* of black, brown, and white.

Similar species: Its pied pattern, though difficult to describe, renders it unmistakable, particularly in breeding dress. Looks small-headed. See Surfbird.

Status and distribution: Common transient and winter resident along both coasts, more numerous on Pacific; rather uncommon but regular in May–August period.

Habits: Though characteristically a bird of pebbly beaches and rocky shores, in Panama the Ruddy Turnstone also occurs regularly in other habitats such as the mudflats at Panama Viejo and even on grassy fields near the coast such as those at Coco Solo. Generally not found any distance inland.

Range: Breeds in arctic; winters from southern United States south coastally to southern South America and in West Indies, in Old World to southern Africa, Asia, Australia, and New Zealand, also on islands in South Pacific.

SURFBIRD
Aphriza virgata　　　　　　　　Plate 5

Description: 9–10. Bill short and stout, dusky with base of mandible yellow; legs yellowish or greenish. Nonbreeding plumage: *mostly dark gray*, with whitish throat and white belly, latter with dusky streaking especially on flanks. Breeding plumage: head and neck whitish streaked gray, with back blackish edged white and with mostly rusty scapulars; *below white heavily marked with black spots and chevrons*. In flight in any plumage shows bold white wing-stripe, *white rump and tail with black triangle near tip*.

Similar species: Ruddy Turnstone (with which this species often occurs) in non-breeding plumage is brown above and on chest, and has bright orange legs. See also very rare Wandering Tattler.

Status and distribution: Fairly common but local along rocky shoreline of Panama Bay from Panama Viejo to Panama City; present throughout the year, but in largest numbers on migration, though rarely are more than 50–75 birds seen together. Single records from Piñas Bay, Darién (H. Loftin), and Playa Coronado, western Panama province (Eisenmann) are the only ones reported away from Panama City, but to be watched for wherever there is appropriate habitat.

Habits: Usually feeds on rocks, but sometimes spreads out onto adjacent mudflats.

Range: Breeds in Alaskan mountains; winters on Pacific coast from western North America south very locally to Tierra del Fuego.

RED KNOT
Calidris canutus　　　　　　　　p.139

Description: 10–11. Bill black; legs dark greenish to black. *Chunky shape* (somewhat plover-like). Nonbreeding plumage: *uniform gray above* with whitish superciliary; white below, somewhat spotted or washed with gray on chest. Juvenile similar but with feathers of upperparts edged white, giving scaly effect. Breeding plumage: grayish brown above, feathers edged buff or whitish; *mostly rich cinnamon-rufous below and on sides of head*. In flight in any plumage shows only a faint wing-stripe, pale grayish white rump, and gray tail.

Similar species: In breeding plumage likely confused only with the dowitchers, which are much longer-billed and have obvious white rump extending up lower back. Non-breeding Red Knots are nondescript; note their stocky plover-like shape (slender bill differentiates from any plover, of course) and overall gray appearance with even the flight pattern relatively featureless. Non-breeding Stilt Sandpiper is perhaps closest in plumage, but it has longer, droopier bill, longer legs, more contrasty white rump in flight, etc.

Status and distribution: Uncommon visitant to both coasts, though more regular and in larger numbers on Pacific (on Caribbean recorded only from Canal area); greatest numbers are recorded during periods of transience (especially September–October and March–April), but a few are now wintering and over-summering regularly (especially in the Juan Diaz/Panama City and Aguadulce areas).

Habits: In Panama found mainly on coastal mudflats and beaches, though during fall passage also feeds on wet short-grass fields (but never recorded at any distance from coast). Usually accompanies larger numbers of dowitchers or Black-bellied Plovers.

Range: Breeds in high arctic; winters mostly in southern South America, with a few north coastally to southern United States; in Old World winters to Africa, Australia, and New Zealand.

SANDERLING
Calidris alba　　　　　　　　Plate 5

Description: 7½–8½. Bill and legs black. Nonbreeding plumage: *pale gray above with black shoulders; superciliary, face, and underparts white*. Juvenile similar but more checkered with black above. Breeding plumage (usually just beginning to be assumed as adults are migrating northward): *head, neck, and breast rusty brown* with black spotting, back blackish with rusty feather edging, and

RED KNOT (nonbreeding plumage), PECTORAL SANDPIPER, and STILT SANDPIPER (nonbreeding plumage)

belly white. In flight in any plumage shows a *very bold white wing-stripe*, and white rump with blackish median band.

Similar species: In nonbreeding plumage, the *palest* of the smaller sandpipers, with characteristic black shoulders (these may be briefly hidden at times). None of the "peeps" shows such a conspicuous wing-stripe. See especially nonbreeding Red-necked Phalarope (not dissimilar in flight, and remember that Sanderlings do at times fly over the ocean far from land), and Baird's Sandpiper (superficially like a Sanderling in breeding plumage, though slimmer and longer-winged, with much less obvious wing-stripe).

Status and distribution: Uncommon to fairly common transient and winter resident along Pacific coast, much less numerous along Caribbean; only report of apparently over-summering birds is a group of six seen on coast south of Pedregal, Chiriquí, on June 27, 1982 (Ridgely).

Habits: Prefers sandy and pebbly beaches, often with flocks of Semipalmated Plovers and Western Sandpipers. A very active feeder, chasing the waves back and forth.

Range: Breeds in high arctic; winters coastally fron United States to Tierra del Fuego, and in southern Europe, Africa, southern Asia, Australia, and islands in South Pacific.

SEMIPALMATED SANDPIPER
Calidris pusilla   Plate 5

Description: 6–6½. Rather short black bill (longer in female) and black legs. Non-breeding plumage: brownish gray above with vague whitish superciliary; white below, with grayish wash on sides of chest. In flight shows faint white wing-stripe and black center to white rump. Juvenile similar but with back feathers blacker but pale-edged, resulting in scaly pattern. Breeding plumage birds are browner above, often showing rufous tinge on crown and ear-coverts, and are streaked with dark brown across chest.

Similar species: Distinguishing this species and the Western Sandpiper in Panama presents a major difficulty. In nonbreeding plumage (at least November–March) they are virtually identical except for calls (see below) and bill length differences, though at close range Westerns can be seen to have a narrow band of gray shaft streaks across chest (lacking in Semipalmated). Typically, the bill of Semipalmated is shorter than that of Western, but because of sexual variation in both species (females have bills longer than males), only extremes can be certainly identified on this basis alone. Thus, a short-billed bird (*often with bill looking shorter than the head*) is a male Semipalmated, while a long-billed bird (*with bill at least equal in length to head*, and often looking decidedly drooped at tip) is a female Western. Thus it is the female Semis and the male Westerns which overlap, and cause the problem. In the hand, birds with exposed culmen of under 20 mm are Semipalmated, while those with over 23 mm are Western; those with exposed culmen of 20–22 mm may be either species. By April, migrating adults of both species are assuming their breeding plumage, and

Westerns are then relatively easy to pick out (see under that species). Semipalmated also resembles Least Sandpiper, which see.

Status and distribution: Fairly common to common transient and winter resident on both coasts, but in much larger numbers along the Pacific; small numbers (relatively) over-summer locally, with greatest concentrations in the Juan Diaz/Panama Viejo area and at Aguadulce, Coclé.

Habits: Feeds mostly on coastal tidal flats, to a lesser extent on beaches and around margins of ponds and marshes; rarely at any distance from coast (then perhaps only as migrants). The usual call heard in flight is a short low harsh *chert* or *churk*.

Range: Breeds in arctic North America; winters mostly along coasts of Panama and South America, very rarely north to Florida.

WESTERN SANDPIPER
Calidris mauri   Plate 5

Description: 6¼–6¾. Rather long black bill (shorter in male), *often with slight but distinct droop at tip* (especially in longer-billed females), and black legs. Virtually identical to Semipalmated Sandpiper in nonbreeding plumage; note, however, that Westerns typically show a *narrow but discrete band of gray shaft streaking across chest* (not shown by Semipalmated), visible at close range. The rusty scapulars shown by many adult Westerns during southward passage in the United States (and featured in North American field guides) *are usually lost before they reach Panama*. However, Westerns assuming breeding plumage during their northward passage (especially April) are seen, and are quite easily identified: they are *decidedly rusty on the crown, ear-coverts, and scapulars* (Semipalmateds look much more uniform), and are more boldly marked across breast, with triangular spots extending down onto flanks (which are almost immaculate white in Semipalmated).

Similar species: See Semipalmated and Least Sandpipers.

Status and distribution: Common to locally abundant transient and winter resident on both coasts, but in very much larger numbers along Pacific; small numbers (still totalling in the thousands) also over-summer, mostly at various sites along Pacific coast (especially Juan Diaz/Panama Viejo and Aguadulce, so far as known). Numbers of this species relative to the Semipalmated in Panama remain somewhat conjectural, though usually

Westerns seem to be in the decided majority. At any rate, the vast throngs of the two combined can at times be staggering: at Juan Diaz I have on several occasions estimated that 200,000 to 300,000 were present. Numbers seems greatest while on spring (northward) passage; southward passage is more protracted, and seem not to produce such large concentrations.

Habits: Feeds mostly on coastal tidal flats, only in much smaller numbers elsewhere. Frequently forages in deeper water than the Semipalmated tends to do, but there is much overlap, and both species often probe and pick in exposed mud. The Western's usual flight call is a shrill, rather high-pitched thin *cheep* or *jeep*, somewhat different from the lower, more guttural *chert* of the Semipal. However, it takes practice to discern the difference, and it is admittedly often difficult to pick out an individual call from among the mass and twitters of even a small flock.

Range: Breeds in northeastern Siberia and western Alaska; winters coastally from southern United States to northern South America.

LEAST SANDPIPER
Calidris minutilla   Plate 5

Description: 5¾–6¼. Slender, slightly drooped black bill; *legs dull yellowish or greenish*. Nonbreeding plumage: brownish gray above with vague whitish superciliary; white below, with band of dusky streaking across chest. In flight shows faint white wing-stripe and black center to white rump. Juvenile has feathers of upperparts boldly edged with bright rufous, and have prominent white "V" on mid-back, but by the time they reach Panama these have mostly faded or abraded (and they resemble winter adults). Breeding plumage birds also have feathers of upperparts edged buff or rufous (resulting in a brighter, more variegated pattern), and are more extensively streaked with brown on throat and breast.

Similar species: In all plumages looks browner (not so gray) than does Western or Semipalmated Sandpiper, and never has black legs (but be careful, as legs of Least can look dark in strong light, or when they are coated with mud). Further points of distinction are Least's thinner bill and its distinctive call (see below); note, too, its typically hunched silhouette, with small head and short neck. See also Pectoral Sandpiper.

Status and distribution: Common transient (mostly September–October and March–April, with largest numbers during fall) and fairly common winter resident along both coasts, with small numbers occurring inland in appropriate habitat. There is no certain evidence that this species ever over-summers in Panama (unlike the Semipalmated and Western), with reports from as late as mid-May presumed to be late stragglers, while those recorded from as early as late July (e.g. 40 at Aguadulce, Coclé, on July 26, 1975; Ridgely *et al.*) are believed to pertain to early-arriving adults.

Habits: Widespread, but tends to avoid the vast coastal tidal flats so favored by Western and Semipalmated Sandpipers, and if present in such a situation usually only at its edge. Elsewhere numbers are usually more equal, and Least is often the commonest species around fresh water and on wet grassy fields. Leasts are often very tame, when finally flushing (sometimes almost virtually at one's feet) often towering with wings not held out as far as other shorebirds, or flying off like a snipe with a zigzag course. Its usual call is a shrill high-pitched grating *kree-eep*, often given as the bird flushes.

Range: Breeds in northern North America; winters from southern United States to South America, and in West Indies.

WHITE-RUMPED SANDPIPER
Calidris fuscicollis

Description: 7–7½. Bill and legs black. Nonbreeding plumage: *uniform brownish gray above*, sometimes showing short white superciliary; mostly white below, but with *distinct brownish gray smudge and streaking across chest*, and *extending down as sparse streaks to flanks*. In flight shows faint wing-stripe and *completely white rump* (with no dark stripe down center). Juvenile browner above and on crown, with buff feather edging. Breeding plumage with whitish and buff streaking and edging on upperparts; white below with *broad band of neat brown streaking across breast and extending down flanks*. At rest wing-tips extend beyond tips of tail (as in Baird's).

Similar species: Easily recognized by the all-white rump, a mark not shared by any other peep, but visible only in flight. At rest White-rumps can be picked out by their slim, attenuated appearance (an impression created by their longer, protruding wings), fairly large size, and, in nonbreeding

plumage (the most often seen in Panama), overall gray plumage. Baird's Sandpiper in nonbreeding plumage is very similar (it too then looks quite gray), but it lacks White-rump's flank streaking and (in flight) has black-centered rump.

Status and distribution: Rare transient on both coasts (mostly September–October and April–May); recorded only from Bocas del Toro, both coasts of Canal area, and eastern Panama province (including one anomalous bird seen at Cerro Azul on September 8, 1979; A. Moore), but probably more widespread. There have also been a couple of reports of presumed over-summerers.

Habits: Reaches Panama in but very small numbers; probably most numerous on coastal mudflats, but also seen on wet grassy areas. Has a distinctive two-noted mouse-like squeak, *jeet-jeet*, often given in flight.

Range: Breeds in high arctic; winters in southern South America, mostly east of the Andes.

BAIRD'S SANDPIPER
Calidris bairdii

Description: 7–7½. Bill and legs black. Nonbreeding plumage: brownish gray above, sometimes showing short white superciliary; mostly white below, with brownish gray wash and streaking across chest. In flight shows faint white wing-stripe and black center to white rump. Juvenile buffier brown above, with *feathers on back and scapulars broadly white-edged giving distinct scaly appearance*; face and breast washed with buff and with sparse dark brown streaking. Breeding plumage birds resemble juveniles, but are splotchier (not as scaly) above. At rest wing-tips extend beyond tips of tail (as in White-rumped).

Similar species: In Panama seen most often in relatively distinctive juvenile plumage, but by October many of these are beginning to molt into more confusing winter dress. In shape the Baird's is very like White-rumped Sandpiper; latter in most plumages is grayer (not buffy), but full nonbreeding adults of the two are very alike except for its lack of White-rump's sparse flank streaking, and its black-centred rump. Pectoral Sandpiper looks distinctly streaked above, and shows high contrast between streaked breast and white belly; its legs are yellow (not dark). Juvenile Buff-breasted Sandpiper also looks buffy and very scaled above, but it never looks even vaguely streaked on breast and has yellow (not dark) legs. See also the smaller peeps, and breeding plumage Sanderling.

Status and distribution: Rare to locally and briefly uncommon as fall transient (September–October); very rare on return passage in spring (reported only in April–May 1966; N. G. Smith). Recorded only from Canal area, where mostly seen on wet short-grass fields on Caribbean side (especially Coco Solo and Gatun Dam).

Habits: In Panama usually associates with Pectoral or Buff-breasted Sandpipers; in Panama it has been seen only in grassy habitats. Its flight call is a low *krrrit*, sometimes doubled and similar in quality to Pectoral Sandpiper's.

Range: Breeds in northeastern Siberia and arctic North America; winters mostly in southern South America, also in Andes from Ecuador south.

PECTORAL SANDPIPER
Calidris melanotos p.139

Description: 8½–9, males considerably larger than females. Bill black, sometimes flesh-colored at base; *legs yellow to greenish yellow.* Above blackish brown with buff to white feather edging, and whitish superciliary; *throat and breast buff densely streaked with brown, ending abruptly against white belly.* Little seasonal variation in plumage. In flight shows faint wing-stripe and black center to white rump.

Similar species: Sharp contrast between streaked breast and pure white belly is characteristic. Small females especially can be confused with Baird's Sandpiper, but latter is always smaller and buffier, usually scaly on back, and has black legs. Least Sandpiper is almost exactly like a Pectoral in plumage, but is hardly half the size. See also Upland Sandpiper. See also Sharp-tailed Sandpiper (below).

Status and distribution: Locally common fall transient (late August–mid-November), but rare to uncommon in spring (mostly March–April, a few occasionally lingering into May and very rarely to June); recorded mostly near either coast, with largest numbers in the Canal area, particularly on Caribbean side.

Habits: Shows strong predeliction for wet grassy fields, and can occur in flocks of hundreds at especially favorable sites such as Coco Solo and Gatun Dam. Numbers during northward passage are much smaller, doubtless in part because these same fields are much drier during those

months, it being the dry season. Only occasionally are Pectorals found on coastal mudflats, then usually at their somewhat grassier margins. Usual flight call is a low throaty *krrik*, sometimes doubled, or a shorter *churk*.

Range: Breeds in northeastern Siberia and arctic North America; winters mostly in southern South America.

Note: Sharp-tailed Sandpiper (*Calidris acuminata*) now occurs regularly in very small numbers in North America (though it is primarily an Asian sandpiper); these presumably are wintering in South America, and thus the species is a definite possibility in Panama. Sharp-tailed resembles Pectoral in size and overall appearance, but juvenile differs in having a much buffier and more sparsely and finely streaked breast which *does not* contrast with the white belly; its cap is rustier and the white superciliary wider and thus much more prominent. Breeding plumage adults are more streaked on breast, but these still do not contrast especially with the belly; additionally there are black chevrons on the flanks. Sharp-tailed usually associates with Pectoral Sandpipers, and the two are similar in habits.

DUNLIN
Calidris alpina

Description: 7½–8½. Casual. *Bill black, stout and rather long, drooped or decurved toward tip*; legs also black. Nonbreeding plumage: *uniform brownish gray above and on breast*, latter sometimes blurrily streaked darker; remaining underparts whitish. Breeding plumage: *mostly bright rusty above*, with some black spotting or streaking; white below, finely streaked dusky on breast and with *conspicuous black patch on belly.* In flight shows bold white wing-stripe and black center to white rump.

Similar species: The drooping bill is the best mark. Nonbreeding Red Knot is larger, paler gray, with straight bill and greenish legs. Western Sandpiper also has drooping bill but is considerably smaller; non-breeding White-rumped Sandpiper is also gray but has straight bill and shows prominent all-white rump in flight. See also nonbreeding Stilt Sandpiper and Curlew Sandpiper (below).

Status and distribution: Only a few records. Wetmore records seeing single birds at Panama Viejo on December 3 and 28, 1955, and five further east at the mouth of the Río Chico, eastern Panama province, on March 5, 1956. More recently, three were seen and one photographed at Coco Solo, on Caribbean side of Canal area, on January 19–24, 1974 (D. Engleman, R. Johnson, J. Pujals), and one was seen at Aguadulce, Coclé, on January 7, 1977 (A. Greensmith *et al.*)

Habits: The Dunlin's favored foraging habitats are similar to those of Western and Semipalmated Sandpipers, i.e. coastal mudflats and lagoons.

Range: Breeds in northern North America and Eurasia; American birds winter mostly in southern United States and Mexico, casually south to Costa Rica and Panama and accidentally to western Peru.

Note: Curlew Sandpiper (*Calidris ferruginea*) occurs regularly in very small numbers in North America (though it is primarily a Eurasian sandpiper), and has been recorded a few times in South America (Argentina and Peru); it is thus a definite possibility in Panama. In nonbreeding plumage it closely resembles nonbreeding Dunlin, but in flight shows an all-white rump (without black stripe down center); its bill is slenderer and more evenly decurved, legs slightly longer, underparts somewhat whiter, and overall stance somewhat more upright with longer neck, but all these points are so subtle as to be useful mostly in direct comparison (not likely in Panama!). Curlew Sandpiper in breeding plumage is unmistakable, with rich chestnut-red underparts and edging to upperparts; birds molting into or out of this plumage are regularly seen.

STILT SANDPIPER
Calidris himantopus p.139

Description: 8–9. Long slender black bill, *slightly decurved and usually showing droop at tip*; long legs dull yellowish to grayish green. Nonbreeding plumage: uniform brownish gray above with narrow white superciliary and some pale edging to back and scapular feathers; whitish below, tinged grayish on breast. Juvenile similar but with darker crown and stronger pale edging on feathers of upperparts. Breeding plumage birds are very different: mostly blackish above with feathers boldly edged white, and *crown and ear-coverts tinged chestnut*; *white below coarsely barred blackish*. In flight shows dark wings, white rump, and pale grayish tail.

Similar species: Confusing when in nonbreeding dress. Most resembles nonbreeding dowitcher (either species), but longer-legged and shorter-billed (and bill not perfectly *straight* as in the dowitchers), whiter below, and with different flight pattern (Stilt lacking dowitchers' white up the lower back). Lesser

Yellowlegs has a straight bill, shows a less prominent superciliary or none at all, and has bright yellow legs and an entirely different manner of feeding. Red Knot is chunkier in build, has shorter bill and legs, and has relatively uniform flight pattern (lacking Stilt's white rump); their feeding behavior also differs markedly. See also very rare Dunlin (and even more, Curlew Sandpiper); both have shorter black (not yellowish or greenish) legs.

Status and distribution: Rare to uncommon transient on or near both coasts (recorded mostly August–September and March–April); a few records from other seasons. Most reports are from the Canal area, the only exception being three seen at Punta Chame, western Panama province, on April 25, 1976 (Ridgely).

Habits: Favors shallow fresh water ponds and rain pools on short-grass fields, though occasionally also noted roosting at high tide with other shorebirds along coast (e.g. at Juan Diaz). Usually associates with dowitchers or Lesser Yellowlegs. Feeds much like a dowitcher, often wading out into water up to its belly, submerging its head and probing the mud below with repeated fast up and down thrusts.

Range: Breeds in arctic North America; winters mostly in southern South America, rarely in southern United States and Middle America.

Note: Formerly placed in the monotypic genus *Micropalama*.

BUFF-BREASTED SANDPIPER
Tryngites subruficollis

Description: 7½–8½. Bill short, black; *legs yellow*. Rather small head and slender neck (somewhat reminiscent of much larger Upland Sandpiper). Above mostly blackish brown, *feathers edged buff giving scaly appearance*; *face and entire underparts buffy*, fading to buffy whitish on belly. Juvenile similar but with feathers above *edged white*, imparting an *even more marked scaly appearance*, and whiter on belly. In flight shows *white underwing-linings*; wings dark above.

Similar species: Somewhat like a small Upland Sandpiper but much more buffy. Baird's Sandpiper is buffy on breast only and has black legs. See also Pectoral Sandpiper.

Status and distribution: Locally fairly common fall transient (August–October) on short-grass fields on both slopes of Canal area; much rarer on spring passage, with a single old report from near Gatun (one seen on March 29, 1912; L. Jewel) and a few seen at Paitilla airport in Panama City in March–April 1966 (N. G. Smith). Not reported from elsewhere in Panama, though it may occur where there is appropriate habitat.

Habits: Very tame. Has a distinctive wide-eyed, innocent-looking appearance. Usually occurs in flocks of its own species, sometimes in fairly large numbers (25–75 individuals). When flushed, usually twists and turns like a snipe, circling several times, often as not returning to the spot from which it was put up.

Range: Breeds in western arctic North America; winters in southern South America; rather a scarce and local transient in between.

RUFF
Philomachus pugnax

Description: ♂ 11–12; ♀ 9–10. Casual. Bill fairly short, straight or slightly drooped at tip, black but often with yellow or orange at base; legs orange to reddish (or sometimes yellow) in adults, brownish to greenish in juveniles. Nonbreeding plumage: *more or less plain grayish brown above*, with *white area at base of bill* and often a partial white eye-ring; white below, washed with grayish brown on breast and sometimes splotched or barred with dusky, especially on sides. In flight shows faint white wing-stripe and *distinctive pair of oval white patches at sides of rump*. Juvenile similar but more scaled with rufous above, and with buffier wash on breast. Dimorphic in breeding plumage: females are blackish brown above, and are *heavily scaled blackish brown on throat and breast*, becoming white on belly; males are unmistakable with their *spectacular erectile ear-tufts and ruff*, variously colored black, white, chestnut, or buff (or some combination thereof).

Similar species: Rather variable in plumage, and often confused, especially as the remarkable males in full breeding regalia are so infrequently seen in the New World. Essentially what one is looking for is a variably sized (male and female a bit smaller than the Greater and Lesser Yellowlegs, respectively), small-headed and short-billed, but rather heavy-bodied, shorebird which in most respects is yellowlegs-like but is always browner and only very rarely has bright yellow legs. Females are somewhat reminiscent of Pectoral Sandpiper but lack the streaked effect above and on breast, and never

show the sharp contrast between streaked breast and pure white belly. See also Upland Sandpiper.

Status and distribution: Two records, both of males in nonbreeding plumage: one seen at Coco Solo, on Caribbean side of Canal area, on September 29–October 2, 1968 (Ridgely and H. Loftin); one seen and photographed at Howard AFB, on Pacific side of Canal area, on November 19–20, 1974 (S. West).

Habits: Both Panama birds were found on wet short-grass fields. Elsewhere Ruffs (females of which are called Reeves) also frequent the margins of shallow ponds, marshes, and sometimes tidal flats. In the New World they usually associate with yellowlegs or dowitchers.

Range: Primarily an Old World shorebird, breeding in northern Eurasia, wintering widely in tropical areas; in the New World known mostly as a rare (but perhaps increasing) migrant in North America, especially on the east coast, with a scatter of records south to Costa Rica, Panama, Colombia, Venezuela, Peru, and the West Indies and Trinidad.

SHORT-BILLED DOWITCHER
Limnodromus griseus   Plate 5

Description: 10–11. *Long straight black bill* (2–2½ in); legs greenish. Nonbreeding plumage: grayish above with white superciliary; throat and breast also grayish, sometimes with a few darker speckles on breast, and belly white with blackish barring on flanks. In flight shows white trailing edge to inner flight feathers, *white rump extending up onto lower back as a wedge*, and tail narrowly barred black and white. Juvenile has feathers of upperparts (including scapulars and tertials) broadly edged and marked with rusty or buff, usually shows some speckling or streaking on breast, and breast is sometimes buff-tinged; this plumage is retained until November–December (at least in some individuals). Breeding plumage varies with race (and is seen in early arriving birds in July–August, and in northward-bound migrants in March–April): *hendersoni* is *uniformly bright rusty red below*, with only a little white below and on crissum, with sparse black spotting on chest and sides (densest across chest); nominate race has much more extensively white belly and is much more densely spotted and speckled with black below, also with more barring on flanks; above both races are blackish brown, feathers edged buff or rusty.

Similar species: Very closely resembles

Long-billed Dowitcher; see under that species for comparison. Most dowitchers in Panama will be difficult to distinguish with certainty. However, from collecting data it is known that Short-billed is by far the commoner of the two here, so a safe general rule is to assume they are Short-bills unless proven otherwise. Dowitchers in the general sense should be easily recognizable by their snipe-like, absolutely straight bills and in flight by their very distinctive white wedge up the lower back; compare especially to nonbreeding Stilt Sandpiper and Red Knot.

Status and distribution: Fairly common to locally common transient and winter resident along both coasts, though in larger numbers on Pacific; recorded mostly August–April, with small numbers of arriving adults having been seen as early as late July (e.g. about 25 birds believed to be *hendersoni* at Aguadulce, Coclé, on July 26, 1975; Ridgely *et al.*), and some first-year birds over-summer (usually in small numbers, with maximum count being 2000 or more, all in nonbreeding plumage, at Panama Viejo on July 7, 1975; Ridgely).

Habits: Prefers mudflats, gathering in rather large flocks where conditions are favorable. Feeds by wading belly-deep into shallow water and rapidly jabbing bill into mud with perpendicular motions, entirely submerging head. The usual call is a metallic *tu-tu-tu*, given in flight or when flushed.

Range: Breeds in northern Canada; winters from southern United States south coastally to Peru and central Brazil.

Note: Has been called Common Dowitcher.

LONG-BILLED DOWITCHER
Limnodromus scolopaceus

Description: 10½–11½. Very closely resembles Short-billed Dowitcher, and often cannot be distinguished in the field. Bill measurements overlap, though *long extremes* of this species (females) can often be picked out. In the hand, birds with an exposed culmen of 68 mm or more are Long-billed, while those with less than 56 mm are Short-billed; Long-billed also has relatively shorter wings, so that difference between wing length and exposed culmen is 77 mm or less, whereas in Short-billed the difference is 77 mm or more. In nonbreeding plumage the two are almost impossible to differentiate on plumage characters alone, but Long-billed has gray on breast darker and more extensive. Juvenile Long-billed have *less ornate pattern on*

tertials and scapulars than do juvenile Short-bills (in which there not only is rusty or buff edging, but also internal markings of the same color), and they are grayer on sides of neck and breast; this plumage is retained until November–December (at least in some individuals). Breeding plumage Long-bills are *brighter and more uniform rusty red below* (extending over belly and crissum) with *dense black spotting on throat and barring on breast and sides.* Their *characteristically different voices* are often the best clue (see below); preferred habitats also differ, but are not invariable.

Status and distribution: Not certainly known due to identification difficulties. Probably a rare winter resident along both coasts, though to date reports are from Caribbean; collected in Bocas del Toro in October, November, and January; sight reports from Canal area from October to March.

Habits: Tends not to be found on tidal mudflats (and has never been found in such a situation in Panama), preferring instead fresh water situations such as pond margins, flooded or wet grassy fields, etc. However, the Short-billed is by no means restricted to coastal flats, and regularly occurs in fresh water situations identical to those favored by the Long-billed. The Long-billed's call is a sharp thin *keek!* or *kik!*, often trebled or in series, especially when taking flight; this is much more strident than the Short-billed's mellower *tu-tu-tu* or *tudulu.* Unlike the Short-billed, Long-billed Dowitchers frequently call when resting or feeding, whereas Short-bills call almost only in flight (K. Kaufman).

Range: Breeds in northeastern Siberia and western arctic North America; winters from southern United States to Central America (regularly in small numbers to Costa Rica, apparently only rarely to Panama), and perhaps casually to South America (a few old records which require modern confirmation; recent sightings from western Peru and a probable specimen from northern Colombia).

COMMON SNIPE
Gallinago gallinago   Plate 5

Description: 10½–11½. *Long straight bill* (2½–2¾ in), blackish with paler base; short greenish legs. Dark brown above, streaked and mottled with buff and white, and with *pale buff and black striped head*; breast buff mottled with brown, belly white barred with blackish. In flight shows dark wings, brown rump, and *usually fanned mostly orange-rufous tail* with dark subterminal stripe and white tip.

Similar species: Rather like a dowitcher in general proportions, but with different habits and with striped head and brown rump. No other shorebird has proportionately such a long bill.

Status and distribution: Locally fairly common transient and winter resident (October–April) in boggy areas and freshwater marshes and wet spots in lowlands on both slopes, ranging up to Volcán Lakes in lower highlands of western Chiriquí. Particularly numerous in coastal eastern Panama province from Juan Diaz east to the Chepo area.

Habits: Cryptically colored and close sitters, snipes are usually not noticed until they abruptly flush (often almost at one's feet) and zigzag away, holding bill angled downward, often uttering a harsh grating *scaip*. Though most often solitary, they regularly concentrate in small loose aggregations at particularly favorable feeding grounds.

Range: Breeds in North America and Eurasia; North American birds winter south to northern South America.

Note: Does not include *G. paraguaiae* (South American Snipe), resident in South America.

WILSON'S PHALAROPE
Phalaropus tricolor

Description: 8½–9½. *Very slender, needle-like black bill*; legs greenish to straw yellow in nonbreeding plumage, black in breeding plumage. Nonbreeding plumage: *above uniform pale gray*; face and *entire underparts pure white*, with dusky stripe through eye accentuating the white superciliary. In flight shows *dark unpatterned wings, white rump*, and whitish tail. Breeding plumage females are beautifully patterned: *crown pale gray becoming white on hindneck, black stripe through eye running down sides of neck, becoming chestnut on lower neck and across chest*, and back gray with broad chestnut stripes. Breeding male similar but duller.

Similar species: Breeding plumage birds should be easy, but have not yet been reported in Panama. Red-necked Phalarope in nonbreeding plumage is darker gray above with white striping, has a distinct black facial patch, and in flight shows a bold white wing-stripe, dark center to white

rump, and darker tail. Compare also to Lesser Yellowlegs (with more spotted upperparts, etc.) and nonbreeding Stilt Sandpiper (with heavier, droopier bill, etc.).

Status and distribution: Rare fall transient (August–September), and apparently only casual during spring passage (only one report, a bird seen on March 29, 1983, at Tocumen, eastern Panama province; A. D. Brewer *et al.*); recorded only from Canal area, with most reports from Caribbean side, particularly at Coco Solo and the Gatun Dam spillway.

Habits: In Panama has usually been seen on muddy or grassy margins of shallow pools; unlike the other two phalaropes, the Wilson's never occurs at sea. Very active and graceful, often dashing about on the mud in a crouched position, stabbing at insects on either side; they also regularly swim lightly on the water, often spinning round and round, picking insects off the surface.

Range: Breeds in western North America; winters mainly in southern South America (especially in the high Andes), occasionally or casually north to Middle America and extreme southern United States; migration routes are poorly documented.

Note: Formerly placed in the monotypic genus *Steganopus*.

RED-NECKED PHALAROPE
Phalaropus lobatus   p.147

Description: 7–7¾. Slender black bill; dark legs. Nonbreeding plumage: dark gray above with *whitish stripes on back* (striping sometimes obscure in immature birds); forecrown, face, and underparts white, with *dark gray patch through and behind eye*. In flight shows bold white wing-stripe, dark center to white rump, and dark tail. Breeding plumage female has white back striping replaced by rufous, and *chestnut patch on sides of neck and chest outlining white throat*. Breeding male similar but duller.

Similar species: Breeding plumage is distinctive; at other seasons marked as a phalarope by the dark patch through the eye. Nonbreeding Wilson's Phalarope is similar but has unpatterned gray back, yellowish legs, and no wing-stripe; the two are not normally found together, the Wilson's not being pelagic. See also Red Phalarope (below).

Status and distribution: Irregular but at times common transient off Pacific coast (August–November, and April–May), usually in much larger numbers during southward passage; usually absent or in very small numbers during northern winter months, but very occasionally can be quite common even at this season. Usually occurs well offshore, but occasionally (especially during fall passage) visible in numbers from shore (Fort Amador seems to be an especially favorable locality). Not recorded from Caribbean coast (or offshore), but seems possible.

Habits: Usually seen as a group; flies rapidly and erratically low over the ocean, all too often continuing on out of sight. They feed while swimming, often spinning around rapidly like a top, daintily picking up small food items from on or near the surface.

Range: Breeds in arctic North America and Eurasia; winters at sea in Atlantic, Pacific, and Indian Oceans.

Note: Formerly placed in the monotypic genus *Lobipes*, and called Northern Phalarope. Red Phalarope (*Phalaropus fulicaria*) has not yet actually been recorded from Panama, but seems likely to occur well offshore, at least on the Pacific (there have been several reports of

RED-NECKED PHALAROPE (nonbreeding plumage)

this species from just beyond what are here considered to be Panama waters, most recently by R. G. B. Brown in October and December 1977) Red's range is much like Red-necked's, but it is more of a high arctic nester, and when not breeding is even more pelagic. In nonbreeding plumage the two are quite similar, though Red is larger (8–8½ in) with stouter bill that often shows yellow at base, and it has paler gray back that is devoid of striping; in breeding plumage both sexes can be instantly known by their rufous underparts with contrasting white face.

SKUAS, GULLS, TERNS, AND SKIMMERS: Laridae (32)

Gulls and terns and their allies are familiar and cosmopolitan birds, most prominent along coasts but also found inland on larger lakes, rivers, and marshes, with a few species well offshore except when they are breeding. Though birds of this family are numerous in Panama, none is known to breed here (three tropical terns may do so very locally), though many individuals of various nonbreeding species do occur year-round. The four subfamilies are easily differentiated; note that the family Laridae has recently been expanded to include not only the gulls and terns but also the skuas (and jaegers) and the skimmers. The skuas and jaegers (Stercorariinae) are often piratic seabirds which breed in polar regions but then usually migrate long distances when not nesting, regularly to tropical waters. They are gull-like but have strong hooked bills (and also a horny cere unlike gulls and terns), long wings showing a flash of white in the primaries, and in breeding plumage jaegers have lengthened central tail feathers. Identification is often difficult, as is taxonomy in the skua group. Gulls (Larinae) are generally larger than terns (Sterninae), heavier somewhat hooked bills, rather broad wings, and usually square tails, while most terns are smaller and slimmer, with slender straight bills, rather narrow pointed wings, and usually (except the noddies) forked tails. Gulls regularly swim (so do skuas and jaegers), while terns rarely do. Most terns dive into the water after small fish (others pluck from the surface while hovering or swooping), while gulls usually scavenge for animal matter or refuse along shores or floating on the water. Species identification is often very difficult, with problems compounded by most species having one or more confusing immature plumages which must be contended with; this sequence of plumages is important, and is emphasized in the species accounts, where appropriate; the term "mantle" is also often used, and signifies the entire back and upper wing surface area. Finally, the skimmers (Rynchopinae) form a very distinctive group of tern-like birds, three species of which are found in the warmer parts of the world (one in America). They are characterized by their unusual bill which is laterally compressed and has the upper mandible markedly shorter than the lower.

POMARINE JAEGER
Stercorarius pomarinus   Plate 6

Description: 18–21. *Distinctly larger than Laughing Gull.* Plumage variable, with breeding plumage adults (infrequently seen in Panama, only on northward passage) having *fairly long (up to 4 in) twisted central tail feathers, rounded at tip (spoon-shaped)*, extending beyond rest of tail. Light phase breeding adult dark grayish brown above with black cap and creamy collar on hindneck; white below with varying amounts (often extensive) of dark brown barring, especially on sides and across breast (typically forming a *distinct broad breast band*); *prominent white flash at base of primaries* is obvious in flight, both from above and below (from below may also show a *distinctive second pale patch at base of primary coverts*, not shared by other jaegers). Dark phase uniform sooty brown with black cap and the same white in wing. Juvenile variable but basically brown, drabber and more grayish on head; *entire underparts, extending to under tail-coverts, usually evenly and boldly barred blackish* (this also on rump); wings as in adult, but under wing-coverts more barred with whitish; central tail feathers barely protrude (rarely noticeable). Immature and nonbreeding adult similar to juvenile but with dark cap, white throat, and more white on belly and rump; nonbreeding adult has under wing-coverts solidly dark.
Similar species: Jaegers are notoriously tricky to identify, and this is especially the case in Panama where the relatively distinctive full breeding adults are rarely seen, but a confusing array of subadult plumages is. These are often hard to distinguish from Parasitic Jaeger; points to look for include the following (but many are subtle, requiring a close look or much experience; many jaegers cannot be identified to species). *Pomarine bulks larger* and looks distinctly larger-headed; its flight is especially powerful and steady, with slow relatively shallow wingbeats, and *wings very broad at their base.* In all plumages the *Pomarine shows more white at the base of the primaries* than does Parasitic. Pomarine's *bill is notably heavier*, and looks pale (usually bluish, less often horn-colored) with *contrasting black tip* (Parasitic's is darker bluish gray basally, with less contrasting black tip). Juveniles and immatures tend to be *more evenly and boldly barred below* than Parasitics of the same age (in which the barring is more obscure or irregular, often wavy especially on under tail-coverts and rump); *Pomarines almost never*

show the pale nape seen on most young Parasitics. Pomarines can also be confused with South Polar Skua, which see.
Status and distribution: Uncommon to at times fairly common transient and winter visitant to offshore waters both in the Pacific and the Caribbean, less numerous during northern summer months. Only occasionally do they come within sight of land, then most often at Colon harbour, where at times a few can be seen roosting on the seawall at Coco Solo (this can provide an excellent, and unusual, opportunity for close scrutiny, though in recent years numbers seen have tended to be smaller than they were in the 1960s and 1970s; Parasitics are also regularly present). Still only one specimen is known from Panama, that a bird taken at Puerto Obaldía, San Blas, on April 15, 1935; a number of others have been photographed.
Range: Breeds in arctic; winters southward, mostly at sea, in New World from off southern United States to Peru and Guyana.

PARASITIC JAEGER
Stercorarius parasiticus   Plates 4, 6

Description: 16–19. Resembles Pomarine Jaeger but smaller (though there is a little overlap in size), especially appearing smaller headed and with slenderer bill; *about the same size as Laughing Gull* (Pomarine looks distinctly larger). Adults have *fairly long* (up to 3½ in) straight, pointed central tail feathers extending beyond end of tail, though these are shorter in nonbreeding plumage birds and in any case are often partially broken off. Light phase is more frequent in adults than it is in Pomarine Jaeger. Light phase breeding adult grayish brown above with black cap and creamy collar on hindneck; white below with grayish brown wash or blotching on breast (*not the complete broad breast band of Pomarine*), usually with no barring on sides; white flash at base of primaries is obvious in flight, both from above and below (but usually *not as prominent as in Pomarine*). Dark phase uniform sooty brown with black cap and the white in the wing. Juvenile variable, but basically brown, often with rusty tones, and almost always showing a *pale buff area on hindneck*, usually showing at least some irregular or wavy barring below and on rump; wings as in adult but with under wing-coverts more barred with whitish; central tail feathers barely protrude (and are rarely noticeable). Immature and nonbreeding adult similar, resembling juvenile but with dark cap, white throat, and more white on belly and rump (under wing-coverts solidly dark in nonbreeding adults).

Similar species: See under Pomarine and Long-tailed Jaegers.

Status and distribution: Generally an uncommon transient and winter visitant to offshore waters both in the Pacific and Caribbean, with only a few reports from northern summer months. Infrequent within sight of land, though entering the Colon harbor fairly regularly (but usually outnumbered by Pomarines there); there have also been a number of sightings of this species from Gatun Lake, and one immature, almost certainly this species, was seen as it flew in and landed on a small pond along the Pan-American Highway west of Penonomé, Coclé, on January 6, 1974 (Ridgely and F. G. Stiles). An indication that much larger numbers than are typically observed do pass by Panama is N. G. Smith's sighting of between 900 and 1300 flying west along the south shore of the Azuero Peninsula off Punta Mala on March 30, 1970.

Habits: The jaegers are predatory, often piratical seabirds with strongly hooked bills and long pointed angled wings; the behavior of the Parasitic Jaegar is typical of the three species. They are aggressive birds with powerful rapid flight and deceptively slow wingbeats; they can easily overtake gulls, terns, or other seabirds, then forcing them to disgorge their food. Dead fish and some carrion are also eaten. Typically jaegers are solitary, winging in rapidly (often well above the water) to harass a group of feeding birds (terns are preferred), then moving on; sometimes they will approach boats, trailing in the stern, waiting for refuse to be thrown overboard.

Range: Breeds in arctic; winters southward, mostly at sea, in New World from off southern United States to Tierra del Fuego.

[LONG-TAILED JAEGER]
Stercorarius longicaudus

Description: 14–16. Only one old, uncertain report. Resembles Parasitic Jaeger but markedly slimmer and narrower-winged; adults have *very long pointed central tail feathers (up to 10 in in length)*, but these are often broken off or shorter because of molt. Dark phase extremely rare. Breeding adult brownish gray above with black cap and creamy collar on hindneck; white below (with no breast band and no barring on sides), gradually becoming gray on lower belly and black on under tail-coverts; *white flash at base of primaries is small and inconspicuous* (showing only on outer one or two primaries, and *showing no white from below*, unlike Parasitic), and with *distinctive contrast between pale grayish wing-coverts and dark primaries and trailing edge to wing*. Juvenile closely resembles juvenile Parasitic Jaeger but typically is grayer, often paler on head, and usually showing *fine but distinct pale barring on back, scapulars, and wing-coverts* (barring more diffuse and warmer in Parasitic); under tail-coverts are coarsely barred with black (more like Pomarine's than Parasitic). Nonbreeding adult less clean-cut than in breeding plumage, with gray upperparts flecked darker, some white on rump, less defined black cap, and variable amount of dark barring below (this often coalescing into a breast band); immatures are more or less similar to this (but plumage sequences still not well understood in this, the least well known of the jaegers).

Similar species: Adults with lengthened tail feathers are unmistakable, though these are so often missing or shortened that they usually are not much help (and in any case are so thin as to almost be invisible except at close range). Without them Long-tails can easily be confused with much more common Parasitic Jaeger (there is some overlap in overall body length). Long-tail's body and particularly its wings are slimmer, and its flight more buoyant (almost tern-like), though still fast. Adults in all plumages and older immatures always show the contrast between pale (usually quite gray) mantle and dark primaries and trailing edge to secondaries (this effect not shown by Parasitic).

Status and distribution: One report without details of a bird seen with other jaegers in Colon harbor on February 9, 1927 (L. Griscom). This report is difficult to evaluate: Griscom was an experienced and careful observer, but the basis for this identification was never published, and the various criteria for distinguishing Long-tailed from Parasitic Jaegers were then not well established (and overlap in the number of primaries showing white then not recognized). Despite the lack of subsequent records, the Long-tailed Jaeger will probably eventually prove to be a rare migrant off Panama, most likely far offshore in the Pacific; it is the most pelagic of the jaegers, only very rarely coming within sight of land when not breeding.

Range: Breeds in arctic; winters southward, apparently mostly or entirely very far from land (distribution not well understood), in New World south to Chile and Argentina.

[SOUTH POLAR SKUA]
Catharacta maccormicki

Description: 20–22. Sight reports from off Pacific coast. A stocky, barrel-chested seabird with broad wings and a *very large patch of white at base of primaries*. Occurs in three phases, apparently about equal numbers of each. Light phase is almost unmistakable, basically two-toned, with *very pale chamois to whitish head and underparts* (whitest on nape) *contrasting with uniform dark brown upperparts*. Intermediate phase also distinctive, mostly dark brown (including underparts) with *conspicuous contrasting pale buff collar on hindneck*, and usually fairly pale head. Dark phase is essentially uniform dark blackish brown, sometimes with a pale area at base of bill. Juveniles of all three phases resemble their respective adults, but tend to be more grayish, especially on head and underparts, and *usually still show the pale area on hindneck*; their bills are pale bluish to flesh with dark tip (all dark in adults).

Similar species: In Panama waters most likely to be confused with Pomarine Jaeger. Overall lengths of the two are not dissimilar, but the skua is a much heavier bird with broader, not as pointed, wings; in flight the skua also differs in profile, with an often quite noticeable hunch-backed look. White patch in wing of skua is even larger than in jaeger (and is visible from very great distances), and in none of the many confusing immature or nonbreeding plumages of the jaeger does it show the conspicuous pale patch on hindneck displayed by virtually all of the skuas (often the latter imparts a somewhat "hackled" look).

Status and distribution: Apparently an uncommon and irregular visitant off Pacific coast, where recorded from Gulf of Panama and off Azuero Peninsula; there are reports from February, March, July, September, and November. No specimens have been taken in Panama waters, and collection remains desirable as other species of southern-breeding skuas are also possible.

Habits: Similar to the jaegers, though tending to pursue larger seabirds, rarely bothering with terns.

Range: Breeds in Antarctica and on the South Shetland Islands, ranging regularly in the nonbreeding season north to the North Pacific and North Atlantic Oceans.

Note: Skua taxonomy is complex and remains controversial. Until recently only one species, *C. skua* (Great Skua), was recognized. Recent studies have concluded that North Atlantic breeders are a species distinct from southern hemisphere forms. The number of full species of the latter continues to be debated; two seem certain, with three or more a distinct possibility. The true Great Skua of the North Atlantic is most improbable in Panama, but other southern forms (especially the Chilean Skua, *C. chilensis*) could occur; *chilensis* is found regularly north to coastal Peru.

LAUGHING GULL
Larus atricilla   Plate 6

Description: 15–17. *By far the commonest gull in Panama*. Slightly drooped bill and legs black, bill dark red when breeding. Nonbreeding adult: head and underparts white with brownish gray wash or mottling on head (especially around eyes and on nape); *mantle leaden gray, blending into black on wing-tips*, with white trailing edge to wing; rump and tail also white. First-year immature similar but with *gray breast and flanks*, brownish-mottled wing-coverts with more black on flight feathers, and broad black subterminal tail band. Second-year immature like adult but with some gray on breast and some dusky on tail. Breeding adult has black hood with prominent white eyelids; this plumage is seen regularly in Panama in March–April prior to their migration to nesting areas.

Similar species: In Panama this slender-winged gull is the one to which all the others must be compared; see especially the Franklin's Gull.

Status and distribution: Very common, often locally abundant, transient and winter visitant on both coasts (especially Pacific) and larger bodies of fresh water; smaller numbers, but still locally common, occur in summer months, especially around Panama City (all birds then being immatures or nonbreeding adults). Does not breed in Panama.

Habits: Easily outnumbers all other gulls in Panama put together, sometimes gathering in very large flocks. Regularly feeds on insects over land. Habitually lands on the heads of pelicans that have just surfaced after diving; they then attempt to rob the pelican of its catch as it attempts to swallow.

Its loud, "laughing" call is often heard in March, prior to northward migration.

Range: Breeds locally along Atlantic and Gulf coasts of North America, in Bahamas and on many Caribbean islands including those off Venezuela, and in southeastern California and northwestern Mexico; winters from southern United States to Peru and northern Brazil.

FRANKLIN'S GULL
Larus pipixcan   Plate 6

Description: 13½–15. Resembles much more numerous Laughing Gull, but somewhat smaller and more compact. Bill slenderer and not so drooped; bill and legs blackish to dull reddish, becoming brighter red (especially bill) in breeding adults. Nonbreeding adult: head and underparts white with *well-defined blackish half-hood from hindcrown to sides of head* and broad white eyelids; mantle gray (slightly paler than in Laughing Gull) with *distinct white bar separating the gray from the black wing-tips*, with outer tips of primaries and trailing edge of wing also white; rump and tail mainly white, with central pair of tail feathers pale gray. Immature similar but tail with blackish subterminal band (*except on outer pair of feathers, which are white*); wing pattern much like Laughing Gull's (thus lacking white in primaries), but with *inner primaries grayish, contrasting with blackish outer primaries and subterminal bar on secondaries*. Breeding adult has black hood with broad white eyelids, and sometimes shows a rosy flush on breast (this plumage seen briefly during northward passage).

Similar species: Nonbreeding adults differ from Laughing Gull in having white in primaries and more discrete blackish area on rear of head. Immatures are whiter below than immature Laughings (which always show at least some, and often considerable, gray on breast and flanks), and in Laughing the black subterminal tail band extends across all the tail feathers (outer pair all-white in Franklin's), though this distinction can be hard to make out except at close range; head patterns also differ (much as in adults of both). See also Gray-hooded and Bonaparte's Gulls.

Status and distribution: Uncommon to fairly common transient (April–May; November–December) and less numerous winter visitant to both coasts, most numerous along shore of Panama Bay

(especially about Panama City); immatures and subadults remain throughout the summer, often showing almost complete black hoods. Also occurs well offshore, and often noted inland on Gatun Lake and other Canal waters, especially on migration.

Habits: Has a more buoyant, graceful flight than Laughing Gull.

Range: Breeds in western North America; winters mainly along Pacific Coast of South Panama in Peru and Chile, in increasingly small numbers north to Mexico; very small numbers also on Caribbean coast of Panama.

[GRAY-HOODED GULL]
Larus cirrocephalus

Description: 16½–17½. One sight report from Pacific coast. Bill and legs dark red, brighter when breeding (both dusky yellowish in immatures); *iris white* in adult. Adult has *pearly gray hood* , darkest along its posterior margin and whitish on foreface; mantle pale gray with mostly black primaries and *large white wedge on leading edge of outer wing*; most of underparts, and rump and tail white. Immature lacks hood but has *dusky patch on ear-coverts*; otherwise much as adult, but with brownish mottling on wing-coverts (*pattern on outer wing similar*), and with narrow blackish subterminal band on tail. Nonbreeding adult has paler gray hood.

Similar species: Franklin's Gull never shows as much white on outer wing as does this species (at most it has a white bar across primaries and tipping); head pattern also differs, Franklin's never showing an earspot (but always with at least a blackish "half-hood"). Immature Ring-billed Gull shows somewhat similar wing and tail pattern, but it too never has a dark earspot (though almost always showing brown streaking at least on head and neck). Bonaparte's Gull is much smaller, etc.

Status and distribution: Only report is a sighting of a nonbreeding adult along Panama city waterfront on September 25, 1955 (M. Moynihan).

Habits: In its normal range a gull of coastal lagoons, harbors, saltworks (and inland saline lakes), etc; usually not on the open ocean. Its numbers in South America may be increasing.

Range: Breeds locally along coast of southern Ecuador and Peru, and in southern Brazil and Argentina; also Africa.

BONAPARTE'S GULL
Larus philadelphia

Description: 12–14. Three records, all from Caribbean coast. Bill slender, usually black, sometimes with reddish base in immatures; legs flesh-colored, orange-red in breeding adults. *A trim, graceful, tern-like gull.* Nonbreeding adult: head and underparts white with *conspicuous blackish spot on ear-coverts* and pale gray hindcrown; mantle pale gray with *long white wedge on front part of outer wing*, and narrow black tipping on primaries. Immature similar but with *narrow black subterminal tail band*, and *distinctive wing pattern*: entire trailing edge of wing bordered with black, broadly black-edged outer primaries, and broad diagonal band of dusky across wing-coverts. Breeding adult has black hood with narrow white eyelids.

Similar species: Sabine's Gull is only other gull in Panama which is as small, but in all plumages it has *black* wedge on front part of wing (where this species is white). See also Common Black-headed and Little Gulls (below).

Status and distribution: Apparently a casual visitor to Panama, with three records, all from Caribbean coast of Canal area: an immature photographed at Coco Solo on December 26–29, 1972 (J. Pujals); an immature at Gatun Dam spillway on January 13, 1974 (C. Leahy and Ridgely); and an adult photographed at Coco Solo on December 11–29, 1984 (D. Engleman *et al.*).

Habits: In Panama has usually associated with Common or Sandwich Terns.

Range: Breeds in Alaska and Canada; winters mostly coastally in United States, Mexico, and Canada, with a few vagrants south to Costa Rica and Panama.

Note: Both the Common Black-headed (*L. ridibundus*) and the Little (*L. minutus*) Gulls have been recorded recently in northern South America, and thus should be watched for in Panama; both are basically Eurasian species, but have been slowly increasing in North America over the past few decades, and both now even breed in small numbers. Black-headed resembles respective plumages of Bonaparte's but has heavier reddish to yellowish bill and more dark on underwing. Little is smaller than Bonaparte's; adults have uniform pale gray upperwing (no white wedge) and mostly blackish underwing, while immature has blackish crown (in addition to the ear-spot) and a bolder "W" pattern across upperwing.

[GRAY GULL]
Larus modestus

Description: 17–18. Two sightings from off Pacific coast. Bill and legs black. Adult *uniform plain gray* with *whitish hood* (hood brown in nonbreeding plumage); flight feathers blackish with secondaries tipped white, forming *broad white trailing edge to wing*; tail gray with black subterminal band and white tip. Immature grayish brown, feathers of mantle narrowly edged paler; tail with black subterminal band and buff tip.

Similar species: Beware immature Laughing Gulls, which can look very uniform gray when perched; however, once they fly, their white rump and basal tail should be obvious (*rump and tail dark in Gray Gull*, tail with *white or buff tip* depending on age). Otherwise not likely to be confused.

Status and distribution: Apparently a casual vagrant to Gulf of Panama. There are two Panama reports: one was reported seen south of Pacific entrance to the Panama Canal on November 28, 1945 (R. C. Murphy); three were seen south of Isla Otoque on February 6, 1956 (Wetmore). Somewhat surprisingly, none were reported during the invasion of other Humboldt Current seabirds in the severe "Niño year" of 1983.

Habits: In its normal range a gull of sandy coastlines, sometimes feeding Sanderling-like on ocean beaches, also offshore (but never far from land).

Range: Breeds in Atacama Desert of northern Chile and probably Peru; disperses north regularly to coast of southwestern Ecuador, and apparently casually to off Colombia, Panama, and Cocos Island.

BAND-TAILED GULL
Larus belcheri

Description: 2–22. Three records from Pacific coast. *Bill very heavy, yellow with outer third red* and black spot on upper mandible; legs yellow. Breeding adult has head, neck, and entire underparts white; entire mantle slaty black with broad white trailing edge to wing; rump and tail white with *broad black subterminal band on tail*. Nonbreeders and subadults similar but with *contrasting blackish brown hood*, duller bill colors. Immature mostly grayish brown, feathers of upperparts edged paler; *head and breast contrastingly dark brown*; tail mostly blackish, with whitish rump; bill mostly yellow with black tip.

Similar species: The heavy, brightly colored bill and band on the tail are distinctive;

Panama birds are most likely to be non-breeders or young birds, in which case their *solid dark-hooded effect* is almost diagnostic.

Status and distribution: Apparently a casual vagrant to Gulf of Panama. There are three Panama reports: one at Panama Viejo on December 20, 1962 (Eisenmann); one at Fort Amador on May 10 and August 24, 1964 (W. Belton and H. Loftin; photographed) one at Albrook AFB on December 2, 1967 (H. Loftin). As with Gray Gull, it seems somewhat surprising that none was reported in 1983, a year when numerous other Humboldt Current seabirds invaded the Gulf of Panama because of a particularly severe and protracted invasion (Niño current) of warm water off the west coast of South America.

Habits: In its normal range a gull of rocky coastlines and harbors, not particularly numerous.

Range: Breeds locally along coasts of Peru and Chile, casually wandering north to Panama and south to Tierra del Fuego; a population on the coast of Argentina, *atlanticus*, probably represents a distinct species (Olrog's Gull).

RING-BILLED GULL
Larus delawarensis Plate 6

Description: 18–20. Rare but increasing nonbreeding visitant. Adult has *yellow bill with conspicuous black band near tip, greenish yellow legs*; in immature *bill pinkish with dusky tip, legs dull pinkish to grayish flesh.* Adult mainly white with pale gray mantle (*much paler than the dark gray of Laughing Gull*); wing-tips black with small subapical white spots on outermost primaries, and white trailing edge to wing. Except when breeding head and neck are variably streaked with brown. Immature has streaking on head and neck more prominent, and also a variable amount of brown spotting and scaling on underparts; its wing-coverts are browner (though back already gray), with more extensive blackish to flight feathers and no subapical spots; tail white with *narrow black subterminal band.* Older (second-year) immatures like adult but still show a trace of the tail band, and lack subapical spots in primaries.

Similar species: Readily told from Laughing Gull, with which it usually associates in Panama, by its larger size and paler overall appearance (even when immature); Laughing Gull's bill and legs are usually black when in Panama, and slenderer

drooped shape to bill is very different. Herring Gull is larger, and young immatures (which are the birds most often found in Panama) are browner overall with much broader dark tail band.

Status and distribution: Rare but regular nonbreeding visitant in small numbers to both coasts of central Panama, rarely seen any distance inland. A few may be present virtually throughout the year, but most regular during northern winter months, especially November–April; up to four birds have been seen at once at favored localities such as Fort Amador. Still no specimen from Panama. The increase in its numbers here (it was not recorded regularly until the 1970s) is probably both genuine, reflecting its marked increase in North America during recent decades, and a result of increased observer coverage and awareness. Only one report away from central Panama, that a single immature at Coiba Island on April 9–14, 1976 (Ridgely).

Habits: Usually spotted as it rests among a large throng of Laughing Gulls.

Range: Breeds in North America; winters mainly in United States, Mexico, and Greater Antilles, in very small numbers south to Costa Rica and Panama.

HERRING GULL
Larus argentatus Plate 6

Description: 22–25. Rare but increasing visitant. *Considerably larger than Laughing Gull*, and easily picked out on that basis alone. Adult has yellow bill with red spot near tip of lower mandible, *flesh-colored legs*; in immature *bill dark* (sometimes with pale base; older immatures have *dull yellowish bill with wide black tip*), legs also flesh. Adult mainly white with pale gray mantle; wing-tips black with small subapical white spots on outermost primaries, and white trailing edge to wing. Except when breeding head and neck are variably streaked with brown. First-year immature *predominantly brown* with paler feather edging; flight feathers entirely brownish black; *tail with very wide blackish band* (often so wide that entire tail looks dark). Second-year immature more like adult, but with browner wings (back is already gray), and *very wide brownish black tail-band* contrasting with white rump. Only immatures seem to have been reported from Panama.

Similar species: Larger and heavier than Ring-billed Gull; immature Ring-bills never look as brown as Herrings in their first year do, and never show nearly as much dark on the tail. See also Lesser Black-backed and Band-tailed Gulls.

Status and distribution: Rare but regular nonbreeding visitant in small numbers to Panama, where recorded mostly from both coasts of central Panama; a few reports from Gatun Lake, and coast of Bocas del Toro. Mostly recorded December–April, with one second-year bird seen at Fort Amador on July 7, 1975 (Ridgely). Still no specimen from Panama; as with Ring-billed Gull, its recent increase here doubtless reflects a large population expansion in North America and more careful and frequent observer coverage.

Range: Breeds in North America and Eurasia; in New World winters south regularly to Mexico, in small numbers in West Indies and to Costa Rica and Panama, and casually to north coast of South America.

LESSER BLACK-BACKED GULL
Larus fuscus

Description: 21–22. Accidental. Resembles Herring Gull (particularly immatures); *adult's legs are yellow*, though these are often dull flesh in younger immatures. Adult easily distinguished by its *dark gray mantle* (much darker than in Herring Gull). Immatures are *very* similar to respectively aged Herring Gulls, and can only be distinguished in flight and at very close range. First-year Lesser Black-backs have an all-dark outer wing and an inner wing showing *two dark bars* (formed by the secondaries and the greater secondary coverts; only the secondaries are so dark in Herring Gull). Second-year Lesser Black-backs will typically have begun to show adult's *dark gray back* (Herring's back markedly paler).

Similar species: Attempting to identify immatures is a hazardous undertaking, and previous experience in their more normal range mandatory. To compound the difficulties, other unrecorded dark-mantled gulls are just about as likely as this mainly Eurasian species (especially the Kelp, *L. dominicanus*, and Western, *L. occidentalis*, Gulls), and the real possibility of hybrids must also be considered.

Status and distribution: What must be presumed to be the same individual has wintered for many years in the Fort Amador area; first seen in the winter of 1979/1980, when it was in second-year plumage, it has occurred each winter since (most recently in 1987/1988); see N. G. Smith (*Am. Birds 36*(3):

336–337, 1982). The bird has been identified as of the European race *graellsii*.

Range: Breeds in northern Eurasia, wintering south to Africa; small numbers have increasingly been found in North America (mainly eastern), with vagrants south to Panama, the West Indies, and northern South America.

SABINE'S GULL
Xema sabini   Plate 6

Description: 13–14. *A small, mostly pelagic gull with shallowly forked tail and striking wing pattern.* Bill black with *yellow tip* (little or no yellow in immature); legs black. Breeding plumage adult has *slaty gray hood margined narrowly with black*; neck, underparts, rump, and tail white; back and wing-coverts pale gray, with *broad black wedge on front part of outer wing and large white triangular area behind that* (formed by inner primaries and secondaries). When not breeding adults lose the hood, it being reduced to a smudge of gray on hindneck; most often seen in Panama are passage birds molting between these plumages. Immature resembles nonbreeding adult but is browner on mantle, this extending up over hindneck to mid-crown, the feathers narrowly pale-edged resulting in delicate scaly effect; the slightly forked tail is *narrowly black-tipped.*

Similar species: Almost unmistakable, this lovely small gull could only be confused with Bonaparte's, which has white (not black) wedge on outer wing, etc.

Status and distribution: Uncommon to at times fairly common transient to offshore waters in the Pacific, very rarely recorded from shore; seen mostly while apparently on passage (mainly September–December and April–June), with very few records from northern mid-winter months. Only record from Caribbean side is of an immature photographed at Coco Solo on October 7–8, 1977 (J. Pujals); other reports are uncertain.

Habits: Has a buoyant, tern-like flight with deep wing-strokes. Often in loosely associated small groups, regularly with terns or other pelagic birds.

Range: Breeds in arctic North America and Eurasia; in New World apparently winters mainly off Peru and Chile (but winter distribution still not well understood).

[SWALLOW-TAILED GULL]
Creagrus furcatus

Description: 21–23. One somewhat uncertain report from off Pacific coast. *A large,* *beautifully marked gull with deeply forked tail.* Bill black, in adult tipped pale greenish and with some red at base; *legs pink*, brightest when breeding. Adult has *slaty gray hood* with white at base of bill, *becoming paler gray on breast and mantle* and white on belly; *flight feathers mainly white* (contrasting with gray wing-coverts), with outer primaries black; narrow white stripe on either side of back (formed by the scapulars). Nonbreeding adult similar but head mostly white with *large blackish patch around eye and on ear-coverts*. Immature has mantle brown with feathers boldly edged white; *wing pattern otherwise as in adult*; head and underparts white with *black patch around eye and another on ear-coverts*; tail with *black terminal band*.

Similar species: Large size combined with bold wing pattern and the forked tail makes this gull almost unmistakable. Wing pattern reminiscent of much smaller Sabine's Gull; Sabine's never shows black around the eye and has much less noticeably forked tail, etc.

Status and distribution: One report of a bird believed this species seen 10 miles north of Piñas Bay, Darién on July 18, 1957 (C. R. Robins).

Habits: Highly pelagic when away from its nesting grounds (primarily the Galapagos). The Swallow-tailed Gull feeds primarily at night; during daylight hours it is usually seen resting on the water.

Range: Breeds on Galapagos Islands and on Malpelo Island off Colombia; ranges to off coast of western South America, perhaps casually to Panama.

GULL-BILLED TERN
Sterna nilotica   Plate 6

Description: 13–14. Locally along coasts (mostly the Pacific). *Heavy, almost gull-like bill black*; legs also black. Looks *very white overall*; *tail rather short, only slightly forked.* Nonbreeding adult and immature mostly white with very pale gray mantle and *dusky patch through eye onto ear-coverts*; narrow dusky tips to primaries. Breeding plumage adults have black crown and nape instead of the ear-patch.

Similar species: The whitest-looking tern normally occurring in Panama. Most resembles Sandwich Tern, but differs in its thicker, all-black bill (remember that Sandwich's yellow tip can be missing or hard to see, but it is always slenderer and longer), shorter and not so deeply forked tail, and in lacking black on hindcrown. Common Tern

is slenderer with more deeply forked tail; it is grayer above with pronounced dark carpal bar and black on hindcrown in nonbreeding plumage. See also Forster's Tern.

Status and distribution: Uncommon to locally common visitor to Pacific coast, seeming somewhat erratic and variable in numbers, with no pronounced season of maximum abundance; much less numerous on Caribbean coast, where known only as a scarce transient, especially September–October. Largest concentrations seem to be found at the salinas at Aguadulce, Coclé, but even here seems irregular (up to 160 have been counted, that on January 6, 1974; Ridgely). Birds in full breeding plumage are noted regularly from at least April–July. Breeding in Panama unrecorded, though not inconceivable: groups of birds in breeding plumage have been seen quite consistently at Aguadulce (a seemingly suitable site) in June–July.

Habits: Unlike most terns, the Gull-bill only occasionally dives into water, more often hawking for large insects over marshes and shallow water (sometimes even capturing them while walking on the ground). Its call is a rasping, sharp *kay-wéck, kay-wéck*, mostly often doubled.

Range: Breeds locally on coasts of southern United States and western Mexico, in the West Indies, and in South America in Ecuador (its breeding site closest to Panama) and from the Guianas to Argentina; nonbreeders occur more widely and range south to Peru; also locally in warmer parts of Old World.

Note: Formerly placed in the monotypic genus *Gelochelidon*.

CASPIAN TERN
Sterna caspia   Plate 6

Description: 21–23. Rare visitant, mostly to Caribbean coast. A large, stocky, broad-winged tern with *very heavy bright red bill* (usually blackish-tipped); legs black (dark reddish in some immatures). Nonbreeding plumage: *entire crown black narrowly streaked with white*; otherwise mostly white with pale gray mantle, primaries edged blackish (*most visible from below*); tail only slightly forked. Breeding plumage birds similar but with crown solid black.

Similar species: Resembles much more numerous Royal Tern; Royal has slimmer more orange bill, white forehead in nonbreeding plumage (black only on rear-crown), more deeply forked tail, and lacks Caspian's blackish underside of primaries.

Status and distribution: Rare but apparently now regular winter visitant, mainly to Caribbean coast (especially in Canal area), but also with a few reports from Panama Viejo/Tocumen area and one from Gatun Lake; recorded only November–March, but a few may occur at other seasons as well.

Habits: In Panama usually found singly, often in association with other terns and gulls. Feeds mostly around lakes, ponds, or harbors, less often over ocean itself. Its commonest call is an often startlingly loud harsh *krra-ark*! and immatures also give a distinctive squealing *squee-you*.

Range: Breeds locally in North America and the Old World; in America winters mostly coastally in southern United States and Mexico, with small numbers south to Costa Rica and Panama, northern South America, and West Indies.

Note: Formerly placed in the monotypic genus *Hydroprogne*.

ROYAL TERN
Sterna maxima   Plate 6

Description: 19–21. A large, generally numerous and widespread coastal tern. *Stout bill reddish orange to yellow-orange* (reddest when breeding); legs usually black. Nonbreeding plumage: mostly white with *rearcrown and nape black* (often with some white streaks), the feathers forming a *bushy crest* which frequently stands out from head; mantle pale gray, primaries edged blackish (*visible mostly from above*); tail moderately forked. For a short period at onset of breeding season entire crown is black (but this condition rarely seen in Panama).

Similar species: Caspian Tern never shows the white forecrown which is almost always very prominent on Royal Terns in Panama; there are other differences as well (see under that species). Sandwich Tern has similar plumage, but is markedly smaller and can easily be known by its slender black bill usually showing a yellow tip. See also the very similar Elegant Tern.

Status and distribution: Fairly common to common and widespread along both coasts, but generally in larger numbers on Pacific; small numbers are also sometimes found on larger bodies of fresh water, particularly Gatun Lake, and this species sometimes wanders well offshore, far beyond sight of land, though it is primarily coastal. Royal Terns occur in Panama waters year-round,

but do not breed; numbers seem greatest during northern winter months.

Habits: Feeds almost entirely by diving for small fish, often plunging down from considerable heights; they usually scatter out when foraging, but tend to gather in flocks when roosting at certain favored sites. Calls are shrill and sharp, a *chirrik* and a *keeyr* being most frequent.

Range: Breeds locally on coasts of southern United States, Mexico, on islands in southern Caribbean (closest site to Panama being the Netherlands Antilles), and in eastern South America south to Argentina; nonbreeders occur widely, and range south to Peru; also in Africa.

Note: Formerly placed in the genus *Thalasseus*.

ELEGANT TERN
Sterna elegans   Plate 6

Description: 16–17. A rare visitant to Pacific coast and offshore waters. Closely resembles the somewhat larger and heavier-built Royal Tern; a good view is necessary to confirm an identification of this species. *Bill longer and more slender* (in shape much like a Sandwich Tern's; Royals' bills can vary somewhat in stoutness, so be careful), *yellow to orange-yellow* (more reddish orange at onset of breeding season). The crest is slightly longer, and the fully solid black crown is retained longer; in nonbreeding plumage the *black of rearcrown extends forward to encompass eye* (in most Royals the black eye stands out in a white face), and cap is solidly black from behind (no white streaking visible as in Royal); a *pink flush* is sometimes evident on breast of breeding plumage birds (never shown by Royals).

Status and distribution: Rare and seemingly irregular visitant to Pacific coast and offshore waters; no pronounced season of maximum abundance, with largest number seen being 55 at Aguadulce, Coclé, on June 26, 1971 (Eisenmann and J. Pujals). No specimens have been taken in Panama, though one was photographed at Fort Amador on January 23, 1969 (Ridgely).

Habits: The Elegant Tern may be mostly pelagic as a migrant to and from its Mexican breeding grounds, and this could account for the relative scarcity of Panama records. Persistent searching of Royal Tern flocks is the best way to find this species.

Range: Breeds mostly on islands off of Baja California and in Gulf of California, also a few in extreme southern California; winters

mostly along coast of Peru and Chile, in smaller numbers north to Guatemala.
Note: Formerly placed in the genus *Thalasseus*.

SANDWICH TERN
Sterna sandvicensis   Plate 6

Description: 15–17. *Long slender black bill with yellow tip* (tip difficult to see at a distance, occasionally even lacking); legs black. Nonbreeding plumage: mostly white with rearcrown and nape black, the feathers forming a slight bushy crest; mantle pale gray, primaries edged blackish (visible mostly from above); tail quite deeply forked. Breeding plumage birds similar but with entire crown solid black.
Similar species: In plumage very like Royal Tern, but markedly smaller with very differently colored and shaped bill and more deeply forked tail. Confusion more likely with Gull-billed Tern, though that has much heavier shorter all-black bill, only slightly forked tail, and lacks black on rearcrown (restricted to ear-coverts) in nonbreeding plumage. Common Tern is somewhat smaller and slighter in build; perched birds can look somewhat alike, but note nonbreeding Common's dark carpal bar, reddish (not black) legs, and reddish at base of bill (usually). Sandwich Tern's mantle is whiter generally than any other Panama tern except the Gull-billed (Common's is distinctly darker).
Status and distribution: Uncommon to locally common visitant to both coasts, though considerably more numerous on Pacific (where often the commonest tern); a few are also sometimes found on larger bodies of fresh water, particularly on Gatun Lake and along the Canal. Sandwich Terns occur in Panama waters year-round, but do not breed; numbers are definitely highest during northern winter months (especially December–April), with 200–300 or even more being regularly encountered at that time at certain favored sites such as Juan Diaz.
Habits: Similar to Royal Tern, but does not seem nearly so prone to wander far out to sea as does that species.
Range: Breeds locally along coasts of southeastern United States, Caribbean Mexico, on West Indies, and along northern and eastern coasts of South America to Argentina; northern breeders winter south on Pacific coast to Peru; also in Eurasia and North Africa.

Note: Formerly placed in the genus *Thalasseus*. *S. eurygnatha* (Cayenne Tern) of southern Caribbean and Atlantic coasts of South America is now considered conspecific with this species; its bill is typically pale lemon yellow, but intergrades between the two are common at certain colonies. ''Cayenne Terns'' could wander west to the Caribbean coast of Panama (there are several records from northern Colombia), and should be watched for.

COMMON TERN
Sterna hirundo   Plate 6

Description: 13–15. *Bill blackish, often with some reddish or* (in immatures) *yellowish near base* (in breeding adults, coral red with black tip); *legs reddish to dull orange* (bright red in breeding adults). Nonbreeding plumage: mostly white with *black hindcrown and nape*; mantle pale gray with *dark bar along leading edge of inner wing* (the ''carpal bar'') and blackish tipping on outer primaries; tail deeply forked, with *outer web of outer pair of feathers blackish*. Breeding plumage birds have solid black crown and nape, and lack the dark carpal bar.
Similar species: Sandwich Tern is whiter generally (this evident especially in flight), and has more slender bill with yellow tip; its legs are black (not reddish or orange), often a useful character among a dense flock of roosting terns. See also Forster's Tern, and Arctic and Roseate Terns (below).
Status and distribution: Fairly common transient and uncommon winter resident along both coasts, numbers usually greater on Pacific; small numbers are found fairly often on Gatun Lake and along the Canal; a few immatures or nonbreeders are present during northern summer, but most numerous October–November and in April. Overall numbers seem to have declined in Panama in recent years.
Habits: Flight is very graceful and buoyant, with deep wing-strokes; often hovers with rapid wingbeats prior to plunging into the water. Usually quiet while in Panama.
Range: Breeds in North America and locally in West Indies and on islands off northern coast of South America, wintering mostly along coast of South America (especially the Caribbean and Atlantic) south to Peru and Argentina, in smaller numbers north to Mexico and in West Indies; also occurs widely in the Old World.
Note: Two other similar terns are possible but unrecorded. Roseate Tern (*S. dougallii*) should be watched for especially on Carib-

bean coast; it breeds very locally on Atlantic coast of North America, in West Indies, on islands off coast of Belize and Honduras, and on islands in southern Caribbean (also in Old World), wintering mainly in the Guianan region, but with a few sightings from northern Colombia and a band recovery from Gorgona Island off Colombian Pacific coast (the latter bird almost had to have passed through Panama). Nonbreeding Roseate Tern resembles nonbreeding Common, but is paler overall with *much longer outer tail feathers* (tail extends well beyond wing-tips on resting birds) with *outer web of outermost pair white like rest of tail* (not blackish), and with *much less prominent carpal bar* above wing. Arctic Tern (*S. paradisaea*) could occur as a transient far offshore in the Pacific (much less likely along the coast), to or from its far southern wintering grounds (it breeds in arctic North America and Eurasia). Arctic Tern is difficult to distinguish from Common when they are in nonbreeding plumage; best points to look for are Arctic's *whiter flight feathers* (especially the secondaries), its *all white tail* (with no dusky on outer web of outermost retrix), and its less distinct dark carpal bar. Thus nonbreeding Arctics also very closely resemble nonbreeding Roseate Tern (also with very white wing and tail, and less prominent carpal bar; note Roseate's slightly longer outer tail feathers). Arctic's bill is slightly shorter and thicker, but best means of separating them is *Roseate's lack of a narrow black trailing edge on underside of outer wing* (narrow and sharply defined in Arctic, wider and less crisp in Common). *Note that Common Terns also migrate far out to sea*; it is *definitely* not safe to assume such birds are Arctics.

FORSTER'S TERN
Sterna forsteri

Description: 13–15. Several recent reports from both coasts of central Panama. Nonbreeding plumage birds closely resemble Common Terns in that plumage. Best points of distinction are: *the absence of Common's dark carpal bar* (in Forster's the entire upper wing is basically pale gray, with only a little blackish tipping on primaries, and often showing an *obvious silvery flash on outer wing*, formed by white edging on primaries); its *blackish eye-patch* (shaped rather like Gull-billed's; Forster's may show some dusky streaks on hind-neck, but never has Common's entirely black hindcrown and nape); and its very pale gray tail with white outer tail feathers (Common's tail mostly white, with outer web of outermost retrix dusky — the reverse of Forster's).

Status and distribution: Only recently reported from Panama, but possibly will prove to be a regular winter visitant in very small numbers. There are six known reports: one at Fort Amador on March 20–24, 1980 (N. G. Smith *et al.*); one at Coco Solo on November 10, 1977 (D. Engleman); two at Panama Viejo on March 2, 1983 (T. Davis *et al.*); one at Isla Margarita on November 26, 1983 (D. and L. Engleman); one at Coco Solo on December 27, 1984 (D. and L. Engleman); and three at Coco Solo (one of them photographed, photos to VIREO) on December 6, 1987 (D. and L. Engleman, P. Akers). All were in nonbreeding plumage. Presumably the recent spate of reports is merely due to more careful observer coverage, though it has only recently been recorded from Costa Rica as well.

Range: Breeds in North America; winters mostly coastally in southern United States, Mexico, and Greater Antilles, rarely south to Costa Rica and Panama.

LEAST TERN
Sterna antillarum Plate 6

Description: 8½–9½. *Panama's smallest tern* (aside from the accidental Yellow-billed). Breeding adult has *bill bright yellow narrowly tipped black*, and orange-yellow legs; birds in nonbreeding plumage and immatures have bill and legs brownish to black. Breeding plumage: mainly white with black crown and nape, and *white forehead extending back as narrow stripe over eye*; mantle pale gray, with outer two primaries black; tail deeply forked. Nonbreeding adult and immature: similar, but with black crown reduced extending back from eye around nape, gray mantle mottled with dusky (especially in immatures), and *dark carpal bar*.

Similar species: Small size and pale overall appearance unique among regularly occurring Panama terns; compare to Yellow-billed Tern (only one record), and Peruvian Tern (below). Black Tern is uniform pale gray above, only notched tail, very different behavior, etc.

Status and distribution: Uncommon to at times fairly common transient on both coasts and also offshore in Panama Bay (and probably elsewhere), with one report from Gatun Lake; recorded mostly August–January and

April–May, with a few birds lingering through northern summer months (doubtless first-summer pre-breeders), most regularly at the Aguadulce salinas in Coclé.

Habits: In Panama often associates with Black Terns, frequently flying and hovering well above the flock of milling Blacks. Usually flies with very rapid wing-beats.

Range: Breeds locally along coasts and rivers in United States, and on Pacific coast of Mexico, Caribbean coast of Belize and Honduras, and in West Indies and on islands off northern South America; northern birds winter south coastally to Peru and Brazil.

Note: The 1983 AOU Check-list separated New World birds, *S. antillarum* (Least Tern), from those of the Old World, *S. albifrons* (Little Tern). Peruvian Tern (*S. lorata*) should be watched for in Pacific waters of Panama though it has not been recorded north of Ecuador (and breeds only in Peru). It resembles Least Tern but has blacker and often somewhat longer bill (only basal part of bill is yellow, even when breeding), and is *grayer generally* (especially on underparts, rump, and tail) with even less black showing on outer primaries.

YELLOW-BILLED TERN
Sterna superciliaris

Description: 10. One record from Caribbean coast of central Panama. Resembles Least Tern, but slightly larger and with *somewhat stouter and longer bill entirely yellow* (slightly duskier in immatures), and legs duller olive yellow. Plumages of the two are very similar but *Yellow-billed has more of outer primaries black* (four or five as opposed to two in Least); its tail is shorter and not as deeply forked.

Status and distribution: Only one record, that a bird photographed at Coco Solo on October 20, 1977 (J. Pujals). As the species is not known to be migratory, and as it basically is not a coastal bird in its normal range (rather favoring rivers and fresh water lakes), the Yellow-billed Tern seems likely to remain at best a casual wanderer to Panama.

Range: South America south to northern Argentina and Uruguay; west of the Andes known only from along the Cauca and Magdalena Rivers (not the coast) in northern Colombia; one Panama record.

BRIDLED TERN
Sterna anaethetus   Plate 6

Description: 14–15. Known only from off Pacific coast. Bill and legs black. Forehead narrowly white, *extending back as narrow superciliary to just behind eye*; crown and nape otherwise black, *separated from dark brownish gray upperparts by whitish collar*; below white, sometimes tinged with gray; tail deeply forked, pale grayish with outer feathers white. Immature similar to adult but crown white streaked blackish, and mantle with pale feather edging.

Similar species: Resembles Sooty Tern; Sooty is, however, black above (lacking the brown or gray tone of Bridled) and lacks a pale nuchal collar (though Bridled's collar often hard to see under normal field conditions); Bridled's forehead patch is a bit smaller than Sooty's, but it does extend back as narrow stripe over eye.

Status and distribution: Probably breeds on Los Frailes del Sur, a pair of rocky islets off Punta Mala, where a substantial number were seen on February 6, 1956 (Wetmore); confirmation of the existence of this colony highly desirable. Flocks have also been seen off Punta Mala by other observers; otherwise known in Panama from small groups in Gulf of Panama from south of Pearl Islands to Darién (rare in Panama Bay), where reported mostly September–November, occasionally in other months. Not reported from Caribbean, though seems likely to occur at least occasionally.

Habits: Normally pelagic when not breeding, but tends not to occur as far offshore as the Sooty Tern. Often seen resting on pieces of flotsam in drift lines. Does not plunge-dive like so many other terns, rather swooping low over water and snatching prey from near the surface.

Range: Breeds locally on islands in tropical oceans, ranging quite widely when not breeding. Closest certain breeding sites to Panama are on islets off southwestern Costa Rica, and also believed to nest on Octavia Rocks off northern Chocó, Colombia.

SOOTY TERN
Sterna fuscata

Description: 15–16. Rare off both coasts (and occasionally blown ashore). Bill and legs black. Forehead white; *otherwise black above and white below*; tail deeply forked, black with white outer tail feathers. Immature mostly dark brown, feathers of mantle tipped white; lower belly and under wing-coverts whitish.

Similar species: Bridled Tern is somewhat smaller ˙and slimmer, with even more attenuated and narrower wings; its upperparts are dark brownish gray (not black) and it has a pale nuchal collar lacking in Sooty (though often not conspicuous even in Bridled); its tail is somewhat paler than back (not concolor, black); and white on forehead extends back as narrow superciliary (lacking in Sooty). *Immature is only basically dark tern with a deeply forked tail.*

Status and distribution: Probably breeds on Los Frailes del Sur, a pair of rocky islets off Punta Mala, were flying birds were seen on March 18, 1962 (Wetmore); confirmation of the existence of this colony highly desirable. Otherwise reported only very occasionally from off Pacific coast (where decidedly less numerous than Bridled), and from occasional storm-driven birds, all of them seemingly having been blown in from the Caribbean (with the likely exception of one picked up at Albrook APB on May 31, 1975; S. West). Several of these storm-driven birds had been banded at the Dry Tortugas off Florida.

Habits: Similar to Bridled Tern. The Bridled, however, seems far less likely than the Sooty to be blown around by storms (and even deposited inland, dead or moribund). Both species seem equally strong flyers.

Range: Breeds locally on islands in tropical oceans, ranging widely at sea when not breeding. Closest certain breeding sites to Panama are on islands off northern Venezuela.

LARGE-BILLED TERN
Phaetusa simplex   Plate 6

Description: 15. A rare wanderer from South America; *large*, with *very stout yellow bill* and dull yellowish green legs. Crown black with a little white at base of bill; back and short, slightly forked (almost square) tail dark gray; *striking wing-pattern, with black primaries, large white triangular area on secondaries and inner primary-coverts, and gray median primary-coverts*; rump and underparts white. Nonbreeding adult has crown mottled white, solid white on forehead. Immature similar but mantle mottled with brownish, less black on crown.

Similar species: The flashing wing-pattern and very long heavy bill render this species virtually unmistakable. See Black Skimmer.

Status and distribution: A rare visitant to both coasts of central Panama, recorded mainly from the Canal area east to Juan Diaz, but also two records from coastal Herrera (the more recent a bird collected on

August 15, 1979; F. Delgado). There is no apparent seasonality component to the reports; as the species is very conspicuous and easily identified, it seems possible that only a few wandering individuals have been involved.

Habits: In its normal range primarily a tern found along rivers, where it plunge-dives much like a Royal Tern for small fish. Its calls are, however, strikingly reminiscent of those of the Laughing Gull.

Range: South America south to northern Argentina and Uruguay, mainly east of the Andes (west of them only in northern Colombia, ranging as close as the lower Magdalena valley, and in western Ecuador), a few wandering to Panama, accidentally to the United States and Cuba.

BLACK TERN
Chlidonias niger   Plate 6

Description: 9–10. A small tern with an *only slightly notched tail*. Bill and legs black. Nonbreeding adult and immature: *mostly smooth gray above*, head white with blackish patch on rear-crown and around eye and on ear-coverts; white below with small dusky patch on sides of breast. Breeding plumage adult (seen only briefly in Panama) very striking with *entire head, neck, and underparts black*; mantle, rump, and tail gray; entire underwing pale gray; under tail-coverts white. Splotchy molting birds and first-summer immatures are regularly seen.

Similar species: Small size (among Panama terns only the Least is as small), mostly gray upperparts, and pied head pattern are distinctive.

Status and distribution: Fairly common to occasionally common transient on both coasts (particularly along the Pacific) and also inland on larger bodies of fresh water; also regular well offshore, especially in Gulf of Panama, where occasionally very numerous, even in winter months (flocks of tens of thousands of birds have been seen); smaller numbers also over-summer. While considerable numbers are still noted in Panama, especially during southward passage, there seems to have been a marked reduction overall as compared with numbers seen in the 1960s; the cause(s) of this decline (or shift in range) remain unknown.

Habits: Has a graceful but erratic, somewhat nighthawk-like flight, sometimes swooping like a swallow, at other times fluttery. Usually dose not dive, rather pausing to hover briefly while it daintily picks up some

morsel from the water's surface. Also catches insects, over both land and water.
Range: Breeds in North America, Europe, and southwestern Asia; in New World winters mostly offshore from Panama to Surinam and Peru (but exact winter distribution still imperfectly known).

INCA TERN
Larosterna inca

Description: 16–17. An accidental vagrant from Peruvian coasts. *Bill rather heavy, red*, with yellow wattle at gape; legs also red. *Mostly bluish gray* with indistinct blackish crown and nape and *conspicuous white plumes springing from base of bill and curving down over neck*; trailing edge of inner flight feathers also white; tail blackish, slightly forked. Immature a much browner and duller version of adult, with much less prominent plumes and grayish trailing edge to inner flight feathers.
Similar species: This large tern could only be confused with Brown Noddy, and that only at a great distance.
Status and distribution: Inca Terns invaded Panama Bay in substantial numbers during 1983, an invasion surely associated with the unusually severe and prolonged "El Niño" inversion of late 1982– early 1983 off western South America. They first appeared in May 1983, and a few lingered until January 1984; several were photographed. Estimating total numbers present was impossible, but up to 65 were counted resting on the rigging of a single shrimp boat during June 1983. Whether they will ever occur again seems problematic.
Habits: In its normal range the beautiful Inca Tern is a coastal species, feeding offshore by swooping low over the water (not diving). They roost on cliffs and in harbors, and are often quite tame.
Range: Breeds along coast of Peru and northern Chile; small numbers wander occasionally north to southern Ecuador, accidentally (under anomalous conditions) to Panama.
Note: For details on the Panama invasion, see J. R. Reed (*Am. Birds 42*(2): 172–173, 1988).

BROWN NODDY
Anous stolidus   Plate 6

Description: 15. Recorded off both coasts. Bill black. *Dark sooty brown* except for *somewhat paler gray crown* (*galapagensis* of

Pacific side), or *forecrown whitish* becoming pale gray on hind-crown (nominate race of Caribbean side); *tail wedge-shaped.* Immature darker with no white on forecrown.
Similar species: Distinctive in its Panama range, where the only tern with wedge-shaped tail; note that Pacific birds have markedly less contrasting crown than Brown Noddies from most of the rest of the species' range. See immature Sooty Tern.
Status and distribution: Probably breeds on Los Frailes del Sur, a pair of rocky islets off Punta Mala, where photographed on May 6, 1949, and seen in February 1961 (E. O. Willis); confirmation of the presence of this colony would be desirable. Otherwise known in Panama from small groups seen quite regularly in Gulf of Panama from south of Pearl Islands to Darién (only very rarely from mainland shore), and from wandering birds along Caribbean coast and offshore (all known reports from July–January period, including single specimens from Bocas del Toro and San Blas, and several sightings from Canal area coast, especially Fort Sherman/San Lorenzo).
Habits: Primarily pelagic when not breeding. Often seen among flocks of Black Terns where its larger size and heavier less graceful flight make it stand out. The noddy, like the Black Tern, does not dive, rather picking up its food from the surface.
Range: Breeds locally on islands in tropical oceans, dispersing at sea when not resting. Closest certain breeding site to Panama is in Pacific on the Octavia Rocks off northern Chocó, Colombia.

[WHITE TERN]
Gygis alba

Description: 11–12. One recent sighting off Pacific coast. Bill black with some blue at base; legs black or bluish with yellow webs. *Entirely snowy white* except for ring of black feathers around eye; iris dark blue; tail slightly forked. Immature shows dusky nape patch, blackish ear-patch, brownish mottling on mantle, and black shafts on outer primaries.
Similar species: Virtually unmistakable: no other tern is so pure white.
Status and distribution: Two were seen 6 miles south of the mouth of the Río Pacora in Panama Bay on June 14, 1983 (N. G. Smith). At this time a marked invasion of unusual birds into Panama Bay (associated

with the strong "El Niño" Current off western South America) was occurring; possibly the presence of the White Terns was in some way correlated, though it is a tropical water species.

Habits: This most ethereal and delicate-looking of all seabirds has a slow, erratic, fluttery flight; the wings are almost translucent.

Range: Ranges widely on islands in tropical oceans, dispersing at sea when not breeding. Closest breeding site to Panama is Cocos Island, 350 km (217 miles) south of Costa Rica.

BLACK SKIMMER
Rynchops niger   Plate 6

Description: 16–18. *Bill compressed, bright red tipped with black, lower mandible longer than upper. Black above* except for white forehead and trailing edge to secondaries; white below. Tail slightly forked, mostly white in nominate *niger* (North America), mostly dark gray in *cinerascens* (northern South America); both of these have occurred in Panama, and can be identified given a good view, but note that *intercedens*, the race of southern South America, also has a white tail and would not be distinguishable in the field (it is not known to occur as far north as Panama). Immature like adult but browner and somewhat streaked above, often with rather pale-looking head.

Similar species: Virtually unmistakable; at a distance resting birds might be confused with Large-billed Tern.

Status and distribution: Rare and apparently irregular visitant to both coasts, always in small numbers, and with no apparent seasonality component; reported from Bocas del Toro, Veraguas, Colon, and Panama provinces, most often from Caribbean coast of of Canal area and along shore from Panama Viejo to Juan Diaz. The only specimen taken was of the North American race (that at Cocoplum, Bocas del Toro on October 28, 1927), and most records from the northern winter months are probably of that race. Two *cinerascens* were present at Coco Solo, Caribbean coast of Canal area, in late June and July 1973 (photographed by J. Pujals), as yet the only definite record of that race.

Habits: Usually seen loafing on sandbars or mudflats with other gulls or terns. Feeds by flying steadily low over the water, skimming the surface for small fish or invertebrates; skimmers fly with a distinctive easy, languid grace.

Range: Breeds on coasts of southern United States and Mexico, and on coasts and along rivers in northern and eastern South America; scattered records of nonbreeders along coasts of Central America and in West Indies. Closest breeding area to Panama is in northern Colombia.

PIGEONS AND DOVES: Columbidae (26)

The pigeons and doves are a widespread group of birds, well represented in Panama. They are heavy-bodied with small heads, rather short necks, and short legs. Most Panamanian species are plainly though attractively attired in various soft shades of brown and gray, often with some irridescence on head or breast (in some of the quail-doves also on back). Most species are found individually or in pairs; however, some of the pigeons (especially the Band-tailed) and the *Columbina* ground-doves regularly flock. They all feed chiefly on various sorts of vegetable matter. The nest is a flimsy structure of twigs usually placed in a bush or tree; young are fed by regurgitating "crop-milk". Several species are considered good gamebirds, and one, the Band-tailed, has been reduced in numbers.

ROCK DOVE
Columba livia

Description: 12–13. The introduced, semi-domesticated, highly variable "pigeon". Birds of the ancestral type are *mostly gray*, paler across mantle with two bold blackish bars across secondaries, and with *white rump* and dark tip to tail; usually shows iridescence on sides of neck. But more frequently seen are the many color variants (a result of selective breeding in captivity), which *range from being white to various shades of brown to blackish*; they may be solidly colored, but more often they show some pied pattern.

Similar species: Native *Columba* pigeons are all basically some shade of brown, and their plumages do not vary intraspecifically.

Status and distribution: Locally common in urban areas, and around towns and villages, sometimes isolated buildings in agricultural areas. Panama birds are at best only marginally feral, and do not occur away from man (and his food). Its date of introduction into Panama is uncertain, and doubtless the ''wild'' population continues to be augmented by escapes from captivity.

Range: Native to the Old World, but now virtually cosmopolitan.

PALE-VENTED PIGEON
Columba cayennensis   Plate 10

Description: 12–13. Bill black. *Mostly deep ruddy brown*, head more grayish and with crown and nape glossed with green and bronze; breast and upper belly reddish brown, *fading to whitish on lower belly and under tail-coverts;* lower back and rump gray.

Similar species: A large dark arboreal pigeon, quite easily confused with Short-billed Pigeon but note larger size, noticeably paler lower belly (not uniformly rufous brown), and different habitats (Pale-vent in lighter woodland and borders, Short-bill in humid forest). Scaled Pigeon is about same size and often occurs with Pale-vent but is conspicuously scaled below and has red bill.

Status and distribution: Fairly common to common in lighter woodland and borders, clearings, mangroves, and residential areas with large trees in lowlands on both slopes, ranging in smaller numbers up into foothills to about 1050 m (3500 ft); common also on Coiba Island, Taboga Island, Pearl Islands, and other islands off Pacific coast.

Habits: Usually rather shy, perching high in tall trees, often in small groups. The usual call is a mournful hooting, *coó-oo, cuk-tu-cóoo, cuk-tu-cóooo*, etc., sometimes with the *coó-oo* omitted or with only one *cuk-tu-cóoo*.

Range: Southeastern Mexico to Bolivia, northern Argentina, and Uruguay.

SCALED PIGEON
Columba speciosa   Plate 10

Description: 12–13. *Bill bright red*, tipped paler. Mostly chestnut with neck, upper back, throat, and breast feathers with white central spots and prominent black edging,

giving *scaled appearance*; lower underparts buffy whitish, feathers edged dusky giving scalloped appearance; tail dark brownish black.

Similar species: In poor light or in flight, scaly effect may not be evident, but red bill can usually be seen.

Status and distribution: Common in forest borders, second-growth woodland, and shrubby clearings in lowlands and foothills on both slopes to about 1200 m (4000 ft); sometimes comes out into more open country to feed.

Habits: Single birds or pairs are often seen perched conspicuously on high branches, and like Pale-vented Pigeon (but unlike Short-billed) frequently seen in high, long-distance flight well above treetop level. Also may occur in small flocks (rarely to 20 or more birds), especially when feeding. The usual call is a deep resonant *whooo, whoó-whooo, whoó-whooo*.

Range: Southern Mexico to Bolivia, northern Argentina, and southern Brazil.

WHITE-CROWNED PIGEON
Columba leucocephala

Description: 13–14. Found only on Bocas del Toro coast and in San Blas Islands. Bill with reddish base and pale tip. *Mostly dark slaty gray with prominent white crown* (pale grayish in female, dusky and barely contrasting in immature).

Similar species: The crown patch can be hard to see, particularly in flight, in which case could be confused with Pale-vented Pigeon (the two occur together in Bocas and San Blas); try to ascertain ground color (dark gray in White-crown, ruddy brown in Pale-vent).

Status and distribution: Fairly common locally along the coast of western Bocas del Toro and on offshore islands (Swan Cay, Escudo de Veraguas); uncommon in San Blas Islands (recently discovered near Porvenir with proof of breeding in August 1984, by J. Guarnaccia and M. Villamil; presumably had been overlooked).

Habits: In Bocas frequents mangroves and adjacent forest, sometimes flighting slightly inland to feed; usually in small flocks. In San Blas seen flying singly between islands, roosting in mangroves that fringe some islands. The call is a deep low *coo-croo* or *coo, cura-croo* with variants. Can be seen in mangroves near Almirante, and on islands east of Porvenir, San Blas.

Range: Southern Florida throughout West Indies to St Lucia; islands off Yucatan,

Belize, Honduras, Nicaragua, and Caribbean western and east-central Panama.

BAND-TAILED PIGEON
Columbia fasciata Plate 10

Description: 13–14. Found only in western highlands. Bill yellow. Dark brown above with conspicuous *white band across hind-neck;* vinaceous below; *basal half of tail dark grayish, outer half pale grayish* (the contrast prominent, especially in flight).
Similar species: Only other large arboreal pigeon found in western highlands is the smaller and more uniformly ruddy brown Ruddy Pigeon.
Status and distribution: Fairly common to common in forest, forest borders, and clearings with large trees in highlands of western Chiriquí (1200–3000 m: 4000–10,000 ft); recorded also from eastern Chiriquí and Veraguas highlands.
Habits: Breeds in mountain forests, descending in flocks from at least March to July. Still locally common, but numbers have decreased in recent decades due to forest destruction and hunting pressure. Most often seen flying high above valleys and mountain slopes. Usually perches in canopy, but may come lower when feeding in fruit-laden trees; generally quite shy. The call is a deep *co-oooh, co-oooh,* and also occasionally gives a guttural *grrrak*, especially in alarm.
Range: Western North America to western Panama; Venezuela and Colombia to northwestern Argentina.

SHORT-BILLED PIGEON
Columba nigrirostris Plate 10

Description: 11. Bill black, very short. *Mostly warm brown*; duller and *darker more olivaceous brown on back, wings, and tail*; under winglinings dull cinnamon.
Similar species: Pale-vented Pigeon is larger, has pale belly, and favors semiopen habitats (not humid lowland forest); behavior also differs markedly. In eastern Panama more apt to be confused with Ruddy Pigeon; the latter is a more uniform rufescent brown (with mantle not as contrastingly darker as in this species), but this is subtle and when possible better to go by voice. See also Dusky Pigeon.
Status and distribution: Common in humid forest and borders in lowlands on entire Caribbean slope; on Pacific slope known

from lowlands and foothills (to about 1350 m: 4500 ft) in Chiriquí and western Veraguas, and from eastern Panama province (Cerro Azul/Jefe area, Bayano River valley) and Darién. Now very local in Pacific west due to deforestation; still fairly common in remaining forests on Burica Peninsula in June 1982 (Ridgely), but no other recent reports. Less numerous in forests of eastern Darién than on Caribbean slope. Widespread and numerous on Caribbean side of Canal area.
Habits: Usually seen in pairs at middle and upper tree levels, sometimes coming lower and out into small clearings to feed. Relatively lethargic, and often quite unsuspicious. Unlike Pale-vented and Scaled Pigeons, rarely perches conspicuously in the open. Heard far more often than it is seen, the far-carrying musical call of this species is one of the characteristic sounds of the Panamanian forest, typically a mellow mournful *ho, cu-cu-coóo* (Eisenmann) or *oh-whit-mo-gó* (Wetmore); also has a growling *grrrr*.
Range: Southern Mexico to northwestern Colombia.

RUDDY PIGEON
Columbia subvinacea

Description: 11–12. Found only in western highlands and eastern Panama. Closely resembles more widespread Short-billed Pigeon. *Entirely ruddy brown*, slightly paler on head, neck, and underparts; some purplish gloss on hindneck.
Similar species: Short-billed Pigeon is very similar, but is slightly less rufescent generally with mantle a more contrasting, darker olivaceous brown. When possible go by their distinctively different voices (once these are learned, far more of both will be heard than are ever seen).
Status and distribution: Uncommon to fairly common in forest and forest borders in highlands of Chiriquí and Veraguas, mostly above 1200 m (4000 ft) in Chiriquí but lower in Veraguas; also locally fairly common in eastern Panama province (upper Bayano River valley; Ridgely), Darién, and eastern San Blas (Puerto Obaldía).
Habits: Primarily a forest bird, usually seen in pairs or small groups perching high in canopy, though rarely fully in the open. The call resembles that of Short-billed Pigeon but is faster and somewhat higher-pitched, with distinctly different rhythm: *cook wo-coó coo* (has been paraphrased as *what do you*

know). Call of *berlepschi* (eastern Panama) is very similar to that of the nominate race in the western highlands (Ridgely). Also gives a growling *krrrow*, similar to equivalent call of Short-billed Pigeon.

Range: Costa Rica to Bolivia and Amazonian Brazil.

[DUSKY PIGEON]
Columba goodsoni

Description: 10½. Found only in eastern Darién. Bill black; iris light bluish gray. *Head and underparts essentially gray,* somewhat paler on throat, tinged vinaceous on sides and more brownish on belly; upperparts dark olive brown, tinged vinaceous; under wing-linings cinnamon-rufous.

Similar species: Much grayer overall than either Short-billed or Ruddy Pigeons, with no rufescent tones at all. Its voice is also distinctive.

Status and distribution: Two were heard and seen in humid lowland forest near Pucuro in the middle Tuira River valley of eastern Darién on March 7, 1981 (Ridgely and V. Emanuel *et al.*; the latter obtained excellent tape recordings, but these were subsequently lost). Actual status here uncertain, but may have been overlooked in the past; this species replaces *C. nigrirostris* in western Colombia and Ecuador.

Habits: Resembles Short-billed Pigeon; usually found singly or in pairs in canopy of humid forest, sometimes coming lower when feeding at borders or in adjacent clearings. The call is characteristically *three-syllabled* (unlike the four-noted calls of both Short-billed and Ruddy Pigeons), *woók, coo-coo*, repeated over and over, usually from a high hidden perch.

Range: Extreme eastern Panama to northwestern Ecuador.

WHITE-WINGED DOVE
Zenaida asiatica   Plate 42

Description: 11. Known only from Herrera and Coclé. Bare blue ocular area. Mostly pale grayish brown with black spot on ear-coverts and slight purplish gloss on neck, grayer on lower underparts; *large white patch on wing-coverts* (visible on perched birds, but *especially conspicuous in flight*); basically square (not pointed) tail mostly gray with black subterminal band and *large white corners* (conspicuous in flight).

Similar species: Easily known by the conspicuous white patch on the wing.

Somewhat resembles the more widespread Mourning Dove.

Status and distribution: Uncommon to fairly common but local in and near mangrove swamps in Herrera and southwestern Coclé (chiefly around the Gulf of Parita); feeds in nearby fields and open scrubby areas. Now known definitely to be resident in Panama, with the endemic Panama subspecies having been recently named *panamensis*; a nest was located by F. Delgado near Parrita, Herrera, on June 18, 1978. Northern migrants are not known south of northwestern Costa Rica, but are not inconceivable in western Panama.

Habits: Rather shy and difficult to locate in Panama. Because so much of its mangrove habitat is difficult of access, White-winged Doves are here most likely to be seen as they wing inland to feed; south of Aguadulce, Coclé, is a good area for them. Their mournful cooing calls are variably phrased, one being *who hoó hoó-ah* (Wetmore), sometimes paraphrased as *who-cooks-for-you*.

Range: Southwestern United States south locally to northern Costa Rica; west-central Panama; western Ecuador to northern Chile; Bahamas and Greater Antilles.

Note: South American birds (*meloda*) may be specifically distinct.

EARED DOVE
Zenaida auriculata

Description: 9–10. Two recent records. Superficially resembles Mourning Dove but *notably smaller and without pointed tail* (tip rounded). Crown gray with small black spot behind eye and a larger one below ear-coverts; olive brown above with black spots on wing-coverts; forehead, sides of head, and underparts vinaceous; *in flight, outer tail feathers show conspicuous cinnamon-rufous corners in northern races.* Female lacks gray crown. Some South American races (less likely in Panama) have white (not cinnamon) in tail.

Similar species: Mourning Dove is larger with pointed, white-bordered tail.

Status and distribution: Two reports of single wandering birds: an immature (still with scaling on back and wing-coverts, and very tame) seen and photographed at Coco Solo on Caribbean side of Canal area on February 3, 1973 (Ridgely, Eisenmann, J. Gwynne, and C. Leahy); and one (not an immature) seen at Tocumen, eastern Panama province, in mid-February 1987 (J. Arvin *et al.*). The first bird was suspected of being an escape from captivity (though its tameness may simply have been a result of its young age; further, the species is unusual in captivity); the second bird seemed definitely of wild origin. In its normal range, Eared Dove is found in open, often quite arid, country.

Range: Most of South America; southern Lesser Antilles; two recent records from Panama.

MOURNING DOVE
Zenaida macroura   Plate 42

Description: 11–12. A slender dove with a *long, pointed white-bordered tail*. Mostly light brown, paler on throat and belly, with small black spot on ear-coverts and black spotting on wings.

Similar species: White-winged Dove has shorter, more rounded tail, and large white patch on wing, prominent in flight. See also the casual Eared Dove.

Status and distribution: Uncommon to locally fairly common in savannas and open scrubby areas with scattered trees in lowlands on Pacific slope from Chiriquí to western Panama province, ranging up occasionally to about 1800 m (6000 ft) in cleared areas in the highlands of western Chiriquí; resident population is augmented during northern winter by migrants from temperate North America (recorded November–early April), at which time it has been recorded once in Bocas del Toro and once on Pacific side of Canal area (a single bird seen at Balboa on February 18, 1941; R. C. Murphy).

Habits: Usually feeds in small groups and rather wary in Panama; sometimes flocks with White-winged Doves. Though there is evidently a resident population in Panama, its unmistakable mournful call (*whoo-ah, whoo, whoo, whoo*), so well known in the United States, seems not to have been heard here.

Range: Breeds from North America south locally to central Panama; Bahamas and Greater Antilles; northern birds winter south to Panama, accidentally to Colombia.

COMMON GROUND-DOVE
Columbina passerina   Plate 42

Description: 6. Found very locally in coastal Herrera and Los Santos. Bill dusky with *some reddish or yellow at base*. Above olive brown, crown paler and grayer; below pale vinaceous, *feathers of neck and breast with dark centers giving a scaly effect*; wing-coverts with

black spots, primaries chestnut (latter flashing conspicuously in flight, as in Plain-breasted Ground-Dove); outer tail feathers black, narrowly tipped white. Female paler and grayer, particularly below, with somewhat less neck and breast spotting.

Similar species: Plain-breasted Ground-Dove always has all-black bill (never showing color), and never shows scaly effect on neck and breast.

Status and distribution: Only recently discovered in Panama. In 1977 collected by F. Delgado near Chitre in coastal Herrera, and by V. H. Tejera at Salinas Villalaz in coastal Los Santos (specimens to GML and University of Panama). Presumably had been previously overlooked. Racial designation of Panama birds unknown, probably close to Central American *neglectus*.

Habits: In Panama mostly found in sandy areas near coast. Behavior similar to other ground-doves, often crouching until almost stepped on, then unexpectedly flushing with a loud whirr. The call in Costa Rica is an endlessly repeated *whoo-oo* or simply *woo*.

Range: Southern United States to northwestern Costa Rica; west-central Panama; Colombia south locally to western Ecuador and northeastern Brazil; West Indies.

PLAIN-BREASTED GROUND-DOVE
Columbina minuta   Plate 10

Description: 6. Small. Head and nape bluish gray; upperparts otherwise grayish brown; *light grayish below*; wing-coverts with a few spots of steel blue, and *primaries chestnut* (flashing conspicuously in flight); outer tail feathers black *narrowly tipped white*. Female duller.

Similar species: Male of more widespread Ruddy Ground-Dove is mostly ruddy brown, with only head gray. Females of the two are sometimes difficult to distinguish, but female Ruddy is more rufescent above than female Plain-breast, and it never shows the narrow white tail corners. Plain-breast is far less widespread than Ruddy (and is usually less numerous). See also Common Ground-Dove.

Status and distribution: Locally common in dry or open areas with extensive grassland in lowlands on Pacific slope from Chiriquí to eastern Panama province; on Caribbean slope recorded locally and infrequently only from Canal area. Rather scarce in Canal area, even on Pacific slope, but numerous in some areas of savanna to east and west.

Habits: Usually in pairs though occasionally gathers in small groups. Generally less confiding than Ruddy Ground-Dove. Calls *whoop, whoop, whoop* . . . from 5 to 30 times without a pause.

Range: Southeastern Mexico locally to Peru, northern Paraguay, and southern Brazil.

RUDDY GROUND-DOVE
Columbina talpacoti   Plate 10

Description: 6–7. Male *mostly ruddy brown with gray head*; wings with a few black spots; primaries and secondaries flash rufous in flight. Female duller brown and paler below, but *back still distinctly brown*.

Similar species: Male's ruddy coloration with contrasting gray head is distinctive; female more easily confused, especially with the grayer Plain-breasted Ground-Dove, but usually can be known by the company they keep. Female Blue Ground-Dove is larger, with chestnut spotting on wings and rufous rump.

Status and distribution: Abundant in clearings, shrubby areas, and around habitations in lowlands on both slopes, ranging up in smaller numbers into foothills and rarely to lower highlands (to about 1590 m: 5300 ft, in Chiriquí); found also on Coiba Island and the Pearl Islands.

Habits: One of the most numerous birds in open and settled parts of Panama. Small flocks gather on grassy lawns and fields where they crouch close to the ground while feeding; at one's approach they walk away with bobbing heads, flying off with a whirr when one gets too close. The male's call is a soft *hoo-whoop, hoo-whoop* . . ., repeated 3 to 10 times at a slower pace than Plain-breasted Ground-Dove's call; it is usually given from a low perch.

Range: Mexico (rarely southern Texas) to Bolivia, northern Argentina, and Uruguay (sight reports); accidental in Chile.

BLUE GROUND-DOVE
Claravis pretiosa   Plate 10

Description: 8. Male unmistakable, *mostly bluish gray*, paler on head and underparts; wings spotted with black; outer tail feathers black. Female buffy brown above and duller brownish below, whiter on throat and lower belly; wings with a few chestnut spots and *two irregular chestnut bands across secondaries; rump and tail rufous*, outer tail feathers black.

Similar species: Female somewhat resembles female Ruddy Ground-Dove but is larger with dark chestnut spots on wing, rufous rump, and bicolored tail. This species is almost always seen in pairs, which simplifies identification.

Status and distribution: Fairly common in forest borders, second growth woodland, and shrubby clearings in lowlands and foothills on both slopes, ranging in small numbers to about 1590 m (5300 ft) in lower highlands.

Habits: Because it usually perches in thick undergrowth or in trees, less often seen than the *Columbina* ground-doves. Pairs sometimes come out onto woodland trails and roads, especially in early morning. The male's call, an abrupt *boop* or *woop*, usually given singly but sometimes in a series, is very difficult to track down to its source; it is usually given from a perch at middle tree heights.

Range: Eastern Mexico to Bolivia, northern Argentina, and southern Brazil.

MAROON-CHESTED GROUND-DOVE
Claravis mondetoura   Plate 10

Description: 8½. Local in western highlands. Male dark gray above with whitish foreface and throat; *large breast patch deep purplish chestnut*, with lower underparts grayish; wings with two violet-black bars; tail grayish with *outer feathers white* (conspicuous in flight). Female olive brown above and buffy below, browner across chest and on flanks; wings marked as in male; outer tail feathers blackish *broadly tipped white* prominent in flight).

Similar species: Handsome male is readily recognized, even in a fleeting view, by the obvious white in tail (more than any other ground-dove). Female resembles female Blue Ground-Dove (little overlap), but lacks rufous rump and tail, has blackish (not chestnut) bands on wing, and shows broad white tail corners (lacking in Blue).

Status and distribution: Rare in forest undergrowth and shrubby forest borders in highlands of western Chiriquí (900–2400 m: 3000–8000 ft, mostly above 1500 m: 5000 ft); also known from Cerro Campana, western Panama province (750–900 m: 2500–3000 ft), where also rare (and considerably outnumbered by Blue Ground-Dove). Not recorded from elsewhere, though seems possible. Temporarily became more numerous above Cerro Punta in January–March 1979, apparently in response to seeding bamboo there.

Habits: Not well known. Seems to favor forest with heavy bamboo understory, and distribution and abundance may be tied to the bamboo's infrequent seeding. At all times reclusive and difficult to observe. Probably feeds on ground, but usually calls from an elevated perch in dense tangled growth 3–9 m (10–30 ft) above ground (where very hard to locate); the call itself resembles that of Blue Ground-Dove, a deep and resonant *whoo-oóp; whoo-oóp* . . ., repeated steadily for long periods.

Range: Southern Mexico south locally to northwestern Venezuela and Bolivia.

WHITE-TIPPED DOVE
Leptotila verreauxi   Plate 10

Description: 11. Grayish brown above, paler on forehead and with *light grayish blue orbital and loral skin; pale pinkish brown below*, becoming white on lower belly; tail blackish, *broadly tipped white*.

Similar species: Gray-headed Dove of western Panama has contrasting bluish gray head, less white on tail. See also Gray-chested Dove.

Status and distribution: Very common in lighter second-growth woodland and borders, shrubby clearings, and (where not overly persecuted) around habitations in lowlands and foothills on entire Pacific slope (in western Chiriquí following clearings up into lower highlands, rarely to 1800 m: 6000 ft); on Caribbean slope found in western Bocas del Toro (where rare) and from western Colon province to western San Blas; found also on Taboga Island, the Pearl Islands, and other islands off the Pacific coast (but not on Coiba). The most widespread and by far the most numerous *Leptotila* dove in Panama; very numerous in Canal area on both slopes, often coming out onto residential lawns.

Habits: Mostly terrestrial, pottering about with head nodding back and forth. Usually rather wary, before one can get too close flushing with an audible wing whirr and an obvious white flash in tail, often landing on a nearby low perch where it may nervously nod head, dip tail, or walk a few steps along branch to better concealment. The call is a soft but deep *hoó-oo*, sometimes doubled (two-syllabled effect is distinctive); recalls sound produced by blowing across top of empty bottle. Locally often called "rabiblanca".

Range: Southern Texas and Mexico to central Argentina and Uruguay.

GRAY-HEADED DOVE
Leptotila plumbeiceps   Plate 10

Description: 10–11. Found only in western Panama. *Crown and hindneck bluish gray*, with red loral and gray orbital skin; otherwise olive brown above; *pinkish white below*, more vinaceous on chest, becoming white on belly; tail dusky with outer feathers narrowly tipped white. Birds from the Pacific slope (*battyi*, possibly a distinct species, Brown-backed Dove) are similar but have *upperparts brighter and more rufous brown*, and breast more strongly tinged with pinkish.

Similar species: White-tipped Dove lacks the contrasting gray crown, is more grayish brown above, and has broader white tail tipping; on the Azuero Peninsula, Gray-headed Dove is found mostly in forest, with the White-tipped favoring more open situations.

Status and distribution: Rather rare in forest and second-growth woodland in coastal lowlands of western Bocas del Toro (Changuinola, Almirante, Isla de Colón); common in undergrowth of forest and second-growth woodland on Coiba Island; uncommon in forest on western side of Azuero Peninsula in southern Veraguas and western Herrera (where doubtless declining rapidly with destruction of forest) and on Cébaco Island.

Habits: Similar to other *Leptotila* doves, though rarely in the open. Usually encountered singly, walking or feeding on the ground inside forest. Often flushes with a whirr to a low branch where it remains motionless or may nod nervously. The call on Coiba Island (*battyi*) is given from a usually hidden perch in lower growth; it is a deep resonant *whoo-oooo*, deeper than that of White-tipped Dove but with same cadence (Ridgely). Wetmore has transcribed the call of Bocas del Toro birds as a low *cwuh-h-h-a* with reedy quality suggestive of a Broad-billed Motmot.

Range: Eastern Mexico to western Panama; western Colombia.

Note: The AOU Check-list (1983) has merged the Middle American and western Colombian *plumbeiceps* groups with *L. rufaxilla* of cis-Andean South America, calling the enlarged species "Gray-fronted Dove". We are not convinced that this is the proper course, and prefer to maintain them as full species. Wetmore (1968) also considered birds from Pacific western slope, *battyi* (Brown-backed Dove) as a distinct, endemic species; if their vocalizations are actually as different as he described, then this split may be warranted.

GRAY-CHESTED DOVE
Leptotila cassinii   Plates 10,42

Description: 10–11. Olive brown above with *gray crown* and *red loral and orbital skin; foreneck, chest, and breast gray*, darkest on breast, pale grayish on throat, belly whitish; tail grayish with outer feathers *narrowly* tipped white. Birds from western Chiriquí (*rufinucha*, formerly sometimes treated as distinct, Rufous-naped Dove, ranging also in southwestern Costa Rica) have nape rufous brown.
Similar species: More numerous White-tipped Dove has more conspicuous white tail-tipping, pinkish brown (not gray) underparts, and bluish eye-ring and loral skin. See also Gray-headed Dove.
Status and distribution: Uncommon to locally fairly common in forest, second-growth woodland, and borders (in continuous forest most often at treefalls) in lowlands on entire Caribbean slope; on Pacific slope in lowlands and foothills of western Chiriquí (*rufinucha*; now rare and very local due to deforestation, with few recent reports though it was fairly common in remaining forests on Burica Peninsula in June 1982; Ridgely), foothills of Veraguas, and in lowlands from Canal area east through Darién. Widespread in Canal area, though considerably more numerous on Caribbean side and never as conspicuous as White-tipped Dove.
Habits: Everywhere less familiar than the common White-tipped Dove. A terrestrial forest dove that either walks away at one's approach, or flies up to a low branch where it nods nervously. The call is a deep low-pitched, low drawn *cooooooh* (E. O. Willis).
Range: Southern Mexico to northern Colombia.

OLIVE-BACKED QUAIL-DOVE
Geotrygon veraguensis   Plate 10

Description: 9–10. Mostly dark olive brown above; *forehead and broad facial stripe white*; hindcrown and nape gray, nape and back glossed purple; brownish gray below, more whitish on throat, becoming buffy on flanks. Female darker, with buffier forehead.
Similar species: A *very dark* quail-dove whose white forehead and (especially) broad facial stripe stand out prominently even in deep forest shade. See Purplish-backed Quail-Dove.
Status and distribution: Rare to locally uncommon (doubtless often overlooked) in undergrowth of humid forest and adjacent dense secondary growth in lowlands on entire Caribbean slope; on Pacific slope known only from eastern Panama province (upper Bayano River valley; pair seen near Aguas Claras on July 21, 1973, by D. Hill) and Darién. Only recently (1968) found in Canal area, but now seen regularly in Pipeline and Achiote Road forests.
Habits: Usually seen walking on forest floor and generally quite unsuspicious. When alarmed usually freezes or walks away very slowly and quietly, but may flush a short distance to a low perch where it will nervously nod its head and raise its rearparts. Usually encountered singly. Seems to favor ravines or dense tangled growth near streams.
Range: Costa Rica to northwestern Ecuador.

CHIRIQUI QUAIL-DOVE
Geotrygon chiriquensis   Plate 10

Description: 11. Found only in western highlands. *Crown and nape dark gray*; otherwise chestnut brown above, glossed purple on back; cheeks and throat buffy, crossed by conspicuous black moustache, with sides of neck giving effect of fine radial lines; *breast cinnamon-rufous, becoming cinnamon-buff on belly*.
Similar species: Buff-fronted Quail-Dove has buff forehead and dark green crown (not an entirely gray crown), and mostly gray underparts (not rufous and cinnamon). Ruddy Quail-Dove (usually found at lower elevations though there is a little overlap) lacks the gray crown, etc.
Status and distribution: Uncommon in undergrowth of forest and forest borders in highlands of Chiriquí and Veraguas (recorded 900–3000 m: 3000–10,000 ft, but mainly 1200–1950 m: 4000–6500 ft). The most numerous quail-dove in the Bambito/Nueva Suiza area, where it sometimes comes out into overgrown coffee plantations.
Habits: Found singly or in pairs on ground; rather shy. When flushed usually flies to a low branch. The call is a mournful one-syllabled *hoooo* (Slud).
Range: Costa Rica and western Panama.
Note: The AOU Check-list (1983) adopted the name "Chiriqui Quail-Dove" for this species, formerly known as Rufous-breasted Quail-Dove.

PURPLISH-BACKED QUAIL-DOVE
Geotrygon lawrencii   Plate 10

Description: 10–11. Mostly olive brown above with *whitish foreface, gray crown and* *hindneck*, and *contrasting triangular purplish area on upper back*; conspicuous black moustache; underparts mostly gray, becoming buffier on belly.

Similar species: See Buff-fronted and Russet-crowned Quail-Doves.

Status and distribution: Rare to uncommon and apparently local in undergrowth of humid forest in foothills on both slopes (perhaps somewhat overlooked); on Caribbean slope known from Bocas del Toro, eastern Colon province (Cerro Bruja), and western San Blas (Nusagandi); on Pacific slope known from Veraguas, Panama province (Cerro Campana, Cerro Azul/Jefe), and Darién (Cerro Tacarcuna; apparently not found on Cerro Pirre); recorded mostly 450–1050 m (1500–3500 ft), occasionally somewhat higher.

Habits: Mostly terrestrial and difficult to observe in the dense undergrowth it favors. The call is a fairly loud, nasal and somewhat hollow *cowh*, repeated steadily for lengthy periods at 3-second intervals, sounding very like a frog (and easily passed over as one); it is usually given from a perch several meters above the ground (J. Guarnaccia).

Range: Southern Mexico; Costa Rica to eastern Panama.

BUFF-FRONTED QUAIL-DOVE
Geotrygon costaricensis   Plate 10

Description: 10–11. Found only in western highlands. *Forehead buff, crown and nape dark green*; otherwise chestnut above, strongly glossed purple on back; cheeks and throat white, crossed by conspicuous black moustache; *underparts mostly gray*, becoming buffier on belly.

Similar species: A beautifully colored quail-dove, partially sympatric with the other quail-dove of the western highlands, the Chiriqui Quail-Dove; the latter is rufous and cinnamon below (not mostly gray), and has entirely gray crown and nape (not buff and green). Pattern of Buff-fronted is quite like that of Purplish-backed Quail-Dove, but note Purplish-backed's white (not buff) forehead, and its gray (not green) crown and nape.

Status and distribution: Uncommon in undergrowth of montane forest in highlands of western Chiriquí (1200–3000 m: 4000–10,000 ft); recorded also from adjacent Bocas del Toro (specimen from Camp Cylindro, 1580 m: 5200 ft; Mönniche), eastern Chiriquí (found above Cerro Colorado on May 23, 1986; J. Guarnaccia), and Veraguas (two specimens from Chitra, 1200–1290 m (4000–

4300 ft); R. Benson). Small numbers can be found in forest above Finca Lerida.

Habits: Much like other quail-doves: mostly terrestrial and shy, usually encountered singly. The call is a rather high-pitched *cwa* repeated steadily and quite rapidly at 1-second intervals for protracted periods, sounding rather like a slow pygmy-owl (J. Guarnaccia).

Range: Costa Rica and western Panama.

RUSSET-CROWNED QUAIL-DOVE
Geotrygon goldmani

Description: 11. Found only in foothills in eastern Panama. *Crown and nape rufous-chestnut*; otherwise dull brown above, glossed purple on back; *forehead and cheeks cinnamon-buff*, the latter bordered below by a narrow black moustache, and with sides of neck giving effect of fine radial lines; throat white, with remaining underparts mostly gray, becoming buffyish on belly.

Similar species: Purplish-backed Quail-Dove has white (not buff) foreface, and gray (not rufous) crown and nape.

Status and distribution: Uncommon in undergrowth of humid forest in foothills of eastern Panama province (Cerro Jefe, where still only known from a single bird seen on July 27, 1973, by D. Hill, and on the Serranía de Majé), western San Blas (seen and photographed on Cerro Brewster in late April 1985 by J. Blake), and foothills and lower highlands of eastern Darién; recorded mostly 750–1500 m (2500–5000 ft). Regularly encountered in cloud forests on Cerro Pirre above Cana (principally above 1050 m: 3500 ft).

Habits: Similar to other quail-doves. Usually encountered singly, walking sedately on the forest floor, generally very wary. The call is a very low-pitched, downward-inflected *woooo* repeated at 4–5 second intervals for several minutes from a perch 3–15 m (10–20 ft) above the ground; it is similar to but longer than Gray-chested Dove's call (M. Robbins).

Range: Eastern Panama and extreme northwestern Colombia.

VIOLACEOUS QUAIL-DOVE
Geotrygon violacea   Plate 10

Description: 9–10. Local in lowland and foothill forests. *Bill, orbital skin, and legs purplish red. Forehead white* and crown gray, becoming *rich reddish chestnut strongly glossed violet on hindcrown, nape, and back*; upperparts otherwise rich chestnut brown; only a faint dusky moustache; sides of head and underparts grayish mauve, whiter on throat and especially on belly. Female duller, more olive brown above with less violet gloss, and grayer on breast.

Similar species: *The only Panama quail-dove lacking a conspicuous moustache.* Its pattern, consequently, is somewhat reminiscent of a *Leptotila* dove, but it lacks white in tail, is more highly colored, etc. Most resembles Purplish-backed Quail-Dove (which see). Female Ruddy Quail-Dove is basically cinnamon-buff below (not grayish and white).

Status and distribution: Rare to locally uncommon (probably often overlooked) in undergrowth of humid forest in lowlands and foothills of central and eastern Panama (recorded up to 1500 m (5000 ft) in Darién); on Caribbean slope known from Canal area and eastern Colon province (Portobelo), on Pacific slope from eastern Panama province (Cerro Azul; no recent reports, however) and Darién (where somewhat more widespread and numerous). Not recorded from western Panama, but should occur on Caribbean slope. In Canal area recorded only from Barro Colorado Island and Pipeline Road (several recent reports from both); also occurs on lower slopes of Cerro Pirre above Cana.

Habits: Usually seen singly on ground inside forest, less often in dense bordering vegetation. When flushed it flies off *without a whirr of wings* (like other quail-doves, but unlike *Leptotila*). Gives a short hollow *cooo*, repeated at several second intervals, from perches usually 3–6 m (10–20 ft) up.

Range: Eastern Nicaragua south locally to Bolivia and northern Argentina.

RUDDY QUAIL-DOVE
Geotrygon montana   Plate 10

Description: 9–10. *Bill, orbital skin, and legs purplish red.* Male *rufous-chestnut above*, glossed with purple on back; *pinkish cinnamon facial stripe* bordered below by chestnut moustache; throat cinnamon, becoming buff on remaining underparts. Female much duller, mostly olive brown above with *cinnamon forehead and facial stripe*; cinnamon to buffy below, sometimes mottled with dusky on breast; tail grayish olive. Immature like female but with dusky bars and rufous spots on back and wings.

Similar species: Rufous-breasted Quail-Dove of western highlands has gray crown.

Status and distribution: Fairly common in undergrowth of forest and second-growth woodland in lowlands and foothills (to about 1200 m: 4000 ft in Chiriquí) on both slopes, less numerous or lacking in dry Pacific lowlands from eastern side of Azuero Peninsula to western Panama province; found also on Coiba Island and reported from Pearl Islands (San José). The most widespread quail-dove in Panama. In Canal area more numerous on Caribbean side.

Habits: A largely terrestrial forest dove which, though shy and infrequently encountered, seems more numerous than other quail-doves. Flushes without whirr of wings so noticeable in the *Leptotila* doves. The call is a low soft resonant *cooo* given at 3–5 second intervals from a usually hidden perch close to the ground; it is similar to but shorter than that of Gray-chested Dove.

Range: Southern Mexico to Bolivia, northeastern Argentina, and southern Brazil.

PARROTS: Psittacidae (22)

Parrots are widespread chiefly in tropical and south temperate areas of the world, but reach their greatest development in the neotropics and Australia. They are noisy and gregarious birds, familiar and widely distributed in Panama, though most numerous in forested lowlands. Most Panamanian species are basically green, the major exception being the macaws, some of which are clad in red or blue and yellow. Macaws are also characterized by their huge bills and bare facial skin; they, like the *Aratinga* parakeets, have long pointed tails. Panama's representatives vary in size from the large macaws with a length of over three feet to the tiny sparrow-sized Spectacled Parrotlet. They all feed mostly on fruit and nuts, and nest in hollows in trees or in termitaries. Many species are still quite numerous and easily seen, especially in the early morning when they fly to their feeding areas, generally in groups numbering in multiples of two, the pairs remaining together throughout the year. Macaws, however, have been greatly reduced throughout Panama, and now occur only in remote mostly unsettled areas, especially in the forested eastern third of the country. Not only have the macaws been affected by the reduction in their habitat, but in some areas they are shot for food and the young are taken from nest holes to be sold as pets or to dealers. Without increased protection, several species will probably become extinct in Panama in the near future: a sad loss, as there are few grander sights than a pair or flock of these great birds flying by with their long tails streaming behind. The sequence of species employed here follows Forshaw (1973), and not the AOU Check-list (1983).

BLUE-AND-YELLOW MACAW
Ara ararauna   Plate 11

Description: 32–34. Found only in eastern Panama. Unmistakable. Very long pointed tail. Bare facial skin white with lines of blackish feathers; bill black. *Rich blue above*; small throat patch black; ear-coverts, sides of neck, and *entire underparts rich orange-yellow*. From below wings and tail yellow.

Status and distribution: Uncommon to locally still fairly common in lowlands on Pacific slope in eastern Panama province (upper Bayano River valley) and Darién. Favors deciduous or swampy forest, often near rivers; usually avoids hilly areas, though found in some numbers in the flat swampy valley at Cana (540 m: 1800 ft). Decreasing in numbers, particularly near partially settled areas, due to combination of increased habitat disturbance, hunting, and capturing of young for the pet trade.

Habits: Most often seen in pairs or small flocks in which the separate pairs are evident. Usually seen in flight, especially during early morning and late afternoon but also at other times of day; it is while flying that they tend to be most vocal, their loud raucous calls (somewhat less so in this species than in Panama's other three large macaws) regularly heralding their approach from very great distances. They are less noisy when perched, however, and usually are virtually silent when feeding; at such times the mere fall of bits of fruit or other debris is often the first indication of their presence in the trees high overhead.

Range: Eastern Panama to Bolivia and eastern Brazil.

GREAT GREEN MACAW
Ara ambigua   Plate 11

Description: 34–36. Very long pointed tail. Bare facial skin usually dull pink (sometimes whitish) with lines of small black feathers; bill black, tip grayer. *Mostly light yellowish green*; forehead red; lower back, rump, and under tail-coverts pale blue; tail (from above) basally red, tips and outer feathers

blue; flight feathers (from above) mostly blue. From below wings and tail olive yellow.

Similar species: Chestnut-fronted Macaw is also mostly green, but is hardly half the size and has underside of wings and tail reddish. In poor light, and especially from below, overall color can be difficult to discern, and this species is then readily confused with the other large macaws, especially the Blue-and-yellow.

Status and distribution: The most widespread and least rare macaw in Panama, though now scarce and decidedly local due to habitat destruction and persecution. In recent years reported from western Bocas del Toro, northern Veraguas, southwestern Azuero Peninsula, eastern Panama province (upper Bayano River valley), and Darién. Favors humid forest, especially in hilly areas; recorded to 1500 m (5000 ft) in Darién. Formerly known to have occurred on Caribbean slope of Canal area, it has not been found here since early in the twentieth century; a re-introduction effort could, however, now be feasible. The most numerous macaw in Darién, where relatively wide-ranging and locally fairly common, but even here declining except in the most remote regions.

Habits: Similar to other large macaws. Usually in pairs or small groups of up four to eight birds, very rarely more. Has extremely loud, far-carrying raucous calls. Notably unwary; feeding birds often allow a remarkably close approach.

Range: Eastern Honduras to western Ecuador.

SCARLET MACAW
Ara macao   Plate 11

Description: 35–38. Now found only on Coiba Island and remote parts of southwestern Azuero Peninsula. Very long pointed tail. Bare facial skin white, with *no* lines of feathers; bill bicolored, maxilla mostly horn, mandible black. *Mostly bright scarlet*; lower back, rump, and under tail-coverts light blue; *wing-coverts mostly yellow* (showing as a prominent band across wing). Flight feathers (from above) mostly dark blue; from below wings and tail red.

Similar species: Red-and-green Macaw (with which the Scarlet does not occur in Panama) is a darker shade of red and has green (not yellow) wing-coverts. Provided light is adequate, otherwise unmistakable at virtually any distance.

Status and distribution: Still common on Coiba Island, but now extirpated from its entire former mainland range except in the remote southwestern Azuero Peninsula; here a few persist, mostly in the still-forested districts inland from the immediate coast (F. Delgado). Now but a fading memory throughout Chiriquí (even on the Burica Peninsula) and most of Veraguas; status on islands other than Coiba, e.g. Cébaco, unknown. Formerly presumed to have been much more widespread on the Pacific slope, and may even have occurred on Caribbean slope of Canal area, though the two nineteenth-century specimens from there could easily have been of captive origin. A few escapees are still seen from time to time in the Canal area. Not known at all from eastern Panama.

Habits: In Panama found in undisturbed deciduous forest (a habitat now largely destroyed in the Republic), though elsewhere also in continuous humid lowland forest and in gallery woodland. Fortunately, Coiba Island remains a penal institute to which access is restricted; as a result its forest is mostly undisturbed, and the island functions as a de facto macaw preserve. Coiba's population is the only "secure" one in Panama, for on the Azuero numbers continue to diminish due to habitat destruction and persecution (the latter mostly for their tail feathers, still in use in certain folkloric dances; F. Delgado). In behavior the Scarlet Macaw resembles the other large macaws, though during the nonbreeding season it sometimes gathers in larger flocks than the others (with the occasional exception of the Blue-and-yellow). Despite their gaudy coloration, Scarlet Macaws are often remarkably difficult to see when perched in a leafy tree.

Range: Southern Mexico south very locally through Central America (numbers now much diminished), and in lowlands of South America south to northern Bolivia and Amazonian Brazil.

RED-AND-GREEN MACAW
Ara chloroptera   Plate 11

Description: 35–38. Found only in eastern

Panama. Very long pointed tail. Bare facial skin white with lines of small red feathers; bill bicolored, maxilla mostly horn, mandible black. *Mostly red*; lower back, rump, and under tail-coverts mostly pale blue; *wing-coverts mostly green*; flight feathers from above mostly pale blue. From below wings and tail red.

Similar species: The similar Scarlet Macaw is a lighter, more scarlet red, and has yellow (not green) wing-coverts. Flying overhead, the two are often not easy to separate, but they do not occur together in Panama.

Status and distribution: Uncommon locally in eastern Panama, where found in remote humid forested areas in Darién, eastern San Blas, and probably eastern Panama province (somewhat uncertain reports from the upper Bayano River valley). May formerly have occurred west to the Caribbean slope of Canal area, though the two nineteenth-century specimens could well have been of captive origin. Favors hilly areas, and in Darién recorded up to at least 900 m (3000 ft).

Habits: Similar to the Great Green Macaw, and in Darién often occurring sympatrically with it, though the two species never seem to mix in the same flock. This and the other large macaws are known locally as "guacamayos", this species as the "guacamayo rojo", etc.; in Costa Rica macaws are called "lapas", while in Honduras they are known as "guaras".

Range: Eastern Panama to northern Argentina, eastern Paraguay, and southern Brazil.

CHESTNUT-FRONTED MACAW
Ara severa   Plate 11

Description: 18–20. Found only in eastern Panama. Long pointed tail. Bare facial skin creamy white with lines of small blackish feathers; bill blackish. *Mostly green*; forehead dull chestnut, crown more bluish green. *Underside of wings and tail dull reddish* (conspicuous in flight).

Similar species: So much smaller than the other Panama macaws that confusion is unlikely; the Great Green is almost twice as large.

Status and distribution; Fairly common and widespread in lowlands of Darién, where found locally up to about 600 m (2000 ft). Reports from eastern Panama province (upper Bayano River valley) are so far unconfirmed. Formerly may have occurred west to Canal area, though the single nineteenth-century specimen from there could easily have been of captive origin; presumed escapees have been seen on a number of occasions during the last few decades. Unlike the larger macaws, there is no evidence to indicate that this species' numbers have declined appreciably in Panama (or elsewhere); it actually seems to favor partially cleared areas, and is only infrequently persecuted.

Habits: Favors forest borders and clearings with scattered large trees; often found along rivers and in swampy areas. Wingbeats faster and somewhat shallower than the larger macaws, and rarely flies high; calls are weaker and shriller, though still far carrying. Most often seen in pairs or small groups of up to 10 or so birds; frequently perch on dead snags.

Range: Eastern Panama to northern Bolivia and Amazonian Brazil.

CRIMSON-FRONTED PARAKEET
Aratinga finschi   Plate 11

Description: 11–12. Found only in western Panama. Bill horn; conspicuous bare white eye-ring. *Green* with *red forecrown*; bend of wing and lesser under wing-coverts red, bordered behind by yellow greater coverts *(flashing conspicuously red and yellow under the wing in flight)*; underside of flight feathers and tail yellowish olive.

Similar species: The largest Panama parakeet. Brown-throated Parakeet is noticeably smaller, lacks all red, has brownish throat and chest, etc. See also Sulphur-winged Parakeet.

Status and distribution: Locally common in lowlands of western Bocas del Toro, Chiriquí, and Pacific slope of Veraguas; since 1980 small numbers have been seen in the hills of southern Herrera, on east side of Azuero Peninsula (F. Delgado). Evidently increasing and spreading eastward (probably on both slopes?). In Chiriquí ranges, probably only seasonally, up into lower highlands (to about 1650 m: 5500 ft).

Habits: An adaptable parakeet, found mostly in forest or woodland borders, and in partially or even mostly cleared areas. Regularly roosts in groves near houses and even in some towns. Quite noisy, with loud screeching calls, *keerr, keerr*, given especially in flight and at roosting sites.

Range: Nicaragua to western Panama.

OLIVE-THROATED PARAKEET
Aratinga nana   Plate 11

Description: 9–10. Known only from Bocas del Toro. Bill horn; conspicuous bare white eye-ring. Green above; *olive brown below*, becoming more olive on belly; flight feathers mostly blue above, slaty below.

Similar species: Rather like Brown-throated Parakeet (a Pacific slope bird), but more olive (not so brown) below, and without Brown-throat's patch of orange feathers below eye. See also Crimson-fronted Parakeet.

Status and distribution: Rare in lowlands of western Bocas del Toro (Almirante/Río Changuinola area), where known from only six specimens, all taken within the April–October period (four in 1927; one in 1961; one in 1963). Perhaps merely an irregular wanderer from Costa Rica; it is difficult to see why this species has not settled and even spread eastward along Panama's Caribbean slope.

Habits: Favors forest borders and clearings with scattered trees, not solid forest. Usually in small flocks of up to 10–15 birds, occasionally more. Frequently voices a high-pitched screech, especially in flight.

Range: Eastern Mexico to western Panama; Jamaica.

Note: Middle American birds, the *astec* group, were formerly considered a distinct species; they are now considered conspecific with the Jamaican form, *nana*, which has priority.

BROWN-THROATED PARAKEET
Aratinga pertinax   Plate 11

Description: 9–10. Bill blackish; bare whitish eye-ring. Green above, the crown more bluish, with *prominent patch of orange feathers below eye; sides of head, throat, and chest buffy brownish*, fading to yellowish green on lower underparts; underside of flight feathers slaty. Immature lacks the orange below the eye.

Similar species: Crimson-fronted Parakeet is larger with red on crown, and red and yellow under wing. See also Olive-throated Parakeet (found only in Bocas del Toro), and the notably smaller and shorter-tailed Orange-chinned Parakeet.

Status and distribution: Locally common in savannas and open scrubby areas with scattered trees in lowlands on Pacific slope from western Chiriquí (west to near the Costa Rica border around La Esperanza) east to western Panama province; in much smaller numbers occurs east to the Panama City/Tocumen area (perhaps mostly in the dry season; no evidence of breeding this far east). Occasional birds, quite likely only escapees, have also been seen on the Caribbean side of the Canal area. Readily seen (especially in early morning) along Pan-American Highway from about Playa Coronado west.

Habits: Usually seen in small flocks flying by rapidly, chattering loudly as they go. Often rather unsuspicious.

Range: Western and central Panama; Colombia to northern Brazil and the Guianas.

Note: The Panama form (*ocularis*) has sometimes been treated as a distinct species, Veragua Parakeet.

SULPHUR-WINGED PARAKEET
Pyrrhura hoffmanni   Plate 11

Description: 9–10. Found only in western highlands. Slender and long-tailed. Bill horn; conspicuous whitish eye-ring. Mostly green, sometimes variably marked with yellowish about face and on breast; *conspicuous patch on ear-coverts dull red; greater wing-coverts, inner primaries, and outer secondaries yellow* (forming a band conspicuous in flight from both above and below, though it is often mostly or entirely hidden when perched); tail tinged brownish red.

Similar species: Crimson-fronted Parakeet is notably larger with red on forecrown and none on cheeks, and no yellow on upperside of wings.

Status and distribution: Fairly common to common in highlands of western Chiriquí, mostly above 1200 m (4000 ft); found also in highlands and foothills of Bocas del Toro (where also once recorded from near sea level, at Cricamola), and small flocks have also been recently reported seen on several occasions in western Veraguas (above Santa Fé).

Habits: Most often noted in small flocks as they wing by rapidly with high-pitched chatters and screeches, *kreey-kreey-kreey* or *keeyik-keeyik-keeyik*. Usually rather wary, but sometimes a feeding group can be approached closely.

Range: Costa Rica and western Panama.

PAINTED PARAKEET
Pyrrhura picta   Plate 11

Description: 9. Recently found in southern Azuero Peninsula. Bill blackish; eye-ring dull sooty. Above mostly green with crown and nape dusky-brown, nape tinged blue; *narrow red frontal band extending to lores and back around ocular area*, becoming duskier red on cheeks, and with *conspicuous pale buff patch on ear-coverts*; throat and chest dusky, *feathers broadly edged with buffy whitish*; lower underparts green with broad area of dull red on mid-belly; lower back and rump also dull red; tail maroon with green toward base on upperside.

Similar species: This surprising recent addition to the avifauna of Panama should be easily recognized in its limited range on the southern Azuero; note especially the *bold scalloping below*.

Status and distribution: Locally common in humid forest and forest borders in hilly areas of southwestern Azuero Peninsula (southwestern Los Santos and adjacent southern Veraguas); though numerous in areas which remain forested, much forest in its range has been cut in recent decades, and its continued existence in Panama will depend on adequate protection of at least some portion of what remains. The species was first discovered in Panama only in 1979, by F. Delgado.

Habits: Similar to Sulphur-winged Parakeet of western highlands.

Range: West-central Panama; northern Colombia; southern Venezuela and the Guianas south to northern Bolivia and Amazonian Brazil.

Note: Though described as a race, *eisenmanni*, of *Pyrrhura picta* (F. Delgado, *Neotropical Ornithology*, P. A. Buckley *et al.* Eds., AOU Monograph No. 36, pp. 17–20, 1985), recent re-examination of specimens in AMNH seems to indicate that they are closer to *Pyrrhura leucotis* (Maroon-faced or White-eared Parakeet) on most plumage characters than they are to *P. picta*, notably in the pattern of breast feather edging. Pending a more thorough analysis, however, *eisenmanni* is here left as a race of *P. picta*. The form it most closely resembles is also the geographically nearest, *caeruleiceps*, found very locally in northwestern Colombia and also currently classified as a race of *P. picta*. Aside from crown color (bluish in *caeruleiceps*), these two forms are very similar in appearance, and they appear to be more closely related to each other than either is to any other form in the *P. picta/P. leucotis* complex.

BARRED PARAKEET
Bolborhynchus lineola   Plate 11

Description: 6½. Found only in western highlands. Tail short, wedge-shaped. Bill pale horn. Green, paler and yellower below, with *feathers of upperparts and sides edged black imparting a generally barred appearance*; bend of wing also black.

Similar species: This species' distinctive black barring is usually difficult to discern (and can almost never be seen in flight). Barred's size and shape is rather like the much more abundant Orange-chinned Parakeet, but note entirely different distributions, very different flight calls, etc. when plumage characters cannot be seen. See also the rare Red-fronted Parrotlet.

Status and distribution: Usually rare (but notably erratic, and locally or briefly can be much more numerous) in forest and forest borders in highlands of western Chiriquí above about 1500 m (5000 ft); also recorded from Bocas del Toro highlands, and down in foothills to about 600 m (2000 ft); one report from Veraguas foothills (group of six seen above Santa Fé on April 8, 1975, by N. G. Smith). Large numbers were present in the mountain forests above Cerro Punta from at least January to March, 1979; this temporary abundance was apparently correlated with the seeding of bamboo in the area.

Habits: Usually in flocks, sometimes large. Most often noted in flight high overhead, and very difficult to see perched, when it "vanishes" into the green foliage of the canopy of towering trees. In flight often gives a distinctive soft musical chattering, *chorreeoweé, chorreeoweé.* . . .

Range: Highlands of southern Mexico south locally to Peru.

SPECTACLED PARROTLET
Forpus conspicillatus   Plate 40

Description: 5. Known only from eastern Panama. A *tiny* parrot, sparrow-sized, with very short, wedge-shaped tail. Male green with *bright blue ocular region* (often not very conspicuous) and *dark blue wing-coverts and rump*. Female lacks the blue, but both sexes have bluish green under wing-coverts.

Similar species: The smallest Panamanian parrot. Orange-chinned Parakeet is larger, with longer tail, lacks the blue, and has brown shoulders.

Status and distribution: Uncommon and rather local in lighter woodland, borders, and clearings in lowlands of eastern Panama province (Bayano River valley; also two recent sightings of small groups on Cerro Azul, by J. Karr *et al.* and R. A. Rowlett *et al.*) and Darién (mostly in the lower Tuira and Chucunaque River valleys, but also

seen once on coast at Piñas Bay, by Ridgely). Perhaps slowly increasing and spreading westward.

Habits: Most often seen flying past in small tight groups, giving their distinctive buzzing or chattering calls, e.g. *tzit, tzit, tzit.* . . . Upon alighting they are often hard to see, though they do often perch in the open (e.g. in *Cecropia* trees). Sometimes feeds in grass on ground, the only Panama parrot to do so.

Range: Eastern Panama through northern Colombia to western Venezuela.

ORANGE-CHINNED PARAKEET
Brotogeris jugularis   Plate 11

Description: 6½–7¼. *Fairly short, wedge-shaped tail* . Mostly green with small spot of orange on chin (usually difficult to see in the field) and *brown shoulders*: under wing-coverts yellow.

Similar species: *Aratinga* parakeets are considerably larger, with long pointed tails. *Touit* parrotlets have square tails and lack the brown shoulders. See also Spectacled Parrotlet (much smaller) and Barred Parakeet (barred with black).

Status and distribution: Abundant and widespread in lowlands on both slopes except in Bocas del Toro and Caribbean slope Veraguas; most numerous in cleared areas with trees and in second-growth woodland, but also found in canopy and borders of humid forest; ranges in reduced numbers up into foothills; found also on Coiba and Taboga Islands, but not known from Pearl Islands.

Habits: The most familiar of Panama's parrots and a popular cage bird, known locally as "perico" (as are the other parakeets). Abundant throughout the Canal area where it roosts in large numbers in stands of banyans or palms. Often occurs in large flocks. Very noisy, flocks give an almost incessant chattering.

Range: Southern Mexico to northern Colombia and northern Venezuela.

RED-FRONTED PARROTLET
Touit costaricensis   Plate 11

Description: 7. Found only in western Panama (mostly in humid foothills). *Tail short and square.* Green with *red forecrown*, lores and narrow streak below eye also red; *leading edge of wing and wing-coverts also red, primaries and outer secondaries black* (both conspicuous in flight from above); tail pale greenish yellow tipped black; *under wing-coverts yellow* (conspicuous in flight from below). Female has much less red on wing.

Similar species: Blue-fronted Parrotlet of eastern Panama is similar but has blue forecrown. Orange-chinned Parakeet has wedge-shaped tail, lacks the red, and has brown shoulders. See also Barred Parakeet.

Status and distribution: Seemingly rare and local (but doubtless somewhat overlooked) in canopy and borders of very humid forest, principally in foothills but does seem to wander. Few Panama records: one taken above Boquete, Chiriquí (1200 m: 4000 ft) on February 7, 1905; another collected at Cocoplum, Bocas del Toro (near sea level) on November 5, 1927; several recent sightings from the Fortuna, Chiriquí, area and the Bocas del Toro foothills immediately to the north (750–1050 m: 2500–3500 ft), in February–March 1976 and July 1982 (Ridgely); and two to three seen above El Copé in western Coclé (on Caribbean slope) on March 8–9, 1986 (Ridgely *et al.*). Probably ranges all along foothill zone of Bocas del Toro, and very likely in Veraguas as well.

Habits: Not well known in Panama; seems more numerous in Costa Rica, but this may merely be a reflection of the difficulty of access of much of its presumptive Panama range. Usually noted in early morning as pairs or small groups hurtle rapidly past, generally low over canopy. Very inconspicuous when perched, rarely in the open. In flight sometimes gives a high soft *ch-weet*, at times almost sounding like the bird's generic name.

Range: Costa Rica and western Panama.

Note: May be a well-marked race of the following species, but the two forms are maintained as full species in the 1983 AOU Check-list. If merged, the enlarged species would be called Red-winged Parrotlet.

BLUE-FRONTED PARROTLET
Touit dilectissima   Plate 11

Description: 7. Known only from eastern Panama. Closely resembles Red-fronted Parrotlet of western Panama (sometimes regarded as conspecific). Male differs in having inconspicuous *blue forecrown* (no red), and more blue and less red below eye. Female resembles male but has less red on wing-coverts

Similar species: See Red-fronted Parrotlet. Spectacled Parrotlet is smaller with no red, has blue rump and wing-coverts.

Status and distribution: Rare in humid forest and forest borders of foothills and lower highlands in eastern Panama province (Cerro Jefe area; also one sighting from El Llano-Carti road on February 16, 1983, by J. Pierson and B. Whitney) and eastern Darién (Cerro Pirre region). Eastern Panama province birds have yet to be collected (one should be), but from photographs the population does not appear to show any approach toward *costaricensis* (Ridgely).

Habits: Similar to Red-fronted Parrotlet.

Range: Eastern Panama to northwestern Venezuela and western Ecuador.

BROWN-HOODED PARROT
Pionopsitta haematotis   Plate 11

Description: 8–9. Rather chunky, with short tail. *Head and throat slaty*, more brownish olive on crown, with small red patch on ear-coverts; otherwise mostly green, with *rosy red collar on foreneck*, and brownish tinge on breast; upper and under wing-coverts pale blue with red axillars, flight feathers darker blue. Female has red patch on ear-coverts and collar on foreneck smaller and less conspicuous. Nominate race (western Panama east to Coclé) lacks the red collar on foreneck found in *coccinicollaris* of rest of Panama range.

Similar species: A small parrot, likely to be confused only with the Blue-headed, though lacking the blue. See also the *Touit* parrotlets.

Status and distribution: Locally fairly common in humid forest and forest borders in lowlands and foothills (to about 1050 m: 3500 ft); on Pacific slopes known from lowlands and (now mostly) foothills of Chiriquí and Veraguas (up to over 1200 m: 4000 ft in western Chiriquí), hilly areas in southwestern part of Azuero Peninsula (where since 1980 recorded by F. Delgado from several localities in southwestern Los Santos and adjacent southern Veraguas), and from Panama province (recorded from Chorrera and Tocumen, but probably no longer occurs in either area due to deforestation; more widespread and numerous from the Cerro Azul/Jefe area and upper Bayano River valley eastward) and Darién). In Canal area quite numerous along Pipeline Road and in the Achiote/Escobal Road area, but here as elsewhere recorded mostly only in flight (infrequently seen perched).

Habits: Usually seen in small groups. Has a distinctive rapid flight, tossing from side to side, lifting wings above the horizontal. The calls are quite high-pitched, a *check-check* or *cheek-cheek*, and a thin *tseek*.

Range: Southern Mexico to northwestern Colombia.

Note: Does not include *P. pulchra* (Rose-faced or Beautiful Parrot) of western Colombia and western Ecuador.

SAFFRON-HEADED PARROT
Pionopsitta pyrilia   Plate 40

Description: 8–9. Known only from eastern Darién. Bill and bare ocular area whitish. *Head, neck, and shoulders orange-yellow*; otherwise green above; chest olive yellow, breast and belly green; bend of wing, axillars, and *under wing-coverts red*.

Similar species: No other Panama parrot has its entire head yellow. Brown-hooded Parrot has only axillars red, not axillars and entire under wing-coverts. See Yellow-crowned Amazon.

Status and distribution: Uncommon in humid forest in lowlands and lower foothills (to at least 690 m: 2300 ft) in eastern Darién. Over most or perhaps all of this area sympatric with *P. haematotis*. Until the 1970s known from only two specimens, both taken in 1915; since then there have been a number of sightings by many observers (from lower Rió Chucunaque, Pucuro, Río Mono, Cerro Quía, above Cana, Enseñada de Guayabo), and three additional specimens (taken in April 1972 by P. Galindo on Cerro Nique; in Gorgas collection). Whether these represent a real increase in numbers, or simply reflect better observer coverage, is uncertain, but the Saffron-headed Parrot does not seem to be of mere "temporary" presence here, as Haffer (1975) suggested.

Habits: Much like Brown-hooded Parrot, but never seen to actually flock with that species. Noted in pairs or small groups, inconspicuous when not flying. Its voice is very similar, some calls seeming to be identical.

Range: Eastern Panama to northern Colombia and northwestern Venezuela.

BLUE-HEADED PARROT
Pionus menstruus   Plate 11

Description: 9½–10. Base of bill reddish; bare ocular area whitish. *Head, neck, and chest blue* with blackish ear-coverts and small red patch on chest (variable in extent); otherwise mostly green, with red under tail-coverts and base of underside of tail.

Similar species: No other parrot has an all-blue head, though in poor light this color can be hard to discern. In extreme western Panama see White-crowned Parrot.

Status and distribution: Common in forest, second-growth woodland, and adjacent clearings with some trees left standing in lowlands on both slopes, in western Chiriquí ranging up to around 1200 m (4000 ft) near Volcán; found also on Coiba Island and the larger Pearl Islands. Widespread in forested areas in the Canal area, though in larger numbers on the Caribbean side.

Habits: In most areas the most numerous of the larger parrots. In flight, easily told from the Amazon parrots (which are larger) by its deeper wing-stroke. Flight calls are relatively high-pitched and characteristically doubled, *keeweenk, keeweenk, keeweenk . . .*; when perched, gives other calls, typically a *krrreeeck*. Often kept in captivity, and known locally as "casanga".

Range: Costa Rica to northern Bolivia, and central Brazil.

WHITE-CROWNED PARROT
Pionus senilis   Plate 11

Description: 9½–10. Found only in western Panama. Bill mostly yellowish horn; bare ocular area dull pinkish. *Forecrown and patch on throat white*; remainder of head, neck, and chest greenish blue; upperparts otherwise mostly green, with *wing-coverts edged and spotted buff*; breast and belly dark green, feathers somewhat edged blue; under tail-coverts and base of tail red. Female usually somewhat duller than male.

Similar species: In form and general coloration resembles better known Blue-headed Parrot, but even in poor light this species' white crown (especially) and throat can usually be picked up.

Status and distribution: Uncommon in forest borders and clearings with scattered large trees in lowlands and foothills of western Chiriquí (where found regularly up to 1200–1500 m: 4000–5000 ft in the Volcán/Santa Clara area), and in lowlands of western Bocas del Toro.

Habits: Similar to Blue-headed Parrot. Like that species, very noisy, with the usual flight call a raucous *krreeck, krreeck, krreeck. . .* (Ridgely). Has a very deep wing-stroke, even deeper than that of Blue-head.

Range: Eastern Mexico to western Panama.

RED-LORED AMAZON (PARROT)
Amazona autumnalis   Plate 11

Description: Bill bicolored, yellowish horn above, dusky below; small bare ocular area whitish. *Red forehead and lores*; otherwise mostly green, *more yellowish green on face* and throat, with crown and nape feathers edged lavender; red speculum on secondaries (prominent in flight, but usually hidden at rest); tail broadly tipped yellowish green, with some red at base.

Similar species: The red area on the forehead is small and not easy to see, which makes this species easy to confuse with the other Amazons, especially in flight; often the yellowish cheeks (a character not shared by other Panama Amazons) are more prominent at a distance. When together can be told from Mealy Amazon by its smaller size.

Status and distribution: Fairly common to common and widespread in forest and more humid woodland (e.g. gallery woodlands) in lowlands and (in smaller numbers) in foothills (to about 900 m: 3000 ft) on both slopes, though absent from drier areas on eastern side of Azuero Peninsula and in southern Coclé and western Panama province; found also on Coiba Island, the larger Pearl Islands, and Escudo de Veraguas. Capable of persisting in partially or even mostly deforested areas provided some trees are left standing, e.g. along watercourses; the Mealy cannot. More numerous in less settled areas, though often outnumbered by Mealy Amazon in extensively forested regions. On Pacific side of Canal area scarce and perhaps only seasonal; much more numerous and widespread on Caribbean side.

Habits: Relatively catholic in its choice of habitat. As with the other amazons, almost invariably seen in multiples of two (pairs), and most conspicuous during their early morning and late afternoon flight periods, when they may pass high overhead. Large numbers (many hundreds) congregate at certain roosts, particularly in the nonbreeding season. Like the other amazons, flies with shallow stiff wing-strokes, obvious in the field and making the genus easy to recognize even if the various species often are not. The Red-lored's flight calls are very loud and harsh, the most strident of Panama's three amazons, and include a characteristic repeated *keekorák, keekorák, . . .* (Ridgely) or *chikák, chikák, oorák, oorák, ooerk* (Chapman).

Range: Eastern Mexico to western Venezuela and western Ecuador; northwestern Brazil (perhaps a separate species, *A. diadema*, Diademed Amazon).

Note: The genus *Amazona* is such a distinctive, well-characterized group that we feel it preferable to employ the group term "amazon", well-known from avicultural usage, rather than simply referring to them as more "parrots". Forshaw (1973) also uses "amazon", but the 1983 AOU Check-list employs "parrot".

YELLOW-CROWNED AMAZON (PARROT)
Amazona ochrocephala   Plate 11

Description: 12. Bill pale horn with dusky tip; small bare ocular area dull grayish. *Forehead to mid-crown yellow*; otherwise mostly green; red along bend of wing, and red speculum on secondaries (latter usually visible only in flight); some red at base of tail.

Similar species: Unless seen clearly, easily confused with other amazons, especially the Red-lored. Yellow-crowned tends to favor more open country in Panama (though it regularly occurs with, and sometimes even flies with, Red-lored), and in flight its somewhat shorter tail and richer more musical voice may suffice to identify it, even when head colors are not apparent.

Status and distribution: Uncommon to locally fairly common in gallery woodland and savannas in lowlands on Pacific slope from Chiriquí (where rare or absent west of David) to Darién (recorded east only to the El Real area, where Wetmore recorded a few sightings); on Caribbean slope known only from western Bocas del Toro (a few Wetmore sightings), Canal area, above Madden Lake, and eastern San Blas (where Wetmore recorded it as the most numerous parrot); found also on the larger Pearl Islands. The scattered nature of the Canal area reports (both slopes) suggests that many refer to escaped cagebirds, though some do persist in the Tocumen area. The Yellow-crowned Amazon is now scarce and declining over much of its Panama range, with numbers probably greatest in the west-central part of the Republic; small numbers can usually still be seen along the Pan-American Highway in Coclé (between Penonomé and Divisa especially).

Habits: Usually outnumbered by the Red-lored Amazon. Its calls are not as raucous as those of the other Panama Amazons, being deeper and more variable, *chuck, week-weeah*, and *chickwah, chickwah*, also a musical *wheeawhit*. Highly prized as a cagebird, and considered the best talker among the Panama parrots; for this reason, it has been much reduced about more populated areas. This and the other Amazons are known collectively as "loros".

Range: Western Panama to northern Bolivia and Amazonian Brazil.

Note: Panama birds (the *ochrocephala* group, including *panamensis*) are now considered by the 1983 AOU Check-list to represent a species distinct from two Middle American forms, *A. auropalliata* (Yellow-naped Amazon) and *A. oratrix* (the true Yellow-headed Amazon).

MEALY AMAZON (PARROT)
Amazona farinosa   Plate 11

Description: 14–15. Bill pale, tip of maxilla dusky; *large bare ocular area whitish. Mostly green*, feathers of crown and nape edged with bluish often giving a powdery look; red speculum on secondaries (visible in flight); tail two-toned, outer half paler yellowish green.
Similar species: Notably larger than Panama's other two Amazons, though this is usually helpful only when direct comparison in possible. Note lack of either red or yellow on the head, and its much more prominent bare eye-ring.
Status and distribution: Fairly common to locally common in humid forest in lowlands and (in smaller numbers) in foothills on both slopes; now largely if not entirely absent from drier open Pacific slope lowlands from western Veraguas to western Panama province; in western Chiriquí at least formerly ranged up into lower highlands to about 1500 m (5000 ft), but few recent reports; common on Coiba Island. In Canal area widespread in forests on Caribbean side, though outnumbered by the Red-lored.
Habits: More strictly a forest bird than the Red-lored Amazon, though the two occur together widely; in extensively forested regions usually the commonest amazon. Only rarely is the Mealy found in gallery woodland in savanna areas, perhaps being mostly seasonal here. Generally similar in behavior to other Amazons. Its very loud flight calls resemble those of the Red-lore, but can usually be recognized by the phrases *chop-chop* or *cookyüp-kyüp*, often repeated. When perched sometimes gives a variety of whistles and throaty gurgles.
Range: Southern Mexico to northern Bolivia and southern Brazil.

CUCKOOS: Cuculidae (14)

The cuckoos are a widespread group of generally rather inconspicuous birds, occurring in a wide range of habitats in Panama. Most Panamanian species are slender, long-tailed birds, rather solitary and of furtive habit. Various Old World species are well known for their parasitic habits; however, most New World cuckoos are not parasitic, the exceptions being the Striped Cuckoo *Tapera* and the two species of *Dromococcyx*. Anis are conspicuous black birds that occur in groups and lay their eggs in large communal nests and then share in the duties of incubation and nestling care. All other American (nonparasitic) species construct flimsy twig nests in bushes and trees. All are largely insectivorous.

[DWARF CUCKOO]
Coccyzus pumilus

Description: 8–8¼. One recent report. Bill black, slightly decurved; iris and narrow eye-ring red. *Tail shorter and not as graduated as in other Coccyzus cuckoos.* Mostly brownish gray above, with crown and nape grayer; *throat and chest rufous*, contrasting with creamy white lower underparts; tail blackish, feathers narrowly tipped white (most visible from below). Immature has brown iris and yellow eye-ring, is browner above with tail tipping often lacking, and has pale gray throat.
Similar species: The short tail often makes it look rather thrush-like. Because of the rufous throat and chest not likely to be confused with other members of the genus.
Status and distribution: One seen at Tocumen marsh, eastern Panama province, on January 9, 1979 (V. Emanuel and D. Wolf *et al*.); see M. Braun and D. Wolf, *Bull BOC 107*(3): 115–117, 1987. It is not inconceivable that it could colonize Panama, for in Colombia its range has expanded greatly in recent years due to deforestation.
Habits: Favors open woodland, shrubby clearings, and thickets, often near water.

Sluggish and furtive, usually foraging alone.

Range: Western Colombia and northern Venezuela; one report from central Panama.

BLACK-BILLED CUCKOO
Coccyzus erythropthalmus

Description: 12. Slender, smooth profile with rather long tail. *Bill all black. Eye-ring red* in adult, dull buffyish in immature. Olive brown above; white below; long graduated tail, *pale gray below, feathers narrowly white-tipped.* Immature may show some yellow at base of lower mandible, a little pale rufous on outer primaries (sometimes visible in flight), buff tinge below.
Similar species: Yellow-billed Cuckoo has yellow lower mandible (except in immatures), a prominent rufous flash in wing, and has tail feathers more broadly tipped white; adult's orbital skin is gray.
Status and distribution: Rare to occasionally uncommon fall transient (mainly late September–early November); one exceptionally late bird was seen at Rodman on Pacific side of Canal area on December 8, 1986, by D. Engelman and A. Sasada), but very rare on return northward passage (only two records, April 20 and 28). Reports scattered, mostly from coastal lowlands with one from western Chiriquí highlands.
Habits: Like the other Panama *Coccyzus* cuckoos rather furtive, rarely leaving dense cover. Can occur almost anywhere on migration, but prefers open woodland and edges, clearings with scattered bushes and trees.
Range: Breeds in eastern North America; winters in northwestern South America.

YELLOW-BILLED CUCKOO
Coccyzus americanus   p.181

Description: 12. Resembles Black-billed Cuckoo. *Lower mandible mostly yellow. Eye-ring gray* in adult, yellowish in immature. Olive brown above; white below; wings with *primaries broadly edged rufous* (conspicuous in flight, but usually visible on perched birds as well); long graduated tail, *black below, feathers broadly white-tipped.* Immature similar but may show less yellow on bill and less black underside of tail (but still much darker than in Black-billed, and pattern remains the same).
Similar species: See Black-billed Cuckoo. Immature Yellow-bill resembles Black-bill but almost always shows at least some yellow

YELLOW-BILLED CUCKOO

on lower mandible and has more white on tail (though somewhat less than as adults). Mangrove Cuckoo has prominent black mask through eyes and is buffy below.
Status and distribution: Uncommon to occasionally fairly common fall transient (mid-September–early December, but most numerous in October; once as early as August 14); less numerous on return northward passage (mostly in April, rarely as late as mid-May); small numbers appear to over-winter at least occasionally, with reports from eastern Panama province (especially Tocumen area) and Canal area but likely also elsewhere. Recorded mostly from lowlands, favoring semiopen shrubby areas, lighter woodland, and forest borders, especially near water.
Habits: Like Black-billed Cuckoo: quiet, secretive, not often seen. Does not seem to call in Panama.
Range: Breeds in North America, Mexico and West Indies; winters mostly in South America, a few in Costa Rica (perhaps) and Panama.

DARK-BILLED CUCKOO
Coccyzus melacoryphus

Description: 11. One recent record. *Bill all black.* Eye-ring yellow in adult, grayish in immature. Mostly olive brown above, grayer on crown and nape, and with *black mask through eyes and onto ear-coverts; mostly rich pale buff below*, with *distinct pale gray area on sides of throat and chest*; long graduated tail, black below, feathers broadly white-tipped (same pattern as Yellow-billed Cuckoo).
Similar species: Most resembles Mangrove Cuckoo, but that species has a yellow lower mandible, lacks the gray area on sides of neck. See also Gray-capped Cuckoo.
Status and distribution: A single record: one was observed and photographed at Tocumen

marsh, eastern Panama province, on January 26, 1980 (P. Scharf, M. and G. Neubauer; photos to VIREO). The extraordinary concentration of "vagrant" cuckoos in 1979 and 1980 in the Tocumen area remains to be explained; no less than three *Coccyzus* species new to Panama were found there during that period.

Habits: In South America favors groves of low woodland and shrubbery. Behavior similar to other *Coccyzus* cuckoos, voice (unlikely to be heard in Panama) most like that of Mangrove.

Range: Colombia to central Argentina; mainly or entirely an austral migrant to Amazonia and most of northern South America, but evidently resident in western Colombia (*fide* Hilty and Brown, 1986), and the date of the Panama record would support this; accidental in Panama and on Grenada.

GRAY-CAPPED CUCKOO
Coccyzus lansbergi

Description: 9½–10. Casual vagrant to eastern Panama; four recent reports. Bill black, sometimes with small spot of yellow at base of lower mandible. Eye-ring yellow (at least in adult). *Head and nape dark gray; otherwise rich rufous brown above; below rufous-buff*, deepest on throat and chest, paling to cinnamon-buff on belly; long graduated tail, black below, feathers broadly white-tipped (same pattern as Yellow-billed Cuckoo).

Similar species: A handsome, richly colored cuckoo, much darker than others in its genus in Panama. Mangrove Cuckoo has a black mask, etc.; see also Dark-billed Cuckoo.

Status and distribution: Uncertain; presumably a casual vagrant, but the four recent reports might lead one to speculate that the species is regular in Panama (and conceivably even colonizing the eastern half of the country). Single birds have been seen on three occasions at Tocumen marsh, eastern Panama province: on February 10, 1980 (V. Emanuel and M. Braun *et al.*); on January 7–8, 1982 (J. and R. A. Rowlett *et al.*); and on December 23, 1985 (L. O'Meallie and T. Meyer); and another was seen at Cana in eastern Darién on January 30, 1985 (D. Wolf and M. Braun *et al.*). See M. Braun and D. Wolf, *Bull BOC 107*(3): 115–117, 1987.

Habits: In South America favors undergrowth in woodland and borders, also shrubby clearings and overgrown gardens.

Apparently migratory, but seems irregular and usually rare everywhere, with details of movements yet to be worked out. Usually forages within 3–4.5 m (10–15 ft) of the ground; secretive behavior similar to other *Coccyzus* cuckoos.

Range: Locally in northern Venezuela, western Colombia, western Ecuador, and western Peru; casual in Panama.

MANGROVE CUCKOO
Coccyzus minor   Plate 12

Description: 12. Lower mandible yellow; upper mandible dusky. Bare orbital skin yellow. Grayish brown above with *broad black mask through eyes and over ear-coverts; buffy below*, varying in intensity; tail feathers broadly tipped white.

Similar species: Black and Yellow-billed Cuckoos both lack black mask and have white (not buffy) underparts.

Status and distribution: Uncertain. Rare and local in lowlands on Pacific slope from Chiriquí to Canal area and Panama City; also a few reports from Caribbean slope in Canal area, and from various islands off Pacific coast. Most records are from northern winter months (especially January–March), and possibly does not nest in Panama; Wetmore, however, did obtain a female in breeding condition in May in Veraguas, and one was seen near Summit Gardens in June (Ridgely). If the Mangrove Cuckoo was only a migrant one would expect more reports from near Caribbean coast.

Habits: Similar to other *Coccyzus* cuckoos. In Panama favors light woodland and borders and shrubby clearings with thickets and scattered trees, with no particular predeliction for mangroves (though most reports are from rather near Pacific coast). Its low guttural call, *gaw-gaw-gaw-gaw-gaw*, should be listened for (and might indicate breeding status), but has not been reported heard in Panama.

Range: Primarily in West Indies; also southern Florida, locally in Middle America, islands in southern Caribbean, Guianas, north-eastern Brazil, Venezuela, and Colombia (uncertain breeding status in many areas).

SQUIRREL CUCKOO
Piaya cayana   Plate 12

Description: 17–19. Larger than other true cuckoos, with *very long tail* that often seems to be loosely connected to the rest of its body. Somewhat decurved bill and *bare orbital skin yellowish green. Chestnut above*; throat and chest pinkish cinnamon, *breast and belly gray*, becoming black on under tail-coverts; underside of tail black with feathers broadly tipped white.

Similar species: This widespread species is easily recognized by its large size, spectacular long tail, and chestnut upperparts. See Little Cuckoo.

Status and distribution: Common in forest borders, second-growth woodland, shrubby clearings with trees, and even groves of trees in rather open country in lowlands on both slopes, ranging in smaller numbers up into foothills, and in western Chiriquí recorded in highlands to over 1800 m (6000 ft).

Habits: Usually rather quiet and furtive, but sometimes runs rapidly along a branch (like a squirrel). Forages at all levels in bushes and trees. Has a number of distinctive and arresting calls, among them a dry *chick, kwah* and a loud *trrt-trrt-trrt-trrt*; also a loud *kikerah* or *geep-kareer*, rather reminiscent of a Great Kiskadee, and others.

Range: Mexico to Bolivia, northern Argentina, and Uruguay.

LITTLE CUCKOO
Piaya minuta   Plate 12

Description: 10–11. Resembles Squirrel Cuckoo but *much smaller* with proportionately shorter tail. Bill greenish yellow; *bare orbital skin red*. Rufous brown above; throat and chest tawny, blending into brownish gray breast, grayish belly, and black under tail-coverts; underside of tail black with feathers tipped white.

Similar species: Squirrel Cuckoo is much larger with longer tail, greenish (not red) orbital skin, and shows more contrast between pinkish cinnamon chest and gray breast.

Status and distribution: Uncommon in damp thickets and tangled areas at edge of woodland or in clearings in lowlands on Pacific slope in eastern Panama province and Darién; on Caribbean slope recorded only from Canal area and eastern Colon province, but perhaps occurs eastward. Small numbers are regularly seen at Tocumen marsh.

Habits: A skulking bird, usually found singly as it sneaks around in dense undergrowth, generally near water. It is a quiet bird, much more so than Squirrel Cuckoo, and thus probably is often overlooked; nonetheless it does have a distinctive call which will sometimes draw attention to the bird (and will often decoy in well to tape playback). This call is an odd soft nasal almost whining, *wyurr, wreh-reh-reh?*, so different from the calls of the Squirrel Cuckoo that it is hard to remember that it comes from a closely related bird.

Range: Central Panama to northern Bolivia and central Brazil.

STRIPED CUCKOO
Tapera naevia   Plate 12

Description: 11–12. *Short bushy crest*; tail fairly long and graduated. *Brown above* streaked with buff and blackish, with whitish superciliary; *whitish below*, buffier on throat and chest.

Similar species: See Pheasant Cuckoo.

Status and distribution: Fairly common in open areas and clearings with scattered bushes and thickets in lowlands on entire Pacific slope (has apparently only recently spread into Darién, where now especially numerous in the lower Tuira River valley, particularly around El Real), ranging in smaller numbers up into the foothills, and in western Chiriquí to the lower highlands (1500 m. 5000 ft); on Caribbean slope found in cleared areas from northern Coclé east through San Blas.

Habits: Usually rather secretive, remaining hidden in dense underbrush. Best known from its calls, the most frequent being a pure melancholy two-noted whistle, the second note a half-tone higher than the first, *püü-peeee*, highly ventriloquial and far-carrying; also has a five- or six-noted call of similar quality, falling off at the end. A calling bird often perches in the open on top of a bush or fencepost, elevating its crest with each vocalization. A parasitic species, apparently mostly on species building domed nests, in Panama especially the Pale-breasted Spinetail, Black-striped Sparrow, *Thryothorus* wrens, and *Myiozetetes* flycatchers (N. G. Smith).

Range: Southern Mexico to Bolivia and central Argentina.

PHEASANT CUCKOO
Dromococcyx phasianellus   Plate 12

Description: 15–16. *Rather small head*, with short pointed crest, and *thin neck* giving unusual profile. *Tail long and wide* (fan-shaped), with *upper tail-coverts greatly elongated*, almost as long as tail itself. Dark brown above, feathers with whitish edgings, and with narrow whitish postocular stripe; mostly whitish below, with *band of dusky spotting across buffyish chest*; tail brown, feathers tipped whitish.

Similar species: Striped Cuckoo is smaller and paler brown above, lacks streaking below, and has more normal tail.

Status and distribution: Uncommon and perhaps somewhat local (though to a large extent merely overlooked) in dense thickets and undergrowth in second-growth woodland and forest borders in lowlands on Pacific slope (recorded Chiriquí, Los Santos, Canal area, eastern Panama province, and Darién); on Caribbean slope known only from Canal area to western San Blas.

Habits: Rarely seen but often heard in proper habitat. The call resembles the short call of the Striped Cuckoo, but with an added third note that is either trilled or broken into two or three short notes, *püü, peee, pr'r'r'r*; also has a long call of four to six whistles much like that of Striped Cuckoo but usually ending in a tremulo and not falling in pitch. Parasitic, mainly on species building cup nests, but also on those constructing closed nests (N. G. Smith).

Range: Southern Mexico south locally to northern Bolivia, Paraguay, northeastern Argentina, and southern Brazil.

RUFOUS-VENTED GROUND-CUCKOO
Neomorphus geoffroyi   Plate 12

Description: 19–20. Unmistakable. *A large, crested, very long-tailed terrestrial cuckoo*, somewhat resembling a roadrunner (*Geococcyx* sp.). Heavy hooked horn-colored bill; bare gray skin around dark eye. *Mostly bronzy olive brown above* with blue-black crest; buffy brown below, with *narrow band of black spots across chest*, becoming rufous on lower belly and under tail-coverts; tail dark bronzy olive.

Status and distribution: Rare and now local in extensive areas of humid forest in lowlands and foothills; recorded locally from entire Caribbean slope, and on Pacific slope locally in foothills from eastern Chiriquí (Cordillera de Tolé) eastward, in Darién also in the lowlands. Rare in Canal area, but has been seen in recent years in Achiote Road area and on a number of occasions along Pipeline Road (various observers); also recently reported from Cerro Campana (a pair with a full-grown young bird on January 6, 1980; P. Donahue).

Habits: Almost entirely terrestrial in areas of extensive little disturbed humid forest. Elusive and infrequently encountered anywhere; most likely to be found at an army ant swarm, particularly very large ones. Also reported to follow White-lipped Peccaries. Usually shy, retreating at first sight of observer, even at an antswarm — but with patience, may return. Snaps bill very loudly, apparently in alarm (reminiscent of *Manacus* but even louder), and also has loud moaning call.

Range: Nicaragua to northern Bolivia and central Brazil.

GREATER ANI
Crotophaga major   p.185

Description: 18–19. *Bill arched only on basal two-thirds of upper mandible* (giving characteristic "broken nose" effect), and laterally compressed. *Eye conspicuously whitish. Glossy blue-black all over*, glossed somewhat greener on wings and purplish on tail.

Similar species: The other two anis are considerably smaller and duller black (without the gloss), and have dark eyes.

Status and distribution: Fairly common in thickets and trees along larger rivers and lakes, and in freshwater swamps and marshes, in lowlands on Caribbean slope from western Colon province east, and on Pacific slope from Canal area (where uncommon) east. Quite numerous on shores of Chagres River and Gatun Lake, also at Tocumen marsh.

Habits: Looks sleek and well-groomed, unlike the other two anis. Usually found in groups of 4 to 12 individuals. The most characteristic call is a bubbling *prrrr* or *brrrr*; also has an almost mammal-like growl *grrwa*.

Range: Central Panama to Bolivia, northern Argentina, and southern Brazil; also recently recorded from specimens supposedly taken in northeastern Mexico (S. Olson, *Auk* 95(4): 766–767, 1978), but actual occurrence there seems improbable.

SMOOTH-BILLED ANI
Crotophaga ani   p.185

Description: 13–14. Bill arched and laterally compressed, with high narrow ridge. Eye dark. Dull black all over.

Similar species: Distinguishing between this species and the Groove-billed Ani is often

Upper left, two GREATER ANIS. Heads: upper, GREATER ANI; middle, SMOOTH-BILLED ANI; lower, GROOVE-BILLED ANI

eeeek?, often given in flight; also has a variety of other whining and clucking vocalizations.
Range: Florida; West Indies and islands in western Caribbean; southwestern Costa Rica to western Ecuador and northern Argentina.

GROOVE-BILLED ANI
Crotophaga sulcirostris   p.185

Description: 11–12. Bill arched and laterally compressed, with upper mandible grooved. Eye dark. Entirely dull black, but somewhat glossier than Smooth-billed Ani.
Similar species: Closely resembles the Smooth-billed Ani; the presence or absence of bill grooving is usually difficult to discern in the field, and the Smooth-bill under some lighting conditions gives an illusion of grooving. A better mark is the Groove-bill's unbroken arc on culmen; the Smooth-bill usually has a thin irregular hump at the base of the culmen, breaking the smooth arc. The Groove-bill is a little smaller and often looks sleeker. The two are generally best differentiated by their rather different calls.
Status and distribution: Common on open fields and pastures and in dry scrubby areas in lowlands on Pacific slope from Chiriquí to eastern Panama province (Chepo/El Llano area; not recorded from farther east, but could spread with clearing of forest); on Caribbean slope common in clearings and open areas in lowlands of western Bocas del Toro (to which it presumably spread from Costa Rica, following clearing for banana cultivation), and in very small numbers in the Canal area; also recorded from Cébaco and Gobernadora Islands off Pacific Veraguas coast. Rather scarce in the Canal area, but numerous in more open regions on Pacific slope just to the east and west. This species occurs sympatrically with the Smooth-billed in some areas, but the two never seem to actually associate in the same flock.
Habits: Similar to Smooth-billed Ani. Like that species, often forages around cattle, feeding on insects disturbed by the animals. Has a variety of guttural clucking calls (some rather similar to certain vocalizations of the Smooth-bill), and a distinctive sharp dry *kwik* or *hwilk*, usually given in a series and often accelerated into an almost flicker-like *wicka-wicka-wicka*.
Range: Extreme southwestern United States to northern Chile, northwestern Argentina, and Guyana; not found in Amazon basin or Brazil.

not easy; see discussion under that species. The Greater Ani is much larger and glossier than either, and has a prominent pale eye.
Status and distribution: Common in open areas, clearings, and residential areas in lowlands on both slopes, ranging in smaller numbers up into the foothills in western Chiriquí, occasionally to about 1500 m (5000 ft); not found in Bocas del Toro or Caribbean slope Veraguas; common also on Coiba Island, and the Pearl Islands. Regularly found in small clearings made in otherwise forested areas. Much the more numerous of the two small anis in the Canal area, less common in drier Pacific lowlands from eastern Veraguas to western Panama province (where probably outnumbered by the Groove-bill).
Habits: Almost always found in small groups, perching in bushes and low trees and on fences and wires. Their flight is labored and awkward, with frequent periods of gliding, the long tail often looking "loose-jointed". Can look incredibly shaggy and disheveled. The most characteristic call is a whining querulous *oooo-*

BARN-OWLS: Tytonidae (1)

The barn-owls are a small but cosmopolitan group, closely allied to the typical owls but differing outwardly in the strongly marked heart-shaped facial disk and the long slender legs. Like the typical owls, barn-owls are mainly nocturnal. They favor the vicinity of human habitations, where they often nest. Agriculturally valuable birds, they feed almost exclusively on various rodents.

COMMON BARN-OWL
Tyto alba   p.186

COMMON BARN-OWL

Description: 14–16. Iris dark brown. *Heart-shaped facial area buffy or white*, encircled by narrow black line. Two phases. Light phase mixed grayish and golden buff above, with a few white and black dots; *white below*, lightly dotted with blackish. Tawny phase darker and grayer above, *buff below* dotted lightly with blackish.

Similar species: Has an unusual narrow profile when perched, with large head and slender body. Characteristic pale ghostly appearance at night. See Great Potoo (which also looks very pale at night).

Status and distribution: Uncommon to locally fairly common in semi-open country in lowlands on entire Pacific slope (though apparently rare or local in Darién), ranging occasionally up into lower highlands in the west; on Caribbean slope recorded only from western Bocas del Toro, and Canal area and Colon province; found also on Pearl Islands (San José). Regularly seen around human habitations where it often obtains diurnal shelter and nesting sites in towers and other structures; also roosts and nests in hollows in trees. Seems particularly numerous on the rice fields at Tocumen.

Habits: Primarily nocturnal, but sometimes active in early morning or late afternoon, when it may be observed perched on fence posts or on the ground, or slowly flapping low over pastures or fields, often with legs dangled. Its calls are varied, a loud rasping shriek (often uttered in flight) being most characteristic. When disturbed at its day roost, will usually crouch, spread its wings, and sway from side to side, all the while hissing and snapping its bill.

Range: Virtually cosmopolitan in temperate and tropical regions.

TYPICAL OWLS: Strigidae (14)

Owls are universally known birds, the nocturnal counterparts to the hawks and eagles. Because many species are so strictly nocturnal (and hence only rarely seen), and because they have a variety of far-carrying vocalizations, owls are the subject of many superstitious beliefs. As a group they are characterized by their forward-facing eyes, strong hooked bill, powerful sharp talons, and fluffy plumage; many species have ear-like tufts (''horns''). Their flight is noiseless. They feed on a variety of small mammals and birds, some of the smaller species mostly on large insects; prey is located primarily through their keen sense of hearing. Food is swallowed whole, the undigestible parts later being cast up as pellets. The nest is placed in a variety of situations; in tree hollows (most Panamanian species), on an old stick nest of another bird, or on the ground.

VERMICULATED SCREECH-OWL
Otus guatemalae   Plate 12

Description: 8. A small owl with *ear-tufts, lacking* conspicuous streaks or bars. Iris yellow. Dark grayish brown above vermiculated with dusky, wing-coverts and scapulars with large white spots; pale brown to whitish below, *densely vermiculated with narrow wavy dusky brown barring*, but with *only a few inconspicuous vertical streaks*. In rufous phase the grayish brown is replaced by rufous-chestnut (and the bird looks more uniform overall), with *underparts vermiculated rufous and white* (the rufous being almost solid on throat and chest).
Similar species: Tropical Screech-Owl has a whitish face with dark rim (no distinct facial rim in this species), well-marked white superciliary (lacking in Vermiculated), and is conspicuously streaked below (not with predominately *horizontal* vermiculations); the calls differ characteristically. Juvenile Tropical and Vermiculated Screech-Owls are both barred with dusky brown above and below, but Tropical already shows black facial rim. In highlands, see also Bare-shanked Screech-Owl.
Status and distribution: Uncommon and local (doubtless somewhat overlooked) in humid forest and mature second-growth woodland in lowlands and foothills (to about 900 m: 3000 ft) on both slopes; on Pacific slope recorded from Chiriquí, Veraguas, and Canal area east locally through Darién; on Caribbean slope recorded only from Bocas del Toro, and from Canal area east into western San Blas (where recorded on Cerro Brewster in April 1985 by J. Blake).
Habits: Not very well known in Panama, and infrequently encountered. On Barro Colorado Island reported to range mostly at lower levels inside forest or at edge (E. O. Willis). The call is a short, guttural *kr-r-r-r-r-o*, repeated at fairly long intervals, rather frog-like in quality (this from a tape recording of a closely observed bird found along Achiote Road; G. Clayton and R. Behrstock). A rapid quavering trill on one pitch with no change in emphasis has also been reported. Frequently seems unresponsive to tape playback.
Range: Mexico south locally to Bolivia and northern Brazil.
Note: Birds from Costa Rica southward (*O. vermiculatus*) may represent a species distinct from Middle American birds (true *O. guatemalae*); their apparently different voices would seem to support this, but more information is needed.

TROPICAL SCREECH-OWL
Otus choliba   Plate 12

Description: 8½–9½. A small grayish brown owl with *ear-tufts*. Iris yellow. *Facial area including superciliary dirty whitish, bordered by black rim*; otherwise grayish to cinnamon brown above, somewhat streaked and vermiculated with dusky; cinnamon mottling and banding on wings; whitish or pale grayish below (bases of feathers golden buff) with *prominent herringbone pattern of dusky streaks and angled bars*. Rare rufous phase is rufous brown above and on face; buffy or cinnamon below, marked as in normal phase.
Similar species: Vermiculated Screech-Owl is smaller and darker, lacks the superciliary and facial rim and the prominent vertical streaking below, and is a forest or humid woodland bird. In highlands see also Bare-shanked Screech-Owl.
Status and distribution: Fairly common in light second-growth woodland, borders, clearings and semiopen areas with scattered trees, and residential areas in lowlands on Pacific slope from Chiriquí to Canal area and Panama City area (probably eastward as well), with a single record from Darién (one collected on Cerro Nique at 2000 ft in April 1972 by R. Hinds; specimen in GML collection); on Caribbean slope recorded only from Canal area and eastern San Blas (Armila); found also on larger Pearl Islands. Has been heard at night at Boquete, in lower highlands of western Chiriquí.
Habits: The commonest owl on the Pacific slope, but strictly nocturnal and hence infrequently recorded except by call at night. The call is a distinctive dry purring trill, *prrrrrrr* or *hoorrrrrr*, usually, but not always, terminating in an abrupt querulous *ook*; or *ook? ook?* — most often heard in the evening soon after dark, also at night and in early morning before dawn.
Range: Costa Rica to Bolivia, northern Argentina, and southern Brazil.

BARE-SHANKED SCREECH-OWL
Otus clarkii   Plate 12

Description: 9–10. Found only in highlands of west and east. A rather large *spotted* screech-owl with *ear-tufts*. Iris yellow. *Facial area cinnamon-tawny with no obvious facial rim*; otherwise *dark reddish brown above* with black mottling, streaks, and vermiculations; large white spots on scapulars and wing-coverts; buffy brownish below with *prominent white* *spotting or short bars* and narrow black streaks, becoming paler on lower belly.

Similar species: Has a big-headed appearance. Rufous phase of Vermiculated Screech-Owl (which usually is found at lower elevations, though there may be some overlap) is smaller, has more black spotting and streaking on upperparts, and lacks the prominent squarish white bars or spots below.

Status and distribution: Apparently rare (doubtless to some extent overlooked) in forest in highlands of Chiriquí, Veraguas (one old specimen from Calobre), and eastern Darién; recorded 1080–2100 m (3600–7000 ft).

Habits: Strictly nocturnal, and not well known in Panama. Apparently largely confined to true cloud forest (e.g. on Cerro Pirre, and along the Continental Divide above Fortuna, Chiriquí). Call is a series of rather low *ooo* or *coo* notes, often irregularly paced and rather pattern-less, but at times holding to a more regular *ooo, ooo-ooo-ooo; ooo, ooo-ooo-ooo . . .* or *coo, coo-cu; coo, coo-cu. . . .* Pairs at times duet (M. Robbins *et al.*).

Range: Costa Rica to extreme northwestern Colombia.

CRESTED OWL
Lophostrix cristata   Plate 12

Description: 16. A large owl with *very long whitish or buffy ear-tufts.* Iris variable, yellow or brown. Sooty brown above mottled with rufous; *prominent white or buffy eye-stripe,* which extends onto ear-tufts in an unbroken line; wings conspicuously spotted with white; underparts buffy to tawny with narrow dusky barring giving mottled appearance.

Similar species: No other Panama owl combines the unstreaked underparts with such spectacularly long ear-tufts.

Status and distribution: Uncommon and seemingly local (though probably to a large extent only overlooked) in forest and second-growth woodland in lowlands and foothills (rarely to over 900 m: 3000 ft) on both slopes. Better knowledge of its voice (see below) has recently shown it to be widespread on the Caribbean slope of the Canal area, with numbers perhaps greatest along Pipeline Road.

Habits: Strictly nocturnal. Birds roost by day in thickets and tangles, often along small forested streams, usually perching only 3–9 m (10–30 ft) above the ground; they have been repeatedly found in such situations along certain streams which cross the middle part of Pipeline Road. The characteristic call is usually given as the bird perches in the canopy of tall trees; it is a low but penetrating and far-carrying *groorrrr* or *bwoorrrr*. A vocalizing bird will sometimes decoy in to a tape of its call, but they are shy and more often then hang back.

Range: Southern Mexico to western Ecuador, Bolivia, and Amazonian Brazil.

SPECTACLED OWL
Pulsatrix perspicillata   Plate 12, p.188

Description: 17–19. A large owl without ear-tufts. Iris yellow. Dark chocolate brown above with *broad white eyebrow extending to lores and area around bill* (the "spectacles"); throat white, *chest band dark brown, lower underparts buffy whitish to buff.* Completely different immature is mostly buffy white with *contrasting blackish face,* brownish wings.

Status and distribution: Uncommon to fairly common in forest and second-growth woodland in more humid lowlands and foothills (to about 1200 m: 4000 ft) on both slopes, but not often seen.

Habits: Nocturnal, resting by day in thick foliage, but occasionally will become active on dark cloudy late afternoons. Its commonest call is a rapid series of six to eight low rattling hoots, *bobobobobobo,* lacking in resonance but far-carrying, sounding almost like a distant machine gun. Decoys readily to a tape of its voice. Juveniles give a slightly hoarse loud whistle, *hweeew.*

Spectacled Owl (juvenile)

Range: Southern Mexico to Bolivia, northern Argentina, and southern Brazil.

GREAT HORNED OWL
Bubo virginianus
Description: 19–21. Very rare. *Panama's largest owl*, with *prominent ear-tufts*. Iris yellow. Sooty brown above mottled with tawny and grayish and streaked with black; facial area buffy bordered by black facial rim; *lower throat and foreneck white*; remaining underparts tawny to whitish, *barred with blackish*.
Similar species: Crested Owl has conspicuous pale superciliary and ear-tufts and lacks the white throat patch; it is much smaller and slenderer than this species. Striped Owl is also smaller and is streaked (not barred) below.
Status and distribution: Uncertain. Only two records: a nineteenth-century specimen taken at Chitra, Veraguas; and one seen perched at the edge of a swamp on Isla Ranchería, off Coiba Island, on February 4, 1956 (Wetmore). Probably a rare and local resident in forests of Pacific western Panama (and possibly elsewhere); Wetmore assigned the Chitra specimen to the Central American race *mesembrinus*.
Range: Northern North America to Tierra del Fuego; rare and very local in tropical Middle and South America.

ANDEAN PYGMY-OWL
Glaucidium jardinii   p.191

Description: 6. Found only in western highlands. Iris yellow. Brown above, *crown with small whitish to buff spots*, back spotted with buff, and wings barred with white and buff; short white eyebrow and small black eye-like spot on either side of nape; mostly white below with irregular brown band across chest (often broken in middle), and with *sides and flanks extensively barred or spotted with brown*; tail blackish with four narrow white bars and white tip. Rufous phase is mostly rufous below with little barring and no streaking; its buff crown spots are larger and blurrier. Immature has grayish crown without spots or with spots restricted to forecrown, sides more streaked.
Similar species: Only pygmy-owl in the western highlands. Both other Panama pygmy-owls have streaking on underparts.
Status and distribution: Rare in forest and forest borders in highland of western

Chiriquí and Veraguas, mostly above 1500 m (5000 ft). Not well known in Panama but can be seen occasionally in the Cerro Punta area.
Habits: Similar to the better known Ferruginous Pygmy-Owl, and likewise partly diurnal. The call in Costa Rica is a long series of whistled *poop* notes given in couplets, but in South America a long series of evenly spaced *poop* notes (much like that of Ferruginous Pygmy-Owl) has also been heard.
Range: Costa Rica and western Panama; Andes of northwestern Venezuela and Colombia to Bolivia.

LEAST PYGMY-OWL
Glaucidium minutissimum   p.191

Description: 5½. Iris yellow. *Head grayish with small white dots, especially on crown*; narrow buff nuchal band terminating on either side of nape in small black eye-like spot; otherwise mostly brown above, sometimes with a few small buffy white spots on wings; white below *broadly streaked rufous brown across breast, sides, and lower belly* ; tail black with three narrow white bars and white tip. Immature lacks white dots on head.
Similar species: Only pygmy-owl in humid forested lowlands (no known sympatry with other pygmy-owls in Panama). Ferruginous Pygmy-Owl's crown is streaked, not dotted (though this can be hard to see in the field), and its tail has more bars; Andean Pygmy-Owl is barred or spotted, not streaked, below.
Status and distribution: Rare to locally uncommon in humid forest in lowlands and lower foothills on both slopes; probably widespread, though often overlooked, and recorded so far from western Bocas del Toro (lower Changuinola River, where seen in April 1980 by Ridgely), Canal area (Pipeline Road, where netted and photographed in May 1977 by N. Brokaw and D. Schemske, and since occasionally recorded by others), eastern Panama province (Río Boqueron above Madden Lake, and in the Bayono River valley at Majé), eastern San Blas (Permé, Puerto Obaldía), and Darién (lower Chucunaque River, and Cana and lower slopes of Cerro Pirre). Reports of pygmy-owls from Pacific side of Canal area (N. G. Smith and others) may refer to this species or to *G. brasilianum*; confirmation needed.
Habits: Like other pygmy-owls, abroad both by day and night. Usually found in canopy

to middle levels of forest. Call is a short series of three to five *poop* notes, sometimes more (up to eight or nine) when the bird is excited; compared to Ferruginous, Least's call usually has a slower tempo, and the series is always shorter. A vocalizing bird can often be decoyed in by imitating its easily whistled call.

Range: Mexico south locally to Peru, Paraguay, and southern Brazil.

Note: More than one species may be involved. Panama birds seem allied to those of northern South America; vocally, those of Mexico and southeastern South America appear to differ.

FERRUGINOUS PYGMY-OWL
Glaucidium brasilianum   p.191

Description: 6½. Found only in Pacific western lowlands. Iris yellow. Two color phases. Either grayish brown or rufous above, *crown narrowly streaked buff or whitish*, and wings with whitish or buff spots; short white eyebrow and black eye-like spot on either side of nape; white below *broadly streaked brown or rufous* (depending on phase), especially across breast and on sides; tail blackish *with five to six narrow whitish bars* and white tip. Immature lacks crown streaks.

Similar species: The only frequently encountered pygmy-owl in Panama, and not known to overlap with other species. In its range, generic characters of small size and chunky shape, black "false eyes" on back of head, and fairly long often cocked tail are distinctive. Both other Panama pygmy-owls have crown spotted, not streaked, but this is not always easy to see.

Status and distribution: Uncommon to locally fairly common in scrubby and light woodland, clearings, and semi-open areas with thickets and scattered trees in lowlands on Pacific slope (chiefly in drier regions) from Veraguas and eastern side of Azuero Peninsula to western Panama province. Reports of pygmy-owls from Pacific side of Canal area (N. G. Smith and others) may refer to this species or to *G. minutissimum*; confirmation needed.

Habits: Often active during the day, perching in the open on fence posts or even on telephone wires. The usual call is a long series of whistled *poop* or *toot* notes, repeated rather rapidly for up to several minutes; it is heard mostly at night, though it also calls by day. Often responds strongly to a whistled imitation (or tape recording) of its call; in areas where it occurs many small birds will also come in to mob it.

Range: Extreme southwestern United States to northern Chile and central Argentina.

BURROWING OWL
Athene cunicularia

Description: 9–10. Accidental. *Long legs*; quite short tail. Iris yellow. Brown above spotted with whitish, forehead and superciliary white; whitish below with blackish band across chest, and barred irregularly with brown on breast and sides. *Terrestrial.*

Status and distribution: Only one record, a bird taken at Divalá, Chiriquí on December 13, 1900.

Habits: Active by day as well as by night, perching on the ground or on low vantage points, bobbing up and down on its long legs when nervous.

Range: Breeds locally in western North America and Mexico, wintering south to Honduras, accidentally to Costa Rica and western Panama; also breeds in Florida, West Indies, and locally in open parts of South America.

Note: Formerly placed in monotypic genus *Speotyto*. Short-eared Owl (*Asio flammeus*) has been recorded in northern winter casually as far south as Costa Rica; it breeds in temperate North America, South America, and the Old World, favoring open marshy and grassy country. It is fairly large (15–16 in) and mostly tawny brown, lightly streaked below, with short ear-tufts; buffy wing-patches and black patch at carpal joint show in low flopping flight.

MOTTLED OWL
Ciccaba virgata   Plate 12

Description: 13–14. A medium-sized owl without ear-tufts. Iris brown (virtually nonreflective at night). Dark brown above mottled with grayish buff and dusky, and with *whitish* eyebrow; wings and tail dark brown barred buffy grayish; *breast buffy heavily mottled and streaked dusky, belly paler buff streaked dark brown.* A dark phase is darker above and more cinnamon below with irregular dusky barring and streaking.

Similar species: Black-and-white Owl is distinctly barred below with black and white. Striped Owl has prominent ear-tufts and is found in open country, not in forest and woodland.

Status and distribution: Fairly common in forest and second-growth woodland on both slopes, mostly in lowlands and foothills, but

Left to right, Unspotted Saw-whet Owl, Andean Pygmy-Owl, Ferruginous Pygmy-Owl, Least Pygmy-Owl

in western Chiriquí ranging well up into highlands (to about 2100 m: 7000 ft); less numerous or absent from drier Pacific lowlands from eastern side of Azuero Peninsula to western Panama province.

Habits: Strictly nocturnal and hence not often seen. Roosts by day in dense thickets, but at night often found at edge of forest or woodland. Rather vocal, the commonest call being a deep muffled *whoo-ow, whoo-ow* or *whooou, whooou*, typically doubled or tripled (sometimes more), but also gives a cat-like screech *keeyóww* or keeeoweéyo.

Range: Northern Mexico to Bolivia, northern Argentina, and southern Brazil.

BLACK-AND-WHITE OWL
Ciccaba nigrolineata   Plate 12

Description: 14–15. A medium-sized owl without ear-tufts. Iris light brown (but reflects a deep red at night). *Above sooty black*, narrowly barred white on upper back; *facial area and throat black*, outlined by speckled white eyebrow; *below white narrowly and evenly barred with black*; tail blackish with several white bars.

Similar species: Mottled Owl is essentially brown and is not barred below.

Status and distribution: Uncommon (doubtless somewhat overlooked) in humid forest and forest borders on both slopes, mostly in lowlands but has also been

recorded up to 2100 m (7000 ft) in western Chiriquí highlands (Ridgely); definitely recorded only from Bocas del Toro, Chiriquí, Veraguas, Canal area, eastern Panama province, and Darién, but likely found elsewhere in suitable habitat. In recent years found to be widespread and fairly numerous on Caribbean side of Canal area, with a few reports from Pacific side as well.

Habits: Strictly nocturnal and rarely seen by day, but calls persistently at night, and can often be lured in for a view by tape-recordings. Has several distinctly different calls, the most frequent being a somewhat nasal whining *keeeów* or *keyów*, and a rather fast *buh-buh-buh-buh-buh-bwóh-bwo*, with accent characteristically on penultimate note (the last note sometimes inaudible or not given). Also gives a very deliberate, deep resonant *whoof, whoof, whoof* (Eisenmann).

Range: Southern Mexico to northwestern Venezuela and northwestern Peru.

STRIPED OWL
Asio clamator   Plate 12

Description: 13–15. A medium-sized owl with *conspicuous, blackish ear-tufts*. Iris light brown to orange-yellow. Tawny-buff above coarsely streaked and vermiculated with blackish; facial area whitish bordered by black rim; whitish to buffy below, *heavily streaked with brownish black*.

Similar species: The only medium-sized owl with ear-tufts that is streaked below. Very rare Great Horned Owl is much larger and is barred below. See also Stygian Owl (below).

Status and distribution: Uncommon and local in open grassy areas and shrubby clearings in lowlands on Pacific slope from Chiriquí to eastern Panama province (not recorded from Darién, but with continued clearings likely will spread there, and may already occur); on Caribbean slope recorded only from Canal area and eastern Colon province (where seen several times in late December 1986 near the Río Claro east of Portobelo by D. Graham); in western Chiriquí ranges up occasionally to about 1050 m (3500 ft).

Habits: Rests by day in low trees or thickets, but nests on the ground. Can sometimes be seen flying low over the ground at dusk; also regularly perches on wires and low trees, peering intently downward. Often quite tame, or so intent on its hunting that it virtually ignores the observer. Has a loud, penetrating, semi-whistled *wheeeyoo*; also a stacatto series of barking hoots *ow, ow, ow, ow* (P. Schwartz).

Range: Southeastern Mexico south locally to Bolivia, northern Argentina, and Uruguay.

Note: Formerly placed in the monotypic genus *Rhinoptynx*. Stygian Owl (*Asio stygius*) may yet be found in the highlands of Panama; very local, it is recorded from Mexico to Belize and Guatemala and in Nicaragua, the Greater Antilles, and South America. Stygian resembles the Long-eared Owl (*A. otus*) of temperate North America and Eurasia (15 in), but *looks very dark*. It is mainly blackish above with dusky (not rufous) facial area; buff below, strongly streaked and barred with blackish; prominent but slender dark ear-tufts.

UNSPOTTED SAW-WHET OWL
Aegolius ridgwayi   p.191

Description: 7. Apparently rare; known only from western Chiriquí mountains. Dark brown above, including face, with *forehead and narrow line above eye white; buff below* with indistinct cinnamon band across breast.

Similar species: A small and plain owl, with no streaking, barring, or spotting (except on inner secondaries). See Andean Pygmy-Owl. In appearance strikingly like juvenile plumage of Northern Saw-whet Owl (*A. acadicus*).

Status and distribution: Known only from one bird taken in a mist-net set in forest on west flank of Volcán Barú, at about 2100 m (7000 ft), on February 17, 1965.

Habits: Little known. Apparently rare throughout its range, though possibly only overlooked. In Costa Rica, the call is reported to be a series of rhythmic whistles of equal pitch, similar to but seemingly somewhat lower in pitch than the call of the Northern Saw-whet, *A. arcadius* (M. S. Foster and N. K. Johnson, *Wilson Bull. 86*(1): 59, 1974).

Range: Southern Mexico to western Panama.

NIGHTJARS: Caprimulgidae (10)

Except for the crepuscular nighthawks, members of this family are strictly nocturnal; by day they are almost never seen except when flushed accidentally. The family is virtually worldwide in occurrence. Most are best known from their calls, in most species readily recognized, given primarily by males during the breeding season. Nightjars as a group are characterized by their short bills, large mouths, which open wide, and loose fluffy plumage; most species resemble each other closely and are difficult to separate on visual characters alone. By day, nighthawks and nightjars rest either on the ground or lengthwise on a branch, their cryptic coloration making them almost invisible. They eat insects, captured on the wing. Eggs are laid directly on the ground, there being no attempt at a nest; *Lurocalis* nests on a branch in forest canopy.

SHORT-TAILED NIGHTHAWK
Lurocalis semitorquatus   p.196

Description: 9–9½. *Very short, square tail*; rather long, somewhat pointed wings. *Black-ish above*, speckled with rufous; throat white, remaining underparts dark brown barred with black; tail dark brown; wings dark *without white band*. At rest, wings extend well beyond tail.

Similar species: Looks very dark in the field, with no white in wings or tail; characteristic silhouette of short tail and long wings is almost reminiscent of a huge swift. *Chordeiles* nighthawks have longer slightly forked tails, more pointed wings with a conspicuous pale band, and usually frequent open country (not forest and adjacent areas).

Status and distribution: Uncommon and apparently local (but possibly increasing and spreading to some extent) in humid forest and forest borders in lowlands and foothills on both slopes; more widespread on Caribbean side, and on Pacific side known only from Veraguas (Cébaco Island), southwestern Los Santos (Río Guánico, Cerro Hoya), and from Canal area (one seen along Chiva Chiva Road on January 24, 1984; Ridgely and J. Vardaman) east into Darién. Noted quite regularly at dusk along Pipeline Road.

Habits: Crepuscular, and almost always seen at dusk or dawn as it feeds in and above the forest canopy, sometimes coming lower out over clearings, roads, or rivers. Roosts by day high in forest trees, and nests on horizontal limbs well above the ground. Flight is erratic and shifting, rather bat-like. Most often silent, but occasionally gives a rather sharp stacatto *cu-it, cu-it, cu-it.*

Range: Honduras (recent sightings) to northern Argentina and southern Brazil.

Note: More than one species is probably involved in South America.

LESSER NIGHTHAWK
Chordeiles acutipennis

Description: 8–9. Long, slender, pointed wings; fairly long, somewhat notched tail. Dark grayish brown to buffy brown above, marbled and spotted with buff, whitish, and black; throat white, remaining underparts buff barred with dusky; *band of white across primaries nearer to tip than to bend of wing*; tail barred whitish and dusky, with white band near tip. Female has throat and wing-band pale buffy (but looks white at any distance) and lacks white tail band. At rest wings reach end of tail.

Similar species: Often difficult to distinguish from Common Nighthawk. Smaller, with wing-band nearer tip of wing (this difference is often hard to discern in the field, however). Sometimes more helpful is the difference in wing shape: in Lesser the outermost primary is shorter than the adjacent inner one (resulting in a somewhat more rounded shape), whereas in Common the outermost primary is the longest

(resulting in a very pointed look). Commons tend to fly higher, and fly with deeper wing-strokes; Lessers fly lower usually, and their wing-strokes are shallower and more fluttery. Female Lesser is the only night-hawk with a buff wing-band, but this too is often not easy to see under normal field conditions. Common Pauraque and other nightjars have broader rounder wings which at rest do not reach the end of the tail.

Status and distribution: Locally fairly common in lowlands on Pacific slope, breeding in drier more open areas, especially in eroded and scrubby savanna country of Coclé and western Panama province; local breeders augmented by northern migrants late July–April, and during this season also occurs on Caribbean slope (particularly on migration) and up into lower highlands.

Habits: Both *Chordeiles* nighthawks have a rapid bounding flight with deep wing-strokes, swerving and changing speeds abruptly. Active in the late afternoon and evening and before dawn, feeding over open areas, usually flying low (not high as in Common Nighthawk). On migration flies higher and in broad daylight, frequently in loose flocks. Generally spends day roosting lengthwise on a tree branch, especially in mangroves and swampy areas. Much less vocal than Common Nighthawk, never booming nor giving that species' nasal *peent*; during breeding season gives a frog-like trilling on the ground, and a bleeting or whinnying call in flight.

Range: Southwestern United States to northern Bolivia, Paraguay, and southern Brazil; northern breeders winter from Mexico to Colombia.

COMMON NIGHTHAWK
Chordeiles minor

Description: 9–10. Very similar to Lesser Nighthawk. Larger and usually somewhat darker and more coarsely marked, particularly below; as in Lesser only male has white throat and only adult male has white tail band; white wing-band in this species is *about midway between tip and bend of wing* (in Lesser it is nearer the tip) and is white in both sexes.

Similar species: Very similar to Lesser Nighthawk. For distinctions in flight, see under that species. When perched the two are often very difficult to separate, but Lesser females and some males have basal half of primaries barred or spotted with buff (this area, aside from the white wing-band, all blackish in Common).

Status and distribution: Fairly common but apparently local breeder (*panamensis*) in open areas in lowlands and foothills on Pacific slope from Chiriquí to eastern Panama province; actual nesting has only been recorded from Cerro Campana and the Canal area, but presumably more widespread. Various northern races occur as transients on both slopes, with numbers apparently largest along Caribbean coast (e.g. "hundreds" were seen passing eastward along the western San Blas coast in September 1985 by J. Jolly). There are *no* confirmed records of Common Nighthawks of *any* race (including *panamensis*) during the northern winter months (November 4– March 24), at which time all nighthawks in Panama (and anywhere in Middle America) can be presumed to be Lessers; at this season all Commons are believed to be in South America.

Habits: Tends to fly high, whereas the Lesser skims low over the ground, but both species fly high overhead when migrating, and this species sometimes forages low. During much of the year (less outside of breeding season) utters an unmistakable nasal *peent* or *beezhnt*; males in courtship display give a loud booming sound when diving toward the ground.

Range: Breeds from North America to Panama; winters in South America.

COMMON PAURAQUE

COMMON PAURAQUE
Nyctidromus albicollis   p.194

Description: 9½–11. Rounded wings; *rather long, rounded tail*. Brownish above, mottled and spotted with dusky and buff; chin dusky, throat buff, remaining underparts buffy, finely barred with dusky; wings with *broad white band across primaries; sides of tail mostly white* (very prominent in flight). Female has narrower white wing-band and white in tail reduced to tipping. At rest wings extend only half the length of the tail.

Similar species: Superficially like a *Chordeiles* nighthawk but with rounded and shorter wings and unforked tail. White-tailed Nightjar is considerably smaller with buff or tawny collar on hindneck and almost square tail. Rufous Nightjar and Chuck-will's-widow are both much ruddier and lack white wing-band.

Status and distribution: Common in clearings, shrubby areas, and secondgrowth woodland in lowlands and foothills on both slopes, more local on Caribbean side, and scarce in mostly forested regions; found also on larger Pearl Islands, and on Cébaco and Gobernadora Islands off coast of Veraguas.

Habits: Strictly nocturnal, this species' true abundance is best indicated during breeding season (February–May) when at night in proper habitat its calls may resound from all around. The typical call is a hoarse *whe-wheéee-oo*; this is sometimes slurred into a *por-weéeeeer* or preceded by a series of *bup* notes; occasionally the *bup* notes are given alone in series. In eastern Panama this well known bird is called the "bujío", an imitation (excellent) of its typical vocalization. At night comes out into more open areas, and then often seen resting on dirt or gravel roads, its bright orange-red eye reflecting car headlights from great distances; at such times it can sometimes be approached very closely. Infrequently encountered by day, usually as it flushes from the ground and flies off like a large moth.

Range: Southern Texas and Mexico to Bolivia, northern Argentina, and southern Brazil.

[OCELLATED POORWILL]
Nyctiphrynus ocellatus

Description: 8½. Hypothetical. *Mostly blackish brown*, with some rufous markings; wing-coverts spotted rufous and with *several large white spots* (sometimes absent); white band across lower throat; some white spotting on belly (hard to see in the field); no white wing-band, but *tail narrowly tipped white*.

Similar species: A small, very dark, forest-based nightjar; note especially the white spotting on wing-coverts (if present; absent in the one Nicaraguan specimen, *fide* Eisenmann) and the white tip to tail.

Status and distribution: One believed seen on Achiote Road on Caribbean side of Canal area on March 15, 1978 (R. Ryan). Specimen verification needed.

Habits: The race most likely to occur in Panama, *rosenbergi* of western Colombia and Ecuador, is poorly known. In eastern Brazil the nominate race is found in humid forest and forest borders in lowlands and foothills (to about 900 m: 3000 ft); its call is a short and rather soft *ddrrrreuw*, somewhat like a weak Pauraque, and is usually delivered from a low perch 3–7.5 m (10–25 ft) above ground inside forest or at edge (Ridgely).

Range: Eastern Nicaragua (one specimen, described as the race *lautus*); Panama (perhaps) to western Ecuador; western Amazonia locally to southeastern Brazil and northeastern Argentina.

Note: More than one species may be involved.

CHUCK-WILL'S-WIDOW
Caprimulgus carolinensis

Description: 11–12. *Rufous brown above*, vermiculated and spotted with buff and black; paler brown below, barred with dusky, lower throat white; no wing-band; inner web of outer three tail feathers buffy white in male (shows conspicuously), rest of tail tawny barred and dotted with black; no white in tail of female.

Similar species: Best told by combination of large size (the largest nightjar in Panama) and dark brown overall appearance. Rufous Nightjar is very similar in plumage but notably smaller; in the hand, note lateral filaments on rictal bristles (lacking in Rufous Nightjar). Common Pauraque has white wing-band.

Status and distribution: Rare to uncommon (probably often overlooked) winter resident (October–April) in forest, second-growth woodland, and at least locally even in residential areas with large trees (e.g. Panama City) almost throughout, though probably most numerous in lowlands and scarcer eastward.

Habits: Strictly nocturnal. By day roosts on the ground in a secluded place, perhaps also high in trees (where it would almost invariably escape detection). At night may come out into semiopen areas to feed; also recorded sallying from perches in forest canopy. At least on migration an occasional predator on small birds (O. Owre).

Range: Breeds in southeastern United States; winters through Middle America to Colombia (once Venezuela), and in Florida and Greater Antilles.

RUFOUS NIGHTJAR
Caprimulgus rufus   p.196

Description: 10. Very similar to the Chuck-will's-widow but *smaller* and ruddier brown, with less white in tail of male. In the hand, note this species' smooth rictal bristles (like other nightjars), without lateral filaments of the Chuck-will's-widow.

Similar species: See Chuck-will's-widow. Common Pauraque, with which this species often occurs, has a white wing-band, more white in tail, and is much less rufous generally.

Status and distribution: Locally fairly common in second-growth woodland and borders in lowlands and foothills on Pacific slope in Canal area and eastern Panama province; elsewhere on Pacific slope apparently less numerous, though recorded from Chiriquí to Darién; on Caribbean slope known only from Canal area (where scarce and local, *fide* J. Pujals), and single Bocas del Toro and San Blas records; found also on Coiba Island (where quite common). During breeding season (late January–early May) can easily be heard in the Curundu/Fort Clayton area on Pacific side of Canal area, and on lower slopes of Cerro Azul.

Habits: Strictly nocturnal. Does not sit on roads as often as Pauraque. During breeding season calls from dusk to dawn, a fast resonant *chuck, wick-wick-weéoo*, the first syllable inaudible except at close range, the entire call reminiscent of that of Chuck-will's-widow but considerably faster and higher pitched. Calling birds usually perch on a branch a few meters off the ground inside woodland, and hence they are hard to see.

Range: Southern Costa Rica (rare) south locally to northern Argentina and southeastern Brazil.

WHIP-POOR-WILL
Caprimulgus vociferus

Description: 9–10. Recorded only from Chiriquí highlands. *Grayish brown above*, vermiculated and spotted with tawny and

Left to right, WHITE-TAILED NIGHTJAR (male), SHORT-TAILED NIGHTHAWK, RUFOUS NIGHTJAR (male)

black; upper throat blackish, *lower throat buffy white*, remaining underparts brownish mottled with dusky; outer tail feathers broadly tipped white in male, more narrowly tipped buff in female.

Similar species: Dusky Nightjar male is blacker, without whitish lower throat. Rufous Nightjar is ruddier generally, as is the larger Chuck-will's-widow.

Status and distribution: Two records from western Chiriquí highlands: one collected on slopes of Volcán Barú above Cerro Punta (1950 m: 6500 ft) on March 8, 1955 (Wetmore); and one seen at Volcán Lakes on January 15, 1974 (Ridgely).

Habits: Like other nightjars, strictly nocturnal; as with Chuck-will's-widow silent on its wintering grounds and hence usually overlooked.

Range: Breeds in eastern North America and from southwestern United States to Honduras; winters from extreme southern United States to Costa Rica (rare), casually to western Panama.

DUSKY NIGHTJAR
Caprimulgus saturatus

Description: 9. Known only from Chiriquí highlands. Male *blackish* spotted throughout with cinnamon-rufous; belly buff barred with blackish. Female has larger cinnamon-buff spots so that general effect is of a *very dark rufous* bird. Outer tail feathers broadly tipped white in male, more narrowly tipped buffy in female.

Similar species: Whip-poor-will is grayer overall (not blackish or dark rufous) with distinct narrow whitish band across lower throat. Rufous Nightjar is more uniform and paler rufous brown, not spotted.

Status and distribution: Uncommon in forest and forest borders in highlands of western Chiriquí around Volcán Barú, mostly above 1500 m (5000 ft).

Habits: Strictly nocturnal, by day resting on branches a few feet off the ground in thickets in humid montane forest. At dusk emerges to forest edge and adjacent clearings, where it often perches on fallen logs, and from which (at least during the January–April dry season) it gives its fast burry call, *cheer-for-weer*. Can regularly be found soon after dusk along the Boquete Trail above Cerro Punta.

Range: Costa Rica and western Panama.

WHITE-TAILED NIGHTJAR
Caprimulgus cayennensis   p.196

Description: 8–8½. Pale grayish above mottled with buffy brown and vermiculated with dark brown; *prominent cinnamon collar across hindneck*; superciliary and throat white; breast buffy with coarse dusky barring and some large white spots, becoming white on belly; wings with broad white band across primaries (like band of a Lesser Nighthawk); tail notched, *mostly white from below* (white also easily seen in flight), central feathers vermiculated gray and dusky above. Female quite different, darker above and buffier below, but with *same cinnamon nuchal collar*; wings more narrowly banded with buff, and tail banded buff and dusky (neither with any white); throat and belly ochraceous buff, breast with dusky barring and white spots as in male.

Similar species: Nighthawks have longer pointed wings that at rest extend to tip of tail; in this species wings are considerably shorter and more rounded, reaching only about midway down the tail. Common Pauraque is larger with rounded tail; it has a paler crown and lacks the distinct nuchal collar. See also Spot-tailed Nightjar (below).

Status and distribution: Uncommon and local (probably somewhat overlooked) in open rather dry grassy areas, bushy savannas, and rather barren hillsides in lowlands on Pacific slope from Chiriquí to western Darién (Santa Fé; seen in April 1967 by Eisenmann).

Habits: Strictly nocturnal, resting by day on the ground, usually under cover of a bush. The call, apparently given mostly May–September, is a long high-pitched whistle, first rising, then going down in pitch at the end, introduced by a short dry note (inaudible at a distance), *tk, chweeeeeeea* or *pick, speeeeeea*, slightly suggestive of a Pauraque but much higher-pitched and without burry quality. It is usually given from a slightly elevated perch such as a fence post or grass stem.

Range: Costa Rica to the Guianas and extreme northern Brazil.

Note: Spot-tailed Nightjar (*C. maculicaudus*) could occur; it is recorded from savannas and pastures, often near water, from Mexico south very locally to Bolivia and Brazil, and has been found apparently breeding very near the Darién border in Colombia (J. Haffer), so perhaps most likely in cleared areas of Darién. In size and pattern it resembles female White-tailed Nightjar. Both sexes have blackish crown and cheeks, buff superciliary, and blackish chest with large buff and white spots, bordered below by band of dense narrow blackish barring (latter not present in White-tailed); male's tail has a broad white tip and small white spots on underside near base (latter visible only in the hand), while female's is banded buff and dusky (without white), like White-tailed's. Its call is a thin high-pitched *pitsweét* or *spit-sweét*, rather insect-like.

POTOOS: Nyctibiidae (2)

The potoos are a small family of exclusively neotropical, rather little known birds. They resemble the nightjars in many respects, especially in their large eyes, cavernous mouths, and nocturnal habits, but differ in their greater size and more or less upright (not horizontal) posture. They are rarely seen by day, for they then rest motionless, often high in a tree, looking like an extension of a dead snag or stump. If the bird is unaware of one's presence, its head is hunched into its body and its bill is in a natural, forward position. Usually, however, the potoo will see the observer before you see it, and it then slowly assumes the typical stretched-out position with the bill pointing skyward. More easily seen at night (especially when the moon is full), when the birds may be calling and may be seen perching on a prominent look-out. They feed on insects caught on the wing, usually returning to their original perch after a sally. The nest is nonexistent: a single egg is laid in the small depression or crevice created by a broken-off branch.

GREAT POTOO
Nyctibius grandis   p.198

Description: 19–20. *Looks very pale, virtually white, in the field.* Eyes large, dark brown, but reflecting orange at night. Pale brownish above, spotted and margined with buffy and whitish; whitish below, finely barred with dusky, spotted with dusky on breast.

Similar species: Common Potoo bulks only half as large and is much darker overall. Common Barn-Owl also looks very pale at night, but has different shape (large head).

Status and distribution: Uncommon (often overlooked) in humid forest, second-growth woodland, and borders in lowlands on Caribbean slope, on Pacific slope in eastern Panama province (upper Bayano River valley) and Darién. In recent years recorded regularly from many forested sites on Caribbean side of Canal area, perhaps in greatest numbers in the Achiote/Escobal region.

Habits: Similar in most respects to the better known Common Potoo. Nocturnal, resting by day high in a forest tree (where nearly invisible), at night coming out more into the open, often to forest borders and even adjacent clearings. The easily recognized call is heard fairly often; it is loud and far-carrying, an explosive bawling *bwarrr*.

Range: Guatemala to northern Bolivia and southern Brazil.

COMMON POTOO
Nyctibius griseus p.198

Description: 15–16. Eyes very large, yellow, *reflecting intense glowing orange at night.* Bill notably small, but opening wide, exposing huge flesh-colored mouth. *Grayish brown to brown,* intricately patterned above and below with tawny, black, and white; a broken band of scattered black spots across chest in some birds. Upstanding feathers above eyes sometimes resemble horns.

Similar species: Most likely to be mistaken for an owl but of different proportions, with smaller head and long tail. Great Potoo is larger and appears much whiter.

Status and distribution: Fairly common but perhaps somewhat local in forest borders, second-growth woodland, and clearings in lowlands on both slopes, ranging up to about 1200 m (4000 ft) in the western highlands; absent from drier and more open parts of western Pacific slope, and seems also to avoid extensively forested regions.

Habits: Active only by night, especially in hours just after dusk and just before dawn. Very difficult to see during the day, then resting motionless but often fully in the open, usually at moderate heights on a bare branch of a tree, relying on its cryptic coloration and lack of movement for protection. The beautiful haunting call is one of the most memorable of Panama bird sounds, and is heard particularly on moonlit nights. It is a deep, melancholy, wonderfully mod-

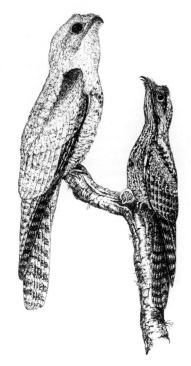

Left, GREAT POTOO; right, COMMON POTOO

ulated series of four to eight wailing notes, falling in pitch, loudest at first and falling off at the end; perhaps most aptly paraphrased as *poor-me-all-alone* (J. Bond).

Range: Mexico to Bolivia, northern Argentina, and Uruguay; Jamaica and Hispaniola.

Note: Two species are likely involved, for the northern Middle American (and Jamaican) *N. jamaicensis* (Northern Potoo) lacks the wailing call so characteristic of southern Middle American and South American *N. griseus.*

OILBIRDS: Steatornithidae (1)

To date, the presence of oilbirds in Panama rests solely on the three records mentioned below, but it is probable that a colony exists in some yet undiscovered cave or grotto in eastern Panama. In South America, oilbirds are found locally, usually in limestone caves, and in some areas are still persecuted, the very fat young being taken as a source of oil. In appearance they are something between a large nightjar and a hawk, with strong hooked bills and sharp claws. When disturbed in their caves, they emit loud screams; in these caves they also utter clicking sounds used as echo-locators, but probably they find their food (various fruits, mostly palm) primarily through their sense of smell (D. Snow). Oilbirds are the only nocturnal fruit-eating birds.

OILBIRD
Steatornis caripensis

Description: 18. Only three records. Eyes reflect bright red. *Heavy, hooked bill. Rufous brown above*, spotted with rusty on head, *spotted with white on wing-coverts*, wings lightly barred with blackish; *pale rusty brown below*, spotted with white; tail long and graduated, brown barred narrowly with blackish.
Similar species: Somewhat nightjar-like, but much larger with hawk-like bill and rather large, white, black-encircled spots.
Status and distribution: Uncertain; only three records: one taken in a mist-net set for bats over the Río Tacarcuna (1750 ft) in eastern Darién on March 19, 1959; one seen and photographed as it rested on a branch in humid forest along Pipeline Road in Canal area on May 11, 1974 (N. Gale, J. Pujals); and one captured in weakened condition as it fluttered around a street lamp in Panama City in early November 1987 (this bird was taken to N. Gale, under whose care it gradually recovered, ultimately to be released in mid-November in apparent good health; photos by M. Letzer to VIREO). Probably a colony exists in some as yet undiscovered cave in eastern Panama, but D. Snow (in letter to M. Letzer) believes it at least equally likely that the Panama records could refer to stragglers from Colombian breeding colonies, such long-range dispersal having been recorded elsewhere, mainly involving young birds.
Range: Eastern Panama locally to Guyana and northern Bolivia.

SWIFTS: Apodidae (12)

The swifts are a distinct group of superficially swallow-like birds, having long very narrow stiff wings, compact bodies, and generally dark plumage (in some species patterned with white or rufous). They are worldwide in distribution, but most species occur in the tropics. True swifts are pre-eminently birds of the air, not perching "normally", usually roosting and nesting on vertical surfaces such as cliffs or the inside of hollow trees (or chimneys); some even copulate in the air (the only birds known to do so), and some species are known to sleep on the wing (D. Lack). All swifts are totally insectivorous, catching insects in their wide-opening mouths during very swift flight. The nest is usually constructed against a vertical surface, its components being held together by a glue-like salivary excretion, in most species a simple cup or half-cup, in some (e.g. Lesser Swallow-tailed Swift) more elaborate. The status of many Panamanian swifts is still very inadequately known. Collection of swifts, while not easy, is still desirable, for field identification of many species is often difficult. Not only does variation in appearance occur because of wear on feathers and dirt accumulated from their roosting sites, but the exact status and distribution of many species is still so uncertain that one can often not safely identify by range.

[BLACK SWIFT]
Cypseloides niger

Description: 6. One recent Chiriquí sighting. Sooty blackish with *inconspicuous whitish frosting on forecrown*, and sometimes with some whitish barring on belly; *tail fairly long and distinctly notched*.
Similar species: Not easy to identify with certainty in the field, but compared to other Panama *Cypseloides* the tail is both longer and more notched (with shallow fork nearly always being visible). White-chinned Swift's tail is shorter and square (or virtually so), but this distinction is subtle so birds must be at close range.
Status and distribution: Only record is a flock of about 40 carefully observed for over an hour as they fed low over savanna country near La Esperanza, Chiriquí, on June 25, 1982 (Ridgely). Specimen confirmation needed, but Black Swift's occurrence in Panama comes as no great surprise given the considerable number recently collected in adjacent Costa Rica, where they apparently breed during the May–June period (see L. F. Kiff, *Condor* 77(1): 102, 1975).
Range: Breeds locally from western North America to Costa Rica and in the West Indies; withdraws during northern winter from North America, and may occur at this

season in northern South America (still no specimens), but range at this season still very imperfectly known.

WHITE-CHINNED SWIFT
Cypseloides cryptus

Description: 5½–5¾. Very rare (or overlooked). *A large uniform dark swift with a short square tail.* Sooty black above with some paler edging on forehead; dark grayish brown below, usually with small whitish area on chin (not visible under normal field conditions). Female often has belly feathers tipped white. Distinguished from other *Cypseloides* swifts in the hand by its shorter tail (41–48 mm) and relatively long tarsus (15–16 mm).

Similar species: Barely distinguishable in the field from female or immature Chestnut-collared Swifts lacking the collar, but larger and with a shorter, square (not notched) tail. See also the even more similar Black Swift and Spot-fronted Swift (below).

Status and distribution: Uncertain. Only two records: one taken at Armila, San Blas, on July 4, 1932; another taken off Coiba Island on March 23, 1957. Perhaps only a visitant from South America, as practically all Middle American records are from austral winter months.

Range: Recorded from Belize to Guyana and Peru, but everywhere apparently scarce and local; breeding area unknown.

Note: Spot-fronted Swift (*C. cherriei*) may occur as it has been recorded from Costa Rica, Colombia, and Venezuela (but only a small number of specimens are known). It is slightly smaller (5 in) than either White-chinned or Black, sooty black with small but distinct white spots in front of and behind eye, also some whitish on chin in some birds; tail short and square. See C. Collins, *Am. Birds 34*(6): 852–855, 1980, for an interesting account of this heretofore little known bird, with fine photographs.

CHESTNUT-COLLARED SWIFT
Cypseloides rutilus

Description: 5. Sooty black with *broad rufous-chestnut collar encircling neck in adult male* (usually incomplete or lacking in females and immatures); tail fairly long, slightly notched.

Similar species: No other Panama swift has the chestnut collar, but this is difficult to see unless the bird flies against a dark background. Overhead, with backlighting from the sky, it becomes almost impossible. Compared to any

Chaetura swift, has longer tail, narrower more swept-back wings, and usually steadier and less fluttery flight with more gliding. Females and immatures lacking the collar are very similar to White-chinned Swift, which see.

Status and distribution: Apparently uncommon and perhaps local, but in recent years recorded more frequently than in the past. Known mostly from the western foothills and highlands; not reported east of Cerro Azul, eastern Panama province, though seems likely to occur. Only one record from Caribbean slope (in western Bocas del Toro, on lower Río Changuinola in April 1980; Ridgely), but perhaps overlooked. Recently recorded on several occasions in coastal Chiriquí and western Veraguas, presumably descending from adjacent mountains to feed. Breeding unrecorded in Panama, but seems likely; nests in Trinidad were on damp protected rock faces, often near (or even behind) waterfalls (C. Collins).

Habits: Usually seen in flocks, occasionally large; up to 200 were reported in western Veraguas in June (D. Wilcove and J. Wall). Often accompany White-collared Swifts, less frequently various *Chaetura*.

Range: Central Mexico south locally to Guyana and Bolivia.

WHITE-COLLARED SWIFT
Streptoprocne zonaris   p.201

Description: 7½–8½. A *very large* blackish swift with *prominent white collar completely encircling neck*; tail distinctly forked (though often not noticeable). Immature has narrower collar, sometimes reduced to patches or entirely lacking.

Similar species: Much larger than any other Panama swift, with unmistakable white collar.

Status and distribution: Fairly common to common in foothills and highlands throughout, also ranging regularly down into the coastal lowlands on entire Caribbean slope, somewhat less often to the Pacific slope lowlands (where also recorded from Coiba Island). In Canal area only small numbers are usually seen, and they are rare on the Pacific side.

Habits: Almost invariably seen in flocks, generally small to moderate-sized, but occasionally gathering in large milling flocks of several hundred or more, these sometimes riding thermals up to great heights. Other swifts often fly with them. White-collareds can fly at terrific speeds, and they

Upper left, two BAND-RUMPED SWIFTS; lower left, VAUX'S SWIFT;
middle, two SHORT-TAILED SWIFTS;
upper right, LESSER SWALLOW-TAILED SWIFT;
lower right, WHITE-COLLARED SWIFT

apparently range over great distances in their daily foraging; they also occasionally soar on stiff outstretched wings, the only Panama swift to do so. A loud hissing screech and various chittering calls are sometimes given, especially when they are chasing each other or near their nesting colonies. Nests are placed on damp cave walls or rock faces, often behind waterfalls, and are usually very inaccessible; no colony seems to have ever been found in Panama, though they surely nest here.

Range: Mexico to northern Argentina and southern Brazil; Greater Antilles.

CHIMNEY SWIFT
Chaetura pelagica

Description: 5¼–5¾. Fairly large. *Dark sooty olive above* with slightly paler rump and upper tail-coverts (but little contrast); grayish brown below, *noticeably paler on throat*; tail short.

Similar species: Most apt to be confused with Chapman's Swift, but not as black or glossy (more olive), and with much more contrast between throat and remaining underparts. Vaux's Swift is smaller and blacker above.

Status and distribution: Probably a regular transient, perhaps common, but specimen records few and most sightings difficult to verify; recorded October–November and March–May. Records are mostly from Caribbean slope, on Pacific slope only from Canal area east; sightings during spring passage from Taboga Island (Wetmore) and Panama Bay (Ridgely).

Habits: Usually seen in groups which move steadily, sometimes in association with transient swallows. In April reported flying north over the open ocean both on the Caribbean and on Panama Bay.

Range: Breeds in eastern and central North America; winters mostly in western Amazonia, also apparently in western Peru; migrates through Colombia and Venezuela, Middle America, and in West Indies.

VAUX'S SWIFT
Chaetura vauxi   p.201

Description: 4¼. *Small.* Sooty black above, with rump and upper tail-coverts grayish brown (showing *little* contrast in highland birds, *richmondi*, but paler with *more* contrast elsewhere in Panama range, *ochropygia*); sooty gray below with *distinctly paler gray throat.*

Similar species: Though this is the only *Chaetura* normally in the Chiriquí highlands, elsewhere in its Panama range this is a confusing swift. Short-tailed has an obviously very short tail, a higher contrast light grayish rump, and a dark throat with virtually no contrast. Gray-rumped and Band-rumped Swifts have longer tails and different rump patterns and color. Chimney Swift is notably larger and not as black above, but is otherwise very similar. See also Ashy-tailed Swift.

Status and distribution: Common in highlands of western and central Chiriquí and adjacent Bocas del Toro (seen north of Fortuna along the oleoducto road in July 1982; Ridgely); also locally numerous in lowlands and foothills of southern Veraguas (including western side of Azuero Peninsula), on Coiba and Pearl Islands, and seen once in coastal Chiriquí (six near Alanje on June 25, 1982; Ridgely). In addition there are a number of sight reports from the eastern side of the Azuero Peninsula, the Coclé foothills, and on both sides of Canal area and around Panama City (specimen verification still desirable, but probably resident throughout).

Range: Western North America to Panama (northern birds wintering from Mexico south, with southern limit still uncertain); northern Venezuela.

Note: It is possible that the two forms in Panama (*richmondi* and *ochropygia*) represent distinct species; their respective ranges and differing rump patterns would seem to suggest this, but additional work is needed. The northern, true *vauxi* group may also be distinct from the Middle American forms.

CHAPMAN'S SWIFT
Chaetura chapmani

Description: 5–5½. Very rare (or overlooked). Black above, *often with blue or green gloss on back and wings*; rump and upper tail-coverts grayish brown, showing some contrast; deep sooty below, *throat only slightly paler* (showing little or no contrast).

Similar species: The most uniform, darkest, and glossiest *Chaetura* swift. Chimney Swift is not as black or glossy, and shows distinctly paler throat. Ashy-tailed Swift has much more contrasting pale rump. Vaux's Swift is smaller, not as black or glossy above, and has pale throat. *Cypseloides* swifts show no contrast at all between back and rump (paler rump of this species is always discernible).

Status and distribution: Uncertain. Only two confirmed records: two collected at Gatun on Caribbean side of Canal area on July 9, 1911; and two taken at Mandinga, San Blas, on January 30, 1957. Several sight reports cannot be confirmed. Wetmore has assigned Panama specimens to the nominate race of northern South America, so local breeding seems likely; austral migrants are also possible.

Range: Northern and central South America, where seemingly local (and poorly known); recorded from Panama.

SHORT-TAILED SWIFT
Chaetura brachyura   p.201

Description: 4¼. Fairly small. Mostly black above with *contrasting pale ashy brown rump and upper tail-coverts*; tail very short, virtually covered by upper tail-coverts, and *often appearing almost tail-less in the field*; below sooty black, very slightly paler on throat (*little or no contrast*), with under tail-coverts gray.

Similar species: Best known by its small size and distinctive very short-tailed silhouette, also by the highly contrasting rump and uniform blackish underparts. Ashy-tailed Swift is larger and not as black, and has contrasting pale throat. Vaux's Swift has longer tail and less contrasting rump (but much more contrasting throat). Chapman's Swift is also mostly blackish, but is larger with a longer tail and much less contrasting rump.

Status and distribution: First recorded only in 1960, but more recently found to be common in fairly open places on Pacific side of Canal area, and locally on Caribbean side as well (east to Río Cascajal east of Portobelo in eastern Colon prov.; D. Graham). May prove to be more widespread, as a few were also recently found in the lower Tuira River valley of eastern Darién in March 1981 (Ridgely et al.). Had apparently been overlooked.

Habits: Flies commonly over residential and semiopen areas, frequently giving a twittering call. Found breeding in a woodpecker hole in the trunk of a dead palm on Chiva Chiva Road (E. S. Morton); in

Bolivia recorded nesting in a chimney (D. Pearson).

Range: Central Panama to Peru, central Brazil, and the Guianas.

ASHY-TAILED SWIFT
Chaetura andrei

Description: 5 ¼ . Very rare (or overlooked). Deep sooty brown above with *contrasting pale brownish gray rump and upper tail-coverts*; tail gray, fairly short, usually covered by upper tail-coverts; sooty brown below with *contrasting pale gray throat*.

Similar species: A confusing swift, best known by combination of fairly large size, overall sooty or dusky coloration, and its contrastingly paler gray rump and throat. Chimney Swift is the same size, but has longer tail and much less contrasting rump. Short-tailed Swift has similar pale rump and upper tail-coverts, but is notably smaller with even shorter tail, and is blacker generally with dark (*noncontrasting*) throat. Vaux's Swift is smaller with proportionately longer tail, and has browner (not so gray) and less contrasting rump.

Status and distribution: Only one specimen from Panama, that a bird collected from a flock of swifts at Juan Diaz, eastern Panama province, on August 4, 1923; also a sighting of a single swift believed this species at Rincón, Herrera, on July 26, 1975 (Ridgely). Apparently an austral migrant to Panama as the Juan Diaz specimen was identified as of the migratory southern race *meridionalis*, which breeds mostly in southern Brazil and northern Argentina.

Range: Venezuela and the Guianas; southeastern Bolivia, Paraguay, and eastern and southern Brazil to northern Argentina; recorded as an austral migrant (July–September) in Venezuela, Colombia, and Panama.

BAND-RUMPED SWIFT
Chaetura spinicauda   p.201

Description: 4 ¼ . Small. Glossy black above with *strongly contrasting narrow whitish band across rump*; upper tail-coverts and *fairly long tail* black; below slaty blackish, throat and chest considerably paler.

Similar species: Gray-rumped Swift (not known to overlap) has same size and shape, but its rump patch is wider and grayer (not obviously narrow and whitish), and its underparts are more uniform. See also Vaux's and Short-tailed Swifts.

Status and distribution: Recorded in foothills from Veraguas (numerous sightings above Santa Fé) eastward, common in more humid lowlands and foothills from around Canal area eastward (*aetherodroma*; known from only sightings west of Canal area); also recorded from western Chiriquí, mostly in lowlands but also occasionally to lower highlands (*fumosa*). The most numerous *Chaetura* on Caribbean side of Canal area.

Habits: The common small swift of the eastern half of Panama. Most often seen in small groups, flying rapidly above forest, sometimes circling and coming lower over clearings, when the white rump band can often be seen to good advantage. Also regularly drops to quiet stretches of water in order to drink, especially early and late. Frequently gives a twittering call in flight, similar to other small swifts.

Range: Costa Rica to western Ecuador and northern Brazil.

GRAY-RUMPED SWIFT
Chaetura cinereiventris

Description: 4 ¼ . Known only from western Bocas del Toro. Small. Glossy black above with *sharply contrasting gray triangular patch on rump* and upper tail-coverts; *tail fairly long*, black; dark gray below, paler on throat.

Similar species: Resembles Band-rumped Swift (same shape, with longish tail) but that species has a narrower and paler (almost white) band across rump only, and is blacker below with more contrasting throat. See also Vaux's Swift.

Status and distribution: Fairly common in lowlands and foothills of western Bocas del Toro.

Habits: Similar to Band-rumped Swift. Usually in groups, flying over forest, but often coming lower over clearings and rivers. Gives a fast twittering in flight, similar to other *Chaetura* swifts.

Range: Nicaragua to Caribbean western Panama; Colombia to Guyana and western Brazil; coastal Brazil, eastern Paraguay, and northeastern Argentina.

LESSER SWALLOW-TAILED SWIFT
Panyptila cayennensis   p.201

Description: 5. A distinctively patterned small swift. Mostly deep black with *white collar around hindneck connecting with white throat and chest*, and a *white patch on flanks*; tail very long and deeply forked, though usually held closed in a point.

Similar species: *Chaetura* swifts, which are similarly sized except for this species' longer tail, lack the sharp black and white pattern of this species, and have shorter squared tails. White-collared Swift is very much larger.

Status and distribution: Locally fairly common in more humid lowlands on both slopes, ranging locally up into the lower highlands at least in western Chiriquí; recently seen also on Coiba Island (a single bird on April 13, 1976; Ridgely). Seems less numerous in extensively forested regions, e.g. Bocas del Toro and Darién, and is apparently absent from the most arid parts of the Pacific slope.

Habits: Attaches its conspicuous, usually tubular felt-like nest on the trunk of a tree or the side of a building (sometimes hung free from a branch or structure); these can be seen at Ancon Heights and at Summit Gardens. Nests are used both for reproduction and for roosting; birds are not often seen near the nests during daylight. Usually observed flying very high, singly or in pairs (not in flocks), occasionally with other swifts. For nesting seems to prefer towns or inhabited areas, though often observed flying over forest.

Range: Southern Mexico to Amazonian and coastal Brazil.

HUMMINGBIRDS: Trochilidae (55)

Within this large family are found the smallest of birds (a few weigh no more than a dime) and perhaps the most brilliantly colored. Found exclusively in the Americas, they reach their highest development in northern South America: the family is well represented in all habitats in Panama, though the more spectacularly ornamented species are lacking. Hummingbirds are renowned for a number of things besides their size. Perhaps most remarkable is their power of flight: the wing is rotated through an angle of 180°, allowing a much greater measure of control, including perfectly stationary hovering and backward flight (of which no other birds are capable). The wings also beat incredibly rapidly, in some species at rates up to 80 beats per second, though notably slower in the larger species; the speed of flight can also be very great, with extraordinarily abrupt starting and stopping. Hummingbirds are most famous for their brilliant iridescent coloring; these brilliant areas are colorful only when bird, observer, and the sun are in perfect juxtaposition, and often change in hue depending on the angle of light (at other times they appear blackish). In many species, a glittering area is found on the throat, which is then termed a *gorget*. Males are almost always more brightly colored than females except in those species in which both sexes are dull (e.g. the hermits). Hummingbirds feed on nectar, tiny insects, and spiders in varying proportions; many are exceedingly belligerent in the defense of their feeding areas. A number of species apparently engage in seasonal movements, the details of which are as yet poorly understood and documented. Males of some species gather to display in communal leks in forest undergrowth where they "sing" interminably. In many other species, males simply select a prominent perch and emit their insignificant "songs", while in some others males have spectacular aerial display flights (especially in the genus *Selasphorous*). The nest is an attractive structure of plant down and spider webs, placed in the fork of a branch or underneath a large leaf; males play no role in the rearing process. Identification of many species is tricky: they are often seen only briefly and the salient characters not observed, and the light may be poor and the iridescent areas may not show up. Females are especially difficult. Bill length and shape are often particularly useful characters.

BRONZY HERMIT
Glaucis aenea   Plate 13

Description: 4. Found only in western Panama. Bill long (1¼ in), decurved, *entirely black*. Sexes similar. *Coppery bronze above* with dusky crown and mask and distinct cinnamon band behind eye; rusty cinnamon below, paler on chin and duller on belly; tail rounded, *chestnut*, with broad black subterminal band and whitish tip.

Similar species: Rufous-breasted Hermit (no known overlap) is larger, greener above (less coppery or bronzy), and has a yellow mandible (not an all-black bill). See also Band-tailed Barbthroat.

Status and distribution: Fairly common in undergrowth of forest borders in lowlands of western Bocas del Toro (Almirante, Río Changuinola), and in western Chiriquí and western Veraguas (recorded once from Zapotillo). Overall numbers on the Pacific slope are doubtless much reduced due to deforestation, but remains locally numerous on the Burica Peninsula and north of Puerto Armuelles (numerous June 1982 sightings; Ridgely).

Habits: Usually found in thick border growth (often along streams), and not inside extensive forest; especially favors thickets of *Heliconia*, where it probes their flowers or inspects the underside of the leaves for insects.

Range: Nicaragua to western Panama; western Colombia to northwestern Ecuador.

RUFOUS-BREASTED HERMIT
Glaucis hirsuta   Plate 13

Description: 4½. Bill long (1¼ in), decurved, lower mandible yellow. Metallic to bronzy green above; *mostly dull rufous below*, whiter or grayer on throat and belly, with some green on sides; *tail rounded, mostly chestnut*, with black subterminal band and white tip. Female similar but brighter and more uniform cinnamon-rufous below. Immature more bronzy above with buff edging, duller below.

Similar species: In western Panama see Bronzy Hermit. Band-tailed Barbthroat is rather similar but is more grayish white below (not so rufous) and lacks chestnut in tail. *Phaethornis* hermits have elongated central tail feathers.

Status and distribution: Uncommon to fairly common in undergrowth of humid forest, woodland clearings, and borders in lowlands and foothills on Caribbean slope from Coclé east through San Blas; on Pacific slope from western Panama province (Cerro Campana) east through Darién. In Canal area more numerous on Caribbean side.

Habits: Favors *Heliconia* thickets and banana plantations, usually remaining low in dense vegetation and not often seen, though regularly caught in mist-nets. In Trinidad one to three females nest in an area along a stream defended by a single male (which does not directly assist in rearing the young, however); the nest is attached to the underside of a *Heliconia* leaf, often directly over the stream (B. Snow).

Range: Central Panama to northern Bolivia and southern Brazil; Grenada.

BAND-TAILED BARBTHROAT
Threnetes ruckeri   Plate 13

Description: 5. Bill long (1½ in), decurved, lower mandible mostly yellow. Bronzy green above, with blackish mask bordered above and below by buffyish stripes; *throat blackish*, contrasting strongly with cinnamon-rufous chest; remaining underparts mostly buffy grayish, more cinnamon-rufous on flanks; tail rounded, basal half white with *broad black subterminal band and white tip*. Immature has throat dull buffy gray.

Status and distribution: Uncommon in humid forest and forest borders in lowlands and lower foothills on entire Caribbean slope; on Pacific slope recorded from Chiriquí lowlands and foothills (but now very local due to deforestation, with recent reports only from Fortuna and Burica Peninsula), Veraguas foothills (above Santa Fé), Cerro Campana, and from Canal area east through Darién. In Canal area considerably more numerous on Caribbean side.

Habits: Much like Rufous-breasted Hermit: inconspicuous, favoring *Heliconia* thickets but also found more regularly inside forest. Males display in loose groups (especially May–July), perching on low branches and emitting a series of short squeaky notes, all the while vibrating their partly fanned tails.

Range: Guatemala and Belize to western Venezuela and western Ecuador.

GREEN HERMIT
Phaethornis guy   Plate 13

Description: 6–7. Bill long (1½ in), decurved, lower mandible mostly reddish. Male *mostly metallic bluish green above*, bluest on rump; mask blackish with narrow buff postocular streak and moustache; throat buffy, but *most of underparts metallic green*, washed with slaty on center of breast and belly; tail long and graduated, central pair of feathers elongated and tipped white. Female similar but not as blue above, and with broader moustachial and postocular streaks; *grayer below* with lower belly buff; central tail feathers tend to be longer than in male.

Similar species: *A very dark-looking hermit.* Long-tailed Hermit is similarly sized and has much the same pattern, but is much browner generally, never so green below, and always has a cinnamon-buff rump.

Status and distribution: Common in undergrowth of humid forest and forest borders in foothills and highlands on both slopes (mostly 600–1650 m: 2000–5500 ft), but not yet recorded from eastern San Blas; on Caribbean slope has been reported locally from lowlands as well, but whether these represent resident birds or postbreeding wanderers remains uncertain (there are lowland records from western Bocas del Toro, Canal area, and eastern Colon province). Numerous on Cerro Campana and in the Cerro Azul/Jefe area.

Habits: Usually seen singly inside forest. A sharp squeak is frequently heard, especially in flight. Males gather in loose groups to display during the breeding season; they then interminably utter short snappy noises (some almost manakin-like), accompanied by moving their tails, and are often frustratingly difficult to see as they perch low in the dense undergrowth.

Range: Costa Rica to northern Venezuela and southern Peru.

LONG-TAILED HERMIT
Phaethornis superciliosus   Plate 13

Description: 6–7. Bill long (1½ in), decurved, lower mandible mostly yellow. *Mostly brownish*, back more bronzy green, with *rump cinnamon-buff* barred with black; mask blackish with narrow whitish postocular streak and moustache; underparts mostly buffy whitish, the throat more brownish with a whitish central streak; tail long and graduated, mostly black with sides edged cinnamon, *central pair of feathers greatly elongated and tipped white.*

Similar species: Pale-bellied Hermit is more uniformly green above and whiter below. Green Hermit is darker and never as brown; it occurs mostly at higher elevations than this species.

Status and distribution: Common in undergrowth of forest, second-growth woodland, and borders in lowland and lower foothills (to about 900 m: 3000 ft) on both slopes, but absent from dry Pacific lowlands from eastern side of Azuero Peninsula to extreme western Panama province.

Habits: One of the characteristic birds of Panama's lowland forests. Most often seen as it dashes by, uttering a sharp squeak; like the other hermits, often seems almost curious, pausing abruptly to hover in front of the observer for a few seconds, then darting off. Groups of males, often large, perform at their ''singing'' assemblies in forest undergrowth

through much of the year, interminably giving a short squeaky note to the accompaniment of tail wagging. The nest, shaped like an inverted cone, is attached to the underside of the tip of a palm or *Heliconia* leaf.

Range: Central Mexico to northern Bolivia and Amazonian Brazil.

Note: More than one species may be involved.

PALE-BELLIED HERMIT
Phaethornis anthophilus   Plate 13

Description: 6–6½. Bill long (1¼ in) but *somewhat less decurved* than in other Panama hermits, lower mandible mostly orange- red. *Dull bronzy green above*, duskier on crown; mask blackish with *contrasting white postocular streak and rather broad moustache; dingy whitish below*, whitest on belly; tail long and graduated, mostly black, central pair of feathers elongated (though not quite as far as in Long-tailed) and white-tipped.

Similar species: Long-tailed Hermit is browner and buffier generally, and has less sharply defined facial pattern.

Status and distribution: Fairly common in woodland undergrowth and in adjacent shrubby clearings on the larger Pearl Islands; on the mainland known only from eastern Panama province (where recorded between Tocumen and Chico), with one record also from eastern San Blas (Puerto Obaldía). Small numbers have been found regularly in recent years in the Tocumen marsh area, particularly in the woodlands past the dike (be aware that Long-tailed Hermits are also found here).

Habits: Seems to forage more in the open and in clearings adjacent to woodland than do the other Panama hermits.

Range: Central Panama through northern Colombia to northern Venezuela.

LITTLE HERMIT
Phaethornis longuemareus   Plate 13

Description: 3½. *Very small*; much of the given length is bill and tail. Bill long (1 in), decurved, lower mandible mostly yellow. Bronzy green above becoming chestnut on rump; mask blackish with buff postocular streak and moustache; *mostly cinnamon below*, with some dusky flecking on chin; tail bronzy tipped with buff, sharply graduated, but with central pair of feathers *not* excessively elongated, tipped white.

Similar species: Much larger Long-tailed Hermit has greatly elongated white-tipped central tail feathers. Rufous-breasted

Hermit and Band-tailed Barbthroat have rounded tails with black subterminal bands.
Status and distribution: Fairly common to common in undergrowth of forest borders, second-growth woodland, and adjacent clearings in more humid lowlands and foothills on both slopes, less numerous or lacking in dry Pacific lowlands from eastern side of Azuero Peninsula to western Panama province. Widespread in the Canal area.
Habits: Usually seen singly, within a few feet of the ground. This species and a few other small hummingbirds regularly fly *through* mist-nets. When perched, often wags tail up and down. Males form "singing" assemblies during the breeding season, perching very low in dense undergrowth where they emit a series of insignificant squeaks.
Range: Southern Mexico to Peru, Amazonian Brazil, and the Guianas.
Note: More than one species may be involved.

Upper, TOOTH-BILLED HUMMINGBIRD, lower, WHITE-TIPPED SICKLEBILL

WHITE-TIPPED SICKLEBILL
Eutoxeres aquila   Plate 43, p.207

Description: 5½. Unmistakable with *very sharply decurved bill, bent almost into a right angle.* Bronzy green above; *below heavily streaked sooty and white;* tail graduated, bronzy green broadly tipped white.
Status and distribution: Rare to locally fairly common (to some extent merely overlooked; true numbers better revealed through mist-netting) in undergrowth of humid forest and forest borders in foothills locally on both slopes, favoring ravines with dense undergrowth and stands of *Heliconia;* recorded mostly 300–900 m (1000–3000 ft); not known from western Chiriquí. In Bocas del Toro and San Blas also recorded, perhaps only seasonally, in lowlands, most often in areas adjacent to hilly country, and there is one recent record from Canal area, a bird netted and photographed on Pipeline Road on March 15, 1984 (J.Karr *et al.*). Regular in small numbers on both Cerro Campana and Cerro Jefe.
Habits: A heavy-bodied hummingbird with slow audible wingbeats. Like a hermit, will often pause to briefly inspect the observer, hovering at eye-level a few yards away. Often feeds in *Heliconia*, clinging awkwardly to the flowers and probing their blossoms with its curious bill.
Range: Costa Rica to northern Peru.

TOOTH-BILLED HUMMINGBIRD
Androdon aequatorialis   p.207

Description: 5¼–5½. Found only in highlands of eastern Darién. *Bill very long* (1½ in) *and straight*, with upper mandible black, lower yellow. Forecrown reddish coppery; otherwise bronzy green above with *prominent white band across rump*; grayish white below, *streaked with blackish especially on throat and breast*; tail rounded, gray with broad dark green band and broad white tipping. Female duller and less streaked below. Immature like female but nape bluish.
Similar species: No other Panama hummer has such a long bill and the streaked underparts.
Status and distribution: Uncommon in lower and middle growth of humid forest and forest borders in foothills and highlands of eastern Darién (600–1560 m: 2000–5200 ft). Regularly encountered in small numbers on the slopes of Cerro Pirre above Cana.
Habits: Rather inconspicuous, usually seen singly as it feeds at flowers up to 7.5 m (25 ft) above the ground, most often in small forest openings. Also occasionally seen making short sallies after minute insects; the minute serrations on the cutting edge of the outer half of the bill might serve in the capture of insects (S. Hilty). The call note is a sharp penetrating *cheet*, sometimes doubled to *cheet-it* (M. Robbins *et al.*).
Range: Eastern Panama to western Ecuador.

GREEN-FRONTED LANCEBILL
Doryfera ludoviciae   Plate 13

Description: 4½. Known only from highlands of west and east. *Bill very long* (1½ in), *straight*, black. *Forecrown glittering green*, hindcrown coppery, with small white postocular spot; otherwise dark metallic green above, glossed with *bluish on upper tail-coverts*; tail blackish tipped with gray; underparts dull grayish green. Female duller, glittering green patch on forehead smaller or lacking.
Similar species: A very dark-looking hummingbird, best recognized by its strikingly long straight bill.
Status and distribution: Rare to locally uncommon in forest and forest borders in highlands of Chiriquí (1620–2250 m: 5400–7500 ft, ranging locally down to 1020 m: 3400 ft near Fortuna; Ridgely), Veraguas (Chitra), and eastern Darién (900–1500 m: 3000–5000 ft).
Habits: An inconspicuous hummingbird, usually seen singly, feeding at flowering shrubs or low trees inside forest and at borders. Seems to favor very shady damp ravines.
Range: Costa Rica to western Venezuela and northern Bolivia.

SCALY-BREASTED HUMMINGBIRD
Phaeochroa cuvierii   Plate 13

Description: 4½–5. Bill rather short (¾ in), straight with basal half of mandible pinkish or whitish. Dull bronzy green above; mostly grayish buffy below, with *yellowish green spots giving scaly effect* except on lower belly; tail bronzy green, *outer feathers broadly tipped white* (giving effect of white corners to tail).
Similar species: A rather plain fairly large hummingbird without many field marks aside from the conspicuous white tail corners. Most apt to be confused with female White-necked Jacobin, which is even more conspicuously scaled below, has white (not buffyish) belly, and much smaller white tail tipping. White-vented Plumeleteer is brighter green above, lacks scaly effect below, and shows conspicuous white vent.
Status and distribution: Fairly common locally in clearings and gardens, woodland borders, and mangroves on Pacific slope from Chiriquí to Herrera and Los Santos, and in Canal area and eastern Panama province (east to lower Bayano River valley); on Caribbean slope locally from around Canal area east through San Blas; also found on Coiba Island.
Habits: Regularly seen at flowering trees in the semiopen. One of the more accomplished singers in its family, uttering an endlessly repeated series of various chips, e.g. *tsup, sst-sst-sst...,* from an exposed perch, often emphasizing each note with a twist of its head.
Range: Southern Mexico to northern Colombia.

VIOLET SABREWING
Campylopterus hemileucurus   Plate 14

Description: 5½. Found only in western highlands. Bill fairly long (1¼ in), *decurved*. Male *mostly brilliant dark violet;* inconspicuous white leg tufts; tail mostly black with *three outer feathers very broadly tipped white* so that when closed from below tail seems white on terminal half. Female metallic green above; mostly gray below, paler on belly, with *patch of violet on throat* and some green on sides; *tail as in male.*
Similar species: Male is spectacular, especially in flight when the white on the tail flashes conspicuously. Female is best known by its large size and prominent white in tail; female Magnificent Hummingbird has long straight bill and lacks white in tail.
Status and distribution: Fairly common in lower growth of forest, forest borders, and small clearings in lower highlands of Chiriquí, Veraguas, and western side of Azuero Peninsula; most numerous 900–1650 m (3000–5500 ft); one old record from lowlands of Chiriquí. Regularly seen along the Santa Clara road west of Volcán.
Habits: Frequently found in small clearings or at borders where there are stands of *Heliconia* or banana plantations, feeding at the inflorescences. Often hovers before the observer like a hermit. Sometimes "sings" rythmically and interminably while perched in forest undergrowth, the voice suggestive of Green Violet-ear but thinner.
Range: Southern Mexico to western Panama.

WHITE-NECKED JACOBIN
Florisuga mellivora   Plate 13

Description: 4½. Bill rather short (¾ in), straight, and black. *Entire head and chest shining blue* with *conspicuous white crescent on hindneck;* otherwise shining green above; breast and belly white, contrasting sharply with blue chest; *tail mostly white,* tipped black. Female green above; throat and chest dusky, *feathers edged white giving scaly effect;* lower underparts white; tail dark green with broad black subterminal band and white tip.

Some females assume varying degrees of the male's plumage, especially the blue head and white tail.

Similar species: Male virtually unmistakable (but see Purple-crowned Fairy). Female somewhat resembles Scaly-breasted Hummingbird, but is even more scaled below, with white (not buffyish) belly, much smaller amount of white in tail.

Status and distribution: Fairly common to common in clearings and borders of forest and second-growth woodlands in humid lowlands on both slopes, ranging in reduced number up into the lower highlands to about 1500 m (5000 ft), more local on Pacific slope and largely absent from dry Pacific lowlands from eastern side of Azuero Peninsula to western Panama province. Apparently moves about seasonally, being mostly absent from Pacific slope of Canal area during dry season.

Habits: Usually seen singly, though small groups may congregate with other hummers at flowering trees. Regularly sallies for flying insects, or may hover in front of a swarm, picking them off one by one; also gleans from leaves or branches. Males have an attractive territorial display during breeding season in which they swoop about and hover at considerable heights, fanning their white tails in a virtual semicircle.

Range: Southern Mexico to Bolivia and central Brazil.

BROWN VIOLET-EAR
Colibri delphinae   Plate 13

Description: 4¼. Bill straight, fairly short (¾ in). *Mostly dull brownish,* somewhat streaked with whitish below; *long violet-blue ear-tuft;* upper throat green, becoming violet-blue on lower throat, *bordered by white moustachial streak;* rump mostly tawny, under tail-coverts rusty. Sexes similar. Immature lacks violet ear-tuft and has rusty tipping on back.

Similar species: A drab hummingbird, best known by the violet ear-patch (though it may be hard to see in poor light), a mark shared only by the otherwise very different Green Violet-ear. Most like Long-billed Starthroat, but without that species' very long bill.

Status and distribution: Apparently rare; recorded from lower highlands of Chiriquí (1050–1350 m: 3500–4500 ft), and foothills of Veraguas (Calovévora, Santa Fé), western Panama province (several seen at Cerro Campana on July 20, 1969; J. Karr and H. Hespenheide), and eastern Darién (Cana, Cerro Quía).

Habits: Not well known in Panama. In South America often seasonal in its appearances, seeming to occur most frequently in partially deforested regions. Usually noted feeding at flowering trees at forest edge or in semiopen; also hawks for flying insects.

Range: Guatemala to Bolivia and northern and eastern Brazil.

GREEN VIOLET-EAR
Colibri thalassinus   Plate 14

Description: 4½. Found only in western highlands. Bill straight (1 in). Sexes similar. Mostly shining green with a *long violet ear-patch* and some violet gloss on chest; tail greenish blue with broad black subterminal band.

Similar species: The violet ear-patch, usually quite conspicuous, distinguishes this hummer from all others in Panama except the otherwise very different Brown Violet-ear.

Status and distribution: Common in forest borders and clearings in highlands of western Chiriquí (mostly above 1500 m: 5000 ft, in smaller numbers down to about 1200 m: 4000 ft); recorded also from foothills and lower highlands of eastern Chiriquí and Veraguas (Chitra, Calovévora), and recently found to be uncommon on Cerro Montuosa, in Herrera (at about 900 m: 3000 ft), with one specimen taken on August 30, 1977 (F. Delgado).

Habits: One of the most numerous hummingbirds in the western Chiriquí highlands. Its voice attracts attention, but the calling bird can be hard to see as it often sits high and motionless. The "song" is endlessly repeated, normally two-noted but with some variation, *tsip-tsup,* or *tsut-tsip,* given as the bird perches motionless on a bare twig, often rather ventriloquial.

Range: Central Mexico to Honduras (one recent record from north-central Nicaragua); Costa Rica and western Panama; Colombia and northern Venezuela to northwestern Argentina.

Note: More than one species may be involved; birds from Costa Rica south into South America have been separated as *C. cyanotus* (Montane) Violet-ear.

GREEN-BREASTED MANGO
Anthracothorax prevostii   Plate 43

Description: 4½. Bill slightly decurved (1 in). Male metallic green above; *brilliant green below,* more bluish on breast and center of belly; *tail mostly purplish maroon* with narrow black tip. Female metallic green above; mostly white below with *broad median stripe of* *greenish blue*; tail mostly blackish with outer feathers tipped white. Immature like female but with underparts adjacent to median stripe (which is more blackish) rufous.

Similar species: Much like Black-throated Mango but male largely green without Black-throat's broad black stripe on underparts; female Green-breast's median stripe is greenish blue (not black).

Status and distribution: Uncommon and local in open areas with trees, shrubby clearings, and along tree-bordered streams in lowlands on Pacific slope from Chiriquí to southern Coclé (Aguadulce). Two immature specimens from Gatun on Caribbean slope of Canal area are attributed to this species by Wetmore (the only ones from so far east or from the Caribbean slope).

Habits: Similar to Black-throated Mango, and like that species often seen feeding at flowering immortelle trees (*Erythrina* sp.). Regularly seen at the airport in David, Chiriquí.

Range: Eastern Mexico to central Costa Rica; western and central Panama; Colombia and northern Venezuela; western Ecuador and northwestern Peru.

Note: Taxonomy of this species (or species complex) has not been firmly established. The disjunct Panama race, *veraguensis*, is rather divergent from all other forms of the species, both to north and south, in lacking black on underparts. It perhaps should be regarded as a distinct species (Veraguan Mango); Wetmore, however, found a trace of black on lower throat of some specimens, the presence of which he viewed as showing a relationship of *veraguensis* with the rest of *A. prevostii.* More study is definitely needed.

BLACK-THROATED MANGO
Anthracothorax nigricollis   Plate 13

Description: 4½. Bill slightly decurved (1 in). Male green with *black throat continuing as broad black stripe down center of underparts; tail maroon-chestnut.* Female metallic green above; white below, with *black stripe down center of underparts* and green on sides: tail as in male but with broad blackish subterminal band and white tip. Immature like female but with some brownish edging above.

Similar species: Female more striking than male as its black median stripe contrasts more strongly with remainder of underparts; male somewhat tricky until seen in good light, but maroon tail usually evident. In Pacific western Panama see Green-breasted Mango.

Status and distribution: Locally fairly common in open areas with scattered trees, in shrubby clearings and around houses, and at woodland borders in lowlands on Pacific slope from southern Veraguas (Santiago) and southern Coclé (Aguadulce) east through Darién; on Caribbean slope from Canal area east through San Blas. Old specimens attributed to "Chiriquí" are dubious.

Habits: Often seen feeding at varying heights in flowering trees, usually in the open. Also captures flying insects. Female-plumaged birds outnumber adult males.

Range: Western Panama to Bolivia, northern Argentina, and southern Brazil.

RUBY TOPAZ
Chrysolampis mosquitus

Description: 3½. A vagrant to Darién. Bill short (½ in), almost straight. Brilliantly colored male unmistakable, but often looks mostly black. *Crown and nape glowing ruby-red, throat and breast glittering orange-yellow* ("topaz"); otherwise mostly dark brown, more blackish above, this extending as narrow stripe up sides of neck to eye; *under tail-coverts and tail bright rufous.* Female dull bronzy to coppery green above and dull pale grayish below; tail bronzy green, *outer feathers mostly rufous with blackish subterminal band and white tip.* Molting immature males with varying amounts of adult plumage are frequently seen.

Similar species: In poor light, when males can look basically all black, the non-iridescent rufous tail is the best mark. Drab females are often confusing, but no other similar hummingbird shares its tail pattern. Both sexes (but especially males) often raise feathers of rearcrown and nape, *imparting a distinctly bushy-headed look.*

Status and distribution: A male was carefully observed and photographed at El Real, Darién, on January 27 and February 3, 1985 (D. Wolf and M. Braun *et al.*; photos in VIREO). See M. Braun and D. Wolf, *Bull. BOC 107*(3):115–117, 1987.

Habits: In its normal range a bird of woodland undergrowth and edge, often coming out into gardens and to feed at flowering trees (but usually feeds and perches fairly close to the ground).

Range: Locally from Colombia, Venezuela, and the Guianas to Bolivia and central and eastern Brazil; perhaps somewhat migratory (but exact pattern not known).

Recorded regularly as close to Panama as the Caribbean coast of Colombia near Cartagena, and also known from Los Katíos National Park on the Darién border in Chocó.

VIOLET-HEADED HUMMINGBIRD
Klais guimeti   Plate 13

Description: 3. Bill straight, short (½ in). Male with *entire head (including throat) violet-blue* and *conspicuous white spot behind eye* (often giving effect of white eye); otherwise bright green above; grayish below flecked with green on breast; tail bluish green tipped whitish. Female similar but with only forecrown blue, pale gray below with some green on sides, broader whitish tail tipping.
Similar species: No other small Panamanian hummingbird has so prominent a white spot behind the eye.
Status and distribution: Uncommon to locally common in lower growth and borders of humid forest and second-growth woodland in foothills on both slopes (mostly 300–1200 m: 1000–4000 ft), ranging down occasionally into the lowlands, mainly on Caribbean slope and in Chiriquí and Veraguas; not recorded from eastern San Blas (but recently found in small numbers at Nusagandi in the west), and seems distinctly uncommon in Darién. Scarce in Canal area, where reported only from Caribbean side, probably only a post-breeding wanderer from foothills; fairly common on Cerro Campana and in the Cerro Azul/Jefe area.
Habits: Usually found singly, feeding low in shrubbery or at small flowering trees at edge of forest. Males gather in singing assemblies (especially January–May), perching in woodland just inside edge some 4.5–7.5 m (15–25 ft) above the ground, there tirelessly repeating a high *tsi-titititititi* and other rapid calls.
Range: Honduras to western Venezuela and Bolivia.

RUFOUS-CRESTED COQUETTE
Lophornis delattrei   Plate 13

Description: 2¾. Bill short (⅓ in), straight. *Minute.* Male with *crown and long bushy crest rufous;* otherwise bronzy green above with *conspicuous white or buff band across rump* and mostly rufous tail; throat glittering green, remaining underparts bronzy green. Female lacks crest, has *dull rufous forecrown;* otherwise bronzy green above with *band across rump as in male;* throat light cinnamon,

upper chest dusky bronze, remaining underparts dull bronzy green; *tail cinnamon* with broad black subterminal band.
Similar species: Tiny rufous-crested males are unmistakable; females are best known by their size, rufous forecrown, and pale rump band (a mark shared by all the coquettes). In western Chiriquí see White-crested Coquette; see also Black-crested Coquette (below).
Status and distribution: Rare to locally uncommon in borders of humid forest and second-growth woodland and in adjacent clearings in lowlands and foothills on both slopes; on Caribbean slope recorded from central Bocas del Toro (Cocoplum; no recent reports), and from Canal area east to western San Blas (one seen at Nusagandi on March 7, 1986; Ridgely and J. Guarnaccia); on Pacific slope recorded from western Chiriquí (Bugaba; no recent reports), Veraguas foothills, and from western Panama province (Cerro Campana) east through Darién. Seemingly not numerous anywhere, with the most reports coming from the Canal area (particularly on Caribbean side), perhaps only because of concentration of observers there.
Habits: Usually seen perched on an exposed branch or twig, often at moderate heights. Usually feeds in low flowers and shrubbery. In flight, the tail is slowly wagged up and down and the pale rump band is conspicuous; often looks strikingly bee-like.
Range: Southwestern Mexico; southwestern Costa Rica south locally to northern Bolivia.
Note: Black-crested Coquette (*Lophornis helenae*) of Caribbean slope lowlands and lower foothills from southern Mexico to Costa Rica remains a possibility in Bocas del Toro. Bill red tipped dusky, duller in female. Male has green crown and long black wispy pointed crest, long buff ear-tufts, brilliant green throat, black breast patch (feathers extended at sides), whitish rump band, mainly rufous tail (central feathers bronzy), and large coppery spots on whitish lower underparts. Female lacks head ornamentation, has dusky cheeks and pale buff throat with small green spots; rump band and spotting below as in male. See Plate 43.

WHITE-CRESTED COQUETTE
Lophornis adorabilis   Plate 14

Description: 3. Found only in western Chiriquí. Bill short (½ in) and straight, red tipped dusky. Ornate male with rufous forecrown, *pointed white crest,* and *very elongated pointed green ear-tufts* (extending out over back); otherwise bronzy green above with *white to pale buff band across rump;* throat glittering green, chest white (often with effect of a pectoral collar), lower underparts cinnamon-rufous with some green on flanks; tail bronzy rufous. Female lacks head ornamentation, is mostly bronzy green above with *white to pale buff band across rump; throat and chest white* flecked with bronze on throat, remaining underparts cinnamon-rufous with some green on sides; tail mostly rufous with broad black subterminal band.

Similar species: The beautiful males cannot be confused; females rather resemble female Rufous-crested Coquette (both have distinctive rump band) but are slightly larger and have white throat and chest (not cinnamon and bronzy).

Status and distribution: Rare in shrubby clearings, forest and woodland borders, and gardens in lowlands and foothills (to about 1200 m: 4000 ft) of western Chiriquí; a specimen supposedly taken on Cébaco Island off the Veraguas coast is considered by Wetmore to have been mislabeled.

Habits: Not well known in Panama (where it is apparently rarer than in Costa Rica), with few recent reports. In Costa Rica often seen feeding at white-flowered *Inga* trees, or at blue-flowered *Stachytarpheta* hedges.

Range: Costa Rica and Pacific western Panama.

GREEN THORNTAIL
Discosura conversii　　　　　　Plate 13

Description: ♂4; ♀3. Bill short (½ in), straight. Male mostly green, more bronzy above; crown, throat, and chest glittering green, with bluer spot on center of breast; *broad white band across rump to flanks* and white leg-tufts; tail bluish black, feathers with white shafts, *extremely long and deeply forked,* with three outer pairs of feathers very narrow (essentially reduced to the shaft). Female green above with *broad white rump band extending around to flanks;* throat black *bordered at sides by broad white malar streak;* breast green, center of belly black with *conspicuous white patch on flanks;* tail much shorter than male's, slightly forked, bluish black tipped white.

Similar species: Though they are very different looking, both sexes are essentially unmistakable; their coquette-like white rump band is especially prominent.

Status and distribution: Rare and local (but possibly somewhat overlooked in the past, with a considerable number of recent reports), with most records from foothills on Pacific slope, mostly 600–1200 m (2000–4000 ft). Recorded from Chiriquí (Fortuna, Cerro Chame), Veraguas (Cordillera del Chucú, Santa Fé, Calovévora), Coclé (El Valle, above El Copé), Panama province (Cerro Campana and Cerro Jefe), and eastern Darién (Cana); likely occurs at similar elevations on the Caribbean slope as well.

Habits: Usually seen singly, though often congregating with other hummingbirds at *Inga* trees or *Stachytarpheta* hedges. Often perches in exposed positions, frequently at the tops of trees. A thorntail's flight is typically leisurely, sometimes with tail slowly wagged up and down like that of a coquette, sometimes (especially in males) held cocked upward at a 30° angle.

Range: Costa Rica to western Ecuador.

Note: Formerly placed in the genus *Popelairia.*

GARDEN EMERALD
Chlorostilbon assimilis　　　　　Plate 13

Description: 3. Bill short (½ in), straight, blackish. Small. Male *entirely green,* glittering on underparts, with white leg-tufts (usually not apparent); tail blue-black, *forked.* Female green above with *dusky mask bordered above by whitish streak behind eye;* pale gray below with some green on sides; tail not forked, mainly blue-black, outer feathers tipped pale gray.

Similar species: Male best known by its small size, all green plumage, and noticeably forked tail. Female best known by its mask, a field mark shared by no other similar Panama hummer.

Status and distribution: Fairly common in open areas, gardens, and clearings and edge of woodland in lowlands and (in smaller numbers) in foothills on Pacific slope from Chiriquí to western Darién (Garachiné); on Caribbean slope recorded only from Bocas del Toro (where rare) and from Canal area; fairly common also on Pearl Islands, Taboga Island, Coiba Island, and many other smaller islands off Pacific coast.

Habits: Usually seen feeding at flowers fairly close to the ground, but will range up higher into trees when these are in flower.

Range: Southwestern Costa Rica and Panama.

Note: The 1983 AOU Check-list considered *C. assimilis* as a species distinct from *C.*

canivetii (Fork-tailed Emerald) of Mexico to northwestern Costa Rica.

CROWNED WOODNYMPH
Thalurania colombica   Plate 13

Description: ♂4; ♀3½. Bill fairly long (1 in), black, essentially straight but slightly decurved at tip. Male in most of its Panama range *(venusta)* has *crown glittering violet-blue;* otherwise bluish green above with bright violet patch on back; *throat and chest glittering green,* contrasting with *glittering violet-blue breast and belly;* tail blue-black, *rather deeply forked.* Male in Darién and eastern San Blas *(fannyi)* has *crown glittering green* and violet back patch lacking or almost lacking. Female green above with bronzier crown; throat and chest pale brownish gray, *breast and belly distinctly darker gray,* with some green on sides; tail not forked, blue-black, outer feathers tipped white.
Similar species: Male in good light is one of Panama's most beautiful hummingbirds, but in its shady habitat it often looks very dark; Violet-bellied Hummingbird is smaller, lacks glittering crown, has rounded tail. Female woodnymph best known by her *distinctly two-toned underparts;* female Violet-bellied is somewhat smaller, and has uniform pale gray underparts and reddish lower mandible (not an all-black bill).
Status and distribution: Fairly common in humid forest, second-growth woodland, and borders in lowlands and (in smaller numbers) foothills on both slopes, but absent from dry open Pacific lowlands from Azuero Peninsula to western Panama province. In Canal area more numerous on Caribbean side.
Habits: Regularly found inside forest, foraging in lower growth, but more often seen along edge of forest clearings and openings, also in *Heliconia* thickets.
Range: Western Mexico; Guatemala to western Venezuela and western Ecuador.
Note: Some authors separate green-crowned birds, *T. fannyi* (Green-crowned Wood-nymph) of eastern Panama to western Ecuador, from blue-crowned birds, true *T. colombica* (Blue-crowned Woodnymph) of Mexico to central Panama and in northern Colombia and western Venezuela. Others (including, with reservations, Wetmore) unite the broad *colombica* group with the dull-crowned *T. furcata* complex of much of South America, and call the whole Fork-tailed or Common Woodnymph. Here the 1983 AOU Check-list is followed in including in *T. colombica* all the glittering crowned birds. There may be additional full species in South America.

FIERY-THROATED HUMMINGBIRD
Panterpe insignis   Plate 14

Description: 4¼. Found only on high western mountains. Bill straight (¾ in), black above, pinkish below except for black tip. Sexes similar. *Crown blue,* with black from lores back over nape and small white spot behind eye; otherwise mostly metallic green above, with *often quite conspicuous blue iridescence on rump;* tail blue-black; *throat golden orange becoming scarlet in center,* chest blue becoming violet in center; remaining underparts bluish green.
Similar species: In good light this hummer is dazzling and not likely to be confused; often the distinctive rump iridescence is easier to see than that on the throat and chest. Magnificent Hummingbird is considerably larger with a proportionately longer bill; their respective glittering colors can be hard to discern except in perfect light.
Status and distribution: Uncommon to (at higher elevations) fairly common in shrubby clearings and forest borders in western Chiriquí (mostly on higher slopes of Volcán Barú), rarely also in adjacent Bocas del Toro; recorded mostly above 2100 m (7000 ft). Small numbers can be found regularly along the upper part of the Boquete Trail, and even more numerous high along road to summit of Barú.
Habits: Usually observed foraging fairly low at flowers (in January–March especially at thistles) and flowering shrubs, often with Magnificent Hummingbirds, Green Violet-ears, and Volcano Hummingbirds. Very active and pugnacious.
Range: Costa Rica and western Panama.

VIOLET-BELLIED HUMMINGBIRD
Damophila julie   Plate 13

Description: 3¼. Bill short (½ in), straight, *lower mandible mostly reddish* (tip black). Male shining green above; throat glittering green, *remaining underparts dark violet-blue;* tail blue-black, rounded. Female green above; pale gray below, becoming whitish on lower belly, sides of chest with some green spots; tail like male's but outer feathers tipped grayish.
Similar species: Smaller than the Crowned Woodnymph, which in both sexes has an all-black bill (not with reddish lower mandible); male woodnymph has forked (not rounded) tail and glittering crown, female had two-

toned grayish underparts (not uniform). Sapphire-throated Hummingbird female is whiter below with green spots on sides, has slightly forked tail.

Status and distribution: Fairly common in forest borders, second-growth woodland, and clearings on both slopes from northern Coclé and western Panama province east through San Blas and Darién; ranges up at least locally into lower foothills (Cerro Campana); one specimen from Taboga Island (in AMNH). Widespread in Canal area, though more numerous on Caribbean side, and may be at least partly seasonal (absent during dry season) on Pacific.

Habits: A widespread but usually not very conspicuous little hummingbird. Usually seen fairly close to the ground, most often at edge or breaks in forest or woodland; sometimes goes higher to feed in flowering trees.

Range: Central Panama to western Ecuador.

Note: Wetmore rejects two old specimens supposedly from Costa Rica as being mislabeled; there are no recent records (*fide* F. G. Stiles).

SAPPHIRE-THROATED HUMMINGBIRD
Lepidopyga coeruleogularis   Plate 13

Description: 3½. Bill virtually straight (¾ in), basal half of lower mandible reddish. Male metallic green above; *throat and chest glittering violet-blue,* remaining underparts bright green; tail distinctly forked, blue-black. Female metallic green above; *white below with green spotting on sides;* tail as in male, but outer feathers tipped whitish and central pair green.

Similar species: Male Blue-chested Hummingbird is duller, with only center of throat and chest blue, and with only slightly forked tail. Female like female Blue-chest but whiter below, without Blue-chest's green spotting on throat or blue spotting on chest.

Status and distribution: Fairly common to common locally in shrubby clearings, light woodland, and in coastal scrub and mangroves in lowlands on Pacific slope from Chiriquí to Darién (lower Tuira and Chucunaque River valleys); on Caribbean slope locally from Canal area east through San Blas; fairly common also on Coiba and Cébaco Islands. Most numerous on or within a few miles of either coast.

Habits: Usually seen rather low, feeding at flowering shrubs or trees; also sometimes gleans insects.

Range: Western Panama to northern Colombia.

BLUE-HEADED SAPPHIRE
Hylocharis grayi

Description: 3¾. Known only from Darién. Bill almost straight, broad at base, *red to reddish* (brighter in male) with black tip (¾ in). Male with *head and chin glittering blue;* otherwise metallic green above; *underparts glittering green;* tail slightly forked, dark green. Female metallic green above; *underparts white lightly spotted with green except on center of breast and belly;* tail as in male but tipped whitish.

Similar species: Male Sapphire-throated Hummingbird has blue only on throat (not on all of head), and only base of lower mandible reddish. Female also somewhat like female Sapphire-throated, but with much more conspicuously reddish bill and more heavily green-spangled underparts.

Status and distribution: Recorded from four specimens taken in 1946 in the coastal lowlands of southern Darién near Jaqué (Wetmore).

Habits: The Jaqué birds were collected as they fed individually "at the border of the mangrove swamps or closely adjacent" (Wetmore).

Range: Eastern Panama to northwestern Ecuador.

BLUE-THROATED GOLDENTAIL
Hylocharis eliciae   Plate 13

Description: 3½. Bill almost straight, broad at base, *mostly coral red with black tip* (¾ in). Green above, becoming *coppery bronze on rump and bright metallic golden bronze to golden green on tail; throat and upper chest violet-blue;* center of remaining underparts dull buff; breast, sides, and flanks bronzy green. Female similar, with dusky margins on throat feathers and more dusky on bill.

Similar species: The much more numerous Rufous-tailed Hummingbird can look quite similar, but has only base of lower mandible pink (not most of bill bright red), nonmetallic rufous-chestnut rump and tail, and lacks blue gorget (though throat can look bluish at certain angles). Male Sapphire-throated Hummingbird also has blue throat and chest, but it has blue-black forked tail.

Status and distribution: Rare to locally uncommon in lower growth of forest, second-growth woodland, and borders in lowlands on entire Pacific slope, ranging in smaller numbers up into lower foothills; absent from eastern side of Azuero Peninsula to western Panama province; on Caribbean slope known only from a very few Canal area records; found also on Coiba Island, where unusually common. Doubtless now much reduced in overall numbers due to deforestation over much of its Panama range, and now very local. Extremely scarce in Canal area, with few if any confirmed recent reports. Can be seen in small numbers along the Boca de Cupe trail in the valley floor at Cana, in Darién.

Habits: Favors lower and middle growth in shady woodland and forest, though it regularly emerges into adjacent clearings to feed. Males gather in loose singing assemblies during the dry season, giving a simple *tsi* or similar note, repeating it interminably from perches 4.5–12 m (15–40 ft) above the ground.

Range: Southern Mexico to northwestern Colombia.

VIOLET-CAPPED HUMMINGBIRD
Goldmania violiceps   Plate 13

Description: 3½. Bill almost straight (½ in). Male has *bright violet blue crown,* otherwise bright metallic green above and below; under tail-coverts with small tuft of stiffened white feathers; *tail forked, rich chestnut, broadly tipped with bronze.* Female green above; mostly white below, with grayish spots on throat and green spotting on sides; under tail-coverts green with white tuft; *tail as in male,* but feathers tipped whitish.

Similar species: Violet-headed Hummingbird has conspicuous white spot behind eye and blue-black tail. See also male Crowned Woodnymph. No similar female hummingbird has deep chestnut on tail.

Status and distribution: Fairly common to locally common in humid forest and forest borders in foothills of eastern Colon province (Cerro Bruja), western San Blas (common on Cerro Brewster in late April 1985; J. Blake), eastern Panama province (Cerro Azul/Jefe), and eastern Darién (Cerro Tacarcuna); recorded mostly 600–1200 m (2000–4000 ft). Quite easily seen in the Cerro Azul/Jefe area, particularly in the elfin cloud forest on the summit of Cerro Jefe, where it is the commonest hummingbird.

Habits: Usually found singly, feeding low in forest undergrowth or at borders. Attracted by squeaking even more than most other hummingbirds.

Range: Central Panama to extreme northwestern Colombia.

RUFOUS-CHEEKED HUMMINGBIRD
Goethalsia bella   Plate 40

Description: 3½. Found only in eastern Darién mountains. Bill almost straight (½ in). Male has *forehead, lores, and lower cheeks rufous-chestnut;* otherwise metallic green above; mostly glittering green below, with cinnamon-buff on chin and flanks; under tail-coverts with stiff tuft of recurved white feathers; *wide band across base of inner secondaries cinnamon-buff,* and *tail mostly cinnamon-buff,* with central feathers green. Female like male above, but with green forehead; *mostly light cinnamon-buff below,* more whitish on chest, with green only on sides; *wings and tail as in male.*

Similar species: The conspicuous buff on wings and tail render both sexes virtually unmistakable in their restricted Darién range.

Status and distribution: Uncommon in lower growth of humid forest and borders in foothills and highlands of eastern Darién (Cerro Sapo and Cana/Cerro Pirre); recorded 600–1500 m (2000–5000 ft), but on Cerro Pirre commonest 1050–1200 m (3500–4000 ft).

Habits: Usually seen individually, often as it feeds at flowering shrubs or small trees in the forest interior (e.g. *Cephalus* sp.); at higher elevations often chased off by the commoner and more aggressive Greenish Puffleg. Appears to replace the Violet-capped Hummingbird on the Cerro Pirre and Cerro Sapo ranges.

Range: Eastern Panama and adjacent Colombia.

BLUE-CHESTED HUMMINGBIRD
Amazilia amabilis   Plate 13

Description: 3½. Bill straight (½ in), lower mandible basally pinkish. Male has *crown glittering green;* otherwise bronzy green above; upper throat dull blackish, *center of lower throat and chest glittering violet-blue* (often with duller edgings); lower underparts brownish gray, sides dull green; tail bronzy or bluish black, slightly forked. Female bronzy green above; pale grayish below with *green spotting on throat and breast (more glittering blue on upper chest);* tail like male's but tipped grayish.

Similar species: Males are duller than other similar male hummingbirds and often look like a female or immature. Male Sapphire-throated has throat and chest *entirely* glittering blue (much more solid and prominent than the blue of the Blue-chested), and has a more deeply forked tail. Female Blue-chests can be known by their conspicuous spotting below (*including throat*), and the touch of blue on chest; compare to female Crowned Woodnymph and Violet-bellied Hummingbird (female Sapphire-throated is much whiter below). In Chiriquí see also Charming Hummingbird (similar, but no overlap).

Status and distribution: Uncommon to fairly common in lower growth of forest borders, second-growth woodland, and clearings in lowlands on entire Caribbean slope; on Pacific slope recorded from Canal area east through Darién (where it ranges locally up into the lower foothills to about 600 m: 2000 ft). In Canal area more numerous on Caribbean side.

Habits: Usually found singly, feeding at flowers in lower growth, but also coming regularly to flowering trees in the semi-open; also gleans insects from foliage. Especially in the dry season males call singly or in small groups from perches 9–15 m (30–50 ft) up, a monotonously repeated *pseik* at a rate of about two calls per second (E. O. Willis).

Range: Eastern Nicaragua to western Ecuador.

Note: Does not include *A. decora* (Charming Hummingbird) of Chiriquí and south-western Costa Rica, now considered a full species.

CHARMING HUMMINGBIRD
Amazilia decora   Plate 43

Description: 3½. Found only in western Chiriquí. Bill straight (¾ in), lower mandible basally pinkish. Resembles Blue-chested Hummingbird (with which formerly considered conspecific; no range overlap), but *bill noticeably longer*. Other described differences (extent of glitter in crown, color of rump and tail) are not likely to be evident in the field, and are barely perceptible in specimens.

Status and distribution: Locally fairly common in humid forest and second-growth woodland borders and adjacent shrubby clearings in lowlands and (sparingly) foothills of western Chiriquí; recorded up to about 1200 m (4000 ft). Now much reduced in overall numbers due to extensive forest destruction over much of its Panama range; the only recent reports seem to be from the

Burica Peninsula, where it was quite numerous in late June 1982 (Ridgely).

Habits: Similar to Blue-chested Hummingbird, but better known in Costa Rican portion of its range than it is Panama. Seems seasonal in its appearances in at least some areas; often feeds at flowering *Inga* trees. Males are reported to sing in loose assemblies, perching on branches inside lower growth of woodland, repeating a sharp thin *tsweet tswe we we we* (A. Skutch).

Range: Southwestern Costa Rica and Pacific western Panama.

Note: The 1983 AOU Check-list regarded *A. decora* as a species distinct from *A. amabilis* (Blue-chested Hummingbird).

SNOWY-BELLIED HUMMINGBIRD
Amazilia edward   Plate 13

Description: 3½. Bill straight (¾ in), black with base of mandible pinkish. Sexes similar. Metallic green above, *becoming coppery bronze on lower back, rump, and tail;* throat and chest glittering green, *contrasting sharply with white breast and belly.* Birds from Chiriquí to eastern side of Azuero Peninsula and western Coclé (*niveoventer*) have greener (less coppery) lower back, and blue-black tail.

Similar species: Rufous-tailed Hummingbird lacks the strong contrast below.

Status and distribution: Common in open woodland, clearings, and gardens in lowlands and foothills on Pacific slope from Chiriquí (where it ranges up in western Chiriquí highlands to over 1800 m: 6000 ft at least seasonally) to Darién (where less numerous, ranging east to the lower Tuira River valley around El Real); on Caribbean slope recorded only from Canal area and eastern Colon province (east to Portobelo), with one specimen from Bocas del Toro (Chiriquí Grande); found also on the Pearl Islands, Taboga Island, and Coiba Island.

Habits: One of the more frequently seen and most numerous hummingbirds in non-forested parts of the Canal area, but seems distinctly seasonal in some places. May concentrate in rather large numbers at flowering trees, notably at Summit Gardens and on Cerro Azul.

Range: Southwestern Costa Rica to eastern Panama.

Note: Formerly known as the Snowy-breasted Hummingbird. Mangrove Hummingbird (*A. boucardi*), known only from Pacific coast mangroves and adjacent areas in Costa Rica, remains a possibility in Chiriquí, though recent searches have failed to turn it up. Bill essentially straight (¾ in), lower mandible reddish; slightly larger (3¾ in) than Snowy-bellied Hummingbird. Male shining green above with some coppery reflections; tail bronzy green; throat and chest glittering green, becoming whitish on lower underparts with some green on sides. Female similar, but more white below with only a little green spotting on throat and sides. Male resembles male Snowy-bellied (and in part overlaps with *niveoventer* race of that species), differing in the lack of a sharp contrast below, tail color (bronzy green in Mangrove, black in Snowy-bellied), also in having rump more or less concolor with rest of upperparts (not contrastingly coppery bronze). See Plate 43.

RUFOUS-TAILED HUMMINGBIRD
Amazilia tzacatl   Plate 13

Description: 3½. Bill almost straight, usually black above with *basal half of lower mandible pinkish* (sometimes upper mandible as well) (¾ in). Green above with *tail rufous-chestnut*, slightly forked; throat and chest glittering green (throat may look quite bluish at some light angles), breast and belly grayish. Female similar but feathers of throat and chest with buffy margins.
Similar species: The much less numerous Blue-throated Goldentail is brighter overall with entire bill pink to red with black tip; its tail is golden-bronzy (not rufous-chestnut), and its throat distinctly blue (beware some Rufous-tails with bluish-looking throats). See also Snowy-bellied Hummingbird.
Status and distribution: Common to very common in open woodland, clearings, and around habitations in lowlands and foothills virtually throughout, though only one recent record from San Blas (a single bird mist-netted at Cangandi on May 16, 1985; J. Blake), and only recently found in Darién (mostly in lower and middle Tuira River valley; occasionally also seen at Cana); found also on Isla Escudo de Veraguas off Bocas del Toro (see below), Coiba Island, Taboga Island, and other small islands off Pacific coast (but not, somewhat strangely, on Pearl Islands). Probably increasing and spreading in eastern Panama due to clearing of forest. In Canal area generally the most numerous and familiar hummingbird, found everywhere except inside forest.
Habits: Perhaps even more active and pugnacious than most other members of its family. Feeds at flowers at virtually all heights (perhaps less often in canopy), and

frequent at feeders in Canal area; also regularly gleans insects.
Range: Eastern Mexico to western Venezuela and western Ecuador.
Note: Included is *A. handleyi* (Escudo Hummingbird), restricted to Escudo de Veraguas off coast of Bocas del Toro, recently described by Wetmore; it is larger and darker than mainland birds, and is possibly best regarded as a full species.

STRIPE-TAILED HUMMINGBIRD
Eupherusa eximia   Plate 14

Description: 3½. Found only in western highlands. Bill straight (¾ in). Male mostly green with white under tail-coverts; wings with *prominent patch of cinnamon-rufous on secondaries and base of inner primaries; tail mostly white, tipped black,* with two central pairs of feathers and outer web of outer pair black. Female like male but with underparts grayish white and green spotting on sides; cinnamon-rufous wing-patch smaller; outer tail feathers without black outer edge.
Similar species: The cinnamon wing-patch (easily visible at rest and in flight) and the mostly white tail are prominent in both sexes. Male Black-bellied Hummingbird (which also has cinnamon wing-patch) is black below and on crown; female Black-belly closely resembles this species but is smaller with less conspicuous cinnamon wing-patch. White-tailed Emerald, also with mostly white tail, is smaller and lacks cinnamon in wings.
Status and distribution: Fairly common in forest, forest borders, and small clearings in highlands of Chiriquí and Veraguas (both slopes), mostly above 1500 m (5000 ft) in western Chiriquí, lower in Veraguas; recorded also from adjacent highlands of Bocas del Toro (upper Río Changuena). Best known from western Chiriquí highlands.
Habits: Regularly forages within forest, in lower growth, but most often seen in shrubbery and low trees at forest edge.
Range: Southern Mexico to western Panama.

BLACK-BELLIED HUMMINGBIRD
Eupherusa nigriventris   Plate 14

Description: 3¼. Found locally in very humid western highlands. Bill straight (½ in). Male bronzy green above, crown feathers edged black; *forecrown, sides of head, and underparts black,* with green on sides and white under tail-coverts; somewhat concealed patch of cinnamon-rufous on

secondaries; *tail mostly white,* with two central pairs of feathers black. Female like male above but has underparts grayish, wing patch more restricted and cinnamon, bronzier upper tail-coverts; tail as in male.
Similar species: Male, with its velvety black underparts, should not be confused. Female very difficult to distinguish from female Stripe-tailed but has notably less conspicuous cinnamon wing-patch, often not visible at all.
Status and distribution: Uncommon locally in forest and borders in very humid highlands of western Panama, probably more widespread on Caribbean slope; recorded 900–1800 m (3000–6000 ft). Known from Bocas del Toro, Chiriquí (Cerro Pando, seen in July 1980 by N. Smith; Fortuna, male collected on March 2, 1976 and others seen then and in July 1982 by Ridgely; specimen to GML), and Veraguas (Cordillera del Chucú, Santa Fé, and Calobre). Largely if not entirely replaced by Stripe-tailed Hummingbird in the less humid highlands around Cerro Punta and Boquete, Chiriquí; one probable sight record of Black-billed from Finca Lerida by Eisenmann.
Habits: Similar to Stripe-tailed Hummingbird.
Range: Costa Rica and western Panama.

WHITE-TAILED EMERALD
Elvira chionura　　　　　　　　　Plate 14

Description: 3¼. Found only in western highlands. Bill straight (½ in). Male all metallic green except for *white center of belly; tail mostly white, broadly tipped black,* with central pair of feathers bronzy green. Female green above; *white below with green sides and flanks,* throat sometimes flecked with green; *tail similar to male's* but feathers narrowly tipped white.
Similar species: Lacks the cinnamon wing-patch so prominent in the otherwise somewhat similar Stripe-tailed Hummingbird. See also Black-bellied Hummingbird, the female of which is grayish (not mostly white) below. Female Snowcap is notably smaller, with underparts entirely grayish white (no green on sides).
Status and distribution: Uncommon to locally fairly common in humid montane forest and forest borders in foothills and lower highlands on Pacific slope from Chiriquí east through Veraguas (where there are a few records from Caribbean slope) to eastern Coclé (above El Valle). Found regularly at Finca Lerida above Boquete, particularly at El Velo.

Habits: Usually seen singly, foraging inside forest in lower growth, often drawing attention to itself by flashing its largely white tail.
Range: Southwestern Costa Rica to central Panama.

SNOWCAP
Microchera albocoronata　　　　　Plate 13

Description: 2½. Known only from western Panama, mostly Caribbean slope. *Tiny.* Bill short and straight (⅓ in). Male has *white crown; upperparts otherwise dark reddish purple,* brightest on rump; *underparts black glossed with purple; tail mostly white* with outer third black, central pair of feathers bronzy. Female green above; *uniform grayish white below; tail as in male* but feathers narrowly tipped white.
Similar species: The spectacular male is unmistakable. Female is best known by combination of diminutive size, mainly white tail, and lack of green spotting on underparts (present in female White-tailed Emerald, which is otherwise very similar except for its larger size).
Status and distribution: Rare to uncommon at borders and in openings of humid forest in foothills and lower highlands in western Panama; very local, with relatively few Panamanian records though it may be more widespread on the still mostly inaccessible Caribbean slope; recorded mostly 600–1650 m (2000–5500 ft). Known from extreme western Chiriquí (seen in July 1980 on slopes of Cerro Pando; N. G. Smith), both slopes of Veraguas (Cordillera de Chucú, Santa Fé), Coclé (above El Copé), western Colon province (Belém; *fide* Eisenmann), and western Panama province (two sightings from Cerro Campana); surely also found in Bocas del Toro, but as yet unrecorded. In Costa Rica reported to engage in seasonal altitudinal movements, occurring in Caribbean lowlands adjacent to the mountains mostly June–September, at other seasons higher (F. G. Stiles); likely does this in Panama as well.
Habits: Forages mostly at lower and middle levels at flowering shrubs and trees along forest edge, less often inside forest. The exquisite male's white cap and tail render it very conspicuous, but they tend to be outnumbered by females and immature males. Both sexes often flick their tails. Small numbers of this splendid but tiny hummer can regularly be found at least during the month of March above El

Copé — certainly the most reliable place to find it in Panama (and perhaps anywhere).
Range: Southeastern Honduras to western Panama.

WHITE-VENTED PLUMELETEER
Chalybura buffoni Plate 13

Description: ♂ 4¾; ♀ 4¼. *Bill black,* almost straight, rather long (1 in). Male metallic green with *conspicuous silky white feathers on under tail-coverts; tail blue-black.* Female similar but smaller, with grayish underparts and outer tail feathers tipped whitish.
Similar species: The enlarged white under tail-coverts are characteristic of the plumeleteers, but distinguishing between the two species is not always easy. Bronze-tail has pale base to lower mandible (not all black), pinkish feet, and a purplish or golden bronzy tail (not steely blue-black). Scaly-breasted Hummingbird and female White-necked Jacobin are also generally similar, but neither shows the white vent, and both have obviously scaly underparts.
Status and distribution: Fairly common in second-growth woodland and forest borders in lowlands on Pacific slope from western Panama province (La Campana) east through Darién; on Caribbean slope known only from Canal area. Widespread though rather inconspicuous in woodland on Pacific side of Canal area.
Habits: Forages primarily in woodland lower growth, only occasionally coming out into adjacent clearings. Usually found singly or in pairs.
Range: Central Panama to northern Venezuela and western Ecuador.

BRONZE-TAILED PLUMELETEER
Chalybura urochrysia Plate 13

Description: ♂ 4½; ♀ 4. Bill almost straight, rather long (1 in), black with *base of lower mandible pale reddish brown to pinkish white. Feet red to pinkish,* this surprisingly conspicuous in the field (black in White-vented). Resembles White-vented Plumeleteer. Male bronzy green above; mostly bluish green below, becoming grayish on lower belly; under tail-coverts enlarged and white (but often mixed with dusky in western Bocas del Toro, *isaurae); rump and tail purplish bronzy.* Birds from southeastern Darién (Jaqué and Cerro Pirre

area, nominate *urochrysia*) have underparts greener without the blue. Female like male but mostly pale grayish below with green on sides, under tail-coverts whitish; tail more greenish bronze with outer feathers tipped white.
Similar species: See White-vented Plumeleteer.
Status and distribution: Uncommmon in lower growth of humid forest and forest borders in lowlands on entire Caribbean slope; on Pacific slope recorded from Veraguas foothills (Santa Fé), western Panama province (Cerro Campana), and in lowlands and lower foothills of eastern Darién. In Canal area found regularly only in the Achiote/ Escobal road region.
Habits: Regularly forages within heavy forest, but also in shrubbery (e.g. *Heliconia* thickets) at forest borders.
Range: Nicaragua to northwestern Ecuador.

WHITE-BELLIED MOUNTAIN-GEM
Lampornis hemileucus Plate 43, p.220

Description: 4. Known locally from very humid western highlands. Bill straight (¾ in). Male metallic green above with *prominent white postocular stripe; throat shining violet-purple,* with *remaining underparts white,* spotted with green on sides; tail bronzy green. Female similar but without gorget, throat white spotted with green.
Similar species: Male is not likely to be confused, but see Long-billed Starthroat. Female can be known by combination of mostly white underparts and bold white streak behind eye.
Status and distribution: Locally fairly common at borders of very humid forest and in adjacent clearings, in Panama recorded 750–1050 m (2500–3500 ft). Until recently known only from two nineteenth-century "Chiriquí" specimens without further data. Found to be quite common at Fortuna in central Chiriquí in February–March 1976 (with two specimens taken, now in GML; Ridgely) and again in July 1982 when it was also seen on the adjacent Caribbean slope in Bocas del Toro. Has also been seen above Santa Fé, Veraguas. Apparently not present in the less humid highlands around Volcán Barú.
Habits: Usually seen foraging singly in lower growth at breaks in forest, less often out into

WHITE-BELLIED MOUNTAIN-GEM (male)

adjacent shrubby clearings; infrequent inside forest itself.

Range: Costa Rica and western Panama.

WHITE-THROATED MOUNTAIN-GEM
Lampornis castaneoventris   Plates 14,43

Description: 4. Found only in western Chiriquí highlands. Bill straight (¾ in). Male has shining green crown, remaining upperparts bronzy green; ear-coverts and sides of head dusky, *bordered above and behind by a prominent white stripe; throat white,* chest bright green, lower under parts brownish gray; tail black. Female metallic green above, sides of head blackish bordered above by a whitish or buff streak; *entire underparts tawny-rufous;* outer tail feathers tipped white. A few males have throat purple (but white in vast majority).

Similar species: No similar hummingbird in the western Chiriquí highlands; further east see Purple-throated Mountain-gem.

Status and distribution: Common in forest lower growth, borders, and shrubby clearings in highlands of western Chiriquí (east only to around Boquete); recorded mostly above 1500 m (5000 ft).

Habits: One of the most numerous hummingbirds of the western Chiriquí highlands, a number often gathering around a single flowering shrub or small tree. Males are outnumbered by female-plumaged birds (many doubtless immatures).

Range: Southern Costa Rica and extreme western Panama.

Note: The 1983 AOU Check-list recognized two species in this complex, white-throated (in the male) *L. castaneoventris* (with similar but gray-tailed *cinereicauda* of Costa Rica as a subspecies), and purple-throated *L. calolaema.* Many authors, including Wetmore, have regarded all forms as con-

specific (as Variable Mountain-gem), and this may still ultimately prove to be the case. A study of their contact zone between Boquete (where most males are white-throated) and Fortuna (where all males seem to be purple-throated) would be of great interest.

PURPLE-THROATED MOUNTAIN-GEM
Lampornis calolaema   Plate 14

Description: 4. Found only in western highlands (but *not* in western Chiriquí). Male similar to male White-throated Mountain-gem, but *throat violet-purple* (not white). Female apparently cannot be distinguished in the field from female White-throated Mountain-gem.

Similar species: Not known to overlap with White-throated Mountain-gem, so identification can be made on the basis of range. Male White-bellied Mountain-gem also has a purple gorget, but its remaining underparts are mostly white (not dark).

Status and distribution: Uncommon to fairly common in lower growth of forest, forest borders, and shrubby clearings in foothills and highlands of central and eastern Chiriquí (west to the Fortuna area in the upper Río Chiriquí valley), Veraguas, and western Coclé (above El Copé); recorded mostly 900–1500 m (3000–5000 ft), lower eastward (to 600 m: 2000 ft in Coclé).

Habits: Similar to White-throated Mountain-gem.

Range: Nicaragua to central Costa Rica; west-central Panama.

Note: See under White-throated Mountain-gem, *L. castaneoventris.*

GREEN-CROWNED BRILLIANT
Heliodoxa jacula   Plate 13

Description: 5¼. Found mainly in highlands of west and east. *Large.* Bill straight (1 in). Male has *glittering green crown, throat, and chest* with spot of glittering violet on center of lower throat; otherwise metallic green above, with small white postocular spot; lower underparts metallic green; *tail fairly long and rather deeply forked,* blue-black in *henryi* of western Panama (east to Coclé), blue-black with bronzy central tail feathers in nominate race of eastern Panama (west to Cerros Brewster and Jefe). Female metallic green above with white postocular spot and *prominent narrow white malar streak;* white below, *heavily spotted with green* especially on throat and breast; *tail as in male* but outer feathers tipped white. Immature resembles female but with *rufous on chin and sides of throat.*

Similar species: No other highland hummer is as boldly spangled below as the female Green-crowned Brilliant (but it could marginally overlap with White-necked Jacobin in foothills). Male has no really obvious marks, but is stunning at close range and in good light; note its large size, long forked tail, and mainly brilliant green foreparts.

Status and distribution: Uncommon to locally fairly common in humid forest, forest borders and adjacent clearings in foothills and highlands on both slopes; recorded from Chiriquí (but rather scarce on slopes of Volcán Barú, particularly its drier west slope), Bocas del Toro (recorded only from upper Río Changuena, but probably more widespread), Veraguas, western Coclé (one seen above El Copé on March 8, 1986; Ridgely, J. Guarnaccia, D. Engleman *et al.*), eastern Panama province (one seen on Cerro Jefe on January 11, 1974; Ridgely), western San Blas (found to be numerous on Cerro Brewster in late April 1985, photos to VIREO; J. Blake), and eastern Darién (Cana/Cerro Pirre and Río Tacarcuna); recorded mostly 900–2100 m (3000–7000 ft) in western Panama, lower in central Panama (600–1050 m: 2000–3500 ft) and eastern Darién (510–1500 m: 1700–5000 ft).

Habits: Despite its size, usually a rather inconspicuous hummingbird, few being seen even where many are being captured in mist-nets. Generally forages at or below eye level, though may ascend to feed with other hummingbirds in flowering trees (e.g. at *Inga* spp.). Displaying males in Costa Rica give an interminable *tseek, tseek, tseek...* with quality and cadence of Black-headed Tody-Flycatcher (B. Whitney).

Range: Costa Rica to western Ecuador.

MAGNIFICENT HUMMINGBIRD
Eugenes fulgens Plate 14

Description: 5½. Found only in western Chiriquí highlands. *Bill long* and straight (1¼ in). *Large.* Male has *brilliant violet-blue to purple crown* and *white postocular spot,* with forehead, sides of head, nape and upper back dull black; lower back and rump bronzy green; *throat glittering green,* contrasting with dark bronzy green breast and sides, center of belly grayish brown; tail forked, bronzy green, dusky toward tip.

Female bronzy green above, feathers of crown edged black; cheeks blackish, bordered above by *conspicuous white postocular streak;* below grayish buffy, washed with green on sides; tail bronzy green, outer feathers tipped pale grayish.

Similar species: Among the Chiriquí hummingbirds, only the Violet Sabrewing and Green-crowned Brilliant are as large as this species. Male Magnificent often looks decidedly black, and then it can be confused with these species (but note its much longer straighter bill), or with the smaller Fiery-throated Hummingbird (which see).

Status and distribution: Fairly common in forest borders and clearings in highlands of western Chiriquí around Volcán Barú massif, usually above 1650 m (5000 ft).

Habits: Usually seen feeding at flowering shrubs and small trees in clearings and at edge of forest; also often investigates bromeliad inflorescences, and sometimes comes to gardens. When seen well the males are spectacular, and both sexes are notably active and pugnacious. Displaying males sing a repeated *cheet-tititi, cheet-tititi...* from exposed perches at forest edge.

Range: Southwestern United States to western Panama.

GREENISH PUFFLEG
Haplophaedia aureliae Plate 40

Description: 4. Found only in eastern Darién highlands. Bill straight (¾ in). Male mostly green, more coppery bronze on head and golden bronze on upper tail-coverts; small white postocular spot; *feathers of underparts narrowly edged whitish* giving somewhat scaly look, becoming entirely whitish on median breast and belly; *fairly prominent white (sometimes buff-tinged) powder puff-like tufts of legs;* tail slightly forked, blue-black. Female similar but with broader whitish feather edging below, and tail tipped whitish.

Similar species: This rather dull-plumaged hummingbird can generally be known by its leg-tufts, though at times these are partially concealed; the scaling below is usually quite obvious. See Rufous-cheeked Hummingbird (often found with this species, even feeding at the same understory tree).

Status and distribution: Fairly common to common in humid forest in foothills and highlands of eastern Darién (Cerro Pirre, Cerro Quía, and Cerro Tacarcuna); recorded 510–1500 m (1700–5000 ft), but most numerous above 900 m (3000 ft).

Habits: In general rather inconspicuous,

usually found singly inside forest, less often at edge. Forages at flowering shrubs and small trees, also at bromeliad inflorescences.
Range: Eastern Panama to Bolivia.

PURPLE-CROWNED FAIRY
Heliothryx barroti   Plate 13

Description: ♂ 4½ ; ♀ 4¾. Bill straight, quite short (⅔ in). Male has *violet-purple crown and black mask* (ending in violet tuft) bordered below by brilliant green cheek stripe; otherwise shining green above; *immaculate white below; tail long and graduated, mostly white,* central feathers blue-black. Female similar but with green crown and without green cheek stripe. Immature has gray spotting on breast.
Similar species: Virtually unmistakable, but see male White-necked Jacobin.
Status and distribution: Uncommon to fairly common in forest, second-growth woodland, and borders in more humid lowlands and (in smaller numbers) foothills on both slopes; absent from eastern side of Azuero Peninsula and southern Coclé; in western Chiriquí recorded sparingly up into the lower highlands, to about 1800 m (6000 ft), though scarce over 1200 m (4000 ft).
Habits: This beautiful hummingbird generally keeps to middle and upper levels of forest and woodland, but sometimes comes lower. The wings beat relatively slowly, and the tail (notably longer in the female than in male) moves from side to side and fans open and shut. Like the hermits, this species often seems somewhat curious, flying in to hover erratically in front of the observer, a lovely picture of flashing green and white.
Range: Southeastern Mexico to western Ecuador.

LONG-BILLED STARTHROAT
Heliomaster longirostris   Plate 13

Description: 4¾. *Bill very long* (1½ in), *straight.* Male has *glittering pale blue crown* and white postocular spot; otherwise bronzy green above with *partly concealed white stripe down lower back and center of rump; throat glittering reddish purple, bordered by whitish malar streak;* remaining underparts grayish with bronzy green on sides and partially concealed white flank patch (often hidden by wings); tail bronzy green, outer feathers tipped white. Female like male but lacks the blue crown and has duller or less complete gorget with *wider white malar streak.*

Similar species: No other Panama hummingbird is really very similar. Brown Violet-ear is browner generally and has a much shorter bill; it too shows a prominent malar streak.
Status and distribution: Uncommon to fairly common in borders of second-growth and open woodland and shrubby clearings in lowlands and foothills on entire Pacific slope; on Caribbean slope more local and uncommon, recorded mostly from Canal area and vicinity, but also from Bocas del Toro and San Blas; ranges up to around 1500 m (5000 ft) in western Chiriquí highlands; found also on Taboga Island.
Habits: Not particularly numerous at any locality, and often seems erratic. Usually seen in the semiopen, often perching on high exposed branches. Feeds mostly at flowering trees, in the dry season frequently at *Erythrina* spp. with other hummingbirds (mangos, emeralds, etc.); also regularly sallies out after small insects.
Range: Southern Mexico to Bolivia and southern Brazil.

MAGENTA-THROATED WOODSTAR
Calliphlox bryantae   Plate 14

Description: 3½. Found only in western highlands. Bill straight, rather short (½ in). Male metallic green above with *white postocular spot* and *whitish patches on either side of rump* (sometimes giving effect of partial rump-band); *throat glittering reddish purple,* bordered below by *broad white pectoral collar;* lower underparts mostly bronzy greenish with white center of belly and conspicuous area of cinnamon-rufous on flanks; *tail black, rather long, narrow, and deeply forked* (though usually held closed). Female like male above; below cinnamon-buff to whitish, with green spotting on sides of breast and cinnamon-rufous sides and flanks; tail short and not forked, cinnamon-rufous basally with broad black subterminal band and buff tips, central feathers green.
Similar species: Male Scintillant and Glow-throated Hummingbirds lack the postocular spot and white on rump, have more pointed gorgets and shorter, unforked, mostly rufous tails. Female woodstar also resembles females of those two species, but lacks throat spotting and has white postocular and rump tufts. In flight style and general appearance also strongly recalls a coquette.
Status and distribution: Uncommon in forest borders and shrubby clearings in lower highlands of Chiriquí and Veraguas;

PLATES

PLATE 1

RAILS, QUAIL, TINAMOUS, HERONS, ETC.

1. COLOMBIAN CRAKE (*Neocrex columbianus ripleyi*). Red legs, gray underparts with no barring. Rare. See Paint-billed Crake (with barred flanks) on Plate 3. *p. 122*
2. SPOTTED RAIL (*Pardirallus m. maculatus*). Barred, streaked, and spotted black and white. Rare. *p. 123*
3. UNIFORM CRAKE (*Amaurolimnas concolor guatemalensis*). Uniform brown, short greenish bill. Local. *p. 121*
4. GRAY-BREASTED CRAKE (*Laterallus exilis*). Small size, gray head and breast, chestnut nape. Rare. *p. 119*
5. YELLOW-BREASTED CRAKE (*Porzana f. flaviventer*). Small size, buffyish underparts, yellow legs. Local. *p. 122*
6. WHITE-THROATED CRAKE (*Laterallus a. albigularis*). Rufous and brown generally, bold belly barring. *p. 119*
7. GRAY-NECKED WOOD-RAIL (*Aramides c. cajanea*). Large size, gray head and neck (outer half of bill greener than portrayed). *p. 120*
8. RUFOUS-NECKED WOOD-RAIL (*Aramides axillaris*). Fairly large size, rufous head and neck, black lower underparts. Local, mangroves. *p. 121*
9. SUNBITTERN (*Eurypyga helias major*). Intricate variegated pattern, orange wing flashes, short legs and long tail. Forest streams. *p. 126*
10. SUNGREBE (*Heliornis fulica*). Striped head and neck, slender form. Aquatic. *p. 125*
11. NORTHERN JACANA (*Jacana s. spinosa*). Three-lobed yellow frontal shield. Western Panama. Shows more white at base of bill. *p. 132*
12. WATTLED JACANA (*Jacana jacana hypomelaena*). Two-lobed purplish frontal shield, yellow on wings, long toes. *p. 132*
13. BLACK-EARED WOOD-QUAIL (*Odontophorus m. melanotis*). Male. Rufous forecrown and underparts (female lacks black face and throat), purplish or blackish orbital skin. Local, foothills. *p. 116*
14. BLACK-BREASTED WOOD-QUAIL (*Odontophorus leucolaemus*). Mostly black head and underparts, usually white throat. Local, western highlands. *p. 117*
15. TACARCUNA WOOD-QUAIL (*Odontophorus dialeucos*). White on face, throat, and chest, blackish crown. Cerro Tacarcuna in Darién. *p. 117*
16. SPOTTED WOOD-QUAIL (*Odontophorus guttatus*). Black throat, spotted underparts. Chiriquí highlands. *p. 117*
17. MARBLED WOOD-QUAIL (*Odontophorus gujanensis marmoratus*). Lacking bold pattern, reddish orbital skin. *p. 116*
18. TAWNY-FACED QUAIL (*Rhynchortyx c. cinctus*). Male: tawny face, gray underparts. Female: narrow eye-stripe, light barring below. *p. 118*
19. HIGHLAND TINAMOU (*Nothocercus bonapartei frantzii*). Blackish head, rufous underparts, large size. Chiriquí highlands. *p. 51*
20. GREAT TINAMOU (*Tinamus major castaneiceps*). Large size, olive brown plumage (more crested in eastern Panama). *p. 51*
21. LITTLE TINAMOU (*Crypturellus soui poliocephalus*). Female. Small size, uniform brown plumage, tinamou shape. *p. 52*
22. CAPPED HERON (*Pilherodius pileatus*). Black crown, blue bill and facial area. Eastern Panama. Often buffier below than depicted. *p. 72*
23. COCOI HERON (*Ardea cocoi*). Like a white Great Blue Heron (see Plate 2); black crown and flanks. Mostly eastern Panama. *p. 69*
24. AGAMI HERON (*Agamia agami*). Long slender bill, chestnut neck and belly, green upperparts. Forest streams. *p. 72*

continued over

1

PLATE 2

HERONS, IBISES, STORKS

1. BOAT-BILLED HERON (*Cochlearius cochlearius panamensis*). Adult. Huge bill, ample crest, large eyes. Nocturnal. *p. 73*
2. BLACK-CROWNED NIGHT-HERON (*Nycticorax nycticorax hoactli*). Adult. Gray wings, all white underparts. *p. 72*
3. YELLOW-CROWNED NIGHT-HERON (*Nycticorax violaceus caliginis*). a) Adult: dark gray body, black and white on head. b) Immature: slaty with fine white streaking, heavy blackish bill. *p. 73*
4. LEAST BITTERN (*Ixobrychus exilis erythromelas*). Male. Very small size, buff wing-coverts. Secretive in marshes. *p. 66*
5. GREAT EGRET (*Casmerodius albus egretta*). Nonbreeding. Large size with long neck, yellow bill, black legs. *p. 69*

6. SNOWY EGRET (*Egretta t. thula*). Nonbreeding. Black legs with yellow feet, slender black bill. *p. 69*
7. CATTLE EGRET (*Bubulcus i. ibis*). Nonbreeding. Chunky with thick neck, some buff when breeding. Often far from water. *p. 71*
8. GREAT BLUE HERON (*Ardea h. herodias*). Nonbreeding. Very large size, mostly gray plumage. See Cocoi Heron on Plate 1. *p. 68*

9. LITTLE BLUE HERON (*Egretta caerulea*). a) Adult: dark plumage (slaty blue and maroon). b) Juvenile: bicolored bill, greenish legs; older birds pied with "blue". *p. 70*
10. TRICOLORED HERON (*Egretta tricolor ruficollis*). Nonbreeding. Contrasting white belly, slender neck, long thin bill. *p. 70*
11. WHITE IBIS (*Eudocimus albus*). Mainly Pacific coast. a) Adult: decurved bill and legs reddish, black wing-tips. b) Immature: decurved bill, white rump and belly. *p. 74*
12. ROSEATE SPOONBILL (*Ajaia ajaja*). Local, mainly Pacific coast. a) Adult: unmistakable spoon bill; plumage showing much pink. b) Immature: same bill; much whiter. *p. 76*
13. GREEN IBIS (*Mesembrinibis cayennensis*). Stocky and short-legged, dark plumage, bushy crest. Local in forested rivers and swamps. *p. 75*
14. GLOSSY IBIS (*Plegadis falcinellus*). Nonbreeding. Long legs, dull chestnut brown, neck flecked whitish (breeding adult glossier and lacking streaks). Scarce. *p. 75*
15. LIMPKIN (*Aramus g. guarauna*). Large size with fairly straight bill, streaking on head and neck. Very local. *p. 126*
16. JABIRU (*Jabiru mycteria*). Huge size, massive bill, red on neck. Very rare wanderer. *p. 77*
17. WOOD STORK (*Mycteria americana*). Large size, bare head and neck, black on wings. Local in marshes, often soars high. *p. 77*

PLATE 1 *continued from previous page*

25. GREEN-BACKED HERON (*Butorides striatus*). Small size. a) Gray neck and underparts (resident nominate race; mostly eastern Panama). b) Chestnut neck and underparts (northern migrant *virescens*; similar birds are resident in western Panama). *p. 71*
26. RUFESCENT TIGER-HERON (*Tigrisoma l. lineatum*). Large size. a) Adult: rufous head and neck. b) Juvenile: coarse black barring, feathered white throat. *p. 67*
27. BARE-THROATED TIGER-HERON (*Tigrisoma mexicanum*). Large size. a) Adult: bare yellow throat, gray sides of head. b) Juvenile: coarse black barring (more banded on wings than previous species), bare yellow throat. *p. 68*
28. FASCIATED TIGER-HERON (*Tigrisoma fasciatum salmoni*). Adult. Very dark overall, slaty sides of head. Along forested streams, scarce. *p. 67*

Note: Cracids are depicted on Plate 41.

Gwynne 12·84

PLATE 3

GREBES, DUCKS, RAILS, JACANA

1. LEAST GREBE (*Tacybaptus dominicus brachypterus*). Small size, thin black bill, yellow eye. a) Breeding adult. b) Nonbreeding. *p. 53*
2. PIED-BILLED GREBE (*Podilymbus podiceps antarcticus*). Larger than Least Grebe, pale and thicker bill. a) Breeding adult. b) Nonbreeding. *p. 53*
3. MASKED DUCK (*Oxyura dominica*). Small, squat, secretive duck; local in marshes. Male: blue bill, black face. Female: parallel dark facial stripes. *p. 82*
4. LESSER SCAUP (*Aythya affinis*). Diving duck of open water. Male: pale grayish with dark head. Female: dark brown with white foreface. *p. 82*
5. BLUE-WINGED TEAL (*Anas discors*). Panama's commonest duck (a northern migrant). Pale blue wing-coverts (in flight); small size. Male: white crescent on face. Female: brown; note size, blue on wing, and her consort. *p. 80*
6. AMERICAN WIGEON (*Anas americana*). Male. Obvious white crown, white wing-coverts (in flight). Female see text. *p. 81*
7. BLACK-BELLIED WHISTLING-DUCK (*Dendrocygna a. autumnalis*). Red bill (dusky in immature), black belly; bold white wing-stripe in flight. *p. 78*
8. COMB DUCK (*Sarkidiornis melanotos sylvicola*). Large size, white head and underparts. Male larger, with comb. Eastern Panama, scarce. *p. 79*
9. MUSCOVY DUCK (*Cairina moschata*). Large size, all dark plumage; white wing-patch in flight. Male larger. Local, mostly Pacific slope. *p. 78*
10. PURPLE GALLINULE (*Porphyrula martinica*). a) Adult: deep violet-blue head and underparts, colorful bill. b) Immature: brownish, lacks flank stripe. *p. 124*
11. AMERICAN COOT (*Fulica a. americana*). Mainly white bill. *p. 124*
12. COMMON MOORHEN (*Gallinula chloropus cachinnans*). White flank stripe, slaty coloration, red bill. *p. 124*
13. WATTLED JACANA (*Jacana jacana hypomelaena*). Yellow on wings, very long toes. a) Adult: mostly black. b) Immature: white underparts and eye-stripe. *p. 132*
14. SORA (*Porzana carolina*). a) Adult: black face, gray breast, barred flanks. b) Immature: buffier below. *p. 121*
15. PAINT-BILLED CRAKE (*Neocrex erythrops olivascens*). Red legs and on bill, barred flanks and crissum. Rare, only western Bocas del Toro (see Colombian Crake on Plate 1). *p. 123*

3

Gwynne 8·84

PLATE 4

BOOBIES, SHEARWATERS, STORM-PETRELS, ETC.

1. MAGNIFICENT FRIGATEBIRD (*Fregata magnificens*). Large size, long narrow pointed wings, long forked tail. Often soars high. Male: all black, red throat pouch. Female: white breast (also a white head in immatures). *p. 65*

2. BROWN PELICAN (*Pelecanus occidentalis carolinensis*). Huge size, pouch on bill. Plunges into water. a) Adult breeding: mainly gray, white on neck. b) Immature: browner. *p. 63*

3. ANHINGA (*Anhinga anhinga leucogaster*). Male and female. Long tail often fanned, silvery wing-patch, sharply pointed bill. Female has brownish head and neck. Fresh water, often soars. *p. 65*

4. NEOTROPIC CORMORANT (*Phalacrocorax o. olivaceus*). Long slightly hooked bill. Both salt and fresh water; often swims. a) Adult: all black; facial skin bordered white when breeding. b) Immature: browner above, whitish underparts. *p. 64*

5. BLUE-FOOTED BOOBY (*Sula n. nebouxii*). Pale head, white below and on rump; bright blue legs. Local on Pacific coast and islands. *p. 61*

6. MASKED BOOBY (*Sula dactylatra granti*). White with black flight feathers (immature see text). Pelagic. *p. 61*

7. BROWN BOOBY (*Sula leucogaster etesiaca*). Pelagic and locally along both coasts. a) Adult male: contrasting white belly (female with less white on face). b) Immature: echoes adult's pattern. *p. 62*

8. PARASITIC JAEGER (*Stercorarius parasiticus*). Nonbreeding adult. White wing flash, pointed and protruding central tail feathers. Hard to distinguish from Pomarine Jaeger; see text and Plate 6. Mainly pelagic. *p. 148*

9. SOOTY SHEARWATER (*Puffinus griseus*). Gliding flight low over ocean on stiff bowed wings. Sooty plumage, whitish underwing. *p. 56*

10. AUDUBON'S SHEARWATER (*Puffinus lherminieri subalaris*). Small shearwater with fluttery flight; white below. Pelagic. *p. 57*

11. LEAST STORM-PETREL (*Oceanodroma microsoma*). Small size, short wedge-shaped tail. Pelagic on Pacific. *p. 59*

12. WEDGE-RUMPED STORM-PETREL (*Oceanodroma t. tethys*). Large triangular white rump patch. Pelagic on Pacific. *p. 58*

13. BLACK STORM-PETREL (*Oceanodroma melania*). Rather large storm-petrel, all dark. Pelagic on Pacific. *p. 58*

4

PLATE 5

SHOREBIRDS

Almost all these species are primarily coastal birds; only a few regularly occur inland around fresh water (e.g. 3, 7, 8, 11, and 12).

1. SEMIPALMATED PLOVER (*Charadrius semipalmatus*). a) Breeding: orange at base of short stubby bill, white nuchal collar. b) Browner and less patterned, blackish bill. *p. 130*

2. WILSON'S PLOVER (*Charadrius wilsonia beldingi*). Male and female. Heavy all-black bill, dull pinkish legs. *p. 129*

3. COLLARED PLOVER (*Charadrius collaris*). Male. Thin black bill, neat trim pattern with some rufous on head; no white nuchal collar. *p. 128*

4. SURFBIRD (*Aphriza virgata*). Nonbreeding. Chunky shape; mostly gray, white rump and basal tail. Pacific coast, on rocks. *p. 138*

5. RUDDY TURNSTONE (*Arenaria interpres morinella*). Nonbreeding. Pied pattern with dark chest (much brighter in breeding), short orange legs, small head. *p. 137*

6. BLACK-BELLIED PLOVER (*Pluvialis squatarola*). Large and chunky, with heavy bill; black axillars and white rump and wing-stripe in flight. a) Nonbreeding: mottled grayish. b) Breeding: black underparts. *p. 127*

7. SOUTHERN LAPWING (*Vanellus chilensis cayennensis*). Unmistakable pattern, wispy crest. Scarce and local resident, mostly eastern Panama. *p. 127*

8. COMMON SNIPE (*Gallinago gallinago delicata*). Long bill, cryptic mottled brown pattern. Inconspicuous in damp areas. *p. 145*

9. SHORT-BILLED DOWITCHER (*Limnodromus g. griseus*). Nonbreeding. Long bill, mainly gray plumage (rufous in breeding); triangular white rump in flight. See text for Long-billed Dowitcher. *p. 144*

10. SANDERLING (*Calidris alba*). Nonbreeding. Very pale plumage, usually showing black on bend of wing; bold white wing-stripe in flight. Mostly sandy beaches. *p. 138*

11. SOLITARY SANDPIPER (*Tringa s. solitaria*). Nonbreeding. White eye-ring, dark upperparts, dark legs. *p. 134*

12. SPOTTED SANDPIPER (*Actitis macularia*). Nonbreeding. Smudge on chest (spotted below in breeding). Often teeters; stiff shallow wing-strokes. *p. 135*

13. WESTERN SANDPIPER (*Calidris mauri*). Long slightly drooped bill. a) Breeding: more rufous shows on upperparts. b) Nonbreeding: grayer; see text. *p. 140*

14. LEAST SANDPIPER (*Calidris minutilla*). Nonbreeding. Small size, yellowish or greenish (not black) legs. *p. 140*

15. SEMIPALMATED SANDPIPER (*Calidris pusilla*). Nonbreeding. Fairly short straight bill; see text. *p. 139*

16. BLACK-NECKED STILT (*Himantopus mexicanus*). Unmistakable black and white pattern, exceedingly long pink legs. *p. 131*

17. WILLET (*Catoptrophorus semipalmatus inornatus*). Nonbreeding. Dingy and gray (browner in breeding), but flashy wing pattern in flight. *p. 135*

18. WHIMBREL (*Numenius phaeopus hudsonicus*). Large and brownish, striped head pattern, long decurved bill. *p. 136*

19. MARBLED GODWIT (*Limosa fedoa*). Nonbreeding. Large size, buffy brownish plumage, long slightly upturned bicolored bill. *p. 137*

20. GREATER YELLOWLEGS (*Tringa melanoleuca*). Nonbreeding. Bright yellow legs, fairly long bill (see text for smaller Lesser Yellowlegs). *p. 133*

Gwynne 11·85

PLATE 6

GULLS, TERNS, JAEGERS, SKIMMER

1. HERRING GULL (*Larus argentatus smithsonianus*). First winter. Large size; younger birds very dark, becoming whiter with age. Uncommon. *p. 153*

2. RING-BILLED GULL (*Larus delawarensis*). Subadult. Paler mantle than Laughing Gull, pink bill with dusky tip (yellow with black ring in adult). Uncommon. *p. 153*

3. FRANKLIN'S GULL (*Larus pipixcan*). Nonbreeding adult. Dark half-hood, white flash on outer flight feathers. *p. 151*

4. LAUGHING GULL (*Larus atricilla*). Panama's commonest gull. a) Nonbreeding adult: dark gray mantle, no white on flight feathers. b) Breeding adult: black head, reddish bill. c) Immature: browner, breast smudge, black terminal tail band. *p. 150*

5. PARASITIC JAEGER (*Stercorarius parasiticus*). Immature. Smaller than next species, usually with pale area on hindneck; hard to distinguish. Mostly pelagic. See also Plate 4. *p. 148*

6. POMARINE JAEGER (*Stercorarius pomarinus*). Immature. Much like previous species; stockier build with heavy bill, barring on underparts. Also mostly pelagic. *p. 148*

7. SABINE'S GULL (*Xema sabini*). Nonbreeding adult. Striking flight pattern, shallow fork in tail. Mostly pelagic, especially on Pacific. *p. 154*

8. ELEGANT TERN (*Sterna elegans*). Nonbreeding. Slender orange bill. Only on Pacific, uncommon. *p. 156*

9. ROYAL TERN (*Sterna m. maxima*). Nonbreeding. Fairly stout orange-red bill. *p. 156*

10. CASPIAN TERN (*Sterna c. caspia*). Nonbreeding. Mostly dark crown, heavy bright red bill. Rare. *p. 155*

11. LARGE-BILLED TERN (*Phaetusa s. simplex*). Heavy yellow bill, black crown, striking flight pattern. Rare. *p. 160*

12. GULL-BILLED TERN (*Sterna nilotica aranea*). Nonbreeding. Heavy black bill, short barely forked tail, dusky ear-patch (black crown when breeding). *p. 155*

13. SANDWICH TERN (*Sterna sandvicensis acuflavidus*). Nonbreeding. Slender black bill with yellow tip, forked tail. *p. 157*

14. COMMON TERN (*Sterna h. hirundo*). Nonbreeding. Black hindcrown, dark carpal bar, reddish legs. *p. 157*

15. LEAST TERN (*Sterna a. antillarum*). Breeding adult. Small size, yellow bill. Uncommon. *p. 158*

16. BRIDLED TERN (*Sterna anaethetus nelsoni*). Brownish gray mantle, white nuchal collar. Pelagic. *p. 159*

17. BLACK SKIMMER (*Rhynchops n. niger*). Unique red and black bill, striking black and white plumage. Very uncommon. *p. 162*

18. BROWN NODDY (*Anous stolidus galapagensis*). Wedge-shaped tail, contrasting pale crown. Mainly pelagic. *p. 161*

19. BLACK TERN (*Chlidonias nigra surinamensis*). Small size, dark mantle and tail (latter slightly notched). a) Molting adult: becoming black on head and underparts. b) Nonbreeding: white underparts, smudge on sides of chest. *p. 160*

6

Gwynne 1·86

PLATE 7

BIRDS OF PREY I

1. BAT FALCON (*Falco r. rufigularis*). Small size and long pointed wings, white throat, very dark underparts. *p. 112*

2. PLUMBEOUS HAWK (*Leucopternis plumbea*). All slaty gray, orange cere and legs, single tail band. Rare. *p. 94*

3. SEMIPLUMBEOUS HAWK (*Leucopternis semiplumbea*). Orange cere and legs, white underparts, single tail band. *p. 94*

4. ROADSIDE HAWK (*Buteo magnirostris petulans*). Small size, gray head and chest, rufous wing-patch. Clearings and savannas. *p. 99*

5. COLLARED FOREST-FALCON (*Micrastur semitorquatus naso*). Lanky shape with long graduated tail, black facial crescent and white (or buffy) collar. *p. 110*

6. SLATY-BACKED FOREST-FALCON (*Micrastur mirandollei*). Slaty upperparts, yellow cere and legs, tail bands (see text). Rare. *p. 109*

7. BARRED FOREST-FALCON (*Micrastur ruficollis interstes*). Small size, even barring below, yellow orbital area. *p. 109*

8. TINY HAWK (*Accipiter superciliosus fontanieri*). Very small size, barred underparts. Rare. *p. 92*

9. BICOLORED HAWK (*Accipiter b. bicolor*). Two-toned gray plumage, chestnut thighs. Rare. *p. 93*

10. GRAY-HEADED KITE (*Leptodon cayanensis*). a) Adult: gray head (rather small), blackish upperparts, whitish underparts. b) Immature (light phase): white head with black crown patch (but plumages variable and confusing; see text). *p. 86*

11. HOOK-BILLED KITE (*Chondrohierax u. uncinatus*). Male: strongly hooked bill, mostly gray plumage, indistinct barring below, usually greenish cere. Female: tawny collar, coarse barring below. *p. 86*

12. DOUBLE-TOOTHED KITE (*Harpagus bidentatus fasciatus*). Male. Dusky throat stripe, more or less rufous underparts (female more uniformly rufous below). *p. 90*

Note: Immatures of the following species on this Plate are depicted on Plate 9: Barred Forest-Falcon, Tiny Hawk, Bicolored Hawk, Hook-billed Kite, Double-toothed Kite.

PLATE 8

BIRDS OF PREY II

[handwritten: Aligmndi River 2/01]

1. GRAY HAWK (*Buteo nitidus blakei*). Mostly pearly gray, narrow barring below, white tail bands. Immature on Plate 9. *p. 98*

2. BARRED HAWK (*Leucopternis princeps*). Dark throat and chest contrasting with pale lower underparts, large size. Foothills and highlands. *p. 94*

3. GREAT BLACK-HAWK (*Buteogallus urubitinga ridgwayi*). Much like Common Black-Hawk, but larger with slaty lores, two white tail bands, white thigh barring (usually). In eastern Panama (nominate race) basal tail all white; see text. *p. 96*

[handwritten: Mogue River 2/01]

4. COMMON BLACK-HAWK (*Buteogallus a. anthracinus*). Caribbean coastal areas (see text for very similar Mangrove Black-Hawk of Pacific coast). a) Adult: yellow lores and cere, single tail band. b) Immature: heavy streaking below, numerous tail bands (see text). *p. 95*

5. ORNATE HAWK-EAGLE (*Spizaetus ornatus vicarius*). Tawny sides of head and neck, long crest, coarsely barred underparts. *p. 106*

6. RED-THROATED CARACARA (*Daptrius americanus*). Bare red face and throat, white belly. Local, declining. *p. 107*

[handwritten: Aligmdi River 2/01]

7. CRANE HAWK (*Geranospiza caerulescens niger*). All slaty, dark cere and lores, long orange reddish legs. *p. 93*

8. YELLOW-HEADED CARACARA (*Milvago chimachima*). Buffy head and underparts, black eye-streak. *p. 108*

9. CRESTED CARACARA (*Polyborus plancus audubonii*). Red facial skin, black crown, white sides of head and throat. *p. 107*

10. SAVANNA HAWK (*Buteogallus meridionalis*). Large size, long legs, mostly tawny-rufous plumage, tail band. *p. 97*

11. BLACK-COLLARED HAWK (*Busarellus n. nigricollis*). Mostly rufous, whitish head, black patch on foreneck. Local in marshes. *p. 97*

8

PLATE 9

BIRDS OF PREY III

1. BARRED FOREST-FALCON (*Micrastur ruficollis interstes*). Immature. Rather small, variable amount of black barring below, usually a pale collar. *p. 109*
2. BICOLORED HAWK (*Accipiter b. bicolor*). Immature. Some shade of buff below, thighs often more rufous, *Accipiter* visage. *p. 93*
3. TINY HAWK (*Accipiter superciliosus fontanieri*). Immature (rufous phase). Small size, showing variable amount of rufous. *p. 92*
4. SHARP-SHINNED HAWK (*Accipiter striatus velox*). Adult. Bluish gray upperparts, rufous barring below, *Accipiter* shape and visage. Immature browner, streaked below. Northern migrant, mainly to west. *p. 92*
5. HOOK-BILLED KITE (*Chondrohierax u. uncinatus*). Immature. Pale spot before eye (as in adult) imparts odd visage, creamy buff underparts with a bit of barring (but variable; see text). *p. 86*
6. SNAIL KITE (*Rostrhamus s. sociabilis*). Strongly hooked bill, red to orange facial skin and legs. Very local and scarce in marshes. a) Adult male: gray with white basal tail. b) Immature: browner and more streaked, same tail pattern. *p. 89*
7. GRAY HAWK (*Buteo nitidus blakei*). Immature. Rather sparse but bold spotting below, thighs often barred, usually pale-headed. Confusing; see text. Adult on Plate 8. *p. 98*
8. DOUBLE-TOOTHED KITE (*Harpagus bidentatus fasciatus*). Immature. Dark median throat stripe (as in adult). *p. 90*
9. BROAD-WINGED HAWK (*Buteo p. platypterus*). Widespread and common northern migrant. a) Immature: brownish upperparts, streaking below; confusing (see text). b) Adult: rufous barring below, two white tail bands. *p. 99*
10. PLUMBEOUS KITE (*Ictinia plumbea*). Gray, long wings protruding beyond tail at rest, rufous patch in wings (mostly visible in flight), banded tail (*contra* migrant Mississippi Kite; see text). *p. 91*
11. WHITE-TAILED KITE (*Elanus leucurus*). Beautiful white, gray, and black kite of open country. Often hovers. *p. 89*
12. PEARL KITE (*Gampsonyx swainsonii leonae*). Small size, yellowish buff on face, white underparts. Recent colonizer to Panama. *p. 87*
13. AMERICAN KESTREL (*Falco s. sparverius*). Female. Small size, ornate facial pattern, mainly rufous tail; male with blue-gray wings. Northern migrant to open areas. *p. 110*
14. APLOMADO FALCON (*Falco f. femoralis*). Complex facial pattern, black and rufous on lower underparts, white trailing edge on wing (in flight). Local in open areas on western Pacific slope. *p. 111*

Note: Adults of the following species on this Plate are depicted on Plate 7: Barred Forest-Falcon, Tiny Hawk, Bicolored Hawk, Hook-billed Kite, Double-toothed Kite.

9

Gwynne 11·86

PLATE 10

PIGEONS

1. BAND-TAILED PIGEON (*Columba fasciata crissalis*). White crescent on nape, two-toned gray tail. Western highlands. *p. 164*

2. SCALED PIGEON (*Columba speciosa*). Scaly underparts, red bill. *p. 163*

3. PALE-VENTED PIGEON (*Columba cayennensis pallidicrissa*). Whitish lower belly and vent. *p. 163*

4. SHORT-BILLED PIGEON (*Columba nigrirostris*). All ruddy brown; in humid forested lowlands. See text for very similar Ruddy Pigeon (of western highlands, and in east). *p. 164*

5. MAROON-CHESTED GROUND-DOVE (*Claravis m. mondetoura*). Male. Gray, purplish chest, white on tail. Western highlands, local. *p. 167*

6. PLAIN-BREASTED GROUND-DOVE (*Columbina minuta alaeodes*). Male: mostly grayish, conspicuous chestnut primaries in flight. Female: duller (see text). *p. 166*

7. RUDDY GROUND-DOVE (*Columbina talpacoti rufipennis*). Male: ruddy brown, gray head. Female: duller, but still brown above. *p. 167*

8. GRAY-HEADED DOVE (*Leptotila plumbeiceps notius*). Gray crown and nape, pinkish underparts (more richly colored on Pacific slope). Very local, western Panama. *p. 168*

9. GRAY-CHESTED DOVE (*Leptotila c. cassinii*). Gray head, foreneck, and breast, narrow white tail-tipping, red orbital skin. See Plate 42 for rather different *rufinucha* form of western Chiriquí. *p. 169*

10. WHITE-TIPPED DOVE (*Leptotila v. verreauxi*). Broad white tail-tipping, pinkish brown underparts, bluish orbital skin. Iris usually yellower than shown. *p. 168*

11. BLUE GROUND-DOVE (*Claravis pretiosa*). Male: all bluish gray. Female: chestnut wing-spots, black and rufous tail. *p. 167*

12. RUDDY QUAIL-DOVE (*Geotrygon m. montana*). Male: rufous upperparts, cinnamon facial stripe and underparts, chestnut moustache. Female: much duller, brown and cinnamon-buffy. *p. 171*

13. VIOLACEOUS QUAIL-DOVE (*Geotrygon violacea albiventer*). Male. Violet-glossed hindcrown and back, white forecrown, lacking obvious moustache. Orbital area and bill purplish red (like Ruddy). Local in humid forest. *p. 170*

14. CHIRIQUI QUAIL-DOVE (*Geotrygon chiriquensis*). Gray crown and nape, rufous and cinnamon underparts. Western highlands. *p. 169*

15. PURPLISH-BACKED QUAIL-DOVE (*Geotrygon lawrencii*). Purplish back, white foreface, gray crown and hindneck. Very local in foothills. *p. 169*

16. BUFF-FRONTED QUAIL-DOVE (*Geotrygon costaricensis*). Buff forehead, green crown and nape, purplish back, mostly gray underparts. Western highlands. *p. 170*

17. OLIVE-BACKED QUAIL-DOVE (*Geotrygon veraguensis*). Conspicuous white facial stripe and forehead. Humid lowland forest. *p. 169*

Note: Mourning Dove, White-winged Dove, and Common Ground-Dove are all depicted on Plate 42.

PLATE 11

PARROTS

1. BLUE-FRONTED PARROTLET (*Touit dilectissima*). Male and female. Small size, short tail; red on upperwing, yellow on underwing, blue forecrown. Local, eastern Panama. *p. 177*

2. RED-FRONTED PARROTLET (*Touit costaricensis*). Male. Like preceding, but forecrown red. Very local, western Panama. *p. 176*

3. BARRED PARAKEET (*Bolborhynchus l. lineola*). Fairly long wedge-shaped tail, black barring (can be hard to see). Scarce, western highlands. *p. 175*

4. ORANGE-CHINNED PARAKEET (*Brotogeris j. jugularis*). Small size, wedge-shaped tail, brown shoulders. Widespread and common. *p. 176*

5. SULPHUR-WINGED PARAKEET (*Pyrrhura hoffmanni gaudens*). Red ear-patch, conspicuous yellow on wing in flight. Western highlands. *p. 175*

6. PAINTED PARAKEET (*Pyrrhura picta eisenmanni*). Scaly breast, red foreface, pale buff ear-patch. Recently discovered, southern Azuero Peninsula. *p. 175*

7. GREAT GREEN MACAW (*Ara a. ambigua*). Very large size, mostly yellowish green. Now very local. *p. 172*

8. CHESTNUT-FRONTED MACAW (*Ara severa*). Small size (compared to other Panamanian macaws), reddish under wings and tail. Eastern Panama. *p. 173*

9. BLUE-AND-YELLOW MACAW (*Ara ararauna*). Unmistakable bright blue and golden yellow. Eastern Panama, local. *p. 172*

10. RED-AND-GREEN MACAW (*Ara chloroptera*). Mostly deep red, wing-coverts green. Eastern Panama, local. *p. 173*

11. SCARLET MACAW (*Ara macao*). Mostly bright red, wing-coverts yellow. Western Panama, now very rare and local (except Coiba). *p. 172*

12. OLIVE-THROATED PARAKEET (*Aratinga nana astec*). Olive brown underparts. Bocas del Toro. *p. 174*

13. BROWN-THROATED PARAKEET (*Aratinga pertinax ocularis*). Brownish throat and chest, orange below eye. Pacific western Panama. *p. 174*

14. CRIMSON-FRONTED PARAKEET (*Aratinga finschi*). Relatively large, long tail; red forecrown, red and yellow under wing. Western Panama. *p. 174*

15. RED-LORED AMAZON (*Amazona autumnalis salvini*). Red forehead and lores. *p. 178*

16. YELLOW-CROWNED AMAZON (*Amazona ochrocephala panamensis*). Yellow forecrown. *p. 179*

17. MEALY AMAZON (*Amazona farinosa inornata*). No red or yellow on head, very prominent eye-ring. *p. 180*

18. BROWN-HOODED PARROT (*Pionopsitta haematotis coccinicollaris*). Male. Slaty brown head, red chest patch. *p. 177*

19. BLUE-HEADED PARROT (*Pionus menstruus rubrigularis*). Mostly blue head, neck, and breast. *p. 178*

20. WHITE-CROWNED PARROT (*Pionus senilis*). Contrasting white forecrown, buffy brownish wing-coverts. Western Panama. *p. 178*

Note: All flying birds are drawn to a smaller scale, the macaws to an even smaller one.

Gwynne '83

PLATE 12

OWLS, CUCKOOS

1. BARE-SHANKED SCREECH-OWL (*Otus clarkii*). Ear-tufts, tawny facial area, reddish brown upperparts. Highlands. *p. 187*
2. TROPICAL SCREECH-OWL (*Otus choliba luctisonus*). Ear-tufts, whitish superciliary, black facial rim, herring-bone pattern below. *p. 187*
3. VERMICULATED SCREECH-OWL (*Otus guatemalae vermiculatus*). Ear-tufts, no facial rim, barred and mottled underparts. *p. 187*
4. MOTTLED OWL (*Ciccaba v. virgata*). No ear-tufts, mostly brown, mottled, barred, and streaked. *p. 190*
5. BLACK-AND-WHITE OWL (*Ciccaba nigrolineata*). No ear-tufts, narrow black barring below. *p. 191*
6. STRIPED OWL (*Asio clamator forbesi*). Prominent ear-tufts, streaked underparts. Semi-open country. *p. 191*
7. SPECTACLED OWL (*Pulsatrix perspicillata chapmani*). Large size, no ear-tufts, white spectacles, black chest. *p. 188*
8. CRESTED OWL (*Lophostrix cristata wedeli*). Conspicuous long pale ear-tufts and eye-stripe. *p. 188*
9. MANGROVE CUCKOO (*Coccyzus minor palloris*). Black mask, buffy underparts, yellow on bill (see text for other *Coccyzus* cuckoos). *p. 182*
10. STRIPED CUCKOO (*Tapera naevia excellens*). Short bushy crest, streaked brown upperparts, whitish underparts. *p. 183*
11. PHEASANT CUCKOO (*Dromococcyx phasianellus rufigularis*). Long graduated tail, elongated upper tail-coverts, chest streaking. *p. 183*
12. LITTLE CUCKOO (*Piaya minuta panamensis*). Smaller than Squirrel Cuckoo; red orbital ring, no gray below. *p. 183*
13. SQUIRREL CUCKOO (*Piaya cayana thermophila*). Mostly chestnut, gray breast and belly, very long tail. *p. 182*
14. RUFOUS-VENTED GROUND-CUCKOO (*Neomorphus geoffroyi salvini*). Large size, crest, bronzy upperparts, very long tail. Rare. *p. 184*

PLATE 13

HUMMINGBIRDS

1. VIOLET-HEADED HUMMINGBIRD (*Klais guimeti merritii*). Male: violet-blue head and throat, white spot behind eye. Female: white spot behind eye. Especially foothills. *p. 211*
2. VIOLET-CAPPED HUMMINGBIRD (*Goldmania violiceps*). Male. Violet-blue crown, chestnut tail. Eastern Panama foothills. *p. 215*
3. BLUE-THROATED GOLDENTAIL (*Hylocharis eliciae earina*). Male. Mostly red bill, bright golden bronzy tail, violet-blue throat. Local, Pacific slope. *p. 214*
4. SAPPHIRE-THROATED HUMMINGBIRD (*Lepidopyga c. coeruleogularis*). Male: blue throat and chest, forked tail. Female: mostly white underparts. *p. 214*
5. CROWNED WOODNYMPH (*Thalurania colombica venusta*). Male: blue crown (green in eastern Panama), forked tail, green throat and chest. Female: two-toned grayish underparts. *p. 213*
6. GARDEN EMERALD (*Chlorostilbon assimilis*). Male: all green, forked tail. Female: blackish mask, white streak behind eye. *p. 212*

Continued over

PLATE 13 *continued from previous page*

7. WHITE-NECKED JACOBIN (*Florisuga m. mellivora*). Male: bright blue head, white nape patch, white tail. Female: very scaly underparts. *p. 208*

8. SCALY-BREASTED HUMMINGBIRD (*Phaeochroa c. cuvierii*). Large whitish tail corners, overall dull greenish plumage. *p. 208*

9. BLUE-CHESTED HUMMINGBIRD (*Amazilia amabilis*). Male: violet-blue patch on lower throat, notched tail. Female: much green spotting below. See Charming Hummingbird on Plate 43. *p. 215*

10. VIOLET-BELLIED HUMMINGBIRD (*Damophila julie panamensis*). Male: mostly violet-blue underparts, graduated tail. Female: uniform pale grayish underparts. *p. 213*

11. WHITE-VENTED PLUMELETEER (*Chalybura buffonii micans*). Male. Prominent white vent, blue-black tail. Female grayish below. Central and eastern Panama. *p. 219*

12. BRONZE-TAILED PLUMELETEER (*Chalybura urochrysia isaurae*). Male. White vent, purplish bronzy tail, pinkish feet and lower mandible. *p. 219*

13. RUFOUS-TAILED HUMMINGBIRD (*Amazilia t. tzacatl*). Male. Rufous-chestnut tail, pinkish base of bill. *p. 217*

14. SNOWY-BELLIED HUMMINGBIRD (*Amazilia e. edward*). Sharp green-white contrast on underparts. *p. 216*

15. PURPLE-CROWNED FAIRY (*Heliothryx barroti*). Male: pure white underparts, much white in long tail. Female: similar, with green crown. *p. 222*

16. BLACK-THROATED MANGO (*Anthracothorax nigricollis*). Male: maroon-purple tail, black throat and median underparts. Female: black stripe down underparts. See Green-breasted Mango on Plate 43. *p. 210*

17. RUFOUS-CRESTED COQUETTE (*Lophornis delattrei lessoni*). Male: rufous crest, pale rump band. Female: pale rump band, rufous forecrown. *p. 211*

18. SNOWCAP (*Microchera a. albocoronata*). Male. White crown, mostly white tail, otherwise very dark. Western Caribbean slope, rare. *p. 218*

19. LONG-BILLED STARTHROAT (*Heliomaster l. longirostris*). Male. Very long bill, reddish gorget bordered by whitish streak. *p. 222*

20. GREEN-FRONTED LANCEBILL (*Doryfera ludoviciae veraguensis*). Male. Very long bill, green frontlet, otherwise quite dark. Highlands, scarce. *p. 208*

21. GREEN THORNTAIL (*Discosura conversii*). Male: long slender tail, white rump-band. Female: black and white underparts, white rump-band. Foothills. Rump-band of both sexes should be wider. *p. 212*

22. GREEN-CROWNED BRILLIANT (*Heliodoxa jacula henryi*). Male: mostly green, violet throat spot, deeply forked tail. Female: large green spots below. Foothills and highlands. Male should have white postocular spot, female a white malar streak. *p. 220*

23. BROWN VIOLET-EAR (*Colibri d. delphinae*). Mostly dull brownish, green gorget bordered by whitish streak, purple ear-tuft. Rare, highlands. *p. 209*

24. LITTLE HERMIT (*Phaethornis longuemareus saturatus*). Long graduated tail, small size. *p. 206*

25. GREEN HERMIT (*Phaethornis guy coruscans*). Female. Bluish green upperparts, slaty underparts (male much greener below). Foothills and highlands. *p. 205*

26. LONG-TAILED HERMIT (*Phaethornis superciliosus cephalus*). Mostly brownish, cinnamon rump, long white-tipped central tail feathers. *p. 206*

27. PALE-BELLIED HERMIT (*Phaethornis a. anthophilus*). Mostly white underparts, rather green upperparts. Pearl Islands, locally in eastern Panama. *p. 206*

28. BAND-TAILED BARBTHROAT (*Threnetes ruckeri darienensis*). Blackish throat, rounded tail with much white but no chestnut. *p. 205*

29. RUFOUS-BREASTED HERMIT (*Glaucis hirsuta affinis*). Female. Much chestnut in rounded tail, dull rufous underparts. Central and eastern Panama. *p. 205*

30. BRONZY HERMIT (*Glaucis a. aenea*). Coppery bronzy upperparts. Western Panama. *p. 204*

Note: White-tipped Sicklebill on Plate 43.

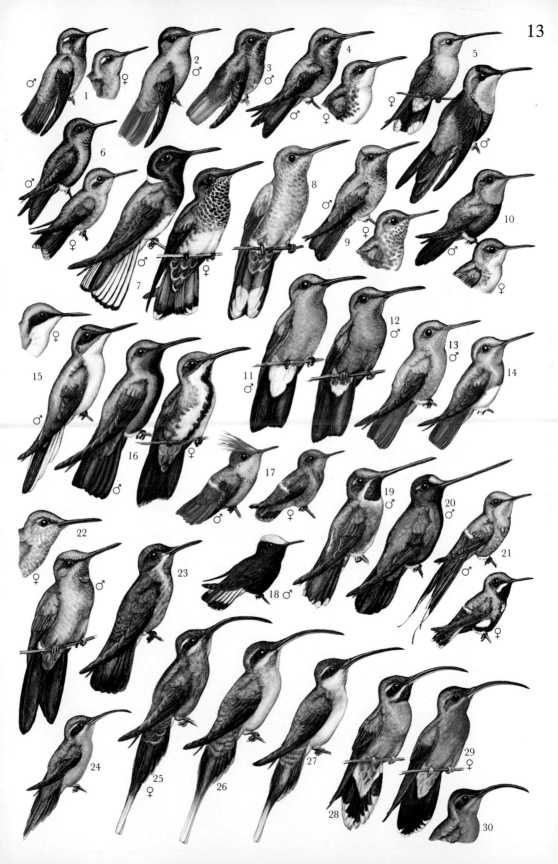

PLATE 14

CHIRIQUI HUMMINGBIRDS, FURNARIIDS

All of the following are found primarily in the western highlands; a few reappear in the Darién highlands.

1. SCINTILLANT HUMMINGBIRD (*Selasphorus scintilla*). Male: small size, bright red gorget, rufous tail. Female: spotted throat, mostly rufous tail. Chiriquí only. *p. 224*

2. VOLCANO HUMMINGBIRD (*Selasphorus flammula torridus*). Male. Dull-colored gorget, mostly black tail. Chiriquí only. *p. 223*

3. GLOW-THROATED HUMMINGBIRD (*Selasphorus ardens*). Male. Bright rose red gorget. Eastern Chiriquí and Veraguas only. *p. 224*

4. MAGENTA-THROATED WOODSTAR (*Calliphlox bryantae*). Male: long deeply forked black tail. Female: unspotted throat, whitish tufts on sides of rump. *p. 222*

5. WHITE-THROATED MOUNTAIN-GEM (*Lampornis c. castaneoventris*). Male: white throat, postocular streak. Female: uniform rufous-tawny underparts. Western Chiriquí only. *p. 220*

6. PURPLE-THROATED MOUNTAIN-GEM (*Lampornis calolaema homogenes*). Male. Like preceding but throat purple. Females very similar. Eastern Chiriquí to Coclé. *p. 220*

7. WHITE-CRESTED COQUETTE (*Lophornis adorabilis*). Male: white crest, green ear-tufts, pale rump band. Female: pale rump band, blackish forecrown, white throat. Chiriquí lowlands and foothills. *p. 211*

8. FIERY-THROATED HUMMINGBIRD (*Panterpe i. insignis*). Orange and red throat, violet-blue chest, blue crown. Chiriquí only. *p. 213*

9. BLACK-BELLIED HUMMINGBIRD (*Eupherusa nigriventris*). Male. Black underparts. Caribbean slope. *p. 217*

10. MAGNIFICENT HUMMINGBIRD (*Eugenes fulgens spectabilis*). Male: large size, overall dark appearance, purple crown. Female: white postocular streak, grayish underparts. Chiriquí only. *p. 221*

11. VIOLET SABREWING (*Campylopterus hemileucurus mellitus*). Male: mostly dark violet, much white in tail. Female: large size, decurved bill, violet throat patch, white on tail. *p. 208*

12. GREEN VIOLET-EAR (*Colibri thalassinus cabanidis*). Violet ear-patch, otherwise mostly green. *p. 209*

13. WHITE-TAILED EMERALD (*Elvira chionura*). Male. Much white in tail, no cinnamon wing-patch. *p. 218*

14. STRIPE-TAILED HUMMINGBIRD (*Eupherusa eximia egregia*). Male: conspicuous cinnamon wing-patch, much white in tail. Female: cinnamon wing-patch, grayish underparts. *p. 217*

15. LINEATED FOLIAGE-GLEANER (*Syndactyla subalaris lineata*). a) Adult: narrow streaks on back and underparts (eye-stripe not as conspicuous as portrayed). See Striped Woodhaunter of lowlands on Plate 20. b) Immature: Orange-tawny on sides of neck, throat, and chest. Western and eastern highlands. *p. 253*

16. RED-FACED SPINETAIL (*Cranioleuca erythrops rufigenis*). Mainly rufous head; rufous wings and tail. Western and eastern highlands. *p. 250*

17. BUFF-FRONTED FOLIAGE-GLEANER (*Philydor rufus rufescens*). Buffy forehead and eye-stripe, plain ochraceous underparts, rufous wings. *p. 254*

18. GRAY-THROATED LEAFTOSSER (*Sclerurus albigularis canigularis*). Pale gray throat. See other leaftossers (Plate 20). Chiriquí only. *p. 257*

Continued over

PLATE 15

TROGONS

1. RESPLENDENT QUETZAL (*Pharomachrus mocinno costaricensis*). Male: spectacular long train. Female: large size, bushy crest, red belly. Western highlands. *p. 229*
2. GOLDEN-HEADED QUETZAL (*Pharomachrus a. auriceps*). Male. Mostly golden green, train slightly longer than tail, dark underside of tail. Darién highlands. *p. 228*
3. BLACK-TAILED TROGON (*Trogon melanurus macroura*). Male. Like more widespread Slaty-tail, but bill yellow, white band across chest. Canal area east. *p. 227*
4. SLATY-TAILED TROGON (*Trogon massena hoffmanni*). Male: orange-red bill, red belly, black underside of tail. Female: reddish on bill, red belly. *p. 228*
5. LATTICE-TAILED TROGON (*Trogon clathratus*). Male: like Slaty-tail, but with pale eye, yellow bill, very narrow bars on underside of tail. Female: yellow on bill, pale eye, tail as in male. Western Caribbean slope, local. *p. 228*
6. COLLARED TROGON (*Trogon collaris puella*). Male: white chest band, red belly, white bars on underside of tail. Female: brown, white eye-ring, pale red belly. Highlands. *p. 226*
7. ORANGE-BELLIED TROGON (*Trogon a. aurantiirostris*). Male: like Collared, but belly orange or orange-red. Female: orange belly, white eye-ring. Pacific western foothills and highlands. *p. 227*
8. BLACK-THROATED TROGON (*Trogon rufus tenellus*). Male: blue eye-ring, yellow belly. Female: brown upperparts and chest, yellow belly. *p. 227*
9. BAIRD'S TROGON (*Trogon bairdii*). Male: blue eye-ring, red belly, white underside of tail. Female: blue eye-ring, slaty upperparts, red belly, barred underside of tail. Western Chiriquí. Belly of both sexes should be less orangey. *p. 225*
10. WHITE-TAILED TROGON (*Trogon viridis chionurus*). Male: blue eye-ring, orange-yellow belly, white underside of tail. Female: blue eye-ring, slaty upperparts and chest, mostly white underside of tail. *p. 225*
11. VIOLACEOUS TROGON (*Trogon violaceus concinnus*). Male: yellow eye-ring, orange-yellow belly. Female: slaty upperparts and chest, barred underside of tail. *p. 226*

PLATE 14 *continued from previous page*

19. SPECTACLED FOLIAGE-GLEANER (*Anabacerthia v. variegaticeps*). Conspicuous eye-ring and eye-stripe, no streaking. Chiriquí only. *p. 254*
20. RUDDY TREERUNNER (*Margarornis r. rubiginosus*). Mostly rufous, white superciliary and throat (breast more rufescent than portrayed). *p. 252*
21. STREAK-BREASTED TREEHUNTER (*Thripadectes rufobrunneus*). Large size, tawny streaks below. *p. 255*
22. BUFFY TUFTEDCHEEK (*Pseudocolaptes l. lawrencii*). Large size, conspicuous tuft on sides of neck. *p. 252*
23. SPOTTED BARBTAIL (*Premnoplex brunnescens brunneicauda*). Small size, prominent spots below, creeping behavior. Foothills and highlands. *p. 251*

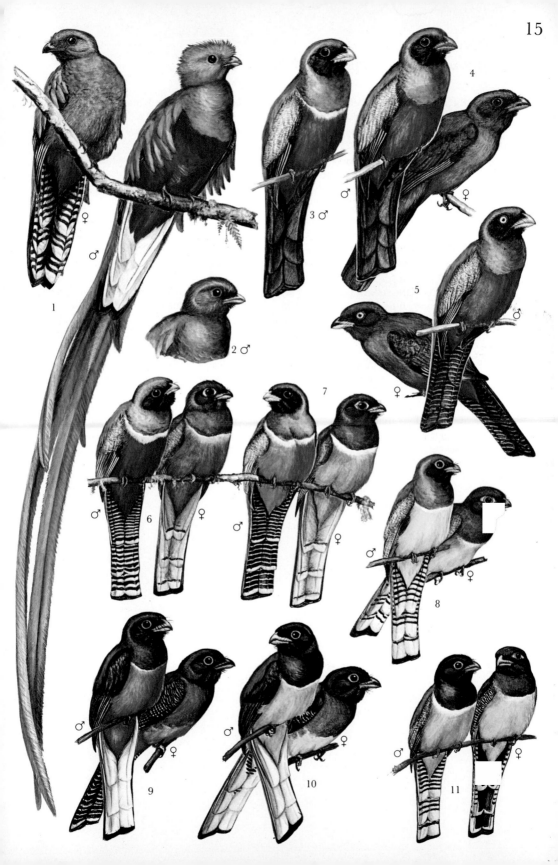

PLATE 16

MOTMOTS, JACAMARS, KINGFISHERS

1. BROAD-BILLED MOTMOT (*Electron platyrhynchum minor*). Like Rufous Motmot, but smaller, with green on underparts extending farther up. *p. 231*

2. RUFOUS MOTMOT (*Baryphthengus martii semirufus*). Large size, rufous head, neck, and most of underparts. *p. 230*

3. BLUE-CROWNED MOTMOT (*Momotus momota conexus*). Conspicuous blue eye-stripe, large size; underparts greener in western Panama. *p. 230*

4. TODY MOTMOT (*Hylomanes momotula obscurus*). Buffy head stripes, small size, no racquet tail-tips. Local. *p. 230*

5. RUFOUS-TAILED JACAMAR (*Galbula ruficauda melogenia*). Male. Long slender bill, rufous underside of tail, glittering green underparts. Male has white throat, female buff. Western Panama and Darién. *p. 237*

6. GREAT JACAMAR (*Jacamerops aurea penardi*). Female. Heavy bill, rufous underparts. *p. 238*

7. AMAZON KINGFISHER (*Chloroceryle amazona mexicana*). Female. Fairly large size, green upperparts, little white in wings and tail. Male has rufous chest band. *p. 232*

8. AMERICAN PYGMY KINGFISHER (*Chloroceryle aenea* spp). Male. Very small size, oily green upperparts, rich rufous underparts. Female with narrow dark band across chest. *p. 233*

9. GREEN-AND-RUFOUS KINGFISHER (*Chloroceryle inda chocoensis*). Male. Essentially a larger version of Pygmy Kingfisher, but no white below. Female with dark chest band. *p. 233*

10. RINGED KINGFISHER (*Ceryle t. torquata*). Male. Large size, blue-gray upperparts, mostly rufous underparts. Female has gray chest band. *p. 231*

11. GREEN KINGFISHER (*Chloroceryle americana isthmica*). Small size, white spots on wings and tail. *p. 232*

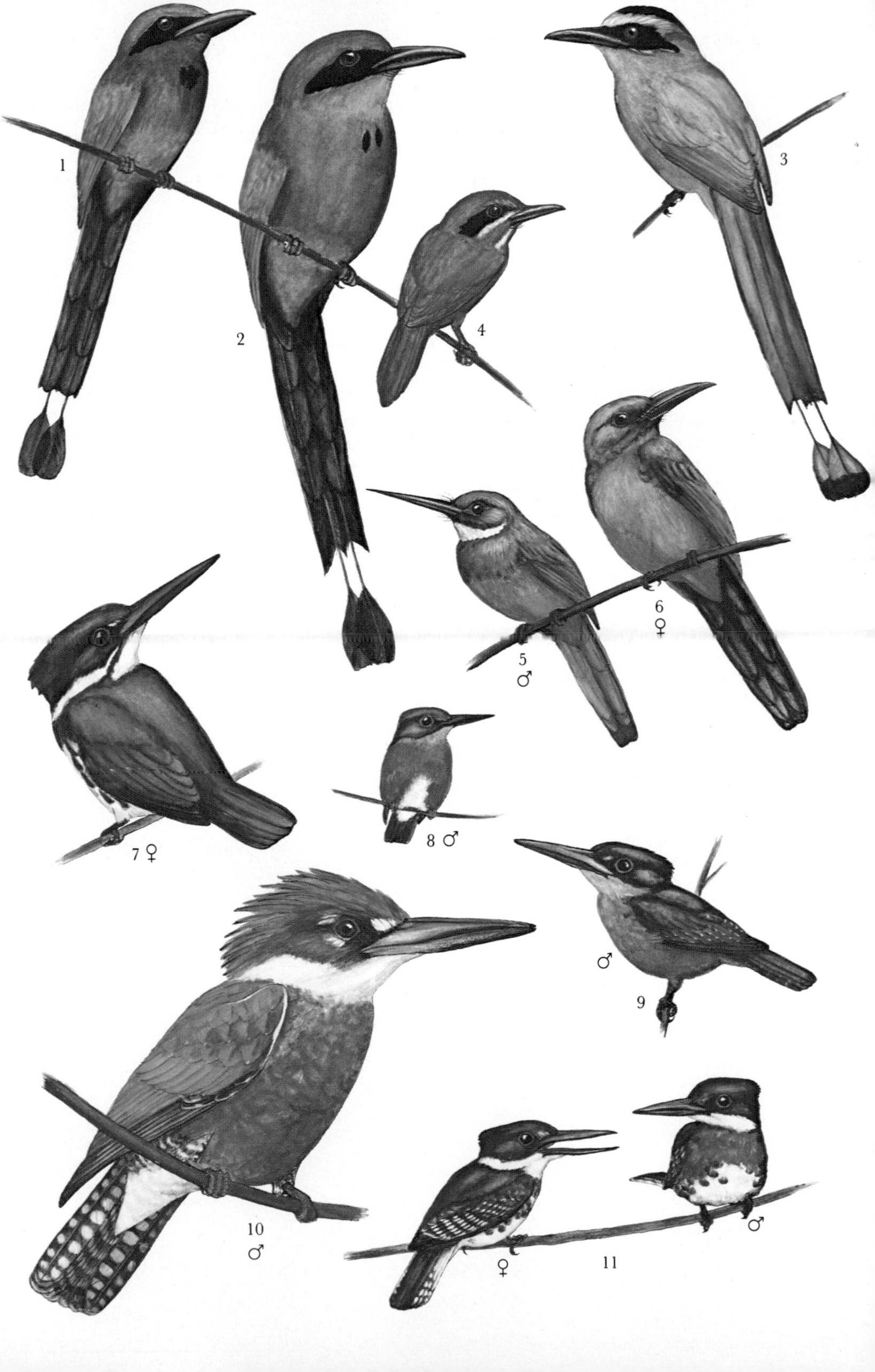
1
2
3
4
5
♂
6
♀
7 ♀
8 ♂
♂
9
10
♂
♀
11
♂

PLATE 17

PUFFBIRDS, BARBETS, TOUCANS, JAYS

1. WHITE-WHISKERED PUFFBIRD (*Malacoptila p. panamensis*). Male. Puffy and brown, white "whiskers". Female grayer above, less streaked below. Lower mandible (except for dusky tip) should be yellowish green. *p. 235*

2. GRAY-CHEEKED NUNLET (*Nonnula ruficapilla stulta*). Slender bill, gray face, rusty breast. *p. 236*

3. RED-HEADED BARBET (*Eubucco bourcierii salvini*). Male: bright red head and neck. Female: bluish sides of head, yellowish breast. Highlands. *p. 239*

4. SPOT-CROWNED BARBET (*Capito m. maculicoronatus*). Male: glossy black upperparts, yellow chest band, black and orange flanks. Female: similar to male, throat and chest also black. *p. 238*

5. PRONG-BILLED BARBET (*Semnornis frantzii*). Thick grayish bill, ochraceous head and breast. Western highlands. *p. 239*

6. EMERALD TOUCANET (*Aulacorhynchus prasinus coeruleogularis*). Mostly green plumage, blue throat. Highlands. *p. 240*

7. YELLOW-EARED TOUCANET (*Selenidera spectabilis*). Male. Yellow ear-patch, black underparts. Female has chestnut crown, lacks ear-patch. Local in humid foothills and lowlands. Bare ocular area should be yellower below eye. *p. 241*

8. CHESTNUT-MANDIBLED TOUCAN (*Ramphastos swainsonii*). Bicolored bill, yellow bib. *p. 242*

9. KEEL-BILLED TOUCAN (*Ramphastos sulfuratus brevicarinatus*). Multicolored bill, yellow bib. *p. 241*

10. COLLARED ARACARI (*Pteroglossus t. torquatus*). Black head and neck, yellow underparts with black and red. Bare ocular area should be all orange-red. Fiery-billed Aracari on Plate 44. *p. 240*

11. SILVERY-THROATED JAY (*Cyanolyca argentigula*). White throat. Chiriquí highlands. *p. 338*

12. AZURE-HOODED JAY (*Cyanolyca c. cucullata*). Pale blue crown and nape. Western highlands, mostly Caribbean slope. *p. 337*

13. BLACK-CHESTED JAY (*Cyanocorax affinis zeledoni*). Black throat and chest, white underparts and tail-tipping. *p. 337*

Note: Other puffbirds are depicted on Plate 23; White-fronted Nunbird and Brown Jay on Plate 44.

PLATE 18

WOODPECKERS

1. SPOT-BREASTED WOODPECKER (*Colaptes punctigula striatigularis*). Spotted underparts, barred back, white sides of head. Eastern Panama, rare. *p. 247*

2. RUFOUS-WINGED WOODPECKER (*Piculus simplex*). Plain olive throat, no cheek stripe, rufous on wings. Western Panama. *p. 246*

3. STRIPE-CHEEKED WOODPECKER (*Piculus callopterus*). Whitish cheek stripe, spotted throat. Foothills. *p. 246*

4. GOLDEN-GREEN WOODPECKER (*Piculus chrysochloros aurosus*). Yellow cheek stripe, boldly barred underparts, unspotted throat. Eastern Panama, rare. *p. 246*

5. GOLDEN-OLIVE WOODPECKER (*Piculus rubiginosus uropygialis*). Gray on crown, whitish sides of head, wings edged with yellow. Western foothills and highlands. *p. 247*

6. GOLDEN-NAPED WOODPECKER (*Melanerpes c. chrysauchen*). Male. Yellow forecrown and nape. Pacific western Panama. *p. 243*

7. BLACK-CHEEKED WOODPECKER (*Melanerpes p. pucherani*). Male. Black sides of head and neck, black barring on lower underparts. *p. 244*

8. RED-CROWNED WOODPECKER (*Melanerpes rubricapillus wagleri*). Male. Evenly barred upperparts, whitish sides of head and underparts. *p. 244*

9. ACORN WOODPECKER (*Melanerpes formicivorus striatipectus*). Male. Clown-like facial pattern, streaked underparts. Western highlands. *p. 243*

10. HAIRY WOODPECKER (*Picoides villosus extimus*). Male. White back stripe, dull brownish underparts. Western highlands. *p. 245*

11. RED-RUMPED WOODPECKER (*Veniliornis kirkii neglectus*). Male. Small size, red rump, barred underparts. Local. *p. 245*

12. SMOKY-BROWN WOODPECKER (*Veniliornis fumigatus sanguinolentus*). All olive brownish, small size. Foothills and highlands. *p. 245*

13. CINNAMON WOODPECKER (*Celeus loricatus mentalis*). Short bushy crest, rufous plumage, heavy black barring. *p. 247*

14. CHESTNUT-COLORED WOODPECKER (*Celeus castaneus*). Male. Long pointed crest, pale head, little black barring. Bocas del Toro. *p. 248*

15. LINEATED WOODPECKER (*Dryocopus lineatus mesorhynchus*). Large size, parallel white back stripes, black facial stripe. *p. 248*

16. CRIMSON-CRESTED WOODPECKER (*Campephilus melanoleucos malherbii*). Large size, white back stripes converging in "V", white at base of blackish bill. *p. 248*

17. PALE-BILLED WOODPECKER (*Campephilus g. guatemalensis*). Large size, whitish bill, white back stripes almost converging in "V". Bocas del Toro and Chiriquí. *p. 249*

18. CRIMSON-BELLIED WOODPECKER (*Campephilus haematogaster splendens*). Male. Large size, mostly crimson underparts, buff facial stripe. Rare. *p. 248*

PLATE 19

WOODCREEPERS, PICULET

1. OLIVACEOUS PICULET (*Picumnus o. olivaceus*). Male. Tiny size, spotted crown. *p. 243*
2. RUDDY WOODCREEPER (*Dendrocincla homochroa ruficeps*). Uniform rufous brown, brightest on crown. *p. 259*
3. TAWNY-WINGED WOODCREEPER (*Dendrocincla anabatina saturata*). Dull olive brown generally, contrasting tawny flight feathers. Chiriquí. *p. 258*
4. PLAIN-BROWN WOODCREEPER (*Dendrocincla fuliginosa ridgwayi*). Dull brown overall with no spotting or streaking, dusky moustache. *p. 258*
5. OLIVACEOUS WOODCREEPER (*Sittasomus griseicapillus veraguensis*). Grayish head and underparts. *p. 259*
6. WEDGE-BILLED WOODCREEPER (*Glyphorhynchus spirurus sublestus*). Small size, short wedge-shaped bill. *p. 260*
7. SPOT-CROWNED WOODCREEPER (*Lepidocolaptes affinis neglectus*). Spotted crown, slender decurved bill. Chiriquí highlands. *p. 263*
8. STREAK-HEADED WOODCREEPER (*Lepidocolaptes souleyetii lineaticeps*). Streaked crown, pale slender decurved bill. *p. 262*
9. BUFF-THROATED WOODCREEPER (*Xiphorhynchus guttatus nanus*). Rather long straight dark bill, buffy throat. Most widespread and frequently encountered woodcreeper. *p. 262*
10. LONG-TAILED WOODCREEPER (*Deconychura longicauda darienensis*). Long tail, eye-stripe and eye-ring (see text). *p. 259*
11. SPOTTED WOODCREEPER (*Xiphorhynchus erythropygius insolitus*). Spotted underparts. Foothills and lower highlands. *p. 262*
12. STRAIGHT-BILLED WOODCREEPER (*Xiphorhynchus picus extimus*). Straight whitish bill, white sides of head and throat. Mangroves, mostly Pacific slope. *p. 261*
13. STRONG-BILLED WOODCREEPER (*Xiphocolaptes promeropirhynchus costaricensis*). Very large size, heavy bill. Western foothills, rare. Usually shows more prominent dark malar than depicted. *p. 260*
14. BLACK-BANDED WOODCREEPER (*Dendrocolaptes picumnus costaricensis*). Large size, barred lower underparts. Western highlands, rare. *p. 261*
15. BARRED WOODCREEPER (*Dendrocolaptes certhia nigrirostris*). Large size, generally barred appearance. *p. 261*
16. BLACK-STRIPED WOODCREEPER (*Xiphorhynchus l. lachrymosus*). Boldly striped appearance. *p. 262*
17. RED-BILLED SCYTHEBILL (*Campylorhamphus trochilirostris brevipennis*). Very long decurved reddish bill. Central and eastern Panama. *p. 263*
18. BROWN-BILLED SCYTHEBILL (*Campylorhamphus pusillus borealis*). Very long decurved dark bill (though often not as dark as protrayed), blackish head. Foothills, lower highlands. *p. 264*

PLATE 20

LOWLAND FURNARIIDS, ANTSHRIKES

1. PALE-BREASTED SPINETAIL (*Synallaxis albescens latitabunda*). Long pointed tail, rufous hindcrown and wing-coverts, whitish underparts. Pacific savannas. *p. 250*

2. SLATY SPINETAIL (*Synallaxis brachyura nigrifumosa*). Very dark overall, with slaty underparts, rufous hindcrown and wing-coverts; long pointed tail. Local. *p. 250*

3. COIBA SPINETAIL (*Cranioleuca dissita*). Coiba Island only. Rufous upperparts, buffy eye-stripe. Arboreal. *p. 250*

4. PLAIN XENOPS (*Xenops minutus ridgwayi*). Short upturned bill, silvery cheek stripe. See text for Streaked Xenops. *p. 256*

5. STRIPED WOODHAUNTER (*Hyloctistes subulatus virgatus*). Streaked upper back and breast, buffy throat, chestnut wings and tail (see text). Local. *p. 253*

6. SLATY-WINGED FOLIAGE-GLEANER (*Philydor fuscipennis erythronotus*). Tawny eye-stripe and underparts, contrasting dusky wings. Especially foothills. *p. 254*

7. BUFF-THROATED FOLIAGE-GLEANER (*Automolus ochrolaemus pallidigularis*). Buff eye-stripe and narrow eye-ring, pale throat, no streaking. *p. 255*

8. SCALY-THROATED LEAFTOSSER (*Sclerurus g. guatemalensis*). Mostly dark brown, whitish scaly-looking throat. *p. 257*

9. TAWNY-THROATED LEAFTOSSER (*Sclerurus mexicanus andinus*). Tawny throat and chest, rufous rump. *p. 257*

10. RUSSET ANTSHRIKE (*Thamnistes anabatinus coronatus*). Heavy hooked bill, buffy eye-stripe and underparts, rufous wings and tail. Especially foothills. *p. 267*

11. BLACK-HOODED ANTSHRIKE (*Thamnophilus bridgesi*). Male: mostly black, slaty belly, white on wing-coverts. Female: lightly streaked head and throat, brown upperparts, Pacific western Panama. *p. 266*

12. BARRED ANTSHRIKE (*Thamnophilus doliatus nigricristatus*). Male: broad black and white barring, yellow eye. Female: rufous upperparts, buffy underparts, yellow eye. *p. 265*

13. SLATY ANTSHRIKE (*Thamnophilus punctatus atrinucha*). Male: mostly slaty gray, black crown, much white on wing. Female: olive brown upperparts, much buff on wing. *p. 266*

14. GREAT ANTSHRIKE (*Taraba major melanocrissus*). Male: black and white, red eye. Female: rufous brown and white, red eye. *p. 265*

15. FASCIATED ANTSHRIKE (*Cymbilaimus lineatus fasciatus*). Male: narrow black and white barring, red eye. Female: narrow buff and dark brown barring, red eye. *p. 265*

Note: Ruddy Foliage-gleaner is depicted on Plate 45.

PLATE 21

ANTWRENS, ANTBIRDS

1. RUFOUS-RUMPED ANTWREN (*Terenura c. callinota*). Male. Rufous rump, gray sides of head and throat, yellow lower underparts. Foothills and highlands, local. Female duller. *p. 271*

2. PLAIN ANTVIREO (*Dysithamnus mentalis septentrionalis*). Male: chunky, big-headed, mostly gray, yellowish belly. Female: russet crown. Foothills and lower highlands. *p. 267*

3. SPOT-CROWNED ANTVIREO (*Dysithamnus p. puncticeps*). Crown with white (male) or tawny (female) spots. Iris pale gray or creamy. *p. 268*

4. STREAKED ANTWREN (*Myrmotherula surinamensis pacifica*). Male: streaked black and white. Female: bright tawny head and underparts. *p. 269*

5. PYGMY ANTWREN (*Myrmotherula brachyura ignota*). Male. Tiny size, streaked upperparts, pale yellow underparts. Canal area east. Female buffier below. *p. 268*

6. SLATY ANTWREN (*Myrmotherula s. schisticolor*). Male: slaty, black throat. Female: dull tawny underparts, no wing-spotting. Especially foothills. *p. 270*

7. CHECKER-THROATED ANTWREN (*Myrmotherula f. fulviventris*). Male: checkered throat. Female: uniform buffy underparts, pale eye. *p. 269*

8. WHITE-FLANKED ANTWREN (*Myrmotherula axillaris albigula*). Male: black, white flank tuft. Female: whitish throat and flanks, dark eye. *p. 269*

9. DOT-WINGED ANTWREN (*Microrhopias quixensis virgata*). Male: white on wing, tipping on rather long tail. Female: rufous underparts, wings and tail as in male. *p. 270*

10. DUSKY ANTBIRD (*Cercomacra tyrannina rufiventris*). Male: uniform gray (blacker in western Panama). Female: uniform tawny underparts. *p. 272*

11. IMMACULATE ANTBIRD (*Myrmeciza immaculata berlepschi*). Female. Chocolate brown, large bare blue ocular area. Local in foothills. Male (all black) shown on Plate 22. *p. 274*

12. BARE-CROWNED ANTBIRD (*Gymnocichla n. nudiceps*). Male: bare bright blue crown and orbital area. Female: bright rufous underparts, bare blue orbital skin. *p. 272*

13. JET ANTBIRD (*Cercomacra nigricans*). Male: black, much white on wings and tail (see text). Female: streaking on throat and chest (variable in extent). *p. 272*

PLATE 22

ANTBIRDS, ANTTHRUSHES, ANTPITTAS

1. IMMACULATE ANTBIRD (*Myrmeciza immaculata berlepschi*). Large bare blue ocular area. Male: all black. Female: mostly chocolate brown. Local, mainly foothills. *p. 274*

2. CHESTNUT-BACKED ANTBIRD (*Myrmeciza exsul*). a) Nominate: Male: bare blue ocular area, black head and underparts. Female: like male but duller, brown below. Central Panama (with similar forms in west). b) *Cassini*: Male. Like above but with white spots on wing-coverts. Female has rufous on breast. Eastern Panama. *p. 273*

3. DULL-MANTLED ANTBIRD (*Myrmeciza l. laemosticta*). No bare blue orbital area, red eye, more chestnut above. Uncommon. *p. 274*

4. WHITE-BELLIED ANTBIRD (*Myrmeciza longipes panamensis*). Male: black throat and chest, white belly. Female: like male, but throat and chest buffyish. Mostly Pacific slope. *p. 273*

5. SPOTTED ANTBIRD (*Hylophylax n. naevioides*). Small size, bright color and pattern. Male: with black-spotted breast. Female: browner. *p. 275*

6. OCELLATED ANTBIRD (*Phaenostictus m. mcleannani*). Ornate pattern with large bright blue ocular area, spotting below. *p. 276*

7. BICOLORED ANTBIRD (*Gymnopithys leucaspis bicolor*). Truly "bicolored" (basically brown above, white below). *p. 276*

8. WING-BANDED ANTBIRD (*Myrmornis torquata stictoptera*). Very short tail, three buff wing-bands. Local in humid forest. *p. 275*

9. BLACK-FACED ANTTHRUSH (*Formicarius analis panamensis*). Crake-like shape, contrasting black face and throat. Widespread. *p. 276*

10. RUFOUS-BREASTED ANTTHRUSH (*Formicarius rufipectus carrikeri*). Chestnut crown and breast. Very local, foothills. *p. 277*

11. BLACK-HEADED ANTTHRUSH (*Formicarius n. nigricapillus*). Entire head to breast black. Local, foothills. *p. 277*

12. SCALED ANTPITTA (*Grallaria guatimalensis princeps*). Large size and tail-less shape, scaly look above, malar streak. Scarce, foothills and highlands. *p. 278*

13. BLACK-CROWNED ANTPITTA (*Pittasoma m. michleri*). Male. Large size and long legs, black crown, boldly scalloped underparts (less prominent in female). Uncommon and local, humid forest. *p. 278*

14. OCHRE-BREASTED ANTPITTA (*Grallaricula costaricensis brevis*). Very small size, ochraceous overall, yellow bill. Local in foothills. *p. 279*

15. FULVOUS-BELLIED ANTPITTA (*Hylopezus dives barbacoae*). Like Spectacled but no eye-ring or wing-spots, much more buff and rufous below. Only Bocas del Toro and Darién. *p. 279*

16. SPECTACLED ANTPITTA (*Hylopezus p. perspicillatus*). Plump tail-less shape, buff eye-ring and spots on wing-coverts, streaking below. Widespread, lowland forest. *p. 278*

PLATE 23

PUFFBIRDS, LARGE TYRANT FLYCATCHERS

1. WHITE-NECKED PUFFBIRD (*Notharchus macrorhynchus hyperrhynchus*). Large size, white foreneck and forehead. *p. 234*

2. BLACK-BREASTED PUFFBIRD (*Notharchus pectoralis*). Moderate size, glossy blue-black color, white ear-patch. Central and eastern Panama. *p. 234*

3. PIED PUFFBIRD (*Notharchus tectus subtectus*). Small size, narrow breast band, white on scapulars. *p. 235*

4. FORK-TAILED FLYCATCHER (*Tyrannus savanna monacha*). Long deeply forked tail, black head (see Scissor-tailed Flycatcher on Plate 46). *p. 316*

5. SIRYSTES (*Sirystes sibilator albogriseus*). Mainly gray and white, blackish head, white-tipped tail. Forest canopy. *p. 308*

6. TROPICAL KINGBIRD (*Tyrannus melancholicus chloronotus*). Gray head, olive breast, notched tail. Very common. *p. 314*

7. GRAY KINGBIRD (*Tyrannus d. dominicensis*). Gray above with dusky ear-patch, whitish below, slightly forked tail. *p. 315*

8. EASTERN KINGBIRD (*Tyrannus tyrannus*). White-tipped tail (*not* notched or forked), blackish head. *p. 315*

9. GREAT CRESTED FLYCATCHER (*Myiarchus crinitus*). Rufous edging on wings and tail; distinctive call. *p. 309*

10. PANAMA FLYCATCHER (*Myiarchus panamensis*). Like preceding but lacking the rufous. *p. 309*

11. GRAY-CAPPED FLYCATCHER (*Myiozetetes g. granadensis*). Gray crown, short white superciliary. *p. 311*

12. SOCIAL FLYCATCHER (*Myiozetetes similis columbianus*). Wing-bars faint but present (often more obvious than shown), no rufous on wings, dusky ear-coverts. Very common. *p. 311*

13. RUSTY-MARGINED FLYCATCHER (*Myiozetetes cayanensis harterti*). Rufous edging on flight feathers (*no* wing-bars), blackish ear-coverts; distinctive calls. Especially near water, more numerous eastward. *p. 310*

14. WHITE-RINGED FLYCATCHER (*Conopias albovittata*). Rather like Social but with longer bill, blacker ear-coverts, broad white superciliary encircling hindneck. Forest canopy. *p. 311*

15. GREAT KISKADEE (*Pitangus sulphuratus guatimalensis*). Rather large size, quite brown upperparts, rufous in wings and tail. Mainly Bocas del Toro and central Panama, still spreading. *p. 310*

16. LESSER KISKADEE (*Philohydor lictor panamensis*). Much like Rusty-margined but with long slender bill; different calls. Near water in central and eastern Panama. *p. 309*

17. DARK PEWEE (*Contopus lugubris*). Uniform and dark, obviously crested. Chiriquí highlands. *p. 299*

18. OLIVE-SIDED FLYCATCHER (*Contopus borealis*). "Vested" look below, white flank patch, short tail. *p. 299*

19. BOAT-BILLED FLYCATCHER (*Megarhynchus pitangua mexicanus*). Very heavy bill, more olive upperparts (no rufous) than Great Kiskadee. *p. 310*

20. GOLDEN-BELLIED FLYCATCHER (*Myiodynastes hemichrysus*). Dusky moustache, vague olive breast streaking. Western highlands, foothills. *p. 312*

21. STREAKED FLYCATCHER (*Myiodynastes maculatus difficilis*). Streaky effect overall, rufous tail (compare to next species). *p. 313*

22. SULPHUR-BELLIED FLYCATCHER (*Myiodynastes luteiventris*). Resembles preceding; belly yellower, dusky chin, whitish edging on wing-coverts. Uncommon migrant. *p. 313*

Continued over

23

Gwynne
1-87

PLATE 24

MID-SIZED TYRANT FLYCATCHERS

1. BLACK-TAILED FLYCATCHER (*Myiobius a. atricaudatus*). Conspicuous yellow rump, mostly yellowish underparts. *p. 298*

2. SULPHUR-RUMPED FLYCATCHER (*Myiobius barbatus aureatus*). Conspicuous yellow rump, tawny chest and sides. *p. 297*

3. YELLOW-MARGINED FLYCATCHER (*Tolmomyias assimilis flavotectus*). White eye-ring and short supraloral, prominent wing-edging. Usually shows dark iris; has pale speculum at base of primaries. Mostly canopy of humid forest. *p. 295*

4. YELLOW-OLIVE FLYCATCHER (*Tolmomyias sulphurescens flavoolivaceus*). Very like preceding; more prominent wing-bars, usually a pale iris. Mostly lighter woodland. *pp. 295, 455*

5. FOREST ELAENIA (*Myiopagis gaimardii macilivainii*). Yellow crown patch, prominent wing-bars and edging, short bill. Central and eastern Panama, especially canopy and borders of humid forest. *p. 285*

6. GREENISH ELAENIA (*Myiopagis viridicata accola*). Very like preceding, but lacks wing-bars (see text). *p. 285*

7. TROPICAL PEWEE (*Contopus cinereus brachytarsus*). Grayish white lores. Closely resembles the two wood-pewees (see Plate 32), and often best identified by voice. *p. 301*

8. YELLOW-BELLIED ELAENIA (*Elaenia flavogaster pallidorsalis*). Upstanding crest showing white, yellow lower underparts. *p. 286*

9. LESSER ELAENIA (*Elaenia c. chiriquensis*). Resembles preceding, but only slight crest shows (with only a little white), less contrast on underparts (see text). *p. 286*

10. MOUNTAIN ELAENIA (*Elaenia f. frantzii*). Very like Lesser Elaenia, but usually showing eye-ring and with rounded head (white not showing), underparts quite uniform (see text). Western highlands. *p. 287*

11. NORTHERN SCRUB-FLYCATCHER (*Sublegatus a. arenarum*). Short bill, supraloral stripe, contrast on underparts. *p. 284*

12. DUSKY-CAPPED FLYCATCHER (*Myiarchus tuberculifer brunneiceps*). Contrasting blackish cap. *p. 308*

13. PANAMA FLYCATCHER (*Myiarchus panamensis*). No rufous in wings or tail except in immatures. See Great Crested Flycatcher (Plate 23). *p. 309*

14. ROYAL FLYCATCHER (*Onychorhynchus coronatus fraterculus*). Hammerhead effect (bright-colored fan-shaped crest rarely showing), ochraceous rump and basal half of tail. *p. 296*

15. BROWNISH TWISTWING (*Cnipodectes subbrunneus panamensis*). Overall brown appearance, rump and tail more rufous (see text). Wing-lifts. Iris often brighter orange than shown. Central and eastern Panama. *p. 293*

16. OLIVE-STRIPED FLYCATCHER (*Mionectes olivaceus hederaceus*). Dark appearance, conspicuous light eye-spot, streaked underparts. *p. 288*

17. OLIVACEOUS FLATBILL (*Rhynchocyclus olivaceus bardus*). Broad flat bill, yellowish wing-bars and edging. Central and eastern Panama. *p. 294*

18. EYE-RINGED FLATBILL (*Rhynchocyclus b. brevirostris*). Resembles previous species, but with more conspicuous eye-ring, no wing-bars, darker olive throat and chest. *p. 294*

Note: Ochraceous Pewee is depicted on Plate 46.

PLATE 23 *continued from previous page*

23. PIRATIC FLYCATCHER (*Legatus l. leucophaius*). Short bill, breast streaking, long white eye-stripe, no rufous in tail. *p. 313*

Note: Other puffbirds are depicted on Plate 17; Black Phoebe on Plate 46.

PLATE 25

SMALL TYRANT FLYCATCHERS

1. RUDDY-TAILED FLYCATCHER (*Terenotriccus erythrurus fulvigularis*). Very small size; cinnamon-rufous underparts, wings, and tail. *p. 297*

2. NORTHERN BENTBILL (*Oncostoma cinereigulare*). Like next species, but throat and chest grayish white. Western Panama. *p. 292*

3. SOUTHERN BENTBILL (*Oncostoma olivaceum*). Bent downward bill, yellowish olive underparts. Central and eastern Panama. *p. 292*

4. MOUSE-COLORED TYRANNULET (*Phaeomyias murina eremonoma*). Drab appearance, pale lower mandible, buffyish wing-bars (see text). Pacific western Panama. *p. 284*

5. BLACK-CAPPED PYGMY-TYRANT (*Myiornis atricapillus*). Minute with very short tail, black cap, mostly whitish underparts. *p. 291*

6. BROWN-CAPPED TYRANNULET (*Ornithion brunneicapillum*). Very small size, brown cap, conspicuous white eye-stripe. *p. 283*

7. PALE-EYED PYGMY-TYRANT (*Atalotriccus pilaris wilcoxi*). Pale eye, olive crown, slender bill (should show brownish chest streaking). *p. 291*

8. OCHRE-BELLIED FLYCATCHER (*Mionectes oleagineus parcus*). Uniform olive upperparts, mostly ochraceous below. Wing-lifts. *p. 288*

9. PALTRY TYRANNULET (*Zimmerius vilissimus parvus*). Slaty cap, conspicuous wing-edging (but no bars), pale grayish underparts. *p. 282*

10. BLACK-HEADED TODY-FLYCATCHER (*Todirostrum nigriceps*). Very small size with short tail, black head contrasting with green back, white throat. *p. 293*

11. COMMON TODY-FLYCATCHER (*Todirostrum cinereum finitum*). Broad bill, slaty head with no contrast, pale eye, all yellow underparts. *p. 293*

12. SLATE-HEADED TODY-FLYCATCHER (*Todirostrum sylvia schistaceiceps*). Slaty head and nape, white supraloral stripe, yellow wing-bars and edging, pale grayish underparts (see text). *p. 292*

13. WHITE-FRONTED TYRANNULET (*Phyllomyias z. zeledoni*). White forehead and eye-stripe, prominent wing-bars. Chiriquí highlands. *p. 282*

14. SOUTHERN BEARDLESS-TYRANNULET (*Camptostoma obsoletum flaviventre*). Brownish crown, narrow whitish eye-stripe, mostly yellow underparts (see text). *p. 283*

15. YELLOW-GREEN TYRANNULET (*Phylloscartes flavovirens*). White eye-ring, yellow wing-bars, all yellow underparts. Local, central and eastern Panama. *p. 289*

16. SEPIA-CAPPED FLYCATCHER (*Leptopogon amaurocephalus faustus*). Brownish cap, dusky patch on ear-coverts. Local, mostly Pacific slope (see Plate 46 for Slaty-capped Flycatcher of foothills). Wing lifts. *p. 288*

17. BRAN-COLORED FLYCATCHER (*Myiophobus fasciatus furfurosus*). Brown upperparts, blurry breast streaking, *Empidonax* size and shape. *p. 298*

18. COMMON TUFTED-FLYCATCHER (*Mitrephanes phaeocercus vividus*). Pointed crest. Foothills and highlands. *p. 299*

19. SCALE-CRESTED PYGMY-TYRANT (*Lophotriccus pileatus luteiventris*). Black and rufous crest (usually laid flat). Foothills and lower highlands. *p. 291*

20. GOLDEN-CROWNED SPADEBILL (*Platyrinchus coronatus superciliaris*). Very small and stubby, wide flat bill, cinnamon-rufous in crown, black facial patches. Lowland forest (see Plate 45 for White-throated Spadebill of foothills and highlands). *p. 296*

21. YELLOW-CROWNED TYRANNULET (*Tyrannulus elatus panamensis*). Slaty crown, yellow crown patch (often visible), grayish sides of head and throat (see text). *p. 284*

Continued over

PLATE 26

BECARDS, TITYRAS, COTINGAS, ETC.

1. WHITE-WINGED BECARD (*Pachyramphus polychopterus similis*). Male: black back, broad white scapular stripe, dark gray underparts. Female: buffy wing-bars and edging, brownish crown. *p. 317*

2. BLACK-AND-WHITE BECARD (*Pachyramphus albogriseus ornatus*). Male: gray back contrasting with black cap, white supraloral stripe, pale gray underparts. Female: chestnut cap, white eye-stripe. Western Panama, rare. *p. 317*

3. ONE-COLORED BECARD (*Pachyramphus h. homochrous*). Male: uniform blackish and slaty gray. Female: no supraloral stripe, upperparts rufous-tawny (including crown), pale buffy underparts (see text). Eastern Panama. *p. 318*

4. BARRED BECARD (*Pachyramphus versicolor panamensis*). Male: yellowish sides of head and throat, lightly barred underparts. Female: much rufous on wings, barring below. Chiriquí highlands. *p. 316*

5. CINEREOUS BECARD (*Pachyramphus rufus*). Male: pale gray back, white underparts. Female: crown darker than back (see text). Canal area east, rare. *p. 316*

6. CINNAMON BECARD (*Pachyramphus c. cinnamomeus*). Pale supraloral stripe, grayish lores (sexes similar). *p. 317*

7. BRIGHT-RUMPED ATTILA (*Attila spadiceus sclateri*). Bull-headed look, hooked bill, yellow rump (usually), streaked underparts. *p. 307*

8. PURPLE-THROATED FRUITCROW (*Querula purpurata*). Male. Purple throat (lacking in female), otherwise black. *p. 323*

9. SPECKLED MOURNER (*Laniocera r. rufescens*). Spotting on wing-coverts, faintly scalloped breast. Usually shows more of a buffy yellowish eye-ring. *p. 307*

10. RUFOUS MOURNER (*Rhytipterna h. holerythra*). Uniform rufous brown. Bill should be blacker. *p. 307*

11. RUFOUS PIHA (*Lipaugus u. unirufus*). Very similar to preceding. Somewhat larger and stockier with rounder head, somewhat stouter bill showing pale at base, throat relatively pale. *p. 320*

12. BLUE COTINGA (*Cotinga nattererii*). Male: shining turquoise blue, distinctive shape. Female: generally spotted and scaled. Central and eastern Panama (see Plate 45 for Turquoise and Lovely Cotingas of far western Panama). *p. 321*

13. THREE-WATTLED BELLBIRD (*Procnias tricarunculata*). Male: three hanging wattles, white head and neck. Female: streaked underparts, olive appearance, fairly large size. Western highlands. *p. 324*

14. MASKED TITYRA (*Tityra semifasciata costaricensis*). Bare red ocular area and bill. Male mostly white, female with brown on upperparts. *p. 319*

15. BLACK-CROWNED TITYRA (*Tityra inquisitor fraserii*). Black crown and bill, female with chestnut sides of head. *p. 319*

Note: Rose-throated Becard and Sharpbill are depicted on Plate 45.

PLATE 25 *continued from previous page*

22. YELLOW TYRANNULET (*Capsiempis flaveola semiflava*). Overall yellow appearance. *p. 289*

23. YELLOWISH FLYCATCHER (*Empidonax f. flavescens*). Mostly rich yellow underparts, conspicuous yellow eye-ring. Western highlands. *p. 304*

24. BLACK-CAPPED FLYCATCHER (*Empidonax atriceps*). Contrasting black cap. Western Chiriquí highlands. *p. 304*

Note: Arcadian Flycatcher is depicted on Plate 32; Rufous-browed Tyrannulet, White-throated Flycatcher, and Torrent Tyrannulet on Plate 46.

26

PLATE 27

MANAKINS, TAPACULO

1. BLUE-CROWNED MANAKIN (*Pipra coronata minuscula*). Male: blue crown. Female: mostly green (not olive). *p. 329*
2. RED-CAPPED MANAKIN (*Pipra mentalis ignifera*). Male: red head. Female: olive, brownish legs. *p. 330*
3. GOLDEN-HEADED MANAKIN (*Pipra e. erythrocephala*). Male. Orange-yellow head. Female see text. Eastern Panama. *p. 329*
4. GOLDEN-COLLARED MANAKIN (*Manacus vitellinus*). a) Central and eastern Panama (nominate *vitellinus*): Male with bright golden collar and throat, both sexes with orange-red legs (should be brighter). b) Bocas del Toro (*cerritus*): Yellow extends to back in male. *p. 327*
5. ORANGE-COLLARED MANAKIN (*Manacus aurantiacus*). Male. Orange collar and throat (female like female Golden-collared). Pacific western Panama. *p. 327*
6. LANCE-TAILED MANAKIN (*Chiroxiphia lanceolata*). Male: blue-black, red crown. Female: projecting central tail feathers, orange-red legs. Mostly Pacific slope. *p. 328*
7. WHITE-CROWNED MANAKIN (*Pipra pipra anthracina*). Male: white crown and hindneck. Female: bluish gray cap and hindneck (iris usually redder). Western foothills, rare. *p. 328*
8. WHITE-RUFFED MANAKIN (*Corapipo a. altera*). Male: white bib. Female: grayish throat. Foothills and lower highlands. *p. 328*
9. BROAD-BILLED SAPAYOA (*Sapayoa aenigma*). Male. Uniform olive above, olive yellowish below, broad bill. Central and eastern Panama, uncommon. *p. 325*
10. THRUSH-LIKE MOURNER (*Schiffornis turdinus*). a) *Dumicola* (foothills): Uniform dark olive brown (see also Plate 45). b) *Panamensis* (lowlands of Central and eastern Panama): More rufescent generally, grayish belly. *p. 325*
11. SILVERY-FRONTED TAPACULO (*Scytalopus a. argentifrons*). Male: dark slaty gray, silvery forehead and eye-stripe (sometimes reduced or lacking). Female: browner, no silvery (see text). Western highlands; other tapaculos in Darién highlands (see text). *p. 280*

Note: White-collared Manakin is depicted on Plate 45.

27

PLATE 28

WRENS

1. PLAIN WREN (*Thryothorus modestus elutus*). Mostly whitish underparts, indistinct wing and tail barring. Western and central Panama. *p. 343*
2. BUFF-BREASTED WREN (*Thryothorus leucotis galbraithii*). Rather buffy underparts, prominent wing and tail barring. Central and eastern Panama. *p. 343*
3. HOUSE WREN (*Troglodytes aedon inquietus*). Dull brownish, no distinctive markings. *p. 343*
4. OCHRACEOUS WREN (*Troglodytes ochraceus ligea*). Bright brown, buffy eye-stripe and underparts. Highlands. *p. 344*
5. TIMBERLINE WREN (*Thryorchilus b. browni*). White eye-stripe, white on wings. High on Volcán Barú, Chiriquí. *p. 345*
6. RUFOUS-AND-WHITE WREN (*Thryothorus rufalbus castanonotus*). Bright rufous upperparts, white underparts. Mostly Pacific slope. *p. 342*
7. RUFOUS-BREASTED WREN (*Thryothorus rutilus hyperythrus*). Streaked sides of head and throat, bright rufous breast, unbarred wings. *p. 342*
8. BAY WREN (*Thryothorus nigricapillus costaricensis*). Black crown and nape, chestnut underparts. Western and central Panama (in eastern Panama, see Plate 40). *p. 341*
9. BLACK-BELLIED WREN (*Thryothorus fasciatoventris albigularis*). White throat and breast, contrasting black belly. *p. 340*
10. WHITE-BREASTED WOOD-WREN (*Henicorhina leucosticta darienensis*). Small size with very short tail, mostly white underparts. *p. 345*
11. GRAY-BREASTED WOOD-WREN (*Henicorhina leucophrys collina*). Mostly gray underparts. Highlands. *p. 345*
12. STRIPE-BREASTED WREN (*Thryothorus thoracicus*). Streaked underparts. Western Caribbean slope. *p. 342*
13. BLACK-THROATED WREN (*Thryothorus atrogularis*). Black throat and chest, otherwise mostly chestnut. Bocas del Toro. *p. 340*
14. RIVERSIDE WREN (*Thryothorus semibadius*). Boldly barred underparts. Chiriquí. *p. 341*
15. SOUTHERN NIGHTINGALE-WREN (*Microcerculus marginatus luscinia*). Dark and unpatterned; long bill, short tail. Near ground in humid forest. *p. 346*
16. SONG WREN (*Cyphorhinus phaeocephalus lawrencii*). Chestnut sides of head, throat, and chest; bare blue ocular area. *p. 346*
17. WHITE-HEADED WREN (*Campylorhynchus albobrunneus*). Large size, white head and underparts. Central and eastern Panama. *p. 339*
18. BAND-BACKED WREN (*Campylorhynchus zonatus costaricensis*). Banded upperparts, mostly spotted underparts, large size. Western Caribbean slope. *p. 339*

PLATE 29

WRENTHRUSH, SILKY-FLYCATCHERS, THRUSHES

1. WRENTHRUSH (*Zeledonia coronata*). Plump with short tail, tawny crown, gray underparts. Western highlands. *p. 384*
2. BLACK-AND-YELLOW SILKY-FLYCATCHER (*Phainoptila melanoxantha*). Male: black head and upperparts, yellow sides. Female: black cap, yellow sides. Western highlands. *p. 358*
3. LONG-TAILED SILKY-FLYCATCHER (*Ptilogonys caudatus*). Male. Sleek and bluish gray with long tail, yellowish crest; female more olivaceous. Chiriquí highlands. *p. 359*
4. BLACK-FACED SOLITAIRE (*Myadestes melanops*). Slaty gray overall, white wing-band, orange bill and legs. Western highlands. See Plate 40 for Varied Solitaire of Darién. *p. 350*
5. ORANGE-BILLED NIGHTINGALE-THRUSH (*Catharus aurantiirostris russatus*). Gray head, brown back, orange bill and legs. Western foothills and lower highlands. *p. 351*
6. RUDDY-CAPPED NIGHTINGALE-THRUSH (*Catharus frantzii wetmorei*). Ruddy cap, brown upperparts. Chiriquí highlands. *p. 351*
7. BLACK-BILLED NIGHTINGALE-THRUSH (*Catharus gracilirostris accentor*). Dark bill and legs, mostly gray head and underparts. Chiriquí mountains. *p. 351*
8. SLATY-BACKED NIGHTINGALE-THRUSH (*Catharus fuscater hellmayri*). Mostly slaty, white eye, orange bill and legs. Foothills and lower highlands. *p. 352*
9. BLACK-HEADED NIGHTINGALE-THRUSH (*Catharus mexicanus fumosus*). Black head, brownish olive upperparts, dark eye. Western foothills, mostly Caribbean slope. *p. 352*
10. PALE-VENTED THRUSH (*Turdus o. obsoletus*). Dark bill, white lower belly and vent. Foothills and lower highlands. *p. 354*
11. SOOTY THRUSH (*Turdus nigrescens*). Sooty brown and blackish, white eye, orange bill and legs. Chiriquí mountains. *p. 354*
12. MOUNTAIN THRUSH (*Turdus p. plebejus*). Dull uniform brown, dark bill. Western highlands. *p. 354*
13. WHITE-THROATED THRUSH (*Turdus albicollis cnephosus*). White throat (with dusky streaks) and upper chest. Foothills and lower highlands. *p. 355*
14. CLAY-COLORED THRUSH (*Turdus grayi casius*). Light-colored bill, sandy brown overall. *p. 355*

Note: Northern migrant thrushes (Wood, Swainson's, Gray-cheeked, and Veery) are depicted on Plate 31.

PLATE 30

GNATCATCHERS, VIREOS, ETC.

1. TROPICAL GNATCATCHER (*Polioptila plumbea bilineata*). Slender and long-tailed; bluish gray upperparts with black crown in male, all-white underparts. *p. 349*
2. SLATE-THROATED GNATCATCHER (*Polioptila schistaceigula*). Dark slaty throat, chest, and upperparts. Eastern Panama, rare. *p. 349*
3. TAWNY-FACED GNATWREN (*Microbates cinereiventris semitorquatus*). Tawny face, black streaks across chest, short tail. *p. 348*
4. LONG-BILLED GNATWREN (*Ramphocaenus melanurus rufiventris*). Long straight bill, long tail often cocked, cinnamon-buffy sides of head and underparts. *p. 348*
5. RUFOUS-BROWED PEPPERSHRIKE (*Cyclarhis gujanensis perrygoi*). Heavy hooked bill, rufous eye-stripe (Chiriquí birds duller). *p. 366*
6. YELLOW-BROWED SHRIKE-VIREO (*Smaragdolanius eximius*). Like next species, but with yellow eye-stripe, entire crown and nape blue. Darién. *p. 365*
7. GREEN SHRIKE-VIREO (*Smaragdolanius pulchellus viridiceps*). Stout hooked bill, brilliant green upperparts, yellow throat. *p. 365*
8. YELLOW-GREEN VIREO (*Vireo f. flavoviridis*). Yellow sides and crissum, gray crown, white eye-stripe. See similar Red-eyed Vireo on Plate 31. *p. 362*
9. YELLOW-WINGED VIREO (*Vireo carmioli*). Yellow spectacles, broad yellow wing-bars. Chiriquí highlands. *p. 361*
10. BROWN-CAPPED VIREO (*Vireo leucophrys chiriquensis*). Brown cap, *Vireo* shape. See similar Philadelphia Vireo on Plate 31. Highlands. *p. 361*
11. SCRUB GREENLET (*Hylophilus flavipes viridiflavus*). Pale eye, pinkish bill, yellow underparts. *p. 363*
12. TAWNY-CROWNED GREENLET (*Hylophilus ochraceiceps pallidipectus*). Brownish wings and tail, tawny crown, pale eye, gray throat. Forest understory. *p. 364*
13. GOLDEN-FRONTED GREENLET (*Hylophilus a. aurantiifrons*). Orangey forehead, brown cap, dark eye. Central and eastern Panama. *p. 364*
14. LESSER GREENLET (*Hylophilus decurtatus*). Puffy-headed, short-tailed. a) Nominate *decurtatus* (western and central Panama): gray head. b) *Dariensis* (eastern Panama): olive head. *p. 364*
15. SWALLOW TANAGER (*Tersina viridis occidentalis*). Male: mostly turquoise blue, black face and throat. Female: bright green overall, barring on lower underparts. Eastern Panama, rare. *p. 407*
16. YELLOWISH PIPIT (*Anthus lutescens parvus*). Slender, brown, streaked, white outer tail feathers. Pacific savannas. *p. 357*

PLATE 31

MIGRANT VIREOS, WOOD-WARBLERS

1. YELLOW-THROATED VIREO (*Vireo flavifrons*). Yellow spectacles, throat, and breast. *p. 360*
2. RED-EYED VIREO (*Vireo o. olivaceus*). Resembles Yellow-green Vireo (Plate 30), but head striping more distinct, greenish (not yellowish) flight feather edging, less yellow below (usually). *p. 362*
3. PHILADELPHIA VIREO (*Vireo philadelphicus*). Grayish crown, dull pale yellow underparts. Mostly western Panama. See Brown-capped Vireo on Plate 30. *p. 361*
4. TENNESSEE WARBLER (*Vermivora peregrina*). a) Immature: plain, yellowish superciliary and underparts, single wing-bar (faint). b) Adult male: whitish superciliary and underparts, gray crown. *p. 367*
5. GOLDEN-WINGED WARBLER (*Vermivora chrysoptera*). Black ear-patch and throat (grayer in female), golden wing-patch. *p. 367*
6. KENTUCKY WARBLER (*Oporornis formosus*). Male. Black crown and sideburns. *p. 377*
7. MOURNING WARBLER (*Oporornis philadelphia*). Male. Black bib, gray hood, no eye-ring; female with brownish hood, partial white eye-ring. *p. 378*
8. WILSON'S WARBLER (*Wilsonia p. pusilla*). Male. Black crown (may be obscure in female and immatures). *p. 380*
9. YELLOW WARBLER (*Dendroica petechia aestiva*). a) Adult male: bright yellow, chestnut streaking below. b) Immature: more yellow-olive, yellow tail-spots; no superciliary. See Plate 33 for "Mangrove" Yellow Warbler. *p. 369*
10. PROTHONOTARY WARBLER (*Protonotaria citrea*). Male. Deep golden hood and underparts, blue-gray wings. *p. 376*
11. CHESTNUT-SIDED WARBLER (*Dendroica pensylvanica*). a) Breeding male: yellow crown, chestnut on sides. b) Immature: bright yellow-olive upperparts, grayish white underparts, white eye-ring. *p. 369*
12. BAY-BREASTED WARBLER (*Dendroica castanea*). a) Breeding male: buff patch on sides of neck; chestnut crown, throat, and chest. b) Immature: pale buffyish underparts (no streaking), usually some chestnut on flanks. *p. 374*
13. BLACKBURNIAN WARBLER (*Dendroica fusca*). Immature. Yellow outlining dark cheeks, yellow throat and breast (latter more orange, and upperparts blacker, in breeding birds, especially males). *p. 372*
14. BLACK-THROATED GREEN WARBLER (*Dendroica virens*). Immature female. Yellow sides of head, mostly white throat and underparts (throat black in adults). *p. 372*
15. CANADA WARBLER (*Wilsonia canadensis*). Male. Necklace of black streaks, blue-gray upperparts. Immatures duller. *p. 381*
16. MAGNOLIA WARBLER (*Dendroica magnolia*). Immature. White on tail, grayish head and chest. Breeding males much brighter (see text). *p. 370*
17. AMERICAN REDSTART (*Serpophaga ruticilla*). Male: unmistakable, black with orange patches. Female: with distinctive yellow patches. *p. 375*
18. OVENBIRD (*Seiurus a. aurocapillus*). Terrestrial and thrush-like, orange crown stripe. *p. 376*
19. NORTHERN WATERTHRUSH (*Seiurus n. noveboracensis*). Buffy yellowish superciliary; teeters near water. See text for Louisiana Waterthrush. *p. 377*
20. BLACK-AND-WHITE WARBLER (*Mniotilta varia*). Female. Streaked black and white (even more in male); creeps on limbs. *p. 375*

Note: Common Yellowthroat is depicted on Plate 48.

Gwynne 12·85

PLATE 32

MIGRANT THRUSHES, TYRANT FLYCATCHERS, EMBERIZIIDS, ETC.

1. SCARLET TANAGER (*Piranga olivacea*). Molting male: black wings and tail, red patches (the red solid in full plumage). Female: dark wings and tail, olive-yellow underparts. *p. 401*

2. SUMMER TANAGER (*Piranga r. rubra*). Rather pale bill. Male: all rosy red. Female: deep yellow underparts. See Hepatic Tanager on Plate 35. *p. 401*

3. GRAY CATBIRD (*Dumetella carolinensis*). Gray, chestnut crissum. *p. 356*

4. ACADIAN FLYCATCHER (*Empidonax virescens*). Bold wing-bars, fairly prominent eye-ring. A confusing genus with numerous species; see text, and Plates 25 and 46. *p. 302*

5. EASTERN WOOD-PEWEE (*Contopus virens*). Drab except for bold wing-bars; upright posture. See text. *p. 301*

6. TROPICAL PEWEE (*Contopus cinereus brachytarsus*). Much like preceding but with pale lores; see text. *p. 301*

7. WOOD THRUSH (*Hylocichla mustelina*). Rufous crown and back, boldly spotted underparts. *p. 354*

8. VEERY (*Catharus f. fuscescens*). Little spotting below, rufescent upperparts. *p. 352*

9. SWAINSON'S THRUSH (*Catharus ustulatus swainsoni*). Buffyish eye-ring and cheeks. *p. 353*

10. GRAY-CHEEKED THRUSH (*Catharus m. minimus*). Rather plain face, grayish cheeks. *p. 353*

11. ORCHARD ORIOLE (*Icterus s. spurius*). Male: dark chestnut and black. Female: oriole shape with slender bill, greenish yellow underparts. *p. 430*

12. NORTHERN ORIOLE (*Icterus g. galbula*). Male: orange and black. Female: orange-yellow on underparts (especially breast). *p. 431*

13. BOBOLINK (*Dolichonyx oryzivorus*). Female. Striped crown, buffy underparts. Breeding male much more patterned, with black underparts, etc.; see text. *p. 426*

14. DICKCISSEL (*Spiza americana*). Female. Rusty shoulders, yellow on chest. Breeding male brighter, with black "V" on breast, etc. *p. 412*

15. INDIGO BUNTING (*Passerina cyanea*). Male: uniform bright blue. Female: brown, streaked below (see text). *p. 412*

16. ROSE-BREASTED GROSBEAK (*Pheucticus ludovicianus*). Male: black and white with rosy chest patch. Female: heavy bill, head striping, streaking below. *p. 411*

17. BLUE GROSBEAK (*Guiraca c. caerulea*). Female. Larger than Indigo Bunting, with heavier bill; prominent buff wing-bars. Male is blue, wing-bars as in female. *p. 411*

1 ♂
♀
2 ♂ ♀
3
4
5
6
7
8
9
10
11 ♂
♀
12 ♀
♂
13 ♀
14 ♀
15 ♂
♀
16 ♂
♀
17 ♀

Gwynne
12·86

PLATE 33

RESIDENT WOOD-WARBLERS, BANANAQUIT, HONEYCREEPERS

1. GREEN HONEYCREEPER (*Chlorophanes spiza aguta*). Male: bright green plumage, black head, yellow bill. Female: uniform paler green, only slightly decurved bill (see text). *p. 390*

2. BLUE DACNIS (*Dacnis cayana ultramarina*). Male: mostly bright blue, short bill. Female: bluish head, short pointed bill. *p. 389*

3. SCARLET-THIGHED DACNIS (*Dacnis v. venusta*). Male: bright blue head and neck, black underparts. Female: buffy underparts. Both sexes usually have bright red eye. Mostly foothills. *p. 389*

4. SHINING HONEYCREEPER (*Cyanerpes lucidus isthmicus*). Male: yellow legs, black throat and chest, long decurved bill. Female: blue chest streaking, decurved bill, short tail. *p. 390*

5. RED-LEGGED HONEYCREEPER (*Cyanerpes cyaneus carneipes*). Male: pale blue crown, red legs, decurved bill. Female: reddish legs, streaked breast, decurved bill. *p. 391*

6. BANANAQUIT (*Coereba flaveola mexicana*). White eye-stripe, gray throat, short decurved bill. *p. 384*

7. TROPICAL PARULA (*Parula pitiayumi speciosa*). Grayish blue upperparts, yellow underparts, wing-bars. *p. 368*

8. FLAME-THROATED WARBLER (*Vermivora gutturalis*). Slaty gray upperparts with black back, bright orange throat and breast. Chiriquí highlands. *p. 368*

9. YELLOW ("MANGROVE") WARBLER (*Dendroica petechia erithachorides*). Male. Rufous-chestnut head (variable in extent, depending on race). Female very dull (see text). See Plate 31 for migrant Yellow Warbler. *p. 369*

10. RUFOUS-CAPPED WARBLER (*Basileuterus rufifrons mesochrysus*). Chestnut crown and ear-patch, long white eye-stripe. *p. 382*

11. THREE-STRIPED WARBLER (*Basileuterus tristriatus melanotis*). Crown stripes, black ear-coverts (much less in eastern Panama), dull yellow underparts. Local, foothills and highlands. *p. 383*

12. GOLDEN-CROWNED WARBLER (*Basileuterus culicivorus godmani*). Orange crown stripe (sometimes yellow), bright yellow underparts. Western foothills and highlands. *p. 382*

13. BLACK-CHEEKED WARBLER (*Basileuterus m. melanogenys*). Chestnut crown, long white eye-stripe, black sides of head. Western highlands. *p. 382*

14. COLLARED REDSTART (*Myioborus torquatus*). Yellow face and underparts, black chest band. Western highlands. *p. 381*

15. SLATE-THROATED REDSTART (*Myioborus miniatus aurantiacus*). Slaty throat and upperparts. Highlands. *p. 381*

16. BUFF-RUMPED WARBLER (*Basileuterus fulvicauda leucopygius*). Buff rump and basal two-thirds of tail (usually fanned). Watercourses. *p. 383*

Note: Masked, Olive-crowned, and Gray-crowned Yellowthroats are depicted on Plate 48.

PLATE 34

TANAGERS I

1. GOLDEN-BROWED CHLOROPHONIA (*Chlorophonia callophrys*). Male. Very gaudy, bright green and yellow. Western highlands. *p. 391*
2. WHITE-VENTED EUPHONIA (*Euphonia minuta humilis*). Male. White lower belly and vent. Especially foothills. *p. 394*
3. FULVOUS-VENTED EUPHONIA (*Euphonia f. fulvicrissa*). Male: tawny center of belly and vent. Female: tawny lower belly, rufous forecrown. Central and eastern Panama. *p. 393*
4. BLUE-HOODED EUPHONIA (*Euphonia elegantissima*). Male. Blue crown and nape. Western highlands. *p. 393*
5. YELLOW-THROATED EUPHONIA (*Euphonia hirundinacea*). Male. Very like next species, but smaller yellow area on forecrown. Female more different (see Plate 48). Chiriquí (somewhat uncertain). *p. 393*
6. THICK-BILLED EUPHONIA (*Euphonia laniirostris crassirostris*). Male: underparts entirely yellow (including throat). Female: yellowish underparts, olive wash on chest.*p. 392*
7. SPOT-CROWNED EUPHONIA (*Euphonia imitans*). Male. Yellow forecrown with dusky spots (see text). Chiriquí. *p. 394*
8. YELLOW-CROWNED EUPHONIA (*Euphonia luteicapilla*). Male: entire cap yellow, lower underparts all yellow. Female: uniform dull yellow underparts. *p. 392*
9. OLIVE-BACKED EUPHONIA (*Euphonia gouldi praetermissa*). Male. Glossy green upperparts, yellow forecrown, tawny center of breast and belly (see text). Western Caribbean lowlands. *p. 394*
10. TAWNY-CAPPED EUPHONIA (*Euphonia a. anneae*). Male. Tawny crown. Foothills. *p. 395*
11. PLAIN-COLORED TANAGER (*Tangara inornata languens*). Mostly gray, small mask and wings black. *p. 386*
12. GOLDEN-HOODED TANAGER (*Tangara larvata fanny*). Golden head with black mask, black breast, blue on wings and sides. *p. 388*
13. EMERALD TANAGER (*Tangara florida*). Mostly bright green, black cheek-patch. Foothills. *p. 386*
14. BAY-HEADED TANAGER (*Tangara gyrola delecticia*). Chestnut head, blue underparts. *p. 387*
15. RUFOUS-WINGED TANAGER (*Tangara lavinia dalmasi*). Male. Chestnut head, rufous wings, yellow hindneck, green underparts. Foothills. *p. 388*
16. SILVER-THROATED TANAGER (*Tangara icterocephala frantzii*). Mostly bright yellow, whitish throat. Foothills and highlands. *p. 387*
17. SPANGLE-CHEEKED TANAGER (*Tangara dowii*). Green and buff spangling, cinnamon lower underparts. Western highlands, uncommon and local. *p. 388*
18. SPECKLED TANAGER (*Tangara guttata eusticta*). Spotted above and below. Foothills. *p. 387*

PLATE 35

TANAGERS II

1. GREEN-NAPED TANAGER (*Tangara fucosa*). Green and blue spangling on sides of neck and breast, cinnamon lower underparts. Darién highlands. *p. 389*
2. BLUE-AND-GOLD TANAGER (*Bangsia a. arcaei*). Blue upperparts, rich yellow underparts, red eye. Foothills, local. *p. 396*
3. GRAY-AND-GOLD TANAGER (*Tangara palmeri*). Mostly bluish gray and whitish, yellow band across chest (sometimes indistinct). Darién. *p. 386*
4. PALM TANAGER (*Thraupis palmarum atripennis*). Olive, black rear half of wing. *p. 395*
5. BLUE-GRAY TANAGER (*Thraupis episcopus cana*). All pale grayish blue. *p. 395*
6. CRIMSON-COLLARED TANAGER (*Phlogothraupis sanguinolenta aprica*). Brilliant red collar, bluish bill. Caribbean western Panama. *p. 402*
7. FLAME-RUMPED TANAGER (*Ramphocelus flammigerus icteronotus*). Male: black, yellow lower back and rump. Female: yellow lower back and rump, mostly yellow underparts, bluish bill. *p. 404*
8. SCARLET-RUMPED TANAGER (*Ramphocelus passerinii*). a) Chiriquí race (*costaricensis*): male black with scarlet lower back and rump; female with bluish bill, rump and chest orange. b) Bocas del Toro race (nominate): male much as above; female with rump and chest duller, more yellowish. *p. 403*
9. CRIMSON-BACKED TANAGER (*Ramphocelus d. dimidiatus*). Male: red lower back and rump, lower underparts; silvery on bill. Female: duller, still with red rump and belly. *p. 403*
10. FLAME-COLORED TANAGER (*Piranga bidentata citrea*). Male: mostly orange-red, streaked back. Female: yellowish head and underparts, streaked back. Chiriquí highlands. *p. 402*
11. WHITE-WINGED TANAGER (*Piranga leucoptera latifasciata*). Male: mostly rose red, broad white wing-bars, black mask. Female: yellowish, bold wing-bars. Western highlands. *p. 402*
12. RED-CROWNED ANT-TANAGER (*Habia rubica vinacea*). Male: scarlet crown with narrow black border. Female: yellow crown with narrow black border. Closely resembles next species (see text). *p. 399*
13. RED-THROATED ANT-TANAGER (*Habia fuscicauda willisi*). Male: mostly dull carmine, bright red throat. Female: brownish olive, contrasting yellow throat. *p. 400*
14. OLIVE TANAGER (*Chlorothraupis carmioli lutescens*). Mostly olive green, yellow throat (see text). Especially foothills. *p. 396*
15. LEMON-SPECTACLED TANAGER (*Chlorothraupis olivacea*). Mostly olive, contrasting yellow spectacles. Eastern Darién foothills. *p. 397*
16. HEPATIC TANAGER (*Piranga flava testacea*). Male: all brick red, blackish bill. Female: bright yellowish underparts, blackish bill (see text). Foothills. *p. 400*

PLATE 36

TANAGERS III

1. WHITE-THROATED SHRIKE-TANAGER (*Lanio leucothorax melanopygius*). Male: heavy hooked bill, black head, white throat. Female: heavy hooked bill, grayish head, brown upperparts (see text). Western Panama, local. *p. 397*
2. WHITE-SHOULDERED TANAGER (*Tachyphonus luctuosus*). a) Most of Panama (*panamensis*): male black with white shoulders; female with contrasting gray head. b) Western Chiriquí (*nitidissimus*): male with golden crown patch, reduced white in wing; female with more olive head. Both sexes of *panamensis* should have pale base to lower mandible. *p. 398*
3. YELLOW-BACKED TANAGER (*Hemithraupis flavicollis ornata*). Male: black above with yellow rump, yellow throat. Female: throat and breast yellow, belly whitish. Eastern Darién. *p. 407*
4. BLACK-AND-YELLOW TANAGER (*Chrysothlypis c. chrysomelas*). Male: bright yellow, black wings and tail. Female: bright yellow underparts in most of Panama range (except in Chiriquí; see text). Foothills. *p. 407*
5. TAWNY-CRESTED TANAGER (*Tachyphonus delatrii*). Male: orange-tawny crest. Female: all dark brown. *p. 399*
6. SULPHUR-RUMPED TANAGER (*Heterospingus rubrifrons*). Gray generally, yellow rump, white tuft on sides of breast. *p. 398*
7. SCARLET-BROWED TANAGER (*Heterospingus xanthopygius*). Male. Glossy black generally, scarlet postocular stripe, yellow rump (female resembles previous species). Darién. *p. 398*
8. GRAY-HEADED TANAGER (*Eucometis penicillata cristata*). Gray head and neck, bright yellow underparts. *p. 397*
9. WHITE-LINED TANAGER (*Tachyphonus rufus*). Male: all black, bluish bill, white under wing-linings. Female: rufous brown and tawny, bluish bill (see text). *p. 399*
10. DUSKY-FACED TANAGER (*Mitrospingus c. cassinii*). Blackish sides of head and throat, yellowish crown, pale eye. *p. 404*
11. ROSY THRUSH-TANAGER (*Rhodinocichla rosea eximia*). Male: rosy red underparts. Female: tawny underparts. *p. 404*
12. SOOTY-CAPPED BUSH-TANAGER (*Chlorospingus pileatus*). Sooty black head, broad white eye-stripe. Western highlands. *p. 406*
13. COMMON BUSH-TANAGER (*Chlorospingus ophthalmicus*). Western highlands. a) Western Chiriquí (*regionalis*): white postocular, head brownish. b) Veraguas and Coclé (*punctulatus*): blackish head, throat speckling, orange tone on chest. *p. 405*
14. PIRRE BUSH-TANAGER (*Chlorospingus inornatus*). Blackish head, yellow underparts. Darién highlands (but not on Tacarcuna). *p. 405*
15. YELLOW-THROATED BUSH-TANAGER (*Chlorospingus flavigularis hypophaeus*). Dull, with no white markings on head, yellow throat. Local in humid foothills, mostly Caribbean slope, western and central Panama. See Ashy-throated Bush-Tanager on Plate 48. *p. 406*
16. TACARCUNA BUSH-TANAGER (*Chlorospingus tacarcunae*). Olive, with no white head markings but has pale eye; yellow throat and breast. Foothills in eastern Panama east to Cerro Tacarcuna in Darién. *p. 405*

Note: Slaty Flowerpiercer and Ashy-throated Bush-Tanager are depicted on Plate 48.

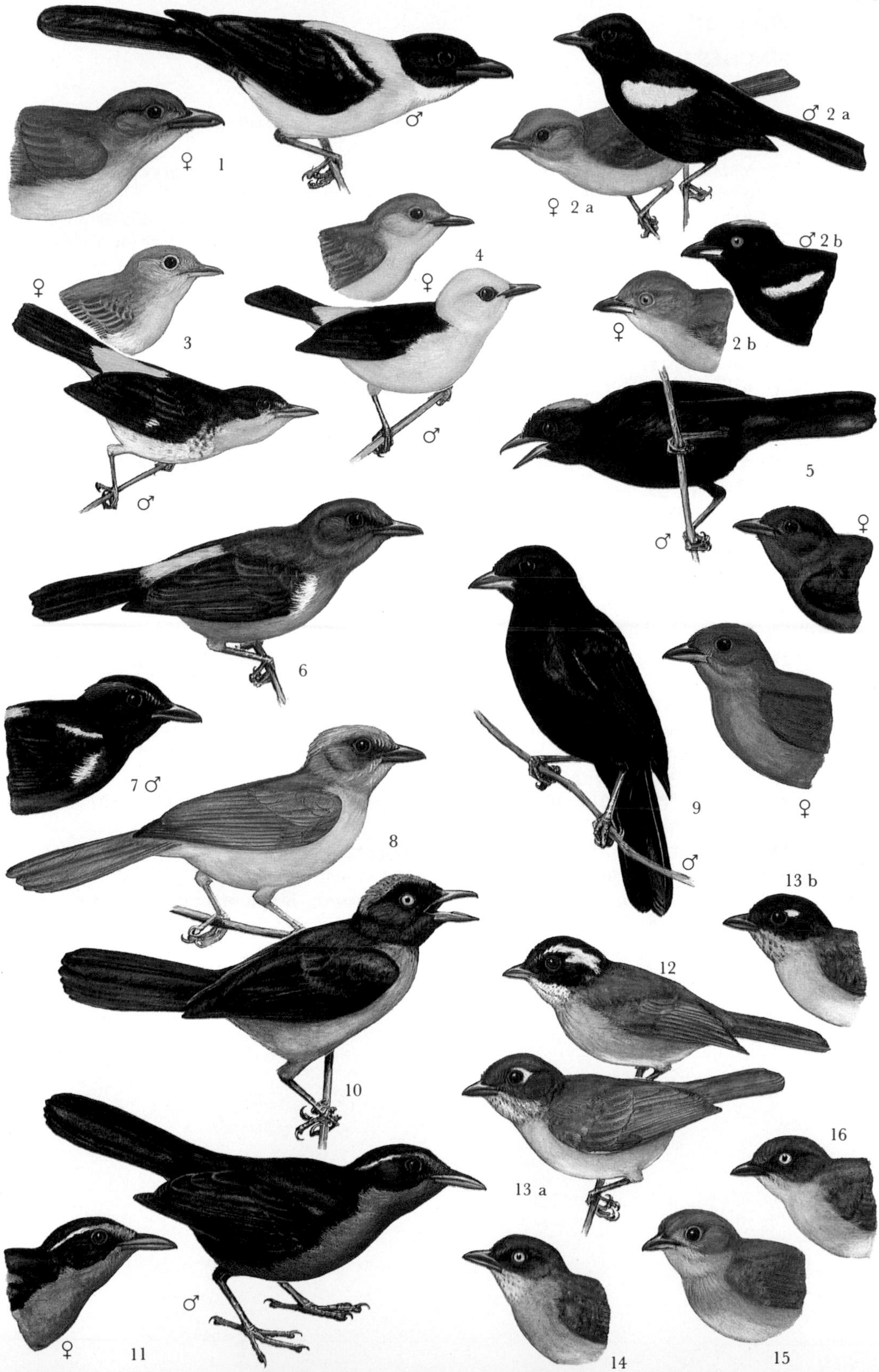

♀ 1
♂
♂ 2 a
♀ 2 a
4
♀
♂ 2 b
♀
3
♂
♀
2 b
5
♂
♂
♀
6
7 ♂
8
9
♀
♂
13 b
12
10
16
13 a
♂
♀
11
14
15

PLATE 37

FINCHES I

1. YELLOW-THIGHED FINCH (*Pselliophorus tibialis*). Dark slaty, conspicuous yellow thighs. Western Chiriquí highlands. *p. 414*
2. YELLOW-GREEN FINCH (*Pselliophorus luteoviridis*). Like preceding, but gray replaced by olive green. Highlands of eastern Chiriquí and Veraguas. *p. 414*
3. BLACK-FACED GROSBEAK (*Caryothraustes poliogaster scapularis*). Mostly yellowish olive, black face and throat, grayish belly. Western Caribbean slope (see text for Yellow-green Grosbeak of eastern Darién). *p. 410*
4. SOOTY-FACED FINCH (*Lysurus c. crassirostris*). Chestnut cap, white moustache, yellow lower underparts. Foothills and highlands locally. *p. 413*
5. SLATE-COLORED GROSBEAK (*Pitylus grossus saturatus*). Male. Mostly slaty, heavy bright red bill. *p. 409*
6. BLACK-THIGHED GROSBEAK (*Pheucticus tibialis*). Male. Very heavy blackish bill, mostly yellow head and underparts (mottled with blackish to varying degrees). Western highlands. *p. 410*
7. STREAKED SALTATOR (*Saltator albicollis isthmicus*). Streaked underparts, no throat patch. *p. 408*
8. BLACK-HEADED SALTATOR (*Saltator atriceps lacertosus*). Large size, black crown and nape, white throat. Western and central Panama. *p. 409*
9. BUFF-THROATED SALTATOR (*Saltator maximus intermedius*). Mostly dark gray head, buffy throat patch. *p. 409*
10. LARGE-FOOTED FINCH (*Pezopetes capitalis*). Mostly unpatterned olive green, slaty head. Chiriquí highlands. *p. 414*
11. YELLOW-THROATED BRUSH-FINCH (*Atlapetes gutturalis brunnescens*). Yellow throat, white underparts, black head. Western highlands. *p. 414*
12. BLACK-HEADED BRUSH-FINCH (*Atlapetes atricapillus tacarcunae*). Mostly white underparts, black head with narrow gray median stripe and superciliary. Foothills and lower highlands, eastern Panama (Chiriquí birds have broader gray head stripes and grayer underparts). *p. 415*
13. CHESTNUT-CAPPED BRUSH-FINCH (*Atlapetes brunneinucha elsae*). Chestnut crown, black chest band. Foothills and highlands. *p. 415*
14. BLACK-STRIPED SPARROW (*Arremonops conirostris striaticeps*). Gray head with black stripes, grayish underparts. *p. 416*
15. ORANGE-BILLED SPARROW (*Arremon a. aurantiirostris*). Bright orange bill, black chest band. *p. 416*

PLATE 38

FINCHES II

1. BLUE SEEDEATER (*Amaurospiza c. concolor*). Male: all dark blue (see text). Female: all tawny brown (see text). Very local. *p. 420*
2. BLUE-BLACK GROSBEAK (*Cyanocompsa c. cyanoides*). Male: all blackish blue, very stout bill. Female: all rich brown, very stout bill. *p. 411*
3. LESSER SEED-FINCH (*Oryzoborus angolensis ochrogyne*). Very thick bill. Male: all black, white wing-spot. Female: mostly rich brown. *p. 420*
4. SLATY FINCH (*Haplospiza rustica barrilesensis*). Male: rather slender bill, uniform slaty gray. Female: rather slender bill, brownish, lightly streaked underparts (see text). Chiriquí highlands. *p. 421*
5. BLUE-BLACK GRASSQUIT (*Volatinia jacarina splendens*). Pointed bill. Male: all glossy blue-black. Female: brownish, streaked underparts. *p. 416*
6. RUDDY-BREASTED SEEDEATER (*Sporophila minuta centralis*). Male: gray upperparts, cinnamon-rufous underparts. Female: buffy to dull cinnamon underparts. Pacific savannas. *p. 419*
7. SLATE-COLORED SEEDEATER (*Sporophila s. schistacea*). Male. Yellow bill, mostly gray plumage, white wing-spot. Very local. *p. 417*
8. YELLOW-BELLIED SEEDEATER (*Sporophila n. nigricollis*). Male. Pale yellow or whitish lower underparts. Female see text. *p. 419*
9. VARIABLE SEEDEATER (*Sporophila americana hicksii*). Male: basically black above and white below (but variable; see text). Female: dull brown to buffyish (see text). *p. 417*
10. YELLOW-BELLIED SISKIN (*Carduelis x. xanthogastra*). Male: mostly black, yellow belly and band on wings. Female: olive, conspicuous yellow wing-band, whitish lower belly. Chiriquí highlands. *p. 435*
11. YELLOW-FACED GRASSQUIT (*Tiaris olivacea pusilla*). Male: yellow eye-stripe, eye-ring, and throat; black bib. Female: echoes facial pattern of male. *p. 421*
12. WEDGE-TAILED GRASS-FINCH (*Emberizoides herbicola hypochondriacus*). Streaked and buffy brownish, long pointed tail, whitish eye-ring. Local, Pacific grasslands. *p. 423*
13. SAFFRON FINCH (*Sicalis f. flaveola*). Male. Bright yellow, orange on head (less in female). Caribbean slope, Canal area. *p. 422*
14. GRASSLAND YELLOW-FINCH (*Sicalis luteola eisenmanni*). Male. Facial area, underparts, and rump yellow. Female duller. Very local, Pacific grasslands. *p. 423*
15. RUFOUS-COLLARED SPARROW (*Zonotrichia capensis costaricensis*). Rufous collar, striped head. Western highlands. *p. 425*
16. VOLCANO JUNCO (*Junco vulcani*). Pink bill, yellow eye. High on Volcán Barú, Chiriquí. *p. 425*

Note: Peg-billed Finch is depicted on Plate 48.

PLATE 39

ICTERIDS

1. YELLOW-TAILED ORIOLE (*Icterus mesomelas carrikeri*). Black back, yellow on tail and wing-coverts. *p. 431*
2. YELLOW-BACKED ORIOLE (*Icterus chrysater giraudii*). Rich orange-yellow (including back), all black wings and tail. *p. 430*
3. ORANGE-CROWNED ORIOLE (*Icterus auricapillus*). Contrasting orange crown and nape. Eastern Panama. *p. 431*
4. BLACK-COWLED ORIOLE (*Icterus dominicensis praecox*). Largely black, yellow lower underparts. Caribbean western Panama. *p. 430*
5. YELLOW-BILLED CACIQUE (*Amblycercus h. holosericeus*). All black, yellowish bill. *p. 432*
6. SCARLET-RUMPED CACIQUE (*Cacicus uropygialis microrhynchus*). Scarlet rump, blue eye. *p. 432*
7. YELLOW-RUMPED CACIQUE (*Cacicus cela vitellinus*). Yellow rump and basal half of tail. *p. 433*
8. CHESTNUT-HEADED OROPENDOLA (*Psarocolius wagleri*). Chestnut head and neck, yellow tail. *p. 433*
9. BLACK OROPENDOLA (*Psarocolius guatimozinus*). Large size, yellow-tipped black bill. Eastern Panama. *p. 434*
10. MONTEZUMA OROPENDOLA (*Psarocolius montezuma*). Large size, mostly chestnut plumage, blue and pink facial skin. Western Caribbean slope to Canal area. *p. 434*
11. CRESTED OROPENDOLA (*Psarocolius decumanus melanterus*). Mostly black, all yellowish bill. Local. *p. 433*
12. RED-BREASTED BLACKBIRD (*Sturnella m. militaris*). Male: red underparts. Female: pink-tinged breast (usually). Pacific slope (mostly) savannas. *p. 426*
13. GREAT-TAILED GRACKLE (*Cassidix mexicanus peruvianus*). Male: long creased tail. Female: buffy brown eye-stripe and underparts. *p. 428*
14. SHINY COWBIRD (*Molothrus bonariensis cabanisii*). Male. Small size, all glossy blue-black plumage. Eastern Panama. *p. 428*
15. BRONZED COWBIRD (*Molothrus a. aeneus*). Male. Ruff (more conspicuous in male), mostly bronzy plumage, red eye. *p. 429*
16. GIANT COWBIRD (*Scaphidura oryzivora*). Male: large size, conspicuous ruff, black bill and frontal shield. Female: smaller, with less prominent ruff. *p. 429*

PLATE 40

SOME DARIÉN SPECIALTIES

All of the following species are known in Panama only from the east, with many being restricted to Darién. Note that a few other species with comparable distributions have been figured on previous Plates.

1. PURPLE HONEYCREEPER (*Cyanerpes caeruleus chocoanus*). Male. Like Shining Honeycreeper (see Plate 33), but more purple (less blue), with smaller throat patch. *p. 390*
2. WHITE-EARED CONEBILL (*Conirostrum l. leucogenys*). Male: small size, short tail, gray plumage, white ear-patch. Female: grayish, rather undistinctive (see text). *p. 385*
3. VIRIDIAN DACNIS (*Dacnis viguieri*). Iris yellow. Male: mostly opalescent green to bluish green. Female: mostly dull greenish, black primaries. *p. 389*
4. RUFOUS-CHEEKED HUMMINGBIRD (*Goethalsia bella*). Male. Cinnamon wing-patch, white vent. Highlands. *p. 215*
5. GREENISH PUFFLEG (*Haplophaedia aureliae caucensis*). Male. Conspicuous whitish leg-tufts. Highlands. *p. 221*
6. DOUBLE-BANDED GRAYTAIL (*Xenerpestes m. minlosi*). Small size, whitish underparts, wing-bars, and eye-stripe. *p. 251*
7. BRONZE-OLIVE PYGMY-TYRANT (*Pseudotriccus pelzelni berlepschi*). Uniform and dark, rufous wing-edging. Highlands. *p. 290*
8. SOOTY-HEADED TYRANNULET (*Phyllomyias griseiceps cristatus*). Brownish cap, no wing-bars, mostly yellow underparts (see text). *p. 282*
9. GOLDEN-CROWNED FLYCATCHER (*Myiodynastes chrysocephalus minor*). Dusky moustache, light chest streaking. Highlands. *p. 312*
10. GRAY ELAENIA (*Myiopagis caniceps absita*). Male. Bluish gray appearance, much white on wing. Female see text. *p. 285*
11. BLACK-BILLED FLYCATCHER (*Aphanotriccus audax*). Slender and long-tailed, mostly yellow underparts, white supraloral stripe. *p. 298*
12. TAWNY-BREASTED FLYCATCHER (*Myiobius v. villosus*). Recalls Sulphur-rumped Flycatcher (see Plate 24) but larger, and darker and more uniformly tawny below. Highlands (Tacarcuna only). *p. 297*
13. VARIED SOLITAIRE (*Myadestes coloratus*). Tawny back and wings, slaty head and underparts, orange bill and legs. Highlands. *p. 350*
14. SPECTACLED PARROTLET (*Forpus c. conspicillatus*). Male. Very small size, short tail, blue rump. *p. 176*
15. SAFFRON-HEADED PARROT (*Pionopsitta pyrilia*). Yellow head and neck. *p. 178*
16. DUSKY-BACKED JACAMAR (*Brachygalba salmoni*). Male. Long slender bill, dark green upperparts, black chest and sides. *p. 237*
17. STRIPE-THROATED WREN (*Thryothorus leucopogon*). Striped sides of head and throat, barred wings, buffyish underparts. *p. 341*
18. SOOTY-HEADED WREN (*Thryothorus spadix*). Mostly chestnut; gray and black head and throat. *p. 340*
19. BAY WREN (*Thryothorus nigricapillus schotti*). Barred underparts, black cap (not barred in central and western Panama; see Plate 28). *p. 341*
20. RUFOUS-WINGED ANTWREN (*Herpsilochmus rufimarginatus exiguus*). Male. Rufous wing-edging, pale yellow underparts, long white superciliary. Female duller. *p. 270*

Continued over

PLATE 40 *continued from previous page*

21. BLACK ANTSHRIKE (*Thamnophilus nigriceps*). Male: all black, no white showing on wings or tail (except under wing). Female: streaked head and underparts. *p. 266*
22. SPECKLED ANTSHRIKE (*Xenornis setifrons*). Male: streaked upperparts, slaty gray underparts. Female: streaked overall effect (should be darker). *p. 267*
23. PIRRE WARBLER (*Basileuterus ignotus*). Greenish yellow eye-stripe (see text). Highlands. *p. 382*
24. GREEN MANAKIN (*Chlorpipo holochlora litae*). Larger and longer-tailed than most manakins, contrasting yellowish belly. *p. 326*
25. SHARP-TAILED STREAMCREEPER (*Lochmias nematura nelsoni*). Leaftosser-like, conspicuous white spotting below. *p. 257*

recorded mostly 900–1500 m (3000–5000 ft).

Habits: Usually seen singly as it forages near the ground, but also sometimes congregates at flowering trees with other hummingbirds. Flight is usually slow (like a coquette, bee-like and often with audible *hmmm*), with tail of male often held cocked up at about a 30° angle, or slowly wagged up and down. Male has a territorial display in which he repeatedly swings diagonally back and forth in front of a selected small tree at forest edge; the end of each trajectory is marked by an audible snap.

Range: Costa Rica and western Panama.

Note: Formerly placed in the genus *Philodice*, as was the following species.

PURPLE-THROATED WOODSTAR
Calliphlox mitchellii

Description: 3¼. Known only from eastern Darién. Bill straight, rather short (½ in). Male dark bronzy green above; *throat glittering rosy violet,* bordered below by a *broad white pectoral collar* extending well up onto sides of neck; lower underparts mostly dusky bronze with patch on flanks chestnut, and with *large white patch on lower flanks* (sometimes partially hidden under wing) *extending up onto sides of rump* (often giving effect of partial rump band). Female like male above; throat buffy whitish speckled dusky, somewhat *smaller and less well indicated white pectoral band* (but still usually evident), and *mostly rufous lower underparts; tail mostly rufous with broad black subterminal band,* not forked.

Similar species: The only woodstar recorded from eastern Panama.

Status and distribution: Known only from two specimens taken at Cana in eastern Darién, both females: one was collected on April 13, 1938 (O. Pearson; specimen in ANSP), the other mist-netted and collected on August 11, 1982 (M. Robbins *et al.*). The collection and identification of the second bird prompted a re-examination of the first, and it too proved to be a female *mitchellii* (and not Gorgeted Woodstar, *Acestrura heliodor,* as originally identified).

Habits: Unknown in life in Panama. In western Ecuador found mainly at forest borders and in shrubby clearings, primarily in foothills and lower subtropical zone. Often seen perched on high exposed branches but regularly comes lower to feed at flowering shrubs or low trees.

Range: Eastern Panama to western Ecuador.

Note: As noted above, Gorgeted Woodstar, *Acestrura heliodor,* should be deleted from the Panama and North American lists (Robbins *et al.*, 1985).

RUBY-THROATED HUMMINGBIRD
Archilochus colubris　　　　　　Plate 43

Description: 3½. Bill straight (¾ in). Male green above with small white spot behind eye: *gorget bright ruby red,* remaining underparts mostly white washed with grayish on sides and flanks; *tail black, forked.* Female lacks gorget, is green above with small white spot behind eye; *whitish below* with buffy flanks; tail unforked, *outer feathers tipped white.*

Similar species: Male should be readily recognized in the Pacific western lowlands where it is most likely to occur. Female-plumaged birds (which are much more numerous, many doubtless being immature males) are most apt to be confused with female Garden Emerald, though Ruby-throat lacks the blackish mask and has a less prominent postocular spot. See also female Sapphire-throated Hummingbird and, in highlands, female Scintillant Hummingbird (which has mainly rufous tail).

Status and distribution: Apparently a rare winter visitant; recorded only from lowlands on Pacific slope, with a few nineteenth-century specimens from western Chiriquí (and a single sighting of a molting male near Concepción on March 4, 1986; Ridgely *et al.*), and one sighting of four or five (including an adult male) at Playa Coronado, western Panama province, on November 25, 1962 (Eisenmann).

Habits: In its winter quarters favors light (often scrubby) woodland, borders, and semiopen areas.

Range: Breeds in eastern and central North America; winters in southern Florida and from Mexico to Costa Rica, rarely to Panama.

VOLCANO HUMMINGBIRD
Selasphorus flammula　　　　　　Plate 14

Description: 2¾. Found only in western Chiriquí mountains. Bill straight (½ in). Male bronzy green above; *gorget dull grayish purple to grayish green and elongated at sides;* chest and middle of breast and belly white, sides and flanks cinnamon; *tail mostly black.* Female like male but without gorget; *throat white with small dusky spots; tail mostly rufous* with broad black subterminal band and *white tip.*

Similar species: Rather closely resembles partly sympatric Scintillant Hummingbird; male Scintillant has bright orange-red (not grayish purple or greenish) gorget and has mostly rufous (not largely black) tail; female Scintillant very similar but has tail tipped with buff (not white) and usually is buffier below.

Status and distribution: Fairly common in forest borders and shrubby clearings in mountains of western Chiriquí on Volcán Barú massif, mostly above 1950 m (6500 ft). Most readily seen along Boquete Trail above Cerro Punta.

Habits: Often allows a remarkably close approach as it sits on a twig in a bush or low tree. Males have a spectacular display given during breeding season (at least January–March), repeatedly diving steeply down from about 15 m (50 ft) up, the dives describing a "U" over a twig, with a whistled sound produced (by the wings?) on both the down and the upswing, and a few clicks at the bottom.

Range: Costa Rica and western Panama.

GLOW-THROATED HUMMINGBIRD
Selasphorus ardens   Plate 14

Description: 2 ¾. Known only from eastern Chiriquí and Veraguas highlands. Bill straight (½ in). Male bronzy green above; *gorget bright rose red to purplish red and elongated on sides;* chest white, lower underparts bronzy green, becoming grayish white on lower belly; tail graduated, black, with rufous inner web of most feathers. Female bronzy green above; throat pale buff finely dotted with dusky; remaining underparts mainly whitish, tinged buff on chest, and buffy on flanks and lower belly; tail mostly rufous, crossed by black band.

Similar species: Closely resembles Scintillant Hummingbird, and note that two specimens of the latter (wandering birds?) have been taken within range of Glow-throated (at Cerro Flores). Males differ in gorget color (reddish orange in Scintillant, rose red in Glow-throated) and in color of tail; female Glow-throat is *very* similar to female Scintillant but has rufous edging to middle (green) tail feathers, and is usually paler below.

Status and distribution: Uncommon in shrubby second-growth of clearings and forest borders in foothills and lower highlands of eastern Chiriquí and Veraguas (Santa Fé, Castillo, and Calovévora); recorded 750–

1800 m (2500–6000 ft). Apparently found regularly above Cerro Colorado in eastern Chiriquí; a few have also been seen on occasion along the road above Santa Fé, Veraguas, though the species there seems to range mainly at higher elevations.

Habits: Not very well known, but basic behavior probably similar to Scintillant Hummingbird.

Range: West-central Panama.

Note: F. G. Stiles (*Auk 100*(2): 311–325, 1983) has shown that this species' closest relative is *S. scintilla* (Scintillant Hummingbird), and not a Costa Rican form, *simoni* (which Stiles demonstrated was actually a race of *S. flammula,* the Volcano Hummingbird). Glow-throated and Scintillant are both species of moderate elevations and have at least mostly allopatric ranges.

SCINTILLANT HUMMINGBIRD
Selasphorus scintilla   Plate 14

Description: 2 ¾. Found only in western Chiriquí highlands. Bill straight (½ in). Male bronzy green above, more rufous on rump; *gorget brilliant reddish orange to orange-red* (in some lights pure red or even golden green) *and elongated at sides;* chest and center of breast white, sides and belly cinnamon-rufous; *tail rufous.* Female bronzy green above; throat buffy with tiny dusky dots; chest and middle of breast white, sides and belly cinnamon; tail mostly rufous with broad black subterminal band and *buff tip.*

Similar species: Resembles the less numerous Volcano Hummingbird. Males differ in their bright gorget and mostly rufous (not black) tail, while females differ in their white (not buff) tail tipping. For the most part they segregate by elevation, with Scintillant mainly between 1200–2100 m (4000–7000 ft), and Volcano above 2100 m (7000 ft). See also Magenta-throated Woodstar and female White-crested Coquette.

Status and distribution: Fairly common to common in forest borders, clearings, and gardens in highlands of western Chiriquí, mostly 1200–2100 m (4000–7000 ft); also known from two specimens taken at Cerro Flores in eastern Chiriquí, presumed to be nonbreeding wanderers (F. G. Stiles) as this is well within the range of Glow-throated Hummingbird.

Habits: Birds in female plumage (many doubtless immatures) are seen much more often that the beautiful males. Usually seen close to the ground, foraging at flowers and flowering shrubs, often perching beside the blossom they are probing. Males have a spectacular aerial display similar in most respects to that of the Volcano Hum-mingbird, but describing a wider "U" shape with pronounced zigzag on the upswing, and more sputtery call at the bottom (F. G. Stiles).

Range: Costa Rica and western Panama.

TROGONS: Trogonidae (11)

Trogons are widely distributed in forested areas in the neotropics, Africa, and southern Asia. They reach their highest diversity and abundance in Middle and South America, and are well represented in Panama. Trogons are among the most beautiful of birds: most males are largely metallic green or blue above with contrasting red, orange, or yellow lower underparts; females are duller, usually brown or slaty above. Despite their bright coloration, trogons are often difficult to see because they perch quietly for long periods; their posture is erect, with the tail hanging straight down. All have loud resonant calls that are characteristic forest sounds, but are often difficult to track down to their source. Trogons eat fruit and insects, procuring both on the wing in spectacular, fluttering flights. The nest is in a tree cavity or in a hole dug out of an arboreal wasp nest. Several Panamanian species resemble each other closely, and care must be taken in distinguishing especially the females. The pattern on the underside of the tail is often the key mark; other important points are the color of the bill, eye-ring, and lower underparts.

WHITE-TAILED TROGON
Trogon viridis   Plate 15

Description: 10–11. Bill bluish gray in male, as is lower mandible in female (upper mandible black); *pale blue eye-ring in both sexes.* Male has upperparts, throat, and chest metallic blue-black with strong violet gloss on head, neck, and chest; *breast and belly orange-yellow; underside of tail essentially white.* Female *slaty above and on throat and chest;* breast and belly orange-yellow; *underside of tail mostly white* but with some irregular black barring or blotching on inner webs and near base of feathers.

Similar species: Males of all other "yellow-bellied" trogons have prominent black and white barring on underside of tail. Female most resembles female Violaceous Trogon but has blue (not yellow) eye-ring and mainly white underside of tail (not prominently barred with black).

Status and distribution: Locally fairly common in humid forest, second-growth woodland, and borders in lowlands on Caribbean slope from central Bocas del Toro (Chiriquicito Grande) east through San Blas; on Pacific slope known from eastern Panama province (where evidently rare or local: one old Panama City record and seen in hills east of Chepo, on road from Platanares to Jesús Maria — Ridgely and Eisenmann) and from Darién (where more numerous). In Canal area quite common on Barro Colorado Island and in the Fort Sherman/San Lorenzo area.

Habits: Similar to other trogons; often perches rather high in forest trees. The call is a series of rather soft *coo* notes, repeated slowly at first, then accelerated into a roll, sometimes ending with several slower notes. Occasionally the call will be varied with three or four *kuh* notes. Also calls *chuck, chuck, chuck,* and twitches spread tail from side to side.

Range: Western Panama to northern Bolivia and central Brazil.

BAIRD'S TROGON
Trogon bairdii   Plate 15

Description: 10–11. Found only in western Chiriquí. A close ally of White-tailed Trogon (possibly conspecific). Both sexes have *bluish bill* and *pale blue eye-ring.* Male like male White-tailed but has *red breast and belly.* Female resembles female White-tailed, but it too has *red lower underparts* and is paler slaty above; underside of tail looks essentially barred, with white bars much narrower than the slaty bars (half the width). In museum specimens color of underparts seems to fade to orange-red.

Similar species: See White-tailed Trogon (with entirely different range, and orange-yellow belly in both sexes). Male Collared Trogon has underside of tail black with numerous white bars (not mostly white), white band separating the green and red on underparts, and vermiculated wing-coverts (lacking in Baird's); it usually is found at higher elevations.

Status and distribution: Rare in forest and forest borders in lowlands and foothills of western Chiriquí; recorded, at least formerly, to about 1200 m (4000 ft). Now very local due to the destruction of forest over most of its limited Panama range (fortunately numbers remain greater in Costa Rica); the only recent report is of two pairs seen on the Burica Peninsula on June 26, 1982 (Ridgely).

Habits: Very similar to White-tailed Trogon; its primary vocalization also appears to be similar.

Range: Southwestern Costa Rica and extreme western Panama.

VIOLACEOUS TROGON
Trogon violaceus   Plate 15

Description: 9½. Male has pale grayish bill and *orange-yellow eye-ring;* female has dusky upper mandible, pale grayish lower, and *prominent broken white eye-ring.* Male mostly metallic green above with *crown, sides of neck, and chest glossy violet-blue;* sides of head and throat black; wing-coverts and secondaries black vermiculated white; vague white band across breast, with *lower underparts orange-yellow;* underside of tail narrowly and evenly barred black and white, with outer feathers broadly tipped white forming three wide bands. Female *mostly gray above and on throat and chest;* lower underparts as in male; underside of tail black, outer webs of outer feathers narrowly barred and broadly tipped white.

Similar species: Male Black-throated Trogon has green (not blue) crown and chest, and pale blue (not yellow) eye-ring. See also male White-tailed Trogon (with blue eye-ring and white, not barred, underside of tail). Female's mostly gray coloration brings to mind female White-tailed, but latter has blue eye-ring and mostly white underside of tail. White-tailed lacks wing vermiculation. Female Black-throated Trogon is brown where female Violaceous is gray.

Status and distribution: Fairly common in forest borders, lighter woodland, and clearings with large trees in lowlands on both slopes, ranging regularly up in foothills to about 900 m (3000 ft); not reported from Azuero Peninsula, and seems less numerous in Darién.

Habits: Not a bird of forest interior. Usually found singly or in pairs, occasionally in small groups. The call is a series of soft *cow* notes or sometimes *kyoo* notes, repeated steadily 10 to 15 times, somewhat higher in pitch and usually faster than Slaty-tailed Trogon's.

Range: Eastern Mexico to northern Bolivia and Amazonian Brazil.

COLLARED TROGON
Trogon collaris   Plate 15

Description: 10. Known only from highlands of extreme west and east. Male has yellow bill and inconspicuous brown eye-ring (red in *extimus* of Darién); female has blackish upper mandible, yellowish lower, and *prominent broken white eye-ring* (feathered). Male metallic green above and on chest, with sides of head and throat black; wing-coverts and secondaries black vermiculated white; *white band across upper breast* separating green chest from *red lower underparts;* underside of tail black with numerous narrow white bars (narrowest in Chiriquí race, *puella*) and outer feathers tipped white forming three bands. Female has *brown* replacing male's green, *red of underparts faded* (often pinker); *tail mostly chestnut above,* pale gray below with outer feathers broadly tipped white forming three bands.

Similar species: Both sexes resemble Orange-bellied Trogon, but lower underparts are obviously red (not orangey). See also Baird's Trogon.

Status and distribution: Fairly common in forest and forest borders in highlands of western Chiriquí (mostly 1200–2400 m: 4000–8000 ft; rarely, perhaps only formerly, down to 690 m: 2300 ft) and adjacent Bocas del Toro (Camp Cilindro), and in eastern Darién (Cerro Tacarcuna, Cerro Quía, Cerro Pirre; recorded 750–1500 m: 2500–5000 ft). Wetmore believes that old published records from eastern Chiriquí and Veraguas are in error; even as far west as the Fortuna area in central Chiriquí only the Orange-bellied Trogon has recently been found.

Habits: Often found in pairs, usually at low or middle levels inside forest. The typical call is a *cow* or *caow* repeated slowly and steadily; also has a two or three-noted call of similar quality, and a churring note which is often uttered in alarm as it quickly raises its tail and then slowly lowers it.

Range: Eastern Mexico to northern Bolivia and Amazonian and eastern Brazil.

Note: More than one species may be involved.

ORANGE-BELLIED TROGON
Trogon aurantiiventris   Plate 15

Description: 10. Closely resembles Collared Trogon. Male differs only in having *lower underparts orange, reddish orange, or orange-red* (never true red). Female likewise differs only in having lower underparts orange to reddish orange.

Similar species: See Collared Trogon. Some males in western Chiriquí are so orange-red that field separation from Collared is difficult; birds on Cerro Campana are definitely orange. Black-throated Trogon is somewhat similar but has bright yellow lower underparts, evenly banded black and white tail (not black with narrow white bands), and blue eye-ring.

Status and distribution: Uncommon to fairly common in humid forest and forest borders in foothills and highlands of Chiriquí, adjacent Bocas del Toro, Veraguas, Coclé (seen above El Copé on March 8–9, 1986; Ridgely, J. Guarnaccia, D. Engleman), and western Panama province (Cerro Campana); recorded mostly 600–1800 m (2000–6000 ft).

Habits: Much like Collared Trogon, though found more commonly at somewhat lower elevations. Probably the most numerous trogon on Cerro Campana (where Collared does not occur). Possibly a partly localized color phase of Collared Trogon; studies are needed of its behavior and to determine whether there is interbreeding in areas of overlap. E. S. Morton considers its vocalization to be like that of Black-throated Trogon.

Range: Costa Rica to central Panama.

BLACK-THROATED TROGON
Trogon rufus   Plate 15

Description: 9½. Male has greenish yellow bill and *pale blue eye-ring;* female has dusky upper mandible, yellowish lower, and inconspicuous pale blue eye-ring and prominent white in front of and behind eye. Male *metallic green above and on chest,* sides of head and throat black; wing-coverts and secondaries black vermiculated white; faint white band across breast, with *lower underparts bright yellow;* underside of tail narrowly and evenly barred black and white, outer feathers broadly tipped white forming three wide bands. Female has brown replacing male's green; *upperside of tail mostly rufous* tipped black, underside as in male.

Similar species: Male resembles male Violaceous Trogon but has blue (not yellow) eye-ring and strong green tones on head and neck (not violet-blue). Female is only brown trogon with yellow underparts. Both sexes resemble Orange-bellied Trogon but have yellow underparts (not orange) and show light blue eye-ring.

Status and distribution: Fairly common in forest and mature second-growth woodland in more humid lowlands on both slopes, ranging up regularly into lower foothills to about 900 m (3000 ft); except in eastern Panama, generally more numerous on Caribbean side; recently recorded from Azuero Peninsula on Cerro Montuosa, Herrera (a pair seen near the summit on November 3, 1979, and another in March 1982; F. Delgado).

Habits: Generally found at low heights within forest and often very tame. The typical call consists usually of two to four well separated *cow* notes (sometimes with rhythm of Chestnut-backed Antbird); also has a sharp *chirr,* often given in alarm and as the bird, having raised its tail, slowly lowers it.

Range: Honduras to eastern Peru, Paraguay, northeastern Argentina, and southern Brazil.

BLACK-TAILED TROGON
Trogon melanurus   Plate 15

Description: 12–13. Found only from Canal area east. Very like better known Slaty-tailed Trogon. Male has *yellow bill* and orange-red eye-ring; female has only *lower mandible yellow* and inconspicuous blackish eye-ring marked with red. Male like male Slaty-tail but with different bill color and *narrow white band separating green chest from red breast and belly.* Female like Slaty-tailed Trogon except for yellowish lower mandible.

Status and distribution: Uncommon and somewhat local in humid forest and second-growth woodland on both slopes in Canal area (more numerous on Caribbean side, where also found locally in mangroves), becoming more numerous eastward through lowlands of San Blas and Darién. Readily found in the upper Bayano River valley of eastern Panama province and in Darién; it probably outnumbers Slaty-tailed Trogon.

Habits: Similar to Slaty-tailed Trogon. The call also is similar, but the notes seem louder, more reasonant, *kwo, kwo, kwo...*

Range: Central Panama to northern Bolivia and Amazonian Brazil.

SLATY-TAILED TROGON
Trogon massena   Plate 15

Description: 12–13. Male had *orange-red bill* and eye-ring; in female only lower mandible and base of bill are reddish. Male mostly metallic green above with area of black and white vermiculations (appearing gray at a distance) on wing-coverts; facial area and throat black, chest metallic green, *breast and belly bright red; underside of tail slaty, with no white.* Female has slaty replacing male's green.
Similar species: Only other Panama trogon with red belly and wholly dark underside of tail is Black-tailed Trogon; male Black-tail has yellow bill (not orange-red or salmon), and narrow white band separating green and red of underparts; female Black-tail differs from this species in having lower mandible yellow (not dull reddish). See also Lattice-tailed Trogon.
Status and distribution: Fairly common to common in forest and second-growth woodland and borders in lowlands and foothills on both slopes, but absent from drier Pacific slope lowlands, and seems scarce across most of Darién (where perhaps largely replaced by Black-tailed Trogon). The common red-bellied trogon of the Canal area, especially widespread and numerous on the Caribbean side.
Habits: Like other trogons, often phlegmatic, perching motionless for considerable periods and then difficult to locate. Though basically a forest bird, it regularly comes to clearings and borders (where it is more easily seen), and also inhabits mangroves. Usually found singly or in pairs, occasionally in small groups. The call is a series of loud *cuh* notes, sometimes 20 or more, usually with a steady tempo and often with a ventriloquial effect.
Range: Southern Mexico to western Ecuador.

LATTICE-TAILED TROGON
Trogon clathratus   Plate 15

Description: 11–12. Known primarily from western Caribbean slope. *Iris yellow or cream-colored* (rarely pale blue). *Bill yellow in male,* upper mandible dusky and *lower mandible yellow in female.* Male resembles male Slaty-tailed Trogon, is metallic green above and on throat and chest, wing-coverts finely vermiculated black and white; breast and

belly red; *underside of tail black with widely spaced very narrow white bars.* Female like female Slaty-tail, slaty above and on throat and chest, becoming brown on breast, red on belly; *underside of tail as in male.*
Similar species: The tail barring is not very prominent in the field. The very similar Slaty-tailed Trogon has dark eye, reddish bill and eye-ring, and all dark underside of tail. Collared Trogon has dark eye, more conspicuous barring on underside of tail, and white band separating green and red on underparts; female Collared is brown (not slaty) above.
Status and distribution: Apparently rare (perhaps somewhat overlooked) in humid forest in lowlands and foothills on Caribbean slope from Bocas del Toro to Coclé (Río Cascajal); locally spills over Divide onto Pacific slope in very humid foothills of central and eastern Chiriquí (pair seen and male collected and photographed, but later lost, at Fortuna on March 2, 1976, by Ridgely; an old record from Cordillera de Tolé) and western Veraguas (Santa Fé); recorded 150–1050 m (500–3500 ft) in Panama, but somewhat higher (to 1350 m: 4500 ft) in Costa Rica (Slud).
Habits: Recalls Slaty-tailed Trogon in appearance and behavior, and regularly occurs sympatrically with it, though Lattice-tail favors more humid areas (especially hilly or lower montane), is more restricted to tall undisturbed forest, and seems almost always to be outnumbered by it. Its call is also similar to that of Slaty-tail, but is somewhat higher-pitched and not as steady or as long, tending to start slowly, speed up in the middle, and then trail off.
Range: Costa Rica and western Panama.

GOLDEN-HEADED QUETZAL
Pharomachrus auriceps   Plate 15

Description: 13–14; male's tail plumes add 3–4 in. Found only in eastern Darién highlands. Bill of male yellow, mottled brownish or grayish in female. Male *metallic golden green above* and on throat and chest; breast and belly red; *elongated upper tail-coverts extending slightly beyond tip of tail;* wings largely black except for elongated green coverts; tail black. Female like male but head and breast bronzy brown, upper tail-coverts shorter than tail, outer tail feathers tipped white.
Similar species: Slaty-tailed Trogon lacks the train and has wing-coverts vermiculated black and white.

Status and distribution: Fairly common in cloud forest on Cerro Pirre in eastern Darién; recorded 1200–1500 m (4000–5000 ft).

Habits: Behavior much like Resplendent Quetzal, often perching quietly for long periods and easily overlooked except when vocalizing or feeding at a fruiting tree. Its far-carrying call is very distinctive, a somewhat modulated ("reedy") hawk-like whistled phrase repeated up to six to eight times, *whe-wheeu, whe-wheeu, whe-wheeu.*

Range: Eastern Panama to northwestern Venezuela and northern Bolivia.

RESPLENDENT QUETZAL
Pharomachrus mocinno   Plate 15

Description: 14–15; male's plumes add 15–30 in. Found only in western highlands. Bill of male yellow, dusky in female. Male unmistakable, *mostly glittering golden green* with rounded and laterally flattened crest and *extraordinary train* consisting of lengthened feathers of upper tail-coverts; *breast and belly scarlet;* tail white from below. Female duller green, with upper tail-coverts usually not extending beyond tip of tail and with bushy crest; green above with head more bronzy; mostly brownish gray below with metallic green chest and red belly; tail slaty, outer feathers barred and tipped with white.

Similar species: Female might possibly be confused with considerably smaller male Collared Trogon; Collared has white band across breast separating green chest from red belly etc.

Status and distribution: Uncommon to locally fairly common in highlands of western Chiriquí, now mostly above 1500 m (5000 ft), formerly lower; recorded also in highlands of Bocas del Toro, eastern Chiriquí, and Veraguas, but actual status in these areas unknown. Inhabits humid mountain forest, but seems to favor forest edge and park-like clearings, regularly nesting in such situations.

Numbers continue to decline, at present mostly because of the clearings of tracts of mountain forest. A certain amount of direct persecution probably still occurs, but this appears to be reduced. Chiriquí residents know the bird well (called "guaco" locally, in imitation of its call, but "quetzal" is generally understood), and can often direct one to areas where it occurs. Quetzals are readily found, especially during the February–May nesting season, along the Boquete Trail above Cerro Punta, particularly at the tract of forest looked after by the Fernandez family (the "trail" is now drivable to this point, and this forest is the first substantial area one comes to above Cerro Punta; one of the family members will usually appear to guide you around, and should be paid for their expertise and interest). Quetzals are also usually readily found around the "Mirador" on Finca Lerida above Boquete; ask at the Hotel Panamonte for directions, etc. Overall, quetzals are probably easier to see here than anywhere else, in part because of Chiriquí's good weather over a relatively great proportion of the year: they have become a quite considerable tourist attraction in the area, and deserve full protection and encouragement as such.

Habits: Considered by many the most beautiful bird in the world — the sight of a male in good plumage, especially in flight with its incredible undulating train shimmering in the sun, is breathtaking. Perched quetzals are, however, often not easy to spot, and they may remain quiet and motionless for long periods. Especially during the breeding season, tape recordings of their calls are often very effective at bringing them in for a view — but moderation in their use is urged. Quetzals have a variety of calls, the most characteristic being a loud *hwaao* or *huaco*, often varied to a *wek-wek-wek-wecko* or simply *wek-wek;* also has a very different throaty whistle, *keeeoo-keeeoo.*

Range: Southern Mexico to western Panama.

MOTMOTS: Momotidae (4)

The motmots are a small neotropical family with the greatest number of species being found in Middle America. Most inhabit lower and middle growth of forest and woodland, though a few are found in more open situations. Despite their fairly large size, they are not conspicuous birds, being active mostly in the early morning and late afternoon, usually resting the remainder of the day. The three large Panama motmots are most often recorded from their far-carrying hooting or nasal calls. Motmots feed mostly on large insects, to a lesser extent on fruit and even small vertebrates. The nest is a burrow dug into an earth bank. The racquet tail tips of the central pair of tail feathers of three of the four Panamanian species are produced as a result of preening (and to some extent perhaps also abrasion), so that the barbs just above the feather tips fall off, leaving the shaft exposed. Birds with new central tail feathers (and no, or only one, racquet) are regularly seen.

TODY MOTMOT
Hylomanes momotula   Plate 16

Description: 7. *A small, large-headed, chunky motmot with no racquet tips on its short tail.* Crown greenish rufous with *short blue superciliary* and narrow black mask through eyes, bordered below by *conspicuous buffy white stripe;* otherwise dull green above, with *olive brownish wedge-shaped tail;* throat buffy bordered by *short whitish stripe;* remaining underparts dull brownish, more greenish on sides and whitish on lower belly.
Similar species: Much the smallest motmot, readily recognized by its striped facial pattern.
Status and distribution: Rare to locally fairly common in undergrowth of humid forest in foothills of Veraguas (Chitra, specimen in AMNH), eastern Colon province (Cerro Bruja), eastern Panama province (specimens from Cerro Azul and Cerro Chucantí, but no recent reports), eastern San Blas (Puerto Obaldía), and eastern Darién; recorded up to 1200 m (4000 ft). More numerous in Darién than elsewhere in its Panama range; regularly seen around Cana, especially along the trail to Boca de Cupe.
Habits: Tody Motmots seem to favor forest or tall woodland with a tangled viny understory. Here they are found singly or in pairs, perching unobtrusively at about eye level and doubtless often overlooked. They may remain motionless for prolonged periods, but do regularly flick their tail from side to side much as do the larger motmots. The call is a far-carrying, resonant *cwa-cwa-cwa-cwa...,* suggestive of a Prong-billed Barbet.
Range: Southern Mexico to northwestern Colombia.

BLUE-CROWNED MOTMOT
Momotus momota   Plate 16

Description: 16. Tail long, usually with *racquet tips. Crown and sides of head black* with *blue forehead and superciliary;* upperparts otherwise green; underparts mostly dull tawny, washed with olive on breast, with black spot on chest. Birds from western Panama east at least to Herrera (*lessonii*) have underparts mostly light olive green.
Similar species: Broad-billed and Rufous Motmots have rufous heads; Tody Motmot is much smaller and lacks tail racquets.
Status and distribution: Fairly common in forest borders, second-growth and gallery woodland, and clearings with dense undergrowth in lowlands and especially in foothills on much of Pacific slope (absent from the most open areas), including Azuero Peninsula, ranging in small numbers up into lower highlands (to about 1800 m: 6000 ft) in western Chiriquí; on Caribbean slope known only from Canal area and extreme eastern San Blas. In Canal area more numerous on Pacific side, where widespread in wooded areas and the commonest motmot.
Habits: Unlike other Panama motmots, not a true forest bird, and especially in the west often found in thickets and hedgerows in pastures. Usually seen in pairs, resting quietly in the lower growth and not very conspicuous, often passed by unnoticed. Dustbathes regularly, and at dusk quite often seen sitting on little-traveled dirt roads. Canal area birds give a rather dove-like single *hoo-oo* (sometimes doubled), somewhat hoarser or more tremulous than the usually tripled hoot of the ʻRufous Motmot; also has a very tremulous *hoorr* or *hrrroo,* softer than corresponding call of Rufous Motmot. Chiriquí birds seem to have a somewhat different vocalization, a *woot* or *woop* repeated two to six or more times.
Range: Eastern Mexico to northern Argentina and southern Brazil.

RUFOUS MOTMOT
Baryphthengus martii   Plate 16

Description: 18. Tail long, usually with *racquet tips. Head, neck, and underparts rufous* with broad black mask through eyes and black spot on chest; otherwise green above with violet-blue on wings; *lower belly bluish green.*

Similar species: Broad-billed Motmot is smaller with bluish green breast and belly (rufous down only to chest), has green chin, lacks violet in wings.

Status and distribution: Fairly common to common in forest and second-growth woodland in lowlands and lower foothills on entire Caribbean slope; on Pacific slope known from hill country of Veraguas and Coclé, in lowlands and lower foothills from western Panama province east through Darién. In Canal area widespread and common in forest on Caribbean side, less numerous on Pacific.

Habits: Found singly or in pairs in lower growth of forest or woodland. Frequently, especially when disturbed, swings its tail back and forth like a pendulum. Often executes an abrupt about-face on its perch. The call, heard most often in the early morning just before dawn, is a loud resonant rhythmic hooting, *hó-hoo-hoo* or *hoó-doo-doo,* often repeated and echoed by other individuals, sometimes varied and accelerated into a roll; the effect is almost owl-like. Another common call is *hoórro.*

Range: Nicaragua to western Ecuador and western Amazonia.

Note: We favor recognizing the *martii* group (Rufous Motmot) of southern Middle America to western Amazonia as a species distinct from true *B. ruficapillus* (Rufous-capped Motmot) of geographically distant southeastern South America; *ruficapillus* has a very different pattern (with rufous much reduced), and never acquires racquet tail

tips. The 1983 AOU Check-list treated them as a conspecific.

BROAD-BILLED MOTMOT
Electron platyrhynchum   Plate 16

Description: 13. Tail long, usually with *racquet tips. Head, neck, and chest rufous* with broad black mask through eyes, green chin, and black spot on chest; otherwise green above; *breast and belly bluish green.*

Similar species: Rufous Motmot is larger with rufous on underparts extending lower, onto breast and belly (bluish green only on lower belly); it has violet on wings.

Status and distribution: Fairly common in forest and second-growth woodland in lowlands and lower foothills on entire Caribbean slope; on Pacific slope found in eastern Chiriquí (San Félix), Veraguas foothills (Santa Fé, Chitra), El Valle and Cerro Campana, and in eastern Panama province and Darién. Widespread in forested areas on Caribbean side of Canal area, though not as numerous as Rufous Motmot.

Habits: Found singly or in pairs, sitting quietly on a horizontal branch or liana. Forages at all levels, but most often in middle or even upper strata. The call is very distinctive, a loud and resonant, somewhat nasal *aahnk* or *cwahnk,* usually given singly, but sometimes repeated rapidly in a series.

Range: Honduras to Bolivia and central Brazil.

KINGFISHERS: Alcedinidae (6)

The kingfishers are a large and cosmopolitan group of birds that reach their highest development in tropical Africa and Asia. Only six species are found in the Western Hemisphere, all of which occur in Panama. Many African and Asian species are brightly colored, but the New World kingfishers are relatively somberly clad in blue-gray or metallic green and white and rufous. In the Old World, kingfishers occupy a variety of niches; however all six American kingfishers are found only near water, where they feed primarily on fish. They are solitary birds, usually seen perched on a branch overlooking some body of water. The nest is frequently in a hole burrowed into a bank. As the result of the introduction of "peacock bass" into Gatun Lake in the early 1970s, populations of three kingfishers (Ringed, Amazon, and Green) have declined drastically.

RINGED KINGFISHER
Ceryle torquata   Plate 16

Description: 15–16. *Panama's largest kingfisher.* Bushy crest. *Bluish gray above,* throat

and collar around hindneck white; *underparts mostly chestnut-rufous.* Female similar but with bluish gray band across chest, bordered below by narrow white band; lower underparts chestnut-rufous.

Similar species: Belted Kingfisher is smaller and mostly white below with band of bluish gray (male) or bands of bluish gray and chestnut (female).

Status and distribution: Fairly common along both coasts and on lakes, rivers, and streams in lowlands on both slopes, ranging occasionally into lower highlands of western Chiriquí; found also on Coiba Island and larger Pearl Islands. Widespread in Canal area.

Habits: Usually seen singly or in pairs, often perched on horizontal branches above water. Frequently flies high overhead between feeding areas, then giving a harsh *keerrek*. Also has a rattle much like Belted Kingfisher's but louder.

Range: Southern Texas and Mexico to Tierra del Fuego.

BELTED KINGFISHER
Ceryle alcyon

Description: 12–13. Ragged crest. *Bluish gray above* with white collar on hindneck; *mostly white below* with *chest crossed by single bluish gray band*. Female similar but with *added band of rufous across breast,* extending down over flanks.

Similar species: Ringed Kingfisher is considerably larger with mostly chestnut-rufous underparts (not mostly white). Amazon Kingfisher is green above (as are all other Panama kingfishers).

Status and distribution: Uncommon winter resident on both slopes, mostly along either coast but also around lakes and larger rivers (particularly on migration); recorded occasionally as high as lower highlands of western Chiriquí; found also on Taboga Island, Pearl Islands, and other smaller Pacific coastal islands. Less numerous in Darién. Recorded mostly September–April, with rare stragglers (?) into June.

Habits: Usually seen singly. Perches on branches over water, staring intently downward; often hovers for a moment or two before diving in.

Range: Breeds in North America; winters from United States to Panama and in West Indies, rarely to Colombia, Venezuela, and the Guianas.

GREEN KINGFISHER
Chloroceryle americana   Plate 16

Description: 7–8. The commonest Panama kingfisher. Dark metallic green above with narrow white collar and *numerous small white spots on wings* and *patch of white on each side of tail* (flashes conspicuously in flight); *white below* with broad chestnut band across chest and green spotting on flanks (male), or with two narrow green bands across chest and green spotting on flanks (female).

Similar species: Amazon Kingfisher is much larger, without conspicuous white on tail and less on wings; female has only one green chest band (not two). Green-and-rufous Kingfisher is rich rufous below and has less white on tail.

Status and distribution: Common along streams and rivers and along shores of lakes in lowlands on both slopes, found also in mangroves and locally on rocky coasts; ranges in reduced numbers up into highlands of western Chiriquí (to about 1590 m: 5300 ft) and foothills of southern Azuero Peninsula (Cerro Hoya) and Darién; found also on Coiba Island and other Pacific coastal islands, but not recorded from islands in Gulf of Panama (Taboga, Pearl Islands, etc.).

Habits: Found singly or in pairs. Often raises its head and jerks its tail. Regularly perches on rocks in streambeds. Gives a clicking *trit-trit-trit* in flight, much like two pebbles being struck together.

Range: Extreme southwestern United States to northern Chile and central Argentina.

AMAZON KINGFISHER
Chloroceryle amazona   Plate 16

Description: 11. *Largest "green" kingfisher.* Somewhat crested. Dark oily green above with narrow white collar on hindneck and a few white spots on wings; *white below,* male with broad rufous chest band and a few green spots on flanks, female with broken band of green spot replacing male's rufous.

Similar species: Green Kingfisher is much smaller and has much more white in wings and tail. Green-and-rufous Kingfisher is rich rufous (not mostly white) below and has buffy (not white) collar.

Status and distribution: Fairly common along larger streams, rivers, and lakeshores in lowlands on both slopes, ranging up in small numbers into foothills in Chiriquí and Darién. Not very numerous in Canal area (virtually extirpated from Gatun Lake), but easily seen at Río Piedras, eastern Colon province.

Habits: Usually not found on coast but may occur in brackish lagoons or tidal rivers and river mouths. Favors wider watercourses, not shady streams (though present in small

numbers in such situations as well). Has a loud harsh *cack* and a higher rapidly repeated note approaching a rattle.
Range: Mexico to central Argentina.

GREEN-AND-RUFOUS KINGFISHER
Chloroceryle inda   Plate 16

Description: 8–9. Male dark shining green above, with *broad collar on sides of neck and entire underparts rich orange-rufous,* somewhat paler on throat; wings and tail lightly speckled white. Females similar but with greenish black chest band, feathers edged whitish.
Similar species: American Pygmy Kingfisher is much smaller and has white on lower belly. Green Kingfisher is mostly white below, and has more white in tail.
Status and distribution: Rare to locally uncommon (doubtless often overlooked) along small forest streams and in swampy forest and mangroves in lowlands on entire Caribbean slope, and on Pacific slope from eastern Panama province (where also found in more open swampy terrain, e.g. at the Tocumen marsh) east through Darién; found also on larger Pearl Islands. Scarce in Canal area, but locally more numerous in Bocas del Toro and Darién.
Habits: Unobtrusive and the least often encountered kingfisher in Panama. This and the Pygmy Kingfisher prefer shady backwaters and swampy areas and only rarely perch in the open, usually remaining hidden from view by a screen of leaves. Has a crackling *trit-trit-trit,* most often tripled.
Range: Nicaragua to northern Bolivia and southern Brazil.

AMERICAN PYGMY KINGFISHER
Chloroceryle aenea   Plate 16

Description: 5. *Panama's smallest kingfisher (by far).* Male dark metallic bronzy green above; broad collar on sides of neck and *most of underparts rich orange-rufous,* paler and buffier on throat; *center of belly and under tail-coverts white;* wings lightly speckled whitish (more in *stictoptera* of Pacific slope east to eastern Panama province). Female like male but with band of greenish black (edged with white) across chest.
Similar species: Not likely to be confused because of its small size. Much larger Green-and-rufous Kingfisher is similarly plumaged but is rufous to the vent and has some white barring on tail.
Status and distribution: Uncommon to locally fairly common along small streams in woodland and forest and in mangroves in lowlands on both slopes, including Azuero Peninsula, but apparently absent from drier areas on Pacific slope from eastern Coclé to Canal area; also found on Coiba Island, but not on islands in Gulf of Panama.
Habits: Shy and unobtrusive, usually perching low over water under the cover of vegetation. Sometimes perches over small forest puddles no more than an inch or two deep, but apparently does not actually sally for aerial insects (these being aborted dives for fish, *fide* J. V. Remsen). The call is a sharp but rather weak *tyeet.* Flight is low and fast, so much so that flying birds are difficult to follow to their next perch.
Range: Southern Mexico to northern Bolivia and southern Brazil.

PUFFBIRDS: Bucconidae (8)

The puffbirds are a rather heterogenous group of exclusively neotropical birds found chiefly in forest and woodland. Most species are characterized by their somber plumage, large heads and short necks, and short tails; many (a striking exception being the nunbirds) are rather inactive. Most puffbirds (nunbirds excepted) are relatively silent, though *Notharchus* puffbirds especially do have loud vocalizations, usually given with long pauses between utterances. They feed on large insects and also small lizards and frogs (and some fruit), often captured in flight. The nest is a burrow in a bank or on level ground, or a cavity in an arboreal termite nest.

BARRED PUFFBIRD
Nystalus radiatus   p.235

Description: 8½. Bill greenish gray: iris yellow. *Tawny to cinnamon buff above coarsely barred black,* with *broad buff collar;* throat whitish, otherwise buff below, *narrowly barred black* especially on sides.

Similar species: Female Fasciated Antshrike is smaller, black above barred with brown, has wholly rufous cap and no buff collar.
Status and distribution: Rare to locally uncommon in humid forest and forest borders in lowlands and lower foothills on Caribbean slope from northern Coclé (possibly Veraguas) east through San Blas;

on Pacific slope recorded mainly from Darién, with one old record from western Panama province (Capira, but probably actually taken in humid foothills north of town). In Canal area known only from two specimens collected in the nineteenth century. Most numerous eastward, particularly in Darién; readily found around Cana.

Habits: Usually found in pairs (sometimes well separated); they often perch quietly and motionless for long periods, frequently at forest edge but also inside. Much more likely to be noticed once its unmistakable call, a far-carrying (but soft), slowly delivered "wolf whistle", is recognized; birds may respond to even a crude imitation of it.

Range: Central Panama to western Ecuador.

Note: Placed in the genus *Bucco* in the AOU Check-list (1983), but we prefer to maintain *Nystalus* for it and several South American species until more is known about all of them. Sooty-capped Puffbird (*Bucco noanamae*) occurs very close to the Panama border in adjacent Colombia along the west shore of the Gulf of Urabá, and should be watched for (especially in eastern San Blas). It is a mid-sized (7½ in), forest-inhabiting puffbird (still little known, and with a very limited range); dark brown above with white forehead and superciliary, and blackish sides of head; throat white, extending back as inconspicuous grayish collar; broad breast band black, with lower underparts buffy white spotted black.

WHITE-NECKED PUFFBIRD
Notharchus macrorhynchus　　　Plate 23, p.235

Description: 10. Heavy black bill. Mostly black above with *white forehead* and broad white collar; mostly white below with *broad black breast band* and black barring on flanks.

Similar species: See Black-breasted Puffbird.

Status and distribution: Fairly common in canopy and borders of forest and second-growth woodland in lowlands on both slopes, though unrecorded from dry open lowlands in southern Coclé and western Panama province, and rare on Azuero Peninsula (F. Delgado). The most conspicuous puffbird in the Canal area, and at least on the Pacific side the most numerous.

Habits: Usually seen perched rather high on an exposed branch. Often remains motionless for long periods, then flying off in pursuit of a large insect, which it captures

with an audible snap, frequently then returning to its original perch where it kills its prey by beating it vigorously against the branch. Generally silent, but has a thin high twittery song, surprisingly weak considering the size of the bird.

Range: Southern Mexico to Bolivia, northeastern Argentina, and southern Brazil.

Note: Placed in the genus *Bucco* in the 1983 AOU Check-list, as were the following two species. We prefer, however, to maintain the genus *Notharchus* for them and a fourth species found in South America, as they seem to form a cohesive group of canopy-inhabiting, black and white puffbirds quite different from the typical *Bucco* group.

BLACK-BREASTED PUFFBIRD
Notharchus pectoralis　　　Plate 23, p.235

Description: 8. Heavy black bill. Mostly glossy blue-black above with *large white patch on ear-coverts* extending back as narrow white collar; *patch on upper throat white*, with *very broad black band across lower throat and breast*; lower underparts white with black barring on flanks.

Similar species: White-necked Puffbird is somewhat larger with white forehead and considerably more white on sides of neck and chest. Pied Puffbird is much smaller with different black and white pattern.

Status and distribution: Fairly common in humid forest and forest borders in lowlands on Caribbean slope from Canal area east through eastern Colon province (seen along Río Cascajal east of Portobelo in January–June 1987; D. Graham) to western San Blas (one below Nusagandi on March 7, 1986; Ridgely and J. Guarnaccia); on Pacific slope from Canal area (where scarce) east through eastern Panama province (mainly in upper Bayano River valley) and Darién. Quite numerous along both Achiote and Pipeline Roads in Canal area.

Habits: Usually perches high, frequently within the concealing foliage of the forest canopy, doubtless often escaping observation. Sometimes, however, comes out into small trees in forest clearings. Its presence is often made known by its distinctive loud song, an often long series of whistles usually ending with three drawling and descending couplets, *kweee-kweee-kweee-kweee-kweee, kweee-a, kwey-a, kyoo-a*; there may be as many as 30 *kweees* before the falling notes.

Range: Central Panama to northwestern Ecuador.

Note: See under White-necked Puffbird.

Left to right, WHITE-NECKED PUFFBIRD, BLACK-BREASTED PUFFBIRD, PIED PUFFBIRD, BARRED PUFFBIRD, LANCEOLATED MONKLET, WHITE-FRONTED NUNBIRD

PIED PUFFBIRD
Notharchus tectus   Plate 23, p.235

Description: 6. *Obviously smaller than other Notharchus puffbirds.* Black above with small white spots on crown and narrow white superciliary; white patch on scapulars; white below with *narrow black breast band* and black barring on flanks; tail feathers broadly tipped white (easily seen from below).

Similar species: White-necked and Black-breasted Puffbirds are larger with broad black breast bands and no white on wings or tail.

Status and distribution: Uncommon (west of Canal area) to fairly common in canopy and borders of humid forest, and in clearings with many scattered trees, in lowlands on entire Caribbean slope (unrecorded from northern Coclé and western Colon province, though surely occurs); on Pacific slope fairly common from eastern Panama province (Bayano River valley) east through Darién. In Canal area most easily found along Achiote Road.

Habits: Usually found in pairs; most likely to be seen perched at low and middle levels at edge of forest (difficult to see when high in forest canopy). More active than other *Notharchus* puffbirds, though it too will perch for long periods without moving. The song is a high, thin, weak whistle, rapidly given though slowing at end, *wee-weeda-weeda-weeda, weee-a weee-a, weee-a*, the slow terminal couplets sometimes replaced by *wheeeer*.

Range: Costa Rica to Peru and Amazonian Brazil.

Note: See under White-necked Puffbird.

WHITE-WHISKERED PUFFBIRD
Malacoptila panamensis   Plate 17

Description: 8. *"Puffy" looking.* Bill dusky above, mostly yellowish green below; iris red. Rufous brown above lightly spotted on back and wings with buff, and with *prominent white preocular area and moustachial tufts* (forming the "whiskers"); throat and chest tawny, lower underparts pale buff *streaked dusky*. Female grayer above and less streaked below.

Similar species: Overall puffy and brown appearance, conspicuous white about bill, and streaked lower underparts are characteristic.

Status and distribution: Fairly common in undergrowth of forest and second-growth woodland in lowlands and in smaller numbers in foothills (to about 1200 m: 4000 ft) on both slopes, but absent from dry Pacific lowlands from eastern side of Azuero Peninsula to extreme western Panama province.

Habits: Most often found in pairs, perching lethargically in the undergrowth; doubtless often overlooked. Once discovered usually very tame, almost "stupid", allowing a close approach. Sometimes follows antwren-dominated forest flocks; also occasionally in attendance at army ant swarms. Captured quite regularly in mist-nets, sometimes living up to its name when handled, fluffing out its feathers until it becomes a veritable puffball. Rather silent birds, they occasionally utter a very thin weak *tseet* or *pseeeu* (probably in alarm); also other squeaky notes (E. O. Willis and Eisenmann).

Range: Southern Mexico to western Ecuador.

LANCEOLATED MONKLET
Micromonacha lanceolata   p.235

Description: 5. Very rare. A *small* puffbird with heavy arched blackish bill and short tail. Rufous brown above and on sides of head and neck, with *narrow white area on forehead, lores, and around bill; below white with bold but rather sparse black streaking;* tail with blackish subterminal band.

Similar species: Small size and streaked underparts should preclude confusion. White-whiskered Puffbird is much larger; Gray-cheeked Nunlet is unstreaked rufous below, has gray (not white) on face.

Status and distribution: Only record is a bird collected at Guaval on Río Calovévora (at 540 m: 1800 ft), Caribbean slope of Veraguas on border with Bocas del Toro, on September 6, 1926.

Habits: Poorly known, and evidently rare throughout its range. Birds seen in western Colombia and western Ecuador have tended to perch quietly without moving for protracted periods, and thus the monklet probably is often passed by unnoticed. They seem to favor borders of humid forest and tall second-growth woodland. Sluggish birds, often a very close approach being permitted.

Range: Costa Rica south very locally to northwestern Ecuador, northeastern Peru, and western Brazil.

GRAY-CHEEKED NUNLET
Nonnula ruficapilla   Plate 17

Description: 6. *Bill rather long, slender, and slightly decurved,* bluish gray. Very narrow eye-ring red. Plain brown above, more rufescent on forecrown, with *sides of head contrastingly gray; bright tawny-cinnamon below,* fading to buffy whitish on belly.

Status and distribution: Rare to uncommon in humid forest borders and second-growth woodland in lowlands on Caribbean slope in northern Coclé and the Canal area (probably also occurs eastward, but as yet unrecorded); on Pacific slope found in eastern Panama province (Tocumen and Chepo area, from whence not recently reported, and in Bayano River valley) and Darién. In Canal area the only place where it appears to be at all regular is along the far end of Achiote Road (just before it enters Colon province).

Habits: Generally seen in lower growth of trees, often in or near dense viny tangles. Regularly joins mixed flocks of antwrens, small flycatchers, etc. Perches quietly with upright posture, occasionally sallying to branches or foliage for insects; often quite tame and approachable. Its call is a long series of up to 20 plaintive measured notes, *weeip, weeip, weeip* . . . (R. A. Rowlett).

Range: Central Panama to northern Colombia; eastern Peru and western Brazil.

Note: Formerly called *Nonnula frontalis*, but this form (found in Panama and Colombia) was considered conspecific with the geographically distant (but similar in plumage) *N. ruficapilla* in the 1983 AOU Check-list.

WHITE-FRONTED NUNBIRD
Monasa morphoeus   Plate 44, p.235

Description: 11. Unmistakable. *Bill bright red,* rather long, slender and somewhat decurved. *Mostly dark slaty* with white forehead; head and neck blacker. Birds from Bocas del Toro (*grandior*) also have chin white, as do some birds from central Panama. Birds from eastern Panama (*pallescens*) are somewhat paler gray, especially on wing-coverts, and black of head extends down over chest.

Status and distribution: Uncommon to locally fairly common in humid forest and to a lesser extent in forest borders in lowlands and foothills (regularly to about 600 m: 2000 ft, rarely to 900 m: 3000 ft) locally on both slopes; recorded from western Bocas del Toro, western Colon province (Chilar on Río Indio), eastern Colon province (drainages of Río Boqueron and Río Pequení into Madden Lake; also seen on Cerro Santa Rita by N. G. Smith), San Blas (recorded only from Cerro Brewster in west and Armila in the east, but probably more widespread), in eastern Panama province (early records from Cerro Azul, but none in recent decades; widespread in upper Bayano River valley), and Darién. Most numerous in eastern Panama, and with an apparent (and inexplicable) gap through much of west-central and central Panama. Only one sighting from Canal area, that of two seen and others heard on Barro Colorado Island on April 6, 1950 (Wetmore).

Habits: Most often seen in small groups perched in middle and upper forest levels, regularly in association with other medium-sized forest birds (caciques, mourners, etc.). Nunbirds are frequently noisy, giving a variety of loud whistled and gabbled notes; groups often excitedly chorus together, with bills pointed upward. Flight often includes characteristic long swooping jay-like glides. The nest in Costa Rica is an angled burrow dug deep into the ground (A. Skutch).

Range: Southeastern Honduras to northern Bolivia and southeastern Brazil.

JACAMARS: Galbulidae (3)

The jacamars form an exclusively neotropical family of slender, attractive birds, most species with very long thin bills. Three species are found in Panama, none of which is particularly numerous or widespread. Especially puzzling is the absence from most of Panama of a jacamar of the genus *Galbula*, at least one of which is found virtually everywhere else in tropical Middle and South America in forested areas. Rather active and conspicuous arboreal birds, they usually perch not too high above the ground, with the bill characteristically angled upward. Jacamars are primarily insectivorous, capturing their prey entirely on the wing; they consume many large butterflies. Their nest is a burrow dug into an earth bank, or sometimes an old wasp nest.

DUSKY-BACKED JACAMAR
Brachygalba salmoni   Plate 40

Description: 7. Found only in eastern Darién. Bill very long (2 in) and slender; tail quite short. *Upperparts, chest, and sides greenish black*, browner on crown; throat white (more buffy in female); center of breast and belly cinnamon.

Similar species: Smaller, shorter-tailed, and duller and darker than Rufous-tailed Jacamar.

Status and distribution: Uncommon to locally fairly common at borders of humid forest and in adjacent small shrubby clearings in lowlands of eastern Darién (lower Chucunaque and Tuira River valleys, ranging up in the latter to the Cana area).

Habits: Often in pairs, usually perching quite high (typically higher than in Rufous-tailed Jacamar) on exposed horizontal branches. Make long looping sallies after passing insects, returning to the same perch or close by. Less vocal than Rufous-tailed Jacamar, but periodically gives a high thin upward-inflected *psee*, sometimes repeated in a long series.

Range: Eastern Panama and northwestern Colombia.

RUFOUS-TAILED JACAMAR
Galbula ruficauda   Plate 16

Description: 9. Found only in far western and eastern Panama (includes *melanogenia*, formerly treated as a distinct species, Black-chinned Jacamar). *Glittering golden green above and on chest*; throat white (buff in female) with small area of black on chin (often hard to see in the field); *breast, belly, and underside of tail rufous*, with central two pairs of feathers green (hidden from below). *Ruficauda* (eastern Panama) lacks the black chin and has only one pair of tail feathers green.

Similar species: The only Panama jacamar with a rufous undertail. Great Jacamar is larger with shorter heavier bill, and has black underside of tail. See also Dusky-backed Jacamar.

Status and distribution: Uncommon in forest borders and secondary woodland in lowlands of western Bocas del Toro; locally fairly common in similar situations in western Chiriquí (where ranges up into lower highlands to about 1200 m: 4000 ft, with overall numbers doubtless much reduced due to deforestation though it remains numerous in the few places where forest and woodland remain reasonably extensive, e.g. on the Burica Peninsula). Also recorded in eastern Panama, where the situation is complicated: nominate *ruficauda* has been collected at El Real and seen around that town on a number of recent occasions, and it was probably this form which has been seen twice in eastern Panama province (one near Ipetí in the upper Bayano valley on April 23, 1976, by Ridgely; and one on Cerro Azul on February 24, 1979, by A. Moore); and a pair of what seemed to be *melanogenia* was carefully observed at Cana, eastern Darién, on March 3, 1981 by Ridgely and V. Emanuel. Conceivably the Rufous-tailed Jacamar is beginning to spread westward toward central Panama (a consequence of partial deforestation across the region?). The presumed contact zone between *melanogenia* and nominate *ruficauda* in Darién merits study; in adjacent Colombia a few hybrids have been recorded (the basis for the two forms now being considered conspecific), and hybridization may be occurring in Panama as well.

Habits: Usually found in pairs, perching alertly in lower or middle growth, but often not very conspicuous (at least in Panama). They make long sallies after flying insects, including butterflies, dragonflies, and bees. The usual call is a loud *peeek*, sharply inflected, while the song is a long series of chippering notes with the same quality, gradually accelerating and ending in a trill.

Range: Southern Mexico to western Ecuador, northern Bolivia, northern Argentina, and southern Brazil.

GREAT JACAMAR
Jacamerops aurea Plate 16

Description: 12. *Bill heavy and slightly decurved.* Brilliant metallic golden green above; upper throat green, lower throat white in male (tawny in female); remaining underparts rich tawny-rufous; underside of tail blue-black.

Similar species: The largest jacamar and the only one without a thin straight bill; note the rufous underparts without a chest band.

Status and distribution: Uncommon in humid forest and mature second-growth woodland in lowlands and lower foothills on entire Caribbean slope; on Pacific slope found only from Canal area east through Darién. Widespread in forested parts of Canal area, though more numerous on Caribbean side; here as elsewhere infrequently recorded until the distinctive call is recognized.

Habits: Found singly or in pairs, perching quietly on branches at lower and middle levels, often not moving for long periods and doubtless often overlooked despite its brilliant coloration. Makes long sallies to branches or foliage, often snapping up its insect prey with an audible puffbird-like click. Occasionally utters a long, eerie, mournful *kleeeeeeee-enhhhhh*, slurred and somewhat hawk-like in quality, gradually fading away; it is far-carrying, but the calling bird often sounds farther away than it actually is. Responds readily to tape playback, sometimes even to crude whistled imitations of its call.

Range: Costa Rica to northern Bolivia and central Brazil.

BARBETS: Capitonidae (3)

Barbets are found in the tropical parts of America, Africa, and southern Asia; three very distinctive species are found in Panama. They are heavy-bodied birds with stout bills. Basically forest birds, barbets are usually found in pairs or small groups, often gathering to feed with other birds in fruit laden trees. They nest in holes hollowed out in dead trees.

SPOT-CROWNED BARBET
Capito maculicoronatus Plate 17

Description: 7. Bill stout, blue-gray tipped black. Male *glossy blue-black above*, center of crown spotted whitish; below mostly white with *broad yellow band across breast* (more orange in center), sides boldly streaked blue-black with *bright orange patch on flanks*. Female like male above but with *throat and breast blue-black*; lower underparts white,

streaked black on sides with *bright orange patch on flanks*. Birds from Darién and San Blas, *rubrilateralis*, have the flank patch *bright scarlet*.

Similar species: Recognized as a barbet by its thick bill and chunky, neck-less appearance; the only Panama barbet with extensive black in plumage.

Status and distribution: Uncommon to locally fairly common in humid forest and forest borders in lowlands and lower foothills (to about 900 m: 3000 ft) on Caribbean slope from Veraguas (seen above Santa Fé by N. G. Smith) and northern Coclé east through San Blas; on Pacific side from eastern Panama province (Cerro Azul, where now rare, with few recent reports) and Darién (where widespread and more numerous). In Canal area most easily seen in Achiote Road/Escobal region.

Habits: Usually seen in pairs or small groups, often following mixed flocks, moving deliberately at middle and upper levels. Generally quiet, but occasionally gives a fairly loud toucan-like croaking; male also has a harsh two-syllabled "throat-clearing" call (Eisenmann).

Range: Western Panama to western Colombia.

RED-HEADED BARBET
Eubucco bourcierii   Plate 17

Description: 6¼. Found only in highlands of west and east. Bill stout, greenish yellow. Male unmistakable: *head and neck bright red* with black around eye and narrow bluish white bar across hindneck; otherwise dull green above; *red of throat passing into orange on chest and yellow on breast and center of belly*, flanks whitish streaked with greenish. Female very different: forehead and area around eyes black, crown olive green washed with yellow, *sides of head grayish blue bordered behind by a yellow bar*; otherwise dull green above; throat grayish yellow, chest orange-yellow, *lower underparts yellowish streaked with greenish.*

Status and distribution: Uncommon to fairly common in humid montane forest and forest borders in foothills and lower highlands of Chiriquí, Bocas del Toro, Veraguas (Santa Fé, Chitra, Calobre), western Coclé (a pair seen above El Copé on March 8, 1986; D. and L. Engelman, Ridgely, J. Guarnaccia), and eastern Darién (Cerro Tacarcuna, Cerro Quía, Cerro Pirre); one sighting of a pair above Puerto Obaldía in eastern San Blas on June 18, 1965 (D. Sheets); recorded mostly 900–1800 m (3000–6000 ft) in western Panama, lower in west-central Panama (600–1200 m: 2000–4000 ft); aside from the San Blas report, somewhat higher again in eastern Panama (mostly 900–1500 m: 3000–5000 ft).

Habits: Forages at all levels, usually at medium heights and lower. Often probes into dead leaf clusters. Most often found singly, frequently accompanying mixed flocks of other highland birds. Although usually silent, the Red-headed Barbet does have an infrequently heard song, perhaps given mainly when breeding; this consists of a short fast series of hollow notes lasting about two seconds, *who-oh-oh-oh-oh-oh*, the quality being rather like a Rufous Motmot or antpitta.

Range: Costa Rica to northern Peru.

PRONG-BILLED BARBET
Semnornis frantzii   Plate 17

Description: 7. Found only in western highlands. *Very heavy bluish gray bill,* tip of lower mandible pronged, upper mandible notched. Yellowish olive above, more tawny on crown; black tuft on nape (absent in female) and black around base of bill; *sides of head, throat, and breast ochraceous tawny*, with patch of bluish gray on sides of breast; flanks grayish, center of belly light yellow.

Similar species: Though without a strong pattern or bright colors, this species should be easily recognized by its thick-set appearance, very stout bill, and the yellowish tawny head and breast. The male's black tuft normally lies flat. Female Red-headed Barbet has blue cheeks, streaks on belly, greenish yellow bill. See also Black-faced Grosbeak.

Status and distribution: Rare to locally uncommon in forest and forest borders in highlands of western and central Chiriquí (mostly 1500–2250 m: 5000–7500 ft, locally down to 1050 m: 3500 ft above Fortuna); also recorded from adjacent Bocas del Toro, eastern Chiriquí (Cerro Flores), and Veraguas (Chitra). Seemingly more numerous in Costa Rica, e.g. at Monteverde.

Habits: Usually found in small groups at low and middle tree levels. Often very tame, especially when feeding in a fruit-laden tree or bush, and generally rather sluggish. Heard considerably more often than it is seen, its very distinctive far-carrying call being one of the characteristic sounds of the humid mountain forest; it is a deep *cwa-cwa-cwa-cwa . . .* repeated many times and often given by two or more birds at once, and which Slud describes as having "a special character, like an Indian yell in which the palm of the hand is rapidly and repeatedly pressed against and removed from the mouth."

Range: Costa Rica and western Panama.

TOUCANS: Ramphastidae (6)

The toucans are a characteristic group of neotropical birds found in forest and woodland. They are best known for their enormously enlarged and multicolored bills (superficially similar to those of the Old World hornbills, Bucerotidae, though the two groups are not closely related). Though the bill makes the birds look awkward, it actually is very light, being largely hollow. Toucans are gregarious birds, usually seen in small flocks, especially at fruiting trees. Though their food is primarily fruit and berries, that diet is supplemented with large insects and small reptiles and amphibians, as well as the eggs and young of other birds. They nest in hollows in trees, the smaller species often roosting as a group in a disused woodpecker hole. The larger toucans are shot for food in some parts of Panama, but are numerous and easily observed in the Canal area.

EMERALD TOUCANET
Aulacorhynchus prasinus　　　　　Plate 17

Description: 13 (bill 2½–3 in). Bill mostly black, with broad area on culmen yellow, and base sharply outlined with white. Inconspicuous bare ocular area slate. *Mostly bright green*, slightly paler below, with brownish crown and *blue throat*; under tail-coverts and underside of tail chestnut.

Similar species: *The only mostly green toucan in Panama*. Compare to slightly larger Yellow-eared Toucanet.

Status and distribution: Common in humid montane forest, forest borders, and clearings with large trees in highlands of Chiriquí, adjacent Bocas del Toro (recorded only from north of Fortuna, Chiriquí, but presumably more widespread), and Veraguas; rare in foothills of Coclé, western Panama province (Cerro Campana), and western San Blas (where known only from a group of five seen at Cerro Brewster on April 25, 1985, by J. Blake); fairly common in foothills and highlands of eastern Darién (Cerro Pirre, Cerro Tacarcuna); in western Chiriquí recorded mostly 1200–2400 m (4000–8000 ft), but lower elsewhere (down to 600–750 m: 2000–2500 ft).

Habits: Found in pairs or small groups, foraging at all levels. Omnivorous, regularly taking eggs and nestlings of other birds. Quite noisy, repeating a variety of loud, harsh, often hoarse *kwack* or *kweck* notes in a series, rising to *queerk* when excited; also a *kee-kee-krrr*, and a repeated *krik*, which can suggest call of Keel-billed Toucan.

Range: Central Mexico to western Venezuela and southern Peru.

COLLARED ARACARI
Pteroglossus torquatus　　　　　Plate 17

Description: 16 (bill 4 in). *Upper mandible mostly ivory whitish*, with blackish culmen, tip, and lower mandible; base of bill sharply outlined with white. Bare ocular area red. *Head, neck, and throat black* with inconspicuous chestnut collar; otherwise dull greenish black above with red rump; *remaining underparts mostly yellow*, more or less stained red, with spot of black on center of breast and *mixed band of black and red across upper belly*. Sanguineus (recently recorded from extreme eastern Darién; formerly considered a distinct species, Stripe-billed Aracari) differs in its bill pattern (with *distinct horizontal black stripe on yellowish upper mandible*, no blackish tip, and more numerous but shallower "tooth marks" along cutting edge of upper mandible), and has *ocular area bluish slate* becoming dark red behind eye (not all red) and *no chestnut collar*.

Similar species: The only aracari in most of Panama. Fiery-billed Aracari of Pacific west has orange-red (not whitish) upper mandible, etc.

Status and distribution: Common in forest, second-growth woodland, and borders in lowlands and foothills (to about 900 m: 3000 ft) on entire Caribbean slope and on Pacific slope from Canal area east through Darién. Some form of aracari (probably this) is found in western Panama province (Cerro Campana and El Valle), but its identity has still not been determined. The situation is complex in eastern Darién: in July 1975 a number of apparently pure or near-pure *sanguineus* were noted near the Colombia border (mouth of Río Mono into Tuira River and lower slopes of Cerro Quía) and no *torquatus* were seen (Ridgely). Further down the Tuira, at Matugantí, an obvious hybrid *torquatus × sanguineus* was taken on July 20 (specimen to AMNH), and later examination revealed a previously unrecognized specimen of "almost pure" (90%) *sanguineus* taken by R. Hinds at Río Mono on February 18, 1969 (in GML collection). J. Haffer (*Am. Mus. Novitates* no.

2294, 1967, p.29) demonstrated that the two forms "hybridize freely" across a narrow zone in northwestern Colombia, and this appears to be occurring in Darién as well.

Habits: Aracaris travel about in groups of up to about a dozen individuals, generally keeping in close contact; they "follow the leader", straggling one by one across clearings and forest openings, flying on a straight line with rapid fluttery wingbeats interspersed with short glides. Usually they stay rather high in trees, often perching in the open in early morning and to a lesser extent in late afternoon. The usual call is a distinctive high squeaky or sneezy *ksíyik, ksíyik*; also a *kecheéf*.

Range: Southern Mexico to northwestern Venezuela and western Ecuador.

Note: *P. sanguineus* is now considered conspecific with *P. torquatus* (with another form, *P. erythropygius*, of western Ecuador also included) by the 1983 AOU Check-list.

FIERY-BILLED ARACARI
Pteroglossus frantzii   Plate 44

Description: 16 (bill 4 in). Known only from Chiriquí and western Veraguas. Similar to Collared Aracari, but has *upper mandible mostly orange-red*, more numerous "tooth marks" along cutting edge of upper mandible, bare ocular area black in front of eye and red behind (not all red), and *broader and more solidly red band across upper belly*, with black restricted to narrow broken line at upper edge.

Similar species: See Collared Aracari.

Status and distribution: Uncommon to fairly common but now very local in forest, second-growth woodland, and borders in lowlands and foothills on Pacific slope in Chiriquí and coastal Veraguas (a 1924 record from Río San Lorenzo); recorded regularly up to about 1200 m (4000 ft), rarely up to 1800 m (6000 ft). Recent decades have seen a marked decline in numbers of this spectacular aracari, a decline entirely attributable to the deforestation which has taken place over most of its Panama range. Nonetheless, they do persist in encouraging numbers in remnant patches of forest and woodland between Volcán and Santa Clara, and on the Burica Peninsula; there are no recent reports except from western Chiriquí.

Habits: Similar to Collared Aracari. The usual call is a *kachíf*, varied to *ksichík* and *weechíf*.

Range: Southwestern Costa Rica and Pacific western Panama.

YELLOW-EARED TOUCANET
Selenidera spectabilis   Plate 17

Description: 15 (bill 3½ in). Bill mostly black, with upper part of upper mandible mostly yellowish green; bare ocular area basically green above eye and yellow below, the green brighter and more bluish in male. Male has *head, neck, and underparts black* with *conspicuous tuft of yellow feathers on ear-coverts*; back and wings olive green; patch of yellow on flanks, under tail-coverts red. Female similar but lacks the yellow ear-tufts and has *crown and hindneck chestnut*.

Similar species: This strongly patterned toucan is not likely to be confused if seen reasonably well; in poor light might be confused with Emerald Toucanet.

Status and distribution: Uncommon and somewhat local in humid forest in lowlands and (mostly) foothills on entire Caribbean slope; on Pacific slope recorded from eastern Chiriquí (Cordillera de Tolé), Veraguas, Panama province (Cerro Campana and Cerro Azul/Jefe), and eastern Darién (Cerro Tacarcuna, Cerro Quía, Cerro Pirre); recorded mostly 450–1050 m (1500–3500 ft), less often down to sea level and up to 1440 m (4800 ft). May engage in seasonal altitudinal movements; perhaps in lowlands mostly during rainy season, after breeding. Rather rare in Canal area, in recent years seen mainly along Pipeline and Achiote Roads.

Habits: Found singly or in pairs, foraging at all levels but most often high. Rather inconspicuous birds, rarely perching fully in the open, generally remaining within the concealment of the canopy. Not particularly vocal, but does give a dry rhythmic repeated *t-krrrk, t-krrrk, t-krrrk . . .* or *ak-tkrrrk, ak-tkrrrk, ak-tkrrrk . . .*, much like Keel-billed Toucan but weaker and usually more distinctly bisyllabic.

Range: Southern Honduras to northwestern Ecuador.

KEEL-BILLED TOUCAN
Ramphastos sulfuratus   Plate 17

Description: 19 (bill 5½ in). *Bill multicolored, mostly yellowish green with red tip, broad orange-red stripe on upper mandible*, and light blue area on lower mandible. Bare ocular area greenish. Mostly black with bright yellow throat and chest, bordered narrowly below by red band; rump white, and under tail-coverts red.

Similar species: Chestnut-mandibled Toucan is larger with a bicolored yellow and chestnut bill.

Status and distribution: Common in forest, second-growth woodland, and borders in lowlands and lower foothills (to about 900 m: 3000 ft) on entire Caribbean slope; on Pacific slope less numerous and more local except in eastern Panama province (Cerro Azul/Jefe area, Bayano River valley) and Darién, ranging in forested foothills from Veraguas eastward and on Azuero Peninsula; absent from dry open lowlands from eastern side of Azuero Peninsula to extreme western Panama province. Conspicuous in forested areas on Caribbean side of Canal area; more local, perhaps irregular, on Pacific side.

Habits: Usually seen in small groups high in trees, often perching fully in the open, especially in early morning and late afternoon. Keel-bills sometimes accompany Chestnut-mandibled Toucans, but more often alone. They look top-heavy in flight because of the long bill. Flight is undulating, with several rapid wingbeats followed by a descending glide on set wings, then more wingbeats to regain some altitude (though they usually seem to steadily lose altitude) — unmistakably a toucan, at any distance, though the two species can often not be distinguished when far away. The typical call is an endlessly repeated, grunting or croaking *kre-ék, kre-ék, kre-ék* . . ., the calling bird often bobbing its head or tossing it from side to side with each note. Also has other croaking or guttural calls.

Range: Eastern Mexico to northern Colombia and northwestern Venezuela.

CHESTNUT-MANDIBLED TOUCAN
Ramphastos swainsonii Plate 17

Description: 23 (bill 6–7 in). Bill *bicolored*: most of upper mandible *yellow*, lower mandible and wedge-shaped area at base of upper mandible *dark reddish chestnut*. Bare ocular area yellowish green. In plumage like Keel-billed Toucan, but often shows a narrow white line at lower edge of yellow bib.

Similar species: In reasonable light easily distinguished from Keel-billed Toucan by differently colored bill; Chestnut-mandibled is also larger overall, and its bill is proportionately even longer.

Status and distribution: Fairly common to locally (in more remote regions) common in forest and forest borders in lowlands and foothills (to about 900 m: 3000 ft) on entire Caribbean slope; on Pacific slope recorded from western Chiriquí (where formerly recorded up to 1650 m: 5500 ft, but has declined drastically in recent decades due to deforestation, with recent reports only from Burica Peninsula), and from western Panama province (Chorrera) east locally through Darién (where generally widespread and numerous; recorded to 1500 m: 5000 ft on Cerro Tacarcuna). Even in areas where substantial forest remains, this toucan may decline due to heavy hunting pressure. Widespread in forested areas on Caribbean side of Canal area.

Habits: Similar to and often occurring with Keel-billed Toucan. The call is, however, entirely different, an almost gull-like repeated yelping *kee-yoo, tedick-tedick-tedick*, the rhythm of the basic phrase being well expressed by the Spanish vernacular name of "Dios-te-dé".

Range: Honduras to western Ecuador.

Note: Choco Toucan (*R. brevis*) of western Colombia and western Ecuador may yet be found in extreme eastern Darién as it has been recorded very close to the Panama border. Plumage closely resembles Chestnut-mandibled Toucan (including bill colors), but is same size as Keel-billed Toucan (19 in) and has similar keel-shaped bill and croaking voice. This form was earlier considered a small race of *R. ambiguus* (Black-mandibled Toucan) of northern South America, but Haffer (1974) has shown that *brevis* is actually closer to the *sulfuratus* group, and that it should be treated as a full species. A specimen was recorded by Ridgway as having been taken at "Loma del León", presumably in eastern Darién, but Wetmore regarded the locality as uncertain.

WOODPECKERS: Picidae (20)

The woodpeckers are a virtually cosmopolitan and well known group of birds, living wherever there are trees (except on oceanic islands), specializing in clinging to trunks and branches. They are heavy-bodied birds with strong, straight, pointed bills and stiffened tail feathers (except in piculets and Old World wrynecks) used to brace themselves against the trunk. They are widely distributed in Panama, though in most areas the number of species is not large. Most species are sexually dimorphic, males usually with more red on head. Woodpeckers are primarily insectivorous, drawing their prey out of bark or wood with their long sticky tongue, but some species also eat fruit, some go to the ground for ants, and a few capture insects on the wing. They nest in holes dug into trunks and branches (usually dead wood); their nests are much used by other birds after the woodpeckers have abandoned them.

OLIVACEOUS PICULET
Picumnus olivaceus   Plate 19

Description: 3½. A *tiny* woodpecker, by far Panama's smallest. *Crown and hindneck black, spotted with orange in front and with white to the rear* (spots all white in female); otherwise dull yellowish olive above with yellowish wing-edging; tail black; buffy yellowish below, indistinctly streaked with brownish olive.

Status and distribution: Uncommon and rather local in lighter woodland, borders, and shrubby clearings in more humid lowlands and foothills on Pacific slope in Chiriquí (where recorded up to 1620 m: 5400 ft, though usually only to about 1200 m: 4000 ft), western Veraguas, southwestern Herrera (Cerro Montuosa: F. Delgado), and southern Los Santos, and on both slopes from the Canal area east through San Blas and Darién (where somewhat more numerous and widespread). Rather scarce in the Canal area.

Habits: Rather inconspicuous as it forages at lower and middle levels, creeping on trunks and limbs much like a nuthatch (*Sitta* sp.), not using its tail for support, often pausing for several minutes to industriously peck on a twig or small branch. Sometimes perches normally like a songbird. Often joins mixed flocks. The call is a distinctive high thin chippering trill, in pattern reminiscent of a Downy Woodpecker's (*Picoides pubescens*) but much weaker.

Range: Guatemala to northwestern Venezuela and western Ecuador.

ACORN WOODPECKER
Melanerpes formicivorus   Plate 18

Description: 8–9. Found only in western highlands. *The "clown face".* Mostly glossy black above with red crown and *yellowish white forecrown*, the latter *extending down in front of eye and connecting with yellowish white band across upper chest*; rump white; upper throat black, lower underparts white *streaked with black on breast and sides*. Small white patch on wings and white rump conspicuous in flight. Female similar but only nape red, with black band across crown separating the white from the red.

Similar species: The unusual facial pattern renders this species virtually unmistakable; no other Panama woodpecker has streaked underparts.

Status and distribution: Common in forest borders and park-like clearings and pastures with large trees in highlands of western Chiriquí, mostly above 1200 m (4000 ft); recorded also from eastern Chiriquí and Veraguas, with one sighting of a group of four on Cerro Campana, western Panama province, on September 7, 1968 (N. G. Smith).

Habits: A conspicuous bird around Cerro Punta and Bambito in western Chiriquí. Active, usually seen in groups of up to a dozen or more, often perching on high dead snags. Regularly sallies after flying insects. Also eats many acorns (which it sometimes stores), and some fruit. A rather noisy woodpecker, with a variety of loud throaty calls.

Range: Western United States to western Panama; Colombia.

GOLDEN-NAPED WOODPECKER
Melanerpes chrysauchen   Plate 18

Description: 7½–8. Found only in Chiriquí and western Veraguas. Resembles Black-cheeked Woodpecker, but has *bright yellow* (not red) *hindneck*, and *broad white stripe down center of back* (back not black with narrow white barring).

Similar species: See Black-cheeked Woodpecker; the two do not occur together. Acorn Woodpecker, which at least formerly occurred sympatrically with this species, is equally boldly patterned and colorful. Hairy Woodpecker also has whitish back stripe.

Status and distribution: Rare and now very local in forest, forest borders, and second-growth woodland in lowlands and (at least formerly) in foothills of western Chiriquí; also recorded from coastal Veraguas (a 1924 record from Río San Lorenzo); recorded up to about 1200 m (4000 ft). Has declined markedly over virtually all of its former Panama range due to deforestation; the only recent report comes from the Burica Peninsula, where a single pair was seen on June 26, 1982 (Ridgely), and even here it appears to have decreased substantially (Wetmore in 1966 considered it "fairly common").

Habits: Much like Black-cheeked Woodpecker, with calls also similar.

Range: Southwestern Costa Rica and western Panama; northern Colombia.

BLACK-CHEEKED WOODPECKER
Melanerpes pucherani   Plate 18

Description: 7½–8. Forehead yellow, crown and nape red, *cheeks and sides of neck black; upperparts otherwise black*, narrowly barred on back and spotted on wings with white, and with white rump; throat and breast olive grayish, *lower underparts buffy whitish barred with black*, with red on center of belly. Female has crown black, only nape red.

Similar species: A much blacker bird than the Red-crowned Woodpecker, with characteristic black face instead of an all-white face. In Pacific western Panama see also Golden-naped Woodpecker.

Status and distribution: Common in forest, forest borders, and second-growth woodland in lowlands on entire Caribbean slope; on Pacific slope found in foothills from Veraguas eastward, and in lowlands from Canal area eastward, with one sighting from eastern side of Azuero Peninsula (seen in gallery woodland south of Llano de Piedra, Los Santos, on July 24, 1964; Eisenmann); recorded up to about 1050 m (3500 ft). In Canal area more numerous and widespread on Caribbean side.

Habits: Usually forages rather high in trees, frequently perching conspicuously on dead snags; comes lower at forest edge and in clearings. Eats much fruit. The calls resemble those of Red-crowned Woodpecker, but are higher-pitched, a *churrr* and a *chiriree*.

Range: Southern Mexico to western Ecuador.

RED-CROWNED WOODPECKER
Melanerpes rubricapillus   Plate 18

Description: 7–7½. Crown and nape red; *remaining upperparts barred black and white*, with white rump; *forehead and sides of head whitish*; grayish white below, tinged with red on center of lower belly. Female similar but with crown grayish buff, only nape red. Immature has yellowish forehead.

Similar species: Likely to be confused only with Black-cheeked Woodpecker but is evenly barred black and white above and lacks black on sides of head.

Status and distribution: Very common in lighter woodland, shrubby clearings, residential areas, and mangroves in lowlands and foothills on Pacific slope from Chiriquí to western Darién (Punta La Sabana); on Caribbean slope found in cleared areas from Coclé east through San Blas; found mostly below 750 m (2500 ft), locally up to about 1200 m (4000 ft). Common also on Coiba and Cébaco Islands, and on the Pearl Islands (but absent from Taboga).

Habits: The most familiar and numerous woodpecker on most of the Pacific slope and throughout the Canal area except in heavy forest. Found singly or in pairs. Rather noisy, the typical calls being a *churr, churr*, rather like the call of its North American congener *M. carolinus* (Red-bellied Woodpecker), and a *wicka, wicka*. Eats fruit as well as insects.

Range: Southwestern Costa Rica through Panama, northern Colombia, Venezuela, and the Guianas.

YELLOW-BELLIED SAPSUCKER
Sphyrapicus varius

Description: 7–8. Male mostly black above white rump and barring on back; *wings with elongated white stripe* (conspicuous at rest); crown and nape patch red, white stripes behind eye and back from bill; throat red, patch on chest black, remaining underparts yellowish white with dusky barring on sides. Female has white throat and mostly black crown. Immature quite different, *mostly brownish*, but already with the *characteristic white wing-stripe*.

Similar species: This scarce northern migrant is most likely to be seen in dull immature plumage. No resident woodpecker has a similar wing-stripe.

Status and distribution: Rare and irregular winter visitant to western and central Panama, especially along Caribbean coast and in foothills and highlands (recorded November–March). Many northern winters pass with no records at all, though there seems to have been some recent increase (perhaps merely due to more complete observer coverage?). Not recorded east of Cerro Azul, eastern Panama province.

Habits: Favors semiopen areas and light woodland or plantations. Usually inconspicuous, but often quite approachable once located. Occasionally draws attention to itself by its slurred squealing call, but in general a quiet bird on its winter quarters.

Range: Breeds in eastern North America, wintering south to Honduras and the Greater Antilles, in small numbers to Panama and the Lesser Antilles.

HAIRY WOODPECKER
Picoides villosus Plate 18

Description: 7–7½. Found only in western highlands. Mostly black above with *brownish white stripe down center of back* and whitish line behind eye and on sides of head; *grayish brown below*. Male has red nape patch; immature male has more red on crown (red sometimes replaced with yellow).

Similar species: Considerably smaller than the North American races of the Hairy Woodpecker (and actually about the size of the Downy Woodpecker, *P. pubescens*), and with its uniform brownish underparts rather different in appearance. See Golden-naped Woodpecker.

Status and distribution: Fairly common in forest, forest borders, and clearings with large trees in highlands of western Chiriquí, mostly above 1500 m (5000 ft) less often down to 1200 m (4000 ft); recorded also from adjacent Bocas del Toro and highlands of eastern Chiriquí (Cerro Flores).

Habits: Found singly or in pairs, foraging at all heights but generally rather high. Not as conspicuous or noisy as the Acorn Woodpecker, with which it is often found; the calls are reminiscent of those of the North American races, though higher-pitched and more subdued. Drums fairly often.

Range: North America to western Panama.
Note: Formerly placed in the genus *Dendrocopos*.

SMOKY-BROWN WOODPECKER
Veniliornis fumigatus Plate 18

Description: 6½. Found only in highlands of west and east. *Small. Uniform smoky brown to tawny-olive*, somewhat grayer below; male with red crown (lacking in female, and only rearcrown red in immature male).

Similar species: The plain, essentially unmarked brownish plumage is characteristic. Red-rumped Woodpecker is somewhat similar but has red rump and barred underparts. Ruddy Woodcreeper is differently shaped and more brightly colored.

Status and distribution: Uncommon in humid forest, second-growth woodland,

and borders in foothills and highlands of Chiriquí (where also one old record from lowlands), Bocas del Toro, Veraguas (Santa Fé), and eastern Darién (Cerro Tacarcuna); recorded mostly 600–1800 m (2000–6000 ft).

Habits: An inconspicuous woodpecker, found singly or in pairs, foraging mostly at middle or lower levels, primarily on smaller branches (less often on trunks). Regularly accompanies mixed flocks. Not very vocal, but its occasional single sharp *peek!* does draw attention to it.

Range: Eastern Mexico to Venezuela and northwestern Argentina.

RED-RUMPED WOODPECKER
Veniliornis kirkii Plate 18

Description: 6½. Found only in western and eastern Panama. *Small*. Crown red more or less speckled with black, and bordered behind by a *narrow yellow band on nape*; upperparts otherwise tawny-olive, often stained red (browner in western race, *neglectus*, than in eastern race, *cecilii*); *rump red* (often concealed by wings); sides of head and throat brownish gray, with remaining *underparts narrowly and evenly barred dull whitish and brown*. Female similar but with brownish crown.

Similar species: Smoky-brown Woodpecker lacks red rump and the barring below.

Status and distribution: Rare to locally uncommon in forest (both humid and deciduous, depending on locality) in lowlands and foothills on Pacific slope; recorded from western Chiriquí (where greatly decreased due to deforestation; the only recent reports are from Burica Peninsula), Veraguas (nineteenth-century specimens from Calobre and Cordillera del Chucú; no recent reports), eastern Panama province (upper Bayano River valley), and Darién; found also on Coiba Island. In Darién recorded up to at least 900 m (3000 ft). Not yet reported from western side of Azuero Peninsula, though seems possible.

Habits: Much like Smoky-brown Woodpecker. Likewise not very vocal, but often first located by tracking down its persistent soft tapping. Forages mostly on smaller branches, at varying heights above the ground, and both inside forest and at edge and in adjacent clearings.

Range: Costa Rica to Venezuela and western Ecuador.

RUFOUS-WINGED WOODPECKER
Piculus simplex   Plate 18

Description: 7¼. Found only in western Panama. Iris bluish white. *Crown, nape, and moustachial streak bright red; sides of head dull olive green*; otherwise dull yellowish olive above, flight feathers barred rufous and black; *throat and chest olive*, latter sparingly spotted with buffy yellowish; lower underparts buffy yellow barred dusky olive. Female similar but with crown and moustachial region dull olive (only the nape red, sometimes also with some red around eyes).

Similar species: Rather like Stripe-cheeked Woodpecker, but lacks that species' cheek stripe and has a plain olive throat (not spotted whitish). Golden-olive Woodpecker has gray crown and white face, and entirely barred underparts.

Status and distribution: Rare in humid forest in lowlands of western Chiriquí (two nineteenth-century specimens, but no modern reports and quite possibly extirpated due to deforestation) and western Bocas del Toro (Almirante area and lower Río Changuinola), and in foothills of Veraguas on both slopes (Calovévora, Santa Fé).

Habits: Not a well known bird in Panama. Usually seen singly, less often in pairs, foraging mostly at middle or lower levels inside forest, occasionally at edge. At long intervals both sexes utter a loud explosive *keeeeeeyr*, sometimes doubled, in quality rather like the common call of Great Kiskadee.

Range: Honduras to western Panama.

Note: The AOU Check-list (1983) treats both *P. simplex* and *P. callopterus* as conspecific with the South American *P. leucolaemus* (White-throated Woodpecker), calling the enlarged species Rufous-winged Woodpecker. We are not convinced that this is the best course (the facial patterns of *simplex* and *callopterus* are quite distinct, and the ranges of the two approach each other quite closely in Veraguas, if indeed they do not actually overlap, with no evidence of any intergradation), and until more definite data is forthcoming, we prefer to maintain all three as allospecies. Preliminary data also indicate that vocalizations differ.

STRIPE-CHEEKED WOODPECKER
Piculus callopterus   Plate 18

Description: 7. Iris pale gray. *Crown, nape, and moustachial streak bright red; a whitish stripe across lower cheeks*; otherwise orange-brown or brassy olive above, rump olive barred yellowish, and flight feathers barred rufous and black; throat and chest olive *spotted with whitish*; lower underparts dull yellowish barred with dusky olive. Female similar but with crown and moustachial region dark gray, only the nape red.

Similar species: Rufous-winged Woodpecker lacks the cheek stripe, and has an unspotted plain olive throat. The larger Golden-green Woodpecker has a yellow cheek stripe, is much more boldly barred and yellower below, and is brighter olive green above.

Status and distribution: Uncommon and local in humid forest and borders, mostly in foothills (300–900 m: 1000–3000 ft); on Caribbean slope recorded from Veraguas (one nineteenth-century specimen of uncertain locality) and eastern Colon province (not recorded from San Blas but may occur); on Pacific slope recorded only from eastern Panama province (Cerro Azul/Jefe area) and Darién (Cerro Pirre). In Canal area known only from one nineteenth-century specimen; there are several recent sightings from near sea level at Río Piedras, eastern Colon province, perhaps having wandered down from adjacent foothills.

Habits: Rather quiet and inconspicuous. Usually found singly or in pairs, foraging at lower or middle levels; sometimes accompanies mixed flocks.

Range: Panama.

Note: See under Rufous-winged Woodpecker.

GOLDEN-GREEN WOODPECKER
Piculus chrysochloros   Plate 18

Description: 8½. Found only in eastern Panama. Crown, nape, and moustachial streak red; *broad yellow streak above red moustache*; upperparts otherwise rather bright olive green; throat golden buff, *remaining underparts golden yellow barred with blackish*. Female similar but with *crown and moustachial region golden yellow*.

Similar species: The brightest of Panama's green woodpeckers. See Stripe-cheeked Woodpecker.

Status and distribution: Evidently rare in deciduous and swampy forest in lowlands of eastern Panama province (Bayano River valley) and Darién (lower Tuira and Chucunaque River valleys).

Habits: The distinctive Panama race *aurosus* (also found in northern Colombia) is poorly known. In South America other races of this

species are found singly or in pairs, usually foraging at middle or upper forest levels (rarely at edge or in the open), and often accompanying mixed flocks.
Range: Eastern Panama to northern Argentina, Paraguay, and southeastern Brazil.

GOLDEN-OLIVE WOODPECKER
Piculus rubiginosus   Plate 18

Description: 8–8½. Known only from western Panama. *Crown gray*; narrow line on either side, nape, and moustachial streak red; *sides of head grayish white*; upperparts otherwise golden olive with dull yellow rump, the wings edged with yellow; throat blackish, streaked with whitish, remaining underparts brownish olive barred with yellowish. Female similar but with only nape red.
Similar species: See other *Piculus* woodpeckers.
Status and distribution: Fairly common in second-growth woodland, forest borders, and clearings with scattered trees in foothills and highlands of Chiriquí, adjacent Bocas del Toro (recorded only from north of Fortuna, Chiriquí, but probably more widespread), Veraguas, Coclé (one specimen taken at Río Guabal), and on southwestern Azuero Peninsula north to southern Herrera (where seen on Cerrol Montuoso; F. Delgado); recorded mostly 600–1500 m (2000–5000 ft), but at least formerly it apparently occurred down to sea level in Chiriquí and Veraguas. Seems generally less numerous in Costa Rica.
Habits: Found singly or in pairs, usually at middle and upper levels. Its calls are somewhat kiskadee or flicker-like, a loud *geep* or *keer*; also has a peculiar *utzia-deek*.
Range: Southern Mexico to western Panama; Colombia to northwestern Argentina and Guyana.

SPOT-BREASTED WOODPECKER
Colaptes punctigula   Plate 18

Description: 7½–8. *Crown black*; hindcrown, nape, and moustachial streak red; *sides of head white*; upperparts otherwise golden olive barred with black; throat white checkered with black, remaining underparts yellowish olive *spotted with black*, chest sometimes tinged orange-red. Female similar but with black moustachial stripe and only nape red.
Similar species: The combination of the black crown and spotted underparts is diagnostic.

Status and distribution: Rare in mangroves, lighter woodland, and semiopen areas with scattered trees in lowlands on Pacific slope locally in eastern Panama province (Juan Diaz, Río Chico) and Darién (Garachiné, El Real). Scarce in Panama (though a relatively numerous and conspicuous bird in South America), Spot-breasteds have been recently seen in the mangroves at Juan Diaz on a few occasions, and also around El Real (including at the airport).
Habits: Not very well known in Panama. In South America forages singly or in pairs, usually not too high above ground and often more or less in the open. Sometimes drops to the ground to feed on ants. Its commonest call is a weak and rather high *whee-whee-whee-whee . . .* (up to 8–10 notes), somewhat reminiscent of the northern flickers.
Range: Central Panama to northern Bolivia, western Brazil, and the Guianas.
Note: Formerly placed in the genus *Chrysoptilus*.

CINNAMON WOODPECKER
Celeus loricatus   Plate 18

Description: 8. Bill greenish yellow. *Distinct but short bushy crest. Head and upperparts cinnamon-rufous*, more or less spotted black (virtually plain in some birds); tail coarsely barred buff and black; male with red moustachial streak and upper throat; cinnamon-buff below, *boldly barred and scaled with black*, the markings sparser on belly. Bocas del Toro birds (*diversus*) are darker rufous above than birds from the rest of Panama (*mentalis*).
Similar species: In Bocas del Toro see Chestnut-colored Woodpecker.
Status and distribution: Uncommon to locally fairly common (though heard much more than seen) in humid forest and forest borders in lowlands on entire Caribbean slope (not recorded between Veraguas and the Canal area, though probably occurs), and on Pacific slope from Canal area (where rare) east through Darién; ranges locally up into foothills, e.g. on Cerro Azul/Jefe. In Canal area perhaps most numerous on Pipeline Road.
Habits: Usually forages singly in or near forest canopy, though occasionally comes much lower. Most often not with flocks. Much more readily found once its distinctive call is recognized, a loud clear semi-whistled *wheeét, wheeet, wheet-it*, sometimes with an introductory *chuweéoo*; overall effect reminiscent of Black-striped

Woodcreeper, but with notes better enunciated.
Range: Nicaragua to western Ecuador.

CHESTNUT-COLORED WOODPECKER
Celeus castaneus Plate 18

Description: 9. Known only from western Bocas del Toro. Bill yellowish with bluish base. *Long pointed crest. Mostly chestnut, shading to paler dull tawny on head*; sparsely barred with black above and below except on head and wings; rump sometimes yellowish; moustachial streak and area below eyes red in male.
Similar species: Cinnamon Woodpecker is smaller, with a shorter bushier crest and with head same color as back (not paler); its black barring is much more noticeable, especially below.
Status and distribution: Uncommon in humid forest and forest borders in lowlands of western Bocas del Toro.
Habits: Less conspicuous and quieter than the Cinnamon Woodpecker, which seems generally to outnumber it. Found singly or in pairs, foraging mainly in middle and upper levels of forest, sometimes following mixed flocks. Its distinctive call is a somewhat nasal *keeyark*, rather soft, sometimes followed by one to two *kuh-kuh* notes; North American birders will be struck by this call's resemblance to that of the Red-headed Woodpecker (*Melanerpes erythrocephalus*).
Range: Southeastern Mexico to Caribbean western Panama.

LINEATED WOODPECKER
Dryocopus lineatus Plate 18

Description: 13–14. *Large.* Mostly black above with crown, *conspicuous pointed crest*, and moustachial stripe bright red; *two virtually parallel white stripes down back* and another from bill to behind eye and down sides of neck; throat and chest black, lower underparts barred buff and blackish. Female similar but with forecrown and moustache black.
Similar species: Superficially much like a Crimson-crested Woodpecker but with white back stripes not converging and different facial pattern. In extreme western Panama see also Pale-billed Woodpecker.
Status and distribution: Fairly common to common (usually conspicuous) in forest borders, second-growth woodland, and clearings with large trees in more humid lowlands on both slopes, ranging up in smaller numbers into foothills to over 1200 m (4000 ft).

Habits: Tends not to occur inside forest, and to avoid extensively forested regions. Found singly or in pairs, climbing up trunks and larger branches at all heights. Frequently seen feeding on *Cecropia* trees, there obtaining ants or their larvae. Its calls are a loud flicker-like *wicka-wicka-wicka* and a lower *keép-grrrr* ; also drums.
Range: Mexico to northern Argentina, Paraguay, and southeastern Brazil.

CRIMSON-BELLIED WOODPECKER
Campephilus haematogaster Plate 18

Description: 13–14. Large. *Entire crown, crest, and neck red*; broad black mask, *bordered above by a narrow yellowish buff line, and below by a much broader one*; otherwise mostly black above (with no white back stripes), lower back and rump dark crimson; upper throat black, *remaining underparts essentially crimson*, with some dusky markings especially on belly; inner flight feathers boldly spotted yellowish buff (usually showing on closed wing), under wing-coverts uniform buff. Female similar but neck black with *buff facial stripe continuing down sides of neck*, and lower underparts more heavily mixed black.
Similar species: Has much more red than Panama's other large woodpeckers, and the only one with buff stripe on face and spotting on wings, and lacking white back stripes.
Status and distribution: Rare in humid forest and forest borders in lowlands and foothills on Caribbean slope from Bocas del Toro (Buena Vista and Laguna de Chiriquí) east locally through San Blas; on Pacific slope found in eastern Panama province (several recent sightings from Cerro Jefe) and Darién (where widespread and perhaps more numerous than westward). Only recently (1968) found in Canal area, where it remains a rare and infrequently seen resident in forests along Pipeline Road.
Habits: This spectacular but inconspicuous woodpecker is usually found inside tall forest, climbing mostly on trunks of large trees at lower levels. Most often encountered in pairs; usually very shy. Gives a very loud whacking double drum, the first stroke stronger.
Range: Western Panama to eastern Peru.

CRIMSON-CRESTED WOODPECKER
Campephilus melanoleucos Plate 18

Description: 14–15. A large woodpecker. *Bill blackish. Conspicuous pointed crest and head largely bright red*, with white spot at base of bill and another small black and white spot on ear-coverts; otherwise mostly black with long white stripes extending down sides of neck and *almost converging in a "V" on lower back*; lower breast and belly barred buffy white and black. Female similar but crown black with white neck stripe starting broadly at base of bill and extending through face.

Similar species: Lineated Woodpecker has almost parallel white stripes down back; female Lineated has white facial stripe narrowing in front of eye. In extreme western Panama see Pale-billed Woodpecker.

Status and distribution: Fairly common in forest, second-growth woodland, and borders in lowlands on both slopes from eastern Bocas del Toro (west to Cricamola) and eastern Chiriquí (west to San Félix and Cerro Chame) east through San Blas and Darién, ranging up in reduced numbers into foothills (to about 900 m: 3000 ft). Replaced westward by the Pale-billed Woodpecker; it is not known whether the two are ever sympatric.

Habits: Often seen in pairs, climbing on trunks and larger branches at all levels, occasionally in isolated trees at considerable distances from actual forest. Like the other large woodpeckers it has a deeply undulating flight. Its loud and far-carrying drumming is typically three or four (or even five)-noted, thus differing from the distinctly two-noted raps of Pale-billed and Crimson-bellied Woodpeckers: the first stroke is much the loudest, with the last two or three being weaker, and thus at a distance often only the first two can be heard. Also gives a loud *chiz-ik* and a rasping *kiarhh*, often followed by a snarling *rai-ai-ai-ai*

E. O. Willis and Eisenmann), but lacks flicker-like call of Lineated Woodpecker.

Range: Western Panama to northern Argentina and southeastern Brazil.

PALE-BILLED WOODPECKER
Campephilus guatemalensis Plate 18

Description: 13–14. Found only in extreme western Panama. *Large. Bill yellowish white. Conspicuous crest, entire head, and throat bright red*; otherwise mostly black with long white stripes extending down sides of neck onto back and *almost converging in a "V" on lower back*; breast and belly buffy barred with black. Female similar but with only face and crest red, crown and throat black.

Similar species: Best told from similar Crimson-crested Woodpecker by its pale (not blackish) bill and somewhat different facial patterns; the two allied species are apparently not sympatric. Lineated Woodpecker has parallel white back stripes and black on face.

Status and distribution: Uncommon in forest, second-growth woodland, and borders in lowlands and foothills (to about 1200 m: 4000 ft, rarely higher) in western Chiriquí (where reduced in overall numbers due to forest destruction); fairly common in lowlands of western Bocas del Toro (east to Chiriquí Grande).

Habits: Though basically a forest bird, this woodpecker does come out into partially cleared areas to feed. Found singly or in pairs, perching at all heights. Has a characteristic double drumming, the first stroke much louder; also gives a nasal *nyuck, nyuck*.

Range: Mexico to western Panama.

OVENBIRDS AND ALLIES: Furnariidae (23)

The ovenbirds or horneros (no group name is especially fitting) are a diverse group of neotropical sub-oscines allied to the woodcreepers, best developed in temperate and montane South America, with only a few species reaching the lowlands of Panama (more in mountain areas of east and west). They are essentially insectivorous, but occupy a great variety of niches. All the Panamanian species have rather dull plumage, mostly in tones of brown, some with buff spotting and streaking. Most of the Panamanian representatives are forest birds; the exception, the two *Synallaxis* spinetails, are found in bushes in open country or border growth. The variety of nests of members of this family is remarkable. The "ovenbirds", or "horneros" as the Argentinians call them, for which the family is named, are found only in South America and get their name from their large domed mud nests which resemble a Dutch oven. Among Panama representatives, the *Synallaxis* spinetails construct large twig nests with a narrow tubular entrance, the Red-faced Spinetail builds a pendant, coconut-shaped globe of more fibrous material, and a number of genera construct nests in holes in banks.

PALE-BREASTED SPINETAIL
Synallaxis albescens   Plate 20

Description: 6. Grayish brown above with gray forehead and *rufous crown and hindneck* and *rufous wing-coverts; white below*, tinged with brownish gray on chest and sides, and with sometimes concealed dusky patch on lower throat; *tail long and graduated*, brown. Immatures lack rufous and are browner below.

Similar species: No similar bird is found with it in most of Panama range; locally occurs with the much darker Slaty Spinetail. Wedge-tailed Grass-Finch is larger and buffier, without rufous on crown and wings.

Status and distribution: Common in open grassy areas with scattered bushes, scrubby areas, and sedgy or wet meadows in lowlands on Pacific slope from Chiriquí to eastern Panama province (lower Bayano River); in Chiriquí ranges up in cleared pastures to around 1200 m (4000 ft); not known from Darién. Very local in Canal area due to absence of much suitable habitat, but common and easily found in the Tocumen/Chepo area.

Habits: Unless singing, usually rather unobtrusive, creeping about in tangles near ground. The song is distinctive, two-noted, *wee-bzü* or *fee-bü*, reminiscent of the *fitz-bew* song of the Willow Flycatcher.

Range: Southwestern Costa Rica to central Argentina.

SLATY SPINETAIL
Synallaxis brachyura   Plate 20

Description: 6. Dark grayish brown above with *crown and hindneck rufous* and *mostly rufous wings; sides of head and underparts slaty* with a few whitish streaks on throat; tail long and graduated, brown.

Similar species: Likely to be confused only with Pale-breasted Spinetail, but much darker overall with uniform slaty (not mostly white) underparts.

Status and distribution: Local in Panama. Uncommon in shrubby overgrown clearings and woodland borders in lowlands and foothills of Bocas del Toro and northern Veraguas (Río Calovévora), and in foothills and lower highlands of western Chiriquí (perhaps formerly also in lowlands but now mainly 600–1200 m: 2000–4000 ft; recorded from Volcán area westward, apparently not present on Boquete side of Volcán Barú); rare on Caribbean side of Canal area (few recent reports, mostly from Achiote Road area), becoming somewhat more numerous east

through eastern Colon province to western San Blas (Mandinga); fairly common locally in lowlands and lower foothills of eastern Darién (Cerro Pirre area, especially at Cana, and in upper Río Jaqué drainage).

Habits: More skulking than Pale-breasted Spinetail, but presence often given away by its calls, a broken, sometimes prolonged, *ch-ch-chirrrrr* or *brrrrr*.

Range: Eastern Honduras to northwestern Peru.

RED-FACED SPINETAIL
Cranioleuca erythrops   Plate 14

Description: 5½. Found only in highlands of west and east. *Front half of head rufous*, hindneck and most of upperparts olive brown except for mostly rufous wings and tail; underparts somewhat paler olive brown, lightest on throat; tail long and graduated. Immature very similar but with olive brown crown, only sides of head rufous, and sometimes showing a vague superciliary.

Similar species: *Synallaxis* spinetails are not arboreal forest birds; foliage-gleaners are considerably larger. In any case, none has the contrasting rufous face.

Status and distribution: Fairly common in forest and forest borders in highlands of Chiriquí, Bocas del Toro (recorded only from north of Fortuna, along oleoducto road, but probably more widespread), Veraguas (Chitra, Santa Fé), and eastern Darién (Cerro Pirre and Cerro Tacarcuna); in western Chiriquí recorded mainly 1200–2100 m (4000–7000 ft), but elsewhere down to about 900 m (3000 ft).

Habits: Usually forages slightly above eye-level, gleaning in dead-leaf clusters, epiphytes, and among twigs. Found singly or in pairs, frequently in flocks of other highland birds. Its frequently given song is a fast, high-pitched, almost stuttering *see-see-see-se-se-e-e-e-e*.

Range: Costa Rica to western Ecuador.

COIBA SPINETAIL
Cranioleuca dissita   Plate 20

Description: 5¾. *Found only on Coiba Island*. In form resembles Red-faced Spinetail but not found with it. *Rusty brown above with rufous crown and narrow buff superciliary*; sides of head brownish lightly streaked with grayish; throat whitish, remaining underparts light olive brown; wings and tail rufous, tail long and graduated.

Similar species: Unlike any other bird on Coiba.

Status and distribution: Fairly common in lower and middle growth of forest and forest borders on Coiba Island.

Habits: General behavior resembles that of Red-faced Spinetail, tending to creep about fairly actively in dense foliage and viny tangles, also sometimes creeping up tree trunks, occasionally and briefly using its tail as a support. Usually found singly, less often in pairs, sometimes with small mixed flocks of other Coiba birds. Its song resembles that of Red-faced Spinetail, being a complicated series of high fast notes, some rather musical, with gradual descending or fading effect.

Range: Coiba Island, Panama.

Note: We prefer to consider this isolated form as a full species, though it was described by Wetmore as a race of the South American *C. vulpina* (Rusty-backed Spinetail). Apart from the most peculiar range (if lumped), *dissita* differs from *vulpina* in its forest habitat (*vulpina* being a bird of riparian thickets), and in voice (the song of *dissita* being more or less typical of the arboreal *Cranioleuca* group, which includes *erythrops*, and quite different from *C. vulpina*); *dissita* also differs in plumage, being browner ventrally than any of the races of *C. vulpina*.

DOUBLE-BANDED GRAYTAIL
Xenerpestes minlosi   Plate 40

Description: 4. Found only in eastern Darién. Dark olive gray above with blackish crown, *yellowish white superciliary*, and *two white wing-bars; yellowish white below*; tail dark gray, graduated. Immature similar but with blackish streaks on throat and breast.

Similar species: Unlike any other Panama Furnariid. Not particularly distinctive, most resembling various nonbreeding wood warblers (e.g. Cerulean or Bay-breasted) in overall color pattern; note its distinctive behavior (below).

Status and distribution: Rare to locally uncommon in canopy and borders of forest and second-growth woodland in eastern Panama province (family party of three seen above Ipetí in upper Bayano valley on April 23, 1976; Ridgely) and Darién.

Habits: Favors mid-level viny tangles where it forages actively but usually remaining within cover so often hard to see clearly. Has characteristic habit of clinging to underside of leaves, twigs and even small branches, moving quite acrobatically, sometimes hanging upside-down or creeping like a xenops. Does not actually seem to associate with mixed flocks very much. Though the genus' inclusion in the Furnariidae has been questioned, a large stick nest with a side entrance found at Cana in March 1981 near where graytails were foraging (Ridgely *et al.*), seems likely to have been this species', though graytails were never seen to actually enter it. No other Cana bird is known to make such a nest. Regularly found along the Boca de Cupe trail at Cana.

Range: Eastern Panama and northern Colombia.

SPOTTED BARBTAIL
Premnoplex brunnescens   Plate 14

Description: 5¼–5½. Foothills and highlands. Dark brown above with indistinct buff superciliary; *tail brownish black*, with stiff protruding spines; throat buffy, *remaining underparts dark brown profusely marked with large oval black-outlined buff spots*.

Similar species: An obscure *dark* brown bird with *conspicuous* spotting below. Its plumage most resembles that of Wedge-billed Woodcreeper, but that species is more slender and has differently shaped bill, rufous (not blackish) tail, etc. In Darién see Beautiful Treerunner.

Status and distribution: Fairly common in undergrowth of humid forest and (less often) forest borders in foothills and highlands on both slopes; recorded from Chiriquí, Bocas del Toro, Veraguas, western San Blas (birds mist-netted on Cerro Brewster on April 23 and 25, 1985; J. Blake), and eastern Darién; recorded mostly 600–2250 m (2000–7500 ft), but mostly above 1200 m (4000 ft) in western Chiriquí and Darién.

Habits: An inconspicuous bird whose true numbers are better reflected by its often frequent capture in mist-nets. Forages quietly, creeping along mossy branches and trunks, only occasionally using its tail for support (despite the protruding "barbs"). Found singly or in pairs, regularly accompanying mixed flocks. Most easily located once its distinctive high sharp *teep*! call note is learned (B. Whitney).

Range: Costa Rica to northern Venezuela and Bolivia.

BEAUTIFUL TREERUNNER
Margarornis bellulus   p.252

Description: 6. Found only in eastern Darién highlands. In form like Ruddy Treerunner. Dull brown above with rufous wing-coverts and tail; *prominent creamy white eye-ring, superciliary, and streaks on sides of head*; throat white, remaining underparts brown with *conspicuous pale yellowish black-edged tear-shaped spots.*

Similar species: A brightly marked species of very limited known range which should be easily identified. Not found with the uniform rufous Ruddy Treerunner. See also Spotted Barbtail.

BEAUTIFUL TREERUNNER

Status and distribution: Rare in cloud forest in highlands of eastern Darién (Cerro Pirre, Cerro Tacarcuna, and Cerro Quía); recorded mostly above 1350 m (4500 ft), but one was observed at 900 m (3000 ft) on summit of Cerro Quía on July 18, 1975 (Ridgely). Small numbers can be found near the summit of Cerro Pirre above Cana.

Habits: Similar to Ruddy Treerunner.

Range: Eastern Panama.

RUDDY TREERUNNER
Margarornis rubiginosus   Plate 14

Description: 6. Found only in western highlands. *Almost entirely rufous, paler below*; buffy superciliary, *whitish throat*, and a few very small buffy dusky-margined spots on chest; buffy wing-band noticeable in flight.

Similar species: Somewhat resembles a woodcreeper as it creeps up branches and trunks often using its tail for support, but small with a short bill and more uniform rufous than any except the Ruddy. Foliage-gleaners only rarely use their tails for support, and they normally do not creep up branches.

Status and distribution: Uncommon in forest and forest borders in highlands of western Chiriquí (mostly above 1800m: 6000 ft); found also in eastern Chiriquí (Cerro Flores) and Veraguas (Chitra, where recorded down to 1200 m: 4000 ft).

Habits: Forages at all levels, hitching itself up tree trunks and branches like a woodcreeper, sometimes also feeding in dead leaf clusters. Found singly or in pairs, often with flocks of other highlands Furnariids, warblers, etc.

Range: Costa Rica and western Panama.

BUFFY TUFTEDCHEEK
Pseudocolaptes lawrencii   Plate 14

Description: 8. Found only in western mountains. Ruddy brown above, more rufous on rump and tail, with cap dusky streaked with buff; wings mostly blackish, edged buff on wing-coverts; *throat pale buff extending over sides of neck into conspicuous tuft*; buffy below, mottled with dusky on chest and becoming rufous on sides.

Similar species: A *large* and rather robust furnariid whose broad moustache-like tufts easily distinguish it. See Streak-breasted Treehunter.

Status and distribution: Uncommon in montane forest of Chiriquí, Bocas del Toro (only one record, a specimen from Camp Cylindro), and Veraguas (two old specimens); best known from western Chiriquí, where rarely recorded below 1800 m (6000 ft), but elsewhere has been recorded down to 1200 m (4000 ft).

Habits: Usually found well above the ground in tall forest trees. Forages mostly by probing into bromeliads and other epiphytes, frequently propping itself up with its tail and rummaging about noisily, sometimes even disappearing inside; also works along major horizontal branches, inspecting moss, crevices, etc. Has a loud metallic *spink!* call note that sometimes draws attention to it. Often with mixed bird flocks. Seen regularly in the Fernandez forest along the Boquete Trail above Cerro Punta.

Range: Costa Rica and western Panama; western Colombia and western Ecuador.

Note: The South American population (*johnsoni*) could be specifically distinct.

Habits: An inconspicuous, furtive foliage-gleaner which is probably often over-looked. Usually found singly or in pairs, sometimes accompanying forest under-story flocks, woodhaunters rummage about and probe in dense often viny vegetation and into epiphytes. The call is a tirelessly repeated series of five to seven fast notes, *kip, yip-yip-yip-yip-yip* (B. Whitney; Ridgely); also gives a sharp *squirp* or *greep!*.

Range: Nicaragua to southern Peru and western Brazil.

Note: Has been called Striped Foliage-gleaner.

STRIPED WOODHAUNTER
Hyloctistes subulatus   Plate 20

Description: 6¼. Bill rather long, slender, and straight. Brown above with *fine buffy streaks on head and somewhat broader streaks on hindneck and upper back; wings, rump, and tail chestnut*; throat buff, edged with olive, *remaining underparts buffy olive with buff streaks on breast*. Birds from eastern Panama (*cordobae*) are grayer above with less distinct streaks on crown, no streaks on back; wings are duller brown; breast is less sharply streaked.

Similar species: A confusing bird, though its most similar relatives are mainly montane in distribution (with woodhaunter in lowlands and foothills). Closely resembles Lineated Foliage-gleaner (especially in western Panama), but woodhaunter differs in its less prominently streaked upperparts (particularly on nape), more olivaceous underparts, and more rufescent wings. See also Buff-throated Foliage-gleaner (which lacks streaks, and has buff superciliary and eye-ring).

Status and distribution: Rare to uncommon in lower growth of humid forest; on Caribbean slope recorded in lowlands and foothills from Bocas del Toro east to Coclé (where known only from an old specimen labeled "Nata"), and in foothills of eastern Colon province (Cerro Bruja) and San Blas (recorded only from Nusagandi in west, Ranchón in east; probably more wide-spread); on Pacific slope in lowlands and foothills of Chiriquí (perhaps only formerly in lowlands; old records from Bugaba, but no recent reports) and foothills of Veraguas, foothills of eastern Panama province (Cerro Jefe), and lowlands and foothills of eastern Darién.

LINEATED FOLIAGE-GLEANER
Syndactyla subalaris   Plate 14

Description: 7½. Found only in highlands. Warm brown above, *streaked narrowly with buff, most prominent on hindneck*; rump and tail rufous; throat pale buff, remaining underparts dull brown *streaked narrowly with buff*, becoming tawny-olive on flanks. Immature much more brightly colored, darker on crown and hindneck with conspicuous orange-tawny streaks on latter; more reddish brown above; *throat, sides of neck, and breast orange-tawny* with paler streaks; belly dull brown.

Similar species: Note the *buff streaking above and below*; the large Streak-breasted Treehunter lacks streaks above. Spectacled Foliage-gleaner has a conspicuous ochre eye-ring and superciliary. See also Striped Woodhaunter.

Status and distribution: Uncommon to fairly common in forest and (less often) forest borders in highlands of Chiriquí, adjacent Bocas del Toro (recorded only from north of Fortuna, along oleoducto road, but probably more widespread; Ridgely), Veraguas (on both slopes), and eastern Darién; in western Chiriquí recorded mostly above 1500 m (5000 ft), but elsewhere ranges down regularly to 900 m (3000 ft), occasionally to 750 m (2500 ft).

Habits: Forages mostly at low and middle levels, gleaning among twigs and in dead leaf clusters. Usually met with singly or in pairs, sometimes accompanying mixed flocks of other highland birds. Its distinctive call is a rather fast series of loud harsh nasal notes which start slowly and gradually accelerate and fade away, *ank--ank--ank-ank-ank-ank-ankankankank*.

Range: Costa Rica to northwestern Venezuela and southern Peru.

SPECTACLED FOLIAGE-GLEANER
Anabacerthia variegaticeps   Plate 14

Description: 6¼. Known only from Chiriquí highlands. Bill rather short. *Crown grayish olive contrasting with ruddy back* (only indistinct buff streaks on crown); *conspicuous ochre eye-ring and superciliary*; throat yellowish white, feathers of lower throat margined with dusky; remaining underparts light brown, darker on flanks; wings and tail ruddy brown.

Similar species: The contrasting crown and prominent eye-ring and eye-stripe make this species relatively easy to identify.

Status and distribution: Uncommon to fairly common in forest and (less often) forest borders in lower highlands of western Chiriquí (recorded mainly 1200–1800 m: 4000–6000 ft), somewhat lower (to 1050 m: 3500 ft) in forests of upper Río Chiriquí valley in central Chiriquí (Fortuna area; Ridgely); only record from eastern Chiriquí is an AMNH specimen taken by L. Griscom at 1200 m (4000 ft) on Cerro Flores.

Habits: Similar to Lineated Foliage-gleaner, but considerably easier to see as it tends to forage higher (more at middle levels) and more in the open, and to be less shy. Feeds actively and acrobatically, clambering along limbs, inspecting foliage and epiphytes, peering inside bromeliads, etc; a frequent member of mixed bird flocks. The call resembles that of Lineated but is longer with individual notes delivered more rapidly and somewhat higher-pitched (B. Whitney).

Range: Southern Mexico to western Panama; western Colombia and western Ecuador.

Note: South American birds (*A. temporalis*, Spot-breasted Foliage-gleaner) may be specifically distinct.

SLATY-WINGED FOLIAGE-GLEANER
Philydor fuscipennis   Plate 20

Description: 6¼. Mostly *plain chestnut above*, more grayish on crown, with rump and tail brighter rufous-chestnut; ear-coverts grayish with *conspicuous long narrow tawny stripe extending back from eye; wings dusky contrasting strongly with back*; throat buffy, remaining underparts tawny buff.

Similar species: An unusually strongly patterned and attractive member of the family. The bold eye-stripe and dark grayish wings are the points to watch for.

Status and distribution: Uncommon to locally fairly common (more numerous in eastern Panama) in lower growth of humid forest; on Caribbean slope recorded from Veraguas (where it also spills over onto Pacific slope foothills) and Coclé, Canal area (regular in small numbers along middle third of Pipeline Road; Ridgely *et al.*), hill country of eastern Colon province (Cerro Santa Rita), and San Blas; on Pacific slope recorded from eastern Panama province (Cerro Azul/Jefe area) and Darién. In Panama most numerous in foothill areas; recorded to at least 1050 m (3500 ft) on Cerro Pirre above Cana, in eastern Darién.

Habits: Usually in pairs or small groups, most often with mixed flocks of other understory species. Forages actively with fast movements, but often perches fairly in the open on lianas or at edge of viny tangles, and usually not difficult to observe. Its call is an infrequently given, sharp *chif*.

Range: Western Panama to western Ecuador.

Note: We favor treating trans-Andean *P. fuscipennis* (with *erythronotus*) as a species distinct from *P. erythrocercus* of Amazonian South America (the true Rufous-rumped Foliage-gleaner, with which it has often been considered conspecific. *P. fuscipennis* seems morphologically and behaviorally closer to Amazonian *P. pyrrhodes* (Cinnamon-rumped Foliage-gleaner) than it does to *P. erythrocercus*.

BUFF-FRONTED FOLIAGE-GLEANER
Philydor rufus   Plate 14

Description: 7½. Known only from western highlands. *Forehead cinnamon-buff*, crown and hindneck brownish gray; *superciliary and cheeks ochre*; back grayish brown; wings and tail rufous; *underparts uniform ochraceous*.

Similar species: The smaller Spectacled Foliage-gleaner has an ochre eye-ring and superciliary and lacks the buff forehead. Slaty-winged Foliage-gleaner has contrasting dark wings, is found only at lower elevations than this species.

Status and distribution: Rare in forest and forest borders in highlands of western Chiriquí and adjacent Bocas del Toro (1200–2100 m: 4000–7000 ft); one old specimen labeled as from "Veragua" probably was taken in Chiriquí; not known from Darién, but possible. In recent years, most frequently noted at Finca Lerida above Boquete.

Habits: Not well known in Panama. Usually feeds well above the ground, foraging in typical foliage-gleaner fashion, mostly along horizontal branches; one or two will sometimes accompany a mixed flock.

Range: Costa Rica and western Panama; Colombia and Venezuela to Bolivia, Paraguay, northeastern Argentina, and southeastern Brazil.

BUFF-THROATED FOLIAGE-GLEANER
Automolus ochrolaemus   Plate 20

Description: 7. Olive brown above with *narrow buff eye-ring and superciliary*; wings somewhat browner, rump and tail chestnut; *throat mostly white*, remaining underparts pale dull brown. Birds from Chiriquí and Pacific slope Veraguas (*exsertus*) have throat pale buff; birds from Bocas del Toro and Caribbean slope Veraguas (*hypophaeus*) have throat deeper buff and remaining underparts darker olive brown.

Similar species: The commonest and most widespread foliage-gleaner in the lowlands; compare to Striped Woodhaunter and Slaty-winged Foliage-gleaner. See also Plain-brown Woodcreeper (somewhat similar overall coloration, but very different behavior, etc.).

Status and distribution: Fairly common in lower growth of humid forest in lowlands and foothills (mostly up to about 900 m: 3000 ft, but to over 1200 m: 4000 ft in western Chiriquí) on both slopes; widespread on Caribbean slope, while on Pacific slope recorded from western Chiriquí (where now very local due to forest destruction), Veraguas (now probably only in foothills), and from eastern Panama province (Cerro Azul/Jefe area, Bayano River valley) east through Darién. Widespread in appropriate habitat on Caribbean side of Canal area, perhaps most numerous on Pipeline Road.

Habits: Usually forages in dense vegetation and dead leaf clusters in lower and middle growth; despite its active and even acrobatic feeding habits, not often seen, mist-netting better revealing its true abundance. One or two often accompany a mixed flock of antwrens and other birds. Its call is a short unmusical descending *ki, ki, ki-ki-kikikrrr*, given mainly in early morning and late afternoon; distinctive once learned, and given fairly often, this is an excellent indication of this furtive species' presence.

Range: Southeastern Mexico to northern Bolivia and Amazonian Brazil.

RUDDY FOLIAGE-GLEANER
Automolus rubiginosus   Plate 45

Description: 7¾. Found very locally in foothills and lower highlands. *Dark and uniform* in appearance; some bare gray skin usually shows around eyes. Western birds (*fumosus*) are *warm* brown above; rufous on rump, tail, and under tail-coverts; *throat and breast rich cinnamon-rufous*, belly somewhat paler cinnamon-tawny. Eastern birds (*saturatus*) are even darker overall, with *blackish tail*.

Similar species: A very dark brown and essentially unpatterned species. See Ruddy Woodcreeper.

Status and distribution: Rare to uncommon and local in undergrowth of humid forest and (especially) forest borders in foothills and lower highlands of western Chiriquí (recorded east only to southern slope of Volcán Barú), foothills of western San Blas (two birds mist-netted and photographed on Cerro Brewster on April 23 and 25, 1985; J. Blake, photos to VIREO where referable to eastern *fumosus* race) and eastern Panama province (a single bird mist-netted on Cerro Jefe on July 17, 1973; D. Hill), and foothills and lower highlands of eastern Darién (Cerro Pirre and Cerro Tacarcuna); in Chiriquí and Darién recorded mostly 600–1350 m (2000–4500 ft), but lower (750–990 m: 2500–3300 ft) at the two localities from which it is known in central Panama.

Habits: A difficult bird to observe, the Ruddy Foliage-gleaner tends to skulk alone or in pairs in dense undergrowth at edge of forest or in ravines. Usually it is located after its distinctive calls are recognized; these include a querulous drawn-out *kreee-yaah?* which vaguely recalls a Smooth-billed Ani, and also a fast scold, *chedit* or *chededit*. Tape recordings will sometimes lure a bird in close, but it likely will remain in heavy cover and be hard to actually see. Small numbers can be found in patches of forest along road west of Volcán toward Santa Clara in western Chiriquí.

Range: Central Mexico south locally to northern Bolivia, extreme northern Brazil, and the Guianas.

STREAK-BREASTED TREEHUNTER
Thripadectes rufobrunneus   Plate 14

Description: 8¼. Found only in western highlands. Rather heavy bill. *Dark warm brown above*, duller on head; rump and tail chestnut; sides of head and throat rufous with dusky scaling, remaining underparts olive brown, *streaked with ochraceous on breast* and with rufescent on under tail-coverts.

Similar species: The largest Furnariid of the western highlands; *has no buff streaks on upperparts*. Lineated Foliage-gleaner is smaller and is streaked with buff on head, hindneck, and upper back. Buffy Tuftedcheek is arboreal and has conspicuous buffy tuft on sides of head.

Status and distribution: Uncommon to locally fairly common in undergrowth of forest in highlands of Chiriquí, adjacent Bocas del Toro, and Veraguas, ranging mostly 1200–2400 m (4000–8000 ft), in Veraguas recorded as low as 750 m (2500 ft).

Habits: An active bird that usually remains in dense undergrowth (though sometimes rising into low tree branches) and hence is not often seen clearly. Favors vicinity of mountain streams where there are high banks for nesting. Its typical call is a harsh sharp *cheyt, cheyt*; also gives a loud grating frantic scold, *tí-chr, tí-chr, tí-chr . . .*, often long-continued.

Range: Costa Rica and western Panama.

PLAIN XENOPS
Xenops minutus   Plate 20

Description: 4½. *Bill short and wedge-shaped*, the lower mandible conspicuously upturned. Brown above with indistinct whitish eye-stripe and *prominent silvery crescentic stripe on cheeks*; rump, tail, and wing-band (visible in flight) rufous; throat whitish, remaining underparts dull brown.

Similar species: Wedge-billed Woodcreeper is larger with buff throat and buff spots on breast, lacks silvery cheek stripe, and creeps up trees. See also Streaked Xenops.

Status and distribution: Common in forest and second-growth woodland in lowlands on both slopes, ranging regularly in smaller numbers well up into the foothills to over 900 m (3000 ft), and recorded once at 1860 m (6200 ft) in western Chiriquí; not recorded from dry Pacific lowlands on eastern side of Azuero Peninsula and southern Coclé.

Habits: Gleans over small branches and twigs, usually at middle and upper heights, often hanging upside-down like a chickadee. Almost always accompanies mixed feeding flocks of antwrens, greenlets, etc.

Range: Southeastern Mexico to northern Bolivia, Paraguay, northeastern Argentina, and southeastern Brazil.

STREAKED XENOPS
Xenops rutilans   p.256

Description: 4½. Found only in highlands, replacing the more common lowland Plain Xenops. Resembles that species but has *cap, hindneck, and upper back streaked with buff*; throat white, remaining underparts brown *streaked with white, most broadly on breast*. Darién birds (*incomptus*) have reduced streaking both above and below (but still more than Plain Xenops).

STREAKED XENOPS

Similar species: See Plain Xenops (*unstreaked*); the two only rarely overlap. Spotted Barbtail is a little larger, lacks the cheek stripe, and is spotted (not streaked) below.

Status and distribution: Rare in forest and forest borders in lower highlands of western Chiriquí (east only to slopes of Volcán Barú above Boquete; mostly 1200–1800 m: 4000–6000 ft), and in eastern Darién (known only from Cana on lower slopes of Cerro Pirre, but probably also on Cerro Tacarcuna; recorded 540–600 m: 1800–2000 ft).

Habits: Similar to Plain Xenops, usually found singly or in pairs, often accompanying mixed flocks.

Range: Costa Rica to northern Argentina and southeastern Brazil.

TAWNY-THROATED LEAFTOSSER
Sclerurus mexicanus Plate 20

Description: 6. Dark rich brown above with rufous rump; *throat and chest tawny-rufous*, lower underparts dark brown.

Similar species: Scaly-throated Leaftosser has white throat with feathers edged black giving scaly appearance, and lacks rufous rump; it too has a tawny chest. Often confused with the much more numerous Song Wren; the wren is best known by its pale blue behind eye, barred wings and tail, and almost constant churring notes. See also Gray-throated Leaftosser.

Status and distribution: Generally rare and local in humid forest in lowlands and foothills on entire Caribbean slope; on Pacific slope known from foothills and lower highlands (720–1500 m: 2400–5000 ft) of Chiriquí, Veraguas, eastern Panama province, and Darién. In Canal area apparently most numerous at Achiote Road.

Habits: Leaftossers are furtive, mostly terrestrial, forest birds, not often seen but frequently captured in mist-nets. They feed on the ground, usually in moist areas, flicking leaves aside with their bills and probing the soil. When disturbed, they usually fly up with a loud and harsh squeak and perch a short distance away on a low and open branch; there they remain motionless for several minutes before flying off, again with a squeak. The song is a high, wheezy, descending series of four to five notes, each slightly shorter than the preceding, *peéeeees-peéeees-peéees-peee* (B. Whitney). They nest in holes burrowed in banks.

Range: Southern Mexico to northern Bolivia and central Brazil.

GRAY-THROATED LEAFTOSSER
Sclerurus albigularis Plate 14

Description: 6¼. Known only from western Chiriquí highlands. Dark rich brown above with *rufous rump* and wing edging; *throat pale gray*, chest tawny-chestnut, lower underparts dull dark brown.

Similar species: Tawny-throated Leaftosser is very similar but has tawny (not gray) throat. Scaly-throated Leaftosser has white throat with feathers edged black giving scaly appearance and lacks the rufous rump.

Status and distribution: Rare in humid forest in lower highlands of western Chiriquí, recorded mostly 1200–1800 m (4000–6000 ft).

Habits: Similar to Tawny-throated Leaftosser. Gray-throated's song in Costa Rica is complex and often long-continued, a series of often trebled notes, *kwee-kwee-kwee, kwu-kwu-kwu, kwee-kwee-kwee . . .*, repeated rapidly with variable pattern and with long musical trills interspersed (G. Diller).

Range: Costa Rica and western Panama; Colombia and northern Venezuela to northern Bolivia.

SCALY-THROATED LEAFTOSSER
Sclerurus guatemalensis Plate 20

Description: 6. Dark rich brown above (*no rufous rump*); *throat white with feathers outlined in black giving scaly effect*; chest tawny, lower underparts dark brown.

Similar species: Both other Panama leaftossers have rufous rumps.

Status and distribution: Uncommon to locally fairly common in humid forest in lowlands and (in smaller numbers) foothills on entire Caribbean slope; on Pacific slope known from lowlands of western Chiriquí, western side of Azuero Peninsula (Cerro Hoya, 780 m: 2600 ft), Cerro Campana, and from Canal area east through Darién. Generally the most numerous Panamanian leaftosser. In Canal area most easily found along Pipeline Road, but there as elsewhere inconspicuous and recorded largely from mist-net captures.

Habits: Similar to Tawny-throated Leaftosser. Scaly-throated's call is an even harsher and sharper *shweek!*, while its song is a distinctive descending series of loud whistled notes, *whit-whit-whit-peet-peet-peet-peet-pert-pert* (E. O. Willis).

Range: Southeastern Mexico to northern Colombia.

SHARP-TAILED STREAMCREEPER
Lochmias nematura Plate 40

Description: 6. Known only from eastern Darién highlands. Bill long and narrow, slightly decurved; rather short tail. Uniform dark warm brown, *spotted conspicuously with white on sides of head and entire underparts*.

Similar species: The habitat and bold white spotting below make this species easy to recognize. Rather like a leaftosser in shape and posture.

Status and distribution: Apparently rare; recorded from undergrowth bordering forested streams in highlands of eastern Darién (Cerro Pirre, Cerro Malí, Cerro Quía).

Habits: Largely terrestrial and usually difficult to see, hopping on ground in dense tangled undergrowth, sometimes on rocks or along edges of streams. Flicks leaves with its bill much like a leaftosser. The song in South America is a dry, unmusical, evenly pitched series of notes which start slowly but gradually accelerate until they end in a run-together chipper, the whole lasting about 5 seconds.

Range: Eastern Panama and locally in Colombia and South America east of the Andes south to Bolivia, Paraguay, northeastern Argentina, and Uruguay.

Note: The 1983 AOU Check-list used the name Streamside Lochmias for this species. We see nothing to be gained by this change, and retain the long-used "Sharp-tailed Streamcreeper".

WOODCREEPERS: Dendrocolaptidae (17)

The woodcreepers are a widespread neotropical family that superficially resembles the smaller brown or tree creepers (Certhiidae) of the Northern Hemisphere. In Panama most inhabit forest; several species are quite rare, thinly spread, and little known. They climb trees and branches at varying heights, always clinging closely, probing for insects in bark, crevices, and epiphytes. Stiffened tails, usually with protruding central shafts, help support them in the manner of woodpeckers. The nests of a number of species remain undescribed; those that are known are in crevices and crannies on tree trunks and branches, often behind a piece of dead bark. All are easily recognized as woodcreepers (though some Furnariids look and act like them), but many are similar in appearance and often confused. The key points to watch for are: 1) total length; 2) shape, length, and color of bill; 3) presence or absence of streaking or spotting on crown and back and/or underparts; and 4) degree of ruddiness on head and upper back. The woodcreepers are now sometimes considered as only a subfamily in the Furnariidae.

PLAIN-BROWN WOODCREEPER
Dendrocincla fuliginosa   Plate 19

Description: 8. Bill straight, blackish. *Cap and back plain dull brown*, duller on crown and wing-coverts, wings slightly more rufous with dusky tips, with *no buff spotting or streaking*; sides of head more grayish, usually showing a *dusky moustachial stripe*; dull brown below with a few inconspicuous buffy streaks on breast; tail rufous.

Similar species: Within its range, the lack of any spotting or streaking above will distinguish it from all similar species except the rather rare Ruddy Woodcreeper, which is uniform rufous (not plain crown), especially bright on crown. In Chiriquí see Tawny-winged Woodcreeper.

Status and distribution: Fairly common in humid forest and second-growth woodland in lowlands and foothills on entire Caribbean slope; on Pacific slope known from foothills of Veraguas (Chitra), Cerro Campana, and eastern Panama province (Cerro Azul/Jefe area, Bayano River) east through Darién.

Habits: A regular army ant follower (half a dozen or more sometimes gathering), the Plain-brown Woodcreeper is also found foraging singly or in pairs at low and middle heights. Unlike most woodcreepers, it often perches "normally", across a branch. Its usual call is a loud squeaky *sweeach* or *scheeah*.

Range: Honduras to northeastern Argentina and southeastern Brazil.

Note: More than one species may be involved in South America.

TAWNY-WINGED WOODCREEPER
Dendrocincla anabatina   Plate 19

Description: 7–7½. Found only in Chiriquí. Bill straight, blackish. *Olive brown above*, sometimes with indistinct, fine streaks on crown, darker on wing-coverts; *tawny streak behind eye*; throat buff, remaining underparts olive brown with indistinct, narrow buff streaks on chest; *flight feathers mainly tawny*, wing-tips dusky; tail rufous. Feathers of nape often look ragged.

Similar species: Resembles Plain-brown Woodcreeper but somewhat smaller, more olive brown generally, with contrasting tawny area on wings; the two do not occur together in Panama. Olivaceous Woodcreeper is considerably smaller and uniform grayish olive on head and underparts.

Status and distribution: Rare in forest in western Chiriquí; recorded mostly from lowlands, but also in smaller numbers to about 1200 m (4000 ft) around Santa Clara. Very few recent records from Panama, where most of its habitat has now been destroyed; probably persists in lowlands only on the Burica Peninsula, where one was seen on June 26, 1982 (Ridgely).

Habits: Similar to Plain-brown Woodcreeper, and like that species a regular army ant follower. Often flicks its wings rapidly. Its usual call is a single loud, rather musical *cheeuw*, repeated slowly.

Range: Southern Mexico to Pacific western Panama.

RUDDY WOODCREEPER
Dendrocincla homochroa   Plate 19

Description: 7½. Bill straight, pale brownish to dull flesh, often with blackish tip. *Uniform deep rufous, brightest on crown* and wing-coverts, somewhat duller below.

Similar species: Many other woodcreepers have rufous wings and tails, but this is the only one that is bright rufous all over. The brown Plain-brown Woodcreeper can be confused, however, especially in the dull light inside forest: note that Ruddy's crown is markedly brighter than rest of its head.

Status and distribution: Rare to locally uncommon in forest in lowlands and (especially) foothills on Pacific slope including the Azuero Peninsula (where recently found south to Cerro Hoya; F. Delgado); on Caribbean slope known only from a few records from foothills of Bocas del Toro and in Canal area lowlands; recorded mostly 300–900 m (1000–3000 ft), with one report from as high as 1350 m (4500 ft) above Fortuna, in central Chiriquí (Ridgely).

Habits: Rather furtive and easily overlooked. A regular army ant follower. Constantly flicks its wings.

Range: Southeastern Mexico to northern Colombia and northwestern Venezuela.

OLIVACEOUS WOODCREEPER
Sittasomus griseicapillus   Plate 19

Description: 6–6½. A small woodcreeper with straight, slender, mostly blackish bill. *Grayish olive head, neck, and entire underparts contrasting with ruddy back*; buff wing-band conspicuous in flight; tail rufous.

Similar species: No other Panamanian woodcreeper has the *mostly grayish plumage* of this species. In Chiriquí, see Tawny-winged Woodcreeper.

Status and distribution: Uncommon and rather local in woodland, forest borders, and adjacent clearings and plantations in lowlands and foothills on Pacific slope from Chiriquí to Darién; on Caribbean slope known from only a few records from northern Veraguas (Calovévora) east to western San Blas (Mandinga). Seemingly not really numerous anywhere in Panama, perhaps most so in lower highlands of Chiriquí (where recorded up to about 1500 m: 5000 ft) and on Azuero Peninsula. At least at Juan Diaz, eastern Panama province, it also occurs in mangrove forests.

Habits: Usually found singly, foraging rather in the open at medium heights. For the most part climbs up main trunks or larger branches, occasionally darting out to capture escaping prey. Its usual song is a short, fast, somewhat musical trill.

Range: Central Mexico to northern Argentina and southeastern Brazil.

LONG-TAILED WOODCREEPER
Deconychura longicauda   Plate 19

Description: 7½–8. *Rather slender straight short bill*. Dull brown above with vague buff superciliary and faint buff streaks on crown; mainly dull brown below, with throat pale buff, large buff spots on chest, and a few buff streaks on breast; wings and tail rufous, the *tail proportionately longer than in other woodcreepers*. Males average significantly larger than females.

Similar species: Often confused, though its slim appearance, accentuated by the long tail, is quite apparent when the bird is seen well. In dim dark light of forest interior this species can look quite plain, potentially causing confusion with Plain-brown Woodcreeper (which see). Buff-throated Woodcreeper is larger with longer bill and conspicuous buff streaking on head and upper back. In plumage Long-tailed is very similar to the diminutive Wedge-billed Woodcreeper (and behavior is also similar), but note difference in bill shape.

Status and distribution: Uncommon in humid forest in lowlands and foothills on entire Caribbean slope; on Pacific slope known from several old specimens from western Chiriquí (Divalá, Bugaba; no recent records, and perhaps extirpated, though may persist in remnant forest on Burica Peninsula), foothills of western Panama province (Cerro Campana), and lowlands and foothills of eastern Panama province (Cerro Azul/Jefe, upper Bayano River valley) and Darién; recorded up to about 1050 m (3500 ft) in Darién. In central Panama most easily seen along Pipeline Road (but even here not regularly encountered).
Habits: Forages singly (less often in pairs), mostly at lower and middle levels. Regularly with mixed flocks of forest understory birds.
Range: Eastern Honduras to eastern Peru and Amazonian Brazil.

WEDGE-BILLED WOODCREEPER
Glyphorhynchus spirurus   Plate 19

Description: 5¾–6. *Panama's smallest woodcreeper. Bill short, wedge-shaped.* Generally dull brown with *buffy whitish superciliary*; throat buffy and with small, wedge-shaped buffy spots on breast; buff wing-band conspicuous in flight; tail rufous.
Similar species: Small size and oddly shaped bill should easily distinguish it from other Panamanian woodcreepers; see especially Long-tailed. Plain Xenops is smaller, has a silvery stripe on sides of head, and does not habitually creep up trunks.
Status and distribution: Uncommon to fairly common in humid forest and mature second-growth woodland in lowlands on entire Caribbean slope, also ranging in smaller numbers up into foothills; on Pacific slope found in western Chiriquí (where recorded up to about 1200 m: 4000 ft, but now very local due to deforestation), hill country of Veraguas, and lowlands and foothills of eastern Panama province (Cerro Azul/Jefe, upper Bayano River valley) and Darién (where surprisingly uncommon).
Habits: Usually found singly, less often in pairs, generally independent of mixed flocks (though sometimes with them). Forages mostly by hitching up main trunks, primarily at low levels. Its call is an explosive but not very loud *chiff!*, often repeated several times (especially in alarm); this frequently reveals the presence of an otherwise often inconspicuous bird.

Range: Southeastern Mexico to northern Bolivia and central Brazil.

STRONG-BILLED WOODCREEPER
Xiphocolaptes promeropirhynchus   Plate 19

Description: 12–12½. Known only from western foothills. *Panama's largest woodcreeper. Bill heavy and long* (2 in), slightly decurved, blackish. Mostly brown above, duskier on crown with narrow buffy whitish streaking on head and upper back; throat buffy whitish bordered by *indistinct dusky moustachial streak*; remaining underparts dull brown narrowly streaked with buff especially on breast, usually with some dusky barring on belly; wings and tail rufous.
Similar species: In plumage most resembles the markedly smaller Buff-throated Woodcreeper, though that species has much less massive bill and never shows a moustachial streak; they are not known to occur together. Black-banded Woodcreeper also quite similar (and these two *do* occur sympatrically), but is a little smaller with straighter less massive bill, lacks the moustache, and is more prominently barred on belly (though even in Black-banded the barring can be hard to see in the field).
Status and distribution: Rare and local in humid forest in foothills on Pacific slope in western Panama. Few Panama records: one old specimen from an uncertain locality in western Chiriquí (presumed by Wetmore to have been taken on lower slopes of Volcán Barú near Boquete); one collected at Fortuna, in central Chiriquí, on February 26, 1976 (Ridgely, specimen to GML), with another seen on February 28; five AMNH specimens from Chitra, Veraguas; and reported seen above El Copé, Coclé, on June 9–11, 1984 (P. Trail).
Habits: Usually seen singly, less often in pairs, typically foraging on trunks and larger branches where they inspect bromeliads and other epiphytes. Occasionally reported to follow swarms of army ants. The song in South America (and presumably also in Panama) is an unmistakable series of paired ("double-stopped"), descending, whistled notes, often beginning with a single higher one; it is given mostly at dawn and dusk, and though far-carrying is delivered at such long intervals as to be very difficult to track to its source.
Range: Mexico to western Panama; Colombia to Guyana, Amazonian Brazil, and northern Bolivia.

BARRED WOODCREEPER
Dendrocolaptes certhia   Plate 19

Description: 10–11. Bill heavy, nearly straight (1½ in), pale dusky, blackish at tip. *Head, back, and underparts brown barred with dusky*, finer on head and neck, coarser below, fainter on back; wings and tail rufous, unbarred.
Similar species: The only Panama woodcreeper that is barred above; see Black-banded Woodcreeper.
Status and distribution: Rare to uncommon in humid forest and tall second-growth woodland in lowlands on entire Caribbean slope, ranging up in smaller numbers into foothills; on Pacific slope known from lowlands and foothills of western Chiriquí (where now much reduced in range and numbers due to deforestation, with no known recent reports), locally in foothills from Veraguas east to western Panama province (Cerro Campana), and in lowlands and foothills of eastern Panama province (Cerro Azul/Jefe, upper Bayano River valley) and Darién. Seems most numerous in Bocas del Toro; scarce in Canal area, where most regularly found in middle Chagres River valley (Madden Forest and Lake area, Pipeline Road).
Habits: Usually solitary and lethargic, often clinging motionless to a trunk for protracted periods, hence doubtless sometimes overlooked. Most frequently found at swarms of army ants; away from antswarms usually found alone in lower growth, less often accompanying a mixed flock. The song is a series of three to six whistled *oówit* notes, falling in strength; the call a nasal *kíyarrr, kíyarrr . . .*, sometimes sped up and squeakier.
Range: Southeastern Mexico to Bolivia and central Brazil.

BLACK-BANDED WOODCREEPER
Dendrocolaptes picumnus   Plate 19

Description: 10½–11. Known only from western highlands. Bill heavy, almost straight, dusky. Brown above, duskier on crown, with narrow buff streaking on head, neck, and upper back; throat buffy whitish vaguely streaked brown, breast brown broadly streaked pale brown, *belly buffy brown narrowly and evenly barred with black*; wings and tail rufous.
Similar species: Strong-billed Woodcreeper is only slightly larger, but it has a longer more massive bill, shows at least a vague dusky moustache, and its barring on belly is at most obscure. Black-banded resembles

Barred Woodcreeper, but has head, neck, and breast streaked (not barred). See also Buff-throated Woodcreeper.
Status and distribution: Rare and local in humid forest in foothills and highlands of western Panama. Few Panama records: two old specimens taken high on slopes of Volcán Barú above Boquete, in western Chiriquí; one seen at Fortuna, central Chiriquí, on February 29, 1976, and another in adjacent Bocas del Toro along the oleoducto road on July 3, 1982 (Ridgely); four old specimens from Veraguas (Chitra); and one nineteenth-century specimen labeled as from Capira, western Panama province (Wetmore regards the locality as "questionable"). In western Chiriquí recorded 1800–2100 m (6000–7000 ft), elsewhere 900–1200 m (3000–4000 ft).
Habits: Forages at all heights in trees, most often independently of mixed flocks. At least in South America single birds or pairs are regularly encountered at swarms of army ants.
Range: Southern Mexico to western Panama; Colombia to the Guianas, Amazonian Brazil, Paraguay, and northwestern Argentina.

STRAIGHT-BILLED WOODCREEPER
Xiphorhynchus picus   Plate 19

Description: 8–8½. Found locally in or near mangroves. *Bill straight, dull whitish or pinkish.* Rufous brown above, duller on crown which is also streaked with buffy; whitish superciliary; *most of sides of head, throat, and large spots on chest whitish*; lower underparts brown with buffy white spots on breast that become streaks on belly; wings and tail rufous.
Similar species: The commonest woodcreeper in mangroves. Distinguished from Buff-throated Woodcreeper by its smaller size, pale straight bill, and prominent whitish (not buffy) throat and sides of head; from Streak-headed by its straight (not slightly decurved) bill, and the whitish sides of head and throat.
Status and distribution: Uncommon to locally fairly common in mangroves and adjacent woodland and semiopen areas on and near Pacific coast from eastern side of Azuero Peninsula to Darién (Garachiné), and locally in mangroves on Caribbean coast of Canal area on Galeta Island and at Fort Randolph; perhaps increasing in Panama (not recorded on Caribbean coast prior to 1972, though possibly only overlooked?).

Habits: Usually found singly, sometimes in pairs, feeding at lower and middle heights. Rather quiet, but has a soft trill somewhat like Streak-headed Woodcreeper's.
Range: Western Panama to northern Bolivia and Amazonian Brazil.

BUFF-THROATED WOODCREEPER
Xiphyorhynchus guttatus   Plate 19

Description: 8½–9½. The most numerous and widespread Panamanian woodcreeper. *Bill fairly heavy, almost straight, rather long, blackish*. Dull brown above, the *head and upper back with buff streaks* margined with black; *throat buffy*, remaining underparts brown, breast with buff streaks somewhat edged with black; wings and tail rufous.
Similar species: Often confused with Streak-headed Woodcreeper, though that species is considerably smaller and has pale and differently shaped bill (slender and distinctly decurved). Long-tailed Woodcreeper is smaller, lacks distinct streaking on head and neck, and has notably long tail. Straight-billed Woodcreeper has shorter pale bill and whitish sides of head and throat.
Status and distribution: Very common and widespread in lowlands and lower foothills (to just over 600 m: 2000 ft) throughout, occurring virtually wherever there are trees, though normally not within extensive heavy forest except at borders or clearings.
Habits: Usually forages at low levels, often in pairs. Rather noisy, calling, especially in early morning and late afternoon, a series of clear whistles that starts fast, then slows down and drops at the end, *pee-pee-pee-pee-pee-pew-pew-pew*.
Range: Guatemala to northern Bolivia and Amazonian and southeastern Brazil.

BLACK-STRIPED WOODCREEPER
Xiphorhynchus lachrymosus   Plate 19

Description: 9½. Bill slightly decurved, dusky. *Blackish above with conspicuous broad streaks of buffy white*; throat buffy, *remaining underparts buffy whitish streaked with black* and with buffy feathers edged with black; wings and tail rufous.
Similar species: No other Panama woodcreeper is so brightly patterned.
Status and distribution: Fairly common in humid forest and forest borders in lowlands and foothills (to about 1050 m: 3500 ft) on entire Caribbean slope; on Pacific slope found in lowlands of western Chiriquí (where now

probably found only on Burica Peninsula, due to deforestation elsewhere), foothills of Veraguas (Santa Fé), and lowlands and foothills of eastern Panama province (Cerro Azul/Jefe, upper Bayano River valley) and Darién. Widespread in forested areas on Caribbean side of Canal area.
Habits: This striking and handsome woodcreeper forages higher than most other members of its family, working mainly along larger horizontal limbs. Its call is distinctive and frequently heard, a series of three or four very loud, far-carrying whistled notes which descend, *whee, hew, hew*, reminiscent of call of Cinnamon Woodpecker but with notes more slurred and rapidly delivered. The song is a series of about 10 (sometimes more) descending notes which starts slowly, then speeds up, with quality of Buff-throated Woodcreeper.
Range: Nicaragua to northwestern Ecuador.

SPOTTED WOODCREEPER
Xiphorhynchus erythropygius   Plate 19

Description: 8½. Bill almost straight, dusky. Olive brown above usually with a few buffy streaks on nape; throat buffy, *remaining underparts olive brown with tear-shaped buffy spots*; wings and tail rufous.
Similar species: Best distinguished by its rather olive overall plumage and the distinct spotting below. Long-tailed Woodcreeper is smaller with buffy superciliary, streaking (not spotting) on belly, and long tail. See Buff-throated Woodcreeper.
Status and distribution: Uncommon to fairly common in humid forest chiefly in foothills on both slopes (recorded mostly 300–1350 m: 1000–4500 ft); a few records from Caribbean lowlands in west and extreme east; one old specimen from Canal area (the La Jagua specimen mentioned by Wetmore was a pen-slip). Quite easily seen on Cerro Campana and in the Cerro Jefe area.
Habits: Usually found singly, often accompanying mixed flocks of insectivorous birds. The call is a nasal descending *ddrreew, ddrreew, ddrreew*, sometimes only doubled.
Range: Central Mexico to western Ecuador.

STREAK-HEADED WOODCREEPER
Lepidocolaptes souleyetii   Plate 19

Description: 7½. *Bill slender and distinctly decurved, pale brownish or flesh*. Warm brown above with *distinct narrow buff streaks on head* (also on upper back in birds from western Panama, *compressus*); throat buffy whitish streaked dusky on sides, remaining underparts dull brown streaked with buffy; wings and tail rufous.

Similar species: Inhabits relatively open areas, not the forests preferred by most other woodcreepers. Frequently confused with Buff-throated Woodcreeper but smaller with a more slender and decurved, paler bill. Straight-billed Woodcreeper is slightly larger with straight whitish bill and whitish sides of head and throat. In western Panama see also the very similar montane Spot-crowned Woodcreeper.

Status and distribution: Locally fairly common in open and gallery woodland and in trees and shrubby clearings and largely cleared areas in lowlands and in smaller numbers in foothills (to about 1500 m: 5000 ft) on Pacific slope (specimens in AMNH from Pacific slope Veraguas; also seen in western Panama province by Eisenmann); on Caribbean slope known from western Bocas del Toro and from Canal area east through San Blas. Seems most numerous in western Chiriquí (e.g. around Puerto Armuelles) and in partially cleared parts of Darién (e.g. around El Real); rather scarce in Canal area.

Habits: Usually found singly, foraging actively at all heights. Frequently gives a rather musical trill or chirring of variable intensity.

Range: Southern Mexico to northwestern Peru, extreme northern Brazil, and Guyana.

SPOT-CROWNED WOODCREEPER
Lepidocolaptes affinis   Plate 19

Description: 7½–8. Found only in Chiriquí highlands. *Bill slender and distinctly decurved, pale. Crown and nape dark brown with small buff spots* (looking more streaky on nape); back rufescent brown, *essentially unstreaked*, with wings and tail rufous; throat buff, remaining underparts brown with *conspicuous pale buff streaking*, streaks narrowly black-edged.

Similar species: Closely resembles Streak-headed Woodcreeper, though for the most part the two species separate out by altitude (Streak-headed at lower elevations). Best points of distinction are Streak-head's streaking (not spotting) on crown, and its blurrier less crisply delineated streaking on underparts.

Status and distribution: Common in forest and forest borders in highlands of western Chiriquí, mostly above 1200 m (4000 ft); only record from eastern Chiriquí is a specimen in AMNH taken on Cerro Flores (1080 m: 3600 ft) by L. Griscom.

Habits: Forages actively at all heights, often joining mixed flocks of insectivorous birds. One call is a rather un-woodcreeper-like (with almost quality of Orange-billed Sparrow), high and sibilant *tsew, tsii-tsii* (sometimes only one, or up to three, *tsii* notes; J. Guarnaccia). One of the more numerous forest birds in the western Chiriquí highlands.

Range: Central Mexico to western Panama; Colombia and northern Venezuela to northern Bolivia.

Note: South American birds (*L. lachrymiger*, Montane Woodcreeper) are sometimes considered specifically distinct from Middle American form.

RED-BILLED SCYTHEBILL
Campylorhamphus trochilirostris   Plate 19

Description: 9–10. *Bill enormously long* (3 in) *and very decurved, reddish.* Brown above streaked with buffy on head and back; throat buffy whitish, remaining underparts brown streaked with buffy; wings and tail rufous. Bill of juvenal browner.

Similar species: Though resembling several other woodcreepers in plumage, will at once be known by its unmistakable bill. Brown-billed Scythebill has a brown bill, blackish crown, and is a foothill or highland bird.

Status and distribution: Rare to locally uncommon in forest borders and second-growth woodland in lowlands on Caribbean slope from northern Coclé (El Uracillo) east through San Blas; on Pacific slope recorded from eastern Panama province (upper Bayano River valley) and Darién (where recorded up to about 1050 m: 3500 ft above Cana). Decidedly scarce in Canal area, where in recent years most often seen in Portobelo area of eastern Colon province.

Habits: Usually found singly or in pairs, foraging alone as often as it accompanies mixed flocks. Probes into holes and crevices, beneath pieces of bark, and in epiphytes, mostly at lower levels (but sometimes higher). On the whole, however, despite its amazing bill its foraging techniques do not seem to differ markedly from those of other woodcreepers with more normally sized bills. In western Ecuador the loud, fast, musical song starts with a rolling trill and ends with eight to ten *tew* notes.

Range: Central Panama to northern Argentina and southern Brazil.

BROWN-BILLED SCYTHEBILL
Campylorhamphus pusillus   Plate 19

Description: 10. *Bill as in preceding species but not quite as long (2½ in) and dull brown. Head blackish* and back brown, both narrowly streaked with buff; throat buff, remaining underparts brown streaked with buff; wings and tail rufous.

Similar species: Red-billed Scythebill is typically found at lower elevations (though the two may meet or even overlap in eastern Darién); its bill is longer and thinner and usually quite reddish (though color differences are often tricky in the field), and it is browner (not so blackish) on head.

Status and distribution: Rare to locally uncommon in humid forest in foothills and lower highlands in western Bocas del Toro (where also one GML specimen from lowlands taken on Río Changuinola in January 1980), Chiriquí (where much more numerous in the Fortuna area than elsewhere), Veraguas (both slopes), eastern Panama province (a specimen and several sightings from the Cerro Azul/Jefe area), and eastern Darién; recorded mostly 600–1500 m (2000–5000 ft).

Habits: Usually found in lower growth, most often accompanying mixed flocks; often rather wary and difficult to see clearly. Its commonest song is a series of four to five rising whistles followed by a lower short note, *tuwee-tuwee-tuwee-twee-twee-tweé-trrr* (B. Whitney).

Range: Costa Rica to Peru and Guyana.

ANTBIRDS: Formicariidae (38)

The antbirds are a large and diverse family of exclusively neotropical birds, well represented in Panama, where there are many species in lowland forests and woodlands, fewer at higher elevations. The term "antbird" is something of a misnomer as very few species are known to feed on ants; the name is derived from the habit of several species of following swarms of army ants (especially *Eciton burchelli*) and feeding on the insects and other arthropods disturbed by them. A majority of antbirds, however, pay scant attention to the swarms, feeding at various strata from the ground to the canopy. Antbirds are not brightly colored, but many are attractively or contrastingly patterned in black, gray, white, and various shades of brown. The sexes differ in most species, females tending to be more rufescent than males. A number have an area of bare blue skin around the eyes, the function of which is unknown. Antshrikes resemble the true shrikes (Laniidae) only in their heavy hooked bills. Antvireos resemble the true vireos in their heavy-headed dull-colored appearance and their relatively lethargic behavior. Antwrens are small spritely birds that roam about forest and woodland usually in mixed flocks; they behave more like wood-warblers than wrens. Antthrushes are plump, terrestrial forest birds that unlike the thrushes usually carry their tails cocked up; they walk rather than hop and really resemble crakes more than they do thrushes. Antpittas are remarkably like the Old World pittas (Pittidae) in shape though not with the latter's gorgeous coloration; they are plump, almost "tail-less", very long-legged, terrestrial or almost terrestrial forest birds. Many antbirds (in the broad sense) are shy and difficult to see, but most have distinctive calls that frequently are the best indication of the species' presence. All members of the family are apparently almost exclusively insectivorous. Breeding habits for many species are unknown, but most of those known construct an open cup nest, rather vireo-like, while some nest in small tree cavities or holes in stubs (e.g. Black-faced Antthrush, Bicolored Antbird). Recent biochemical studies seem to indicate that the antbirds do not represent a single family unit: the antthrushes and antpittas may not belong in the same family as the rest of the antbirds (which would be called the family Thamnophilidae). As some results are still pending, however, the traditional single-family arrangement is retained, in accordance with the 1983 AOU Check-list.

FASCIATED ANTSHRIKE
Cymbilaimus lineatus   Plate 20

Description: 6½–6¾. Heavy hooked bill. *Iris red.* Male *black narrowly barred with white* except on crown. Female blackish above *narrowly barred with buff*, with chestnut crown; buff below *narrowly barred with black*.
Similar species: The more familiar Barred Antshrike has male *broadly* barred black and white, female very different and bright rufous above and buffy below with no barring; both have yellow (not red) eyes. Female has pattern somewhat reminiscent of the considerably larger Barred Puffbird.
Status and distribution: Uncommon to fairly common in dense viny tangles at borders of humid forest and in second-growth woodland in lowlands and lower foothills on entire Caribbean slope; on Pacific slope recorded locally from more humid lowlands and foothills from central Chiriquí east to Coclé (but recently reported only from Veraguas foothills above Santa Fé), and from Canal area east through Darién; in Darién recorded up to about 3500 ft, but usually below 600 m (2000 ft); no records from Azuero Peninsula. Widespread but never especially numerous in wooded areas on both sides of Canal area.
Habits: Generally inconspicuous, and apt to be overlooked unless they are calling, though pairs sometimes accompany mixed flocks of *Myrmotherula* antwrens and other forest understory birds. Tend to be shy, and to move about slowly, deliberately peering about in dense foliage, searching for large insects. The song is a series of six to eight steadily repeated soft whistled notes, *cü, cü, cü, cü* . . ., with notably ventriloquial quality.
Range: Southeastern Honduras to northern Bolivia and Amazonian Brazil.

GREAT ANTSHRIKE
Taraba major   Plate 20

Description: 7½–8. Heavy, hooked bill. *Red iris.* Sometimes shows a loose crest. Male *black above* with white edging on wing-coverts forming two white bars; *white below*, tinged gray on flanks and under tail-coverts. Female *rufous brown above; white below*, tinged buff on flanks and under tail-coverts.
Similar species: Large size, prominent red eye, and two-toned color pattern are diagnostic. Bicolored Antbird is smaller, with dark eye and black on face, and is a bird of forest interior (not clearings or borders).

Status and distribution: Uncommon to fairly common in dense undergrowth and viny tangled thickets in clearings and forest and woodland borders in more humid lowlands on both slopes (ranging locally up into lower foothills to about 600 m: 2000 ft), but more local on Pacific slope west of Canal area, and entirely absent from drier areas and Azuero Peninsula. Occurs in only very small numbers in extensively forested regions, doubtless because of limited availability of suitable habitat.
Habits: Usually in pairs and difficult to see as it remains concealed in dense tangles even when calling. The call is a series of fairly loud hoots, usually increasing in tempo, sometimes ending in a snorting or whining nasal *nyaah*; the total effect is quite trogon-like except for the contrasting ending.
Range: Southeastern Mexico to northern Argentina and Uruguay.

BARRED ANTSHRIKE
Thamnophilus doliatus   Plate 20

Description: 6–6¼. Fairly thick, hooked bill. *Iris yellow or white.* Loose crest elevated especially when excited. Male *black broadly barred with white* throughout except for wholly black crown (white bases of feathers sometimes showing). Female very different, *bright rufous above*, hindneck and sides of head deep buff streaked with black; *buffy below*. Immature male barred dark brown and buff.
Similar species: Male Fasciated Antshrike is *narrowly* barred with white and has a red (not yellow) eye.
Status and distribution: Fairly common to common in dense thickets and lower growth of woodland borders, overgrown clearings, gardens, and hedgerows in lowlands on Pacific slope from Chiriquí to eastern Panama province (lower Bayano River valley); on Caribbean slope known only from northern Coclé (El Uracillo) east into eastern Colon province, with one report from western San Blas (a pair at Nusagandi on March 7, 1986; Ridgely and J. Guarnaccia); ranges up in reduced numbers into lower foothills to about 600 m (2000 ft); common also on Coiba Island and most of larger Pearl Islands (but not on San José). On Coiba Island also found inside tall deciduous forest, regularly even ranging high up in the trees.
Habits: Usually in pairs; often the bright female is easier to see than the barred male. Heard much more often than seen, the call being a series of rapidly accelerating notes a

whinnying effect, but ending with a length-ened emphasized nasal note on a rising inflec-tion, *heh-heh-heh-heh-heh-heh-heh-heh-weng*; also has a growling *ahrrrr* and a repeated *enk*.
Range: Eastern Mexico to Bolivia, northern Argentina, and southern Brazil.

BLACK ANTSHRIKE
Thamnophilus nigriceps   Plate 40

Description: 5¾. Known only from eastern Panama. Fairly thick hooked bill. Male *entirely black* with white under wing-coverts. Female has *black head streaked with buffy whit-ish; back, wings, and tail chestnut*; slaty below, *broadly streaked with buffy whitish*; thighs and under tail-coverts cinnamon.
Similar species: Male Slaty Antshrike is slaty (not black), has white spotting and edging on wings, and tail tipped white. Male Immaculate Antbird has bare pale blue to whitish orbital skin. Male Jet Antbird has much white on wings and tail; female is slaty (not chestnut) above and also has white on wings and tail.
Status and distribution: Rare to uncommon in dense undergrowth of overgrown clear-ings and woodland and forest borders in lowlands of eastern Panama province (middle and upper Bayano River valley) and Darién. Perhaps locally more numerous (Griscom, for example, in 1927 recorded it as "abundant at Cape Garachiné"); found regularly at Majé Island in the Bayano Lake of eastern Panama province.
Habits: Similar to Barred Antshrike, which it seems to replace in Darién, though appar-ently favoring taller and less shrubby growth in more humid regions. Wetmore reports it to be less shy than that species.
Range: Eastern Panama and northern Colombia.

BLACK-HOODED ANTSHRIKE
Thamnophilus bridgesi   Plate 20

Description: 6–6¼. Found only in Pacific western Panama. Fairly thick, hooked bill. Male *mostly black*, slaty on lower underparts; *wing-coverts lightly spotted with white*. Female similar to male but *head, throat, and breast narrowly streaked with white*; back brown; lower underparts tinged with olive.
Similar species: Slaty Antshrike is not found in this species' range. The smaller Jet Antbird has male with much more white on wing and also on tail, female with white streaking only on underparts (not on head) and brown (not slaty black) back.

Status and distribution: Uncommon to locally fairly common in lower growth of forest, second-growth woodland, gallery woodland, and mangroves in lowlands on Pacific slope from Chiriquí east to eastern side of Azuero Peninsula (Río Pedasí in Los Santos); at least formerly it ranged up in foothills to about 1110 m (3700 ft) (these areas now mostly deforested). Forest destruction over most of its Panama range has been so complete that this species is now very local, and there are few recent reports (this despite the fact that it seems capable of persisting in quite degraded patches of woodland). Its Panama stronghold is now on the Burica Peninsula from around Puerto Armuelles south.
Habits: Similar to Slaty Antshrike, though seems somewhat more prone to forage on its own (as a pair), rather than accompany small mixed flocks of understory birds. Its fast song is also similar, an accelerating roll, *eh-eh-eh-eh-eh-eh-eh-énh*; while calling almost always shivers its tail, and sometimes the rather shaggy expressive crown feathers are raised.
Range: Costa Rica and Pacific western Panama.

SLATY ANTSHRIKE
Thamnophilus punctatus   Plate 20

Description: 5¾–6. Fairly thick, hooked bill. Male *slaty gray above with black crown*, wings and tail; *much white spotting and edging on wings* and tail tipped white; slaty gray below. Female *olive brown above with dull chestnut crown; wings with much buff spotting and edging* and tail tipped buff; dull brownish olive below.
Similar species: Male Dusky Antbird is smaller and more uniform slaty gray, and has more slender bill and less white on wing; female Dusky has uniform tawny under-parts. In eastern Panama see also Black Antshrike.
Status and distribution: Very common in lower growth of forest and second-growth woodland in lowlands and lower foothills on entire Caribbean slope; on Pacific slope found from Cerro Campana and Canal area east through Darién. Wetmore believes an old record from Santiago, Veraguas (on Pacific slope), is in error.
Habits: Normally occurring in relatively open undergrowth within forest and often bold and inquisitive, this species is much easier to observe than other Panama antshrikes. Usually in pairs, often on the

periphery of a mixed foraging flock of antwrens, etc. Its song is one of the characteristic sounds of the Panamanian forest, an accelerating roll, the last note accented and with an upward inflection; rather like Barred Antshrike's song but more nasal.
Range: Guatemala and Belize to Bolivia and southern Brazil.
Note: More than one species is probably involved. E. O. Willis has pointed out that trans-Andean birds differ markedly from birds found east of the Andes in vocalizations and some aspects of behavior. If split, Panama birds would belong with *T. atrinucha* (Western Slaty Antshrike).

SPECKLED ANTSHRIKE
Xenornis setifrons   Plate 40

Description: 6¼–6½. Known only from eastern Panama. Bill heavy and hooked. Male has *crown and upperparts dark brown with short tawny streaks; wings with two prominent deep buff wing-bars*; tail dark gray, outer feathers tipped whitish; *sides of head and entire underparts dark slaty gray.* Female *like male above*; upper throat whitish edged with buff, remaining underparts brown, deepest on belly, mottled with buff on breast.
Similar species: Color and pattern more reminiscent of a foliage-gleaner than an antshrike, but lacks their rufous tails. See female Slaty Antshrike.
Status and distribution: Rare in lower growth of humid forest in lowlands and lower foothills of San Blas (where recorded in the east from hills above Armila, and more recently from Nusagandi in the west, where first found by J. Blake from a female mist-netted and a few others seen in April–May 1985, photos to VIREO; since seen by a few other observers) and eastern Darién (recorded only from middle slopes of Cerro Tacarcuna); recorded mainly (150–600 m: 500–2000 ft. Seemingly very local in Panama (which comprises the major portion of its range), perhaps more just overlooked.
Habits: Not very well known. Birds seen at Nusagandi have foraged mostly as pairs, generally not with mixed flocks, favoring dense viny tangled growth. The song is a series of three to nine (most often five) high-pitched and evenly spaced notes which rise steadily in pitch, the call a fairly loud fast *chak-chak-chak* (sometimes only one or up to five or more syllables); both song and call are given by both sexes (B. Whitney and G. Rosenberg).

Range: Eastern Panama and northwestern Colombia.
Note: The 1983 AOU-Check-list opted to use Wetmore's suggested name of Spiny-faced Antshrike for this distinctive species, this instead of the Speckled Antshrike used in most other references. We favor continuing to use the latter, in part because the short black bristles at the base of the bill and below the eye are so inconspicuous, in part because *Xenornis* is the only antshrike with a speckled pattern.

RUSSET ANTSHRIKE
Thamnistes anabatinus   Plate 20

Description: 5½. *Bill stout and hooked. Brown above*, more rufous on crown and particularly on wings and tail, with *buffy eye-stripe*; concealed patch of orange-buff on back (absent in female); *yellowish buffy brown below*, tinged grayish on sides.
Similar species: A somewhat confusing bird; note especially its stocky bull-headed appearance accentuated by its heavy bill, and its arboreal behavior. Most apt to be confused with various foliage-gleaners though it is smaller with shorter tail which lacks pointed feathers. See also Cinnamon and female One-colored and Cinereous Becards (all with different behavior, and with nowhere near as stout or hooked bill).
Status and distribution: Uncommon to locally fairly common in humid forest in foothills on entire Caribbean slope (most numerous 300–900 m: 1000–3000 ft), in lowlands from Canal area eastward; on Pacific slope recorded locally in foothills from Chiriquí (where found recently only in the Fortuna area), Veraguas, Panama province (Cerro Campana and Cerro Azul/Jefe area), and Darién, in lowlands only from western Chiriquí (recent reports only from Burica Peninsula). In Canal area seen most regularly along Pipeline Road (but even here in very small numbers).
Habits: Often forages considerably higher than other antshrikes, frequently in association with a mixed flock of insectivorous birds. Quite active, gleaning in the foliage. The usual call is a *wee-tsip*, often repeated.
Range: Southeastern Mexico to western Venezuela and Bolivia.

PLAIN ANTVIREO
Dysithamnus mentalis   Plate 21

Description: 4¼–4½. Bill heavy. Male *mostly dark olive gray*, darkest on crown and cheeks; two narrow white wing-bars; somewhat paler olive gray below (palest on throat), fading to *buffy yellowish on belly*. Female more olive above with *distinct russet crown* and a whitish eye-ring; two narrow buff wing-bars; throat whitish, breast and sides grayish olive, lower belly yellowish.

Similar species: Note thick-set, heavy-headed appearance with short tail and stout slightly hooked bill. Antwrens are smaller and slighter with narrower bills and more active behavior. Spot-crowned Antvireo of lowland forests is similar but both sexes have spots on crown. See also Tawny-crowned Greenlet (which lacks wing-bars).

Status and distribution: Uncommon to fairly common in lower growth of humid forest in foothills and lower highlands on both slopes, mostly 600–1500 m (2000–5000 ft), occasionally somewhat lower or higher. In central Panama known only from Cerro Campana and the Cerro Azul/Jefe area and uncommon at both localities.

Habits: Usually in pairs, often foraging independently of mixed flocks, normally within a few meters of the ground. Their deliberate behavior is somewhat reminiscent of the larger vireos. Has an accelerating call similar in pattern to those of the *Thamnophilus* antshrikes but higher; also has a nasal but rather soft *nyoot, nyoot* and a *choot-nyoo*.

Range: Southeastern Mexico to northern Bolivia, Paraguay, northeastern Argentina, and southern Brazil.

SPOT-CROWNED ANTVIREO
Dysithamnus puncticeps   Plate 21

Description: 4¼–4½. Bill heavy; iris pale grayish. Rather like Plain Antvireo. Male *mostly slaty olive*, the *crown black with small white spots*; two narrow white wing-bars; somewhat paler gray below, breast narrowly streaked with dusky, fading to buffy on belly. Female brownish above with *bright tawny crown streaked and spotted with black*; two narrow buff wing-bars; buffy below, with narrow black streaks on throat and breast.

Similar species: Plain Antvireo lacks crown spots and occurs in foothills and highlands (not mostly lowlands). Antwrens, with which this species often occurs, are smaller and more active.

Status and distribution: Uncommon in lower growth of humid forest in lowlands and lower foothills (to about 600 m: 2000 ft) on entire Caribbean slope; on Pacific slope recorded only from eastern Darién (primarily in lower foothills, up to about 750 m:

2500 ft). In Canal area most readily found along Pipeline Road and on Barro Colorado Island.

Habits: Similar to Plain Antvireo. Its song is a series of soft purring notes which gradually accelerate but do not end with an accented note (rather, it has effect of fading away), *hu hu-hu-h-h-h-h-h-h-u-u-u-u*; overall quality is similar to a screech-owl.

Range: Southeastern Costa Rica to western Ecuador.

PYGMY ANTWREN
Myrmotherula brachyura   Plate 21

Description: 2¾. *Tiny and virtually tail-less.* Male *black above, streaked with white*, rump pale gray; two white wing-bars; black line through eye and another on cheeks; throat white, *cheeks and remaining underparts pale lemon yellow*. Female very similar but crown sometimes streaked with buff, not white.

Similar species: Combination of streaked upperparts and pale yellow underparts make identification of this minute but very attractive bird easy. Only possible confusion is with considerably larger male Streaked Antwren (which is streaked below); see also the equally small Black-headed Tody-Flycatcher (unstreaked above).

Status and distribution: Uncommon to locally fairly common in canopy and borders of humid forest and taller second-growth woodland in lowlands on Caribbean slope in Canal area and San Blas (where recorded only at Mandinga, but probably more widespread), and on Pacific slope in lowlands and lower foothills (to about 600 m: 2000 ft, e.g. around Cana in Darién) in eastern Panama province (middle or upper Bayano River valley) and Darién. A difficult bird to collect, now known to be considerably more numerous than had been realized. In Canal area most frequent along Achiote Road, but there as elsewhere much more likely to be recorded once its distinctive vocalization is known.

Habits: Favors dense foliage and viny tangles at middle levels of forest borders, *not* particularly associated with water's edge. Usually in pairs, gleaning and fluttering in foliage, not easy to see (in part due to their small size); they regularly follow mixed flocks, but sometimes also forage independently. Its characteristic song is a repeated single note which accelerates and ends in a short trill, *chree, chree-chre-chre-che-che-che-che-ee-ee-e-e-e*; this is given frequently, almost throughout the day, and often reveals the bird's presence as it moves about unseen in leafy growth overhead.

Range: Central Panama to northern Bolivia and Amazonian Brazil.

STREAKED ANTWREN
Myrmotherula surinamensis   Plate 21

Description: 3½. Male *black above streaked with white*; two white wing-bars: *white below streaked with black.* Female with *head bright orange-rufous* lightly streaked with black; remaining upperparts black streaked white, two white wing-bars; *pale orange-buffy below*, unstreaked.

Similar species: Color pattern of male is reminiscent of Black-and-white Warbler though it is very different in shape and behavior. The pretty female should be easily recognized. Pygmy Antwren is smaller, with shorter tail and pale yellow underparts.

Status and distribution: Locally fairly common in shrubby clearings and woodland and forest borders, often near water, in lowlands on entire Caribbean slope (west to western Bocas del Toro around Almirante), and on Pacific slope in lowlands and lower foothills (to about 600 m: 2000 ft, e.g. around Cana in Darién) in eastern Panama province (west to around Tocumen) and Darién. In Canal area most frequent along Achiote Road.

Habits: Not a forest bird, rarely if ever associating with other antwrens. Usually found in pairs foraging in tangled vines and foliage at low and middle levels, most often independent of other birds. The call is a fast, accelerating chipper, rising lightly as it goes along, *chee-chee-chee-chee-chee-chee;* also has a nasal *nyee deea.*

Range: Western Panama to eastern Peru and Amazonian Brazil.

CHECKER-THROATED ANTWREN
Myrmotherula fulviventris   Plate 21

Description: 4. *Iris pale in both sexes.* Male olive brown above with blackish wing-coverts and two buffy wing-bars; *white throat, feathers edged with black, giving checkered appearance*; remaining underparts brownish buffy. Female similar but lacks checkered throat; *uniform plain brownish buffy below.*

Similar species: Male easily recognized by checkered throat. Female closely resembles female White-flanked Antwren, but has pale (not dark) eye (this usually not too prominent in the field) and uniform buffy underparts (no whitish throat and flank tufts). Female Slaty Antwren is more tawny

below; it is more of a foothill bird (not lowlands), though there is some overlap.

Status and distribution: Uncommon to locally very common (less numerous westward) in lower growth of humid forest and second-growth woodland in lowlands and in smaller numbers in lower foothills (to about 750 m: 2500 ft) on entire Caribbean slope; on Pacific slope recorded locally from Veraguas foothills (above Santa Fé), and from western Panama province (Cerro Campana, Chorrera) east through Darién. In Canal area more numerous on Caribbean side; especially common on Barro Colorado Island.

Habits: Almost always in pairs or small groups which frequently associate with mixed flocks of other understory birds (especially other antwrens and Slaty Antshrike). An active feeder which specializes in probing into hanging dead leaf clusters; usually forages somewhat closer to the ground than White-flanked Antwren. Its calls are sharp, squeaky, and high-pitched, and include a single *pseeyk!* and a loud *tseek-seek-seek-seek.* Disputing males occasionally perch very close to each other (a foot or two apart) and bow back and forth with throats puffed out, constantly repeating a squeaky, hummingbird-like *syip-syip-syip* . . . (E. O. Willis; Ridgely).

Range: Honduras to western Ecuador.

WHITE-FLANKED ANTWREN
Myrmotherula axillaris   Plate 21

Description: 3½. Iris dark. Male mostly *black*; wing-coverts spotted lightly with white, tail (usually) tipped white; *long silky white tuft on flanks* (sometimes partly concealed under wings); under wing-coverts also white. Female grayish brown to grayish olive above with some buff spots on wing-coverts; *throat whitish*, remaining underparts buffy, with buffy whitish flanks.

Similar species: Female Checker-throated Antwren has pale (not dark) eye and is deeper buff below with no white on throat or flanks. Female Slaty Antwren is tawny below and lacks spots on wings.

Status and distribution: Uncommon to locally very common (much less numerous westward) in lower and middle growth of humid forest and second-growth woodland in lowlands and in smaller numbers in foothills (to about 900 m: 3000 ft) on entire Caribbean slope; on Pacific slope recorded from western Panama province (Cerro Campana, where scarce) and Canal area east through Darién. On Pacific side of Canal area even less numerous and more local than Checker-throated Antwren, but common and widespread in forest on Caribbean side.

Habits: Almost invariably found in a mixed foraging flock, and often the numerically dominant species in such groups. Tends to forage higher than the Checker-throat and is even more active. A frequently heard call is a descending *chee-doo* or *chee-chee-doo*; less often heard is its song, a measured series of six to ten descending whistled notes, *pyee, pee, piy, pey, peh, pu* (E. O. Willis; Ridgely).

Range: Honduras to northern Bolivia and southeastern Brazil.

SLATY ANTWREN
Myrmotherula schisticolor   Plate 21

Description: 3¾. Male *slaty with black throat and chest*; wing-coverts and tail tipped white. Female olive brown above; *sides of head and throat buff, remaining underparts dull tawny*.

Similar species: In most areas where it occurs, the only antwren present. Male White-flank is black (not slaty) with the white tuft on flanks always at least partially visible. Female Checker-throats and White-flanks have buff spots on wings (lacking in Slaty) and buff (not tawny) underparts.

Status and distribution: Uncommon to fairly common in lower growth of humid forest and second-growth woodland in foothills and lower highlands (mostly 600–1500 m: 2000–5000 ft) locally on Pacific slope from Chiriquí to Darién, spilling over onto Caribbean slope foothills at least in Veraguas (Río Calovévora) and probably elsewhere (e.g. in Bocas del Toro); in western Chiriquí and on western and southern sides of Azuero Peninsula also recorded in lowlands down to near sea level (but few or no recent reports, and may be virtually extirpated from such areas by deforestation). In central Panama recorded only from Cerro Campana and the Cerro Azul/Jefe area, and scarce at both localities.

Habits: Usually in pairs, often accompanying small mixed flocks of other understory birds such as Plain Antvireos, various *Basileuterus* warblers and foliage-gleaners, etc. Its calls include a nasal *nyeeah* scold and a sharp *pseeyt*.

Range: Southern Mexico to northern Venezuelan and southern Peru.

RUFOUS-WINGED ANTWREN
Herpsilochmus rufimarginatus   Plate 40

Description: 4½. Found only in eastern Panama. Male with *crown and narrow stripe through eye black*, and *long white superciliary*; back gray with some black mixed in; wings black with two white wing-bars and broad rufous edging to flight feathers (forming *large conspicuous rufous patch on primaries and most of secondaries*); tail dusky broadly tipped white; throat whitish, *remaining underparts pale yellow*. Female similar but with *crown and stripe through eye rufous*, more grayish olive black.

Similar species: No other vaguely similar Panama bird shows the prominent rufous in the wing. See Pygmy Antwren (also with mainly yellow underparts, and with somewhat similar call).

Status and distribution: Fairly common in canopy and borders of forest and second-growth woodland in lowlands and lower foothills (recorded in small numbers up to about 1050 m: 3500 ft) of eastern Panama province (middle and upper Bayano River valley) and Darién. Quite readily found around Cana, in eastern Darién, once its distinctive call is learned; as with the Pygmy Antwren, this species is relatively difficult to collect, and has proven in recent years to be considerably more numerous than had been earlier assumed the case.

Habits: Particularly favors viny tangles at mid-levels along forest borders or in openings. Usually in pairs, regularly accompanying mixed flocks of various tanagers, Lesser Greenlets, etc., but inconspicuous, tending to forage inside dense foliage. Its characteristic call is a fast, smoothly accelerating series of rather nasal notes (with somewhat an antshrike-like quality), the last accented, *chu, chu, chu-chu-ch-ch-chchchch-chít*; it is given by both members of the pair, usually the male first, almost always with rapidly shivering tail.

Range: Eastern Panama locally to northern Bolivia, northeastern Argentina, and southern Brazil.

DOT-WINGED ANTWREN
Microrhopias quixensis   Plate 21

Description: 4½. Tail proportionately longer than in *Myrmotherula* antwrens, *often held somewhat cocked and fanned*. Male *glossy black*, with white spots and *broad white bar on wing* and *broad white tipping on tail*; usually concealed white dorsal patch revealed when excited. Female slaty or black above, *rich rufous below*, with wings, tail, and white dorsal patch as in male.

Similar species: Female easily recognized. Male White-flanked Antwren is smaller, with white tuft on flanks and less white on wings and tail.

Status and distribution: Fairly common to common in humid forest, second-growth woodland, and borders in lowlands and (in smaller numbers) lower foothills on entire Caribbean slope (somewhat less numerous westward); on Pacific slope recorded from western Chiriquí (no recent records; perhaps extirpated due to deforestation, but may survive in remaining forest on Burica Peninsula), western Veraguas (one nineteenth-century specimen from Soná in AMNH; no recent records, and likely extirpated due to deforestation), and from Canal area east through Darién (where seems more numerous in foothills, and recorded up to about 1050 m: 3500 ft). In Canal area considerably more numerous and widespread on Caribbean side.

Habits: Very active and spritely, gleaning among foliage at lower and middle levels. Though often found in mixed flocks of *Myrmotherula* antwrens and other birds, also regularly forages in pairs and small groups of exclusively its own species. Also more apt to be seen at forest edge than the *Myrmotherula* antwrens, often in tangled viny or thickety growth. Its calls include a rapid series of five to ten whistled notes going upscale, *pu-peh-pey-pih-pee-pyee?*, sometimes alternated with rough *zhaiet* notes, a falsetto *peep* and *chew*, and a tinny buzzy note reminiscent of the chirr of Spotted Antbird (E. O. Willis).

Range: Southeastern Mexico to Bolivia and Amazonian Brazil.

Status and distribution: Fairly common in lower growth of woodland and borders on larger Pearl Islands; not found on mainland.

Habits: Usually found singly or in pairs, feeding in bushes and low branches of trees, often fanning their tails from side to side, and drooping their wings. Its calls include a soft mellow *tu, tr-r-r-r* and a sharper *tru-ík, tru-ík . . .*; sometimes both are merged into one vocalization.

Range: Pearl Islands; Colombia to the Guianas and Amazonian and southeastern Brazil.

WHITE-FRINGED ANTWREN (male above, female below)

WHITE-FRINGED ANTWREN
Formicivora grisea   p.271

Description: 4¾. *Found only on Pearl Islands.* Male brownish gray above, wings blackish with single white bar and white spotting on shoulders, rounded tail blackish and broadly tipped white; *black sides of head and most of underparts, separated from upperparts by broad white eye-stripe continuing down sides of neck and widening on sides and flanks.* Female dull brown above with short white superciliary, wings and tail as in male; *mostly buff below*, deepest on chest, whiter on throat and lower belly.

Similar species: One of just three antbirds on the Pearl Islands (others being Barred Antshrike and Jet Antbird); there should be no problem in recognition. Recalls Dotwinged Antwren in shape and behavior.

RUFOUS-RUMPED ANTWREN
Terenura callinota   Plate 21

Description: 4¼. Local in *very humid foothills.* Male has *black crown* and narrow stripe through eye, and narrow white superciliary; back olive green with *contrasting bright rufous rump*; wings blackish with bright yellow on bend of wing, *two broad pale yellowish wing-bars*, and olive edging on flight feathers; tail olive grayish very narrowly tipped white; sides of head pale gray, becoming *grayish white on throat and chest*, and pale yellow on lower underparts. Female duller than male, with grayish olive crown and back.

Similar species: Rufous-winged Antwren is somewhat larger and longer-tailed, with rufous on wings instead of rump; the two occur together only marginally, in foothills of eastern Darién.

Status and distribution: Locally uncommon to fairly common in middle levels and canopy of very humid foothill forest in central Chiriquí (Fortuna area) and adjacent Bocas del Toro (along the oleoducto road north of Fortuna), Caribbean slope of Veraguas (known only from one specimen from Calobre, but likely more numerous and widespread), and eastern Darién (Cerro Tacarcuna, Cerro Pirre, and Cerro Quía); recorded mostly 750–1200 m (2500–4000 ft). Many of the above records represent recent sightings (though LSUMZ obtained a specimen on Cerro Pirre in 1982, and two specimens were taken at Fortuna in 1976 by Ridgely for GML, though both seem now to have been lost); the Rufous-rumped Antwren is a difficult bird to collect, and the paucity of earlier records is doubtless merely a reflection of this.

Habits: Typically in pairs, and almost always seen as they accompany mixed flocks of tanagers and other insectivorous birds, usually well above the ground (occasionally lower at forest edge). They glean very actively, mostly in foliage and along smaller branches on outer edge of trees; they also habitually turn upside-down to examine the underside of leaves, and at such times the rufous rump often flashes out conspicuously. Its call is a high thin *ti-ti-ti-i-i-i-i-i-i-i-tzz-tzz-tzz*, initially with quality of Plain Xenops, and with number of buzzy syllables at end being variable (B. Whitney).

Range: Costa Rica to northwestern Venezuela and Peru; Guyana and Surinam.

DUSKY ANTBIRD
Cercomacra tyrannina   Plate 21

Description: 5½. Male *uniform slaty gray* (*blackish slate* in birds from western Panama east to northern Veraguas, *crepera*); wing-coverts and tail tipped white; usually concealed white dorsal patch. Female olive brown above with some buffy tipping on wing-coverts; *sides of head and underparts tawny*, tinged olive on flanks.

Similar species: Male most likely to be confused with male Slaty Antshrike, which is larger with heavier bill, black crown, and more white spotting on wings. Male Jet Antbird is uniform glossy black (in area of overlap, Dusky is slaty gray). Female Slaty Antshrike has brownish olive (not tawny) underparts; female Bare-crowned Antbird has brighter orange-rufous underparts and bare blue orbital area.

Status and distribution: Common in thickets and undergrowth of shrubby clearings, second-growth woodland, and forest borders in lowlands and lower foothills on both slopes; absent from drier Pacific slope lowlands.

Habits: Almost always in pairs, usually rather difficult to see clearly. The call is distinctive and frequently heard, a series of whistled notes, the first two given slowly, the remaining three to five fast and rhythmic, usually on a rising scale, *pü, pü, pí-pipi*. Also has a *dididit*, and a *wheeerrr*.

Range: Southeastern Mexico to western Ecuador and northern and eastern Brazil.

JET ANTBIRD
Cercomacra nigricans   Plate 21

Description: 5½. Male *glossy black with two broad white wing-bars* and broad white tip to tail; usually concealed white dorsal patch. Female slaty above with wings and tail as in male; *throat and chest slaty prominently streaked with white*, remaining underparts slaty gray (in some females white streaks extend to belly).

Similar species: Male Dusky Antbird in central and eastern Panama is slaty gray and shows very little white on wing. Male Immaculate Antbird has bare blue orbital skin and white only on shoulder. Female's white-streaked throat and chest distinguishes her from other Panama antbirds except female Black Antshrike (which is chestnut above) and female Black-hooded Antshrike (which is brown above).

Status and distribution: Uncommon and rather local in thickets and undergrowth in shrubby clearings and woodland borders in lowlands on Pacific slope from Veraguas and through Darién; on Caribbean slope recorded locally from western Colon province (Río Indio) east to western San Blas (Mandinga); more numerous on some of larger Pearl Islands (Rey, Cañas, Viveros).

Habits: Usually in pairs, often along streams or in damp areas. Like so many other antbirds, often difficult to see, though the bird's presence is frequently revealed by its distinctive call, a repeated *tch-ker, tch-ker, tch-ker, tch-ker*.

Range: Western Panama to western Ecuador and extreme northern Brazil.

BARE-CROWNED ANTBIRD
Gymnocichla nudiceps   Plate 21

Description: 6. Male *black with bare, bright*

blue crown and orbital area; white spotting on wing-coverts and white tip on tail. Female has *only orbital area bright blue* (crown is feathered); olive brown above with some buff spotting on wing-coverts; *bright rufous below*.

Similar species: Male Immaculate Antbird lacks blue crown; female Immaculate is brown (not rufous) below. Female Chestnut-backed Antbird is also brown below.

Status and distribution: Uncommon in dense undergrowth at edge of second-growth woodland and forest, and in adjacent shrubby regenerating clearings in lowlands on entire Caribbean slope; on Pacific slope recorded only from lowlands of Chiriquí (*erratilis*; no recent records, and with deforestation now doubtless very local if not totally extirpated, though some may survive in remaining forests on Burica Peninsula), Veraguas (known only from one nineteenth-century specimen without precise locality), and eastern Panama province (middle and upper Bayano River valley), and lowlands and lower foothills (to about 600 m: 2000 ft) of Darién. Scarce in Canal area, where reported mostly from near Caribbean coast, especially in Achiote/Escobal Road area; more numerous in eastern Panama province and Darién.

Habits: A confirmed army ant follower, though occasionally seen away from them. Usually in pairs, and rather skulking or shy; they often pound their tail downward, perhaps especially when nervous. Their song is a loud series of about eight ringing notes, accelerating slightly in the second half but all on the same pitch, *chew-chew-chew-chew-cheep-cheep-cheep-cheep*, given with rapidly vibrating tail; it is rather like song of Immaculate Antbird.

Range: Guatemala and Belize to northern Colombia.

Note: The monotypic genus *Gymnocichla* should probably be merged with *Myrmeciza*.

able in extent (in some birds this looks like a wing-bar, sometimes two of them); crown browner and *cheeks dusky*; whitish below, *strongly washed with buff on breast*.

Similar species: Chestnut-backed Antbird has bare blue orbital skin and all dark underparts (no white or whitish belly). Bicolored Antbird has only cheeks black (underparts mostly white) and likewise has blue orbital area.

Status and distribution: Fairly common to common in undergrowth of deciduous forest and second-growth woodland, gallery woodland, and dense scrub in lowlands (and sparingly in foothills up to about 600 m: 2000 ft) on Pacific slope from western Coclé (seen above El Copé on March 9, 1986; Ridgely, J. Guarnaccia, D. Engleman) east to central Darién (recorded as far east as Yaviza); old specimens labeled "Veragua" require modern confirmation, but seem possible; on Caribbean slope recorded mainly from middle Chagres River valley (e.g. along first part of Pipeline Road), but since 1986 a few have also been present in the France Field/Coco solo area near Caribbean coast (D. Engleman, J. Guarnaccia, G. Vaucher *et al.*), and in January–June 1987 they were also found east into eastern Colon province in the Portobelo area (D. Graham). Numerous in virtually any wooded area on Pacific side of Canal area, though always heard much more often than it is seen.

Habits: Feeds almost entirely on or very near the ground. The call is loud and distinctive, often given as the bird perches on a fallen log, a fast accelerating crescendo, tailing off markedly at the end, typically, *cheer, cheer, cheer-cheer-cheercheercheecheer, chew, chew, chew*.

Range: Central Panama to northern Colombia, Venezuela, Guyana, and northeastern Brazil.

WHITE-BELLIED ANTBIRD
Myrmeciza longipes   Plate 22

Description: 5¾. Rather long flesh-colored legs; small area of bare blue skin around eye. Male *mostly bright rufous-chestnut above*, grayer on crown, flight feathers edged somewhat paler; *sides of head, throat, and breast black*, bordered by *gray superciliary and sides of neck and breast*; *lower underparts white*, flanks washed with buff. Female similar but duller, lacking the black throat and breast; wing-coverts with subterminal black spots, vari-

CHESTNUT-BACKED ANTBIRD
Myrmeciza exsul   Plate 22

Description: 5½. *Bare ocular region pale blue*; iris brown. Male has *head, neck, and underparts slaty black, contrasting with chestnut back, wings, and tail*; flanks and (sometimes) lower belly dull brown. Female like male above but duller; sides of head and throat slaty, with remaining underparts dark brown. Birds from Darién (*cassini*) have conspicuous white spots on wing-coverts, and females are brighter below, almost rufous on breast;

wing spots are also seen in some birds from farther west (as far as around Cerro Jefe and on Caribbean side of Canal area).

Similar species: Rare Dull-mantled Antbird lacks blue orbital skin, has red eye (not brown), and has upper back olive brown. See also White-bellied Antbird.

Status and distribution: Common in undergrowth of humid forest and second-growth woodland in lowlands and lower foothills (to about 900 m: 3000 ft) on entire Caribbean slope; on Pacific slope recorded in lowlands from Chiriquí east to western side of Azuero Peninsula (*occidentalis*, now very local due to deforestation, though it remains numerous on the Burica Peninsula), and from Canal area (where uncommon and local) east through Darién. Widespread and numerous on Caribbean side of Canal area, though always heard far more often than it is seen.

Habits: Typically seen alone or in pairs low in forest undergrowth, but usually not on ground itself, often perching sideways on small vertical saplings. Does not regularly follow army ant swarms, but is sometimes attracted to them. The call is a series of two or three emphatic whistles, easily imitated, *peh, peh, peeéa*, or *peh, peeea*; Chapman paraphrases it as "come-right-hére" or "come-here". Black-faced Antthrush's call is similar but more hesitant and less emphatic. Also has a soft *chirr*.

Range: Southern Honduras to western Ecuador.

scapular patch (absent in Chestnut-backed); occasionally this is visible in the field, when a Dull-mantled is excited and has raised its back feathers.

Status and distribution: Rare to locally uncommon in undergrowth of humid forest in lowlands and foothills on entire Caribbean slope (not recorded from Bocas del Toro, though seems likely to occur); on Pacific slope recorded from foothills of Veraguas (Santa Fé), Panamá province (Cerro Campana and Cerro Azul/Jefe; also a 1949 specimen from Chepo taken by Wetmore), and Darién (mostly in foothills, a few records from lowlands). Found only recently (1969) in Canal area, with most reports from Pipeline Road (especially along streams crossing its middle third, e.g. Río Pelón), a few from Achiote Road.

Habits: Particularly fond of shady streamsides and dark ravines in heavily forested areas, especially in the foothills. General behavior similar to Chestnut-backed Antbird, like that species often clinging to vertical saplings as they hop through the undergrowth. Occasionally attracted to army ant swarms. Their song is not nearly as noticeable as that of the Chestnut-backed, being a series of about six high clear notes, *beet, beet, beet-beet-beet-beet*, dropping a bit at end; female sometimes follows with a slightly softer *beet-beet, chutu* (B. Whitney; Ridgely).

Range: Costa Rica to northwestern Venezuela.

DULL-MANTLED ANTBIRD
Myrmeciza laemosticta   Plate 22

Description: 5 ½ . *No* bare blue ocular region; *iris red*. Male has head and neck slaty, *olive brown upper back and wings, wing-coverts with small buff and white dots*; lower back, rump, and tail chestnut; throat and upper chest black, remaining underparts slaty, with some brown on flanks and lower belly. Female similar but with *throat checkered black and white*, and all spots on wing-coverts buff.

Similar species: Easily confused with Chestnut-backed Antbird, especially birds of that species with white wing-spotting. Chestnut-backed differs in its brown (not red) eye, having prominent bare blue skin around the eye (in both sexes), and in having solid chestnut mantle (with no olive), thus showing more contrast with slaty head. In the hand note further that both sexes of Dull-mantled have a large concealed white inter-

IMMACULATE ANTBIRD
Myrmeciza immaculata   Plates 21, 22

Description: 7. A *large*, long-tailed antbird; *large area of bare skin around eye pale blue in front, whitish behind*. Male *uniform jet black*, with bend of wing white. Female *uniform chocolate brown* with blackish sides of head and throat, and dusky tail; bend of wing white.

Similar species: Notably larger than other *Myrmeciza* antbirds in Panama. Male most resembles male Bare-crowned Antbird, but lacks that species' bare bright blue crown; see also male Black Antshrike (very different behavior, no bare ocular area, etc.). Female Chestnut-backed Antbird is smaller and more chestnut above and on tail, etc.

Status and distribution: Rare to uncommon in undergrowth of humid forest, second-growth woodland, and borders in foothills and lower highlands on Caribbean slope in Bocas del Toro, Veraguas, and Coclé (above El Copé), spilling over locally onto Pacific slope in central Chiriquí (Fortuna area in upper Río Chiriquí valley) and Veraguas (Santa Fé), and in foothills and highlands of eastern Darién (Cerro Pirre, Cerro Tacarcuna); recorded mostly 300–1200 m (1000–4000 ft). No confirmed records from central Panama.

Habits: Usually in pairs, less often in small groups, Immaculate Antbirds are frequent attendants at swarms of army ants but are otherwise shy and difficult to see, though they are often heard. Their tails are constantly slowly raised and then rapidly lowered. The call is a distinctive series of loud clear whistled notes, delivered rapidly and with slight emphasis on first note, *peer-peer-peer-peer-peer-peer-peer-peer*, somewhat slower toward end.

Range: Costa Rica to northwestern Venezuela and western Ecuador.

SPOTTED ANTBIRD
Hylophylax naevioides   Plate 22

Description: 4¼. Tail short and often fanned. Male *reddish brown above with head and nape ashy gray*; wings with chestnut and black bars and white spots; throat black, remaining underparts white, *breast crossed by band of large black spots*. Female echoes pattern of male but is duller and buffier, head brownish, mostly whitish below with breast crossed by band of less distinct brownish spots.

Similar species: Small size and bright coloration facilitate recognition of this common species. Only possible confusion is with larger Wing-banded Antbird, which has black and gray (in male), or rufous and gray (female), underparts.

Status and distribution: Fairly common to common in undergrowth of humid forest and second-growth woodland in lowlands and foothills on entire Caribbean slope; on Pacific slope recorded in foothills from Veraguas eastward, in lowlands from western Panama province and Canal area (where local in areas of more humid forest and woodland) eastward; recorded up to around 900 m (3000 ft). Widespread in forested areas on Caribbean side of Canal area, perhaps most numerous along Pipeline Road.

Habits: A faithful attendant at army ant swarms but also often found foraging independently, alone or in pairs. Its distinctive song is a series of high wheezy, falling slightly in pitch and with fading effect, *peezee, wheezee, wheezee, wheezee, wheeya*. Frequently flicks its often spread tail upward.

Range: Honduras to western Ecuador.

WING-BANDED ANTBIRD
Myrmornis torquata   Plate 22

Description: 6. *Looks virtually tail-less*. Bill rather long; bare orbital area pale blue. Male dull chestnut above faintly scaled dusky; wings slaty with *three distinct tawny bands across coverts and another broader area near tip of flight feathers*; throat and chest black, with *area on sides of neck whitish vermiculated with black*; remaining underparts slaty gray with rufous under tail-coverts. Female similar but with throat and chest tawny, only the cheeks black.

Similar species: Oddly proportioned and not likely to be confused. Easily told from any antthrush or antpitta by the banding on the wings, etc. See also much smaller Spotted Antbird.

Status and distribution: Apparently rare and local in undergrowth of humid forest in lowlands on Caribbean slope in Canal area and eastern San Blas (Permé and Puerto Obaldía; probably more widespread), and on Pacific slope in eastern Panama province (recorded only Cerro Chucantí, but probably more widespread) and in lowlands and foothills (to over 1200 m: 4000 ft) of Darién. In Canal area recorded only from Pipeline Road; more numerous in Darién (seen regularly in small numbers on slopes of Cerro Pirre above Cana).

Habits: Almost entirely terrestrial, and rather tame (especially for an antbird), often hopping about unconcernedly only a few feet away, or flushing only a short distance to land on a low perch. Found singly or in pairs, less often in small groups; they forage independently of other antbirds (and seem never to be attracted to antswarms), probing in ground litter and flicking leaves aside with their bill (like a leaftosser). A nasal *chirr* similar to call of Bicolored Antbird is often given in alarm. Less often heard is their song, a long series (lasting for 8–10 seconds) of insistent emphatic whistled notes, very gradually ascending in pitch and increasing in intensity, *tueee, tueee-tueee-tueee-tueee . . . . . tweetweetweetweetwee*; this is usually delivered from a perch some 3–6 m (10–20 ft) above the ground.

Range: Eastern Nicaragua; central Panama south locally to northeastern Peru and Amazonian Brazil.

BICOLORED ANTBIRD
Gymnopithys leucaspis   Plate 22

Description: 5½. Sexes similar. *Bare ocular area grayish blue. Chestnut brown above* with *black cheeks* and gray band stretching from above eye to sides of neck; *white below*, with sides and flanks brown. Birds from Chiriquí and Bocas del Toro (*olivascens*) lack the gray above eye and on sides of neck.

Similar species: Basically two-toned brown and white plumage is distinctive among forest antbirds. Female Great Antshrike is also brown above and white below but is larger, with prominent red eye, and lacks black cheeks. Black-bellied Wren is also superficially similar but has black across all of lower underparts.

Status and distribution: Uncommon to fairly common in undergrowth of humid forest in lowlands and foothills on entire Caribbean slope; on Pacific slope recorded from lowlands and foothills of western Chiriquí (few or no recent reports, and now very local or even extirpated due to deforestation), foothills from Veraguas eastward, and lowlands of eastern Panama province (upper Bayano River valley) and Darién; in Chiriquí and Darién recorded in small numbers to over 1500 m (5000 ft), elsewhere below 900 m (3000 ft). More numerous from Canal area eastward; widespread in forested areas on Caribbean side of Canal area, perhaps commonest along Pipeline Road.

Habits: An inveterate follower of army ants and rarely seen away from them; in such assemblages, it is usually the most numerous of the several attendant species. A distinctive whining *chirrrr* is the most frequently given call; also has a nasal *nyap-nyap*.

Range: Honduras to northern Peru and northern Brazil.

Note: Birds from west of the Andes are sometimes considered specifically distinct (as *G. bicolor*, Bicolored Antbird) from birds of upper Amazonia (*G. leucaspis*, White-cheeked Antbird), but they were treated as conspecific in the 1983 AOU Check-list.

OCELLATED ANTBIRD
Phaenostictus mcleannani   Plate 22

Description: 7½–7¾. Rather long-tailed. *Large area of bare bright blue skin around eyes* and *generally spotted appearance* preclude confusion. Sexes similar. Olive brown above with large black spots; ear-coverts, throat, and chest black; remaining underparts chestnut with large black spots.

Status and distribution: Uncommon in undergrowth of humid forest in lowlands and lower foothills on entire Caribbean slope; on Pacific slope recorded in foothills from Veraguas eastward, and in lowlands from western Panama province (a 1910 specimen from Chorrera; no recent reports from here, or from Pacific side of Canal area) and eastern Panama province (middle and upper Bayano River valley; early records from the Chepo area) east through Darién; recorded up to around 900 m (3000 ft). Less numerous in western Panama; in Canal area probably commonest along Pipeline Road.

Habits: This spectacular antbird is the least numerous of central Panama's faithful trio of persistent army ant following antbirds (with the Bicolored and Spotted), and only infrequently is it seen away from them. It is often wary (more so than the others), even at antswarms. The tail is frequently jerked upward and then slowly lowered. Its song is an infrequently heard series of high penetrating whistles which rises rapidly, *peee-peee-pee-pee-pee-ee-ee-ee-ee-ee-ee-ee-eer-eer*, usually dropping on the last several notes; a subdued shorter version of this is sometimes given at antswarms, when its sharp *dzerrr* alarm notes are also regularly heard (B. Whitney; Ridgely).

Range: Southeastern Honduras to northwestern Ecuador.

BLACK-FACED ANTTHRUSH
Formicarius analis   Plate 22

Description: 6½–7. Short tail, usually cocked. Sexes similar. Bare bluish skin before and behind eye. *Olive brown above*, more rufous on sides of head and neck; *cheeks and throat black*, chest slaty gray, remaining underparts paler gray with tawny under tail-coverts.

Similar species: The most numerous and widespread antthrush in Panama. Black-headed Antthrush has entirely black head and neck; Rufous-breasted Antthrush has crown, nape, and chest obviously chestnut.

Status and distribution: Common in undergrowth and on floor of humid forest and second-growth woodland in lowlands and lower foothills on entire Caribbean slope; on Pacific slope recorded in lowlands and foothills of Chiriquí (*hoffmanni*; few or no recent records, though seems likely to persist in forest patches above Santa Clara and on Burica Peninsula), in foothills from Coclé (El Valle) eastward, and in lowlands from western Panama province and Canal area eastward; recorded up to about 900 m (3000 ft). Widespread in forested areas on Caribbean side of Canal area; considerably more local on Pacific side (where restricted to more humid forests).

Habits: An almost completely terrestrial bird that walks slowly and deliberately (almost like a little rail) over the forest floor, often with its tail cocked practically straight up in the air. Regularly found at the periphery of army ant swarms. Not easy to see, but its call is a characteristic sound of the Panamanian forest, a series of three (sometimes many more) plaintive and deliberate whistles, the first longer and a little higher in pitch, followed after a hesitation by the next two (or more) slightly lower pitched notes, *pee; pü, pü,* . . . Sometimes the last note is repeated (occasionally as many as 10–15 times), giving a very different effect. The three-noted call resembles call of Chestnut-backed Antbird but is unemphatic and hesitant, with accent on first note (not last). A calling bird can often be drawn in very close by a whistled imitation of its call. Sings most persistently during the rainy season.

Range: Southeastern Mexico to northern Bolivia and Amazonian Brazil.

Note: More than one species may be involved; birds from Mexico south to northern Honduras (*F. moniliger*, Mexican Antthrush) differ morphologically and vocally from birds of southern Middle America.

BLACK-HEADED ANTTHRUSH
Formicarius nigricapillus   Plate 22

Description: 6½. Rather like a very dark Black-faced Antthrush. Narrow bluish white eye-ring (broadest before and behind eye). *Entire head, neck, throat, and chest black*, merging into slaty gray on breast and paler gray on belly, with under tail-coverts chestnut; above otherwise dark brown, with black tail. Female slightly tinged olive below.

Similar species: Black-faced Antthrush has

brown crown and nape and is not as dark below. *This species looks very dark in the field*, virtually black below.

Status and distribution: Rare to locally fairly common in very humid forest in foothills and lower highlands on both slopes (but mainly Caribbean); very local (but likely somewhat overlooked), recorded from Bocas del Toro, both slopes of Veraguas, Panama province (Cerro Campana, and since 1984 has also been recorded on Cerro Jefe, where first found by R. Behrstock), and western San Blas (Nusagandi, where first found in March 1986 by Ridgely and J. Guarnaccia); recorded 450–1500 m (1500–5000 ft). On Cerro Campana syntopic with Black-faced Antthrush (but much less numerous than that species) but restricted to areas around 900 m (3000 ft); on Cerro Jefe found on north side of peak in elfin forest.

Habits: Similar to Black-faced Antthrush, basically terrestrial and difficult to see (even harder than Black-faced), favoring very dense vegetation. Its distinctive song is a series of about 10 slightly accelerating short whistled notes, becoming a little louder then stopping suddenly, *hü-hü-hü-hü-hü-hü-hü-hü-hü-hü*, lasting about 5 seconds, with a pause of about 10 seconds before another repetition.

Range: Costa Rica to western Ecuador.

RUFOUS-BREASTED ANTTHRUSH
Formicarius rufipectus   Plate 22

Description: 7–7½. Resembles Black-faced Antthrush. *Crown, nape, sides of neck, and breast chestnut;* cheeks and throat black; otherwise dark olive brown above; belly dark olivaceous with chestnut under tail-coverts.

Similar species: Black-faced Antthrush has brown crown and nape and slaty gray chest.

Status and distribution: Uncommon in very humid forest and forest borders in foothills and lower highlands on both slopes, but very local (though probably at least somewhat overlooked); recorded only from Chiriquí (only recent records are from Fortuna area), central Bocas del Toro (several heard along oleoducto road north of Fortuna in July 1982; Ridgely), Veraguas (two nineteenth-century specimens without precise locality; recently heard at Santa Fé by B. Whitney), and eastern Darién (Cerro Pirre, Cerro Tacarcuna); recorded mostly 750–1500 m (2500–5000 ft). In Bocas del Toro (along oleoducto road) occurs slightly higher than Black-headed Antthrush (mostly 990–

1200 m: 3000–4000 ft, vs. 750–990 m: 2500–3300 ft for latter), though on a few occasions in July 1982 the two species could be heard singing simultaneously.

Habits: Much like Black-faced and Black-headed Antthrushes, but even harder to see (almost impossible without the use of tape playback). Seems to favor thick damp *Helionia* thickets at edge of undisturbed forest, usually on very steep slopes. The song is a short, flat, fast two-noted whistle, *hü-hü*, the second note either a semi-tone above the first or on the same pitch but often seeming slightly shorter; at and soon after dawn it is often repeated steadily at 10–20 second intervals (B. Whitney; Ridgely).

Range: Costa Rica to eastern Peru.

BLACK-CROWNED ANTPITTA
Pittasoma michleri   Plate 22

Description: 7¼–7½. Panama's most spectacular antbird; unmistakably *large* and essentially tail-less, with *very long legs. Crown and nape glossy black* contrasting with chestnut cheeks; otherwise brown above with two rows of inconspicuous buff spots on wing-coverts; throat mostly black, *remaining underparts white boldly and broadly scalloped with black*. Female similar but without black throat, and more buffy whitish below, with sparser black scalloping.

Status and distribution: Rare and local (but more numerous in eastern Panama, particularly in Darién) in undergrowth and on floor of humid forest in lowlands and foothills on entire Caribbean slope; on Pacific slope recorded locally in humid foothills from Veraguas (Santa Fé) eastward, and in lowlands of eastern Panama province (upper Bayano River valley) and Darién; recorded up to about 1050 m (3500 ft). Most recent Canal area reports are from along Pipeline Road, also seen a few times along Achiote Road; here as elsewhere most often encountered when attending a swarm of army ants.

Habits: Almost entirely terrestrial, hopping or bounding rapidly over the forest floor, but flushing up to low branches when disturbed. Its most often heard call is a sudden series of 10–16 harsh notes, slowing slightly toward end, *wakwakwakwakwakwakwakwakwak-wak-wak-wak*; this call may be given mostly in alarm. The song is a long level series of high clear penetrating *tu* notes which start rapidly, and gradually slow down; the entire song can last over a minute (B. Whitney).

Range: Costa Rica to northwestern Colombia.

SCALED ANTIPITTA
Grallaria guatimalensis   Plate 22

Description: 7. Found only in highlands of west and east. Plump, short-tailed, and very long-legged. Crown and nape slaty, otherwise brownish olive above, *feathers of all of upperparts edged with black producing scaled effect*; buffy whitish malar streak; *mostly rufous* below with some blackish mottling on throat and upper chest. Foregoing applies to *princeps* of western Panama; *chocoensis* of eastern Darién is similar, but darker above, and has breast narrowly streaked with buff.

Similar species: Large size and scaly upperparts should make recognition of this beautifully marked antpitta easy.

Status and distribution: Apparently rare in forest in foothills and highlands of Bocas del Toro, Chiriquí, Veraguas, and eastern Darién; in Chiriquí recorded mostly above 1500 m (5000 ft), though considerably lower elsewhere (570–1290 m: 1900–4300 ft).

Habits: Mostly terrestrial, hopping on forest floor or up onto fallen logs, rarely flying; when flushed may land on a low branch. Very shy and hard to see. Its song is a fast series of low hollow notes, rather quavering and almost reminiscent of a screech-owl, *huhuhuhuhuhuhuhúhú-dudu-hu*, most often delivered from a low perch.

Range: Central Mexico to extreme northern Brazil and Bolivia.

SPECTACLED ANTPITTA
Hylopezus perspicillatus   Plate 22

Description: 5½. *A plump, short-tailed, very long-legged terrestrial forest bird.* Crown and nape gray with *large and prominent buff eye-ring*; otherwise olive brown above with *two rows of small buff spots on wing-coverts*, and usually with a few buff shaft streaks on back; white below, chest tinged buff, with *breast and sides boldly streaked black*.

Similar species: The only numerous antpitta in the lowlands. Only likely confusion is with the much rarer Fulvous-bellied Antpitta, which see.

Status and distribution: Uncommon to fairly common (less numerous westward) in lower growth and on floor of humid forest in lowlands and lower foothills (to about

750 m: 2500 ft) on entire Caribbean slope; on Pacific slope recorded from lowlands and foothills (to about 1200 m: 4000 ft) of western Chiriquí (*lizanoi*; few or no recent records, and probably virtually if not in fact extirpated due to deforestation), foothills of Veraguas, and lowlands and foothills of eastern Panama province (middle and upper Bayano River valley) and Darién; old specimens from lowlands of western Panama province and Pacific side of Canal area, but no recent records. Widespread in forested areas on Caribbean side of Canal area, with numbers probably greatest along Pipeline and Achiote Roads.

Habits: A solitary bird which seems to favor areas of forest with relatively little undergrowth. Mostly terrestrial, hopping or walking quietly on the forest floor, usually escaping detection by freezing but sometimes flushing to a low perch. Heard *far* more often than it is seen, the usual song is a slow series of melancholy whistled notes, rising slightly at first, the last three lower and fading away, *deh, dee-dee-dee-dee-dee-dee, deu, deu, deu*; sings mostly during the rainy season. Usually calls from an elevated perch such as a fallen log or even a branch up to ten or more feet above the ground, and when singing usually not too shy or difficult to approach (though the song is ventrioquial, and the bird thus often frustratingly difficult to track down!).

Range: Nicaragua to western Ecuador.

Note: Formerly called the Streak-chested Antpitta in most literature, the 1983 AOU Check-list opted for the name "Spectacled Antpitta".

FULVOUS-BELLIED ANTPITTA
Hylopezus dives   Plate 22

Description: 6. Known only from far western and far eastern Panama. Recalls Spectacled Antpitta. Crown and nape slaty, becoming slaty olive on back and olive brown on wings, wings with flight feathers edged rufescent (but *no* dots on coverts); *lores buff, but no evident eye-ring*; throat white, *remaining underparts ochraceous buff with blurry dusky streaking on breast and sides, deepening to quite bright cinnamon-rufous on flanks and lower belly*. *Barbacoae* (of Darién) more brownish olive, less slaty, on back and brighter below than *dives* (of Bocas del Toro).

Similar species: Spectacled Antpitta has bold buff eye-ring and buff spots on wing-coverts

(both lacking in this species), and is basically white below (no pronounced rufous or buff effect) with much bolder and more discrete breast streaking.

Status and distribution: Uncommon to locally fairly common in very dense undergrowth at forest borders and in adjacent overgrown clearings and in lowlands and lower second-growth foothills in western and central Bocas del Toro (Almirante, lower Río Changuinola, oleoducto road south of Chiriquí Grande) and eastern Darién (lower slopes of Cerro Pirre and Cerro Tacarcuna, upper Tuira River valley at mouth of Río Mono); recorded up to about 750 m (2500 ft). Quite numerous in dense thickets around the airstrip at Cana, in eastern Darién.

Habits: Tends to remain in very dense, often damp, tangled thickets, and almost impossible to see unless one decoys the bird in through a whistled imitation (or tape recording) of the bird's distinctive vocalization. Even then much patience will probably be required, for it will usually remain frustratingly just out of sight; watch for its slow rocking motion as it stands on its perch. The song is a series of six to eight whistled notes of a quality similar to the Spectacled Antpitta, but more rapidly given and ending abruptly (not trailing off as in that species), *oh-oh-ou-ou-ou-uu-uu-uu*.

Range: Southern Honduras to western Colombia.

Note: Trans-Andean birds are here treated as a species distinct from true *H. fulviventris* (White-lored Antpitta), found in eastern Ecuador and southeastern Colombia. Voices differ dramatically, and these are several marked plumage differences.

OCHRE-BREASTED ANTPITTA
Grallaricula flavirostris   Plate 22

Description: 4–4½. Found only in highlands of west and east. *A tiny, almost tail-less antpitta. Bill yellow* with some dusky on culmen. Olive brown above with bold tawny eye-ring and lores; *sides of head and entire underparts rich ochraceous*, fading to whitish on belly, usually with a few indistinct blackish streaks on sides.

Similar species: So much smaller than any other Panama antpitta that confusion is unlikely.

Status and distribution: Rare in undergrowth of humid forest in foothills and lower highlands of Bocas del Toro, Chiriquí (recent reports only from the Fortuna area), Veraguas, and eastern Darién (Cerro Pirre,

Cerro Quía); recorded 900–1500 m (3000–5000 ft). Small numbers have been encountered quite regularly in recent years on the slopes of Cerro Pirre above Cana (mostly above 1200 m: 4000 ft).

Habits: Usually solitary, perching in undergrowth but rarely actually on the ground.

Active and unsuspicious, almost fearless, but hard to see because of its small size and sudden manakin-like movements (S. Hilty). The song in western Ecuador is a simple melancholy whistled *peeeu*, repeated steadily at 8 to 10-second intervals (M. Robbins).

Range: Costa Rica to northern Bolivia.

TAPACULOS: Rhinocryptidae (3)

The tapaculos are a small family of neotropical birds, allied to the antbirds, found mostly in temperate areas of South America (especially Chile) and in the Andes, with only one species ranging as far north as Costa Rica. Four forms of one genus (*Scytalopus*) occur in the highlands of Panama, each in a different area, and their relationship to each other has been disputed (depending on the author, from two to four species being recognized). Most tapaculos are terrestrial or semi-terrestrial, the Panama species occurring in dense thickets in humid forest. Many are fast runners but fly poorly. They tend to carry their tails cocked up over their backs. Tapaculos are insectivorous. Their nesting situation is varied, though always well hidden: in burrows, in banks, in hollows or crevices of trees, or in dense tangled vegetation on or near the ground. The nesting of the Panama species is unknown, however. The name "tapaculo", according to Darwin (*Voyage of the Beagle*), refers to the birds' habit of exposing their rear end, but according to Johnson (*Birds of Chile*, Vol. II: 212, 1967) is an onomatopoeic version of the call of one Chilean species.

SILVERY-FRONTED TAPACULO
Scytalopus argentifrons   Plate 27

Description: 4½. Found only in western highlands. Male *sooty black above* with rump feathers tinged rusty and *silvery forehead and superciliary* (often absent; present only on older birds); *throat dark slaty, remaining underparts slaty gray*, becoming silvery on belly, with flanks tipped rusty. Female lacks the silver, and has feathers margined with brown above and below. Juvenile dark brown above narrowly margined with black (giving barred effect), dark brown below margined with tawny. Males from eastern Chiriquí and Veraguas (*chiriquensis*), formerly considered a distinct species, have only forehead silvery (no superciliary behind eye) and are uniformly blackish slate below.

Similar species: An obscure little bird of forest undergrowth, somewhat wren-like but without wing and tail barring, and mostly gray and black (not brown). Like a wren, it often carries its tail cocked. See also Wrenthrush.

Status and distribution: Uncommon to fairly common in undergrowth of humid forest in highlands of Chiriquí, adjacent Bocas del Toro (along the oleoducto road

north of Fortuna, where several were heard in July 1982; Ridgely), and Veraguas (Chitra); in western Chiriquí recorded mostly above 1800 m (6000 ft), elsewhere lower, 1050–1650 m (3500–5500 ft).

Habits: Prefers shady, dark thickets on forested hillsides and in ravines. Very secretive and difficult to observe, creeping about in dense tangles near the ground. Its frequently heard song is a series of loud sharp notes which start rapidly and gradually reach a crescendo as they slow toward the end, the whole lasting 5–7 seconds, sometimes longer (B. Whitney, Ridgely), while its call is a sharp *ch-ch-ch-ch-chit*, often given in alarm or as it scolds the intruder.

Range: Costa Rica and western Panama.

TACARCUNA (PALE-THROATED) TAPACULO
Scytalopus panamensis

Description: 4½. Found only on Tarcarcuna range in eastern Darién. Resembles Silvery-fronted Tapaculo of western highlands. Male differs in having forehead black, *broad silvery superciliary* (above and behind eye), throat not as dark slaty, lower breast and belly mottled with pale gray, and rump, flanks, and crissum brown barred with black. Female similar to male but browner above.

Similar species: Narino Tapaculo is found only on Cerro Pirre; males lack the silvery supercilliary. See also Silvery-fronted Tapaculo.

Status and distribution: Common in forest in highlands of eastern Darién (Cerro Tacarcuna, Cerro Malí); recorded 1020– 1380 m (3400– 4600 ft).

Habits: Usually in pairs, low down or on the forest floor, often around fallen tree trunks; a piping song, a repetition of a single note, *tseety, seety seety seety*, is occasionally given (Wetmore).

Range: Eastern Panama and adjacent north-western Colombia.

Note: As this species is found only on Cerro Tacarcuna, it would seem especially helpful to so indicate in its English name; in fact, its throat, while paler than in other Panama tapaculos, is not strikingly "pale".

NARINO TAPACULO
Scytalopus vicinior

Description: 4¾. Found only on Cerro Pirre

in eastern Darién. Male has *crown blackish*, becoming blackish brown on upper back and dark chestnut brown on lower back; below gray, becoming somewhat paler on belly; rump, flanks, and crissum cinnamon brown barred with black; wings and tail brownish black. Female brighter brown above except for dark brownish gray crown, somewhat paler gray below.

Similar species: Tacarcuna Tapaculo has distinct silvery eye-stripe, lacking in this species; the two do not occur together.

Status and distribution: Uncommon in dense tangled undergrowth in humid forest, forest borders, and elfin woodland on Cerro Pirre in eastern Darién; recorded 750– 1500 m (3500–5000 ft).

Habits: Similar to Silvery-fronted Tapaculo. The song is a rapidly uttered series of loud notes which often continues for at least 30 seconds, *keh-keh-keh-keh-keh*; in alarm or in response to tape playback gives a shorter series *thu-tu-tu-tu-tu-tutu*, or a single explosive *pzeert* (M. Robbins *et al.*).

Range: Eastern Panama to northwestern Ecuador.

Note: The systematics of this species remains uncertain (T. Schulenberg).

TYRANT-FLYCATCHERS: Tyrannidae (99)

There are many more species of flycatchers in Panama than there are in any other bird family, and this total was recently increased by the action of the 1983 AOU Check-list Committee, in which several genera formerly placed with the Cotingidae were transferred to the Tyrannidae. Three genera (*Attila, Rhytipterna,* and *Laniocera*) are now believed to be allied to the myiarchine flycatchers (though recent information indicates that *Laniocera* is probably a cotinga after all), and the *Pachyramphus* becards and *Tityra* tityras are now held to be a subfamily in the Tyrannidae. The family is strictly American in distribution, and is most diverse in tropical areas; however, a good number of species nests in either temperate North or South America, most of these migrating to the tropics during their respective winters. The family exhibits tremendous size and form variation, which reaches its culmination in South America but still is quite marked in Panama. Most Panama flycatchers have rather dull plumage, though some are more boldly patterned and colored; usually the sexes do not differ markedly. Many genera have a usually concealed crown patch of a bright color (most often yellow or red), the function of which is still debated. Identification is often very difficult, with the tyrannulets and elaenias being especially tricky among the resident species, while several of the migrant *Empidonax* and *Contopus* can be virtually impossible. Most Panamanian species are essentially arboreal, though they may differ greatly in the degree to which they expose themselves: thus some are very conspicuous and cannot be missed (e.g. Tropical Kingbird and Social Flycatcher) while many others ars obscure, skulking in undergrowth (e.g. Slate-headed Tody-Flycatcher) or remaining hidden in foliage high in trees (Black-capped Pygmy-Tyrant). The food of the group as a whole consists chiefly of insects and other arthropods, but unlike the situation in temperate North America many are not sallying flycatchers, rather gleaning more like wood-warblers or vireos in foliage. Some (including a few migrants such as the Eastern Kingbird and Great Crested Flycatcher) also eat a large amount of fruit, and a few (e.g. Piratic Flycatcher and Olive-striped Flycatcher) have an almost totally fruit diet as adults. Several others, notably the Great Kiskadee, also take small reptiles and amphibians, even fish and small birds. The nesting situation of flycatchers is equally varied, with some species building a simple cup nest, while others construct untidy globular affairs or pensile nests with a side entrance; a few nest in holes, notably the myiarchine assemblage. All in all, the family is an exceptionally interesting and diverse one, representing the most remarkable radiation and diversification of any bird group in the neotropics (or really, of any bird group anywhere in the world).

WHITE-FRONTED TYRANNULET
Phyllomyias zeledoni   Plate 25

Description: 4¼. Found only in Chiriquí highlands. Olive above with slaty cap and *white superciliary distinctly broader in front of eye and on forehead*; cheeks flecked with slaty and white; dusky wings edged with yellowish and with *two yellowish wing-bars; mostly pale yellow below*, with whitish throat and chest mottled with olive.

Similar species: Somewhat resembles Yellow-crowned Tyrannulet (of lowlands) except for the broader white eyestripe and lack of a yellow crown patch. Paltry Tyrannulet lacks wing-bars and has grayish (not pale yellow) underparts.

Status and distribution: Rare in borders of humid forest and in adjacent shrubby clearings with scattered taller trees in lower highlands of western Chiriquí (recorded mostly 1200–2100 m: 4000–7000 ft); one was also mist-netted and collected (specimen to GML) at Fortuna in central Chiriquí (1050 m: 3500 ft) on March 3, 1976 (Ridgely).

Habits: Not very well known, either in Panama or elsewhere in its range; perhaps often overlooked or not identified. Usually seen singly as they forage actively in middle and upper tree levels, regularly accompanying mixed flocks. Posture is quite horizontal, and occasionally they flick up a wing over the back. In Costa Rica heard to give an excited-sounding insistent *psss psss psss* (Slud).

Range: Costa Rica and western Panama; locally from Colombia and Venezuela to southern Peru.

Note: Formerly placed in the genus *Acrochordopus. Zeledoni* of Costa Rica and Chiriquí, together with *leucogonys* of Venezuela to Peru, is here considered a species distinct from *P. burmeisteri* (Rough-legged Tyrannulet) of southeastern South America; they were considered conspecific in the 1983 AOU Check-list, but two species were also recognized by Wetmore.

SOOTY-HEADED TYRANNULET
Phyllomyias griseiceps   Plate 40

Description: 4. Known only from eastern Darién. Slightly crested. *Cap brownish becoming gray on sides of head and neck*, whitish superciliary, and fine whitish streaks on ear-coverts; otherwise greenish olive above, wings duskier with *narrow* paler edging (*no wing-bars*); throat white, *remaining underparts pale yellow*, breast washed with olive.

Similar species: Paltry Tyrannulet has pale grayish underparts (no yellow), conspicuous yellow wing-edging, slaty cap. See also Southern Beardless and Yellow-crowned Tyrannulets, both of which have wing-bars.

Status and distribution: Locally fairly common in borders and canopy of humid forest, second-growth woodland, and clearings with tall trees in lower foothills of eastern Darién (recorded only from around Cana, but likely more widespread); two birds believed this species were also seen just east of the bridge over the Bayano River in eastern Panama province on January 1, 1975 (Ridgely), but no other reports from so far west.

Habits: Often in pairs, perching quite upright, making short fluttering sallies to foliage, less often gleaning. Generally does not forage with mixed flocks. Much more likely to be noticed once its distinctive call is learned, a rather loud, bright, rhythmic *whip, whip-dip-irip* or *whit, whit-wheeu*, both with very characteristic cadence. Even after this is recognized, this tyrannulet will likely remain a hard bird to see well, for it tends to remain high in trees.

Range: Eastern Panama south locally to eastern Peru and Amazonian Brazil.

Note: Has sometimes been called Sooty-crested Tyrannulet.

PALTRY TYRANNULET
Zimmerius vilissimus   Plate 25

Description: 4. Short blackish bill; pale iris. Slaty cap and whitish superciliary contrasting with olive back; *wings conspicuously edged with yellow (but no wing-bars); pale grayish below*, slightly tinged yellowish olive on sides.

Similar species: All other forest-based tyrannulets have predominantly yellow underparts; see especially Yellow-crowned and White-fronted Tyrannulets. Slate-headed Tody-Flycatcher is also pale grayish below but has very different fairly long flat bill, and yellow wing-bars as well as wing-edging; it inhabits thickets.

Status and distribution: Fairly common to common in canopy and borders of forest and second-growth woodland, and in adjacent clearings, in lowlands and foothills on both slopes, but absent from eastern side of Azuero Peninsula to southern Coclé; recorded mostly below 1200 m (4000 ft), but in western Chiriquí ranges regularly to over 2100 m (7000 ft). Especially numerous in the western Chiriquí highlands, and seemingly less common in Darién. In Canal area much more numerous and widespread on Caribbean side.

Habits: Not always easy to see, as it often forages high in trees, but also comes low. Tail is often carried "half-cocked", well above horizontal. The call is frequently heard, a semi-whistled *peeayik* or *peee-yip*, rather similar to a call sometimes given by the Thick-billed Euphonia. Eats many mistletoe berries.

Range: Southern Mexico to northwestern Colombia.

Note: Formerly placed in the genus *Tyranniscus*. Here Middle American birds are considered a separate species from those of northern South America (*Z. improbus*, Venezuelan Tyrannulet); they were treated as conspecific in the 1983 AOU Check-list.

BROWN-CAPPED TYRANNULET
Ornithion brunneicapillum   Plate 25

Description: 3. *Tiny*, with very short tail. Olive green above with *dark brown cap* and *prominent short white superciliary*; wings duskier with indistinct olive green edging; *entirely bright yellow below*.

Status and distribution: Fairly common in canopy and borders of humid forest and second-growth woodland in lowlands and lower foothills (to about 750 m: 2500 ft) on both slopes from western Colon province and western Panama province east through San Blas and Darién; also occurs west in Caribbean lowlands in diminishing numbers to western Bocas del Toro (where it is

distinctly rare, with westernmost record being a bird recorded on several dates in late April 1980 on the lower Río Changuinola; Ridgely). In Canal area more numerous and widespread on Caribbean side.

Habits: Usually seen foraging in middle and upper levels, sometimes joining mixed flocks of insectivorous birds. Heard far more often than it is seen, it has a distinctive high piping whistled call with characteristic pause after the first note, the latter three to four notes descending, *plee, pih-pey-peh-puh*.

Range: Costa Rica to northern Venezuela and western Ecuador.

Note: Yellow-bellied Tyrannulet (*O. semiflavum*) of Mexico to Costa Rica has been found very close to the Panama border in southwestern Costa Rica, and likely occurs in the adjacent lowlands of Chiriquí. It resembles Brown-capped Tyrannulet but has slaty (not brown) crown. See Plate 46.

SOUTHERN BEARDLESS-TYRANNULET
Camptostoma obsoletum   Plate 25

Description: 3¾. Very small, *usually with somewhat bushy-crested look*. Mostly dull grayish olive above, somewhat darker and browner on crown and with fairly distinct whitish superciliary; wings with two yellowish white wing-bars; *clear yellow below* except for white upper throat and a faint tinge of olive on chest. Immature has buffier wing-bars.

Similar species: Yellow-crowned Tyrannulet has slaty cap with yellow in crown, gray superciliary, and yellow restricted to lower underparts (entire throat whitish, chest distinctly olive). Mouse-colored Tyrannulet is larger and longer-tailed, dull brownish on back with buffy wing-bars, and has mostly pinkish lower mandible. See also Yellow-green Tyrannulet.

Status and distribution: Fairly common to common in shrubby clearings, pastures and agricultural areas with hedgerows and scattered trees, and in borders of second-growth woodland in lowlands and lower foothills (occasionally to just over 600 m: 2000 ft) on entire Pacific slope, though less numerous and more local in Darién; on Caribbean slope known only from Canal area and in San Blas (Permé, Puerto Obaldía); found also on Coiba and Cébaco Islands and the Pearl Islands.

Habits: Forages actively like a warbler among outer twigs and foliage, occasionally making aerial sallies. Often cocks tail well

above horizontal. The usual call is a very distinctive, rather melancholy series of three to five (most often four) *pee* or *twee* notes, sometimes dropping slightly in pitch and varying in speed; also gives a *tooreé tooreé*.
Range: Costa Rica to northern Argentina and southeastern Brazil.

MOUSE-COLORED TYRANNULET
Phaeomyias murina   Plate 25

Description: 4¾. Local in scrub on Pacific slope. Bill rather thick, *lower mandible flesh-colored at least at base*. Grayish brown to brownish olive above with *dull whitish superciliary* and *two pale buff wing-bars*; throat whitish becoming dull olive grayish on breast and pale yellowish on belly.
Similar species: A very drab tyrannulet. Confusion most likely with Southern Beardless-Tyrannulet, but that species is smaller and often cocks its relatively shorter tail, has a smaller all-black bill, and shows little or no superciliary and whitish (not buff) wing-bars. See also Northern Scrub-Flycatcher and Lesser Elaenia.
Status and distribution: Uncommon to locally fairly common in scrub and agricultural areas with hedgerows and scattered trees in lowlands on Pacific slope from Chiriquí (recorded west to around Estero Rico, south of Concepción; Ridgely) east locally to eastern Panama province (now regular in the Tocumen area, with two also seen as far east as Majé in Bayano River valley on January 15, 1976; F. G. Stiles). May have only recently spread to Chiriquí and eastern Panama province (though possibly only overlooked?).
Habits: An inconspicuous small flycatcher, likely to be overlooked until its distinctive dry gravelly call is learned, a harsh fast chattering *je je je je jé jew* or *je je je je jéw*. Usually perches quite upright, but does glean for insects and takes some fruit.
Range: Panama (may spread to southwestern Costa Rica); Colombia to northwestern Argentina, Paraguay, and southern Brazil.

NORTHERN SCRUB-FLYCATCHER
Sublegatus arenarum   Plate 24

Description: 5½. *Bill short, blackish.* Brownish gray above with *whitish supraloral stripe* and a narrow, broken, grayish eye-ring; wings with two whitish bars (sometimes a third visible); *throat and chest gray contrasting with light yellow lower underparts*.
Similar species: In pattern similar to

Panama Flycatcher but much smaller with short bill and whitish supraloral stripe. Yellow-bellied Elaenia has a conspicuous crest and is more olive on chest (not pure gray); Lesser Elaenia has mostly grayish olive underparts with little contrast. Mouse-colored Tyrannulet is smaller and more slender, with brownish wings and buffy wing-bars, and it too shows less contrast on underparts.
Status and distribution: Uncommon to locally fairly common in scrub, dry woodland, and mangroves in lowlands on Pacific slope from Chiriquí east to western Darién (Garachiné), especially in more arid areas and most numerous near coast; on Caribbean slope recorded only (and rather uncertainly) from middle Chagres River valley; also found on Coiba and Cébaco Islands, Taboga Island, the Pearl Islands (where more numerous than on mainland), and some other smaller islands off Pacific coast. Quite common in the Tocumen marsh area.
Habits: An unobtrusive and quiet bird, generally remaining in thickets and shrubs. Perches quite upright. The call is a soft clear whistled *peep*, often doubled.
Range: Costa Rica to Venezuela and the Guianas.
Note: The taxonomy of M. A. Traylor (*Fieldiana, Zool.*, New Series, no. 13, 1982) is followed here, in which he split off *S. modestus* (with *obscurior*) from more northern *S. arenarum*; the 1983 AOU Check-list, however, considered all forms as conspecific. We have slightly modified *S. arenarum*'s English name so as to reflect its distribution vis-a-vis *S. modestus* (which, with the inclusion of *obscurior*, cannot be called "Short-billed").

YELLOW-CROWNED TYRANNULET
Tyrannulus elatus   Plate 25

Description: 4. Bill short. Olive above with *slaty cap* and *often revealed yellow crown patch* (very rarely tawny) and *grayish superciliary* above darker line through eye; wings edged with yellow and with two yellowish wing-bars; *pale yellow below* except for *grayish throat* and tinge of olive on chest. Juvenile lacks crown patch.
Similar species: Can be confusing, though behavior and (especially) voice very helpful (see below). Forest Elaenia is larger without as stubby a bill, is not as gray on face, etc. Southern Beardless-Tyrannulet has notably different mannerisms (more horizontal pos-

ture, often cocked tail, bushy crest), is browner on crown and lacks yellow patch, etc. Sooty-headed Tyrannulet is superficially quite similar except that it lacks wing-bars and a crown patch.

Status and distribution: Fairly common to common in gardens, clearings, lighter woodland, and forest borders in lowlands on entire Pacific slope; on Caribbean slope known from northern Coclé (El Uracillo) east through Canal area (where common) to western San Blas (Mandinga).

Habits: Usually solitary, perching inconspicuously in foliage at low to moderate heights; generally does not accompany mixed flocks. Posture is quite vertical, and does not cock tail. Heard more often than seen, its distinctive call, subdued but far-carrying, is given at intervals even through the heat of the day: it is clear melancholy *pray-teér* (Wetmore) or *pee-peeu* (Ridgely). Often reveals its yellow crown patch when vocalizing.

Range: Southwestern Costa Rica to northern Bolivia and Amazonian Brazil.

FOREST ELAENIA
Myiopagis gaimardii   Plate 24

Description: 5. Bill short. Above mostly olive, grayer on head and with indistinct whitish superciliary; crown darker gray with *usually concealed canary yellow crown patch*; wings dusky with *two prominent yellowish wing-bars*; throat whitish, breast pale yellow *mottled with olive* (often with effect of streaking); belly fairly bright pale yellow.

Similar species: Easily confused and probably often overlooked; note also its very distinctive voice (see below). Greenish Elaenia is similar but has virtually plain wings (no bars); it tends to perch more vertically. Yellow-margined Flycatcher has broader more flattened bill (not short and quite slender), lacks crown patch and effect of blurry breast streaking, etc. See also Yellow-olive Flycatcher and female Gray Elaenia.

Status and distribution: Fairly common in canopy and borders of humid forest and second-growth woodland in lowlands on Caribbean slope from Coclé (El Uracillo) east through San Blas; on Pacific slope recorded from Canal area (where scarce and local) east through Darién (where recorded locally up into lower foothills). Widespread on Caribbean side of Canal area, though there as elsewhere usually overlooked until its voice is learned.

Habits: A hard bird to see, usually remaining in upper parts of trees, gleaning in foliage or among twigs. Most often recorded by voice; its frequently heard call is a sharp and emphatic *pitchweét* or *pitchéw*, usually with a long pause between repetitions.

Range: Central Panama to northern Bolivia and southern Brazil.

GRAY ELAENIA
Myiopagis caniceps   Plate 40

Description: 5. Male *bluish gray above* with usually concealed white crown patch; *wings black with prominent white edging and two white wing-bars*; throat and breast paler gray, becoming grayish white on belly. Female very different, *mostly bright olive above* with only head gray (same white coronal patch as in male); wings as in male, but with *markings bright pale yellow*; throat grayish white, with remaining underparts pale greenish yellow, brightest on belly.

Similar species: No other vaguely similar Panama flycatcher is even remotely so gray as the male. Females, however, present more of a problem as they resemble the Forest Elaenia; they are only to be distinguished by female Gray's brighter olive upperparts and bolder and yellower wing-markings.

Status and distribution: Apparently rare in canopy of humid forest and tall second-growth woodland; probably overlooked to some extent, there are records only from Caribbean side of Canal area (sightings by various observers from Pipeline Road; no specimens), and from eastern Darién (Cana and Cerro Tacarcuna); recorded up to about 600 m (2000 ft). A few have been seen fairly regularly around Cana in recent years (especially along the trail to Boca de Cupe).

Habits: Similar to Forest Elaenia, like that species tending to perch more horizontally than does the Greenish Elaenia. Often accompanies mixed flocks.

Range: Central Panama to northern Argentina, Paraguay, and southern Brazil.

GREENISH ELAENIA
Myiopagis viridicata   Plate 24

Description: 5¼. Bill short. Mostly olive above, grayer on crown with usually concealed yellow crown patch, and with *indistinct whitish superciliary*; wings duskier with narrow yellowish edging but *wing-bars obscure or lacking*; throat pale grayish, becoming grayish olive on breast and pale yellow on belly.

Similar species: Easily confused. Forest Elaenia is similar, but it shows conspicuous yellowish wing-bars; the two normally are found in different habitats, and Greenish usually perches much more vertically. Yellow-olive Flycatcher has broader bill and much more boldly marked wing (including wing-bars). *Elaenia* elaenias lack the superciliary, have whitish wing-bars, etc. See also the smaller Sooty-headed Tyrannulet (with similar overall pattern, but yellower below, etc.)

Status and distribution: Uncommon to locally fairly common in lower and middle growth of second-growth woodland and borders, gallery woodland, adjacent clearings with scattered trees in lowlands on Pacific slope from Chiriquí (where it ranges up to around 1200 m: 4000 ft in Volcán/Santa Clara area) to western Darién (Garachiné); on Caribbean slope recorded only from Canal area; found also on Coiba Island and some of the Pearl Islands.

Habits: Usually inconspicuous, tending to perch vertically (almost like a pewee) inside shady woodland. Most often alone, not accompanying mixed flocks. Its usual call is a buzzy *cheerip* (Ridgely) or *screechit* (E. S. Morton), more slurred and less emphatic than call of Forest Elaenia (which sounds distinctly two-noted).

Range: Mexico to northern Argentina and southeastern Brazil.

younger second-growth woodland, gardens, and agricultural areas with hedgerows and scattered trees in lowlands and foothills on entire Pacific slope (though only in small numbers and very local in more extensive cleared areas in Darién; but doubtless increasing), in western Chiriquí ranging sparingly well up into the highlands (recorded to over 1800 m: 6000 ft); on Caribbean slope recorded only from lowlands of western Bocas del Toro (small numbers found in lower Río Changuinola area in April 1980, likely spreading in from adjacent Costa Rica), and from northern Coclé (El Uracillo) east through Canal area to western San Blas (Mandinga); common also on larger Pearl Islands, Coiba Island, Taboga Island, and other smaller islands off Pacific coast.

Habits: Noisy and conspicuous wherever found, one of the more numerous birds in open areas on Pacific slope. Usually seen singly or in pairs, but sometimes gathers in larger groups at fruiting trees. When excited, the crest is especially noticeable. The calls are varied, but usually rather hoarse, typically a *week-krreeup*, second syllable sometimes repeated; also a *freeee* and a *wrrreee*. The nest is an open cup placed in the fork of a branch.

Range: Eastern Mexico to northern Argentina and southeastern Brazil; Lesser Antilles.

YELLOW-BELLIED ELAENIA
Elaenia flavogaster   Plate 24

Description: 6–6¼. Bill quite short; tail rather long and slender. Usually shows a *distinct, upstanding* (bifurcated) *crest*, often revealing partly concealed white center. Olive or brownish olive above with narrow white eye-ring and two yellowish to whitish wing-bars; pale gray throat merging into grayish olive on chest and sides; *lower underparts yellow, usually contrasting with grayish chest.* Immature browner above with buff wing-bars, no white in crown.

Similar species: Lesser Elaenia lacks the conspicuous crest (though it can show some) and is more uniform and darker grayish olive below. Northern Scrub-Flycatcher has no crest at all and has gray throat and chest with no tinge of olive. Panama Flycatcher is considerably larger with longer heavier bill, lacks the prominent crest, and also has distinctly gray throat and chest with no olive.

Status and distribution: Common to very common in shrubby regenerating clearings,

LESSER ELAENIA
Elaenia chiriquensis   Plate 24

Description: 5¼–5½. Much like Yellow-bellied Elaenia, but shows *only a slight crest* (at times giving back of head a squared-off appearance) that sometimes reveals a *partly concealed white center*. Often has pinkish or flesh base of lower mandible. Grayish olive above with narrow whitish eye-ring and two whitish wing-bars; throat gray, somewhat tinged with yellowish, *blending into olive on chest, sides, and flanks*, and pale yellow on center of breast and belly. Immature browner above with brownish wing-bars, no white in crown.

Similar species: Yellow-bellied Elaenia is larger with more conspicuous crest, and has more contrast in coloration below. Mountain Elaenia has a rounded head with no visible white in center of crown, lacks the grayish effect on the throat, and is more uniformly yellowish below. Northern Scrub-Flycatcher has sharply contrasting gray and yellow underparts, lacks white in crown.

Status and distribution: Fairly common in scrubby and shrubby areas, and open fields and pastures with small trees in lowlands and foothills on Pacific slope from Chiriquí to eastern Panama province (lower Bayano River; not reported from Darién), ranging up to at least 1500 m (5000 ft) rarely 1800 m (6000 ft), in Chiriquí highlands; on Caribbean slope uncommon and found only in more open parts of Canal area and adjacent Colon province; found also on Coiba and Cébaco Islands and some of the Pearl Islands. Especially numerous on the open eroded hillsides of Cerro Campana.

Habits: Has a vareity of calls, all lacking the raucous quality of the Yellow-bellied Elaenia, a buzzy *dzbew* or *peb-zü*, a soft *weeb* or *beebzb* repeated at intervals, and a burry *freeee* or sweeter *feeee*.

Range: Costa Rica to northern Bolivia and southern Brazil.

MOUNTAIN ELAENIA
Elaenia frantzii   Plate 24

Description: 5½–5¾. Found only in western highlands. Very like Lesser Elaenia, but ranges overlap only in part. Often has pinkish or flesh base of lower mandible. Greenish to brownish olive above with narrow yellowish eye-ring, wings with broad white edging and two pale yellowish or whitish wing-bars; *practically uniform light yellowish olive below (with no grayish throat)*, passing to pale yellow (sometimes whitish) on belly. Immature browner above with buffy wing-bars, and often whiter on breast and belly.

Similar species: Lesser Elaenia sometimes shows a slight crest revealing white in center (Mountain Elaenia's head usually looks rounded and never shows white); Lesser is also grayer above and on throat, and not so uniformly yellowish below. Yellow-bellied Elaenia is larger, distinctly crested, and shows more contrast in color below.

Status and distribution: Very common in farmland with hedgerows and scattered trees, shrubby regenerating clearings, and borders of forest in highlands of western Chiriquí (recorded mostly 1200–2400 m: 4000–8000 ft, occasionally higher); much less numerous elsewhere in the western highlands, where recorded only from eastern Chiriquí (Cerro Flores), Veraguas (Chitra), and western Herrera (Cerro Montuosa, where recorded lower, to 750 m: 2500 ft). The most frequently seen flycatcher in the western Chiriquí highlands.

TORRENT TYRANNULET

Habits: The usual calls are a whistled *peeee-oo* or *twee-oo* and a drawn out *peeee-err*, the latter suggestive of call of Western Wood-Pewee. What is apparently its full song (heard infrequently, mainly soon after dawn during nesting season) is a very different, burry and fast *cheeree, chi-gwee*, sometimes interspersed with a *trrrr* trill.

Range: Guatemala to western Panama; Colombia and western Venezuela.

TORRENT TYRANNULET
Serpophaga cinerea   Plate 46, p.287

Description: 4. Found only in western highlands *along rivers and streams. Mostly gray*, whiter below; *crown black* with small, usually concealed white crown patch; wings and tail blackish.

Similar species: Black Phoebe is also found along highland streams; it is considerably larger and predominantly black, not gray.

Status and distribution: Fairly common to common along streams and rivers in foothills and highlands of Chiriquí, Bocas del Toro, and both slopes of Veraguas; in western Chiriquí recorded mostly 1200–1950 m (4000–6500 ft), but lower (to about 750 m: 2500 ft) elsewhere; one report of a single bird seen at *much* lower elevation along lower Río Changuinola in western Bocas del Toro (about 120 m: 400 ft) on April 23, 1980 (N. G. Smith). Conspicuous along the Río Chiriquí Viejo between Volcán and Cerro Punta.

Habits: A perky little bird, usually seen perched on a rock out in the middle of the stream or on a twig over the water. Often very tame. Jerks its tail up and down like so many other river-haunting passerines. The common call is a repeated *tsip*.

Range: Costa Rica and western Panama; Colombia and northwestern Venezuela to northern Bolivia.

OLIVE-STRIPED FLYCATCHER
Mionectes olivaceus   Plate 24

Description: ♂5; ♀4½. Rather long, slender bill; fairly long tail; slim appearance with smallish head. Dark greenish olive above with *usually prominent short whitish spot behind eye*; paler olive below, *finely streaked with yellowish on throat, breast, and flanks*, becoming uniform pale yellow on center of belly. Adult male has 9th primary shortened and very narrowed terminally.

Similar species: In shape most resembles the Ochre-bellied Flycatcher, though that species lacks the postocular spot and is unstreaked and buffy below. See also the larger flatbills.

Status and distribution: Uncommon to locally common in lower growth of humid forest and second-growth woodland in lowlands and foothills (to about 1200 m: 4000 ft) on entire Caribbean slope, though less numerous in Bocas del Toro; on Pacific slope recorded from foothills throughout (though apparently absent from Azuero Peninsula), ranging up in highlands of western Chiriquí to over 1800 m (6000 ft), and in lowlands from Canal area eastward; always seems most numerous in foothill zone (300–1200 m: 1000–4000 ft). In Canal area considerably more numerous on Pacific side, perhaps commonest along Pipeline Road.

Habits: Favors shady ravines with heavy thickety growth. Quiet and inconspicuous, its true abundance is revealed by the frequency with which it is caught in mist-nets. Infrequently flicks up one wing at a time like Ochre-bellied Flycatcher. Eats mainly fruit. Males in apparent display give a high sibilant call with a hummingbird-like quality, *ts-ts-ts-tsu*, repeated several times, then a pause, followed by another series; several males may sing within earshot of each other in open but shady forest lower growth.

Range: Costa Rica to northern Venezuela and southern Peru.

OCHRE-BELLIED FLYCATCHER
Mionectes oleaginea   Plate 25

Description: 5. Fairly long slender bill, base of lower mandible often pinkish. Olive above, browner on wings and tail; *sides of head and throat olive grayish* with *remaining underparts yellowish ochre*. Birds from western Colon and western Panama provinces eastward (*parca*) are paler generally and have ochraceous edging on wings and two indistinct ochraceous wing-bars. Often recognized by its habit of *quickly lifting up a wing up over back*, one after the other.

Similar species: Combination of rather slim, small-headed appearance and the mostly ochraceous underparts is distinctive, but often first identified by its frequent wing-lifting. Ruddy-tailed Flycatcher is smaller with short stubby bill, has mostly rufous wings and tail, etc. See also Olive-striped Flycatcher.

Status and distribution: Common in lower growth of forest, second-growth woodland, borders, and adjacent clearings in lowlands on both slopes, ranging in reduced numbers into foothills to about 1050 m (3500 ft); absent from dry Pacific lowlands from eastern side of Azuero Peninsula to western Panama province; found also on Coiba and Cébaco Islands and the larger Pearl Islands.

Habits: Usually seen singly, though often accompanying a mixed flock. Ochre-bellied Flycatchers eat a combination of insects, obtained by gleaning, and fruits, especially mistletoe. Males during the breeding season sing interminably from perches in their small territories, *twich, twich, twich . . .*, with variations, sometimes bisyllabic, *tit-twich* or *tsyick*, all the while flicking their wings. The nest is ball-shaped with a side entrance and is usually covered with moss; it is suspended from a slender vine or root, hung over a stream or from the side of a bank or tree trunk. The female alone raises the young.

Range: Southern Mexico to Bolivia and Amazonian and eastern Brazil.

Note: Formerly placed in the genus *Pipromorpha*.

SEPIA-CAPPED FLYCATCHER
Leptopogon amaurocephalus   Plate 25

Description: 5¼. Rather long slender bill; fairly long tail. *Crown brown*, with *facial area dull buff* grizzled dusky, and *dusky patch on ear-coverts*; otherwise mostly olive above, tail decidedly brownish; wings dusky with *two broad buff wing-bars* and yellowish buff edging on flight feathers; throat pale grayish, becoming dull olive on breast and pale yellow on belly. Coiba Island birds (*idius*) are duller and grayer above with more yellowish wing-bars, and paler yellow on lower underparts.

Similar species: Slaty-capped Flycatcher has dark gray (not brown) cap, and inhabits mainly foothills and highlands (though there is some overlap with this species). The duller Coiba Island form can be confused with Greenish Elaenia.

Status and distribution: Rare to uncommon and quite local in undergrowth of second-growth woodland, gallery woodland, and deciduous forest in lowlands on Pacific slope from Chiriquí east to eastern Panama province (an old record from "savanna east of Panama City"), ranging sparingly up in lower foothills to about 660 m (2200 ft) on Cerro Montuosa, in Herrera; on Caribbean slope known only from two nineteenth-century specimens apparently taken in middle Chagres River valley; also fairly common in lower growth of forest on Coiba Island. Only recent reports in Canal area are from Chiva Chiva Road and vicinity. Overall numbers in Panama must have declined very substantially due to the removal of virtually all of its favored wooded habitat on Pacific slope.

Habits: Usually seen perched quietly in undergrowth inside woodland, sometimes with mixed flocks. Twitches up one wing at a time like Slaty-capped Flycatcher. Its most frequently heard call is a fast series of rough chattering notes, *dreh, dreh, deedeedee-deedeedeeuw.*

Range: Southern Mexico to northern Argentina and southeastern Brazil.

SLATY-CAPPED FLYCATCHER
Leptopogon superciliaris　　　　　Plate 46

Description: 5 ¼. Found only in humid foothills of west and east. Rather long slender bill; fairly long tail. *Crown slaty*, with *facial area whitish grizzled dusky*, and *dusky patch on ear-coverts*; otherwise mostly olive above, tail more brownish; wings dusky with *two prominent yellowish buff wing-bars* and yellowish buff edging on flight feathers; throat pale grayish, becoming olive on breast and pale yellow on belly.

Similar species: Sepia-capped Flycatcher has brown (not slaty) cap, buffyish (not whitish) facial area, and occurs mainly in Pacific lowlands (not in humid foothill forest).

Status and distribution: Rare to locally uncommon in lower growth of humid forest and forest borders in foothills and lower highlands of Chiriquí, Bocas del Toro (known only from north of Fortuna, Chiriquí, but presumably more widespread), Veraguas (Calovévora), western Coclé (several seen above El Copé on Caribbean slope on March 8–9, 1986; Ridgely, J. Guarnaccia, D. Engleman), and

eastern Darién (Cerro Pirre and Cerro Tacarcuna); recorded in Panama mostly 450–1350 m (1500–4500 ft), with one nineteenth-century specimen reported taken near sea level at Bugaba in western Chiriquí (when there was still much forest in the area).

Habits: Seen singly or in pairs, usually as they accompany a mixed flock. Rather active and conspicuous, perching erectly and sallying out to foliage; quite often they will be seen to lift a wing over the back much like an Ochre-bellied Flycatcher. The call is a sharp but spiritless *skeeey, di-i-i-i-i-ír.*

Range: Costa Rica to Venezuela and northern Bolivia.

YELLOW TYRANNULET
Capsiempis flaveola　　　　　Plate 25

Description: 4. Slender and rather long-tailed. *Yellowish olive above* with two yellow wing-bars; *forehead, superciliary, and entire underparts yellow.*

Similar species: No other Panama tyrannulet is so yellow overall.

Status and distribution: Fairly common in thickets in clearings and overgrown pastures and in woodland borders in lowlands on Pacific slope from Chiriquí to eastern Panama province (Bayano River valley, at least occasionally as far upriver as Majé); on Caribbean slope recorded locally from western Bocas del Toro (one specimen from Almirante), and from Coclé (El Uracillo) east through Canal area to eastern Colon province, with one recent report from western San Blas (a pair at Nusagandi on March 7, 1986; Ridgely and J. Guarnaccia); ranges up sparingly to about 1150 m (3800 ft) in western Chiriquí highlands; found also on Coiba Island. Probably spreading in eastern Panama due to deforestation.

Habits: Found in pairs or small groups, foraging within 3 m (10 ft) of the ground. Gleans actively like a warbler, but also sometimes perches quite upright. Calls frequently, a pleasant-sounding rollicking which speeds up and lacks discernible pattern, but distinctive once learned.

Range: Eastern Nicaragua to northern Bolivia, eastern Paraguay, and southeastern Brazil.

YELLOW-GREEN TYRANNULET
Phylloscartes flavovirens　　　　　Plate 25

Description: 4¼. Slender longish bill; rather long tail. Olive green above with *conspicuous* *white eye-ring* (but no superciliary); wings dusky edged with yellow and with *two bright yellow wing-bars; entire underparts (including throat) yellow*, slightly tinged olive on chest.

Similar species: Readily confused with a number of species, but shape and behavior often distinctive. Yellow-crowned Tyrannulet differs in having distinctly slaty cap (when crown patch not exposed), narrow yellowish wing-bars, and grayish throat. Yellow-olive and Yellow-margined Flycatchers are larger, stouter birds with fairly broad bills; the former has no eye-ring and is rather olive on chest, the latter lacks bright wing-bars and is quite gray on chest. See also Forest Elaenia and Southern Beardless-Tyrannulet.

Status and distribution: Uncommon to locally fairly common in canopy and borders of second-growth woodland and forest in lowlands and lower foothills on Pacific slope from Canal area east locally to Darién (Garachiné; also a sighting of total of three on slopes of Cerro Quía, in extreme eastern Darién on the Colombia border, on July 18, 1975; Ridgely); on Caribbean slope recorded only from middle Chagres River valley. Regularly seen in small numbers on Chiva Chiva Road and at Madden Lake.

Habits: Usually seen singly or in pairs, often with mixed flocks of warblers, other flycatchers, etc. They perch very horizontally with long tail held cocked in manner reminiscent of a gnatcatcher, and frequently droop their wings (simultaneously) or flick them straight up over their back (one at a time). The most frequently heard call is a very rapid *dree-di-di-dít*.

Range: Central and eastern Panama.

RUFOUS-BROWED TYRANNULET
Phylloscartes superciliaris   Plate 46

Description: 4½. Found locally in humid foothills. Slender fairly long bill; rather long tail. Crown and nape slaty with *narrow rufous frontal band and superciliary*; spot at base of bill and *ear-coverts white, latter narrowly encircled with black*; otherwise mostly olive above, wings and tail duskier with narrow yellowish olive edging; throat and breast pale grayish, becoming white on belly.

Similar species: Though the rufous in the face is dark and thus often hard to discern, the black and white pattern on the ear-coverts is striking and makes recognition of this attractive tyrannulet easy.

Status and distribution: Locally uncommon to fairly common in canopy and borders of humid forest in foothills of central Chiriquí and central Bocas del Toro (first recorded in the Fortuna area in February–March 1976, with one specimen being taken on March 4; then also found north of there on the Caribbean slope of the Divide in July 1982; Ridgely), both slopes of Veraguas (Santa Fé, Calovévora, Chitra), Coclé (seen above El Copé in June 1984; P. Trail), and eastern Darién (Cerro Tacarcuna); recorded mostly 600–1200 m (2000–4000 ft). Had doubtless been overlooked until recently: this species is simple enough to see and identify, but is not an easy one to collect.

Habits: Forages actively in foliage, often toward the outside of trees, perching horizontally with long tail partially cocked. Regularly accompanies mixed flocks of tanagers, other flycatchers, etc. In Costa Rica reported to give a lively, arresting *wiss, wreewreewreewreewreewree* or *wree titititíti* (S. Hilty).

Range: Costa Rica locally to northwestern Venezuela and southern Ecuador.

BRONZE-OLIVE PYGMY-TYRANT
Pseudotriccus pelzelni   Plate 40

Description: 4¼–4½. Found only in eastern Darién highlands. Iris reddish brown to dark red. *Uniform dark olive brown above*, wing and tail feathers edged with rufous; throat whitish, becoming dull olive on breast and sides, pale yellowish on middle of belly.

Similar species: A relatively uniform-looking small flycatcher of dark forest tangles. Overall aspect something like a *Myiobius* flycatcher, but of course lacks yellow rump, etc. See also various female manakins (chunkier, much more olive, etc.).

Status and distribution: Fairly common in undergrowth of elfin woodland and humid forest in highlands of eastern Darién (Cerro Pirre and Cerro Tacarcuna); recorded mostly 1200–1500 m (4000–5000 ft), occasionally a little lower.

Habits: Usually found singly, foraging actively in undergrowth, often alone but sometimes with mixed flocks of various antbirds, Furnariids, *Basileuterus* warblers, etc. Tends to perch quite upright, making frequent short abrupt flights from one perch to another; wings often whir audibly as it flies, and often a sharp snapping noise is also heard, this presumably made by its bill.

Range: Eastern Panama to southern Peru.

BLACK-CAPPED PYGMY-TYRANT
Myiornis atricapillus   Plate 25

Description: 2¾. *Tiny* and *looks virtually tailless*; the smallest Panamanian passerine. *Cap black* with *prominent white supraloral spot and eye-ring*, the black shading to slaty gray on hindneck and sides of head; otherwise bright olive green above, wings blackish edged with yellowish; mostly white below, with gray on sides and yellow lower belly. Most of female's cap is dark slaty, only forehead black.
Similar species: Minute size and black cap distinguish it from all but the Black-headed Tody-Flycatcher, which has mostly yellow underparts and lacks white on face.
Status and distribution: Uncommon to locally fairly common (unquestionably much overlooked) in mid-levels and canopy of humid forest, forest borders, and second-growth woodland in lowlands on entire Caribbean slope (recorded only Bocas del Toro, Canal area, eastern Colon province, and San Blas but range almost surely continuous); on Pacific slope recorded only from eastern Panama province (middle and upper Bayano River valley) and Darién; ranges at least locally up into lower foothills (e.g. on Cerro Santa Rita, in eastern Colon province, and around Cana on lower slopes of Cerro Pirre).
Habits: Combination of its diminutive size and habit of generally remaining rather high in trees and not moving very much makes the Black-capped Pygmy-Tyrant a difficult bird to observe. Usually found singly or in pairs, apart from mixed flocks. The call is a sharp high-pitched *tseeyk!* or a buzzier *tzzzzt, trrreép?*; both can be given singly or repeated several to many times.
Range: Costa Rica to western Ecuador.

SCALE-CRESTED PYGMY-TYRANT
Lophotriccus pileatus   Plate 25

Description: 3½. A very small flycatcher with a *transverse crest of black rufous-tipped feathers*; the crest is usually not carried erect, but even when laid flat, the color pattern is apparent and a small tuft extends on back of head. Olive above with brownish forehead and rusty-tinged ear-coverts; wings with two narrow yellowish bars; yellowish below, indistinctly streaked with grayish olive on throat and chest. Females and immatures have reduced crest, more brownish head.
Similar species: The unusual head markings should preclude confusion.

Status and distribution: Common in lower growth of humid forest, forest borders, and second-growth woodland in foothills and lower highlands on both slopes (though not recorded from Azuero Peninsula); most numerous 600–1200 m (2000–4000 ft), but in smaller numbers somewhat lower and higher. There are very few actual records from Caribbean slope, but its range is presumed to be as continuous there as it is on the Pacific. Numerous on both Cerro Campana and in the Cerro Azul/Jefe area; unlike many other foothill birds of forest understory, the Scale-crested Pygmy-Tyrant seems capable of persisting in substantial numbers even in degraded, isolated woodlots, etc.
Habits: As with the royal-flycatcher, this species' crest is most likely to be seen erect when it is handled after being mist-netted. Not a particularly difficult bird to observe, the Scale-crested Pygmy-Tyrant is nonetheless heard far more often than it is seen (in many areas it is by voice one of the commonest forest birds). Male's calls are astonishingly loud for so small a bird, and include various harsh sharp notes, e.g. *kree-eek* or *trit*, either run together in a series (often rising) or given separately, often with long pauses between bouts of vocalizing (B. Whitney; Ridgely).
Range: Costa Rica to northern Venezuela, and southern Peru.

PALE-EYED PYGMY-TYRANT
Atalotriccus pilaris   Plate 25

Description: 3¾. Very small. Pale yellowish iris. Above mostly bright olive, with whitish lores and *narrow buffy eye-ring and sides of head*; wings dusky with two yellowish wing-bars; mostly whitish below, with *indistinct brownish streaking on throat and chest*, flanks and crissum tinged pale yellow.
Similar species: Often confused. Slate-headed Tody-Flycatcher has differently shaped bill (longer and wider) and has obviously gray head with no buff on facial area; it is unstreaked on throat and chest. Vocally the Pale-eyed Pygmy-Tyrant resembles the Scale-crested Pygmy-Tyrant, though the two do not occur together and Pale-eyed lacks crest ornamentation, etc. *Note that many other small Panama flycatchers also have pale irides*; this species' yellow eye is, in fact, *not* especially conspicuous in the field.
Status and distribution: Uncommon to locally fairly common in scrubby thickets and lower growth of deciduous woodland in

lowlands on Pacific slope from western Chiriquí (Alanje, David, La Caldera area) east to eastern Panama province (east to Tocumen area); most numerous in lowlands (locally even to inland edge of mangrove swamps), but once recorded up to 1080 m (3600 ft) at Chitra, Veraguas.

Habits: Usually inconspicuous, perching upright within cover, making abrupt short flights to new perches, often hard to follow. Its calls are loud and strident, in quality and pattern reminiscent of Scale-crested Pygmy-Tyrant, typically a *kip-kip, t-t-trrr* or *kip-kip-t-t-t-tr-tr-r-rreép.*

Range: Western Panama to Venezuela and Guyana.

NORTHERN BENTBILL
Oncostoma cinereigulare   Plate 25

Description: 3¾. Known only from western Panama lowlands. Rather like the more widespread Southern Bentbill, with the same *peculiar bent downward bill.* Iris pale. Olive above, adults usually (but not always) with grayish cap, wings edged with grayish though usually (but not always) without wing-bars; *throat and chest grayish white streaked with gray*; lower underparts pale yellow tinged with olive on flanks. Immature has olive cap and narrow wing-bars.

Similar species: Resembles Southern Bentbill (the two are not known to occur together); best distinguished by the grayish throat and chest (in Southern olive yellowish like rest of underparts). Otherwise easily known by the unusual bill.

Status and distribution: Uncommon in undergrowth at borders of humid forest and in second-growth woodland in lowlands of western and central Bocas del Toro (east to Chiriquí Grande), and in western Chiriquí (no recent records). Possibly occurs eastward in Bocas del Toro and northern Veraguas toward range of Southern Bentbill, or may intergrade with that form.

Habits: Very similar to Southern Bentbill (including vocalizations).

Range: Southern Mexico to western Panama.

SOUTHERN BENTBILL
Oncostoma olivaceum   Plate 25

Description: 3½. The odd, rather thick, *distinctly bent downward bill* prevents confusion with all except the previous species. Iris color variable, usually pale. Olive above

with narrow yellowish wing-bars; *yellowish olive below*, sometimes indistinctly streaked with olive on breast.

Similar species: See Northern Bentbill of western Panama.

Status and distribution: Fairly common to common in thickets and dense undergrowth in second-growth woodland and forest borders in lowlands on Caribbean slope from Coclé (Río Indio) east through San Blas, and on Pacific slope from Canal area east through Darién (where occurs up into lower foothills, e.g. around Cana). Widespread in wooded areas throughout Canal area.

Habits: Usually hard to see, sitting quietly in dense low cover, then darting off to a new perch. Its guttural, rather toad-like trill, *grrrr* or *chiurrrrrrrr*, is given more or less continuously. The nest is a small rounded structure of light-colored fibers, the entrance on the side, suspended from a small branch within 4.5 m (15 ft) of the ground.

Range: Central Panama to northern Colombia.

SLATE-HEADED TODY-FLYCATCHER
Todirostrum sylvia   Plate 25

Description: 3¾. Bill flat and rather long; iris color variable. *Crown slaty gray with contrasting white supraloral and eye-ring* (broken in front); otherwise bright olive above, wings blackish with *two prominent yellow wing-bars* and edging; *grayish white below,* grayest across breast.

Similar species: Other Panama tody-flycatchers have bright yellow underparts. Slate-headeds with pale irides (seemingly a minority, in Panama at least) are somewhat similar to Pale-eyed Pygmy-Tyrant but are grayer on head and brighter olive on back with sharper wing-bars (Pale-eyed is really a quite drab bird by comparison), and lack any trace of streaking below.

Status and distribution: Uncommon to locally fairly common in dense regenerating clearings and thickets at woodland borders in lowlands on Pacific slope from Chiriquí east to eastern Panama province (Tocumen/La Jagua area), but largely absent from Azuero Peninsula; on Caribbean slope recorded from western Bocas del Toro (Almirante, Changuinola) and from western Colon province (Río Indio) to Canal area (perhaps somewhat more widespread, and could increase with clearing of forest); recorded sparingly in foothills of western Chiriquí up to 810 m (2700 ft). Very scarce in immediate Canal area, but quite readily found in Tocumen area (if you know the voice).

Habits: A very difficult bird to observe clearly, usually remaining inside dense thickets within 3–4.5 m (10–15 ft) of the ground, moving restlessly. It calls a rather soft croaking *trrp* (often doubled), a *thaa-trrr*, and a trill *trrreee*, often reveals the bird's presence.

Range: Southeastern Mexico to the Guianas and northeastern Brazil.

COMMON TODY-FLYCATCHER
Todirostrum cinereum   Plate 25

Description: 3¾. Bill flat and rather long. *Conspicuous pale iris. Forecrown and face black shading to slaty on nape and grayish olive on back*; wings black edged with yellow, tail black tipped white; *entire underparts yellow.*

Similar species: See Black-headed Tody-Flycatcher.

Status and distribution: Common in clearings, shrubby areas, woodland borders, and gardens in lowlands on both slopes, ranging up in reduced numbers in suitable habitat into the foothills, and to about 1500 m (5000 ft) in Chiriquí; found also on Coiba Island.

Habits: A droll little bird, usually found in pairs, foraging in foliage at low and middle levels in shrubs and smaller trees. Its tail is constantly in motion, often held flopped to one side, sometimes flipped around in an almost circular manner. Active and not at all hard to see, unlike Panama's other tody-flycatchers. The pear-shaped pendant nest is generally in plain sight. The usual calls are a short unmusical trill, *srrrr*, and a repeated ticking note.

Range: Southeastern Mexico to Bolivia and southeastern Brazil.

BLACK-HEADED TODY-FLYCATCHER
Todirostrum nigriceps   Plate 25

Description: 3. *Tiny*, with *short tail*. Bill rather long and flat. *Iris dark. Cap and sides of head glossy black, contrasting sharply with bright olive back*; wings black with yellowish green edging and two yellow wing-bars; *throat white*, remaining underparts yellow.

Similar species: Common Tody-Flycatcher is notably larger and has prominent pale eye, black of forecrown merging into gray on nape and upper back (without contrast), and entirely yellow underparts (no white

throat). Black-capped Pygmy-Tyrant is even smaller, also has contrasting black head but with conspicuous white supraloral spot and eye-ring, and with mostly white (not yellow) underparts.

Status and distribution: Uncommon to locally fairly common in borders of humid forest and second-growth woodland, and in clearings with scattered tall trees in lowlands and lower foothills on entire Caribbean slope (though not recorded from Veraguas or San Blas, seems certain to occur); on Pacific slope recorded from Canal area (where local) east through Darién; recorded in reduced numbers up to 900–1050 m (3000–3500 ft). In Canal area more numerous on Caribbean side (perhaps especially at Achiote Road), but there as elsewhere much more likely to be recorded once voice is learned (see below).

Habits: Small size, and habits of foraging in dense foliage and moving abruptly and rapidly, usually rather high up, all combine to make observation quite difficult. Its distinctive call is a series of eight to ten loud notes, *jyip, jyip, jyip . . .*, with slow measured cadence and each note well enunciated; a calling bird usually remains motionless, and thus is often hard to spot even though it may be at least partially in the open (and often surprisingly unresponsive to tape playback).

Range: Costa Rica to western Venezuela and western Ecuador.

BROWNISH TWISTWING
Cnipodectes subbrunneus   Plate 24

Description: ♂ 7; ♀ 6. *Mostly dull brown, more rufous on rump and tail*, paler on throat and breast, becoming pale buffy yellowish on belly; wings dusky with *buffy edging and buffy brown wing-bars*. Adult male has stiffened and peculiarly twisted outer primaries (function unknown).

Similar species: Bran-colored Flycatcher is smaller, has blurry breast streaking and more conspicuous buffy wing-bars, and is a bird of more open habitats (not forest interior). More likely to be confused with Thrushlike Mourner, with which it regularly occurs; the latter is not as bright brown on tail, lacks the buffy wing-edging and the longish tail, and in central and eastern Panama lowlands has breast and belly grayish olive. The twistwing can often easily be known by its *wing-lifting habit* (see below).

Status and distribution: Uncommon to locally fairly common in undergrowth of humid forest and second-growth woodland, most often near shady streams, in lowlands on Caribbean slope from Coclé (Rio Cascajal, El Uracillo) eastward, and on Pacific slope from Canal area eastward. In Canal area perhaps most numerous along Pipeline Road, particularly in vicinity of the many small streams which cross the road.

Habits: Favors areas where the forest floor is open and dark, and, for a bird of the forest interior, not too hard to see. Shares with Ochre-bellied and the *Leptopogon* flycatchers the habit of frequently lifting wings above body, one at a time; in this species the movement is so leisurely that it seems as if the bird is stretching its wing. The call is a distinctive sharp and emphatic whistle, usually doubled (sometimes single or triple), *kuuuu-wit! kuuuu-wit!*, often preceded by a bill snap or two; sometimes wing-lifts simultaneously. May continue to call off and on throughout the day.

Range: Central Panama to northern Peru and western Amazonian Brazil.

Note: Primaries of male are so unusually twisted that we have opted to highlight this in the name of what is otherwise a rather obscure brownish bird. The name "twist-wing" was long ago employed by various authors (e.g. Hellmayr), but for some reason was then dropped in favor of the far more prosaic "Brownish Flycatcher", used in the 1983 AOU Check-list and in most recent literature.

EYE-RINGED FLATBILL
Rhynchocyclus brevirostris   Plate 24

Description: 6. Found chiefly in highlands. Very like Olivaceous Flatbill, the Eye-ringed differing in its *much more conspicuous white eye-ring, more solidly olive throat and breast* (with less yellowish flammulation), and less prominent wing-bars.

Status and distribution: Uncommon to fairly common in lower growth of humid forest on Pacific slope in Chiriquí (where recorded from sea level up in highlands to over 1800 m: 6000 ft; now very local in lowlands, with only recent report being birds seen on Burica Peninsula in June 1982; Ridgely), Veraguas (mostly in foothills, also spilling over Continental Divide onto Caribbean slope; also at least formerly in lowlands, but now much reduced in numbers or extirpated due to deforestation), western side of Azuero Peninsula (including Cerro Montuosa in Herrera), western Panama province (Cerro Campana), and eastern Darién (Cerro Tacarcuna, Cerro Pirre, Cerro Quía, Cerro Nique); recorded in Panama mostly 600–1500 m (2000–5000 ft); not yet found in Bocas del Toro but seems almost certain to occur.

Habits: Much like Olivaceous Flatbill.

Range: Southern Mexico to northwestern Colombia.

Note: Does not include *R. pacificus* (Pacific Flatbill) of western Colombia and northwestern Ecuador, considered conspecific with *R. brevirostris* in the 1983 AOU Check-list.

OLIVACEOUS FLATBILL
Rhynchocyclus olivaceus   Plate 24

Description: 6. Heavy-headed, with *very broad, flat bill*. Mostly olive above with an *indistinct whitish eye-ring; wings broadly margined with yellowish and with yellow wing-bars*; throat and chest olive, indistinctly streaked with pale yellow, lower underparts pale yellow.

Similar species: See Eye-ringed Flatbill of highlands. The fairly large size, broad flat bill, and generally dull olive plumage set it apart from other flycatchers; see the smaller slender-billed Olive-striped Flycatcher. Broad-billed Sapayoa lacks the eye-ring, wing-bars, and wing-edging, and is yellower on chest with no streaking.

Status and distribution: Uncommon to fairly common in forest and second-growth woodland in lowlands on Caribbean slope from western Colon province (Chilar) east through San Blas, and on Pacific slope from Canal area east through Darién (where ranges up to at least 600 m: 2000 ft at Cana and Cerro Sapo); one old record from "Veragua" is only report from western Panama. In central Panama more numerous on Caribbean slope.

Habits: Somewhat phlegmatic, usually seen sitting quietly inside forest at low and middle heights. Sometimes joins mixed foraging flocks of insectivorous birds. Its characteristic call is a loud harsh *tsheet* or *bzeeyp*; the infrequently heard song is a very thin, high, but musical *tee-tee-tee-tee*. The nest is a very bulky pear-shaped structure with projecting spout entrance at bottom on side, similar in shape to those of *Tolmomyias* but larger and covered with coarse (not fine) plant material.

Range: Central Panama to northern Bolivia and Amazonian and eastern Brazil.

YELLOW-OLIVE FLYCATCHER
Tolmomyias sulphurescens   Plates 24, 46

Description: 5½. Rather heavy-headed, with *fairly broad somewhat flattened bill*. Lower mandible pale, grayish white to pale flesh; *iris typically rather pale*, either grayish or brownish. Mostly bright olive above with grayish crown and whitish supraloral and narrow eye-ring; wings blackish with two yellowish wing-bars and prominent edging on flight feathers; throat whitish, becoming olive on breast and flanks, and pale yellow on belly.
Similar species: *Closely* resembles Yellow-margined Flycatcher; for distinctions see under that species. Forest Elaenia has shorter unflattened bill, a dark iris, and a yellow crown patch (often concealed); voices of the two differ characteristically, as does their posture. See also Olivaceous Flatbill.
Status and distribution: Uncommon to fairly common in second-growth woodland and woodland borders and adjacent clearings, especially along streams (above which it often nests) in lowlands and foothills on entire Pacific slope (though less numerous in Darién, where easternmost report is apparently one seen at El Real on March 5, 1981; Ridgely *et al.*); on Caribbean slope recorded from western Bocas del Toro (one seen on lower Río Changuinola on April 25, 1980, this likely pertaining to the Middle American subspecies *cinereiceps*; Ridgely), and from northern Coclé (El Uracillo) and western Colon province (Chilar) east to western San Blas (Mandinga); in western Chiriquí recorded up to about 1650 m (5500 ft), but elsewhere mostly below 900 m (3000 ft).
Habits: Usually forages at middle heights, gleaning in the foliage and often difficult to see clearly. The call is somewhat similar to that of the Yellow-margined but is thinner and not as penetrating, usually of only one or two notes, a high sibilant *dzz, dzz* or *tsit, tsit*, sometimes followed by a fast musical rattle. The foot-long, hanging, purse-shaped nest with a downward extending tube, made of fine hair-like fibers, is conspicuous (rarely more than 6 m: 20 ft above ground) and can be regularly seen at Summit Gardens.
Range: Southern Mexico to northern Argentina and southeastern Brazil.

YELLOW-MARGINED FLYCATCHER
Tolmomyias assimilis   Plate 24

Description: 5¼. Very like Yellow-olive Flycatcher. Best points of distinction are: its *typically dark iris*, brownish to grayish; *usually quite prominent pale speculum at base of outer primaries* (lacking in Yellow-olive); and usually different habitat and vocalizations (see below). All previously described differences are variable, and seem to break down under close scrutiny of series of specimens and photographs.
Similar species: Best distinguished from Yellow-olive Flycatcher by the eye-ring, contrasting gray cap, broad yellow wing-edging and no bars, and greater contrast on underparts; the Yellow-margined is a brighter, cleaner-cut bird. Also resembles Greenish Elaenia but is smaller with broader flatter bill, and different voice and habitat. See also Yellow-green Tyrannulet.
Status and distribution: Common in canopy and borders of humid forest in lowlands and lower foothills (to about 750 m: 2500 ft) on entire Caribbean slope (seems somewhat less numerous westward); on Pacific slope recorded locally from western Chiriquí (one specimen from Cerro Pando; and two pairs seen at Río Algarrobos on June 30, 1982; Ridgely), and from western Panama province (Cerro Campana) and Canal area (locally) east through Darién. In Canal area widespread and much more numerous on Caribbean side.
Habits: Forages at middle and upper levels of forest in *humid* areas (tending to avoid more deciduous woodland favored by Yellow-olive), often joining mixed flocks of insectivorous birds. Gleans from foliage, often carrying tail partly cocked up; tends to perch vertically less often than Yellow-olive. Yellow-margined's frequently heard call is a series of harsh and buzzy notes, given deliberately and often with a distinct pause after the first note, *zhweek; zhweek, zhweek, zhweek;* there often is a long interval before the call is given again, thus it sometimes is hard to track to its source.
Range: Costa Rica to northern Bolivia and Amazonian Brazil.

WHITE-THROATED SPADEBILL
Platyrinchus mystaceus   Plate 46, p.296

Description: 3½–3¾. *Tiny* and stubby, with *broad flat bill* and short tail. Olive brown above with usually concealed yellow crown patch (small or absent in female and immature), *buffy supraloral stripe and eye-ring*, and a patch of dusky with buff center on ear-coverts; *throat white*, chest and sides buffy brownish, remaining underparts pale yellow.

Similar species: No highland species at all resembles it. Golden-crowned Spadebill has more strongly marked facial pattern, golden-rufous crown, and lacks the conspicuous white throat; the two are found together only very locally.

Status and distribution: Uncommon in undergrowth of humid forest in foothills and highlands on both slopes; recorded from Chiriquí, Bocas del Toro, Veraguas, western Panama province (Cerro Campana), western San Blas (three individuals mist-netted on Cerro Brewster on April 23 and 25, 1985; J. Blake, photos to VIREO), and eastern Darién; recorded mostly 750–1800 m (2500–6000 ft), but there are also single records from coastal lowlands of Bocas del Toro (near Almirante) and Darién (Garachiné).

Habits: Seems even harder to see than Golden-crowned Spadebill, favoring dense undergrowth. Usually seen singly, independent of mixed flocks, remaining motionless for long periods, then flying abruptly to a new perch. Its frequent calling often reveals its presence, and include a sharp *squeep!* or *squip*, sometimes doubled or in series.

Range: Costa Rica to northern Bolivia, Paraguay, northeastern Argentina, and southeastern Brazil.

Note: More than one species may be involved in South America.

GOLDEN-CROWNED SPADEBILL
Platyrinchus coronatus   Plate 25

Description: 3½–3¾. A *tiny* stubby flycatcher with a *broad flat bill* and a *very short tail. Crown cinnamon-rufous* bordered with black, superciliary yellowish, *a black spot in front of eye and another on ear-coverts*; otherwise olive above; pale yellow below, tinged with olive on breast and sides.

Similar species: In shape, not unlike a manakin. The complex facial pattern and very broad bill should preclude confusion.

Status and distribution: Uncommon to fairly common in lower growth of humid forest in lowlands on entire Caribbean slope, ranging up in smaller numbers into foothills to about 1050 m (3500 ft); on Pacific slope recorded from lowlands of western Chiriquí (where now very local due to deforestation, with only recent report being several seen on the Burica Peninsula in June 1982; Ridgely), foothills of Veraguas and western Panama province (Cerro Campana), and in lowlands and lower foothills of eastern Panama province

WHITE-THROATED SPADEBILL

(now mainly in middle and upper Bayano River valley, formerly west to around Panama City) and Darién. More numerous from around Canal area eastward; fairly common in Pipeline Road forests, though as always inconspicuous.

Habits: Similar to White-throated Spadebill, though tending to favor areas with more open understory so not quite so difficult to see. Their call is a distinctive weak thin buzzy trill, *bzee-ee-eeép*, often so faint as to be nearly inaudible which, though weak, does often reveal the bird's presence.

Range: Honduras to Peru and Amazonian Brazil.

ROYAL FLYCATCHER
Onychorhynchus coronatus   Plate 24

Description: 6½–7. The remarkable *fan-shaped crest* for which this bird is famous is unfortunately not often seen. Bill long and broad. Brown above with *small buffy spots on wing-coverts; rump and tail tawny-ochraceous*, becoming brown toward tip of tail; yellowish buffy below with indistinct olive mottling or barring on chest (more obvious in immatures). When closed (almost always), the crest lies flat but protrudes to the rear, giving a *distinct hammerhead effect*; when spread, the crest is a full semi-circle of scarlet (yellow-orange in female) with black spots and steel blue tips, held perpendicular to axis of body; only rarely does any color show through when crest is folded.

Similar species: No other similar bird has the hammerhead effect. Might be confused with Brownish Twistwing or a *Myiarchus*.

Status and distribution: Uncommon in lower growth of forest borders and second-growth woodland, usually near streams, in lowlands and (in smaller numbers) foothills on both slopes, recorded up to 1110 m (3700 ft) in western Chiriquí; more numerous on Pacific slope but absent from driest areas on eastern side of Azuero Peninsula to western Panama province.

Habits: Rather an inconspicuous bird generally, most often alone or in pairs and not foraging with mixed flocks. When handled (as after capture in a mist-net), the bird raises its crest to its fullest glory and rhythmically twists its head from side to side and up and down, almost contorting its neck, at the same time opening and closing its bill. This display is so rarely seen under natural conditions that its function remains debated, though it has been observed while preening, in courtship and after copulation, and in agonistic displays. Usually rather quiet, but sometimes gives a repeated sharp clear *pree-o* or (B. Whitney) *kéy-up*, sounding rather like a *Manacus* manakin or a jacamar. The nest is very long and slender (1–2 m: 2–6 ft), loosely constructed with entrance on the side, and hung from the tip of a drooping branch, usually over a small shady stream.

Range: Southern Mexico to northern Bolivia and southeastern Brazil.

Note: The 1983 AOU Check-list considers trans-Andean populations, which were formerly often separated as a distinct species (Northern Royal-Flycatcher, *O. mexicanus*), as conspecific with birds found east of the Andes.

RUDDY-TAILED FLYCATCHER
Terenotriccus erythrurus   Plate 25

Description: 3½–3¾. *Small.* Short rather stubby bill. Head and back grayish olive; *rump and tail cinnamon-rufous; most of wings and entire underparts ochraceous.*

Similar species: Likely to be confused only with the larger Ochre-bellied Flycatcher, which is mostly olive above and on throat, and has a rather long and slender bill.

Status and distribution: Common in second-growth woodland and forest in lowlands and in smaller numbers up into lower foothills (to about 780 m: 2600 ft) on both slopes; absent from dry Pacific lowlands from eastern side of Azuero Peninsula to western Panama province.

Habits: Forages at lower and middle levels, often perching in the open and not difficult

to see. Sometimes twitches wings rapidly up over its back, both going up simultaneously. Its calls are a thin *pseeoo-see* and a *seeoo-bzeew*.

Range: Southeastern Mexico to northern Bolivia and central Brazil.

TAWNY-BREASTED FLYCATCHER
Myiobius villosus   Plate 40

Description: 5½. Known only from eastern Darién highlands. *Conspicuous yellow rump;* graduated tail. *Dark olive above* with usually concealed yellow crown patch (dull cinnamon in female); throat whitish, *most of underparts tawny brown*, center of belly pale yellow.

Similar species: Sulphur-rumped Flycatcher is smaller, shows much more yellow on underparts (including throat), with only chest and sides suffused with brighter tawny, and is not as dark above. Black-tailed Flycatcher lacks tawny altogether; both species are essentially lowland birds.

Status and distribution: Recorded from two specimens taken in forest in highlands of eastern Darién (Cerro Tacarcuna, 1200–1440 m: 4000–4800 ft). As yet there is no definite evidence that this species occurs on Cerro Pirre.

Habits: Similar to Sulphur-rumped Flycatcher, though generally much less numerous and less often seen even in its main Andean range.

Range: Eastern Panama to northwestern Venezuela and northern Bolivia.

SULPHUR-RUMPED FLYCATCHER
Myiobius barbatus   Plate 24

Description: 5. *Conspicuous yellow rump;* rather rounded *black tail.* Olive above with usually concealed yellow crown patch in male; throat yellow, becoming *bright tawny on breast and flanks*, yellow on middle of belly.

Similar species: Black-tailed Flycatcher has buffy-olive instead of bright tawny on breast. In eastern Darién see also Tawny-breasted Flycatcher.

Status and distribution: Uncommon to fairly common in lower growth of humid forest in lowlands and lower foothills on entire Caribbean slope (less numerous westward); on Pacific slope recorded from lowlands and foothills of western and central Chiriquí (now quite local due to deforestation, in lowlands probably persisting only in remaining forests on Burica Peninsula), and in foothills locally from Veraguas eastward, in lowlands in eastern Panama province (mainly middle and upper Bayano River valley) and Darién. In Canal area perhaps most numerous in forests along Pipeline Road.

Habits: Always seems to be showing off its yellow rump by drooping its wings and fanning its tail. Usually found singly, often accompanying a mixed foraging flock moving through the lower growth of the forest. The nest is an irregular, closed structure attached to the end of a slender branch, the entrance on the side; it often hangs over a small stream.

Range: Southeastern Mexico to Bolivia and southern Brazil.

Note: The 1983 AOU Check-list considers trans-Andean populations as a distinct species, *M. sulphureipygius*. We prefer to treat all forms of *M. barbatus* as conspecific, mainly because variation within the *barbatus* group east of the Andes is equally as great as that between *sulphureipygius* and *barbatus*.

BLACK-TAILED FLYCATCHER
Myiobius atricaudus   Plate 24

Description: 4¾–5. Resembles Sulphur-rumped Flycatcher but has *chest washed with buffy-olive* (not suffused with bright tawny on chest and sides).

Similar species: See Sulphur-rumped Flycatcher.

Status and distribution: Fairly common in lower growth of forest borders, second-growth woodland, and gallery woodland in lowlands and lower foothills on both slopes, though somewhat local; scarce in Bocas del Toro, and seems unrecorded from western and central Chiriquí (though found in adjacent Costa Rica) and absent from dry lowlands from eastern side of Azuero Peninsula to western Panama province. Normally not found *within* humid forest, where the Sulphur-rumped takes over.

Habits: Very active and spritely, moving about restlessly, displaying its yellow rump and fanning its tail. Found especially near streams.

Range: Southwestern Costa Rica to Peru and southern Brazil.

BRAN-COLORED FLYCATCHER
Myiophobus fasciatus   Plate 25

Description: 4½–4¾. Suggests an *Empidonax* in size and shape. *Brown above* with usually concealed yellow crown patch (smaller in female; absent in immature);

wings and tail dusky with *two broad buffy whitish wing-bars*; buffy yellowish below with *indistinct brownish streaks on breast*.

Similar species: Superficially resembles White-throated Flycatcher except for the blurry breast streaking and concealed crown patch, and lack of an eye-ring.

Status and distribution: Uncommon and rather local in overgrown pastures and other shrubby areas in lowlands on Pacific slope from Chiriquí to eastern Panama province (lower Bayano River valley at Puerto San Antonio), but not recorded on Azuero Peninsula; on Caribbean slope recorded only from Canal area and eastern Colon province (where decidedly scarce and local); in western Chiriquí ranges sparingly up to about 1200 m (4000 ft) in the lower highlands; found also on some of the Pearl Islands.

Habits: Perches low on fences and in bushes, often in pairs. Usually rather inconspicuous. Its song is a loud but unemphatic, monotonous *weeb, weeb, weeb, weeb . . .*, sometimes sound like *weeup* or *tweep*.

Range: Southwestern Costa Rica to northern Chile and northern Argentina.

Note: More than one species may be involved in South America.

BLACK-BILLED FLYCATCHER
Aphanotriccus audax   Plate 40

Description: 5¼. Found only in eastern Panama. *Short all-black bill.* Bright olive above, somewhat grayer on crown and with *whitish supraloral stripe and narrow eye-ring broken in front and behind*; wings duskier with two pale buff wing-bars; throat whitish, sides of chest clouded with olive, becoming clear yellow on lower breast and belly.

Similar species: In plumage somewhat like an *Empidonax*, but these never show a supraloral stripe and always have a pale lower mandible. Shape and posture are reminiscent of a *Leptopogon* flycatcher, though their facial patterns are quite different. See also Yellow-olive Flycatcher.

Status and distribution: Uncommon and seemingly local (perhaps mostly just overlooked) in lower growth of humid forest and shady second-growth woodland in lowlands and lower foothills of eastern Panama province (upper Bayano River valley) and Darién; recorded up to about 600 m (2000 ft). Small numbers can be regularly found near Cana in eastern Darién, especially along the trail to Boca de Cupe.

Habits: An inconspicuous and rather drab

small flycatcher, perching quietly in undergrowth, making short sallies to foliage, usually not joining mixed flocks. Its call is an infrequently given, sharply enunciated but burry *jee-jee-jew*.

Range: Eastern Panama and northern Colombia.

COMMON TUFTED-FLYCATCHER
Mitrephanes phaeocercus   Plate 25

Description: 4¾–5. *Conspicuous pointed crest* is unique among small Panama flycatchers. Olive above with whitish loral spot and very inconspicuous eye-ring; wings and tail duskier, with two indistinct grayish olive wing-bars; *tawny below*, becoming pale yellow on belly. Foregoing applies to birds of western and central Chiriquí (*aurantiiventris*); eastward they gradually become paler and buffier below (*vividus*), culminating in the pale washed-out underparts of *eminulus* on Cerro Pirre in Darién.

Similar species: Not likely to be confused, but see the considerably larger (and *much* rarer) Ochraceous Pewee.

Status and distribution: Common in borders of humid forest and in adjacent clearings with scattered trees in foothills and highlands of Chiriquí (in western Chiriquí mostly 1200–2400 m: 4000–8000 ft, lower eastward), Bocas del Toro (recorded only along the oleoducto road north of Fortuna, but probably more widespread), Veraguas, Coclé, and western Panama province (Cerro Campana), and eastern Darién (Cerro Tacarcuna and Cerro Pirre); recorded mostly 600–1500 m (2000–5000 ft). Curiously, has never been found in the Cerro Azul/Jefe area.

Habits: Acts like a diminutive wood-pewee. Perches conspicuously at low and middle heights, sallying out after passing insects, often returning to its original perch, and characteristically shivering its tail sideways upon alighting. Frequently gives a piping whistle, *pee-pee-pee-pee*... (up to eight notes).

Range: Northern Mexico to northwestern Ecuador.

Note: Excludes *M. olivaceus* of the east slope of the Andes in Peru and Bolivia, following the 1983 AOU Check-list. However, so as to associate the two allospecies, it seems preferable to call the widespread, numerous *M. phaeocercus* the "Common Tufted-Flycatcher" and *M. olivaceus* the "Olive Tufted-Flycatcher".

OLIVE-SIDED FLYCATCHER
Contopus borealis   Plate 23

Description: 6¾. A rather large flycatcher with a *short tail* and a *bull-headed look*. Lower mandible mostly yellowish. Dark grayish olive above; wings and tail dusky, wings with only indistinct pale grayish wing-bars; throat and median underparts whitish to yellowish white, with *sides and flanks olive grayish*, sometimes with streaked effect, *this almost extending all the way across breast* (suggesting a "dark unbuttoned vest over a white shirt"); *a tuft of white often protrudes from behind wing onto sides of rump* (but may be hidden).

Similar species: Most easily confused with the wood-pewees but larger, darker below, with relatively shorter tail and less distinct wing-bars. See also Dark Pewee (almost uniformly dark).

Status and distribution: Uncommon transient throughout except in very open areas (late August–mid-November; mid-March–late May); a few individuals overwinter in foothills and highlands.

Habits: Typically seen perched on a high, exposed, dead branch or tall stub, flying out for long distances after passing insects, usually returning to its original perch. Its unmistakable loud whistled *hic-three-beers* is occasionally heard, especially on spring migration; also gives a *whip-whip-whip*, like Dark Pewee.

Range: Breeds in northern and western North America; winters from Venezuela and Colombia to Bolivia, a few in Middle America.

Note: Formerly placed in the monotypic genus *Nuttalornis*.

DARK PEWEE
Contopus lugubris   Plate 23, p.300

Description: 6½. Found only in Chiriquí highlands. *Distinctly crested.* Lower mandible yellowish. *Uniform dark olive-slaty*, paling somewhat on upper throat and lower belly.

Similar species: Should be readily recognized on account of its conspicuous crest and uniform dark coloration. Confusion is most likely with Olive-sided Flycatcher, which is shorter-tailed and not so prominently crested (though it does look large-headed), and is nowhere near as uniform looking (especially below).

Status and distribution: Uncommon to fairly common in canopy and borders of humid montane forest, and in clearings with

DARK PEWEE

scattered large trees, in foothills and high-lands of western and central Chiriquí (recorded east to the Fortuna area); in western Chiriquí recorded primarily 1200–2250 m (4000–7500 ft), but occurs somewhat lower eastward (900–1500 m: 3000–5000 ft).

Habits: Quite reminiscent of Olive-sided Flycatcher, usually perching high on dead branches and making long sallies into the air, shivering its tail as it returns to its perch. Has several short calls, the most frequent being a loud *pip-pip-pip*. A. Skutch also describes an infrequently heard dawn song, given mainly or entirely during the April–May breeding season, as a *fréd-rick-fear*, repeated over and over.

Range: Costa Rica and western Panama.

Note: Sometimes considered conspecific with *C. pertinax* (Greater Pewee) of southwestern United States to Nicaragua, and *C. fumigatus* (Smoke-colored Pewee) of South America. Here the 1983 AOU Check-list is followed in considering all three as allospecies.

OCHRACEOUS PEWEE
Contopus ochraceus   Plate 46

Description: 6½. Known only from Chiriquí highlands. Lower mandible yellowish. *Ochraceous olive above* with duskier crown, wings, and tail, *wings with two prominent buff*

bars; *mostly yellow below*, tinged with ochraceous olive on sides of neck and chest.

Similar species: Common Tufted-Flycatcher is markedly smaller, has conspicuous pointed crest but lacks obvious wing-bars, and is much tawnier (not so yellow) on underparts.

Status and distribution: Only recently confirmed for Panama, one or two birds have been seen quite regularly along the upper part of the Boquete Trail above Cerro Punta since about 1980; one was recognizably photographed by R. Behrstock on February 25, 1981 (photos to VIREO; here recorded mainly 2100–2400 m (7000–8000 ft). Another, much more surprising report is of a bird reported seen at much lower elevation (ca 1200 m: 4000 ft) north of Fortuna in central Chiriquí near the oleoducto road on January 9, 1985 (D. Gardner and R. Johnson). The provenance of the nineteenth-century AMNH specimen labeled only as having been taken in "Chiriquí" is thus given substantially more credence, as is Eisenmann's February 29, 1960, sighting of a bird in almost exactly the same area from whence come all the recent reports from western Chiriqí.

Habits: Usually seen singly, mostly perching at the edge of forest some 6–12 m (20–40 ft) above the ground. Sometimes seems to move with mixed flocks, but more often rather sedentary, repeatedly returning to the same perch after its short aerial sallies. Usually shivers its tail upon alighting. The only call heard has been a typically pewee-like *pip-pip-pip*.

Range: Costa Rica and western Panama.

WESTERN WOOD-PEWEE
Contopus sordidulus

Description: 5½–6. Very similar to Eastern Wood-Pewee and, unless calling, usually not safely distinguished in the field (nor sometimes in the hand). Averages grayer or browner above and more extensively dark below (often without white on center of breast); *bill sometimes entirely or almost entirely dark* (in Eastern, lower mandible always largely yellowish or pinkish except at tip); wing formulae similar.

Status and distribution: Transient and perhaps occasional winter resident (early August–late November; early March–May; one specimen from February 15); exact status and abundance uncertain due to identification problem. Specimens chiefly from western foothills and highlands, where on migration it generally outnumbers Eastern Wood-Pewee and where Tropical Pewee does not usually occur.

Habits: Like Eastern Wood-Pewee. Calls fairly often both while on migration and on its South American wintering grounds, a melancholy burry *preeer* or *freeer* with different quality from the typical call of Eastern Wood-Pewee, but remember that the latter does occasionally give a burrier-sounding call (*pee-ur*).

Range: Breeds from western North America to Honduras (possibly to Costa Rica); winters in northern and western South America, a few occasionally in Costa Rica and Panama.

EASTERN WOOD-PEWEE
Contopus virens   Plate 32

Description: 5¾. Lower mandible yellowish, sometimes tipped dusky. Dark grayish olive above, wings and tail duskier with two distinct pale grayish to whitish wing-bars; throat whitish, more grayish on sides, becoming olive grayish on breast and flanks, and whitish on mid-belly; under tail-coverts often yellowish. Immatures have buffier wing-bars and tend to be yellower below; they may have an all-dark bill.

Similar species: A drab flycatcher, easily confused; its voice is generally the best clue (see below). Often cannot be safely distinguished in the field from Western Wood-Pewee and Tropical Pewee; see respective species for distinctions. *Empidonax* flycatchers are smaller than wood-pewees, usually have a complete eye-ring (sometimes faintly indicated in wood-pewees, especially in front of eye), and have shorter wings in proportion to tail (in wood-pewees, the wings usually extend more than halfway down tail), but longer tarsus (14.5–17.5 mm in *Empidonax*, 12.0–14.5 in wood-pewees). Olive-sided Flycatcher is larger with short tail, darker below.

Status and distribution: Common transient throughout, mostly in lowlands (recorded mainly September–November, with a few reports as early as late August and as late as mid-December; and March–mid-May); recorded also from Pearl Islands, Taboguilla Island, and on Escudo de Veraguas. A few may possibly over-winter, but there are *no* definite records between late December and early March (and relatively few at any time in December or March).

Habits: Usually seen perched at low- and mid-heights in clearings and at edge of second-growth woodland and forest, sallying out, sometimes for long distances, after passing insects. Calls frequently during migration, most often a sweet plaintive *pee-weé?*, sometimes slurred downward to *pee-ur*; much less often heard (mostly during northward passage) is its full song, *pee-a-wee*, with quality of the first call.

Range: Breeds in eastern North America; winters in northern and western South America, possibly in southern Middle America.

TROPICAL PEWEE
Contopus cinereus   Plates 24, 32

Description: 5½. Closely resembles Eastern and Western Wood-Pewees. Grayish olive above with *whitish lores*; wings and tail dusky, wings with two whitish to pale grayish wing-bars; throat whitish, breast and flanks olive grayish, with mid-belly whitish to pale yellowish. Birds from Coiba Island (*aithalodes*) are much darker generally.

Similar species: Compared to the two wood-pewees, Tropical is somewhat smaller and proportionately shorter-winged and longer-tailed; the best and most consistent mark, however, is Tropical's whitish lores, quite easily seen at close range. The calls of the three species also differ characteristically. Also easily confused with several of the *Empidonax* flycatchers, especially the "Traill's"; these are all about the same size, and "Traill's" can show some whitish on lores (and often does not have an eye-ring). Tropical Pewee has less well delineated wing-bars and is grayer overall (not so brown or olive), but often vocalizations are the most helpful point to check for. "Traill's" also habitually flick their tail upward, a mannerism not shared by any of the pewees.

Status and distribution: Locally fairly common in shrubby areas and overgrown pastures with scattered trees or small shrubs in lowlands (occasionally to 900 m: 3000 ft) on both slopes east to eastern Colon province and western Darién (Garachiné); more widespread on Pacific slope, though apparently absent from driest areas in eastern Herrera, southern Coclé and western Panama province; on Caribbean slope only where clearings are fairly extensive; found also on Coiba Island.

Habits: Similar to those of the two wood-pewees, but tends to perch lower. Makes short sallies and often quivers its tail upon alighting. The call is a rapid *sreerrip* or variants, often repeated, very different from the wood-pewees.

Range: Southeastern Mexico to northern Argentina and southern Brazil.

YELLOW-BELLIED FLYCATCHER
Empidonax flaviventris

Description: 5–5¼. Lower mandible pale orange to yellowish. Brownish olive above with *relatively wide pale yellowish eye-ring*; wings and tail dusky, wings with two prominent whitish or pale yellowish bars; *throat yellowish*, becoming olive across breast, and pale yellow on belly. Immature duller with buffier wing-bars.

Similar species: Easily confused with Acadian Flycatcher, *which can be just as yellow below*, even on throat. Yellow-bellied is slightly smaller and has somewhat broader and more yellow-tinged eye-ring, but probably the best way to differentiate them is through their calls (given especially often by Yellow-bellied; see below). Remember, too, that their ranges in Panama mostly differ. Yellow-bellied usually has difference between longest and 6th primary of 5 mm or less (in Acadian usually 6 mm or more) and has 10th (outer) primary usually equal to or longer than 5th; outer web of 6th primary sometimes slightly emarginate (cut out or narrowed toward tip); total wing length 62–70 mm. See also Yellowish, Yellow-olive, and Yellow-margined Flycatchers.

Status and distribution: Uncommon to fairly common winter resident (early September–late April) in lower growth of humid forest and second-growth woodland and in adjacent clearings and coffee plantations in Chiriquí, Bocas del Toro, Veraguas, and on the western side of Azuero Peninsula; most numerous in the foothills and highlands (especially 600–1500 m: 2000–5000 ft), but also recorded from the lowlands, perhaps mostly as transients. Eastward in Panama there are only two confirmed records: a nineteenth-century specimen taken by McLeannan from the Caribbean side of the Canal area, and a specimen taken at Cana, Darién (both in AMNH); various sightings are regarded as unconfirmed.

Habits: Usually solitary, perching at low- and mid-heights, making short sallies to foliage and into the air; they often quiver their tails as they alight on their perch. The Yellow-bellied's most characteristic call, fortunately quite often heard in Panama, is a spiritless whistle *chu-wee* or *per-wee* with a rising inflection (R. T. Peterson), often decidedly suggestive of the short call of Eastern Wood-Pewee. This differs strikingly in both quality and pattern from call of Acadian Flycatcher.

Range: Breeds in northern North America; winters from eastern Mexico to Panama.

ACADIAN FLYCATCHER
Empidonax virescens   Plate 32

Description: 5½. Lower mandible yellowish. Olive above with fairly prominent yellowish white eye-ring and whitish lores; wings and tail dusky, wings with two bold whitish wing-bars; throat grayish white, becoming pale olive gray on breast, white on mid-belly, and pale yellow on flanks and under tail-coverts. Immature has buffier wing-bars, and often is yellower below (even on throat).

Similar species: Yellower fall individuals are very easily taken for a Yellow-bellied Flycatcher (see discussion under that species). Duller individuals are sometimes very hard to separate from Traill's Flycatcher but are usually greener above and yellower below, slightly larger, and have slightly differing wing formula. Acadian usually has difference between longest and 6th primary of 6 mm or more (in Yellow-belly usually 5 mm or less; in Traill's usually less than 6 mm), and has 10th (outer) primary usually equal to or longer than 5th; total wing length 67–81 mm.

Status and distribution: Fairly common transient and winter resident (mostly September–late April) in borders of humid forest and in shady second-growth woodland on both slopes, mainly in lowlands but in smaller numbers (and perhaps especially as a transient) in foothills and highlands; recorded also from Pearl Islands and Taboguilla Island. *By far* the most numerous wintering *Empidonax* in the Canal area.

Habits: Behavior on its wintering grounds, where it is apparently territorial, is much like on the breeding areas: Acadian is usually found inside woodland or forest, often in fairly open areas, perching on exposed branches. Attention is often drawn to them by their sharp, inflected *wheep!* call note, but they do not seem to sing very much away from their nesting areas.

Range: Breeds in eastern United States; winters from Costa Rica to Venezuela and western Ecuador.

TRAILL'S FLYCATCHER
Empidonax traillii

(Includes Alder (*E. alnorum*) and Willow (*E. traillii*) Flycatchers.)

Description: 5½. Brownish olive to grayish olive above with *inconspicuous narrow whitish eye-ring* (often altogether lacking), sometimes with some whitish on lores; wings and tail dusky, wings with two bold whitish to pale buff wing-bars (buffier in immatures); throat whitish, breast grayish to brownish olive, belly pale yellowish white. The two species, here combined into one account, are essentially indistinguishable in the field on morphological characters, though Alder is said to show slightly more of an eye-ring than Willow, and to be somewhat greener above; better, unless they are vocalizing, to simply leave them as "Traill's".

Similar species: Acadian Flycatcher is very similar, but usually shows a more obvious eye-ring, and is greener above and yellower below; it favors more wooded terrain (though this could break down on migration), and its calls also differ. See also White-throated Flycatcher, and Eastern Wood-Pewee. In the hand, Traill's usually has difference between 6th and longest primary of 6 mm or less, and has 10th primary usually equal to or longer than 5th in eastern-breeding birds (usually equal to or a little shorter in western-breeding birds); total wing length 64–78 mm.

Status and distribution: Fairly common to common transient in open shrubby areas and woodland borders in lowlands throughout, occurring in smaller numbers up into foothills and lower highlands in appropriate semiopen habitat (recorded mostly September–November, and in April–mid-May). Small numbers, apparently all Willow Flycatchers (as evidenced by their voice; see below) also over-winter at least locally in semiopen areas, mostly on Pacific slope, but also reported from shore of Gatun Lake (E. O. Willis).

Habits: Usually perches low in bushes or small trees, often near water. Habits of the Willow and Alder Flycatchers are essentially identical in Panama. Alder apparently winters virtually entirely in South America, to the south of the wintering range of Willow, and thus is seen in Panama only on migration; chances for identification are greatest during northward passage, when they fairly often can be heard to give their distinctive song, a rather burry *free-breéo*, with accent on the *second* syllable. Willow also evidently winters mainly in South America, but small numbers remain in Panama and Costa Rica; listen for their sharp snappy *fitz-bew* which they give both on their winter territory and on northward passage. Call of Willow, a dry *whit*, is distinctly different from that of Acadian. Alder's call is reported to be a fairly loud, flat *peert* or *peet* (B. Whitney).

Range: Breeds in North America; winters from Guatemala to northern Argentina.

WHITE-THROATED FLYCATCHER
Empidonax albigularis   Plate 46

Description: 4¾–5. *Olive brown above* with indistinct or partial yellowish buffy eye-ring and *buffy wing-bars*; throat whitish, breast and sides brownish olive, belly buffy yellowish, deepening to buff on under tail-coverts; under wing-coverts buffy brown. Immature has wing-bars broader and more cinnamon.

Similar species: The brown upperparts, buffy wing-bars, and buff tone to lower underparts should set it apart from all the migrant *Empidonax* except immatures of the larger Traill's Flycatcher, which are also often brown above with brownish buffy wing-bars. White-throated's 10th primary is distinctly (3–5 mm) shorter than 5th (in Traill's at most only slightly shorter); inner web of 6th primary slightly emarginate; total wing length 55–63 mm. See also Bran-colored Flycatcher.

Status and distribution: Apparently a rare resident in highlands of western Chiriquí, mostly 1200–1800 m (4000–6000 ft). Two specimens from lowlands (one taken at Chiriquicito, Bocas del Toro, on March 26, 1926; one nineteenth-century McLeannan specimen from Canal area) represent either wanderers from highlands or possibly migrants from farther north in Middle America.

Habits: Favors rather open shrubby areas. Its song is an explosive, but not loud, buzzy *pseeyp* or *kseeyip*.

Range: Mexico to western (casually central) Panama.

LEAST FLYCATCHER
Empidonax minimus

Description: 4¾. Very rare. Lower mandible mostly yellowish (dusky toward tip). Grayish olive above with *conspicuous white eye-ring*; wings and tail dusky, wings with two whitish bars; *mostly dull whitish below*, tinged gray on breast and pale yellow on belly. Immature browner above and on breast, and with buffyish wing-bars.

Similar species: Resembles the two Traill's and Acadian Flycatchers, but smaller with more prominent eye-ring and grayer above and more uniformly whitish below. Yellow-bellied Flycatcher also has a bold eye-ring (though it is yellower), but is much yellower below and not as gray above (more brownish olive). Least has notched tail and 10th (outer) primary equal to or shorter than 5th; outer web of 6th primary is distinctly emarginate; total wing length 57–68 mm.

Status and distribution: Apparently a very rare winter visitant; few records, but perhaps somewhat overlooked. Records include: a specimen taken at David, Chiriquí, on October 16, 1900; a bird mist-netted, measured by Eisenmann, and released on October 19, 1965, at Almirante, Bocas del Toro; three nineteenth-century specimens taken by McLeannan in the Canal area; and a specimen taken at Farfan Beach, on Pacific side of Canal area, on October 5, 1953.

Habits: Favors woodland borders and shrubby areas; usually found singly. Its call is a dry *whit*, soft but sharp, rather resembling call of Willow Flycatcher; seemingly does not give (or gives very rarely) its song while on its winter quarters.

Range: Breeds in eastern North America; winters from Mexico (a few in extreme southern United States) to Panama.

[HAMMOND'S FLYCATCHER]
Empidonax hammondii

Description: 5¼. One recent report from western Chiriquí highlands. Closely resembles Least Flycatcher, and barely distinguishable in the field, but slightly larger; bill very short and thin, essentially all black (whereas Least generally shows obvious orange-yellow on lower mandible); somewhat darker below.

Status and distribution: One was carefully observed and photographed (photos to VIREO) at Finca Lerida above Boquete, western Chiriquí, on February 22, 1982 (B. Whitney *et al.*). While the photos themselves cannot be considered incontrovertible (*fide* K. Kaufman), B. Whitney is confident that the bird was indeed a Hammond's. Unfortunately, it did not call.

Habits: Favors woodland and forest understory, during winter perhaps most often at or near edge. Its distinctive call is a sharp *peek* or *peep*, quite different from the softer drier *whit* of the Least.

Range: Breeds from Alaska to western United States; winters mainly in highlands from Mexico to Honduras, probably to Nicaragua, with one report from western Panama.

YELLOWISH FLYCATCHER
Empidonax flavescens   Plate 25

Description: 5. Found only in western highlands. *Yellowish olive above* with *very prominent yellowish eye-ring*, broader to the rear; two buffy wing-bars; *rich yellow below* (with an almost brassy tone), tinged with olive on chest and sides. Immature is browner above with cinnamon wing-bars; buffier on chest, but becoming almost whitish on belly.

Similar species: Much yellower than any other *Empidonax*, including the Yellow-bellied, and with more prominent eye-ring. Immature might be confused with Bran-colored Flycatcher but is much yellower and lacks Bran-color's breast streaking.

Status and distribution: Fairly common in forest borders and clearings with trees in highlands of Chiriquí and Veraguas, mostly 1050–2100 m (3500–7000 ft). Can be found regularly at the edge of coffee groves and gardens in the valley of the Río Chiriquí Viejo around Nueva Suiza and Bambito, in Chiriquí's western highlands.

Habits: Generally stays fairly low in shrubs and small trees, usually within 3 m (10 ft) of ground. Very unsuspicious. The common call is a simple *seee* (A. Skutch); generally a rather quiet bird.

Range: Southern Mexico to western Panama.

BLACK-CAPPED FLYCATCHER
Empidonax atriceps   Plate 25

Description: 4¼. Found only in western mountains. *Cap black* contrasting with otherwise olive upperparts; prominent but often broken white eye-ring and indistinct grayish wing-bars; throat white, chest and sides brownish, fading to pale yellow on flanks; outer web of outer pair of tail feathers white. Immature has cap more sooty but it still contrasts with back.

Similar species: No other similar flycatcher has the contrasting black or sooty cap.

Status and distribution: Fairly common in brushy clearings in mountains of western Chiriquí and adjacent Bocas del Toro, mostly above 2100 m (7000 ft). Quite easily found in the shrubby regenerating clearings along the upper part of the Boquete Trail above Cerro Punta, especially above the Fernandez farm.

Habits: Usually stays at or below eye-level, perching conspicuously on the top of a small bush, fence post, or low tree. Often shivers tail sideways. Very unsuspicious. The call is a simple *tsip*.

Range: Costa Rica and western Panama.

BLACK PHOEBE
Sayornis nigricans   Plate 46

Description: 6¾. *River and stream borders. Slaty black* with *contrasting white belly*, and white outer tail feathers. Birds of western Panama (*amnicola*) have wings margined with gray, while those from eastern Panama (*angustirostris*) have wing-edging white, and also two fairly prominent white wing-bars and less white on belly.

Similar species: Torrent Tyrannulet is smaller and mostly pale gray. Dark Pewee is slaty gray (not black), conspicuously crested, lacks the white belly, and perches high on dead branches.

Status and distribution: Fairly common along streams and rivers in foothills and highlands of western and central Chiriquí (east to Fortuna area), mostly 900–1800 m (3000–6000 ft). recorded locally along Río Changuinola in western Bocas del Toro down virtually to sea level (sightings in April 1980 by N. G. Smith, Ridgely); local in hill country of eastern Colon province (Cerro Bruja, Río Boquerón above Madden Lake; also at least occasionally down to near sea level, where seen along Río Guanche in early 1987 by D. Graham) and eastern Panama province (Cerro Chucantí; also locally along upper Bayano River, at least formerly, with numbers now probably reduced due to flooding from Bayano Lake), and in foothills of eastern Darién (Cerro Tacarcuna and near Cana).

Habits: Often sits on a rock out in the middle of the torrent, flying out after passing insects. Often pumps its tail while perched, sometimes spreading the feathers as well. Nests in rock crevices and under bridges and eaves. The song in Chiriquí is a *peep-feebreew*.

Range: Southwestern United States to northern Venezuela and northwestern Argentina.

VERMILION FLYCATCHER
Pyrocephalus rubinus

Description: 5¾–6. Casual vagrant. Somewhat bushy-crested. Male unmistak-able, with *crown, lower face, and entire underparts brilliant scarlet*, contrasting with sooty blackish upperparts and broad mask through eye. Female ashy brown above, sootier on wings and tail; throat and breast whitish, *breast with variable amount of dusky streaking*, becoming *pink to reddish pink on flanks and lower belly*. Younger immatures resemble female but have lower belly yellowish. Females of southern nominate race (which migrate north in austral winter at least to Amazonia, and are possible in Panama) usually show little or no pink below, and have *dusky streaking extending down over belly*.

Status and distribution: Casual, with a scatter of reports, most but not all from northern winter period. Known records include: male photographed at Playa Coronado, western Panama province, on August 19, 1947 (Eisenmann); subadult male seen and photographed at Gatun Dam, on Caribbean side of Canal area, January 16–March 20, 1974 (D. Engleman, Mrs Kani Myers *et al.*); female seen at Hotel Washington in Colon on February 11, 1982 (R. Behrstock and B. Feltner *et al.*); male seen at Boquete, western Chiriquí, on April 2, 1983 (J. Grugan); and a male seen at Ft. Gulick, on Caribbean side of Canal area, February 8–March 30, 1984 (J. and S. Follett *et al.*). It is still not known whether Panama records pertain to either migratory northern or southern populations (or both): males are indistinguishable in the field, but females and immatures often can be, and an effort should be made to at least photograph them.

Habits: Favors open country with scattered bushes and trees. Often very conspicuous, perching on fences, phone wires, etc.

Range: Southwestern United States to Nicaragua; Colombia to northern Chile and central Argentina; a few records from Panama.

PIED WATER-TYRANT
Fluvicola pica   p.306

Description: 5. *A small black and white flycatcher*, unmistakable in the marshy areas where it occurs. Mostly white, with black nape and center of back, black wings margined with white, and black tail tipped white.

Status and distribution: Locally common around freshwater marshes and ponds and in adjacent brushy areas in lowlands of eastern Panama province (mainly from

PIED WATER-TYRANT

Juan Diaz east to the mouth of the Bayano River, also a few recent reports from Bayano Lake and from Panama City), with small numbers also reported in recent years from the middle Chagres River valley (Gamboa area, Madden Lake); no reports from Darién, surprisingly. May be slowly increasing in range and numbers.

Habits: An attractive and unsuspicious bird, usually seen feeding on or near the ground, on emergent vegetation, or in shrubs; gleans rather than flycatches. Its call is a nasal *zhweeoo*.

Range: Central Panama to Venezuela, the Guianas, and northern Brazil.

Note: *F. albiventer* (Black-backed Water-Tyrant) of central and southern South America is here regarded as a species distinct from *F. pica*.

LONG-TAILED TYRANT
Colonia colonus   p.306

Description: ♂9–10; ♀7–8. Unmistakable. *Mostly black* with *white forehead and superciliary* whitish streaking on lower back and rump (often concealed); *central pair of tail feathers greatly elongated* (up to 4 in beyond rest of tail) in males, somewhat shorter in females and molting males.

Similar species: Fork-tailed Flycatcher is larger, has white underparts, and has *outer* tail feathers elongated; it is an open country (not a forest-based) bird.

Status and distribution: Fairly common in forest borders and small clearings adjacent to humid forest in lowlands and foothills (to about 900 m: 3000 ft) on entire Caribbean slope; on Pacific slope recorded from foot-

hills of Veraguas (Santa Fé), and in lowlands and foothills of eastern Panama province (Cerro Azul/Jefe, middle and upper Bayano River valley) and Darién (where recorded up to about 1200 m: 4000 ft on the slopes of Cerro Pirre). Widespread on Caribbean side of Canal area, with greatest numbers near the coast (e.g. Achiote Road, Fort Sherman/San Lorenzo).

Habits: Generally perches conspicuously on an exposed stub or dead branch, sallying out after passing insects, often returning to its original perch. Seen singly or in pairs. Nests in tree holes, typically in a dead, burned tree in a clearing. The calls are a distinctive soft *twee* or *chweet*; also has a musical humming *drüü*, accompanied by whipping the long tail.

Range: Honduras to Bolivia, Paraguay, northeastern Argentina, and southeastern Brazil.

[CATTLE TYRANT]
Machetornis rixosus

Description: 8. Casual vagrant to Darién. Looks rather like a kingbird, but more or less *terrestrial* and *long-legged*; *iris red*. Mainly pale olive brown above, somewhat grayer on crown and with usually concealed fiery orange crown patch; narrow dusky line through eye; wings and tail browner, *tail tipped paler*; mostly bright yellow below.

Similar species: Tropical Kingbird is much grayer above (not so brown), is markedly olive on chest, has differently shaped tail without a pale tip; it is not habitually terrestrial.

LONG-TAILED TYRANT

Status and distribution: One was seen in the clearing at Cana, in eastern Darién, on June 18, 1981, by P. Scharf and G. L. Vaucher. The species ranges very close to the Panama border in recently deforested parts of northwestern Colombia, and could conceivably colonize Panama in the future.

Habits: In its normal range found in semi-open country, most often in pastures and savannas where it habitually associates with cattle and other domestic animals. Feeds mostly on the ground, often running rapidly for considerable distances; when resting, perches low in trees or on buildings.

Range: Colombia to northern Argentina and Uruguay.

BRIGHT-RUMPED ATTILA
Attila spadiceus   Plate 26

Description: 7¾. Bill heavy and prominently *hooked*, pinkish basally; *rather bull-headed.* Variable in color. Olive to brownish olive above (rarely grayish) with *yellow rump* (sometimes buffy yellow or even bright tawny); wings and tail brownish edged with buff; olive yellow below, fading to whitish on lower belly, *streaked with dusky on throat and breast.*

Similar species. When the yellow rump cannot be seen, this can be a confusing bird. Its very upright posture suggests various large flycatchers but the obviously hooked bill marks it as an attila. Panama mourners and the piha are much more uniform brown and have very different bills.

Status and distribution: Fairly common (though heard much more often than seen) in forest, second-growth woodland, and borders in lowlands and foothills on both slopes including the western side of the Azuero Peninsula; absent from drier more open lowlands on Pacific slope between eastern side of Azuero Peninsula to western Panama province; ranges up in highlands of western Chiriquí to over 1800 m (6000 ft), and to at least 1500 m (5000 ft) in eastern Darién; found also on Coiba Island, where uncommon.

Habits: Usually found singly at low and middle levels, both inside forest and at borders. Often lifts its tail slowly and about-faces abruptly. The call is a series of loud and emphatic whistles, down-sliding at the end, *wheédip, wheédip, wheédip, wheédip, wheedip, wheeeeer,* or *whit, whit, weeda, weeda, weedoo;* very distinctive but also quite ventriloquial.

Range: Western and southern Mexico to northern Bolivia and southeastern Brazil.

SPECKLED MOURNER
Laniocera rufescens   Plate 26

Description: 8. *Mostly rufous brown*, feathers of breast often scaled with dusky (more pronounced in immatures, which may also show a few black spots); *wing-coverts dusky,* feathers with *large rufous tips.* Pectoral tuft pale yellow in male (but often hidden behind wing), usually lacking in female and immature (rarely orange-ochraceous?).

Similar species: Not always easy to identify. Rufous Mourner is more uniformly rufous brown, lacks contrasting spots on wing, vague barring on breast, and yellow pectoral tufts. See also larger Rufous Piha and smaller Cinnamon Becard.

Status and distribution: Rare to locally uncommon in humid forest and second-growth woodland in lowlands on entire Caribbean slope (only record from Bocas del Toro being several seen and one collected along lower Río Changuinola in late April 1980, with specimen to GML; Ridgely); on Pacific slope recorded from Canal area (where decidedly rare) east through Darién (where recorded up to 1350 m: 4500 ft on slopes of Cerro Tacarcuna).

Habits: Usually seen singly, perching quietly in trees at middle levels inside forest, sometimes at borders. Seems to favor vicinity of swampy places or streams. Its song is a ringing, clear *tlee-yeeí; tlee-yeeí; tlee-yeeí . . .* (or *tee-wheeít*), the couplets repeated up to 12–15 times, then a pause before another sequence; given periodically throughout the day, the Speckled Mourner's call has an odd, high-pitched and ventriloquial quality.

Range: Southeastern Mexico to northwestern Ecuador.

Note: Formerly placed in the Cotingidae, the genus *Laniocera* was transferred to the Tyrannidae in the 1983 AOU Check-list. Recent anatomical evidence is beginning to indicate that the genus is not properly placed in the Tyranninae subfamily, but as its precise relationships remain uncertain, it is left where the 1983 AOU Check-list suggested.

RUFOUS MOURNER
Rhytipterna holerythra   Plate 26

Description: 8. *Uniform plain rufous brown,* paler and more tawny below.

Similar species: *Easily* confused, especially with Rufous Piha. Mourner is somewhat smaller and slimmer with less heavy bill that seems not to show pink, its throat and breast are more uniform cinnamon-rufous (not paler on throat), and its crown and wing-coverts are slightly duller than remaining upperparts (not uniform or slightly brighter). Voice is often the most helpful distinction. Speckled Mourner shows rufous spotting on dusky wing-coverts. See also Cinnamon Becard, and female One-colored Becard.

Status and distribution: Uncommon and rather local in humid forest and second-growth woodland in lowlands and foothills on entire Caribbean slope (perhaps most numerous in Bocas del Toro); on Pacific slope recorded from lowlands and foothills of Chiriquí (no recent reports from lowlands, where doubtless now much reduced or even extirpated by deforestation), and locally in foothills from Veraguas eastward, in lowlands in eastern Panama province (middle and upper Bayano River valley) and Darién; not recorded from Azuero Peninsula.

Habits: Inconspicuous, usually encountered singly, perched on a branch inside forest (less often at edge) at most any height; sometimes accompanies mixed flocks, but more often alone. Frequently hunches far forward on its perch, raising its tail. Heard more often than seen, its usual call is a clear mournful whistle *wheeeip, wheeeer* (sometimes likened to a minor-keyed "wolf-whistle") or *wheee-per, wheeúr*. In southwestern Costa Rica and Chiriquí another call is also given, a loud steady series of clear ringing notes, *wheé-oo, wheé-oo . . . weé-oo, weé-oo* or *treeeo, treee, treeé, treeéo, treeé . . .* (B. Whitney; Ridgely). No nest of this species has ever been found, but given its apparently close relationship to the *Myiarchus* flycatchers (W. E. Lanyon), one suspects that it may nest in holes, perhaps dug into banks.

Range: Southeastern Mexico to northwestern Ecuador.

SIRYSTES
Sirystes sibilator   Plate 23

Description: 7–7½. A distinctive white, gray, and black flycatcher of the forest canopy. *Cap black, shading to slaty gray on sides of head*; back light gray, *rump white*; wings black with white edging and two broad, white wing-bars; *rather long, square-tipped tail black tipped whitish*; pale gray below, becoming whitish on belly.

Similar species: Shaped, but not colored, like a *Myianchus* flycatcher. Vaguely recalls a tityra but much more slender and not as white; also somewhat resembles an imma-

ture Fork-tailed Flycatcher lacking lengthened central tail feathers.

Status and distribution: Uncommon in canopy and borders of humid forest in lowlands on Caribbean slope from Canal area eastward, and on Pacific slope in eastern Panama province (Bayano River valley) and Darién (where it ranges up into the foothills to at least 1050 m: 3500 ft); early specimens from "Veragua" may have been mislabeled (there is one labeled even as having been taken in the Pacific lowlands at Soná), and there are no recent records from anywhere west of the Canal area. In Canal area most numerous along Pipeline Road.

Habits: Often in pairs, sometimes accompanying mixed foraging flocks high in forest trees. In shape and actions rather like a *Myiarchus* flycatcher. Frequently utters a rather loud *chup-chup-chup . . .* or *prip-prip-prip . . .*

Range: Panama to northern Bolivia, Paraguay, northeastern Argentina, and southeastern Brazil.

DUSKY-CAPPED FLYCATCHER
Myiarchus tuberculifer   Plate 24

Description: 6. Mostly grayish olive above with *contrasting blackish cap*; throat and chest pale gray, lower underparts light yellow. Birds from western Panama east to Veraguas (*bangsi*) have narrow cinnamon edging on wings and tail. Immatures throughout show this cinnamon edging, and have dusky cap.

Similar species: The sooty black cap sets it apart from other similar flycatchers; noticeably smaller than other Panama *Myiarchus*.

Status and distribution: Fairly common to common in canopy and borders of humid forest, second-growth woodland, and adjacent clearings in lowlands and foothills on both slopes, ranging up to about 1800 m (6000 ft) in highlands of western Chiriquí; apparently absent from drier Pacific lowlands from eastern side of Azuero Peninsula to western Panama province; most numerous in foothills, and seems rather scarce in Caribbean slope lowlands of western Panama. In Canal area more numerous on Caribbean side.

Habits: Characteristic and often heard is a whistled, long-drawn, plaintive *whee-eew*, often slightly burred or throaty in quality; also gives a thin *pheeeee* or *seeeee* (suggestive of Rusty-margined Flycatcher) and an unmusical *wheerrrrp*.

Range: Extreme southwestern United States to northwestern Argentina, Paraguay, and southern Brazil.

PANAMA FLYCATCHER
Myiarchus panamensis   Plates 23, 24

Description: 7½. Very like Great Crested Flycatcher and often confused with it, but *adults lack rufous in wings and tail.* Grayish olive above, the head usually *not* giving a crested appearance, wings with pale grayish wing-bars; throat and chest pale gray, lower underparts light yellow. Immature shows some narrow rufous edging on wings and tail.

Similar species: Immature Panama Flycatcher is very like Great Crested but underside of tail is dusky (not rufous). See also Dusky-capped Flycatcher. Northern Scrub-Flycatcher resembles adult of this species in pattern but it is markedly smaller with a shorter bill. Tropical Kingbird lacks gray on underparts and has slightly forked tail.

Status and distribution: Fairly common in semiopen and scrubby areas, clearings, light woodland, and coastal growth and mangroves in lowlands and foothills (to about 1350 m: 4500 ft) on entire Pacific slope (local and uncommon in Darién); on Caribbean slope found in western Bocas del Toro (Almirante, Cocoplum) and from northern Coclé east through San Blas; found also on the Pearl Islands, Coiba Island, Taboga Island, and many other smaller islands off the Pacific coast.

Habits: Similar to Great Crested Flycatcher, but much more a bird of semiopen situations. Its vocalizations are softer and less arresting than the Great Crested's: the dawn song is a fast whistled *tseeédew* or *wheédee-dew*; another call is a semi-whistled twittering *tee, deedeedeedeedeedee* with variations; also has a soft clear whistled *wheee* and a *prrt*.

Range: Southwestern Costa Rica to northern Venezuela.

GREAT CRESTED FLYCATCHER
Myiarchus crinitus   Plate 23

Description: 8. Plain olive above, head browner and often appearing distinctly crested; wings with indistinct whitish wing-bars, and with *rufous edging on primaries; tail with much rufous edging (whole underside looks rufous)*; throat and chest gray, lower underparts light yellow.

Similar species: See Panama Flycatcher.

Status and distribution: Fairly common to common winter resident in canopy and borders of forest and second-growth woodland in lowlands throughout, occurring in smaller numbers up into lower foothills to about 1050 m (3500 ft) (recorded mostly October–April, with a few records from as early as 20 September and as late as May 25); recorded also (perhaps mostly as a transient) on the Pearl Islands (Saboga), and on Coiba and Cébaco Islands.

Habits: Usually solitary. Often eats small fruit in Panama. Its most distinctive call, a whistled *wheeeep*, is often heard; also gives a throaty rolling *prrrrreet* (R. T. Peterson).

Range: Breeds in eastern North America; winters in southern Florida and from Texas to Colombia and northern Venezuela.

LESSER KISKADEE
Philohydor lictor   Plate 23

Description: 6½. *Bill long and slender.* Like Great Kiskadee in plumage except for somewhat less rich rufous on wings and less rufous in tail.

Similar species: Best distinguished from Great Kiskadee by its smaller size and different calls (see below). Also resembles the somewhat smaller Rusty-margined Flycatcher but has long slender (not stubby) bill.

Status and distribution: Fairly common in shrubby growth and low trees near water (especially in marshy areas and along sluggish rivers) in lowlands on both slopes from around Canal area eastward through San Blas and Darién. Rather scarce on Pacific side of Canal area, though widespread in appropriate habitat on Caribbean side; particularly numerous in what remains of the Tocumen marsh.

Habits: Usually in pairs, often in the same areas as the Rusty-margined Flycatcher; rather retiring. Its usual calls are vigorous and rather nasal, often a buzzy *dzay, drwey* or *dzai-dey-dzéy-daha;* sometimes a *keekzi-deeée* suggesting Great Kiskadee.

Range: Panama to northern Bolivia and southern Brazil.

Note: W. Lanyon (*Am. Mus. Novitates 2797*: 1–28, 1984) is followed in separating this species generically from *Pitangus*; it differs very markedly in its syrinx and its cup-shaped nest.

GREAT KISKADEE
Pitangus sulphuratus   Plate 23

Description: 8½–8¾. A *large* flycatcher, almost the size of a Boat-bill, and like that species with a *heavy* (but not as broad) *bill. Brown above with much rufous on wings and tail;* crown black with usually concealed yellow-orange crown patch, broad white superciliary that just meets at nape, and black ear-coverts; throat white, remaining underparts yellow.
Similar species: Best told from Boat-billed Flycatcher by its brown (not olive) upperparts with prominent rufous in wings and tail. Lesser Kiskadee is considerably smaller with more slender bill.
Status and distribution: Fairly common to common but still rather local around habitations and in clearings and shrubby areas, especially near water, in lowlands on Caribbean slope in western and central Bocas del Toro (east to Cocoplum), and in Canal area and eastern Colon province (east to Portobelo); on Pacific slope known mainly from Canal area and adjacent Panama province (in latter west at least to Playa Coronado, and east at least to Tocumen), with 1982 reports also from western Chiriquí in the Puerto Armuelles/ Burica Peninsula area (Ridgely; also a February 1973 sighting from Volcán Lakes in lower highlands by C. Leahy and A. Morgan), and from Chitré, Herrera (F. Delgado). Great Kiskadees have been increasing and steadily expanding their Panama range during the last few decades, and there is no reason to think that they will not continue to do so; an aggressive bird and frequent commensal of man, the puzzle is why it was until recently so scarce and local in Panama.
Habits: An adaptable bird that will eat almost anything. Has a variety of loud characteristic calls, some of them buzzy. One of the most distinctive is reflected in its common name, *kisk-a-deé*; others include a *geep* and a *cheekaw* (the last resembling a call of the Squirrel Cuckoo).
Range: Southern Texas and Mexico to central Argentina.

BOAT-BILLED FLYCATCHER
Megarhynchus pitangua   Plate 23

Description: 9–9¼. A *large* flycatcher with a *heavy, broad bill. Olive above* with black crown and usually concealed orange-yellow crown patch, white superciliary, and black ear-coverts; throat white, remaining underparts yellow. Immature has some rufous edging on wings.
Similar species: Much like a Great Kiskadee in size and pattern, but olive (not more or less rufous) above, with wider bill. Social Flycatcher is also olive above but is much smaller with shorter and narrower bill and shows indistinct wing-bars.
Status and distribution: Fairly common to common in clearings, second-growth woodland, and forest borders in lowlands on both slopes, with smaller numbers up into the foothills and to about 1800 m (6000 ft) in highlands of western Chiriquí; recorded also from Cébaco Island.
Habits: Very noisy, with a variety of harsh grating vocalizations, typical being a rattling *keerrrrrr-eék*; also has shorter calls such as a *kirr-wick* and *krrrrreek*. Usually found singly or in pairs, often high in trees; regularly captures quite large insects, often repeatedly whacking them on a branch like a puffbird. Generally a very conspicuous bird, especially from its vocalizations. Boat-bills build cup nests, unlike most flycatchers with its color pattern (except for the Lesser Kiskadee).
Range: Mexico to Bolivia, Paraguay, northeastern Argentina, and southeastern Brazil.

RUSTY-MARGINED FLYCATCHER
Myiozetetes cayanensis   Plate 23

Description: 6–6¼. *Olive brown above* with *rusty edging on flight feathers*; crown blackish or sooty with usually concealed orange crown patch, prominent white superciliary, *blackish ear-coverts*; white throat, remaining underparts yellow. Immature lacks crown patch, has more rusty edging on wing and rusty edging on tail.
Similar species: Often difficult to distinguish from Social Flycatcher (*immature Socials show some rusty on wings and tail*). Best told by its brown (not olive) tone above, lack of indistinct wing-bars, blacker crown and ear-coverts, and (usually most useful of all) its different calls (see below). Lesser Kiskadee is somewhat larger, brighter rufous brown above, has distinctly longer and slenderer bill, and also has different calls.
Status and distribution: Fairly common to common in shrubby areas and clearings, almost always near water, in lowlands on both slopes from western Colon and western Panama provinces east through San Blas and Darién (especially numerous in semi-open, cleared parts of the latter, where Social Flycatcher is absent); apparently an

isolated population is found in lowlands of eastern Chiriquí and southern Veraguas, where it seems distinctly uncommon. In Canal area more numerous and widespread on Caribbean side, though it is fairly common around Tocumen.

Habits: Generally not as familiar as the abundant Social Flycatcher, and usually not around houses. Much less vocal than the Social, its most characteristic and frequent call being a high thin whining long-drawn *feeee* or *wheeeeeee*, lasting 2–3 seconds, often repeated several times. Some other calls are more like those of Social, a *cheepcheeree-chew* and a rapid, repeated *keéwit*.

Range: Western Panama to northern Bolivia and southern Brazil.

SOCIAL FLYCATCHER
Myiozetetes similis   Plate 23

Description: 6–6½. *Olive above* with *indistinct, pale wing-bars*; crown brownish gray with usually concealed vermilion (sometimes orange-red) crown patch, prominent white superciliary, and *dark brownish gray ear-coverts*; throat white, remaining underparts yellow. Immature lacks crown patch, has grayish brown upperparts, and shows pale rusty edging on wings and tail.

Similar species: Rather resembles the less numerous White-ringed and Rusty-margined Flycatchers; see both species for distinctions. See also Gray-capped Flycatcher.

Status and distribution: Abundant around houses, in shrubby areas and clearings, and in lighter woodland and forest borders in lowlands and foothills on both slopes east to eastern Colon province (Río Guanche) and eastern Panama province (Bayano River); not recorded from Darién and only sightings from San Blas (at Puerto Obaldía on June 16–18, 1965; D. Sheets), which require confirmation; also ranges well up into western highlands; not recorded from offshore islands.

Habits: This species, the Yellow-bellied Elaenia, and the Tropical Kingbird are the three most widespread and numerous flycatchers in the open and semiopen parts of Panama. Often forages on lawns, though usually at middle heights and occasionally in forest canopy. At times it is distinctly "social", usually where there is a good supply of food. Eats much fruit as well as the more standard flycatcher fare of insects. The nest is a rather untidy large, domed ball with the entrance on one side near the top, often in a thorn tree or near a bee or wasp nest, occa-sionally using the nest of another bird as a foundation. A very noisy bird, with a variety of loud and harsh calls, most commonly *kree-yoo*; also *tsiyoo* and *kree-kree-kree-kree*. This species and the many other fairly large fly-catchers with mostly yellow underparts are called "pechi-amarillo" by Panamanians.

Range: Northern Mexico to Boliva, Paraguay, northeastern Argentina, and southeastern Brazil.

GRAY-CAPPED FLYCATCHER
Myiozetetes granadensis   Plate 23

Description: 6¼. Recalls Social Flycatcher. Mostly olive above and yellow below (throat whitish), but with different pattern on head; instead of Social's broad white superciliary, has *gray crown with white restricted to forehead and short, narrow superciliary only extending slightly behind eye*; ear-coverts blackish; only adult males have usually concealed orange-yellow crown patch (greatly reduced when present in females). Immature has more olive crown and pale tawny edging on wings and tail.

Similar species: Tropical Kingbird is larger with no white on head, and has pale gray throat and chest.

Status and distribution: Locally fairly common to common in shrubby areas and clearings, usually near water, in lowlands on entire Caribbean slope (though seems unac-countably scarce in Canal area); on Pacific slope recorded in lowlands and foothills of western Chiriquí (in small numbers regu-larly up to just over 1200 m: 4000 ft), less commonly and more locally in lowlands from eastern Chiriquí east to southern Coclé, and in lowlands and lower foothills (to about 600 m: 2000 ft) in eastern Panama province (Bayano River valley) and Darién (where quite numerous). In Canal area most numerous in eastern Colon province.

Habits: Often occurs with Social Flycatcher, which it resembles in actions. Gray-cap's call somewhat suggest those of Social but are sharper and usually shorter, as *keep, geer-geer* (much like Great Kiskadee) or *kip-kee-kew*, with variations.

Range: Honduras to northern Bolivia and western Brazil.

WHITE-RINGED FLYCATCHER
Conopias albovittata   Plate 23

Description: 6. Olive above; crown sooty brown with usually concealed yellow crown patch, bordered below by *broad white supercil-iary that extends around nape*, ear-coverts black-ish; throat white, remaining underparts yellow.

Similar species: Strongly resembles Social Flycatcher but has distinctly longer bill, lacks even indistinct wing-bars, and always shows broader white eye-stripe meeting at back of head. Both kiskadees also have white eye-stripes meeting at back of head, but they have longer and more pointed bills, are markedly rufescent above, and usually occur in a different habitat.

Status and distribution: Uncommon to fairly common in canopy and borders of humid forest in lowlands and foothills on Caribbean slope from around Canal area east through San Blas, and on Pacific slope in eastern Panama province (Cerro Azul/Jefe, upper Bayano River valley) and Darién (where it ranges regularly up to about 1350 m: 4500 ft on Cerro Pirre); as yet not found in Caribbean slope lowlands west of Canal area, though as it is known from Caribbean slope of Costa Rica it may well occur there. In Canal area most numerous along Pipeline Road, though there as elsewhere much more likely to be found once its characteristic vocalization is learned; also relatively numerous in Darién.

Habits: Usually found in pairs high in forest trees. The common call is a whirring trill *wherr-r-r*, with several variations. Nests in holes or crevices in trees.

Range: Southern Honduras to northwestern Ecuador.

Note: Placed in the genus *Coryphotriccus* in the 1983 AOU Check-list, but W. Lanyon (*Am. Mus. Novitates 2797*: 1–28, 1984) has since shown the two genera to be very similar anatomically, and suggested their merger. Formerly the species occurring in Panama was often (though incorrectly, due to name priority) called *C. parva*. Note that we here consider the birds found east of the Andes in South America as a separate species, *C. parva* (Yellow-throated Flycatcher).

GOLDEN-BELLIED FLYCATCHER
Myiodynastes hemichrysus   Plate 23

Description: 7¾–8. Found only in western highlands. Looks rather like a cross between Streaked and Boat-billed Flycatchers. Bill somewhat broader than in Streaked. *Olive brown above* with blackish crown and usually concealed yellow crown patch; white supercil-iary, blackish ear-coverts, white submalar stripe, and *prominent dusky moustache stripe*; wings edged inconspicuously with rufous; throat

white, *remaining underparts yellow* (immature has buffy tinge) with indistinct light olive streaking on sides of breast.

Similar species: Boat-billed Flycatcher is larger, with broader bill, lacks the mous-tachial stripe and streaking below. Golden-crowned Flycatcher is found only in Darién highlands.

Status and distribution: Uncommon to locally fairly common in forest borders and adjacent clearings, often along streams, in foothills and highlands of Chiriquí, Bocas del Toro, and Veraguas; in western Chiriquí recorded mostly 1200–1800 m (4000–6000 ft), but elsewhere usually lower, more 750–1500 m (2500–5000 ft). Small numbers can usually be found in the valley of the Río Chiriquí Viejo around Nueva Suiza and Bambito in western Chiriquí, but it is more numerous further east in the Fortuna region.

Habits: Much like Streaked Flycatcher, though never seems as numerous. Usually in pairs, often noisy and conspicuous. Its wheezy and emphatic calls are more like Sulphur-bellied Flycatcher in quality (but are less nasal), and include a *skeé-eey* or *skweey*, and a more involved *skeé-kit, skeé-lit, skeé-kit, chwit-chwit-ti-ti-tit-twit* (B. Whit-ney).

Range: Costa Rica and western Panama.

GOLDEN-CROWNED FLYCATCHER
Myiodynastes chrysocephalus   Plate 40

Description: 8. Found only in eastern Darién highlands. Resembles Golden-bellied Fly-catcher of western highlands but has *dis-tinctly buff throat and chest* and is more *definitely streaked and mottled with olive on breast*.

Similar species: See Golden-bellied Fly-catcher. Streaked and Sulphur-bellied Flycatchers are brown and heavily streaked above. Boat-billed Flycatcher is larger with broader bill, lacks the moustache stripe, buff throat and chest, and streaking below.

Status and distribution: Uncommon in forest borders in upper foothills and lower highlands of eastern Darién (Cerro Tacarcuna, Cerro Pirre); recorded above 1200 m (4000 ft).

Habits: Similar to Golden-bellied Fly-catcher, but in its limited Panama range seems not so tied to the vicinity of streams, and essentially restricted to the higher ridge tops. Golden-crowned is also a noisy bird with several calls, the most frequent being a loud forceful *kyíss-yu*, often repeated numerous times.

Range: Eastern Panama to northern Venezuela and northern Bolivia.

STREAKED FLYCATCHER
Myiodynastes maculatus   Plate 23

Description: 8. Bill long and heavy, with base of lower mandible pinkish. *Mostly brown above streaked with dusky*, and with *mostly rufous rump and tail*; usually concealed yellow crown patch, whitish superciliary, broad blackish area across face and ear-coverts bordered below by white lower cheeks and then a prominent dusky malar streak; wings dusky with narrow *rufous or buff edging on wing-coverts*; *whitish or dingy yellowish below, broadly streaked with dusky especially on breast, sides, and under tail-coverts.* Insolens (breeding in northern Middle America south at least to Honduras, wintering south to Panama and northern South America) has more olivaceous crown (not so rufescent), more yellowish superciliary, and unstreaked under tail-coverts.
Similar species: See very similar Sulphur-bellied Flycatcher. Piratic Flycatcher is smaller with shorter bill, has no rufous in tail, etc.
Status and distribution: Common in open second-growth woodland, forest borders, and clearings with scattered tall trees in lowlands and foothills on both slopes, but more numerous in humid regions; ranges up into highlands (to about 1650 m: 5500 ft) in western Chiriquí; found also on Pearl Islands and on Coiba and Cébaco Islands. Northern migratory race *insolens* recorded only February–April, but presumably present much earlier as well (probably arriving in September–October period).
Habits: Noisy and conspicuous birds, often around habitations. Its calls are harsh and nasal, *chup* and *eéchup* being frequent, but also has a squeaky and unexpectedly musical dawn song (also given at dusk), a loud *wheeé-cheederee-wheé* repeated over and over, often well before first light. Nests in natural cavities, under eaves of buildings, on ledges, etc.
Range: Eastern Mexico to Bolivia, northern Argentina, and southeastern Brazil; northernmost (*insolens*) and southernmost (*solitarius*) breeders withdraw to the tropics when not nesting.

SULPHUR-BELLIED FLYCATCHER
Myiodynastes luteiventris   Plate 23

Description: 8. Closely resembles much more numerous Streaked Flycatcher. Differs in having more brownish gray or olive crown (not tawny brown), *whitish edging on wing-coverts* (not rufous or buff), dusky moustachial streak *joining across chin* (with effect of a "strap"; this sometimes hard to clearly discern in the field, but is diagnostic as in all Streakeds this area is whitish), and often with *lower underparts distinctly clear sulphur yellow* (not whitish or dull pale yellowish; do note, however, that some Sulphur-bellies, especially immatures, may be quite whitish on belly), and always with *unstreaked under tail-coverts* (in race of Streaked resident in Panama this is boldly streaked, but note that in its migrant *insolens* race it is unmarked, as in Sulphur-bellied).
Similar species: A close look is usually required in order to distinguish the Sulphur-bellied and Streaked Flycatchers, and the rather different migrant race of the latter only complicates affairs. Note that certain other ascribed differences between the two (such as bill colors, and color of superciliary) have been shown, after comparison of photographs and study skins, not to be reliable.
Status and distribution: Uncommon transient in wooded or forested areas throughout (mostly September–October, once to November 20; and March–April, once to May 1); no evidence of over-wintering birds. In Costa Rica breeds both in humid-forested montane areas (such as Monteverde), and in gallery woodland in Guanacaste.
Habits: Similar to Streaked Flycatcher. Sulphur-bellied's calls are squeaky or angry-sounding, in quality more like the Golden-bellied than the Streaked, e.g. a *squeez-ya*, often repeated or with several *kip* notes in succession.
Range: Breeds from southeastern Arizona and Mexico to Costa Rica; winters in Ecuador, Peru, and Bolivia.

PIRATIC FLYCATCHER
Legatus leucophaius   Plate 23

Description: 6–6¼. Bill rather short. Olive brown above with usually concealed yellow crown patch, *whitish superciliary*, dusky ear-coverts, a whitish submalar streak, and a dusky moustachial stripe; throat white, remaining underparts pale yellow, brightest on belly, with *dusky streaking on breast*.
Similar species: In pattern and colors much like Streaked and Sulphur-bellied Flycatchers, but much smaller with stubbier bill and *no rufous in tail*.

Status and distribution: A common breeding bird in clearings and forest and woodland borders in lowlands on both slopes, ranging up to about 1500 m (5000 ft) in Chiriquí highlands; apparently migrates to South America during the late rainy season: no Panama records from November or December and very few for October.

Habits: Appropriates domed or closed nests of various species (oropendolas, caciques, becards, some other flycatchers, etc.) for its own use, driving away the rightful owners by its constant pestering; virtually every oropendola or cacique colony has a pair of these birds. The call consists of a whining *weé-yee*, often followed, after a pause, by a rising *pirrirriree*, and is endlessly repeated from late January through September, even in the heat of the day. It usually calls while sitting on a bare twig at the top of a leafy tree, where often hard to see from below. Adults eat exclusively fruit throughout the year (though fledglings are fed some insects); the species apparently leaves Panama during the height of the rainy season (October–December) because of the scarcity of available fruit at that season, and returns first (in January) to the Pacific side of the Canal area because fruit ripens earlier there than it does on the wetter Caribbean slope, where Piratics do not settle in until February–March (E. S. Morton).

Range: Eastern Mexico to northern Argentina and southeastern Brazil; Middle American birds evidently migrate to South America during nonbreeding season.

TROPICAL KINGBIRD
Tyrannus melancholicus Plate 23

Description: 9–9½. Head gray with dusky ear-coverts and usually concealed reddish orange crown patch; *otherwise grayish olive above* with dull brown wings and *slightly forked tail*; throat whitish, *remaining underparts yellow*, chest tinged with olive.

Similar species: Both other kingbirds known from Panama have white underparts. Great Crested and Panama Flycatchers both have wing-bars and distinctly gray throats and breasts. See also the casual Western Kingbird.

Status and distribution: An abundant and widespread bird, most common in open and semiopen country, but also in residential areas, roadsides, and clearings in generally forested areas; occurs virtually wherever there is adequate habitat, even ranging well into highlands (to about 1860 m: 6200 ft) in

clearings; occurs on all large and most small islands off both coasts.

Habits: One of the most conspicuous Panama birds, often sitting on wires and other exposed perches. Like the other kingbirds, a typical sallying flycatcher, sometimes following an insect in almost swallow-like pursuit. Its dawn song, a couple of short *pip* notes followed by a rising twitter, *piririree*, is often the first bird sound heard in the morning, frequently being given well before first light. Also gives a *feet-feet-feet*.

Range: Southern Arizona and Mexico to central Argentina; southern breeders migrate north at least to Amazonia during austral winter, and northernmost breeders also withdraw southward during northern winter.

Note: Does not include Couch's Kingbird (*T. couchii*) of southern Texas, eastern Mexico, and Belize, regarded as a full species in the 1983 AOU Check-list. Couch's is not known to be migratory.

[WESTERN KINGBIRD]
Tyrannus verticalis

Description: 8¾. One recent sighting. Closely resembles omnipresent Tropical Kingbird. Differs in its *shorter bill*, less apparent (or completely absent) dusky patch on ear-coverts, *paler and grayer throat and chest*, and black (not dusky brown) tail with *distinct white outer web of outer pair of feathers* (normally lacking in Tropical, but note that some birds in fresh plumage may appear to have a pale outer web, and that some worn Westerns may lack them); tail also is *essentially square*, lacking the slight fork usually apparent in Tropicals.

Status and distribution: Only report is of a single bird carefully studied along Chiva Chiva Road, Pacific side of Canal area, on January 21, 1988 (D. Wolf *et al.*). Westerns should especially be watched for in western Panama, particularly near Pacific coast.

Habits: General behavior similar to Tropical Kingbird, but usually silent on its wintering grounds. In western Costa Rica and (especially) western Nicaragua, where it is much more numerous, it regularly associates with over-wintering flocks of Scissor-tailed Flycatchers.

Range: Breeds in western North America; winters mainly from southern Mexico to western Costa Rica, small numbers north to extreme southern United States, and casually as far south as Panama.

EASTERN KINGBIRD
Tyrannus tyrannus   Plate 23

Description: 8–9. *Blackish above* with usually concealed orange-red crown patch; white below; rather rounded *tail tipped conspicuously with white.* Immature is duller above with less white in tail.
Similar species: Gray Kingbird is gray (not blackish) above and has forked tail without any white. Tropical Kingbird shows much yellow on underparts.
Status and distribution: Common transient in lowlands (to about 750 m: 2500 ft) on entire Caribbean slope (sometimes abundant on northward migration) and common transient on Pacific slope from Canal area eastward, apparently less numerous westward with only a few reports from Veraguas and Chiriquí (where perhaps irregular); a few may winter on Pacific slope; recorded also from Pearl Islands (especially on northward migration) and Taboga and Taboguilla Islands; recorded in Panama mostly early September–late November and late March–mid-May.
Habits: Sometimes occurs in large flocks of many hundreds, occasionally even more, especially on spring migration. On its breeding grounds found in open country, but in Panama more often in border growth. While migrating, often occurs in flocks in the forest canopy, feeding on fruit; often flies in compact groups, like waxwings. Usually silent in Panama.
Range: Breeds chiefly east of the Rockies in North America; winters mainly in western Amazon basin of South America, possibly northward to Costa Rica.

GRAY KINGBIRD
Tyrannus dominicensis   Plate 23

Description: 9–9½. Thick bill and heavy head and body give characteristic *bull-headed effect. Gray above* with dusky ear-coverts and usually concealed orange crown patch; wings and tail more brownish, *tail slightly forked*; white below with gray wash on chest.
Similar species: Eastern Kingbird is smaller and slenderer, blacker above, with tail tipped white. Tropical Kingbird also has forked tail, but shows much yellow below, is more olive above, and is smaller with less heavy bill.
Status and distribution: Uncommon to locally fairly common winter resident along both coasts and in residential and semiopen residential areas in lowlands on both slopes (late August–late April); recorded mostly

from central Panama, but there are recent reports from as far west as near Santiago, Veraguas (though none as yet from Chiriquí), and from as far east as Darién (several sightings at El Real), as well as several specimens from San Blas. Breeding in Panama is not inconceivable, and should be watched for, having only recently been documented for Venezuela and also suspected in northern Colombia; displaying "pairs" have been seen in late April in parks along the waterfront in Panama City.
Habits: Usually seen perched on fences or telephone wires, often with the much more numerous Tropical Kingbird. The call is a rolling throaty *pe-cheer-ry* (R. T. Peterson).
Range: Breeds in coastal southeastern United States, West Indies, and Venezuela (on mainland as well as on offshore islands), perhaps also in northern Colombia; winters in southern West Indies, Panama, and northern South America (migrants have also been noted a few times in recent years along Caribbean cost of Costa Rica, and recorded casually in Nicaragua).

SCISSOR-TAILED FLYCATCHER
Tyrannus forficatus   Plate 46

Description: ♂ 12–14; ♀ 10–11½. A beautiful, *silvery gray* bird with a *very long and deeply forked tail* (longer in male). Pale gray above, wings black, edged with whitish and with orange-red to salmon patch under wing; white below, becoming *pale salmon on belly.* Immatures have red replaced with creamy buff; they and molting adults lack the very long outer tail feathers.
Similar species: The far more numerous Fork-tailed Flycatcher lacks the red or salmon, has a distinct black cap, and is darker gray above.
Status and distribution: An apparently irregular winter visitor (November–March) to open country in lowlands on Pacific slope, most numerous in western Panama (in some years fairly common in Herrera and southern Coclé) but with only a few reports from Canal area, the farthest east being one seen at Tocumen on January 23, 1980 (D. Finch *et al.*); only record from Caribbean slope is of several seen around Almirante, Bocas del Toro, in October 1962, with one collected on October 31 (R. Hinds). More numerous as a winterer from Costa Rica northward.
Habits: In Panama usually noted as straggling individuals or in small groups, perching low on fences or bushes; larger numbers may gather at roosts. Incomparably graceful in the

air as they pursue insects, in Panama Scissor-tails are also known to eat some fruit.

Range: Breeds in south-central United States; winters from southern Mexico (a few also in southern Florida) to central Panama.

Note: Formerly placed in the genus *Muscivora*.

FORK-TAILED FLYCATCHER
Tyrannus savana   Plate 23

Description: ♂ 13–16; ♀ 10½–12½. *Very long deeply forked tail* (longer in male). *Head and nape black* with usually concealed yellow crown patch; back pale gray, wings darker gray, tail black; *white below*. Immatures (with more brownish caps) and molting adults lack the very long outer tail feathers.

Similar species: See Scissor-tailed Flycatcher.

Status and distribution: Common in low-lands on Pacific slope (numbers fluctuating seasonally and locally) in savannas and dry scrubby areas, extensive lawns, and residential areas from Chiriquí (where ranges up to about 1350 m: 4500 ft) to eastern Panama province (lower Bayano river around El Llano); not recorded from Darién. On Caribbean slope reported only from Canal area, where usually uncommon and probably not breeding; one also seen at Puerto Obaldía, San Blas in mid-June 1965 (D. Sheets). Also once reported (January) from Coiba Island (Wetmore), and once (July) from Taboga Island (Eisenmann). Birds nesting on Pacific slope (*monachus*) gather in post-breeding flocks, and apparently engage in some movement away from nesting areas, but whether in true migration uncertain. Birds of the same race which breed farther north in Middle America probably occur in Panama as migrants. On Caribbean coast of Canal area birds seeming to be migrants have been seen in late August and September. The highly migratory southern South America race (nominate *savana*) may also reach Panama, though as yet no specimen has been taken (perhaps the San Blas sighting was of a bird of this race); it regularly migrates to northern South America during the austral autumn and winter (March–October), and individuals rarely even reach the United States. In the hand this race can be known by its much darker gray back than *monachus*.

Habits: Often occurs in sizable flocks, at times gathering in large numbers to roost. Usually seen perched on low bushes or trees, sometimes on the ground. Most of its food,

insects, is obtained by flycatching; also eats royal palm fruit taken in flight. At its best in the air, when the long tail is spread and whipped around to aid in maneuverability.

Range: Southern Mexico to central Argentina.

Note: Formerly placed in the genus *Muscivora*, and called *M. tyrannus*.

BARRED BECARD
Pachyramphus versicolor   Plate 26

Description: 5. Known only from western Chiriquí highlands. Male *glossy black above* with gray rump; wing-coverts and inner flight feathers boldly spotted and edged with white; *lores, eye-ring, sides of head and necks, and throat greenish yellow*, fading to whitish on remaining underparts, *all with light dusky barring*. Female has *slaty crown*; otherwise olive above and on sides of head and neck, with *yellow eye-ring*; wings blackish with *wing-coverts mostly rufous-chestnut*, and rufous edging on inner flight feathers; mostly pale yellow below with faint dusky barring.

Similar species: Smaller and chunkier than any other Panama becard, and *the only one with barred underparts*.

Status and distribution: Uncommon in forest, lighter woodland, and borders in highlands of western Chiriquí, mostly above 1500 m (5000 ft).

Habits: Found singly or in pairs, usually not too high up except in tall forest. More active than other becards, frequently joining mixed foraging flocks. Males have a soft pretty song, usually given at quite long intervals, *pee-pee-pee-pee-pipipipeh*, sometimes varied to a fast rising *trrrdididee?*

Range: Costa Rica and western Panama; Colombia to northwestern Venezuela and northern Bolivia.

CINEROUS BECARD
Pachyramphus rufus   Plate 26

Description: Rare in eastern Panama. Male *pearly gray above* with *black crown and white forehead and lores*; wings blackish *narrowly edged with white*; tail slaty very narrowly (if at all) tipped with white; *white below* tinged gray on breast. Female bright cinnamon-rufous above, crown darker and more chestnut and with *whitish lores; mostly whitish below*, washed buff on chest.

Similar species: Male closest to male Black-and-white Becard but latter has wings with much more white and tail conspicuously tipped white. Male White-winged Becard is blacker above with much more white in wings, broadly white-tipped tail, lacks white on lores and forehead, and is grayer below. Female whiter below than other becards with rufous upperparts. Cinnamon Becard has gray (not whitish) lores as well as cinnamon-buff underparts; female One-colored Becard is obviously larger, etc.

Status and distribution: Apparently rare in clearings with groves of large trees, and in woodland and forest borders in lowlands on both slopes of Canal area (though, curiously, there seem to be no recent records), and locally in eastern Panama province (lower and middle Bayano River valley) and Darién (recent sightings from Matuganti and Cana; Ridgely, N. G. Smith *et al.*).

Habits: Found singly or in pairs, rarely or never with mixed flocks of other birds. The song in South America is a fast series of rising musical notes, almost trilled at end, *twee, twee, twee-twee-tweetweeteeteetititi?*

Range: Central Panama to northeastern Peru and Amazonian Brazil.

CINNAMON BECARD
Pachyramphus cinnamomeus   Plate 26

Description: 5½. Sexes alike. Chestnut-rufous above, somewhat darker on crown, with *slaty lores bordered above by pale buff supraloral; cinnamon-buff to tawny-buff below*, whitest on throat.

Similar species: Resembles females of several other less numerous becards. Female One-colored is slightly larger and more bull-headed (frequently looking bushy-crested) and lacks Cinnamon's distinct pale supraloral. Female Cinereous is smaller and has whitish (not slaty) lores, also lacks a supraloral, and is distinctly more whitish below. Rufous Mourner is considerably larger and more uniform rufous. See also female White-lined Tanager.

Status and distribution: Fairly common but somewhat local in woodland and forest borders and clearings with scattered trees (sometimes also in mangroves) in lowlands and lower foothills (to about 750 m: 2500 ft) on entire Caribbean slope; on Pacific slope found very locally from western Chiriquí (pair seen at Estero Rico on March 6, 1976; Ridgely) eastward, becoming more numerous in eastern Panama province (Cerro Azul/Jefe, Bayano River valley) and Darién (where recorded to over 1200 m: 4000 ft on Cerro Tacarcuna).

Habits: Favors trees in partly cleared areas, often near water. Its song is a loud fast series

of musical notes, typically *teedeedee-deedeedee*, sometimes shorter and slower; occasionally begins or ends with a downsliding *tew* and at times given so fast as to become a musical trill.

Range: Southeastern Mexico to northwestern Venezuela and western Ecuador.

WHITE-WINGED BECARD
Pachyramphus polychopterus   Plate 26

Description: 5¾. Male *mostly black above* with slaty rump and usually showing a gray nuchal collar; *scapulars white and wing-coverts broadly edged white*; tail black broadly tipped white; *below uniform gray*. Female brownish olive above, brownest on crown and with narrow broken white eye-ring; wings dusky with *broad cinnamon-buff edging on scapulars and wing-coverts*; tail black broadly tipped cinnamon-buff; below pale dull yellowish, tinged olive on breast and sides.

Similar species: The most widespread Panama becard. Note that male lacks white lores, shown by male Black-and-white Becard (which also lacks white on scapulars and has gray, not black, back) and by male Cinereous Becard (smaller and paler generally, with much less white in wing, etc.). Female has much duller facial pattern than female Black-and-white Becard.

Status and distribution: Fairly common in lighter woodland, forest borders, and clearings with scattered trees in lowlands on both slopes, ranging up in smaller numbers into the lower foothills and in western Chiriquí to the lower highlands (to about 1200 m: 4000 ft around Volcán); apparently less numerous in Darién and unrecorded from eastern San Blas.

Habits: Found singly or in pairs, foraging at low and middle levels. One vocalization is a rhythmic tittering with some musical quality *tut-tut-tut-tut-tut-tut*; male also has a pretty, mellow song consisting of three slow-paced introductory notes followed by three or four shorter and faster ones, slightly higher in pitch.

Range: Guatemala and Belize to Bolivia and northern Argentina.

BLACK-AND-WHITE BECARD
Pachyramphus albogriseus   Plate 26

Description: 5½. Known definitely only from western Panama. Male has *white supraloral stripe* extending narrowly over forehead and *black cap contrasting strongly with gray back*; wings black with broad white edging and tipping, forming one or two wing-bars; tail black broadly tipped white; *pale gray below, becoming whitish on throat and pure white on belly*. Female has *striking chestnut cap margined below and behind by a black line, and narrow white eye-stripe*; otherwise olive above, wings duskier with broad buff bands; tail dusky tipped buff; pale yellow below, tinged olive on chest.

Similar species: Male best distinguished from male of much more numerous White-winged's Becard by its white supraloral stripe, black cap contrasting with gray back (not uniform black above), and by lacking White-winged's white scapular stripe. Cinereous Becard male is smaller and shows much less white in wing; the two are not known to occur together. Female has by far the most striking head pattern of any female becard.

Status and distribution: Apparently rare in humid forest and forest borders in highlands of Chiriquí and Veraguas (Calovévora, Chitra); recorded mostly 900–2100 m (3000–7000 ft). There are nineteenth-century specimens labeled as having been taken in the lowlands of western Chiriquí (e.g. at Bugaba), but no recent records below the foothill level. Specimens recorded from eastern Panama province and Darién are regarded as misidentified or uncertain (Wetmore).

Habits: In Panama essentially a bird of humid montane forest. Found singly or in pairs, sometimes accompanying mixed foraging flocks of warblers, tanagers, etc. Its song is a fast series of clear whistled notes with quality similar to Cinnamon Becard, *syoo-syoo-syoo-syoo-syoo-swee?* (B. Whitney; Ridgely).

Range: Northwestern Costa Rica to western Panama; Colombia to northern Venezuela and northern Peru.

ROSE-THROATED BECARD
Pachyramphus aglaiae　　　　　　Plate 45

Description: 6½. Several recent sightings from lower highlands of western Chiriquí. Male *mostly uniform dark slaty gray above*, blackest on crown and sides of head; uniform paler gray below. Some birds may show a trace or patch of rosy pink on center of throat, but most males in southern Middle America *lack* this color. Female mostly dark rufous brown above with *contrasting sooty crown*, and sometimes showing a narrow buff nuchal collar; uniform buff below.

Similar species: Male lacking pink on throat would probably not be safely distinguished from male One-colored Becard, but seems unlikely ever to occur with that species, and is otherwise not apt to be confused. Female's contrasting dark crown is unlike that of any other female Panama becard.

Status and distribution: Apparently a casual winter visitant to lower highlands of western Chiriquí in the Volcán/Santa Clara region, with at least four recent reports: female seen above Santa Clara on January 17, 1977 (A. Greensmith *et al.*); male and female seen west of Volcán on February 18, 1981 (R. A. and J. Rowlett *et al.*); male and female seen at Volcán Lakes on December 23, 1983 (D. Engleman and M. Cooper); male seen at Volcán Lakes on February 28, 1987 (R. Behrstock *et al.*). Status in Panama remains to be clarified; all reports are from northern winter months, so could be presumed to have been migrants (and northernmost breeding birds are known to be migratory). However, as "pairs" have twice been noted, and as the males in neither case had pink on the throat (raising the possibility of their actually having been one or the other of the two southern Middle American races, *latirostris* or *hypophaeus*), resident status is not inconceivable, though made less likely by their apparent absence from adjacent Costa Rica.

Habits: In Panama seen in patches of secondary woodland or forest in partially cleared terrain. Like the One-colored Becard, the Rose-throated often raises its crown feathers into a somewhat bushy crest, resulting in a silhouette quite different from the typical (i.e. non-"*Platypsaris*" becards). What is evidently the song of nesting birds in northwestern Costa Rica is a thin, almost squeaky *tseeuw*, sometimes preceded or followed by some twittery notes; on the whole, though, this and the One-colored Becard seem considerably less vocal than are the true *Pachyramphus* becards.

Range: Extreme southwestern United States and Mexico to western Costa Rica, casually (?) to western Panama.

Note: This and the following species were formerly placed in the genus *Platypsaris*. That genus was merged into *Pachyramphus* in the 1983 AOU Check-list, a move which we follow here, though we are not entirely convinced that this was the correct course.

ONE-COLORED BECARD
Pachyramphus homochrous　　　　Plate 26

Description: 6½. Found mostly in eastern Panama. Male *mostly slaty gray above*, blackest on crown, wings, and tail; *below uniform gray.* A few males show a wash of pink on lower throat. Female *uniform rufous-tawny above,* often with some dusky around eye, and with primaries dusky edged cinnamon; uniform cinnamon-buff below, somewhat whiter on throat and center of belly. Immature males are regularly seen; juvenals first look like adult females, but gradually acquire male's gray, first on the crown and back, last on wings and tail; these latter birds are particularly striking, being mostly slaty and gray but with contrasting rufous wings and tail.

Similar species: Neither sex is really "one-colored": rather, both are basically *two-toned,* paler below. Male should be readily recognized, but female can cause problems; latter is especially like Cinnamon Becard, though that species is markedly smaller, never looks high-crowned or bushy-crested the way this species so often does, and has quite conspicuous pale buff supraloral lacking in One-colored.

Status and distribution: Uncommon to locally fairly common in canopy and borders of forest, and in adjacent clearings with scattered large trees, in lowlands on Pacific slope in eastern Panama province (Bayano River valley) and Darién; there are also a few records from farther west, including two nineteenth-century McLeannan specimens presumed to be from the Caribbean side of the Canal area, three specimens taken above Madden Lake on the Río Pequení in 1964 (Wetmore), and a male seen near Summit on December 19, 1981 (T. Fuqua). In Panama seems to be most numerous in the deciduous forest and woodland of the Bayano valley; in Darién apparently more local and not as common.

Habits: Usually in pairs, foraging at middle and upper levels (occasionally lower at edge), sometimes accompanying mixed bird flocks. Often nods head like a *Myiarchus* flycatcher and frequently raises its crown feathers giving a distinctive high-crowned or somewhat bushy-crested look. Its presumed song is a loud sharp sputtering *stet-ee-ee-teet-tsit-tsit-ts-tsít,* variable but lacking the clear melodic quality of the typical *Pachyramphus* becards.

Range: Central Panama to northwestern Venezuela and northwestern Peru.

Note: Formerly placed in the genus *Platypsaris.*

MASKED TITYRA
Tityra semifasciata   Plate 26

Description: 7¾. Male *mostly white,* tinged pearly gray above, with wings and basal half of tail black; forehead and facial area black with *bare skin around eye and most of bill red.* Female similar, *retaining red bill and bare skin around eyes* but with head brown and back tinged brownish.

Similar species: Both sexes of Black-crowned Tityra lack red on face and bill and have black crowns. See also female Snowy and Yellow-billed Cotingas.

Status and distribution: Common and widespread in wooded lowlands and foothills (in Chiriquí small numbers to over 1800 m: 6000 ft) on both slopes except in dry scrubby lowlands of southern Coclé and adjacent western Panama province; found also on Coiba and Cébaco Islands.

Habits: Can occur almost anywhere in wooded or forested areas, but prefers clearings and borders with tall dead trees for perching and nesting places. Usually in pairs, quite high up, gathering in small groups at fruiting trees. Has an odd, grunting, almost pig-like call, *querp,* sometimes doubled.

Range: Northern Mexico to Bolivia and Amazonian Brazil.

BLACK-CROWNED TITYRA
Tityra inquisitor   Plate 26

Description: 7¼. *Bill black above, bluish to leaden gray below.* Birds from western and central Panama (east to Canal area; *fraserii*) have *crown and sides of head black*; otherwise mainly pearly gray above, white tinged gray below; wings and terminal half of tail black. Female with *black crown* and buff forehead contrasting with *rufous-chestnut sides of head*; back and scapulars brown, with some white on nape; otherwise like male, but slightly grayer below. Birds from eastern Panama (*albitorques*) have males similar (back somewhat paler gray), but females quite different with back and scapulars rather dark gray (not brown).

Similar species: Both sexes of Masked Tityra have bill and bare orbital skin red, have only forehead black (male) or crown brown (female). See also female Snowy and Yellow-billed Cotingas.

Status and distribution: Uncommon to locally fairly common in canopy and borders of forest and second-growth woodland and in clearings with some large trees left standing in lowlands and foothills (to about 1200 m: 4000 ft) on both slopes, but absent from drier lowlands of southern Coclé and adjacent western Panama province. Almost everywhere outnumbered by the Masked Tityra.

Habits: Similar to the Masked Tityra, the two occasionally nesting in the same dead tree. Its call is drier and less grunty, *zick-zick-zick.*

Range: Eastern Mexico to Bolivia, eastern Paraguay, northeastern Argentina, and southern Brazil.

COTINGAS: Cotingidae (10)

The cotingas form a diverse group of neotropical birds which reaches its highest development in South America, though it is quite well represented in Panama. Several genera formerly placed in the family Cotingidae have recently been shown to be closer to other groups: the *Pachyramphus* becards are now placed with the tityras in a subfamily, the Tityrinae, in the family Tyrannidae; and the attilas as well as the *Rhytipterna* and *Laniocera* mourners are now associated with the *Myiarchus* flycatchers, in the Tyranninae subfamily (but *Lipaugus* pihas remain with the Cotingidae). While recognizing that these shifts are confusing, they are followed here, as they were in the 1983 AOU Check-list. What remain as "true" cotingas are a variable but often colorful or ornamented lot of medium-sized to large birds. All are mostly or entirely frugivorous: in fact, some species are among the very few birds known even to feed their nestlings a diet composed exclusively of fruit (which, being relatively deficient in protein as compared with insects, makes rapid growth difficult). In most species it appears that no true pair bond is formed, with females having exclusive care of the young; nests, so far as known, are flimsy shallow twig platforms.

RUFOUS PIHA
Lipaugus unirufus　　　　　　　　Plate 26

Description: 9½. Bill blackish with some pinkish buff or buffy brown on basal half of lower mandible. *Uniform cinnamon brown*, slightly brighter on crown, palest on throat.

Similar species: Not always easy to distinguish from Rufous Mourner but piha is larger and heavier looking, with rounder head (mourner looks "flat-crowned") and somewhat heavier bill; crown and wings are slightly brighter or uniform with back (not duller). These are all tricky points; often the two are most easily told by their distinctly different vocalizations.

Status and distribution: Uncommon to fairly common in humid forest and mature second-growth woodland in lowlands and lower foothills on entire Caribbean slope; on Pacific slope recorded from lowlands of western Chiriquí (where now very local due to extensive deforestation, but common in remaining untouched forests on Burica Peninsula in June 1982; Ridgely), and in lowlands and lower foothills of eastern Panama province (Cerro Azul/Jefe area, middle and upper Bayano River valley; earlier records from as far west as Panama City area) and Darién (where recorded up to about 1200 m: 4000 ft on Cerro Pirre). Widespread in small numbers in forested areas on Caribbean side of Canal area.

Habits: Active at times, but also sits quietly for long periods, often hunched forward, on a branch within forest, usually rather high. The call is a loud explosive whistled *peeeéa* or *wheéoo;* also has a *chooweeéoo*, sometimes the two combined. It is very difficult to track down, for not only does it have a ventriloquial quality but the calls are given at very long intervals, frequently in response to another abrupt noise such as a shout, hand-clap, or the slamming of a car door.

Range: Southeastern Mexico to western Ecuador.

TURQUOISE COTINGA
Cotinga ridgwayi　　　　　　　　Plate 45

Description: 7½. Found only in western Chiriquí. Very like the Blue Cotinga. Male differs in having patch on throat and upper chest more purple (less black) and larger patch of purple on center of lower breast and belly. Female very similar to female Blue Cotinga but somewhat paler, margined with buffy whitish above, generally buff below with dark brown spots.

Similar species: See Blue Cotinga.

Status and distribution: Uncommon and local in canopy and borders of humid forest

and second-growth woodland in lowlands and foothills of western Chiriquí (recorded up to about 1350 m: 4500 ft). Widespread deforestation has now very much reduced overall range and numbers of this cotinga in Panama; recent reports are all from the Santa Clara area west of Volcán, where small numbers can be seen fairly regularly in remaining patches of forest and in tall trees shading coffee plantations. Should also survive on the Burica Peninsula, though none were encountered there in June 1982 (Ridgely).
Habits: As in Blue Cotinga.
Range: Southwestern Costa Rica and Pacific western Panama.

[LOVELY COTINGA]
Cotinga amabilis   Plate 45

Description: 7½. One recent sighting from western Bocas del Toro. Male resembles male Blue Cotinga, but lacks that species' black eye-ring, has a more purplish (not so black) and slightly wider dark throat patch, a *markedly larger patch of purple on breast*, and longer blue upper tail-coverts (almost concealing the black tail). Female closely resembles female Blue Cotinga, but somewhat more spotted (less scaled) below; were they to occur together (which there is no evidence that they do), the two would be very difficult to distinguish in the field.
Similar species: See Blue Cotinga.
Status and distribution: One sighting of a male near Changuinola, Bocas del Toro, on November 24, 1978 (D. Engleman and R. Johnson). Possibly only a wanderer to Bocas from eastern Costa Rica; even there it is not numerous.
Habits: Similar to Blue Cotinga.
Range: Southeastern Mexico to eastern Costa Rica, one report from western Panama.

BLUE COTINGA
Cotinga nattererii   Plate 26

Description: 7½. Rather short bill and small head give somewhat dove-like expression. Male unmistakable in its range, *mostly shining blue* with black patch (faintly tinged purple) on throat and upper chest and rounded purple patch on center of belly; black eye-ring; wings and tail black broadly edged with blue. Female very different, dark brown above with buff edging, lighter brown below with buff edging, giving *overall scaly effect*.
Similar species: Even the gorgeous males can look dull when seen against the light. Females are best known by their distinctive silhouette and scaly appearance. Turquoise Cotinga is very similar but has different range.
Status and distribution: Uncommon to locally fairly common in canopy and borders of humid forest and taller second-growth woodland in lowlands and lower foothills (to about 900 m: 3000 ft) on both slopes from western Colon province and western Panama province (Chorrera) east through San Blas and Darién. In Canal area most numerous along Pipeline Road; also frequently noted at the clearing on Barro Colorado Island.
Habits: Generally seen high in trees, often on an exposed snag above the canopy, where may remain for protracted periods without moving. Usually more or less solitary, but small groups may concentrate at fruiting trees (and may then also come closer to the ground); fruit is plucked in flight, the bird often hovering briefly. Cotingas of this genus apparently make no vocal sounds, but wings of males (in display?) are sometimes heard to whirr or rattle in flight.
Range: Central Panama to northwestern Venezuela and northwestern Ecuador.

BLACK-TIPPED COTINGA
Carpodectes hopkei   p.322

Description: 9–10. Known only from eastern Darién. Iris dark red; bill black. Male *pure white*, with outer primaries very narrowly tipped black and (in younger birds) central tail feathers also black-tipped (neither of these black markings is very noticeable in the field). Female grayish brown above with wings and tail brownish black, *wing-coverts and inner flight feathers broadly edged white*; throat and breast pale gray, becoming white on belly.
Status and distribution: Uncommon and local in canopy and borders of humid forest in lowlands and foothills (up to about 900 m: 3000 ft) of eastern Darién (Piñas Bay, Cerro Sapo, Cana/Cerro Pirre area, Cerro Quía, and Alturas de Nique). Perhaps moves about seasonally. A few are sometimes in evidence around the Cana airstrip or on the slopes of Cerro Pirre above.
Habits: Males are exceptionally conspicuous birds, visible from tremendous distances, especially as they perch on high protruding branches or in their slow bounding flight just above the canopy. Males usually seem more numerous as they stand out so much more than females. *Carpodectes* cotingas are

Left to right, SNOWY COTINGA (male, immature male, and female); YELLOW-BILLED COTINGA (male); BLACK-TIPPED COTINGA (male)

generally more active and gregarious than *Cotinga*; small groups (composed of both sexes) may move about together, swooping on their broad rounded wings from tree to tree. Not known to make any vocal sounds.

Range: Eastern Panama to northwestern Ecuador.

Note: Sometimes called White Cotinga.

YELLOW-BILLED COTINGA
Carpodectes antoniae   p.322

Description: 8. Known only from western Chiriquí. Like Snowy Cotinga but *bill mostly yellow* (culmen is black). Male *almost immaculate pure white*, with crown tinged pearly gray. Female similar to female Snowy Cotinga, but with *mostly yellow bill* as in male.

Status and distribution: Uncertain. Recorded in mangroves (at least formerly) and canopy and borders of humid forest in western Chiriquí. Possibly occurs (or more likely, occurred) farther east: R. Benson told Eisenmann that he had collected one in the 1920s in mangroves near Aguadulce, Coclé, but this specimen was lost. Only two Panama specimens can now be accounted for, both taken by W. W. Brown, Jr, in 1901 at Pedregal. There are also two sight reports from the Burica Peninsula, the more recent of a male seen on June 26, 1982 (Ridgely); N. Smith records seeing seven *Carpodectes* sp.

(which we presume to have been *antoniae*) in the Río Cotón valley above Santa Clara in July 1980. What seems certain is that this species, probably never very numerous in Panama, is now very rare and localized; as it is also reported to be scarce in Costa Rica (though more numerous than in Panama), the species probably deserves to be officially classified as of "threatened" status. There is some evidence that this species breeds inland in foothill areas (though most reports from throughout its range are from on or near coast); virtually complete deforestation across all of its potential range in Chiriquí suggests that the continued survival of even a remnant population here would be tenuous indeed (aside from, possibly, the Burica Peninsula).

Habits: Not well known, but general behavior apparently similar to Black-tipped and Snowy Cotingas. A. Skutch observed what were presumed to be swooping courtship display flights in Costa Rican foothill forests at about 750 m (2500 ft). In June 1987, Yellow-billed Cotingas were numerous in mangroves and adjacent fringing lowland forest along the Río Sierpe near the base of the Osa Peninsula, both sexes (but mostly males) perching in the open high in trees and flying back and forth over the river, often quite low over the water.

Range: Southwestern Costa Rica and Pacific western Panama.

SNOWY COTINGA
Carpodectes nitidus   p.322

Description: 8. Found only in western Bocas del Toro. *Bill bluish gray. Male looks pure white*, but is tinged with very pale bluish gray above. Female brownish gray above with white eyering, wings grayer edged with white; grayish white below, whitest on throat and belly.

Similar species: Almost identical to Yellow-billed Cotinga of Chiriquí but with bluish gray bill. Female might be confused with the two tityras but has different bill and no black or brown on head.

Status and distribution: Uncommon in canopy of humid forest, forest borders, and adjacent clearings with scattered large trees in the lowlands and lower foothills (to about 450 m: 1500 ft) of western Bocas del Toro.

Habits: Similar to Black-tipped Cotinga; as with that species, the stunning males are almost unbelievably conspicuous and are noted more often than the drabber, though still handsome, females. The species is not particularly well known in Panama, and whether it actually engages in altitudinal movements (as it apparently does in Costa Rica) is uncertain; it may simply engage in post-breeding wandering of a general nature.

Range: Honduras to Caribbean western Panama.

PURPLE-THROATED FRUITCROW
Querula purpurata   Plate 26

Description: ♂ 11½; ♀ 10½. *Black with reddish purple throat.* Females and immatures lack the purple throat. Broad wings and short tail very evident in flight.

Status and distribution: Common in humid forest and second-growth woodland in lowlands on entire Caribbean slope; on Pacific slope recorded from around Canal area east through Darién (where recorded up to around 600 m: 2000 ft, though usually not above about 300 m: 1000 ft). Widespread in forested and wooded areas of Canal area, though considerably more numerous on Caribbean side.

Habits: Noisy and conspicuous, these fruitcrows typically troop about in groups of from three to six birds, swooping through middle and upper levels of forest; they sometimes accompany flocks of oropendolas, toucans, nunbirds, or other large birds. A variety of loud calls are given, some harsh, others quacking, still others almost whistled, e.g. *wak-wak-wheéawoo* or *cher-kaw* or *kwick-oo, oooo-waa* or simply *ooo*.

BARE-NECKED UMBRELLABIRD

Range: Costa Rica to northern Bolivia and Amazonian Brazil.

BARE-NECKED UMBRELLABIRD
Cephalopterus glabricollis   p.323

Description: ♂ 18; ♀ 15. Found only in west, mostly in highlands. Male unmistakable, *black with upstanding umbrella-shaped crest over head and bill; throat and neck bare, vivid scarlet when expanded*, with short narrow wattle hanging from neck (usually not too prominent). Female less spectacular, blackish above with much smaller crest, neck feathered and no wattle; brownish black below.

Similar species: Even female should be easily identified; only possible confusion lies with substantially smaller Purple-throated Fruitcrow of lowlands.

Status and distribution: Rare in humid forest in foothills and highlands of Chiriquí, Bocas del Toro, and Veraguas; apparently descends in nonbreeding season to lowlands on Caribbean slope, at least in Bocas del Toro; recorded mainly 900–2100 m (3000–7000 ft) when presumed to be breeding (no nest has ever been found), about April to September. Presumed to be more numerous on Caribbean slope, though even here there are relatively few reports (perhaps due mainly to the inaccessible nature of most of this area); at any rate, very rare in western Chiriquí highlands. Small numbers have been found in recent years in the Fortuna area of the upper Río Chiriquí valley in central Chiriquí, especially in the drainage of the Quebrada de Arena.

Habits: Not very well known in Panama, nor indeed is it anywhere in its rather small range, over most of which it is seemingly rare; because of deforestation over significant portions of this range, this remarkable and spectacular cotinga may deserve to be officially classified as of "threatened" status. When encountered, usually seen perched high in forest trees; during nonbreeding season they sometimes accompany fruitcrows, nunbirds, etc. At that time they are usually quiet and inconspicuous, but at the onset of the breeding season they are reported to be more conspicuous and easier to see. Males at that time are quite noisy, chasing each other with chuckling sounds and a throaty *oooah*, and displaying on low perches, spreading their crests and distending their scarlet air sac on chest, and emitting a deep booming sound (C. Cordier). This sound has been likened to the low moaning bellow of a bull, and doubtless for this reason the umbrellabird is known locally as *bramón* (in South America a related species, *C. ornatus*, is the "pájaro de toro").

Range: Costa Rica and western Panama.

THREE-WATTLED BELLBIRD
Procnias tricarunculata   Plate 26

Description: ♂ 12; ♀ 10½. Found only in west, mostly in highlands. Male unmistakable, *mostly bright chestnut-rufous*, with *striking white head and neck; three worm-like wattles hang limply from base of bill*. Female olive above, feathers margined with yellowish; *yellow below streaked with olive*; no wattles. Immature males have short wattles with plumage of female.

Status and distribution: Locally fairly common in forest in foothills and highlands of Chiriquí, Bocas del Toro, and Veraguas; recorded in western Chiriquí mostly 1200–2100 m (4000–7000 ft), down to about 750 m (2500 ft) elsewhere; present in highlands for what is presumed to be the breeding season (no nest has ever been found) mostly

March (small numbers sometimes earlier) to September, after which they descend to the lowlands, mostly on Caribbean slope at least in recent years (doubtless most now prevented from descending into Chiriquí lowlands by that area's near-total deforestation). Also recorded from hill country of Azuero Peninsula, where breeding seems possible (especially in the mountainous Cerro Hoya area at southwestern tip) but remains unconfirmed; and was common, with many calling males, through much of the hilly interior of Coiba Island in April 1976 (Ridgely). In recent years a few bellbirds have even wandered as far east as the Canal area (J. Pujals, N. Smythe, N. Gale *et al.*), giving rise to some speculation that ongoing destruction of forest habitat in its normal range is displacing some individuals. In any case there can be little doubt that the bellbird, like so many other western highland specialties, is gradually losing ground, a discouraging prospect indeed. For now they remain relatively numerous during the breeding season on the Boquete side of Volcán Barú (e.g. on Finca Lerida); bellbirds seem always to have been less common on the Cerro Punta side, perhaps because it is drier.

Habits: The presence of bellbirds in an area will usually be obvious from the male's unmistakable and far-carrying call. The bird hunches forward and opens its cavernous mouth so that lower mandible practically touches breast and emits a harsh resonant grunt (not at all bell-like), *ihrk*, then pauses for about a second (mouth still wide open) before giving a louder sharper croak, *kyahrrk* or *krreeak*. Either note may be given alone. At the conclusion, he often jumps a short distance into the air and then returns to his perch with a reversed orientation. Males may be calling from all around but can often be frustratingly difficult to see as they perch high in the canopy often hidden from the ground. Females are, not unexpectedly, less conspicuous and are much less often observed. Chiriquí residents know the bird by the inappropriate name of "calandria", the Spanish name for lark!

Range: Honduras to western (rarely central) Panama.

MANAKINS: Pipridae (12)

Manakins are small, strictly neotropical birds found in forests and woodland, mostly at low elevations with a few species higher. Typical manakins are plump birds with short bills and short tails (though several species have lengthened tail feathers); most males are brightly or contrastingly colored, while females usually are drab olive. Several aberrant genera (represented in Panama by *Sapayoa* and *Schiffornis*), at present generally placed in the Pipridae, may not actually belong here. Typical manakins are best known for their elaborate courtship behavior in which males gather to display in groups; here they perform a variety of stereotyped actions, and emit an astonishing array of loud, often cracking or whirring, noises, in some species made mechanically. In typical manakins, so far as known, females build the nest and rear the young alone, constructing a small shallow cup nest in a tree fork, usually not far above the ground. Manakins feed primarily on fruit, to a lesser degree on insects.

THRUSHLIKE MOURNER (MANAKIN)
Schiffornis turdinus   Plates 27, 45

Description: 6½. Sexes similar. *Essentially brown or olive brown*, without distinctive markings. In lowlands of central and eastern Panama (*panamensis*) lighter, with brighter brown cap, wings, and tail; *throat and chest light cinnamon-rufous contrasting with grayish olive breast and belly*. In lowlands and foothills of western and central Panama (*dumicola*), and at higher levels on Cerro Tacarcuna in eastern Darién (*acrolophites*; but note that only *panamensis* occurs on Cerro Pirre, even at high levels), darker and more olive brown generally, more uniformly colored both above and below.

Similar species: Broad-billed Sapayoa is basically a yellowish green (not brownish) bird, and has a broad flat bill. Brownish Twistwing has more slender build with relatively longer tail, has buffy wing-edging and fairly distinct wing-bars, brighter brown tail; it has wing-lifting habit.

Status and distribution: Fairly common in lower growth of humid forest and shady second-growth woodland in lowlands and foothills on Caribbean slope from northern Veraguas eastward (not known from Bocas del Toro except at Guaval on Veraguas border); on Pacific slope recorded from Chiriquí, Veraguas, and western side of Azuero Peninsula (but no recent reports from Chiriquí or Veraguas lowlands, where perhaps extirpated by deforestation), in foothills of Coclé and western Panama province, and in lowlands and foothills from Canal area eastward. Recorded mostly below 1200 m: 4000 ft, though small numbers occur a little higher in the western highlands and in Darién. No specimens are available from foothills of Panama province (Cerro Campana, Cerro Azul/Jefe), but birds occurring here are certainly not *panamensis* (the form occurring in lowlands below), and are probably very close to western *dumicola*. This distribution, with two morphologically distinct populations replacing each other altitudinally, together

with distinct vocalization differences (see below), strongly suggests that two species are involved, though to date definitive work establishing this has not been done. These species would be: *S. veraepacis* (Brown Mourner; represented in Panama by western *dumicola*, the birds on Cerro Campana and Cerro Azul/Jefe, and *acrolophites* of Cerro Tacarcuna), and *S. turdinus* (Thrushlike Mourner; represented in Panama by *panamensis*, mainly of lowlands and lower foothills).

Habits: Not often seen except when caught in mist-nets. Perches rather low, sometimes clinging to upright stems, peering about with a wide-eyed look; rarely with mixed flocks. Utters distinctive loud musical whistled songs, but often at long intervals, and usually hard to track to their source (but often will decoy to tape playback). In the Canal area and in lowlands eastward *panamensis* gives a four-noted rhythmic phrase, *wheeuu, wheet-wheet, wheet?* In the west and in foothills of central Panama (east to Nusagandi in western San Blas) *dumicola* or *dumicola*-type birds give a three-noted phrase of recognizably similar quality but much more drawn-out, *wheeeeeeee-oweee; téw*. The voice of *acrolophites* (only Cerro Tacarcuna, Darién) appears from Wetmore's description to be similar to that of *dumicola*.

Range: Southeastern Mexico to Bolivia and southeastern Brazil.

Note: The genus *Schiffornis* appears not to be allied to the true manakins, and certainly does not look or act like them. Recent evidence (R. Prum, pers. comm.) indicates that the genus is closest to *Laniocera*; he suggests that the members of the genus be called "mourners", and this is adopted here. As noted above, more than one species is likely involved; the situation seems clear enough in Panama, but as so often is the case becomes more complicated in South America.

BROAD-BILLED SAPAYOA (MANAKIN)
Sapayoa aenigma   Plate 27

Description: 6–6¼. *Broad flat bill* noticeable only at close range; *rather long tail. Uniform* *fairly bright olive*, duskier on wings and tail, somewhat yellower on throat and mid-belly. Males have a usually concealed yellow crown patch.

Similar species: A confusing bird, probably often overlooked. Like many female manakins in coloration but much larger and with longer tail and different bill. Thrushlike Mourner is basically brown, not olive green. Olivaceous Flatbill is similar in color and proportions, but has broad, yellowish margins on wings, an eye-ring, and indistinct dusky streaking on chest. Olive Tanager has different bill and rather contrasting yellow throat; it troops about in noisy, active flocks.

Status and distribution: Rare and seemingly local (perhaps in part just overlooked) in lower growth of humid forest in lowlands on Caribbean slope from Canal area eastward; on Pacific slope recorded from foothills of eastern Panama province (one 1949 specimen from Cerro Azul; no further reports), and lowlands and lower foothills of eastern Darién (where perhaps slightly more numerous, and recorded up to about 600 m: 2000 ft). In Canal area known only from along Pipeline Road, where most often seen by walking up one of the many streams which cross the road.

Habits: Found singly or in pairs, often near streams, foraging in a manner reminiscent of a flatbill at low and middle levels inside forest, sallying out after insects. Often joins mixed foraging flocks of antwrens, small flycatchers, etc. Seems to favor areas near forest streams. Sometimes utters a soft, somewhat nasal, and vaguely Long-billed Gnatwren-like trill, or a slightly louder *chip, ch-ch-ch* (J. Guarnaccia).

Range: Central Panama to northwestern Ecuador.

Note: As this species is evidently not a true manakin, it would seem more accurate to refer to it as the Broad-billed Sapayoa. Its actual affinities are still uncertain; probably it is a tyrant-flycatcher (R. Prum).

GREEN MANAKIN
Chloropipo holochlora Plate 40

Description: 4¾. Found only in eastern Panama. Bill black above, gray below; legs grayish to brown. Dull olive green above; throat and breast grayish olive *contrasting with yellowish belly*. Sexes similar. Race found in Panama (*litae*, extending to northwestern Ecuador) is markedly duller above than the nominate race found east of Andes.

Similar species: Easily confused. Best told from females of other manakins by its larger size and proportionately longer tail. Female Lance-tailed lacks the contrast below, and has protruding central tail feathers and reddish (not dull) legs; they are unlikely ever to occur together. See also the even larger Broad-billed Sapayoa, which also lacks contrast below, etc.

Status and distribution: Apparently rare to uncommon in undergrowth of humid forest in lowlands and (especially) foothills in San Blas (where recently recorded as far west as Cerro Brewster, where mist-netted and photographed in late April 1985 by J. Blake, and also seen at Nusagandi) and eastern Darién. May be more numerous in the Cerro Tacarcuna area than elsewhere.

Habits: A poorly known bird throughout its range, most often recorded from mist-net captures. When seen usually moving about alone in forest understory, in manner reminiscent of a Thrushlike Mourner. Like the latter it does not seem to be especially attracted to the fruiting trees so favored by many other manakins.

Range: Eastern Panama to eastern Peru.

WHITE-COLLARED MANAKIN
Manacus candei Plate 45

Description: 4–4¼. Found recently in extreme western Bocas del Toro, where locally it replaces Golden-collared Manakin. *Reddish orange legs*. Male has *white collar and throat*, feathers of former lengthened and stiffened; otherwise mostly black above with lower back and rump olive; *lower underparts bright canary yellow*. Female dull olive green above and on throat and breast, becoming *fairly bright yellow on belly*.

Similar species: The striking males are hardly to be confused, though beware the possibility of hybrids with Golden-collared Manakin (as yet not recorded). Female resembles female Golden-collared Manakin, but is notably yellower on belly (female Golden-collar more uniform olive yellowish below).

Status and distribution: Fairly common at forest borders and in dense overgrown clearings in lowlands of western Bocas del Toro (lower Río Teribe and lower Río Changuinola valleys). First recorded in Panama by W. Martinez and J. Pujals in October 1978, with a male specimen taken on February 17, 1979 (Martinez and W. Booth), both in the Río Teribe area; several more specimens were taken by GML personnel in January 1980 near the projected damsite on the lower Río Changuinola. In neither area is there any evidence of hybridization with *M. vitellinus cerritus*; furthermore, what appeared to be a perfectly pure *cerritus* was displaying, alone (though there were *candei* not too far away), near the Changuinola damsite in April 1980 (Ridgely). More study is needed.

Habits: Similar to Golden-collared Manakin.

Range: Southern Mexico to Caribbean western Panama.

Note: This and the following species are sometimes considered conspecific with *M. manacus* (White-bearded Manakin) of South America; if expanded, the species' English name is Bearded Manakin.

GOLDEN-COLLARED MANAKIN
Manacus vitellinus Plate 27

Description: 4–4 ¼. *Reddish orange legs*. Male has *bright golden yellow collar and throat*, the feathers lengthened and stiffened; otherwise mostly black above with center of back and rump olive; lower underparts olive. Female dull olive green above, paler and more yellowish olive green below. Males from western Bocas del Toro, formerly often regarded as a distinct species (*M. cerritus*, Almirante Manakin), have a more lemon yellow collar and throat, and this extends to upper back and lower on underparts.

Similar species: See Orange-collared Manakin of western Pacific slope. Female Golden-collar resembles several other female manakins, but can be known by its reddish orange legs; female Lance-tail also has orange-red legs but is larger with projecting central tail feathers.

Status and distribution: Common in undergrowth of borders of humid forest, second-growth woodland, and in dense regenerating clearings in lowlands and lower foothills (recorded sparingly up to about 450 m: 2500 ft) on entire Caribbean slope (west to coastal western Bocas del Toro in the Changuinola/Almirante area); on Pacific slope recorded from foothills of Veraguas eastward, and in lowlands from western Panama province east; common also on Escudo de Veraguas, off eastern Bocas del Toro. Common and widespread on both sides of Canal area.

Habits: This and its congeners are the noisiest Panama manakins, the males producing a variety of sounds. The most striking is an almost firecracker-like snap produced by the wings; also has a softer *chee-póo* or *pee-yóo*, and a ripping sound like cloth tearing. Small groups of males display in woodland undergrowth throughout the prolonged breeding season; each male has its own "court", a small area where the ground is cleared of leaves and other debris. Calling and wing-snapping is especially intense at the approach of a female; often the lengthened throat feathers are puffed out away from the body to form a "beard".

Range: Western Panama to western Colombia.

Note: See under White-collared Manakin.

ORANGE-COLLARED MANAKIN
Manacus aurantiacus Plate 27

Description: 3 ¾–4. Found only on Pacific western slope. *Orange legs*. Similar to Golden-collared Manakin, replacing it in its range, and by some considered conspecific. Male has *more orange collar and throat*, extending over upper back, with lower underparts yellow (not olive) and tail olive (not black); otherwise as in Golden-collar. Female more golden olive green above, more yellowish below.

Similar species: See Golden-collared Manakin.

Status and distribution: Fairly common in undergrowth of forest borders, second-growth woodland, gallery woodland, and regenerating clearings in lowlands and lower foothills (to about 750 m: 2500 ft) on Pacific slope in Chiriquí, southern Veraguas, and on the Azuero Peninsula (including its eastern side, in Herrera and Los Santos). Numbers have declined substantially due to deforestation over much of its Panama range: though the species can persist in quite degraded, purely secondary habitats, even where these are patchy, it cannot survive in areas mostly or entirely cleared for pasture or large-scale agriculture. Remains numerous around Puerto Armuelles and on the Burica Peninsula, in Chiriquí.

Habits: Similar to Golden-collared Manakin.

Range: Southwestern Costa Rica and Pacific western Panama.

Note: Though regarded as a race of *M. vitellinus* (Golden-collared Manakin) by the 1983 AOU Check-list, we prefer to maintain it as a distinct species. No hybridization has been demonstrated across the zone of possible intergradation in Veraguas, where they seem likely to at least at one time have been in contact (*vitellinus* occurring west along the foothills to Santa Fé, *aurantiacus* occurring in southern Veraguas in the Soná/Santiago area, etc.).

WHITE-RUFFED MANAKIN
Corapipo leucorrhoa Plate 27

Description: 3½–3¾. Mainly in foothills. Legs dark. Male *mostly glossy blue-black; throat white*, feathers lengthened at the sides to form a ruff. Female mostly olive green, somewhat paler below, with *throat and sides of head grayish*, belly pale yellowish. Males from western Chiriquí (*heteroleuca*) have black of underparts protruding as a "V" into middle of lower throat (rounded effect in *altera* of the rest of Panama).
Similar species: Female resembles female Red-capped Manakin but is brighter green above and has distinctly grayish throat. Female White-crowned Manakin has mostly gray head.
Status and distribution: Fairly common to common in undergrowth of humid forest in foothills and lower highlands on both slopes including the Azuero Peninsula (as far south as Cerro Hoya); recorded mostly 450–1200 m (1500–4000 ft), occasionally (in Chiriquí) to over 1500 m (5000 ft), or as low as sea level (a few records from Bocas del Toro and San Blas, these perhaps being an indication of post-breeding altitudinal migration). Not definitely recorded from Canal area, but numerous in remaining habitat on Cerro Campana and in Cerro Azul/Jefe area.
Habits: Similar to other manakins, like them perhaps most often seen at fruiting trees with other birds. The usual call, given by both sexes, is a sharp *prrrreep*. Males have a marvelous display: groups of from three to six of them gather in the vicinity of a selected fallen mossy log or buttressed root, either approaching extremely slowly (looking as if they'll surely stall) with flailing wings and puffed out throats, or more rapidly and normally and landing with an indistinct snap. The slow flight seems to be given mostly in the presence of a female. On the whole, this display seems almost eerily quiet (especially as compared with *Manacus* and some *Pipra* displays), but Skutch has heard them give several different harsh vocalizations. Even more remarkable, an aerial display in which males mount some 15–30 m (50–100 ft) into the air has been reported from Cerro Jefe (R. A. Rowlett).
Range: Eastern Nicaragua to western Colombia and northwestern Venezuela.
Note: Birds from Middle America to northwestern Colombia were formerly often considered a distinct species (*C. altera*, White-ruffed Manakin) from those of northeastern Colombia and western Venezuela (*C. leucorrhoa*, White-bibbed Manakin), and may yet prove to be, but the two were considered conspecific by the 1983 AOU Check-list, which we follow. Structure of their outer primaries differs, and this may effect their respective displays; but as yet true *leucorrhoa* seems not to have been studied in the field.

LANCE-TAILED MANAKIN
Chiroxiphia lanceolata Plate 27

Description: 5–5¼. *Orange-red legs; projecting, pointed central tail feathers*, somewhat longer in male. Male black with *red crown* and *sky blue back*. Female olive green above, sometimes with some red on crown; somewhat paler olive green below, fading to whitish on belly. Immature male is like female but with red crown.
Similar species: Female larger than female Golden- and Orange-collared Manakins, with protruding central tail feathers.
Status and distribution: Common in thick scrub and lower growth of dry and second-growth woodland in lowlands on Pacific slope from western Chiriquí (ranging up to about 1200 m: 4000 ft, rarely to 1590 m: 5300 ft) to western Darién (Garachiné); on Caribbean slope known only from middle Chagres River valley (Gamboa, Madden Dam area, near Summit Gardens); found also on Coiba Island and Cébaco Island.
Habits: Even the lovely males are often frustratingly difficult to see in the dense undergrowth this species favors. The Lance-tail's vocalizations are very unlike those of other Panama manakins, most characteristic being a mellow semi-whistled *doh* or *tee-o*, often repeated and sometimes accelerated into a roll, *dowee-oh*; also gives a very different nasal snarl, *nyaah*. As with many other manakins, males gather to display in courtship assemblies during the breeding season; two males often perch side by side on the same branch, calling steadily and occasionally jumping up and down in alternation.
Range: Southwestern Costa Rica to northern Venezuela.

WHITE-CROWNED MANAKIN
Pipra pipra Plate 27

Description: 3¾. Known only from very humid western foothills. *Iris red* in both sexes (more conspicuous in female). Male velvety black with *striking white crown and hindneck*. Female has *crown and hindneck slaty gray* contrasting with olive green upperparts; somewhat paler olive green below, more yellowish on belly.

Similar species: Female's distinctly gray cap (often looking quite bluish) distinguishes her from other female manakins (see especially female White-ruffed, with grayish throat).

Status and distribution: Rare and seemingly local in lower growth of humid forest in foothills and lower highlands of central and eastern Chiriquí (old specimens from Cordillera de Tolé; also one female collected at Fortuna on March 3, 1976, specimen to GML; Ridgely), both slopes of Veraguas, and Caribbean slope of Coclé (Río Guabal); recorded mostly 600–1200 m (2000–4000 ft). Not yet found in Bocas del Toro, but almost certain to occur there.

Habits: Little known in Panama. In South America males vocalize from perches mostly 3–6 m (10–20 ft) above the ground, often in small loose groups. Most frequent call a somewhat buzzy *dreee-ee-ew* (recalling Golden-crowned Spadebill); displaying males often fly back and forth between several branches, with crown patch spread and flattened.

Range: Costa Rica and western Panama; Colombia to eastern Peru, Amazonian and eastern Brazil, and the Guianas.

BLUE-CROWNED MANAKIN
Pipra coronata   Plate 27

Description: 3½. Legs dark; iris dark red. Male all velvety black except for *bright blue crown*. Female *rather bright grass green above*; somewhat paler green below, more grayish on throat and pale yellowish on belly.

Similar species: Female is distinctly greener above, less olive, than other female manakins in Panama. In eastern Panama, see the larger Green Manakin.

Status and distribution: Uncommon to locally common in undergrowth of humid forest and mature second-growth woodland in lowlands and lower foothills on Caribbean slope in western and central Bocas del Toro (east to Cricamola), and from Canal area eastward; on Pacific slope recorded from lowlands and foothills of western Chiriquí (numbers now much reduced by deforestation, though found still to be numerous in remaining primary forest on Burica Peninsula in late June 1982; Ridgely), foothills of Veraguas (specimens

in AMNH from Santa Fé), and locally in lowlands and lower foothills (to about 750 m: 2500 ft) from Canal area eastward (most numerous in Darién). In Canal area much more numerous on Caribbean side; most easily seen along Pipeline Road.

Habits: Seems to favor forested areas with relatively sparse undergrowth, often near streams. Not as noisy as most other typical manakins, though both sexes do often give a musical trill, *treereereeree*. Displaying males alternate this trill with a harsher *chiwrrr*, often repeated several times; they call from a low perch in shady understory, often inclining slightly forward. No loud snapping noises are given, nor do calling males seem to interact with other males, though often one or several are within hearing distance. They may display mostly during the rainy season.

Range: Costa Rica to northern Bolivia and Amazonian Brazil.

GOLDEN-HEADED MANAKIN
Pipra erythrocephala   Plate 27

Description: 3½–3¾. Found only in eastern Panama. *Bill whitish; legs pinkish to whitish; iris white in adult male, yellowish in female,* darker in immatures. Male black with *glistening yellow-orange head*, and red and white thighs (usually hidden). Female olive green above, paler yellowish olive below.

Similar species: Male Red-capped Manakin has red head and yellow thighs; female Red-cap closely resembles female Golden-head but has dark bill and legs, somewhat longer tail. See also female Golden-collared Manakin.

Status and distribution: Uncommon to rare (at western edge of range) to common (eastward) in humid and deciduous forest and second-growth woodland in lowlands and lower foothills of eastern San Blas, eastern Panamá province (now mainly in upper Bayano River valley; early specimens from near the Bayano's mouth, but almost certainly long since extirpated from this region by deforestation), and Darién (where regularly ranges higher, up to at least 1200 m: 4000 ft, at least on Cerro Pirre). On the Pacific slope there is a zone of overlap with the Red-capped Manakin in eastern Panamá province; around Majé, for example, both species occur though the Red-capped is considerably more numerous (P. Galindo), and there is at least one known hybrid (J. Strauch). On the Caribbean slope the zone of overlap or replacement is unknown, there being a considerable gap through central San

Blas from whence neither has been reported (though this likely is only because the area has never been ornithologically surveyed). **Habits:** Similar to Red-capped Manakin in habitat and behavior. The voice, however, is rather different, with a variety of whirring, buzzy, and humming sounds, but without the loud snaps (D. Snow). **Range:** Eastern Panama to eastern Peru, northern Brazil, and the Guianas.

RED-CAPPED MANAKIN
Pipra mentalis   Plate 27

Description: 3¾–4. *Legs brownish*; iris white in adult male, dark brown in female and immatures. Male black with *glistening red head* (base of feathers yellow, showing through at times) and yellow thighs (usually hidden except in display). Female olive green above, paler yellowish olive below. **Similar species:** Female Golden-collared Manakin is similar but has reddish orange (not dark) legs; female Blue-crowned Manakin is smaller with distinctly green (not olive) upperparts. In eastern Panama see also Golden-headed Manakin. **Status and distribution:** Common in humid forest and second-growth woodland in lowlands (rare above 600 m: 2000 ft) on Caribbean slope east to western San Blas (Mandinga); on Pacific slope recorded from Chiriquí (where now very local due to deforestation, though still numerous in remaining primary forests on Burica Peninsula in June 1982; Ridgely), southern Veraguas (no recent reports, and likely nearly extirpated due to deforestation), and in Panama province and Canal area (recorded east in eastern Panama province to middle Bayano River valley and Cerro Chucantí). Widespread in Canal area, though more numerous on Caribbean side. **Habits:** Often one of the most abundant forest birds on the Caribbean slope, though usually not very conspicuous, flying rapidly from perch to perch, then remaining motionless, their black or olive plumage blending into the shadows and foliage. Especially during the dry season, males gather to display in small loose groups, and at such times the forest may resound with their long-drawn rising *sick-seeeeeee* and other loud snapping and clicking noises (the latter made mostly with the wings, perhaps also with the bill). Each male has its own display perch, located 4.5–15 m (15–50 ft) or more above the ground, which is the center of its activity. On and around it, the male performs a variety of stereotyped actions, including rapid to-and-fro flights to a nearby branch, sidling quickly up and down the display branch, abrupt "aboutfaces", and wing quivering, all the while accompanied by a variety of loud noises, both vocal and mechanical. **Range:** Southeastern Mexico to northwestern Ecuador.

SHARPBILLS: Oxyruncidae (1)

The one species in this family has a highly disjunct, relictual distribution from Costa Rica to southeastern South America, mostly in humid foothill forests. Its taxonomic position is unclear, and though it seems allied to both the Tyrannidae and the Cotingidae, the 1983 AOU Checklist maintained it in its own separate family.

SHARPBILL
Oxyruncus cristatus   Plate 45

Description: 6¼. Found locally in humid foothills of west and east. Plump and stocky, with *sharply pointed bill*; eyes orange. Mostly olive above, head and neck mainly whitish with narrow blackish scaling and with *black-edged flame-colored crest* (usually laid flat, the orange-red often concealed); throat whitish narrowly scaled blackish; remaining underparts pale yellow, *profusely spotted with black*. Darién birds (*brooksi*) are more yellowish white below. **Similar species:** Speckled Tanager is spotted above as well as below and has different bill and facial pattern. **Status and distribution:** Rare to locally fairly common in canopy and borders of humid forest in foothills and lower highlands of Chiriquí (where known only from one old specimen from Boquete, though seems likely to occur in the Fortuna area), Bocas del Toro (known only from sighting of one bird along oleoducto road north of Fortuna on July 4, 1982; Ridgely), both slopes of Veraguas, and eastern Darién (Cerro Sapo, Cerro Pirre, Cerro Quía, and Cerro Tacarcuna); recorded 750–1350 m (2500–4500 ft). Regularly seen on the slopes of Cerro Pirre above Cana, particularly once its call is recognized.

Habits: Usually quite inconspicuous, most often seen singly as it accompanies mixed flocks of tanagers and other birds. They seem to forage mostly by searching for insects along major limbs and in outer foliage, regularly clinging upside-down like a chickadee (*Parus* sp.); less often fruiting trees are visited. Its song is a drawn-out high thin somewhat buzzy trill that gradually slides down in pitch, *zheeeeeeeeeeuuuuu'u 'u'u'u'u*.

Range: Locally in Costa Rica, Panama, southern Venezuela, Guyana, eastern Peru, Amazonian and southeastern Brazil, and eastern Paraguay.

SWALLOWS: Hirundinidae (15)

The swallows are a familiar group of highly aerial birds found virtually throughout the world, with many highly migratory species (including over half the recorded Panama species). With long pointed wings and rapid graceful flight, they differ most obviously from the swifts in their frequent perching on exposed branches and wires and their more maneuverable flight. Most species are dark above and light below, many with notched or forked tails. All but a few are gregarious, some gathering in large flocks (in Panama especially the martins); a number are colonial breeders as well. Swallows are essentially insectivorous, capturing prey in flight in their wide gape. Nesting sites are rather varied, with many favoring man-made structures: several species (non-Panamanian breeders) nest on cliff ledges, but most nest in holes or crevices, either in trees, on buildings, or in banks.

PURPLE MARTIN
Progne subis

Description: 7–8. Male *entirely glossy blue-black*. Female and immature sooty brown above with *forecrown usually gray margined with whitish, giving a hoary effect*; sooty brown below, fading to white on breast and belly (which are usually streaked, sometimes heavily, with dusky), with *patches of whitish to dull buff on sides of neck*, sometimes extending around hindneck to form a narrow whitish collar.

Similar species: Female-plumaged birds resemble Gray-breasted Martin but have gray forehead (sometimes absent), pale areas on sides of neck, darker underparts, and usually streaked lower underparts (in Gray-breasted at most faint shaft streaks). Adult male easily distinguished from Gray-breasted Martin, but cannot be separated in field from adult male Southern Martin. Female Southern Martin resembles a very dark female Purple, but lacks grayish forehead and pale sides to neck, and has entire underparts dusky, usually with pale edging (the effect being more like scaling than streaking).

Status and distribution: Locally common fall transient along immediate Caribbean coast (mostly early August–late September); uncommon but perhaps regular around Gatun Lake, but seemingly not recorded from elsewhere on Caribbean slope; apparently rare in lowlands on Pacific slope, with only a few sightings (southern Coclé to eastern Panama province). Apparently much less numerous as spring transient (mostly mid-February–mid-March), when also recorded primarily from along Caribbean coast.

Habits: Usually in small flocks (occasionally large), feeding over open areas, often with other martins or migrating swallows. Many probably migrate past Panama unnoticed, either flying very high or streaming past just offshore in the Caribbean; steady, heavy rains will often "ground" them, however, and they may then gather in large milling flocks and perch on dead snags or wires.

Range: Breeds in North America; winters in south-central South America; recorded spottily as a transient from Middle America and West Indies.

Note: Sinaloa Martin (*P. sinaloae*, breeding in northwestern Mexico), Caribbean Martin (*P. dominicensis*, breeding in most of West Indies), and Cuban Martin (*P. cryptoleuca*, breeding in Cuba) all vacate their nesting grounds during northern winter, and presumably migrate to South America though there are few if any records (in part because of identification difficulties). All would be hard to confirm without specimens, but should nonetheless be watched for, especially on northward passage when they would be in fresher plumage. Sinaloa Martin male has contrasting and sharply demarcated white on median lower underparts; Caribbean Martin male similar but with white median area narrower (thus more broadly blue-black on flanks); Cuban Martin male like Purple but has some white feathers on belly. Females would be impossible in the field. Taxonomic status of these forms is still disputed, though all were treated as full species in the 1983 AOU Checklist.

GRAY-BREASTED MARTIN
Progne chalybea   Plate 47

Description: 6¼–7¼. Male *steely blue-black above (including forehead)*; throat, breast, and sides grayish brown, lower underparts white. Female similar but duller with less glossy upperparts and sooty forehead, paler gray throat. Immature like female but more sooty brown above, with grayish of breast blending into white of lower underparts.
Similar species: The commonest martin in Panama; see other martins for distinctions. Immature Gray-breast can be confused with Brown-chested Martin but lacks clearly marked chest band and white throat.
Status and distribution: Very common to locally abundant in flocks that gather after breeding season in lowlands on both slopes, more numerous and widespread on Pacific side; ranges up in smaller numbers into foothills and where widely cleared into lower highlands (to about 1500 m: 5000 ft); found also on Coiba Island. Numbers seem much larger after breeding season — the local population is probably augmented by migrating birds from farther north in Middle America.
Habits: Not found in extensively forested areas, this species appears soon after clearings are made. It favors towns and habitations, especially near water. Nests in crevices and under eaves of houses and in hollow trees; colonial martin houses like those used in the United States would probably also be suitable, but seem not to have been tried in Panama. Males give a musical gurgling song similar to that of Purple Martin.
Range: Mexico (casually southern Texas) to

central Argentina; birds from northern Middle America are at least in part migratory, but their winter range is unknown; southernmost nesters (nominate *chalybea*) are highly migratory, wintering north to Venezuela and the Guianas.

SOUTHERN MARTIN
Progne modesta

Description: 7–8. Apparently very rare, though quite possibly overlooked. Male *entirely glossy blue-black* (tail more deeply forked than in Purple Martin). Female and immature blackish above; *sooty brown to dusky below (including belly) with pale edging* (some adult females look almost uniformly dark below).
Similar species: Adult male cannot be distinguished in the field from adult male Purple Martin. Female-plumaged Southern Martin can be distinguished from Gray-breasted and female-plumaged Purple Martin by its lack of white lower underparts.
Status and distribution: Probably a casual austral migrant. Still only one definite record, an immature taken at Puerto Obaldía, San Blas on July 14, 1931. Other sightings of all dark presumed males of this species include: one at Coco Solo on June 20, 1958 (J. Ambrose); one near Gamboa on July 15, 1970 (Eisenmann and E. S. Morton, both of these in the former Canal Zone); and two with Brown-chested Martins on the Bayano Lake in eastern Panama province on April 24, 1976 (Ridgely).
Range: Breeds in Argentina and southern Bolivia, migrating north during austral winter to Amazonia (mostly), also recorded from Suriname and casually (?) to Panama.
Note: Here the highly migratory southern form *elegans* (the race which occurs in Panama) and resident *murphyi* of coastal Peru and northern Chile (Peruvian Martin) are considering conspecific with *P. modesta* (the nominate form of which is resident on the Galapagos; if split it would be called Galapagos Martin). The 1983 AOU Checklist considered all three full species.

BROWN-CHESTED MARTIN
Phaeoprogne tapera

Description: 6½–7½. *Grayish brown above*; white below with *distinct grayish brown band across chest* and a line of small brownish spots below the chest band. White feather of under tail-coverts long and silky, often visible from above along edge of rump and base of tail.

Similar species: Almost a replica of the Sand Martin, but much larger and with different shape and swooping (not fluttery) flight style. Other adult Panama martins are blue-black or blackish above (not brown), and even the more brownish immatures never show a distinct chest band contrasting with white throat.

Status and distribution: Variable in numbers and rather local. Uncommon to (in some years) abundant austral winter visitant from southern South America (mid-April–late September, most numerous May–August; four presumed stragglers seen near Antón, Coclé, on January 2, 1974, by Ridgely) in lowlands on both slopes, recorded west to western Bocas del Toro (where irregular) and western Chiriquí. Seems much more numerous in some years than others, sometimes noted in very large flocks of hundreds of birds. Found in open areas, often in association with smaller numbers of Gray-breasted Martins.

Range: Breeds in South America south to central Argentina; southern breeders (*fusca*) winter in northern South America and Panama, casually to Costa Rica (one sight report).

TREE SWALLOW
Tachycineta bicolor

Description: 5–6. Rare. *Steely blue-black or green-black above;* immaculate white below. Immature dusky brown above; whitish below, with indistinct and incomplete dusky band on sides of chest.

Similar species: Mangrove Swallow is smaller with prominent white rump. Blue-and-white Swallow is very similar but has prominent black under tail-coverts (white in Tree). Immature Trees can be confused with Northern Rough-winged Swallow and Sand Martin.

Status and distribution: A highly erratic, usually rare and local winter visitant to lowlands on both slopes, some years passing without any records while in others (notably in early 1976) it is relatively numerous and widespread; recorded mostly January–March, a few lingering birds into early April. Recorded mostly from central Panama, especially along Caribbean coast of Canal area, around Gatun Lake, and in eastern Panama province (Juan Diaz to La Jagua, especially at Tocumen); 50 or more were seen near Rincón, Herrera, on

January 23, 1976 (Ridgely).

Habits: Sometimes mixed with other migratory swallows, but more often seems to occur in groups comprised solely of its own species. Usually found in open areas near water.

Range: Breeds in North America; winters from southern United States to Nicaragua and in Greater Antilles, casually or irregularly to Costa Rica, Panama, Colombia, and Guyana.

MANGROVE SWALLOW
Tachycineta albilinea   Plate 47

Description: 4½. *Glossy greenish to steel blue above* (greener in fresh plumage, becoming bluer with wear) with narrow white supraloral stripe and *white rump; immaculate white below.* Immature more grayish above except for white rump, tinged with brownish on sides of chest.

Similar species: Blue-and-white Swallow lacks white rump and has black under tail-coverts. See very rare Tree and Violet-green Swallows. See also White-winged Swallow (below).

Status and distribution: Locally common, almost always near water, in lowlands on Caribbean slope east to western San Blas (Mandinga, Cangandi); on Pacific slope somewhat less numerous and more local, but recorded from western Chiriquí to eastern Darién (lower and middle Tuira River valley); found also on Cébaco and Coiba Islands.

Habits: Usually seen in small groups skimming low over the water of lakes, ponds, rivers, and in mangroves, sometimes over damp fields and meadows, even over salt water just beyond the shoreline. Perches low on snags and dead branches. Its call is a *dzreet, dzreet,* often given in flight.

Range: Mexico to eastern Panama; northwestern Peru.

Note: White-winged Swallow (*T. albiventer*) of South America (occurring as close as northwestern Colombia) is possible in San Blas; it resembles Mangrove Swallow but has large white patches on wings (visible at rest, very prominent in flight) and lacks white supraloral stripe.

VIOLET-GREEN SWALLOW
Tachycineta thalassina

Description: 5–5½. Very rare. Steely green above, glossed with violet and with *white of underparts extending up and behind eyes; broad*

white patch on each side of rump (leaving only a narrow dark central stripe); immaculate white below.

Similar species: Tree Swallow lacks white on face and the white rump patches. Mangrove Swallow also lacks white on face and has an all-white rump.

Status and distribution: Very rare or irregular winter visitant to western highlands east to western Panama province; has been reported during only three winters. Panama records include: at least 50 seen above Boquete, Chiriquí (1350 m: 4500 ft) on February 20–21, 1960 (Eisenmann and J. Linford), with the same observers then seeing 70–100 birds each afternoon in the Volcán/Cerro Punta area on February 23–27; up to 40 seen at Cerro Campana, western Panama province on December 27–29, 1976 (A. Greensmith *et al.*), with the same observers then seeing up to 80 birds near the Volcán Lakes in western Chiriquí on 13–14 January, 1977; and about 15 seen near Boquete on March 17, 1983 (R. Behrstock *et al.*).

Habits: As with the Tree Swallow, evidently in some years groups of Violet-greens move south of their normal wintering range; the Violet-green tends not to be so closely associated with areas close to water.

Range: Breeds in western North America; winters from Mexico to Honduras, casually to Costa Rica and Panama, accidentally to northern Colombia (one sighting).

BLUE-AND-WHITE SWALLOW
Notiochelidon cyanoleuca   Plate 47

Description: 4¾–5. Glossy, steely blue above; white below, usually with a few small blackish spots on chest, with *black under tail-coverts*. Migrants from southern South America (*patagonica*) are larger and have gray under wing-coverts (not blackish) and black on under tail-coverts not extending so far up.

Similar species: Tree Swallow has white under tail-coverts; Mangrove Swallow has white rump.

Status and distribution: Common in open areas and around habitations in highlands of western Chiriquí (mostly above 900 m: 3000 ft), and also recorded more locally eastward through the rest of Chiriquí, Veraguas (Calovévora), Coclé (above El Copé, El Valle), and western Panama province (Cerro Campana); these represent the resident nominate race. The migratory race *patagonica* has been recorded as an irregular, but occasionally common, visitant to eastern

and central Panama during the austral winter months (recorded in Panama at least April–August); most reports are from Canal area, probably because of greater observer coverage there (with maximum number seen being about 400 at Gatun Dam spillway on July 4, 1983; D. Engleman), but there are a number of sightings from eastern Panama province, and Goldman saw "hundreds" and collected two at Cana, Darién, on May 22, 1912.

Habits: A common and familiar bird in the western highlands, often around towns and habitations. Can also be seen regularly flying over the open, grassy hillsides of Cerro Campana. Sometimes nests semi-colonially, depending upon site availability, in eaves under buildings, holes dug into banks, and other crevices.

Range: Costa Rica to central Panama, and widely in highlands and temperate zone of South America; southernmost breeders winter north across much of northern South America to central Panama, casually to Nicaragua and southern Mexico.

Note: Here placed in the genus *Notiochelidon*, following general usage (e.g. Meyer de Schauensee 1966, 1970), but the 1983 AOU Check-list retained it in the monotypic *Pygochelidon*.

WHITE-THIGHED SWALLOW
Neochelidon tibialis   Plate 47

Description: 4–4½. *Small. Dark brown above, paler grayish brown below*; thighs white (difficult to see in the field).

Similar species: No other Panamanian swallow is so uniformly dusky. Superficially suggests a *Chaetura* swift but note different shape, flight, and perching habit.

Status and distribution: Uncommon to locally fairly common in forest borders and adjacent small clearings in humid lowlands and foothills from Coclé (above El Copé, head of Río Guabal, above El Valle) and Caribbean side of Canal area east through San Blas; on Pacific slope recorded from foothills of eastern Panama province (Cerro Azul/Jefe area; but seemingly unrecorded from Bayano River valley), and from lowlands and foothills of Darién; found up to about 900 m (3000 ft). In Canal area seen most often flying over forest and along roads at Fort Sherman/San Lorenzo, and along Pipeline Road.

Habits: Usually in small groups which generally do not associate with other swallows (though occasionally with Southern Roughwings). Perch in dead trees or branches at edge of forest or along streams. Flight is fast and erratic; usually silent. They apparently nest in holes in dead trees.

Range: Central Panama locally to eastern Peru and Amazonian and eastern Brazil.

NORTHERN ROUGH-WINGED SWALLOW

Stelgidopteryx serripennis   Plate 47

Description: 5½. Only migratory to Panama. *Uniform drab grayish brown above; throat and breast washed dingy pale grayish brown,* becoming whitish on lower underparts; wings and slightly notched tail blackish.

Similar species: Southern Rough-winged Swallow (now regarded as a distinct species) is similar but smaller, and has contrasting pale rump and distinctly cinnamon throat. Sand Martin is even smaller, has white throat sharply demarcated from its brown chest band. See also White-thighed Swallow.

Status and distribution: Fairly common transient and winter resident to lowlands and foothills on both slopes of western and central Panama (recorded September–April); few if any definite reports from San Blas or Darién.

Habits: Usually occurs in small groups, rarely associating with Southern Rough-wings though sometimes with other migrant swallows. Its usual call is a short harsh *brrrt.*

Range: Breeds from southern Canada south to central Costa Rica (where mostly in foothills and highlands, the race *fulvipennis* nesting sympatrically with Southern Rough-winged along north slope of the Central Volcanoes); winters from southern United States to Panama, probably a few also in northern South America (no confirmed records, but what appear to be transients are regularly seen in central Panama, near the southern edge of its recorded wintering range).

Note: Following the 1983 AOU Check-list and F. G. Stiles (*Auk 98*(2): 282–293, 1981), *S. serripennis* is considered a species distinct from mostly South American, true *S. ruficollis* (represented in Middle America by the race *uropygialis*), formerly called simply the Rough-winged Swallow.

SOUTHERN ROUGH-WINGED SWALLOW

Stelgidopteryx ruficollis   Plate 47

Description: 5. Mostly drab grayish brown above, duskier on crown and with *contrasting whitish rump; throat and upper chest cinnamon,* breast and sides pale grayish brown, fading to whitish on belly; wings and slightly notched tail blackish.

Similar species: Northern Rough-winged Swallow (recently split from this species) lacks the pale rump and has dingy throat (no cinnamon). Southern Rough-wing is the only basically brown swallow in Panama with a pale rump; young Mangrove Swallows are grayer above, and purer white below. See also White-thighed Swallow.

Status and distribution: Fairly common to common in open areas and clearings, especially near water, in lowlands and foothills on both slopes, ranging up in smaller numbers well into the highlands of western Chiriquí (to 1500–1800 m: 5000–6000 ft).

Habits: Usually found in pairs or small groups, though larger flocks are sometimes noted when not breeding. Nests in holes dug into banks, typically along rivers or in road cuts; some are dug by the swallows themselves, while others are former kingfisher burrows. Its usual call is an upslurred *djreeet.*

Range: Eastern Honduras to northern Argentina.

SAND MARTIN (BANK SWALLOW)

Riparia riparia   Plate 47

Description: 4¾. Rather small. *Uniform grayish brown above,* wings and slightly notched tail duskier; white below, *including throat,* with *grayish brown band across chest* (often extending down as a line of spots on mid-breast).

Similar species: Very like Brown-chested Martin in pattern but much smaller. Neither species of Rough-winged Swallow shows either a white throat or a distinct brown chest band.

Status and distribution: Fairly common transient on both slopes (recorded mostly September–October and March–April, with a few arrivals as early as early August, and stragglers lingering into May and rarely even early June), and rather rare and local winter resident, when recorded mostly from eastern Panama province with a few reports from elsewhere in semiopen to open parts on Pacific slope.

Habits: Usually seen flying low over open country, particularly near coast; frequently accompanies Barn Swallows. Its usual call is a dry gravelly *drrt,* sometimes given in series.

Range: Breeds in North America, Europe, northern Africa, and southern Asia; in New World winters mainly in South America, a few in Panama.

Note: Known in American literature, including the 1983 AOU Check-list, as the Bank Swallow. However in the Old World it is universally known as the "Sand Martin" and B. L. Monroe, Jr., has convinced us that the Americans need to synchronize with the rest of the world.

CLIFF SWALLOW
Hirundo pyrrhonota

Description: 5–5¾. Mostly dull, steely blue-black above, with *buff to whitish forehead*, buffy grayish collar on hindneck, and narrow white streaks on back; *rump buffy; cheeks and throat chestnut*, with black patch on center of lower throat; remaining underparts grayish buff, fading to whitish on lower belly; *tail almost square-tipped*. One race (*melanogaster*) has forehead chestnut like throat. Immature duller above, but often with deep rufous forehead; throat dull grayish buffy, usually lacking black patch on lower throat.
Similar species: Barn Swallow lacks this species' conspicuous pale buffy rump, and most have tail deeply forked (lacking in immature and molting winter adult). See also the very rare Cave Swallow.
Status and distribution: Uncommon to fairly common transient (late August–late October; early March–early May) throughout, but especially in coastal lowlands; one sighting of two as early as July 29 (Ridgely and J. Karr); small numbers apparently over-winter at least occasionally, usually among the flocks of Barn Swallows in Pacific slope lowlands.
Habits: Most often seen migrating, often with Barn Swallows, low over the ground in open areas.
Range: Breeds in North America; winters mostly in southern South America.
Note: Formerly placed in the genus *Petrochelidon*.

[CAVE SWALLOW]
Hirundo fulva

Description: 5½. Two recent sight reports. Closely resembles far more numerous Cliff Swallow. Differs in having *rufous-chestnut forehead* (not buffyish, but beware Cliffs of the race *melanogaster*, which also have chestnut foreheads; this race *does* occur in Panama on migration); *cheeks, throats, and upper chest cinnamon to pale buff* (not chestnut, and *lacking* Cliff's black on lower throat). Immatures duller, and would probably be hard to identify with certainty in the field.

Status and distribution: One was seen perched with other migrant swallows at Juan Diaz, eastern Panama province, on March 10, 1976 (Ridgely); another was noted with other over-wintering swallows at Tocumen, eastern Panama province, on February 10, 1980 (V. Emanuel *et al.*). The species is doubtless usually overlooked; all Cave Swallows breeding in northern Middle America presumably pass through Panama en route to their still uncertain South American wintering grounds.
Range: Breeds from southwestern United States to southern Mexico, and in Greater Antilles; at least some northern birds presumably winter in South America (but West Indian races are believed to be resident).
Note: Formerly placed in the genus *Petrochelidon*. Does not include Chestnut-collared Swallow (*H. rufocollaris*) of southwestern Ecuador and western Peru.

BARN SWALLOW
Hirundo rustica   Plate 47

Description: 6–7½. *Long deeply forked tail.* Steely blue-black above with chestnut forehead; throat chestnut, remaining underparts cinnamon-buff; tail blue-black with band of white spots on inner webs. Immature and molting adult may lack the long outer tail feathers.
Similar species: The only Panama swallow with a deeply forked tail. Cliff Swallow is superficially similar (especially to Barns without the long tail streamers) but has buffy rump.
Status and distribution: Very common to occasionally abundant transient (late August–late November; early March–mid-May; a few as early as late July and as late as May) virtually throughout (less numerous in highlands above 1800 m: 6000 ft) but especially in coastal lowlands; rare to locally fairly common winter resident in more open areas, most numerous in Pacific western Panama; a few scattered individuals occasionally spend the entire northern summer. By far the most numerous migrant swallow in Panama.
Habits: During migration, small groups are almost constantly visible in open country, flying swiftly and steadily low over the ground. Often flies directly over Panama Bay. Can be seen anywhere, but in greatest numbers along either coast, flying generally eastward in September–November, westward on return passage.
Range: Breeds in North America, Europe, northern Africa, and Asia, with a very small

number having also recently commenced nesting in eastern Argentina (Buenos Aires); in New World winters primarily in

South America, small numbers in southern Middle America, a few northward.

JAYS, MAGPIES, AND CROWS: Corvidae (4)

Of this varied and widespread family, only jays are found in Panama (and South America), typical crows not occurring south of Nicaragua. Only one of the four Panamanian species, the Black-chested Jay, is at all widespread in the country. Jays are typically found in small often noisy groups, moving through the trees at all heights. They are virtually omnivorous. Jay nests are usually large open structures of twigs, lined with finer material, generally well hidden in bushes and trees; however, virtually nothing seems to have been recorded about nesting in Panama.

BLACK-CHESTED JAY
Cyanocorax affinis   Plate 17

Description: 12½–14½. Panama's only widespread jay. *Head, throat, and chest black* with small bright blue patches above and below eye and on cheeks; otherwise blue above, more brownish violet-blue on back; *breast and belly creamy white; tail broadly tipped creamy white.*
Similar species: The only jay in most of its Panama range. Brown Jay of Bocas del Toro is mostly brown.
Status and distribution: Locally uncommon to fairly common in forest and forest borders, second-growth woodland, gallery woodland, and even dry deciduous woodland in lowlands on both slopes including Azuero Peninsula and up into foothills at El Valle in Coclé, ranging into lower highlands in western Chiriquí (sparingly to 1620 m: 5400 ft). In Canal area rare or irregular in middle Chagres River valley, but numerous near Caribbean coast (e.g. Achiote and Escobal Roads, Fort Sherman/San Lorenzo).
Habits: Travels about in small active groups, usually of no more than half a dozen individuals. Calls frequently, a loud and distinctive *chowng, chowng* or *kyoo-kyoo*, with a ringing metallic quality.
Range: Costa Rica to northern Colombia and Venezuela.

BROWN JAY
Cyanocorax morio   Plate 44, p.338

Description: 15–16. Regular only in Bocas del Toro lowlands. Considerably larger than other Panama jays, with long tail. Bill black in adult, with yellow base in immature (some variation). *Uniform brown above; some-*

what paler brown on throat and chest; breast and belly white; tail brown with broad white tips to outer feathers, very prominent in flight. An inflatable airsac on the chest can sometimes be seen, especially as the bird calls; it makes an odd, quite loud, popping sound.
Similar species: Panama's other jays are largely blue above, not brown.
Status and distribution: Uncommon in forest borders, lighter woodland, and shrubby clearings in lowlands of western and central Bocas del Toro; two recent sightings of a group of about six individuals one mile north of Achiote, western Colon province (just over Canal area border), the first on January 21, 1969, and again in early 1970 (both N. G. Smith), but not observed since.
Habits: A noisy and conspicuous bird, trooping about in groups of half a dozen or more. Often heard is its loud raucous call, *keeyah, keeyah*, sometimes given at the approach of a human.
Range: Southern Texas and eastern Mexico to Caribbean western (casually central) Panama.
Note: Formerly placed in the monotypic genus *Psilorhinus*. Wetmore *et al.* (1982) argue that the unique airsac justifies its continued separation from the other *Cyanocorax* jays at the genus level, but we follow the 1983 AOU Check-list in placing it in *Cyanocorax.*

AZURE-HOODED JAY
Cyanolyca cucullata   Plate 17

Description: 11. Known only from western highlands. *Mostly dark blue; rearcrown and nape contrasting pale blue*; forecrown and sides of head and neck black.
Similar species: See Silvery-throated Jay.

BROWN JAY

Status and distribution: Uncommon to locally fairly common in humid forest and forest borders in foothills and highlands of Bocas del Toro (900–2100 m: 3000–7000 ft), crossing over Divide into central Chiriquí in the Fortuna area (where first recorded in February–March 1976 by Ridgely, with one specimen to GML); also recorded from Veraguas (Chitra). Absent from the western Chiriquí highlands, and still little known and seemingly local throughout its Panama range.
Habits: Generally found in groups of from two to (rarely) eight individuals, moving about actively in middle and upper tree levels; its call is an arresting, rather nasal *renk* or *renk-ee-renk*.
Range: Central Mexico to western Panama.

SILVERY-THROATED JAY
Cyanolyca argentigula   Plate 17

Description: 10. Found only in western Chiriquí highlands. Head and neck black with *bluish white forecrown extending as narrow stripe over eye*; remaining upperparts purplish blue; *throat pale silvery blue*, chest black, shading into dusky purplish blue on lower underparts. Juvenile lacks blue stripe on head and has bluish dusky crown.
Similar species: See Azure-hooded Jay.
Status and distribution: Uncommon in forest and forest borders in highlands of western Chiriquí, recorded 1500–3000 m (5000–10,000 ft). In recent years a pair or two has been found regularly in the Fernandez area along Boquete Trail above Cerro Punta.
Habits: Usually rather inconspicuous, in pairs or small groups, remaining high in forest canopy. The call is a moderately loud, nasal *chaak, cheuk, cheh*.
Range: Costa Rica and western Panama.

WRENS: Troglodytidae (22)

The wrens are an essentially American family, with only one species having spread into the Old World via Alaska; the family is most abundant and diverse in the neotropics. Most wrens are rather small, compact birds, largely brown with paler underparts, often with a short tail, in most species with wings and tail conspicuously barred with blackish. Many species are skulking, rarely coming into the open, though most are curious and the patient observer will usually eventually be rewarded with at least a brief view. Most wrens have well developed and often very attractive songs; many in the genus *Thryothorus* sing antiphonally, each member of the pair giving part of the total phrase. Wrens are essentially insectivorous; most species construct closed domed nests, while a few nest in cavities of some sort. In some species a number of individuals roost communally in a "dormitory", either another nest (often built specifically for the purpose) or a natural cavity; other species roost individually in a cavity. Note that the Donacobius is now considered to be a member of the Wren family.

BLACK-CAPPED DONACOBIUS
Donacobius atricapillus   p.339

Description: 8. Known only from eastern Darién. Slender and sleek in appearance. *Iris conspicuously yellow. Head black; upperparts otherwise dark chocolate brown;* wings black with white patch in primaries; tail black tipped white; *buffy below,* sometimes with fine black barring on sides; a bare orange area on sides of neck is usually concealed but can be expanded.
Status and distribution: Uncommon in overgrown marshes and wet meadows with rank vegetation in eastern Darién, where it has been found around El Real and in the swampy valley at Cana (but may possibly occur elsewhere).
Habits: Usually seen in pairs or small groups, often perching in the open and not difficult to observe. In display one bird perches a few inches above another and gives a *whtm,* flashing (and partly spreading) tail from side to side; the lower bird then answers with a louder semi-whistled *kweéa, kweéa;* both birds also sometimes expose the orange skin on the neck.
Range: Eastern Panama to Bolivia and northern Argentina.
Note: Formerly placed in the Mimidae, but now considered to belong in the Troglodytidae, probably closest to *Campylorhynchus.*

WHITE-HEADED WREN
Campylorhynchus albobrunneus   Plate 28

Description: 7½. Unmistakable. *Very large. Head and entire underparts white;* back, wings, and tail dark brown. At least during the dry season white parts of plumage in many birds looks soiled (throat often appears brown); this condition probably is derived from their frequent dust-bathing at that season.
Status and distribution: Uncommon to locally common (more numerous eastward) in canopy and (especially) borders of forest and adjacent clearings in lowlands on both slopes; rather local, on Caribbean slope known from northern Coclé and western Colon province (Río Indio) east into Canal

area (where recorded in recent years only from Achiote Road), and in eastern San Blas (Puerto Obaldía); on Pacific slope known from eastern Panama province (middle and upper Bayano River valley) and Darién (where it ranges well up into foothills, having been found to about 1200 m: 4000 ft on Cerro Pirre).
Habits: Favors forest borders, where it forages in small groups in lianas and epiphytes, mostly at middle levels. The call is a harsh *churk,* the song a *ch-ch-ch-ch-ch-kaw-kaw,* with last notes semi-musical.
Range: Central Panama to western Colombia.
Note: Perhaps conspecific with Band-backed Wren; a population from southwestern Colombia may represent hybrids between the two forms, for now still treated as two species.

BAND-BACKED WREN
Campylorhynchus zonatus   Plate 28

Description: 7½. Known only from western Panama. *Very large.* Crown black broadly edged with brownish gray, superciliary whitish; *upperparts otherwise boldly banded black and buffy whitish; throat, chest, and breast white conspicuously spotted with black;* belly tawny. Juvenile has plain black cap, back black spotted or streaked with brown (wings and tail banded as in adult), underparts mostly dull whitish mottled with gray.

BLACK-CAPPED DONACOBIUS

Similar species: Large size and striking banded and spotted appearance render this species virtually unmistakable.

Status and distribution: Uncommon to locally fairly common in canopy and borders of humid forest, and in adjacent clearings with larger trees, in lowlands and foothills of Bocas del Toro (recorded up to around 1000 m: 3300 ft along the oleoducto road north of Fortuna, Chiriquí), and in foothills on both slopes in western Veraguas (Santa Fé). In Panama seems more numerous in hill country than in the lowlands.

Habits: Usually found in pairs or small groups that forage at all levels, often climbing about among vines and epiphytes. Has a variety of harsh scratchy rhythmical calls such as *zikarúk-tzikadarik* and *zick-urr* (Slud).

Range: Eastern Mexico to western Panama; northern Colombia; northwestern Ecuador.

SOOTY-HEADED WREN
Thryothorus spadix   Plate 40

Description: 5½. Known only from eastern Darién foothills. *Crown sooty gray, becoming black on sides of head, throat, and upper chest*; narrow white superciliary and ear-coverts lightly streaked white; *otherwise rufous*, becoming duller brown below; wings and tail barred with black. Juvenile duller with face and throat more slaty.

Similar species: Black-throated Wren of Bocas del Toro has crown chestnut brown and lower underparts mostly dull brown (breast not rufous).

Status and distribution: Uncommon in undergrowth of humid forest, forest borders, and adjacent heavily overgrown clearings in foothills of eastern Darién (Cerro Tacarcuna, Cerro Pirre, Cerro Quía); recorded about 450–1200 m (1500–4000 ft).

Habits: Rather more closely associated with forest undergrowth than other *Thryothorus* wrens; here it skulks in pairs, favoring very dense viny or tangled undergrowth, occasionally accompanying mixed bird flocks. Its song is loud and vigorous, rather rich in quality, a phrase being slowly repeated a number of times before going on to a different one, e.g. *wee-chee, weecheereeo* or *weechoaweeawee, chuwoo* (Ridgely, M. Robbins *et al.*).

Range: Eastern Panama to western Colombia.

BLACK-THROATED WREN
Thryothorus atrogularis   Plate 28

Description: 5½. Found only in western Bocas del Toro. Chestnut above, dull brown below, with *sides of head, throat, and upper chest black*; wings barred with black; tail black, faintly barred with brown. Juvenile entirely dull brown with some dusky on sides of head and throat, tail as in adult.

Similar species: Sooty-headed Wren of Darién has entire head dark sooty gray and lower underparts mostly rufous (not dull brown). Superficially rather antbird-like.

Status and distribution: Uncommon to locally fairly common in tangled second-growth woodland, shrubby overgrown clearings, and swampy woodland in lowlands and foothills of western Bocas del Toro; recorded primarily from the Almirante/lower Río Changuinola area, but also up to about 720 m (2400 ft) on the Río Changuena.

Habits: Found singly or in pairs, usually in dense undergrowth and often hard to even glimpse. The song is a short but rich and melodious phrase *treeeoo-treee? treeeoo*, rapidly delivered, often followed by a throatier chatter or trill.

Range: Nicaragua to Caribbean western Panama.

BLACK-BELLIED WREN
Thryothorus fasciatoventris   Plate 28

Description: 6. Chestnut brown above with narrow white superciliary and dusky ear-coverts; *throat and chest white contrasting with black breast and belly*, belly more or less barred with white; tail barred brown and black. Juvenile much duller with throat and chest gray, lower underparts brownish somewhat barred with dusky.

Similar species: Note sharp contrast between upper and lower underparts. In pattern somewhat antbird-like.

Status and distribution: Fairly common in thickets and dense undergrowth of woodland and forest borders and damp woodland in lowlands of western Chiriquí (*melanogaster*), and on Caribbean slope from northern Coclé and western Colon province eastward, and on Pacific slope from Canal area eastward; records from Veraguas are considered uncertain by Wetmore.

Habits: Quite partial to the vicinity of water. Usually the most difficult *Thryothorus* wren to observe. Its song is very fine, rich and mellow, rather low-pitched and slow-paced, often ending with a characteristic *wheeowheét* or "cream of wheat" (F. O. Chapelle) with an upward inflection; it has a large repertory of phrases, each phrase repeated many times before changing.

Range: Costa Rica to western Colombia.

BAY WREN
Thryothorus nigricapillus   Plates 28, 40

Description: 5 ½ . *Bright chestnut above* with *black crown and nape*, white spot on ear-coverts, and black and white stripes on sides of head, wings and tail boldly barred chestnut and black; birds from western Caribbean slope east to eastern Colon province (formerly considered a distinct species, the *T. castaneus* group) have white throat, remaining underparts tawny rufous with a little black barring on sides and flanks; birds from San Blas and Darién (the *nigricapillus* group, formerly called Black-capped Wren) are *mostly white below boldly barred with black*, tinged chestnut on flanks and under tail-coverts. Intermediates between the two types occur in eastern Colon and Panama provinces (Portobelo, Cerro Jefe area, Bayano River valley) with mostly rufous underparts and black barring.
Similar species: The main divisions of this species are very different looking below, but both should be easily recognized. Riverside Wren of Chiriquí rather resembles eastern populations of Bay Wren but has chestnut crown and nape (like back) and narrower barring below.
Status and distribution: Common in rank undergrowth near streams and roadsides through forest and in overgrown clearings in humid lowlands on entire Caribbean slope; on Pacific slope found in humid foothills from Veraguas (Santa Fé), Coclé (El Valle), and eastern Panama province (Cerro Jefe area) eastward, in lowlands from south-western Canal area (scarce) and eastern Panama province (Bayano River valley) eastward; found also on Escudo de Veraguas off coast of Bocas del Toro.
Habits: Seems especially fond of *Heliconia* thickets. Usually remains hidden from view, but often inquisitive and will regularly come out to look over the patient observer. A very vocal bird, with a variety of calls and rich musical songs, one of the best singing wrens; the song consists of loud ringing whistled phrases, each phrase repeated rapidly many times, then switched to another often very different phrase, e.g *see-me, how-wet-I-am.*
Range: Nicaragua to western Ecuador.

RIVERSIDE WREN
Thryothorus semibadius   Plate 28

Description: 5½. Found only in western Chiriquí. *Bright chestnut above* with white superciliary and sides of head streaked black and white, wings and tail prominently barred pale rusty and black; throat white, *remaining underparts conspicuously barred black and white.*
Similar species: Eastern races of Bay Wren have black crown and nape and coarser black barring below; they have an entirely different range. Otherwise unmistakable.
Status and distribution: Uncommon to locally fairly common in dense thickets and shrubby woodland and forest undergrowth, mostly near streams, and at edge of mangroves, in lowlands of western Chiriquí, ranging up in reduced numbers to around 1200 m (4000 ft) near Volcán. Regularly encountered in appropriate habitat around Puerto Armuelles (though outnumbered there by Black-bellied Wren); nonetheless, overall numbers in Chiriquí have probably declined as a result of deforestation.
Habits: Like other members of the genus, usually hard to glimpse, generally skulking in dense low damp thickets. Its song is similar to Bay Wren's but perhaps somewhat higher-pitched.
Range: Costa Rica and Pacific western Panama.

STRIPE-THROATED WREN
Thryothorus leucopogon   Plate 40

Description: 5. Found only in eastern Panama. Iris pale hazel to auburn. Olive brown above with narrow white superciliary and *black barring on wings* and tail; *sides of head and throat white streaked with black; remaining underparts deep tawny brown.*
Similar species: Stripe-breasted Wren of Caribbean western Panama has most of underparts streaked with black (not merely the throat). Rufous-breasted Wren is rather similar but has unbarred wings and is brighter rufous below, especially on chest; it is not known from Darién.
Status and distribution: Fairly common in tangled viny growth, mostly at middle levels and at edge, in forest and second-growth woodland in lowlands and lower foothills in San Blas (where recorded mostly from eastern portion, but recently found also in extreme west at Nusagandi; Ridgely *et al.*), extreme eastern Panama province (Cerro Chucantí), and Darién; recorded up to about 750 m (2500 ft) on slopes of Cerro Pirre. Easily seen at Cana, Darién.
Habits: Relatively easy to see for a *Thryothorus* wren, foraging higher above ground and more often in the open than most; pairs frequently accompany mixed flocks of antwrens, etc. Its call is a distinctive *chu,*

ch-chu, or *chu, ch-chu, ch-chu;* the song is a repetition of a simple phrase, e.g. *tee-peee, teeo-peee . . . .* or *wurree-tu, wurree-tu . . . .*
Range: Eastern Panama to western Ecuador.

STRIPE-BREASTED WREN
Thryothorus thoracicus   Plate 28

Description: 5. Found mainly in Caribbean western Panama. Plain brown above, more olive on head, with narrow white superciliary and black barring on wings and tail; *sides of head and most of underparts whitish conspicuously streaked with black,* dull brown on sides and flanks.
Similar species: No other Panama wren has such boldly *streaked* (not barred) underparts.
Status and distribution: Uncommon in borders of humid forest and in second-growth woodland in lowlands on Caribbean slope from Bocas del Toro (where recorded up into foothills to about 720 m: 2400 ft on the Río Changuena) to northern Coclé and locally to Caribbean side of Canal area (where a few have been recorded regularly in recent years from Achiote Road); spills over Divide onto Pacific slope above Santa Fé, Veraguas (where recorded in March 1974 by A. Skutch *et al.*).
Habits: Usually in pairs or small groups, foraging chiefly at low and middle tree levels, often among vines and lianas. Its call is a characteristic single whistled note, regularly repeated at short intervals, heard especially soon after dawn; the song resembles that of other *Thryothorus* wrens, consisting of a variety of rich phrases, each usually repeated several times before going on to another, often given antiphonally between members of a pair.
Range: Nicaragua to central Panama.

RUFOUS-BREASTED WREN
Thryothorus rutilus   Plate 28

Description: 5. Plain brown above (*wings unbarred*), more rufous on crown, with white superciliary; *sides of head and throat black speckled with white; remaining underparts tawny-rufous, brightest (almost orange) on chest;* tail grayish brown barred with black.
Similar species: No other Panama *Thryothorus* wren has unbarred wings, and none shows such a contrast between the speckled throat and the bright orange-rufous chest. In eastern Panama see Stripe-throated Wren.
Status and distribution: Fairly common in dense thickets and undergrowth of lighter or drier second-growth woodland in lowlands

and (especially) foothills on Pacific slope from Chiriquí (where it ranges up in small numbers into the lower highlands to about 1500 m: 5000 ft) to eastern Panama province (lower Bayano River valley); on Caribbean slope recorded locally and in smaller numbers in thickets in clearings and at edge of secondary woodland from Canal area and eastern Colon province (Portobelo); apparently absent from drier lowlands from eastern side of Azuero Peninsula to extreme western Panama province.
Habits: Often found with Rufous-and-white Wren but usually in somewhat less dense areas. Normally not as difficult to see as most other *Thryothorus* wrens. The song is rollicking and musical (though less rich than that of most other species), very variable, typically a five or six-syllabled phrase repeated rapidly over and over, often with a slurred downward ending, such as *whee-ha-chweéoo* and *weeper-cheepeereéyoo.* Like most other *Thryothorus* wrens, frequently sings antiphonally. A distinctive call is similar to the mechanical sound made by rubbing one's finger against the tines of a comb.
Range: Costa Rica to central Panama; northeastern Colombia to northern Venezuela.

RUFOUS-AND-WHITE WREN
Thryothorus rufalbus   Plate 28

Description: 5¾. *Bright rufous above* with sharp white superciliary and white cheeks streaked with black; wings and tail prominently barred with dusky; *white below,* tinged with brown on sides and flanks.
Similar species: Note the striking contrast between rufous upperparts and white underparts. See Plain Wren.
Status and distribution: Fairly common in shrubby clearings and undergrowth of deciduous woodland in lowlands and foothills on Pacific slope from Chiriquí to eastern Panama province (lower and middle Bayano River valley), in western Chiriquí ranging up in small numbers up into lower highlands to 1200–1500 m (4000–5000 ft) in partially cleared areas; on Caribbean slope recorded only from Canal area, where found in small numbers from the middle Chagres River valley to Fort Sherman.
Habits: Very shy and furtive, heard far more often than seen. Its song is unmistakable, a series of very low-pitched "hooting" whistles, often with four or more notes on same pitch followed by another on a different pitch, sometimes with interposed trilling,

exceptionally hard to describe but one recurring phrase is a *hoo, hoo-hoo-hoo-whit*.
Range: Southern Mexico to Colombia and northern Venezuela.

BUFF-BREASTED WREN
Thryothorus leucotis   Plate 28

Description: 5 ¼. Brown above with white superciliary and whitish cheeks streaked with dusky; *distinctly barred with black on wings and tail*; throat white, *remaining underparts buffy*, brightest on flanks and belly.
Similar species: Often confused with Plain Wren in central Panama. Plain Wren has less distinct barring on wings and tail (not sharply black) and is mostly white below (not mostly buff); in zone of overlap the two also tend to segregate out by habitat; the songs are also very different.
Status and distribution: Fairly common in thickets and dense undergrowth and woodland borders (usually near water) in lowlands on both slopes from Canal area eastward; fairly common also on some of the Pearl Islands (Rey, Víveros, Puercos, and Cañas).
Habits: Rather shy and often hard to see well, but has a loud rich musical rollicking song with one phrase of one or two parts repeated over and over and then changed to another phrase, typically *choreéwee, choreéwee, choreéwee . . . wheeooreé-tickwheeoo, wheeooreé-tickweeoo . . .* and so on.
Range: Central Panama to Peru and central Brazil.

PLAIN WREN
Thryothorus modestus   Plate 28

Description: 5 ¼. Rather like Buff-breasted Wren. Brown above, tinged slightly grayish especially on crown, with white superciliary; *wings and tail indistinctly barred with dusky; mostly white below*, tinged buffy brown on sides, becoming richer buff on flanks and lower belly. Birds from western Bocas del Toro (*zeledoni*) are larger (5 ½ – 5 ¾ in) and heavier-billed, and are considerably darker overall, more dark grayish olive above (not so brown) and tinged grayish olive on sides and under tail-coverts.
Similar species: See Buff-breasted Wren. Somewhat larger Rufous-and-white Wren is brighter rufous above and purer white below and has sharp barring on wings and tail. House Wren is smaller and less distinctly marked, with only vague buffy superciliary (not white) and buffy brownish underparts.

Status and distribution: Fairly common to common in thickets and bushes in clearings and grassy areas and in gardens in lowlands and foothills on Pacific slope from Chiriquí (where it ranges up to over 1800 m: 6000 ft in suitable cleared habitat) to eastern Panama province (Cerro Azul/Jefe, lower Bayano River valley); on Caribbean slope known only from lowlands of western Bocas del Toro (*T. m. zeledoni*), and from Canal area and eastern Colon province (east at least to Portobelo area).
Habits: Generally shy, remaining in thick cover. The song, though musical, lacks the rich mellow quality of the Buff-breasted Wren's, consisting of a variety of repeated phrases, the most common being variants of *cheéncheereegwee*. The *churr* call resembles that of other *Thryothorus* wrens but is exceptionally loud and sharp. The voice of *zeledoni* seems generally similar to that of typical Plain Wren, with the *cheéncheereegwee* also being frequently given; at least in Costa Rica may be somewhat shriller and higher-pitched.
Range: Southern Mexico to central Panama.
Note: There exists a large gap between the recorded ranges of *T. m. zeledoni* and *T. m. elutus* in west-central Panama; whether this is an artifact of inadequate collecting, or represents a real absence, is uncertain. Wetmore and the 1983 AOU Check-list treated *zeledoni* and *modestus* as conspecific, and this course is followed here. Formerly *T. zeledoni* had often been considered a full species, Canebrake Wren, and the situation still warrants further study.

HOUSE WREN
Troglodytes aedon   Plate 28

Description: 4 ½. *Mostly brown*, somewhat paler and buffier below, becoming buffy whitish on throat; indistinct buffy brown superciliary; some indistinct dusky barring on wings and tail. Birds from Coiba Island (*carychrous*) are markedly brighter brown above and brighter buff below.
Similar species: Among Panamanian wrens only the very dark Southern Nightingale-Wren of humid forest is quite so devoid of distinctive markings. Most likely to be confused with larger Plain Wren, which has more prominent white eye-stripe and contrastingly whitish underparts. See also Ochraceous Wren.
Status and distribution: Generally common in open country, clearings, and especially around habitations in lowlands and foothills on both slopes, in western Chiriquí ranging

up in small numbers to over 2100 m (7000 ft) where there are suitable clearings; somewhat local, and on the whole less numerous in Bocas del Toro and Darién than elsewhere (but likely will increase with clearing?); common also on Coiba Island (where in addition to its usual habitats, also ranges commonly in forest undergrowth) and on Pearl Islands.

Habits: An energetic and friendly bird, often nesting in crannies of buildings. Its bubbly gurgling song will at once be recognized by anyone familiar with House Wrens in North America, but it is perhaps even more pleasing and musical, less raspy; also gives a musical *chew-chew-chew* . . . .

Range: North America to Tierra del Fuego; Lesser Antilles.

Note: Formerly two species were recognized, *T. musculus* (Southern House-Wren, the form in Panama) and *T. aedon* (Northern House-Wren).

OCHRACEOUS WREN
Troglodytes ochraceus   Plate 28

Description: 4. A highland bird. Small and rather short-tailed. Tawny brown above with *conspicuous ochre superciliary* above dusky line through eye; *buffy-ochre below*, fading to whitish on belly.

Similar species: Small size and bright brown coloration with prominent superciliary simplify identification. House Wren is duller brown with indistinct superciliary.

Status and distribution: Fairly common to common in forest and forest borders in highlands of Chiriquí, adjacent Bocas del Toro (where reported only from along oleoducto road north of Fortuna, but probably more widespread), Veraguas, and eastern Darién (Cerro Pirre and Cerro Tacarcuna); a few sightings from near the summit of Cerro Campana, western Panama province, in the 1960s (E. O. Willis, N. G. Smith), and one was seen in August 1984 (J. Guarnaccia); in western Chiriquí found mainly above 1500 m (5000 ft), elsewhere lower (mostly 750–1650 m: 2500–5500 ft). Particularly numerous in the Fernandez forest area along the Boquete Trail above Cerro Punta.

Habits: Generally forages well up in the trees, feeding among the epiphytes and other air plants so numerous on larger branches and trunks. The song is a fairly musical trilling *seerrrrrrrr*, sometimes introduced by a more musical *tswee-tswee*, at times somewhat reminiscent of the holarctic Winter Wren (*T. troglodytes*).

Range: Costa Rica to eastern Panama.

GRASS (SEDGE) WREN
Cistothorus platensis

Description: 4¼. Very rare; known only from western Chiriquí. *Crown brown streaked with buff; back blackish broadly streaked with buffy whitish*; wings and tail rufous brown barred black; buffy whitish below, whitest on throat and median belly.

Similar species: Small size, streaked back, and habitat (see below) should distinguish this species from other Panama wrens, in the event it is ever found again. North American observers should note that the tail of the Panama race (*lucidus*, also in Costa Rica) is *markedly longer* than in northern birds, resulting in rather different shape and overall appearance.

Status and distribution: Very rare in grassy or sedgy marshes, boggy areas, and wet meadows in western Chiriquí; not recorded in Panama since early in the twentieth century. At that time it may have been locally numerous in appropriate habitat (which must always have been local), with specimens being recorded from Bugaba in lowlands, around Boquete at several different sites, and on Volcán Barú (at 2700 m: 9000 ft). Drainage and over-grazing may have so altered its limited Panama habitat that it may be extirpated from the country, though one hopes a colony or two may survive somewhere. Numbers in Costa Rica are also very much reduced; the subspecies *lucidus* certainly deserves endangered status.

Habits: Elsewhere secretive and difficult to observe unless singing or calling, which fortunately it frequently does. Usually creeps around in grassy or sedgy growth, on or near the ground, rather mouse-like; they flush reluctantly, and fly only short distances before diving back into cover. They sometimes are curious, however, and may be enticed into view by squeaking. In Costa Rica its call has been described as a grasshopper-like *tzrrr*, and the song as a *chyip-chyip-chyip-chyip-chyip*, sometimes with a gurgling quality (Slud).

Range: Eastern and central North America south locally to Tierra del Fuego.

Note: More than one species is surely involved, but actual species limits remain uncertain, as is the position of the Panama race, *lucidus*; the latter has usually been placed with the northern *stellaris* group (Sedge Wren), as its southernmost representative, but actually in most respects seems closer to the southern true *platensis* group (which itself may consist of more than one species). For simplicity's sake, the 1983 AOU Check-list, which continued to lump all populations in one species, is followed here.

TIMBERLINE WREN
Thryorchilus browni Plate 28

Description: 4. Found only high on Volcán Barú. Rather short-tailed. Tawny brown above with *broad white superciliary; primaries edged with white; mostly white below*, chest flecked with brown, flanks tinged with tawny-olive.
Similar species: Ochraceous Wren has an ochre superciliary and is buffy-ochre below. The only Panama wren with white on the wings.
Status and distribution: Fairly common on higher slopes of Volcán Barú in western Chiriquí, only above about 2700 m (9000 ft); also occurs on summit of Barú's major spur, Cerro Copete, at about 3000 m (10,000 ft). Readily found along upper part of the tele-communications tower access road (which ascends Barú's east flank, from above Boquete).
Habits: Found in dense low forest with extensive bamboo understory at levels below timberline, in scattered low bushes above timberline. Its complex song begins as a whisper, then steadily builds into a complex jumble of high *cheedle* notes and twitters, *chee-deet-tee-deé, deedle-deét-doo, chee-deét-tee-dee, deedle-deet-doo* . . . and so on until hopelessly jumbled with high peeps, rougher scolding notes, and warbles (B. Whitney; Ridgely). Overall the song is quite suggestive of the Winter Wren (*Troglodytes troglodytes*) of North America, though nowhere near as loud or far-carrying, and not quite so musical. Its alarm call is a distinctive high and un-wrenlike *speee*.
Range: Costa Rica and western Panama.

WHITE-BREASTED WOOD-WREN
Henicorhina leucosticta Plate 28

Description: 4. Small with *very short tail*, usually cocked up. Mostly brown above with *prominent white superciliary*; sides of head and neck streaked black and white; wings and tail barred with black; *mostly white below*, grayish on sides, brownish on lower belly. Birds from western Panama (*pittieri*) have crown *dark chestnut* brown, while those from San Blas, eastern Panama province (Bayano River valley eastward), and Darién (*darienensis*) have *deep black* crown; birds from central Panama (e.g. the Canal area) are intermediate, though closer to *pittieri*.
Similar species: Very like Gray-breasted

Wood-Wren except for white (not gray) underparts and shorter tail.
Status and distribution: Fairly common to common in undergrowth of humid forest and mature second-growth woodland in lowlands and foothills on entire Caribbean slope; on Pacific slope found widely in foothills (especially 600–1050 m: 2000–3500 ft), in lowlands recorded only from western Chiriquí (recent records only from the Burica Peninsula area), and from Canal area (where local) east through Darién (where widespread and numerous). In Canal area particularly common at Fort Sherman/San Lorenzo.
Habits: Particularly fond of steep, forested hillsides and ravines and the tangled undergrowth that springs up after the fall of a forest tree creates an opening in the canopy. Usually in pairs, keeping very low in undergrowth; often curious so normally not too hard to observe. The song is variable, quite rich and melodic, with short repeated whistled phrases; characteristic is a *pretty-pretty-bird* (F. O. Chapelle) or *churry-churry-cheer*; others include a somewhat shrike-vireo-like *teea-teea-teeoo*, and a *wheé-tew-tew*. The call is a peculiar *bweeer*, somewhat reminiscent of call of Swainson's Thrush.
Range: Mexico to central Perú, northern Brazil, and the Guianas.

GRAY-BREASTED WOOD-WREN
Henicorhina leucophrys Plate 22

Description: 4½ . *Highlands*. Small and short-tailed (but tail longer than in White-breasted Wood-Wren). Rather like White-breasted Wood-Wren and in a few areas found with it. Rufous brown above, more blackish on crown (especially on its sides), wings and tail lightly barred with black; superciliary white, sides of head and neck streaked black and white; *underparts mostly gray*, more whitish on throat (which is heavily streaked with dark gray in western *collina*, essentially unstreaked in nominate race of eastern half of Panama), washed with rufous brown on flanks and lower belly.
Similar species: White-breasted Wood-Wren has mostly white underparts, is a lowland bird.
Status and distribution: Common to very common in dense undergrowth of montane forest and forest borders, coffee plantations, and heavily overgrown clearings in highlands of Chiriquí, adjacent Bocas del Toro, Veraguas, Coclé (above El Copé and El

Valle), western Panama province (Cerro Campana), eastern Panama province (Cerro Jefe), extreme western San Blas (Cerro Brewster, where found in April 1985 by J. Blake), and eastern Darién (Cerro Pirre and Cerro Tacarcuna); recorded mostly above 900 m (3000 ft), locally a little lower in central Panama.

Habits: Like the White-breast this is an inquisitive little bird that often will come out to look over the patient observer. The song has much longer phrases but is not as rich as that of the White-breasted Wood-Wren; a typical example is *cheerooeecheé-cheeweé-cheerooeéchee*, and variations, repeated over and over; the call is a mild *chirrrr*.

Range: Mexico to northern Venezuela and northern Bolivia.

SOUTHERN NIGHTINGALE-WREN
Microcerculus marginatus   Plate 28

Description: 4¼. *Bill rather long and slender;* legs quite long; *tail very short*, often cocked. *Dark brown above*, wings and tail unbarred; throat whitish to pale gray, *remaining underparts dull grayish* with some brown on flanks and lower belly, sometimes with some pale scalloping on belly.

Similar species: A dark, essentially unpatterned little wren of forest undergrowth.

Status and distribution: Locally fairly common, but rarely seen, in undergrowth and on ground in humid forest and mature second-growth woodland in lowlands and foothills on entire Caribbean slope; on Pacific slope recorded from lowlands and foothills of western Chiriquí (in lowlands reported only from Burica Peninsula; in recent years has also been heard quite regularly in highlands up to 1800–2100 m: 6000–7000 ft), locally in foothills eastward through Darién, and in lowlands of eastern Panama province (upper Bayano River valley) and Darién; recorded mostly below about 1050 m (3500 ft). In Canal area most numerous along Pipeline Road.

Habits: Prefers steep, forested hillsides, ravines, and dense undergrowth near streams. Very furtive and inconspicuous; when glimpsed, its never ceasing habit of bobbing its hind end up and down like a waterthrush will at once be apparent. The unmistakable song is the usual indication of this species' presence; after a rather short, fairly rapid, and irregular opening phrase (often not heard at a distance), it consists of a long series (usually 10 or more) of almost sibilant single long-drawn whistles (each lasting about a

second), progressively very slightly lower in pitch and less loud, with even longer pauses between notes (almost tantalizing toward end when each pause may last more than 10 seconds).

Range: Southern Costa Rica to northern Bolivia and Amazonian Brazil.

Note: Birds from southern Mexico to northern Costa Rica are now recognized as a distinct species, *M. philomela*; see F. G. Stiles, *Wilson Bull 95*(2): 169–183, 1983. The basic split suggested by Stiles was adopted in the 35th Supplement to the AOU Check-list (*Auk 102*(3): 683, 1985). Taxonomy within *M. marginatus* is complex (note that Stiles called Panama birds *M. luscinia*), with more than one species perhaps being involved in South America, but more research is needed. English names also present various difficulties. Stiles suggested restricting "Nightingale Wren" to *M. philomela*, though admitting that it was a somewhat unfortunate choice given that neither it nor any other member of the *marginatus* complex really sounds very much like a nightingale! He called Panama birds (separated as *M. luscinia*) the "Northern Whistler-Wren", and *M. marginatus* would presumably have become the "Southern Whistler-Wren". The AOU Check-list, when it formally accepted the proposed split, suggested calling *M. marginatus* (in which the *luscinia* group was lumped) the "Scaly-breasted Wren", this despite the fact that most of its component forms do *not* have scaly breasts. This all seems unduly complex. A far simpler course, and one which reflects the undoubted close relationship of all forms, and the fact that all have long been called Nightingale Wrens, is to use that as the group name and then apply geographical modifiers. *Microcerculus philomela* would become the "Northern Nightingale-Wren", and *M. marginatus* (including the *luscinia* group) the "Southern Nightingale-Wren"; this is the course followed here. Should *M. luscinia* be split, it might best be called the "Panama Nightingale-Wren".

SONG WREN
Cyphorhinus phaeocephalus   Plate 28

Description: 5. Bill rather long and ridged. Mostly warm brown with *sides of head and neck, throat, and chest bright rufous-chestnut; patch of pale blue bare skin around eye*; wings and tail barred with black. Female more grayish on lower belly.

Similar species: The pale blue skin around the eye brings to mind several antbirds, but none has barred wings and tail; see especially female Bare-crowned Antbird. Tawny-throated Leaftosser almost duplicates this species in general pattern, but it lacks the pale blue skin and the wing and tail barring.

Status and distribution: Fairly common to common in undergrowth of forest and second-growth woodland in lowlands on entire Caribbean slope; on Pacific slope known from more humid lowlands and lower foothills (to about 900 m: 3000 ft) from Cerro Campana and Canal area east through Darién. In Canal area more numerous and widespread on Caribbean side.

Habits: Usually seen in pairs or small groups, on or near the ground, individuals often pausing briefly on a stump or low branch to look over the observer, then moving on, all the while "churring" distinctively. Sometimes follows army ants. The song is a characteristic and far-carrying mixture of harsh *churr* notes and other guttural notes, interspersed with clear musical whistles of varying pitches; some songs consist of three pure music whistles that may leap or fall a full octave. The overall effect can be enchanting! A frequently heard call is simply a harsh non-musical *cutta, cutta, cutta* (Eisenmann).

Range: Honduras to western Ecuador.

DIPPERS: Cinclidae (1)

The dippers are remarkable in their aquatic habits, being the only truly aquatic passerine. The family is small and has a discontinuous distribution: two species are found in the Old World, three in the New, all similar except in color pattern. Dippers are restricted to clear, rapid, rocky streams. They are chunky, short-tailed, rather wren-like birds, fully capable of swimming underwater in even very fast currents and of walking on the bottom of the stream or river. Dippers feed on a variety of small aquatic life, mostly procured underwater. The nest is a large, domed structure placed on a ledge on a rock or steep bank or cliff along the watercourse, sometimes behind a waterfall.

AMERICAN DIPPER
Cinclus mexicanus p.347

Description: 6½. Found only *along streams in western highlands*. Chunky and short-tailed. *Entirely slaty gray*. Juvenile has pale gray underparts and narrow white wing-bars.

Status and distribution: Uncommon along clear rocky streams in highlands of Chiriquí and Veraguas, chiefly 1200–2100 m (4000–7000 ft) though occurs lower in Veraguas (to 750 m: 2500 ft). Most readily seen along Chiriquí Viejo River between Cerro Punta and Bambito, but even there pairs are widely spaced and can be difficult to locate. In Panama seems to have been found only on Pacific slope.

Habits: Usually seen singly, perched on a rock in the middle of the torrent, bobbing up and down, or flying rapidly low over the water. Utters a sharp *bzeet*, frequently in flight.

Range: Western North America to western Panama.

Note: A dipper may occur in eastern Darién; Dr C. R. Schneider (a chemist) believes he saw one on the Cana River near Cana, Darién (at over 900 m: 3000 ft), in July 1965 (*fide* Eisenmann). If any dipper does occur in Darién, it might be either this species, or the allied White-capped Dipper (*C. leucocephalus*) of the South American Andes, or

AMERICAN DIPPER

possibly an undescribed form. Despite much recent field work in this area, there have been no reports of any dipper; possibly the 1965 sighting referred to *Lochmias*.

OLD WORLD WARBLERS, KINGLETS, AND GNATCATCHERS: Sylviinae (4)

The taxonomic position of the two exclusively American groups placed in this subfamily is uncertain; the usual treatment, adhered to by the 1983 AOU Check-list, is to associate the gnatcatchers and gnatwrens with the Old World Warblers, and this is done here, placing the Sylviinae subfamily in the vast Muscicapidae family. Others disassociate the gnatcatchers and gnatwrens as a separate subfamily in the Muscicapidae, the Polioptilinae, or break up the vast Muscicapid assemblage, treating the various units as full families. Gnatcatchers are tiny, slender, mainly gray birds whose long tails constantly flip around in an animated fashion; arboreal birds, they favour forest borders and woodland. Gnatwrens inhabit forest and woodland undergrowth and borders, where due to their small size, rather dull brown plumage, and retiring behavior they are difficult to see. Both groups are insectivorous, and construct a pretty open-cup nest in a bush or tree.

TAWNY-FACED GNATWREN
Microbates cinereiventris   Plate 30

Description: 4. Bill long but proportionately shorter than in Long-billed Gnatwren; tail short, usually cocked. Dark brown above with *sides of head and neck bright tawny*; throat white *bordered by broad broken black stripe; partial collar of black streaks across chest*; remaining underparts gray. Birds of eastern Darién (nominate race) have *prominent blackish postocular streak*, this lacking in those from elsewhere in Panama (*semitorquatus*).
Similar species: Superficially like several wrens but without wing and tail barring; in dark light of forest undergrowth, the collar can be hard to see, but the tawny face is usually not. See Long-billed Gnatwren.
Status and distribution: Uncommon to locally fairly common but always inconspicuous in undergrowth of humid forest in lowlands and lower foothills (to about 900 m: 3000 ft) on entire Caribbean slope; on Pacific slope recorded only from foothills of Veraguas (Santa Fé) and Panama province (Cerro Campana and Cerro Azul/Jefe), and lowlands and foothills of eastern Darién.
Habits: Usually in pairs or small family groups which actively hop through lower growth, typically remaining close to the ground but sometimes foraging in viny tangles up to 4–6 m (13–20 ft) above it. Their tail is almost constantly being jerked or flipped around, and sometimes is almost held in a right angle. They regularly accompany mixed flocks of antwrens or tanagers, but at least as often move independent of them. The most often heard call is a nasal complaining scold *nyeeeh*, but also gives a fast chattering *chrichrichrichrichri*.
Range: Nicaragua to southern Peru.
Note: Sometimes called Half-collared Gnatwren.

LONG-BILLED GNATWREN
Ramphocaenus melanurus   Plate 30

Description: 4¾. *Very long, slender, straight bill*; tail narrow and long, often cocked. Mostly grayish olive above with crown and hindneck brown; sides of head and neck cinnamon; *mostly buffy below*, throat whitish with indistinct dusky streaks; tail blackish with feathers tipped white. Immature brownish above.
Similar species: Somewhat wren-like but easily known by its very long bill. Tawny-faced Gnatwren is smaller with a shorter bill and is mostly gray below (except for white throat) with broad broken black stripe along sides of neck.
Status and distribution: Fairly common in lower growth (especially where there are viny tangles) of forest borders, second-growth woodland, light scrubby woodland, and densely overgrown clearings in more humid lowlands on both slopes, ranging locally up to 1050–1200 m (3500–4000 ft) in foothills and lower highlands; apparently absent from drier areas on Pacific slope from eastern side of

Azuero Peninsula to western Panama province; at least locally found also in elfin cloud forest, e.g. near summit of Cerro Jefe, and the Quebrada de Arena area above Fortuna.

Habits: Rather skulking and often difficult to see. Usually in pairs, frequently calling back and forth to each other with a distinctive clear musical trill usually only on one pitch, sometimes rising in intensity and then softening toward end. At times joins mixed foraging flocks of insectivorous birds.

Range: Southeastern Mexico to eastern Peru and Amazonian and eastern Brazil.

Note: The 1983 AOU Check-list is followed in considering the trans-Andean *R. rufiventris* (Straight-billed Gnatwren) as conspecific with *R. melanurus*.

TROPICAL GNATCATCHER
Polioptila plumbea   Plate 30

Description: 4. A slender little bird with a rather long tail, often cocked up. Male *bluish gray above* with *glossy black crown and hindneck*; superciliary, sides of head, and entire underparts white; tail black with outer feathers white. Female similar but without black cap. Coiba Island birds (*cinericia*) are darker gray above, and grayer on breast and flanks.

Similar species: Warbler-like in its spritely behavior. See Slate-throated Gnatcatcher.

Status and distribution: Fairly common and widespread in forest canopy and borders, second-growth woodland, shrubby clearings, and locally even in scrubby areas in lowlands and foothills on both slopes, ranging up to around 1200 m (4000 ft), occasionally higher; found also on Coiba Island; one sight report of a pair on Pearl Islands (Rey) on February 11, 1970 (Ridgely).

Habits: Seen singly or in pairs, often with mixed foraging flocks of insectivorous birds. Very active, constantly moving its tail about. Has a rather thin but musical song consisting of a series of simple notes with decreasing intensity, *sweet, weet, weet, weet, weet,* sometimes faster and more sibilant; the usual call is a *tzeet-tzeet.*

Range: Southeastern Mexico to central Peru and central Brazil.

Note: More than one species may be involved in South America.

SLATE-THROATED GNATCATCHER
Polioptila schistaceigula   Plate 30

Description: 4. Known only from eastern half of Panama. Sexes alike. *Mostly blackish slate above* with narrow white eye-ring and a little white on lores; *throat and chest also blackish slate*, contrasting with white lower breast and belly; tail black, outer tail feathers only very narrowly fringed white.

Similar species: Much commoner Tropical Gnatcatcher is paler more bluish gray above, and *entirely* white below.

Status and distribution: Rare in canopy and borders of humid forest; recorded only from Río Boquerón above Madden Lake in eastern Colon province (a specimen collected by Wetmore on February 27, 1961), and locally from eastern Darién (Cerro Quía, Cerro Pirre), where recorded 450–750 m (1500–2500 ft), but to be looked for elsewhere.

Habits: Behavior similar to Tropical Gnatcatcher, usually found singly or in pairs as they accompany mixed flocks of tanagers and other insectivorous birds.

Range: Central Panama to northwestern Ecuador.

Note: Birds from Panama and northern Colombia are blacker generally than those from southwestern Colombia and northwestern Ecuador and lack latter's vague whitish superciliary, malar streak, and some mottling on throat. As Ecuador is the type locality, more northern (including Panama) birds appear to represent an as-yet unnamed subspecies, but more specimen material is needed in order to fully clarify the situation.

SOLITAIRES, THRUSHES, AND ALLIES: Turdinae (16)

The thrushes are a large and widespread group of birds, most diverse in the Old World, though there are many familiar American species. Most American thrushes are rather subdued in color, though many are handsome birds; a number are, however, exceptionally fine songsters. Three genera are especially important in Panama. Thrushes of the genus *Turdus* are especially well represented from the foothills to above timberline with one species, the Clay-colored

Thrush, being widespread in the lowlands. The genus *Catharus* contains three temperate North American breeding migrants and five species resident in the highlands (mostly in the west); several members of this genus are among the finest singing birds in the world, with hauntingly beautiful clear whistled phrases. The solitaires (genus *Myadestes*) are also excellent songsters; they differ from *Catharus* in their broader bills. Many Panama thrushes are primarily terrestrial feeders, though their open-cup nests are placed in a tree or bush; solitaires, however, are mainly arboreal but like *Catharus* nest on or near the ground. Thrushes have a varied diet, some species taking mainly fruit, others mostly animal matter. The thrushes and allies are here considered a subfamily (Turdinae) in the enlarged muscicapid assemblage (Muscicapidae), following the 1983 AOU Check-list; some consider the thrushes to be worthy of full family rank, the Turdidae.

BLACK-FACED SOLITAIRE
Myadestes melanops   Plate 29

Description: 7. Found only in western highlands. *Rather broad bill and legs bright orange. Mostly slaty gray* with *forehead, facial area, and chin deep black*; wings black with *whitish band showing along base of flight feathers* (conspicuous in flight); tail black with outer pair of feathers mostly gray. Juvenile blackish with prominent large buff spots.
Similar species: Slaty-backed Nightingale-Thrush is blacker generally (not so gray) and has pale eye with orange eye-ring and whitish belly. Sooty Thrush is much larger and blacker (not so gray) with prominent whitish eye.
Status and distribution: Fairly common to common but hard to see (recorded much more often by voice) in montane forest and forest borders in highlands of Chiriquí, adjacent Bocas del Toro, Veraguas, and western Coclé (seen twice above El Copé in February and March 1985 by D. Engleman *et al.*); best known and perhaps most numerous in western Chiriquí, where recorded mainly above 1500 m (5000 ft); elsewhere found lower, down to 750–900 m (2500–3000 ft), and once recorded at sea level in Almirante, Bocas del Toro, on October 28, 1963 (perhaps a partial altitudinal migrant).
Habits: Often sits rather upright, almost like a trogon. Generally sluggish, remaining motionless for some time and allowing a close approach, then flying off abruptly with a flash of white in the wings. The song is a series of loud, very clear, liquid whistles, given deliberately with rather long pauses between phrases, *teedleedleé . . . tleedleeé . . . lee-dah . . . lee-doo*, with variations; also has a liquid *tlee-loo*, and other two- and three-note phrases given alone. Though often sharply brassy in quality and generally with an inconclusive ending, the best songs have a beautiful ethereal quality.
Range: Costa Rica and western Panama.

VARIED SOLITAIRE
Myadestes coloratus   Plate 40

Description: 7. Found only in highlands of eastern Darién. Resembles Black-faced Solitaire. Bill and legs yellow-orange. *Head, neck, and underparts mostly slaty gray* with forehead, facial area, and chin deep black; *mantle mostly bright rufous brown*; wings with *silvery gray band along base of primaries* (flashing in flight), and tail black with *outer three pairs of feathers silvery gray*.
Similar species: Not likely to be confused in its limited range; see Slaty-backed Nightingale-Thrush.
Status and distribution: Fairly common in cloud forest in foothills and highlands of eastern Darién (Cerro Pirre, Altos de Nique, Cerro Quía, and Cerro Tacarcuna); recorded mostly above about 1200 m (4000 ft), occasionally somewhat lower and found at about 900 m (3000 ft) on the summit of Cerro Quía.
Habits: Similar to Black-faced Solitaire, but perhaps even more difficult to see. Singing birds can be particularly frustrating as they then perch virtually motionless, rarely fly, and because of the ventriloquial nature of the song; often more readily spotted when foraging, and sometimes joins tanagers and other birds at fruiting trees. Its leisurely song especially resembles that of South America's Andean Solitaire (*M. ralloides*), consisting of a series of drawn-out single notes or flute-like phrases with long intervening pauses, sometimes with a few less musical notes interspersed.
Range: Eastern Panama and adjacent northwestern Colombia.
Note: Sometimes considered conspecific with *M. melanops* (Black-faced Solitaire) of Costa Rica and western Panama, though they were treated as separate species in the 1983 AOU Check-list; *M. ralloides* (Andean Solitaire) of South America is also closely related.

BLACK-BILLED NIGHTINGALE-THRUSH
Catharus gracilirostris Plate 29

Description: 6. Found only in Chiriquí highlands. *Bill and legs blackish.* Mostly plain brown above, somewhat more rufescent on back and rump, and distinctly grayer on forecrown and face; *mostly plain gray below*, more whitish on throat and becoming whiter on median lower belly, and with *band of dull olive brown across chest*. Birds from eastern Chiriquí (*bensoni*) are darker and more rufescent brown above and on chest band than western Chiriquí birds (*accentor*).
Similar species: The only nightingale-thrush with an all-dark bill.
Status and distribution: Fairly common to common in undergrowth of montane forest, forest borders, and regenerating clearings in highlands of western Chiriquí (mostly above 2100 m: 7000 ft, a few occasionally wandering lower, to about 1500 m: 5000 ft); recorded also from eastern Chiriquí (Cerro Flores or Santiago, and Cerro Bollo), where found at 1800–2100 m (6000–7000 ft). Easily seen along the Boquete Trail above Cerro Punta, especially above the Fernandez patch of forest.
Habits: Often very unsuspicious, sometimes hopping about almost at one's feet or perching at very close range; much easier to see than the Ruddy-capped Nightingale-Thrush (which tends to remain more in forest), regularly emerging into the semi-open or even feeding at the edge of recently plowed fields. Its song suggests that of the Ruddy-capped, but is thinner, higher, and inferior; call is a distinctive loud, rapidly rising *sweeeeeee?* (B. Whitney).
Range: Costa Rica and western Panama.

ORANGE-BILLED NIGHTINGALE-THRUSH
Catharus aurantiirostris Plate 29

Description: 6½. Found only in western foothills and highlands. *Bill and legs orange.* Brown above with *gray head* and narrow orange eye-ring; light gray below, fading to whitish on throat, middle of breast, and belly.
Similar species: Ruddy-capped and Black-billed Nightingale-Thrushes have dark bills and legs. Black-headed Nightingale-Thrush has obviously black (not gray) head.
Status and distribution: Fairly common in forest borders, lighter woodland, and less-disturbed gardens with dense shrubbery in foothills and lower highlands on Pacific slope in Chiriquí, Veraguas, western Coclé (above El Copé; one specimen taken by Wetmore on February 25, 1962), and recently recorded also from mountains of Azuero Peninsula, both on Cerro Montuosa in Herrera and on Cerro Hoya near its southwestern tip (F. Delgado); recorded mostly 900–1650 m (3000–5500 ft), but at least formerly found lower, virtually to sea level, in eastern Chiriquí and southern Veraguas. Regularly found in gardens around the Panamonte Hotel in Boquete (where seems tamer and easier to see than elsewhere).
Habits: Usually hard to see, keeping to dense low vegetation. For a nightingale-thrush, its song is poor and unmusical with varied phrases, some twangy, others squeaky; a short *tsip, wee-ee, tsirrip-tsip* is one of several.
Range: Northern Mexico to western Panama; Colombia and Venezuela.

RUDDY-CAPPED NIGHTINGALE-THRUSH
Catharus frantzii Plate 29

Description: 6½. Found only in western Chiriquí highlands. Bill dusky above, pale salmon below; legs brown. Brown above with *russet cap*; pale grayish below, fading to whitish on throat and belly.
Similar species: The only Panama nightingale-thrush with a russet cap (in others gray or black). Veery is slightly spotted on chest and is more uniform tawny above.
Status and distribution: Common in undergrowth of forest and forest borders in highlands of western Chiriquí, recorded 1200–2400 m (4000–8000 ft) but mostly 1500–2100 m (5000–7000 ft). The most numerous nightingale-thrush in the Bambito and Cerro Punta area.
Habits: Usually on or near the ground, sometimes hopping out into clearings but never far from cover. Has a beautiful far-carrying ethereal song consisting of many phrases and sometimes very long, in quality rather like a Hermit Thrush (*C. guttatus*) but in phrasing like a Wood Thrush (C. Hartshorne). The solitaire's song has a somewhat similar liquid quality but it is richer, louder, less varied, and is usually much shorter in duration and with longer pauses between phrases. A distinctive call is a sweet but burry, upslurred *ooeerrrp?*.
Range: Central Mexico to western Panama.

SLATY-BACKED NIGHTINGALE-THRUSH
Catharus fuscater   Plate 29

Description: 6½. *Bill and legs orange; iris whitish. Slaty blackish above*, blackest on head and with narrow orange eye-ring; *mostly slaty gray below*, fading to whitish to pale yellowish buff on center of lower breast and belly. Birds from eastern Panama (*mirabilis* on Cerro Pirre, evidently nominate *fuscater* on Cerro Tacarcuna and likely west to Cerro Jefe) have throat, breast, and flanks duller and more olive-gray than western birds (*hellmayri*), and have *yellower median lower underparts* (but fading to whitish in older museum specimens). Juveniles have dark irides, and bill and legs blackish with varying amounts of orange.
Similar species: The only nightingale-thrush known from central or eastern Panama. Black-headed Nightingale-Thrush has dark eye and black head contrasting with olive upperparts; Orange-billed Nightingale-Thrush is brown above (no slaty) with gray head, dark eye. Black-faced Solitaire has broader bill and more upright posture, is uniform gray below. See also the larger Sooty Thrush.
Status and distribution: Locally fairly common though always difficult to see (most often recorded by voice) in undergrowth of humid montane forest and cloud forest in foothills and lower highlands of Chiriquí, adjacent Bocas del Toro (where recorded only from along the oleoducto road north of Fortuna, but probably more widespread), Veraguas, very locally in eastern Panama province (Cerro Jefe) and extreme western San Blas (Cerro Brewster, where mist-netted and photographed on Cerro Brewster in April 1985 by J. Blake), and eastern Darién (Cerro Tacarcuna, Alturas de Nique, and Cerro Pirre); recorded mostly 900–1500 m (3000–5000 ft). The common nightingale-thrush of the Fortuna area in central Chiriquí; early in the twentieth century it was apparently equally numerous further west around Boquete (W. W. Brown collected 21 specimens here), but there are few or no recent reports, probably because of extensive clearing (the species has never been found on western, drier side of Volcán Barú).
Habits: A shy and inconspicuous bird, when seen usually hopping alone on the forest floor, occasionally curious and coming into a squeak or in attendance at small ant swarms. Much more often heard than seen, its song is a series of beautiful short phrases with a pure liquid quality, e.g. *toh-toh-tee, tee-*
toh or *toh-tee, tee-toh-toh-tee* with some variation (local dialects?); the effect is solitaire-like but notes are clearer, and phrasing simpler.
Range: Costa Rica to northwestern Venezuela and northern Bolivia.

BLACK-HEADED NIGHTINGALE-THRUSH
Catharus mexicanus   Plate 29

Description: 6. Known only from western foothills. *Bill orange*; legs orange-yellow. *Iris dark. Head black* with prominent narrow orange eye-ring; otherwise *brownish olive above;* whitish below with grayish chest and sides. Female has crown somewhat more brownish.
Similar species: Note black head contrasting with olive back and dark eye. Slaty-backed Nightingale-Thrush is all dark slaty gray above and has prominent pale eye. Black-billed Nightingale-Thrush has dark bill and legs, and gray head.
Status and distribution: Locally fairly common in undergrowth of humid forest in foothills on Caribbean slope in Bocas del Toro and Veraguas, in the latter spilling over Divide onto Pacific slope around Santa Fé; recorded mostly in a narrow zone between 750 and 1050 m (2500 and 3500 ft), locally a few a little higher and lower. Quite numerous (by voice) along oleoducto road north of Fortuna, Chiriquí, in early July 1982 (Ridgely); small numbers were seen hopping along roadside in early mornings and late afternoons.
Habits: Similar to Slaty-backed Nightingale-Thrush, and equally reclusive. Its song is short and rapidly delivered, the notes with a clear flute-like quality, e.g. *dleét-dloo-dlee-dlee* or *beéry-tlurrr*, while its call is sharply inflected, as if asking a question (B. Whitney).
Range: Eastern Mexico to western Panama.

VEERY
Catharus fuscescens   Plate 32

Description: 7. *Uniform tawny brown above*; white below, washed with buff on throat and chest and *very indistinctly spotted with dusky on chest.*
Similar species: Wood Thrush is much more prominently spotted below and is rufous only on crown and nape. Swainson's and Gray-cheeked Thrushes are usually olive brown above (but some Swainson's are almost as russet above) and are more dis-

tinctly spotted below. See also Ruddy-capped Nightingale-Thrush.

Status and distribution: Uncommon fall transient in lower growth of forest and second-growth woodland in lowlands on Caribbean slope, recorded mostly along immediate coast (late September–mid-November), and so far only from Bocas del Toro, Canal area, and San Blas but doubtless more widespread; rare fall transient elsewhere, with one report from western Chiriquí highlands and two from Pacific slope of Canal area (Fort Clayton); very rare spring transient, with only two reports (early March and early April), both from Bocas del Toro.

Habits: A shy and reclusive bird in Panama, rarely seen, with by far the majority of the birds recorded having been mist-netted; some may be presumed to be overlooked, but it seems certain that northward passage must be mainly via another route.

Range: Breeds in North America; winters in northern South America; a scarce transient, apparently, in both Middle America and West Indies.

GRAY-CHEEKED THRUSH
Catharus minimus   Plate 32

Description: 7. Dull olive brown above with *grayish cheeks* and *no distinct eye-ring*; white below, washed with buffy grayish on chest and spotted lightly with dusky on chest and breast.

Similar species: Often very difficult to distinguish from Swainson's Thrush. Gray-cheeks tend to be duller above than most (but not all) Swainson's and have grayish (not buffy) cheeks and show no distinct buffy eye-ring or loral stripe. In the hand, Gray-cheek's tail (except in immature) is longer than bend of wing to tip of secondaries (not longer in Swainson's), and Gray-cheek's 6th, 7th, and 8th primaries are sinuate on inner web (in Swainson's usually only 7th and 8th primaries have inner web sinuate).

Status and distribution: Uncommon to locally fairly common fall transient in lower growth of forest and second-growth woodland in lowlands, mainly on Caribbean slope, on Pacific slope mostly from Canal area eastward (but also recorded on Cerro Campana, western Panama province), mostly late September–late November; rare winter resident and spring transient, when recorded only from central and eastern Panama (as late as mid-April).

Habits: As with the Veery, the Gray-cheeked Thrush's shy and reclusive nature make it difficult to detect in Panama (and often to identify), and doubtless it passes under-recorded; it is best known from mist-net captures, especially from Bocas del Toro. E. O. Willis found it regularly following swarms of army ants on Barro Colorado Island.

Range: Breeds in northern North America and northeastern Siberia; winters mostly in northern South America, rarely in Middle America.

SWAINSON'S THRUSH
Catharus ustulatus   Plate 32

Description: 7. Brownish olive to rather russet brown above with *buffy brown cheeks* and a *usually prominent buffy eye-ring and supraloral area*; white below, throat and chest tinged buffy and lightly spotted with dusky. The race *swainsoni* (with olive brown upperparts, breeding in eastern north America) is by far the commonest form in Panama, though grayer-backed *almae* and the more rufescent nominate race, both of which breed in western North America, have also been collected (as has *oedicus*, the third western breeding race, intermediate in dorsal coloration between *swainsoni* and nominate).

Similar species: Gray-cheeked Thrush is very similar, but it never shows the buff supraloral and eye-ring of Swainson's (occasionally a very narrow whitish eye-ring is present), and its cheeks usually look grayish (and in any case are never buffyish as in Swainson's).

Status and distribution: Common to locally abundant fall (mostly October–November, a few as early as mid-September) and fairly common to common spring (mostly March–April, a few straggling to mid-May) in lower growth of forest, second-growth woodland, and borders throughout, ranging up in western Chiriquí highlands to at least 1800 m (6000 ft), and occurring also on Pearl Islands and Coiba Island; uncommon to rare winter resident in lowlands and foothills, mostly in central and eastern Panama; one anomalous specimen taken on July 4 at Permé, San Blas, presumably had not migrated. Apparently most numerous in Caribbean lowlands, with greatest numbers having been recorded in coastal Bocas del Toro (3120 were mist-netted during fall passage in 1963 by P. Galindo and E. Mendez).

Habits: Like other migrant thrushes, usually keeps to rather dense cover and shy, so not visible in large numbers; at times, however, the number mist-netted is staggering. Easily the most numerous migrant thrush in Panama. During April can sometimes be heard to sing. E. O. Willis has found it regularly following swarms of army ants on Barro Colorado Island.

Range: Breeds in North America; winters mainly from Mexico to northern Argentina.

WOOD THRUSH
Hylocichla mustelina   Plate 32

Description: 7½. Brown above shading to *rufous on crown and nape*; white below with *numerous large black spots*.

Similar species: No other adult thrush has such conspicuous spotting below. Veery is uniform tawny above; Swainson's and Gray-cheeked Thrushes are uniform olive brown above.

Status and distribution: Uncommon to rare winter resident in more forested lowlands of western and central Panama, also ranging regularly into highlands of western Chiriquí (mostly mid-October–mid-April); most numerous in Bocas del Toro (but even there the least numerous of the four migrant thrushes), becoming rare in Canal area, and only a few reports from farther east (including one mist-netted by Wetmore at Tacarcuna Village, Darién, on March 10, 1964).

Habits: Usually seen singly on or near the ground in forest or second-growth woodland. Its distinctive call is a rapid *whip-whip-whip*.

Range: Breeds in eastern North America; winters from Mexico to Panama, accidentally to northwestern Colombia and Guyana; a rare transient in West Indies.

SOOTY THRUSH (ROBIN)
Turdus nigrescens   Plate 29

Description: 10. Found only *high* in western Chiriquí mountains. *Bill, legs, and eye-ring bright orange to yellow-orange; iris whitish. Dark sooty brown all over*, blackest on head, wings, and tail.

Similar species: Panama's only "black" thrush. Mountain Thrush is duller and more olivaceous, with dark eye, bill, and legs. Slaty-backed Nightingale-Thrush is rather similar but is notably smaller and has white belly. See also Black-faced Solitaire.

Status and distribution: Uncommon to fairly common (greater numbers at higher elevations) in clearings, forest borders, and semiopen lava fields on higher slopes of Volcán Barú in western Chiriquí; found mostly above 2250 m (7500 ft), occasionally

wandering as low as 1830 m (6100 ft) on the rocky Llanos del Volcán. In Panama most readily found along the telecommunications tower access road above Boquete; a pair or two is sometimes present near crest of Boquete Trail above Cerro Punta.

Habits: Usually seen on or near the ground in pairs or small groups. Reported to have a poor but still somewhat thrush-like song (Slud); the calls are a *trrrr* and a harsh *tchweerp, tchweerp.*

Range: Costa Rica and western Panama.

Note: The 1983 AOU Check-list called some of the Panama *Turdus* (including this species) "Robins", and others "Thrushes", with no consistency. So as to avoid confusion, it would seem preferable to use the group name "Thrush" for all of the *Turdus* genus in America except *T. migratorius* (whose name of American Robin seems too ingrained to change, however inappropriate it may be).

MOUNTAIN THRUSH (ROBIN)
Turdus plebejus   Plate 29

Description: 10. Found only in western highlands. *Bill blackish.* Dark dull olive brown above; dark dull brownish gray below, throat inconspicuously streaked with dusky.

Similar species: *Nondescript.* Clay-colored Thrush is smaller, paler and sandier with greenish yellow bill. Sooty Thrush has bright orange bill, legs, and eye-ring, and is dark sooty brown. Pale-vented Thrush is more rufescent brown with white belly.

Status and distribution: Fairly common to common in montane forest, forest borders, and small clearings in highlands of western Chiriquí (mostly 1200–2400 m: 4000–8000 ft), and in foothills and highlands of central and eastern Chiriquí and adjacent Bocas del Toro (down in small numbers to about 900 m: 3000 ft).

Habits: Found singly or in small groups, usually well up in the trees. Sings very little, and its song is inferior to that of its allies, being faster, more repetitious and monotonous, with few pitch changes; its calls are a repeated *cack* or *kick* and a mournful *oóoooreee.*

Range: Southern Mexico to western Panama.

Note: See under Sooty Thrush.

PALE-VENTED THRUSH (ROBIN)
Turdus obsoletus   Plate 29

Description: 9. *Bill blackish. Almost uniform, warm reddish brown,* somewhat streaked with dusky on throat and duller below, with *contrasting white belly and under tail-coverts*.

Similar species: Much more numerous Clay-colored Thrush has pale greenish bill and lacks white belly. Mountain Thrush is duller and also lacks white belly.

Status and distribution: Uncommon and seemingly local (perhaps mostly just overlooked) in humid forest and forest borders in foothills on both slopes; recorded from Bocas del Toro (possibly locally crossing Divide into Chiriquí but no definite records, even from Fortuna area), Veraguas (Santa Fé), Coclé (seen north of El Copé on March 7, 1986; Ridgely *et al.*), Panama province (Cerro Campana and Cerro Azul/Jefe), extreme western San Blas (found on Cerro Brewster in April 1985; J. Blake), and eastern Darién, mostly 450–1500 m (1500–5000 ft). The type specimen, without precise locality, has been attributed to the Canal area (Lion Hill or Panama Railroad), but this is almost certainly in error as there have been no subsequent records.

Habits: A rather shy, essentially arboreal bird. The song is somewhat like Clay-colored Thrush's but is faster and less rich and is interspersed with *chrrrrs* and squeaky notes.

Range: Costa Rica to western Ecuador.

Note: See under Sooty Thrush. We consider *T. hauxwelli* of upper Amazonia (Hauxwell's Thrush) to be a species distinct from *T. obsoletus*; they were considered conspecific in the 1983 AOU Check-list (but as far as we are aware, there are *no* intermediate specimens in the Colombian Andes, and habitat, elevation, and behavior differ quite strikingly).

CLAY-COLORED THRUSH (ROBIN)
Turdus grayi   Plate 29

Description: 9–10. *Bill greenish yellow or olive* (dusky in immature). Brownish olive above; *dull light buffy brown below*, inconspicuously streaked with dusky on throat.

Similar species: Mountain Thrush of western highlands has blackish bill and is darker and duller throughout than the Clay-color. See also Pale-vented Thrush.

Status and distribution: Very common in clearings, gardens, lighter woodland, and generally in more open areas in lowlands and foothills on both slopes, though not recorded from Darién or from far eastern Panama province (easternmost limit as of 1986 seems to be around El Llano, but likely will spread eastward along Pan-American Highway in clearings); in western Chiriquí ranges well up into highlands in cleared areas, regularly to

around Cerro Punta at 1800–1950 m (6000–6500 ft). Most numerous in Canal area, where the extensive lawns provide ideal habitat.

Habits: A very familiar and conspicuous bird, the Panamanian replacement for the well known American Robin (*T. migratorius*) of temperate North America. The song is a whistled caroling, reminiscent of the northern bird but clearer and more melodic; in addition to typically robin-like cackles, it also utters a characteristic long-drawn, nasal, whining *wee-eé-gwa*, and a querulous *keyaah*.

Range: Central Mexico (casually southern Texas) to northern Colombia.

Range: See under Sooty Thrush.

WHITE-THROATED THRUSH (ROBIN)
Turdus assimilis   Plate 29

Description: 9. *Bill and narrow eye-ring yellow.* Mostly dark brownish olive to grayish olive above; *throat white boldly streaked with dusky, white continuing below as a white patch on upper chest* contrasting strongly with dull brown of adjacent underparts; lower belly white. Darién (*daguae*) and Coiba Island (*coibensis*) birds have blackish bill, are ruddier above than western mainland birds (*cnephosus*).

Similar species: No other Panama thrush has contrasting white throat.

Status and distribution: Fairly common to common (locally and seasonally) in humid forest and forest borders in foothills and lower highlands on Pacific slope from Chiriquí east to western Panama province (Cerro Campana), and in hill country and mountains on western side of Azuero Peninsula; apparently uncommon in highlands of eastern Darién (Cerro Pirre and Cerro Tacarcuna); very common on Coiba Island (where one of the most numerous forest birds). Small numbers apparently disperse on a fairly regular basis to both slopes of Canal area (but mostly on Caribbean side), with reports mainly November–January, a few times as early as October or as late as April; E. S. Morton found it to almost completely disappear from Cerro Campana during the dry season.

Habits: Mostly arboreal, often in small groups, occasionally a larger number gathering to feed in a fruiting tree. Western mainland birds have a good typical *Turdus*-like song, and another of loud and rich repeated phrases recalling a thrasher (*Toxostoma*). Calls include a characteristic and peculiar short guttural or nasal *enk* or *urrnk*, almost frog-like in quality, and a screechy *dzee-yoo*. Song of Coiba birds is suggestive of Clay-colored Thrush, but higher and slower (Wetmore).

Range: Northern Mexico to northwestern Ecuador.

Note: See under Sooty Thrush. Sometimes considered conspecific with *T. albicollis* (White-necked Thrush) of South America east of the Andes, but treated as two species in the 1983 AOU Check-list.

MOCKINGBIRDS, THRASHERS, AND ALLIES: Mimidae (2)

This family of rather slender, long-tailed birds is found only in the New World; the typical thrashers are found mostly in southwestern United States and Mexico and none occurs in Panama. Mimids are usually dull in color, shades of brown and gray predominating; most have loud and vigorous songs of repeated phrases. The group is most insectivorous, some fruit also being taken; species whose nesting is known build an open, often bulky, cup nest in a dense bush or tree. Note that the Donacobius has been transfered from the Mimidae to the Troglodytidae (Wrens).

GRAY CATBIRD
Dumetella carolinensis   Plate 32

Description: 8. Slender, with rather long blackish tail. *Mostly slaty gray* with black cap and *chestnut crissum*.

Status and distribution: Locally common transient and winter resident in lowlands of Bocas del Toro (mostly October–April, a few arriving in September and lingering into May), becoming less numerous eastward on Caribbean slope to San Blas (where uncommon, though probably regular), and uncommon on Pacific slope from Chiriquí (a few reports from lower highlands) east to eastern Panama province (farthest east being a bird seen at Cerro Azul on March 11, 1979, by Ridgely *et al.*); once seen on Taboga Island.

Habits: Often skulks in thickets and shrubbery; its characteristic cat-like mewing note will often reveal its presence.

Range: Breeds in North America; winters from southern United States to central Panama (accidentally to Colombia) and in West Indies.

TROPICAL MOCKINGBIRD
Mimus gilvus   p.356

Description: 10. Rather slender, with long blackish tail. *Pale brownish gray above* with dusky patch through eye; wings blackish with two white bars; tail blackish tipped white; *whitish below*. Immature browner above and buffier below but still easily recognizable.

Status and distribution: Apparently introduced from Colombia, first seen in 1932 in Balboa by H. Deignan. Now common in cleared and residential areas on both slopes of Canal area; on Caribbean slope it had spread as far west as western Colon province (Río Indio) as early as 1952 (and may have spread farther by now), and occurs regularly as far east as Portobelo area, eastern Colon province (and could easily spread to San Blas); on Pacific slope it is resident west to western Panama province (Chorrera area), with an apparently isolated population established about 1980 around Chitre, Herrera (F. Delgado), and has spread as far east as the Canita/El Llano area in eastern Panama province; single records from above Boquete and near David, Chiriquí, probably represent isolated cage bird escapees.

TROPICAL MOCKINGBIRD

Habits: Like its northern relative, noisy, conspicuous, and aggressive. Especially fond of areas where extensive lawns are maintained. The song is a series of various notes and phrases, reminiscent of the Northern Mockingbird (*M. polyglottos*) but less rich, without tendency to repeat a phrase several times, and with more churring notes; there seems to be no tendency to imitate other birds.

Range: Southern Mexico to El Salvador and Honduras; Colombia to the Guianas and northern Brazil and south along Brazilian coast; Lesser Antilles; introduced in central Panama.

PIPITS AND WAGTAILS: Motacillidae (1)

Only pipits occur in the New World, except in Alaska where two species of wagtails breed. Two species of pipits are found in North America and seven others in South America, with one of these extending to the Pacific slope of Panama. Pipits are slender terrestrial birds of open country, general streaked in plumage, with slender bills and rather long dark tails with outer feathers white. Unlike most passerines, they usually walk rather than hop. Pipits are mainly insectivorous, and the Panama species, like most of the others, nests on the ground in grass.

YELLOWISH PIPIT
Anthus lutescens   Plate 30

Description: 5. A small, slender bird of Pacific grasslands. Brown above streaked with buffy and black and with narrow pale buffy whitish eye-ring; *yellowish white below* streaked with dusky on chest; tail blackish with *outer feathers whitish*, prominent in flight.

Similar species: The only small brownish bird of Pacific grasslands that walks on ground. Female seedeaters are not streaked; Grasshopper Sparrow is more furtive, never walking in open.

Status and distribution: Locally common in short grass savannas and fields in lowlands on Pacific slope from western Chiriquí (west to near the Costa Rican border in the La Esperanza area) east to eastern Panama province (Chepo area); a few have been reported seen on grassy slopes of Gatun Dam spillway since about December 1982 (P. Harger *et al.*), the only report from the Caribbean slope.

Habits: Found in well-scattered colonies, the birds blending into the ground and often difficult to spot until flushed. The male's song is distinctive and attractive, initially a series of *dzee* notes on a rising pitch, usually given as the bird ascends in a looping manner into the sky, then a long slurred *dzeeeeeeeeeeee* given as it slowly glides back to earth, often with a *dzip* at end. Also sings from ground, a shorter *tsitsirrit*.

Range: Western and central Panama; South America east of the Andes south to northern Argentina, west of them in coastal Peru and northern Chile.

WAXWINGS: Bombycillidae (1)

The waxwings are a small group of but three species breeding in temperate North America and Eurasia, with one species irregularly migrating to Panama. Their common name is derived from the wax-like red tips to the secondaries. They are gregarious, rather unsuspicious birds, feeding mostly on fruit and berries, with some insects captured in the air at least during the breeding season.

CEDAR WAXWING
Bombycilla cedrorum   p.358

Description: 7. Rare. A *sleek* brownish bird with a *conspicuous pointed crest. Mostly soft pinkish brown* with black around face, paler below fading to yellowish on belly; wings more grayish with *secondaries tipped waxy scarlet;* tail gray *tipped yellow.* Immature similar but duller and grayer, more whitish below with light brownish streaking, crest shorter, generally without waxy red wing tipping.
Similar species: Long-tailed Silky-Flycatcher has somewhat similar sleek and crested appearance but is distinctly gray in male (olive in female) with notably long tail.
Status and distribution: A rare and very irregular winter visitant (January–March), with records few and scattered; reported from Chiriquí highlands, western Panama province, both slopes of Canal area, and Pearl Islands. Not recorded during many northern winters.
Habits: In its normal range, usually in compact flocks, often quite large, but has occurred in Panama as scattered individuals or in small groups. Has a very distinctive high

CEDAR WAXWING

thin sibilant *tseeee,* frequently given in flight.
Range: Breeds in North America; winters south increasingly irregularly to central Panama and in Greater Antilles, accidentally to Colombia and Venezuela.

SILKY-FLYCATCHERS: Ptilogonatidae (2)

The silky-flycatchers form a group of only four species found from southwestern United States to western Panama. They are usually considered most closely related to the waxwings, and have at times been given only subfamily status within the Bombycillidae. The suggestion (C. G. Sibley, *Auk 90*: 394–410, 1973) that the *Myadestes* solitaires be placed in the Ptilogonatidae was not followed by the 1983 AOU Check-list (in part because of nesting differences; see L. Kiff, *Auk 96*: 198–199, 1979). The name "silky-flycatcher" is something of a misnomer for, while they are indeed "silky", they are not at all related to the Tyrannidae. Three of the four species are conspicuous and gregarious birds, the exception being the Black-and-yellow, which usually is found in pairs and tends to remain within shrubby cover. All apparently eat both fruit and insects, and construct shallow cup-shaped nests placed in forks or crotches of trees and shrubs.

BLACK-AND-YELLOW SILKY-FLYCATCHER
Phainoptila melanoxantha   Plate 29

Description: 8½. Found only in western highlands. Male *mostly glossy black above* with *yellow rump; throat also black, contrasting with yellowish olive chest;* lower underparts gray with *bright yellow sides and flanks.* Female olive above, yellower on rump, with *glossy black cap;* throat grayish, chest olive, *lower underparts as in male.*
Similar species: Does not at all resemble Long-tailed Silky-Flycatcher. Both sexes are best known by their characteristic yellow

sides and glossy black on head (at least). Rather thrush-like in proportions and posture. See also Yellow-thighed Finch.
Status and distribution: Rare to uncommon in montane forest and shrubby forest borders in highlands of western Chiriquí (above 1650 m: 5500 ft); found locally also in adjacent Bocas del Toro, central and eastern Chiriquí, and in Veraguas (Chitra), where ranges lower (down to 1050 m: 3500 ft). Seems most numerous at higher elevations (above about 2250 m: 7500 ft), and quite readily seen along telecommunications tower access road ascending Volcán Barú's eastern flank above Boquete.

Habits: Usually seen singly or in pairs, feeding sluggishly and quietly on fruit in dense foliage, mostly at low levels, especially shrubbery at forest edge. Regularly accompanies mixed flocks. Very quiet, only a thin weak *tsip* call having been heard.

Range: Costa Rica and western Panama.

Note: Sometimes called Black-and-yellow Phainoptila.

LONG-TAILED SILKY-FLYCATCHER
Ptilogonys caudatus   Plate 29

Description: 9½. Found only in western Chiriquí highlands. *Sleek and slender*, with *prominent bushy crest* and *long graduated tail*. Male *soft bluish gray above* with *crest and most of head olive yellowish*; wings and tail black, latter with white patch and central feathers somewhat elongated; throat yellowish olive, remaining underparts gray becoming yellow on lower belly and under tail-coverts. Female similar but with upperparts mostly olive.

Status and distribution: Common in canopy and borders of montane forest, and in adjacent clearings and pastures with large trees left standing, in highlands of western Chiriquí (mostly above 1500 m: 5000 ft); small numbers were found above Fortuna (down to about 1050 m: 3500 ft) in central Chiriquí in February–March 1976 (Ridgely), the farthest east and lowest it has been recorded in Panama.

Habits: Very attractive birds, somewhat variable in numbers but at times one of the more conspicuous birds in the western Chiriquí highlands. Generally in small groups perched high in the trees, sometimes lower in fruiting trees. The call is a frequently uttered dry *cheerink* varied to *seerip* or *chirrip*. Also has a quiet soft song consisting of *seet* and chirring notes interspersed with *chirrip* calls, audible only at close range with effect almost "as if bird was talking to itself" (B. Whitney).

Range: Costa Rica and western Panama.

STARLINGS AND ALLIES: Sturnidae (1)

Widespread and numerous in the Old World, particularly in tropical regions, no member of the Starling family occurs naturally in the Americas, though several have been introduced, one (the European Starling) so successfully that it has become a major pest and one of the more numerous North American birds. One can only hope that the single Panama record of this bold aggressive species is not a harbinger of things to come. Thankfully, however, it is a temperate zone inhabitant and, unlike the House Sparrow, has so far shown no evidence that it can establish itself in tropical climates such as that of Panama.

[EUROPEAN STARLING]
Sturnus vulgaris

Description: 8. One record from Canal area. A *short-tailed*, chunky bird with a *long pointed bill* (yellow when breeding, otherwise dusky); legs yellowish. *Mostly blackish*, in breeding plumage showing iridescent purple on head and neck and green on back and rump. Birds in fresh plumage (molts August–October) have feathers broadly tipped with pale buff or whitish, *resulting in boldly speckled effect*; these tips gradually wear off, leaving only the black. In flight shows *pointed wings*.

Similar species: Not likely to be confused in Panama; male Red-breasted Blackbird vaguely similar when seen from the rear.

Status and distribution: A single bird was seen on lawns at Albrook AFB, Pacific side of Canal area, on February 10, 1979 (J. Rowlett *et al.*), and was also observed 2 days later (R. A. Rowlett *et al.*). One has to suspect the provenance of this bird; presumably it was either ship-assisted, or had been deliberately released by someone ignorant of the damage a population of these birds could do to Panama's native avifauna.

Habits: Consumes a variety of food, procured primarily on the ground. Highly gregarious when not nesting.

Range: Native to Eurasia; introduced to North America, where now widespread and occurring regularly south to northern Mexico in northern winter, with populations also established on Jamaica and Puerto Rico.

VIREOS: Vireonidae (16)

The vireos are a strictly American family of rather plain, arboreal, primarily (but not exclusively) insectivorous birds, represented in Panama by both migrant and resident species. Typical vireos of the genus *Vireo* are olive above, with or without wing-bars, and with either a superciliary (most Panama species) or an eye-ring. Greenlets of the genus *Hylophilus* (all of which are resident) are smaller, with more slender bills; they lack wing-bars and superciliary, though most have crown (at least) either tawny, brownish, or gray in contrast to remaining upperparts. Typical vireos differ from wood-warblers in their usually larger size, somewhat heavier bills, and less active behavior; greenlets are more warbler-like in size and actions, but resemble none in plumage details and are somewhat stockier larger-headed birds. Nests of the genus *Vireo* are rather deep cups suspended between two forking horizontal branches; little is recorded about the nesting of *Hylophilus*, though it appears to be similar to *Vireo*. Note that the somewhat larger and heavier-billed shrike-vireos and peppershrikes are now considered subfamilies in the Vireonidae.

WHITE-EYED VIREO
Vireo griseus

Description: 4½–5. Casual. *White iris* in adult only, dark in immature. Olive above with *yellow eye-ring and supraloral stripe*, wings dusky with two white wing-bars; whitish below *tinged with yellow on sides and flanks*.
Similar species: Yellow-throated Vireo has yellow spectacles but also has bright yellow throat. In color pattern somewhat like a number of small flycatchers but differs in bill shape, posture, and actions.
Status and distribution: Apparently a casual winter visitant to lowlands on Caribbean slope. Three records: two from western Bocas del Toro, both of birds mist-netted and collected (specimens to USNM), one at Punta Vieja on Isla Bastimentos on February 7, 1963 (C. O. Handley and F. M. Greenwell), and one at Almirante on October 16, 1964 (D. L. Hicks); and one from Canal area, a bird seen at Fort Davis on January 3, 1987 (D. and L. Engleman).
Habits: Favors dense thickets and low trees in shrubby clearings and woodland borders.
Range: Breeds in eastern United States and northeastern Mexico; winters from southern United States to Honduras, rarely to Nicaragua, casually to Costa Rica and Panama.

SOLITARY VIREO
Vireo solitarius

Description: 5–6. Three recent sightings. *Head blue-gray with conspicuous white "spectacles"*; bright olive back, wings duskier with *two whitish wing-bars; underparts white* with yellowish green sides and flanks.
Similar species: Only vireo with blue-gray head; note contrast of head with olive back and snowy white throat. See also the *Tolmomyias* flycatchers, both of which have contrasting gray heads.
Status and distribution: Apparently a casual winter visitor to Panama, with three reported sightings: one seen at Volcán in lower highlands of western Chiriquí on March 17, 1972 (C. Leahy and R. Forster); one seen at precisely the same spot on January 16, 1974 (C. Leahy and Ridgely); and one seen at Fort San Lorenzo on Caribbean side of Canal area on January 24, 1977 (R. Rodriguez). Likely the same individual was involved in the two Volcán sightings.
Range: Breeds in northern and western North America and south through Mexican highlands to Honduras; winters from southern United States southward through remaining part of breeding range, with eastern North American breeders (nominate *solitarius*) occurring casually as far south as Costa Rica and Panama.

YELLOW-THROATED VIREO
Vireo flavifrons   Plate 31

Description: 5¼–5½. Bright olive above with *prominent yellow eye-ring and supraloral area* and two prominent white wing-bars; *throat and breast bright yellow*, belly white.
Similar species: The brightest and most clean-cut vireo. In pattern recalls several winter-plumaged wood warblers but can always be known by the combination of yellow spectacles and yellow throat and breast.
Status and distribution: Fairly common transient and winter resident in canopy and borders of forest and woodland virtually

throughout (mainly late October–early April; once as early as 11 October); during northern mid-winter months numbers seem largest in foothills and lower highlands.

Habits: Usually found singly, often in mixed flocks with wood-warblers. Lethargic and slow-moving even for a vireo. Its burry, phrased song is quite often heard, especially shortly before it departs to breed.

Range: Breeds in eastern North America; winters from southern Mexico to Colombia and northern Venezuela, also in Cuba.

YELLOW-WINGED VIREO
Vireo carmioli   Plate 30

Description: 4½. Found only in Chiriquí highlands. Olive above with *yellowish eye-ring and short superciliary*, and *broad yellow wing-bars* and wing-edging; *mostly yellow below*, whitish on throat, tinged olive on sides.

Similar species: No other Panamanian vireo has *yellow* wing-bars. Golden-winged and Chestnut-sided Warblers do, but both are whitish below. Overall pattern most resembles Yellow-throated Vireo.

Status and distribution: Fairly common in canopy and borders of montane forest, and in adjacent clearings with scattered large trees, in highlands of western Chiriquí, mainly above 1800 m (6000 ft). Easily seen in forest patches along the Boquete Trail above Cerro Punta; not known to range east of the Boquete area.

Habits: Forages mostly at high levels, sometimes with mixed flocks. The song consists of short, leisurely phrases with a hoarse quality somewhat suggestive of a Solitary Vireo, often with distinctive, accented terminal phrase, *cheéyah . . . cheéyou . . . chipcheeweé*, or sometimes *chewit, chweéoo*.

Range: Costa Rica and western Panama.

BROWN-CAPPED VIREO
Vireo leucophrys   Plate 30

Description: 4½. Found only in western highlands (*chiriquensis*) and in eastern Darién. Dull olive above with *brown cap* and whitish superciliary; throat whitish, remaining underparts pale yellowish. Darién birds (*dissors*) have more grayish brown crown and paler underparts.

Similar species: No other "vireo" has a brown cap; Philadelphia Vireo is otherwise very similar. Tawny-crowned Greenlet also has brown cap, but is smaller and essentially brown (not olive green) above; it is a slenderer, more active, warbler-like bird.

Status and distribution: Common in forest borders, more open woodland, and shrubby clearings in highlands on Pacific slope in Chiriquí and Veraguas (mostly 1200–2100 m: 4000–7000 ft in western Chiriquí, somewhat lower eastward); known also from one specimen taken on Cerro Malí (a spur of Cerro Tacarcuna), Darién, at about 1425 m (4750 ft) by P. Galindo on June 4, 1963.

Habits: Often in small groups, associating with other highland birds. The song, a fairly continuous warble, is reminiscent of the Warbling Vireo (*V. gilvus*) but is shorter and less varied. Its frequently given call is also distinctive, a buzzy *dzeee-ip . . . dzeee-ip*, usually doubled with the two notes well separated (sometimes up to four notes).

Range: Southern Mexico to northern Venezuela and northwestern Bolivia.

Note: The 1983 AOU Check-list assigned resident birds from Mexico to Honduras to *V. leucophrys* rather than to *V. gilvus* (Warbling Vireo), in which they are sometimes placed. Warbling Vireos breeding in North America winter south rarely to Honduras and Nicaragua (with one sighting from Costa Rica), and could occur in Panama. It resembles Brown-capped but is more grayish olive above (including the crown), and more uniformly whitish below (yellowish at most on sides and flanks).

PHILADELPHIA VIREO
Vireo philadelphicus   Plate 31

Description: 4¾. Dull olive above, grayer on head, with whitish superciliary; *dull pale yellow below*, somewhat brighter on chest, palest on belly. Immatures are more uniformly yellowish below, adults have whitish belly.

Similar species: Lacks Brown-capped Vireo's brown cap though otherwise very similar. Yellow-green Vireo is larger, with more pronounced eye-stripe, and with yellow restricted to sides and under tail-coverts. See also Tennessee Warbler.

Status and distribution: Fairly common to locally common winter resident (mostly October–early April) in foothills and highlands of Chiriquí and Veraguas (mainly 900–2100 m: 3000–7000 ft), with smaller numbers in lowlands of western and central Panama, especially on Pacific slope, east to Canal area; easternmost report is of a bird seen at Majé, in Bayano River valley of eastern Panama province, on January 10, 1976 (J. Pujals).

Habits: On its Chiriquí wintering grounds frequents brushy clearings and forest borders, often foraging at little more than eye-level.

Range: Breeds in northern North America; winters from southern Mexico to central Panama, casually to Colombia.

RED-EYED VIREO
Vireo olivaceus   Plate 31

Description: 5½–6¼ . Olive above with *gray crown and white superciliary bordered above by a thin black line and below by a dusky streak*; whitish below, sometimes tinged yellowish on flanks and under tail-coverts (especially in fall and in immatures). Red iris visible only at close range.

Similar species: Very like Yellow-green Vireo but with a sharper, cleaner-cut facial pattern and at most only a little yellow below (Yellow-green has bright greenish yellow sides, flanks, and vent). In the hand, a helpful distinction is that the Red-eye's 9th primary is usually distinctly longer than its 6th and always distinctly longer than its 5th. See also the Black-whiskered Vireo. Philadelphia and Brown-capped Vireos are smaller and duller, with less distinct white eye-stripes and no bordering black lines.

Status and distribution: Very common transient in forest and woodland canopy and borders and in clearings with trees virtually throughout, including the western Chiriquí highlands; recorded mostly September–mid-November, and March–early May, with a few arriving as early as mid-August and lingering later into May; very small numbers may overwinter, with a few sightings (but as yet no specimens) from Canal area and Darién at that season.

Habits: Apparently mostly frugivorous away from its North American nesting grounds, the Red-eyed Vireo is one of the more numerous transient birds in Panama, and often occurs in marked "waves". Singing is very rarely heard here (in contrast to Yellow-throated Vireo), and in fact their silence can help to distinguish migrant Red-eyeds during their northward passage from the Yellow-green Vireos which at that season are nesting and singing persistently.

Range: Breeds in North America; winters mostly in the Amazon basin of South America.

Note: D es not include Yellow-green Vireo (*V. flavoviridis*), regarded as conspecific with Red-eyed Vireo in the 1983 AOU Checklist, but since re-split.

YELLOW-GREEN VIREO
Vireo flavoviridis   Plate 30

Description: 5¼–6. Much like the Red-eyed Vireo. Olive above with grayer crown and whitish or pale grayish superciliary, bordered above and below by thin dusky lines (sometimes absent); whitish below with *bright greenish yellow sides, flanks, and under tail-coverts.* Iris never as bright or deep red as in Red-eyed Vireo.

Similar species: Closely resembles Red-eyed Vireo but brighter olive above, head stripes less distinct, and with much more yellow on sides and vent. Note also its yellow or yellowish edging on flight feathers (not greenish or grayish). See also the Black-whiskered Vireo. Philadelphia Vireo also has considerable yellow below but is smaller with olive (not gray) crown and shorter less distinct eye-stripe.

Status and distribution: Common to very common breeder in lighter woodland, shrubby clearings with scattered trees, coastal scrub and mangroves, and in gardens in lowlands on Pacific slope from Chiriquí east to eastern Panama province (lower Bayano River valley; east of there in Panama province and in Darién, Yellow-green's status as a breeder is uncertain, and it may only be a transient); on Caribbean slope known to breed only in Canal area and perhaps eastward in eastern Colon province to around Portobelo (but elsewhere apparently occurs only as a migrant); in western Chiriquí ranges up in lower highlands to about 1650 m (5500 ft), and breeding appears likely in suitable habitat (e.g. around Volcán and Boquete); also a very common breeder on Pearl Islands and Coiba Island, on the latter ranging frequently up into the canopy of tall deciduous forest. Birds which breed in northern Middle America are numerous as transients in Caribbean lowlands (especially near coast) in September–October and again in March. Birds which breed in Panama apparently migrate to South America during the height of the local rainy season: they are much less numerous and conspicuous by July–August, and have all left by the end of October. Their return, marked by much singing, usually occurs in January (sometimes a few in late December), with full numbers present by March; in the Canal area they appear first on the Pacific slope.

Habits: One of the most numerous and widespread birds in open and semiopen country on Pacific slope. Its song is much like the Red-eyed Vireo's, an endlessly repeated (even during the heat of the day) series of abrupt phrases, but is slower and more monotonous with shorter individual phrases and longer intervening pauses.

Range: Breeds from southern Texas and Mexico to Panama, migrating to Amazon basin in South America during nonbreeding season.

Note: Though considered conspecific with *V. olivaceus* (Red-eyed Vireo) in the 1983 AOU Check-list, the Yellow-green Vireo was recently re-split (*Auk 104* (3): 593–594, 1987).

BLACK-WHISKERED VIREO
Vireo altiloquus

Description: 6. Very much like Red-eyed Vireo but with heavier bill and *dusky malar stripe* (the "whisker") *on side of throat.* Olive above, tinged with grayish or brownish gray on crown, and with white superciliary bordered below by blackish stripe; whitish below, tinged pale yellowish olive on flanks. Immature duller and buffier below.

Similar species: The definite whisker is the diagnostic mark, but one must be very careful because some molting fall Red-eyed and Yellow-green Vireos may also *seem* to show a whisker.

Status and distribution: Uncertain; probably a rare transient or winter resident in lowlands on Caribbean slope, perhaps mostly on or near coast. Few records: a nineteenth-century specimen taken by McCleannan, labeled only as from "Isthmus of Panama"; one taken by R. R. Benson at Guaval on Río Calovévora (300 m: 1000 ft), Caribbean slope of Veraguas, on August 31, 1926; one taken by H. von Wedel at Puerto Obaldía, San Blas, on September 12, 1930. There are also some recent sightings: one seen at Achiote Road on September 29, 1968 (Ridgely); one at Gatun Dam on January 29, 1970 (E. S. Morton); and at least three seen on small island off Porvenir, San Blas on August 23, 1984 (J. Guarnaccia and M. Villamil). May well be more numerous than these few records seem to indicate, but at least in western Panama it must be at best very rare or casual, for in the seasons of intensive banding effort for migrants in the 1960s not one was recorded.

Habits: Similar to Red-eyed Vireo normally; the Porvenir birds were foraging mostly in palms, but occasionally dropped to the ground.

Range: Breeds in Florida, West Indies, and on islands in southern Caribbean; winters from Lesser Antilles south into Amazonia, with a few occurring in Panama and one record from Caribbean coast of Costa Rica.

SCRUB GREENLET
Hylophilus flavipes   Plate 30

Description: 4½–4¾. Somewhat stockier than other greenlets, often perching more upright. *Bill pale pinkish* and *iris conspicuously whitish* in adult; both dark in immature. Above mostly olive, more brownish on crown; throat pale grayish, *remaining underparts bright pale yellow.* Coiba Island birds (*xuthus*) have heavier bill and are darker olive above and much darker and buffier below.

Similar species: A somewhat confusing bird, often looking quite flycatcher-like or resembling a little peppershrike. Most apt to be confused with Golden-fronted Greenlet (and the two often occur together), especially when immature; note Scrub's heavier bill, brighter yellow underparts, and very different calls.

Status and distribution: Fairly common to common in scrubby areas, shrubby clearings, and borders of light woodland in lowlands on Pacific slope from Chiriquí to eastern Panama province (lower Bayano River valley); on Caribbean slope found only in Canal area and adjacent eastern Colon province (east to Portobelo); ranges sparingly up into lower highlands of western Chiriquí (e.g. around Boquete); fairly common also on Coiba Island, where found more in forest lower growth and borders.

Habits: Less active than other greenlets, in this respect more resembling the true vireos. The call is easily recognized and often heard, a melancholy *tuweé, tuweé, tuweé . . .* , often repeated up to 20 times without pausing.

Range: Southwestern Costa Rica to northern Colombia and Venezuela.

Note: The form found in Panama and adjacent Costa Rica (*viridiflavus*) is quite distinct and disjunct from other populations of Scrub Greenlet found in South America; it may ultimately be best regarded as a full species (Panama, or Yellow-green, Greenlet). Wetmore has also suggested that Coiba Island birds differ so markedly from mainland birds that they too might be specifically distinct; it would be called *H. xuthus*, Coiba Greenlet.

TAWNY-CROWNED GREENLET
Hylophilus ochraceiceps   Plate 30

Description: 4½. *Iris pale grayish to whitish. Crown tawny,* somewhat yellower on forehead; remaining upperparts brownish olive with *wings and tail more russet brown;* throat pale grayish, breast pale olivaceous strongly washed with buff, becoming pale yellowish on belly. Foregoing applies to *nelsoni* of most of Panama range; birds from Chiriquí and Bocas del Toro (*pallidipectus*) are decidedly browner above and buffier on breast, while birds from eastern Darién and perhaps eastern San Blas (*bulunensis*) are much more olive (less brownish) above and have breast and belly more olivaceous (less buff and yellow).
Similar species: The *only* Panama greenlet found in understory of humid forest. Golden-fronted Greenlet is much more olive above (never showing the brown wings and tail always shown by this species), never shows the buff tinge on breast, and has dark (not pale) iris. See also female Plain Antvireo.
Status and distribution: Rare to uncommon in lower growth of humid forest and mature second-growth woodland in lowlands and foothills on both slopes, ranging up in lower highlands of western Chiriquí to about 1500 m (5000 ft); apparently only one record from Bocas del Toro (a bird mistnetted, examined by Eisenmann, and released at Almirante on October 19, 1965), and on Pacific slope found only in foothills except in eastern Panama province (upper Bayano River valley) and Darién. Rather scarce in Canal area, where most likely to be encountered in forest along Pipeline Road.
Habits: Usually occurs within forest, where it forages actively at low and middle levels, often accompanying mixed flocks of antwrens, etc. The call is very different from that of other greenlets, a harsh nasal note, constantly uttered, *nya, nya.* Its presumed song, much less often heard, is a loud clear penetrating *teee-yeeé,* with second note rising.
Range: Southeastern Mexico to northern Bolivia and Amazonian Brazil.

GOLDEN-FRONTED GREENLET
Hylophilus aurantiifrons   Plate 30

Description: 4¼. *Iris dark. Forehead orange-yellow; cap brown contrasting with olive of remaining upperparts;* pale yellow below, tinged buffy on chest and olive on sides.
Similar species: Most apt to be confused with Scrub Greenlet, with which it regularly

occurs; Golden-fronted looks dull and faded, always has a dark iris (conspicuously pale in all but immature Scrubs), and is not as bright yellow below; calls also differ characteristically. Tawny-crowned Greenlet is found in very different habitat (humid forest undergrowth), has whitish iris, is much browner above, etc.
Status and distribution: Fairly common to common in dry scrubby areas and shrubby clearings in lowlands on Pacific slope from Herrera and southern Coclé east to western Darién (Garachiné); on Caribbean slope recorded only from middle Chagres River valley (Frijoles, etc.), where scarce.
Habits: Usually remains fairly low in bushes and small trees. The call resembles the Lesser Greenlet's, an often-heard, usually four-noted whistled phrase, *cheetsacheéyou,* sometimes shortened to three or lengthened to five notes.
Range: Central Panama to northern Colombia and Venezuela.

LESSER GREENLET
Hylophilus decurtatus   Plate 30

Description: 3¾–4. *A puffy-headed, very active little bird with a short tail,* widespread and numerous in forested areas. Birds from western and central Panama (nominate *decurtatus*) have *crown and nape gray with whitish eye-ring,* fading to pale grayish on sides of head; upperparts otherwise bright olive; *grayish white below,* tinged greenish yellow on flanks. Birds from eastern Panama (*darienensis,* found mainly in eastern Panama province, San Blas, and Darién; some intergrades with nominate found in Canal area) have *crown bright olive,* concolor with upperparts. Immatures of both tinged buff below.
Similar species: Different shape (big head, short tail) from any wood warbler, many of which have superficially similar color patterns (see especially Tennessee Warbler). Other greenlets have yellow on underparts.
Status and distribution: Common to very common in humid forest, forest borders, and second-growth woodland in lowlands and foothills on both slopes, though absent from drier lowlands from eastern side of Azuero Peninsula to western Panama province; in western Chiriquí found regularly up to 1200–1500 m (4000–5000 ft) in lower highlands.
Habits: One of the most numerous birds of forested country. Usually seen at middle and upper levels, often in small groups and

as one of the more abundant species in mixed foraging flocks of insectivorous birds. The call is a rapid, musical phrase suggestive of a single phrase of the Yellow-green Vireo but even more monotonous, constantly repeated, typically *deedereét* or *itsacheét*.

Range: Southern Mexico to western Ecuador.

Note: Formerly two species were recognized, *H. decurtatus* (Gray-headed Greenlet, found from Mexico to central Panama) and *H. minor* (with *darienensis* as a race, Lesser Greenlet, found from eastern Panama to Ecuador), but it is clear that they intergrade extensively in central Panama, and all recent authorities consider them conspecific.

GREEN SHRIKE-VIREO
Vireolanius pulchellus   Plate 30

Description: 5½. Heavy-headed, with *stout hooked bill*. *Bright grass green above* except for inconspicuous blue band on hindneck; *throat bright yellow*, remaining underparts pale yellowish green, yellower on under tail-coverts. Foregoing applies to *viridiceps* of most of Panama range; *verticalis*, found in Bocas del Toro and Veraguas lowlands and foothills (intergrading with *viridiceps* in Veraguas or Coclé) similar but with an additional and *more conspicuous blue band on forehead*.

Similar species: Brilliantly colored but difficult to see. Golden-browed Chlorophonia of western highlands is generally similar in color but mostly bright yellow below with contrasting green throat (the reverse of this species) and has yellow eye-stripe and short wide bill. Green Honeycreeper is also bright green but has slimmer proportions and slenderer, slightly decurved bill, lacks yellow on throat.

Status and distribution: Fairly common to common (though most often recorded only by voice) in canopy of humid forest and second-growth woodland in lowlands and foothills on both slopes (though specimen records are comparatively few); recorded from entire Caribbean slope east to western San Blas (where heard above Nusagandi on March 7, 1986; Ridgely); on Pacific slope much more local, but known from a few reports from western Chiriquí , in foothills from Veraguas east to eastern Panama province (Cerro Azul/Jefe), and in lowlands of Canal area and eastern Panama province (east at least to the middle Bayano River valley around Majé). Widespread in forested areas on both slopes of Canal area.

Habits: Deliberate behavior, green plumage blending into the foliage, and habit of usually remaining high in forest trees, all combine to make this beautiful bird exasperatingly difficult to see. Sometimes, however, it joins a mixed flock of insectivorous birds and then may descend much lower. Heard far more often that it is seen, its true abundance is best indicated by its distinctive song consisting of a phrase of three whistles, tirelessly repeated, *peeea, peeea, peeea . . .* , the notes sometimes lacking the downward slide (then *pee-pee-pee . . .*), reminiscent of song of Tufted Titmouse (*Parus bicolor*) of temperate North America.

Range: Southeastern Mexico to eastern Panama.

Note: Formerly placed in the genus *Smaragdolanius*. Until recently the shrike-vireos were usually given full family rank (Vireolaniidae), but all recent authorities (including the 1983 AOU Check-list) agree that they are best considered a subfamily of the Vireonidae.

YELLOW-BROWED SHRIKE-VIREO
Vireolanius eximius   Plate 30

Description: 5½. Known only from eastern Darién. Resembles Green Shrike-Vireo, replacing it eastward. Differs in having *entire crown and nape blue* (not just a band on the hindneck), *conspicuous bright yellow superciliary*, and small yellow spot below eye.

Status and distribution: Rare to uncommon in canopy of humid forest in foothills of eastern Darién (480–930 m: 1600–3100 ft); recorded only from slopes of Cerro Pirre above Cana (where seemingly absent from the valley itself), and from Cerro Quía (where two separate individuals were seen on July 17, 1975; Ridgely). Possibly ranges farther east, or into lowlands; any shrike-vireo found in western Darién, eastern San Blas, or extreme eastern Panama province should be carefully checked (and if possible collected) so as to determine whether intergradation between this species and the Green Shrike-Vireo is occurring.

Habits: Behavior, including vocalizations, similar to Green Shrike-Vireo.

Range: Eastern Panama to northwestern Venezuela.

Note: Formerly placed in the genus *Smaragdolanius*. *V. eximius* is perhaps conspecific with *V. pulchellus*, but was considered distinct in the 1983 AOU Check-list.

RUFOUS-BROWED PEPPERSHRIKE
Cyclarhis gujanensis   Plate 30

Description: 5 ¾. Heavy-headed, with *stout strongly hooked bill*. Olive above with brownish gray crown, *prominent broad rufous superciliary*, and gray sides of head; mostly yellow below, fading to whitish on chin and lower belly. Chiriquí birds (*subflavescens*) are duller above and below, and have more extensive white on belly; Coiba Island birds (*coibae*) are darker and duller olive above.
Similar species: In proportions like a shrike-vireo but with very different color pattern and habitat. Vireos are slimmer, have less heavy bill, lack rufous eye-stripe.
Status and distribution: Fairly common in forest borders, second-growth woodland, and clearings with scattered trees in foothills and lower highlands of western and central Chiriquí (mostly 900–1800 m: 3000–6000 ft; easternmost record is a bird south of Fortuna on the Hornito ridge on July 4, 1982; Ridgely), and in lighter woodland and gallery forest in lowlands on Pacific slope locally from southern Veraguas to western Panama province, including eastern side of Azuero Penin-sula; found also in mangroves and adjacent coastal scrub in eastern Panama province (seemingly local, but more likely just over-looked; recent sightings from as far west as Juan Diaz) and western Darién (Garachiné); fairly common in canopy and borders of forest on Coiba Island.
Habits: An arboreal and rather lethargic bird; when singing usually sits quietly in the foliage and often very hard to see. The song is monotonous, consisting of short but musical rather oriole or grosbeak-like whistled phrases, sometimes repeated without change for 5–10 minutes, then changed to a new phrase which is likewise repeated for a long period, and so on. Characteristic phrases are *tootoo-wheétee, tooweeoo* and *chee-weech, awatweéa*; one bird may sing for hours, going through a repertory of numerous dif-ferent phrases.
Range: Eastern Mexico to central Argentina.
Note: Until recently the peppershrikes were usually given full family rank (Cyclar-hidae), but all recent authorities (including the 1983 AOU Check-list) agree that they are best considered a subfamily of the Vireonidae.

WOOD-WARBLERS: Parulinae (51)

The wood-warblers are a rather large group of lively, and often very pretty, chiefly insectivorous birds found only in the New World. They were formerly considered as a full family, but the 1983 AOU Check-list gave them only subfamily rank in the vastly expanded Emberizidae family; for ease of reference we have retained a separate group heading for them. Most Panama species are migrants from temperate North America, mainly from east of the Rockies; Panama's resident species are found primarily in the highlands. A large proportion of the migrants arrive in Panama as dull-plumaged and often very confusing immatures (and a few species have adult nonbreeding plumages as well). However, by the time they leave for their northern nesting grounds, all but a few have attained full adult breeding plumage, though they rarely or never sing. They are especially numerous during their periods of transience, mostly September–early November and March–April, less so during the intervening northern winter months. With few exceptions they shun the interior of forest in favor of second-growth woodland, borders, shrubby clearings, and even residential areas. In woodland they often join mixed foraging flocks of resident species. Identification is often a real challenge, for not only are many of the species easy to confuse with each other, but they also resemble some resident groups such as the greenlets, a few small tanagers, and certain small flycatchers. The resident warblers fall into three main groups. The three native species of yellowthroats resemble the familiar northern species in appearance and behavior. The two redstarts (genus *Myioborus*) are attractive birds of highland forests, reminis-cent in their lively behavior of the American Redstart, though the two genera are not closely related. The six Panama *Basileuterus* warblers are rather plain birds of forest and woodland undergrowth, occurring mostly in the highlands; one, the Buff-rumped, is very different, occupying a niche similar to that of the waterthrushes. Recent evidence indicates that the distinctive Wrenthrush, though until recently considered a monotypic family (Zeledoniidae) is actually not too distantly related to the *Basileuterus* warblers. Nests of the yellowthroats are open cups of grass placed on or near the ground, while *Myioborus*, *Basileuterus*, and *Zeledonia* all (so far as known) build domed or partially domed nests with a side entrance, these also being placed on or near the ground.

BLUE-WINGED WARBLER
Vermivora pinus

Description: 4½–5. Male with bright yellow crown, face, and underparts, with *narrow black line through eye*; hindneck and back bright olive, *wings bluish gray with two bold white wing-bars*. Female somewhat duller, with more whitish under tail-coverts.

Similar species: Female and immature Yellow and Wilson's Warblers lack both the black eyeline and the white wing-bars.

Status and distribution: Rare winter visitant (mid-October–late March) to woodland and forest borders in lowlands and foothills of western and central Panama, with easternmost record being a bird collected at Chepo, eastern Panama province, on March 7, 1927; in western Panama reported mainly from Caribbean slope.

Range: Breeds in eastern United States; winters mostly from southern Mexico to Nicaragua, in small numbers to Costa Rica and Panama, casually to Colombia.

Note: Hybrids between this species and the Golden-winged Warbler are well known in North America; the two primary phenotypes were originally described as full species. "Brewster's Warbler" is essentially like a Blue-wing in pattern but it has yellow wing-bars and mostly white underparts with a variable amount of yellow on breast. The rarer "Lawrence's Warbler" resembles a Golden-wing but its wing-bars are white or whitish and underparts yellow. Various intermediates are known. "Brewster's" type birds have been reported seen in the highlands of western Chiriquí and in Bocas del Toro.

GOLDEN-WINGED WARBLER
Vermivora chrysoptera   Plate 31

Description: 4½–5. Male gray above with yellow forecrown and *large patch of yellow on wing*; sides of head and underparts white with *black patch through eye and black throat*. Female similar but with eye-patch and throat pale gray.

Similar species: Male is easily recognized; some females and immatures show only a trace of the characteristic facial pattern but always have prominent and characteristic yellow wing-patch.

Status and distribution: Uncommon to fairly common transient and winter visitant (mostly October–April, a few arriving in September or lingering into May) in woodland and forest borders throughout, but in smaller numbers in eastern Panama, and not reported from drier more open lowlands on Pacific slope; most numerous in foothills and lower highlands of western Panama. The decline in numbers which has been noted on its North American breeding grounds has not yet been noted in Panama.

Habits: Forages at all levels, often with mixed flocks of various insectivorous birds. Frequently feeds in dead leaf clusters.

Range: Breeds in eastern North America; winters from Guatemala to Colombia and northern Venezuela.

TENNESSEE WARBLER
Vermivora peregrina   Plate 31

Description: 4½. Adult male bright olive above with gray crown and nape, *narrow white superciliary*, and dusky line through eye; below entirely white. Female similar but more olive on crown and nape, superciliary tinged yellow, and throat and chest washed with pale yellow. Immature uniform olive above with *narrow yellowish superciliary* and usually a *single whitish wing-bar*; below more or less yellowish, brightest on breast and palest on belly and under tail-coverts (*latter usually white*). By mid-winter most birds have assumed adult plumage.

Similar species: Immatures can be confused with dull immature Yellow Warblers, but these never show an eye-stripe and have yellow spots in tail. Philadelphia Vireo is larger with proportionately heavier bill and never shows a wing-bar; its behavior is more lethargic. Adults might be confused with Lesser Greenlet, but latter is chunkier and shorter-tailed, shows an eye-ring instead of a superciliary, etc.

Status and distribution: Common to very common transient and winter resident throughout, from lowlands to highlands (regular to about 2100 m: 7000 ft in western Chiriquí); recorded mostly October–April, a few arriving in September or lingering into May. Found virtually anywhere there are trees, but especially in clearings, woodland,

and forest borders; less numerous in continuous forest, and apparently not as common in eastern Panama as farther west.

Habits: Often occurs in quite large flocks of its own species, more so than other wintering warblers do. Large numbers often concentrate at flowering immortelle trees (*Erythrina* spp.).

Range: Breeds in northern North America; winters from southern Mexico to Colombia and northern Venezuela.

[NASHVILLE WARBLER]
Vermivora ruficapilla

Description: 4½. Accidental. *Head gray with narrow but conspicuous white eye-ring*, and usually concealed chestnut crown patch; otherwise uniform olive above; *underparts uniform bright yellow*. Female slightly duller than male, immatures even more so, with buffy whitish eye-ring and more brownish gray head.

Similar species: See especially immature Tennessee and Yellow Warblers.

Status and distribution: Only one report, a single bird seen with a large mixed species flock along the Santa Clara road some 25 km by road west of Volcán in lower highlands of western Chiriquí on January 2, 1980 (P. Donahue and J. Van Oss).

Range: Breeds in northern and western North America; winters mostly from Mexico to Honduras, rarely in Greater Antilles, with one report from western Panama.

NORTHERN PARULA
Parula americana

Description: 4½. Casual visitant to Caribbean coast. Male *mostly blue-gray above* with *narrow but conspicuous broken white eye-ring*, and suffused greenish yellow patch on upper back; wings with two bold white wing-bars; throat and breast bright yellow, with *band of mixed black and orange-rufous across chest*; belly white. Female similar but not so brightly marked, with chest band reduced or lacking. Immatures can be considerably duller (upperparts paler and grayer, etc.), but have same overall pattern.

Similar species: Resembles the far more numerous Tropical Parula. Tropical lacks Northern's broken eye-ring, and has black on foreface, wider area of yellow on sides of throat, and is more extensively yellow below (extends to upper belly, whereas in Northern the yellow stops on the breast) and

never shows the distinct chest band (at most an ochraceous suffusion).

Status and distribution: Known in Panama from a few sightings of individual birds near the Caribbean coast of Canal area, including birds seen at Coco Solo on March 15, 1972 (D. Engleman and A. Ramirez), at Fort Sherman on March 25, 1972 (same observers), and at Galeta Island on January 21, 1976 (J. Pujals *et al.*) and March 4, 1977 (J. Pujals and S. Stokes). To be watched for elsewhere.

Range: Breeds in eastern North America; winters mainly in Florida and West Indies, sparingly along Gulf/Caribbean coasts of Mexico and Central America.

TROPICAL PARULA
Parula pitiayumi   Plate 33

Description: 4½. Sexes similar. *Grayish blue above* with black facial area and *patch of olive green on back*; two white wing-bars, one sometimes indistinct; *yellow below*, somewhat tawnier on throat, becoming whitish on lower belly.

Similar species: Likely confused only with Flame-throated Warbler, which see; Flame-throat is confined to western Chiriquí highlands. See also the casual Northern Parula.

Status and distribution: Fairly common to common in canopy and borders of forest and second-growth woodland in foothills and lower highlands of Chiriquí, adjacent Bocas del Toro (recorded only from along oleoducto road north of Fortuna, but likely more widespread), Veraguas, western side of Azuero Peninsula (where recently found as far south as Cerro Hoya by F. Delgado), and in lowlands of eastern Panama province (upper Bayano River valley) and foothills of Darién; in western Panama recorded mainly 300–1500 m (1000–5000 ft), in Darién up only to 1050 m (3500 ft); common also on Coiba Island.

Habits: Small size and habit of usually foraging at considerable heights sometimes make observation difficult, but readily attracted by squeaking. Its song is a buzzy trill, typically *tsip-tsip-tsip-tsip-tsip-tsrrrrrrrrrip*, with variations.

Range: Southern Texas and Mexico to Bolivia, northern Argentina, and Uruguay.

FLAME-THROATED WARBLER
Parula gutturalis   Plate 33

Description: 4½. Found only in Chiriquí

highlands. Sexes similar. *Slaty gray above* with black patch on cheeks and *on back; throat and chest bright orange*, lower underparts white. Immature similar but duller, throat and chest buffier.

Similar species: The Tropical Parula is more bluish above with greenish patch on back and is mostly yellow (not orange) below; it also shows at least one white wing-bar.

Status and distribution: Fairly common in montane forest and forest borders in highlands of western Chiriquí, mostly above 1500 m (5000 ft).

Habits: A very active and pretty warbler, usually foraging quite high in trees but occasionally dropping low. Pairs or small groups often join mixed foraging flocks. Its song is a weak dry buzz, *zeeeeeoo* (R. Ward).

Range: Costa Rica and western Panama.

Note: Formerly placed in the genus *Vermivora*.

YELLOW WARBLER
Dendroica petechia   Plates 31, 33

Description: 4½–5. Includes both North American migrant forms (the true "Yellow Warbler"), and resident forms (the "Mangrove Warbler"). Male "Yellow" *mostly yellow, more olive on back; wings and tail dusky*, wings with yellow edging, tail with *yellow patches on inner webs* (conspicuous in flight); *breast and flanks with variable amount of chestnut streaking*. Female similar but duller overall, with chestnut streaking faint or absent; immatures are even drabber and more olive generally. Male "Mangrove" has *entire head, throat, and chest rufous-chestnut*, except that on coast of Darién the race *jubaris* has rufous-chestnut more or less restricted to crown, with sides of head and throat at most tinged rusty; otherwise like male "Yellows". Female "Mangrove" resembles migratory females, but often is more *grayish above* and *whitish below*; this tendency is even more pronounced in immatures, which are often quite dingy and grayish, showing little or no yellow or even olive.

Similar species: Males of all races should be easily recognized, but females and immatures both of resident and migratory forms can be confusing. Migrants usually look quite yellow, or at least yellowish olive, and no other similar warbler shares their yellow in tail; immature Tennessee Warbler is most similar, but it also always shows a superciliary. Drab, grayish-looking "Mangrove Warblers" are often best known by accompanying bright males, and by their mangrove or island habitat.

Status and distribution: Migrants are common to very common transients and winter residents in semiopen and open areas and lighter woodland (including mangroves) in lowlands on both slopes; recorded mostly September–April, a few arriving as early as mid-August or lingering into early and even mid-May. Resident "Mangrove Warblers" are common in appropriate mangrove habitat along both coasts, and are also numerous on various islands off both coasts, on many of which (e.g. the Pearl Islands and Fortified Islands at Fort Amador) it also ranges into woodland and scrub habitats; on Coiba Island, however, it seems to be restricted to mangroves.

Habits: Migrants are numerous, familiar, and widespread in nonforested localities. Though they give their *tsip* or *chip* call notes almost incessantly, especially when excited by squeaking (as they easily are), they seem rarely or never to actually sing in Panama. Residents behave in a generally similar way (and the two often occur together during northern winter months), but are much more restricted in habitat. Male "Mangroves" have a bright lively song, rather variable but often consisting of a fast series of its *tsit* call notes with an emphasized terminal note (the effect being rather different from the song of northern birds).

Range: North America, West Indies, and coasts of Middle and South America south to northwestern Peru and western Venezuela; northern migrants winter south to Peru, northern Bolivia, and Amazonian Brazil.

Note: Birds resident in Middle and South America (the *D. erithachorides* group; Mangrove Warbler) are now usually considered conspecific with birds which breed in North America (the *D. aestiva* group), under the name of *D. petechia* (the name of group breeding in West Indies and southern Florida; Golden Warbler). The numerous races comprising the resident *erithachorides* and *petechia* groups do seem best considered conspecific, but migratory races united in the *aestiva* group are quite different, and perhaps deserve full species status.

CHESTNUT-SIDED WARBLER
Dendroica pensylvanica   Plate 31

Description: 4¼–4¾. Nonbreeding plumage: *yellowish olive green above*, somewhat grayer about head and with narrow white eye-ring; wings duskier with two yellowish wing-bars; sides of head and underparts grayish white, adult usually with *some chest-*

nut on sides. Breeding plumage birds have complex pattern with *yellow crown,* black striping on back, a black stripe below eye, and *prominent chestnut sides and flanks* (less in females).

Similar species: Immatures (most of which lack any chestnut on sides) can be known by their bright, unstreaked, lemon green upperparts in conjunction with the whitish underparts.

Status and distribution: Common to very common winter resident in forest borders and woodland in lowlands and foothills on both slopes in western and central Panama, but becoming decidedly less numerous in eastern Panama; recorded mostly late September–early April, occasional individuals as early as early September or as late as early May.

Habits: Usually noted as they forage with mixed species flocks of other warblers, tanagers, etc. Active and spritely, Chestnut-sided Warblers almost invariably cock their tail at a characteristic angle, and often droop their wings as well. Occasionally one will give a brief snatch of its song just prior to their departure.

Range: Breeds in eastern North America; winters from Guatemala to Panama, casually to Colombia and Venezuela.

MAGNOLIA WARBLER
Dendroica magnolia Plate 31

Description: 4½–5. Nonbreeding plumage: olive green above with grayish head and white eye-ring, two white wing-bars, and *broad white band across middle of tail* (lacking on middle pair of feathers), rump patch yellow; mostly yellow below with a little black streaking on sides and flanks, and usually a *grayish band across chest.* Breeding plumage much brighter (especially in male): bluish gray above with black face patch and back (latter streaked with olive in female); bright yellow below *with heavy black streaking* except on throat.

Similar species: In any plumage the white tail band combined with the mostly yellow underparts is distinctive. See Prairie Warbler.

Status and distribution: Uncommon to rare winter resident in forest borders, second-growth woodland, and clearings in lowlands on Caribbean slope east to Canal area and eastern Colon province (Portobelo area); also regular in small numbers on Pacific slope east into eastern Panama province (Tocumen/Chepo area and Bayano River valley); only one sighting from as far east as Darién (a bird seen by Wetmore at Jaqué on March 29, 1946); recorded mostly October–April, a few lingering into May.

Habits: Usually seen singly, feeding at low levels, often with mixed foraging flocks in second-growth woodland. Sometimes fans its tail as if to display the characteristic white tail band.

Range: Breeds in northern North America; winters from Mexico to Panama and in West Indies (rarely Florida), casually in Colombia.

CAPE MAY WARBLER
Dendroica tigrina

Description: 4½–5. Very rare. Nonbreeding plumage: olive green above (sometimes more grayish), with dull yellowish rump and *small indistinct* (but nearly always visible) *yellowish patch behind ear;* wings duskier with two whitish wing-bars; whitish or pale yellowish below, *rather uniformly* (often heavily) *streaked with dusky.* Breeding plumage male very different and quite unmistakable, with *chestnut cheeks* and bright yellow underparts boldly streaked with black. Breeding plumage female resembles nonbreeders but is brighter with more distinct yellow neck-spot and yellower underparts.

Similar species: Though older males retain varying degrees of their breeding plumage pattern through the winter, many nonbreeding birds are dull, and are readily confused with several other warblers. These include the Yellow-rumped, which is larger and browner, distinctly streaked above, and with much more conspicuous clear yellow rump, and the Palm, which has distinctive yellow under tail-coverts and wags its tail almost incessantly.

Status and distribution: Very rare but now probably annual winter visitant in small numbers to clearings, woodland borders, and residential areas in lowlands of western and central Panama (not definitely recorded east of Canal area), with several reports also from lower highlands of western Chiriquí; recorded December–March. Seems most regular near Caribbean coast of Canal area. Increased observer activity over the past 10–20 years has doubtless played a role in the upsurge of Cape May Warbler reports over the same period, but it also seems virtually certain that the warbler has undergone an actual population increase, apparently correlated with insect outbreaks on its breeding grounds.

Habits: On its wintering grounds, found mostly at flowering trees, also often in ornamental palms.

Range: Breeds in northern North America; winters mostly in West Indies, in very small numbers in Florida and Middle America.

BLACK-THROATED BLUE WARBLER
Dendroica coerulescens

Description: 5–5½. Casual. Male very clean cut, *dark grayish blue above* with prominent white speculum at base of primaries; *sides of head, throat, and sides black*; breast and belly white. Female very dull, brownish olive above with narrow whitish superciliary and the *same prominent white speculum as in male*; dull pale brownish yellow below, sometimes buffier, sometimes more whitish.

Similar species: Dapper male is easily recognized; female is more difficult but can be known by the speculum, a mark shared by no other similar bird.

Status and distribution: Apparently a casual winter visitant, with several recent sight reports, all of males: one near Gatun Locks, Caribbean side of Canal area, on January 14, 1973 (D. Engleman *et al.*); one at Volcán, Chiriquí, on February 19, 1984 (K. Weber); one near Gatun Dam on Tiger Trail on December 20, 1984 (D. Engleman and D. Gardner; seen again on December 29); and one at Bambito, Chiriquí, on February 16, 1986 (W. Martinez). Photographic confirmation desirable.

Habits: Favors undergrowth in woodland and forest; the Tiger Trail bird noted above was accompanying a flock of White-flanked and Checker-throated Antwrens, etc.

Range: Breeds in eastern North America; winters mostly in Greater Antilles, more rarely in Lesser Antilles, with a few scattered records from Middle America and northern South America.

YELLOW-RUMPED WARBLER
Dendroica coronata

Description: 5–5½. Nonbreeding plumage: brownish above streaked with dusky; two white wing-bars and *conspicuous yellow rump; throat white, remaining underparts whitish* with grayish on chest and sides and *yellow patch on sides*. Breeding plumage male brighter, *bluish gray above* streaked with black and with *yellow crown patch*; white below with broad black band across chest and down sides, and yellow patch on sides; *conspicuous yellow rump*. Breeding plumage female similar but duller. Forms breeding in western North America (*auduboni* group) are similar but

have *throat yellow* and larger white patch on wings; these differences may be obscure on some birds, and there is some intergradation.

Similar species: The bright yellow rump will in any plumage distinguish this species from most other warblers; Magnolia and Cape May (both of which do show yellowish rumps) are mostly yellow (not whitish) below. Another good point is the Yellow-rumped's frequently heard call, a loud *tchek*; this is varied to a distinctly different, fast *whit* in birds of the *auduboni* group.

Status and distribution: An erratic winter visitant to western and central Panama, numbers being large in some years (Wetmore relates that in January–February 1958 it was one of the most abundant birds in the Almirante/Changuinola region of Bocas del Toro), but virtually absent in others; occurs in largest numbers in Bocas del Toro and Chiriquí, and becomes decidedly rare in eastern Panama, with only one reported sighting from San Blas and only a few from Darién; recorded early November–late March. Only report of *auduboni* race (which usually winters farther north in Middle America) is a single bird seen and heard near Volcán, Chiriquí, on February 5–6, 1976 (R. Foroter and Ridgely).

Habits: In Panama usually feeds on the ground in fairly open areas, flying up to trees when disturbed. Often occurs in small flocks of only its own species.

Range: Breeds in North America; winters from central United States to Panama and in West Indies, casually to Colombia.

TOWNSEND'S WARBLER
Dendroica townsendi

Description: 4½–5. Casual visitant to Chiriquí highlands. Adult male has striking head pattern, with *black crown and ear-patch, latter surrounded by bright yellow*, and *black throat and chest*; otherwise olive above, back streaked with black; wings duskier with two white wing-bars; *breast bright yellow*, becoming white on lower belly, with bold black streaking on sides and flanks. Adult female similar but with more olive crown, duskier ear-patch, mostly yellow throat, and less back streaking; immature even duller (especially females), with more olive ear-patch, plain olive back, and less black on chest.

Similar species: Female and immature Black-throated Green Warblers lack black streaks on crown, show only a trace of an olive or dusky cheek patch (their entire face looks yellow), and usually have whitish throat and breast (male sometimes has some yellow on breast). Female and immature Blackburnian Warblers have striped back and less yellow on face.

Status and distribution: Casual winter visitant to highlands of western Chiriquí. Four known records: an adult male seen repeatedly at Nueva Suiza on November 19–30, 1967 (T. V. Heatley and V. M. Kleen); an adult female seen and photographed near Volcán on March 21–22, 1979 (Ridgely and J. Baird *et al.*; photos to VIREO); an adult male seen along Boquete Trail above Cerro Punta on March 21, 1979 (Ridgely and J. Baird *et al.*); and an adult female seen on summit of Volcán Barú on January 21, 1988 (Ridgely and T. Richards *et al.*).

Habits: The few birds which reach Costa Rica and western Panama seem to favor forest borders and tall trees in clearings, and also regularly forage in the exotic junipers and cypresses which are planted in gardens around houses.

Range: Breeds in northwestern North America; winters mainly from Mexico to Costa Rica (especially in highlands), casually to western Panama and accidentally to northern Colombia.

HERMIT WARBLER
Dendroica occidentalis

Description: 4½–5. Casual visitant to Chiriquí highlands. Adult male has *bright golden yellow head; otherwise mostly gray above*, back streaked with black, wings duskier with two white wing-bars; throat black, *remaining underparts white*, with a little dusky streaking on sides. Adult female similar but duller, with black throat patch reduced. Immature resembles female but often has black throat patch entire lacking.

Similar species: Male easily known by its all-yellow head; female and immature can be known from respective stages of Black-throated Green by their gray (not olive) back and less streaking on sides. Male's black throat patch is considerably smaller than that of male Black-throated Green.

Status and distribution: Casual winter visitant to highlands of western Chiriquí: what was likely the same adult male was seen at the same garden in Nueva Suiza on December 22, 1973 (D. Gardner), on January 15, 1974 (Ridgely and C. Leahy *et al.*), on January 16, 1976 (J. Pujals *et al.*), and on March 6, 1976 (P. Miliotis *et al.*); an adult female was seen in Bambito on February 25, 1986 (T. Meyer *et al.*).

Specimen or photographic confirmation remains desirable.

Range: Breeds in western United States; winters mainly from Mexico to Nicaragua (especially in highlands), casually to Costa Rica and western Panama.

BLACK-THROATED GREEN WARBLER
Dendroica virens　　　　　　Plate 31

Description: 4½–5. Adult male olive above with *sides of head mostly bright yellow* (cheeks faintly outlined with olive); wings and tail blackish, with two bold white wing-bars; *throat and chest black*, extending down as black streaking on sides; otherwise white below, sometimes tinged yellow on under tail-coverts. Female similar but duller overall, with less black below (throat usually yellowish); immatures even duller (especially females), often showing almost no black on throat or chest, and with black streaking on sides faint or absent.

Similar species: Can be recognized in any plumage by its yellow cheeks. Some birds (especially immature) show little black on throat and chest and might be confused with an immature Blackburnian but have much more yellow on face and no streaking on back. See also Townsend's and Hermit Warblers.

Status and distribution: Common to very common winter resident in montane forest, woodland, and borders in foothills and highlands of western Panama, with largest numbers in Chiriquí; occurs in smaller numbers in foothill areas of central Panama, and a few apparently winter regularly in highlands of eastern Darién (Cerro Pirre, Cerro Tacarcuna), but evidently occurs in lowlands only or mainly as a transient (with few reports, for example, from former Canal area); recorded mostly October–April, with a few arriving in mid or late September.

Habits: An arboreal warbler, usually occurring as a member of mixed foraging flocks in second-growth woodland, borders, and clearings.

Range: Breeds in eastern North America; winters from Mexico (rarely southern United States) to Panama and in West Indies, casually to Colombia and Venezuela.

BLACKBURNIAN WARBLER
Dendroica fusca　　　　　　Plate 31

Description: 4¾–5¼. Adult male unmistakable: *mostly black above* with white striping on back and large white wing patch; *fiery orange on center of crown, as broad stripe encircling the black ear-coverts, and (especially bright) on throat and chest*; underparts fade to pale yellow on breast, and white on lower belly, with sides streaked black. This plumage can be seen except soon after the species' arrival in Panama, when even older males are somewhat duller below and mottled with olive above. Adult female and immatures are *similar in pattern* but much duller; they are mostly grayish olive above streaked with blackish (most solidly black in immature males), have the *bright orange replaced by orange-yellow to dull yellow* (dullest in immature females), and have two white wing-bars rather than a solid patch.

Similar species: Nonbreeding Black-throated Green Warbler has more or less solid yellow face and mostly white underparts (not yellow on throat and chest). See also Yellow-throated Warbler.

Status and distribution: Fairly common transient and winter resident in montane forest, woodland, and borders in foothills and highlands throughout, but recorded from lowlands only or mainly as a rare to uncommon transient; recorded mostly September–April. Numbers seen in western and central Panama during northern mid-winter months seem to vary; in some years almost as numerous as the Black-throated Green in western Chiriquí, while in others it is virtually absent as an over-winterer. Seems consistently fairly common during mid-winter in eastern Darién highlands (e.g. on Cerro Pirre).

Habits: Usually met singly in mixed foraging flocks. Feeds primarily at middle and high tree levels.

Range: Breeds in eastern North America; winters from Costa Rica to Venezuela and Peru.

YELLOW-THROATED WARBLER
Dendroica dominica

Description: 5–5½. Casual. Sexes similar. *Gray above* with *white stripe over eye and another on cheeks*; two prominent white wing-bars; *throat and upper chest yellow*, bordered with a black stripe; remaining underparts white, streaked with black on sides.

Similar species: Nonbreeding Blackburnian Warbler is less sharply patterned, has striped back and yellow stripes on head.

Status and distribution: Casual or very rare winter visitant to western and central Panama, with scatter of records. Five known reports: one seen at Almirante, Bocas del

Toro, on February 3, 1958 (Wetmore); one seen and photographed at Summit Gardens on February 2, 1973 (Ridgely and C. Leahy *et al.*; photos to VIREO); one seen at Cerro Azul, eastern Panama province, on January 20, 1978 (R. Forster and J. Baird *et al.*); one seen at Achiote Road on February 24, 1983 (R. Behrstock *et al.*); and one seen below Volcán along road to Concepción, Chiriquí, on January 16, 1988 (Ridgely and T. Richards *et al.*).

Habits: In Panama has most often been seen in gardens or residential areas with planted palms and Caribbean Pines.

Range: Breeds in eastern United States and on several of the Bahamas; winters from Florida and Texas to Nicaragua and in the Greater Antilles, rarely to Costa Rica, casually to Panama, northern South America, and the Lesser Antilles.

PRAIRIE WARBLER
Dendroica discolor

Description: 4¾. Casual. Male mostly olive above with faint chestnut streaking on back; *bright yellow below and on face*, with *bold black stripes through eye and on malar area*, and *prominent black streaking on sides*; wings and tail dusky, wings with two yellowish bars. Female similar but duller, with stripes on face dusky-olive, little or no chestnut on back. Immature even duller, with grayer and less strongly patterned facial area.

Similar species: Immature most resembles immature Magnolia Warbler, but lacks its grayish breast band, white median tail band, and yellowish rump. Prairie's habit of *frequently pumping its tail* is also helpful. Palm Warbler also wags its tail (even more persistently, in fact), but is more generally streaked and is never so bright yellow below.

Status and distribution: Apparently a casual winter visitant, with several recent sight reports: one seen at Volcán, Chiriquí, on January 23, 1973 (R. Brownstein and W. George); one to two birds present at Isla Margarita (formerly Fort Randolph), on Caribbean coast of Canal area, from November 19, 1983, to January 2, 1984 (D. Engleman, D. Scott, *et al.*); one seen near Fortuna, Chiriquí, on January 20, 1986 (T. Meyer *et al.*). Photographic confirmation desirable.

Habits: During northern winter favors light woodland, scrub, and gardens; the Isla Margarita birds were found in a small area of mangroves.

Range: Breeds in eastern United States; winters mostly in Florida and the West Indies, in smaller numbers on islands off Yucatan Peninsula and Honduras, and casually to Costa Rica, Panama, and northern South America.

PALM WARBLER
Dendroica palmarum

Description: 5–5½. Nonbreeding plumage: brownish above indistinctly streaked with dusky; wings with two indistinct whitish or yellowish wing-bars; whitish or pale yellowish below, indistinctly streaked with dusky; *lower belly and under tail-coverts yellow.* Breeding plumage birds have chestnut cap, and some races become quite bright yellow below. Often first recognized by its *almost constant tail-wagging.*

Status and distribution: Rare but perhaps regular winter visitant in very small numbers to open or semiopen areas in lowlands on both slopes; so far recorded mostly from near Caribbean coast of Canal area, and from near coast of eastern Panama province (Panama City to La Jagua), also one report from Chiriquí (one seen along La Caldera road below Boquete on January 19, 1988; Ridgely and T. Richards *et al.*); recorded mid-November–mid-March.

Habits: Usually feeds on or near the ground, often in small groups of its own species. Shows no preference for palms! (unlike Yellow-throated and Cape May Warblers, which do regularly feed in them).

Range: Breeds in northern North America; winters from central United States to Honduras, and in Greater Antilles, rarely to Costa Rica and Panama.

BAY-BREASTED WARBLER
Dendroica castanea   Plate 31

Description: 5–5½. Nonbreeding plumage: olive above *streaked with blackish on crown and mantle*; wings dusky with two white wing-bars; *buffy whitish below with at most very indistinct dusky streaking on breast* (most often showing none); most adults, particularly males, show a *trace of chestnut on flanks* (seen on virtually all birds by January–February). Breeding plumage male entirely different, looking very dark: *cap, throat, chest, and sides dark chestnut*; forehead and face black, with *conspicuous pale buffy patch on sides of neck*. This plumage is assumed in March. Breeding plumage female has same pattern but is duller.

Similar species: Except for the extremely rare Blackpoll Warbler, the only warbler with combination of streaked back and essentially unstreaked underparts. Look for the tinge of chestnut on flanks.

Status and distribution: Fairly common to common transient and winter resident in lowlands and foothills on entire Caribbean slope, on Pacific slope from eastern Veraguas eastward; not reported from Chiriquí or western Veraguas, nor from any of Pacific offshore islands; recorded mostly late September–mid-April, a few arriving in mid-September and lingering into early May; in winter, more numerous eastward.

Habits: Usually occurs in light woodland and borders or in clearings with trees, often foraging rather high.

Range: Breeds in northern North America; winters from Costa Rica (rare) to Colombia and western Venezuela.

BLACKPOLL WARBLER
Dendroica striata

Description: 5–5½. Very rare, but probably overlooked among the hordes of Bay-breasted Warblers which over-winter in Panama. Nonbreeding plumage: extremely similar to the much more numerous Bay-breasted Warbler, the main (but subtle) differences being: *underparts more pale greenish yellow to pale yellowish* (with no buff tone), with whiter belly and *immaculate white under tail-coverts* (latter at least tinged buff in Bay-breast); some *fine dusky-olive streaking across breast and down flanks* usually shows (lacking in Bay-breast); legs typically pale (but can be dusky to blackish, as in Bay-breast). Breeding plumage male very different (and easily recognized); *crown black contrasting sharply with white cheeks*, grayish olive and black streaking on upperparts, *white underparts with black malar stripe*, and bold black streaking down sides. This plumage is assumed in March. Breeding plumage female similar to nonbreeding birds, but more sharply streaked blackish below.

Similar species: See Bay-breasted Warbler.

Status and distribution: Apparently a very rare, perhaps irregular, transient and winter visitant, with few records. One undated McLeannan skin from the Canal area is the only specimen record from Panama. More recently, there have been a few sightings of birds on both slopes of the Canal area and in eastern Panama province (B. Whitney *et al.*), and one bird was recognizably photographed along Chiva Chiva

Road on February 15, 1982 (B. Whitney; photo to VIREO); these have been noted at least January–March. Two birds were also banded and released on October 19 and 29, 1964, at Almirante, Bocas del Toro (D. L. Hicks). Further specimen confirmation desirable, but it now appears that the Blackpoll Warbler does indeed occur at least semi-regularly in Panama, albeit in very small numbers (there are also a few recent Costa Rican records).

Habits: Similar to Bay-breasted Warbler.

Range: Breeds in northern North America; winters mainly in Amazonia, migrating mostly through West Indies; casual or very rare in Costa Rica and Panama.

CERULEAN WARBLER
Dendroica cerulea

Description: 4¾. Male *azure blue above*, brightest on crown, and streaked black on back; wings and tail dusky, former with two white wing-bars; white below with *narrow black band across chest* (sometimes incomplete) and some black streaking on sides. Female *more bluish green above* with *narrow pale yellowish superciliary* and no streaking on back; wings and tail as in male; below pale yellowish to whitish, usually devoid of streaking (at most a little on sides). Immatures similar to female, but males may already show a faint chest band, and females tend to be greener (less blue) above and yellower below.

Similar species: The pretty male is easily recognized; duller female and immature are more difficult. They resemble a female Tennessee Warbler but have prominent white wing-bars; also resemble female Bay-breasted Warbler but are unstreaked above with more prominent eye-stripe and are whiter below. See also the very rare Blackpoll Warbler.

Status and distribution: Uncommon transient in canopy of humid forest, second-growth woodland, and borders (mostly late August–early October, and mid-March– mid-April), with a few reports of apparently over-wintering individuals (these latter mostly in foothills); not recorded from Pacific slope of western Panama.

Habits: This inconspicuous warbler may often be overlooked in Panama as it tends to forage very high above the ground. During September and again in late March and early April small "waves" may be encountered, however, often accompanying other migrating warblers and other small birds.

Range: Breeds in eastern United States; winters from Colombia and Venezuela to northern Bolivia.

BLACK-AND-WHITE WARBLER
Mniotilta varia   Plate 31

Description: 4¾–5¼. *Striped black and white all over*, center of belly white; male has black cheeks and throat; female has underparts whiter than male. *Creeps over tree branches* and even up tree trunks.

Similar species: No other warbler really resembles it, but see breeding plumage male of extremely rare Blackpoll Warbler, also black and white but with solid black (not striped) crown. See also male Streaked Antwren.

Status and disbribution: Fairly common transient and winter resident in second-growth woodland and forest borders throughout, but most numerous in lowlands and foothills (mostly late August–early April, once as early as 14 August); recorded also on Pearl Islands.

Habits: Generally found singly, often accompanying mixed foraging flocks, creeping over larger limbs and branches, the only Panama warbler to habitually do this.

Range: Breeds in eastern North America; winters from southern United States to northern South America (casually to Peru), and in West Indies.

AMERICAN REDSTART
Setophaga ruticilla   Plate 31

Description: 5. Adult male *mostly black*, with *large orange patches on wings, sides, and at base of tail*; belly white. Female and immatures grayish olive above, grayest on head and with narrow white spectacles; mostly whitish below; patches on wings, sides, and at base of tail as in male but *yellow instead of orange*. Immature males require 2 years to acquire full adult plumage; they gradually become blacker (first on face and foreneck, often looking blotchy), and their patches become more orange.

Similar species: Readily distinguished by its orange or yellow patches, regardless of plumage. Behavior also distinctive (see below). Does not resemble the *Myioborus* redstarts at all.

Status and distribution: Uncommon to fairly common transient and winter resident in forest borders and second-growth woodland, also mangroves, throughout; numbers are highest during migration, and as an over-winterer seems most numerous in foothills and mangroves; recorded mostly late August–late April, a few tardy migrants sometimes into May.

Habits: Extremely active, constantly drooping its wings, fanning its tail, and flitting out after passing insects. Usually seen with mixed flocks of other warblers, tanagers, etc.

Range: Breeds in North America; winters in Florida, West Indies, and from Mexico to Peru, northern Brazil, and the Guianas.

PROTHONOTARY WARBLER
Protonotaria citrea   Plate 31

Description: 5 ¼. Male has *head and underparts bright orange-yellow* (brightest on head and foreneck); back olive, *wings and tail uniform blue-gray*, latter with white patch on inner web conspicuous in flight; lower belly and under tail-coverts white. Female similar but duller, less orange, head tinged olive.

Similar species: Yellow Warbler also has head and underparts bright yellow but has yellowish (not blue-gray) wings. Male Black-and-yellow Tanager has vaguely similar pattern.

Status and distribution: Locally common transient and winter resident in mangroves and shrubbery and trees usually near water in lowlands throughout (a few in foothills and even lower highlands on migration); recorded mostly September–March, but small numbers regularly arrive in August, and a male was seen on the anomalous date of June 30, 1982 (early arrival? over-summering bird?), along the Río Algarrobos in western Chiriquí (Ridgely). Of the warblers commonly over-wintering in Panama, the Prothonotary departs the earliest.

Habits: Regularly found in small groups, with even larger numbers being found together on migration or at what appear to be favored "roosting" sites. Generally forages rather low, but sometimes goes higher, foraging in flowering *Erythrina* trees, etc.

Range: Breeds in eastern United States; winters from southern Mexico to northern Colombia and Venezuela, casually to Ecuador and Surinam.

WORM-EATING WARBLER
Helmitheros vermivorus

Description: 5 ¼. Sexes similar. Head pale buff with *broad black stripe on either side of crown and narrower black line through eye*; otherwise brownish olive above; *plain buff below*.

Similar species: The striped head pattern and otherwise dull coloration sets it apart

from other migrant warblers. Resembles several *Basileuterus* warblers, particularly the Three-striped, except for its buffy (not yellowish) underparts.

Status and distribution: Uncommon to rare winter resident in lower growth of forest and second-growth woodland on both slopes in western and central Panama, becoming less numerous eastward with easternmost records being one seen on San Blas coast near El Porvenir on October 14, 1985 (J. Jolly), and a specimen from Puerto San Antonio on lower Bayano River in eastern Panama province; on Pacific slope of western Panama recorded mainly from foothills and lower highlands; recorded mostly October–April, a few arriving in late September.

Habits: Generally very unobtrusive, remaining near the ground in thick undergrowth.

Range: Breeds in eastern United States; winters from Mexico to Panama and in West Indies.

OVENBIRD
Seiurus aurocapillus   Plate 31

Description: 5½–6. This species and the waterthrushes have a more horizontal posture than most other warblers. Olive above with *white eye-ring* and *orange crown bordered by narrow black stripe*; white below streaked with black on breast and sides. Crown of immature is less bright orange.

Similar species: Waterthrushes have eye-stripes (not eye-rings), lack the orange crown, and bob up and down when walking. Vaguely reminiscent of several of the migrant thrushes.

Status and distribution: Fairly common on ground and in undergrowth of humid forest and second-growth woodland in lowlands of western Bocas del Toro and in foothills and lower highlands of western Chiriquí (where also regularly in shady coffee groves), becoming less numerous eastward, rather rare in central Panama, and only two records from Darién and none in San Blas; recorded late September–late April.

Habits: Solitary and quite unobtrusive. Usually seen walking sedately on the ground inside forest or woodland; readily attracted by squeaking.

Range: Breeds in eastern and central North America; winters in Florida and the West Indies, and from Mexico to Panama, rarely to Colombia and Venezuela.

NORTHERN WATERTHRUSH
Seiurus noveboracensis Plate 31

Description: 5½–5¾. Olive brown above with *prominent long yellowish to buff superciliary*; pale yellowish to whitish below, *boldly streaked with dark brown* except on throat (where spotting faint) and lower belly.

Similar species: The less numerous Louisiana Waterthrush is very similar; see under that species for the distinctions between the two. The Ovenbird has the same shape but has prominent orange crown and a white eye-ring instead of a superciliary.

Status and distribution: Very common transient and common winter resident in lowlands on both slopes, including Pearl Islands; in highlands occurs mostly on migration (late September–late April, a few arriving in mid-September and lingering into May).

Habits: Usually in mangroves or along streams, but on migration may appear almost anywhere. Near water it is a common sight, walking with a teetering gait much like a Spotted Sandpiper. Its loud and easily recognized metallic call, *tchink*, is often heard, especially when the bird is alarmed or as it flies.

Range: Breeds in northern North America; winters in Florida and the West Indies and from Mexico to northern Peru, Venezuela, and the Guianas.

LOUISIANA WATERTHRUSH
Seiurus motacilla

Description: 5¾–6. Very similar to much more numerous Northern Waterthrush. Slightly larger, with longer bill and brighter pinkish legs. Main differences are: *wider and whiter superciliary*, notably broader and whitest behind eye (not uniformly narrow and tinged buffyish); *often quite obvious contrast between buffy flanks and white of rest of underparts* (Northern can look buffy yellowish below, but always more or less uniform, never with flanks in contrast); central area of throat pure white without dusky streaking (Northern's is flecked with dusky; this character often hard to discern in field, however).

Similar species: See Northern Waterthrush.

Status and distribution: Rare to uncommon transient and winter resident along forested or wooded streams throughout, over-wintering birds seeming to be most numerous (but by no means common) in foothills and lower highlands; recorded mostly August–March, a few lingering into early April. The

earliest migrant warbler to regularly arrive in Panama.

Habits: Very like the Northern Waterthrush but prefers running streams to quiet water.

Range: Breeds in eastern United States; winters mostly from Mexico to Panama and in West Indies, in very small numbers to northern South America.

KENTUCKY WARBLER
Oporornis formosus Plate 31

Description: 5¼. Olive above with *black forecrown and sides of head and neck* (forming "sideburns"), and *prominent yellow supraloral stripe and incomplete eye-ring*; entirely bright yellow below. Female similar but with less extensive black on face (crown often looks flecked, and is grayer), while in immatures the black is sometimes entirely lacking.

Similar species: Most apt to be confused with immature Canada Warbler (which may lack the diagnostic necklace), but Canada is basically gray (not olive) above; note that facial patterns of the two can be quite similar. Male yellowthroats also show black on face, but none has yellow around the eye; their semiopen habitat differs from Kentucky's.

Status and distribution: Fairly common but inconspicuous winter resident on or near ground in humid forest and second-growth woodland in lowlands and foothills throughout, though decidedly less numerous in eastern Panama than it is in central and western portions; on migration also recorded in small numbers up into highlands (e.g. in Chiriquí); recorded early September–late April.

Habits: A skulker, infrequently seen on its wintering grounds, though regularly captured in mist-nets. At least on Barro Colorado Island often found in attendance at army ant swarms (E. O. Willis).

Range: Breeds in eastern United States; winters mostly from southern Mexico to Panama, in very small numbers in northern South America.

CONNECTICUT WARBLER
Oporornis agilis

Description: 5½. Very rare. In all plumages shows a *conspicuous complete white or buffy whitish eye-ring*. Male mostly olive above with *gray hood* (palest on throat, purest gray on chest); lower underparts dull yellow. Female similar but *hood more grayish brown or* *even brownish buff*, palest on throat. Immatures similar to female but hood duller and even browner, and upperparts more brownish olive.

Similar species: Adult males are relatively easily distinguished, but other plumages are easily confused with much more numerous Mourning Warbler. In most Mournings (but not all) the eye-ring is incomplete, and it usually is not as prominent as in Connecticut. Further points to watch for are Connecticut's larger size, browner hood, duller yellow underparts, and its longer under tail-coverts (which reach more than halfway down underside of tail, imparting a short-tailed appearance). A good look will, however, be required, and this is usually not easy to obtain. In the hand, note that wing of Connecticut is longer than that of either Mourning or MacGillivray's (64–74 mm, av. 70 mm), with wing minus tail equalling 19 mm or more (W. E. Lanyon and J. Bull, *Bird Banding 38*: 187–194, 1967).

Status and distribution: Rare fall and spring transient in western Bocas del Toro lowlands (late September–late October; late March–early April). Three specimens have been taken, all in fall; spring specimens would be desirable. Mist-netting may reveal that it also occurs as a very rare transient elsewhere in Panama.

Habits: Poorly known outside of North America. Favors dense shrubby thickets and woodland borders; hard to see well. Sometimes *walks* on the ground (Mourning hops), often bobbing its head and raising its tail.

Range: Breeds in north-central North America; winters in Venezuela, eastern Colombia, and northern Brazil; migrates through (or over) West Indies, with a few records from Panama.

MOURNING WARBLER
Oporornis philadelphia   Plate 31

Description: 5. Male has *gray hood which becomes black on chest and sometimes on throat* (often with scaly effect on throat and chest); otherwise olive above, yellow below. Female similar but duller, with no black on bib and often with throat tinged yellowish buff; it may show an incomplete white eye-ring. Immatures often entirely lack the hooded effect, or the hood is *tinged brownish* and most pronounced on sides of chest; an eye-ring is usually present, *generally broken in front and often behind the eye*, but occasionally virtually complete.

Similar species: Adult male with its black bib and *lack of an eye-ring* is readily distinguished, as are those females which lack any eye-ring. Connecticut Warbler (very rare) has a complete eye-ring in all plumages; thus immature Mournings which show a more or less complete eye-ring can be quite similar (for distinctions see under that species). Male MacGillivray's Warbler (rare) resembles male Mourning but has an incomplete white eye-ring; females and immatures of these two are indistinguishable except in the hand (see under MacGillivray's).

Status and distribution: Fairly common transient and winter resident in dense shrubby woodland and forest borders and overgrown grassy and bushy clearings throughout, but most numerous as an overwinterer in the Chiriquí highlands; recorded mid-September–mid-May.

Habits: Usually skulks in dense vegetation, rarely allowing a protracted view, but can sometimes be coaxed into the open by squeaking. Favors areas near water. Often hops on the ground.

Range: Breeds in northern North America; winters from Nicaragua to Ecuador and Venezuela.

MACGILLIVRAY'S WARBLER
Oporornis tolmiei

Description: 5. Very rare except in Chiriquí highlands. Male very similar to male Mourning but has *prominent though incomplete white eye-ring* (broken in front of and behind eye); also has black lores and less solidly black bib (but bibs of some Mournings can be very similar). Female and immatures indistinguishable in the field from female and immature Mournings. In the hand, wing of MacGillivray's averages slightly shorter than Mourning's (55–65 mm, av. 61.5 mm; Mourning 55–67 mm, av. 62 mm), and its tail slightly longer (47–63 mm, av. 52.5 mm; Mourning 43–53 mm, av.48 mm), so that wing-minus-tail equals only 2–10 mm (av. 6.5 mm), versus Mourning's wing-minus-tail of 10–18 mm (av. 13 mm).

Similar species: See Mourning and Connecticut Warblers; latter shows a complete eye-ring in all plumages.

Status and distribution: Uncommon to rare winter resident in overgrown clearings and shrubby woodland borders; recorded only from Chiriquí (mostly in lower highlands, also one specimen from Puerto Armuelles) and Canal area (three old specimens, including one originally identified as a Mourning), but perhaps more widespread; recorded mid-October–mid-May. Most likely to be found around Volcán; has been seen recently near the Dos Rios Hotel.

Habits: As in Mourning Warbler.

Range: Breeds in western North America; winters from Mexico to western Panama (casually farther east).

COMMON YELLOWTHROAT
Geothlypis trichas   Plate 48

Description: 4½–5. Male olive above with *black mask extending over forehead and bordered above by whitish or pale grayish band*; throat and breast yellow, *fading to whitish on belly*. Female lacks black mask (sides of head olive), and has *yellow more restricted to throat*, with lower underparts more brownish. Immature resembles female but is often rather brownish above.

Similar species: Both sexes of Masked and Olive-crowned Yellowthroats have underparts *entirely* yellow. Male Masked Yellowthroat further differs in having gray (not whitish) border to mask, male Olive-crowned lacks any border at all.

Status and distribution: Rare winter resident in low shrubby or grassy areas in lowlands of western and central Panama (also recorded from lower highlands of Chiriquí), with only one report from San Blas (at least two seen at Mandinga in January and February 1957; Wetmore) and one from Darién (two seen at El Real on March 5, 1981; Ridgely and V. Emanuel *et al.*); recorded mostly mid-October–late April, with one surprising report of an amazingly early male at Tocumen on September 7, 1980 (A. Moore). Small numbers are now seen regularly on both slopes of Canal area, where it was perhaps mostly overlooked until recently.

Habits: Typically forages near the ground in shrubbery near water. Its distinctive husky call note, *tchep*, often gives away the bird's presence, but other yellowthroats have similar calls.

Range: Breeds in North America and Mexico; winters from southern United States to Panama and in West Indies, casually to Colombia and Venezuela.

OLIVE-CROWNED YELLOWTHROAT
Geothlypis semiflava   Plate 48

Description: 4½–5. Known only from Bocas del Toro lowlands. Male olive above with *black mask extending over forecrown onto sides of head* (more extensive than in other Panama yellowthroats), but *without gray or whitish border*; bright yellow below, tinged olive on sides and flanks. Female olive above and *bright yellow below* with more olive on sides and flanks than in male. Immature like female but buffier below (no brownish tone above as in the immature Common Yellowthroat).

Similar species: Common Yellowthroat always has whitish belly. Masked Yellowthroat is found only in Chiriquí.

Status and distribution: Common in tall grass, bamboo thickets, and low bushes especially near water in lowlands of western Bocas del Toro (in Costa Rica ranges up into lower highlands).

Habits: Similar to other yellowthroats. The song is a loud rich musical warbling which starts slowly and ends in a jumbled twitter, more complex than song of Masked (Chiriquí) Yellowthroat.

Range: Honduras to Caribbean western Panama; western Colombia and western Ecuador.

MASKED YELLOWTHROAT
Geothlypis aequinoctialis   Plate 48

Description: 4½–5. Found only in western Chiriquí highlands. Resembles Common Yellowthroat. Male has *bluish gray mid-crown and border above black mask* (not whitish); both sexes have *entire underparts yellow*. Female has gray forehead and sides of head, but lacks black mask. Immature like female but with olive crown and sides of head.

Similar species: See Common Yellowthroat. Gray-crowned Yellowthroat is somewhat larger with heavier bill, has gray crown but no black mask (even in the male). Olive-crowned Yellowthroat has entirely different range.

Status and distribution: Fairly common in damp meadows and low shrubby growth near streams in lower highlands of western Chiriquí (1050–1350 m: 3500–4500 ft). Very local, but regularly found in appropriate habitat around Volcán, and west along the road from there toward Santa Clara; one traditional spot has been the area near the Dos Rios Hotel. Deforestation in this region over the past few decades may have permitted an increase in its local population.

Habits: Similar to Common Yellowthroat. Rather skulking except when males mount to an exposed but low perch when singing. Its song is a sweet warbled phrase, e.g. *twicheetwee-tweetweeo, tweecheétee*, somewhat variable.

Range: Southwestern Costa Rica and Pacific western Panama; South America south locally to northern Argentina and Uruguay.
Note: The form found in Chiriquí, *chiriquensis*, has often been considered a full species (Chiriqui Yellowthroat), but was treated as a race of the Masked Yellowthroat in the 1983 AOU Check-list.

GRAY-CROWNED YELLOWTHROAT
Geothlypis poliocephala   Plate 48

Description: 5¼–5½. Found only in Chiriquí. Somewhat larger than other yellowthroats, bill heavier and with arched culmen, *tail longer* and somewhat more graduated. Male grayish olive above with *gray crown* and *black lores and ocular region* (but *no mask*); below bright yellow, fading to buffy whitish on lower belly. Female similar but has crown tinged olive and lacks black on face (lores dusky, ocular area olive). Immatures lack gray on crown.
Similar species: Female resembles female Common Yellowthroat (both have dingy whitish lower bellies), and is best distinguished by its larger size and different proportions (longer tail, longer bill with arched not straight culmen). See also female Masked Yellowthroat (smaller, with all-yellow underparts, gray on face).
Status and distribution: Rare to uncommon and local in grassy pastures and savannas with scattered bushes in foothills and highlands (900–2250 m: 2300–7500 ft) of western and central Chiriquí; recently found as far east as the Río Algarrobos area east of La Caldera, and in savannas along road to La Caldera (east of the David–Boquete highway).
Habits: Much less tied to the vicinity of water than the other Panama yellowthroats, often in quite dry areas. Frequently pumps and swivels its long tail. Its song is a clear, fast, rather high warbled phrase, usually delivered from a somewhat elevated perch.
Range: Northern Mexico (formerly southern Texas) to Pacific western Panama.
Note: Formerly separated in the monotypic genus *Chamaethlypis*, and we are not entirely convinced that it does not deserve generic separation, though for now we follow its placement in *Geothlypis* by the 1983 AOU Check-list.

HOODED WARBLER
Wilsonia citrina

Description: 5½. Rather rare. Male unmistakable with *striking black hood enclosing bright yellow forehead and face*; otherwise olive above, bright yellow below; *inner web of outer tail feathers mostly white* (flashing conspicuously in flight). Female lacks the hood (or it shows merely as a scattering of a few black feathers), but is otherwise like male (including bright yellow underparts extending to forehead and face, and the *white in tail*).
Similar species: Female Wilson's Warbler is smaller and lacks white in tail. See also Prothonotary and Canada Warblers.
Status and distribution: Rare winter visitant to lower growth of humid forest and second-growth woodland in lowlands of western and central Panama (late September–early May); recorded only from western Bocas del Toro, Coiba Island, and both slopes of Canal area, but perhaps more widespread. The genuine rarity of the Hooded Warbler in Panama is reflected in the fact that only three or four were mist-netted in two entire seasons of banding at Almirante, Bocas del Toro (H. Loftin).
Habits: Forages actively, usually inside woodland or forest, often making short aerial sallies after fleeing prey. The tail is frequently flicked open, exposing the white.
Range: Breeds in eastern United States; winters mostly from eastern Mexico to Nicaragua, in smaller numbers in Costa Rica and Panama, casually to northern South America.

WILSON'S WARBLER
Wilsonia pusilla   Plate 31

Description: 4½–4¾. Male olive above with *characteristic black cap*; bright yellow below and on face. In female and immatures black cap is reduced or replaced by olive, otherwise like male.
Similar species: Female Hooded Warbler is larger and flashes white in tail. Best distinguished from female yellowthroats with entirely yellow underparts by its yellow forehead and face and different actions. Female Yellow Warbler is also rather similar but lacks yellow forehead and face and has yellow edging on wings and spots in tail.
Status and distribution: Very common winter resident in highlands of Chiriquí above 1050 m (3500 ft), recorded mid-September–mid-May, becoming progressively less numerous in highlands and foothills eastward; rare in central Panama, with only three sightings, all of males; one on Cerro Campana on September 14, 1961 (R. Ryan), and single individuals on Cerro Azul on December 30, 1967 and December 28, 1973 (both Ridgely); so far not definitely

reported from lowlands, though a possibility on migration.

Habits: One of the most numerous and conspicuous birds in the Chiriquí highlands during the northern winter months. Very active and noisy, feeding at low and middle levels in bushy clearings and woodland borders, chipping constantly.

Range: Breeds in northern and western North America; winters from Mexico to western (rarely central) Panama.

CANADA WARBLER
Wilsonia canadensis   Plate 31

Description: 5¼. Male *bluish gray above* with black forecrown and sides of head, and *prominent yellow spectacles*; below bright yellow with *chest crossed by a conspicuous necklace of black streaks*; under tail-coverts white. Female similar but paler (not so blue) above, with fainter necklace and reduced black facial markings. Immatures have even fainter necklace (sometimes virtually lacking), and may be tinged olive on back.

Similar species: The necklace is the mark; when it is missing, look for combination of gray upperparts and yellow spectacles.

Status and distribution: Fairly common to occasionally common transient in lowlands throughout, with smaller numbers up into highlands (most numerous late September–early October, and late April–early May, but recorded as early as early September and as late as mid-May); rare winter resident, when found mostly in foothills.

Habits: Favors lower growth and shrubby borders of humid forest and woodland. Forages quite actively, sometimes making short aerial sallies; regularly accompanies mixed flocks, and has been seen in attendance at army ant swarms (E. O. Willis). In Ecuador has been heard to sing during northward passage.

Range: Breeds in eastern North America; winters mostly from Venezuela to Peru, in very small numbers in Panama, and increasingly rarely northward in Middle America.

SLATE-THROATED REDSTART
Myioborus miniatus   Plate 33

Description: 4¾–5. Highlands. *Slaty gray above and on throat*, with chestnut crown patch (sometimes concealed); remaining underparts bright yellow; *outer tail feathers and tail tipping white*.

Similar species: Collared Redstart has all of

underparts yellow with chest crossed by black band.

Status and distribution: Common to locally very common in forest, woodland, borders, and adjacent clearings in highlands of Chiriquí and Bocas del Toro (*aurantiacus*; in latter apparently recorded only from along oleoducto road north of Fortuna, but doubtless more widespread), in smaller numbers in Veraguas and recently seen as far east as western Coclé (two north of El Copé, on Caribbean slope, on March 8, 1986; Ridgely, D. Engleman *et al.*); rather uncommon in highlands of eastern Darién (*ballux*; on Cerro Pirre and Cerro Tacarcuna), with apparently this race also ranging east to Cerro Jefe, eastern Panama province (one July 1973 sighting by D. Hill; no subsequent reports), and to Cerro Brewster, western San Blas (two mist-netted by J. Blake on April 26, 1985); in western Chiriquí mostly 900–1800 m (3000–6000 ft), ranging lower (to about 600 m: 2000 ft) elsewhere in western Panama; in eastern Darién mostly above 1200 m (4000 ft).

Habits: Rather similar to American Redstart, very active, making short flycatcher-like sallies, and spreading its tail exposing the white. Has several usually squeaky or sibilant songs, sometimes suggestive of American Redstart, *tseeweech, sweeswee, sweech-sweechee,* or *tseeoo-tseeoo, cheewee-cheewee-tsee*.

Range: Northern Mexico to Guyana, northern Brazil, and Bolivia.

COLLARED REDSTART
Myioborus torquatus   Plate 33

Description: 4¾–5. Found only in western highlands. Slaty above with rufous cap (sometimes raised); *face and underparts bright yellow, chest crossed by a narrow black band*; outer tail feathers and tail tipping white.

Similar species: Not likely to be confused. Slate-throated Redstart lacks black chest band and contrasting yellow face and throat.

Status and distribution: Common in forest and woodland borders in highlands of Chiriquí and adjacent Bocas del Toro, mostly above 1800 m (6000 ft), sometimes down to 1200 m (4000 ft); found also in Veraguas highlands where regularly ranges lower, to 1050–1200 m (3500–4000 ft).

Habits: Similar to Slate-throated Redstart, and sometimes found with it, though in general replacing it at higher elevations. Usually seen in pairs, often accompanying mixed flocks, generally foraging rather low. Often charmingly tame, sometimes appearing almost curious. The song is a rather soft, slightly musical *tsit-tsit-tsee*, repeated; also has another sweeter and more elaborate song.

Range: Costa Rica and western Panama.

GOLDEN-CROWNED WARBLER
Basileuterus culicivorus   Plate 33

Description: 5. Found only in western highlands. Head with *yellow or orange crown stripe enclosed by broad black stripes* and olive superciliary with a dusky spot in front of and behind eye; otherwise olive above (*including cheeks*); yellow below (*including throat*).

Similar species: Three-striped Warbler in western Panama has buffy crown stripe (not yellow or orange), black ear-coverts, and is duller yellow below with whitish throat.

Status and distribution: Uncommon to locally fairly common in lower growth of forest and woodland in highlands on Pacific slope, mainly in Chiriquí (mostly 1050–1650 m: 3500–5500 ft) but also known from Veraguas and the western side of Azuero Peninsula in Herrera; only one report from Caribbean slope, that a single (perhaps wandering) bird seen along oleoducto road north of Fortuna in Bocas del Toro on July 3, 1982 (Ridgely).

Habits: Usually forages actively near the ground, most often in pairs or small (family) groups, regularly with mixed flocks. Has a chattering contact note and rather frequently given song consisting of several fast *wee* notes ending with distinct upslur.

Range: Central Mexico to western Panama; western Colombia to Bolivia, northern Argentina, and Uruguay.

RUFOUS-CAPPED WARBLER
Basileuterus rufifrons   Plate 33

Description: 5. *Crown and ear-coverts bright rufous-chestnut with intervening long white superciliary*; otherwise olive above; bright yellow below.

Similar species: The only *Basileuterus* warbler (apart from the very different Buff-rumped) in most of its Panama range.

Status and distribution: Fairly common in shrubby regenerating clearings and undergrowth of woodland in lowlands on Pacific slope east to eastern Panama province (lower Bayano River valley; no definite records from Darién); on Caribbean slope recorded only from Canal area and Colon province; in Chiriquí ranges regularly up into the lower highlands to 1200–1350 m (4000–4500 ft), rarely higher; found also on Coiba Island, where it is common and

ranges regularly in undergrowth of undisturbed tall forest.

Habits: Usually found in thickets not far above ground. Often cocks tail in a perky manner. Its song is a fast, dry *chit-cha-chup-cha-chu weep*, sometimes ending with a *chee-weecha*, in pattern reminiscent of a Canada Warbler but in quality rather more like a Chestnut-sided or Yellow.

Range: Northern Mexico to Colombia and northwestern Venezuela.

Note: Chestnut-capped Warbler (*B. delatrii*), formerly often considered a distinct species and found from Guatemala southward, is now considered conspecific with *B. rufifrons*, with "Rufous-capped Warbler" being the name used for the expanded species.

BLACK-CHEEKED WARBLER
Basileuterus melanogenys   Plate 33

Description: 5¼. Found only in western highlands. *Chestnut crown* narrowly margined with black; *long white superciliary above black sides of head*; otherwise grayish olive above; grayish white below, darkest on breast and sides, tinged slightly with pale yellow. Birds from Veraguas (*bensoni*) have slatier back, lack the yellowish tinge on belly, and have more distinct and darker band of grayish across breast.

Similar species: Sooty-capped Bush-Tanager lacks the chestnut crown and has stockier build.

Status and distribution: Fairly common in lower growth of humid montane forest and second-growth woodland, to a lesser extent also at borders, in highlands of western Chiriquí (east only to slopes of Volcán Barú above Boquete), recorded mostly 1500–2400 m (5000–8000 ft); also recorded from Veraguas (Chitra, where much lower, 1200–1500 m: 4000–5000 ft); should occur in eastern Chiriquí (probably *bensoni*). Readily found in forests above Finca Lerida.

Habits: Usually seen in pairs or small groups, sometimes with mixed foraging flocks, moving rapidly through the undergrowth. Often quite unsuspicious.

Range: Costa Rica and western Panama.

Note: Birds from Veraguas (and probably eastern Chiriquí), *bensoni*, have been considered a distinct species (Benson's, or Veraguan, Warbler).

PIRRE WARBLER
Basileuterus ignotus   Plate 40

Description: 5¼. Found only in eastern Darién highlands. Resembles Black-cheeked

Warbler but *superciliary pale greenish yellow* (not white), sides of head greenish yellow mottled with black (not solid black), upperparts greener, and underparts considerably yellower.

Similar species: Black-cheeked Warbler.

Status and distribution: Uncommon in lower growth of humid elfin woodland and forest in highlands of eastern Darién (Cerro Pirre, Cerro Tacarcuna); recorded mostly 1350–1650 m (4500–5500 ft).

Habits: Similar to Black-cheeked Warbler, though reported to forage somewhat higher above the ground.

Range: Eastern Panama and adjacent northwestern Colombia.

Note: Sometimes considered conspecific with *B. melanogenys* (Black-cheeked Warbler) of Costa Rica and western Panama, though they were treated as separate species in the 1983 AOU Check-list.

THREE-STRIPED WARBLER
Basileuterus tristriatus   Plate 33

Description: 5. Foothills and highlands locally. Birds from western Panama (*melanotis*) have head with *narrow buffy crown stripe enclosed by broad black stripes*, and *buffy superciliary over black ear-coverts*; otherwise olive above; mostly pale yellow below, whitish on upper throat and washed with olive on chest. Birds from eastern Panama (*tacarcunae*) have crown stripe more orange and *black on ear-coverts reduced to a thin line behind the eye*.

Similar species: Golden-crowned Warbler (found only in western Panama) has yellow or orange crown stripe (not buffy), lacks black ear-coverts, and is entirely yellow below. Also vaguely recalls Worm-eating Warbler.

Status and distribution: Locally fairly common to common in lower growth of humid montane forest and woodland in highlands of Chiriquí and Bocas del Toro (where recorded mostly 1200–2250 m: 4000–7500 ft), and in Veraguas (where it ranges lower, mostly 600–1350 m: 2000–4500 ft); found also (*tacarcunae*) in elfin forest on Cerro Jefe, eastern Panama province (numerous sightings of small numbers in the 1970s, but seemingly fewer since), and on Cerro Brewster in western San Blas (where J. Blake found it to be quite common in April 1985, photos to VIREO), and in highlands of eastern Darién (Cerro Tacarcuna; 900–1500 m: 3000–5000 ft). Decidedly scarce around Volcán Barú in

western Chiriquí, but much more numerous in the Fortuna area, where it is one of the commoner forest understory birds.

Habits: Usually in mixed flocks which forage actively and conspicuously in lower growth (and are generally not difficult to see well, unlike so many other forest understory birds); frequently with mixed flocks. They draw attention to themselves by their nearly incessant calling, various high-pitched notes being given, also a very fast jumbled song of twittery notes.

Range: Costa Rica to northern Venezuela and northern Bolivia.

BUFF-RUMPED WARBLER
Basileuterus fulvicauda   Plate 33

Description: 5½. Waterthrush-like in general appearance. Birds from western and central Panama (*leucopygius*) are olive brown above with buff superciliary and *buff rump and basal two-thirds of tail; pale buffyish below*, somewhat mottled with olive on chest. Birds from eastern Panama (*semicervinus*) lack the olive mottling on chest, are paler olive above, and have a more prominent superciliary; most Canal area birds are intermediate between the two races.

Similar species: Waterthrushes are streaked below, lack contrasting rump.

Status and distribution: Uncommon to fairly common along rivers and streams, usually rapid and stony, inside forest and second-growth woodland in lowlands and foothills on both slopes; found also in mangroves in Bocas del Toro. Somewhat local, at least in central Panama, and absent from some areas that would appear suitable.

Habits: In many ways reminiscent of a Louisiana Waterthrush, repeatedly flushing ahead when disturbed, finally circling around to its point of origin. Unlike waterthrushes, does not teeter up and down, rather swings its fanned tail from side to side. Also unlike waterthrushes, seems only to hop, rarely if ever actually to walk. The male's song is a rising crescendo of loud notes, loud enough to be heard over the roar of turbulent streams.

Range: Honduras to Peru and western Brazil.

Note: The 1983 AOU Check-list included this species in the genus *Phaeothlypis*. We prefer to retain it in *Basileuterus*, however, because there are apparently "intermediate" species in South America.

WRENTHRUSH
Zeledonia coronata   Plate 29

Description: 4½–5. Found only in western highlands. A plump little bird with a rather short tail. *Golden tawny crown* margined with black, otherwise dark olive brown above; *face, sides of neck, and entire underparts slaty gray.*
Similar species: Somewhat suggests a small plump nightingale-thrush with a short tail and crown patch, or a heavy-bodied *Basileuterus* warbler. Gray-breasted Wood-Wren lacks crown patch and has white superciliary and black and white-streaked sides of neck and throat. See also Silvery-fronted Tapaculo.
Status and distribution: Rare to locally uncommon in dense undergrowth of humid forest and forest borders in highlands of western Chiriquí (above 1800 m: 6000 ft), with single reports from above Fortuna at 1620 m (5400 ft) (Ridgely) and at Cerro Colorado (N. G. Smith), in central and eastern Chiriquí, respectively; also known from highlands of Veraguas (Chitra, 1050–1200 m: 3500–4000 ft). Probably underrecorded due to its reclusive habits; once its voice is recognized, small numbers will be heard regularly along the upper part of the Boquete Trail above Cerro Punta, but it is always a hard bird to see (particularly without tape-recording).
Habits: Lives near the ground in thick vegetation, hopping in dense tangles but rarely actually descending to the ground, and rarely or never flying more than a few feet. Its distinctive and quite often heard call is a very high, piercing, sibilant *seeeeeeeeep* (G. Tudor) or *pseeee* (Ridgely); the song is a somewhat squeaky *tseét, tsoo-tseét, tseé-tee-too* (B. Whitney). As they hop around Wrenthrushes often flick their wings simultaneously (J. Hunt).
Range: Costa Rica and western Panama.
Note: This distinct, monotypic genus was formerly considered related to the muscicapid assemblage and placed in its own flamily, the Zeledoniidae, but recent evidence indicates it is more allied to the woodwarblers, closest to *Basileuterus*. It has been suggested, therefore, that it might better simply be called the "Zeledonia" (Wetmore *et al.*, 1984, p. 331); for now, however, we continue to follow the 1983 AOU Check-list and retain its traditional name of "Wrenthrush".

YELLOW-BREASTED CHAT
Icteria virens

Description: 6½–7¼. Considerably larger than other warblers. *Heavy bill.* Olive green above with *conspicuous white "spectacles"*; throat and breast bright yellow, belly white.
Similar species: The yellowthroats are much smaller.
Status and distribution: Uncommon winter resident in lowlands of western Bocas del Toro (early October–late April); only other report is a sighting of one bird on Cerro Campana on September 14, 1961 (R. Ryan and N. Boyajian).
Habits: Generally remains hidden in dense undergrowth of brushy areas and woodland borders. Most readily noted through mist-net captures.
Range: Breeds in United States and Mexico; winters from southern United States to Caribbean western (casually central) Panama.
Note: Some authors doubt this species' inclusion in the Parulinae.

BANANAQUITS: Coerebinae (1)

The sole remaining member of the former Honeycreeper family, now considered only a subfamily in the expanded Emberizidae, the Bananaquit is distinctive on account of its bill and unusual (compared to its purported relatives) globular nest with a side entrance. Though it has a very wide range throughout the warmer parts of the neotropics, the Bananaquit tends to be most numerous on island or in coastal areas, occurring in smaller numbers or even absent from many inland areas.

BANANAQUIT
Coereba flaveola   Plate 33

Description: 3¾. *Rather short, slender, decurved bill,* often with some pink or pale brownish at base of lower mandible. Mostly dark olive gray above, with black crown, *prominent long white superciliary*, and yellow on rump; small white wing speculum; throat pale gray, *remaining underparts yellow*. Pearl Island birds (*cerinoclunis*) are blacker above, hardly contrasting with crown.

Similar species: Combination of decurved bill and long white eye-stripe distinctive.

Status and distribution: Uncommon to locally common in gardens, shrubby clearings, lighter woodland, and forest borders in lowlands and foothills on both slopes, principally in more humid areas, ranging up commonly into lower highlands of western Chiriquí in the Volcán/Santa Clara area (1200–1350 m: 4000–4500 ft), to which it may have only spread subsequent to the destruction of most of that area's forest cover; common also on Coiba Island, the Pearl Islands (where perhaps the most abundant resident landbird), and other islands off Pacific coast. Seems inexplicably scarce on Pacific side of Canal area. Generally seems more numerous in the foothills than in the lowlands (even occurring locally in elfin woodland and cloud forest), but reaches its maximum Panama abundance in lowlands of western Chiriquí in the Puerto Armuelles/Burica Peninsula area.

Habits: A very active, tame little bird that will feed wherever there are flowers; also extremely fond of sugar. Has a high, sibilant song, rather warbler-like, *tsee, tsee, tsee, tsee* . . . .

Range: Southeastern Mexico to northern Bolivia, Paraguay, and northeastern Argentina; West Indies (except Cuba) and most Caribbean islands, rarely in southern Florida.

TANAGERS: Thraupinae (65)

The tanagers are a large group of birds found only in the New World, now considered as a subfamily within the expanded Emberizidae. The great majority of species are found in the tropics, with only four mainly migratory species having spread as far north as the United States to breed. Many tanagers are exceptionally attractive birds, exhibiting a great variety of bright colors and striking contrasts; a few are duller, notably the genera *Chlorospingus* and (in South America) *Hemispingus*. Most tanagers are arboreal birds, and many occur in mixed flocks; several inhabit forest and woodland undergrowth, while one species, the thrush-tanager, is partly terrestrial. In most tanagers song is poorly developed, chief exceptions in Panama being the various *Piranga* spp., the ant-tanagers, and the thrush-tanager. In Panama the two most important subgroups are the euphonias and allied chlorophonia, small chunky birds with short tails and stubby bills, and the genus *Tangara*, containing the typical multi-colored tanagers, most diverse in the Andes but well represented in Panama, especially in foothill areas. With the dismemberment of what was formerly considered the Honeycreeper family (Coerebidae), most of its genera have now been assigned to the Tanagers. These include the *Conirostrum* conebills (by some considered to have affinities with the warblers as well, hence they are placed first in the tanager sequence), and the *Dacnis* dacnises and *Cyanerpes* and *Chlorophanes* honeycreepers (all of which are considered rather closely allied to the *Tangara* tanagers); however, the *Diglossa* flower-piercers have now been placed with the Emberizine finches (though there is still debate on this point). In addition, the Swallow Tanager, formerly placed in a monotypic family (Tersinidae), is now treated merely as a tribe within the Thraupinae subfamily. Tanagers as a whole eat mostly fruit, though most species also take at least some insects (especially to feed their young), and some species are primarily insectivorous. The euphonias and chlorophonias specialize in eating mistletoe berries, while the honeycreepers consume a great deal of nectar when this is available (some other tanagers are also nectarivorous to a lesser extent). The nests of most tanagers are open, often shallow cups placed in bushes and trees; euphonias, chlorophonias, and the Blue-and-gold Tanager all build covered nests with a side entrance, however (and there may be others which do this), while the *Thraupis* tanagers may place their untidy nests inside a cranny of some sort. It should be noted that the nests of many species, even genera, remain unknown.

WHITE-EARED CONEBILL
Conirostrum leucogenys   Plate 40

Description: 3¾. Found only in eastern Panama. Conical pointed bill; *rather short tail* (a helpful character when high in trees). Male *bluish slate above* with black crown, *conspicuous white ear-coverts*, and usually some white on rump; inconspicuous white wing speculum; *paler bluish gray below*, with under tail-coverts rufous. Female rather different, dull bluish gray above, usually with some white on rump but *no* black on crown or white on ear-coverts; *face and entire underparts pale yellowish buff*, somewhat darker on breast.

Similar species: See female Scarlet-thighed Dacnis.

Status and distribution: Uncommon to locally fairly common in canopy and borders of forest and woodland in lowlands of eastern Panama province (middle and upper Bayano River valley) and Darién. Seems most numerous in deciduous (rather than humid) forest, particularly where cuipo trees (*Cavanillesia*) are numerous; thus, for example, readily found around Majé, in eastern Panama province, but rather scarce (or perhaps irregular) in more humid Cana area in Darién.

Habits: Usually seen in pairs or small groups which feed high in forest canopy, sometimes gleaning in terminal foliage and branches, but also often at flowering trees (including cuipos and *Erythrima*), where it may feed with other tanagers, orioles, etc.

Range: Eastern Panama to Colombia and northern Venezuela.

PLAIN-COLORED TANAGER
Tangara inornata   Plate 34

Description: 4¾. Unusual among the colorful and highly patterned *Tangara* tanagers is this dull-plumaged species. *Leaden gray above* with some black through eyes; wings and tail black with usually concealed blue lesser wing-coverts; *paler gray below,* fading to white on lower belly. Birds of western Bocas del Toro (*rava*) have lower underparts tinged pinkish buff (rather than the whitish shown by birds from elsewhere in Panama, *languens*).

Similar species: Sulphur-rumped Tanager is also mostly gray with blackish wings and tail but is larger, shows a tuft of white feathers on the sides, and has a yellow rump. The larger Blue-gray and Palm Tanagers can look gray when seen against the light.

Status and distribution: Common in clearings, second-growth woodland, and forest borders in lowlands on Caribbean slope in western Bocas del Toro (where somewhat less numerous) and from northern Coclé and western Colon province eastward, and on Pacific slope from western Panama province (Cerro Campana area) eastward; ranges in reduced numbers up into foothills (to 600–750 m: 2000–2500 ft).

Habits: Seems almost always to occur in groups of four to six individuals, frequently independent of other species. Often feeds in *Cecropia* trees.

Range: Costa Rica to northern Colombia.

GRAY-AND-GOLD TANAGER
Tangara palmeri   Plate 35

Description: 5¾. Found only in eastern Panama. *A rather large, mostly gray and black Tangara tanager.* Above mostly pale gray with small black mask and pale opalescent green back; wings and tail black broadly edged gray; mostly whitish below, with *sprinkling of black spots down sides of neck and across chest* (with necklaced effect), an *opalescent gold tinge on chest*, and some gray on sides.

Similar species: See Golden-hooded Tanager.

Status and distribution: Rare to locally uncommon in canopy and borders of humid forest in foothills of eastern Panama province (recorded only from two independent sightings near Nusagandi on the El Llano–Carti road on February 12 and 16, 1983, possibly involving the same bird; D. Engleman and L. Gomez, and J. Pierson and B. Whitney) and eastern Darién (Cerro Tacarcuna, Cerro Quía, Cerro Pirre, and Cerro Sapo); in Darién recorded 540–1020 m (1800–3400 ft), but lower (450 m: 1500 ft) at Nusagandi.

Habits: Usually seen in pairs or small groups which often are noisy and conspicuous, frequently perching in the open for long periods. At least in western Colombia (S. Hilty) they are considered to be one of the "nuclear" species around which foraging flocks of other tanagers form.

Range: Eastern Panama to northwestern Ecuador.

EMERALD TANAGER
Tangara florida   Plate 34

Description: 5¼. *Mostly golden emerald green*, male with yellow nape; back streaked with black and with black spot in front of eye and black patch on ear-coverts; lower belly yellow.

Similar species: No other Panama tanager is so predominantly *bright* green.

Status and distribution: Uncommon to locally common in canopy and borders of humid forest in foothills on entire Caribbean slope, mostly 300–900 m (1000–3000 ft); on Pacific slope found in foothills of eastern Panama province (Cerro Azul/Jefe area eastward) and Darién. More numerous on actual Caribbean slope: this is one of the commonest *Tangara* at appropriate elevations along the oleoducto road north of Fortuna in Bocas del Toro, and around Nusagandi in western San Blas, but it is rather scarce on Cerro Azul/Jefe and on Cerro Pirre.

Habits: Usually seen in small numbers, feeding quite high in the trees, generally accompanying large mixed flocks of other frugivorous birds.

Range: Costa Rica to northwestern Ecuador.

SILVER-THROATED TANAGER
Tangara icterocephala Plate 34

Description: 5¼. *Mostly bright golden yellow,* streaked with black on back; wings and tail black, broadly edged with green; *throat grayish silvery white,* bordered at sides by long narrow black malar streak. Female similar but duller, often with streaky crown; immature even dingier, but already showing adult's pattern.

Similar species: The pretty male is easily identified; duller female and immature may possibly be confused with female of smaller Black-and-yellow Tanager, but are streaked above and always show at least a vaguely whitish throat.

Status and distribution: Common in forest and forest borders in foothills and highlands on both slopes from 600–1800 m (2000–6000 ft); occasionally as high as 2250 m (7500 ft) in Chiriquí; one record from lowlands of western Bocas del Toro, a specimen taken at Almirante, Bocas del Toro, on November 2, 1962 (R. Hinds), doubtless a postbreeding wanderer down the mountains.

Habits: Particularly numerous on Cerro Campana; there it is often one of the most common birds present, sometimes occurring in large flocks of several dozen or more individuals. Elsewhere it is less dominant but still widespread, usually accompanying mixed flocks of other tanagers, honeycreepers, etc. Its call is a characteristically sharp buzzy *bzeet*, rather different from its congeners.

Range: Costa Rica to western Ecuador.

SPECKLED TANAGER
Tangara guttata Plate 34

Description: 5¼. Unmistakable; no other Panama tanager is *conspicuously spotted above and below*. Bright emerald green above spotted with black, and with black lores and short

yellow superciliary and ocular area; wings black broadly edged blue; mostly white below, profusely spotted black, with flanks and under tail-coverts tinged yellowish green.

Status and distribution: Fairly common in humid forest and forest borders in foothills on entire Caribbean slope (mostly 450–1050 m: 1500–3500 ft); on Pacific slope recorded locally from western Chiriquí (in the Santa Clara area and at least formerly east to Volcán; 1050–1350 m: 3500–4500 ft), Veraguas (above Santa Fé), eastern Panama province (Cerro Azul/Jefe area), and eastern Darién (750–1500 m: 2500–5000 ft). Small numbers can still be found in the Cerro Jefe area (though it seems to have declined recently, probably due to increased deforestation); more numerous above El Copé, Coclé, and north of Fortuna, Chiriquí, along the oleoducto road (in both cases on the Caribbean slope).

Habits: Much like the Emerald Tanager, and often with it, though tending to occur at somewhat higher elevations.

Range: Costa Rica to Venezuela and extreme northern Brazil.

BAY-HEADED TANAGER
Tangara gyrola Plate 34

Description: 5. *Head bright reddish chestnut,* with narrow yellow collar on hindneck (sometimes not apparent); otherwise mostly bright grass green above; rump and *most of underparts bright turquoise blue,* with green on flanks and under tail-coverts. Female like male but duller and paler, particularly below. Immature much duller, often mostly green, but some brown on head and blue on underparts usually show.

Similar species: See Rufous-winged Tanager.

Status and distribution: Fairly common to common in canopy and borders of forest and in adjacent clearings in foothills and lower highlands on both slopes, including hill country and mountains on western side of Azuero Peninsula south to Cerro Hoya in southwestern Los Santos (*fide* F. Delgado); recorded mainly 600–1500 m (2000–5000 ft), locally in small numbers down into lowlands of western Chiriquí (no recent reports, and perhaps no longer occurs due to extensive deforestation) and on Caribbean slope in Canal area (where most numerous along Pipeline Road).

Habits: A typical *Tangara* tanager, gregarious, often found among mixed flocks of frugivorous birds. Seems more tolerant ecologically than its foothill congeners in

Panama, remaining relatively numerous even in quite severely disturbed areas such as Cerro Azul/Jefe.

Range: Costa Rica to northern Bolivia and Amazonian Brazil.

RUFOUS-WINGED TANAGER
Tangara lavinia   Plate 34

Description: 5. Male has *bright reddish chestnut head* with *broad bright yellow collar on hindneck extending down over upper back*; otherwise mostly bright grass green above and below, with *wings mainly bright rufous*. Birds from western and central Panama (*dalmasi*) have small blue spot on mid-throat, whereas nominate race (recorded only from eastern Darién) have somewhat variable blue stripe extending from mid-throat down median underparts to belly. Female and (especially) immature much duller, often basically green, but almost always showing *at least some rufous on head and wings.*

Similar species: The beautiful male is unmistakable, but some females have only a trace of rufous on wings and virtually no chestnut on head, and can be easily passed over. These dull birds most resemble an immature Bay-headed Tanager, but the Bay-head never shows any rufous on wings (a little is almost always present in Rufous-wing).

Status and distribution: Uncommon and quite local in canopy and borders of humid forest in foothills on Caribbean slope east to western San Blas, mostly 300–900 m (1000–3000 ft); on Pacific slope known only from eastern Panama province (Cerro Azul/Jefe area) and eastern Darién (where seemingly very scarce, with only definite report being a sighting of a single male on Cerro Quía at 810 m: 2700 ft on July 18, 1975; Ridgely); one specimen was taken by R. Benson on August 8, 1931, in what is now the Madden Forest, presumably a wanderer from foothills to the east; seems likely on Cerro Tacarcuna, as known from Colombian side of that mountain. Though recorded by Wetmore *et al.* (1984, p. 430) from Chiriquí, we are not aware of any definite records from there. Perhaps commonest and most easily seen around Nusagandi in western San Blas; small numbers can still be found in the Cerro Jefe area.

Habits: Very similar to Bay-headed Tanager and often occurs with it, but seems always to be outnumbered by it.

Range: Guatemala to northwestern Ecuador.

GOLDEN-HOODED TANAGER
Tangara larvata   Plate 34

Description: 5. *Head mostly golden buff with black facial mask bordered with blue*; back and wings black, latter edged with blue; lower back and rump turquoise; *chest and breast black*, center of belly white, *sides and flanks turquoise*. Immature similar but duller with head light bluish green instead of buff.

Status and distribution: Fairly common to common in clearings, second-growth woodland, and forest borders in lowlands and foothills (to about 750 m: 2500 ft) on entire Caribbean slope; on Pacific slope recorded widely in foothill zone (300–900 m: 1000–3000 ft), in western Chiriquí also regularly up into lower highlands (to about 1200–1350 m: 4000–4500 ft) and in lowlands, at least formerly also in lowlands of western Veraguas (Montijo Bay), and widely in lowlands of eastern Panama province (Bayano River valley; formerly west to Tocumen area) and Darién.

Habits: Usually found in small groups, sometimes among mixed flocks of frugivorous birds. Frequent calls are a single or doubled *tssp* and a repeated *tsit-tsit-tsit-tsit* often given in flight as it moves from tree to tree.

Range: Southeastern Mexico to western Ecuador.

Note: This species is called the Golden-masked Tanager in the 1983 AOU Checklist; however, as the mask is *not* golden, but rather is *black* (it is the hood which is golden), we continue to prefer using the more accurate name of Golden-hooded Tanager.

SPANGLE-CHEEKED TANAGER
Tangara dowii   Plate 34

Description: 5. Found only in western highlands. *Mostly black above and on throat and chest; spangled on head and especially on ear-coverts with pale green* and with rusty patch on nape, *spangled on chest with buff*; wings edged with blue, rump opalescent green or blue; *lower underparts cinammon.*

Status and distribution: Rare to locally uncommon in forest and forest borders in highlands of Bocas del Toro, Chiriquí, and Veraguas, mostly 1350–2100 m (4500–7000 ft). In Panama seems decidedly erratic in all areas, and on the whole less numerous than it is in Costa Rica.

Habits: Similar to other *Tangara* tanagers, usually in pairs and small groups, often associating with flocks of other highland frugivorous birds.

Range: Costa Rica and western Panama.

GREEN-NAPED TANAGER
Tangara fucosa   Plate 35

Description: 5. Found only in Darién highlands. Closely resembles Spangle-cheeked Tanager but has *pale green* (not rusty) *patch on nape*, and *blue* (not buff) *spangling on chest*.
Similar species: See Spangle-cheeked Tanager of western highlands.
Status and distribution: Fairly common in forest and forest borders in highlands of eastern Darién (Cerro Pirre, Cerro Tacarcuna); recorded mostly above 1350 m (4500 ft), rarely down to about 600 m (2000 ft) at Cana (but the record from El Real given by Wetmore *et al.*, 1984, p. 433, is in error).
Habits: Similar to Spangle-cheeked Tanager, with which it has been considered conspecific.
Range: Eastern Panama (probably occurs in adjacent Colombia but not yet recorded).

SCARLET-THIGHED DACNIS
Dacnis venusta   Plate 33

Description: 4¾. Iris bright red in male, duller red in female. Male unmistakable with *bright turquoise blue crown and nape, sides of head and neck, center of back, rump, and scapulars*; forehead, lores, sides of back, *wings and* tail, and *mid-throat and entire remaining underparts black*; the thighs are scarlet, but these are usually hidden. Female *dull greenish blue above*, brightest on cheeks, scapulars, and rump, duskier on back, wings, and tail; *below dingy buffy grayish*, buffiest on belly and under tail-coverts.
Similar species: Dull female can be confusing, but nothing of similar size and shape combines the bluish tone above with the buffyish underparts; female Blue Dacnis is much greener overall, while female Viridian lacks the blue above, is more olive below, and has a yellow (not red) eye.
Status and distribution: Uncommon to fairly common in canopy and borders of humid forest in foothills on both slopes (especially 300–1200 m: 1000–4000 ft), ranging down in smaller numbers down into lowlands on Caribbean slope and in Darién, and regularly occurring up into lower highlands of western Chiriquí (mainly to 1200–1350 m: 4000–4500 ft, occasionally somewhat higher). In Canal area most numerous along Pipeline Road, but even there seemingly erratic, at times occurring in quite large numbers (perhaps especially when *Miconia* trees are fruiting), at other times virtually absent.
Habits: Usually in small groups, with marked tendency not to associate with other species.
Range: Costa Rica to northwestern Ecuador.

BLUE DACNIS
Dacnis cayana   Plate 33

Description: 5. Straight pointed bill usually shows some pale pinkish brown at base; legs pinkish flesh. Male *mostly bright blue*, with black lores, back, wings and tail, and throat; wings prominently edged with blue. Birds from Chiriquí and Veraguas (*callaina*) are paler more turquoise blue than the deeper ultramarine blue of birds from the rest of Panama (*ultramarina*). Female *mainly bright green*, paler below, with *contrasting bluish head* and grayish throat.
Similar species: Honeycreepers have decurved bills. Female Scarlet-thighed Dacnis is buffy (not pale green) below. Female most resembles female White-shouldered Tanager but is a little smaller, brighter green (less olive) above, and not as yellow below, with bluish (not grayish) head. In Darién, see also female Viridian Dacnis.
Status and distribution: Common in second-growth woodland, forest borders, and clearings with scattered trees in more humid lowlands on both slopes, with no reports from eastern side of Azuero Peninsula and drier adjacent areas; ranges sparingly up into foothills to about 900 m (3000 ft). Numerous and widespread on both slopes of Canal area.
Habits: Usually in pairs or small groups, foraging actively at all heights, often with mixed flocks of tanagers, etc.
Range: Southern Honduras to eastern Bolivia, northeastern Argentina, and southern Brazil.

VIRIDIAN DACNIS
Dacnis viguieri   Plate 40

Description: 4½. Found only in eastern Darién. *Iris yellow* in both sexes. Male *mostly bluish green*, bluer on rump; lores, upper back, and tail black; *wings mainly green with contrasting black primaries*. Female dull green above; pale greenish yellow below, tinged olive on sides; wings dull green with contrasting blackish primaries; tail black.
Similar species: Male quite similar in pattern to male Blue Dacnis, and the difference in color can be difficult to discern depending on light angle; best distinguishing points are

Viridian's yellow (not dark) iris, its *lack of a black throat patch*, and the *bicolored* (green and black) *effect* on the wings. Female is much duller than female Blue Dacnis, lacks its blue on head, has yellow eye, different wing pattern, etc. See also female Green Honeycreeper.

Status and distribution: Rare in canopy and borders of humid forest in lowlands and lower foothills (to about 600 m: 2000 ft) of eastern Darién, where recorded from near El Real, the Cana valley, and Jaqué. Has been seen recently along the Boca de Cupe trail near Cana, but always in very small numbers (seems genuinely rare there).

Habits: Similar to other dacnises. Has been seen feeding in flowering *Erythrina* trees (D. Wolf); tends to remain high in the forest canopy.

Range: Eastern Panama and northwestern Colombia.

GREEN HONEYCREEPER
Chlorophanes spiza   Plate 33

Description: 5½. *Bill stouter and less decurved* than in other honeycreepers, *bright yellow* with black ridge in male, *duller uniform yellow* in female. Male *mostly bright emerald green* with *contrasting black head*; wings and tail duskier. Female *mostly bright green*, paler below, with yellower throat, around eye, and mid-belly; wings and tail duskier.

Similar species: Male is easily identified; female is brighter and more uniform green than other honeycreepers, and it has a less decurved bill. Female Blue Dacnis is somewhat smaller with shorter straight bill and bluish head. Female Green perhaps most likely confused with certain basically all-green immature *Tangara* tanagers (e.g. Bay-headed and Rufous-winged), but note bill's different shape and its yellowish color. See also Green Shrike-Vireo.

Status and distribution: Fairly common in canopy and borders of forest and second-growth woodland in more humid lowlands and foothills on both slopes; ranges regularly up to about 900 m (3000 ft), occasionally somewhat higher; apparently absent from drier lowlands from eastern side of Azuero Peninsula to western Panama province.

Habits: Usually seen singly or in pairs (not in groups), remaining quite high in the trees, often accompanying mixed flocks of tanagers, etc.

Range: Southeastern Mexico to northern Bolivia and southern Brazil.

SHINING HONEYCREEPER
Cyanerpes lucidus   Plate 33

Description: 4¼. *Bill long, slender, and decurved; legs bright yellow in male, greenish in female.* Male *mostly bright purplish blue*, somewhat paler on crown and sides of head; wings and tail, lores, and *throat and chest black.* Female mostly green above with head strongly tinged bluish gray and dusky lores; wings and tail duskier; throat buffy, bordered by narrow blue malar stripe; remaining underparts buffy whitish, *boldly streaked blue on breast*, and washed greenish on sides.

Similar species: Red-legged Honeycreeper also has slender decurved bill, but *Shining is smaller with shorter tail*; male also differs in obvious yellow (not red) legs, black throat and chest patch, and in lacking Red-leg's pale blue crown; female also differs in its greenish (not reddish) legs and crisp blue breast streaking (not blurry and olive). In eastern Darién see also the very similar Purple Honeycreeper.

Status and distribution: Fairly common to common in canopy and borders of humid forest in foothills on entire Caribbean slope (mostly 300–1200 m: 1000–4000 ft), ranging down in smaller numbers into lowlands; on Pacific slope rather more local, with apparently no definite reports from Chiriquí and only a few from Veraguas (including locally on western side of Azuero Peninsula), but more numerous in eastern Panama province (especially Cerro Azul/Jefe), and ranging in small numbers east to eastern Darién (specimens from the Cana area, Cerro Tacarcuna, and Cerro Sapo). In Canal area much more numerous on Caribbean slope, especially along Pipeline Road, but small numbers also are found (erratically?) on Pacific slope, e.g. in Madden Forest and around Rodman.

Habits: Typically forages rather high in trees, often in small groups and accompanying mixed flocks of tanagers.

Range: Southeastern Mexico to northwestern Colombia.

PURPLE HONEYCREEPER
Cyanerpes caeruleus   Plate 40

Description: 4¼. Known only from eastern Darién. Closely resembles the far more widespread (in Panama) Shining Honeycreeper. Male is particularly difficult, but is darker and more uniformly purplish blue, and with *black of throat not extending down over chest.* Female easier: it is greener on crown (not so grayish) and *buffier on sides of head* *and especially lores* (dusky in female Shining), and has deeper buff throat, and *green* (not blue) *streaking on breast.*

Similar species: See Shining Honeycreeper.

Status and distribution: Locally fairly common in canopy and borders of humid forest in lowlands and lower foothills (to about 600 m: 2000 ft) of eastern Darién; recorded from specimens from Río Jaqué valley and at Cerro Quía, and from recent sightings at Cana. It is worth noting that at the latter site Shining Honeycreepers have been collected, but there are also several recent sight reports (D. Wolf *et al.*; Ridgely *et al.*) of Purples, indicating that the two species are locally sympatric (but whether both actually breed there remains to be determined).

Habits: Much like Shining Honeycreeper.

Range: Eastern Panama to northern Bolivia and Amazonian Brazil.

RED-LEGGED HONEYCREEPER
Cyanerpes cyaneus Plate 33

Description: 4¾. Bill long, slender, and decurved; *legs bright red in male, reddish in female.* Male *mostly purplish blue* with *contrasting pale turquoise blue crown,* lores, back, wings, and tail black; *under wing-coverts bright yellow.* Female dull green above with *indistinct whitish superciliary;* pale yellowish below with *blurry greenish streaking* (especially on throat and breast); under wing-coverts yellow. Male has a non-breeding "eclipse" plumage (July–September) in which it resembles female except for retaining black wings and tail.

Similar species: Shining Honeycreeper is smaller with shorter tail; male has yellow (not red) legs, lacks pale blue crown, has black throat and chest patch; female has greenish (not reddish) legs and blue malar streak and breast streaking, lacks a superciliary, etc. Dacnises have shorter straight bills. See also female Green Honeycreeper (brighter green without streaking).

Status and distribution: Common to very common in residential areas, clearings, shrubby areas, second-growth woodland, and forest borders in lowlands and foothills (mostly below 900 m: 3000 ft) on both slopes, though apparently unrecorded from western Bocas del Toro, the Bayano River valley in eastern Panama province, and much of Darién (though present along the coast); very common on Coiba Island and the Pearl Islands. In some areas seasonal or erratic in its appearances, but generally numerous and familiar throughout the Canal area.

Habits: The most widespread and familiar honeycreeper in Panama; comes to feeding trays. Often occurs in flocks of up to a dozen or more individuals, sometimes alone but frequently joining mixed groups of other birds.

Range: Southern Mexico to northern Bolivia and southern Brazil; Cuba.

GOLDEN-BROWED CHLOROPHONIA
Chlorophonia callophrys Plate 34

Description: 5½. Found only in western highlands. Chunky shape, with short bill and tail. Male *mostly bright green above* with pale blue crown and nape arching around as partial nuchal collar; *bright yellow forehead and superciliary;* tail and flight feathers duskier edged with green; *throat and upper chest bright green,* bordered below by thin black line; *remaining underparts bright yellow,* with contrasting bright green sides and flanks. Female and immature male *like male above* but lacking the yellow superciliary and with less blue on crown; *pattern below similar* but with less contrast, and without the black line separating green of chest from yellow of lower underparts.

Similar species: This species is such a bright green overall that confusion is most unlikely. Green Shrike-Vireo has totally different range, etc. See Blue-hooded Euphonia.

Status and distribution: Uncommon in clearings and forest borders in highlands of Chiriquí and Veraguas, mostly above 1500 m (5000 ft) in Chiriquí, lower (to about 750 m: 2500 ft) in Veraguas.

Habits: Usually remains well up in trees, often in small groups. The brilliant adult males are greatly outnumbered by females and young males. The chlorophonia's commonest call is a soft, melancholy *ooo,* often repeated after a pause, very distinctive once learned. Also has a characteristic nasal call, to some suggestive of the yapping of a small dog, *enk-enk-enk-enk.*

Range: Costa Rica and western Panama.

YELLOW-COLLARED CHLOROPHONIA
Chlorophonia flavirostris

Description: 4¼. Recently recorded from eastern Darién. Both sexes have *iris white with yellow eye-ring, orange-yellow bill with dusky tip,* and *orange-yellow legs.* Male *mostly bright green above* with *broad bright yellow collar on* *hindneck and upper back* and yellow rump; throat and upper chest bright green bordered below by chestnut band; remaining underparts bright yellow, with sides and flanks bright green. Female and immature male *mostly uniform bright green*, with middle of breast and belly bright yellow.

Similar species: Gaudy males are unmistakable, and even the less patterned females and young birds (which usually predominate) can be easily recognized by the combination of their basically uniform bright green plumage and distinctive softpart colors.

Status and distribution: Known from only one record: three birds (with two males photographed) mist-netted and released on January 31, 1983, on the slopes of Cerro Pirre (1200 m: 4000 ft) above Cana, Darién, by R. Baker and D. Hafner (A. Capparella, *Am Birds 40*(2): 194–195, 1986). Cerro Pirre is a full 400 km north of its previous northernmost known locality in western Colombia; whether the species is merely a casual visitant to Panama remains to be determined.

Habits: In its normal range usually in small groups which usually remain inconspicuous in canopy of humid foothill forest; it does seem to show some propensity toward wandering.

Range: Southwestern Colombia and northwestern Ecuador, once in eastern Panama.

YELLOW-CROWNED EUPHONIA
Euphonia luteicapilla   Plate 34

Description: 3¾. Male has *entire crown yellow*; upperparts otherwise steel blue; throat and chest steel blue, lower underparts yellow *with no white or tawny*. Female yellowish olive above, *uniform dull yellow below*.

Similar species: Male Spot-crowned Euphonia of Chiriquí has only forehead (not whole cap) yellow, and black (not steel blue) throat and chest. Otherwise male Yellow-crown is only dark-throated male euphonia with all yellow underparts. Female resembles female Thick-billed Euphonia but is more uniform yellow below with typical euphonia bill (not slightly thicker); this hard to see in the field, however. In Darién see also Orange-bellied Euphonia.

Status and distribution: Fairly common to common in dry scrubby and shrubby areas, savannas, and extensive clearings with scattered trees in lowlands on Pacific slope from western Chiriquí east to eastern Darién (Yaviza/El Real area, with one sighting from up the Tuira River valley as far as near Boca

de Cupe), scarcer in more wooded or forested areas; on Caribbean slope found in small numbers only in lowlands of western Bocas del Toro and in Canal area; ranges sparingly up in foothills to about 900 m (3000 ft) in Chiriquí and Veraguas.

Habits: Typically forages in small flocks of its own species. Calls almost incessantly, a usually double or triple-noted high-pitched *beem-beem*, from which the species' local name "Bim-bim" is derived. Also has a thin, wiry song. A popular cagebird.

Range: Nicaragua to eastern Panama.

THICK-BILLED EUPHONIA
Euphonia laniirostris   Plate 34

Description: 4. Has thicker bill than most euphonias, but this is difficult to see in the field. Male has yellow forecrown and steel blue upperparts; *entire underparts, including throat, yellow*. Female olive above; yellow below with *olive wash on breast*. Immature males with black areas but otherwise like females are often seen.

Similar species: In most of Panama, male is the only adult male euphonia with all yellow underparts; in western Chiriquí see the rare Yellow-throated Euphonia. Female resembles female Yellow-crowned Euphonia, but note latter's uniform yellow underparts (no olive on breast).

Status and distribution: Fairly common to common in clearings, gardens, second-growth woodland, and forest borders in lowlands on entire Pacific slope (though seemingly less numerous in Darién and the upper Bayano River valley of eastern Panama province), and on Caribbean slope from northern Coclé eastward; ranges regularly well up into foothills and lower highlands (to about 1200 m: 4000 ft) where suitable broken forest habitat exists.

Habits: As with other euphonias, often in small groups, feeding especially on mistletoe berries. In most humid lowland areas (e.g. both slopes of Canal area) this is the most numerous and most frequently encountered euphonia. Its usual calls are a sweet *chweet*, a *wheep*, and a clear *peet* or *peet-peet*, the latter much like common note of the Yellow-crowned Euphonia. Males often incorporate snatches of other bird's calls in their songs. Euphonias are much-favored cagebirds in Panama, and this is the most popular and frequently seen; to date, however, no dimunition in their numbers in the wild has been noted.

Range: Costa Rica to Bolivia and Amazonian Brazil.

[YELLOW-THROATED EUPHONIA]
Euphonia hirundinacea   Plates 34, 48

Description: 4. Found only in western Chiriquí. Thick bill as in previous species. Male very like male Thick-billed Euphonia but with *smaller yellow patch on forecrown (extending back only to eye);* like that species, has *entirely yellow underparts.* Female, however, is quite different; olive green above, *grayish white below,* with yellowish restricted to sides.
Similar species: Female Thick-billed Euphonia has mostly dull yellow underparts (no whitish). See also female White-vented Euphonia.
Status and distribution: Apparently rare in lower highlands of western Chiriquí (900–1200 m: 3000–4000 ft). However, there exists some uncertainty as to its Panama status: only one specimen record has ever been published, that of two males taken above Boquete by W. W. Brown in 1901, but these cannot now be located in the MCZ (having perhaps been subsequently re-identified as Thick-billed?). There also are a few sightings from the Volcán/Santa Clara area, but these require further confirmation; in this connection it might be mentioned that the Yellow-throated Euphonia is apparently unknown from adjacent southwestern Costa Rica.
Habits: Similar to Thick-billed Euphonia, but less accomplished vocally.
Range: Eastern Mexico to Costa Rica, perhaps extreme western Panama.

BLUE-HOODED EUPHONIA
Euphonia elegantissima   Plate 34

Description: 4½. Found only in western highlands. Male mostly steel blue above with *contrasting bright turquoise blue crown and hindneck* and a chestnut frontlet; throat black, *remaining underparts rather bright orange-tawny.* Female echoes male's pattern: above mostly bright olive with *contrasting bright turquoise blue crown and hindneck* and tawny frontlet; throat buffyish, remaining underparts olive yellow.
Similar species: No other Panama euphonia has a light blue crown and nape.
Status and distribution: Uncommon to locally fairly common in clearings with scattered trees and woodland borders in lower highlands on Pacific slope in Chiriquí and Veraguas (mostly 1050–1500 m: 3500–5000 ft, sparingly to 1950 m: 6500 ft), also one old record from Coclé (an AMNH specimen from Nata). Quite readily found in the Volcán/Santa Clara area, having perhaps

increased (due to clearing?) in recent decades.
Habits: Like other euphonias usually in small groups. Rather quiet, but both sexes sometimes give a leisurely series of clear ringing *cheeyu* or *chu* notes.
Range: Mexico to western Panama.
Note: Sometimes considered conspecific with *E. musica* (Antillean Euphonia) of the West Indies and *E. cyanocephala* (Golden-rumped Euphonia) of South America, though the three were treated as separate species in the 1983 AOU Check-list. If combined, the name *E. musica* has priority, and the English name is Blue-hooded Euphonia.

FULVOUS-VENTED EUPHONIA
Euphonia fulvicrissa   Plate 34

Description: 4. Male has mostly steel blue upperparts with bright yellow forecrown; throat and upper chest also steel blue; remaining underparts bright yellow, with *usually prominent tawny wash on mid-belly and under tail-coverts.* Female olive above with rufous forecrown, often tinged grayish blue on nape; yellowish olive below with *tawny wash on mid-belly and under tail-coverts.*
Similar species: No other male euphonia with standard pattern has tawny on lower belly. Female probably indistinguishable in the field from female Spot-crowned Euphonia of Chiriquí. Female also resembles both sexes of Olive-backed Euphonia (no known overlap).
Status and distribution: Fairly common to common in shrubby growth and lower trees in forest borders and clearings in lowlands on Caribbean slope from northern Coclé eastward, and on Pacific slope from western Panama province (Cerro Campana area) eastward; ranges locally and sparingly up into foothills (to about 900 m: 3000 ft). Old specimens from Chiriquí and "Veragua" are regarded as uncertain; there are no modern records from so far west, and re-examination will likely prove they were either *E. imitans* or *E. gouldii.*
Habits: Usually in small groups, often feeding at around eye-level (other Canal area euphonias are generally higher up). The usual call is a chattering *treah-treah,* and locally called "Ren-ren" on account of this frequently given note. Sometimes accompanies mixed flocks of *Myrmotherula* antwrens, etc., in forest lower growth.
Range: Central Panama to northwestern Ecuador.

SPOT-CROWNED EUPHONIA
Euphonia imitans   Plate 34

Description: Found only in western Chiriquí. Male has *yellow forecrown with a few dusky spots*; otherwise steel blue above and on throat and upper chest; remaining underparts bright yellow. Female glossy olive above, somewhat tinged blue, with rufous forecrown; yellowish olive below with *tawny wash on mid-belly and under tail-coverts.*

Similar species: Male's crown spots are small, and visible only at close range; in range it would most likely be confused with male Yellow-crowned Euphonia (which has much larger area of yellow on crown) or male White-vented (which also has yellow back to only just above eye, but which differs in its white on lower underparts). Female is more easily recognized, as it is the only euphonia in its range with tawny on lower underparts.

Status and distribution: Rare to locally uncommon in forest and forest borders in western Chiriquí, ranging from lowlands (no recent reports) up to lower highlands (to around 1200 m: 4000 ft). A few can be regularly found at the edge of woodland and forest patches west of Volcán along the road to Santa Clara.

Habits: Similar to Fulvous-vented Euphonia, with unmistakable *treeah-treeah* call virtually identical. The song is a protracted series of weak, often sputtering notes, common ones being a *weyoo-tsít* or *weeweewee-tsít.*

Range: Southwestern Costa Rica and Pacific western Panama.

OLIVE-BACKED EUPHONIA
Euphonia gouldi   Plate 34

Description: 3¾. Found only in western Caribbean Panama. Male departs from standard euphonia colors, and looks "hen-plumaged". *Dark glossy olive green above*, sometimes tinged bluish, with *yellow forecrown*; yellowish olive below, with tawny mid-belly and under tail-coverts. Female similar but less glossy above and with *chestnut forehead* (dark and often hard to see in the field); below entirely yellowish olive, *tawny only on under tail-coverts.*

Similar species: No female-plumaged euphonia has the contrasting yellow forecrown (but beware certain immature males of other species, as these may acquire their yellow forecrowns before completely molting out of their olive immature plumage). Female Olive-backed resembles female Fulvous-

vented Euphonia (not known to occur together, but additional work in western Caribbean lowlands may close the apparent gap), differing in its darker forecrown patch and in having tawny restricted to under tail-coverts (*not* extending up onto mid-belly).

Status and distribution: Common in humid forest, forest borders, and adjacent clearings with scattered trees in lowlands of Bocas del Toro and western Veraguas (Calovévora); old specimens from farther east (e.g. McLeannan specimens from Canal area) or Chiriquí are either unsubstantiated or were misidentified; ranges sparingly up in foothills to about 600 m (2000 ft).

Habits: Similar to Fulvous-vented Euphonia. The calls are also similar, *treeuh-treah*; it is also known to Panamanians as "Ren-ren".

Range: Southeastern Mexico to Caribbean western Panama.

WHITE-VENTED EUPHONIA
Euphonia minuta   Plate 34

Description: 3¾. Above steel blue with *small patch of yellow on forehead* (extends back to only just above eye); throat and upper chest steel blue, remaining underparts yellow with *white lower belly and under tail-coverts.* Female olive above; throat grayish white; *broad breast band, sides, and flanks olive-yellow; mid-belly and under tail-coverts whitish.*

Similar species: The smallest Panama euphonia, and the only species with white on lower underparts (aside from female of very rare Yellow-throated Euphonia, which see).

Status and distribution: Uncommon to locally fairly common in canopy and borders of humid forest in lowlands and (especially) foothills on entire Caribbean slope; on Pacific slope considerably more local and less numerous, known only from western Chiriquí (two old specimens from Bugaba in lowlands, but no records since), Veraguas (foothill zone above Santa Fé), eastern Panama province (Cerro Azul/Jefe), and Darién (where surprisingly uncommon). In immediate Canal area most often seen along Pipeline Road, but even there it seems to be irregular and numbers always small.

Habits: Usually seen high in trees, often accompanying mixed flocks of other frugivorous birds. The calls are much like those of other euphonias, especially that of the Yellow-crowned, *beem.*

Range: Southeastern Mexico to northern Bolivia and Amazonian Brazil.

TAWNY-CAPPED EUPHONIA
Euphonia anneae   Plate 34

Description: 4¼. Foothills. Male has *distinctive rich tawny crown*; remaining upperparts, throat, and upper chest steel blue; remaining underparts yellow (in nominate race of Bocas del Toro and Chiriquí) to orange-yellow (in *rufivertex* of remainder of Panama range); with under tail-coverts white. The rather dark and dingy female is mostly greenish olive above with *dull rufous forecrown* and gray tinge on hindcrown; throat and breast gray, becoming pinkish buff on mid-belly and greenish yellow on sides and flanks.
Similar species: Female Fulvous-vented, Spot-crowned, and Olive-backed Euphonias all also have rufous forecrowns, but are yellowish below (not gray) with tawny on lower belly. No other male Panama euphonia has a wholly tawny cap.
Status and distribution: Uncommon to locally common in lower growth and borders of humid forest and second-growth woodland in foothills on both slopes, mostly 450–1200 m (1500–4000 ft), occasionally somewhat higher, with two records from Caribbean lowlands (a male mist-netted and collected along lower Río Changuinola, Bocas del Toro, on January 15, 1980, by R. Hinds, specimen to GML; and one seen along Río Guanche in eastern Colon province on January 18, 1987, by D. Graham). In eastern Darién recorded only from Cerro Tacarcuna (apparently being replaced on Cerro Pirre by the allied Orange-bellied Euphonia). Particularly numerous in the Fortuna area of central Chiriquí and adjacent Bocas del Toro.
Habits: Usually forages within 6 m (20 ft) of the ground, in pairs or small groups. Has rather harsh conversational notes, but usually silent.
Range: Costa Rica to extreme northwestern Colombia.

ORANGE-BELLIED EUPHONIA
Euphonia xanthogaster

Description: 4¼. Found only in eastern Darién. Mostly steel blue above with *yellow forecrown* (extending back to behind eye), blacker on sides of head and nape; throat black tinged purple; remaining underparts yellow. Female has *dull yellow forehead*, olive mid-crown, and *gray hindcrown and nape*; otherwise olive above; *mostly buffy grayish below*, buffiest on belly, with sides and flanks yellowish olive.
Similar species: Male most resembles male

Yellow-crowned Euphonia, but in that species yellow on crown extends further back; habitat and range (as well as respective females) differ substantially. Female Orange-bellied most resembles female Tawny-capped Euphonia but has yellowish rather than dull rufous forehead; these two species apparently replace each other, and are never sympatric.
Status and distribution: Fairly common in lower growth and borders of humid forest in foothills and highlands of eastern Darién (Cerro Sapo, Cerro Pirre, Cerro Quía and Río Jaqué valley); recorded mostly 450–1500 m (1500–500 ft); not found on Cerro Tacarcuna (where Tawny-capped Euphonia is present).
Habits: Similar to Tawny-capped Euphonia, foraging at various levels but principally inside forest, coming to edge to eat fruit.
Range: Eastern Panama to northern Bolivia and Amazonian and eastern Brazil.

BLUE-GRAY TANAGER
Thraupis episcopus   Plate 35

Description: 6½. *Mostly pale grayish blue*, contrastingly darker on back; *lesser wing-coverts bright cobalt blue*, remaining *wing feathers edged bright blue*; tail feathers also edged bright blue. Races found on Coiba Island (*cumatilis*) and on Isla Escudo de Veraguas off Bocas del Toro (*caesita*) are darker, especially below, but otherwise resemble birds of mainland and other offshore islands (*cana*).
Similar species: Similar in size, shape, and actions to the Palm Tanager, and often found with it. The olive Palm Tanager can always be known by the black outer half of its wing. See also Plain-colored Tanager.
Status and distribution: Abundant in gardens, shrubby clearings, second-growth woodland, and borders virtually throughout, up to around 1800 m (6000 ft) in western highlands; common also on Pearl Islands, Coiba Island, and other islands off Pacific and Caribbean coasts.
Habits: One of the most familiar Panama birds. Noisy and active, often becoming very tame around habitations, and frequently coming to feeding trays. Its song is an unpatterned series of squeaky notes.
Range: Eastern Mexico to the Guianas, Brazil, and northern Bolivia.

PALM TANAGER
Thraupis palmarum   Plate 35

Description: 6. *Generally grayish olive*, with glossy violaceous overtones in some lights;

forehead and lower underparts more yellowish olive; *outer half* (flight feathers) *of closed wing black*; tail sooty blackish. Females lack the glossy sheen.

Similar species: Blue-gray Tanager normally looks blue; if not, Palm Tanager can always be known by its black on the wing. Plain-colored Tanager is smaller, leaden gray (not olive), and entire wing is blackish.

Status and distribution: Common in gardens, shrubby clearings, and woodland and forest borders in more humid lowlands, more numerous on Caribbean slope; absent from drier areas in Pacific lowlands from southern Veraguas to western Panama province; ranges up in foothills to about 1200 m (4000 ft) in Chiriquí.

Habits: Generally associates with the usually more numerous Blue-gray Tanager. Most frequent near habitations, where it often forages under eaves and on screens; also frequently feeds in palms.

Range: Southern Honduras to Bolivia, Paraguay, and southern Brazil.

BLUE-AND-GOLD TANAGER
Bangsia arcaei   Plate 35

Description: 6. *Iris red. Above rich indigo blue,* brightest on head; wings and tail blackish, feathers broadly edged with dark blue; throat blackish blue, contrasting with *rich yellow remaining underparts,* some dusky mottling on sides.

Similar species: No other Panama tanager (other than the much smaller euphonias) is blue above and yellow below.

Status and distribution: Locally fairly common in canopy and borders of very humid forest in foothills of western and central Panama (mostly 750–1050 m: 2500–3500 ft); recorded from central Chiriquí (upper Río Chiriquí valley in the Fortuna area; Ridgely *et al.*), central Bocas del Toro (along the oleoducto road north of Fortuna; Ridgely *et al.*), both slopes of Veraguas, western Coclé (seen recently on several occasions north of El Copé on the Caribbean slope; D. Engleman *et al.*), eastern Panama province (Cerro Jefe area, though few if any recent reports), and western San Blas (seen and photographed on Cerro Brewster on April 24 and 26, 1985, by J. Blake; photos to VIREO); may well occur eastward in San Blas and even on slopes of Cerro Tacarcuna, Darién.

Habits: Usually in pairs or small groups, sometimes accompanying flocks of other tanagers, almost always quite high in trees.

At times rather sluggish and inactive, then often flying considerable distances. Its call is a distinctive loud sharp *tseee, teh-teh-teh,* sometimes with only one *teh* (or up to four of them) being given.

Range: Costa Rica to central Panama.

Note: Placed by the 1983 AOU Check-list in the genus *Buthraupis*; however, based on the South American members of the two genera, *Bangsia* and *Buthraupis*, we still believe it is best to maintain them both as distinct.

OLIVE TANAGER
Chlorothraupis carmioli   Plate 35

Description: 6¾. Bill blackish. *Generally olive green,* somewhat yellower below, especially on throat.

Similar species: Like female Hepatic Tanager but darker olive overall, especially below. Female Red-crowned Ant-Tanager is olive brown above (not olive green) and has tawny yellow crown patch. Female Red-throated Ant-Tanager is even browner above, with more orange-yellow throat that contrasts with rest of underparts. Ant-tanagers are almost always in pairs or small groups, very rarely alone, so there is usually a male present to confirm their identification.

Status and distribution: Fairly common to common in lower growth of humid forest and forest borders in foothills on entire Caribbean slope; on Pacific slope recorded locally from Veraguas (above Santa Fé), eastern Panama province (Cerro Azul/Jefe, and Cerro Chucantí), and eastern Darién (Cerro Tacarcuna; not recorded from Cerro Pirre); recorded mostly 300–1200 m (1000–4000 ft), but locally down into coastal lowlands on Caribbean slope in somewhat smaller numbers (e.g. in western Bocas del Toro and along Pipeline Road in the Canal area, also in eastern Colon province and San Blas). Numerous around Nusagandi in western San Blas.

Habits: Typically troops about in larger bands of up to several dozen individuals. Their incessant calling brings to mind the chattering of Clay-colored Thrushes.

Range: Nicaragua to extreme northwestern Colombia, and locally on Andean slopes from southern Colombia to Bolivia.

Note: Formerly usually called the Carmiol's Tanager, the 1983 AOU Check-list opted for using the name Olive Tanager.

LEMON-SPECTACLED TANAGER
Chlorothraupis olivacea Plate 35

Description: 6¾. Found only in eastern Darién. Resembles Olive Tanager, but easily known by its *bright yellow lores and prominent eye-ring* (forming "spectacles"). Male is darker olive generally than Olive Tanager, especially on most of underparts (which contrast with yellow on the throat); female Yellow-spectacled is, however, about the same olive tone as Olive Tanager.
Similar species: See Olive Tanager.
Status and distribution: Uncommon to locally fairly common in lower growth of humid forest in lowlands and (especially) foothills of eastern Darién (Cerro Sapo, Cana/Cerro Pirre, Cerro Quía, and Jaqué; not found on Cerro Tacarcuna massif, where evidently replaced by Olive Tanager); recorded up to about 1200 m (4000 ft).
Habits: Similar to Olive Tanager, but tends to move in much smaller groups (only two to four birds being the norm), and more often found accompanying true multi-species foraging flocks. Like the Olive Tanager, the Lemon-spectacled is a noisy bird, with excited-sounding calls being given rapidly in series but rather higher-pitched and not as harsh.
Range: Eastern Panama to northwestern Ecuador.
Note: Though this species has traditionally been called the "Lemon-browed" Tanager, it does *not* have a yellow brow, but rather shows yellow only on the lores and around the eye (the "spectacles").

GRAY-HEADED TANAGER
Eucometis penicillata Plate 36

Description: 6¾. *Head, neck, and throat gray* contrasting with olive green upperparts and *bright yellow underparts*.
Similar species: Female White-shouldered Tanager in central and eastern Panama has same general pattern but is smaller and duller; it is primarily arboreal while the Gray-head is a bird of undergrowth.
Status and distribution: Uncommon in undergrowth of humid second-growth woodland and forest in lowlands and (locally) in foothills on Caribbean slope from northern Coclé (El Uracillo) eastward, and on Pacific slope in Chiriquí (where in west it ranges up sparingly into lower highlands to 1200–1500 m: 4000–5000 ft), Veraguas, and western side of Azuero Peninsula, and from western Panama province (La Campana) eastward.

Habits: An active and rather excitable bird which regularly raises its crown feathers into a short bushy crest. Seen singly or in pairs, rarely with mixed flocks though they often are seen in attendance at army ant swarms. The song is a jumbled series of sputtery high notes, not too often heard.
Range: Southeastern Mexico to Bolivia and southern Brazil.

WHITE-THROATED SHRIKE-TANAGER
Lanio leucothorax Plate 36

Description: 7–7½. Found locally in western Panama. *Bill heavy and hooked at tip.* Striking male is *mostly black above* with *conspicuous triangular patch of bright yellow on upper mantle*; innermost wing-coverts white (sometimes hidden); *throat white, remaining underparts mostly yellow*, tinged buff on chest, and with black lower belly and under tail-coverts. Foregoing applies to *melanopygius* of most of Panama range; *ictus* (recorded only from foothills of western Bocas del Toro) similar but with rump feathers black *broadly tipped yellow*. Female much duller, with mostly brownish olive head, duskier on ear-coverts; otherwise *mostly brown above*, brightest on rump; wings and tail dusky, *feathers broadly edged brown; throat and chest pinkish buff* tinged gray, with remaining underparts dull yellow, tinged brown on flanks and under tail-coverts.
Similar species: The boldly patterned male is easily recognized; superficially it looks (but does not act) more like an oriole than a tanager. Female bears a slight resemblance to Gray-headed Tanager but is brown (not olive green) above and not so bright yellow below.
Status and distribution: Rare and local in humid forest and forest borders in western Panama; recorded from lowlands of western Chiriquí (where it probably survives only on the Burica Peninsula, with several pairs seen there in June 1982; Ridgely), foothills of western Bocas del Toro (450–690 m: 1500–2300 ft along the old trail to Boquete; no recent records), foothills on both slopes in Veraguas (mostly 600–900 m: 2000–3000 ft), and foothills on Caribbean slope of western Coclé (one male seen north of El Copé at about 450 m: 1500 ft on March 8, 1986; Ridgely, D. Engleman, J. Guarnaccia *et al.*).
Habits: Most often seen in pairs, foraging at all levels both inside forest and at edge; seems to favor, even in the lowlands, areas with broken terrain. Almost always found

with mixed flocks, appearing to be one of the species around which such flocks form. Usually quite noisy and conspicuous, with a variety of loud calls which draw attention to its presence; further, males, at least in Costa Rica, also give a very complex song consisting of a somewhat subdued jumble of various *chip* and *peep* calls, with warbles (often seeming to be imitations of other birds) interspersed with an occasional loud *pyeer!-pyeer!-pyeer!* . . . (B. Whitney, Ridgely).

Range: Honduras to western Panama.

SULPHUR-RUMPED TANAGER
Heterospingus rubrifrons   Plate 36

Description: 6¼. *Mostly plumbeous gray*, paler below and tinged with yellow on under tail-coverts; wings and tail blackish; *pectoral tuft white* (usually protrudes from under wing); *rump yellow* (usually hidden at rest, but conspicuous in flight).

Similar species: Plain-colored Tanager is also mainly gray, but is smaller, lacks the white tuft and yellow rump, etc. Flame-rumped Tanager also has (at least in Panama) a yellow rump, but otherwise is totally different in behavior and appearance.

Status and distribution: Uncommon to locally fairly common in canopy and borders of humid forest in lowlands and foothills (to about 900 m: 3000 ft) on entire Caribbean slope (east to eastern San Blas at Puerto Obaldía); on Pacific slope recorded only from Veraguas foothills (seen above Santa Fé in June 1977; D. Wilcove and J. Wall), and in eastern Panama province (Cerro Azul/Jefe, and in upper Bayano River valley). Records in the literature from Darién are apparently in error for female Scarlet-browed Tanager, though it remains possible that the Sulphur-rumped ranges east at least to western Darién in the upper Río Chucunaque valley; as yet the two species have not been found to occur together. In Canal area found most readily along Pipeline Road; also frequent around Nusagandi in western San Blas.

Habits: Usually forages at high and middle levels, coming lower in clearings. Generally in small groups, often accompanying large mixed flocks of other tanagers, etc.

Range: Costa Rica to eastern Panama.

SCARLET-BROWED TANAGER
Heterospingus xanthopygius   Plate 36

Description: 7. Known only from eastern Darién. Male *mostly black*, with narrow white

line above eye broadening into *conspicuous scarlet postocular tuft* (often seeming to protrude outward); small patch on shoulders and *rump bright yellow; pectoral tuft white* (usually protrudes from under wing). Female closely resembles Sulphur-rumped Tanager, and probably not safely distinguished in the field (the two are not known to occur together), differing only in its larger size, somewhat darker gray plumage overall, and less yellow on under tail-coverts.

Status and distribution: Uncommon in canopy and borders of humid forest in lowlands and foothills of eastern Darién (various localities in the Tuira River drainage including El Real and Cana/Cerro Pirre; also Cerro Sapo and Río Jaqué valley); recorded up to about 900 m (3000 ft).

Habits: Similar to Sulphur-rumped Tanager. Usually seen in pairs, generally remaining high in forest canopy with mixed flocks of other tanagers, etc.; sometimes comes lower in clearings.

Range: Eastern Panama to northwestern Ecuador.

WHITE-SHOULDERED TANAGER
Tachyphonus luctuosus   Plate 36

Description: 5–5¼. At least base of mandible bluish gray (both sexes). Male of widespread *panamensis* race *glossy black* with *conspicuous white area on wing-coverts* and white under wing-linings. Female olive above with *rather contrasting gray head* (sometimes tinged olive on crown); throat grayish white, remaining underparts quite bright yellow, tinged olive on sides. Birds from western Bocas del Toro (*axillaris*) are similar, but male has reduced white on wing-coverts; female has *head olive* and throat yellowish. Birds from western Chiriquí (*nitidissimus*) are slightly larger, and both sexes have pale grayish iris and larger pale (flesh?) area on mandible; male has *conspicuous crown patch of yellow-tawny* and reduced white in wing like *axillaris*; female like female *axillaris* but somewhat brighter yellow below.

Similar species: Male of larger White-lined Tanager shows no white on closed wing; male Dot-winged Antwren is smaller and slimmer, with white spots on wing (no solid patch) and tail-tips; male Jet Antbird has two broad white wing-bars and white tail-tipping. Females from most of Panama look like miniature Gray-headed Tanager but are duller and have much more arboreal habits; female Blue Dacnis is smaller, with bluish (not gray) head and slender bill. Chiriquí males resemble male Tawny-crested Tanager except for white on shoulders.

Status and distribution: Common in canopy and borders of second-growth woodland and forest in lowlands on Caribbean slope from northern Coclé eastward, and on Pacific slope from Canal area eastward, ranging up in smaller numbers into the foothills to about 750 m (2500 ft) (*panamensis*); rare to uncommon in lowlands of western Bocas del Toro (*axillaris*), with birds believed to be this race seen east to foothills of central Bocas del Toro along the oleoducto road north of Fortuna, Chiriquí, in July 1982 (Ridgely); rare in western Chiriquí (*nitidissimus*). There are no twentieth century reports of *nitidissimus* from Panama, and it may well now be extirpated due to the felling of most lowland forest in Chiriquí. Some form seems likely to occur in intervening area between Bocas del Toro and Coclé, but as yet unrecorded.

Habits: Forages at all levels, but especially at medium heights, and in many areas one of the characteristic members of the mixed foraging flocks of insectivorous birds.

Range: Honduras to northern Bolivia and central Brazil.

Note: It remains possible that *T. nitidissimus* will prove to be a species distinct (Chiriquí Tanager) from wide-ranging *T. luctuosus*, as it is quite divergent morphologically; on the other hand, *axillaris* does show some "intermediate" characters (though it is not intermediate in range).

TAWNY-CRESTED TANAGER
Tachyphonus delatrii   Plate 36

Description: 5½. Male *black* with *orange-tawny crest*. Female *dark olive brown above, brown below*. Immature like female; molting immature male sometimes shows tawny crown before becoming black.

Similar species: In its range not likely to be confused; female is darker brown than any other Panama tanager. Male White-shouldered Tanager from Chiriquí has both tawny crest and white shoulders.

Status and distribution: Fairly common to locally common in lower growth of humid forest and forest borders in lowlands and foothills on entire Caribbean slope; on Pacific slope recorded only from Veraguas foothills (a few seen above Santa Fé in January 1974; Ridgely and F. G. Stiles), eastern Panama province (road above El Lano toward Cartí, also a few in upper Bayano River valley), and Darién (surprisingly few records, seemingly not at all from

the Cana/Cerro Pirre area or elsewhere in the upper Tuira River valley, at least; may be found only along the Cerro Tacarcuna ridge). In Canal area most easily seen along Pipeline Road, though numbers are much greater in lower foothill areas such as around Nusagandi, western San Blas, where it is one of the more numerous birds.

Habits: Very active and conspicuous, usually foraging at low and middle levels, usually moving rapidly, not affording protracted views. Seen in good-sized groups of 6 to 12 individuals; generally they are the only species in the flock, but occasionally they are joined by others, particularly the Carmiol's Tanager. Very noisy, with a variety of sharp squeaky notes.

Range: Eastern Honduras to western Ecuador.

WHITE-LINED TANAGER
Tachyphonus rufus   Plate 36

Description: 6¾. Bill bluish. Male *black*, with white under wing-linings (usually visible only in flight). Female *rufous brown above, tawny below*.

Similar species: Male White-shouldered Tanager is also black but shows much more conspicuous area of white on shoulders when perched. Female somewhat resembles female Cinnamon Becard but has typical pointed tanager bill (becard's is stouter and slightly hooked), is larger, and forages at lower levels; it also lacks becard's buffy supraloral stripe. See also Shiny Cowbird.

Status and distribution: Uncommon to locally fairly common in clearings, shrubby areas, and around houses in lowlands on entire Caribbean slope; on Pacific slope less numerous and more local, with a few records from western Chiriquí (seen once at Puerto Armuelles by Wetmore, and a few other sightings from Boquete), and small numbers from western Panama province east through Darién.

Habits: As a rule seen in pairs, which facilitates identification. Usually forages rather low.

Range: Costa Rica south locally to northeastern Argentina and southern Brazil.

RED-CROWNED ANT-TANAGER
Habia rubica   Plate 35

Description: 7. Bill blackish. Male *mostly brownish red,* paler below and somewhat brighter on throat; *crown scarlet bordered by narrow black line.* Female olive brown above with *tawny yellow crown* bordered narrowly with black; yellowish olive below, the throat tawny yellowish.

Similar species: Closely resembles Red-throated Ant-Tanager and often confused with it. Male Red-crowns are duller red, more brownish, and usually lack male Red-throat's red throat; Red-throat's red crown is not as conspicuous nor is it bordered with black. Female Red-crowns are more olive above (not so brown), have a distinct tawny yellow crown (lacking in Red-throat), and lack Red-throat's prominent yellow throat. See also Olive and Hepatic Tanagers.

Status and distribution: Uncommon to locally fairly common in undergrowth of second-growth woodland and forest in lowlands and foothills on entire Pacific slope, though seemingly quite local in Darién, where found mainly in less humid areas; has been recorded in small numbers up to about 1200 m (4000 ft) in western Chiriquí; in Canal area also found locally on Caribbean slope (middle Chagres River valley in the Madden/Summit region). Decidedly scarce and local anywhere in Canal area, though small numbers occur along tracks leading off Chiva Chiva Road; somewhat more numerous in western Panama, but here numbers have doubtless declined substantially due to widespread deforestation.

Habits: Tends to forage somewhat higher above ground than Red-throated and not to travel in as large groups. The usual call is a rapid chatter of staccato notes, *chit chit chit* . . . , quite unlike Red-throat's harsh, tearing scolds.

Range: Central Mexico to Bolivia, northeastern Argentina, and southeastern Brazil.

RED-THROATED ANT-TANAGER
Habia fuscicauda   Plate 35

Description: 7½. Bill blackish. Male *mostly dull carmine,* with narrow red crown patch; grayer below, tinged with red, but *bright red on throat.* Female more or less brownish above and below with *contrasing ochre-yellow throat.* Nominate *fuscicauda* (western Bocas del Toro) differs from birds of rest of Panama range (*willisi*) in having male's throat less bright red, crown more orange-red, and even grayer underparts; female differs in having throat less contrastingly yellow.

Similar species: Easily confused with Red-crowned Ant-Tanager; in Canal area, the Red-throat is *much* the commoner of the two. Male Red-throat is somewhat redder above and lacks the narrow black line bordering the red crown; it has more prominent red throat. Female Red-throat is browner above

than Red-crown and lacks yellow crown patch; its yellow-ochre throat is its most distinguishing feature. Difference in vocalizations is also helpful. See also Olive and Hepatic Tanagers.

Status and distribution: Common in undergrowth of second-growth woodland and forest borders in lowlands on Caribbean slope in western Bocas del Toro and from northern Coclé to western San Blas (Mandinga), and on Pacific slope more locally from Veraguas (Soná) to eastern Panama province (middle Bayano River valley), but absent from drier areas from eastern side of Azuero Peninsula to western Panama province; ranges in smaller numbers up into lower foothills. Numerous and widespread on both slopes of Canal area.

Habits: Usually in small groups of four to eight individuals which scold at you in harsh nasal tones, *ahrr* (like paper being torn), from hidden perches in the underbrush; they sometimes appear briefly in the open, only to soon drop back out of sight. Males have a pretty song, usually of three clear notes, *do, cheh, wheet,* but not too often heard. Neither this species nor the Red-crowned Ant-Tanager seem to be regular followers of army ants in Panama, despite their English names.

Range: Eastern Mexico to northern Colombia.

HEPATIC TANAGER
Piranga flava   Plate 35

Description: 7¼. *Foothills. Blackish bill,* somewhat paler below, in both sexes. Male *mostly dark brick red,* somewhat paler and brighter below, and more orange-red on throat, mid-belly, and under tail-coverts. Female dusky-olive above, *rather bright olive yellow below,* greenest on breast and sides. Panama race (*testacea*) *lacks* the dusky auricular patch of United States/Mexico birds.

Similar species: Both sexes of Summer Tanager are quite similar, and during their sojourn in Panama they do *not* always show an obviously pale bill, though it is never as dark as it is in the Hepatic. At close range both sexes of Hepatic can be seen to have a notch in upper mandible (lacking in Summer) and *distinctly dusky lores;* male Summers are a paler, rosier hue than the dark carmine of male Hepatic. Female Hepatic also superficially resembles Olive Tanager, but behavior differs very markedly.

Status and distribution: Fairly common but quite local in borders of montane forest and second-growth woodland and in clearings with scattered trees in foothills on both slopes (but much more widespread on the Pacific), ranging mostly 600–1350 m (2000–4500 ft), but apparently also taken at or near sea level at "Cape Garachiné" in Darién. Often persists in substantial numbers in quite disturbed areas. Numerous on Cerro Campana, and in the Cerro Azul/Jefe area.

Habits: Generally found singly or in pairs, usually independent of mixed flocks, feeding rather high in trees, though in clearings occasionally coming lower. Its call is distinctive and often heard, a fast *chúp, che-teh* or *chup-chitup*. The burry song is a rapidly delivered series of phrases which goes up and down in pitch (Slud aptly calls it "jerky"), much more run together than song of Flame-colored Tanager.

Range: Southwestern United States south locally to northern Argentina and southern Brazil.

Note: More than one species may be involved. Panama birds (*testacea*) are part of the *lutea* group found mainly in Andes and highlands of northern and western South America (Highland Hepatic-Tanager), with the *flava* group being found in the lowlands of eastern and south-central South America (Lowland Hepatic-Tanager). Birds of the United States and northern Middle America, the *hepatica* group, seem close to the *lutea* group, but may deserve to be specifically separated as well (Northern Hepatic-Tanager). Morphological differences are quite pronounced in South America, and there appear to be vocal differences as well, but more study is needed.

SUMMER TANAGER
Piranga rubra   Plate 32

Description: 7. Bill usually *dusky-horn* in color, but somewhat variable (can be darker in presumed immatures). Adult male *mostly rosy red*, duskier on wings and tail. Female olive above with duskier wings and tail; *yellow below*. Immature male like female but tinged brownish red; some adult females are similarly tinged.

Similar species: Both sexes of Hepatic Tanager show darker bills and dusky lores (pale in Summer), but the two species are quite similar (especially females) and often can be distinguished only with care. Female resembles female Scarlet Tanager but is brighter yellow below and lacks obviously blackish wings.

Status and distribution: Common to very common transient and winter resident in shrubby areas, clearings with scattered trees, second-growth woodland, and forest borders throughout; most numerous in lowlands, particularly during northern winter months, but widespread as a transient; recorded early September–late April, with most birds leaving by the end of March.

Habits: Usually seen singly, foraging in the semiopen for insects, but small numbers may gather at a fruiting tree. Its distinctive call is often heard, a staccato *pitichuck* or *pituck*.

Range: Breeds from central United States to northern Mexico; winters mainly from Mexico to northern Bolivia and Amazonian Brazil.

SCARLET TANAGER
Piranga olivacea   Plate 32

Description: 6¾. Bill bluish gray in male, dull olive gray in female. Breeding plumage male unmistakable, but seen only on spring migration: *intense scarlet with jet black wings and tail*. Nonbreeding male olive green above, yellower on head, with *black wings and tail*; yellow below. Molting males may show splotches of scarlet; first-year males are duller, more orangey red and have more brownish black wings and tail. Female resembles nonbreeding male but is duller olive above, less yellow on head, duller yellow below, and with duskier wings and tail. Immatures may show pale wing-bars (usually faint).

Similar species: Female Summer Tanager has heavier paler bill, its wings are less dark, and its head and underparts are typically a warmer orange-yellow.

Status and distribution: Uncommon transient and rare winter resident in canopy and borders of forest and woodland in lowlands throughout (may also occur in highlands on migration, but as yet unrecorded); recorded mostly October–November and in April, with one report from early May and a few from northern winter months.

Habits: Much less apt to be seen in the open than the far more numerous Summer Tanager. May therefore often pass unnoticed, though its distinctive throaty *chip-burr* call is regularly uttered.

Range: Breeds in eastern North America; winters mainly in western Amazonia, a few north to Panama.

WESTERN TANAGER
Piranga ludoviciana

Description: 6½. Rare winter visitant to Chiriquí highlands. Stout pale bill. Male has *bright red face* which merges into *bright yellow of hindneck and underparts; back black*, rump yellow; wings and tail black, wings with two broad bars, upper one yellow and lower one white. Nonbreeding males may show little or no red on face and have black back mottled with olive. Female basically olive above, more yellowish on head and neck *contrasting with dusky olive back*; wings and tail dusky, *wings with two pale yellowish to whitish wing-bars*; usually yellow below, but some birds mostly grayish white below with yellow restricted to belly.

Similar species: Immature male Flame-colored Tanager is rather similarly colored to male Western but Flame-colored is larger and has proportionately longer tail with outer feathers tipped whitish (all black in Western); its back always looks distinctly streaked (never solid or mottled as in Western). Females of the two species differ in similar ways. Note that some immature Scarlet Tanagers also show wing-bars. See also female White-winged Tanager.

Status and distribution: Rare but apparently regular winter visitant in very small numbers to second-growth woodland and forest borders in lower highlands of western Chiriquí, where it has principally been found along the road to Santa Clara west of Volcán; recorded late November–late March.

Habits: Similar to Summer Tanager. Its often heard call is also similar, a dry *pi-tick* or *pit-i-tick*.

Range: Breeds in western North America; winters mostly from Mexico to Costa Rica, a few to western Panama.

FLAME-COLORED TANAGER
Piranga bidentata   Plate 35

Description: 7. Found only in western Chiriquí highlands. Bill whitish. Male *orange-red*, back duller *streaked with dusky*; wings dusky with two white wing-bars; tail dusky, *tipped white*. Female olive above, *back streaked with dusky;* dull yellowish below; wings and tail as in male. Young male resembles female but is brighter; immature male is often rather orange, and usually becomes colored first on head.

Similar species: White-winged Tanager is smaller, rosier red, and lacks back streaking and white tail-tips. See also the rare Western Tanager.

Status and distribution: Fairly common to common in forest borders, second-growth woodland, and clearings with scattered trees in highlands of western Chiriquí, with easternmost report being a family group of five seen on the Hornito ridge south of Fortuna on July 4, 1982 (Ridgely); recorded mostly 1200–2100 m (4000–7000 ft).

Habits: Most often in pairs, foraging at all levels, generally low only at edge or in clearings; often surprisingly unsuspicious. The song is a series of clipped, well-separated phrases with a burry or throaty quality similar to that of a Scarlet or Western Tanager (and much less run together than song of Hepatic Tanager). The call is a loud *prreck.*.

Range: Northern Mexico to western Panama.

WHITE-WINGED TANAGER
Piranga leucoptera   Plate 35

Description: 5½. Found only in western highlands. Bill dark. Male *bright rose red* with *black through eyes*; wings and tail black, *wings with two broad white wing-bars*. Female yellowish olive above with the same *broad white wing-bars; bright yellow below*. Immature male more orange than adult male.

Similar species: Both sexes can be distinguished from Flame-colored Tanager by their smaller size, unstreaked back, and tail without white tips; males are rosier red. See also Western Tanager.

Status and distribution: Uncommon to fairly common in canopy and borders of forest in highlands of Chiriquí and Veraguas (mostly 900–1800 m: 3000–6000 ft); recently reported also from near summit of Cerro Montuosa in Herrera (F. Delgado). Seems inexplicably absent from the Caribbean slope, and from eastern Panama.

Habits: Usually forages well up in trees, generally accompanying mixed foraging flocks of other tanagers, warblers, Furnariids, etc. The call is a distinctive *tsupeét* or *wheet, tsupeét*; it apparently has no real song.

Range: Eastern Mexico to western Panama; Colombia and Venezuela to northern Bolivia.

CRIMSON-COLLARED TANAGER
Phlogothraupis sanguinolenta   Plate 35

Description: 6½. Found mainly on western Caribbean slope. Unmistakable. Sexes similar. Bill pale bluish. Mostly black, with *blood red hindcrown, neck and chest* (forming the "collar"); small rump patch also red. Immature duller, the black duskier, the red more brownish.

Similar species: The distinctive pattern of the immature, though less clear than in adults, should preclude confusion.

Status and distribution: Uncommon and rather local in shrubby clearings, second-growth woodland, and borders of humid forest in lowlands of western Bocas del Toro, foothills on Pacific slope in Veraguas (above Santa Fé), foothills on Caribbean slope in Coclé (north of El Copé, where seen in June 1984 by P. Trail), and in lowlands on Caribbean slope north of Cerro Campana in western Panama province (where seen in March 1966 by N. G. Smith); probably more widespread in appropriate, most often hilly, terrain.

Habits: Usually seen singly or in pairs, remaining within 6 m (20 ft) of the ground; generally does not accompany mixed species flocks. Its song, often delivered from an exposed perch, is a leisurely series of rather penetrating, sibilant short phrases randomly interspersed with high-pitched "sissing" notes (Slud).

Range: Southeastern Mexico to central Panama.

Note: Placed in the genus *Ramphocelus* in the 1983 AOU Check-list. We prefer to maintain it in the monotypic *Phlogothraupis*, for it differs in behavior, is not sexually dimorphic in plumage, etc.

CRIMSON-BACKED TANAGER
Ramphocelus dimidiatus   Plate 35

Description: 6¾. *Most of lower mandible gleaming silvery white in male*, duller and grayer in female. Male has head, upper back, throat, and chest deep crimson maroon, becoming *blood red on lower back, rump, and lower underparts*; an inconspicuous area of black on mid-belly; wings and tail black. Female much duller, basically brownish red where the male is crimson maroon, almost blackish on throat and chest, but *retaining the bright red rump and lower underparts*.

Similar species: Males of both ant-tanagers are largely brownish red and somewhat resemble female Crimson-back, but lack the red on rump and belly.

Status and distribution: Common in gardens, scrub, shrubby areas, and clearings in lowlands on both slopes (more numerous on the Pacific) from northern Veraguas and Chiriquí (where decidedly uncommon in the west) eastward; ranges up in smaller numbers into suitable cleared habitat in the foothills, and very sparingly to 1620 m (5400 ft) in highlands of western Chiriquí; common also on Coiba Island (where one of the more numerous birds, ranging regularly through lower growth and even canopy of forest, as well as in more typical semiopen terrain), and on the Pearl Islands.

Habits: Conspicuous and noisy, often trooping about in groups of three to six individuals, usually with only one fully adult male per group. In Panama frequently called the "sangre de toro" (meaning blood of the bull).

Range: Western Panama to Colombia and western Venezuela.

SCARLET-RUMPED TANAGER
Ramphocelus passerinii   Plate 35

Description: 6¾. Found only in west. Male unmistakable, *velvety black* with *brilliant scarlet lower back and rump*; bill pale bluish with black tip. Chiriquí female (*costaricensis*) mostly brownish above, becoming yellowish olive on back and *orange on rump*; throat brownish, *chest orange, lower underparts yellowish olive*. Bocas del Toro female (nominate *passerinii*) duller, with rump dull yellow and chest usually yellowish olive like rest of lower underparts (occasionally with a trace of orange).

Similar species: Female resembles female Flame-rumped Tanager but is more olive below (Flame-rumped is entirely lemon yellow below), and has orange on rump.

Status and distribution: Common to very common in shrubby areas, woodland borders, clearings, and gardens in lowlands of western Bocas del Toro and western Chiriquí, ranging east in smaller numbers to central Bocas del Toro (Cricamola) and through Chiriquí to western Veraguas (a specimen taken by Wetmore near El Zapotillo on June 9, 1953; no recent reports); ranges in moderate numbers up into lower highlands of western Chiriquí in Volcán/Santa Clara area (to about 1350 m: 4500 ft). Particularly abundant around Puerto Armuelles, Chiriquí.

Habits: Much like Crimson-backed Tanager. Males often perch conspicuously in the open and puff out their vivid scarlet rumps. Males from Chiriquí have a variable but rather pretty song, while Bocas del Toro birds sing less often and less forcefully (A. Skutch).

Range: Southeastern Mexico to western Panama.

FLAME-RUMPED (YELLOW-RUMPED) TANAGER
Ramphocelus flammigerus   Plate 35

Description: 7. Male unmistakable, *velvety black* with *bright yellow lower back and rump*; bill pale bluish with black tip. Female grayish brown above with *yellow lower back and rump*; throat whitish, *remaining underparts lemon yellow.*
Similar species: See female Scarlet-rumped Tanager.
Status and distribution: Fairly common to very common (more numerous eastward) in shrubby areas, clearings, and gardens, most often near water, in lowlands on Caribbean slope from central Bocas del Toro (Cricamola) eastward; on Pacific slope recorded sparingly from foothills of Veraguas (above Santa Fé) and Coclé (above El Copé and at El Valle), and in lowlands from Canal area (where decidedly rare, perhaps only seasonal in the rainy season) eastward, becoming much more numerous in eastern Panama province (upper Bayano river valley) and Darién.
Habits: Found in pairs and small groups, usually near ground. Less often in gardens than Scarlet-rumped Tanager, at least in Panama.
Range: Western Panama to western Ecuador.
Note: What was formerly known as the Yellow-rumped Tanager (*R. icteronotus*) is now usually, e.g. by the 1983 AOU Check-list, considered to be conspecific with *R. flammigerus* of western Colombia; the two have been shown to hybridize extensively. This merger causes an unfortunate English name problem, for the rump color of *flammigerus* is flame scarlet; calling the enlarged species ''Flame-rumped'' seems the only, albeit inadequate, recourse. In light of the hybridization between *flammigerus* and *icteronotus* in western Colombia, further investigation of the reported overlap between *R. passerinii* and *R.f. icteronotus* in the Cricamola, Bocas del Toro, area would seem warranted; these two forms differ from each other in much the same way as do *flammigerus* and *icteronotus*, and they too may be found to hybridize.

ROSY THRUSH-TANAGER
Rhodinocichla rosea   Plate 36

Description: 7¾. Male slaty black above with rose red superciliary; *underparts mostly rose red*, flanks and lower belly slaty. Female similar but with *tawny replacing male's rose red*; superciliary white behind the eye, and some white on lower belly.

Status and distribution: Uncommon to fairly common in dense thickets and undergrowth in second-growth woodland and overgrown clearings in lowlands on Pacific slope from Chiriquí to eastern Panama province (lower Bayano River valley); on Caribbean slope known only from Coclé (El Uracillo), Canal area, and eastern Colon province; recorded sparingly up to about 1200 m (4000 ft) in partially cleared areas of western highlands. In Canal area most easily found in woodland along trails leading off Chiva Chiva Road.
Habits: Shy and hard to see in its dense tangled habitat. Mostly terrestrial (hence the group name), and apt to be found from the noise made by its scuffling in dry leaves, or while it is flicking leaves aside with its bill. Not only is this one of Panama's loveliest birds, it also has an excellent rich song, in quality reminiscent of a Black-bellied Wren's, a loud ringing *cho-oh, chowee* or *wheeo-cheehoh, chweeoo* being most frequent. These songs and calls are given persistently, and by both members of a pair; they regularly sing antiphonally, the only tanager known to do so.
Range: Western Mexico; Costa Rica to northern Colombia and northern Venezuela.

DUSKY-FACED TANAGER
Mitrospingus cassinii   Plate 36

Description: 6¾. *Prominent pale iris. Crown olive yellow*, remaining upperparts gray with *blackish mask from sides of head onto forehead and throat*; underparts otherwise olive yellow.
Similar species: Not likely to be confused; one's impression is of an almost comical bird, with its excitable disposition, blackish mask, and staring pale eye.
Status and distribution: Fairly common in dense lower growth at borders of humid forest and woodland in lowlands on entire Caribbean slope; on Pacific slope found locally in foothills of Veraguas (above Santa Fé), and in foothills and lowlands of eastern Panama province (Cerro Jefe area and in upper Bayano River valley) and Darién. Regularly seen along Achiote Road, and well out along Pipeline Road.
Habits: Prefers thickets along forested streams or at forested borders; there noisy groups of from 4 to 12 individuals can be found, usually independent of other species. Often difficult to see clearly as they gener-

ally remain in dense cover and move very rapidly, but at other times quite bold.
Range: Costa Rica to northwestern Ecuador.

COMMON BUSH-TANAGER
Chlorospingus ophthalmicus Plate 36

Description: 5½. Found only in western highlands, with three rather different appearing races. Proceeding from west to east, *regionalis* (western Chiriquí east only to the Volcán/Cerro Punta region) is mostly olive above with mainly *brown head* (crown rather strongly tinged grayish) and *conspicuous white spot behind eye;* throat whitish, somewhat inconspicuously dotted with brown; band across breast dull yellowish, becoming yellowish olive on sides and flanks; center of breast and belly white. *Novicius* (central Chiriquí from Boquete area east at least to Fortuna region, also in adjacent Bocas del Toro) is similar but has darker and browner head (lacking gray on crown), buffier throat with more prominent speckling, and more orange-tinged breast band. *Punctulatus* (Veraguas and Coclé, on both slopes; probably also in eastern Chiriquí) has *very dark blackish brown head,* buffy-orange throat with conspicuous black speckling, and *rather orange band across breast.*
Similar species: Regardless of the color of the head and the breast, and of the extent of speckling on the throat (all of which vary clinally), this species can always be easily known by its prominent white postocular spot. Tacarcuna and Pirre Bush-Tanagers both lack this (though they do have pale irides). Sooty-capped Bush-Tanager has long white *stripe* extending back from eye to sides of neck.
Status and distribution: Common to locally abundant in canopy and borders of humid forest and in shrubby clearings with scattered trees in foothills and highlands of Chririquí, Bocas del Toro, Veraguas, and Coclé; in western Chiriquí most numerous 4500–6500 ft, where it is one of the commonest birds; elsewhere it mostly ranges lower, being most numerous 900–1200 m (3000–4000 ft), lowest (down to about 600 m: 2000 ft) in Coclé.
Habits: Rather noisy and active, traveling in flocks, sometimes quite large, often joined by other species. Forages at all levels, but most frequently low. Often very unsuspicious. Frequently gives a loud piercing "toute suite" (as in French), sometimes followed by a jumble of twittery notes.

Range: Central Mexico to western Panama; Colombia and northern Venezuela to northwestern Argentina.

TACARCUNA BUSH-TANAGER
Chlorospingus tacarcunae Plate 36

Description: 5½. Found only in foothills and highlands of eastern Panama. *Iris whitish or pale orange-yellow.* Dark olive above, lacking white spot behind eye; *throat and chest dull yellow,* becoming greenish on sides and flanks and dull yellowish white on middle of breast and belly.
Similar species: Pirre Bush-Tanager, which also has a pale iris, differs in having a dark gray head (not olive, essentially concolor with rest of upperparts), and in being much yellower below; the two do not overlap. Yellow-throated Bush-Tanager is now known to occur sympatrically with the Tacarcuna (on Cerro Brewster in San Blas — and may be found to do so elsewhere as well); it differs in having a dark iris, bright yellow throat contrasting with buffyish breast, etc. See also Olive Tanager (notably larger, and with dark eye), and various female euphonias.
Status and distribution: Uncommon to locally common in canopy and borders of humid forest and elfin woodland in foothills and highlands of eastern Panama; rather local, and known only from Cerro Azul/Jefe in eastern Panama province, Cerro Brewster in western San Blas (where found in April 1985 by J. Blake), and eastern Darién (only on Cerro Tacarcuna); recorded 750–1500 m (2500–5000 ft).
Habits: Much like other bush-tanagers, usually in small groups, sometimes with other tanagers.
Range: Central Panama to extreme northwestern Colombia.

PIRRE BUSH-TANAGER
Chlorospingus inornatus Plate 36

Description: 5¾. Found only in highlands of eastern Darién. *Iris creamy white to pale orange-yellow.* Head dark gray; otherwise olive above; throat dull yellow, becoming deeper yellow on breast; sides and flanks greenish yellow, brighter yellow on middle of breast and belly.
Similar species: The only bush-tanager in its limited range. In any case, should be easily known by combination of its pale eye, lack of a white postocular spot, and predominantly yellow underparts.
Status and distribution: Common in canopy and borders of humid forest and elfin wood-

land in highlands of eastern Darién (Cerro Sapo, Cerro Pirre, and Alturas de Nique); recorded 780–1560 m (2600–5200 ft). Readily seen on slopes of Cerro Pirre above Cana, but you must go quite high (to 1200 m: 4000 ft or so) to be sure of finding it.

Habits: Similar to Common and Tacarcuna Bush-Tanagers (which see). Usually forage rather high above ground, gleaning from leaves and searching moss and other epiphytes.

Range: Eastern Panama (not yet known from adjacent Colombia).

SOOTY-CAPPED BUSH-TANAGER
Chlorospingus pileatus   Plate 36

Description: 5¼. Found only in western highlands. *Head sooty black* with *broad white stripe extending back from over eye to sides of neck*; otherwise olive above; throat buffy whitish faintly speckled with dusky, remaining underparts yellowish olive fading to whitish.

Similar species: Common Bush-Tanager has merely a white spot behind eye, not a long eye-stripe. Black-cheeked Warbler has chestnut crown and long white stripe beginning at bill, but it and this bush-tanager can look deceptively similar and often occur together.

Status and distribution: Fairly common in montane forest, forest borders, and clearings with scattered trees in highlands of Chiriquí; in western Chiriquí recorded mostly above 2100 m (7000 ft), occasionally down to about 1650 m (5500 ft), in eastern Chiriquí known from somewhat lower. Apparently not certainly recorded from Veraguas, nor from Bocas del Toro.

Habits: Forages actively at all levels but usually fairly low. Often a numerous member of mixed foraging flocks.

Range: Costa Rica and Pacific western Panama.

YELLOW-THROATED BUSH-TANAGER
Chlorospingus flavigularis   Plate 36

Description: 5½. Found locally in foothills. *Iris dark brown*. Entirely olive above; *throat ochraceous yellow, contrasting with drab buffy brownish breast*; sides and flanks grayish olive, middle of breast and belly whitish.

Similar species: Common Bush-Tanagers, of whatever race, always show a prominent white postocular spot. Tacarcuna Bush-Tanager has pale iris, lacks contrast between throat and breast, etc. See also Ashy-throated Bush-Tanager.

Status and distribution: Fairly common to common but very local in foothills on Caribbean slope (mostly 450–900 m: 1500–3000 ft) in Bocas del Toro (along trail up to Boquete, and along the oleoducto road north of Fortuna, Chiriquí), Veraguas (locally extending to Pacific slope above Santa Fé), Coclé (recently found to be regular on Caribbean slope above El Copé), and in western San Blas (where, in a major surprise, it was found by J. Blake in April 1985 on Cerro Brewster, photos to VIREO).

Habits: Similar to other bush-tanagers, usually seen in small groups, often with other tanagers, generally at middle and upper heights.

Range: Western and central Panama; Colombia to northern Bolivia.

Note: The form found in Panama, *hypophaeus*, is geographically disjunct from other races of this species, and stands apart in plumage as well (dark brown as opposed to pale amber or hazel iris, buff as opposed to gray breast, etc.). It may deserve full species status (Drab-breasted Bush-Tanager).

[ASHY-THROATED BUSH-TANAGER]
Chlorospingus canigularis   Plate 48

Description: 5½. One recent sight report from Bocas del Toro. Iris dark brown. *Head mostly gray*, but with crown rather strongly tinged olive; otherwise rather bright olive above; *throat pale grayish white*, set off by *bright greenish yellow band across chest*, extending down as yellowish olive on sides and flanks; middle of breast and belly whitish.

Similar species: Quite unlike any other Panama bush-tanager. Common Bush-Tanager always shows a white postocular spot. Yellow-throated Bush-Tanager has a contrasting yellow throat, lacks gray on head, etc.

Status and distribution: Known only from sightings along the oleoducto road in central Bocas del Toro north of Fortuna, Chiriquí; here about eight, including a pair feeding fledged young, were seen on July 3, 1982, with at least three more the next day (Ridgely); recorded 810–900 m (2700–3000 ft).

Habits: Similar to other bush-tanagers, but in general more arboreal than most, usually foraging well above the ground, actively inspecting foliage and mossy limbs for insects. Usually in pairs or small groups, often accompanying mixed flocks of other tanagers, etc.

Range: Costa Rica and western Panama; Colombia and extreme western Venezuela to northern Peru.

Note: The Costa Rican form *olivaceiceps* (to which Panama birds are presumed to belong, though specimen material could reveal they are subspecifically distinct) is geographically disjunct from South American forms of the species, and is different in plumage as well. It perhaps deserves full species status (Olive-crowned Bush-Tanager).

YELLOW-BACKED TANAGER
Hemithraupis flavicollis   Plate 36

Description: 5. Known only from eastern Darién. Male *mostly black above* with *lower back and rump rich orange-yellow;* a small white wing speculum; *throat and upper chest rich orange-yellow*; remaining underparts white, tinged gray on sides and with yellow under tail-coverts. Female yellowish olive above; wings and tail duskier, feathers edged yellowish olive; *sides of head, throat, and chest lemon yellow, becoming whitish on remaining underparts* except for yellow under tail-coverts.
Similar species: Male should be easily recognized, but female is quite like female Black-and-yellow Tanager except that in that species underparts are essentially uniform bright yellow (not whitish on belly).
Status and distribution: Uncommon in canopy and borders of humid forest and second-growth woodland in lowlands and foothills (to about 1000 m: 3300 ft) of eastern Darién (Cana and lower slopes of Cerro Pirre, Boca de Cupe, mouth of Río Paya, and Jaqué).
Habits: Usually found in pairs, often with mixed flocks of other insectivorous birds, usually foraging well above the ground.
Range: Eastern Panama locally to northern Bolivia and southeastern Brazil.

BLACK-AND-YELLOW TANAGER
Chrysothlypis chrysomelas   Plate 36

Description: 5. Mainly foothills on both slopes. Male *mostly bright yellow*, with *black eye-ring* (imparting a "big-eyed" look), *back, wings, and tail.* Ocularis (east of Canal area) has part of loral area black (all yellow in birds from rest of Panama range). Female yellowish olive above; wings and tail duskier, feathers edged with yellowish olive; *uniform bright yellow below* except tinged greenish on sides and flanks. Birds which are clearly referable to the recently described race *titanota* of Costa Rica have been seen recently (Ridgely) in the Fortuna area of

central Chiriquí and along the oleoducto road in adjacent Bocas del Toro (but females of this race have yet to be collected in Panama); they differ strikingly from females of nominate race (found elsewhere in the species' western Panama range) in being *mostly whitish below with yellow confined to a rather broad band across breast.*
Similar species: Stunning male is virtually unmistakable. Female can be more difficult, but as the species usually travels about in groups can usually be known by the company she keeps. Most resembles female Yellow-backed Tanager, though in area of overlap (only Darién) this species shows uniform yellow underparts (as opposed to Yellow-backed's yellow throat and chest, whitish breast and belly). See also female White-shouldered Tanager (which in most of its Panama range shows a contrasting gray head).
Status and distribution: Locally fairly common to common in canopy and borders of humid forest and second-growth woodland in foothills on both slopes, though in Chiriquí known only from the Fortuna area; recorded mostly 450–1200 m (1500–4000 ft). Usually readily found on both Cerro Campana and Cerro Jefe; especially numerous in the Nusagandi area of western San Blas, where one of the commonest tanagers.
Habits: A very active and spritely arboreal tanager, recalling a wood-warbler. Usually occurs in groups of its own species, which regularly associate with flocks of other tanagers, particularly Silver-throats and Bay-heads.
Range: Costa Rica to eastern Panama (not yet known from adjacent Colombia, but almost surely occurs as it has been found virtually on the border on both Cerro Tacarcuna and Cerro Quía, Darién).

SWALLOW TANAGER   Plate 30, p.408
Tersina viridis

Description: 5½–5¾. Known only from eastern Panama. Broad flat bill. Male *mostly turquoise* with *black mask and throat;* wings and tail black, broadly margined with blue; flanks barred with black, center of belly white. Female *mostly bright grass green* with grayish brown face and throat; wings and tail blackish, broadly margined with green; belly pale yellow with *conspicuous green barring on flanks.*

SWALLOW TANAGER (male)

Similar species: Not likely to be confused. Male might carelessly be mistaken for a male Blue Cotinga, female for a green tanager.

Status and distribution: Uncommon to locally (or seasonally?) fairly common in

lighter woodland and forest borders of eastern Darién (Cana, Tapalisa); evidently a few occasionally wander westward, whence there is one report of a flock of 11 seen in hills north of El Llano, eastern Panama province, on September 3, 1973 (N. G. Smith). While there is no definite evidence as yet of breeding in Panama, from the spread of dates available (spanning virtually the entire year), there seems little reason to believe that it does not do so here.

Habits: Swallow Tanagers are gregarious and conspicuous birds, usually occurring in flocks of its own species and often perching in the open. They eat both fruit and insects, the latter caught on the wing, often after a long pursuit. Its characteristic call is a loud sharp *tseet*. The nest is unusual for a tanager, being placed at the end of a burrow dug into a bank, or in a hole in a wall or similar structure.

Range: Eastern Panama to northern Bolivia, Paraguay, northeastern Argentina, and southeastern Brazil.

Note: Formerly placed in a monotypic family, the Tersinidae.

CARDINALS, GROSBEAKS, AND ALLIES:
Cardinalinae (13)

This group of species, formerly considered part of the Fringillidae family, is now treated as a subfamily within the expanded Emberizidae family. They are fairly large "finches", typically with quite stout bills, but otherwise rather variable in appearance. The resident Panama species are mainly birds of forest and woodland; a few others are northern migrants typically found in more open areas. All the resident species are quite accomplished vocalists; they eat mostly fruit and other vegetable matter.

STREAKED SALTATOR
Saltator albicollis   Plate 37

Description: 7½. Mainly olive above, somewhat grayer on head and tail, with short white superciliary and often a vague whitish eyering; whitish below, *broadly streaked with olive to dusky-olive* except on throat. Of the six described Panama races, *furax* of Chiriquí is the most strongly yellow-tinged below, *scotinus* of Coiba Island is generally the darkest and grayest, and *striatipectus* of Darién is the whitest below; *isthmicus* of most of its mainland Panama range is intermediate in most respects.

Similar species: Both other Panama saltators have throat patches margined with black and lack streaks below. See female Rose-breasted Grosbeak.

Status and distribution: Common in shrubby clearings, gardens, and lighter woodland in lowlands on Pacific slope from Chiriquí east to eastern Panama province (lower Bayano River valley), and locally in eastern Darién (where it appears to be scarce, with old records but no recent ones from Cana, and a few recent reports from lower Tuira River valley); ranges up in smaller numbers and in appropriate habitat in foothills and lower highlands, (in western Chiriquí regularly to about 1200 m (4000 ft), occasionally to 1800 m (6000 ft); on Caribbean slope known only from lowlands of Canal area east into western San Blas (Mandinga); common also on Coiba Island (where in addition to being found in typical habitats, it also ranges into lower growth of forest), Taboga Island, and the Pearl Islands.

Habits: Like Buff-throated Saltator, usually found singly or in pairs except at fruiting trees where small groups often gather. Its frequently heard song is a somewhat variable series of three or four sweet whistled notes, *tchew-tchew-tchew-tcheeér*, with distinctive slurred and prolonged final note.

Range: Southwestern Costa Rica to northern Venezuela and western Peru; Lesser Antilles.

BUFF-THROATED SALTATOR
Saltator maximus   Plate 37

Description: 8. *Head mostly dark gray* with some olive on crown and a short white superciliary; otherwise yellowish olive above; chin white, becoming *buff on lower throat*, both bordered by black malar area (in western Panama this also extending around and below the buff throat as a *broad black collar*); remaining underparts mainly gray, tinged buff especially on lower belly and under tail-coverts. *Magnoides* of Bocas del Toro has black area surrounding the buff throat most extensive, while in *intermedius* of western Pacific slope (east to Coclé) it is somewhat lesser in extent; *tungens* of San Blas and Darién has black restricted to a malar stripe, while birds from geographically intermediate area in central Panama (an unnamed population) are variable in the extent of this character. Juvenile has whitish superciliary obscure or lacking.

Similar species: Black-headed Saltator is distinguished by its notably larger size, more black on head, and white throat (though throats of some Buff-throats can look very pale). See also Streaked Saltator.

Status and distribution: Common in lighter woodland, forest borders, and shrubby clearings in lowlands on both slopes, ranging in smaller numbers up into foothills and (in western Chiriquí) in lower highlands, occasionally to 1800 m (6000 ft). Widespread on both slopes of Canal area, but in general a less familiar bird than the Streaked Saltator, ranging mainly in woodland and less often around houses.

Habits: Often found with the Streaked Saltator, but normally outnumbered or even replaced by it in drier areas (which the Buffthroat tends to avoid). Usually found singly or in pairs in lower growth, but also often sings and feeds quite high in trees. The song is a series of repeated sweet musical phrases, *cheéaweet, cheyoo,* or *cheeareet chweyoo,* sometimes suggestive of a *Turdus* thrush.

Range: Southeastern Mexico to northern Bolivia and southern Brazil.

BLACK-HEADED SALTATOR
Saltator atriceps   Plate 37

Description: 9¾. Considerably *larger than other Panama saltators. Crown and hindneck black,* superciliary whitish, sides of head dark gray; upperparts otherwise bright yellowish olive; *throat white,* bordered on sides and below with black; remaining underparts mostly gray with brownish sides and bright orange-tawny under tail-coverts.

Similar species: Buff-throated Saltator is smaller and has a buffy throat.

Status and distribution: Uncommon to locally fairly common in shrubby thickets in clearings and at forest and woodland borders in lowlands on Caribbean slope from Bocas del Toro east to western San Blas (Mandinga); on Pacific slope local and in very small numbers, with reports from Chiriquí (one specimen collected at Boquete in 1901), Coclé (El Valle, where it may be regular), Panama province (a few reports from Cerro Campana, and one 1972 sighting of a pair from middle Bayano River valley), and Darién (a surprising sighting of a pair at Cana from February 28 to March 5, 1981, by Ridgely and V. Emanuel *et al.*, but not found here since). In Canal area found mainly near Caribbean coast, most easily seen in the Achiote/Escobal area.

Habits: Noisy and quite conspicuous, often in small groups. The usual call is an arresting harsh smacking note, *tsaak,* much louder than other saltators; also has a cackling and squawking song.

Range: Central Mexico to eastern Panama.

SLATE-COLORED GROSBEAK
Pitylus grossus   Plate 37

Description: 8. *Heavy coral red bill. Mostly dark bluish gray;* center of throat white, with black foreface and broad margin around the throat patch. Female similar but paler and slightly more olivaceous gray below, and lacking black on face and around throat.

Status and distribution: Uncommon to fairly common in middle and upper levels of humid forest and mature second-growth woodland in lowlands and lower foothills (to about 900 m: 3000 ft) on entire Caribbean slope; on Pacific slope found locally in foothills from Veraguas (Santa Fé) eastward, and in lowlands from Canal area (where local) eastward. Widespread in forested areas on Caribbean side of Canal area.

Habits: Usually forages at middle and upper tree levels, dropping lower at forest borders. Seen singly or in pairs, sometimes joining mixed foraging flocks of various birds. Its fine song is a rather variable series of loud deliberate whistles, one version being *witcheeweeoo-cheéoo-cheer*, often questioning at the end. The frequently heard call is a sharp metallic *speek*, quite reminiscent of the call of the Northern Cardinal (*Cardinalis cardinalis*).

Range: Eastern Honduras to northern Bolivia and Amazonian Brazil.

BLACK-FACED GROSBEAK
Caryothraustes poliogaster   Plate 37

Description: 7. Found mainly on western Caribbean slope. *Facial area and throat black; crown and sides of head dark yellow*, shading into yellowish olive on remaining upperparts except for gray rump; breast yellow, *belly and under tail-coverts gray*.

Similar species: Should not be confused in western Panama; Yellow-green Grosbeak of Darién is similar but the two are not known to occur together. Streaked Saltator is also mostly olive but lacks the black and is streaked below. See also Prong-billed Barbet.

Status and distribution: Fairly common in middle and upper levels of humid forest and forest borders, sometimes coming out into adjacent clearings with large trees, in lowlands and foothills (to about 1050 m: 3500 ft) on Caribbean slope in Bocas del Toro, Veraguas (where it locally spills over into Pacific slope foothills), and Coclé (a few reports from Río Guabal and north of El Valle); there also are nineteenth-century specimens from Capira in western Panama province and from Caribbean side of what is now the Canal area, but no confirmed recent records from so far east. Numerous (at least seasonally) along the oleoducto road in Bocas del Toro north of Fortuna, Chiriquí, and in foothills above Santa Fé, Veraguas.

Habits: Usually found in noisy flocks of varying size, sometimes quite large. Often forages at high levels in trees, but also comes lower in clearings. Its distinctive call is a loud and arresting *dzzzt-weét*, often given as a contact note between members of a flock as they forage.

Range: Southeastern Mexico to western Panama.

YELLOW-GREEN GROSBEAK
Caryothraustes canadensis

Description: 6¾. Known only from eastern Darién. Resembles Black-faced Grosbeak (the ranges of the two are not known to approach each other), but somewhat smaller, and with *entire lower underparts yellow like breast* (no gray), and no gray on rump.

Status and distribution: Common in upper and middle levels of humid forest on slopes of Cerro Pirre above Cana in eastern Darién, where it has been found to range in a narrow zone between 750 and 1200 m (2500 and 4000 ft). These Darién birds (described as the race *simulans*) have an extraordinarily circumscribed range so far as known, and are amazingly isolated from the rest of the species' range (especially considering that they are so similar in appearance).

Habits: Similar to Black-faced Grosbeak, like that species usually in small groups, sometimes accompanied by other birds such as various tanagers, Sharpbills, etc. Above Cana this is one of the dominant and most conspicuous birds in the narrow elevational range it is found in. Their loud and distinctive calls often draw attention to them from considerable distances; these resemble Black-faced's, but often the *dzreet* call is followed by a *chew-chew-chew-chew* series, or the series is given alone.

Range: Eastern Panama; locally in eastern Amazonia, and in eastern Brazil.

Note: Sometimes called the Green Grosbeak (including by the 1983 AOU Check-list), though the normally used (e.g. Meyer de Schauensee 1966, 1970) name of Yellow-green Grosbeak is a better description of the bird's color.

BLACK-THIGHED GROSBEAK
Pheucticus tibialis   Plate 37

Description: 8½. Found only in western highlands. *Very heavy blackish bill. Male mostly rich yellow*, with *black back, wings, and tail*; sides of neck and breast sometimes mottled with blackish; small white speculum at base of primaries; lores and thighs black (latter hard to see in the field). Female similar but less bright yellow. Immature even duller and more olive on head.

Status and distribution: Uncommon in canopy and borders of forest and in adjacent shrubby clearings with scattered trees in foothills and highlands of Chiriquí, adjacent Bocas del Toro, Veraguas, and Coclé (only one report, a single bird seen above El Copé on March 8, 1986, by L. and D. Engleman, J. Guarnaccia, and Ridgely); in western Chiriquí mostly above 1800 m (6000 ft), but elsewhere much lower, usually 750–1200 m (2500–4000 ft). A few are quite regularly found along the Boquete Trail above Cerro Punta.

Habits: Usually seen singly, less often in pairs, perching stolidly at varying heights above the ground, allowing a close approach until flushed, when may fly a long distance. Usually not with mixed flocks. Its *pink* call note closely resembles that of Rose-breasted Grosbeak, but its musical phrased song, while of good quality, seems weaker, jerkier, and less rich than that of the Rose-breasted.

Range: Costa Rica and western Panama.

Note: Sometimes considered conspecific with *P. chrysopeplus* (Mexican Yellow-Grosbeak, or simply Yellow Grosbeak) of Mexico, some also including *P. chrysogaster* (Southern Yellow-Grosbeak, or Golden-bellied Grosbeak) of South America. We follow the 1983 AOU Check-list in considering all three as allospecies.

ROSE-BREASTED GROSBEAK
Pheucticus ludovicianus   Plate 32

Description: 7¼. Large whitish bill. Breeding plumage male (seen in Panama from February–March onward) unmistakable: *head, upperparts, and throat black*, with *rosy red patch on breast*; rump, lower underparts, and large patches in wing white; under wing-coverts pale rosy red. Nonbreeding male has buff superciliary, coronal stripe, and mottling on upperparts; below whitish, tinged buff on throat and breast with some blackish speckling, and only a *hint of the rose* (but some always present). Female resembles nonbreeding male but is browner above with *whitish superciliary and coronal stripe*, and *brown cheeks*; below whitish, *lightly streaked brown*, never showing any pink; under wing-coverts yellow.

Similar species: Females and nonbreeding males can be known by their chunky grosbeak-shape, heavy bill, the head striping, and the streaking below. See Streaked Saltator.

Status and distribution: Fairly common transient and uncommon winter resident in forest borders, second-growth woodland, and clearings with scattered trees virtually throughout, recorded up to 1500–1800 m (5000–6000 ft) in the western Chiriquí highlands (mostly October–early April, a few as early as late September or lingering to late April); also recorded on Pearl Islands.

Habits: Often in small groups, especially when migrating. Usually forages rather high in trees. Its call, a distinctive, metallic *pink*, is frequently given.

Range: Breeds in eastern and central North America; winters from Mexico to Colombia and Venezuela, rarely to Peru and Guyana.

BLUE-BLACK GROSBEAK
Cyanocompsa cyanoides   Plate 38

Description: 6¼. Very stout black bill. Male *mainly blackish blue*, brightest and palest on superciliary and malar area. *Toddi* (western Panama in Bocas del Toro, and east on Pacific slope to western side of Azuero Peninsula) darker overall than nominate race (of rest of Panama range). Female *uniform deep chocolate brown*, slightly paler below.

Similar species: Both sexes of scarce Blue Grosbeak have prominent tan wing-bars; it favors semiopen scrub, not the forest undergrowth of Blue-black. Indigo Bunting is much smaller with less stout bill; see also female Lesser Seed-Finch.

Status and distribution: Common in undergrowth of humid forest, second-growth woodland, and borders in lowlands on entire Caribbean slope; on Pacific slope found locally from Chiriquí (where due to deforestation may now only occur on Burica Peninsula) to western side of Azuero Peninsula, and from western Panama province east through Darién; ranges in smaller numbers up into foothills and lower highlands (to about 1200 m: 4000 ft) in Chiriquí and Darién. Widespread on both slopes of Canal area.

Habits: A shy and retiring forest grosbeak, much more often heard than seen. Usually in pairs, which generally forage independently of mixed flocks. Its frequently heard call is a loud sharp *chink*, given by both sexes; the song is a series of rich clear notes, at first slow, hesitant, and rising, then falling off and more jumbled.

Range: Southeastern Mexico to Bolivia and Amazonian Brazil.

BLUE GROSBEAK
Guiraca caerulea   Plate 32

Description: 6¾. Rather rare. Stout dusky bill. Male *mostly deep blue* with black lores and around base of bill; wings and tail dusky, with *two prominent tan wing-bars*. In poor light can look quite black. Female brown above, often washed bluish gray on rump; wings and tail dusky, with *two prominent tan to buff wing-bars;*

buffy brown to olive brown below. Immature male like female but often a richer brown; older immatures show splotches of blue and brown.

Similar species: Both sexes of the much more numerous and widespread Blue-black Grosbeak lack the tan or buffy wing-bars prominent in this species. Indigo Bunting is smaller and slenderer, with less stout bill, also lacks the wing-bars.

Status and distribution: Rare winter resident (early October–late March) in open scrubby areas and shrubby clearings with scattered bushes and trees in lowlands on both slopes in western and central Panama; not recorded east of the Canal area.

Habits: Favors dense growth, usually near the ground, but sometimes takes prominent perches on top of bushes or on wires or fences along roads. Sometimes in small loose groups. Often twitches its tail to one side. The call is a distinctive sharp metallic *chink*.

Range: Southern United States to northern Costa Rica; winters from Mexico to central Panama, accidental south to Colombia and Ecuador.

INDIGO BUNTING
Passerina cyanea   Plate 32

Description: 5. Small, conical bill. Breeding plumage male *entirely deep rich blue.* In nonbreeding plumage, male mostly brown (like female) but usually with a few patches of blue, becoming bluer as the season progresses. Female and immatures are olive brown above, buffy whitish below with some *indistinct brownish streaks on breast.*

Similar species: Blue and Blue-black Grosbeaks are both larger with much heavier bills; the former also has conspicuous buffy wing-bars (female Indigos do sometimes show a trace of these); the latter is a forest bird with which the Indigo does not normally occur. More likely to be confused with the smaller Blue-black Grassquit, which has somewhat slenderer bill and males of which are blacker, females more distinctly streaked below (Indigo's streaks are blurrier). See also Blue Seedeater.

Status and distribution: Uncommon to locally common winter resident in shrubby clearings and semiopen areas in lowlands on both slopes in western and central Panama (mostly October–April, a few to mid-May); much more numerous in western Panama (especially in Bocas del Toro), distinctly uncommon in Canal area; only known reports from eastern Panama are individuals

mist-netted at Majé, in Bayano River valley of eastern Panama province, on January 26, 1973, and April 22, 1976.

Habits: Often in small flocks which feed on the ground in grassy areas, retreating to dense cover when disturbed. Quiet and inconspicuous in Panama, probably often overlooked.

Range: Breeds in eastern and central North America; winters in Florida, West Indies, and from Mexico to Panama, rarely in Colombia and Venezuela.

PAINTED BUNTING
Passerina ciris

Description: 5. Small conical bill. Gaudy male unmistakable: *head purplish blue, back bright green*, wings and tail dusky, rump red; *bright red below.* Female and immature male plain dull green above, pale olive yellowish below, becoming yellower on lower belly.

Similar species: Female is simply an all-greenish finch, devoid of any markings. Female Yellow-faced Grassquit is most like it, but it is duller (more olive) and has yellowish facial markings.

Status and distribution: Rare to uncommon winter resident in overgrown fields, shrubby areas, and woodland borders in lowlands on both slopes in western Panama (recorded principally from coastal western Bocas del Toro), with a few reports eastward on Pacific slope to southern Coclé (a male mist-netted at Aguadulce on February 12, 1971; R. Cooke) and western Panama province (seen twice at Playa Coronado by Eisenmann; two on November 25, 1962, and one on March 25, 1967); recorded late October–late April.

Habits: Similar to Indigo Bunting, but usually even shyer and more difficult to observe; even more than that species, doubtless often overlooked.

Range: Breeds in southeastern United States and northern Mexico; winters in Florida, Greater Antilles, and from Mexico to Panama.

DICKCISSEL
Spiza americana   Plate 32

Description: 6. Breeding plumage male has pale gray head with *yellow superciliary* and malar streak; above otherwise brown with dusky streaking on back and *usually prominent rusty shoulders*; upper throat white, with *V-shaped black bib on lower throat and chest; breast yellow*, fading to whitish on belly. Nonbreeding male duller, with yellow less extensive and not as bright; its bib is obscure or lacking. Female like nonbreeding male, but with less rusty on shoulders and no bib; still has *band of yellow across chest*. Immature like female but more nondescript, and usually with fine dusky streaking on breast; usually shows some yellow on breast and face and rufous on the shoulders.

Similar species: Males are distinctive, but duller immatures and females can resemble female House Sparrow; latter never shows any yellow on breast or rufous on wing, never shows streaking below, and lacks Dickcissel's bluish gray bill. See also female Bobolink, and Grassland Yellow-Finch.

Status and distribution: Fairly common to locally common transient and less numerous and very erratic winter resident in open country on Pacific slope (late August–May, but mostly September and April); on Caribbean slope, occurs only as an erratic transient in much smaller numbers.

Habits: Often occurs in very large compact flocks, sometimes of a thousand birds or more. Calls constantly, a distinctive low raspy *ddrrt* and assorted twitters; a large flock will generate considerable noise.

Range: Breeds in central United States; winters mostly in northern South America, erratically in Panama, and in much smaller numbers northward in Middle America and in eastern United States.

Note: The affinities of this monotypic genus remain uncertain. Some believe it to be an icterid; we follow the 1983 AOU Check-list in considering it to be a Cardinaline.

EMBERIZINE FINCHES: Emberizinae (32)

These are the typical American finches and sparrows, considered a subfamily of the expanded Emberizidae family in the 1983 AOU Check-list. As with its other subfamilies (Parulinae, Coerebinae, Thraupinae, Cardinalinae, and Icterinae), this group is here treated separately, for clarity's sake. Note that the Yellow-bellied Siskin and Lesser Goldfinch remain in the family Fringillidae, in which the Emberizinae and Cardinalinae subfamilies were formerly placed. Most Panama members of the Emberizinae have stout more or less conical bills (notable exceptions being the Slaty and Peg-billed Finches, and the Slaty Flowerpiercer); otherwise they exhibit considerable variation in size, shape, and habits. In many species vocalizations are well developed, and some are often kept as cagebirds, frequently as much for their attractive plumage as for their pleasant songs. Most finches eat primarily seeds, but many also consume some insects, and feed them to their young. The nests of most Panama species, so far as known, are open cups placed on the ground, attached to grass stems, or set in a bush or tree. However, the Yellow-faced Grassquit and Black-striped and Orange-billed Sparrows build domed nests with side entrances, while the Saffron Finch nests in cavities or under the eaves of buildings.

SOOTY-FACED FINCH

Lysurus crassirostris   Plate 37

Description: 6. Found only in humid foothills and highlands, mostly on Caribbean slope. *Mostly dark olive green; crown chestnut;* sides of head and throat blackish, with *conspicuous white malar streak;* center of breast and belly bright yellow. *Eurous* (of Darién) has darker crown, slightly paler sides of head and throat, and less extensive yellow below.

Similar species: Chestnut-capped Brush-Finch has white throat with prominent black band across chest. See also Large-footed Finch.

Status and distribution: Uncommon and rather local (but to some extent just overlooked) in undergrowth of humid forest and forest borders in foothills and lower highlands on Caribbean slope in Bocas del Toro, Veraguas (where occurs on both slopes), and Coclé (one nineteenth-century specimen from Río Cascajal); in Chiriquí very local, and largely if not entirely absent from all but very humid areas, with records from Cerro Pando (N. G. Smith), old records from Boquete and "Volcán de Chiriquí" (but none recently), and the Fortuna area in upper Río Chiriquí valley (where fairly common; Ridgely *et al.*); also known from a single specimen from eastern Darién (Cerro Tacarcuna); recorded mostly 600–1200 m (2000–4000 ft) (but old records supposedly from much higher on Volcán Barú).

Habits: Usually found in pairs or small groups on or near the ground in dense tangled undergrowth of ravines and near streams; often not easy to see, though sometimes decoys well to squeaking. The characteristic call is a sharp thin whistled *pu-peee*, generally uttered when hidden in dense undergrowth.

Range: Costa Rica to eastern Panama.

YELLOW-THIGHED FINCH
Pselliophorus tibialis　　　　　Plate 37

Description: 7. Found only in western Chiriquí highlands. *Entirely dark slaty*, blacker on head, throat, wings and tail, sometimes tinged olive on breast; *conspicuous thigh tufts bright yellow.* Immature lacks the yellow thighs.
Similar species: The yellow thighs are readily seen and make this species very easy to recognize. Immatures can be known by their uniform dark slaty plumage; they are usually found with adults.
Status and distribution: Common in forest undergrowth and borders and clearings in highlands of western Chiriquí, mostly above 1500 m (5000 ft).
Habits: Very active and noisy, usually in pairs or small family groups, often joining mixed flocks of other birds. Forages mostly at lower levels. Its song is a fast, very jumbled, almost sputtery series of musical notes, sometimes given by two birds at once.
Range: Costa Rica and western Panama.

YELLOW-GREEN FINCH
Pselliophorus luteoviridis　　　　Plate 37

Description: 7. Known only from highlands of eastern Chiriquí and Veraguas. *Head and throat black*, back dark olive, wings and tail also black; *lower underparts yellowish green*, darkest on flanks; *conspicuous thigh tufts yellow.*
Similar species: The much better known Yellow-thighed Finch of western Chiriquí is essentially gray and black, being slaty where this species is olive and yellowish green. More likely confused with Sooty-faced Finch (and these two could occur together), but that species shows conspicuous white malar streak, chestnut crown, and more yellow on underparts.
Status and distribution: Recorded from highlands of eastern Chiriquí (Cerro Flores area) and Veraguas (Santa Fé and Chitra); recorded 1200–1800 m (4000–6000 ft). Has been seen recently above Cerro Colorado (D. Engleman).
Habits: Poorly known, but apparently much like Yellow-thighed Finch.
Range: West-central Panama.
Note: The possibility of intergradation with

Yellow-thighed Finch in central Chiriquí remains to be investigated.

LARGE-FOOTED FINCH
Pezopetes capitalis　　　　　　Plate 37

Description: 8. Found only on higher mountains of western Chiriquí and Bocas del Toro. *Crown, stripe extending back on either side of nape, and throat black, becoming dark gray on rest of head;* otherwise dark olive above and somewhat paler yellowish green below, darker and more olive on flanks.
Similar species: A notably large finch that appears very dark in the field. Like a brush-finch in shape and habits. See also Sooty-faced Finch.
Status and distribution: Fairly common in undergrowth of clearings and forest borders in higher mountains of western Chiriquí and adjacent Bocas del Toro, mostly above 2100 m (7000 ft), locally down to 1500 m (5000 ft). Small numbers can regularly be found along the upper part of the Boquete Trail above Cerro Punta and along the tele-communications tower road above Boquete.
Habits: Usually seen on the ground, sometimes in the open (especially on recently ploughed fields) but never far from cover. Scratches with both feet at once, like a towhee (Pipilo spp.); also hops with both feet at once, giving it a peculiar bouncing gait. Generally found singly or in pairs. The song is a series of phrases with scratchy musical quality somewhat reminiscent of Orange-billed Night-ingale-Thrush, e.g. *tít-wol-dit, tdleédle-dit, tuawol-dee, teseé-dit . . .*, the sequence often varying (B. Whitney), then occasionally bursts into a series of jumbled and louder, clear ringing notes, or sometimes a loud, descending melodic series, *cleeu-cleeu-cleeu-cleeu-cleeu-cleeu*, usually ending with a *chichichichichi*. The effect is startling and delightful!
Range: Costa Rica and western Panama.

YELLOW-THROATED BRUSH-FINCH
Atlapetes gutturalis　　　　　　Plate 37

Description: 7. Found only in western highlands. *Head black* with narrow white central stripe on crown; upperparts otherwise blackish olive (browner in *azuerensis* of Azuero Peninsula); *throat bright yellow*, remaining underparts white, shaded with olive on flanks.

Similar species: Prominent yellow throat and basically black and white plumage make identification of this common species easy.

Status and distribution: Common to very common in shrubby clearings and forest borders in highlands on Pacific slope in Chiriquí, Veraguas, western side of Azuero Peninsula (south to Cerro Hoya), and western Coclé (one nineteenth-century specimen from Río Cascajal); in western Chiriquí recorded mostly above 1200 m: 4000 ft, but lower down to 750–900 m: 2500–3000 ft) elsewhere in its Panama range.

Habits: Active and conspicuous birds, usually found in pairs or small family groups. Forages on or near the ground like other brush-finches, but much less of a skulker.

Range: Southern Mexico to western Panama; Colombia.

BLACK-HEADED BRUSH-FINCH (spp. *costaricens*)

be almost inaudible except at close range.

Range: Central Mexico to southern Peru.

CHESTNUT-CAPPED BRUSH-FINCH
Atlapetes brunneinucha Plate 37

Description: 7½. Found only in foothills and highlands. *Crown mostly chestnut*, with forehead and sides of head black, forehead with three inconspicuous white vertical stripes; above otherwise dark olive; *throat white*, bordered below by *narrow black chest band;* remaining underparts whitish, sides and flanks olive grayish. Birds from western Panama (*elsae*) have gray on sides and flanks much more extensive than in birds from Darién (*frontalis*).

Similar species: A handsome bird, easily recognized by the chestnut crown and black chest band. Sooty-faced Finch also has a chestnut crown, but has breast and belly yellow, black throat.

Status and distribution: Fairly common in forest undergrowth in foothills and highlands on both slopes, usually above 900 m (3000 ft); recorded from Chiriquí, Bocas del Toro, Veraguas, Coclé (above El Copé and El Valle), western Panama province (Cerro Campana), and eastern Darién (Cerro Tacarcuna, Cerro Pirre, Cerro Quía).

Habits: Though often fairly numerous (as attested to by mist-netting), this shy and inconspicuous species is not seen very frequently. Usually found on the ground, singly or in pairs, inside forest. Flicks leaves aside with its bill, not scratching with its feet. Often best located through its distinctive, very high-pitched vocalizations; the song consists of several thin squeaky notes, e.g. *sweéa-see-seeeé, sweea-seeéa* (B. Whitney), the call a simple *pseet* or *seet*, so high-pitched as to

BLACK-HEADED BRUSH-FINCH
Atlapetes atricapillus Plate 37, p.415

Description: 7½. Local in foothills and highlands. Rather variable. Proceeding from west to east, *costaricensis* (found in Panama only in Chiriquí) has head mostly black with broad gray median crown stripe and superciliary; otherwise olive above, with yellow on bend of wing; *below mostly white*, with gray on sides and olive on flanks. *Tacarcunae* (recorded from Cerro Azul/Jefe, Cerro Brewster in San Blas, and Cerro Tacarcuna in Darién) similar but with *narrower gray median crown stripe and superciliary* (sometimes quite obscure), while in nominate *atricapillus* (found in Panama only on Cerro Pirre in Darién) the *head is virtually black* (with at most a trace of the gray).

Similar species: Black-striped Sparrow is somewhat similar, especially to Chiriquí birds, but is considerably smaller with merely a narrow cheek *stripe* (cheeks not entirely black).

Status and distribution: Rare to uncommon in thickets and forest borders in foothills and lower highlands of western and central Chiriquí (east to the Hornito ridge along road to Fortuna; recorded 300–1200 m: 1000–4000 ft); uncommon to fairly common in dense undergrowth of elfin cloud forest and forest borders in foothills of eastern Panama province (Cerro Azul/Jefe) and western San Blas (where found on Cerro Brewster in late April 1985 by J. Blake, photos to VIREO), recorded 750–990 m (2500–3300 ft); and uncommon in foothills and lower highlands of eastern Darién (Cerro Tacarcuna, and around Cana and on lower slopes of Cerro Pirre).

Habits: Rather skulking and difficult to view in its thick tangled habitat, but can sometimes be lured into the open by squeaking. The song of *costaricensis* is weak and high-pitched (in quality reminiscent of an Orange-billed Sparrow), consisting of sputtery phrases repeated over and over, e.g. *tsu-tsee, ts-ts-ts-ts-tseét? tsu-tsee, ts-ts-ts-ts-tsú . . .* and so on.

Range: Southwestern Costa Rica to western Colombia.

Note: We follow the 1983 AOU Check-list in considering *A. atricapillus* as a species distinct from *A. torquatus* (Stripe-capped Brush-Finch) of South America. It has been suggested, however, that *costaricensis* be placed with *A. torquatus* (which in plumage it quite closely resembles), or that all forms be considered conspecific (as *A. torquatus*, Striped Brush-Finch), this despite the fact that in Colombia *A. atricapillus* and several races of *A. torquatus* occur in virtual sympatry (*atricapillus* at lower elevations) with no indication of intergradation.

ORANGE-BILLED SPARROW
Arremon aurantiirostris   Plate 37

Description: 6. *Bill bright orange. Head mostly black* with narrow gray stripe down median crown and *white superciliary*; some gray on nape, otherwise olive above with bend of wing yellow to orange-yellow; mostly white below with *broad black chest band*, flanks broadly gray.

Similar species: Unusually boldly patterned for a species of the forest interior; the orange bill should at once make the bird known. Both Black-headed Brush-Finch and Black-striped Sparrow have black bills and lack black chest band.

Status and distribution: Fairly common but unobtrusive in undergrowth of forest and second-growth woodland in more humid lowlands on both slopes, ranging up in smaller numbers into foothills to about 1200 m (4000 ft); now very local on Pacific western slope due to deforestation in that area.

Habits: Usually in pairs, hopping and scratching on the ground (rarely at any height above it), generally independent of mixed flocks. Its song is very high and sibilant, a short fast series of notes that to some is reminiscent in pattern to that of the Brown Creeper (*Certhia americana*); also has a very high thin *tsip* call note.

Range: Southeastern Mexico to northern Peru.

BLACK-STRIPED SPARROW
Arremonops conirostris   Plate 37

Description: 7. *Head gray with black stripe on either side of crown and black line through eye onto cheeks*; otherwise olive above, with bend of wing yellow; below pale gray, whitest on throat and center of belly. *Viridicatus* (Coiba Island) is darker generally, especially grayer below, than birds from mainland Panama (*striaticeps*).

Similar species: Though not brightly colored, this neat dapper bird can be easily recognized by its black-striped gray head with contrasting olive back. Somewhat resembles Black-headed Brush-Finch (especially Chiriquí race), but is smaller and has much less black on head.

Status and distribution: Common in shrubby clearings, woodland borders, and thickets in lowlands on both slopes, ranging up in smaller numbers into the foothills, to about 1650 m (5500 ft) in the highlands of western Chiriquí; found also on Coiba Island.

Habits: Usually seen singly or in pairs, on or near the ground; generally rather shy, not venturing far into the open. The male's song is easily recognized and often heard, a series of accelerating notes, *cho; cho; cho, cho, cho, cho-cho-cho-ch-chchch*, with rhythm of ball bouncing to a halt. Also has a sharply accented whistle, *ho, wheét*, vaguely suggestive of a bobwhite, and several other less distinctive calls. Heard more often than seen.

Range: Honduras to Venezuela, extreme northern Brazil, and western Ecuador.

BLUE-BLACK GRASSQUIT
Volatinia jacarina   Plate 38

Description: 4–4¼. *Bill rather slender and pointed.* Male *uniform glossy blue-black*; axillars (and sometimes entire wing-lining) white, often visible in flight. Female dull brown to brownish olive above; whitish to pale buff below, with *breast and flanks streaked dusky*. Immature male resembles female but more blackish above; subadults are mottled blackish and brown (and at times are frequently seen).

Similar species: Seedeaters have stouter bills, and no Panama seedeater is streaked below. Indigo Bunting is larger, male is much brighter blue, female more uniform buffy brown with less streaking below. See also female of rare Slaty Finch.

Status and distribution: Very common to abundant in grassy areas, clearings and gardens, and all types of semiopen and agricultural terrain in lowlands on both slopes, but particularly numerous and widespread on the Pacific; ranges in smaller numbers up into the foothills, and sparingly to over 1500 m (5000 ft) in lower highlands of western Chiriquí; common also on Coiba Island and the Pearl Islands. Much less numerous in mainly forested areas, but does seem to colonize newly cleared areas quite rapidly, and quickly becomes numerous if the extent of suitable terrain permits.

Habits: One of the most frequently observed birds in open areas in the lowlands. Males often perch on top of a bush or grass stem and repeatedly come out with an explosive buzzy *dzee-ew*, at the same time jumping a foot or so into the air (sometimes almost seeming to somersault), then dropping back to its original perch. They sometimes call without jumping. Unlike the Yellow-faced Grassquit, this species builds a small shallow cup nest.

Range: Mexico to northern Chile and central Argentina.

SLATE-COLORED SEEDEATER
Sporophila schistacea   Plate 38

Description: 4¼. *Bill rich yellow* (male), or graylsh (female). *Mostly slaty gray*, usually with *small whitish patch on sides of neck* (sometimes hard to see, or even lacking in younger males); wings and tail blackish, wings with white speculum and usually showing a *single upper wing-bar*; median breast and belly white. Female olive brown above, paler buffy brown below, more creamy whitish on mid-belly.

Similar species: Male is only Panama seedeater with a yellow bill, and should be easily recognized by this and its predominantly gray plumage. Female much more difficult, and perhaps not safely distinguished from other female seedeaters (but can usually be known by the company she keeps).

Status and distribution: Rare and local in second-growth woodland and forest borders in more humid lowlands on both slopes, ranging locally up into foothills to about 900 m (3000 ft); best known from both slopes of Canal area (though here as elsewhere decidedly rare and erratic), but has also been recorded from Bocas del Toro (Almirante), Chiriquí (Bugaba and Fortuna), San Blas (Puerto Obaldía), and Darién (Cana and Pucro).

Habits: Usually found singly or in pairs, rarely or never associating with other seedeaters. Often quite arboreal, more so than other

Panama seedeaters (though be aware that Variables do sometimes feed quite high in trees). Its song is very different from that of other Panama seedeaters, being a high, fast, sibilant, and unmusical *zit-zit-zee-zee-zee-ze-ze-z-z-z-z*, with variations.

Range: Southern Mexico; northern Honduras; Costa Rica south locally to western Ecuador, northern Bolivia, and northern Brazil.

VARIABLE SEEDEATER
Sporophila americana   Plate 38, p.418

Description: 4½. *Easily the most numerous and widespread seedeater in Panama*; males quite variable in plumage, but usually *basically black and white*. In most of Panama (*hicksii*) mainly glossy black above with white wing speculum and usually a white rump (latter often intermixed with gray); throat white, *extending up on sides of neck to form a partial collar* (often shows some black on upper throat); *broad breast band black*, lower underparts white, with often extensive gray and black mottling on sides. Birds from Chiriquí and Coiba Island (*hoffmanni*) similar but with throat usually black (retaining white partial nuchal collar). Much more different are birds from western Caribbean slope east at least to Veraguas (*corvina*) which are *all black* except for the white wing speculum; intergrades between this and *hicksii*-type birds occur east to Caribbean side of Canal area (where a few birds still look essentially black except for some white on belly or sometimes collar). Female olive brown above, paler buffy brown below, becoming somewhat more yellowish buff on belly.

Similar species: See White-collared Seedeater (only in western Panama) and Lesson's Seedeater (a casual wanderer to Darién); note too that all-black *corvina*-type male Variables closely resemble male Lesser Seed-Finch aside from latter's much heavier, squared-off bill. Female very like female Yellow-bellied Seedeater, but tends to be yellower below.

Status and distribution: Very common to abundant in semiopen and agricultural country, gardens and shrubby clearings, and woodland and forest borders in lowlands on both slopes, ranging up in smaller numbers in suitable habitat into foothills and in lower highlands of western Chiriquí; found also on Coiba Island.

Habits: One of Panama's more familiar and frequently seen birds. Usually found in small flocks, birds in female plumage (many

Left to right (all males): NICARAGUAN SEED-FINCH, WHITE-COLLARED SEEDEATER, VARIABLE SEEDEATER (spp. *corvina*)

doubtless immatures) predominating, feeding in grassy areas, clinging to stems. Often associates with Blue-black Grassquits, less frequently with Yellow-bellied Seed-eaters. Birds also sometimes feed quite high in trees, usually on flowers or buds. Male's song is a sweet and fast musical twittering, usually delivered from an exposed perch (most often not very high); both sexes also frequently give a characteristic sweet *cheeeu* or *sweeeu* call. *Corvina*'s song is squeakier and less musical (Slud).

Range: Southeastern Mexico to northwestern Peru, Amazonian Brazil, and the Guianas.

Note: We consider Middle American birds (*S. aurita*, the "true" Variable Seedeater) conspecific with birds found east of the Andes in South America (which if split would be called Wing-barred Seedeater), following most recent authors but not the 1983 AOU Check-list. The two most phenotypically different members of the complex (*corvina* and *hicksii*) appear to hybridize freely where they come into contact in central Panama, this despite reported vocal differences.

WHITE-COLLARED SEEDEATER
Sporophila torqueola   p.418

Description: 4½. Found only in western Panama. Male mostly black above with pale buff to white rump; wings with *two white wing-bars* and white speculum; throat white, extending onto sides of neck to form partial collar; broad and irregular (often splotchy) breast band black; lower underparts white. Subadult males (which sing and are able to breed, and which nearly always seem to

outnumber birds in fully adult plumage) are *much buffier below and on collar,* and are more brownish above. Female brownish olive above, wings duskier with *two whitish to pale buff wing-bars*; cinnamon-buff below, palest on belly.

Similar species: The only Panama seedeater with wing-bars. Most likely confused with Variable Seedeaters of Chiriquí (the two are sometimes together, though Variable always seems more numerous), but these have throat mainly or entirely black (never entirely white or buff), and do not show wing-bars.

Status and distribution: Fairly common in clearings, gardens, and semiopen agricultural terrain in lowlands of western Bocas del Toro (Changuinola and Almirante), and in western Chiriquí (east to around David). Apparently this represents a recent range extension from Costa Rica: it was first reported from Bocas del Toro in 1956 (but by then was already not uncommon), from Chiriquí in 1962. The species could spread farther east, and should be watched for.

Habits: Similar to Variable Seedeater, occurring in flocks, often with the Variable. Male's song is quite different, slower, richer, and sweeter, without the twittering effect of the Variable, the last notes resembling those of a canary.

Range: Southern Texas and Mexico to western Panama.

[LESSON'S SEEDEATER]
Sporophila bouvronides

Description: 4¼. Three recent sightings from eastern Darién. Bill blackish (male), or *mostly yellowish*, especially below (female). Mostly black above, with *broad white malar streak* and a white wing speculum; throat black, remaining underparts white, with sides and sometimes chest mottled black. Female pale olive brown above, buffy to buffy yellowish below.

Similar species: Male Variable Seedeater shows white throat and partial collar, and lacks this species' malar streak. Females of the two are very similar, but note Lesson's Seedeater's yellowish (not dusky) bill.

Status and distribution: Evidently a casual (possibly more regular?) visitant to grassy clearings in eastern Darién, with three recent sight reports: four at Yaviza on April 30, 1979 (J. Pujals *et al.*); 12 at Cana on April 29–May 1, 1980 (P. Scharf); two at Cana on June 18–19, 1981 (also P. Scharf). In each case the Lesson's were accompanying flocks of Variable Seedeaters. Its status in Darién remains to be clarified; seems absent during the dry season.

Range: Northern Colombia and the Guianas south locally to northeastern Peru and Amazonian Brazil (apparently at least partially migratory); casual in eastern Panama.

Note: Here regarded as a species distinct from Lined Seedeater (*S. lineola*). Male of true Lined Seedeater is similar in appearance, differing only in having a narrow white coronal stripe as well as the malar, and in lacking the black mottling on white lower underparts.

YELLOW-BELLIED SEEDEATER
Sporophila nigricollis   Plate 38

Description: 4½. Male has *black head and neck*; otherwise olive above, and *pale yellow to whitish below*. Female olive brown above, buffyish below. Some males have a small white wing speculum.

Similar species: Male is unlike any other Panama seedeater in pattern, though whiter-bellied individuals may seem poorly named. Female is more difficult and is especially hard to distinguish from female Variable, but tends to be more brownish below and usually (but not always) has slaty (not dusky) bill. The problem is simplified by the flocking habit of both species, when some males are almost invariably present.

Status and distribution: Common in open grassy and shrubby areas in lowlands on entire Pacific slope (though less numerous in Darién), ranging up in suitable habitat into the foothills and lower highlands (to 1200–1500 m: 4000–5000 ft) of western Chiriquí; on Caribbean slope recorded only from Canal

area and Colon province; found also on Taboga Island and the Pearl Islands. Disappears from many areas during the dry season, when it apparently gathers in flocks which range in more humid regions (e.g. in damp grassy areas along Caribbean coast).

Habits: Similar to Variable Seedeater, though generally a less familiar bird, and somewhat less partial to residential areas. Male's song is sweet and pretty, shorter than Variable's, often ending with two buzzy phrases, *tzee-tzee-bzeeoo, bzee-bzee.*

Range: Costa Rica to northern Bolivia, northeastern Argentina, and southern Brazil.

RUDDY-BREASTED SEEDEATER
Sporophila minuta   Plate 38

Description: 4. Male *mostly brownish gray above* (varying from grayish brown to quite pure gray), wings and tail duskier with indistinct small whitish wing speculum; rump and *entire underparts cinnamon-rufous*, deepest on throat. Female buffy brown above, wings and tail duskier, feathers with pale buff edging; below pale dull cinnamon to buffy brown.

Similar species: Notably *smaller* than other Panama seedeaters. Attractive males should be easily recognized, while females can generally be known by their size, overall buffy appearance, and pale edging on wing feathers.

Status and distribution: Locally fairly common to common in open savannas and pastures in lowlands on entire Pacific slope; on Caribbean slope considerably less numerous, and known only from Canal area east to western San Blas (Mandinga). This species essentially disappears from its Pacific slope breeding areas in about October, and does not reappear in numbers until about March–April; where most go at this time is uncertain, but the tendency may be to gather in large flocks in damper grassy areas.

Habits: The common and (when breeding) conspicuous seedeater of the Pacific slope savannas. Its song is the best of the Panama seedeaters, fairly long, sweet, and deliberate, typically *weet, weet, weet, weet, weet, too-weet-tew*, often given from an exposed perch such as a telephone wire.

Range: Western Mexico to northwestern Ecuador, Venezuela, the Guianas, and lower Amazonian Brazil.

Note: Does not include *S. hypoxantha* (Tawny-bellied Seedeater) of southern South America, considered a full species by most recent authors (though not in the 1983 AOU Check-list).

NICARAGUAN SEED-FINCH
Oryzoborus nuttingi   p.418

Description: 5¾. Found only in western Bocas del Toro. *Bill enormously thick, flesh-colored in male (sometimes with dusky streaks), dusky in female. Male entirely black.* Female rich dark brown above; somewhat paler rich reddish brown below.

Similar species: Male Lesser Seed-Finch is similar but smaller, with proportionately smaller bill (though its bill is not "small"!); it shows a white wing speculum lacking in this species. Female closely resembles female Lesser, except for her larger size and huge bill. See also female Blue-black Grosbeak (a forest bird, with differently shaped bill).

Status and distribution: Rare in damp shrubby or grassy areas, usually near open shallow water, in lowlands of western Bocas del Toro (Almirante, Changuinola). There is some evidence that this species has only recently spread into Panama (the first record was in 1965), and it also seems to have spread through Caribbean slope Costa Rica during about the same period (F. G. Stiles).

Habits: Similar to Lesser Seed-Finch, though always seems to be scarcer than that species. Usually seen singly or in pairs, feeding in semiopen grassy or sedgy areas, sometimes associating with Lesser Seed-Finches or Variable Seedeaters. The song resembles that of Lesser Seed-Finch, but reportedly slower and richer (F. G. Stiles).

Range: Eastern Nicaragua to western Panama.

Note: Here considered as a species distinct from the *O. crassirostris/maximiliani* complex (Large-billed and Great-billed Seed-Finches, respectively) of South America, following the suggestion of F. G. Stiles (*Condor 86*(2): 118–122, 1984). This was adopted in the 36th Supplement to the AOU Check-list (*Auk 104* (3): 594, 1987).

LESSER SEED-FINCH
Oryzoboros angolensis   Plate 38

Description: 5. *Bill very heavy* (the tip forming a right angle), black in both sexes. Male *all black*, with small white wing speculum and white under wing-linings (latter visible only in flight). Female dull brown above, richer fulvous brown below, with white under wing-linings (but no speculum).

Similar species: Except in western Bocas del Toro (where see also Nicaraguan Seed-Finch), no other similar bird has such an enormously large bill. In western Caribbean lowlands males of this species resemble males of the local race of Variable Seedeater (*corvina*) except for their larger size and much bigger bills. See also Blue-black Grosbeak and Blue Seedeater.

Status and distribution: Locally fairly common in shrubby clearings and woodland and forest borders in more humid lowlands on both slopes, though it seems relatively less numerous in Chiriquí, San Blas (where known only from the west), and Darién (where it may only be a recent immigrant, with the first report from as late as 1978); ranges up locally and in small numbers into foothills; found also on Coiba Island and the Pearl Islands.

Habits: Usually found singly or in pairs, not flocking as do the seedeaters. More arboreal than most seedeaters. Male has a fine song, very long and musical, somewhat Indigo Bunting-like; it is usually delivered from a high exposed perch. Unlike the seedeaters, this species seems regularly to continue singing through the dry season.

Range: Southeastern Mexico to western Ecuador, northern Bolivia, and southern Brazil.

Note: We consider Middle American birds (*O. funereus*, Thick-billed Seed-Finch) conspecific with birds found east of the Andes in South America (which if split would be called Chestnut-bellied Seed-Finch), following most recent authors but not the 1983 AOU Check-list. S. Olson (*Auk 98*(2): 379–381, 1981) presented evidence indicating that there is some intergradation between the two "types" occurring in Colombia west of the Andes; vocally both types appear to be similar.

BLUE SEEDEATER
Amaurospiza concolor   Plate 38

Description: 5. Locally on Pacific slope in western and central Panama. Male *dull dark blue*, foreface slightly blacker. Female *rather bright tawny brown*, slightly paler below. Some birds (perhaps immature males) are a deeper more rufous brown.

Similar species: Male somewhat resembles male Blue-black Grassquit, but is larger and bluer, with distinctly heavier bill; note habitat differences (the seedeater in woodland and forest undergrowth). Female resembles female Lesser Seed-Finch in color, but bill not nearly as heavy, and under wing-coverts dark (not white as in seed-finch); it is larger, and more uniform and brighter brown, than female *Sporophila* seedeaters. See also Indigo Bunting. Male Slaty Finch is obviously grayer, and has much more slender and sharply pointed bill.

Status and distribution: Rare and very local in lower growth of forest, woodland, and borders; best known from highlands of western Chiriquí, where recorded from 600–2700 m (2000–9000 ft) but mainly 1500–2100 m (5000–7000 ft); also recorded from Veraguas (one sighting of two seen above Santa Fé on April 7, 1975; N. G. Smith), Herrera (one collected on Cerro Largo at about 350 m: 1200 ft on July 13, 1925; R. Benson), western Panama province (one sighting of two seen at Cerro Campana on January 3, 1981; R. A. Rowlett and B. Whitney), and Pacific side of Canal area (a few records from the Paraiso/Curundu/Chiva Chiva area). Best looked for around Nueva Suiza and above Finca Lerida in western Chiriquí, but not regularly encountered even at these localities.

Habits: An inconspicuous seedeater (probably often overlooked), usually found singly or in pairs as it feeds quietly just inside forest or woodland, sometimes associating with mixed flocks. In Chiriquí seems partial to stands of *Chusquea* bamboo, but this does not seem to be the case elsewhere. Often perches and feeds some 3–9 m (10–30 ft) above the ground. In Ecuador the song is a short sweet warbled *sweet sweet sweet sa-weet*.

Range: Southern Mexico south locally to western Ecuador.

YELLOW-FACED GRASSQUIT
Tiaris olivacea   Plate 38

Description: 4. Male olive above except for *black crown, sides of head, and breast,* with *contrasting bright yellow superciliary and throat patch*; black of breast fades into grayish olive on belly. Female much duller, with olive replacing all the black, and *yellow face markings* less prominent (but still visible). Immatures resemble female; subadult males have less extensive black on breast than older birds. Birds from Coiba Island (*ravida*) are darker generally, with more extensive black on head (extending to nape) and underparts (extending to belly).

Similar species: Even females have enough facial pattern to be readily recognized. See female Painted Bunting.

Status and distribution: Common in grassy areas and clearings in foothills and highlands of western and central Panama, especially on Pacific slope (ranging up to about 1800 m (6000 ft) in western Chiriquí; uncommon and more local in similar habitat in lowlands on both slopes, somewhat more numerous on Pacific side (especially in coastal areas), but decidedly scarce in San Blas and Darién; common also on Coiba Island.

Habits: The male's song is a thin weak trill delivered from a low perch. Usually seen in flocks, often associating with seedeaters and Blue-black Grassquits. Builds a globular or dome-shaped nest with a side entrance (very unlike the open cups of *Sporophila* seedeaters and the Blue-black Grassquit).

Range: Eastern Mexico to Colombia and Venezuela; Greater Antilles.

SLATY FINCH
Haplospiza rustica   Plate 38

Description: 5. Found mainly in Chiriquí highlands. *Bill rather slender and sharply pointed.* Male *all slaty gray,* slightly darker above and paler below. Female olive brown above, wings duskier with flight feathers narrowly edged rufous; dull yellowish white below, with *blurry dusky streaking on throat and breast*, washed with brownish olive on flanks.

Similar species: Male is only uniform gray small finch in Panama. Female most like female of far more numerous Blue-black Grassquit (and bill shape of the two quite similar); the finch is considerably larger, however, and has streaking extending up over throat (which is unstreaked in grassquit). Forest-based habitat of the finch also very different from that of the grassquit.

Status and distribution: Rare in undergrowth and borders of forest (occasionally out into adjacent clearings) in highlands of western Chiriquí (mainly 1500–1800 m: 5000–6000 ft); one was collected at Fortuna in central Chiriquí (900 m: 3000 ft) on August 14, 1976 (R. Hinds, specimen to GML); another was taken at Aguacate, near Capira at base of Cerro Trinidad, in western Panama province on July 16, 1979 (H. Montenegro, specimen to AMNH), for only central Panama record.

Habits: A rather inconspicuous small finch, usually found just inside forest, where it forages on or near the ground. Most often found singly or in pairs, occasionally in small groups. In South America its song is a fast complex burst of chips, buzzes, and trills which often ends in a long fading buzzy trill.

Range: Southern Mexico south locally to Venezuela and Bolivia.
Note: Formerly placed in the genus *Spodiornis*.

PEG-BILLED FINCH
Acanthidops bairdi Plate 48

Description: 5. Invaded western Chiriquí highlands in 1979, but not recorded before or since. *Bill narrow, sharply pointed, and somewhat upturned; bicolored in both sexes*, black above and *yellow below* (duller in female). Male *all dark slaty gray*, somewhat paler below and tinged buff on lower belly and under tail-coverts; wings and tail blackish. Female olive brown above, duskier on wings and tail and with *two fairly prominent tan wing-bars*; below dull buffy grayish olive with indistinct dusky streaking on throat and breast, buffier on mid-belly and under tail-coverts, browner on flanks.
Similar species: Slaty Finch has all dark bill in both sexes; further, female Slaty lacks Peg-bill's wing-bars. Peg-billed Finch is considerably more arboreal. Slaty Flower-piercer has distinctly differently shaped bill (with hook at tip); male is bluer than male Peg-bill, while female lacks wing-bars, has less prominent streaking below, etc.
Status and distribution: Recorded only from forest and forest borders along upper part of Boquete Trail above Cerro Punta in highlands of western Chiriquí (2100–2400 m: 7000–8000 ft); here it was briefly common between January and March 1979 (first noted by B. Feltner, then seen by many other observers; recognizably photographed by D. Galinat, photos to VIREO). Its unexpected appearance in Panama (especially in such numbers: up to 200 were estimated seen in a day) was presumably tied to the seeding of *Chusquea* bamboo in that area at the time.
Habits: Essentially arboreal, gleaning actively in foliage, among epiphytic growth, and along mossy limbs; has also been observed feeding on flowers (J. Arvin). In Costa Rica no association with bamboo has been noted, but the association could be tied to actual bamboo seeding (i.e. the finches may take advantage of a temporarily super-abundant food source). No breeding activity was noted during its Panama invasion, and there was no song.
Range: Costa Rica; casually to western Panama.

SLATY FLOWERPIERCER
Diglossa plumbea Plate 48

Description: 4¾. Found only in western highlands. Unusual bill with *lower mandible upturned and upper mandible hooked at tip*; lower mandible usually pale, especially at base. Male *above dark bluish slate*, blackest on head; wings and tail blackish, feathers edged gray; *paler slaty gray below*. Female olive-gray above; wings and tail dusky, feathers edged gray; below pale grayish olive, *indistinctly streaked dusky-olive*, becoming buffier on lower belly and under tail-coverts.
Similar species: In Panama the curious bill is unique. See Peg-billed Finch (extremely rare), and Slaty Finch.
Status and distribution: Common in shrubby clearings and forest borders in highlands of western Chiriquí (mostly above 1500 m: 5000 ft); eastward less well known, with only one sighting from eastern Chiriquí (three seen above Cerro Colorado on May 16, 1986; J. Guarnaccia), and a few specimens taken at Chitra in eastern Veraguas (1380–1500 m: 4600–5000 ft).
Habits: Very active, most often seen in pairs, usually remaining low. Punctures the corolla of certain flowers to obtain nectar; also flycatches. Has a weak, rapidly given warbler-like song.
Range: Costa Rica and western Panama.
Note: The genus *Diglossa* was formerly placed in the Coerebidae (Honeycreeper) family; this family has since been dismembered, with most genera transferred to the Tanagers. The taxonomic affinities of *Diglossa* are still being debated (some feel that it too may belong with the Tanagers), but here the 1983 AOU Check-list is followed in placing it with the Emberizine Finches, close to *Acanthidops* and *Haplospiza*.

SAFFRON FINCH
Sicalis flaveola Plate 38

Description: 5¼. Found only in Caribbean coastal region of Canal area. Male *mostly bright golden yellow, becoming orange on front of head*; more olive on back and streaked with dusky; wings and tail dusky, edged with olive. Female similar but with orange reduced or lacking. Immature grayish above streaked with dusky, hindneck and back tinged with yellow; wings dusky edged with olive; whitish below with *broad yellow band across chest* and brownish on sides.
Similar species: No similar bird occurs in the restricted area where this bird is found. Grassland Yellow-Finch is known only from Pacific slope grasslands.

Status and distribution: First noted in 1951, presumably having been introduced; now locally common in residential and park-like areas near Caribbean coast of Canal area from near Gatun Dam to Coco Solo; there are occasional reports of wanderers from the Chagres valley up to the Gamboa vicinity, but still none from the Pacific side of the Canal area (to which it might have been expected to spread by now).

Habits: Usually seen feeding on lawns, often in small groups. The male's song is an endlessly repeated but rather musical *tzip-tzip-tzee-tzee.*

Range: Colombia south locally to central Argentina; introduced into central Panama, and on Jamaica and Puerto Rico.

Note: More than one species may be involved in South America.

GRASSLAND YELLOW-FINCH
Sicalis luteola   Plate 38

Description: 4¾. Known primarily from Coclé grasslands. Male mostly olive brownish above, streaked with dusky on crown and back; rump plain yellowish olive; *lores and ocular area bright yellow*, *wings and tail brownish* edged with pale buff; *below mostly bright yellow*, tinged olive on breast. Female similar but browner above and buffier below with clear yellow only on belly.

Similar species: No other similar bird in its restricted range is so predominately yellow; female Lesser Goldfinch is smaller with white in wings. Saffron Finch is known only from Canal area.

Status and distribution: Locally fairly common in grasslands in lowlands on Pacific slope of Coclé (the endemic race *eisenmanni*); occasionally birds apparently wander elsewhere in Pacific lowlands, e.g. there are two sightings from La Jagua in eastern Panama province (but as that area has since been converted to rice cultivation they seem unlikely to re-occur), and one was seen near Las Lajas in eastern Chiriquí on August 19, 1984 (D. Engleman and J. Guarnaccia).

Habits: Seems to gather in loose colonies during the breeding season and is often absent from other apparently suitable areas. Male has a thin buzzy trill, at times somewhat musical, delivered from an exposed perch, sometimes in flight.

Range: Southern Mexico south locally through Middle America and most of South America to southern Chile and central Argentina; introduced into Lesser Antilles.

Note: More than one species may be involved in South America.

WEDGE-TAILED GRASS-FINCH
Emberizoides herbicola   Plate 38

Description: 7½. Locally in Pacific grasslands. *Bill mostly yellow*, with black ridge; *very long tail, graduated and extremely pointed.* Pale olive brown above streaked with black, wings more olive with bend of wing yellow (often hidden); *lores and conspicuous eye-ring whitish*; underparts whitish, tinged buffy on breast and sides.

Similar species: Much larger and with much longer tail than Grasshopper Sparrow; also lacks crown stripes and has pale bill. Rather like female or nonbreeding male Bobolink but with longer pointed tail and no dark brown on crown.

Status and distribution: Uncommon and very local in less disturbed grasslands and on grassy hillsides on Pacific slope in western and central Panama; recorded only from Chiriquí (in llanos along road to Boquete near base of Volcán Barú; and at Cerro Flores), Veraguas (recorded in August 1981 at Laguna de la Yaguada, and in May 1982 at Buenos Aires de Cañazas; F. Delgado), and in Panamá province (in west at Cerro Campana, in east in the Tocumen/Chepo area); recorded up to about 1050 m (3500 ft). Quite readily found on grassy slopes below Cerro Campana, and has also been recently seen in Chiriquí along the La Caldera road (off the main Boquete highway), but in general a scarce and infrequently encountered bird in Panama, with overall numbers perhaps depleted by overgrazing and excessive burning.

Habits: Usually rather inconspicuous, remaining hidden in long grass, sometimes perching on fences or the top of shrubs. Has two songs, a musical *tleedeé, tleedeé, tleedeé,* with variations, and a very different buzzy *tzit-zeereéa* or *zipzirrree.*

Range: Southwestern Costa Rica south locally to northeastern Argentina and southern Brazil.

GRASSHOPPER SPARROW
Ammodramus savannarum

Description: 4¾. *A flat-headed little sparrow with short and pointed tail found very locally in grasslands.* Buffy brown above streaked with blackish on back; crown dusky with *buff stripe down its center*, usually prominent *yellowish buff lores*, and *buff superciliary*; rich ochraceous yellow below, fading to whitish on belly. Three races occur in Panama: *bimaculatus* is found in most of its Pacific slope range, with the very pale *beatriceae* (with pale pinkish buff underparts, whitish crown stripe, etc.) being restricted to Coclé; northern migrant *pratensis* (indistinguishable from *bimaculatus* in the field, but with longer wing, etc.) has also been recorded in Bocas del Toro. Immatures of all races have dusky breast streaking.

Similar species: Small size, short pointed tail, and crown striping should clinch identification. No female seedeater has stripes on head. Wedge-tailed Grass-Finch is much larger with long tail, lacks head striping.

Status and distribution: Uncommon and very local in less disturbed grasslands on Pacific slope in western and central Panama; recorded only from western Chiriquí (four specimens taken in 1905 at Francés in llanos at base of Volcán Barú; no recent reports), southern Coclé, and eastern Panama province (Chepo and Pacora area, with no reports since the late 1960s). Also known from two mist-netted birds captured at Almirante, Bocas del Toro: one taken by GML personnel in November 1963 (specimen to USNM), another netted and released on November 4, 1967 (V. Kleen). Local populations of the Grasshopper Sparrow are now much reduced by over-grazing and burning.

Habits: Normally very hard to see, crouching in long grass, flushing for short distances with feeble fluttery flight. Most easily noted when males are singing, then perching in the open and emitting an insignificant *pi-tup-tzeeeeeeeeeeeeee*, the first notes inaudible at a distance, very like temperate North American birds.

Range: United States south locally through Middle America to northwestern Ecuador, with northern breeders wintering south at least casually to Costa Rica and western Panama; Greater Antilles.

[LARK SPARROW]
Chondestes grammicus

Description: 6–6½. Accidental. *Crown mostly chestnut* with narrow white median line, broad whitish superciliary, *chestnut cheeks*, white malar area above black submalar streak; otherwise brown above streaked blackish; whitish below with *bold black breast spot; tail with large white corners*, conspicuous in flight. Immature similar, but pattern duller.

Similar species: The complex but attractive head pattern, black "stick-pin" on breast, and extensive white in tail render this species virtually unmistakable — in the unlikely event that it is ever found again in Panama.

Status and distribution: One report, an adult observed at close range and in flight near the Tocumen marsh, eastern Panama province, on February 22, 1985 (J. Rowlett and S. Hilty *et al.*). This is surely the most amazing in the long series of vagrant birds found at Tocumen during the past decade or so.

Habits: In its normal range favors open grassy terrain, usually in arid regions.

Range: Breeds mainly in western United States, wintering south to southern Mexico, casually (only one record) to Honduras; accidental in Panama.

LINCOLN'S SPARROW
Melospiza lincolnii

Description: 5½. Casual. Grayish brown above streaked with blackish; crown rusty brown with narrow buffy median stripe, *pale whitish eye-ring, sides of head grayish*; whitish below, *strongly washed with buff on chest and finely streaked with dusky on breast and sides* (the streaks sometimes coalescing into a central spot).

Similar species: Though a troublesome bird to identify in its normal North American range, in Panama there are few birds much like it. Immature Rufous-collared Sparrow is the most similar; note especially the gray on the sides of the head of the Lincoln's and its fine (but *distinct*, not blurry) breast streaking; the Lincoln's has a slim, trim look to it and, unlike the Rufous-collar, is a great skulker.

Status and distribution: Casual winter visitant to western and central Panama. Only three records (but probably overlooked): a nineteenth-century specimen taken by McLeannan in what is now the Caribbean side of the Canal area; a bird mist-netted and released at Almirante, Bocas del Toro, on October 31, 1967 (V. Kleen); and one closely studied at El Velo on Finca Lerida in highlands of western Chiriquí (1500 m: 5000 ft) on January 20, 1988 (Ridgely and T. Richards *et al.*).

Habits: A quiet and unobtrusive bird, favoring dense lower growth in shrubby clearings and woodland borders.

Range: Breeds in northern and western North America; winters from southern United States to Honduras, casually to Costa Rica and Panama.

RUFOUS-COLLARED SPARROW
Zonotrichia capensis   Plate 38

Description: 5½. Often appears slightly crested. Head mostly gray with a broad black stripe on either side of crown, a narrow black stripe behind eye, and a black "moustache"; *rufous collar on hindneck and sides of chest*; upperparts otherwise brown with blackish streaking; throat white, black patch on either side of upper chest, remaining underparts whitish. Immature much less sharply marked above, with only a trace of rufous collar; buffier below, lightly streaked with dusky on breast.

Similar species: Pert, attractive adults are easily identified by their gray and black-striped heads and prominent rufous collars; immatures are duller and less distinctive but are the only more or less streaked sparrow-like bird in the areas they inhabit. See Lincoln's Sparrow.

Status and distribution: Abundant on shrubby hillsides, fields, and around habitations in highlands of western Chiriquí (where it is one of the most frequently seen birds), mostly above 1200 m (4000 ft); also recorded from highlands of eastern Chiriquí (Cerro Flores, Cerro Colorado) and Veraguas (Chitra, Calovévora, and Castillo), but here apparently less numerous and more local; one old specimen in the USNM is marked as having been taken at "Cascajal, Coclé", but not otherwise known from that province; common again on grassy slopes of Cerro Campana (and also known from nearby Cerro Chame) in western Panama province, where recorded down to 540 m (1800 ft); not known from Azuero Peninsula, or from eastern Panama.

Habits: Very tame and familiar. In Panama the song is a pretty whistle, *teéeo, cheéo,* suggesting song of Eastern Meadowlark; it is one of the most pleasant and characteristic sounds of the western highlands. Also has an interminably uttered *tsip . . .tsip . . . tsip . . .*

Range: Southern Mexico to Tierra del Fuego, mainly in highlands; Hispaniola and Netherlands Antilles.

WHITE-CROWNED SPARROW
Zonotrichia leucophrys

Description: 7. Accidental. *Bill yellowish pink.* Often looks "puffy-crowned". *Crown boldly striped black and white*; above otherwise brownish gray, grayest on nape and brownest on rump, with dusky streaking on back; wings and tail duskier with two white wing-bars; *below uniform light gray.* Immature has similar pattern, but *crown boldly striped brown and pale buff,* and the gray below is tinged with buff.

Similar species: This handsome sparrow (even when in immature plumage) is unlikely to be confused in Panama, in the unlikely event that it should occur again; no local sparrow-like bird shows such a striking head pattern.

Status and distribution: An immature was seen and photographed on the grounds of the Hotel Washington in Colon, on Caribbean coast of Canal area, on January 17–22, 1982 (J. and R. A. Rowlett *et al.*; photographed by B. Whitney, photos to VIREO). The bird was apparently of the eastern nominate race. One of Panama's more extraordinary vagrant records.

Range: Breeds in northern and western North America, wintering from United States to Mexico, rarely in Greater Antilles; accidental in Panama.

VOLCANO JUNCO
Junco vulcani   Plate 38

Description: 6½. Found chiefly above timberline on *Volcán Barú.* Bill pink; conspicuous *yellow or orange iris.* Mostly grayish olive, grayest on sides of head, hindneck, and lower underparts; back more olive, streaked with black; wings and tail dusky edged with olive; outer tail feathers with pale spot toward tip. Young birds are more streaked.

Similar species: The bright yellow or orange eye is unusual among Panama "finches"; note also the pink bill, overall grayish coloration. Unlikely to be confused at the high elevations at which this species occurs.

Status and distribution: Fairly common in semiopen areas and low shrubbery on highest slopes of Volcán Barú; recorded mainly above 3000 m (10,000 ft), once down to about 2700 m (9000 ft).

Habits: Rather unsuspicious. Forages mostly on the ground. The most southern and dullest of the junco group. Seeing it in Panama requires driving the difficult road to the telecommunications towers on the summit of Barú; in Costa Rica the task is much easier, for there it is readily found on the summit of Volcán Irazú, and even along the Pan-American Highway on Cerro de la Muerte.

Range: Costa Rica and western Panama.

AMERICAN ORIOLES AND BLACKBIRDS: Icterinae (21)

This is a varied group, confined to the New World, with most species in the tropics; formerly given full family rank, the icterids are now considered a subfamily within the expanded Emberizidae family. They are medium-sized to fairly large birds with rather long pointed bills, in many species with the male larger or more brightly colored. Many species are wholly or predominantly black, some with varying amounts of yellow, orange, chestnut, or red. Many species also have good songs, though others have only harsh strident vocalizations. Great diversity exists in social habits and breeding behavior. Oropendolas and the Yellow-rumped Cacique are gregarious birds whose conspicuous colonies with their long, pendant nests are a characteristic site in more wooded areas. Other Panamanian caciques are more solitary, usually nesting singly. The Panamanian cowbirds are all brood parasites on other birds, the Giant Cowbird specializing on the colonial oropendolas and caciques, under certain conditions to the host's advantage (N. G. Smith, *Nature 219*: 690–694, 1968). The orioles are the most attractive members of the family in Panama, both resident and migrant species being found in good numbers. Most species have a varied diet of various combinations of fruit and insects, some seeds, with the grackle also taking some small vertebrates (washed up fish, even nestling birds). The arboreal members of the family construct large beautifully woven pouches hanging from branches (sometimes palm fronds, and in some places even radio antennas and wires); the more terrestrial species nest on the ground, while the Great-tailed Grackle constructs a large deep cup nest.

BOBOLINK
Dolichonyx oryzivorus   Plate 32

Description: 6½–7½. Rather short conical bill. Tail somewhat graduated. Female and nonbreeding male brownish buffy above streaked with blackish and with *buffy and dusky stripes on head; yellowish buffy below* with a little brownish streaking on sides. Male in breeding plumage mostly black with *buffy yellow patch on back of neck, white lower back and rump*, and broad white stripe on scapulars. In fresh plumage, feathers broadly tipped with buff, obscuring the pattern; bright plumage is slowly acquired through wearing off of these tips (mostly complete by May).
Similar species: Eastern Meadowlark is chunky, with short tail and long slender bill, and is mostly yellow below; female Red-breasted Blackbird is darker above without head striping, and is tinged pinkish on breast. Wedge-tailed Grass-Finch lacks stripes on head and has longer more pointed tail.
Status and distribution: Uncommon fall and rare spring transient (mid-September–late October; mid-April–early May), mostly along Caribbean coast but also recorded on Pacific slope of central and eastern Panama. Usually noted flying over; when perched, favors clearings with grass and in grassy fields.
Habits: Often in small groups, but decidedly erratic and scarce in Panama at any time. In flight overhead attention is often drawn to it by its characteristic *ink* call; passing males during northward migration also occasionally give snatches of song.

Range: Breeds in North America; winters in south-central South America; migrates mostly via West Indies, small numbers reaching Middle America.

RED-BREASTED BLACKBIRD
Sturnella militaris   Plate 39

Description: 7–7½. Male in breeding plumage unmistakable, mostly black with *bright red throat and breast*; lesser wing-coverts and bend of wing also red (red in wing largely hidden at rest, but quite evident in flight). Nonbreeding males (September–March) have most feathers edged buff or dark brown, producing a mottled effect and obscuring the red (may even show a female-like superciliary and coronal stripe); this edging is gradually worn off, revealing the bright nuptial pattern. Female mostly blackish brown above with feathers edged buff producing a streaked effect; *buff superciliary and coronal stripe usually prominent*; below mainly buff, streaked with brown on sides and belly, and *tinged pink on breast*; usually a bit of pink shows on bend of wing; tail brown narrowly barred with dusky.
Similar species: Female and nonbreeding male Bobolinks are much paler generally, have a spiky pointed tail, and never show pink on breast.
Status and distribution: Locally fairly common to common on savannas and extensive grassy fields in lowlands on Pacific slope

EASTERN MEADOWLARK

from Chiriquí to Darién (El Real/Yaviza area, also rarely wandering to Cana); recently (since 1972) also resident at several localities on Caribbean slope of Canal area and Colon province; small numbers also found in suitable areas up into lower highlands of western Chiriquí (Volcán/Santa Clara area). Overall numbers and range of this species in Panama have doubtless increased due to clearing, but it remains rather local in many areas.

Habits: Rather like a meadowlark, and like it gathering in fair-sized flocks during non-breeding season. Even in breeding season seems somewhat gregarious, nesting in loose "colonies" in particularly favorable habitat. The male's song, given from a slightly elevated perch such as a fence post or low bush, consists of two short introductory notes followed by a long rather buzzy trill.

Range: Southwestern Costa Rica south locally to Bolivia and Amazonian Brazil.

Note: Formerly placed in the genus *Leistes*. Does not include *S. superciliaris* (White-browed Blackbird) of southern South America, sometimes regarded as conspecific.

EASTERN MEADOWLARK
Sturnella magna   p.427

Description: 8–9. Chunky, with long slender bill and short tail. Brown above streaked with black and buff; head striped blackish and white; *yellow below, chest crossed by broad black "V"*. When flushed, *white outer tail feathers* flash out conspicuously. Young birds are duller but still easily recognized as meadowlarks.

Similar species: Given a reasonable view, easily recognized. See female and non-breeding male Red-breasted Blackbird.

Status and distribution: Fairly common to common in savannas and grassy fields in lowlands on Pacific slope from Chiriquí east to eastern Panama province (east to around El Llano; may spread farther with continued forest clearance); ranges up in reduced numbers into highlands of western Chiriquí (to about 1800 m: 6000 ft); has recently (as of the early 1980s) begun to colonize Caribbean slope, with small numbers now evidently resident in suitable habitat locally in the Canal area and eastern Colon province (where in early 1987 found to be present as far east as the Portobelo area; D. Graham).

Habits: Mostly terrestrial, walking about as it feeds, crouching when alarmed and flicking its tail open and shut. In flight alternates several flaps with short sails on stiff wings. Meadowlarks are often not very conspicuous unless they are singing, when they mount to a fence post or low tree branch. The song has much the same slurred pattern as have Eastern Meadowlarks from eastern North America, but in its liquid melodious quality seems more reminiscent of the Western Meadowlark (*S. neglecta*) of western North America, though there is some (individual?) variation; the overall effect is often to combine the best qualities of both! The usual call, often given as a bird flushes, is a harsh *zhueet*.

Range: Eastern North America to Colombia, Venezuela, the Guianas, and northern Brazil.

YELLOW-HEADED BLACKBIRD
Xanthocephalus xanthocephalus

Description: ♂ 11; ♀ 9. A few recent records. Male mainly black with *contrasting bright yellow head and breast*; small black mask from bill to around eye; *large white patch on primary coverts* is partially hidden at rest (though always visible) but conspicuous in flight. Female smaller than male and much less striking in color: mostly dusky brown with *short superciliary, throat and breast yellow*; some white streaking on upper belly.

Similar species: Not likely confused, except with unrecorded (but possible) Yellow-hooded Blackbird (see below).

Status and distribution: A casual vagrant: an immature male was collected on the Gatun Dam spillway, Caribbean side of Canal area, on November 1, 1972 (J. Strauch, Jr.); and up to five or six were seen at Tocumen marsh, eastern Panama province, on at least January 19–24, 1980 (D. Finch, P. Donahue *et al.*).

Habits: Usually in flocks, often large in its normal range, often associating with water. Also regularly feeds on agricultural fields.

Range: Breeds in western North America; winters in southwestern United States and Mexico, small numbers in eastern United States; a few records from West Indies, Costa Rica, and Panama.

Note: Yellow-hooded Blackbird (*Agelaius icterocephalus*) of northern South America could occur in eastern Panama; it is known to be numerous in northwestern Colombia, and has been taken within a few miles of the Panama border. Male superficially resembles male Yellow-headed Blackbird, but is *much* smaller (7 in), lacks white in wing, and has black only on lores. Female is more olive above (not so brown) with obscure dusky streaking on back; its yellow on underparts is duller and more restricted to throat, upper chest, and superciliary; lower underparts more olive brown, with no white streaking. There have been a few birds reported as this species from Tocumen marsh, but as yet no confirmatory critical description or photograph has been obtained, and confusion with Yellow-headed Blackbird seems likely.

GREAT-TAILED GRACKLE
Cassidix mexicanus   Plate 39

Description: ♂ 17; ♀ 13. Long, rather stout, pointed bill. Iris bright golden yellow in male, duller yellow in female, and brown in immatures of both sexes. Male glossy black with purple sheen on head, neck, back, and breast; *tail very long, folded down the middle to form keel shape.* Female much smaller, brown above with *pale buff superciliary* and throat; *remaining underparts buffy brown* becoming grayish brown on belly; black tail much shorter and less keel-shaped than in male.

Similar species: Male could only be confused with Giant Cowbird which, however, has tail of proportionately normal length and shape, has small head and obviously pointed wings, etc. Other cowbirds are very much smaller.

Status and distribution: Locally common to abundant along shorelines and in towns and cities on Pacific slope from Chiriquí (where scarce) to Darién (where also scarce), with numbers particularly great in and around the Canal area; on Caribbean slope found mainly from Canal area eastward along San Blas coast, but recently found also around Changuinola in western Bocas del Toro (April 1980; Ridgely), where it had previously been absent; also numerous on shorelines of most Pacific offshore islands, though much less so

or absent off Chiriquí and Veraguas (e.g. numbers very small on Coiba Island in April 1976; Ridgely), and numerous on islands off San Blas as well. Numbers have increased tremendously over the last three to five decades in the area of the former Canal Zone, Panama City, and Colon, and it is now here virtually omnipresent, roosting in staggering numbers at certain sites (to the point where they sometimes become a public nuisance). Elsewhere, however, their numbers have not increased anywhere near so dramatically, though some recent range expansion is evident.

Habits: Feeds mostly on the ground, also as a scavenger along coasts. Roosts in very large, noisy flocks in trees. Male displays, often on ground, with bill up and long neck extended. Has many vocalizations; both sexes have a harsh *chack*; male gives a long strident whistle, *weeek, week*, sometimes drawn out to *weeeeek*, and both sexes also give a rattling *trit-trit-trit.*

Range: Southwestern United States to northwestern Venezuela and northwestern Peru.

SHINY COWBIRD
Molothrus bonariensis   Plate 39

Description: 8–8½. Short, conical bill. *Iris dark in both sexes.* Male *entirely glossy violet blue-black.* Female dull grayish brown above; *much paler grayish brown below,* with faint dusky streaks on breast. Immature resembles female but is edged with brownish buff above; *yellowish buff below,* streaked with dusky in males.

Similar species: Not always easy to distinguish from Bronzed Cowbird though both sexes lack that species' ruff and red eye; female Shiny is paler and grayer, especially below. Somewhat resembles male White-lined Tanager, but that species has longer bluish bill, lacks glossy violet tones, and has white under wing-linings.

Status and distribution: Now locally uncommon to fairly common in semiopen country and agricultural areas in central and eastern Panama, with small numbers being reported regularly from a few localities on both slopes of the Canal area; this is as far west as the species has been confirmed, but there have been a few as yet unsubstantiated reports of Shiny Cowbirds from western Panama (e.g. Chiriquí) as well. The species is evidently increasing and gradually expanding its range in Panama, but whether its spread northward will be checked by the presence of the ecologically and behaviorally similar Bronzed Cowbird remains to be seen. Prior to the late 1970s the Shiny Cowbird was known in Panama only from a few records from eastern San Blas and eastern Darién.

Habits: Similar to Bronzed Cowbird, also feeding mostly on the ground, often among cattle. Likewise a brood parasite on various small birds. Males have a rather pretty whistled song.

Range: Central Panama to southern South America; in recent decades has spread rapidly northward through the West Indies, and by the mid-1980s a few had even reached southern Florida.

BRONZED COWBIRD
Molothrus aeneus   Plate 39

Description: 8–8½. Stout, somewhat conical black bill. *Red iris in both sexes*, but this is often difficult to discern except in strong light, and is apparently duller and browner in non-breeding season; iris brown in young birds. Male *glossy black with green or bronze sheen on body plumage*; a *thick ruff* on nape and upper back is often apparent, giving bird a small-headed or hunch-backed look. Female similar but duller and blacker, lacking the male's sheen, and sometimes browner below; the ruff is less prominent. Immature like female but often somewhat grayer overall.

Similar species: Shiny Cowbird is confusingly similar, especially when birds are not breeding. Shiny never shows a ruff, and never has red eyes; Bronzed is never as pale as female or immature Shinies often are. Care is needed, however, especially when the birds are at any distance. See also female Giant Cowbird.

Status and distribution: Locally fairly common in semiopen country, agricultural areas, and around towns in lowlands on Pacific slope from Chiriquí east to eastern Panama province (Tocumen/Chepo area); on Caribbean slope known only from lowlands of western Bocas del Toro, and some recent reports from Canal area east into eastern Colon province; ranges up in usually small numbers (or erratically) in suitable cleared terrain into lower highlands of western Chiriquí (mostly in the Volcán/Santa Clara area, rarely as high as around Cerro Punta). In recent years has been reported in variable (usually small, but occasionally substantial) numbers on both sides of Canal area, especially the Pacific side, but has not shown any tendency to move into eastern Panama (on the contrary,

it is the Shiny Cowbird which is giving evidence of moving westward).

Habits: Usually seen feeding on the ground, often with tails held partly cocked. When not breeding frequently in flocks, often large, but rather erratic in most areas. Sometimes associates with cattle, but at least as often seen away from them. The species is a brood parasite on various small birds.

Range: Southwestern United States to central Panama; northern Colombia.

Note: Includes *M. armenti* (Bronze-brown Cowbird) of Colombia, until recently considered a distinct species.

GIANT COWBIRD
Scaphidura oryzivora   Plate 39

Description: ♂ 14; ♀ 11½. Iris red in western and central Panama, becoming more yellowish orange in eastern Panama. *Thick bill and bare frontal shield black* (occasional juvenals have bill pale flesh or yellowish in whole or in part). Male glossy purplish black with *conspicuous ruff on neck* (often giving it a curiously "small-headed" appearance). Female and immatures duller black with much less prominent ruff. Flight profile, with rather long pointed wings and small head, distinctive, as is its somewhat undulating flight style, a few flaps followed by a short glide in which wings are closed.

Similar species: Male recalls male Great-tailed Grackle but has heavier bill, ruff on neck, and shorter rounded tail; female Giant Cowbird is so much smaller than male grackle that confusion is unlikely. Bronzed and Shiny Cowbirds are considerably smaller than even female Giant Cowbird and have conical bills without frontal shields.

Status and distribution: Uncommon to locally fairly common in semiopen country and forest borders in more humid lowlands on both slopes, but absent from eastern side of Azuero Peninsula east through most of western Panama province, and scarce generally on the Azuero Peninsula (*fide* F. Delgado); ranges up in small numbers into lower foothills (e.g. in the Cana valley in Darién). Seems most numerous in the partially cleared lower Tuira and Chucunaque River valleys of Darién. In general, numbers are closely tied to the presence and abundance of oropendolas and caciques, on which it is a brood parasite (see below).

Habits: A brood parasite, its hosts being exclusively the colonial oropendolas and caciques. Most easily seen in the vicinity of these colonies, espcially when the hosts are laying. At other seasons, disperses widely and thinly, feeding primarily on the ground in fields or along open banks or sandbars of rivers, also in flowering trees (sometimes with its hosts). The grassy slopes of Gatun Dam are a good place to look for them at this time; there they often forage near, or even with, Great-tailed Grackles.

Range: Southeastern Mexico to Bolivia, northeastern Argentina, and southern Brazil.

BLACK-COWLED ORIOLE
Icterus dominicensis   Plate 39

Description: 7½–8. Found only in western Bocas del Toro lowlands. *Mostly black (including tail)*, with yellow wing-coverts, rump, breast, and belly; a tinge of chestnut between black chest and yellow breast. Immature similar but with yellowish back. In juvenile black is restricted to forehead, sides of head, throat, most of wings, and tail; remaining areas yellowish, brighter below.

Similar species: Juvenile resembles Yellow-tailed Oriole but is smaller, much duller yellow below, and never has yellow in tail. It is also smaller and much duller than Yellow-backed Oriole (not known from Bocas del Toro). Adult is only breeding Panama oriole with wholly black head and neck.

Status and distribution: Uncommon along forested rivers, and in woodland and forest borders, clearings with scattered trees, and in banana plantations in lowlands of western Bocas del Toro; usually found near water.

Habits: Not well known in Panama. In Costa Rica generally found in pairs, during the dry season sometimes seen feeding with migrant orioles in flowering *Erythrina* trees. Has a metallic *plink* call note (Wetmore), as well as a whistled song consisting of a series of sweet and rapid, but not very loud, phrases.

Range: Southeastern Mexico to Caribbean western Panama; Greater Antilles (except Jamaica) and some of the Bahamas.

Note: Middle American forms (the *prosthemelas* group) were considered conspecific with birds from the Greater Antilles (the *dominicensis* group) in the 1983 AOU Checklist.

ORCHARD ORIOLE
Icterus spurius   Plate 32

Description: 6¾. Male *mostly chestnut*, with black head and neck, back, and bib; wings and tail also mainly black, with chestnut lesser coverts and whitish wing-edging.

Female olive above, brightest on head and rump; wings and tail dusky olive, with two whitish wing-bars; *greenish yellow below*. First-year male like female but with *black bib*, often with some chestnut just below it.

Similar species: This small oriole is the only Panama member of its genus with deep chestnut, not orange or yellow, in its plumage. Female resembles female Northern Oriole, but is smaller and it lacks any trace of orange on underparts (which instead are a uniform greenish yellow).

Status and distribution: Common winter resident (early August–early April, a few sometimes arriving by late July, most departing by mid-March) in semiopen and residential areas with scattered trees, and in lighter woodland and forest borders in lowlands on both slopes; numbers seem greatest on Pacific slope of central Panama, with fewer on Pacific slope of western Panama, or in extensively forested areas (where it occurs mainly as a transient); recorded occasionally as a transient from Pacific offshore islands, and from western highlands up to about 1650 m (5500 ft).

Habits: Widespread in semiopen areas but especially numerous in residential areas, where it congregates in rather large groups to roost, and to feed in flowering trees, notably *Erythrina*. Adult males seem to predominate numerically. Males are occasionally heard to give a snatch of their rich warbled song; both sexes often give their distinctive *chack* call note.

Range: Breeds from eastern and central United States to central Mexico; winters from southern Mexico to Colombia and northwestern Venezuela.

YELLOW-BACKED ORIOLE
Icterus chrysater   Plate 39

Description: 8½–9. *Mostly rich orange-yellow* with black throat and chest, wings, and tail. In many individuals, the yellow areas adjacent to the black bib are more or less tinged with brown.

Similar species: Yellow-tailed Oriole is yellower, has black (not yellow) back, and has yellow in wings and tail (not solid black). In eastern Panama see also Orange-crowned Oriole.

Status and distribution: Fairly common in forest and woodland borders and clearings, and shrubby areas with trees in lowlands on both slopes from Veraguas eastward; ranges up in smaller numbers into foothills to about

900 m (3000 ft). Curiously, no resident oriole has ever been found in Chiriquí; this species would be the most likely. The commonest and most widespread resident oriole in the Canal area, particularly numerous on the Pacific side.

Habits: Often in pairs or small family groups. The song is a series of four to eight loud clear musical whistles moving in a disconnected manner up and down so that it sounds off-key. The usual call is a *teea, cheep-cheep, cheep* (the *cheep*'s nasal); also has a part-chatter, part buzzy whistle *kzwee-kzwee-kzwee-kzwee-kzwee* and a nasal *nyeh-nyeh-nyeh-nyeh*.

Range: Southeastern Mexico to Colombia and northern Venezuela, though not known from Costa Rica.

ORANGE-CROWNED ORIOLE
Icterus auricapillus Plate 39

Description: 8. Found only in eastern Panama. *Crown, nape, and sides of neck orange*; forehead, sides of head, throat, chest, back, wings and tail black; wing-coverts, rump, and lower underparts orange-yellow. Juvenile has crown and nape yellowish olive, back and tail dull olive, wings dusky with pale yellow edging; pale yellow below, brighter on throat, with some dusky on lower throat.

Similar species: An especially attractive oriole. More orange, especially on head, than Yellow-tailed Oriole and with no yellow on tail. Lacks brownish tinge shown by many Yellow-backed Orioles and with black (not yellow) back.

Status and distribution: Uncommon to locally fairly common in woodland and forest borders and shrubby clearings in lowlands of eastern Panama province (middle and upper Bayano River valley) and Darién, with single reports from adjacent western San Blas (a pair seen near Nusagandi on March 7, 1986; Ridgely and J. Guarnaccia) and from Canal area (group of three seen near Gamboa on November 19, 1983; H. Stockwell *et al.*).

Habits: Most often seen in pairs, sometimes feeding high in flowering trees with other orioles. Its simple song consists of a single whistled note or short phrase repeated endlessly for up to 15–20 minutes, with only very infrequent changes (the new note or phrase may also be tirelessly repeated); it is usually delivered from an exposed perch, most often in the early morning.

Range: Eastern Panama to northern Venezuela.

YELLOW-TAILED ORIOLE
Icterus mesomelas Plate 39

Description: 9. *Mostly bright yellow*, with *black back*, wings (except *yellow wing-coverts*), center of tail (with *outer feathers yellow*), and throat and chest.

Similar species: Yellow-backed Oriole has, as name implies, a yellow (not black) back and all black wings and tail, and is more orange-yellow generally. In Bocas del Toro, see juvenile Black-cowled Oriole.

Status and distribution: Fairly common in thickets near water, woodland borders, and clearings with trees in lowlands on entire Caribbean slope; on Pacific slope found in smaller numbers from western Panama province (a pair seen several times near base of Cerro Campana in 1969–1970, but not since) and Canal area eastward, becoming more common in Darién, where it is regularly found well up into lower foothills (e.g. at Cana). In Canal area much more numerous and widespread on Caribbean slope.

Habits: Everywhere seems to prefer the vicinity of water. The song is a series of very rich mellow whistled phrases, each phrase usually repeated several times before going on to the next. Usual and distinctive calls are *chup-cheet* or *chup-chup-cheet*, and a *weechaw*.

Range: Southeastern Mexico to northwestern Venezuela and northwestern Peru.

NORTHERN ORIOLE
Icterus galbula Plate 32

Description: 7¼. Male *mostly bright orange and black:* entire hood, back, and most of wings and tail black; lower back and rump, most of underparts, and sides of tail bright orange; wings with bright orange lesser coverts and single white wing-bar and edging. Female somewhat variable: olive brown to brownish gray above, grayest on back and browner (sometimes almost golden) on crown, nape, and rump, all except rump sometimes mottled with dusky; wings duskier with two white wing-bars; *below usually orange-yellow, brightest and most orange on breast* and under tail-coverts, but sometimes yellower below with only a tinge of orange on breast and whiter on belly. First-winter males resemble bright adult females; by the time they migrate northward they have molted into a duller and somewhat splotchy version of the fully adult male.

Similar species: Male is only truly orange and black oriole in Panama; Black-cowled Oriole also has entire head and neck black, but it is clear yellow (not orange) on wings, rump, and lower underparts. Female Orchard Oriole resembles female, but is *always uniform greenish yellow below* (never showing the orange of the vast majority of female Northerns; in the few Northerns which lack the orange, the belly is always contrastingly whitish).

Status and distribution: Common winter resident throughout (early October–late April, a few sometimes arriving in late September and lingering into early May), mostly in lowlands, but in Chiriquí also in highlands to over 1800 m (6000 ft); recorded also on Pacific islands. Favors woodland borders and fairly open areas with trees.

Habits: Usually does not feed in such large flocks as Orchard Oriole, but may gather in groups to fly to roost or on migration. Like the Orchard Oriole, feeds a great deal in flowering trees.

Range: Breeds in North America; winters sparingly in eastern and southern United States, mostly from Mexico to Colombia and northern Venezuela.

Note: The form breeding in western North America (*bullockii*), formerly considered a distinct species (Bullock's Oriole) but now usually treated as conspecific, could occur during northern winter months; its normal wintering range is in Mexico and Guatemala, rarely south to northwestern Costa Rica. Adult male differs from eastern form (Baltimore Oriole) in its orange face and large white patch on wing, female in its olive gray back and whitish belly. Considerable hybridi-zation occurs where the breeding ranges of the two forms overlap, hence sight reports of birds other than adult males must be viewed with some caution. One such female exhibiting the characters of *bullockii* was seen on Barro Colorado Island November 13, 1972 (M. Perrone).

YELLOW-BILLED CACIQUE
Amblycercus holosericeus   Plate 39

Description: ♂ 10; ♀ 9. *Bill yellowish white or greenish yellow.* Iris pale yellow. *All black.*
Similar species: Perched Scarlet-rumped Cacique, with red rump hidden, looks like this species but has pale blue eye. Male White-lined Tanager is smaller with heavier, shorter, mostly bluish bill, and flashes white under wing-linings in flight.
Status and distribution: Fairly common in thickets and dense undergrowth of clearings and woodland borders in lowlands on both slopes, ranging up in smaller numbers in suitable habitat into the foothills and lower highlands.

Habits: A great skulker, rarely coming into the open, and often difficult to even glimpse. Normally forages close to the ground, but occasionally goes higher to feed in flowering or fruiting trees. Has a variety of liquid whistles and harsh churring notes: a repeated loud clear whistle *pur-weé-pew*; a rather sweet *wreeeeoo* and a harsher *queeyoo*; and an almost duck-like *quack-quack-quack*, varied to *kwok* or a buzzy *kzaak*. Heard more often than seen.
Range: Eastern Mexico to northern Venezuela and Bolivia.

SCARLET-RUMPED CACIQUE
Cacicus uropygialis   Plate 39

Description: ♂ 10; ♀ 9. Rather long bill, greenish white. Iris pale blue. Glossy black with *scarlet rump* (more orange-scarlet in female). Rump patch concealed when perched, but conspicuous in flight. Birds from eastern Darién (*pacificus*) have a larger bill than those from the rest of its Panama range (*microrhynchus*).
Similar species: When rump color cannot be seen, this species can be confused with other all or mostly black forest birds. Yellow-billed Cacique, in particular, is similar in such a situation but is normally found in dense underbrush of clearings and borders.
Status and distribution: Uncommon to locally fairly common in humid forest, second-growth woodland, and borders in lowlands on entire Caribbean slope; less numerous and more local in more humid areas on Pacific slope from Chiriquí (where now very local due to deforestation; now perhaps found only on Burica Peninsula, where fairly numerous in late June 1982) east to eastern Panama province (upper Bayano River valley), though absent from drier areas and all of the Azuero Peninsula; uncommon in eastern Darién (Jaqué/Piñas Bay area and Cerro Pirre southward; not recorded from western Darién); ranges up locally in foothills to about 900 m (3000 ft). Widespread in forested parts of Canal area, though more numerous on Caribbean side.
Habits: Usually nests solitarily, though occasionally in small groups (this perhaps most frequent in eastern portion of its range, *fide* N. G. Smith), hanging its squarish bag-shaped nest from a tree at edge of forest, sometimes even from a bridge or other structure. At other seasons, Scarlet-rumped Caciques troop about the forest in bold noisy bands, often accompanying oropendolas,

fruitcrows, toucans, or nunbirds; they forage at all levels, but mostly rather high, often probing into bromeliads. A variety of loud musical whistled calls is given, among them one with a throaty quality, *shreeo-shreeo*, and another quite human-sounding *wheew-whee-whee-whee-wheet*. *Pacificus* gives a whistled *teeo* or *keeo* without the burry quality of corresponding call of *microrhynchus*, and its other calls may also differ from those of *microrhynchus*, but the significance (if any) of this variation has not been established.

Range: Eastern Honduras south to southwestern Ecuador and Andes of eastern Peru.

Note: More than one species is probably involved, at least in South America. Nominate *uropygialis* of the Andes from Colombia to Peru (Subtropical Cacique) is markedly larger than *microrhynchus* group of Central American and trans-Andean lowlands, and has different vocalizations; it almost surely represents a separate species. Full species status for *pacificus* (Pacific Cacique) also seems possible; this would leave Central American birds as *C. microrhynchus* (Scarlet-rumped Cacique).

YELLOW-RUMPED CACIQUE
Cacicus cela   Plate 39

Description: ♂ 11; ♀ 9½. Bill pale greenish. Iris pale blue. Mostly *glossy black* with *orange-yellow patch on wing-coverts, lower back, rump, basal half of tail, and under tail-coverts.*

Similar species: Oropendolas have yellow only on tail, not on rump, vent, and wings.

Status and distribution: Fairly common to common in canopy and borders of forest and second-growth woodland, and in clearings with scattered trees in lowlands on Caribbean slope from western Colon province (Río Indio) eastward, and locally on Pacific slope from southern Veraguas (Soná, Paracoté) eastward, becoming more numerous in eastern Panama province (Bayano river valley) and especially in Darién; ranges locally up into lower foothills (to almost 600 m: 2000 ft), at least in Darién.

Habits: Similar to the oropendolas and often associating with them, particularly the Chestnut-headed. Frequently nests with oropendolas, but generally in a small group somewhat removed from the main body of their colony. Cacique nests are shorter and more oblong than the long, conical ones of oropendolas, and are often clumped together inches apart or even touching each other. Has a variety of calls ranging from cackles and squawks to squeaks and rather liquid notes.

Range: Western Panama to northern Bolivia and central Brazil.

CRESTED OROPENDOLA
Psarocolius decumanus   Plate 39

Description: ♂ 17; ♀ 15. *Bill ivory yellow to greenish yellow.* Iris blue (more grayish in female, and especially in immatures). *Mostly black (including head)* except for dark chestnut lower back, rump, and under tail-coverts; tail yellow except for central pair of feathers. Not really crested; the "crest" consists merely of a few hair-like feathers that protrude from the crown. In flight looks long-necked and long-tailed, quite "stretched-out".

Similar species: Smaller and chunkier Chestnut-headed Oropendola has chestnut head and neck. Most resembles Black Oropendola of eastern Panama, but that species has bicolored black-tipped yellow bill and bare facial area.

Status and distribution: Uncommon to locally common in canopy and borders of forest and woodland, and in clearings with large trees, in lowlands on Pacific slope from western Chiriquí (from which there are few or no recent reports) eastward, including western side of Azuero Peninsula; on Caribbean slope found from western Colon province and northern Coclé east through Canal area (still not reported from San Blas, though seems likely to occur); ranges locally up in foothills to about 900 m (3000 ft). Rather scarce and local in most of Panama, but becomes numerous in Darién (where the commonest oropendola).

Habits: Similar to the more common Chestnut-headed Oropendola and frequently nests nearby, though apparently not in the same tree; also sometimes nests in association with Yellow-rumped Cacique. Often nests in smallish *Cecropia* trees. Breeding season much like that of Chestnut-headed, but in Canal area seems to extend a little later, into late June.

Range: Western Panama to Bolivia, northern Argentina, and southeastern Brazil.

CHESTNUT-HEADED OROPENDOLA
Psarocolius wagleri   Plate 39

Description: ♂ 14; ♀ 11. Bill whitish ivory to pale greenish yellow (often with dusky tip). Iris pale blue. *Head and neck chestnut;* otherwise mostly black, merging to chestnut on rump and lower belly; tail yellow except for dusky central pair of feathers and outer web of outermost pair. Males have inconspicuous crest consisting of a few hair-like feathers.

Similar species: No other Panama oropendola has a chestnut head and neck (can be hard to see in poor light, however). See Crested Oropendola.

Status and distribution: Common in more humid lowlands on both slopes in forest, second-growth woodland, borders, clearings, and even roadsides with trees; ranges up in reduced numbers in the foothills to about 1350 m (4500 ft); more local on Pacific slope and absent from drier parts of Azuero Peninsula and southern Coclé; not found on Pacific islands. Seems somewhat less numerous in Darién. This species is especially common in the Canal area, and is Panama's most widespread and familiar oropendola.

Habits: This species' nesting colonies of up to a hundred (usually 25–50) nests, hung in an isolated or well-exposed tree or grove, are a characteristic sight in much of the lowlands and present a fascinating spectacle throughout the breeding cycle (roughly January to May, occasionally later). At other seasons the birds disperse and wander widely. Both sexes, but especially males in display, emit a variety of loud slashing croaks and gurgling notes, similar to those of other Panama oropendolas. The gurgling notes are rather musical, and suggest dripping water, *plup, plup, plup, plup-loo-upoo.*

Range: Southeastern Mexico to western Ecuador.

Note: Formerly placed in the monotypic genus *Zarhynchus.*

MONTEZUMA OROPENDOLA
Psarocolius montezuma   Plate 39

Description: ♂ 20; ♀ 16. Known mainly from western Caribbean lowlands. *Bill black with bright orange tip; large area of bare skin below eye blue*, with narrow pink strip below that; iris brown. Head, neck, throat, and breast black; *otherwise bright chestnut above*, darker chestnut on belly; tail yellow except for black central pair of feathers.

Similar species: The Montezuma's impressive size alone normally distinguishes it from other oropendolas within its range; in any case, the bicolored bill and largely chestnut body are diagnostic. See Black Oropendola.

Status and distribution: Locally fairly common to common in canopy and borders

of humid forest and second-growth woodland, and in clearings with scattered tall trees, in lowlands of Bocas del Toro, extending eastward in small numbers on Caribbean slope to Canal area (mainly in Escobal/Achiote region, a few wanderers elsewhere); occasionally also wanders to Pacific slope (e.g. seen above Santa Fé, Veraguas, and in Canal area; both N. G. Smith), with one surprising specimen also having been taken near Chepo, eastern Panama province, in March 1921 by M. J. Kelly (*fide* Wetmore).

Habits: Similar to those of other oropendolas, sometimes nesting in the same tree with them. The nests are larger and longer than those of the Chestnut-headed Oropendola. Males in display give a series of loud slashing gurgling notes, the bird often leaning forward and sometimes doing a partial forward somersault with wings drooped. The calls resemble those of the Chestnut-headed but are louder and even harsher.

Range: Eastern Mexico to central Panama.

Note: Formerly placed in the genus *Gymnostinops.*

BLACK OROPENDOLA
Psarocolius guatimozinus   Plate 39

Description: ♂ 18; ♀ 16. Known only from Darién. *Bill black with bright orange tip; large area of bare skin below eye blue*, with narrow pink strip below that; iris brown. *Mostly black* with only the mid-back to rump, under tail-coverts, and a little on wing-coverts dark chestnut; tail yellow except for black central pair of feathers.

Similar species: Crested Oropendola is similar but has entirely greenish yellow bill, lacks bare facial skin, etc. The somewhat larger Montezuma Oropendola has a different range, is mostly chestnut except for black head and neck.

Status and distribution: Fairly common at borders of humid forest and in clearings with scattered tall trees in lowlands of Darién (mostly in lower Tuira and Chucunaque River valleys, also taken west to Santa Fé); may range west into upper Bayano River valley of eastern Panama province (unconfirmed sightings).

Habits: Similar to those of other oropendolas and often with them.

Range: Eastern Panama and northern Colombia.

Note: Formerly placed in the genus *Gymnostinops.*

FRINGILLINE AND CARDUELINE FINCHES AND ALLIES: Fringillidae (2)

These two species are members of the Cardueline finch subfamily, now classified as part of the Fringillidae (which formerly also incorporated all the Emberizine finches). Both Panama species are small, predominantly yellow birds found in semiopen country, notable for their bounding flight and pretty twittery songs. In Costa Rica both are much reduced in numbers because of persecution for the cagebird traffic, but this is not a serious problem in Panama, where they remain numerous (and in fact may even be increasing).

YELLOW-BELLIED SISKIN
Carduelis xanthogaster   Plate 38

Description: 4½. Found only in Chiriquí highlands. Male *mostly black* with *lemon yellow breast and belly*; large patch of yellow on flight feathers and another at base of tail. Female olive above, wings blackish with *light yellow patch*; light yellowish olive below, somewhat grayer on throat, *fading to white on lower belly*.
Similar species: Resembles Lesser Goldfinch, but male has black throat and chest (not all yellow below); female has yellow (not white) patch on wing and white lower belly (not uniform yellow below).
Status and distribution: Fairly common to common in clearings and forest borders in highlands of western and central Chiriquí (farthest east report being a group of six seen on Hornito ridge along road to Fortuna on July 4, 1982; Ridgely); recorded mostly 1200–2400 m (4000–8000 ft). Particularly numerous in Volcán area; seems to have increased in recent years.
Habits: Almost always seen in small flocks, usually feeding well up in the trees. The song is a thin but musical warbling twitter, long continued and without distinct form.
Range: Costa Rica and western Panama; Venezuela and Colombia to western Ecuador; northern Bolivia.
Note: Formerly placed in the genus *Spinus*.

LESSER GOLDFINCH
Spinus psaltria   p.435

Description: 4. Male *glossy black above, bright yellow below*, with *white patch at base of flight feathers* (forming a band in flight) and on inner remiges, and near tip of inner webs of rectrices. Female olive above (sometimes streaked with dusky), the *wings black with white patches as in male; uniform lemon yellow below*.
Similar species: Male Yellow-bellied Siskin has black throat and chest; female siskin has yellow (not white) patch in wing and is more olive below with white belly (not uniform yellow). Euphonias lack light patches in wings; a flock of goldfinches (or siskins) in flight can always be distinguished by their undulating flight (direct in euphonias).
Status and distribution: Common locally (but somewhat erratic in places) in open country with scattered trees, gardens, and in lighter woodland in lowlands and (especially) foothills on Pacific slope in western and central Panama, most numerous from Chiriquí to Coclé; in central Panama recorded mainly from Pacific side, though there are some reports from the Caribbean as well (some of which may pertain to escaped cagebirds), with small populations now apparently established as far east as eastern Panama province (Cerro Azul, Tocumen/Pacora area). Particularly numerous around Boquete.
Habits: Usually found in small flocks in semiopen country. The song is long and musical, rather irregular, with interspersed twittering phrases.
Range: Western United States to Venezuela and northern Peru.
Note: Formerly placed in the genus *Spinus*, and often called the Dark-backed Goldfinch.

LESSER GOLDFINCH (male)

OLD WORLD SPARROWS: Passeridae (1)

One member of this Old World family has recently appeared in Panama, where it is in the process of establishing itself in towns and cities; it was introduced into North America and southern South America.

HOUSE SPARROW
Passer domesticus

Description: 6. Now locally established in towns and cities in western and central Panama. Male has *gray crown, chestnut nape, white cheeks and sides of neck*, and *black bib on throat and chest*; otherwise brownish above streaked black, with plain gray rump and single white wing-bar; below whitish. Female much drabber: pale grayish brown above, with *whitish superciliary* and dusky-streaked back; single whitish wing-bar; below dingy whitish.

Similar species: Can generally be known by its urban surroundings; males actually have quite attractive plumage, and are easily recognized, while the nondescript females are usually accompanying males. Compare especially to female Dickcissel.

Status and distribution: First recorded on March 6, 1976, when about 20 were seen in David, Chiriquí (Ridgely and C. Myers); has since spread locally into urban areas on Pacific slope, most numerous east through eastern side of Azuero Peninsula (*fide* F. Delgado), in smaller numbers east as far as Panama City (where first noted in March 1979); on Caribbean slope so far known only from Changuinola, Bocas del Toro, where seen in April 1980 (Ridgely), but may spread (recently, in 1988, seen in Colon). It appears that the House Sparrow is now extending its range naturally, without any direct assistance from man; over the past few decades it has spread rapidly through much of Middle and South America, and it no longer appears that it is incapable of persisting in humid tropical climates (as had previously been thought). In the tropics, however, House Sparrows so far seem confined to towns and cities, and they are not establishing themselves in agricultural areas.

Habits: A familiar and often aggressive little bird usually found in small flocks. Elsewhere its spread has often had a decidedly negative impact on populations of certain native small birds (especially hole-nesters and, in South America, the Rufous-collared Sparrow). In Panama, however, no such impact is (yet?) apparent, perhaps because its urban niche is essentially vacant.

Range: Native to Eurasia, but widely introduced elsewhere, then gradually spreading on its own.

ADDITIONAL SPECIES OF COSTA RICA, NICARAGUA, AND HONDURAS

Accounts of the 162 species of birds which have occurred in Costa Rica, Nicaragua, and Honduras, but which have not been found in Panama, follow. These are two additional families, the Thick-knees (Burhinidae) and the Creepers (Certhiidae). The information presented on each species is somewhat abridged compared with the Panama section of this book (hereinafter "main text"). Included, in a single paragraph but in approximately uniform sequence, is a description of the bird in question (employing the same terminology), brief comments on other species with which it is most likely confused, its habitat and range (including extralimital), and some information on behavior and vocalizations where appropriate. A few other species found in this area which also occur in Panama but which look dramatically different in the latter, are also mentioned. Northern migrants are included, though often their accounts are somewhat abbreviated. A few species which remain possible but unrecorded in Panama, and are mentioned in a "Note" in the main text, are referred to again here, but are not redescribed. The few species which are considered hypothetical are marked in brackets. Birds found only on Cocos Island or its vicinity are not included.

A substantial number of these birds are illustrated on Plates 41 to 48. Unfortunately, all species could not be included. Selected for depiction were comparatively widespread and numerous species, particularly if they range in Costa Rica (where ornithological interest is now so great; note that the subspecies selected is usually the one found in Costa Rica). Species restricted to northern or western Honduras (and ranging northward in Middle America) were usually, but not always, excluded. We also took advantage of this new illustration opportunity to include some species which should have been portrayed on a color plate in the first edition of *Birds of Panama*, but which for lack of space were not. Examples would include the four Panamas cracids, a number of swallows, Turquoise and Lovely Cotingas, Fiery-billed Aracari, and so on. Virtually all of these also are found in Central America, but a few anomalies have resulted. For example, the endemic Panama form of the Green-breasted Mango is illustrated here — it was considered useful to show it next to the Costa Rican form, and it had not been shown before. As will be seen, we have cross-referenced back and forth between the two sets of plates as much as is practicable in order to reduce the potential for confusion and to facilitate comparison. We recognize that this final arrangement is not optimal, but it at least permitted the opportunity to provide color illustrations for many species (better than none at all). Creating a completely new set of plates for this new edition was impossible — being both prohibitively expensive and time-consuming.

One of us (RSR) now has a fair amount of experience in many parts of all three of these countries involved — the greatest amount of time being spent in Costa Rica, and (regrettably) the least in Nicaragua. Consequently (as in all such efforts), a certain amount of the information presented herein has been built upon from information derived from other sources. In this regard two seminal works of the recent era must be noted: Paul Slud's *Birds of Costa Rica* (1964) and Burt Monroe's *Distributional Survey of the Birds of Honduras* (1968), both of which were referred to (at least in a general way) continually. A number of more specific articles are referred to in individual species accounts. We should also acknowledge the particular usefulness of John Guarnaccia's recent (1987) trip to Honduras, when he obtained much information and some fine tape recordings, which he placed at our disposal, and to John Arvin's thorough and helpful review of this part of the manuscript.

THICKET TINAMOU
Crypturellus cinnamomeus   Plate 41

10–11. Often numerous mid-sized tinamou found mainly in *deciduous woodland and scrub on Pacific slope. Legs red. Predominantly rufescent* (its former English name of Rufescent Tinamou was not entirely inappropriate), with usually bold *dark barring on upperparts and wings*, also on crissum. Female also has barring on flanks and (in some races, especially *praepes* of Costa Rica) breast. Uncommon to locally common on Pacific slope from Honduras to north-western Costa Rica, mostly below 1500 m (5000 ft), lower southward, also on Caribbean slope in arid interior valleys of Honduras; ranges north to northern Mexico. Hard to see, usually in thick cover and rarely lingering long in the open, walking on the ground. Call is an abrupt and loud, basically single-noted *hoo-oo* with slight upward inflection, given at rather long intervals (this in Costa Rica; more northern races may call differently?). Taxonomy is complex, with more than one species possibly being involved in Middle America and their relationship to various South American forms still unclear.

SLATY-BREASTED TINAMOU
Crypturellus boucardi   Plate 41

10–11. Mid-sized *dark* tinamou of *humid forests on Caribbean slope. Legs red. Head, neck, and breast slaty gray*, becoming more grayish brown on remaining upperparts and brownish on belly, with some blackish barring on flanks and crissum. Female has *conspicuous rufescent and black barring on wings, rump, and flanks*. Uncommon to locally common inside humid forest (occasionally out to forest borders or into adjacent cocoa plantations) in lowlands on Caribbean slope, mostly below 600 m (2000 ft), south to central Costa Rica, locally onto Pacific slope in northwestern Costa Rica (Cordillera de Guanacaste); ranges north to southern Mexico. Infrequently seen and rather shy, walking on forest floor, usually freezing when alarmed (and thus doubtless often passed by), very rarely flying. Call is a

mournful, hollow *cooooo, coooooooooo?*, given especially during calm late afternoons and perhaps mostly during the rainy season. Quite numerous but elusive at La Selva Biological Station. Note that hybrids with *C. cinnamomea* are known from central Honduras.

GREATER SHEARWATER
Puffinus gravis

Single record of washed-up remains found on beach at Tortuguero in northeastern Costa Rica in June 1977 (G. S. Carr, *Condor 81*(3): 323, 1979). See main text under Cory's Shearwater (p.56).

PINNATED BITTERN
Botaurus pinnatus

Recorded very locally from freshwater marshes in Costa Rica (one site being at Palo Verde in Guanacaste), where it presumably breeds. The species likely also occurs in Honduras and Nicaragua in appropriate habitat. See main text under American Bittern (p.67).

GREEN-WINGED TEAL
Anas crecca

Recorded as a rare winter visitor from North America to northern Honduras and accidental as far south as central Costa Rica (where there is only one record, of a recovered banded bird); has also strayed to Colombia. See main text under Blue-winged Teal (p.80).

CANVASBACK
Aythya valisineria

A rare winter visitant from North America to Honduras. 19–22. *Forehead slopes gradually to long black bill*. Male has *chestnut head and neck*, black breast, and *mainly white body*. Female has *pale brown head and neck*, brown breast, and *pale grayish body*. Both sexes *lack* obvious pale wing stripe in flight (unlike Lesser Scaup, Ring-necked Duck, etc.) A diving duck, favoring open water, both fresh and salt.

RUDDY DUCK
Oxyura jamaicensis

A rare winter visitant from North America to northern Honduras (also single possible reports from Nicaragua and Costa Rica); also resident in South America (but whether latter is the same species remains uncertain). 15–16. General form recalls Masked Duck (see main text, p.82), but larger and *long stiff tail* more apt to be *held half-cocked out of the water*. In nonbreeding plumage both sexes have *whitish* (not buff) *cheeks*, in female crossed by *single dark horizontal line* (not two of them); otherwise brownish and whitish. Breeding plumage male (unlikely in Central America) *mostly rufous* with black head and neck and *striking white cheeks*. Both sexes *lack* white wing patch in flight (unlike Masked Duck). A diving duck, in Honduras reported on freshwater lakes.

WHITE-BREASTED HAWK

WHITE-BREASTED HAWK
Accipiter chionogaster   p.439

Resident in highlands of Honduras and Nicaragua (and north into southern Mexico), the form *chionogaster* was treated as a race of *A. striatus* (Sharp-shinned Hawk) in the 1983 AOU Check-list, but has often been considered a full species and is so treated here. 10–14. Adult has *cheeks and entire underparts white* with some fine blackish streaking on cheeks, throat, and chest, and buff thighs; upperparts slaty, tail crossed by several broad grayish bands. Streaking on underparts browner and more prominent and extensive in immatures. Uncommon in cloud forest, pine-oak woodland, and borders in highlands of Honduras, and northern Nicaragua, mostly above 900 m (3000 ft). Behavior much as in typical Sharp-shinned Hawk, and the two occur together during northern winter.

COOPER'S HAWK
Accipiter cooperii

Recorded as a rare winter visitor from North America to Honduras, with single records also from Costa Rica and Colombia. See main text under Sharp-shinned Hawk (p.93).

PLAIN CHACHALACA
Ortalis vetula   Plate 41

19–21. Replaces Gray-headed Chachalaca (see main text) *northward on Caribbean slope*. Olive brown above, grayer on head and darker more bronzy green on tail which is tipped pale buff; small bare red dewlap; underparts pale olive brownish, becoming more rufescent on crissum. *Lacks the chestnut in wings of Gray-headed Chachalaca*. Fairly common in a variety of wooded, second-growth, forest edge, and scrub habitats on Caribbean slope in Honduras and northern Nicaragua (Matagalpa region), with an apparently isolated population on Pacific slope in northwestern Costa Rica (Guanacaste, e.g. at Santa Rosa National Park); ranges north to northeastern Mexico and southern Texas. Gray-headed Chachalaca is more restricted to Caribbean lowlands. Behavior much like Gray-headed Chachalaca; mainly arboreal, often in small groups. Its calls are very loud and raucous, typically a repeated three-noted *cha-cha-lac!* . . .

WHITE-BELLIED CHACHALACA
Ortalis leucogastra

19–20. Replaces other two Central American chachalacas in *Pacific lowlands of Honduras and northern Nicaragua*. Resembles

Plain Chachalaca, but with *ashy gray head and neck*, browner breast (which is scaled whitish) *contrasting with pure white belly*, and *tail feathers tipped white*. Uncommon in deciduous woodland and gallery forest; ranges north to southern Mexico. Behavior as in Plain Chachalaca. Considered conspecific with *O. vetula* (Plain Chachalaca) in 1983 AOU Check-list, but this later changed (*Auk 102* (3): 681, 1985).

HIGHLAND GUAN
Penelopina nigra   Plate 41

21–25. Also called Black Penelopina, or Black Chachalaca. A sexually dimorphic cracid of Honduras and Nicaragua highlands. Male's bill and *legs coral red*; female's *legs coral red*, but bill brown. Male *all shiny black*, with *large red dewlap*. Female *rufous brown*, intricately barred with black above, *more broadly barred on tail*; throat reddish (unfeathered); buffy brown below, with faint or no barring. Does not occur with the blue-faced (no red) Black Guan. Female somewhat chachalaca-like, but none of these is barred above or has red legs. Uncommon and rather local in cloud forest, less often out into adjacent pine-oak woodland, in highlands of Honduras and northern Nicaragua, mostly above 1200 m (4000 ft); ranges north to southern Mexico. Basically arboreal, and inconspicuous and shy (and much hunted), most often encountered when flushed by chance, or when males are displaying (especially February–May). Call an unmistakable, sharply rising (and at close range piercing) whistled *who-o-o-e-e-ee-ee-ee?*, and also has a rattling descending wing whirr given in flight.

BUFFY-CROWNED WOOD-PARTRIDGE
Dendrortyx leucophrys   Plate 41

12–14. A *large, long-tailed* quail of highland forests. Long legs orange-red, as is the orbital area. *Forehead and upper throat pale buff to whitish* (despite its name, the entire crown is not buffy), remainder of crown and neck chestnut streaked white, *mantle bluish gray streaked chestnut*; wings, rump, and tail mainly olive brown; *below mostly bluish gray, broadly streaked chestnut on breast. Hypospodius* of Costa Rica differs from nominate race (remainder of range) in having streaks on breast narrower and *blackish*. Uncommon in cloud forest in highlands of Honduras and northern Nicaragua; rare in northwestern and central Costa Rica; ranges north to southern Mexico. Terrestrial and

very shy, slipping away at the slightest alarm; may occur mainly in pairs (not coveys). Voice not known to us; "gabbles" have been reported from one alarmed individual (P. Slud).

SINGING QUAIL
Dactylortyx thoracicus

8–9. Male mostly olive brown, darkest on crown, upperparts mottled with blackish; *superciliary and throat cinnamon-rufous*, breast finely streaked white. Female like male but with grayish face, *whitish throat*, richer cinnamon-buff on breast. Uncommon in cloud forest in highlands of western Honduras above 1200 m (4000 ft); ranges north to northeastern Mexico, more numerous northward, and locally occurring down to sea level. An inconspicuous, terrestrial forest quail, usually in small coveys. Presence most often made known by its loud clear rollicking call: after several introductory *prreer* notes, starting slowly but gradually becoming faster and louder, it breaks into a fast *chí-cheeroweer, chí-cheeroweer*, . . . latter repeated three or four times. The Singing Quail has exceptionally long claws, but their function is unknown.

OCELLATED QUAIL
Cyrtonyx ocellatus

7½–8. *Small, beautifully patterned plump quail of pine forests. Complex, "harlequin" black-and-white pattern on head and throat*, bushy crest pale brownish (sometimes laid flat); above grayish olive, blotched and spotted with black; breast buff, *belly chestnut, sides gray spotted with buff*, flanks barred with blackish. Female much duller, *mostly vinaceous brown barred and spotted with black*, superciliary and throat whitish spotted black, irregular blackish collar across foreneck. Uncommon in highlands of Honduras and northern Nicaragua, mainly above 750 m (2500 ft); ranges north to southern Mexico. A very secretive quail which favors less disturbed areas with tall grass or heavy shrubby undergrowth. Resembles the Montezuma Quail (*C. montezumae*) of southwestern United States and Mexico, of which it may be only a race.

CRESTED BOBWHITE
Colinus cristatus   Plate 41

8–9. Until recently the bobwhites found from Guatemala to northwestern Costa Rica were considered a full species by most authorities, *C. leucopogon* (Spot-bellied Bobwhite), but this was treated as conspecific with *C. cristatus* (Crested Bobwhite) in the 1983 AOU Check-list. There are numerous subspecies in both groups. "Spot-bellied" Bobwhites are generally similar to "true" Cresteds, but they *usually show no obvious crest*; this is variable, however, both individually and on a population basis, and some birds from Central America have crests fully as long as any from Panama. Further, males have *throat whitish or black bordered with white* (not buff to rufous); all populations, including "true" Cresteds, have the large white spots on the belly. Fairly common in semiopen grassy country with scattered shrubs and scrub on Pacific slope south to western Costa Rica (especially in Guanacaste), also reaching the western side of the Central Plateau), ranging locally onto Caribbean slope in Honduras. Former refers only to range of Spot-bellied group; "true" Cresteds have only recently (in the 1970s) spread into southwestern Costa Rica from Panama and the two could conceivably come into contact in the future. Behavior of both groups, including their distinctive *quoit bob-white?* call, similar. All bobwhites are much more in evidence when they are vocalizing (especially April–June).

BLACK-THROATED BOBWHITE
Colinus nigrogularis

8–9. Only in *lowland pine savanna of eastern Honduras and northeastern Nicaragua* (also from Yucatan to northern Guatemala). Male has no crest, *black throat and superciliary* (both bordered with white); above mottled and barred brown, rufous, and gray; breast and upper belly white, *feathers broadly margined black giving a bold scalloped look*; lower belly cinnamon. Female has throat and superciliary buff; below white, barred and streaked with black and rufous. Behavior, including voice, much as in the "Spot-bellied"/Crested complex; it is fairly common locally.

OCELLATED CRAKE
Micropygia schomburgkii

Single record of a bird collected in savanna (since destroyed to make way for a huge pineapple plantation) near Buenos Aires in southwestern Costa Rica on March 9, 1967 (R. Dickerman, *Bull BOC 88*(1): 25–30, 1968); otherwise known very locally from South America. See main text under Yellow-breasted Crake (p.122).

RUDDY CRAKE
Laterallus ruber   Plate 41

6. A *small*, mainly rufous crake which replaces the White-throated Crake northward in Middle America. Rather heavy blackish bill; iris red; legs olive greenish. *Head and nape blackish slate*; throat whitish; *otherwise mostly rufous-chestnut*, darkest and brownest on wings, rump, and tail. Uniform Crake is considerably larger with red legs and green bill, no slaty on head. Locally common in freshwater marshes and damp grassy areas in lowlands on both slopes in Honduras (ranging east to the Mosquitia), and on Pacific slope of Nicaragua, with one published sighting from northwestern Costa Rica (slopes of Miravalles Volcano; P. Slud); ranges north to northwestern Mexico. Inconspicuous skulking behavior is much like that of White-throated Crake (see main text, p.119), and so is its frequently heard *descending churring call*.

THICK-KNEES: Burhinidae

A small family in the "shorebird" group (Charadriiformes), though our single species is found only on open plains and short grass areas far from water. Distribution of the family is pantropical, with most species in the Old World, only two in America. They are notable for their large yellow eyes (an indication of their mainly nocturnal habit), cryptic brownish plumage, and large "knee" joint.

DOUBLE-STRIPED THICK-KNEE
Burhinus bistriatus   Plate 41

18–20. A *large*, long-legged shorebird of *open savannas and pastures. Large yellow eye*; bill blackish, basally gray; legs dull greenish yellow. Above mainly brownish with rufescent feather edging, with *"double stripe" formed by black lateral crown stripe and white superciliary*; foreneck and breast grayish brown, belly white. White patch at base of primaries flashes in flight. Virtually unmistakable in its dry habitat, though vaguely plover-like. Locally fairly common in Pacific lowlands south to northwestern Costa Rica (Guanacaste), also in arid interior valleys on Caribbean slope in Honduras (where found up to about 1500 m: 5000 ft); ranges north to southern Mexico also in northern South America and on Hispaniola. Terrestrial, often in pairs (small groups when not breeding), *mostly crepuscular and nocturnal*, during mid-day often resting in shade of bush or low tree; look for their eyeshine at night, when regularly found on little-traveled dirt roads. Often crouches when disturbed (relying on its cryptic plumage for concealment), or may walk away, sometimes trotting off surprisingly rapidly. Rather vocal, especially at night, with variety of loud strident calls, some lapwing-like, e.g. *krree-krree-krree-krree* . . . , or *prrrip, prrrip, prrrip, pip-pip*, etc.

ROSEATE TERN
Sterna dougallii

Recorded as breeding in small numbers on an islet in the Bay Islands off northern Honduras (M. Udvardy *et al.*, *Auk 90* (2): 440-442, 1973); found locally on tropical and temperate coastlines. For nonbreeding plumage see main text under Common Tern (p.157). Breeding plumage Roseates resemble Common Tern, but typically have *blackish bill; tail "streamers" strikingly long*, extending well beyond wings when at rest. Listen for Roseate's distinctive "chivy" or "churree" calls when they are around their nesting areas (these calls seemingly rarely given when not breeding).

RED-BILLED PIGEON
Columba flavirostris   Plate 42

13–14. Widespread, mainly on Pacific slope, *dark* pigeon of semiopen areas. *Bill red basally, ivory yellowish terminally*; legs reddish; iris reddish to orange-yellow. Head, neck, upper back, breast, and upper belly vinaceous, becoming brown on mid-back; rump, wings, tail, and *lower belly gray*. Resembles Pale-vented Pigeon but *lower belly not noticeably paler than rest of plumage*; also note Red-billed's brightly colored bill (dark in Pale-vented). Fairly common in woodland, forest borders, and areas with scattered tall trees on Pacific slope of Honduras (where also in interior valleys on Caribbean slope), Nicaragua, and northwestern and central Costa Rica (south to eastern part of Central Plateau around Turrialba, also spreading locally into deforested Caribbean slope lowlands, e.g. around Puerto Viejo); ranges north to northern Mexico and southern Texas. An arboreal pigeon, often occurring in towns and even in cities such as San José, Costa Rica, and regularly along roads (sometimes even perching on wires). Avoids extensive areas of humid forest. Call is a deep, rich *who-ooo; whoo, cu-cu-coo; whoo, cu-cu-coo.*

INCA DOVE
Columbina inca   Plate 42

7½–8½. *A small, scaly dove with long tail and rufous flash in wings.* Pale grayish overall, somewhat darker and browner above, *feathers throughout edged black giving obvious scaly appearance*; wings with *much rufous in primaries*, tail with *white outer corners and edging*, both most conspicuous in flight. Common Ground-Dove is also scaly looking, but only on head and breast; it also differs in its smaller size, shorter tail with much less white, and has pink or yellow at base of bill. Inca Dove is common in open and semiopen areas, often near habitations, in lowlands on Pacific slope from Honduras (where also found in arid interior valleys on Caribbean slope) to northwestern Costa Rica (south to western part of Central Plateau); ranges north to southwestern United States. Potters about in small groups on open ground but usually not too far from cover, tail often raised high at characteristic angle. Generally tame, flushing with a whirr when pressed to perch in low trees. Call is a monotonous, often interminably repeated (even during heat of day), *who-whoóp . . . who-whoóp . . . who-whoóp . . .* , sometimes paraphrased as "no hope." Formerly (and perhaps more correctly) separated in genus *Scardafella*.

CARIBBEAN DOVE
Leptotila jamaicensis

12–13. In our area found only on *two small islands off north coast of Honduras*. Resembles White-tipped Dove (which does not occur on these offshore islands), differing in its purplish red orbital skin, grayer crown, *whiter face*, more purplish iridescence on sides of neck, and *mostly white underparts* (only tinged buffy pinkish on breast), with *rather prominent vertical white band in front of wing*. Occurs on Barbareta Island in the Bay Islands group, and on Little Hog Island is the Cayos Cuchinos (but inexplicably absent from other islands in these groups); different races are also found on Yucatan Peninsula, Jamaica, Cayman Islands, and San Andrés Island. Mainly terrestrial in low scrubby woodland, walking about with nodding head. Call (on Cayman Islands) "a long mournful *cru-cru-crooooo-coa* descending to a sobbing echo, repeated three times" (P. Bradley).

WHITE-FACED QUAIL-DOVE
Geotrygon albifacies   Plate 42

11–12. *Forecrown, face, and throat white*, with remainder of crown gray and *prominent scaly or "lined" effect on sides of neck*; above mainly rich rufous brown, highly glossed with purple on back; breast grayish, becoming cinnamon-buff on remaining underparts. Uncommon in cloud forest in highlands of Honduras and northern Nicaragua, above 1200 m (4000 ft); ranges north to southern Mexico. Locally sympatric with Ruddy Quail-Dove (which see). Inconspicuous and shy, walking about on ground inside forest, usually alone. Call is a deep *whoo-oo* given at fairly long intervals, generally from a somewhat elevated perch, and resembling calls of the other members of the *G. linearis* group (which in Middle America includes this species, and the Chiriquí and Russet-crowned Quail-Doves).

GREEN PARAKEET
Aratinga holochlora   Plate 42

10½. *A numerous red-throated parakeet of interior highlands of Honduras and Nicaragua*. Conspicuous bare whitish eye-ring; bill pale horn. Mostly green, paler and yellower below, with *throat and foreneck red* (extent of red variable, some birds also with a scattering of red feathers on sides of head and neck). Immatures lack the red. Widespread and common in partially wooded terrain in highlands of Honduras (where it favors pine woodland, but also occurs elsewhere) and northern Nicaragua; ranges north to northern Mexico (other, rather different, races being involved; it has been suggested that the red-throated form, *rubritorquis*, is a distinct species, Red-throated Parakeet). Often occurs in large noisy flocks, and these are regularly seen flying past high overhead on their way to and from roosts in early morning and late afternoon.

PACIFIC PARAKEET
Aratinga strenua   Plate 42

11½. Much less numerous replacement of Green Parakeet found in *Pacific lowlands of Honduras and Nicaragua*. Soft-part colors similar. Pacific differs in being larger, and is *entirely green* (lacking the red). Rare to locally uncommon in semiopen country and gallery woodland; ranges north to southern Mexico. Closely related to the Green Parakeet, sometimes being considered conspecific, though treated as a full species in the 1983 AOU Check-list. Behavior is similar, but nowhere in its range does Pacific Parakeet seem to be anywhere near as numerous.

ORANGE-FRONTED PARAKEET
Aratinga canicularis   Plate 42

9. *The common parakeet of the Pacific lowlands*. Bare eye-ring pale yellowish; bill pale horn. Mostly green above with bluer crown and *bright orange frontal band*; throat and breast pale brownish olive, becoming pale yellowish green on belly; wings show much blue, especially evident in flight. Larger than Orange-chinned Parakeet, with longer tail; note differences in head and wing patterns. In Central America most likely confused with Olive-throated Parakeet; the two species have basically allopatric ranges, with Olive-throated on Caribbean slope, but they may overlap locally in interior Honduras. Olive-throated has darker throat and breast, and shows merely a trace of orange above the bill (very different from the *prominent* orange band of this species). Orange-fronted Parakeet is locally common in semiopen country and woodland in lowlands on Pacific slope from Honduras (where locally ranges onto Caribbean slope in interior valleys) to northwestern Costa Rica (where numerous in Guanacaste, small numbers to western side of Central Plateau); ranges north to northern Mexico. A conspicuous and noisy parakeet, the Orange-fronted is usually seen in small groups (less often in large flocks than the Green Parakeet); unlike the latter species, Orange-fronteds usually do not fly too high above the ground.

WHITE-FRONTED AMAZON (PARROT)
Amazona albifrons   Plate 42

10–10½. *Common small amazon of semiopen Pacific lowlands. Bill yellowish. Mostly green, feathers of neck, breast, and back scaled black; forecrown white*, midcrown blue, *lores and ocular area red; primary coverts red* (forming a conspicuous patch in flight, with some showing even on perched birds), much blue in flight feathers; some orange-red at base of tail feathers. Female and immatures show little or no red on wing and have duller facial pattern. Cf. Yellow-lored Amazon (no overlap in our area); other sympatric amazons are markedly larger, fly with shallower wing-beats, and none has white on crown. White-crowned

Parrot (in genus *Pionus*) has much more white on crown, also a white throat, shows no red on face, etc. White-fronted Amazon is widespread and locally common in lowlands on Pacific slope from Honduras (where it also occurs on Caribbean slope in arid interior valleys and locally in lowlands) to northwestern Costa Rica (Guanacaste south to Puntarenas region); ranges north to northern Mexico. Occurs mostly below 1200 m (4000 ft), locally higher. Usually in flocks, sometimes large, which fly about conspicuously in early morning and late afternoon; unlike the larger amazons their flight is quite erratic, with frequent changes in direction. Calls are exceptionally loud and harsh, a repeated *chak-chak, chak-chak* or *cha-cha-chák, cha-cha-chák* being typical.

YELLOW-LORED AMAZON (PARROT)
Amazona xantholora

10–10½ . Only on *Roatán Island* off northern Honduras. Closely resembles much more widespread White-fronted Amazon (which is not found on Roatán). Differs in having *yellow lores* (this in addition to the white forecrown and red around the eye) and dusky earcoverts; body plumage tends to be *more heavily scaled black*. Female and immatures show little red on either head or wings; their entire crown is bluish, but *lores are yellow*. Apparently rare on Roatán Island (recent reports?), where "reportedly confined to the pine ridges" (B. L. Monroe, Jr.); ranges also on Yucatan Peninsula and in northern Belize, where at least locally more numerous. Behavior much as in White-fronted Amazon.

YELLOW-NAPED AMAZON (PARROT)
Amazona auropalliata   Plate 42

13–14. A *large* parrot found locally in *Pacific lowlands*. Bill mainly dark gray. Mostly bright green with *yellow band across hindneck and nape* (variable in width); large red speculum on secondaries (visible most in flight). Nominate *auropalliata* (most of range) has no red on bend of wing, but this is present in *parvipes* found in the Mosquitia region of northwestern Nicaragua and extreme eastern Honduras and on the Bay Islands off northern Honduras. Situation in the Sula valley of northwestern Honduras is confused and complex, with apparently *both* a

yellow-naped and a yellow-crowned form being found there (the latter similar to Yellow-crowned Amazon, of Panama southward; see main text). Yellow-naped Amazon is rare to locally fairly common in gallery forest, deciduous woodland, and in ranchland where some large trees have been left standing, in lowlands on Pacific slope from Honduras (where locally also on Caribbean slope, as noted above) to northwestern Costa Rica (Guanacaste), mostly below 600 m (2000 ft); ranges north to southern Mexico. Declining in numbers, due both to excessive trapping (they are very popular as pets) and to habitat destruction; now extirpated from many regions. Yellow-naped is closely related to Yellow-headed Amazon (*A. oratrix*) of Mexico, and to Yellow-crowned Amazon (*A. ochrocephala*) of South America and Panama; until recently these were all considered conspecific, but they were treated as three species in the 1983 AOU Check-list. The behavior of all three is similar, as are their voices; Yellow-naped's commonest call is a rich throaty *korrow* or *karrow*, lacking the harsh raucous quality of many other amazons.

LESSER GROUND-CUCKOO
Morococcyx erythropygus   Plate 42

11. A *secretive* cuckoo of arid Pacific slope lowlands. Bill rather heavy, *mostly bright yellow*, with dusky culmen; *conspicuous bare ocular area mostly blue*, with some yellow in front of eye. Mainly olive brown above with *whitish superciliary* and black surrounding the ocular area and extending back from eye as a thin stripe; rump more rufous, with blackish barring; *below uniform cinnamon-rufous*; tail bronzy brown, feathers pale-tipped. See Striped Cuckoo (streaked above, etc.), and the more arboreal Mangrove Cuckoo. Lesser Ground-Cuckoo is uncommon in undergrowth of woodland and scrub in lowlands from Honduras (where also found on Caribbean slope in arid interior valleys) to northwestern Costa Rica (Guanacaste and western side of Central Plateau); ranges north to northern Mexico. Usually on or near the ground in dense cover, and infrequently seen (and doubtless much overlooked); sometimes hops out onto dirt roads, and regularly dust-bathes. Its call is very distinctive, but is usually given at very long intervals and thus is hard to track to its source, an extended series of slightly shrill trilled notes, starting fast then slowing noticeably, sounding much like a policeman's or referee's whistle.

PLATES

PLATE 41

ADDITIONAL TINAMOUS, QUAIL, RAILS; THICK-KNEES AND CRACIDS

1. THICKET TINAMOU (*Crypturellus cinnamomeus praepes*). Mid-sized tinamou with red legs, mostly rufous brown plumage. Mainly Pacific slope. *p. 438*

2. SLATY-BREASTED TINAMOU (*Crypturellus boucardi costaricensis*). Mid-sized dark tinamou with red legs, gray foreparts. Mainly Caribbean slope. *p. 438*

3. DOUBLE-STRIPED THICK-KNEE (*Burhinus b. bistriatus*). Large, nocturnal shorebird of dry open plains; head striping. *p. 441*

4. CRESTED BOBWHITE (*Colinus cristatus*). a) *Dickeyi* (''Spot-bellied'' Bobwhite, until recently considered a full species): Throat whitish or black bordered white (varies racially), length of crest also varies. Pacific slope south to northwestern Costa Rica. b) *Panamensis* (''true'' Crested Bobwhite): Throat buff to rufous, always with long crest. Pacific slope from southwestern Costa Rica south into Panama. *pp. 118, 440*

5. BUFFY-CROWNED WOOD-PARTRIDGE (*Dendrortyx l. leucophrys*). Large scarce quail of highland forests, long-tailed; contrasting forehead, chestnut streaking on gray breast (streaking blackish in Costa Rican race). *p. 440*

6. RUDDY CRAKE (*Laterallus ruber*). Small, mostly rufous crake with slaty head. Honduras and Nicaragua. *p. 441*

7. GREAT CURASSOW (*Crax rubra*). Very large size, unique curly crest. Male: black and white with yellow bill knob. Female: mainly rufous brown. Remote forests and woodlands (much persecuted). *p. 115*

8. CRESTED GUAN (*Penelope purpurascens aequatorialis*). Very large size (but slenderer than curassow); only slight bushy crest, red dewlap, breast streaking. Remote forests and woodlands (persecuted, but usually more numerous than curassow). *p. 114*

9. BLACK GUAN (*Chamaepetes unicolor*). Chachalaca-sized cracid of highland forests in Costa Rica and western Panama; all black plumage, blue face. *p. 113*

10. HIGHLAND GUAN (*Penelopina nigra*). Small guan of highland forests in Honduras and northern Nicaragua. Male: black with red dewlap. Female: rufous brown with blackish barring. *p. 440*

11. PLAIN CHACHALACA (*Ortalis v. vetula*). Much like next species, but lacking chestnut in wings. Caribbean slope of Honduras and northern Nicaragua, also locally on Pacific slope in northwestern Costa Rica. *p. 439*

12. GRAY-HEADED CHACHALACA (*Ortalis cinereiceps*). Small cracid with grayish brown plumage, chestnut in wings (most evident in flight), pale tail tipping. Caribbean lowlands from eastern Honduras south through Panama (also Pacific slope in southwestern Costa Rica and Panama). *p. 113*

Gwynne
7·87

PLATE 42

ADDITIONAL PIGEONS, PARROTS, CUCKOOS

1. RED-BILLED PIGEON (*Columba f. flavirostris*). Large dark vinaceous pigeon with red and yellow bill. Open wooded areas south to central Costa Rica. *p. 442*

2. COMMON GROUND-DOVE (*Columbina passerina neglecta*). Small size, scaly breast, red or yellow at base of bill (often obscure). Open areas south to central Costa Rica, also an isolated population in west-central Panama. *p. 166*

3. INCA DOVE (*Columbina inca*). Rather long tail with much white at its edge, scaly overall appearance. Open areas mainly on Pacific slope south to northwestern Costa Rica. *p. 442*

4. WHITE-FACED QUAIL-DOVE (*Geotrygon albifacies sylvestris*). White foreface, dark lines on neck. Undergrowth of highland forest in Honduras and northern Nicaragua. *p. 443*

5. MOURNING DOVE (*Zenaida macroura marginella*). Long pointed tail broadly bordered white, no white on wing. Northern migrant south to west-central Panama, mainly on Pacific slope (also resident?). *p. 166*

6. WHITE-WINGED DOVE (*Zenaida asiatica panamensis*). Much white on wing, squared tail with white corners. Local resident and northern migrant in drier and more open areas on Pacific slope south to northwestern Costa Rica, also resident in west-central Panama. *p. 165*

7. GRAY-CHESTED DOVE (*Leptotila cassini rufinucha*). Contrasting rufous nape. This race only in southwestern Costa Rica and western Chiriquí, Panama; typical birds widespread on Caribbean slope from Honduras to Panama (see Plate 10). *p. 169*

8. YELLOW-NAPED AMAZON (*Amazona auropalliata*). Yellow nape patch. Mainly Pacific slope south to northwestern Costa Rica. *p. 444*

9. WHITE-FRONTED AMAZON (*Amazona albifrons nana*). Male. White forehead, red around eyes and on wing-coverts. Common, mainly on Pacific slope south to northwestern Costa Rica. *p. 443*

10. GREEN PARAKEET (*Aratinga holochlora rubritorquis*). Variable amount of red on throat (sometimes more extensive than shown). Interior of Honduras and northern Nicaragua, often numerous. *p. 443*

11. PACIFIC PARAKEET (*Aratinga strenua*). Scarce, all green parakeet of Pacific lowlands south to southwestern Nicaragua; larger than preceding species. *p. 443*

12. ORANGE-FRONTED PARAKEET (*Aratinga c. canicularis*). Orange forehead, brownish breast. Common, mainly Pacific slope south to northwestern Costa Rica. *p. 443*

13. LESSER GROUND-CUCKOO (*Morococcyx erythropygus*). Yellow bill, bare mainly blue ocular area, rufous underparts. Secretive in scrubby woods, mainly on Pacific slope south to northwestern Costa Rica. *p. 444*

Note: Other pigeons on Plate 10; other parrots on Plate 11; other cuckoos on Plate 12.

Gwynne 8·87

PLATE 43

ADDITIONAL HUMMINGBIRDS

1. EMERALD-CHINNED HUMMINGBIRD (*Abeillia abeillei aurea*). Male. Short bill, mainly green with blackish breast (female gray below). Highlands Honduras and northern Nicaragua. *p. 447*

2. FORK-TAILED EMERALD (*Chlorostilbon canivetii salvini*). Male: glittering green plumage, mostly red bill, deeply forked tail. Female: mostly red bill, white postocular, dusky ear-coverts. Lowlands on both slopes south to central Costa Rica (similar Garden Emerald occurs from southwestern Costa Rica south into Panama; see Plate 13). *p. 447*

3. WINE-THROATED HUMMINGBIRD (*Atthis ellioti*). Male: pointed rosy-violet gorget. Female: small throat spots, rufous sides. Highlands in western Honduras. *p. 451*

4. SPARKLING-TAILED HUMMINGBIRD (*Tilmatura dupontii*). Male: boldly banded and deeply forked tail. Female: tiny size, cinnamon-buff underparts. Highlands Honduras and northern Nicaragua. *p. 451*

5. WHITE-EARED HUMMINGBIRD (*Hylocharis leucotis pygmaea*). Male: mostly red bill, bold white postocular. Female: white postocular, heavy green spotting below. Highlands Honduras and northern Nicaragua. *p. 447*

6. COPPERY-HEADED EMERALD (*Elvira cupreiceps*). Male: decurved bill, white tail, coppery effect above. Female: decurved bill, white tail. Endemic to Costa Rican highlands. *p. 449*

7. BLACK-CRESTED COQUETTE (*Lophornis helenae*). Male: wispy black crest, buff ear-tufts, pale rump band, tiny size. Female: pale rump band, dusky cheeks, buff throat, tiny size. Caribbean lowlands south to Costa Rica. *p. 447*

8. CINNAMON HUMMINGBIRD (*Amazilia r. rutila*). Male. Uniform cinnamon-buff underparts, rufous tail. Mainly Pacific slope south to northwestern Costa Rica. *p. 449*

9. CHARMING HUMMINGBIRD (*Amazilia decora*). Male. Much like Blue-chested Hummingbird (see Plate 13) but bill appreciably longer. Charming only in southwestern Costa Rica and western Chiriquí, Panama (Blue-chested on Caribbean slope from Nicaragua south). *p. 216*

10. STEELY-VENTED HUMMINGBIRD (*Amazilia saucerottei hoffmanni*). Male. Green, with bronzy upper tail-coverts and blue-black tail. Southwestern Nicaragua to central Costa Rica. *p. 449*

11. BLUE-TAILED HUMMINGBIRD (*Amazilia c. cyanura*). Male. Like preceding but with bronzy chestnut on wings. Pacific slope of Honduras and Nicaragua. *p. 449*

12. BERYLLINE HUMMINGBIRD (*Amazilia beryllina devillei*). Male. Purplish chestnut tail, chestnut on wing-coverts. Honduran highlands. *p. 449*

13. MANGROVE HUMMINGBIRD (*Amazilia boucardi*). Male. Bronzy green tail, no coppery on rump, little contrast below (compare to Snowy-bellied Hummingbird, on Plate 13). Local on Pacific coast of Costa Rica. *p. 448*

14. AZURE-CROWNED HUMMINGBIRD (*Amazilia cyanocephala guatemalensis*). Male. Blue crown, pure white throat. Highlands Honduras and northern Nicaragua. *p. 448*

15. WHITE-BELLIED EMERALD (*Amazilia c. candida*). Male. Almost pure white underparts. Mainly Caribbean slope of Honduras and Nicaragua, rarely northern Costa Rica. *p. 448*

16. RUBY-THROATED HUMMINGBIRD (*Archilochus colubris*). Female. Rather plain (male has red gorget), lacking female *Chlorostilbon* emerald's postocular and masked effect. Northern migrant, mainly to Pacific lowlands south to Costa Rica (scarce in Panama). *p. 223*

17. AMETHYST-THROATED HUMMINGBIRD (*Lampornis amethystinus salvini*). Male. Rosy gorget, gray remaining underparts (female has buff throat). Highlands Honduras. *p. 450*

Continued over

43

PLATE 44

ADDITIONAL TROGONS, MOTMOTS, WOODPECKERS, JAYS, ETC.

1. BLACK-HEADED TROGON (*Trogon m. melanocephalus*). Blue eye-ring, yellow belly; black head, throat, and chest (gray in female). Common in lowlands on both slopes south to northwestern Costa Rica. *p. 452*

2. ELEGANT TROGON (*Trogon elegans lubricus*). Red belly, alternating barred and white underside of tail, female with white back of eye. Pacific lowlands south to northwestern Costa Rica. *p. 452*

3. KEEL-BILLED MOTMOT (*Electron carinatum*). Mostly green, with short blue eye-stripe. Rare in humid forest on Caribbean slope south to northern Costa Rica. *p. 453*

4. TURQUOISE-BROWED MOTMOT (*Eumomota superciliosa australis*). Blue-bordered black throat patch, mostly blue tail with very obvious racquets. Mainly Pacific slope south to northwestern Costa Rica; less confined to forest than other motmots. *p. 453*

5. WHITE-FRONTED NUNBIRD (*Monasa morphoeus grandior*). Mostly gray with heavy red bill, variable amount of white on face. Local in humid forest in Costa Rica and Panama. *p. 236*

6. GOLDEN-FRONTED WOODPECKER (*Melanerpes aurifrons santacruzi*). Male. Barred back, red hindcrown. Honduras and northern Nicaragua. *p. 454*

7. HOFFMANN'S WOODPECKER (*Melanerpes hoffmannii*). Barred back, yellow hindcrown. Endemic of southern Honduras to central Costa Rica. *p. 453*

8. FIERY-BILLED ARACARI (*Pteroglossus frantzii*). Mainly red upper mandible, broad red belly band. Endemic to southwestern Costa Rica and western Panama on Pacific slope (Collared Aracari on Caribbean slope north through Honduras; see Plate 17). *p. 241*

9. BUSHY-CRESTED JAY (*Cyanocorax melanocyaneus*). Bushy crest, black head and underparts. Highlands Honduras and western Nicaragua. *p. 459*

Continued over

PLATE 43 *continued from previous page*

18. GREEN-BREASTED MOUNTAIN-GEM (*Lampornis sybillae*). Male: mainly grayish white tail, green underparts. Female: tail as in male, pale buff throat. Endemic to highlands of central Honduras and northern Nicaragua. *p. 450*

19. GREEN-THROATED MOUNTAIN-GEM (*Lampornis viridipallens*). Male. Like preceding but with contrasting green throat, blackish tail (no white); female has white (not buff) throat. Western Honduran highlands. *p. 450*

20. WHITE-BELLIED MOUNTAIN-GEM (*Lampornis hemileucus*). Male. White postocular and underparts, purple gorget. Local, highlands Costa Rica and western Panama. *p. 219*

21. WHITE-THROATED MOUNTAIN-GEM (*Lampornis castaneoventris cinereicauda*). Male. White throat, gray tail. Highlands southwestern Costa Rica (black-tailed nominate race of western Panama on Plate 14). *pp. 220, 450*

22. WHITE-TIPPED SICKLEBILL (*Eutoxeres aquila salvini*). Sharply decurved bill, streaked underparts. Costa Rica and Panama, favoring *Heliconia*. *p. 207*

23. PLAIN-CAPPED STARTHROAT (*Heliomaster c. constantii*). Long bill, white postocular, never a blue crown (unlike Long-billed Starthroat; see Plate 13). Mainly Pacific slope south to northwestern Costa Rica. *p. 450*

24. GREEN-BREASTED MANGO (*Anthracothorax prevostii*). a) *gracilirostris* (Honduras to central Costa Rica): Male: black stripe down mid-throat and chest (only), green to its sides and below. Female: rufous on face and sides, black median stripe below. b) *veraguensis* (western Panama only): Male: no black on underparts. *pp. 209, 447*

25. WEDGE-TAILED SABREWING (*Campylopterus curvipennis pampa*). Male. Large size, long graduated tail, gray underparts. Local in eastern Honduras. *p. 447*

1 ♂ ♀

2 ♂ ♀

3 4

5

6 ♂ 7 ♂ ♀

8

9 10 11 12

Gwynne 10·87

PLATE 45

ADDITIONAL FURNARIIDS, MANAKINS, COTINGAS, BECARDS, ETC.

1. IVORY-BILLED WOODCREEPER (*Xiphorhynchus flavigaster eburneirostris*). Pale bill, prominent streaking above and below. Lowlands south to northwestern Costa Rica. *Note*: Other woodcreepers on Plate 19. *p. 454*

2. RUDDY FOLIAGE-GLEANER (*Automolus rubiginosus fumosus*). Dark brown overall with no streaking, rufous throat and breast. Local in Costa Rica and Panama. *Note*: Other foliage-gleaners on Plates 14 and 20. *p. 255*

3. RUFOUS-BREASTED SPINETAIL (*Synallaxis erythrothorax*). Rufous breast, no rufous on crown (compare to Slaty Spinetail on Plate 20). Lowlands northwestern Honduras. *p. 454*

4. STREAK-CROWNED ANTVIREO (*Dysithamnus striaticeps*). Streaked crown and anterior underparts (compare to other antvireos on Plate 20). Endemic to Caribbean slope from southern Honduras to Costa Rica. *p. 455*

5. THRUSH-LIKE MOURNER (*Schiffornis turdinus veraepacis*). Uniform dark appearance, wide-eyed look (other races on Plate 27). *p. 325*

6. WHITE-COLLARED MANAKIN (*Manacus candei*). Male: white collar and throat. Female: reddish legs, yellow on belly. Replaces Golden-collared Manakin (see Plate 27) on Caribbean slope from Costa Rica northward. *p. 326*

7. LONG-TAILED MANAKIN (*Chiroxiphia linearis fastuosa*). Male: much elongated central tail feathers. Female: protruding central tail feathers. Pacific slope south to northwestern Costa Rica (compare to shorter-tailed Lance-tailed Manakin on Plate 27; Lance-tailed from southwestern Costa Rica south into Panama). *p. 458*

8. GRAY-HEADED PIPRITES (*Piprites griseiceps*). Chunky shape, gray head with white eye-ring, olive-yellow underparts. Local in humid forest on Caribbean slope from eastern Honduras to Costa Rica. *p. 458*

9. LOVELY COTINGA (*Cotinga amabilis*). Male. Brilliant blue, large dark purple throat and belly patches. Replaces similar Blue Cotinga (see Plate 26) on Caribbean slope from Costa Rica northward. *p. 321*

10. TURQUOISE COTINGA (*Cotinga ridgwayi*). Male. Resembles Lovely and Blue Cotingas (see text); best known by its range in southwestern Costa Rica and Pacific western Panama (where the only *Cotinga*). *p. 320*

11. ROSE-THROATED BECARD (*Pachyramphus aglaiae latirostris*). Male: dark gray, blackest on head (in our area usually does *not* show pink on throat). Female: rufous brown upperparts except for blackish crown. On both slopes south mainly to northern Costa Rica (recently also in western Chiriquí, Panama). *p. 318*

12. GRAY-COLLARED BECARD (*Pachyramphus major australis*). Male: pale gray nuchal collar and underparts. Female: rufous edging on wing-coverts, buff nuchal collar. Highlands Honduras and northern Nicaragua. *p. 457*

13. SHARPBILL (*Oxyruncus cristatus frater*). Sharply pointed bill, scaly head and throat, spotted underparts. Local in humid foothills, Costa Rica and Panama. *p. 330*

Note: Other becards on Plate 26.

PLATE 44 *continued from previous page*

10. STELLER'S JAY (*Cyanocorax stelleri suavis*). Pointed crest, mainly blue plumage. Highlands Honduras and northern Nicaragua. *p. 459*

11. BROWN JAY (*Cyanocorax morio cyanogenys*). Large and brown, white belly and tail-tips. Mainly Caribbean slope, Honduras to western Panama. *p. 337*

12. WHITE-THROATED MAGPIE-JAY (*Calocitta formosa pompata*). Very long tail, long loose crest, white underparts. Mainly Pacific slope south to northwestern Costa Rica. *p. 459*

Note: Other trogons on Plate 15; other motmots on Plate 16; other woodpeckers on Plate 18; other jays on Plate 17.

Gwynne 9·87

PLATE 46

ADDITIONAL TYRANT-FLYCATCHERS

1. YELLOW-BELLIED TYRANNULET (*Ornithion semiflavum*). Very small size, gray crown, white superciliary. Caribbean slope lowlands of Honduras to northern Costa Rica, also in southwestern Costa Rica (compare to Brown-capped Tyrannulet on Plate 25). *p. 455*

2. STUB-TAILED SPADEBILL (*Platyrinchus cancrominus*). Small size, very wide bill, white throat. Closely resembles next species, best distinguished by voice and range (see text). Lowlands south to northern Costa Rica. *p. 455*

3. WHITE-THROATED SPADEBILL (*Platyrinchus mystaceus neglectus*). Male. Like preceding, differing especially in voice and montane forest habitat; Costa Rica and Panama. *p. 295*

4. NORTHERN BEARDLESS-TYRANNULET (*Camptostoma imberbe*). Dull-plumaged, showing little yellow below (unlike Southern Beardless-Tyrannulet; see Plate 25). Lowlands south to northern Costa Rica. *p. 455*

5. YELLOW-OLIVE FLYCATCHER (*Tolmomyias sulphurescens cinereiceps*). Broad flat bill, pale iris, contrasting gray crown and nape (see text for similar Yellow-margined Flycatcher). This race from Costa Rica northward. *pp. 295, 455*

6. SLATY-CAPPED FLYCATCHER (*Leptopogon superciliaris hellmayri*). Gray crown, blackish patch on ear-coverts (compare to Sepia-capped Flycatcher on Plate 25). Humid montane forest, Costa Rica and Panama. *p. 289*

7. RUFOUS-BROWED TYRANNULET (*Phylloscartes s. superciliaris*). White ear-coverts encircled with black, slender shape (cocking tail and wing-lifting). Local in humid foothill forest, Costa Rica and Panama. *p. 290*

8. TAWNY-CHESTED FLYCATCHER (*Aphanotriccus capitalis*). Obvious tawny wing-bars, tawny breast and sides. Endemic to eastern Nicaragua and northeastern Costa Rica, scarce. *p. 456*

9. WHITE-THROATED FLYCATCHER (*Empidonax a. albigularis*). Rather brown upperparts, buff wing-bars, distinctly white throat. Local in highlands Honduras to western Panama. See text for other very similar *Empidonax*. *p. 303*

10. BROWN-CRESTED FLYCATCHER (*Myiarchus tyrannulus brachyurus*). Large *Myiarchus* showing rufous in wings and tail, dark bill. Lowlands Honduras and on Pacific slope south to northwestern Costa Rica. See text for other very similar *Myiarchus*. *p. 457*

11. NUTTING'S FLYCATCHER (*Myiarchus n. nuttingi*). Closely resembles preceding species (and often with it); slightly smaller and paler, but best identified by voice (see text). Pacific lowlands south to northwestern Costa Rica. *p. 457*

12. OCHRACEOUS PEWEE (*Contopus ochraceus*). Ochraceous olive upperparts, buff wing-bars, yellowish belly. Scarce and local in highlands of Costa Rica and western Panama. *p. 300*

13. GREATER PEWEE (*Contopus pertinax minor*). Prominent bushy crest, mainly grayish olive plumage. Highlands Honduras and northern Nicaragua. *p. 456*

14. COMMON TUFTED-FLYCATCHER (*Mitrephanes phaeocercus nicaraguae*). Conspicuous crest, uniform rufous-tawny underparts. This race (and similar *quercinus*) in highlands of Honduras and Nicaragua. *p. 456*

15. SCISSOR-TAILED FLYCATCHER (*Muscivora forficata*). Very long deeply forked tail, mostly pearly gray and white plumage. Northern migrant, common south to northwestern Costa Rica, a few to western Panama. *p. 315*

16. BLACK PHOEBE (*Sayornis nigricans amnicola*). Mostly black, with white lower belly. Usually near water, wags tail. Mainly highlands, Honduras through Panama. *p. 305*

17. TORRENT TYRANNULET (*Serpophaga cinerea grisea*). Small size, pale grayish plumage with black head, wings, and tail. Near water in highlands, Costa Rica and western Panama. *p. 287*

Gwynne 2·87

PLATE 47

SWALLOWS; ADDITIONAL WRENS, ORIOLES, ETC.

1. MANGROVE SWALLOW (*Tachycineta a. albilinea*). Green-blue upperparts with white rump and underparts. Usually near water. *p. 333*
2. BLUE-AND-WHITE SWALLOW (*Notiochelidon c. cyanoleuca*). All blue upperparts, black crissum. Mainly highlands, Costa Rica and western Panama. *p. 334*
3. GRAY-BREASTED MARTIN (*Progne c. chalybea*). Male. Large size, contrastingly pale belly but with no pale areas on neck (see text for similar but less numerous Purple and Southern Martins). *p. 332*
4. BARN SWALLOW (*Hirundo rustica erythrogaster*). Deeply forked tail. Common northern migrant. *p. 336*
5. SAND MARTIN (*Riparia r. riparia*). Grayish brown upperparts and distinct chest band, small size. Fairly common northern migrant. *p. 335*
6. WHITE-THIGHED SWALLOW (*Neochelidon tibialis minima*). Small size, uniform dusky plumage. Forest-based, central and eastern Panama only. *p. 334*
7. NORTHERN ROUGH-WINGED SWALLOW (*Stelgidopteryx s. serripennis*). Uniform grayish brown above, dingy brownish wash on throat and chest. Breeds south in highlands to central Costa Rica, winters to Panama. *p. 335*
8. SOUTHERN ROUGH-WINGED SWALLOW (*Stelgidopteryx ruficollis uropygialis*). Like preceding but with whitish rump and cinnamon throat. Resident in lowlands north to eastern Honduras and southwestern Costa Rica. *p. 335*
9. ROCK WREN (*Salpinctes obsoletus guttatus*). Dark wren of rocky or open highlands south to northwestern Costa Rica. Usually coarsely marked below, outer tail feathers tipped buff. *p. 461*
10. RUFOUS-NAPED WREN (*Campylorhynchus rufinucha capistratus*). Large size, black crown, white eye-stripe, rufous upper back. Common conspicuous wren of Pacific lowlands south to northwestern Costa Rica. *p. 460*
11. BANDED WREN (*Thryothorus pleurostictus ravus*). Coarse black barring on lower underparts. Pacific lowlands south to northwestern Costa Rica. *p. 461*
12. SPOT-BREASTED WREN (*Thryothorus maculipectus umbrinus*). Densely spotted breast, unbarred wings. Caribbean lowlands south to northern Costa Rica. *p. 461*
13. WHITE-LORED GNATCATCHER (*Polioptila a. albiloris*). Entire crown black, with lores and tiny postocular white (both absent in breeding males). Pacific lowlands south to northwestern Costa Rica. Compare to Tropical Gnatcatcher on Plate 30. *p. 462*
14. MANGROVE VIREO (*Vireo pallens semiflavus*). Yellow eye-ring and supraloral, pale yellow underparts. South along either coast to southwestern Costa Rica and southeastern Nicaragua. See other vireos on Plate 30. *p. 464*
15. ALTAMIRA ORIOLE (*Icterus gularis gigas*). Large and very brightly colored, solid black back, no breast spots. Lowlands south to Honduras and western Nicaragua. *p. 473*
16. SPOT-BREASTED ORIOLE (*Icterus p. pectoralis*). Black breast spotting. Mainly Pacific slope south to northwestern Costa Rica. *p. 473*
17. STREAK-BACKED ORIOLE (*Icterus pustulatus sclateri*). Streaked back (sometimes obscure), much white edging on wing feathers. Mainly Pacific slope south to northwestern Costa Rica. *p. 473*

Note: Other wrens on Plate 28; other orioles on Plate 39.

Gwynne 12·87

PLATE 48

ADDITIONAL WOOD-WARBLERS, TANAGERS, FINCHES

1. MASKED YELLOWTHROAT (*Geothlypis aequatorialis chiriquensis*). Blue-gray border to mask, all yellow underparts (both sexes). Local in lower highlands of western Chiriquí, Panama, and adjacent Costa Rica. *p. 379*

2. OLIVE-CROWNED YELLOWTHROAT (*Geothlypis semiflava bairdi*). Male. No border to mask, olive crown, all yellow underparts (both sexes). Caribbean lowlands from eastern Honduras to western Panama. *p. 379*

3. COMMON YELLOWTHROAT (*Geothlypis trichas brachydactylus*). Male. Whitish border to mask, belly whitish (male) or pale brownish (female). Northern migrant. *p. 379*

4. GRAY-CROWNED YELLOWTHROAT (*Geothlypis poliocephala ridgwayi*). Male. Black only on lores and ocular area. Both slopes south to Costa Rica, extending to western Chiriquí in Panama. *p. 380*

5. CRESCENT-CHESTED WARBLER (*Parula superciliosa*). Chest patch, plain gray wings and tail. Highlands Honduras and northern Nicaragua. *p. 465*

6. SCRUB EUPHONIA (*Euphonia a. affinis*). Male: small crown patch, dark throat (see text). Female: blue-gray nape, olive on breast. Mainly Pacific slope south to northwestern Costa Rica. *p. 468*

7. YELLOW-THROATED EUPHONIA (*Euphonia l. lauta*). Male: small crown patch, yellow throat (compare to Thick-billed Euphonia on Plate 34). Female: whitish underparts. Lowlands south to northern Costa Rica (locally to western Panama). *p. 393*

8. BLACK-CHEEKED ANT-TANAGER (*Habia atrimaxillaris*). Blackish upperparts (blackest on cheeks), red throat. Endemic to southwestern Costa Rica. Compare to other ant-tanagers on Plate 35. *p. 468*

9. ASHY-THROATED BUSH-TANAGER (*Chlorospingus canigularis olivaceiceps*). Plain gray head with olive crown, whitish throat, yellowish chest band. Local in humid foothills, Costa Rica and western Panama (Bocas). *p. 406*

10. SLATY FLOWERPIERCER (*Diglossa plumbea*). Hooked and upturned bill, male slaty gray, female browner and streaked below. Highlands Costa Rica and western Panama (see text for Cinnamon-bellied Flowerpiercer of Honduras). *p. 422*

11. PEG-BILLED FINCH (*Acanthidops bairdii*). Very sharply pointed and bicolored bill. Male: all gray. Female: with tan wing-bars. Local in highlands of Costa Rica (mainly) and western Panama. *p. 422*

12. GRAYISH SALTATOR (*Saltator coerulescens grandis*). Grayish upperparts, white throat not bordered with black below. Lowlands south locally to central Costa Rica. *p. 469*

13. PREVOST'S GROUND-SPARROW (*Melozone biarcuatum cabanisi*). Complex head pattern, back breast patch. Highlands western Honduras and central Costa Rica. *p. 470*

14. WHITE-EARED GROUND-SPARROW (*Melozone l. leucotis*). Ornate head pattern, yellow on sides of neck, mostly black throat and chest. Highlands Nicaragua and Costa Rica. *p. 470*

15. STRIPE-HEADED SPARROW (*Aimophila r. ruficauda*). Bold head striping, bicolored bill, whitish underparts. Pacific lowlands south to northwestern Costa Rica. *p. 471*

16. RUSTY SPARROW (*Aimophila rufescens discolor*). Chestnut crown striping, rusty wings and tail, black submalar streak. Local in grassy areas south to northeastern Nicaragua and northwestern Costa Rica. *p. 471*

17. OLIVE SPARROW (*Arremonops rufivirgatus superciliosa*). Brown head striping, dingy buffyish underparts. Lowlands of northwestern Costa Rica. Compare to Black-striped Sparrow on Plate 37. *p. 469*

18. BOTTERI'S SPARROW (*Aimophila botterii petenica*). Nondescript, streaky above and dingy grayish to whitish below (see text). Local in grassy or rocky areas south to northeastern Nicaragua and northwestern Costa Rica. *p. 471*

48

LESSER ROADRUNNER

LESSER ROADRUNNER
Geococcyx velox   p.445

18. *Unmistakable large terrestrial cuckoo of semiopen areas*. Black and dark brown above *prominently spotted and streaked with white; very long tail* bronzy brown, feathers broadly tipped white; *below pale buff*, with brown streaking on sides of chest. Differs from Greater Roadrunner (*G. californianus*), not found south of Mexico, in being slightly smaller and in having buff (not whitish) underparts without streaking across breast. Locally fairly common in scrubby or open areas on Pacific slope south to central Nicaragua, in Honduras also extending widely onto Caribbean slope where it may even be gradually moving into deforested areas in humid regions (e.g. the Olancho); ranges north to northern Mexico. Usually seen singly on the ground, often with its long tail cocked high; capable of running very rapidly, with tail then usually held horizontally and neck outstretched.

PACIFIC SCREECH-OWL
Otus cooperi

9. Very similar in appearance to Tropical Screech-Owl (see main text, p.187), but *eartufts often appear longer*; the two do not overlap. Fairly common in deciduous woodland and shade trees around ranch buildings or along roads in lowlands on Pacific slope from Honduras to northwestern Costa Rica (where numerous in Guanacaste, in smaller numbers extending to the Central Plateau); ranges north to southern Mexico. Pacific Screech-Owl's voice is quite different from that of Tropical, being an even fast series of 10 to 12 guttural, almost rattled notes, less musical and trilled than Tropical's, and without that species' accented final note or two.

WHISKERED SCREECH-OWL
Otus trichopsis

8. Very similar in appearance to both Tropical and Pacific Screech-Owls, but averages smaller than either, and with coarser (wider) black streaks on underparts. None of the three species overlap, and each is best distinguished by voice. Whiskered's commonest call is a series of rather high-pitched hoots with *characteristic variable syncopation*, resembling Morse Code; also has a less distinctive series of short whistled notes. Whiskered Screech-Owl is uncommon in pine and pine-oak woodland in highlands of Honduras and northern Nicaragua; ranges north to Mexico and extreme southwestern United States.

NORTHERN PYGMY-OWL
Glaucidium gnoma

7. Similar to Least Pygmy-Owl (see main text, p.189), but appreciably larger, and with whitish spotting on sides and more numerous (usually four or five, not three) narrow white tail bands. Rufous phase is relatively frequent in the race found in Honduras, *cabanense*. Uncommon in pine woodland and cloud forest in highlands of western and central Honduras; ranges north to western North America. In Honduras the Least Pygmy-Owl occurs only in humid lowland forest, the Ferruginous Pygmy-Owl in a variety of semiopen (often arid) habitats.

FULVOUS OWL
Strix fulvescens

16. *A fairly large, round-headed owl of highland forests*. Iris dark. Mostly rufous brown above with blackish and white markings; *prominent pale buff facial discs* outlined with blackish; throat buffy whitish, *breast buff prominently barred blackish*, lower underparts tawny boldly streaked blackish. Mottled Owl is smaller, with dark facial discs outlined paler, no barring across breast, etc. Fairly common (but reclusive and strictly nocturnal, hence not often seen) in cloud forest and pine-oak woodland in highlands of Honduras; ranges north to southern Mexico. Commonest call is a loud, comparatively high-pitched hooting (with quality similar to the Barred Owl, *S. varia*, of North America), e.g. *hoo, hoo-hoo, hoo,*

hoo, usually (always?) lacking the Barred Owl's final drawled note.

STYGIAN OWL
Asio stygius

Apparently rare and local, recorded from north-central Nicaragua, perhaps also occurring in Honduras and Costa Rica. See main text under Striped Owl (p.192).

TAWNY-COLLARED NIGHTJAR
Caprimulgus salvini

10. A *large and dark* nightjar with *rufous collar* and *large white spots or splotches on breast and belly. Tail corners broadly white* (male), *or buff* (female), angled forward at sides (not squared). Whip-poor-will (which is resident south to Honduras highlands, the very dark, blackish brown race *vermiculatus*) is smaller (9 in, but grayer northern migrants are larger, 9½ in) and lacks the rufous collar, etc. Found mainly from eastern Mexico to Belize and northern Guatemala, with one record from Nicaragua (a vagrant?); apparently favors forest borders. Call is a very rapidly repeated *chuck-will, chuck-will, chuck-will . . .*

BUFF-COLLARED NIGHTJAR
Caprimulgus ridgwayi

8¾. A mottled grayish brown nightjar of brushy or rocky areas, mainly in highlands. *Buff collar* shows in both sexes (though it can be inconspicuous), and distinguishes this species from Whip-poor-will (of which both resident and northern migrant races are present, both mainly in association with cloud forest or pine-oak woodland). Flight feathers show some rufous (both sexes), and male has white tail corners, both most likely seen as the bird flushes. Uncommon in arid interior valleys and slopes in highlands (mainly) of Honduras and northern Nicaragua; ranges north to northern Mexico and extreme southwestern United States. Most easily identified from its unmistakable call, an accelerating series of fast *cuk* notes ending with a loud *kuhchayuh* phrase.

SPOT-TAILED NIGHTJAR
Caprimulgus maculicaudus

Recorded locally from savannas in the Mosquitia region of northeastern Nicaragua (and likely also occurs in adjacent extreme eastern Honduras), with one record (of two specimens) from western Honduras (Lake Yojoa); ranges also in southern Mexico, and locally in South America. See main text under White-tailed Nightjar (p.197). With conversion of so much lowland humid forest to cattle pasturage (which can provide favorable habitat for this species), the Spot-tailed Nightjar may perhaps increase in Central America.

SPOT-FRONTED SWIFT
Cypseloides cherriei

A very rare swift with a still imperfectly known range; has been recorded in Costa Rica from specimens taken on Volcán Irazú and near Helechales in Puntarenas Province, otherwise recorded only very locally from northern South America. Perhaps more widespread, but accurate field identification is difficult; see main text under White-chinned Swift (p.200).

WHITE-THROATED SWIFT
Aeronautes saxatalis

6½. A fairly large, *boldly patterned* swift of highlands. Mainly dusky above, browner on crown; *throat, breast, and mid-belly white*, with *large blackish area on sides* and white patch on flanks; tail somewhat forked. Both Greater and Lesser Swallow-tailed Swifts have a different pattern below, with large white throat patch contrasting with mostly blackish remaining underparts; their tails are longer, and are usually held closed in a point. White-throated Swift is an uncommon resident in highlands of western and central Honduras, usually near cliffs (but foraging more widely); ranges north to western United States.

GREAT SWALLOW-TAILED SWIFT
Panyptila sanctihieronymi

7½. Resembles Lesser Swallow-tailed Swift (see main text, p.203), but considerably *larger* and showing *fairly conspicuous white margin on trailing edge of wing* (absent or virtually so in the Lesser). Great Swallow-tailed Swift is fairly common in highlands of Honduras, and is also recorded from Nicaragua, with a few sightings (northern migrants?) also from Costa Rica; ranges north to Mexico. In Honduras this species occurs at elevations above those recorded for Lesser Swallow-tailed Swift (which is found in association with humid lowland forest), and it is most often noted in small flocks (whereas Lesser is usually seen singly or in pairs).

WEDGE-TAILED SABREWING
Campylopterus curvipennis   Plate 43

5¼. An isolated population of this *rather large*, mainly northern Middle American species is found in eastern Honduras. Bill fairly long (1 in), slightly decurved, blackish. Mostly shining green above with glittering violet-blue crown and small white postocular spot; *tail strongly graduated*, central feathers shiny bluish or bronzy green, outer feathers duskier and narrowly edged and tipped whitish; *dull pale grayish below*. Female has less blue on crown, broader white tipping on outer tail feathers. Recorded from Olancho forests of eastern Honduras lowlands; otherwise ranges from eastern Mexico to northern Guatemala and Belize, where often numerous in lower growth of forest, woodland, and borders.

GREEN-BREASTED MANGO
Anthracothorax prevostii   Plate 43

The race of this species (*gracilirostris*) found from central Costa Rica north to Honduras and El Salvador differs markedly from the form in Panama (*veraguensis*); they may or may not be conspecific, but were so treated in the 1983 AOU Check-list, the course followed here. Male here has *narrow stripe of black down center of throat and upper chest*, sharply demarcated from green on sides of throat but blending with dark bluish green of breast; recall that *veraguensis* lacks *any* black below. Female has *rufous on lower face and sides of breast*, variable in extent, sometimes faintly indicated but often very prominent; this is lacking in female *veraguensis*. Remember that Black-throated Mango (see main text, p.210) is not found north of Panama. Taxonomic situation complicated, with nominate *prevostii* group (with *gracilirostris*) of Mexico to Costa Rica being very similar to *viridicortatus* of arid northern Venezuela and northern Colombia, but separated geographically by the quite different *veraguensis* (the position of *iridescens* of western Ecuador seems problematic, but at present it is assigned to *A. prevostii*).

EMERALD-CHINNED HUMMINGBIRD
Abeillia abeillei   Plate 43

2¾–3. *Very small. Bill very short* (⅜ in), straight. Male shining green above with small white postocular spot; *gorget glittering green,*

breast blackish, belly grayish green; tail with small whitish corners. Female like male above; *uniform pale gray below*, some bronzy green on sides. Locally fairly common in cloud forest in highlands of Honduras and northern Nicaragua, mostly above 900 m (3000 ft); ranges north to southern Mexico. Occurs mostly inside forest in lower growth, less often at edge.

BLACK-CRESTED COQUETTE
Lophornis helenae   Plate 43

The *northernmost ranging coquette* except for a rare localized form of Rufous-crested found in southern Mexico. Black-crested ranges in lowlands and lower foothills on Caribbean slope north to southern Mexico and south to central Costa Rica (possibly ranging farther south?). See main text under Rufous-crested Coquette (p.211). Like that species, found mainly at edge of humid forest.

FORK-TAILED EMERALD
Chlorostilbon canivetii   Plate 43

3¼. Bill fairly short (½ in), straight, *red with black tip in both sexes* (duller in female). Male shining bronzy green above, crown more glittering green; *brilliant glittering green below*; rather large white leg-tufts; tail blue-black, *quite deeply forked*. Female shining green above, bronzier on crown, with *white postocular streak* and dusky ear-coverts; *uniform pale grayish below*, some green on sides; tail less deeply forked than in male, outer feathers narrowly tipped pale grayish. Widespread and often common in a variety of semiopen habitats in lowlands on both slopes south to Nicaragua, and on Pacific slope south to Costa Rica (mainly Guanacaste and slopes of northwestern cordilleras, smaller numbers on Central Plateau); ranges north to northern Mexico. Often in gardens, or seen feeding in flowering trees. *C. canivetii* was treated as a full species in the 1983 AOU Check-list, separate from *C. assimilis* (Garden Emerald) of southwestern Costa Rica and Panama; ranges of the two approach each other in Costa Rica but they are not known to be in contact. Garden Emerald is slightly smaller with less deeply forked tail, all-black bill, and males lack glitter on crown.

WHITE-EARED HUMMINGBIRD
Hylocharis leucotis   Plate 43

3½. Bill essentialy straight (½ in), *coral red with black tip in both sexes*. Male has glittering violet-blue forecrown and chin, *long white postocular streak*; otherwise bronzy green above, bronziest on tail; lower throat glittering green, remaining underparts grayish white with considerable green on sides. Female bronzy green above with *long white postocular streak* and *blackish ear-coverts*; outer tail feathers tipped whitish; below whitish spotted with green on throat, *heavily speckled or barred with green on sides and flanks* (this sometimes almost solid). Female Fork-tailed Emerald is grayer below with much less green, but otherwise the two are rather similar. White-eared Hummingbird is common in cloud forest, pine-oak woodland, and borders in highlands of Honduras and northern Nicaragua above about 900 m (3000 ft); ranged north through Mexico, small numbers reaching extreme southwestern United States.

WHITE-BELLIED EMERALD
Amazilia candida   Plate 43

3¼. Bill straight (½ in), lower mandible reddish. Above uniform metallic green, outer tail feathers with dusky subterminal band and grayish tip (both inconspicuous); *below pure white*, with some green on sides. A rather plain, small hummer without notable field marks, but whiter below than most others with which it occurs. Common in forest borders and clearings in lowlands on Caribbean slope south to Nicaragua (where it also occurs locally on Pacific slope), with a few records from northern Costa Rica (perhaps occurring only as a wanderer?); ranges north to eastern Mexico.

HONDURAN EMERALD
Amazilia luciae

3½. Bill essentially straight (¾ in), lower mandible mostly reddish. Uniform metallic green above, tail bronzier with blackish subterminal band; *throat and chest glittering blue to greenish blue* (feathers often edged paler), sides and flanks green, mid-belly to crissum white. An enigmatic bird, the only species endemic to Honduras where it is recorded locally from Caribbean lowlands from Cofradía east to Catacamas. In June 1988 found to be common in arid thorn forest and scrub in the upper Río Aguan valley in Yoro Department (S. N. G. Howell and S. Webb).

MANGROVE HUMMINGBIRD
Amazilia boucardi   Plate 43

Found only along Pacific coast of Costa Rica from the Gulf of Nicoya region south to around Golfo Dulce in the southwest (but could possibly occur south into adjacent western Panama). See main text under Snowy-bellied Hummingbird (p.216).

AZURE-CROWNED HUMMINGBIRD
Amazilia cyanocephala   Plate 43

Formerly known as the Red-billed Azurecrown. 3¾. Bill essentially straight (¾ in), lower mandible mainly red. Mostly bronzy green above with *glittering blue crown* (in most of Cental American range; *guatemalensis*); *throat white*, sides and flanks extensively bronzy green, mid-belly also white. Birds of the Mosquitia region (*chlorostephana*) differ strikingly in having *crown glittering green* (not blue); this could prove to be a distinct species, Mosquitia Hummingbird. Larger and longer-billed than White-bellied Emerald, with considerably more green below, and (in most of range) blue on crown. Common in pine-oak woodland in highlands of Honduras and northern Nicaragua, mostly above 600 m (2000 ft) but occasionally wandering lower on Caribbean slope, in nonbreeding season wandering into other edge habitats; occurs also in Mosquitia pine savanna region of extreme eastern Honduras and northeastern Nicaragua; ranges north to northern Mexico.

INDIGO-CAPPED HUMMINGBIRD
Amazilia cyanifrons

3¾. Resembles Steely-vented Hummingbird, but male with *deep blue crown* (green in females of both species), somewhat less bronzy on upper tail-coverts, and tail not quite so bright blue-black. Indigo-capped is still known in Middle America only from a single specimen taken on Volcán Miravalles in northwestern Costa Rica; it otherwise is known locally from semiopen areas and forest borders on lower Andean slopes in western Colombia. Whether the Costa Rica bird represents a resident population (it was described as a separate species, *A. alfaroana*, but is very similar to the nominate form), or was merely a wandering bird, remains unknown.

BERYLLINE HUMMINGBIRD
Amazilia beryllina   Plate 43

3¾. Bill essentially straight (¾ in), lower mandible reddish. Shining green above, becoming bronzy on lower back and rump; *tail purplish chestnut; greater wing-coverts chestnut* (variable in extent); *underparts mostly glittering green*, lower belly more grayish. Sexes nearly alike, female slightly duller below. Resembles Blue-tailed Hummingbird aside from strikingly different tail color, and less chestnut in wing of Berylline. Uncommon in pine and pine-oak woodland in highlands of Honduras above 600 m (2000 ft); ranges north to northern Mexico, rarely wandering to extreme southwestern United States.

BUFF-BELLIED HUMMINGBIRD
Amazilia yucatanensis

3¾. Bill essentially straight (¾ in), coral red with dusky tip. Above shining bronzy green; *tail mostly rufous*, central feathers more bronzy green; throat and breast glittering green, *rather sharply contrasted from pale dull buff belly*. Resembles much more numerous Rufous-tailed Hummingbird, but in that species glittering green of the breast *merges* into dull *grayish* belly; bill of Rufous-tailed generally shows less red. Buff-bellied is apparently only a rare visitant to Caribbean slope lowlands of northern Honduras (where Rufous-tailed is much more numerous). It ranges north, much more commonly, to northern Mexico and southern Texas.

BLUE-TAILED HUMMINGBIRD
Amazilia cyanura   Plate 43

3½. Bill essentially straight (¾ in), lower mandible reddish tipped dusky. Shining green above, becoming coppery bronze on lower back and rump, and purplish bronze on upper tail-coverts; *tail rather bright blue-black; wing-coverts and base of flight feathers conspicuously coppery bronze*; below mostly glittering green, crissum bluish gray edged white. Resembles slightly larger Steely-vented Hummingbird aside from its having bronzy to chestnut on wings. Blue-tailed is found in similar habitats as that species, but *only northward on Pacific slope* (mainly in Honduras and western Nicaragua; casual in northwestern Costa Rica); in Honduras the Blue-tailed also occurs locally and in small numbers in Caribbean slope lowlands; ranges north to southern Mexico.

CINNAMON HUMMINGBIRD
Amazilia rutila   Plate 43

4. Bill essentially straight (¾ in), mostly red with dusky tip. Rather dull bronzy green above; tail mostly rufous, feathers tipped darker; *below uniform cinnamon-buff*. Common in open dry woodland and borders, pastures with scattered shrubs, and in scrub in lowlands on Pacific slope south to northwestern Costa Rica (mainly in Guanacaste and slopes of northwestern cordilleras, rarely south onto the Central Plateau); in Honduras also occurs in smaller numbers in interior valleys to over 1500 m (5000 ft), and even locally in Caribbean slope lowlands; also numerous in the Mosquitia pine savanna region of extreme eastern Honduras and northeastern Nicaragua. Ranges north to northern Mexico.

STEELY-VENTED HUMMINGBIRD
Amazilia saucerottei   Plate 43

3¾. Bill essentially straight (⅔ in), lower mandible reddish tipped dusky. Shining green above, becoming *coppery-bronze on upper tail-coverts; tail rather bright blue-black; below mostly glittering green*, crissum bronzy grayish edged white. Fairly common to common in deciduous woodland and borders and in shade trees around houses or in coffee plantations in lowlands and lower highlands (to about 1200 m: 4000 ft) on Pacific slope in southwestern Nicaragua and northwestern Costa Rica (south over much of the Central Plateau, also rarely wandering to Caribbean slope). Ranges also in western Colombia and northern Venezuela.

COPPERY-HEADED EMERALD
Elvira cupreiceps   Plate 43

3. Bill rather short (½ in), *distinctly decurved*. Male shining coppery green above, *the coppery most pronounced on crown and upper tail-coverts* (but even here often not easy to discern); *tail mainly white*, central feathers and tips to outer feathers bronzy; below glittering green, white on crissum. Female like male above and on tail, but with no coppery on crown; *whitish below* with a little green on sides. Lacks the conspicuous cinnamon wing-patch of larger Stripe-tailed Hummingbird. Female Snowcap is only slightly larger than this species, and is very similar, but it has a straight bill and is not as extensively white on lateral tail feathers. Endemic to Costa Rica, the Coppery-headed

Emerald is uncommon to locally fairly western cordilleras (e.g. at Monteverde) to Caribbean slope of central volcanoes; most numerous 600–1200 m (2000–4000 ft). Feeds at flowers at all heights, sometimes at *Stachytarpheta* hedges or *Inga* trees.

GREEN-THROATED MOUNTAIN-GEM
Lampornis viridipallens   Plate 43

4¼. Bill straight (¾ in). Male bronzy green above with *white postocular streak*; tail blackish; *throat glittering green*, feathers edged white giving scaly look, *contrasting with white remaining underparts*, with some green on sides. Female like male but more shining (less bronzy) green above, and *mostly white below*, with some green on sides. Both sexes resemble Green-breasted Mountain-gem, males differing in their *contrasting* green gorget (both throat *and* breast green in Green-breasted), females in their white throats (pale buff in Green-breasted), both sexes in lacking Green-breasted's white tail flash. Green-throated is fairly common in lower growth of cloud forest in highlands of western Honduras, mostly above 1200 m (4000 ft), with smaller numbers in pine-oak woodland; southward it is replaced by Green-breasted Mountain-gem. The Green-throated ranges north to southern Mexico.

GREEN-BREASTED MOUNTAIN-GEM
Lampornis sybillae   Plate 43

4¼. Bill straight (¾ in). Male shining green above with white postocular streak; *tail mostly grayish white* (flashing conspicuously in flight), central feathers blackish; *below mostly glittering green*, feathers edged white giving somewhat scaly look, more whitish on lower belly and crissum. Female like male above *and on tail; throat pale buff*, remaining underparts whitish, some green on sides. Cf. Green-throated Mountain-gem (these two closely related species are not known to occur together, Green-throated being more northerly in distribution). Green-breasted Mountain-gem is endemic to lower growth of cloud forest and borders in highlands of central Honduras and northern Nicaragua, where it is locally fairly common. It occurs in La Tigra National Park near Tegucigalpa.

AMETHYST-THROATED HUMMINGBIRD
Lampornis amethystinus   Plate 43

4½. Bill slightly decurved (¾ in). Male above rather dark shining green with postocular streak surmounting dusky ear-coverts; tail black, slightly paler grayish on corners; *throat glittering rosy-magenta, remaining underparts dull sooty gray*, somewhat tinged green on breast. Female resembles male above, with *somewhat more conspicuous pale gray tail corners; throat and upper chest tawny-buff, uniform gray on remaining underparts*. Female resembles female Green-breasted Mountain-gem, but is much grayer (not pure white) below, with more extensive and deeper buff on throat, and different tail pattern. Uncommon in lower growth and borders of cloud forest in highlands of western and central Honduras, mainly above 1500 m (5000 ft); ranges north to northern Mexico.

WHITE-THROATED MOUNTAIN-GEM
Lampornis castaneoventris   Plate 43

The race of this species (*cinereicauda*) found in southern Costa Rica (from around Cerro de la Muerte south through the Cordillera de Talamanca to near the Panama border) has a *gray tail*, whereas in birds found in Chiriquí, Panama, the tail is black. The difference is quite apparent in the field.

GARNET-THROATED HUMMINGBIRD
Lamprolaima rhami

4½. One of the more spectacular Middle America hummingbirds, even in poor light both sexes of the Garnet-throated can be known by their *mainly rufous wings*. Bill straight (¾ in). Male above brilliant green with small white postocular spot; *tail deep violet-purple*; throat patch glittering rosy-magenta surrounded by black, *breast glittering violet-blue*, belly sooty. Female shining green above with small white postocular spot; *tail dark purple with pale corners; below uniform dark sooty*. Uncommon to locally fairly common in lower growth and borders of cloud forest in highlands of Honduras, mainly above 1650 m (5500 ft); ranges north to central Mexico.

PLAIN-CAPPED STARTHROAT
Heliomaster constantii   Plate 43

5. Closely resembles Long-billed Starthroat (see main text, p.222), but both sexes lack male Long-billed's blue crown and have *longer white postocular streak* (not just a spot). For the most part the two starthroats segregate out geographically

and ecologically. Plain-capped is uncommon to locally fairly common in lowlands on Pacific slope from Honduras to northwestern Costa Rica (where it occurs mainly in Guanacaste, with smaller numbers on the Central Plateau and a few reports from the southwest as well); Long-billed in this region is essentially a Caribbean slope bird found in more humid regions. The two are reported to occur sympatrically in the Olancho valley in interior Honduras (B. L. Monroe, Jr.). Plain-capped occurs north to northern Mexico, casually wandering to extreme southwestern United States. Behavior of the two, particularly their habit of frequently perching on high exposed branches and flycatching, is similar.

SLENDER SHEARTAIL
Doricha enicura

♂ 4½ , ♀ 3¼ . Bill slightly decurved (¾ in). Male shining green above; tail blackish, *outer feathers very much elongated resulting in deeply forked effect* (though often the two sides are *held closed in a point*); *throat glittering violet-purple* bordered below by a *broad buffy whitish pectoral collar*; lower underparts whitish, sides broadly bronzy green. Female shining green above, duller on crown with buff postocular streak; *tail forked, outer feathers rufous with broad black median band*, central feathers green; *below uniform cinnamon-buff*, with white leg-tufts. Sparkling-tailed Hummingbird is markedly smaller, shows partial rump band, etc. The sheartail is evidently rare in highlands of western Honduras; it ranges north to southern Mexico.

SPARKLING-TAILED HUMMINGBIRD
Tilmatura dupontii   Plate 43

♂ 3½ , ♀ 2½ . Bill straight, quite short (½ in). Male shining green above with *conspicuous white patch on either side of rump;* tail elongated and deeply forked, outer feathers boldly banded brown and white; *throat glittering blue*, chest white, lower underparts shining dark green. Female shining dark green above with *buffy-white rump patches as in male*; tail short, barely forked, outer feathers black tipped buff or whitish; *face and entire underparts uniform cinnamon-buff*. Male unmistakable, female reminiscent of a female coquette (but none of those is found in the highlands, and none is so uniform below). Sparkling-tailed is locally fairly common in cloud forest borders and pine-oak woodland in highlands of Honduras and northern Nicaragua above about 1050 m

(3500 ft); ranges north to central Mexico. It is usually quite a conspicuous hummingbird, both sexes frequently cocking their tails (male's obviously being much more evident), and slowly wagging it as they hover at flowers.

WINE-THROATED HUMMINGBIRD
Atthis ellioti   Plate 43

2¾ . Bill straight, very short (⅜ in). Male shining bronzy green above with small white postocular spot; tail feathers basally rufous, terminally black, with corners of outer feathers buffy-white; *throat rosy-violet, the gorget extended to a point on either side*; remaining underparts whitish with some bronzy green on sides. Female like male above (except tail corners are buff); throat whitish with *small but discrete bronzy green spots*; breast and mid-belly white, *sides broadly rufous*. A *tiny* hummingbird, with nothing else really very similar in Honduran part of its range. Fairly common in shrubby areas and borders of cloud forest in highlands of western Honduras, mainly above 1500 m (5000 ft); ranges north to southern Mexico. Erratic or seasonal in some areas.

VOLCANO HUMMINGBIRD
Selasphorus flammula

F. G. Stiles (*Auk 100*(2): 311–325, 1983) has shown that *Selasphorus simoni* (Cerise-throated Hummingbird), formerly considered most closely related to *S. ardens* (Glow-throated Hummingbird) of Panama, is actually best considered as a race of the Volcano Hummingbird. Found only on the upper slopes of Volcán Poás and Volcán Barba in Costa Rica's Central Cordillera, *simoni* differs from other races of Volcano Hummingbird in male's having a rosy red gorget. Note that nominate race of Volcano Hummingbird, found on Volcán Irazú and Volcán Turrialba (just to east, also in the Central Cordillera), has a reddish purple gorget. It is the race *torridus*, found on the Cordillera de Talamanca from around Cerro de la Muerte south into Chiriquí, Panama, which has the *dull* gorget (grayish purple to grayish green). All three races breed at high elevations (above about 1800 m: 6000 ft) but may descend lower at other seasons. They thus basically occur *above* the elevational range of the Scintillant Hummingbird (*S. scintilla*), which in Costa Rica ranges north to the Cordillera de Tilarán in the northwest.

BLACK-HEADED TROGON
Trogon melanocephalus   Plate 44

10½. A common trogon of lowlands on both slopes, mainly in *non-humid forested areas*. Male has bluish gray bill and *bright blue eye-ring*, female with dusky maxilla and duller eye-ring. Male's *head, throat, and chest black*, becoming glossy bluish green on back and violet-blue on rump and upperside of tail; lower underparts yellow, separated from black chest by white band; underside of tail black, *feathers broadly tipped white* (at times almost obscuring the black). Female has *dusky gray* replacing the male's black and glossy violet and green; *pattern on underside of tail similar*, but white tipping slightly narrower. Widespread and often (especially for a trogon) conspicuous in deciduous forest and borders, semiopen woodland, and even in mostly scrubby or cleared terrain if there are a few large trees in lowlands on both slopes, south on Pacific side to northwestern Costa Rica (Guanacaste), on Caribbean side to southeastern Nicaragua and adjacent northern Costa Rica in the Río Frío region, mostly below 600 m (2000 ft); ranges north to northern Mexico. Usually in pairs, quite tame, often perching rather low. Commonest call is an accelerating roll, *chuk, chuk, chuk-chuk-chuk-cho-cho-cho-cho-cho-cho*.

MOUNTAIN TROGON
Trogon mexicanus

12. Rather long-tailed. Male has yellow bill and very narrow red eye-ring; dusky maxilla, dull yellowish eye-ring in female. Male brilliant metallic green above and on chest, with face and throat black; *lower underparts bright red*, separated from green chest by conspicuous white band; upperside of tail blue-green, underside black *crossed by three wide bands* (formed by tips of feathers). Female brown replacing male's green, white breast band as in male but then more brown below it, becoming pale red on lower belly; tail dusky below, *outer webs of feathers mainly white with dusky barring*. Collared Trogon is quite similar to both sexes except for differences in pattern on underside of tail (male Mountain lacking male Collared's *narrow* white barring, female with much more white on sides of undertail than in female Collared). See also Elegant Trogon (which is not montane). Mountain Trogon is uncommon in pine-oak woodland and cloud forest in highlands of western and central Honduras, mainly above 1200 m (4000 ft); ranges north to northern Mexico. Commonest call is a rather slow, well-enunci-

ated *cow-cow-cow-cow-cow-cow* (usually six or seven *cow* notes). Can be found in La Tigra National Park above Tegucigalpa.

ELEGANT TROGON
Trogon elegans   Plate 44

11. Both sexes have yellow bill and narrow red eye-ring, latter less prominent in female. Male brilliant metallic green above and on chest, with face and throat black; *lower underparts bright red*, separated from green chest by conspicuous white band; upperside of tail bronzy green, *underside mostly white with narrow dusky barring*. Female has brown replacing male's green, white breast band as in male, but then some brown and whitish below that, pale red only on lower belly; *prominent elongated ("tear-shaped") white patch below and behind eye*; tail mostly dusky below, outer webs of feathers mainly white with dusky barring. Uncommon in gallery forest and woodland in lowlands on Pacific slope south to northwestern Costa Rica (Guanacaste); ranges north to Mexico and extreme southwestern United States. Almost always greatly outnumbered by the often sympatric Black-headed Trogon, and much less conspicuous than that species. Elegant's presence in an area often made known, at least when breeding, by its unmistakable low, throaty, guttural call, *cowah, cowah, cowah, cowah, cowah*, very unlike calls of other trogons.

BLUE-THROATED MOTMOT
Aspatha gularis

10½. A *mostly green, montane* motmot which does *not* acquire racquet tail-tips. All green above with *tawny around eye* and black ear-coverts; *throat pale blue*, breast pale buffy olive with black spot in center, fading to pale turquoise bluish on belly; crissum ochraceous. Uncommon to rare in cloud forest in highlands of Honduras, mainly above 1650 m (5500 ft); ranges north to southern Mexico. Forages mostly in lower growth, infrequently at borders; rather stolid and reclusive, not often seen. More apt to be found once its voice is known, that being a quite distinctive and high-pitched ringing *ook . . . ook . . . ook*, the *ook* notes given at rather long (about 5-second) intervals, usually three or four in a series, then an even longer pause before the next series. Ventriloquial and hard to track to its source, but this motmot sometimes will respond to tape playback of its voice.

KEEL-BILLED MOTMOT
Electron carinatum   Plate 44

13. *A rare and local motmot of humid forests. Mostly green*, with rufous on forehead and a black mask surmounted by a *short blue superciliary*; throat pale bluish green, remaining underparts brownish olive green with large black chest spot; has a typical motmot tail *with racquets*. The northern replacement of Broad-billed Motmot, with similar broad bill, but *much greener generally* (very little rufous). Blue-crowned Motmot is larger and tawnier below, has black on crown, etc.; Turquoise-browed has large black throat patch, much bluer tail, more prominent superciliary, etc. Both Turquoise-browed and Blue-crowned are found in more open or deciduous habitats. Keel-billed Motmot is rare and local inside humid forest in lowlands and foothills on Caribbean slope south to northern Costa Rica (where there are few records, though it has been recently found in the Peñas Blancas area north of Monteverde, *fide* R. Law; here sympatric with Broad-billed Motmot), perhaps to southern Costa Rica. Ranges north to southern Mexico. May be somewhat more numerous in northern Honduras than it is elsewhere (and may range higher here, recorded to at least 1500 m: 5000 ft). Behavior of this enigmatic motmot remains virtually unknown, but is likely similar to Broad-billed Motmot. Voice recently found to be a nasal ringing *ohring*, very similar to that of Broad-billed Motmot (S. G. N. Howell and S. Webb).

TURQUOISE-BROWED MOTMOT
Eumomota superciliosa   Plate 44

13. A strikingly *beautiful* motmot, more often in the open than other species. Mostly green above with *conspicuous pale blue superciliary*, black patch through eye and extending back onto lower cheeks, rufous area on back, and much blue in flight feathers; *tail mostly turquoise blue*, the terminal half of the large and conspicuous racquets black; mainly green below with *large turquoise-bordered black patch on lower throat and upper chest*, lower belly fulvous. Fairly common to common in deciduous and gallery woodland, borders, and even hedgerows in lowlands on Pacific slope south to northwestern Costa Rica (Guanacaste), also in interior valleys of Honduras highlands (where even spreads locally into cleared areas in Caribbean lowlands); ranges north to southern Mexico. Often conspicuous and surprisingly confiding, regularly perching on fences or even phone wires, switching its tail from side to side. Oft-heard voice is very similar to Broad-billed

Motmot's, a nasal far-carrying *cwaw* or *cwaanh*, sometimes repeated several times in succession.

EMERALD TOUCANET
Aulacorhynchus prasinus

Race of Emerald Toucanet found in highlands of Honduras and Nicaragua, *virescens*, has throat white (not the blue of Costa Rican and Panama birds); otherwise they are similar.

RED-VENTED WOODPECKER
Melanerpes pygmaeus

7. A *small* version of Golden-fronted Woodpecker, in our area occurring *only on Guanaja Island in the Bay Islands off northern Honduras*; ranges also on Yucatan Peninsula and in Belize. Resembles Golden-fronted, but has proportionately smaller bill and more yellow on chin (in addition to substantial size difference). Reportedly numerous in all wooded habitats (except in pines) on Guanaja Island.

HOFFMANN'S WOODPECKER
Melanerpes hoffmannii   Plate 44

7½. *The common "zebra-backed" woodpecker of Pacific slope lowlands.* Forecrown mainly white, mid-crown red, *hindcrown yellow*; otherwise coarsely barred black and white above; below drab grayish with some yellow on belly, crissum barred black and white. Female similar but lacks red on crown. Golden-fronted Woodpecker has mid- *and hindcrown red (with no yellow)* and is more narrowly barred above. Red-crowned Woodpecker shows no yellow on nape; it is found only from southwestern Costa Rica south into Panama, never occurring sympatrically with Hoffmann's. Hoffmann's is common on Pacific slope from southern Honduras to western and central Costa Rica (where it extends across most of the Central Plateau, locally even into Caribbean drainage). Inhabits virtually any area with trees of reasonable size; often in semiopen regions, or around buildings and in towns. Has frequent loud churring calls (similar to those of Golden-fronted and Red-crowned).

GOLDEN-FRONTED WOODPECKER
Melanerpes aurifrons   Plate 44

8¼–9. *The widespread "zebra-backed" woodpecker of Honduras and northern Nicaragua.* Forehead whitish with frontal area yellow, *mid- and hindcrown red*; otherwise black above *rather narrowly barred white*; below drab grayish with some yellow on lower belly, crissum barred black and white. Female has *only* hindcrown red. *Pauper* of northern Honduras lowlands somewhat smaller than other races. *Canescens* (found on Roatán Island in the Bay Islands off Honduras) rather strikingly different, being *much whiter* on forehead, face, and underparts, and with red (not yellow) on frontal area and belly. Hoffmann's Woodpecker is smaller and always shows yellow (not red) on hindcrown, and is more coarsely barred above. Golden-fronted is common in virtually all wooded habitats (avoiding extensive humid forest) in Caribbean lowlands and interior highlands of Honduras (where probably the most numerous woodpecker), and ranges south into northern Nicaragua; ranges north (some races rather different looking) through Mexico into southwestern United States.

LADDER-BACKED WOODPECKER
Picoides scalaris

6¼–6½. A *small* woodpecker with boldly barred upperparts and *spotting below*. Crown red (black in female), face whitish with *bold black stripes forming a triangle around ear-coverts*; otherwise coarsely barred black and white above, wings black with white spotting, central tail feathers all black; below whitish to pale grayish with *sparse black spotting on sides and flanks*. Hairy Woodpecker is confined to highlands, and has browner underparts, a solid white mid-back, never has fully red crown, etc.; remember that Central American races of Hairy are smaller than North American birds. Ladder-backed is fairly common but very local in Honduras (recorded from Pacific lowlands and at scattered localities in interior valleys) and northeastern Nicaragua (where known only from Mosquitia region; probably also in adjacent Honduras); ranges north into southwestern United States. In the Mosquitia found in pine woodland, elsewhere in deciduous woodland or scrub, locally even in mangroves. Voice is a whinny similar to that of Smoky-brown Woodpecker (J. Arvin).

NORTHERN FLICKER
Colaptes auratus

11. A large and conspicuous, *basically brownish woodpecker* of highlands. *Upperparts barred buffy brown and black, rump white* barred with black; *crown plain russet brown*; sides of head and neck and throat gray with broad red malar stripe (russet brown in female); *large chest patch black*, lower underparts buffy whitish boldly spotted black; *underwing linings and undertail pinkish orange* (conspicuous in flight). Fairly common in pine and pine-oak woodland in highlands of Honduras and northern Nicaragua above 600 m (2000 ft). The local race, *mexicanoides*, rather closely resembles the "Red-shafted" Flickers of western North America south through Mexico (the *cafer* group, now considered conspecific with *C. auratus*). Behavior, including frequent feeding on the ground, of all forms is basically similar, as are varied vocalizations, most characteristic being a loud clear *kee-ah* and a long *wik-wik-wik-wik* . . . series.

RUFOUS-BREASTED SPINETAIL
Synallaxis erythrothorax   Plate 45

5¾. The *northernmost Synallaxis* spinetail. Mostly olive brown above, with *long tail* tinged rufous and *wings mainly rufous-chestnut*; throat dark gray narrowly streaked white, with *band of solid blackish across chest contrasting with rufous breast*; flanks olive brown, mid-belly pale grayish. Fairly common in shrubby borders and dense second-growth in lowlands up to about 600 m (2000 ft) in northwestern Honduras; ranges north to southern Mexico. Replaced eastward in northern Honduras by the Slaty Spinetail (see main text p.250), the two occurring together at least in the Lancetilla area. Usually in pairs, generally secretive and inconspicuous though its characteristic call is given frequently, a repeated rather emphatic *whit, whit, wheét-u, whit-whit-wheét-u* . . . Can be found around the Lancetilla Botanical Garden.

IVORY-BILLED WOODCREEPER
Xiphorhynchus flavigaster   Plate 45

9¼. A rather large and boldly striped woodcreeper with quite long (1¼ in) slightly decurved *ivory to horn-colored bill*. Above brown, more blackish on crown, with *prominent black-edged buff striping extending down over back and wing-coverts*; wings and tail rufous; throat pale buff with narrow blackish malar streak; remaining underparts pale olive brown *with wide black-edged buff streaks*. Compared to Buff-throated Woodcreeper (see main text, p.262), Ivory-billed has paler bill and is much more profusely and conspicuously striped on mantle (especially) and underparts; Buff-throated also lacks the malar streak. Streak-headed Woodcreeper is smaller with slenderer bill, etc. Ivory-billed is widespread and generally common (especially in Honduras) in a variety of forested and wooded habitats on both slopes of Honduras, mainly on Pacific slope in Nicaragua, and in Costa Rica only in northwest (where generally scarce and local); it ranges north to northern Mexico. Behavior similar to that of Buff-throated Woodcreeper, as is its primary vocalization, a series of loud clear whistled notes which starts rapidly and then gradually slows down. Call is an abrupt loud *cleer* which has been likened to a sudden laugh (J. Arvin).

STREAK-CROWNED ANTVIREO
Dysithamnus striaticeps   Plate 45

4¼. Closely resembles Spot-crowned Antvireo (see main text, p.268); this species replaces Spot-crowned northward on Caribbean slope. Male differs in having *crown gray streaked with black* (no white spotting), and in being *more boldly and profusely streaked black on throat and (especially) breast*. Female much like female Spot-crowned but paler, less buffy, below. Streak-crowned is uncommon in lower growth of humid forest in lowlands and and foothills (to about 600 m: 2000 ft) on Caribbean slope from extreme southeastern Honduras to southeastern Costa Rica. It and the Spot-crowned overlap in the Río Sixaola region of southeastern Costa Rica near the Panama border, but Streak-crowned is much the scarcer of the two here (P. Slud). Behavior and vocalizations of the two are very similar. Pairs can sometimes be found accompanying mixed understory flocks at the La Selva Biological Station.

YELLOW-BELLIED TYRANNULET
Ornithion semiflavum   Plate 46

3. Resembles Brown-capped Tyrannulet (see main text, p.283) but *crown gray* (not brown). Yellow-bellied replaces the Brown-capped northward in Middle America and is uncommon in canopy and borders of humid forest and woodland in lowlands on Caribbean slope from Honduras to extreme northern Costa Rica (south of Lake Nicaragua), and it reappears in southwestern Costa Rica (e.g. on the Osa Peninsula); it ranges north to southern Mexico. In Costa Rica the Brown-capped Tyrannulet occurs only on the Caribbean slope, north to Alajuela (Province) where it may be sympatric with Yellow-bellied. Behavior of the two is similar, as are their vocalizations, though that of Yellow-bellied has a characteristically different cadence: after three or four intial *dee* notes, either on same pitch or falling

slightly (less run together than in Brown-capped), there is a pause followed by a final rising and accented *wheet?* This lacks the pause after the initial note, so distinctive in Brown-capped's call.

NORTHERN BEARDLESS-TYRANNULET
Camptostoma imberbe   Plate 46

3¾–4. Closely resembles Southern Beardless-Tyrannulet (see main text, p.283). Difficult to distinguish on the basis of plumage, but presents an *overall more faded, paler, and washed out appearance* (with belly at most pale yellowish, instead of the pale clear yellow of Southern). Northern Beardless-Tyrannulet replaces the Southern northward in Middle America, and is fairly common in semiopen areas with scrub, gallery woodland, gardens, and in borders of secondary woodland in lowlands and interior valleys on both slopes in Honduras, and mainly on Pacific slope in Nicaragua and northwestern Costa Rica (primarily in Guanacaste, locally also south of Lake Nicaragua); ranges north to Mexico and extreme southwestern United States. Northern and Southern Beardless-Tyrannulets are reportedly sympatric in parts of southern Guanacaste (P. Slud), with Southern occurring south on Pacific slope from there into Panama. Behavior of the two is very similar, as are their vocalizations. Northern's song is a series of four or five clear melancholy descending notes, while its call is a rather loud and sharp *pee-yeép*.

YELLOW-OLIVE FLYCATCHER
Tolmomyias sulphurescens   Plates 24, 46

Birds found from Costa Rica northward (and perhaps also in extreme western Panama), *cinereiceps*, differ from Panama birds (*flavo-olivaceus*) in having distinctly gray crown and nape contrasting with rather bright olive back, and much more grayish throat and breast (not nearly so olive).

STUB-TAILED SPADEBILL
Platyrinchus cancrominus   Plate 46

3¾. Closely resembles White-throated Spadebill (see main text, p.295). Averages larger, and males have crown patch very small (White-throated's patch is considerably larger, and is often displayed by calling birds). Stub-tailed replaces White-throated Spadebill northward in Middle America from northern Costa Rica; the two were long considered to be conspecific, but P. Slud demonstrated that they were locally sympatric in northwestern Costa Rica and that they differed vocally (see below). They mostly separate out by range, with Stub-tailed in Costa Rica being restricted to lower growth inside lowland woodland and gallery forest in Guanacaste, south of Lake Nicaragua, and on slopes of northwestern cordilleras up to about 1200 m (4000 ft); White-throated in Costa Rica is mainly montane, and occurs only from Monteverde area southward. Stub-tailed ranges north on both slopes of Nicaragua and Honduras to Gulf slope of southern Mexico. Behavior of Stub-tailed Spadebill is very similar to that of White-throated, but its commonest call, a fast chippery *tídadit*, differs characteristically from that of White-throated in Costa Rica and Panama (the race *neglectus*).

TAWNY-CHESTED FLYCATCHER
Aphanotriccus capitalis   Plate 46

An obscure, scarce tyrannid endemic to eastern Nicaragua and northeastern Costa Rica. Bill all black. Brownish olive above, grayer on head, and with whitish supraloral spot and eye-ring; wings with *two broad tawny wing-bars*; throat pale grayish, *breast and sides ochraceous-tawny*, remaining underparts pale clear yellow. Favors dense viny and thickety borders of humid forest, ranging in lowlands and up in foothills to about 1050 m (3500 ft). Not a well known bird, but Slud (1964) wrote of encountering this bird singly, most often perched upright like an *Empidonax* flycatcher. It calls frequently, a chippering *choot, choot, choot, ch-ch-ch-chtttreéih*, sometimes lacking the introductory notes. Present in small numbers at the La Selva Biological Station, but not often seen.

COMMON TUFTED-FLYCATCHER
Mitrephanes phaeocercus   Plate 46

Common Tufted-Flycatchers found in the Honduras and Nicaraguan highlands (*guercinus* and *nicaraguae*) are considerably darker and more richly colored below than those from Costa Rica and Panama, and show much less yellow on belly (in some individuals almost none).

BUFF-BREASTED FLYCATCHER
Empidonax fulvifrons

4½. In the notoriously difficult *Empidonax* genus this species stands out as being unusually distinctive: *its breast is a rich cinnamon-buff* (but looks faded and duller in worn plumage). Otherwise it resembles many of its congeners: basically brownish olive above with prominent whitish eye-ring and wing-bars; throat and belly whitish to buffy whitish. Common Tufted-Flycatcher is much more deeply colored below and shows a prominent pointed crest. Buff-breasted is a fairly common resident of pine-oak woodland in highlands of Honduras above about 600 m (2000 ft); it ranges north to Mexico and southeastern Arizona. Song of birds in Arizona is a quite musical but abrupt *pullick-chew*, its call a short dry *pit* (S. Terrill); presumably the voice of Honduran birds is similar.

GREATER PEWEE
Contopus pertinax   Plate 46

6½. Bill black above, *yellow-orange below. Mostly grayish olive*, somewhat paler below, becoming pale yellowish on belly; loral area white; wings and tail duskier, wings with two indistinct whitish to pale buffyish wing-bars. Often shows *slender, somewhat bushy-pointed crest*. The race resident in Honduras and Nicaragua, *minor*, is markedly smaller than the nominate race found from southwestern United States to Guatemala, and thus comes to resemble other pewees (especially Tropical), though Greater always looks more crested; calls also differ characteristically. Olive-sided Flycatcher is shorter-tailed, shows more contrasting pattern below, and white "tufts" usually protrude from behind wing. Greater Pewee is fairly common to common in pine and pine-oak woodland in highlands, mainly above 600 m (2000 ft), of Honduras and northern Nicaragua. The species ranges north to Mexico and southwestern United States, with related forms (sometimes considered conspecific, though not in the 1983 AOU Check-list) in Costa Rica and Panama (Dark Pewee, *C. lugubris*) and South America (Smoke-colored Pewee, *C. fumigatus*). Greater Pewees are usually conspicuous birds, often perching on high exposed branches from which they sally into the air. Frequently heard is a *pip* or *pip-pip-pip* call, similar to that of Dark Pewee and Olive-sided Flycatcher; whether *minor* gives the distinctive *ho-sáy-ma-ri-a* song of Greater's nominate race is not known to us.

ASH-THROATED FLYCATCHER
Myiarchus cinerascens

An uncommon winter visitor to Pacific slope of Honduras, occurring casually south to western Nicaragua and northwestern Costa Rica; breeds north to western United States. 7½–8. Closely resembles Nutting's Fly-catcher, barely distinguishable in the field though Nutting's averages smaller. From below, rufous on inner webs of tail of Nutting's can sometimes be discerned to extend all the way to the tip, whereas in Ash-throated (except in briefly held juvenile plumage) both webs are narrowly dusky-tipped. In the hand, mouth lining of Nutting's is orange (pink in Ash-throated). Nonbreeding call is a dry *pit*, drier than more liquid *quit* of Brown-crested Flycatcher (J. Arvin); but mostly silent out of breeding season.

NUTTING'S FLYCATCHER
Myiarchus nuttingi   Plate 46

6¾–7. A rather small, pallid *Myiarchus* of Pacific slope. Pale grayish brown above; wings and tail duskier, wings with blurry whitish wing-bars and rufous edging to flight feathers, inner webs of tail feathers mainly rufous; throat and breast pale gray, contrasting with pale yellow belly. Resembles Brown-crested Flycatcher (and the two often occur together), but considerably smaller and paler generally; note also their characteristic voices (see below). See also the scarce Ash-throated Flycatcher. Nutting's is uncommon to locally fairly common in deciduous woodland, gallery forest, and scrub on Pacific slope south to northwestern Costa Rica (Guanacaste), mainly in lowlands; ranges north to northern Mexico. Behavior similar to other *Myiarchus* species, but on the whole more retiring and less vocal than most (especially compared to the conspicuous, noisy Brown-crested). Commonest call of Nutting's is a smooth rising *wheep peep?* somewhat reminiscent of Great Crested Flycatcher. The rough rolling *pwerrt* call (common to most members of genus) are high-pitched and metallic in Nutting's, and somewhat resembles calls of White-throated Magpie-Jay.

BROWN-CRESTED FLYCATCHER
Myiarchus tyrannulus   Plate 46

8. A rather large *Myiarchus* of typical coloration, often best identified by voice (see below). Plumage closely resembles Nutting's Flycatcher, but Brown-crested is usually slightly darker above and on throat, and brighter yellow on belly. Panama Flycatcher (which in Costa Rica, at the northernmost limit of its range, is restricted to near Pacific coast, most often in mangroves) *lacks* rufous in wings and tail (except in juvenile plumage). Great Crested Flycatcher (a northern migrant which occurs in much of Middle American range of Brown-crested, though favoring more forested habitats) differs in being more olive above and in having lower mandible (at least at base) pale horn. Brown-crested is widespread and usually common in a variety of semiopen or lightly wooded habitats in lowlands on both slopes of Honduras, and on Pacific slope of western Nicaragua and northwestern Costa Rica (Guanacaste); ranges north to southwestern United States, and also occurs in drier parts of tropical South America. It is rather a noisy *Myiarchus*, with several short sharp calls often drawing attention to the bird including a *whip* or *hurrip*, often run together as an excited-sounding series, or a *peert!* Behavior, including the leaning forward, head nodding, and puffing of throat feathers, is typical of the genus.

CASSIN'S KINGBIRD
Tyrannus vociferans

A casual winter visitant from western United States and Mexico to highlands of Honduras, from which there is only one published record (but perhaps overlooked among large numbers of wintering Western Kingbirds there). Cassin's differs from Western Kingbird in being darker generally but especially in its *darker bluish gray on breast and head* (which contrasts with the small whitish throat and yellow lower underparts), and in *lacking* white outer tail feathers. Differs from Tropical Kingbird in having much slighter bill, darker and grayer (less olive) breast, lacking the dusky ear-patch, and in having a more or less square tail (not notched) with a buffy tip if not in worn plumage. Call is a loud, nasal *chick-queér* (J. Arvin).

GRAY-COLLARED BECARD
Pachyramphus major   Plate 45

6–6¼. Male with *glossy black crown* and inconspicuous whitish supraloral spot; *nuchal collar pale gray*, mid-back mostly black, rump also gray; wings black broadly margined and edged with white, scapulars also white; tail black, feathers broadly tipped white; *below uniform pale gray*. Female has *blackish crown* and buffyish supraloral spot; *nuchal collar yellowish buff*, back and rump rufous; wings black, *feathers broadly edged rufous-buff*; tail mostly rufous-buff, lateral feathers extensively black toward base; *buffy yellowish below*, yellowest on belly. Male White-winged Becard is blacker above and darker gray below, also lacks the nuchal collar (females of these two species are strikingly different); White-winged mainly occurs at lower elevations than Gray-collared. Female Rose-throated Becard rather resembles female Gray-collared, but latter is somewhat smaller with much more conspicuous patterning on wing (which thus does not appear virtually uniform rufous, as in Rose-throated). Gray-collared Becard is uncommon in cloud forest and pine-oak woodland in highlands of Honduras and northern Nicaragua, perhaps descending lower in nonbreeding season; it ranges north to northern Mexico. Behavior similar to that of other becards. Song a sweet *seer, piti; seer, piti* with rising inflection.

GRAY-HEADED PIPRITES (MANAKIN)
Piprites griseiceps   Plate 45

4¾. An atypical "manakin" (likely not a manakin at all), looking more like a small becard or large-headed tyrannulet. Chunky shape with very round head, rather long-tailed (for a "manakin"). Sexes alike. *Entire head gray* with *prominent white eye-ring*; otherwise olive above, wings and tail blackish, wing feathers broadly margined with olive; *olive-yellow below*, brightest yellow on throat and belly and most olive on breast. Does not resemble any other manakin in Middle America. Looks more like a female Barred Becard (but lacks that species' rufous on wings, barring below, etc.) or a *Tolmomyias* flycatcher (but note different shape, bill, behavior, etc.). The Piprites is rare in lower and middle growth of humid forest, second-growth woodland, and borders in lowlands and foothills in southeastern Honduras (only one published record), eastern Nicaragua, and northeastern Costa Rica; also one record from eastern Guatemala. Behavior differs from that of other Middle American manakins (but is much like the allied and better-known Wing-barred Piprites, *P. chloris*, of South America) in that it often accompanies mixed flocks of antwrens and flycatchers, and appears to be mainly insectivorous. Generally rather inactive, it is more likely to be found once its very distinctive call is learned, a loud rollicking *whip-whip-whip-whirr-r-r-r-r-whip!* (D. Wolf recording). With persistence this scarce species can be found in Braulio Carillo National Park, Costa Rica (especially along trail leading back from headquarters); also recorded from La Selva Biological Station. In view of the likelihood of this genus not being a member of the Pipridae (R. Prum, pers. comm.), we prefer using the group name of "Piprites".

LONG-TAILED MANAKIN
Chiroxiphia linearis   Plate 45

♂ 9; ♀ 5. Both sexes have *reddish orange legs* and *elongated central tail feathers* (much longer in males, up to 4–5 in; much shorter, *but still prominent*, in female). Male black with *scarlet crown patch* and *pale sky blue back*. Female plain olive above, somewhat paler olive below, especially on belly. Immature males are olive; red on crown comes in first, then they gradually become blacker, with blue on back last. Male unique and unmistakable, while the dull female can be told from other female manakins (few of which, in fact, overlap in range) by her protruding tail feathers. Fairly common to common in gallery forest and taller deciduous woodland in lowlands on Pacific slope south to northwestern Costa Rica (where found mainly in Guanacaste, also up slopes of northwestern cordilleras to about 1200 m: 4000 ft, e.g. at Monteverde; occurs sparingly on the Central Plateau); ranges north to southern Mexico. Doubtless much diminished in overall numbers due to despoilation of much of its habitat. Long-tailed Manakins are inconspicuous birds, in most areas often heard but not easy to actually see. Males give a far-carrying clear, mellow, whistled *toweeo* (delivered synchronously by two displaying males), and a very different *wrrreh* call; locally called "toledo" because of this first vocalization. Also has a loud *peér-deer*. Quite easily seen in forest along the entrance road to Costa Rica's Santa Rosa National Park.

BLACK-CAPPED SWALLOW
Notiochelidon pileata

5. A rare swallow of western Honduran highlands. *Above mainly dusky brown*, with head black and neck slightly glossed purple; wings and tail duskier, *tail rather deeply forked*; mainly white below, with *rather prominent dusky spotting on throat*, some brown on sides, and a *black crissum*. Resembles Blue-and-white Swallow (not recorded from Honduras, but could occur as a casual austral migrant), but that species is glossy blue above (no brown except in very young birds) and has less forked tail; note that

the highly migratory southern race (*patagonica*) of Blue-and-white which might occur also shows some dusky throat flecking. Black-capped Swallow has been recorded only once in western Honduras (La Esperanza), perhaps merely as a nonbreeding visitant from farther north (though the species is not known to be migratory); ranges north to southern Mexico. Inhabits semiopen country in highlands.

STELLER'S JAY
Cyanocitta stelleri   Plate 44

12. A large, *mainly dark blue* jay with *pointed crest of a brighter, paler blue* (crest length varies); rather black on face and sides of throat, and with some whitish on chin, upper and lower eyelids also sometimes white (individually variable); wings (especially) and tail obscurely barred with black. *The only crested jay in our area* (other than the very different magpie-jay). Fairly common in pine woodland in highlands above 1200 m (4000 ft) of Honduras and northern Nicaragua; ranges north into western North America.

WHITE-THROATED MAGPIE-JAY
Calocitta formosa   Plate 44

18–22. A *spectacular* large jay of Pacific slope; *tail very long*, accounting for over half the bird's total length. Mainly grayish blue above with *long, loose and somewhat recurved black crest; face and entire underparts white*, with some black on sides of neck and *narrow black band across breast*; outer tail feathers broadly white-tipped. Common and conspicuous in semiopen and lightly wooded areas in lowlands on Pacific slope south to northwestern Costa Rica (south to western edge of Central Plateau), ranging up to about 1200 m (4000 ft), and locally onto Caribbean slope in interior valleys of Honduras; ranges north to southern Mexico. Usually in small flocks, often bold and noisy, regularly seen flying low in loose straggling formation, one after the other, their long tails streaming behind with unmistakable silhou-ette. Has a variety of loud and arresting calls, the commonest being a harsh grating *wrah!* sometimes given in series; numerous other calls in varying quality are also uttered.

GREEN JAY
Cyanocorax yncas

11–12. Unmistakable, with *unique green and yellow coloration*. Mostly green above, bluer on tail, with bright blue crown, malar area, and spot above eye, and some milky white on forecrown; face, throat and chest black, lower underparts and *outer tail feathers bright yellow*

(latter flashing conspicuously in flight). Uncommon to locally fairly common in borders of humid forest, second-growth woodland, and clearings with scattered trees in lowlands on Caribbean slope of northern Honduras, ranging up to about 1500 m (5000 ft); ranges north to Mexico and southern Texas, and also occurs in mountains of northwestern and western South America (rather different, more montane forms). Green Jays usually move about in small groups, and despite their flashy coloration they can often be rather furtive and inconspicuous, quietly slipping through dense lower growth; at other times, however, they may call boldly from the open. Vocalizations are numerous and variable, the most frequent being a rapid repetition of a single note, e.g. as a throaty *cheh-cheh-cheh-cheh*.

BUSHY-CRESTED JAY
Cyanocorax melanocyaneus   Plate 44

11–12. *Iris yellow. Head, neck, and underparts black*; remaining upperparts and tail purplish blue. Color of underparts varies in Honduras and Nicaragua (*chavezi*): in most birds nearly uniform black or blackish, but in some the belly is dark purplish blue (though rarely or never as intense a blue as in nominate race of Guate-mala). *Bushy-crested Jay often elevates its crown feathers into a bushy crest* (not shown by any other Central American jay). Black-throated Jay, aside from lacking the crest, is smaller and sleeker, has dark eyes, and is black only on face and throat. Bushy-crested is fairly common to common in pine-oak woodland, cloud forest borders, and partially cultivated areas in highlands of Hon-duras and northern Nicaragua mostly above 900 m (3000 ft), sometimes a bit lower. These are conspicuous and usually noisy jays with a loud querulous *queert!* call, often repeated in series. Numerous in La Tigra National Park above Tegucigalpa.

BLACK-THROATED JAY
Cyanolyca pumilo

9½. A *rather small* jay, *mostly dark but fairly bright blue*, with *black forehead, face, and throat*; forehead and above eye faintly outlined with white. Unicolored Jay is larger and *uniform* blue (with no black on face or throat); Bushy-crested Jay shows crest and has yellow eye and black hood and underparts. Black-throated is fairly common in cloud forest, pine-oak woodland, and borders in highlands of western Honduras above about 1800 m (6000 ft); ranges north to southern Mexico. Usually in pairs or small groups, often quite secretive (like its congeners, generally less conspicuous than the *Cyanocorax* jays). Its commonest call is a fast *skeeysh-skeeysh . . . skeeysh-skeeysh* . . ., almost reminiscent of an *Aratinga* parakeet, also a repeated querulous *zzhweee?*

UNICOLORED JAY
Aphelocoma unicolor

12–13. *Uniform purplish blue*, slightly blacker on face. The *largest* of the Honduran highland jays, and *the most uniformly blue*, showing little discernible black. Uncommon to locally fairly common in cloud forest and cloud forest borders, and in pine-oak woodland, in highlands of Honduras above about 1500 m (5000 ft); ranges north to southern Mexico. Behavior much like the other forest-based jays, usually in pairs or small groups and foraging at all tree levels. Generally rather noisy, a repeated quite nasal *wrenh, wrenh, wrenh . . .* being most frequent, but often hard to locate when not vocalizing. Occurs in La Tigra National Park above Tegucigalpa.

COMMON RAVEN
Corvus corax

23–27. *Very large* and *all black* with massive bill and often showing shaggy throat feathers; tail wedge-shaped (this most evident in flight). Unmistakable in our area, the Common Raven is the southernmost ranging true "crow" in the Western Hemisphere. Uncommon and local in open (sometimes virtually barren) areas in highlands of Honduras and northern Nicaragua, occasionally wandering down to near sea level on Pacific slope; the species occurs widely, mostly in montane areas, in North America and Eurasia. Forages mostly on the ground, ranging widely in its search for food (often carrion). A very loud, low croak will often draw attention to a bird flying past.

CREEPERS: Certhiidae

A small family of slender streaked brown birds which characteristically creep up tree trunks using their tail for support. They superficially resemble woodcreepers, but are much smaller and not closely related. Mainly temperate Old World in distribution, the sole American species reaches its southern limit in our area.

BROWN CREEPER

BROWN CREEPER
Certhia americana   p.460

5. *An unmistakable small slender streaked brown bird which creeps up tree trunks. Very thin decurved bill*. Above streaked blackish brown and buffy whitish, with vague white superciliary; rump rufous-chestnut and *long stiff tail brown*; below dingy buffy grayish, whitest on throat. Very much smaller than any of the woodcreepers. Fairly common in pine forest and pine-oak woodland in highlands of Honduras and northern Nicaragua, mostly above 900 m (3000 ft); ranges north into Canada. Found singly or in pairs, spiralling up tree trunks, probing into crevices in bark, etc.; often with mixed flocks of wood-warblers, etc. Usually quite inconspicuous, and much more apt to be recorded once its vocalizations are recognized. Most often given is a distinctive high thin *tseee*; song of breeding birds in Honduras is similar to that of North American birds, a more melodic but still very high-pitched *tseee, tee-toh-wee-towee* with variations.

RUFOUS-NAPED WREN
Campylorhynchus rufinucha   Plate 47

7–7¼. An unmistakable *large* wren of semi-open areas on Pacific slope. *Crown black, long bold white superciliary*, ear-coverts blackish; *upper back rufous*, becoming browner on remainder of back; wings boldly barred buffy whitish and dusky; tail blackish boldly barred whitish, and with *broad white tips; creamy white below*. Foregoing applies to widespread *capistratus* of Pacific slope; *castaneus* (found only in Río Sula valley, on Caribbean slope of northwestern Honduras) similar but with uniform dark brown back. Common and conspicuous in semiopen and lightly wooded areas in lowlands on Pacific slope south to northwestern Costa Rica (Guanacaste), also locally on Caribbean slope in northwestern Honduras; ranges north to central Mexico. A characteristic and familiar bird in this region, often foraging in the open but rarely dropping to the ground. Usually in pairs or small family groups; tail often cocked, and regularly fanned or swivelled around. Has a varied vocal repertoire consisting of repeated loud phrases, some harsh and some more melodic, frequently given as a duet; one particularly common phrase in Guanacaste is a *wodo-chóp, wodo-chóp* . . . repeated up to five or six times, also a *cheeyor-chowík, cheeyor-chowík* . . .

ROCK WREN
Salpinctes obsoletus   Plate 47

5¾–6. Restricted to *high barren slopes*, often on *volcanoes. Mainly dark grayish brown above*, variably marked with dusky or blackish and with small whitish spots; somewhat *rufescent on rump,* and with *outer tail feathers broadly tipped buff*; below buffy whitish, but *usually so coarsely marked with dusky as to virtually obscure the pale color*, flanks generally heavily barred with dusky. Central American birds have variable appearance, but are always much darker overall, and more spotted or barred below, than the pale-breasted birds of North America. Uncommon and rather local in highlands of Honduras, Nicaragua and northwestern Costa Rica (very local, on slopes of certain volcanoes in the northwestern cordilleras), favoring open often boulder-strewn slopes with sparse vegetation (even on lava flows); ranges north to western North America. Occurs in pairs, sometimes in places otherwise virtually devoid of birdlife. Mostly terrestrial, often perching on top of rocks, surveying its barren surroundings. Song is a series of trills or simple semimusical whistles, each sometimes repeated several times but with little discernible pattern and often separated by long pauses.

SPOT-BREASTED WREN
Thryothorus maculipectus   Plate 47

5. Above rufous brown, with *unbarred plain wings*; superciliary white, cheeks streaked black and white; tail boldly barred brown and dusky; *throat and breast white thickly spotted with*

black, lower underparts buffy brown. Common in dense undergrowth and shrubbery of forest borders and second-growth woodland in lowlands on Caribbean slope south to extreme northeastern Costa Rica (Los Chiles area), ranging up in small numbers to about 900 m (3000 ft); also found north to northeastern Mexico. Usually in pairs, as a rule foraging within 3–4.5 m (10–15 ft) of the ground, sometimes hopping up higher in viny tangles. Has a loud, rollicking quite musical song similar to that of its ally the Rufous-breasted Wren (found in southwestern Costa Rica, Panama, etc.); distinctive call, likened to snapping the tines of a comb, also much alike. Sometimes considered conspecific is the disjunct *T. sclateri* (Speckle-breasted Wren), found locally in northwestern South America.

BANDED WREN
Thryothorus pleurostictus   Plate 47

5–5¼. Mostly rufous brown above with narrow white superciliary, wings and tail barred with black; white below, *coarsely barred with black on sides, flanks, and crissum*. No other similar wren has such bold black markings on its lower underparts. Fairly common to common in scrub and thickets, and in woodland undergrowth in lowlands on Pacific slope south to northwestern Costa Rica (mainly in Guanacaste), small numbers as far south as the western side of the Central Plateau; ranges north to central Mexico. A typical *Thryothorus* wren in behavior, usually in pairs and often rather skulking and difficult to see, tending to remain within thick cover. Has an exceptionally rich, complex, and musical song consisting of a series of repeated whistled notes or short phrases on varying pitches and with varying strengths; the Banded Wren is considered by many to be among the best singers in a vocally gifted genus.

CAROLINA WREN
Thryothorus ludovicianus

5¼. Above rufous brown with long white superciliary, wings barred with black, *tail dusky barred with grayish brown; below pale dingy buffy brownish*. Plain Wren (*zeledoni* form of Caribbean slope) similar but more olivaceous (not so rufescent) above, and more grayish (not so buffy brownish) below. Carolina Wren is known in our area from one specimen, the type of *subfulvus*, taken near what is now known as Darío in northern Nicaragua, and three recently obtained in deciduous forest on Volcán San Cristóbal; other races occur north into eastern United States. The Nicaraguan race, which also occurs locally in central Guatemala, is allied to the *albinucha* group found locally from Yucatan Peninsula to northern Guatemala. This has been considered a full species (White-browed Wren) by some, but was treated as conspecific with *T. ludovicianus* in the 1983 AOU Check-list (but note that Phillips, 1987, emphatically disagrees). Vocally the two forms are similar (J. W. Hardy).

RUFOUS-BROWED WREN
Troglodytes rufociliatus

4. A *small* wren of cloud forest. Rufous brown above with *prominent buff superciliary* and white eye-ring; wings and short tail barred with blackish; *throat and breast rich rufous*, extending to sides of head and neck, becoming dull buff on lower underparts, browner and barred with dusky on flanks. Darker and much more richly colored than House Wren, with bolder superciliary, etc. Rufous-browed is fairly common to common in cloud forest and cloud forest borders in highlands of Honduras and north-central Nicaragua (one recent record) above 1250 m (4100 ft); ranges north to southern Mexico. Forages at all levels, not only in tangled lower growth but also regularly creeping up quite high in trees, hopping in epiphytes and on mossy trunks and branches. Its song is a complex and very musical phrase of warbled and trilled notes, reminiscent of Ochraceous Wren (of Costa Rica and Panama) but even more melodious and not so thin.

WHITE-BELLIED WREN
Uropsila leucogastra

3½. Rare in northern Honduras. Above uniform dull brown with narrow white superciliary, wings and *very short tail* faintly barred with blackish; *below uniform whitish*, tinged gray on sides and becoming buffy brown on flanks and crissum. White-breasted Wood-Wren is more rufescent above, has boldly streaked cheeks (instead of the rather plain face of White-bellied), and an even shorter tail which is usually held cocked (White-bellieds tend not to cock their tails). White-bellied Wren is known in our area only from a disjunct population found near Coyoles in Caribbean lowlands of northern Honduras; otherwise it ranges from northeastern Mexico to northern Guatemala and Belize, and locally in western Mexico. In Honduras recorded from humid forest. Elsewhere the species ranges inside forest, both in undergrowth and up into middle levels, less often at borders; generally quite inconspicuous. Rather fond of thickets of terrestrial bromeliads (*Bromelia*). Song is a mellow, low-pitched, short

phrase repeated over and over, often for very long periods; it has been transcribed as *pink-i-doo* (J. Arvin).

NORTHERN NIGHTINGALE-WREN
Microcerculus philomela

4¼. A *very dark, almost unpatterned* wren of humid forest undergrowth. Bill rather long, *tail very short*. Above dark umber brown, feathers faintly edged black but with no wing or tail barring: *mostly sooty brown below*, throat faintly paler. Uncommon inside humid lowland forest on Caribbean slope south to northeastern Costa Rica (south to base of the Central Cordillera, near Guacimo, also ranging locally onto Pacific slope on volcano slopes in northwestern cordilleras), mostly below 900 m (3000 ft); ranges north to southeastern Mexico. The closely related Southern Nightingale-Wren (*M. marginatus*) ranges north from Panama into southern Costa Rica, on Pacific slope to southern edge of Central Plateau, on Caribbean slope north to Río Revantazón drainage. Until recently these two forms were considered conspecific, and they are very similar in appearance and behavior, aside from their dramatically different songs. Northern's song is a long series of pure whistled notes, seemingly random in pattern and often out of key with respect to each other, unmistakable once learned.

WHITE-LORED GNATCATCHER
Polioptila albiloris   Plate 47

4. Resembles Tropical Gnatcatcher in general form (see main text, p.349). Male differs in having black crown in which the *black—white demarcation extends back as a straight line* (not with white arching up on superciliary and face, as in Tropical); in nonbreeding plumage has white lores and tiny streak back of eye, but still looks basically *black-capped*. Female has head pattern as in male, but black is replaced by gray (concolor with remaining upperparts), this differing from female Tropical in not looking "white-faced". Fairly common to common (more numerous northward) in deciduous woodland and scrub in lowlands on Pacific slope south to northwestern Costa Rica (Guanacaste); ranges north to central Mexico and Yucatan Peninsula. Favors more arid habitats and regions than Tropical Gnatcatcher, but in some places the two are sympatric. Behavior similar to that of Tropical, but usually forages lower (Tropical being more arboreal). Song and call notes are weaker, squeakier, and

higher-pitched than that of Tropical, and its song in particular lacks that species' descending and rather musical quality.

EASTERN BLUEBIRD
Sialia sialis   p.463

6–6½. Male essentially *uniform bright deep blue above; throat and breast rich rufous*, extending up onto sides of neck; belly white. Female similar but duller and more grayish, especially on head and back. Juvenile more spotted with whitish. In our area the Eastern Bluebird is virtually unmistakable, even females and young birds showing considerable blue, *particularly on wings, rump, and tail* (very obvious in flight). Fairly common in semiopen pine and pine-oak woodland in highlands of Honduras and northern Nicaragua, also in lowland pine savanna of Mosquitia region in northeastern Nicaragua and extreme eastern Honduras (the latter inhabited by *caribaea*, the species' smallest race; all Middle American races are somewhat smaller than those found in North America); ranges north into eastern North America. Bluebirds are generally quite conspicuous, often taking prominent perches, from there dropping to the ground in pursuit of insect prey. Their hunched, round-shouldered silhouette is characteristic. Commonest call is a rich, liquid, musical *churlee*, extended into more of a warble in male's song.

BROWN-BACKED SOLITAIRE
Myadestes obscurus

7½–8. A slim, long-tailed thrush of western Honduran highlands. Bill short. *Head, neck and most of underparts gray*, with *brownish back* and *rufous brown wings*; tail grayish with *pale outer feathers*; eye-ring, malar streak, and throat white, with black submalar streak. Slate-colored Solitaire shows no brown or rufous, favors more humid areas. Brown-backed is fairly common in pine-oak woodland and cloud forest borders in highlands of western Honduras, mostly above 900 m (3000 ft); ranges north to northern Mexico. Mostly arboreal, seldom leaving cover, hence relatively inconspicuous except when singing. That song is a lovely, complex, and jumbled series of high but musical notes which starts slowly but then speeds up as it cascades downward; the overall effect is very distinctive and memorable. Call is a metallic *ling?* (J. Arvin).

EASTERN   BLUEBIRD   AND   SLATE-COLORED   SOLITAIRE

SLATE-COLORED SOLITAIRE
Myadestes unicolor   p.463

7½. Similar to Brown-backed Solitaire in overall conformation. *Uniform plumbeous gray above* (with *no brown or rufous*), with narrow and incomplete white eye-ring but no malar streaks; *slightly paler gray below*; outer tail feathers broadly tipped silvery whitish. Juvenile shows buff spotting on crown and wing-coverts. Fairly common to common in cloud forest in highlands of Honduras and northern Nicaragua, mostly above 900 m (3000 ft); ranges north to southern Mexico. Like the other solitaires, basically arboreal and rather inconspicuous, heard far more often than seen. The song of this species is superb, and were it a better known bird it would surely receive worldwide acclaim. It consists of a series of very pure and melodic whistled or trilled notes and short phrases, far-carrying and ethereal. Numerous in La Tigra National Park above Tegucigalpa.

SPOTTED NIGHTINGALE-THRUSH
Catharus dryas

7. *Bill, legs, and narrow eye-ring orange. Head black*, remaining upperparts grayish olive; throat white, *breast and mid-belly buffy-orange or apricot color with large dusky spots*, sides and flanks broadly grayish. Note that in older museum specimens upperparts become darker and grayer, while underparts fade to whitish. Black-headed Nightingale-Thrush lacks the spotting and the apricot color below,

and in Honduras occurs mainly at lower elevations than Spotted. Spotted is rare inside cloud forest in highlands of western Honduras above about 1800 m (6000 ft); it ranges north to southern Mexico, and reappears in Andes of South America. Forages mainly on the ground or low in forest undergrowth; shy and inconspicuous, most often recorded from its far-carrying song. That song (in Mexico) is a series of beautiful, pure-noted short phrases, e.g. *treee; treloweetu; trelotuwee; trulee?; treee?; treedeetu* . . ., hard to track to its source (will usually slip away at your approach, often continuing to sing), but will sometimes respond to tape playback.

BLACK THRUSH (ROBIN)
Turdus infuscatus

8½–9. Male has *bill and legs bright yellow*, narrow red eye-ring; female has *dull yellowish bill and legs*, no eye-ring. Male *all glossy black*. Female dark brown above, somewhat paler brown below, with throat streaked buff and dark brown. Male should be easily recognized, but the dull female resembles Mountain Thrush except for the latter's dark (not yellowish) bill and legs; note that in our area Black Thrush generally occurs at somewhat higher elevations than Mountain (with some overlap). Black Thrush is fairly common in cloud forest and cloud forest borders in highlands of western Honduras above about 1800 m (6000 ft); ranges north to southern Mexico. An arboreal thrush, usually remaining well above the ground. Its song is a series of rich musical phrases with little discernible pattern, the overall effect being quite *Piranga* tanager-like.

RUFOUS-COLLARED THRUSH (ROBIN)
Turdus rufitorques

9½. Bill and legs yellow, bill tipped dusky. Male unmistakable: *mostly black* with *contrasting rufous breast extending up to encircle neck as a broad nuchal collar*; throat streaked black and rufous. Female a duller version of male, the black being more brownish and the rufous paler; some birds (immatures?) are much dingier, showing only a trace of the rufous-collared effect. Rare in borders of pine-oak woodland and in second-growth in highlands of western Honduras above about 1800 m (6000 ft); ranges north to southern Mexico. Very few Honduras records, but seen recently (April 1987) in La Tigra National Park above Tegucigalpa (P. Kastner).

BLACK CATBIRD
Melanoptila glabrirostris

8. One somewhat uncertain report from northern Honduras. Rather long and slender, slightly decurved bill; iris red. *Entirely glossy blue-black*. Superficially quite like a blackbird. Only record from our area is an undated specimen (the type) taken at Omoa in northwestern Honduras in either 1855 or 1856; otherwise found on Yucatan Peninsula, Belize, and in northern Guatemala (most numerous on islands just offshore such as Cozumel). The Honduras specimen may have been mislabeled, and actually taken in Belize; the species' presence in Honduras needs to be confirmed. Favors lower growth of woodland coastal scrub, generally secretive.

BLUE-AND-WHITE MOCKINGBIRD
Melanotis hypoleucus   p.464

10½. Iris red. *Mostly grayish blue above* with *broad black mask; below mainly white*, with lower flanks and crissum dark bluish gray. Not likely to be confused. Uncommon in dense second-growth and shrubby woodland borders in highlands of Honduras above 1200 m (4000 ft); ranges north to southern Mexico. Found singly or in pairs, creeping about secretively in dense undergrowth, rarely in the open. Its song is a series of rather abrupt, loud musical notes or short phrases; does not "mock" other birds.

MANGROVE VIREO
Vireo pallens   Plate 47

4¼. Only in mangroves and adjacent growth along either coast. Iris grayish to brown. Above olive with *yellow eye-ring and supraloral stripe*; wings with two pale yellowish wing-bars; *below mostly pale yellow*, somewhat clouded olive on breast. Foregoing applies to *semiflavus* of Caribbean

BLUE-AND-WHITE MOCKINGBIRD

slope; nominate *pallens* of Pacific slope is duller olive above and not so yellow below. White-eyed Vireo, an uncommon northern migrant to Central America, differs in having whiter eye (at least in adults) and is *much whiter below* (with yellow restricted to sides and flanks). Mangrove Vireo is uncommon to locally common resident in mangroves and adjacent shrubbery and low woodland along both coasts, on Pacific south to northwestern Costa Rica (around the Gulf of Nicoya), on Caribbean south to southern Nicaragua (Bluefields area); ranges north to the Yucatan Peninsula and northwestern Mexico. On the Yucatan Peninsula and in the Peten of Guatemala the Mangrove Vireo ranges inland far from mangroves, but in our area seems more or less tied to them (especially on Pacific side). Usually forages rather low, often quite bold. Its song is a simple chattering series, rapidly uttered, of similar notes, *jew-jew-jew-jew-jew-jew-jew* (R. D. James recording).

BELL'S VIREO
Vireo bellii

A casual winter visitor (nominate race) from North America to Pacific slope of Honduras and northern Nicaragua. 4½. Grayish olive above with *whitish supraloral stripe and* (usually) *eye-ring*; wings with two whitish wing-bars, the upper one often indistinct; mainly whitish below, broadly washed with yellow on sides and flanks. White-eyed Vireo (also a northern migrant to Central America, more numerous than Bell's; see main text, p.360) has yellow (not whitish) supraloral and eye-ring, and adults have white eyes (iris always dark in Bell's). Favors riparian growth and dense scrub.

WARBLING VIREO
Vireo gilvus

A very rare or casual winter visitor (nominate race) from North America to Pacific slope of Honduras and Nicaragua, with one sighting also from northern Costa Rica (La Selva). 4¾. Resembles much more numerous Philadelphia Vireo (also a northern migrant; see main text p.361), but *much whiter below* (with yellow, if present at all, restricted to wash on sides and flanks), and with pale lores (not dusky) and crown essentially concolor with back (not distinctly grayer).

YUCATAN VIREO
Vireo magister

5½. *Islands off northern Honduras. Notably heavy bill.* Above dull olivaceous gray with *broad buffy whitish superciliary* and dusky line through eye; *below dingy grayish buff.* A very dull, large-billed vireo which somewhat recalls the Red-eyed and Yellow-green Vireos, though lacking their yellow and olive tones. Yucatan Vireo is a common resident in scrub and woodland on Bay and Hog Islands off Honduras; also ranges also along coast and (mainly) on islands off Yucatan Peninsula and Belize, and on Grand Cayman Islands. Its song is similar to that of Yellow-green Vireo, a fairly fast series of musical phrases (J. C. Barlow and R. D. James recording).

ORANGE-CROWNED WARBLER
Vermivora celata

An accidental vagrant from North America to Caribbean coast of Costa Rica; otherwise not known south of Guatemala and Belize. Very similar to immature Tennessee Warbler (see main text, p.367), but more grayish olive above and more uniformly yellowish below (*including the crissum, which even in the yellowest Tennessee is white*). Orange-crowned usually shows *some blurry olive breast streaking* (lacking altogether in Tennessee), but its orange crown patch is small and inconspicuous (even absent in some females and immatures). The one published report from our area (F. G. Stiles and S. Smith, *Brenesia 17*: 150, 1980) is of a bird picked up dead at Limón on October 26, 1974; it had been banded in New York in September 1972 (unusually early for it there).

CRESCENT-CHESTED WARBLER
Parula superciliosa   Plate 48

4½. Head and neck gray with *bold white superciliary*; back and rump bright olive green *contrasting with gray wings and tail*; throat and breast bright yellow with *prominent chestnut crescentic patch on chest*; belly grayish white. Tropical and Northern Parulas both have wing-bars, lack superciliary. Crescent-chested is fairly common in cloud forest, pine-oak woodland, and borders in highlands of Honduras and northern Nicaragua above 900 m (3000 ft); ranges north to northern Mexico. An arboreal warbler, gleaning actively in foliage. Its frequently heard song is a simple fast, dry, buzzy trill *tz-z-z-z-z-z-z*. Formerly placed in the genus *Vermivora*.

GOLDEN-CHEEKED WARBLER
Dendroica chrysoparia

An uncommon to rare winter visitant to highlands of Honduras and northern Nicaragua; breeds in Texas, wintering mainly in Mexico and Guatemala. 5. Resembles Black-throated Green Warbler (see main text, p.372). Male differs in having *solid black crown and back* (not olive), irregular black line through face back from eye, and no yellow on lower underpart. Female very similar to female Black-throated Green, but showing some black on crown and back, and with at least some indication of a dark eyeline (instead of Black-throated Green's olive area on ear-coverts). Favors pine-oak woodland.

GRACE'S WARBLER
Dendroica graciae

4¾–5. *Mostly gray above* with *yellow supraloral stripe* and some black streaking on crown; wings with two white wing-bars; *throat and chest bright yellow*, becoming white on lower underparts with some black streaking on sides. Female similar but slightly duller and browner above. *Decora* of the Mosquitia slightly smaller and with more orange tinge to yellow throat and breast than *remota* of the highlands; both lack the black back streaking and white behind eye of northern nominate race. Yellow-throated Warbler is similar but larger, with white superciliary and large white patch on sides of neck, bolder black streaking on sides. Grace's Warbler is fairly common resident in pine woodland in highlands of Honduras and northern Nicaragua above 600 m (2000 ft), and also occurs in lowland pine savanna of Mosquitia region of extreme eastern Honduras and northeastern Nicaragua; ranges north to southwestern United States. Usually remains well above ground in pines, often foraging along horizontal branches. Song is an accelerating musical trill, often starting with several slower notes.

[PINE WARBLER]
Dendroica pinus

An accidental vagrant from eastern North America to Costa Rica; not otherwise known south of extreme northern Mexico (and even there decidedly rare), and Hispaniola. Adult basically *unstreaked olive above*; wings with two white wing-bars; *throat and breast yellow* with dusky streaks on sides, lower underparts white. Female duller, especially below. Immature browner above (especially in females), below dull yellowish (males) or buffy whitish (females) with little or no streaking and usually a buff wash on flanks. The one published report from our area (F. G. Stiles and S. Smith, *Brenesia 17*: 150, 1980) is of two birds seen at separate localities in central Costa Rica in late August 1976, one of them lingering to September 4. Needs further confirmation.

[SWAINSON'S WARBLER]
Limnothlypis swainsonii

An accidental winter visitant from southeastern North America to northwestern Honduras; winters mainly in the West Indies, smaller numbers on Yucatan Peninsula and in Belize. 5¼. Rather long and sharply pointed bill. *Brown above*, more rufescent on crown, and with *conspicuous whitish superciliary* and dark eyeline; *dingy buffy grayish below*. Skulks in lower growth of woodland, where easily overlooked. The one published report from our area (Monroe, 1968, p. 323) is of a bird seen at Lake Yojoa in northwestern Honduras in January 1956. Needs further confirmation.

RED-FACED WARBLER
Cardellina rubrifrons

An uncommon to rare winter visitant to highlands of western Honduras; ranges north to Mexico and extreme southwestern United States. 5. Unmistakable, with *bright red forehead, foreface, throat, and upper chest*, extending up onto sides of neck to form a partial collar; remainder of crown black, extending down over sides of head; some white on nape, *otherwise gray above*, with white rump; remaining underparts grayish white. Immatures duller than adult. Favors pine-oak woodland.

PAINTED REDSTART
Myioborus pictus

5. *Mostly glossy black* with *bright scarlet breast and mid-belly*, lower belly and crissum mixed black and white; small white crescent below eye, *large white patch on wing-coverts*, and mostly white outer tail feathers. Juvenile lacks the red. A spectacularly beautiful bird, virtually unmistakable. Note that race of Slate-throated Redstart occurring in Honduras and Nicaragua (*connectens*) is *orange* on breast and belly, and further differs from Painted in being grayer above, lacking white in wing, etc. Painted Redstart is fairly common resident in pine-oak woodland in highlands of Honduras and northern Nicaragua, mostly above about 900 m (3000 ft); it ranges north to

Mexico and extreme southwestern United States. An active, even acrobatic forager, moving rapidly from perch to perch, constantly drooping its wings and fanning its tail widely. Song is a very pretty fast rich warbling.

FAN-TAILED WARBLER
Euthlypis lachrymosa   p.467

5¾. Mostly slaty gray above, blacker on crown and with semiconcealed yellow coronal patch and *white supraloral spot and crescents above and below eye; rather long tail conspicuously white-tipped*; mostly bright yellow below with *strong tawny wash across breast and down flanks*, crissum buffy whitish. No *Basileuterus* warbler shows the tail tipping or the tawny below. Uncommon to locally fairly common in undergrowth of woodland and drier forest on Pacific slope in Honduras and northwestern Nicaragua, ranging up to about 1500 m (5000 ft); occurs north to northern Mexico. Fan-tailed especially favors ravines and slopes with dense viny growth; here it hops about on or near the ground, often on boulders, frequently spreading and flicking the tail exposing the white tips. Regularly attends swarms of army ants, often in substantial numbers (J. Arvin). Its song is a sweet and musical phrase, rather deliberate and somewhat variable, e.g. *swi-swee-swee-sweechu*.

GOLDEN-BROWED WARBLER
Basileuterus belli

5. Mostly olive above with *chestnut crown and ear-coverts* separated by a *long bright yellow superciliary* (latter bordered above by black); below yellow, mottled with olive on sides and flanks. Rufous-capped Warbler is rather similar but it has white (not yellow) superciliary; it is found in scrubbier growth at lower elevations than this species. Golden-browed is fairly common in lower growth of cloud forest and in pine-oak woodland in highlands of western Honduras; ranges north to northern Mexico. Forages in pairs or small groups, often with mixed flocks. Its song is a fast jumbled series of spritely chippering notes. Call is a ringing metallic *zzzink* (J. Arvin).

OLIVE WARBLER
Peucedramus taeniatus

4¼. Long thin slightly decurved bill. Male has *head, neck, and throat golden tawny* with *conspicuous black ear-patch*; otherwise dark gray

FAN-TAILED WARBLER

above, wings and tail blackish, wings with two broad white wing-bars and a white speculum, outer tail feathers with white on inner webs; lower underparts grayish white. Female has yellowish olive crown and nape and *mostly buffy yellowish face, throat, and upper chest with dusky ear-patch*; otherwise like male. Fairly common in pine and pine-oak woodland in highlands of Honduras and northern Nicaragua above about 1200 m (4000 ft); ranges north to Mexico and extreme southwestern United States. Race in our area, *micrus*, is smaller and more golden on head and neck than northern birds. Olive Warblers are arboreal, and mostly forage well above the ground; they are usually not very conspicuous. Attention is often drawn to them by their loud, descending, whistled calls, e.g. *sheeu, peeuw, wheeu* or simply *cheeu* (rather strange for a warbler); the song is a loud repeated warbled note, quite chickadee (*Parus*)-like. Affinities of the Olive Warbler are debated; it may not be a true wood-warbler.

BLUE-CROWNED CHLOROPHONIA
Chlorophonia occipitalis

5¼. Resembles Golden-browed Chlorophonia of Costa Rica and Panama (see main text, p.391), males differing especially in lacking Golden-browed's yellow forehead and superciliary, both sexes further in having blue on crown paler and more restricted to top of head (not on nape). Uncommon in canopy and borders of cloud forest in highlands of Honduras and northern Nicaragua, mainly above 900 m (3000 ft), sometimes lower in northern Honduras when not breeding; ranges north to southern Mexico. Behavior and vocalizations much like Golden-browed Chlorophonia, which has been considered a race of this species.

SCRUB EUPHONIA
Euphonia affinis   Plate 48

4. Male steel blue with *small* patch on forecrown golden yellow (reaching back to only just above eye); *throat dark violet-blue* (looks black), remaining underparts golden yellow; some white on inner webs of flight feathers. Female mostly grayish olive above, *grayest on hindcrown and nape*, slightly more yellowish on forecrown; *mostly yellowish olive below*, becoming bright yellow on mid-belly and crissum. Male resembles White-vented Euphonia but *lacks* white on lower underparts and its yellow is of a paler more lemon hue; there is little or no range overlap between the two. Yellow-crowned Euphonia male has *much* larger area of yellow on crown; female Yellow-crowned is much more yellow below (lacking this species' olive). Female Yellow-throated Euphonia shows some whitish on underparts. Scrub Euphonia is fairly common in semiopen areas and woodland borders in lowlands on Pacific slope south to northwestern Costa Rica (mainly in Guanacaste, smaller numbers reaching western part of Central Plateau); ranges north to northern Mexico. Behavior similar to that of other euphonias, though more apt to occur in more or less open country with only a few scattered trees (less tied to woodland). Like them it feeds heavily on mistletoe berries. Its distinctive call is a typically trebled, high-pitched *dee-dee-dee.*

YELLOW-WINGED TANAGER
Thraupis abbas

6¾–7. The northern "replacement" of the Palm Tanager. Mainly olive, but *head (especially), throat and breast dull violet-blue*; back with black speckling; wings mainly black with *broad yellow stripe across base of flight feathers* (prominent even on perched birds), olive on wing-coverts; tail black. Common in forest borders and clearings in lowlands on Caribbean slope below about 900 m (3000 ft) in Honduras and northeastern Nicaragua, less numerous in woodland and borders in Pacific slope lowlands of Honduras; ranges north to northeastern Mexico. Palm Tanager occurs north to southeastern Nicaragua (Isler and Isler, 1987), and is also recorded from southeastern

Honduras in the Olancho area (see 1983 AOU Check-list). A familiar bird in its range, the Yellow-winged Tanager often occurs with Blue-gray Tanagers, and is found regularly around houses and in cultivated areas. Unlike the Palm Tanager it shows no particular preference for palms. Song of Yellow-winged is very different from Palm's, being a fast dry almost rattled trill, sometimes ending with a few more musical notes.

BLACK-THROATED SHRIKE-TANAGER
Lanio aurantius

7½–8. Resembles White-throated Shrike-Tanager (see main text, p.397), replacing that species northward in Middle America. *Heavy hooked bill.* Male has *head and throat black*, contrasting with *bright yellow back and remaining underparts*, chest tinged orange-brown; wings black with some white on lesser wing-coverts; tail black. Female *mostly olive brown above*, more grayish on head; *throat gray*, contrasting with olive-yellow of remaining underparts. Rare to locally uncommon in canopy of humid forest in lowlands on Caribbean slope of northwestern Honduras (east to around La Ceiba), below about 450 m (1500 ft); ranges north to southern Mexico. East and south of that area in Honduras is found the nominate race of White-throated Shrike-Tanager; as yet the two have not been found together. Males of the two differ as their English names indicate, while female White-throated has a drab brown throat (not gray). Behavior similar to that of White-throated Shrike Tanager.

BLACK-CHEEKED ANT-TANAGER
Habia atrimaxillaris   Plate 48

7½–8. Only in southwestern Costa Rica. *Mainly sooty blackish above, and extending down over sides of head and neck*, semiconcealed coronal patch orange-red; *below dull reddish, brightest on throat*, and extensively grayish on sides and flanks. Female similar but duller overall, often more orange below, and lacking the red coronal patch. Fairly common in undergrowth of humid lowland forest and second-growth woodland in lowlands on Pacific slope in southwestern Costa Rica, essentially around the Golfo Dulce and on the Osa Peninsula; the only ant-tanager in this area. Usually in pairs or small groups, often with mixed understory flocks. Vocally this striking and highly localized endemic seems quite close to the Red-throated Ant-Tanager, and it has the same distinctive "tearing" scold. Easily found in forest at the Marenco Biological Station at the northern end of the Osa, just outside Corcovado National Park.

SOOTY-CAPPED BUSH-TANAGER
Chlorospingus pileatus

What was long known as *Chlorospingus zeledoni* (Zeledon's or Volcano Bush-Tanager) is found on the higher slopes of Volcán Irazú and Volcán Turrialba in central Costa Rica. It was, however, shown to be only a localized color phase of the Sooty-capped Bush-Tanager (N. K. Johnson and A. H. Brush, *Systematic Zoology 21*: 245–262, 1972). It is very similar in appearance, differing mainly in having pale yellowish olive breast and sides (not yellow, and not contrasting so much with the white throat).

GRAYISH SALTATOR
Saltator coerulescens   Plate 48

8½. *Mostly dull gray above* with short white superciliary; *center of throat white* bordered with blackish, breast drab olivaceous gray, becoming olivaceous buff on flanks and uniform buff on lower belly and crissum. Buff-throated Saltator is olive (not gray) above and has wide black margin to its buff (not white) throat patch. Grayish Saltator is fairly common locally in woodland and forest borders, clearings, and scrub in lowlands on both slopes south to central Costa Rica (on the Central Plateau, e.g. around San José), but evidently not recorded from Pacific slope of Nicaragua; ranges north to northern Mexico, then reappears, after an inexplicable gap through Panama, in South America. Behavior similar to that of other saltators. Has a rich and melodic song, rather variable, a common phrase being *chew, chew, chooóweet*, often starting with sputtering or smacking notes (or the latter may be given alone).

[BLACK-HEADED GROSBEAK]
Pheucticus melanocephalus

An accidental vagrant from western North America to southwestern Costa Rica; otherwise not known south of southern Mexico. Size and shape, including *heavy bill*, much like Rose-breasted Grosbeak (see main text, p.411). Adult male unmistakable, with *rich cinnamon-rufous underparts* (yellower on midbelly), nuchal collar, and rump; otherwise mostly black, back streaked with rufous, wings with two bold white wing-bars. Female and immature much like respective plumages of Rose-breasted but *streaking below is finer and sparser*, mainly restricted to sides and flanks. The one published report from our area (F. G. Stiles and S. Smith, *Brenesia 17*: 153, 1980) is of a female-plumaged bird seen at San Isidro del General on December 22, 1977. Needs further confirmation, but a pattern of extreme vagrancy in this species is established, with one report from Curaçao.

BLUE BUNTING
Cyanocompsa parellina

5½. Fairly heavy bill. Male *mainly very dark blue* with brighter paler blue on crown and nape (especially forecrown), malar area, shoulders, and rump. Female uniform rich brown above, paler and buffier brown below. Blue-black Grosbeak is similar but larger with proportionately more massive bill; it is more restricted to interior of humid forest. Blue Bunting is fairly common locally in shrubby lower growth of forest and woodland borders and clearings, both in humid and quite arid regions, in foothills and interior valleys of Honduras and northern Nicaragua (apparently not in lowlands below 300 m: 1000 ft); ranges north to northern Mexico, occasionally wandering to southern Texas. Usually in pairs, rather inconspicuous. Song a weak, rather patternless *wheat, wheat, witchy-witch-teer-deer*, the last few notes somewhat rushed and jumbled (J. Arvin).

OLIVE SPARROW
Arremonops rufivirgatus   Plate 48

5¼–5½. In our area in *northwestern Costa Rica* (reappears in northern Middle America). Head grayish with *dark brown lateral crown stripe and stripe back from eye*; otherwise dull olive above, yellow on bend of wing; *throat and breast dingy pale buffyish*, this extending up onto lower face, becoming grayish white on belly and dingy buffyish again on crissum. Black-striped Sparrow is larger with black (not brown) head striping and much grayer underparts; at least for the most part the two do not occur together. Olive Sparrow is fairly common locally in lower growth of deciduous woodland and thickety borders in northwestern Costa Rica (Guanacaste); ranges also from southern Texas and Mexico to northern Guatemala and Belize. Often hopping on the ground in dense cover, the Olive Sparrow is quite secretive and inconspicuous unless singing. The song is a simple series of somewhat musical notes which starts slowly and then accelerates, *chew, chew, ch-ch-ch-ch-ch-ch-ch.*

GREEN-BACKED SPARROW
Arremonops chloronotus

5¾–6. In our area only in northern Honduras, the more northern replacement of the Black-striped Sparrow (see main text, p.416). Closely resembles that species but somewhat smaller and with different voice. Green-backed is fairly common in shrubby forest borders and second-growth in lowlands below 600 m (2000 ft) on Caribbean slope of northern Honduras (mainly in the Sula valley and south to Lake Yojoa, also locally in the Aguán and Agalta valleys to the east); it ranges north to southern Mexico. Black-striped Sparrow is found farther east in northern Honduras (ranging as far west as the Tela/La Ceiba region); it is numerous from eastern and southern Honduras southward. Green-backed's song is a loud and ringing series of musical notes *tew, tew, chu-chu-chu-chu-chu-chu-chu-chu*, with some variation but lacking the characteristic long hesitating start-up of Black-striped Sparrow.

PREVOST'S GROUND-SPARROW
Melozone biarcuatum   Plate 48

5¾–6. Two very different-appearing forms in our area, currently considered conspecific though two could be involved. *Cabanisi* of Costa Rica has *complex facial pattern*: black forecrown and lower cheeks, extensive white loral area, rufous-chestnut hindcrown, nape, and sides of neck, and black submalar streak; otherwise plain olive brown above; mostly white below with *large black patch on breast*, some gray and olive brown on sides and flanks. Nominate *biarcuatum* (Honduras) has *much more white on face* (encompassing the entire ocular area, resulting in very different "look"), and *lacks* the black submalar streak and breast patch. See White-eared Ground-Sparrow and Chestnut-capped Brush-Finch. Prevost's is uncommon to locally fairly common in scrubby lower growth of woodland, hedgerows, and coffee plantations in western Honduras (east only to the Sula and Comayagua valleys), and in central Costa Rica (basically on the Central Plateau, including immediate environs of San José); ranges north to southern Mexico. Found singly or in pairs, hopping on or near the ground. Song in Honduras is a short musical warbled phrase, often preceded by one or two *tsit* notes, repeated over and over at about 5-second intervals; in Costa Rica the song is described as "a rapid series of chirping *chep* notes" (P. Slud), seemingly rather different (?).

WHITE-EARED GROUND-SPARROW
Melozone leucotis   Plate 48

6½–7. *Ornate pattern on foreparts: head, throat, and chest mostly black* with large white ocular spot, upper and lower eyelids, and area on ear-coverts, and *bright yellow patch on sides of neck*, white patch with some rufous across center of lower throat; otherwise mainly olive brown, grayer on back; lower underparts whitish, washed broadly with gray on sides and flanks, crissum buffyish. Foregoing is nominate *leucotis* of Costa Rica; *nigrior* of Nicaragua similar but with white on lower throat reduced or lacking. Uncommon to locally fairly common in thick undergrowth at edge of woodland and montane forest in highlands of Nicaragua and Costa Rica (in latter mainly on Central Plateau, but also numerous at Monteverde); found also from southern Mexico to El Salvador. Moves about on or near the ground, in pairs or small groups, sometimes out into gardens or coffee plantations but rarely far from cover. Call or song is a simple, repetitive, non-musical *tsit, tsi-wee; tsit, tsi-wee; tsit, tsi-wee . . .*, repeated a number of times, sometimes becoming more jumbled.

CINNAMON-BELLIED FLOWERPIERCER
Diglossa baritula

4½. *Distinctive sharply hooked and upturned bill* as in Slaty Flowerpiercer of Costa Rica and Panama (see main text, p.422); lower mandible paler. Male *bluish gray above and on throat* (somewhat blacker on head), *remaining underparts cinnamon-rufous*. Female plain olive brown above, paler buffy brown below. Fairly common in borders of cloud forest and adjacent shrubby clearings and gardens in highlands of Honduras and north-central Nicaragua (one recent record) above 1400 m (4600 ft); ranges north to central Mexico. Forages singly or in pairs at all levels but most often rather low, typically probing into or piercing flowers.

STRIPE-HEADED SPARROW
Aimophila ruficauda   Plate 48

7. A handsome large sparrow of Pacific lowlands. Bill strongly bicolored, *lower mandible yellow-orange. Bold black and white head pattern*, with white median crown stripe and superciliary, black lateral crown stripes and cheeks; otherwise buffy brown above, grayer on sides of neck and upper back, with back streaked blackish and tail somewhat more rufescent; some rufous

on shoulders, wing feathers broadly edged pale buff; throat white, chest and sides gray vaguely streaked whitish, becoming whitish on lower underparts and tinged ochraceous on flanks and crissum. Rusty Sparrow lacks black and white head striping, has bold black submalar mark, etc. Stripe-headed is fairly common to common but somewhat local in shrubby grasslands and arid scrub on Pacific slope south to northwestern Costa Rica (Guanacaste), up to about 1350 m (4500 ft); ranges north to central Mexico. Often in small groups, feeding mainly on the ground but perching readily in low trees and bushes, and on fences; an easy sparrow to see. Vocalizations are undistinguished (unusually so for this genus); song in northwestern Costa Rica is a high-pitched squeaky *wít-it-tee, wít-it-tee, wít-it-tee*, delivered with a pumping quality (J. Arvin).

BOTTERI'S SPARROW
Aimophila botterii   Plate 48

5½–6. A *nondescript* sparrow, *very local* in open grassy or rocky areas. *Above streaked brown and grayish* (the streaking more pronounced in freshplumaged birds) with vague grayish superciliary, faint dark submalar streak, and solid brown tail, bend of wing yellow (but usually hidden); *below dingy grayish or buffy whitish*, whitest on throat and mid-belly. Grasshopper Sparrow is smaller, much more ochraceous on face and underparts, etc. Botteri's is uncommon to locally fairly common in tall grassy savannas with a few scattered shrubs in Mosquitia region of extreme eastern Honduras and northeastern Nicaragua, and uncommon and very local on open boulder-strewn volcano slopes (often where there is little or no vegetation) in western Nicaragua and northwestern Costa Rica; ranges north very locally to extreme southwestern United States. Generally an inconspicuous sparrow, the Mosquitia birds remaining in tall grass cover, volcano birds hopping about on rocks with their tails cocked. P. Slud (1964) recorded no real song from the volcano birds. Though morphologically very similar, the various populations of this species may prove not to all be conspecific.

RUSTY SPARROW
Aimophila rufescens   Plate 48

7. Mid-crown gray with *two broad chestnut lateral crown stripes*; face mainly gray with white supraloral spot and black line back from eye; otherwise essentially brown above, back streaked blackish, *wings (especially) and tail quite rufescent*; throat white *bordered by broad black*

submalar streak, chest dingy buffy grayish becoming whitish on lower underparts, tinged ochraceous on flanks and crissum. See Stripe-headed Sparrow. Rusty Sparrow is fairly common to common in grassy and shrubby understory of pine woodland in highlands of western Honduras, and in Mosquitia region of extreme eastern Honduras and northeastern Nicaragua; it is also found, apparently disjunctly (*hypaethrus*), on grassy boulder-strewn slopes of volcanoes along Pacific side of Cordillera de Guanacaste in northwestern Costa Rica; ranges north to northern Mexico. Like the Stripe-headed Sparrow (which is found in shrubbier areas) the Rusty is a fairly bold bird, easy to observe. Its loud musical song (in Honduras) attracts attention, though it is somewhat repetitious (e.g. *tsup-tsirup-tsip-tsiru*); it has something of quality of a *Piranga* tanager or a grosbeak.

CHIPPING SPARROW
Spizella passerina

5¼. Adult has *rufous crown bordered below by prominent straight white superciliary* and thin black line through eye; nape gray, back brown streaked black, rump gray; wings blackish, feathers edged buff or rufous; tail dusky and *distinctly notched* (often noticeable as bird flushes); *below pale gray*. Nonbreeding birds have dusky-streaked crown, more grayish superciliary, and brownish ear-coverts; juveniles are more streaked generally. Fairly common to common resident (*pinetorum*) in pine woodland in highlands of western Honduras above about 900 m (3000 ft), and in Mosquitia region in lowlands of eastern Honduras and northeastern Nicaragua; also one record of a presumed northern migrant in central Costa Rica (one seen and then collected on September 9–13, 1977, near San José; F. G. Stiles and S. Smith, *Brenesia 17*: 153, 1980); ranges north widely into North America. Feeds mostly on the ground, but often takes an elevated perch when singing. Song is a long, fast, dry trill on one pitch.

SAVANNAH SPARROW
Passerculus sandwichensis

A casual winter visitant from North America to northern Honduras. Basically brown above streaked with dusky and gray; *whitish median crown stripe* and usually *some yellow above and in front of eye*; rather short notched tail; *below white boldly streaked with dark brown* except on midbelly, the streaks sometimes coalescing into a spot on center of breast. Lincoln's Sparrow (another rare northern migrant; see main text, p.424) has finer streaking below on buffier ground color, grayer face (no yellow), etc. Savannah favors open grassy areas.

RED-WINGED BLACKBIRD
Agelaius phoenicius   p.472

♂ 7½–8½. ♀ 7–7½. Sharply pointed bill. Male virtually unmistakable, glossy black with *bright red shoulders broadly tipped buffy yellow* (the colors can be obscured on perched birds, but are very obvious in flight). Female dark brown above streaked dusky and rufous, and with whitish superciliary; *whitish below coarsely streaked with dusky brown*. Locally fairly common to common resident in marshes and damp grasslands in semiopen (not forested) country in lowlands on both slopes south to northern Costa Rica (Guanacaste and in Río Frio region); ranges north widely across most of North America and in Greater Antilles. Usually conspicuous and often gregarious, foraging mainly on the ground. Male's song is a distinctive liquid, gurgling *konk-la-reeee*, somewhat variable and often guttural; Costa Rica birds sound much like those of North America.

RED-WINGED BLACKBIRD

MELODIOUS BLACKBIRD
Dives dives

10–10½. Rather heavy dark bill; *dark iris* (both sexes). Male *all glossy black*. Female similar but slightly duller and sootier. Great-tailed and Nicaraguan Grackle males have obvious pale eyes, keeled tails, and are more glossed with violet-blue; Great-tailed also much larger, Giant Cowbird has different profile (small head, neck ruff), red eye, etc. Melodious Blackbird is fairly common to common in a variety of semiopen habitats, often around houses and in towns (but avoiding forested regions) on Caribbean slope in Honduras and northern central Nicaragua; ranges north to northeastern Mexico. A conspicuous and noisy bird, with a wide variety of loud and far-carrying whistled vocalizations.

NICARAGUAN GRACKLE
Cassidix nicaraguensis

♂ 12; ♀ 10. *A small version of Great-tailed Grackle* (see main text, p.428), the two being sympatric *around Lakes Managua and Nicaragua*. Male has straw yellow iris, dark in female (both sexes as in

Great-tailed). Male further differs in having somewhat less creased (or keeled) tail. Nicaraguan Grackle is a locally fairly common endemic in freshwater marshes and nearby agricultural land in western Nicaragua and extreme northern Costa Rica (where known only from southern shore of Lake Nicaragua in the Los Chiles area). Note that larger numbers of Great-tailed Grackles occur through much or all of the same region. Behavior of the two is similar, and they sometimes forage together.

BLACK-VENTED ORIOLE
Icterus wagleri

8½. *Mainly black with orange-yellow rump, shoulders, and belly*; lower border of black bib often shows some chestnut. Patterned much like Black-cowled Oriole (see main text, p.430), but that species has yellow crissum (black in Black-vented) and a more lemon tone to its yellow (more orangey in Black-vented). Black-cowled is found in Caribbean lowlands, whereas Black-vented is fairly common in deciduous and pine-oak woodland in highlands of Honduras and northern Nicaragua, mostly 750–1800 m (2500–6000 ft); ranges north to northern Mexico. Usually in pairs, often showing a marked predilection for palms.

STREAK-BACKED ORIOLE
Icterus pustulatus   Plate 47

8–8¼. Mostly orange-yellow with *black streaking on back* (in some birds so extensive as to be almost solid), also a black ocular area and small bib; wings and tail black, wing feathers with *much broad white edging*, tail feathers narrowly tipped whitish. Intensity of the yellow seems to vary individually, but is always deepest (most orange) on head and foreneck. Altamira Oriole is larger, more intensely orange, has solid black back, etc.; Streak-backed lacks the spots on sides of breast of somewhat larger Spot-breasted Oriole. Streak-backed Oriole is fairly common in arid scrub, gallery woodland, and groves of trees in agricultural or ranching areas on Pacific slope south to northwestern Costa Rica (Guanacaste), and in arid interior valleys on Caribbean slope in Honduras; ranges north to northern Mexico, rarely to extreme southwestern United States. Usually in pairs, and in part because of the open nature of its habitat, rather an easy oriole to observe. A poor vocalist, the Streak-backed seemingly has nothing that can be truly classed as a song; most often heard are wren or even woodpecker-like chatters and scolds.

SPOT-BREASTED ORIOLE
Icterus pectoralis   Plate 47

8½. Mostly yellow-orange with *solid black back*, most of wings (except for orange shoulders and *large area of white on inner flight feathers*), tail, ocular area, and bib; *distinctive and conspicuous black spotting on sides of breast*. Female slightly pale and duller; immatures much duller, with more olive back, wings, and tail, and often little or no breast spotting. Altamira Oriole is larger and more intense orange, and never shows breast spotting. Streak-backed Oriole is smaller, has back streaked black (though in some individuals so heavily that only a little yellow may show), also lacks breast spots. Spot-breasted is locally fairly common in deciduous woodland and scrub, and in shade trees of towns and around ranch buildings in lowlands on Pacific slope from Honduras (where also ranges locally onto Caribbean slope, mostly in less humid regions) to northwestern Costa Rica (Guanacaste, where decidedly scarce, perhaps because of trapping pressure); ranges north to southern Mexico, and introduced into southern Florida. Seen singly or in pairs, this striking oriole has a fine song, basically a long-continued series of rich melodic whistled or gurgled notes.

ALTAMIRA ORIOLE
Icterus gularis   Plate 47

9–10. *Mainly bright orange*, with *solid black back*; wings and tail black, wings with orange shoulders and white tipping to greater coverts and edging on flight feathers; black ocular area extending down as bib over throat and upper chest. Immature yellow instead of orange, and olive instead of black, and lacking the black bib (but usually shows dusky lores). *Altamira is the largest and brightest of the three resident Pacific slope orioles*; cf. especially the Spot-breasted Oriole. Fairly common to common in a variety of lightly wooded habitats, especially in arid regions (but locally under more humid conditions as well), on Pacific slope in Honduras and northern Nicaragua; also ranging widely onto Caribbean slope in western Honduras (where it occurs up to about 1800 m: 6000 ft); found north through Mexico to southern Texas. Often in pairs or small (family?) groups. Song is a series of short whistled notes interspersed with lower harsher ones; also has a raspy call. Formerly sometimes called Black-throated Oriole.

RED CROSSBILL
Loxia curvirostra

5¾–6. *Mandibles cross unmistakably near tip of bill*, but this is often not easy to see at any distance. Male *mostly brick red* (brightness of the red variable individually, apparently deepening with age), brightest on rump and crown, irregularly mottled with dusky; wings and quite short notched tail dusky brown. Female yellowish olive to grayish, irregularly mottled darker, typically brightest on rump and underparts. Juvenile like female but much more heavily streaked with dusky. Not likely to be confused in its Central American range. Fairly common but very erratic in pine woodland in highlands of Honduras and northern Nicaragua, also occurring in lowland pine savanna of Mosquitia region in northeastern Nicaragua (and probably adjacent Honduras); ranges north locally through North America, and in Eurasia. Crossbills usually occur in flocks and are highly nomadic and irregular in their occurrences at any one site; they feed mostly by extracting seeds of pinecones using their specialized bills. Distinctive flight call is a series of *jip* notes.

BLACK-HEADED SISKIN
Carduelis notata

4¼. *Head, throat, and center of chest black* (forming an extensive "hood"); back olive, rump yellow;

wings and tail black, wings with *large yellow patch on flight feathers* (shows as stripe in flight), tail with yellow at base of outer feathers; below mostly greenish yellow. Female slightly duller than male, with less yellow on wings and tail. Immature lacks the "hood", the head being yellowish olive. Fairly common to common in pine and pine-oak woodland in highlands of Honduras and northern Nicaragua, also occurring in lowland pine savanna or northeastern Nicaragua (and probably also adjacent Honduras); ranges north to northern Mexico. Usually in flocks, feeding on seeds and flowers, sometimes near ground but more often high in trees.

FINDING BIRDS IN PANAMA

By Dodge and Lorna Engleman, and Robert S. Ridgely

Birds abound in Panama. Many species can be seen with little effort in many places, but others will be found only by searching them out in their favored haunts. This section suggests some accessible areas proven to be productive recently. Localities in central Panama are emphasized, for the vast majority of residents and visitors will spend most of their time here. Localities outside the Canal area can undergo sudden habitat deterioration — even in National Parks. It is best to check their status before trying them. Good sources for up to date information are: the Panama Audubon Society, Box 2026, Balboa, Republic of Panama; the Smithsonian Tropical Research Institution, APO Miami 34002, USA; Asociación Nacional para la Conservación de la Naturaleza (ANCON), Box 1387, Zone 1, Panama, Republic of Panama; and INRENARE (the National Institute of Renewable Resources), Dept. de Parques Nacionales y de Vida Silvestre, Box 2016 Paraiso, Ancon, Republic of Panama.

Accommodation is plentiful and good in Panama City. In Colon and cities west of Panama City it is readily available, but east of Panama City accommodation is limited and arrangements should be made in advance. English is widely spoken in the Canal area, less so in the interior of Panama. Knowledge of Spanish is certainly a convenience, but not a necessity for birding in Panama. Food and water are generally safe, but one should not drink water from rivers and streams. Malaria and other infectious tropical diseases are now rare in Panama; you may prefer to take malarial prophylaxis (but RSR does not, except when visiting truly remote areas such as Darién). Restaurants, markets, and supermarkets abound, but it is often difficult to find a restaurant open early in the morning. Inexpensive public transport is readily available throughout, but usually does not go to the best areas. Renting your own car will be more convenient; various agencies have offices at Torrijos International Airport, some of the major hotels, and even in some shopping centers in Panama City. Agencies are also found at the David, Chiriquí airport. Cars are not expensive, especially at weekly rates. Fuel is readily available throughout, at twice the US price. Four-wheel drive is not generally necessary; if it is not available through the rental agencies, the new car dealers who sell four-wheel drive vehicles will also rent them.

Birding is good year round. Migrants from the north generally arrive in September and October, during the rainy season, though many of them have passed through before the dry season begins in December. Most migrants have left Panama by the start of the rainy season in late April. The dry season is, on balance, the better time to visit Panama not only because of the presence of migrants but also because only then are some roads passable without four-wheel drive vehicles. The dry season starts two weeks later on the Caribbean side, where rainy days continue sporadically throughout February. A folding umbrella is often very useful during the rainy season.

There are two basic types of tropical forest birding: at the forest edge, for example along roadsides or in clearings; and within the forest interior. Results at the forest edge are best early in the morning, when birds are vocalizing and often perching in the open. In the forest interior it is too dark to see well until at least an hour after dawn, and forest interior birds remain more active throughout the day. In general, we cannot over-emphasize the importance of *getting out early*: you will likely record more in the first few hours after dawn than in all the rest of the day. Cloudy dull afternoons are especially likely to be unproductive. Most experienced observers try to be at their observation site just before dawn. Walking streams in the forest (e.g. along Pipeline Road) has the advantages of both forest edge and interior birding, plus the chance to find species associated with the stream itself. A few special birds are found only at army ant swarms. Swarms are most active from about 9.30 a.m. until shortly after noon. Although chiefly a forest interior phenomenon, swarms do cross roads, and swarms just inside forest areas can be located by recognizing the calls of the attendant birds.

Many birds tend to associate in mixed-species flocks. Consequently forest birding, be it at edge or in the interior, can be slow between flocks. Long periods may pass without the sight or sound of birds, especially at mid-day and in the afternoon. A tree in fruit or flower with birds on it is a rewarding place to linger. In general, do not attempt to cover too much ground; you will see more if you move slowly and quietly (with a minimum of talking). Once you locate activity, stay with it — do not always be in a rush to move on.

Birding by ear is crucial in woodland and forest where so many species are difficult to see. One should learn as many vocalizations as possible, especially of common species, in order to pick out the unusual sound and track it down. A tape recorder is extremely useful as it is often possible to lure a calling bird out of concealment by replaying its call. Observers are cautioned not to do this excessively but we are convinced that except under unusual circumstances no serious disturbance to the bird results.

Night birding presents special challenges and rewards. It is often especially productive in the Canal area, where the good road system permits easy access into a variety of habitats. Cruise slowly, scanning for eyeshine or shapes with a strong light. Stop occasionally to listen, and try to lure in calling birds with tape recordings (now commercially available from ARA Records); use judiciously!

Choice of clothing is highly personal. Lightweight cotton dries quickly and is more comfortable. Some birders prefer long pants because of rough vegetation and mosquitoes; others favor shorts. Most Panama birders prefer sneakers to Jungle boots due to their light weight. Subdued colors are much to be preferred over bright ones or bold patterns. Hummingbirds often seem attracted to a red item, such as a bandana or cap.

The greatest danger when birding in the forest is getting lost. This cannot be overemphasized, and is surprisingly easy to do. In unfamiliar areas always break branches if you leave the trail. Constantly be aware of obvious forks in the trail so you do not inadvertently take a wrong fork when returning. Get an idea of the lay of the land before leaving your vehicle so if you are lost you know which way to follow a stream — should you come upon one — back to the road. Plan to be out in the cool of the early morning (when birding is much better anyway) and unless you know you will back at the car within two hours, carry water and snack items with you.

The danger from poisonous snakes has been greatly exaggerated. They are very rarely seen and are not aggressive; you will be lucky to see one. In the unlikely event that you are bitten, assume the snake is poisonous, as non-venomous snakes will not bite unless molested. Do not, however, assume you were envenomated. Try to stay calm, walk back to your car, and drive sanely to the nearest hospital. Even if you are envenomated, you will have several hours before your condition becomes serious, and most towns in Panama have a hospital or clinic where you can find personnel with snake bite expertise, or evacuation facilities.

Insects pose more of a problem. Although mosquitoes are usually not numerous, the tiny 'no-see-ums' or sandfleas of the lowlands and the black flies of the highlands can be annoying. All can be adequately discouraged with repellant. Spraying repellant on your legs should deter chiggers; it is strongly recommended that you spray your legs and lower clothing before each day's outing (usually that once will suffice). Some people also prefer to tuck their pants inside their socks. Chiggers are most numerous in grassy areas, especially (but not always) where there are cows. Wasps, ants, scorpions and stinging caterpillars can be avoided by being careful where you put your hands and sit down. Be especially careful if you try to make your way through a fresh tree fall. The newest entomological danger in Panama is the aggressive African(ized) bee which is more of a threat in the dry season. Assume all honeybees are Africanized and give them wide berth. If you are stung do not simply swat the bee; immediately run back to your car, preferably through bushy vegetation en route, as this tends to confuse the bees.

Above all else, please do not let the above cautionary notes deter you. In all the time he has spent in Panama, RSR has never really gotten lost, has seen only a handful of poisonous snakes (those mostly at night when actually looking for them), has never been stung by bees, has seen only a couple of scorpions, etc. Chiggers — now there you have a problem (but even that hardly life-threatening), and even they can be thwarted if you can just remember to use repellent each day afield.

An unattended automobile in Panama is as safe as it is in the United States. Except for some areas in the Chiriquí highlands it is very unlikely your vehicle will be broken into unless unseen eyes observe you locking something inside. The best precaution is to avoid leaving anything valuable within site to tempt a potential thief.

Good maps of Panama and Panama City may be purchased at the Instituto

Geográfico Nacional Tommy Guardia on the Trans-Isthmian Highway in Panama City acrosss from the National University, but the maps on the end papers of this book should be satisfactory for most birding needs.

The law requires that all automobiles must stop at Guard checkpoint stations, marked "Alto" (stop).

The following sequence of birding localities begins on the Pacific side of the Canal area and moves north across the isthmus to Colon and environs. Next, Panama east of the Canal area is covered, and then western Panama.

CENTRAL PANAMA
PANAMA CITY AREA

Shorebirds

Stretching for 15 km along the Pacific coast, Panama City provides excellent shorebirding; the area is one of the most important for shorebirds in the Western Hemisphere. Although some are present throughout the year, largest numbers begin to arrive in August and peak in the next two months. Numbers remain high throughout the northern winter but the best time for rarities is certainly from September through to early November. The tidal change at Panama City can be as high as 4.8m (16 ft). The times of high and low tides are published daily in Panamanian newspapers. Birding is best within two hours of high tide. Then the birds congregate on coastal rocks and sandbars where they are much more easily observed. At low tide extensive mudflats are exposed and most birds are far away.

Two good sites in Panama City itself are at the east end of Avenida Balboa, and Panama Viejo. Park off the road in an Avenida Balboa restaurant parking lot and walk to the rocks. Going east from the Marriot Hotel on Via Cincuentenario leads to the ruins of Panama Viejo where one can walk along the main road and scan the shore.

Another good area is the Juan Díaz marsh and beach area. Continue from Panama Viejo on Cincuentenario away from the ocean. In a little over 1 km one comes to a major intersection, Vía España. Turn right (east) and proceed to the racetrack. Take the first right after the track (Calle 24 Este) at the La Pacífica supermarket. The road goes for 4 km first through a residential area and rice fields, then pasture and marsh, then a strip of coastal black mangrove forest before forking, the left fork continuing on to the Juan Díaz river, the right fork (the one to take) to the beach. At highest tide the birds will usually have gone elsewhere, so it is best to be here several hours before high tide. The trees along the shore often have a wintering Peregrine Falcon and the mangroves you pass through before reaching the shore have various good birds, including Mangrove Black-Hawks and a few Spot-breasted Woodpeckers, the latter here at the western limit of their range.

West of Panama City lies Fort Amador and the Fortified Islands. From Balboa Street in the old Canal Zone get on Vía Amador by the YMCA (at the the entrance to Fort Amador). After the checkpoint behind a large military building take the first possible left and you will find yourself in a parking lot overlooking a small bay. The sandbar just beneath the parking lot is often thronged with birds at high tide. If you do not turn left off the main road but instead continue on it, you will find yourself on the causeway road out to the islands; bear right at the one major intersection. This area is now under control of the Panama Defense Forces (National Guard) and is sometimes closed to vehicular traffic. The last building before the start of the actual causeway is the Officer's Club. Just beyond it is a gravel drive that goes down to the shore on the left. A walk along the shore here is often productive. You can leave your car in the parking lot of the Officer's Club.

Pacific Townsites

Between downtown Panama City and the Canal lie Balboa, Ancon, and Diablo Heights, all Canal area townsites which reverted to Panama in the early 1980s. Here are well kept lawns, shade trees, and fruit trees, as well as wooded slopes of Ancon Hill and the mangroves of Diablo Heights. Many common species can be found by strolling the avenues: swifts, especially Short-tailed and Lesser Swallow-tailed, work overhead; Tropical Screech-Owls call at night. The best spots are along Gorgas Road between the Administration Building and Gorgas Hospital in Ancon, and along the service road that parallels the Curundu River in Diablo Heights. To get to Diablo Heights continue on Balboa Street past the piers and turn left at the first opportunity. Take the second left on that street and park behind the school. There are mangroves around the river which are good for warblers during the appropriate season and for Straight-billed Woodcreepers all year. Keep a look-out for hummingbird feeders. Most feeder owners do not mind if you stop and watch the activity of Bananaquits, Blue Dacnis, Red-legged Honeycreepers, and orioles as well as various hummingbirds.

Metropolitan Nature Park

Parque Natural Metropolitano, on the edge of Panama City, is the only city park in Latin America containing tropical semideciduous forest. Covering over 500 acres, it has a birdlist of more than 200 species. It has nature trails within the forest, and birds and wildlife are easily visible. Many of the species mentioned for Fort Clayton in the main text (including Lance-tailed Manakins) can be seen here.

To reach it get on the Ricardo J. Alfaro Ave. and turn off into the Juan Pablo II Ave. which passes the park entrance. Juan Pablo II can also be reached via Curundu Road from Gaillard Highway. A guard house is located at the entrance. Hours are from 8.00 a.m. to 5.30 p.m. daily. For permission to visit earlier contact personnel at CONAMA (National Commission for the Environment) at telephone 32-6055.

GAILLARD HIGHWAY

The Gaillard Highway begins at the Ancon terminal of the Panama railroad and continues to Gamboa. There are several good birding spots along the highway, including Chiva Chiva Road, Summit Gardens, the old Gamboa Road, and Plantation Road.

Chiva Chiva Road

About 2 km beyond the Fort Clayton entrance on Gaillard Highway are a cluster of three ponds. Chiva Chiva Road takes off between the two ponds on the right. The first part of the road borders the pond. From vantage points along the road one can scan the pond for Masked Ducks and other freshwater and marsh birds. The roadside woods also provide good birding. After 3 km on the road there is a large field with several large antennae. Pacific grassland birds such as Red-breasted Blackbirds, Eastern Meadowlarks, and occasionally Savanna Hawks can be found. Large power lines cross the road 2 km beyond the entrance to the antennae farm. A little further an overgrown road goes off to the left; further on it leads into better woodland. Along this trail look for Pale-eyed Pygmy-Tyrant, Yellow-green Tyrannulet, Slate-headed Tody-Flycatcher, Red-crowned Ant-Tanager, and Rosy-Thrush Tanager. The remainder of Chiva Chiva Road beyond this trail is no longer very good for birding.

Summit Gardens

Summit Gardens is a botanical garden with a small zoo maintained by INRENARE. Although crowded on weekends, it is a pleasant picnic area during the week. There are no specialties here, but it remains popular with birders in part because of other facilities (such as the zoo and picnic grounds). Hummingbirds are often numerous and easy to see, and it it a good place for migrants. To get to Summit, turn left at the Gamboa turnoff (the roadsign says "Parque Summit"); the park entrance will be seen about 1.5 km from the turnoff.

Old Gamboa Road

Gaillard Highway is the main drive to Gamboa; paralleling it on the left is the old road to Gamboa. To get on the old road, turn left off Gaillard Highway crossing the tracks instead of turning right into Summit Gardens. A few hundred meters beyond the tracks turn right onto old Gamboa Road. The old Gamboa Road continues for 4.4 km through pleasant second-growth woodland, crossing several streams, before again joining Gaillard Highway. Some good birds are found here, including many Pacific woodland species and a few species that are spillovers from the Caribbean side.

Plantation Road

The turnoff to Plantation Road is 2.5 km along Gaillard Highway from Summit Gardens. A blacktop road takes off to the right from the highway, and continues 1.8 km up a hill to end at the observatory and tower at the summit. This road in itself provides good birding. Plantation Road no longer opens onto the highway. To get on it follow the dirt tracks (often not driveable) to the left about 30 meters from the start of the blacktop road. This takes you over a low ridge and down into a valley to Plantation Road. This is one of the better birding areas in the Canal environs, but you must walk it as it is no longer passable to vehicles because of wash-outs and tree falls. Paralleling the road to the left is a stream which can be approached by various steep trails leading to it from the road above. Some of the humid forest birds of Pipeline Road are found in this forest; Royal Flycatcher, Golden-crowned Spadebill, Blue-crowned Manakin, and all three motmots are regular.

Gamboa

Continuing along Gaillard Highway one crosses a bridge over the Chagres River. Turn right immediately after crossing the bridge and follow the road, scanning the edge of the river for freshwater and marsh species such as the Masked Duck and Least Grebe. On the opposite side of the road is a silted-up pond with marsh vegetation. A trail, worth taking, goes around this marsh, mostly through the woodland. Rufescent Tiger-Heron has been seen here.

If, instead of turning right after crossing the bridge, you go straight ahead, you enter Gamboa. Stay left where the road divides, passing the train station and a gas station. A few hundred meters after a Guardia building farther along on the right, the road forks. The right-hand fork ends immediately at an ammunition storage facility. From the parking area at the enclosure here scan the pond to the left and a swamp to the right — both are good for water and marsh birds such as Rufescent Tiger-Heron and Muscovy Duck and White-throated Crakes are frequent at the water's edge just before dark. A trail follows the fence around the ammunition site and is worth taking.

Pipeline Road

Passing through the heart of Soberanía National Park, Pipeline Road is only 45 minutes from Panama City. This forest is rated as one of the most accessible tropical forests in the world; over 380 species of birds have been recorded here.

Enter Pipeline Road from Gamboa. Continue through Gamboa, bearing left at the intersection past the Guardia station, passing a large pond on the right. The road curves right beyond the pond and goes uphill. Take the first right turn which is Pipeline Road. A gate here is sometimes locked; it is wise to check with one of the organizations mentioned on p.475 regarding the current situation. For the first 6 km the road is of gravel and fairly flat, passing through scrubby habitat, mature second-growth, and some patches of old forest. Birding is good here but even better further along. The road becomes a single lane blacktop and after about 1 km becomes quite hilly. After passing the "Alamo" clearing before the first big hill, you enter spectacular old growth humid forest.

The hills beyond the "Alamo" are an extension of the foothills of eastern Colon province and provide an opportunity to find eastern Panama and foothill species, as well as virtually all of the birds favoring central Panama's humid forests. These include rarities such as Yellow-eared Toucanet, Crimson-bellied Woodpecker, Slaty-winged Foliage-gleaner, Russet Antshrike, Sirystes, Gray Elaenia and Olive, Sulphur-rumped, and Tawny-crested Tanagers. Various forest raptors are regularly noted, and even a Harpy Eagle has been sighted on a few recent occasions.

There are three main ways to bird Pipeline Road: to drive and walk the main road; to walk the trails; or to wade the streams. Greatest activity along the road occurs just after first light when many species join in the "dawn chorus". By about 10.00 a.m. activity has usually started to wane. Since one cannot be everywhere along the road at once, one needs several days to do it justice.

There are three areas with trails. One is at the Limbo Camp. Watch for a narrow but driveable track through tall grass bearing off to the right and up a slight gradient just beyond the Río Limbo bridge (fifth bridge), immediately after the blacktop starts. The camp is beside a stream about 100 meters into the forest and there is an extensive network of trails on both sides of the stream. Another set of trails can be entered behind the "Alamo", a ransacked cement block structure on the left side of the road several hundred meters beyond the Limbo Camp turnoff. A third network of trails is on the left side of the road at the opposite end of the clearing that starts at the "Alamo". Of late, these latter trails have not been maintained and can be difficult to find from the road. Once on them, exercise caution to avoid becoming lost. They are the best places to find forest interior birds such as the Buff-throated Foliage-gleaner, Brownish Twistwing, Speckled Mourner, and Tawny-faced Gnatwren. They are also much cooler than the road itself as noon approaches!

Another productive birding procedure involves coasting quietly down the hills listening for the calls of antswarm specialists such as the Bicolored Antbird. Your best chance of seeing the Rufous-vented Ground-Cuckoo and the Black-crowned Antpitta is to patiently stay with swarms as long as possible — but even then you'll need to be very lucky! Coasting of course also permits one to better hear the calls of other species.

Walking the streams is recommended for birding during the heat of the day. Agami Heron, Sunbittern, Great Curassow, Dull-mantled Antbird, Broad-billed Sapayoa, and Buff-rumped Warbler are among the stream-side specialties. In dry season, there is more overall activity along the streams. Probably any stream on Pipeline Road is worth exploring, but the most success recently has been found downstream on the Frijolito (second bridge), both ways on the Frijoles (third bridge), upstream on the Mendoza (sixth bridge), Sirystes (seventh), Guacharo (tenth), and both ways on the Agua Salud (eleventh).

Night birding on Pipeline Road can also be very productive. At dusk

Short-tailed Nighthawks can be seen flying over the canopy; the eyeshine of both potoo species is frequently seen when the birds perch within sight of the road, while six species of owls including the Vermiculated Screech-Owl and the Crested Owl can be seen and heard.

In the dry season Pipeline Road can be driven in a conventional two-wheel drive car as far as the Agua Salud (17.5 km), where the Panama Canal Commission maintains a hydrographic station. In the rainy season four-wheel drive may be required because of deep and slippery pot holes on the first third of the road. Bridges should be checked before crossing as some are in poor repair. It is best to keep a saw or machete in the car in case a tree has fallen across the road. As your vehicle may be the only one on Pipeline Road, that day, one cannot expect help. This slight ''risk'' should not be a deterrent to exploring this fascinating area, surely one of the best birding spots in all of the Americas.

TRANS-ISTHMIAN HIGHWAY

The recommended two birding areas along the Trans-Isthmian Highway are the forests on Madden Highway, and on the south shore of Madden Lake (Lago Aajuela).

Madden Forest

On pre-1980 maps this forest is indicated as a forest preserve. Madden Forest is now part of Parque Nacional Soberanía and new maps no longer designate it as Madden Forest. The forest here is old, tall, and is easily birded if side roads (of which there are many) and trails are used. Birding from the main road is hazardous and not particularly productive due to heavy traffic.

Coming from Panama City on Gaillard Highway, stay straight on Madden Road (unmarked) instead of turning left on Gaillard Highway toward Summit and Gamboa at the Parque Soberanía sign. The road shortly enters forest. Coming from Panama City on the Trans-Isthmian Highway, turn left immediately upon crossing the viaduct over Madden Road; it is the only such viaduct on the highway, and is 20.1 km from Panama City. Coming from Colon, take the same turnoff, 11 km from the checkpoint where Madden Road rejoins the Trans-Isthmian Highway.

Madden Lake

On the south shore of Madden Lake is an abandoned Boy Scout Camp and a Panama Canal Commission maintenance road. Both are good birding spots, the latter being the better of the two. To reach this area from Colon take the left branch at the highway fork just beyond Salamanca. There is a Guardia checkpoint at the fork to facilitate recognition. A large bridge over the Chagres indicates that one has gone too far. A half kilometer after leaving the bridge over Madden Spillway turn left onto the old blacktop road to the Scout

Camp. Coming from the Pacific side from Madden Forest, stay on Madden
Road going under the viaduct. The Scout Camp turnoff is seen to the right
just as the spillway bridge entrance comes into view. A short cut avoiding the
slow traffic on Madden Road is recommended, however. Get on the Trans-
Isthmian Highway at the viaduct and continue towards Colon for 6.5 km to a
sign for Bodega Mario. Here follow a connecting road of several hundred
meters to Madden Road. Turn left on Madden Road and continue 1.6 km to
the Scout Camp road.

The first part of the Scout Camp road passes through scrubby habitat and
second-growth forest but is a good place for skulkers such as wrens, Yellow-
billed Caciques, and Rosy Thrush-Tanagers. Check for Green-and-rufous
Kingfishers on the stream. The road then forks, with the Scout Camp on the
left and the maintenance road continuing straight. The maintenance road
goes through excellent forest with many cuipos for 2.5 km and affords views of
backwater bays of Madden Lake. Bird activity is unusually good here with a
mixture of species from both slopes such as Black-tailed Trogons, Rufous-
breasted and Rufous-and-white Wrens, Yellow-green Tyrannulets, and
Black-headed Saltators. The Royal Flycatcher is fairly common here, and the
bays should be checked for Anhingas and other wetlands species.

Another interesting birding spot in the area is the trail down the hill from
the parking area just beyond the north entrance to the spillway. Birding along
the highway is also good north of the parking area as there is very little traffic.

A two-wheel drive vehicle will suffice in all seasons but care must be taken
on some of the steep grades. Being only a little more than 30 minutes from
either Panama City or Colon, the area is good for a day trip.

COLON

The Caribbean side of the Canal area is the butt of many isthmian jokes
stemming from its all-too-evident neglect and socioeconomic problems, but
its relative lack of development has meant continued excellent birding. Every
year since 1976 the "Atlantic" area has logged more than 300 species on its
Christmas Bird Count.

There are two good hotels in Colon, the Carlton and the Washington.
When you enter Colon on the causeway (a continuation of the Trans-
Isthmian Highway) you will be on Central Street heading north. When you
come to 10th Street (there is a cathedral on the northeastern corner), turn
right; the Carlton Hotel and restaurant are at the next stop sign. To reach the
Washington Hotel continue on Central until it ends at the beach. Turn left
and follow the winding road (1st Street) to the Washington. The Washington
Hotel is the more luxurious and more expensive, but has an excellent view of
the bay and occasionally rare vagrants are seen on the hotel grounds. **Do not
walk outside the grounds** as there is a real and ever present danger from
muggers.

Coco Solo

Instead of going straight into Colon at the stop light before the causeway, turn right on Randolph Road. Proceed for 4.3 km, passing Cristobal High School and Colo Solo townsite on its left, and an airfield and extensive black mangrove forest on its rights. Scan the playing fields and meadows of Cristobal High School as these are excellent for migrant shorebirds in season, especially after rain. The cement waterfront and seawall behind the high school are worth checking for vagrant coastal species and jaegers. The ditch between the road and the mangroves on the right is rewarding for spotlighting at night for Boat-billed and Yellow-crowned Night-Herons.

Randolph Road then forks: the left hand leading to Isla Margarita (formerly Fort Randolph), now a municipal park and nature reserve; the right hand continuing through mangroves and second-growth to Galeta Naval Station and Galeta Island Research Marine Lab. The best birding at Isla Margarita is in the mangroves around its perimeter. There, and in the mangroves along Galeta Road, look for Straight-billed, Streak-headed and Olivaceous Woodcreepers and "Mangrove" Yellow Warblers. Olivaceous Piculets and Black-tailed Trogons are also possible, and all six species of kingfishers have been seen at the start of Galeta Road and along streams in the mangroves. Migrants, including rarities, are also numerous.

Margarita

Margarita townsite, a suburb of Colon, has spacious lawns and large trees making it a good birding area for the more common residential species. Adjacent to Margarita are two woodlands: Rancho Ramos and Margarita Tank Farm, both of them excellent birding spots. To reach the Margarita townsite turn left at the stoplight before entering the causeway. Shortly the road forks; keep straight ahead for Rainbow City and Colon, turn left onto Diversion Road and, after passing a Chinese vegetable market on the right, you join Bolivar Highway coming out of Colon. This borders the diversion canal and continues southeast to Fort Davis and Gatun townsite.

Rancho Ramos can be reached by taking the second left after entering Bolivar Highway. The sign at this intersection indicates Fort Espinar. Continue towards Fort Espinar until a blacktop road angles off to the right. Immediately cross a small bridge. Just before the next bridge is a gravel road to the left. Turn in here and go about 30 meters to a pipeline valve. Park here and follow the pipeline — using it as a bridge at the first stream —into the woods. One can also reach the pipeline by continuing on the blacktop road to the Rancho Ramos picnic area on the left, parking in the parking area, and walking along the roadside hedge to the pipeline.

To reach the Margarita Tank Farm instead of turning left on to Espinar Road, turn right crossing a small bridge and park in the grassy area in front of the perimeter fence. For the best birding follow the perimeter fence to the left and the drainage ditches through the woods. Both these areas are good for migrant warblers, notably uncommon ones such as Blue-winged, Golden-winged, and Worm-eating, as well as resident birds such as Black-tailed Trogon, Olivaceous Piculet, smaller woodcreepers, Jet Antbird, and wrens. The diversion canal itself has Boat-billed Herons (best seen at night) and American Pygmy Kingfishers. Either area can be birded in an hour and activity is usually good all day.

Fort Sherman/San Lorenzo

The 20-km route from Gatun Locks to Fort San Lorenzo is the most scenic drive in central Panama. From the road you will see the remnants of the old sea level French Canal, drive through wooded hills, cross the Mojinga Swamp, skirt the coast of Limon Bay, and traverse a mangrove swamp before arriving at Fort Sherman. From Fort Sherman an all weather gravel road takes you along a sinuous course through wooded hills to the ruins of Fort San Lorenzo. This partially restored sixteenth-century Spanish fort is a beautiful spot for a picnic, high on a promontory overlooking the Chagres River estuary.

To reach the Gatun Locks continue on Bolivar Highway, turning right at the first opportunity after passing the maintenance buildings just beyond the railroad crossing. After several hundred meters turn right again, at the entrance to the drawbridge across the locks. The bridge is closed when ships are transiting the locks; this can result in a wait of up to 30 minutes. Upon leaving the bridge continue straight ahead, not turning off on any gravel side roads, to reach Fort Sherman after 12 km. Upon entering Fort Sherman you have a short drive down a residential street. To get to San Lorenzo take the next two left turns. Alternatively, proceed straight ahead onto a little-used landing strip which can be good for migrant shorebirds. The road out to San Lorenzo has numerous side roads. Though birding can be good on any of them, the best are the drive up to Fort San Lorenzo itself, the road just before the San Lorenzo turnoff, and the Rio Congo road which is the last left before the boat launch at the estuary. Of the roads off the highway to Fort Sherman the best are Black Tank Road (2 km from the French Canal bridge) and Skunk Hollow Road (7 km from the bridge).

The woodland along the road is noted for trogons, motmots, and numerous other forest and woodland birds. The forests on this route lack some of the wetter forest species seen on the Achiote Road route. Night birding is often productive.

Escobal Road

Immediately after crossing the Gatun locks turn left and continue along the edge of the Canal following the blacktop road which then goes along the base of the grass-covered Gatun Dam. The road soon crosses a single-lane bridge over the spillway. Just before the bridge is the Tarpon Club Restaurant which opens at 10.00 a.m. and serves excellent food. Red-breasted Blackbirds and sometimes a few other savanna species frequent the grass on the dam. It can also be worthwhile to park and scan the spillway for shore and wading birds; watch for Peregrine Falcons and Merlins.

After crossing the bridge the road turns left and continues along the crest of the dam, giving views out over the lake. At the end of the dam the gravel road to the right leads to Tiger Trail. After a couple of hundred meters the road has been obliterated by a huge landslide so one must park here and follow the poorly indicated trail around the slide to the right. Tiger Trail is an easily walked path (after traversing the grassy growth on the now obliterated road beyond the landslide) beside an old railway embankment dating from French construction days. The forest is not old but huge trees are scattered throughout. The trail is canopied and undergrowth is sparse, resulting in good visibility and making walking off the trail easy. This is a good place to find forest-floor and lower-level forest birds such as quail-doves, leaftossers, antpittas, and gnatwrens. Because of the canopy it remains comfortably cool even in the heat of the day. In the rainy season mosquitoes can be obnoxious, however.

Continuing beyond the dam you are on Escobal Road. The side of the road away from the lake has been cleared for power lines and its birding qualities have suffered, but three side roads to the right still offer good birding. The S-9 Road, 3.8 km after the dam, is the best, and has the most shade.

Escobal Road leaves the forest 11 km after the dam and enters cattle country. It continues several kilometers beyond the lakeshore town of Escobal and Pacific slope grassland species such as Savanna Hawk are now present.

Achiote Road

As soon as Escobal Road leaves the forest there is a gravel road to the right which reaches the town of Achiote after 7 km. Clearing along the north side of the road for installation of power lines in 1984 had a deleterious effect on its birding qualities but it is still the only place in the Canal area where many species can be found, including regulars such as White-headed and Stripe-breasted Wrens and Montezuma Oropendolas and rarities such as Gray-cheeked Nunlet. It is also an excellent place to find species such as Spot-crowned Barbet, Pied Puffbird, Streaked and Pygmy Antwrens, and Sulphur-rumped and Dusky-faced Tanagers. Perhaps no other single area in the Canal area and vicinity is as rich in diurnal raptors. At night it is very good for Great Potoos and owls, including the Vermiculated Screech Owl. Count the bridges as you drive along the road. The 500 m between the second and third bridge are the best area for White-headed Wrens. Stripe-breasted Wrens can be found by wading the stream at the third bridge. Just after the fourth bridge is a dead-end road to the left. Seven hundred meters down this road, at the edge of the pasture on the left, is a tree with a large Montezuma Oropendola colony active in the dry season.

Achiote Road has a gravel surface and in the dry season presents no problem to a conventional two-wheel drive vehicle. In the rainy season there can be deep mud holes so a car with high clearance is a decided advantage. It takes about 45 minutes to reach the start of Achiote Road from Margarita or Colon (assuming there are no delays at Gatun locks) so an early start is mandatory. However, it is well worth it: this area and Pipeline Road remain the two premier birding sites in the former Canal Zone.

Barro Colorado Island
Barro Colorado Island is an island in Gatun Lake which was created with the rising of lake waters soon after the turn of the century. It has since been protected as a biological research station. The island has, unfortunately, lost many bird species still found in the Pipeline Road area because of its isolation as an island, its limited size (approximately 3 × 5 km), and the absence of year-round running water. Still, because of its strictly protected status, its many trails, and its relatively sparse undergrowth, some birds are more easily seen here than elsewhere, among them Crested Guan, Great Tinamou, White-whiskered Puffbird, and Black-striped Woodcreeper. It is also excellent for mammals.

Arrangements for day trips as well as longer stays on the island must be made through the Smithsonian Tropical Research Institute office. The phone number is 62-6315. Tuesdays are recommended for day trips. For longer stays make arrangements in advance by writing to the Office of the Director, STRI, APO Miami 34002, USA.

EASTERN PANAMA

There are still numerous good birding areas in the eastern half of the Republic of Panama, but some of the region, including well known locales such as Tocumen, La Jagua, the and Bayano River valley, has suffered from development schemes and deforestation, and are now mere shadows of their former selves.

Tocumen Marsh
Once a well known haven for savanna and marsh species, Tocumen Marsh has deteriorated terribly since its conversion to a rice plantation around 1983. Most of the roadside ditches and marshy ponds have been drained, and many species are now hard to find. Still, because of its proximity to the airport hotel and the lack of accessible better habitat nearby, it is recommended as a half day birding trip on your day of arrival or departure from Panama.

To get to the marsh, drive from the airport towards Panama City and take the new highway to Chepo at the Riande Airport Hotel on the right hand side of the airport highway. After 6.8 km there is an intersection with a small guardia station. Turn right here and 700 m later the road forks. Keep left and at 2.7 km a dirt road turns off to the left into Tocumen Marsh. Shortly after passing through a gate you will arrive at some maintenance buildings (to ensure that you will not be locked in, check with the people at the maintenance buildings for their departure time, since they may lock the gate when they leave). Here the road forks; going right is best. Almost immediately you pass between two ponds, both worth checking; then continue through rice fields to a dike. Going left along the dike leads to broken woodland; going right leads to a lake. The dirt roads are merely bumpy in the dry season, but in rainy season vehicles with high clearance are necessary to avoid getting stuck. Specialties of the area (some present only during the rainy season) include Cocoi and Capped Herons, Least Bittern, Lesser Yellow-headed Vulture, American Pygmy and Green-and-rufous Kingfishers, Glossy Ibis, Pearl Kite, several species of rails, Pied Water-Tyrant, Little Cuckoo, Straight-billed Woodcreeper, and Lesser Kiskadee. Nearby scrub has Pale-bellied Hermit and this is the easternmost place (in Panama) for Mouse-colored Tyrannulet. Various raptors remain fairly numerous. Driving the roads at dusk can yield Common Pauraque, White-tailed Nightjar, Common Barn-Owl, and Striped Owl.

Sadly, the superbly situated La Siesta Hotel has recently been converted into a private country club.

Cerro Azul/Cerro Jefe

This area is within an hour's drive from Panama City, and half an hour from the airport. The elevation is between 450 m and 950 m (1500 ft and 3100 ft). It is well worth exploring for foothill species including some from the Darien. In the dry season a two-wheel drive vehicle with good clearance is sufficient, but in the rainy season four-wheel drive is necessary to get to Cerro Jefe as the roads are steep and slippery. The Cerro Jefe ridge is windy, cool, wet, even in the dry season, so take appropriate clothing.

Take the new Pan-American Highway (Chepo road) where it begins at the Riande Airport Hotel. Turn left at the small guardia station after 6.8 km, onto the old road to Chepo. Continue for 2 km, to a surfaced road on the left beside a Chinese pavilion. After crossing some savanna, this starts to ascend toward Cerro Azul. Take it for 11.5 km where the road forks to the left to Monte Fresco, a new residential development that has good birding in the roadside woods, especially near the start of the road. Then continue straight ahead to Goofy Lake after 1 km and Avenida de los Nimbos 2.5 km further on, going to the left. One option is to park at the end of this street (650 m: 2100 ft) and hike down the undriveable dirt road through woodland that is steep but good for eastern foothill birds. The habitat is not as good as on Cerro Jefe, however, so it is best covered only when weather conditions further along are discouraging. The next 6 km along the main road are surfaced and pass through patches of woodland which can be surprisingly active, especially during the dry season when *Miconia* (Melastomacea) trees are in fruit. At the end of the blacktop the road becomes dirt and continues 6.1 km to the microwave tower atop Cerro Jefe; some portions are quite steep. The last kilometer or so is through a fascinating elfin forest dominated by a unique species of palm. Park in front of the fence around the tower and hike around it to the right on a network of dirt roads cut through the elfin forest. Although it can be quiet for long periods, this forest holds Tacarcuna Bush-Tanager, Black-headed Brush-Finch, and

Violet-headed and Violet-capped Hummingbirds, among others. About 800 m before the main road ends at the tower there is a turn off to the right that descends steeply through various types of forest and continues for miles. Only the most daring would try to drive it; walking it may yield Blue-fronted Parrotlet, White-tipped Sicklebill, White-ruffed Manakin, Slaty-backed Nightingale-Thrush, Striped Woodhaunter and Slaty-winged Foliage-gleaner as well as Emerald, Speckled, Rufous-winged, Olive, Sulphur-rumped, and Black-and-yellow Tanagers.

Nusagandi

In response to the incursion of transmigrant settlers into the foothills of Panama province bordering San Blas, the Kuna Nation set aside part of their Comarca bordering Panama province as a forest reserve. PEMASKY, the park's administration, encourages birders to visit and to stay at the modest facilities established at the park's headquarters in Nusagandi. Arrangements must be made in advance through the PEMASKY office in Panama City (Box 2012 Paraiso, Ancon, Republic of Panama). For updates on the PEMASKY office phone number and location inquire at the STRI office (see section on Barro Colorado Island).

Nusagandi, a two-hour drive from Panama City, is situated at 450 m (1500 ft) on the El Llano-Cartí Road just on the Caribbean side of the continental divide. The park contains 40,000 hectares of mostly primary forest ranging from submontane wet forest on Cerro Brewster at 650 m (2100 ft) to tropical humid forests near sea level. Guides are available to lead you along trails into the different life zones. To reach Nusagandi travel east on the Pan-American Highway to El Llano, 55 km from the Riande Airport Hotel. Just before reaching the village of El Llano the El Llano-Cartí Road takes off to the left. Though easy for two-wheel drive cars in dry season, it is difficult in rainy season so a four-wheel drive vehicle, or at least one with high clearance is then recommended. The PEMASKY office can advise you on the state of the road.

Formerly the entire El Llano-Cartí Road provided excellent birding, but with the advance of transmigrants the forest has all but disappeared on the first half of the 20 km drive road. Your time will therefore, would best be spent going more or less directly to park headquarters. The avifauna here is very rich and includes foothill and eastern Panama species as well as some rare Canal area birds. Birding the main road through the park can be very productive and the trails are very birdable; the undergrowth is not so thick as to obscure the forest floor skulkers. This is the best spot in Panama to look for the Speckled Antshrike, Black-headed Antthrush, and Black-crowned Antpitta; Stripe-throated Wrens occur, and various tanagers (including Rufous-winged) are numerous. To be hoped for are curassow and Crested Guan, ground-cuckoo, and Purplish-backed Quail-Dove.

Majé

The research station of the Gorgas Memorial Laboratory on Isla Majé in the

Bayano Lake well east of Chepo provides an opportunity to see some of the birds of the forests of the upper Bayano valley. Visits can be arranged through the Gorgas Laboratory, or through the Panama Audubon Society; spending at least one night is recommended. Birds especially to watch for include Cocoi Heron, White-fronted Nunbird, Red-rumped Woodpecker, Red-billed Scythebill, Black Antshrike, Rufous-winged Antwren, One-colored Becard, Golden-headed Manakin, White-eared Conebill, and Orange-crowned Oriole.

Darién

Some of the best birding in Panama is found in the province of Darién. In the early 1980s the Pan-American Highway was extended east from the Bayano Dam to Yaviza, Darién, within 50 km of the Colombian border. Pavement ends at Chepo and the road beyond the Bayano essentially constitutes a logging road on which high clearance is a necessity. Lodging is available in Yaviza. Travelling by road to Darién is not recommended as habitat destruction has been so severe that binoculars are needed just to see the forest on distant hillsides.

Part of eastern Darién is now protected as the Darién National Park, a swath of forest at least 20 km wide abutting the entire Colombian boundary. The Chocó Indians are allowed to continue to live in the area, and they help maintain and protect this exceptionally rich park.

There are two main sites for visitors to the park, Cana in the foothills on the east slope of the Pirre ridge, and Pirre Station in the lowlands on the west slope of Cerro Pirre. Cana is the name of a gold mining camp and its adjacent landing strip. Presently birding is superb. Around the landing strip four species of macaws, Black-tipped Cotinga, and Red-throated Caracara can be seen. On the trail east from the strip toward Boca de Cupe are Tody Motmot, Dusky-backed Jacamar, Barred Puffbird, Fulvous-bellied Antpitta, Double-banded Graytail, and many others. The trail from camp up to the ridge is excellent for the highland endemics such as Pirre Bush-Tanager, Pirre Warbler, Varied Solitaire, and Rufous-cheeked Hummingbird, plus Sharpbill, Golden-headed Quetzal, Gray-and-gold Tanager, and numerous other specialties. About 60 Panama species are found only in Darién National Park, and numerous others can be found much easier here than elsewhere.

To fly into Cana requires written permission from INRENARE and requires charter of a plane. Camping gear and food must be brought in. There are no communications with the outside world. As there are no navigational aids at the airstrip, the plane may not be able to make its appointed return in the event of inclement weather. To arrange permission to use the mining camp facilities write to (at present): Office of Chief Geologist, Freeport Exploration Company, PO Box 1911, Reno, Nevada, USA. Telephone contact with the Reno office is (702) 323-2251.

The other access point into Darién National Park is at Pirre Station (Rancho Frío), and this is the official Park campsite which is open to the public. To reach

Rancho Frío take a commercial flight from Paitilla Airport in Panama City to El Real. A road out of El Real can be taken to Piji Baisal. In rainy season this road might not be passable, and you must get to Piji Baisal by boat. From Piji take a trail through broken forest to the park boundary, just inside of which is the barracks where lodging, but not food or utensils, is available. Once in the park there are numerous trails, including one which climbs up to the Cerro Pirre ridge. The foothills and highlands are too distant for a one-day trip with time for birding. To reach the highlands via this route camping gear must be carried. It is strongly advised to have a guide on any of the trails as they are not well marked and the topography is confusing. Arrangements for guides (Spanish speaking only) are easily made through the INRENARE office in El Real.

The lowland Darién birds are the specialties of Rancho Frío. These include White-fronted Nunbird, Crimson-bellied Woodpecker, Striped Wood-hunter, Stripe-throated Wren, Viridian Dacnis, Lemon-spectacled, Scarlet-browed, and Yellow-backed Tanagers (all of these can be found at Cana as well). Of course following the trail to Cerro Pirre ridge may yield the foothill and highland species.

To make advance arrangements to visit Rancho Frío write (preferably in Spanish) to INRENARE, Dept. de Parques Nacionales Y de Vida Silvestre, Box 2016 Paraiso, Ancon, Republic of Panama or, the Director, Parque Nacional Darién, INRENARE, El Real, Darién, Republic of Panama. Upon arrival in El Real you will be met by a representative of the town's only hotel. He also has a general store, a four-wheel drive vehicle, and is the representative for the airline serving El Real. Through him one makes arrangements for transportation to Piji Baisal, mules to take your gear on to Rancho Frío, the guide, return to El Real, and flight back to Panama City.

Whereas arrangements for Rancho Frío are easily made and independent travel there is relatively cheap, independent travel to Cana is expensive and arrangements difficult. It is therefore advisable, though not essential, to join a commercial bird tour if you wish to go to Cana.

WESTERN PANAMA

A 500 km drive west from Panama City takes you to the Costa Rican border and presents the opportunity to see a variety of different habitats. The main faunal areas are lowland savanna and agricultural areas, the western foothills, the marshes and salt flats, and the western Chiriquí highlands. Driving to Chiriquí non-stop is an eight-hour venture, so those with limited time are advised to fly to David, the capital of Chiriquí, and there rent a car. Four-wheel drive vehicles are available from Hertz, Budget, and Econocar, but are not necessary except as mentioned below for specific places. Accommodation is available on the Pan-American Highway at Antón, Penonomé, Aguadulce, Santiago, San Félix, and David and at various places in the highlands.

Lowland Savannas

The specialties in the western lowlands are raptors. Crested and Yellow-headed Caracaras are common throughout as are White-tailed Kites, and Roadside and Savanna Hawks. The White-tailed Hawk and the scarce Aplomado Falcon should also be looked for, particularly west of Penonomé. Crested Bobwhite, Brown-throated Parakeet, and Yellow-crowned Amazon can also be seen here. Grassland Yellow-Finches occur in fields between Antón and Penonomé. In the scrub and fields behind the west end of the truck stop in San Juan, Chiriquí, can be found Mouse-colored Tyrannulet and Yellowish Pipit. From San Juan to the border you should encounter White-collared Seedeaters.

Cerro Campana

In Altos de Campana National Park on Cerro Campana agricultural inroads have decreased the forest area but the park still boasts an avifauna rich in foothill species not found in the lowlands of the Canal area. Lodging is not available presently at Cerro Campana, but there is a campground and it is less than a 90-minute drive from Panama City. The turnoff to the park is 44 km beyond the start of the autopista at Arraiján, 5.5 km from the Queso Chela refreshment stop/gas station outside of Capira. It is an unmarked road that goes to the right steeply uphill, and though rough, is passable with a two-wheel drive vehicle with reasonably high clearance. A National Park Sign is located at 5.2 km from the turnoff and 3.5 km further along a fork in the road. The right-hand fork is the old entrance into the forest, but because of a washout one must park and walk in. If one continues on the main road 1 km beyond the fork one finds a road to the right with a small sign that says "Townshend". Turn here and ascend 1 km passing the microwave tower, to enter the forest from the new entrance.

Amongst the highland/foothill birds you are almost certain to see are: Scale-crested Pygmy-Tyrant, White-ruffed Manakin, Blue-and-white Swallow, White-throated Thrush, and Silver-throated and Black-and-yellow Tanagers. Other likely species include Orange-bellied Trogon, Yellow-eared Toucanet, Plain Antvireo, and Chestnut-capped Brush-Finch. The list of rare possibilities includes Purplish-backed Quail-Dove, White-tipped Sicklebill, Slaty Antwren, and Black-headed Antthrush. Of course other more widespread species are here as well.

El Valle

Another good area for foothill birds within a two-hour drive from Panama City is El Valle. This picturesque little town has two hotels and is well known for its Sunday market. The road up to El Valle is paved but stretches of it are in poor condition. It starts just under 100 km from the Panama Canal and is well marked with signs where it turns to the right from the Pan-American Highway. Once on it there are no forks or intersections until El Valle 28 km later. To find the cloud forest continue on the principal road through town past the market and the church on the left. Turn right at the next intersection and immediately cross a bridge.

Here the road forks; stay on the right fork and after 6 km forest is visible. Here the road again forks and to get to the best birding keep right. After 1.2 km there is a Ganadería sign and the road turns very sharply to the right. Half a kilometer beyond the sign there is another turn to the right. You can drive on this road for about 400 m to a wash-out. Park here and follow the undriveable road on foot. This trail goes along the ridge of Cerro Gaital, which attains on altitude of over 900 m (3000 ft).

Birding is good anywhere in the forest. Foothill species you can expect to see include most of those listed for Cerro Campana plus Common Bush-Tanager, Black-faced Grosbeak, and various hummingbirds such as Green Hermit, Violet-headed Hummingbird, and White-tailed Emerald. Other more widespread species can also be seen.

El Copé

The forests of the El Copé region are among the most beautiful in Panama and provide excellent birding. From just before the Continental Divide and beyond to the Caribbean coast the forest stretches almost unbroken: montane forest near the divide, tall humid forest beyond it. Its birdability is hindered only by the area's chronically inclement weather. Only in March are you reasonably assured of sun, at other times of the year rain and/or fog will likely present a problem.

To reach El Copé continue west along the Pan-American Highway from Penonomé for 20 km. About 1 km before the large bridge over the Río Grande and just as it comes into view there is an asphalt road to the right. After 27 km on this road you come to El Copé, where you continue straight on the gravel road and in 4 km reach a school, Escuela de Barrigón. From here the road ascends and becomes difficult. Four-wheel drive is recommended but pick-up trucks can make it. The road ends at an abandoned sawmill site, 4.5 km beyond the school. This is on the Continental Divide; the trail to the left goes on the Pacific side of the divide, the one on the right descends into the Atlantic slope and is the better trail for birds. Another undriveable road/trail can be found 300 m along the left-hand trail; this ascends rapidly and crosses the divide at a beautiful lookout. The forest begins at the sawmill site at about 600 m (2000 ft). It is about one hour's drive from Penonomé to the sawmill. The El Típico restaurant in Penonomé, across the street from the market, opens at 5.30 a.m. and is the only recourse for an early breakfast.

El Copé is best known for its hummingbirds, the exquisite Snowcap and Green Thorntail being regulars. The foothill species you can expect to see at Cerro Campana and El Valle can also be seen here, as well as toucanets, Slaty-winged Foliage-gleaner, Slaty-capped Flycatcher, Emerald, Speckled, and Blue-and-gold Tanagers, and Yellow-throated Bush-Tanager. Other rarities recorded in the area are Red-fronted Parrotlet, Red-headed Barbet, Golden-olive Woodpecker, Strong-billed Woodcreeper, Immaculate Antbird, Pale-vented Thrush, White-throated Shrike-Tanager, Black-thighed Grosbeak, and many other foothill and western Panama specialties.

Aguadulce

The salt flats south of Aguadulce are excellent for marsh and shore birds especially from late August to November. Aguadulce is 200 km west of Panama City. To find the salt flats continue on the Pan-American Highway; at the approach to Aguadulce is an intersection with a blinking traffic light, a dance hall on the right and a hotel on the left. Turn left here and continue until the street ends. Turn left again and then take the third turn right (which is a four-lane street with a tiny plaza at its start). Stay on this street until you come to the main plaza. Diagonally across the plaza is the post office; turn right between the post office and the pool hall, and after a block turn left. At the first opportunity turn right again and when that road forks keep left, immediately crossing a small bridge. You will soon come to a five-way intersection; take the gentle left and pass a soccer field on your right. A large pond is on the right 3 km down this asphalt road. A dike, worth walking, extends part way across it. To reach the salt flats continue on the asphalt road for 1 km. Here the asphalt turns left and crosses the salt flats for 3.3 km before reaching the sea. You should see hundreds of shorebirds from the asphalt road and the gravel roads at each end of it and along the beach and on the exposed mudflats. Roseate Spoonbill and Wood Stork are best seen early in the morning before pedestrian traffic in the flats picks up. Non-shorebirds you can expect to encounter on and in the brush around the flats are Mangrove Black-Hawk, Plain-breasted Ground-Dove, White-winged Dove, Northern Scrub-Flycatcher, "Mangrove" Yellow Warbler, and during migration, various grosbeaks and finches.

Santa María Marsh

Going west 22 km from Aguadulce you arrve at Divisa where the highway divides. Turn south and in 9.3 km you will cross the Río Escota, a tributary of the Río Santa María. The marshes are along the Escota and many are within sight of the bridge. Dirt roads through marshy areas take off from El Rincón (before the bridge) and París (beyond it). Black-bellied Whistling-Duck, Masked Duck, Lesser Yellow-headed Vulture, Plain-breasted Ground-Dove, Ferruginous Pygmy-Owl, Pale-breasted Spinetail, and other western lowland specialties can be found here.

Santa Fé

About 50 km north of Santiago (250 km west of Panama City on the Pan-American Highway) in the shadow of the Continental Divide lies Sante Fé. In the montane forests of the Divide and the adjacent Caribbean slope, many specialties of eastern Chiriquí and Veraguas can be found. The road through the area of the Divide ranges from 650 m (2100 ft) to 800 m (2600 ft), but trails up through the forest to the ridge reach an altitude of 1350 m (4500 ft).

The road from Santiago to Santa Fé is paved but beyond Santa Fé it is gravel and then dirt; the last is extremely difficult when wet. A ford 1.1 km beyond Santa Fé is passable with two-wheel drive in the dry season but requires four-wheel drive in the rainy season. Alto de Piedra, a forestry school, is 3.5 km further along the road. Beyond the school there is a fork to the left which is passable for only 1 km but it skirts some good forest and has good birding potential (Rufous-winged Woodpecker and Crimson-collared Tanager have been seen). Staying on the main road you cross three ridges before coming to a fourth, the Continental Divide. At the end of the first ridge (approximately 1 km) it is not advisable to continue in two-wheel drive, but with four-wheel drive, and preferably a winch, one can continue to the Divide and even beyond.

Although the forest along the road has been partly cleared it provides excellent birding for forest edge foothill species. Forest interior species and higher altitude birds can be found by taking trails to the left from the road up to the intact forest at higher altitudes. The two best begin about 150 m beyond the fork and just beyond the next stream. Look for Barred Hawk, White-tipped Sicklebill, Snowcap, Green Thorntail, Lattice-tailed Trogon, Striped Woodhaunter, and Spangle-cheeked Tanager, as well as many species listed for El Copé.

Although there is a small Residencia in Santa Fé, it is best to plan to camp if you are going to bird the area. March reportedly has the best weather but be prepared for rain and mud at any time of the year.

Cerro Colorado

The road to Cerro Colorado is worthwhile for finding the birds of eastern Chiriquí Province. Though the forest along it is not extensive, it is the only accessible place in Panama to find the endemic Glow-throated Hummingbird and Yellow-green Finch. The finch is scarce even here, but is readily found. The remaining forest is in the 1200–1500 m (4000–5000 ft) range but the Continental Divide cannot be attained by road.

The road begins at San Félix, 116 km west of Santiago and 74 km east of David. The Hotel Castillo is just beyond San Félix towards David and there is a 24-hour restaurant and gas station at the San Félix turnoff. There is a bridge over the San Félix river 9 km from the turnoff. A guardpost at the bridge may ask for a permit to continue. Though usually not necessary, this can be obtained by writing to Director, RTZ Development Enterprises Limited, Panama Beach, 6-3497 El Dorado, Panama 6, Republic of Panama.

The road beyond the bridge is gravel but in good condition. For 21 km it climbs through devastated habitat to Hato Chamí at 975 m (3200 ft). Here the road divides, both forks going to Campo de Cerro Colorado; keep right, the "high road". The road forks again 14 km beyond Chamí, the left descending to Cerro Colorado, the right continuing 2 km before ending at a landslide. The best birding is along the 10 km before this last fork and along the 2 km dead-end. Besides the aforementioned birds are highland species such as Prong-billed Barbet, Buffy Tuftedcheek, and Azure-hooded Jay.

The 24-hour restaurant on the Pan-American Highway is only an hour's drive from birding habitat, making the area very convenient for a one-day birding trip en route to western Chiriquí.

Fortuna

The central Chiriquí highlands between the Fortuna Reservoir and the Continental Divide are among the best birding locales in Panama. The forest of the reservoir's watershed is rigidly protected and includes cloud forest and very humid montane forest. The presence of the reservoir and a trans-isthmian oil pipeline makes access easy because of good service roads. Camping is the only way to stay overnight in the forest preserve but lodging is available at David 1½ hours away, and 1 hour away in Rambala, Bocas del Toro (see the Chiriquí Grande account on p.500).

To get to Fortuna turn off the Pan-American Highway at the village of Chiriquí, about 20 km east of David, on the well marked road to Gualaca and the Fortuna Reservoir. After passing through Gualaca, at 18 km is a surfaced road. Turn right here and continue for another 18 km through mostly cut-over terrain, passing the IRHE townsite on your left just before coming to a fork. Take the right fork and ascend rapidly, crossing a ridge leading into the forest preserve. Good birding begins at a cement bridge about 8 km from the fork; here the Black-headed Brush-Finch has been found. Another 5 km further is the IRHE camp where a steeply descending road to the right goes to the bridge over the reservoir. After crossing the bridge the road climbs again and where it levels off there is a gravel road to the left. This road is referred to as Umbrellabird Road because of the occasional sightings of that spectacular but rare cotinga along its first part. Look also for Magenta-throated Woodstar, Lattice-tailed Trogon, Resplendent Quetzal, Black-and-white Becard, Sooty-faced Finch, and numerous other montane species.

About 6 km beyond this fork on the main road is the Continental Divide with another Guardia checkpoint. A few yards before the checkpoint there is a gravel road to the left which descends to a stream, turns back right, and ascends towards an abandoned construction camp. At about 3 km from the main road the gravel road curves right and on the left side of the road at the curve are some derelict trucks. There is a 4.5 m (15 ft) mudbank cliff behind the trucks with a partially concealed trail up the near side. This trail continues for miles along the Continental Divide through cloud forest and is the home of such rarities as Black Guan, barbets, many furnariids, Strong-billed Woodcreeper, Rufous-rumped Antwren, Rufous-breasted Antthrush, and Azure-hooded Jay. Higher up are Silvery-fronted Tapaculo and Wrenthrush. Shortly after the start of the Continental Divide trail a landslide covers the road but it is worth strolling the 2 km to where the road ends overlooking a beautiful vista of Atlantic slope forest and the Caribbean Sea. Birding along the road is excellent with White-bellied Mountain-gem, Yellow-eared Toucanet, Three-wattled Bellbird, Spangle-cheeked and Blue-and-gold Tanagers, and Yellow-throated Bush-Tanager not uncommon.

The Fortuna road continues on down into Bocas del Toro (see account on p.500).

Boquete
This attractive town 35 km due north of David at about 1050 m (3500 ft) provides a fine base from which to bird the surrounding mountains and to drive to the summit of Volcán Barú at 3300 m (11,000 ft). A checklist of the Volcán Barú area is available through the Panama Audubon Society.

The best birding in the highlands above town is on Finca Lérida, now owned by the Collins family. Permission to enter the area must be obtained at the Panamonte Hotel in Boquete, either in person, or by writing to: Fritz and Inga Collins, c/o Hotel Panamonte, Entrega General, Boquete, Chiriqui, Republic of Panama (phone: 70-1327). Maps and instructions to find and explore the Finca (especially good is the El Mirador area) can be obtained at the Panamonte. A four-wheel drive vehicle is required to enter the Finca.

To find the road to the summit of Volcán Barú, turn west on Calle 2a Norte and continue on this asphalt road for 7.5 km, until it forks. Take the left fork which forks again in 600 m and here you take the gravel road to the right. The road continues without any turnoffs for 14 km to end on the summit at a communications relay installation; the road is extremely rough and steep in places, and four-wheel drive is required for the uppermost part. Forest is patchy at first but after 2100 m (7000 ft) becomes extensive. The last 2 km pass through elfin/ bamboo forest, habitat of Timberline Wren, Black-and-yellow Silky-Flycatcher and Large-footed Finch and others. Near the summit are scattered low bushes with few birds, but this is the only Panama habitat of the Volcano Junco. Birding anywhere along the road is good, with different species compositions as you ascend. Permits to enter the road are at times necessary. For information call INRENARE in David or Panama City or Mrs Collins at the Panamonte.

Volcán
The village of Volcán is 23 km north of Concepción (25 km west of David on the Pan-American Highway) at 1200 m (4000ft) at the western base of Volcán Barú; this is the starting point for most western highlands birding. The best birding areas are the Volcán Lakes (1200 m: 4000 ft), Bambito to Cerro Punta 1500–1900 m (5000–6200 ft), and Volcán Barú National Park (2100–2400 m: 7000–8000 ft). There are many hotels, restaurants and service stations in the area; the Hotel Bambito is the most luxurious (and expensive), and the Dos Ríos Hotel can also be recommended (very birdy grounds). Public transport to Cerro Punta is good, but for getting to the birding spots it is almost essential to have a private vehicle. For the areas covered in this section a two-wheel drive vehicle is adequate.

To reach the Lakes turn left at the fifth street, Calle El Valle, beyond the Guardia Station in the center of Volcán (the road into Volcán forks at the Guardia Station, the right fork going to Bambito, Cerro Punta, and the National Park, the left towards the lakes and Santa Clara). Here is a sign indicating the airport (Pista de Volcán). Stay on Calle El Valle until another Pista sign indicates to turn right. One block after turning right, turn left at another Pista sign. In 300 m the road forks, the right going to the pista (now being expanded), the left going several kilometers to the lakes. The road is flat and gravel-surfaced. There are no turnoffs before the lakeside woodland. The best birding is along the fork to the left. Do not leave your car out of sight for long. On the lakes look for Masked Duck (irregular), Northern Jacana, and other water birds. Bird life in the woodland around the lakes is rich and includes Pale-billed Woodpecker, mixed flocks of furnariids, flycatchers, and antbirds, the rare Rose-throated Becard, and several tanagers.

To reach the National Park and locales en route keep right at the Guardia Station. The first 6 km is a straight ascending road over a treeless lava plain. Beyond that, broken woodlands begin and you enter Bambito. At 3.8 km beyond the Bambito Hotel a gravel road takes off to the left and parallels the river. From a swinging foot bridge over the river at this point you can see Torrent Tyrannulet, Black Phoebe, American Dipper, and numerous hummingbirds. Walking the gravel road should yield a variety of species, and Blue Seedeater can be located in the bamboo understorey of woods at the end of the road. Continuing on the paved road for 700 m is another gravel road to the left with good birding in the woodlands here.

Cerro Punta is 7 km from the Bambito Hotel along the paved road. Just beyond the town is a dairy farm; immediately past that the road descends, crosses a small bridge, and forks in three directions. Stay on the asphalt, the gentle right, and proceed up through farm land to where the asphalt ends in 3.5 km. The house here belongs to the Fernández Family where often you can hire one of the family members as a (very useful) bird guide to the area.

With their help you can usually find Quetzals and sometimes Black Guan, Andean Pygmy-Owl, Prong-billed Barbet, Buffy Tuftedcheek, Ochraceous Pewee, Silvery-throated Jay, Wrenthrush, and many hummingbirds and other commoner highland specialties. The road becomes gravel beyond the Fernández house and ascends 240m(800 ft) in 2.4 km to the top of a ridge. Birding is excellent along this road; it is best walked. There is a parking area at the start (unmarked) of the National Park 100 m beyond the end of the asphalt (do not leave valuables in the car). Even in the dry season it may drizzle or rain during the afternoon, so carry a rain jacket and umbrella.

Santa Clara is 40 km west of Volcán on an asphalt road which passes through partially cleared terrain. Throughout are patches of roadside scrub and woodland that are well worth birding. Keep scanning the tops of trees for White-crowned Parrot, Fiery-billed Aracari and Turquoise Cotinga, especially early in the morning. At 23.1 km beyond the Guardia Station in Volcán a gravel road takes off to the left descending through good forest for 1.5 km to 1050 m (3500 ft). Here you have the opportunity to see foothill species of this elevation.

Bocas del Toro

Bocas del Toro is the Province of western Panama on the Caribbean slope of the Continental Divide. To the west it borders Costa Rica and therefore it has some birds of the Caribbean coast of Central America that are not found elsewhere in Panama. There are three ways to enter Bocas del Toro: driving across the isthmus from the Pan-American Highway on the Fortuna Road to Chiriquí Grande; flying to the island town of Bocas del Toro; and flying to Changuinola on the mainland near the Costa Rican border. You can also reach Changuinola by road from Limón, Costa Rica.

Chiriquí Grande

The Fortuna Road described above (p.497) continues over the Continental Divide and descends steeply through the Caribbean foothills to the coast paralleling an oil pipeline; in the main text this bird-rich road is referred to as the "oleoducto road". At the beginning of the flat lowlands is the village of Rambala where with a rustic but very comfortable little hotel and restaurant (Hotel Rambala). A few kilometers further along the main road you will enter Chiriquí Grande, a coastal town that is the terminus of the pipeline. Be forewarned that gas is at times not available at Rambala.

Beginning at the Divide the asphalt road descends through cloud forest, then humid foothill forest until reaching the bridge over the Guarumo River. The forest is protected to preserve the watershed and is one of the loveliest in Panama. The steep road has numerous switchbacks but there are frequent places along it to pull off and park. It provides excellent birding (if the weather co-operates), and there is little traffic; amongst a host of good birds, it is Panama's only known site for the Ashy-throated Bush-Tanager.

After crossing the Guarumo one is in the lowlands with the land now sloping gently to the coast. Most nearby forest has been cut but remnant patches of woodland along the road provide good birding. From Rambala into Chiriquí Grande the terrain is marshy with woodland on areas of higher ground. The best remaining lowland woodland which is easily accessible is along the dirt road in front of the hotel after it passes the airstrip.

Almirante/Changuinola

The new road connecting these two towns is good for birding but the forest along it is, as usual, rapidly being cut. Car rental is not possible so it is best to hire a cab to drop you far out on the road and to return for you at a predetermined time. Also worthwhile is a motor launch trip to Swan Key at the west end of Isla Colon (where the town of Bocas del Toro town is situated) to look for Red-billed Tropicbirds and White-crowned Pigeons. A launch may be hired in Almirante or Bocas.

From Changuinola good forest with Bocas specialities can be found be ascending the Changuinola or Teribe Rivers. The forest along the latter is very extensive and in many ways reminiscent of the Darién National Park, even supporting nesting Harpy Eagles and Great Green Macaws. It is essential to have a guide. Guide services can be arranged through Panama Nature Tours, Box 1223, Colon, Republic of Panama; tel: 42-1340, the only birding tour company with extensive experience in Bocas del Toro.

BIBLIOGRAPHY

American Ornithologists' Union. 1983. *Check-list of North American Birds*, 6th edition. Allen Press, Lawrence, Kansas.

Bennet, Charles F. 1968. Human Influences on the Zoogeography of Panama. *Ibero-American 51:* 1–112.

Blake, Emmet R. 1953. *Birds of Mexico: A Guide for Field Identification.* University of Chicago Press, Chicago.

——. 1958. Birds of Volcan de Chiriqui, Panama. *Fieldiana: Zool.*, Vol. 36, No. 5: 499–577. Field Mus. Nat. Hist., Chicago.

Bond, James. 1971. *Birds of the West Indies.* 2nd ed. Houghton Mifflin Co., Boston.

Chapman, Frank M. 1929. *My Tropical Air Castle.* D. Appleton & Co., New York.

——. 1938. *Life in an Air Castle.* Appleton-Century Co., New York.

Davis, L. Irby. 1972. *A Field Guide to the Birds of Mexico and Central America.* University of Texas Press, Austin, Texas.

Dickey, Donald R., and A. J. van Rossem. 1938. The Birds of El Salvador. *Field Mus. Nat. Hist.*, Zool. Ser. 23, Publ. 406: 1–609.

Edwards, Ernest P. 1972. *A Field Guide to the Birds of Mexico.* E. P. Edwards, Sweetbriar, Virginia.

——, and Horace Loftin. 1971. *Finding Birds in Panama.* 2nd ed. E. P. Edwards, Sweetbriar, Virginia.

Eisenmann, Eugene. 1955. The Species of Middle American Birds. *Trans. Linnaean Soc. N. Y., 7:* 1–128.

——, and Horace Loftin. 1972. *Field Checklist of Birds of Panama Canal Zone Area.* 2nd ed. Russ Mason's Flying Carpet Tours, Inc., Kissimmee, Florida.

——, and ——. 1972. *Field Checklist of Birds of the Western Chiriqui Highlands, Panama*, 2nd ed. Russ Mason's Flying Carpet Tours, Inc., Kissimmee, Florida.

ffrench, Richard. 1974. *A Guide to the Birds of Trinidad and Tobago.* Livingston Publ. Co., Wynnewood, Pennsylvania.

Forshaw, Joseph M. 1973. *Parrots of the World.* Doubleday & Co., Garden City, New York.

Griscom, Ludlow. 1935. The Ornithology of the Republic of Panama. *Bull. Mus. Comp. Zool.*, No. 3: 261–382. Harvard Univ., Cambridge, Massachusetts.

Haffer, Jurgen. 1974. *Avian Speciation in Tropical South America.* Publ. Nuttall Ornithol. Club no. 14. Cambridge, Massachusetts.

Hancock, James, and Hugh Elliott. 1978. *The Herons of the World.* Harper and Row, New York.

Harrison, Peter. 1983. *Seabirds: An Identification Guide.* Houghton Mifflin Co., Boston.

Hayman, Peter, John Marchant, and Tony Prater. 1986. *Shorebirds: An Identification Guide to the Waders of the World.* Houghton Mifflin Co., Boston.

Hellmayr, C. E. *et al.* 1924–1949. Catalogue of Birds of the Americas. *Field Mus. Nat. Hist.*, Zool. Ser. 13, pts 1–11.

Hilty, Steven L., and William L. Brown. 1986. *A Guide to the Birds of Colombia.* Princeton University Press, Princeton, New Jersey.

Howell, Thomas R. An ecological study of the birds of the lowland pine savanna and adjacent rain forest in northeastern Nicaragua. *The Living Bird*, Tenth Annual (1971): 185–242. Cornell Laboratory of Ornithology, Ithaca, New York.

Isler, Morton L., and Phyllis R. Isler. 1987. *The Tanagers: Natural History, Distribution, and Identification*. Smithsonian Institution Press, Washington, D.C.

Land, Hugh C. 1970. *Birds of Guatemala*. Livingston Publ. Co., Wynnewood, Pennsylvania.

Meyer de Schauensee, Rodolphe, 1964. *The Birds of Colombia*, Livingston Publ. Co., Wynnewood, Pennsylvania.

——. 1966. *The Species of Birds of South America with their Distribution*. Acad. Nat. Sci., Philadelphia.

——. 1970. *A Guide to the Birds of South America*. Livingston Publ. Co., Wynnewood, Pennsylvania.

Monroe, Burt L., Jr. 1968. *A Distributional Survey of the Birds of Honduras*. American Ornithologists' Union Monograph No. 7.

Murphy, Robert Cushman. 1936. *Oceanic Birds of South America*, Vols. 1–2. Amer. Mus. Nat. Hist., New York.

Peters, J. L. *et al.* 1933–1986. *Check-list of Birds of the World*. Vols. 1–15. Harvard University Press, Cambridge, Massachusetts.

Peterson, Roger Tory. 1947. *A Field Guide to the Birds (East)*. Houghton Mifflin Co., Boston.

——. 1961. *A Field Guide to Western Birds*. Houghton Mifflin Co., Boston.

Peterson, Roger Tory, and Edward L. Chalif. 1973. *A Field Guide to Mexican Birds and Adjacent Central America*. Houghton Mifflin Co., Boston.

Philips, Allan R. 1987. *The Known Birds of North and Middle America. Part I: Hirundinidae to Mimidae; Certhiidae*. Denver Museum of Natural History, Denver, Colorado.

Rand, Austin L., and Melvin A. Traylor. 1954. *Manual de las Aves de El Salvador*. University of El Salvador.

Ridgway, Robert (and Herbert Friedmann, Parts 9–11). 1901–1950. The Birds of North and Middle America, Parts 1–11. *U.S. Natl. Mus. Bull.* 50.

Ripley, S. Dillon. 1977. *Rails of the World: A Monograph of the Family Rallidae*. David R. Godine, Boston.

Robbins, Chandler S., Bertel Brunn, and Herbert S. Zim. 1966. *Birds of North America: A Guide to Field Identification*. Golden Press, New York.

Robbins, Mark B., Theodore A. Parker III, and Susan E. Allen. 1985. The Avifauna of Cerro Pirre, Darién, Eastern Panama. In P. A. Buckley et al. (eds), *Neotropical Ornithology*. Ornithol. Monogr. no. 36: 198–232.

Russell, Stephen M. 1964. *A Distributional Study of the Birds of British Honduras*. American Ornithologists' Union Monograph No. 1.

Skutch, Alexander. 1954–1960–1967. *Life Histories of Central American Birds*, Vols. 1–3. Cooper Ornithological Society. Pacific Coast Avifauna Series, Nos. 31, 34, and 35.

——. 1967. *Life Histories of Central American Highlands Birds*. Publ. Nuttall Ornithological Club, No. 7.

——. 1972. *Studies of Tropical American Birds*. Publ. Nuttall Ornithological Club, No. 10.

Slud, Paul. The Birds of Costa Rica, Distribution and Ecology. *Bull. Amer. Mus. Nat. Hist., 128:* 1–430.

Smithe, Frank B. 1966. *The Birds of Tikal*. Natural History Press, Garden City, New York.

Sturgis, Bertha B. 1928. *Field Book of Birds of the Panama Canal Zone*, G. P. Putnam's Sons, New York.

Wetmore, Alexander. 1960. A classification for the birds of the world. *Smiths. Misc. Coll.*, 139: 37pp.

——. 1965–1968–1973. The Birds of the Republic of Panama, Parts 1–3. *Smiths. Misc. Coll.*, Vol. 150, pts 1–3.

——, Roger F. Pasquier, and Storrs L. Olson. 1984. *The Birds of the Republic of Panama*, Part 4. Smithsonian Institution Press. Washington, D.C.

INDEX OF ENGLISH NAMES

Illustration references are given in **bold type**, e.g. **Pl.20** for color plate 20, and **230** for a drawing on page 230 of the text.

INDEX OF SCIENTIFIC NAMES

Library of Congress Cataloging-in-Publication Data

Ridgely, Robert S., 1946–
   A guide to the birds of Panama: with Costa Rica, Nicaragua, and
Honduras / by Robert S. Ridgely and John A. Gwynne, Jr.—2nd ed.
     p.   cm.
   Bibliography: p.
   Includes index.
   ISBN 0-691-08529-3 (alk. paper): $49.50.
    1. Birds—Panama—Identification.   2. Birds—Central America—
Identification.   I. Gwynne, John A.   II. Title
QL887.P3RB   1989
598.297287--dc 19   88-29309
                                                CIP